THE BURNHAM INDEX TO ARCHITECTURAL LITERATURE

IN TEN VOLUMES

Garland Publishing, Inc.

4

THE
BURNHAM INDEX
TO
ARCHITECTURAL LITERATURE

Dehaudt, M.G. – Gargoyle

PREFACE BY Jack Perry Brown

Ryerson and Burnham Libraries
The Art Institute of Chicago

Garland Publishing, Inc.

NEW YORK AND LONDON 1989

LIBRARY OF CONGRESS CATALOGING–IN–PUBLICATION DATA

The Burnham index to architectural literature.

"Ryerson and Burnham Libraries, The Art Institute of Chicago."
1. Architecture—United States—Bibliography—Indexes.
2. Architecture—Bibliography—Indexes.
3. Burnham Library of Architecture—Indexes.
I. Art Institute of Chicago. Ryerson Library.
II. Burnham Library of Architecture.
Z5944.U5B87   1898   [NA705]   016.72'0973   89–16850
ISBN 0–8240–2664–0 (v. 4 : alk. paper)

Printed on acid-free, 250–year–life paper.

MANUFACTURED IN THE UNITED STATES OF AMERICA

Deilmann, Harald, 1920-
    Architektenhaus in Münster, Westfalen
[plans, section & detail] Harald Deilmann, archt.

Arch & Wohnform
67:172-77 Ag 1959

del Barrio, Alberto Gonzales
see
Gonzales del Barrio, Alberto

Dehaudt, M. G.
see
Lille (Fr.) Department Stores

Deilmann, Harald, 1920-
    Kurklinik in Salzburg [plans, section &
details] Harold Deilmann, archt.

Arch & Wohnform
66:356-67 N 1958

Del Fabro, Eduard
    Primarschulhaus "Im Feld", Wetzikon
[plans & sections] Ed. del Fabro & Bruno
Gerosa, archts.

Bauen& Wohnen
12:320-22 O 1958

STACK
709.3   Dehio,2
351j   Die basilika des Hl.Martin in Tours und ihr
einfluss auf die entwickelung der kirchlichen
bauformen des mittelalters.

Jahrbuch der k. preussischen
kunstsammlungen. 10:13-38
1899

Deilmann, Harald, 1920-
    Theatre de Munster, Allemagne (plan and
section) Harold Deilmann et al., archts.

Aujourd'hui
3:90 My 1958

Del Fabro, Eduard
    Projekt für ein schulhaus in Wetzikon
[plan] Ed. del Fabro & Gerosa, Bruno, archts.

Bauen & Wohnen
#11:398-9N 1956

STACK
709.4   Dehio,G
351j   Zwei Cistersienserkirchen: ein beitrag zur
geschichte der anfänge des gotischen stils.

Jahrbuch der k. preussischen
kunstsammlungen 12:91-103.
1891

Deimal, Johannes
see
Urban and Deimal

720.5   Del Gaudio, Matthew W
A67f   Williamsburg houses, Brooklyn,N.Y. assoc.
archts: Richmond H. Shreve, chief; Matthew W.
Del Gaudio, Gurney and Clavan, Arthur C.Hol-
den, Holmgren, Volz and Gardstein, John W.
Ingle,Jr., William Lescaze, Paul Trapani,
Harry Leslie Walker.

Architectural forum 67: 495
December 1937

Dehn-Rotfelser, Heinrich von
    Das rathus zu Posen.

Jahrbuch der k. preussischen
Kunstsammlungen 7:20-22
1886

DeJarnette, James T.
see
Moundville (Ala.) Mound state museum

710.5   Del Mar (Cal.) Harding (Marston) house
C955   Medieval modernity: a paradox in stucco
in Del Mar, Cal. Residence of Marston
Harding. Richard S. Requa, archt.

Country life (U.S.) 57: 52-53
February 1930

Deilmann, Harald, 1920-
    Architectes d'apres-guerre I; Harald
Deilmann [plans] Harald Deilmann, archt.

Zodiac
2:169-71 My 1958

DeKlerk, Michel
see
Klerk, Michel de

Del Marle, Félix, 1889-1952
    Boutique moderne, à Dinard. A.F. Del Marle,
archt.

Encyclopedie de l'architecture;
Constructions modernes. 12 vols.
Paris: Albert Morancé, 1928-39.
1:pl. 71

Deilmann, Harald, 1920-
    Architect's own house at Munster, West Germany
[plans & sections] Harold Deilmann, archt.

Archl Design
28:371-73 S 1958

MICROFILM
Deknatel, William Ferguson, 1907-

in SCRAPBOOK ON
ARCHITECTURE p. 21
(on film)

Del Marle, Félix, 1889-1952
    Intérieur, 1926. (Interior, 1926.) A.F.
Del Marle, archt.

L'architecture vivante: pl. 11
Spring 1927

Del Monte (Cal.) Del Monte Hotel
    Del Monte Hotel, Del Monte, Cal. Lewis P.
Hobart and Clarence A. Tantau, archts.

            Architectural forum 51:613-616
            December, 1929

7PO.5   Delmaire,
A67r   Lees, Frederic
            The house of the four cardinals: Hotel Rohan
         Paris, Delmaire, archt. No plans.

            Architectural record 24: 31-44
            July 1908

Delano and Aldrich   (Card 6)

    see also

New York (NY)   70th Street, E. No. 121-123
  "   "   "   Union Club
Northport (LI)   Perkins (R.P.) House
Oakland (CA)   City Hall. Competition
Oyster Bay (LI)   Work (B.G.) House
Paris (FR)   U.S. Embassy
Pocantico Hills (NY) Rockefeller (J.D.) Estate
Roslyn (LI)   Whitney (Mrs. H.P.) Studio
Santa Barbara (CA)   Herter House

                            (See Card 7)

Del Monte (Cal.) Del Monte Hotel
    Guest Cottage no. 2 and 8, Del Monte Hotel,
Del Monte, Cal. Lewis Hobart, Clarence A. Tantau,
assoc. archts. Plans

A   Architectural digest 6:44-45
        Number 3, (1930)

Deland (Fla.),
    Stetson University, Hall of Science.
Wm. Chas. Hayes, Arch.

            Inland Arch.
            37, No.2, pl.fol.p. 16
            March 1901

Delano and Aldrich   (Card 7)

    see also

Stapleton (NY)   Staten Island Savings Bank
Syosset (LI)   Burden (J.A.) House
  "   "   Winthrop (E.L.) House
  "   "   Wood (Chambers) House
Wallingford (PA)   Philadelphia orphanage
Washington (DC)   Red Cross House
Williamstown (MA)   Williams College. Dormitory.
                     Competition.
Woodbury (LI)   Hoyt (Lydig) House

                            (See Card 8)

---

del Moral, Enrique

    see

Moral, Enrique del

Delano and Aldrich

    see also

Ardsley (N.Y.) houses
Baltimore (Md.) Abell building
  "   "   Walters Art Gallery
Bayville (L.I.) Williams (Harrison) estate.
                Tennis court and swimming pool
Chicago, IL. Lincoln Park. Eugene Field Memorial
Cincinnati (O.) Carew Tower
  "   "   Starrett's Netherland-Plaza
                    (see card 2)

Delano and Aldrich   (Card 8)

    see also

Woodbury (LI)   Morawetz (Victor) House

---

del Pozo de Lans, Margot

    see

Pizarro, Lans and del Pozo

Delano and Aldrich   (card 2)

    see also

Clinton (N.J.) Farms. Chapel
Cold Spring Harbor(L.I.) Kahn (O.) house
Dater, Alfred W, house, Fishers Island, N.Y.
East Norwich (L.I.) Hammond (Paul) house
East Norwich (L.I.) Swann (Arthur) house
Hartford (Conn.) Christ Church. Parish house
Huntington (L.I.) Chateau des Beaux Arts
Ithaca (N.Y.) Cornell Univ. Willard Straight Hall
Lenox (Mass.) house

                    (see card 3)

Delano and Aldrich

    Members of firm:

Aldrich, Chester Holmes, 1871-1940
Delano, William Adams, 1874-

Del Rio (Tex.) Abbey (W.M.) house
    Residence of W.M. Abbey.
Atlee B. Ayres, arch.

        Architecture 52:312
        Sept. 1925

Delano and Aldrich   (card 3)

    see also

Miami (Fla.) Pan-American Airways
Mill Neck (L.I.) Airdrie
Morristown (N.J.) Thorne (W.V.) house
Mt. Kisco (N.Y.) Borland (W.G.) house
  "   "   "   house
New Haven (Conn.) Hooker (E.R.) house
  "   "   "   house
  "   "   "   Yale Univ. Library
  "   "   "   Memorial Quadrangle
                    (see card 4)

MICROFILM

Delano and Aldrich
    Proposed Gen. Theodore Roosevelt, Jr.
Memorial Library.

                in SCRAPBOOK ON
                ARCHITECTURE p. 474
                (on film)

Delacroix, Ch   and   H

    see

Paris, Fr. Housing

Delano and Aldrich   (card 4)

    see also

New Haven (Conn.) Yale University. Sterling
                  Chemistry laboratory
New Haven (Conn.) Yale University. Wright
                  Memorial Dormitory
New York (N.Y.) Brewster (R.S.) house
  "   "   "   Brown Bros. and Company
  "   "   "   Colony Club
  "   "   "   (3rd) Church of Christ Scientist
                    (see card 5)

Delano and Aldrich
    The R. Fulton Cutting Group.
Delano and Aldrich, archts.

                The Architect (N.Y.) 4:pl.116
                Aug. 1925

Delahalle, R.   R.

    see

Paris (Fr.) Theatre de l'oeil

Delano and Aldrich   (card 5)

    see also

New York (N.Y.) Delano and Aldrich Offices
  "   "   "   Iselin (E.) house
  "   "   "   Knickerbocker club
  "   "   "   Palmer (F.S.) house
  "   "   "   Park Ave. (no. 925) apts.
  "   "   "   Pratt (H.I.) house
  "   "   "   Prince George Hotel
  "   "   "   Straight (Willard) house
                    (see card 6)

Delano & Aldrich
    Russell Sage Hall, Northfield Seminary. Plan

                West. Arch.
                16: pl.fol.p. 108
                Oct. 1910

720.5
A67r
Delano and Aldrich
Bottomley, W.L.
  A selection from the works of Delano and
Aldrich. Drawings by Chester B. Price.

Arch rec 54: 3-71
Jl '23

Delano, William Adams   1874-

See also

Delano and Aldrich

DeLario, John

see

Beverly Hills (Cal.) Lloyd (R.B.) house

Delano and Aldrich and Charles Higgins

see

Cortlandt (N.Y.) Valeria home

Delano, William Adams
  ...credo: "Traditional".

Magazine of art
33: 234
Ap 1940

Delaunay, Nicolas, the elder, 1739-1792
  Two Louis XVI interiors from the
etched states of contemporary French engravings

Old furniture
5: 178-180, N 1928

Delano and Aldrich office

see

New York (N.Y.) Delano & Aldrich office

710.5
C855
Delano, William Adams   1874-
  An interview with W.A. Delano.

Country life (U.S.)52: 66-7
August 1927

Delavan Lake (Wis)

see also

Lake Delavan (Wis)

720.6
A5loc
Delano and Aldrich scholarship. 1930
Butler, Charles
  The Delano and Aldrich scholarship winner,
1930, Pierre Mathé.

The Octagon 2: 10
October 1930

D19.66
V88
Delano,William Adams   1874-
Wood,R.R.
  "Little Ipswich", home of Mr.and Mrs.Chalmers
Wood. W.A.Delano,archt.

Vogue 74: 80-84, 118
October 26,1929

Delavan Lake (WI) Lagorio (A) Summer Home
Victor Andre Matteson, archt. plan

West. Archt.
22: 41-2
Nov, 1915

MICROFILM
Delano, Frederic Adrian, 1863-1953

    obituary notice

in SCRAPBOOK ON
ARCHITECTURE p. 726
(on film)

Delany, J. F.

see

New York (N.Y.) Manhattan college: gymnasium.

Delaware. Architecture, HABS survey

see

New Castle (Del.) Johns (Kensey) house
"   "   "   Van Dyke House
"   "   "   Amstel house
Wilmington (Del.) Holy Trinity Church

Delano, Frederick A.
  Railway terminals & their relation to city
planning. illus.

West Arch.
15: 5-6, 8, 10, 11
Jan. 1910

720.54
A67
Delaon Concours. 1925
Risler, Charles
  Concours Paul Delaon. (Paul Delaon Competit-
ions, 1st class.)

L'architecture 36:182
June 25, 1925

720.5
B84
Delaware county (Pa.) house
  House in Radnor Township, Delaware
County, Pa. George Bisphan Page, Architect.
Plans.

Brickbuilder 19: pls. 73-75
Je '10

Delano, Ward P.,   -1915

see:

Fuller and Delano

Delaporte, Edouard
  Hôpital Avicenne, Rabat, Karokko [plans]
J. K. Bonnemaison, éd. Delaporte & F. Robert,
archts.

Bauen & Wohnen
12:150-54 My 1958

Delaware County (Pa.) St. Vincent's Home
  New St. Vincent's Home, Delaware County, Pa.
Paul Monghan, archt. Photograph and plan.

A   Architecture 44; pl. 107-8.
           July, 1921.

Delaware, Ohio. St. Mary's church (1886).
Illustration. A. Druiding, architect.

Building budget
II: 150 and plate
Dec., 1886

710.5
H84

Delehanty, Bradley
A house and garden for a bride.
Bradley Delehanty, architect. Isabella
Pendleton, landscape architect.

House and garden 63: 20-21
June 1933

Delhi, India. Architecture
The cities of Delhi and their monuments.

Builder
106: 6-8
Ja 2'14

Delaware River. Bridge
The Delaware River Bridge - abutment:
Paul Cret, archt.; no plan.

Federal architect 8:22-23
January, 1938

710.5
H84

Delehanty, Bradley
The house with 10 exposures: the octagonal
house by Bradley Delehanty, archt. Plans.

House and garden 70:54-55,72
July 1936

Delhi, India. Architecture
Delhi, Agra, Sikri. [illus.]

Marg
20: whole issue
S 1967

Delaware Title and insurance company building, Wilmington, (Del.)

see

Wilmington, (Del)-Delaware title and insurance company building

---

DeLeuw-Cather building, Chicago

see

Chicago, Ill. Sargent building

Delhi, India. Architecture
Lee, H.O.
Impressions of Delhi Fort. Diwan-iKhas or
privy council chamber and the Pearl Mosque

Arch jour
56: 271-2
Ag 30, 1922

Delbridge, Harry C   1874(?)-1947
[obituary]

Nat'l arch 3:11
F '47

Delfaute, Charles
Projekt einer wohnüberbauung in Firminy
(Loire) [plans] Marcel Roux, Andre Sive, Charles
Delfaute and Pierre Tyr, archts.

Bauen and Wohnen
No. 6: 213-216
Je 1956

Delhi, India. Jamma Masjid
...the great mosque of Delhi is closer to the
Moslem shrines of Meshed and Samarkand than to
Madura's temples...

National geographic mag.
82: 467
October 1942

Delehanty, Bradley

see also

Easton, Md. "Cape Centaur"
Locust Valley (L.I.) Cravath (P.D.) house
North Castle (N.Y.) Slater,(Mrs. W.A.) estate

Delft, Neth. Technische hogeschool "Stylos"
Kramer, E.
De plaats van stylos.

Forum 9:50-53 F 1954

Ryerson

Delhi, India. Kutb Minar
"The Tower of Victory, Kutb Minar, tops
all the monuments of the eight Delhis - This
238 foot sandstone shaft, built in the 12th
century, marks the Moslem conquest of Hin-
dustan-"

National Geographic Mag.
82: Plate VIII
Oct 1942

710.5
H84

Delehanty, Bradley
Architects lead such interesting lives.

House and garden 72:22-23,61-63
January 1938

Delft, Neth. Technische hogeschool. "Stylos"
Greiner, Otto
Het contact "stylos" - "Poorters"

Forum 9:54-55
F 1954

Delhi, India. Pearl mosque
...The tiny Pearl mosque is a favorite with
visitors to the Mogul gardens and pavilions in the
Fort at Shahjahanabad, the seventh Delhi.

National geographic
magazine 82: 492
October 1942

Delehanty, Bradley
Details of entrance doorway, residence at
Great Neck, L.I.

Archt (N.Y.)
7: front.
January 1927

Delft, Neth. Technische hogeschool. "Stylos"
Rave, J. J.
Excursies

Forum 9:56-62
F 1954

Delhi, India. Planning

see

New Delhi, India. Planning

Delhi, New, India

see

New Delhi, India

Delk, Edward Buehler

see

Bartlesville (Okla.)"La Quinta"
Cimarron, (N.M.) (Near) Villa Philmonti
Tulsa (Okla.) Philtower building
Kansas City (Mo.) Kelley (W.) house

Della Sala, D'Ambrosio, Salvatori

see

Naples (It.) Bar Francesco Cino

---

della Sala, Francesco

see also

Trecase, It. Stazione Circumvesuviana

Dellemann, O
Aus der arbeit der Niedersächischen heimstätte [plans & sections] O. Dellemann, archt.

Baumeister
57:292-300 My 1960

Dellenburg & Zucker

see

Chicago (Ill.) Holy family church

Delmenhorst (Ger.) Market bldg.
Market house in Delmenhorst. Heinz Stoffregen, archt.

Wasmuths 11:71
Heft 2, 1927

Delmenhorst, Ger. Stadthalle & theater. Competition. 1960
Wettbewerb für stadthalle mit theater in Delmenhorst [plans & sections]

Baumeister
57:732-40 O 1960

720.54   Delorme,Philibert   1512/15-1570
A67   Adhémar,M
La Coupole en charpente de la Halle au Blé et l'influence de Philibert Delorme au XVIIIᵉ siécle. (The spherical vault in timber-work of the Corn Exchange, and the influence of Philibert Delorme in the eighteenth century.)

L'Architecture 46: 249-252
July 15,1933

RYERSON LIBRARY
705.4   Delorme,Philibert 1512/15-1570
G28   Berty, Adolphe
Philibert de L'Orme, sa vie et ses oeuvres.

140-149
Gaz.des beaux arts Per.I,v.4,p.78-91;
October;November 1859

RYERSON LIBRARY
705.4   Delos
G28   Jardé,Auguste
Une Pompei Hellenique: Delos. Plan, plates.

Gazette des Beaux Arts 39: 5-16
January 1908

720.5   Delos,Mosaic pavement
A67r   Mosaic floor in Delos Island, Greece.
Andre' Leconte, del.

Architectural record 66: front.
August 1929

720.5   Delphi.Architecture
A67r   Schopfer,Jean
The Greek temple: plot plan of the sanctuary of Delphi; plan of the treasury of the Athenians at Del-hi.

Architectural record 17:461-470
May 1905

Delphi, Greece
Stanton, W. M.
Delphi and the oracle, Greece

Architecture 44: 231-4 pl 121
Ag 1921

Delray Beach, Fla. Ladew, Harvey house,

see

Delray Beach, Fla. "Pied à Mer"

Ryerson
Delray Beach, Fla. "Pied à mer" card house
House of cards: The annex, for parties only, of Mr. Harvey Ladew's "Pied à Mer" at Delray Beach

Vogue
131:136-9, Ap 1, 1958

Delville Wood, S. Af. South African National
Memorial
South African National Memorial, Delville Wood. Sir Herbert Baker, archt. Alfred Turner, sculptor.

Architect 116:pl.fol.p.450
October 15, 1926

Démaret, Jean
Magasins et services d'exécution des Messageries Hachette, a Paris. Plan. J. Démaret, archt.

Encyclopedie de l'architecture;
constructions modernes. 12 vols.
Paris: Albert Morancé, 1928-39.
5:pls.26-8

Demarmels, Hans
Häuser aus vorfabrizierten betonelementen Demarmels-Steiger Building System [plans & section] Hans Demarmels, archt.

Bauen & Wohnen
#2:54-5 F 1957

DeMars, Vernon

see also

Woodville (Cal.) F.S.A. community for Agricultural workers.
Vallejo (Cal.) Carquinez Heights defense project

DeMars, Vernon and Burton D. Cairns

see

Chandler (Ariz.) F.S.A. Community for agricultural workers
Yuba City (Cal.) F.S.A. Community for agricultural workers

720.5
A67f   Demchick, Israel
     Linton restaurant, Philadelphia, Penna.
Israel Demchick, archt. Plan
 	
     Architectural forum 66: 455
     May 1937
	Demonstration houses
	
	see
	
	Model houses
		Denby, Edwin H
		     Exhibition of architectural water colors
		by Edwin H. Denby in the Gallery adjoining
		his office at 333 Fourth Avenue, New York
		City.
		
		     Architectural digest 9: 123
		     Number 3, [1936-37]

720.5
A67f   Demchick, Israel
     A quintet of taxpayers from Philadelphia:
one of the neatest expressions of land util-
ization. Israel Demchick, archt. Plan.
 	
     Architectural forum 67:68
     July 1937
	Demoriane, R Patouillard-
	
	see
	
	Patouillard-Demoriane, R
		720.52
		A67c Denby, Elizabeth
		     Kensal house, Ladbroke Grove,
		Kensington. Executant architect: E. Maxwell
		Fry. Plans.
		
		     A Architect(Lond.)149:345,349,381-384
		     March 19,1937

DeMeurou, F. A.
 	
see
 	
Hamburg (Ger.) Blumenstrasse (no. 9) house
	Dempster, J.A.
	
	see
	
	Polkemmet pithead baths, Scot.
		720.52 Denby, Elizabeth
		A67c Rehousing (abstract of paper read before the
		R.I.B.A. on November 16.)
		
		     Architect and Building News 148:233-235
		     November 20, 1936

Deming, E. W. Sculpture: "The First Inhabitants
of Pittsburg." Selections from Pittsburg
Architectural Club Exhibition, 1907.
 	
     Inland Arch. 50:
     pl. fol. p 76
     D, 1907
	Dempwolf, J. A.
	
	see
	
	Spring Grove (Pa.) Gladfelter (R.L.) and(P.H.)
	houses
		720.5
		I56 Denell, R A
		     Residence of Floyd J. Smith, Chicago,
		Illinois. R. A. Denell, archt.
		
		     Inland architect and news record 34: pl.opp
		     January 1900 p.48

Democracy and architecture
 	
see
 	
Architecture and democracy
	Denbigh, N. Wales, Howell's School
	     Howell's School, Denbigh, North Wales.
	Sir Aston Webb and Son, archts.
	
	     Builder 135:302-3
	     August 24, 1928
		Deneux, Henri Louis, 1874 –
		     Cathédrale de Reims. Charpente de la nef.
		H. Deneux, archt.
		
		     Encyclopedie de l'architecture;
		     constructions modernes. 12 vols.
		     Paris: Albert Morancé, 1928-39.
		     2:pls. 5-6

Demmler, Theodor, 1879-1944
Bange, E.F.
     Theodor Demmler [Obituary]
 	
     Zeitschrift für
     kunstwissenschaft.
     V. 2: 39-30
     1948
	Denbigh (Wales) North Wales counties Mental
	                 hospital
	     The North Wales Counties Mental Hospital.
	Lockwood, Abercrombie and Saxon, archts. Plans.
	
	     Architect (Lond.) 136: 304-308
	     December 15, 1933
		Deneux, Henri Louis, 1874 –
		     Henri-Louis Deneux
		
		     Académie des beaux-arts
		     Bulletin No.3:92-94
		     January-June 1926

DeMoney, Frank, 1873?-1947
     Obituary.
 	
     Illinois society of
     architects bulletin
     31:8
     Mr-Ap 1947
	Denbigh (Wales) North Wales Counties Mental
	                 Hospital
	     North Wales Counties Mental Hospital, Denbigh,
	North Wales. Lockwood, Abercrombie and Saxon,
	archts. Plans.
	
	     Builder 145: 938,944,946-950
	     December 15, 1933
		Denham, B. W. -1946
		     [obituary]
		
		     Nat'l arch 2:15
		     Jl '46

710.5
C85　Denham, Eng. Architecture
　　C.H.
　　　　Unspoiled Denham - where dogs may sleep on
roads.

　　　　　　Country life(London)57:721-3
　　　　　　May 9, 1925

Denivelle, Paul E.　　　-1936

see also

Palo Alto (CA)　Stanford Univ. Women's Dormitory

720.52
B95　Denmark. Architecture
　　Goodden, R. Y.
　　　　The A. A. excursion, 1930.

　　　　　　Builder 139: 350-352
　　　　　　August 29, 1930

Denham (Eng.) Golf Club house
　　Golf club house, Denham, Bucks.
Melville Seth-Ward, archt. Plan.

　　　　　　Builder 109 pl.
　　　　　　November 5, 1915

720.5
A67f　Denivelle, Paul E.　　　-1936
　　Obituary.

　　　　　　Architectural forum 65: sup. 44
　　　　　　November 1936

720.52
B95　Denmark. Architecture
　　The Architectural Association excursion
to Sweden and Denmark. No. illus.

　　　　　　Builder 139: 910
　　　　　　November 28, 1930

Denham (Eng.) Golf Club house
　　Denham, Bucks.
Melville Seth-Ward, F.R.I.B.A., arch.

　　　　　　Builder 129: 629
　　　　　　Oct. 30, 1925

Denman & Son

see

Rickmansworth (Eng.)　　　Royal
Masonic Institution for girls. Competition

705.942
W46　Denmark. Architecture
　　Slothouwer, D. F.
　　　Danish architecture

　　　　　　Wendingen 8:3-18
　　　　　　No.4, 1927

750.54
A67au　Denham (Eng.) London film productions
　　Studios de la London film a
Denham. (plans, sect.)

　　　　　　L'Arch d'aujourd'hui
　　　　　　9: 61-66
　　　　　　Ap.'38

Denman, C. K.

see also

Holmby Hills (Cal.) Johnson (L.H.) house

720.52
A67　Denmark. Architecture
　　Marnus, L.
　　　Denmark. pts.1-2

　　　　　　Architects' jour.61:803-806;
　　　　　　May 27 June3, 1925　847-848

720.52　Denham, Eng. Restoration
B95　　　Restoration work in Buckinghamshire by
Francis Bacon.

　　　　　　Builder 144: 406-408,412
　　　　　　March 10,1933

Denmark. Architecture

see also

Baroque architecture, Denmark
Domestic architecture, Denmark
Manor houses, Denmark

720.52
A67　Denmark. Architecture
　　Marnus, L.
　　　Neo-classicism in Denmark.

　　　　　　Architects' jour. 64: 295-302
　　　　　　September 8, 1926

720.54
A67　Denis, Paul
　　V., G.
　　　Maison de rapport. (Apartment house.)
11 bis, Rue Valentin-Haüy. Paris. Paul Denis,
architect. Plan.

　　　　　　L'architecture. 36:314-316
　　　　　　September 25, 1923

720.52
A67　Denmark. Architecture
　　Marnus, M. L.
　　　Danish architecture.

　　　　　　Architects journal 57:963-4
　　　　　　Je 6 '25

720.52
A674　Denmark. Architecture
　　　Old Danish architecture: Halsteinburg
Castle,Sleevig; Oeskerkirke,Bornholm;Brande-
kilde church,Funen; Rosenborg Castle,Copen-
hagen.

　　　　　　Architecture (Lond.)4: 142-143,147
　　　　　　August 1925

Denison university

see

Granville (O.) Denison university

Denmark. Architecture

　　　　　　Bancroft, Hubert Howe.
　　　　　　Achievements of civilization....
　　　　　　10 vols. New York: The Bancroft
　　　　　　Company, publishers. 1896.
　　　　　　5:Chapter 14

720.52
B95　Denmark. Architecture
　　Robertson, Manning
　　　Some impressions of...Denmark

　　　　　　Builder 129: 8-9
　　　　　　Jl 3 '25

Denmark, Architecture
Birnstingl, H   J
With the architectural association in
Denmark and Sweden

Architects' Jour
62: 138-143
Jl 22, 1925

Denmark. Architecture. 20th century
Portfolio of current Danish architecture:
work by Helweg-Möller and others.

Architectural record 66:235-252
September, 1929

Dennis, C. P.

see

Owensmouth (CA) Owensmouth High School & Open Air
Greek Theater

Denmark. Architecture. 16th century
Brochner, Georg
Sixteenth century Danish architecture.   2 pts.

Builder 121: 378   128:860-1
September 23, 1921 Je 5, '25

Denmark, Architecture. 20th c.
Santi, Carlo
La tradizione nell'architettura contemporanea
danese

Domus 255: 45-48
F 1951

Dennis, Langton

see also

Crowborough (Eng.) Bell (W.L.) house

705.944   Denmark. Architecture, 20th century
W98   Dänische Architektur. [special number]

Das Werk 35: special number
May, '48

Denmark. Architecture. 20th century. Exhibitions
Robertson, Howard
Exhibition of modern Danish architecture.

Architect (Lond.) 117:887-898
May 27, 1927

Dennis, W. H. and O. P.

see

Olympia (WA)   State Capitol Design, Third Prize

Denmark. Architecture. 20th cent.
Enevoldsen, Christian
Danish architecture.

Archl Design
29:91 Mar 1959

Denmark Hill, London

see

London, Eng.

Dennis, William P. -1917
obit.

West. Archt.
26: 46
Dec, 1917

720.52   Denmark. Architecture, 20th century
A67c   [Modern architecture]

The Architect 114: 271
O 16 '25

Denmark's pavilion, Paris exposition, 1937

see

Paris, Fr.   Exposition 1937. Pavillon du Danemark

Dennison and Hirons

see also

Atlantic City (N.J.) Marine trust company
Blairsville (Pa.) First nat'l bank
Bridgeport (Conn.) City national bank & trust co.
Charleston (W.Va.) houses
   "   "   Ward (C.E.) house
   "   "   Thomas (James R.) house
   "   "   Kanawha banking & trust co.
East Orange (N.J.) Essex county trust co.
Erie (Pa.) Erie trust company
Hartford (Conn.) Phoenix national bank

720.53   Denmark. Architecture. 20th century
W31   The modern architecture of Denmark.

Wasmuths 9: 173-85
Heft 5, 1925

Dennis & Farwell

see also

Los Angeles (CA)   Dennis (O.P.) Residences
Los Angeles (CA)   Freeman (Archie) House
   "   "   Marshall Residence
   "   "   Residence
   "   "   Steny (C.N.) Residence
   "   "   Wilson (Erasmus) Residence
Redland Hills (CA) Hill (Mrs. C.S.) Residence
Redlands (CA)   Fisher (Henry) Residence

Dennison and Hirons

see also

Hartford (Conn.) Society for savings. Banking
   room.
New City (N.Y.) Rockland county court house
New Haven (Conn.) Mechanics bank
New York (N.Y.) State bank and trust company
Purcellville (N.J.)   nat'l bank
Rye (N.Y.) Rye national bank
Watertown (Mass.) Union market nat'l bank
Waynesburg (Pa.) Citizens national bank
Wilmington (Del.) Del. title & insurance co.
   office bldg.

720.5   Denmark. Architecture. 20th century
W52   Marnus, L.
        Modern Danish architecture.

Western architect 37:front.,99-100 &
May 1928   pl. 73-87

720.5   Dennis and Farwell
W52   Residence at Los Angeles, California.
        Dennis and Farwell, archts.

Western architect 10: 1pl.fol.p.14
January 1907

Dennison and Hirons

Members of firm:

Dennison, Ethan Allen 1881-
Hirons, Frederick Charles 1882-1942

Dennison, Ethan Allen   1881-

See

Dennison and Hirons

720.5
P50   Dens
         Man's study for a country house, designed
by Ralph T. Walker, archt.
         Man's den designed by Joseph Urban.

         Pencil points 10: 200-201
         March 1929

Denver (CO)
     Apartment Bldg.
W.E. Fisher, Arch.

         Inland Arch.
         37, No.4: pl.fol.p. 32
         May 1901

Dennison, Hirons & Darbyshire

see also

New York (N.Y.) Fire engine house. Vermilye Ave.

Dental buildings

see

Medical and dental buildings

Denver (Col)
     Apartment Building
Boal & Harnois, Arch.

         Inland Arch.
         42: pls. fol. p. 16
         Sept. 1903

720.5
A51   Dennison, Hirons and Darbyshire
             Fire engine house, Vermilye Ave.,
New York. Dennison, Hirons and Darbyshire,
archts.

         American architect 113:pl.201-203
         June 5, 1918

Dentists' offices

see

Medical and dental buildings

Denver (Colo.) Apartment Houses
     Apartment houses.
Denver. Fisher, William E. and Arthur A. Fisher,
archts.

         Western architect 28.pl.
         December, 1919

Denny, Willis F.

see also

Atlanta (Ga.) Dubignon (F.G.) house

Denton, Tex. Stoker (Spencer) Apts.
     Apartment house for Dr. Spencer Stoker,
Denton, Texas. Preston M. Geren, archt. Plan

         Architectural forum 66: 403
         May, 1937

Denver (Col.) Architects

see

Fisher, William E. and Arthur A.

---

ffo
720.6
A51q   Denny, Willis F   1883-1905
             Obituary: Willis F. Denny, A.A.I.A.

         American institute of architects-Quarterly
         October 1906   bulletin v.6: 174

Dentz, J.G.
     A governor's house in a state capital.
Competition of the Society of Beaux-Arts
architects, 1902. Medal - J.G. Dentz

         Archl.review
         9, n.s.4: pl.32-34
         June 1902

Denver (Col) Architectural Sketch Club

         Inland Architect
         21: 39
         Apr, 1893

Deno (Norman) house, Highland Park, Ill.

see

Highland Park (Ill.) Deno (Norman) house

Denver (Co.) Agnes Memorial Sanatorium
     Gove and Walsh, Archts.

         Inland Architect
         45: 8 + pl. fol.
         Feb, 1905

Denver (Co) Architectural Sketch
     club competition
Harry Thomas - 1st prize for sketch
         of House

         Inland Arch 24,
         No. 2: pl. fol. p. 20
         Sept. 1894

710.5
C855   Dens
             Down to the land in ships. A ship room
in the residence of Robert D. Huntington at
Mill Neck, L.I.

         Country life (U.S.) 62: 40
         October 1932

Denver (Colo.) Apartment building
     Sketch of apartment building perspective view,
Denver, Colo. N.B. Wheelock, archt.
R.B. Hotchkin, del.

         Building budget 3:pl.fol.p.110
         September 30, 1887

Denver (CO)   Architectural Sketch Club
Competition. Suburban Railroad Station. Sketch
by Harry Thomas, Jr.

         Inland Arch. 21:
         pl. fol. p 18
         F, 1893

Denver (CO) · Architectural Sketch Club Competition. Suburban Railroad Station. Sketch by T. A. Green, Jr. Inland Arch. 21: pl. fol. p 18 F, 1893	Denver (CO) Bell (Dr.) Residence Varian & Sterner, Archs. Inland Arch. 19: pl. fol. p 66 Je., 1892	Denver (Colo.) Campion(John F.) house Residence of John F. Campion, Denver, Colo. Gove and Walsh, archts. Inl archt 34:pl.fol.p.40 D 1899
Denver (CO) Architectural Sketch Club Competition. Suburban Railroad Station. Sketch by W. Pell Pulis. Inland Arch. 21: pl. fol. p 18 F, 1893	Denver (CO) Broadway Etching by Lester E. Varian. West. Arch. 30: 33 April 1921	Denver, Colo. Cathedral H.S. and Convent Cathedral High School and convent, Denver, Colo. H.J. Manning, architect Western architect 32:pl.10-14 May, 1923
Denver (CO) Architectural Sketch Club Competition. A Village Church in the 13th Century, English Gothic style. Design by Harvey Pridham Inland Arch. 21: pl. fol. p 66 Je., 1893	710.5 H84 Denver (Colo.) Bromfield (A.S.) house Rocky Mountain home, Denver, Colorado of Mr. and Mrs. Alfred S. Bromfield, Jr. Burnham Hoyt, archt. House and garden 74: 56-57 D '38 sec 2	Denver (CO) Cathedral of Immaculate Conception Gove & Walsh, Arch. Plan. West. Arch. 12: pls.fol.p. 52 Oct. 1908
Denver. Architecture see also Brickwork, U.S. Col., Denver	Denver (CO) Brooks (Charlotte) Residence. W.E. & A.A. Fisher, Archs. Plans. West. Arch. 16: 84 August 1910	Denver. Cathedral of St. John in the Wilderness Swartwout, Egerton Cathedral of St. John, Denver, Colorado Tracy, Swartwout, and Litchfield, archts. Plan. A New York architect 2:315-316,366-367 December, 1908
720.5 W 52 Denver (Col.) Architecture Fisher, A. A. The architecture of Denver and vicinity West. Arch. 30:31-6 & pl Ap '21 :47-8 May, 1921	710.5 H54 Denver (Col.) Brownfield (A.J.) Jr. house Rocky Mountain home of Mr. and Mrs. Alfred J. Brownfield, Jr. Burnham Hoyt, archt. A House and garden 74: 56-57 December 1938 section 1	Denver, Col. Cathedral of St. John in the wilderness Cathedral of St. John. Western Arch. 30:pl.11 Apr. 1921.
711 C58 Denver. Architecture Civic center, Denver. Business center, Denver. Major street plan, city and county, Denver. City planning 4: front.,185-188 July 1928	Denver (Co.) Bulkley (F.G.) Residence Gove and Walsh, Archts. Inland Archt. vol. 29, No.3,pl.fol.p. 30 Apr, 1897	720.5 A67 Denver (Colo) Cathedral of St. John in the Wilderness. Competition. Accepted design...Tracy and Swartwout, archts. Competitive designs...Cram, Goodhue and Ferguson, archts. Plans. Arch rev 12: 287-289 O '05
720.5 W52 Denver. Architecture Residence of Dr. J.J. Waring, Denver, Col. J. B. Benedict, archt. Residence of Mrs. R.C. Campbell; J.B. Benedict, archt. Residence of John Evans; J.B. Benedict, archi Other residences of Denver designed by J. B. Benedict. Western archt. 37: pls. 1-18 January 1928	Denver (CO) Busby (F.E.) House A.M. Stuckert, Arch. Inland Arch. 20: pl. fol. p 30 O, 1892	720.5 I56 Denver (Col.) Chamberlin (A.W.) house Residence for A.W.Chamberlin, Denver, Colorado. Kidder and Humphreys, archts. No plan. A Inland architect 14:10,pl.fol.p.13 August 1889

Denver, Col. Chamberlin (A.W.) house
Residence of A.W. Chamberlin, Denver, Colo.
(plan) Kidder and Humphreys, archts.

Inland architect
v. 16 no. 7
pls. fol. p. 82
D 1890

720.5 M59c
Denver. City and County building
Municipal building metalized: City and
County building, Denver, Colorado. Roland
Linder, archt.

Metalcraft 8: 227-230,239
June 1932

Denver (Col.) club house
Denver Club House, Denver, Col. [plan]
Varian & Sterner, archts.

Inland architect
v. 12 no. 9: 78-79, 93-94
pls. at end of vol.
Ja 1889

Denver (Col.) Cheesman Memorial
Marean + Norton, archts.

West. Archt.
30: pl. 2
Apr, 1921

Denver, Col. Civic Center
R., C. M.
Opening the Center of Denver

Arch rec 19: 365-7
My '06

Denver (Col.) College of Divine Science. Auditorium
Auditorium of College of Divine Science,
Denver, Colo.
J.B. Benedict, architect

Arch. record 53:13-14
Jan., 1923

Denver, col. Cheesman Memorial
Cheesman memorial, Marean and Norton, architects

Architectural record 53:233
March, 1923

720.6 A51j
Denver (Col.) Civic center
Read, Henry
Civic planning work in Denver

A.I.A. jour. 3:497-500
N '15

Denver (Col.) Colonnade of civic benefactors
see

Denver (Col.) Civic center. Colonnade of civic
benefactors and open air theater

720.5 A67f
Denver. Children's hospital
Children's hospital, Denver, Colorado. Burnham Hoyt, archt. Plan

A

Architectural forum 65: 354-355
October 1936

720.6 A51j
Denver (Col.) Civic center
Lubschez, B. J.
The Denver Civic Center. E. H. Bennett,
archt.

A.I.A. 5:178-9
Ap '17

Denver (Col.) Colorado National Bank
Colorado National Bank of Denver

Arch. and Bldg. 48:6-7
Jan. 1916

Denver (Col.) Chrysler Garage
Chrysler Garage, Denver, Colo. J.B. Benedict,
archt. Plan.

Western architect 39: pl.144
September, 1930

720.5 A67r
Denver, (Colo.) Civic center
Fisher, T.M.
The Denver civic center. archt. E.H. Bennett, Plans.

Arch rec 53: 189-201
Mr '23

720.5 A67a
Denver. Colorado national bank
Colorado national bank, Denver, Colo.
W.E. and A. A. Fisher, archts. Plans.

A

Architecture 36: pl. 167-172
October 1917

Denver, Colo., Church (William) Residence
with floor plan. Lang and
Pugh, archts.

Inland Archt.
vol.26, no. 2,pl.fol.p. 20
Sept, 1895

Denver (Col.) Civic Center
Colonnade of Civic Benefactors and Open
Air Theater. Marean and Norton, Archts.

West. Archt.
30: pl. 2
Apr. 1921

Denver (Col.) Colorado National Bank
Colorado National Bank.

Western Arch. 30:pl.5.
Apr. 1921.

720.52 A67
Denver. City and county building
City and county building of Denver; by the
Allied Architects' Association.

Architects' journal 68: 233-235
August 15, 1928

720.5 A67r
Denver (Col.) Civic Center. Colonnade
of civic benefactors and open air theater.
Open air Theater. Denver civic
centre, Denver, Colo. Marean and Norton,
archts.

Arch. rec. 53:190,193-4,
197,199-200 Mr'23

Denver (Col.) Cooper building
Cooper building, Denver, Colorado.
F. E. Edbrooke & Co., archts.

Ornamental iron 2:51-52, 58-59
N 1894

720.5
A51
Denver (Col.) Cranmer (G.E.) house
House of G.E.Cranmer,Denver,Colorado. J.B.
Benedict,archt. Plans.

American architect 118: 690,pls.fol.p.
November 24,1920   690

A

720.5
W52
Denver (Col.) Essex apts.
Essex apts. Fisher bros., archts.

West archt 25: pl. 1
D 1919

Denver (Co.) First Ave. Presbyterian Church
with floor plan. William Cowe, Archt.

Inland Archt.
vol.29,No.6,pl.fol.p. 60
Jul, 1897

Denver (Col.) Cranmer (G.E.) House
J. B. Benedict, archt. Plan.

West. Archt.
30: pl. 7-8
May, 1921

---

ffo
720.6
C55
Denver (Col.) Evans (John) house
Residence of John Evans, Esq., Denver,
Colo.; W.E. and A.A. Fisher, archts.;
no plan.

A   Chicago architectural club 27:18
1914

Denver (CO)
First Church of Christ Scientist
Varian & Sterner, Arch.

Inland Archt.
41: pls. fol.p. 28
April 1903

Denver (Colo.) Custom house
United States custom house, Denver, Colo.
Office of Supervising Architect, archts.

Federal architect 2:2
October, 1931

Denver (Col.) Evans (John) House
William E. Fisher and Arthur A. Fisher,
Archts. Plan.

West. Archt.
30: 47, pl. 1-3
May, 1921

720.5
B93b
Denver. First Swedish Baptist Church
First Swedish baptist church, Denver,Colo.
S. Linderoth, archt.

A   Building budget 6: pl.fol.p.34
March 21, 1890

Denver (Col.) Daniels and Fisher Stores Co.
Sterner and Williamson, archts.

West. Archt.
30: 32
Apr, 1921

710.5
C855
Denver (Col.) Evans (John) house
Residence of John Evans at Denver, Colo.
William Fisher & Arthur Fisher, archts.

Country life (U.S.) 50: 66-7
October 1926

720.5
A51
Denver (Colo.) Flower (J.S.) house
House for J.S. Flower...Wm. Cowe, archt.

Amer archt and bldg news
55: pl fol 88
S 12, 1896

Denver (Col.) Denver Gas and Electric Bldg.
F.E. Edbrooke, Archt.

West. Archt.
18: pls.fol.p. 73
Jun, 1912

Denver (Col.) Federal Building
Tracy, Swartwout and Litchfield, archts.

West. Archt.
30: 34
Apr, 1921

Denver (Col.) Foster Bldg.
W. E. and A.A. Fisher, archts.

West. Archt.
17: pls.fol.p. 76
Aug, 1911

720.5
B52
Denver (Col.) El Tovar apts.
El Tovar apartments. Fisher bros., archts.

West archt 25: pl 3-4
D 1919

Denver. Federal Reserve Bank of Kansas City
Denver Colo. Branch, Federal Reserve Bank of
Kansas City. 1925. Graham, Anderson, Probst and
White, archts. No plan

Graham, Ernest R. Architectural work
of Graham, Anderson, Probst and White.
2 vols. London: B.T. Batsford, 1933.
v.2:228

Denver (Col.) (near) 4-L Ranch
A log cabin homestead, the 4-L ranch near
Denver, Colorado. J.B. Benedict, archt. Plan.

Country life (U.S.) 58:41-44
August, 1930

Denver, Colo., Equitable Bldg
Showing Entrance Detail, and interior
views of main corridor, Law Library,
main Stairway and elevators. Andrews,
Jaques and Rantoul, archts.

Inland archt
vol.26, no.5 pl.fol.p. 54
Dec, 1895

Denver (Col.) Fifteenth Street
Etchings by Lester E. Varian.

West. Archt.
30: 32-3
Apr, 1921

720.5
A67a
Denver (Col.) Gano (George) house
House of Geo. Gano, Denver, Col. W.E.
Fisher & A.A. Fisher, archts.

Architecture 55: 343-4
June 1927

Denver (Co.) Gilbert (E.A.) Residence Varian and Sterner. Inland Archt. vol.29,No.3,pl.fol.p. 30 Apr, 1897	Denver (Col.) High St. (360) House J.B. Benedict, archt. West. Arch. 32: pl. 11-12 Feb, 1923	Denver (Col.) Hughes (L.M.) Residence William E. Fisher and Arthur L. Fisher, archts. plans. West. Archt. 28: pl. 6 Dec, 1919
Denver (Col.) Gano (Merritt W. Jr.) Residence M.H. Hoyt Archt. West. Archt. 30: pl. 14-15 Jul, 1921	Denver (Co.) Hobson (Henry W.) Residence and Stable Varian and Sterner, Archts. Inland Archt. vol.29,No.3,pl.fol.p. 30 Apr, 1897	Denver (Col.) International Trust Co. Bldg. W.E. and A.A. Fisher, archts. West. Archt. 30: pl. 5 Apr, 1921
Denver (CO) Grant Residence David Boal, Arch. Inland Arch. 41: pls.fol.p. 28 April 1903	Denver (CO) Hollister House Hollister residence, Denver, (CO) Wm. S. Fisher and Arthur A. Fisher, Archs. Plans. West. Arch. 15: pl.fol.p. 56 May 1910	Denver (Colo.) J.C. Penney Co. Old and new are skillfully combined in Penney's. Raymond Harry Ervin, archt. Northwest archt. 16.no. 5:20,22 S-O 1952
Denver (Co.) Gross Apartment Building Gove and Walsh, archts. Incl. plans. Inland Architect 46: pl.fol.p. 60 Dec, 1905	Denver (Col.) Rosa Lodge J.B. Benedict, archt. Built for City of Denver in Denver Mountain Parks. Plan. West. Archt. 32: pl. 1-2 Feb, 1923	720.5 A67a Denver (Col.) Johnson (J.) house House of J. Johnson, Denver, Colorado. W. E. Fisher and A. A. Fisher, archts. [plan] Arch 52:461-465 D '25
720.5 W52 Denver (Col.) Hannington (Robert, house Residence of Robert Hannington,Denver, Colorado. Gove and Walsh,archts. Western architect 14: pl.fol.p.26 September 1909	Denver (CO) House (Geo.)Residence W.E. & A.A. Fisher, Archs. Plans. West. Arch. 16: 86-7 Aug. 1910	Denver (CO) Kistler (W.H.) Stationery Co. H.W.J. Edbrooke, Arch. West. Arch. 30: 32 April 1921
Denver (Col.) Hendrie (E.B.) Residence Biscoe and Hewett, archts. West. Archt. 30: pl. 4 May, 1921	Denver, Colo., Houses Wm. Cove, Sketcher House at Race St. House at 13 Ave. Inland Archt. Vol. 24, No. 5, pl. Fol. p. 52 Dec. 1894	Denver (Col.) Kountze (Harold) Residence Wm. E. Fisher and Arthur L. Fisher, archts. Plan. West. Archt. 28: pl. 5 Dec, 1919
Denver (Co) High School (New) D.W.Dryden, Archt. Inland Archt. 46: pl.fol.p. 12 Aug, 1905	Denver (Col.) Howard (J.H.) Residence Maurice Biscoe, archt. West. Archt. 30: pl. 11 May, 1921	Denver (CO) McMurtrie Building. F.E. Edbrooke & Co., Archts. Inland Arch. 28: pl. fol. p 30 O, 1896

Denver (Col.) (near) Mayo (Mrs. Paul T.) Mountain
Lodge
(Bear Creek Canyon).
J.B. Benedict, archt. Plan.

West. Archt.
32: pl. 3-5
Feb, 1923

Denver (Col.) Municipal Center
Opening the Center of Denver. Plan of the
center of Denver.

Architectural record 19:365-368
May, 1906

710.5
H84   Denver (Col.) Owen (W.R.) house
A Cornish manor house in Colorado. Home
of W.R. Owen. M.& B. Hoyt, archts.

House and garden 53: 68-9
January 1928

Denver, Colo. Mile high center
Mile High Center in Denver, Colorado
[plans & details] Ieoh Ming Pei & Assocs.,
archts.

Arch & Wohnform
67:16-21 Jan 1959

Denver (Col.) Municipal Center
Civic Center, Denver, Colorado. Arnold Brunner,
archt. Frederick Law Olmstead, landscape archt.

Architectural league of N.Y. 29: 40
1914

Denver (CO) Park Pavilion
W.E. Fisher, Arch.

Inland Arch.
37: No.5: pl.fol.p. 40
June 1901

Denver (CO) Millett, Esq. (Nelson) House
A. Morris Stuckert, Arch.

Inland Arch. 19:
pl. fol. p 78
Jl., 1892

Denver (Col.) National Jewish Hospital for
Consumptives.
National Jewish hospital for Consumptives,
Denver, Col. W.E. and A.A. Fisher, archts.

Architect (N.Y.) 9: 631-3
February, 1928

Denver, (CO)
Patars (E.A.) Residence
Wm. Ellsworth Fisher § Bros. Arch.

West. Arch.
13: pl.13-14
Apr. 1909

Denver, Co. Morey (C.S.) Mercantile Co. Bldg.
Gove and Walsh, Archts.

Inland Archt.
vol.29,No.1,pl.fol.p. 10
Feb, 1897

Denver (Col.) National Safety Vault Co.
W.E. and A.A. Fisher, archts.

West. Arch.
30: 31
Apr, 1921

Denver (Col.) (near) Phelan (Agnes B.) Mountain Cabin
J.B. Benedict, archt. Plan

West. Arch.
32: pl. 6-8
Feb, 1923

Denver (Co.) Morey (C.S.) Residence
Gove and Walsh, Archts.

Inland Archt.
vol.29,No.1,pl.fol.p. 10
Feb, 1897

Denver, Colo. Olmsted, C.H., house.
Sketch. George W. Maher, architect.

Building budget
5: pl. fol. p.6
January 31, 1889

710.5
C855   Denver (Col.) Phipps (L.C.) house
The L.C.Phipps' estate in Denver,Colorado.
William E. and Arthur A. Fisher, archts.

Country life (U.S.) 70:24-29
May 1936

A

Denver (Co.) Mount St.Vincent's Orphanage
Gove and Walsh, archts.

Inland Architect
45: pl.fol.p. 8
Feb, 1905

Denver (Col.) open air theater

see

Denver (Col.) civic center. Colonnade of civic
benefactors and open air theater

Denver, Col. Pioneer monument (1911)
MacMonnies Pioneer memorial much criticized.
[illus.]
MacMonnies explains Pioneer fountain design.

Monumental news
19: 434, 500
Jl, Ag 1907

Denver (Col.) Mountain State's Telephone and
Telegraph Company
Denver's tallest building. The Mountain
States telephone and telegraph company's new home.

Through the ages 8:37-42
July, 1930

705.1
A79   Denver (Col.)(near)Owen (W.R.) estate
A Cornwall manor house in Colorado, not
England. Estate of W.R.Owen near Denver.
Archt.not given.

Arts and decoration 30: 77,114
November 1928

Denver. Colo. Pioneer monument (1911)
Denver's pioneer monument. [illus.]
F. MacMonnies, sculptor

Monumental news
27: 101
F 1915

Denver (Col.) Plan
   Carhart, A.H.
Denver makes a plan.

City planning 6:front;73-85
April, 1930

720.5
A67a
Denver (Col.) Post Office and Courthouse
   Post office and courthouse. Tracy,
Swartwout & Litchfield, architects. Plans.

Architectural record 54:361-375
O '23

Denver, Col. Public Library, Branches
   Reese, Rena
Denver's branch library system. Illustrations
Plans.

Architecture 51:41-48
February, 1925

Denver (Col.) Planning
   Civic Center, Denver.
Business Center, Denver.
   Major street plan, city and county, Denver.

City planning 4:front., 183-188
July, 1928

720.5
A67a
Denver (Colo.) Post office and court house.
   Competition
Competition for U.S. Post office & court
house, Denver, Col. Plan. Tracy, Swart-
wout and Litchfield, archts.

Architecture 19: 65-6, pls.
XXXVIII-XLVI fol 80
My '09

Denver (Col.) Public Library, Dickinson Branch
   Maurice B. Biscoe, Archt.

West. Archt.
20: pls.fol.p. 57
May, 1914

Denver (Col.) Porter (W.H.) Residence
   Varian and Varian, archts. Plan.

West. Archt.
30: pl. 12
May, 1921

Denver (Col.) Presbyterian Hospital
   WE. and AA.Fisher, archts. Sketches.

West. Archt.
30: pl. 12
Apr, 1921

Denver (Col) Public library. Henry White
Warren branch
   Warren branch, Denver, Colo.

West arch 20: pl.fol.16
F'14

Denver (Col.) Post Office and Courthouse
   U.S. Post Office and Court House, Denver, Colo.
Tracy, Swartwout and Litchfield, archts.

A   Architectural record 29: 337
April, 1911

Denver (Colo) Public library
   Denver public library. Ackerman and
Ross, archts. No plan.

Nat. arch 4; pl 49,
N'14

Henry White
Denver (Colo) Public library. Warren Branch
   William E. Fisher and Arthur A. Fisher
Archts.

Amer. arch. 107 pl.fol. 32
Ja 13, '15

Denver (Col.) Post Office and Court house

Arch. and building 48:69-72
April, 1916

Denver (Colo) Public LIbrary
   Public Library, Denver, Colorado.
Ackerman and Ross, archts., No plan.

West archt. 30: pl. 3
Ap '21

Denver (Colo) Public library. Henry White
Warren branch library.
   Henry White Warren branch library,
Denver, Colorado. W.E. and A.A. Fisher,
archts.

West arch 30; pl 9
Ap'21

Denver (Col.) Post Office and Courthouse
   New Post Office and Court house, Denver

Architecture 34:236, 247-248,pl.164-
Nov. 1916   175.

Denver (Colo) Public library, Branch
   Branch library, Denver, Colorado. Varian
and Varian, archts.

West arch 30;   pl. 9
ap '21

Denver (Col.) Public library. Highland park
branch
   see
Denver (Col.) Public library. Woodbury branch

720.52
A67
Denver (Col.) Post office & court house
   United States post office and court
house, Denver, Colorado. Tracy, Swartwout,
and Litchfield, archts.

Arch & bldrs. jour 44:pl. for
p. 271-2
D 15, '16

Denver (Col) Public Library, Branch at 34th
and High Street
   Wm. E. and Arthur A. Fisher, Archts.

West. Archt.
20: pls.fol.p. 57
May, 1914

Denver (Colo) Public library. Park hill
branch
   Park hill branch library, Denver, Colo.
M.H. Hoyt. archt.

West arch 30; pl 7-8
Ap'21

Denver (Colo) Public library. Sarah Platt Decker branch. Sarah Platt Decker library, Denver, Colo. Kareen and Norton. archts. Plan. Nat. arch. 4: pls 55-4 N° 14	Denver (CO) Residence Varian & Sterner, Archs. Inland Arch. 20: pl. fol. p 20 S, 1892	Denver (CO) Residence Thomas, Drydon & Thomas, Arch. Inland Arch. 40: pl.fol.p. 16 Sept. 1902
Denver, Col. Public library. Warren branch Warren branch library. W.E. Fisher, archt [plan] Amer arch 107: pl 2038 Ja 13, 1915	Denver (CO) Residence. Sketch by McCurdy & Pulis, Archs. Inland Arch. 21: pl. fol. p 78 Jl., 1893	Denver (CO) Residence F.J. Sterner, Arch. Inland Arch. 40: pl.fol.p. 24 Oct. 1902
Denver (Col.) Public Library. William H. Smiley Branch. William H. Smiley branch public library, Denver. Mountjoy, French and Frewen, architects. Western arch. 29:pl.5-6. May, 1920	Denver, Colo., Residence Inland Archt. Vol. 24, No. 6, pl. Fol. p. 64 Jan. 1895	Denver (CO) Residence F.J. Sterner, Arch. Inland Arch. 42: pls. fol.p. 40 Dec. 1903
Denver (Col.) Public Library, Woodbury Branch J. B. Benedict, Archt. West. Archt. 20: pls.fol.p. 23 Feb, 1914	Denver (CO) Residence W.E. Fisher, Arch. Inland Arch. 37, No.6:pl.fol.p. 48 July 1901	Denver (CO) Residence Gove & Walsh, Arch. Inland Arch. 43: pls.fol.p. 48 July 1904
Denver (Col.) Public Library. Woodbury Branch Highland Park Branch, Denver, Colorado. J.Benedict, archt. Plans. American architect 105:2 pls.fol.p.120 March 18, 1914	Denver (CO) Residence Varian & Sterner, Arch. Inland Arch. 38: pl.fol.p.8 Aug. 1901	Denver (CO) Residence W.E. & A.E. Fisher, Archs. Plans. West. Arch. 16: pl.fol.p. 100 Sept. 1910
Denver (Col.) Public library, Woodbury branch Highland Park branch, Denver public library. J.B.Benedict, archt. Plan. Nat. Arch. 4: pls. 56, 60. N° 14	Denver (CO) Residence W.E. Fisher, Arch. Inland Arch. 38: pl.fol.p.8 Aug. 1901	Denver (Col.) Residence Marean and Norton, archts. plan West. Archt. 17: pls.fol.p. XVII May, 1911
Denver (Colo) Public library. Woodbury branch. Highland Park branch, Denver public library, Denver, Colorado. J.B.Benedict, archt. West. archt. 30: pl. 7-8 Ap' 21	Denver (CO) Residence Inland Arch. 39: pl. fol. pg. 52 July 1902	Denver (Col.) Residence W.E. and A.A. Fisher, archts. plans West. Arch. 17: 68 Jul, 1911

Denver (Col.) St. Thomas Aquinas Seminary
Benedict, J.B.
The symbolism used in the architecture of St.Thomas
Aquinas Seminary, Denver, Colorado. J.B. Benedict,
archt.

Western architect 37: pl.199-201,
December, 1928   P.259-262

Denver, Colo., Stratton (C.E.) House

William Cowe, Archt.

Inland Arch.
Vol. 25, No. 2, pl.
Fol. p. 23
Mar. 1895

Denver (Colo.) Union Station
Union Station, Denver, Col. Gove and Walsh,
archts.

Western architect 30:pl.4
April, 1921

720.5
A67f   Denver.Security building
Security building, Denver. W.E. and
A.A. Fisher, archts. View and plans.

A   Architectural forum 49:49-51
July 1928

Denver (CO) Symes (G.G.) Residence
F.Louis Harnois, Arch. Plan.

West. Arch.
16: pl.fol.p. 100
Sept. 1910

Denver, Colo., U.S. Mint
Wm. Martin Aiken, Archt.

Inland Arch.
vol.31,No.3, pl.fol.p. 30
Apr, 1898

Denver (Col.) Sewer Pipe and Clay Co.
Denver Sewer Pipe and Clay Co. building.
M. H. and B. Hoyt, archts.

Architectural record 66:153-155
August, 1929

Denver, Col. Thatcher memorial fountain (1918)
Denver unveils fine memorial fountain.
[illus.] Lorado Taft, sculptor.

Monumental news
30: 487
N 1918

Denver (CO) U.S. Mint
James A. Wetmore, Sup. Arch.
(Errata: Tracy, Swartwout & Litchfield misidentified
as architects in April issue).

West. Arch.
30: 35,Apr. 1921
correction: 64, June 1921

720.5
W52   Denver (Col.) Snyder (I.T.) house
Residence of Mrs. Irving T. Snyder,
Denver, Colorado. J.B. Benedict, archt.

West. archt. 30: pl. 15
N '21

Denver, Colo. Thatcher memorial fountain (1918)
Progress in recent memorials; Denver's
Thatcher memorial. [illus.] Lorado Taft,
sculptor.

Monumental news
31: 19-21
Ja 1919

720.5
A67f   Denver(Colo)U.S.national bank building
U.S. national bank building, Denver.
Plans. W.E. and A.A. Fisher, archts.

A   Architectural forum 41:140
September 1924

720.5
W52   Denver (Col.) Sorrento apts.
Sorrento apts. Fisher bros. archts.

West archt 25: pl 2
D 1919

Denver (Col.) Thatcher Memorial Fountain (1918)
Lorado Taft, Sculptor
Detail of Loyalty Group.

West. Arch.
33: pl. 2
Apr, 1924

Denver (Co.) University Club
Varian and Sterner, Archts.

Inland Arch.
vol.29,No. 3,pl.fol.p. 30
Apr, 1897

Denver (Col) State Capitol
View of State Capitol Building from the Colonnade
of Civic Benefactors, Civic Centre.

West. Arch.
30: pl. 1
Apr, 1921

720.5
B84   Denver (Colo.) Trinity Memorial church
Trinity Memorial church, Denver,Colorado.
Cram, Goodhue and Ferguson, archts.

Brickbuilder 18: pls.131-132
October 1909

Denver, Colo., University Club Bldg .

Wm. Cowe, archt.

Inland arch.
vol.26, no.2,pl.fol.p. 20
Sept, 1895

Denver (Col.) State Office bldg.
State office building, Denver, Colo.
William M. Bowman Co., architects.

Architectural record 53:228-9
March, 1923

Denver (Col.) Turner (D.B.) Residence
J.B. Benedict, archt.

West. Archt.
30: pls. 5-6
May, 1921

Denver (Col.) Vail (Mrs. J.F.) Residence
J.B. Benedict, archt. plan.

West. Archt.
30: pl. 14
May, 1921

Denver (Col.) Voorhies Memorial WE. and AA. Fisher, archts. Sketch West. Archt. 30: 33 Apr, 1921	Denzinger, Josef Autoreparaturwerkstätte für die amerikani- schen Streitkräfte in Kornwestheim [plans and sections] Baumeister 53: 236-237 (Tafeln 30-31 at end of issue) Ap 1956	720.52 A67c Department stores The Grinnell prize award for shop prem- ises for a departmental store. Architect (Lond.) 119: 104 January 13, 1928
Denver (Col.) (near) Waring (James J.) Mountain Lodge J.B. Benedict, archt. Plan. West. Archt. 32: pl. 9-10 Feb, 1923	Déols, Fr. Abbaye Hubert, Hean L'Abbaye de Déols et les constructions monastiques de la fin de l'époque Carolingienne [plans] Cahiers archéologiques 9:155-64 1957	Department Stores New department store design [sect] Nat'l arch 3:6-7 S '47
Denver (Col.) Warren Branch Library Wm. E. and Arthur A. Fisher, Archts. West. Archt. 20: p. 17 and pl.fol.p. 23 Feb, 1914	Department stores see also names of individual stores,i.e.: New York (city) Saks fifth ave. Berlin, Ger. Warenhaus Karstadt Paris, Fr. Bon marché etc.	Department Stores The planning of department stores. Builder 118:326-8. Mar. 19, 1920
Denver (CO) Whitney (Dr.) House. 16th & Downing Ave., Sketch by W. Cowe Inland Arch. 22: pl. fol. p 32 O, 1893	Department stores Zietzschmann, Ernst Bauten des verkaufs: das warenhaus [plans] Bauen & Wohnen no. 4 p. 238-240 1954	720.6 B88 Department stores Shop premises for a department store, by Alfred Geeson. Prize winning design in R.I.B.A. competition. R.I.B.A. 35: 175 January 28, 1928
Denver (Col.) Wood (Guilford) Residence Biscoe and Hewett, archts. West. Archt. 30: 48 May, 1921	720.6 B38 Department stores Beaux-arts institute of design: "A de- partment store". Awards. B.A.I.D. 5: 6-12 January 1929	720.5 A51 Department stores, Canada. Toronto Building for T. Eaton Company, Ltd., Toronto, Canada. Ross and Macdonald,archts. American architect 135: 139 January 20, 1929
Denver (Col.) (near) Wyldemere Farm J.B. Benedict, archt. West. Archt. 32: pl. 13 Feb, 1923	720.5 W52 Department stores Department store project. Pierre A. Bezy, University of Illinois. Western architect 38: pl.64 April 1929	Department Stores, England Dickins and Jones new premises. Henry Tanner, architect Academy architecture: 33-47 1922
Denver (Col.) Y.M.C.A. Marean and Norton, Archt. West Archt. 20: pls.fol.p. 23 Feb, 1914	Department Stores Bennett, F. E. The departmental store. Builder 135:630-631;672-3;712-13 Oct. 19,26; Nov. 2, 1928	720.52 A67 Department stores. England New premises for Harvey Nichols & Co,Ltd. An example of rapid rebuilding. Williams & Cox, architects Architects journal 58:148-150 July 25, 1923

720.52 A67e — Department stores, England New premises for John Barker & Co., Ltd. Sir Reginald Blomfield, archt. Architect 116: 621-5 & pls. November 26, 1926	720.52 A67 — Department stores. England. London Messrs. Selfridge's New Extension Graham, Anderson, Probst, & White, and Sir John Burnet & partners, associate archts. Architects' Jour. 62: 863-66 Dec. 9, 1925	Department Stores, England, London Selfridge and Co., Ltd., London, England. 1909-1928. D.H. Burnham and Co., Graham, Burnham and Co., Graham, Anderson, Probst and White, archts. Plan. Graham, Ernest R. Architectural work of Graham, Anderson, Probst and White. 2 vols. London: B.T. Batsford, 1933. v.1: 149-152
720.52 A67 — Department stores, England. Kingston-upon-Thames Bentall's, Kingston-upon-Thames. Sir Aston Webb & Son, archts. Architects' journal 77: 178-179, supp. February 1, 1933	720.52 A67 — Department stores, England. London A modern London store. Designed by Wimperis, Simpson, and Guthrie. Architects' journal 69: 383-388 March 6, 1929	720.52 A67 — Department stores, England. London Selfridge's new extension. Graham, Anderson, Probst and White, and Sir John Burnet and partners, archts. Plans. Architects' journal 57: 84-87 January 3, 1925
720.52 B93 — Department stores, England. Lewisham "Tower House," Lewisham. New store for the Royal Arsenal Cooperative Society, S.W. Ackroyd & J.O'H. Hughes, archts. Plan. Builder 145: 778, 789-790 November 17, 1933	720.52 A67c — Department stores, England. London New entrance hall for Messrs. Selfridge & Co. Sir John Burnet & Partners and Graham, Anderson, Probst & White, assoc. archts. Architect and contract reporter 117: 25 January 7, 1927	720.5 N56 — Department stores, England. London Store of Selfridge and Co., Ltd., London, England. Archt. not given. New York architect 4:63 August 1910
Department stores, England. London see also London (Eng.) River plate house	720.52 B93 — Department stores, England. London New store building for Messrs. John Barker & Co., Ltd., High-street, Kensington. H. L. Cabuche, archt. to the company. Builder 131: 903-4, 911 December 3, 1926	Department stores. France. Paris Insolera, Italo I grandi magazzini di Parigi [plans & sections] Casabella #224:43-53 F 1959
720.52 A67c — Department stores, England. London Derry and Toms' store, Kensington. Bernard George, archt. Plan. Architect (Lond.) 134: 38-43 April 14, 1933	720.52 A67c — Department stores, England. London Proposed central entrance, Messrs. Selfridge & Co's. premises, Oxford street. Sir J. J. Burnet & Partners, archts. Graham, Anderson, Probst, & White, associated archts. (Ink drawing) Architect 115: pl.fol. p. 442 May 7-21, 1926	720.5 B84 — Department stores, Germany Mowel, W.L. The architecture of the German department stores. [plans] Brickbuilder 23: 205-210 S '14
720.52 A67 — Department stores, England. London The limited competition for Daniel Neal's new store. E. Berry Webber, archt. Architects' Journal 71: 714-720 May 7, 1930	720.52 B93 — Department stores, England. London Remodelling of the Wallis store, Holborn Circus. Builder 135: 553-555 October 5, 1928	Department stores. Germany Neubauten der Kaufhof AG in Köln [plans] Wunderlich, archt. Baumeister 56:11-15 Jan 1959 Tafel 5-6
720.52 B93 — Department stores, England. London Messrs. Selfridge's new extension, Graham, Anderson, Probst & White, and Sir John Burnet, A.R.A. & Partners, arch. Builder 124:812 May 18, 1923	720.52 A67 — Department stores, England. London The roof gardens at Selfridge's. Designed by Allen and Sudell, archts. Architects' journal 77: 469 April 5, 1933	720.53 N68 — Department stores, Germany Three department stores for Schocken in Nuremberg, Stuttgart. Moderne bauformen 29: 461-484 November 1930

720.55 W51 — Department stores,Germany. Breslau / Zwei neubauten von Hermann Dernburg. (Two new buildings by Hermann Dernburg.) Wertlein department store in Breslau. Plan. / Wasmuths monatshefte 14: 315-320 / July 1930 / A	Department Stores, Netherlands. The Hague / Robertson, Howard and Yerbury, F.R. A / Modern Dutch department stores; P. Kramer, archt. / Architect (Lond.) 119: 227-231 / February 10, 1928	**721.97 A67c** — Department stores, U.S. (Ariz.) Bisbee / Lescher, R.W. / Store for Phelps Dodge, Bisbee, Arizona. Designed by Lescher and Mahoney, archts. / A Architectural concrete 7: 6-7 / No. 3 [1941]
720.55 W51 — Department stores,Germany. Chemnitz / Hegemann,Werner; DuVinage,Charles / Erich Mendelsohn's kaufhaus Schocken-Chemnits (Erich Mendelsohn's department store, Schocken-Chemnitz.) Plans. / Wasmuths monatshefte 14: 345-356 / August 1930 / A	**720.5 A67f** — Department stores,Remodeled / Department store in a remodeled hotel building.J.Black and Sons,Birmingham,Alabama. Warren,Knight and Davis,archts.Plans / A Architectural forum 65: 310 / October 1936	**720.5 A67c** — Department stores,U.S.(Calif.) Glendale / Carr, O.R. / Four stores for Sears; Glendale, Calif.; Highland Park, Mich.; Baltimore, Md.; and Chicago, Ill. Simons, Carr, and Wright, archts. Section. / A Architectural concrete 4:cover-8 no.2[1938]
720.5 W52 — Department stores, Germany. Chemnitz / The Schocken department store, Chemnitz, Germany. Erich Mendelsohn, archt. / Western architect 40: pl.8 / January 1931 / A	**720.55 B35** — Department stores,Switzerland. Basle / Umbau eines konfektionsgeschäftes in Basel. (Reconstruction of a store in Basle.) Bräuning,Leu and Düring,archts. Plans. / Der Baumeister 31: 310-314 / September 1933	**721 T53** — Department stores, U.S. (Calif.) Los Angeles / The Bullock's Wilshire Store of Los Angeles. John Parkinson and Donald B. Parkinson, archts. / Through the ages 8: 19-24 / June 1930 / A
720.52 A67 — Department stores, Germany. Chemnitz / The Schocken Store, Chemnitz. Erich Mendelsohn, archt. / Architects' journal 76: supp. / October 5, 1932 / A	**720.6 R88** — Department stores, U. S. / Hall, H. A. / Planning of American department stores. Illus. / RIBA jour. 27:237-49 / Ap 10, '20	**720.5 W52** — Department stores. U.S. (Calif.)Los Angeles / Milton G. Cooper dry goods company building, Los Angeles, Cal. Curlett & Beelman, archts. / Western architect 36: pl.159 / September 1927
720.55 W51 — Department stores,Germany. Frankfurt on Main / Umbau eines geschäftschauses in Frankfurt am Main. (Reconstruction of a department store in Frankfurt a.M.) D.Cohn,Jr.,Karl Wilhelm Ochs,archts. Plans. / Wasmuths monatshefte 13: 240-242 / June 1929 / A	**720.6 C53** — Department stores,United States / Proposed store building, Howard Shaw, archt.; no plan. / A Chicago architectural club 13:59 / 1900	**721.97 A67c** — Department stores, U.S. (Calif.) Pasadena / Gardner, A.B. / Broadway store for Pasadena. / A Architectural concrete 7: 12-14 / No. 3 [1941]
Department stores, Germany. Leipzig / Das Warenhaus Theodor Althoff. Leipzig. / Moderne Bauformen 20: 93-6. / May, 1921.	Department stores, U.S. / Revolutionary improvements aid the department store to come. Antonin Raymond and Ladislav L. Rado, archts. / Interiors 106, pt. 2:68-69 / Ja 1947	**720.5 A67f** — Department stores,U.S. (Calif.) San Francisco / Escalator,Emporium department store,San Francisco,Calif. Eleanor Le Maire,designer; John R.Keber,archt. Pittsburgh Glass institute competition. Section drawing. / A Architectural forum 67:139 / August 1937
720.52 A67 — Department stores, Germany. Stuttgart / Staircase in a Stuttgart store; housed in a semicircular window bay feature, constructed of steel and glass. Eisenlohr and Pfennig, archts. / Architects' journal 74: pls. / July 15, 1931	**720.5 A67f** — Department stores,U.S. (Ala) Birmingham / Department store in a remodeled hotel building.J.Black and Sons,Birmingham,Alabama. Warren,Knight and Davis,archts. Plans. / A Architectural forum 65: 310 / October 1936	**721.97 A67c** — Department stores,U.S. (Calif.) Santa Rosa / Concrete for the modern store: Rosenberg's department store, Santa Rosa, Calif. Hertzka and Knowles,archts. No plan. / A Architectural concrete 6:23 / No.4[1940]

720.5
A67d
Department stores,U.S. (Calif.) Westwood
Bullock's Westwood. John and Donald B.
Parkinson,archts.

A   Architectural digest 8: 47
Number 4   [1932-33]

Department Stores, U.S. (Mich.) Detroit
Fyfe store building, Detroit. Smith, Hinchman
and Grills, architects.

Arch. forum 32:pl.90-2.
June, 1920.

Department Stores, U.S., N.Y., New York
The Gimbel store, 32nd to 33rd St. on Sixth Ave.,
New York. D.H. Burnham and Co., archts.

A   Architecture and building 43:71-74
November, 1910

Department Stores, U.S. (IL.) Evanston
Marshall Field and Company, Evanston, IL.
1929.Graham, Anderson, Probst and White, archts.

Graham, Ernest R. Architectural work
of Graham, Anderson, Probst and White.
2 vols. London: B.T. Batsford, 1933.
v.1:130-132

720.5
A67c
Department stores,U.S.. (Mich.) Highland Park
Carr, G.W.
Four stores for Sears: Glendale, Calif.;
Highland Park, Mich.; Baltimore, Md.; and
Chicago, Ill. Nimmons, Carr, and Wright, archts.
Section.

A   Architectural concrete 4:cover-6
No.2[1938]

720.5
A67b
Department stores. U.S. (NY) New York
Kurman store building, New York. D. M.
Oltarsh, architect.

Arch.& building 59: pl. 38
February 1927

720.5
A67f
Department stores, U.S. (Ind.) Indianapolis
Department store, Indianapolis, Indiana.
Vonnegut, Bohn and Mueller, Pereira and
Pereira, and Kenneth C. Welch. archts. Plans.

A   Architectural forum 65: 517-520
December 1936

Department Stores, U.S. (Minn.) Minneapolis
L.S. Donaldson Co., Minneapolis, Minn. 1924.
Graham, Anderson, Probst and White, archts.

Graham, Ernest R. Architectural
work of Graham, Anderson, Probst
and White. 2 vols. London: B.T.
Batsford, 1933. v.1:160

720.5
A67a
Department stores, U.S. (NY) New York
Lord and Taylor store, Fifth Avenue and
38th Street, New York. Starrett and Van
Vleck, architects.

A   Architecture 29:pls.42-51
April 1914

720.5
A67ar
Department stores, U.S. (La.) Shreveport
Feibleman's department store, Shreveport,
La., Jones, Roessle, Olscher & Wiener, archts

Architect (N.Y.)7: 607
February 1927

Department Stores, U.S. (Mo.) St. Louis
Retail store for Carletin Dry Goods Co.
St. Louis, Missouri. Mauran, Russell and Garden,
archts.

A   Western architect 9:pl.
February, 1906

720.5
A67a
Department stores, U.S., (NY) New York
Saks and Company
Starrett and Van Vleck, architects

A   Architecture 50:pl. 156-160
Oct. 1924

720.5
A67c
Department stores,U.S. (Md.) Baltimore
Carr, G.W.
Four stores for Sears: Glendale, Calif.;
Highland Park, Mich.; Baltimore, Md.; and
Chicago, Ill. Nimmons, Carr, and Wright, archts.
Section.

A   Architectural concrete 4:25
No.2[1938]

Department stores. U.S. (NJ) Newark
Kresge department store, Newark. Starrett and
Van Vleck, archts.

A   Arch. and building 59:pl.29-34
February, 1927

Department Stores, U.S., N.Y., New York
Saks new department store, New York City.
Starrett and Van Vleck, architects

Arch. and Building 56:91-92, plates
Oct., 1924   188-191

720.5
B84
Department stores,U.S. (Mass.) Boston
The new Filene store building,Boston,Massa-
chusetts. Daniel H.Burnham,archt. Plans.

A   Brickbuilder 21: 247-250
September 1912

720.5
A67ar
Department stores. U.S. (NY.) New York
Department store, Saks & Company, Fifth
Avenue and Fiftieth Street, New York.
Starrett & Van Vleck, architects.

A   Architect 2:pl.143-44
Sept. 1924

720.5
A67r
Department stores, U.S. (NY) New York
The Wanamaker Building, New York City.
D.H.Burnham and Company, archts. No plan.

A   Architectural record 18:394-395
November 1905

Department Stores, U.S. (Mass.) Boston
Wm. Filene's Sons Company, Boston, Mass.
1912. D.H. Burnham and Co., archts. Plan

Graham, Ernest R. Architectural work
of Graham, Anderson, Probst and White.
2 vols. London: B.T. Batsford, 1933.
v.1:162-163

720.5
A67r
Department stores,U.S.. (NY) New York
Department stores in New York: Macy and
Company,plan;Siegel-Cooper Company(plan only)
De Lemos and Cordes,archts. Saks and Company
Buchman and Fox,archts. No plan. Adams and
Company department stores,De Lemos and Cordes
archts.

A   Architectural record 12:286-303
June   1902

Department Stores, U.S. (Ohio) Akron
M. O'Neil Company for May Department Stores
Company, Akron, Ohio. 1927. Graham, Anderson,
Probst and White, archts. Plan

Graham, Ernest R. Architectural work
of Graham, Anderson, Probst and White.
2 vols. London: B.T. Batsford, 1933.
v.1:153-154

720.5 B84 Department stores, U.S., (Ohio) Cleveland Higbee store building, Cleveland, Ohio. Abram Garfield, archt. A Brickbuilder 21: pl.60 May 1012	Deperthes, M. American high buildings as conceived by the French. Ecole de Beaux Arts prize awarded to M. Deperthes for "une maison à fourteen étages". Inland Architect 19: 48-9 May, 1892	Derby and Robinson see Concord (Mass.) Peter Bulkeley school
Department Stores, U.S. (Ohio) Cleveland The May Company, Cleveland, Ohio. 1914. Graham, Burnham and Co. archts. Graham, Ernest R. Architectural work of Graham, Anderson, Probst and White. 2 vols. London: B.T. Batsford, 1933. v.1:155	Depew memorial fountain. Indianapolis see Indianapolis, Ind. Depew memorial fountain	Derby (Eng.) Council Offices Extension George C. Conestick archt. Academy Archt. 51: 3-4 1920
720.5 A67b Department stores, U.S.,(Ohio) Cleveland The May Company store, Cleveland, Ohio. Graham, Burnham & Co., archts. A Architecture & building 47: 412-416 November 1915	710.5 C855 Depreciation of houses The building of the home Country Life 47:59-60 Dec. 1924	Derby, Eng. The London, Midland & Scottish railroad. School of transport. The London, Midland & Scottish (Rly.) School of Transportation. (plans) William H. Hamlyn,archt. RAIC jrl 16:84 Ap 1939
720.5 A67b Department stores. U.S. (Pa.) Philadelphia Gimbel Bros. store, Philadelphia. Graham, Anderson, Probst & White, archts. Arch. & building 59:pl. 75-75 ,IID April 1927 A	Deptford, Eng. see London, Eng. Deptford	Derby (Eng.) Power Station The power station, Derby. Architect (Lond.) 120: 251 August 24, 1928
720.5 A67r Department stores,U.S. (Pa.) Philadelphia A modern department store. The construc- tion and equipment of the Philadelphia Wana- maker building. D.H.Burnham and Co. archts. No plan. A Architectural record 29: 277-288 March 1911	DeQuares and Watton see New York (N.Y.) McLean (Alice house	Derby, Nelson L House for Oscar Schmidt, Esq., Huntington, L.I. [plan] Nelson L. Derby, archt. Amer arch 1: pl.fol.p.252 Ag 5, 1876
720.5 A67f Department stores,U.S. (Pa.) Pittsburgh Department store,Kaufmann,Pittsburgh, Pennsylvania.Laszlo Gabor,designer.Plan A Architectural forum 65: 308-309 October 1936	Der el-Bahri Egypt. Mortuary temple of Hatshepsut. Le grand temple de Deir-el-Bahari d'apres les releves de M. Sommers-Clarke. (plan and section) Vue d'ensemble. Terrasse central: colonnade nord. Encyclopedie de l'architecture, constructions de Style. 2 vols. Paris: Albert Morancé, 1928- ? Tome 2 pls.85-87	Derby, Richard B. see Derby and Robinson
721 T55 Department stores, U.S.,Pa., Pittsburgh Interiors of the Kaufman Department store, Pittsburgh, Pa. Janssen and Cocken, archts. No plan. Through the ages 9: 23-27 September 1931	Der el-Bahri, Eg. Mortuary Temple of Hatshepsut The mortuary temple of Hatshepsut at Der el Bahari. Architects' journal 74: 360 September 16, 1931	Derby, Robinson & Shepherd see also Boston (Mass.) Common. Parkman memorial band stand

Card 1 (row 1, col 1)
720.5
A67r
Derby, Robinson and Shepard
Price, C.M.
Returning to Classic precedent, 5 houses by
Derby, Robinson and Shepard. Residences of Dr.
Frederick E. Cheney; Murray Ballou; Mrs. E.S.
Barrett; Francis Shepley; Concord, Mass.

Architectural record 32:355-360
October 1912

(row 1, col 2)
720.53
W31
Dernburg, Hermann
Aufstockung der Darmstädte und National-
bank. Hermann Dernburg, archt.

Wasmuths monatshefte 8: 146-148
Heft 5/6, 1924

(row 1, col 3)
720.5
A67f
Des Granges, Donald
The designing of power stations.

Architectural forum 51: 361-372
September 1929

(row 2, col 1)
Derbyshire, Eng.

see

Derby, Eng. (county)

(row 2, col 2)
720.53
W31
Dernburg, Hermann
Kunst gewerbehaus, Berlin.
Warenhaus für Breslau, Hermann Dernburg,
archt.
Bank-Aufstockung in Berlin.

Wasmuths monatshefte 12: 342-344
Heft 8, 1928

(row 2, col 3)
Des Jardins and Hayward
see also
Cincinnati (OH) Busch (S.) residence
"   "   Durrell Residence
"   "   Goldsmith (M.) Residence
"   "   Jones (T.D.) Residence
"   "   Kramer (Adam) Residence
"   "   Miller (J. Leslie) Residence
"   "   Mougey (Peter) Residence
"   "   Mulhauser Residence

(See Card 2)

(row 3, col 1)
Dercum & Beer

see also

Cleveland (OH) Bungalow
"   "   Cottage
Shaker Heights (OH) Baker (Mrs. A. M.) Cottage

(row 3, col 2)
720.53 Dernburg, Hermann
W31   Vorschlag zur erweiterung des Reichstags-
hauses. (Proposal for the extension of the Imperial house; administration building, Berlin.)
Plan.

Wasmuths monatshefte 14: 390-391
September 1930

(row 3, col 3)
Des Jardins and Hayward   (Card 2)

see also

Cincinnati (OH) Residence
"   "   Seventh Presbyterian Church
"   "   Stern (William) Residence
"   "   White Residence

(row 4, col 1)
Dercum & Beer
House for O. Dercum, Cleveland, Ohio
[plans] Dercum & Beer, archts.

Western Arch't
13: 50-51
My 1909

(row 4, col 2)
721.97 Derrah, Robert V
A67c   The building with a sparkle: Coca Cola
warehouse, Pasadena, Calif. R.V.Derrah, archt.

Architectural concrete 3:30-31
No.2, 1937

(row 4, col 3)
720.5   Des Jardins and Hayward
I56   Sketch of residence for John H. Law,
Cincinnati, Ohio. Des Jardins and Hayward
archts.

Inland architect 6:118,pl.fol.120
January 1886

(row 5, col 1)
Derham, J. C.

see

Blackpool (Eng.) Olympia cinema

(row 5, col 2)
Derrah, Richard Vincent   1895(?)-1946
[obituary]

Nat'l Arch 2: 15
N '46

(row 5, col 3)
Des Jardins, S.E.
Development of Architecture in France.

West. Arch.
11: 3-5
January 1908

(row 6, col 1)
Dernburg, Hermann

see also

Berlin (Ger.) Theater der zehntausend
Berlin (Ger.) Langenbeck-Virchow-haus
"   "   Brauerei Schultheiss-Patzenhefer

(row 6, col 2)
Derrick, Robert O., Inc.

see

Dearborn, Mich. Henry Ford Museum
Detroit (Mich.) Derrick (R.O.) house
Grosse Pointe (Mich.) Barbour (E.H.) house
"   "   "   Club
"   "   "   Elementary School
"   "   "   Gabriel Richard School
"   "   "   Kidner (F.C.) house
Grosse Pointe Farms (Mich.) Miller (S.) house
Mentor (O.) Hanna, Leonard, estate

(row 6, col 3)
Des Jardins, S.E.
"Development of Secular
Architecture in France"

West Arch 10:
111-113
Nov. 1907

(row 7, col 1)
720.53 Dernburg, Hermann
W31   Architecture of...

Wasmuths, Monatshefte für Baukunst 4:351-74. Heft 11-12,
1919-20.

(row 7, col 2)
720.54 Dervaux, Adolphe
A67   Sabin, Marcol
La gare de la rue Verte, à Rouen (The railway
station - Rue Verte at Rouen). Plans. M.Adolphe
Dervaux, archt.

L'Architecture 43: p.13-18
January 15,1930

(row 7, col 3)
Des Jardins, S.E.
The Gallic ancestry of the skyscraper.

West. Arch.
12: 56-9
Nov. 1908

Des Jardins, Samuel Eugene -1916 obit. West. Archt. 24: VII. fol. Dec, 1916 issue	Des Moines (Ia) Chamberlain (Lowell) Flats photo Liebbe, Nourse, and Chamberlain Archts. West. Archt. 4: pls.fol.p. 12 Dec, 1905	Des Moines (IA) Electric Co. Sub-Station Sawyer and Watrous, archts. plan West. Archt. 17: pls.fol.p. 112 Dec, 1911
Des Moines (Ia.) Allen (B.F.) houses 1818-1898 Sketch of residence for B.F. Allen, Des Moines. W.W. Boyington, archt. Plans Inland architect 6:7,pl.fol.10 August 1885	Des Moines (IA) Citizens National Bank Liebbe, Nourse and Rasmussen, archts. plan West. Archt. 17: pls.fol.p. 94 Oct, 1911	Des Moine, Ia. Federal building Federal building, Des Moines, Iowa. Supervising Architect's office. Federal architect 1:9 July 1930
| MICROFILM Des Moines, Ia. Art Center in SCRAPBOOK ON ARCHITECTURE p. 882 (on film)	Des Moines (IA) Coffin, (N.E.) Residence Rendering. Smith and Gage, Archts. West. Archt. 1: pl.fol.p. 22 Dec, 1902	Des Moines (IA) First National Bank Liebbe, Nourse and Rasmussen. plan West. Archt. 17: pls.fol.p. 94 Oct, 1911
Des Moines (Ia.) Art Center Contemporary design and dignified simplicity combined in new Des Moines Art Center. Eliel Saarinen and Robt. F. Swanson, archts. Northwest archt 14: 1P-13,cover No. 5 1950	Des Moines (IA) Colonial Flats for Clinton Nourse Photos & floor plans Libbe,Nourse and Rasmussen, arhcts. West. archt. 4: pl. fol. p. 10 Nov 1905	Des Moines (Iowa) Harris (Emery) Dept. Store Rendering, Liebbe, Nourse, and Rasmussen, Archts. West. Archt. 1: pl.fol.p. 22 Dec, 1902
Des Moines (Ia.) Bishops Cafeteria Bishops cafeteria, Des Moines, Iowa. Proudfoot- Rawson, Brooks and Borg, archts. Plan Architectural forum 66: 452 May 1937	Des Moines (Ia.) Crawford (R.A.) Residence Entrance photo. Liebbe Nourse and Rasmussen, Archts. West. Archt. 3: pls.fol.p. 30 Apr, 1904	Des Moines (Ia.) Harter (Geo. W.) Double House Hallett and Rawson. Photo. West. Archt. 3: pls.fol.p. 30 Apr, 1904
Des Moines (Ia.) building The Des Moines building, Proudfoot, Rawson, Souers and Thomas, archts. No plan. Through the ages 9: 3-7 December 1931	Des Moines (Iowa) Drake University. Chancellor's Residence Floor Plan and Photo, C.E. Eastman, Archt. Western Arch. 1: pls.fol.p. 22 Dec, 1902	720.5 B84 Des Moines (Ia.) house House, Des Moines, Iowa. William G. Ran- toul. archt., plans. Brickbuilder 12:1 pl.fol.p.264 December 1903.
720.5 B95b Des Moines. Catholic Church Sketch of new Roman Catholic church, Des Moines, Iowa. James J. Egan, archt. A Building budget 6: pl. fol. p. 22 February 28, 1890	Des Moines (Ia.) Drake university. Fitch Hall of pharmacy Benton, Byre E. Fitch hall of pharmacy, Drake university. Eero Saarinen and assos., archts. Plans. Amer.school & univ. 25: 335-338 1951-1952	710.5 H84 Des Moines (Ia.) Hume (J.C.) house Home of J. C. Hume at Des Moines, Iowa. Charles E. Cope, archt. House and garden 54: 45-6 July 1928

720.5
A51
Des Moines, Iowa State Capitol
Obituary, the late A. H. Piequenard.
No illustration.

American architect 1: 599
December 9, 1876

Des Moines (Ia.) St. Joseph's Academy. Nursery
school.
Model nursery school. Dighton H. Smith, Grant
W. Voorhees, archts.

Northwest archt 15:14,16,35
No. 3 1951

Des Moines (Ia) Weaver (J.B.) Residence
photo. Liebbe, Nourse, and Rasmussen
Archt.

Western Archt.
1: pls.fol.p. 22
Dec, 1902

720.5
I56
Des Moines, Iowa state capitol
Note on the new state capitol building at
Des Moines, Iowa. No illustration.

Inland architect 6:55
November 1885

Des Moines (Ia) Salisbury house
Salisbury House, the residence of Carl
Weeks, Esq. William Whitney Rasmussen, archt
Tudor interiors.

Country life (U.S.) 54: 44-7
O'28

Des Moines (IA) Weaver (J.B.) Residence
Liebbe, Nourse and Rasmussen. Plan

West. Archt.
17; pls.fol.p. 94
Oct, 1911

Des Moines (Ia.) Iowa State Capitol. Lunettes
Lunettes in the Iowa State Capitol at Des
Moines, Iowa. By Kenyon Cox.

Western archt 9: 46, pls;
68, pls.
Ap; Je, 1906

Des Moines (IA), State Capitol. Mural
"Westward" by Edward Howland Blashfield.

West. Arch.
9:Wpl.fol.p. 14
Jan. 1906

Des Moines, Iowa. Weeks (Carl) house

see

Des Moines, Iowa. Salisbury house

Des Moines, Iowa. Iowa state education association

see

Des Moines, Iowa. Salisbury house

Des Moines (IA) Unitarian Church
Liebbe, Nourse and Rasmussen. plans

West. Archt.
17: pls.fol.p. 94
Oct, 1911

Des Moines (Ia.) Wetherell (F.E.) house
Architect's own house at Des Moines, Iowa.
Frank B. Wetherell, archt. Plans.

Architectural record 40:247
September 1916

Des Moines (Ia.) Marsh (W.W.) house
House of W.W. Marsh, Des Moines, Iowa.
Frank E. Wetherell, archt. Plans.

Architectural record 40:315
October 1916

Des Moines (IA) U.S. Post Office
James Knox Taylor, Arch.

West. Arch.
12: pl.fol.p. 20
Aug. 1908

720.5
W95b
Des Moines(Iowa)White(W.L.) house and barn
Residence and barn for W. L. White.
C. H. Lee, archt.

Building budget
3:5 in supp
My 31, 1887

Des Moines (Ia.) Planning
Weaver, J.B., Jester,L.A., Darling,J.N.,
Bell, J.H.
Des Moines comprehensive city plan, its
background and promise.
Des Moines experience with zoning.
Des Moines parks and civic center.
City planning future for Des Moines.

City planning 6: front.,155-183
July 1930

Des Moines (IA) Vanevera (G.M.) Residence
Liebbe, Nourse and Rasmussen, Plan

West. Archt.
17: pls.fol.p. 94
Oct, 1911

Des Moines, (IA), Witmer (W.W.) Residence.
photo.
Liebbe, Nourse, & Rasmussen, Arch.

West. Arch.
9:24,pl.fol.p. 24
Feb. 1906

Des Moines (Ia.) Princess theater
Princess theater, Des Moines, Iowa.
Hallett and Rawson, archts.

Brickbuilder 23:57
Supp. to February 1914

Des Moines (IA) Warehouse
Wetherel and Gage, Archts.

West. Archt.
17: pls.fol.p. 26
Feb, 1911

Des Moines (IA) Wittmer (W.W.) Residence
Liebbe, Nourse and Rasmussen. Plan

West. Archt.
17: pls.fol.p. 94
Oct, 1911

Desbarats, Guy

see

Affleck, Desbarats, Dimakopoulos, Lebensold,
and Sise

Design
Rogers, Ernesto N.
Memoria e invenzione nel "Design" Conferenza
scritta in occasione della "World Design Conference
in Japan"

Casabella
239: 1-3, My 1960

720.5
A67f
Deskey, Donald   1894 -
    Interior doorway, apartment in New York.
Donald Deskey, designer. Pittsburgh plate
glass institute competition.

Architectural forum 67:133
August 1937

Deschermeyer, Josef
    Zwei einfamilienhäuser bei Nürnberg
[plans] Josef Deschermeyer, archt.

Baumeister
Vol. 51:362-364
June 1954

Design, Architectural

see

Architecture. Design

720.5
A67f
Deskey, Donald   1894 -
    Penthouse solarium, Chicago, Ill. Donald
Deskey, designer. Pittsburgh glass institute
competition. Plan.

Architectural forum 67:131-132
August 1937

Desdemona's house. Venice

see

Venice. Palazzo Contarini-Fasan

Design, House

see

Domestic architecture. Design

720.52
A67c
Desks
    Details of staircase and work desk.
House at Crockham Hill, Kent. Minoprio
and Spencely, arch. Plans.

A   Architect(Lond.)149:opp.p.286
        February 26,1937
        Architect portfolio no.379

Desert architecture, U. S.

see

Domestic architecture, U. S. California

Designers' offices.
    Design-coordinator. [plan] Muller-Berringer,
designers.

Interiors
104, pt. 1: 89
Ja 1945

720.5
N56
Desmond, G   Henri
    State capitol, Augusta, Maine. G.H.Des-
mond, archt. No plan.

New York architect 5:197
March 1911

Desert gardens
see also
Cactus gardens

Designs, Architectural

see

Architecture. Designs and plans

720.53
M68
Desmoulins, Jean
    Some sketches by Jean Desmoulins.

Moderne bauformen 1:pls.6,15,27
1902

Desert Gardens
    When desert plants spring up from seed.

House and garden 61:48-49
April, 1932

Designs, House

see

Domestic architecture. Designs and plans

DeSoissons and Wornum

see

Penzance (Eng.) Douglas Haig memorial homes

Deshong (Alfred O.) memorial art gallery,
            Chester, Pa.

see

Chester (Pa.) Alfred O. Deshong memorial art gallery

Desjardins
    Monument de la place des Victoires

La construction mod. 29:   362-4
May 3, 1914

DeSoissons, Louis

see also

London (Eng.) Duchy of Cornwall estate
  "   "   Wilcove place housing scheme
Welwyn Garden City, Eng. Howard memorial

710.5 C85 De Soissons, Louis Phillips, Randal Loo water, Heacham, Norfolk. Additions and alterations by L. de Soissons and G. Wornum. Country life (Lond.) 89: 464-465 April 11, 1931	Despradelle, Constant Desire -1912 obit. West. Archt. 18: 103 Oct, 1912	720.54 A67v Dessau. Architecture Maisons jumelées, Dessau, 1925. (Model of "joined house", Dessau, 1925.) Walter Gropius, archt. L'architecture vivante: pl.37 Winter 1927
DeSoissons, Louis and Arthur W. Kenyon see Welwyn (Eng.) theater " " housing Weybridge (Eng.) housing scheme Leeds (Eng.) Public library	Despradelles, D. see Baltimore (MD) Baltimore Courthouse Competitive Design Berkeley (CA) Univ. of Calif., Phoebe A. Hearst Arch. Plan	720.54 A67v Dessau. "Bauhaus" Le "Bauhaus" de Dessau. (The "Bauhaus" school at Dessau, Germany.) Walter Gropius, archt. Plan. L'architecture vivante : 18,pl.3-4; pl.36 Spring; Winter - 1927
Despradelle, Constant Desire see also Codman and Despradelle	Despree, Jean Louis see Desprez, Louis Jean, 1743-1804	720.54 A67 Dessau. The "Bauhaus" La "Bauhaus" de Dessau,1927. (The"Bauhaus" of Dessau,1927.) Walter Gropius,archt. L'Architecture Vivante: pl.9 1929 - Autumn
Despradelle, Constant Désiré, 1862-1912 Beacon of progress (proposed). Konurert to the glory of the American people Arch rev 7: 94-5 Ag 1900	Després, Jean Louis see Desprez, Louis Jean, 1743-1804	Dessau (Ger.) Bauhaus Gropius, 1925. Bauhaus, Dessau. Museum der gegenwart 2: 35 Heft 1, 1931
ffo 720.6 A51q Despradelle, Constant Desiré 1862-1912 Constant Désiré Despradelle, A.I.A. American institute of architects-Quarterly October 1912 bulletin 13: 251-253	Desprez, Jean Louis see Desprez, Louis Jean, 1743-1804	720.54 A67v Dessau. "Bauhaus" Bauhaus, à Dessau, 1926. (Bauhaus at Dessau, 1926: side elevations, etc.) Fenêtre métallique au "Bauhaus" à Dessau. (Metal window at Bauhaus, Dessau.) L'Architecture vivante :p.10-12,22 Autumn - Winter 1931
Despradelle, Constant Désiré, 1862-1912 Swales, F.S. Master draftsmen, XI:Désiré Despradelle, 1862-1912 Pencil points 6:59-70 My '25	Desprez, Louis Jean, 1743-1804 Un dessin de Desprez, architecte L'Architecture 38: 351-52 Oct. 10, 1925	Dessau, Ger. Bauhaus. Wohnungen der bauhausmeister Maisons jumelées, Dessau, 1925. (Model of double house, Dessau,1925) Walter Gropius, archt. L'architecture vivante: pl.37 Winter 1927
Despradelle, Constant Désiré, 1862-1912 A monument to the American nation Archts & builders jour 37: 205- F 19, 1913	Desprez, Louis Jean, 1743-1804 Wollin, Nils G. Peterskyrkan och Piazza del Quirinale;Deprez-Vedutor i Nationalmuseum. Nationalmusei Krsbok [Stockholm] 3: 70-89 1933	Dessau, Ger. Bauhaus. Wohnungen der bauhausmeister Maison jumelée (Double house) Habitations de "Bauhaus" à Dessau, 1926. Le Maison de Gropius. (Residences of "Bauhaus" at Dessau, 1926. The home of Gropius.) Plan.Walter Gropius, archt. L'Architecture vivante: p.13, pl.1 Autumn - Winter 1931

Dessau (Ger.) Baumeistersiedlung haus
Doppelwohnhaus der bauhausmeistersiedlung,
Dessau. (Double residence building of the
architects' settlement in Dessau.) Walter
Gropius, archt. Plans.

Der Baumeister 28: 61
February 1930

Details, Architectural

see

Architecture. Details

Detroit (MI) Acme White Lead and Color Works
Donaldson & Meier, Archs.

Inland Arch. 50:
pl. fol. p 44
O, 1907

Dessau (Ger.) Housing
Zechlin, H.J.
Siedlungen von Adolf Loos und Leopold
Fischer (Residences (colonies) by Adolf Loos
and Leopold Fischer.) Plans.

Wasmuths monatshefte 13: 70-73,77-78
February 1929

Detention homes

see

Names of individual detention homes, i.e.:
Santa Barbara, Cal. county detention home
etc.

Detroit (Mich.)Air Terminal Midway bldg.
Midway building, Detroit Air terminal,
Michigan. Jesse L. Bowling and Isadore Shank,
archts.

Architectural record 65: 489
May 1929

720.54
A67v
Dessau, Labor building
La maison du travail, à Dessau, 1929.
(The labor building at Dessau, 1929.) Plans.
Walter Gropius, archt.

L'Architecture vivante:p.16,pls.21-22
Autumn - Winter 1931

Detmar, Blou, and Billery

see also

Salisbury (Eng.) Wilsford house

Detroit (MI) Aldrich (Ralph L.) Residence
Stratton and Baldwin, archts.

West. Archt.
24: 141
Oct, 1916

720.54
A67v
Dessau-Torten (Ger.) Housing
Habitations, à Dessau-Torten, 1926.
(Residences at Dessau-Torten, 1926) Walter
Gropius, archt.

L'Arch vivante: 18-20, pl.23
Autumn '31

720.5
A67
Detmar,Blow and Billery
Wilsford house, Salisbury, England, Det-
mar, Blow and Billery, archts.

Architectural review 19 n.s.2: pl. 151
November 1913

Detroit (MI) "Alhambra"
Errata: misidentified in Oct. 1896 issue
as Mouat Flats, Mason & Rice, archts.
Actually "Alhambra", William S. Joy, arch.

Inland Arch.
28: pl.fol.p. 30
Oct. 1896
correction: 28: 52, Dec. 1896

Dessex, Leon E.
see also

Washington (DC) Fire Engine House No. 2
"   " Hamilton (G.E.) Residence

Detroit free press better homes competition 1928
$500.00 prize designs, The Detroit Free Press
Better Homes Competition.

Architect (N.Y.) 11: 36,38
October 1928

Detroit (Mich.) Allen Corp. factory
Factory, Allen Corporation, Detroit, Mich.
The Austin Co., engineers. Plan.

Architectural forum 65: 333
October 1936

720.5
B84
Dessez, Leon E
Engine house No. 2, Washington, D.C.
Leon E. Dessez, archt.

Brickbuilder 20:pl55-50
April 1911

705.1
A79
Detroit (MI)
Detroit becomes a city of architectural
beauty.Sketches by Frederick Polley.

Arts and decoration 30: 64-65
February 1929

Detroit (Mich.) Amer. Auto Trimming Co.
Factory for the American Auto Trimming
Company at Detroit, by Mildner and Eisen,
Archts.

West. Archt.
24: pls.fol.p. 141
Oct, 1916

720.5
A67r
Destailleur, André
Destailleur,André
Restoration of a French chateau: Chateau de
Champs, near Paris. Restored by A.Destailleur.
No plan.

Architectural record 14:1-12
July 1903

710.5
C855
Detroit
View of business district in Detroit from
the balcony of Detroit's City Hall.

Country life (U.S.) 73: 68-69,insert
January 1938

720.5
B95b
Detroit. American building
Design of American building, Detroit,Mich
G.H.Edbrooke, archt., Chicago.

A   Building budget 3: pl.fol.p.128
October 31, 1887

Detroit (MI) Anderson (George) Residence Rogers & McFarlane, Arch Inland Arch 38: pl.fol.p.40 Dec. 1901	720.6 A512j Detroit. Architecture Archives of Detroit architecture ASAH j1 2 no 3: 32 J1 '42	Detroit (Mi) Atcheson (Norman S.) Residence Norman S. Atcheson, archt. West. Archt. 24: 141 Oct, 1916

Detroit (MI) Anthony (Mrs. E.S.)
Residence
A.C. Varney, Arch.
 	
Inland Arch. 38:
pl.fol.p.24
Oct. 1901
	720.5
	A67rev Detroit (Mich.) Architecture
	     Jenkins, C.E.
	     Detroit.
	
	Architectural reviewer: 2 pls
	preceding 1, 1-18
	S 1897
		Detroit (Mich.)Athletic Club
		Kahn, Albert
		    Detroit athletic club, Detroit, Mich.Albert
		Kahn, archt., Ernest Wilby, assoc. archt.
		
		Architecture 32: 174-176,182-184,
		July 1915 pls.71-77 fol.p.192

720.5
B93b   Detroit(Mich) apt. bldg.
     3 story flat building.
     Billings, M. T., archt.
 	
Building budget
3:3 in supp
J1 30, 1887
	720.6
	A512j Detroit. Architecture
	     Rickins, Buford L.
	     Detroit reviews its architecture
	
	ASAH j1 2 no 4: 42-44
	O '42
		Detroit (Mich.) Athletic Club
		    Detroit athletic club. Albert Kahn, archt.,
		Ernest Wilby, assoc. archt.
		
		American architect 108:17-23 & pls.
		July 14, 1915 fol. p.32

Detroit (Mi) Apartment Bldg.
B.C. Wetzel and Co., Archts
 	
West. Archt.
17: pls.fol.p. 68
Jul, 1911
	720.5
	A67a Detroit. Architecture
	     Embury,Aymor II
	     Impressions of three cities: Pt.II. Detroit.
	
	Architecture 31:77-80
	March, 1915
		Detroit (Mich.) athletic club
		    Detroit athletic club. Albert Kahn,
		archt. Ernest Wilby, associate.
		
		Arch and bldg 47: 445-448, 455
		D'15

Detroit (Mi) Aghitectural Club Exhibition 1900
Swales, Francis S.
The 1st exhibition of the Detroit archt. Club.
 	
Inland Architect
35: 34-5
June, 1900
	720.5
	A51 Detroit. Architecture
	     The skyline of the center of the automo-
	tive industry—Detroit.
	
	American architect 134: 749
	December 5, 1928
		Detroit (Mich.) athletic club
		    Athletic Club
		
		British arch. 85:133, 139, & pl.
		Mar. 1916

Detroit, Mich., Architectural Club
Exhibition 1900
Sketches of Residences, Churches and Commercial
Bldg.
 	
Inland Archt.
vol.35,No.5,pl.fol.p. 44
Jun, 1900
	720.5
	W52 Detroit (Mich.) Architecture
	     [Special number]
	
	West arch 24: 125-41
	O '16
		Detroit (Mich.) Athletic Club
		    Detroit Athletic Club, Detroit, Mich.
		Albert Kahn, archt.,Ernest Wilby, assoc. archt.
		
		Western architect 24:pl.fol.p.141
		October 1916

Detroit, Architecture
Fairbrother, F. A.
Architecture of Detroit
 	
Art and archaeology 17:115-119
March 1924
	720.5
	A87f Detroit.Arts and crafts society building
	     Building of the Arts and crafts society,
	Detroit,Michigan. Smith,Hinchman and Grylls
	and William B.Stratton,archts. Plans.
	
	Architectural forum 30:28
	January 1919
		Detroit (Mich.) Athletic Club
		    Detroit Athletic Club, Detroit, Mich.
		Albert Kahn, archt., Ernst Wilby, assoc.
		archt.
		
		Architects and builders Journal 47: pls.fol.
		January 9, 1918 p.22

Detroit (Mich.) Athletic Club garage
Detroit athletic club

Amer. arch. 109: pl.2100
Mar. 22, 1916

Detroit (MI) Belle Isle Park. Casino
Van Leyen and Schilling, archts.

West. Archt.
24: 132
Oct, 1916

Detroit (MI) Book Building
Louis Kamper, archt.

West. Archt.
24: 130
Oct, 1916

Detroit (MI) Bagley Building
Donaldson & Meier, Archs.

Inland Arch. 23:
pl. fol. p 24
Mr., 1894

Detroit, Mich., Belle Isle Park.Police Station.
Mason + Rice, Archts.
Inland Archt.
Vol. 27, No. 6, pl. Fol. p. 60
July 1896

Detroit (Mich.)Book Tower (Proposed)
Proposed Book Tower, Detroit.

Architects' Jour. 64: 771
December 22, 1926

Detroit (MI) Bagley Fountain
   Architect mis-identified as Wm. B. Stratton
Corrected: H.H. Richardson.

West. Archt.
24: 127;Oct, 1916
correction: 147;Nov, 1916

Detroit (Mi.) Belle Isle Park Stables
Mason and Rice, Archts.

Inland Archt.
vol.29,No.6,pl.fol.p. 60
Jul, 1897

720.5
A67a
Detroit (Mich.) Borgman (M.G.) house
   House and Plans, M.G. Borgman, Detroit,
Mich. John Scott & Co., Architects.

Architecture 25: 81
My '12

Detroit, Mich., Bagley (John N.) Residence

Rogers and MacFarlane, Archts.

Inland Archt.
Vol. 24, No. 3, pl.
   Fol. p. 30
Oct. 1894

Detroit, (Mich.) Belle Isle Public Shelter.
Edw. A. Schilling, Archt.

Inland Archt.
vol.32,No.3, pl.fol.p. 30
Oct. 1898

Detroit, Mich., Bourne (Allen) Residence

W.T. Smith, Archt.

Inland Archt.
Vol. 24, No. 5, pl. Fol.
   p. 52
Dec. 1894

720.5
A67a
Detroit(Mich.)Bankers trust company
   Bankers trust company, Detroit, Mich.
Views and plans. Smith, Hinchman and
Grylls, archts.

A   Architecture 57:221-4
April 1928

Detroit (MI) Biddle Residence
Rogers & MacFarlane, Archs.

Inland Arch. 38:
pl.fol.p.24
Oct.1901

Detroit (Mich.) Breitmayer (John)sons floral
                              shop
   Floral shop for John Breitmeyer's sons,
Detroit, Michigan
   Marcus R. Burrowes and Dalton R.
Wells, archts.

Western Arch. 30: Pl. 14.
June 1921.

Detroit, Mich. Belle Isle bath house
   Bath house, Belle Isle, Detroit, Mich.
Stratton and Baldwin, archts

Brickbuilder
9: pl 33
Mr 1910

720.5
A67
Detroit (Mich.).   Boat club
   Clubhouse of the Detroit boat club;
Alpheus Williams Chittenden, archt.

Arch rev 10 (n.s.5): 18-19
F '03

Detroit, Mich, Bridge

   (no further definition given)
Archit. not named.

Inland archt.
vol.28,No.3,pl.fol.p. 30
Oct, 1896

Detroit (MI) Belle Isle Park. Bridge
Edw. A. Schilling, archt.

West. Archt.
24: 140
Oct, 1916

Detroit (Mich.) Bonstelle Playhouse
   Baird, D.G.
   Unique community theater:the Bonstelle play-
house, Detroit, Michigan.Archt.Not given.
Exterior view.

Poster 17:16-17
April, 1926

Detroit (MI) Brown (J.H.) Terrace. Sketch.
E.C. Van Leyen.

Inland Archt.
21:pl.fol.p. 78
Jul, 1893

720.5
A67f

Detroit(Mich.)Buhl building
Buhl building, Detroit. Smith,
Hinchman and Grylls, archts. Plans.

A   Architectural forum 45:30-2,pl.9-14
July 1926

Detroit (Mich.) Cadillac motor co. bldg.
Sales room and building for Cadillac Motor
Car Co.,Detroit, Michigan.
Albert Kahn, inc. archt.

Western architect 34: pls.9-10
August, 1925

Detroit, Mich., Central Christian Church

Malcolmson + Higginbotham, Archts.

Inland Archt.
Vol. 24, No. 6, pl.
Fol. p. 64
Jan. 1893

720.5
R88

Detroit, Buhl building
Buhl building; Smith, Hinchman, and Grylls
archts.

R.I.B.A. 36: 110
December 8, 1928

Detroit (Mich.)Cadillac Square
Cadillac Square, Detroit

Amer. arch. 115:pl.128-132
Apr. 16, 1919

Detroit (MI) Central Methodist Episcopal Church.
House and Woman's Exchange.
Smith, Hinchman and Grylls, archts.

West. Archt.
24: 133
Oct, 1916

Detroit (MI) Buhl Land Co. Office Bldg.
R.E. Raseman, archt.

West. Archt.
24: 137
Oct, 1916

Detroit (MI) Campan (Mrs. R.McD.)
Residence
John Scott & Co., Arch.

Inland Arch 38:
pl.fol.p.32
Nov. 1901

Detroit (MI) Chalmers Motor Co. Factory Bldg.
Albert Kahn, archt.

West. Archt.
24: pls.fol.p. 141
Oct, 1916

Detroit Builders' Show

see

Model houses, U.S. Detroit

Detroit, Mich. Casgrain (Charles W.) house
Residence of Charles W. Casgrain, Detroit, Mich.
Mason & Rice, archts.

Inland Architect
v. 11 no. 7
pl. at end of vol.
Je 1888

Detroit (MI) Chamber of Commerce
Competition

Design by E. T. MacDonald, Archt.

Inland Archt
21: pl.fol.p. 54
May 1893

Detroit (Mich.) Butler (C.J.) house
House of C.J. Butler, Detroit, Michigan.
Albert Kahn, archt. No plan.

Architectural record 40:front,321
October 1916

Detroit (MI) Cass Avenue M-E Church
Malcomson & Higginbotham, Archs.

Inland Arch. 23:
pl. fol p 24
Mr., 1894

Detroit (MI) Chamber of Commerce
Competition

Design by John Scott and Co., Archts.

Inland Archt.
21: pl.fol.p. 54
May, 1893

720.5
B95b

Detroit(Mich.) Caddy(J.H.) house
2-story double-house on Fourth Ave. for
J. H. Caddy. Caddy, J. H.,archt.

Building budget
5:4 in supp
My 31, 1887

Detroit, Mich. Cass (Lewis) monument
The Cass monument, Detroit. Ware and Van
Brunt, archts.

Amer arch
1: 132, pl.fol.p.132
Ap 22, 1876

Detroit (MI) Chamber of Commerce
Competition

Design by Malcomson and Higginbotham,
Archts.

Inland archt.
21: pl.fol.p. 54
May 1893

Detroit, Mich., Cadillac Hotel

John Scott + Co., Archts.

Inland Archt.
Vol. 24, No. 4, pl.
Fol. p. 40
Nov. 1894

Detroit (MI) Catholic Club
E. C. Van Leyen, Arch.

Inland Arch. 23:
pl. fol. p 36
Ap., 1894

Detroit (MI) Chamber of Commerce
Competition

Design by Mortimer and Son, Archts.

Inalnd Archt.
21: pl.fol.p. 54
May 1893

Detroit (MI) Chamber of Commerce, Competition.

Design by Rogers and McFarlane, Archts.

Inland Arch.
21: pl.fol.p. 54
May, 1893

720.8   Detroit (Mich.)Church of the Holy Redeemer
A51   Church of the Holy Redeemer, Detroit,Mich.
         Donaldson & Meier, architects.

American architect 125:8pl..
May 7, 1924

Detroit(Mich.)Coe Terminal Warehouse
     Coe terminal warehouse company building,
Detroit, Michigan. S.Scott Joy, archt.

Architecture 59: 69
February 1929

Detroit (MI) Chamber of Commerce.
Competition

Design by Spier and Rohns, archts.

Inland Archt.
21: pl.fol.p. 54
May 1893

Detroit (Mich.) Civic center
     One of the designs for Detroit's Civic
center. Saarinen, Saarinen and Associates,
archts. [drawing only]

Nat'l arch 4:1,5
F '48

Detroit (Mich.)Coe Terminal Warehouse
     Coe Terminal warehouse, Detroit
S.Scott Joy, archt.

Architectural forum 51: 281
September 1929

Detroit (MI) Chamber of Commerce
     Competition

Design by William S. Joy, Archt.

Inland Archt.
21: pl.fol.p. 54
May 1893

Detroit (Mi) City Hall, Competition

Inland Architect
20: 60
Jan, 1893

Detroit (Mich.) Colby (F.L.) house
     Concrete House of Mr. F. L. Colby,Detroit,
Mich. Mr. Albert Kahn, Architect.

Amer. archt. 101: pls
Jan. 24, 1912

Detroit (MI) Chase (Richard B.) Residence
     Richard H. Marr, Arch.

West. Arch.
27: pl. 15
Jan. 1918

Detroit, (Mich.) Civic Center
     Saarinens show Detroit's proposed civic
center. Saarinen, Saarinen and Associates,
archts.

Nat'l Archt.
5:8
F '49

Detroit (Mi) Colton (Arthur) Co. Factory
     Mildner and Eisen, archts.

West. Archt.
24: 138,pls.fol.p. 141
Oct, 1916

Detroit (Mich.)Chrysler Corp. DeSoto Plant
               Press Shop
     Press shop, De Soto Plant, Chrysler Corpora-
tion Detroit, Mich. Albert Kahn, Inc., archts.
Pittsburgh glass institute competition. No
plan.

Architectural forum 67:113
August 1937

Detroit (Mich.) Civic center
     ....portion of the model of Detroit's
civic center. Eliel Saarinen, consultant

National arch 6: 6
Mr 1950

Detroit, Mich., Columbus Buggy Co. Building.

Mason + Rice, Archts.

Inland Archt.
Vol. 27, No. 3, pl. Fol. p. 30
Apr. 1896

Detroit, Mich. Church of Christ Scientist
     Detroit, Mich.

Arch. forum 27:pl.88-21
Nov. 1917

Detroit (Mich.) civic center. Veteran's memorial
     Veteran's memorial, first unit completed in
Detroit's civic center. Harley, Ellington and Day,
inc., archts.

Natl arch 6: 1,5
N 1950

Detroit, Mi. Continental Motors Co.
     Factory building for Continental Motors Company.
Albert Kahn, archt.

West. Archt.
24: pls.fol.p. 141
Oct, 1916

Detroit, Mich. Church of Christ Scientist
     Detroit, Mich.

Arch. bldrs. Jour.47:pl. for
Jan. 30,1918

Detroit (Mich.)Clara Ford Nurses home
     Clara Ford nurses' home, Detroit.
Albert Kahn, Inc., archts.

Architectural forum 50: pls.36-42
February 1929

Detroit, Mich. Convent of the Sacred Heart
     Convent of the Sacred Heart, Detroit,Mich.

American architect 122:2 pl.
Nov. 8, 1922

Detroit, Mich., Coronado Apartment Bldg. W. W. Joy, Archt. Inland Archt. Vol. 25, No. 2, pl. Fol. p. 23 Mar. 1895	Detroit (Mi) Danziger (Jacob) Residence B. Wetzel, archt. West. Archt. 24: 140 Oct, 1916	Detroit (MI) Detroit Club Wilson Eyre Jr. and John Scott & Co., Joint Archs. Inland Arch. 23: pl. fol. p 24 Mr., 1894
Detroit (Mich.)Cosgrain (C.B)house Residence for Mr. C.B.Cosgrain, Detroit, Mich. J.I.Dise & C.W.Ditchy, archts. West.arch.35:pl. 109-10 Jul. 1926	Detroit (Mi) Darmstaetter (Herman) Residence Louis Kamper, archt. West. Archt. 24: 140 Oct, 1916	Detroit (Mi) Detroit Legal News Bldg. Geo. D. Mason, archt. West. Archt. 24: pls.fol.p. 141 Oct, 1916
Detroit (Mi) Crane (C. Howard) Residence C. Howard Crane, archt. West. Archt. 24: page facing p. 130 Oct, 1916	Detroit (Mi) David Whitney Bldg. Graham, Burnham and Co., Archts. West. Archt. 24: 130, 136 Oct, 1916	Detroit (Mi) Detroit Saturday Night Bldg. Smith, Hinchman and Grylls, archts. West. Archt. 24: pls.fol.p. 141 Oct, 1916
Detroit (Mi) Crane (C.Howard) Residence Entrance C. Howard Crane, archt. West. Archt. 26: pl. 15 Dec, 1917	Detroit. David Whitney building David Whitney building, Detroit, Mich. 1915. Graham, Burnham and Co., archts. Plans Graham, Anderson, Probst and White works. 2 vols. London: B.T. Batsford, 1933. v.2: 352-353	720.5 A67a Detroit. Detroit savings bank. Branch Detroit savings bank, Detroit, Michigan. Albert Kahn, archt. Plan. A Architecture 37:pl.52 March 1918
Detroit (Mi) Crowley (W.C.) Residence R.E. Raseman, archt. Plans West. Archt. 24: pls.fol.p. 141 Oct, 1916	Detroit, Mich., Dean (Edgar S.) Residence Edw. C. Van Leyen, Archt. Inland Archt. Vol. 26, No. 2, pl. Fol. p. 20 Sept. 1895	Detroit (Mi) Diamond Manufacturing Co. Factory Smith, Hinchman and Grylls, archts. West. Archt. 24: pls.fol.p. 141 Oct, 1916
Detroit (Mi) Dakin (H.W.) Residence Stratton and Baldwin, archts. plan West. Archt. 17: pls.fol.p. XVII May, 1911	720.5 A67a Detroit (Mich.) Derrick (R.O.) house House of R. O. Derrick, Detroit, Mich. R. O. Derrick, inc., archts. Architecture 52: 457-8 D '25	Detroit. Dime Savings Bank building Dime Savings Bank building, Detroit, Mich. 1912-1913. Graham, Burnham and Co., archts. Graham, Anderson, Probst and White works. 2 vols. London: B.T.Batsford, 1933. v.2:283-284 A
Detroit (Mich.)Dakin (H.W.)house House, Henry W. Dakin, Detroit,Michigan Stratton & Baldwin, archts., plans. Architecture 25: p.12-13 January 1912	Detroit, Mich., Detroit Boat Club House (interior and exterior views) Donaldson + Meier, Archts. Inland Archt. Vol. 25, No. 1, Plates Fol. p. 11 Feb. 1895	720.5 A67a Detroit.Dime savings bank.Oakland Holbrook branch Dime savings bank (Oakland Holbrook branch) Detroit, Michigan. Weary and Alford, archts. Plans. A Architecture 37:57, 61 March 1918

V. 4

Detroit (MI) Dining Room. Mason & Rice, Archs. Inland Arch. 21: pl. fol. p 30 Mr., 1893	Detroit (MI) Donaldson (John M.) Semi-Detached Houses. Donaldson & Meier, Archts. Inland Arch. 27: pl. fol. p 60 Jl., 1896	Detroit (Mich.) Eaton Tower Eaton Tower, Detroit, Mich. Louis Kamper, archt. and Paul L. Kamper, associate. Architecture 56:82 August 1927
Detroit, Mich. Dixon (S.B.) house Residence of S. B. Dixon, Detroit, Mich. Mason & Rice, archts. Inland Architect v. 11 no.1 pl at end of vol. F 1888	Detroit, (MI) Ducharme (Charles A.) residence. Mason & Rice, archts. (mis-identified as J.M. McMillen residence in Oct. 1896 issue). Inland Arch. 28:pl.fol.p. 30 Oct. 1896 Correction: 28:52 Dec. 1896	Detroit (Mi) Edison Co. Connor's Creek Power House Engineering Dept., archts. West. Archt. 24: pls.fol.p. 141 Oct, 1916
Detroit (Mich.) Dodge Bros. factory Factory plant of Messrs Dodge Bros., Detroit, Michigan. Albert Kahn, archt. Ernest Wilby associate. Views of interior, exterior and plan. American architect 99: pl.fol.p.244 June 14, 1911	Detroit (Mich.)Durant bldg. The Durant Building.Albert Kahn, architect Architecture and building 52: 43-4 & pl.37-9 Apr.1920	720.5 A67a - Detroit.Edison service building Edison service building,Detroit. Smith, Hinchman and Grylls, archts. A Architecture 52:pl.169-171 November 1925
Detroit (Mich.)Dodge bros. factory Dodge factory, Detroit, Michigan. Albert A. Kahn, archt. Architects' Journal 68:271 August 22, 1928	Detroit, Mich., Dwyer (Frank T.) house double residence (brick) on Jefferson Ave. Edw. C. Van Leyen, Arch. Inland Arch. Vol. 25, No. 5, pl. Fol. p. 54 June 1895	Detroit (MI) Edison Shop Interior design.Geo. M. Niedecken, interior Archt. photos West. Archt. 23: 23-6 Mar, 1916
Detroit (MI) Dodge Brothers Office Bldg. Smith, Hinchman and Grylls, archts. West. Archt. 24: pls.fol.p. 141 Oct, 1916	720.5 D52 Detroit (Mich) Dwyer (J.N.) house Residence of John N.Dwyer,Detroit,Michigan. George Hunt Ingraham,archt. Plans. Western architect 13: 3pls.fol.p.12 January 1909	720.5 A67ar Detroit (Mich.) Edwards (Allen) house Residence of Allen Edwards, Detroit, Mich. Chas. A. Platt, archt. Architect (N.Y.)9: 562 February 1928
Detroit (Mich.) Dodge Half-Ton Truck Plant Dodge Half-Ton Truck Plant, Mound Road, Detroit, Michigan. 1938. Albert Kahn Associated Architects and Engineers, Inc. Mock, Elizabeth, ed. Built in the USA. New York: Museum of Modern Art, 1944. 94-95	Detroit (Mich.) Dyar (J.B.) house The John B. Dyar house, Detroit, Mich. Mason and Rice, archts. Plan. Sheldon, George William. Artistic Country Seats. 2 vols. New York: D. Appleton and Co., 1871. v. 2, pt. 5:p. 169-172, pl.45	Detroit (Mich.) Effingham Apartment Bldg. Edw. C. Van Leyen, Archt. Inland Arch. vol. 32, No.4,pl.fol.p. 40 Nov. 1898
Detroit (MI) Donaldson (John M.) Residence. Library View. Donaldson & Meier, Archts. Inland Arch. 28: pl. fol. p 10 Ag., 1896	Detroit, Mich., Dyar (John B.) Residence Mason and Rice, archts. Inland archt. vol.28,No.3,pl.fol.p. 30 Oct, 1896	Detroit (MI) Eisenberg (Edw. N.) Residence Mildner and Eisen, Archts. plans. West. Archt. 24: pls.fol.p. 109 Jun, 1916

Detroit (Mi) Electric Co. Garage
Mildner and Eisen, archts.

West. Archt.
24: pls.fol.p. 124
Sept, 1916

Detroit (Mi) Farwell Bldg.
Rogers, Bonnah and Chaffee, archts.

West. Archt.
24: 131
Oct, 1916

Detroit (Mich.)Fire Alarm telegraph bldg.
(Central)

Central fire alarm station, Detroit, Mich.
Donaldson and Meier, archts.

American architect 121: pls. fol. p.286
March 29, 1922

720.5   Detroit (Mich.) Elks' club
A67a   Elks' club, Detroit, Mich. Van Leyen
          and Schilling, archts.

Architecture 36: 198-9 pls 175-7
O '17

Detroit (Mich.)   Federal Reserve Bank
                            of Chicago
Detroit branch of the Chicago Federal
Reserve bank. Graham, Anderson, Probst &
White, archts.

Architect (N.Y.) 9: 302
December 1927

Detroit (MI) Fire Department Headquarters.
Donaldson & Meier, Archs.

Inland Arch.21:
pl. fol. p 18
F, 1893

Detroit, Mich., Engine House No. 18

Mason + Rice, Archts.

Inland Archt.
Vol. 27, No. 6, pl. Fol. p. 60
July 1896

Detroit. Federal Reserve Bank of Chicago
Detroit, Michigan Branch. Federal Reserve Bank
of Chicago. 1927. Graham, Anderson, Probst and White,
archts. No plan

Graham, Anderson, Probst and White.
Works. 2 vols. London: B.T. Batsford,
1933. v.2:227
A

Detroit (MI) Fire Engine House.
Donaldson & Meier, Archs.

Inland Arch. 21:
pl. fol. p 30
Mr., 1893

Detroit (Mich.) evening news bldg.
"Evening News" building, Detroit, Mich.
Albert Kahn, archt.

Architectural record 52: 488-491
December 1922

Detroit (Mich.) Ferguson (Harry) inc.
Model factory. New postwar tractor plant cuts
down on waste motion and "handling" of supplies.

Life articles on art 1949: 300-301
My 23, 1949

Detroit, Mich., Fire Engine House

Donaldson and Meier, archts.

Inland archt.
vol.28:no.6,pl.fol.p. 64
Jan, 1897

Detroit (Mich.)evening news bldg.
Detroit Evening News,
Albert Kahn, archt.

West. arch. 34
pl. 1-3
Aug. 1925

Detroit (Mi) Ferry Avenue Baptist Church
J. Will Wilson, archt.

West. Archt.
24: 141
Oct, 1916

Detroit, Mich., Fire Engine House

Mason and Rice, Archts.

Inland Arch.
vol. 30, No.1, pl.fol.p.10
Aug, 1897

Detroit, Mich. Fanny E. Wingert school
The Fanny E. Wingert School [plans]
Malcolmson & Higginbotham, archts.

Western Arch't
13: 2 pls. fol. p. 24
F 1909

Detroit (Mi) Fine Arts Theater
C. Howard Crane, archt.

West. Archt.
24: pls.fol.p. 141
Oct, 1916

Detroit (Mi) First Church of Christ Scientist
Smith Hinchman and Grylls,Archts.

West. Archt.
24: 133
Oct, 1916

Detroit (MI) Farrand (J.S., Jr.) Residence
Mason & Rice, Archs.

Inland Arch. 20:
pl. fol. p 70
Ja., 1893

Detroit (Mich.)Fire Alarm Telegraph bldg.
Central
Part elevation of central Fire Alarm
Telegraph building, Detroit, Michigan

Architectural review 3: 40,pl.26
September 1894

Detroit (MI) 'First' Congregational Church
John Lyman Faxon, Arch.

Inland Arch. 21:
pl. fol. p 18
F, 1893

Detroit (Mich.)First Congregational church
Full size detail of ornament and lectern
and pulpit of First Congregational Church,
Detroit, Mich. John Lyman Faxon, archt.

Architectural review 3: pl.31-32
October 1894

Detroit (Mich.)Fisher building
The Fisher building at West Grand and
Second boulevard, Detroit, Michigan.
Albert Kahn, Inc., archts.

Arch. and building 61: 41,54-55
February 1929

Detroit (MI) Flats
Six-family flats for Louis Katz. Mildner &
Eisen, Archs; Plans.

West. Arch.
15: pl.fol.p. 36
March 1910

Detroit (Mich.) First national bank
First National Bank Building, Detroit,Mich.
Albert Kahn, architect.

Arch. & building 54: pl.87-93
June. 1922.

720.5
M59a

Detroit. Fisher building
Bronze elevator doors, Fisher building,
Detroit, Mich. Albert Kahn, archt.

Metal arts 2: pl.8
February 1929

A

Detroit (MI) Flynn (James B.) Residence
Smith, Hinchman & Grylls, Archs.

West. Arch.
25: pl.fol.p. 38
May 1917
26: pl.16
Oct. 1917

Detroit, Mich. First Presbyterian church
First Presbyterian church, Detroit, Michigan.
Mason & Rice, archts.

Inland architect
20, no. 5
pl. fol. p. 58
D 1892

Detroit (Mich.)Fisher building
Grilles of bronze over entrance doors,
Fisher building, Detroit, Mich.Albert Kahn,
Inc., archts.

Metal arts 2: pl.18
April 1929

Detroit. Ford building (1908)
Ford building, Detroit, Mich. 1908. D.H. Burnham
and Co., archts.

Graham, Anderson, Probst and White
works. 2 vols. London: B.T. Batsford,
1933. v.2:369

Detroit, Mich., First Unitarian Church

Donaldson + Meier, Archts.

Inland Archt.
Vol. 24, No. 5, pl.
Fol. p. 52
Dec. 1894

721
T43

Detroit. Fisher building
The new Fisher building in Detroit. Albert
Kahn, Inc., archts.

Through the ages 6: front.,3-5,8-19,
April 1929   24

A

720.5
A67

Detroit (Mich.). Ford (J.B.) house
Residence for J.B. Ford, Esq., Detroit,
Michigan. Alpheus W. Chittenden, architect.
Plan.

Arch rev 12: 18-20
F '05

Detroit (Mich.)Fisher building
Study, Fisher building, Detroit. Albert
Kahn, inc. archts.

Architect (N.Y.)9: 298
December 1927

720.53
W31

Detroit. Fisher building
Gerson, Ernst
Amerikanische geschäftsbauten und wohnhäuser.
(American business and residence buildings.)
Fisher building,Detroit,Michigan. (Rendering)

Wasmuths monatshefte 14: 25
January 1930

Detroit (Mi) Ford (J.B.) Residence
Incl. plans
Alpheus W. Chittenden, arhct.

Inland Architect
46: pl.fol.p. 36
Oct. 1905

721
T 55

Detroit. Fisher Building
Model on a small scale of the lobby of the
new Fisher Building. Albert Kahn,Inc.,
archts.

A   Through the ages 6: front., 28
June 1928

Detroit (Mich.)Fisher theater
The Fisher theatre: Graven and Mayger,
archts.

American archt. 135: 269-276
February 20, 1929

Detroit (Mich.) Ford Motor Co. Factories
Robertson, Howard
The factories of Henry Ford, Albert Kahn,
archt.

Architect (Eng.) 117: 441
March 11, 1927

Detroit (Mich.)Fisher bldg.
Kahn, Albert
Fisher building, Detroit.Albert Kahn,archt.

American archt.135: 211-280
February 20,1929

Detroit (Mich.)Fisher bldg. garage
Fisher building garage. Albert Kahn, Inc.,
archts.

American archt. 135: 264-268
February 20,1929

Detroit (Mich.)Ford Motor Company factory
Kahn, Albert
The Ford Motor Company Factory, Detroit,Mich.
Albert Kahn, archt.

Architects and builders mag. 43:113-117
December 1910

Detroit (MI) Ford Motor Co. Factory Albert Kahn, archt. West. Archt. 24: 129 Oct, 1916	Detroit, Mich. Fort Shelby hotel Illustrations and plans. Schmidt, Garden and Martin, architects. Architectural forum 32: plates 26-28 February 1920	Detroit, Mich. Freer (W.M) Residence Mason and Rice, Archts. Inland Arch. vol.28, no. 1, pl.fol.p.10 Aug, 1896
Detroit, Michigan Ford motor co. factory Ford factory plant at Detroit, Mich. Arts et métiers graphique 16: 90 March 1930	Detroit (MI) Fort Street Presbyterian Church O. and A. Jordan, archts. West. Archt. 24: 128 Oct, 1916	Detroit (Mich.)Fyffe building Fyffe store building, Detroit. Smith,Hinchman and Grills, archts. Architectural forum 32:pl.90-92 June 1920
Detroit (MI) Ford Office Bldg. D.H. Burnham & Co., Arch. Sketches. Plans. West. Arch. 9: 134+pls.fol. Dec.1906	Detroit, Mich. Fort Street Union depot Fort Street Union Depot, Detroit, Michigan. [plan] James Stewart & Co., architects Inland architect v. 16 no. 1 pl. fol. p. 13 Ag 1890	Detroit (Mich. Fyffe bldg. Fyffe building Western Arch. 31: 5-7 Jan. 1922
Detroit (MI) Forest Lawn Cemetery, Gate Lodge. Sketch by Edward C. VanLeyen, Arch. Inland Arch. 22: pl. fol. p 40 N, 1893	Detroit (Mich) Free Press Bldg. Albert Kahn, Archt. West. Archt. 19: p. 13-14, 23 pls.fol.p. 24 Feb, 1913	Detroit (MI) Garden Court Apts. Albert Kahn, archts. West. Archt. 24: 134 Oct, 1916
Detroit (MI) Fort Ponchartrain du Detroit(old) Drawing. West. Archt. 24: 126 Oct, 1916	Detroit (MI) Free Press Bldg. Albert Kahn, archt. West. Archt. 24: pls.fol.p. 141 Oct, 1916	Detroit (Mich.) gas company. Bldg. Office building for the Detroit Gas company, Detroit, Michigan [plan and elevation] John Scott & Co., archts. Western Arch't 13: 2 pls. fol. p. 24 F 1909
microfilm Detroit, Mich. Fort Shelby hotel Schmidt, Garden and Martin, architects Fort Shelby hotel, Detroit, Michigan, 1917-8. Roll 5, frames 365-89	Detroit (Mich.)free press bldg. Free Press building. Detroit, Mich. A.Kahn, archt. Architect(N.Y.)5:pl.93-95 Jan. 1926	Detroit (MI) Gas Company John Scott and Co., Archts. West. Archt. 24: pls.fol.p. 141 Oct, 1916
Detroit, Mich. Fort Shelby hotel Illustrations. Schmidt, Garden, and Martin, architects. American Architect 114: plates 82-86 September 11, 1918	Detroit, Mich. Freer, C.L., house Residence of C.L. Freer, Detroit, Mich. Wilson Eyre, archt. Inland architect 20, no.5 pl. fol. p. 58 D 1892	Detroit (Mich.)General Motors Co. Bldg. General motors building, Detroit, Mich. Arch. & building 53: 88 & pl.181-3 Nov. 1921

Detroit(Mich.)General Motors Company Bldg. Central motors company. Detroit. Amer. Arch. 120: 393-400 & 8 pl. Nov. 23, 1921	Detroit (Mich.) Greater Penobscot bldg. The Greater Penobscot building in Detroit. Smith, Hinchman and Grylls, archts. Through the ages 7: 22-30 November 1929	720.5 A51 Detroit, Harper Nurses' Home Harper Nurses' home,Detroit,Mich. Plans. Albert Kahn and associates, archts. A American architect 124:420.& 6 pls. Nov. 7, 1923
Detroit (Mich) General Motors Technical Center, Advanced Engineering Section. Office Building Engineering staff offices, G.M. Technical Center, Detroit, Mich. Saarinen, Saarinen and Assos. Archts. Natl' archt. 7: 1,2 Sept, 1951	Detroit (MI) Greenfield Union School Van Leyen and Schilling, archts. West. Archt. 24: 132 Oct, 1916	Detroit, (Mich.) Harris (L.S.) Residence Nettleton and Kahn, Archts. Inland Archt. vol.32, No.5,pl.fol.p. 50 Dec, 1898
Detroit, Mich. General motors technical center General Motors Technical Center, Detroit/ USA [plot plan] Saarinen, Saarinen and Assocs., archts. Bauen and wohnen No. 5: 145-150 My 1956	Detroit (MI) Greusel, (Joseph) Block of Residences Edw. C. Van Leyen, Arch. Inland Arch. 22: pl.fol.p. 64 Jan. 1894	Detroit,(Mich.) Harris (Mrs.) Residence Rogers and MacFarlane, Archts. Inland Archt. vol.32, No.4,pl.fol.p. 40 Nov, 1898
Detroit (MI) Goettman (F.P.) Residence Roland C. Gies., Archt. West. Archt. 24: 140 Oct, 1916	Detroit, (Mich.) Griggs (S.A.) Residence Nettleton and Kahn, Archts. Inland Archt. vol.32, No.5,pl.fol.p. 50 Dec, 1898	Detroit (Mich.) Headley (George) Residence Exterior plus views of dining room, Library, and Hall. Nettleton and Kahn, Archts. Inland Archt. vol. 32, No.4,pl.fol.p. 40 Nov, 1898
Detroit (Mich.) golf club Detroit golf club, Detroit, Michigan. Albert Kahn, archt. No plan. American architect 120: 7 pl. November 23, 1921	Detroit (MI) Grinnell Brothers Store Albert Kahn, archt. West. Arch. 24: 137 Oct, 1916	Detroit (MI) Hecker (F.J.) Residence John Scott & Co., Archs. Inland Arch. 20: pl. fol. p 70 Ja., 1893
Detroit (Mich.) golf club Detroit Golf club, Detroit, Albert Kahn, architect Architectural forum 38:pl.17-20 Feb. 1923	Detroit (MI) Haas (Julius) Residence A. M. Chittenden, Archt. Inland Arch. 48: pl. fol. p 12 Ag., 1906	Detroit (Mich.) Henry Ford hospital Henry Ford Hospital Amer. architect 122:294-5 & 7 pl. Sept. 27, 1922
Detroit (Mich.) Grace hospital,home for nurses Home for nurses, Grace hospital, John R. Street, Detroit, Mich. No plan. Architectural record 14:423-424 December 1903	720.5 A51 Detroit (Mich.) Hamilton (James) house House of James Hamilton,Detroit,Michigan. Stratton and Baldwin,archts. Plans. American architect 93: pl.fol.p.66 February 19,1908	Detroit (Mich.) Henry Ford hospital Henry Ford hospital Albert Wood, arch. Western arch. 34: pl.10-14 Apr. 1925

Detroit (Mi) Herbert (Leo) Residence
Alvin E. Harley, archt.
 	
West. Archt.
24: 140
Oct, 1916
	720.5
	B95b Detroit(Mich.) house
	      2-story dwelling. Glaser, William, Archt.
	
	      Building budget
	      5:5 in supp.
	      Jl 30, 1927
		Detroit (Mi) Hudson Motor Car Co. Office Bldg.
		Albert Kahn, archt.
		
		West. Archt.
		24: pls.fol.p. 141
		Oct, 1916

Detroit (Mi) Hirt (R., Jr.) Residence MacFarlane, Maul and Lentz, archts. West. Archt. 24: page facing p. 130 Oct, 1916	Detroit, Mich., House (unnamed) Stratton and Baldwin, archts. Inland archt. vol.28,No.4,pl.fol.p. 44 Nov, 1896	Detroit (Mi) Ingleside Club Donaldson and Meier, archts. plan. West. Archt. 24: pls.fol.p. 141 Oct, 1916

720.5
I56   Detroit (Mich.) Holland (M.K.) house
      Residence of Mrs.M.K.Holland. Rogers and
MacFarlane,archts.
 	
      Inland architect 49: 1 pl.fol.p.54
      April 1907
	720.5
	I56 Detroit (Mich.) house
	      Residence t Detroit, Mich.
	
	      Inland archt. 49: 2 pls pre-
	      ceuing p. 25
	      Ja '07
		Detroit (MI) Inglis (Dr.) Residence
		Stratton & Baldwin, Archts.
		
		Inland Arch. 28:
		pl. fol. p 10
		Ag., 1896

721
I55   Detroit(Mich.)Hollywood theater
      Lobby Hollywood theater, Detroit.
 	
Through the ages 5:19-21
N '27
	720.5
	B84 Detroit (Mich.) house
	      House at Detroit,Michigan. George Hunt
	Ingraham,archt. Plans.
	
	      Brickbuilder 20: pls.fol.p.136
	      June 1911
		Detroit (Mich.) Institute of Arts
		    Detroit Institute of Arts. Paul P.Cret,
		Zantzinger, Borie and Medary, archts.
		
		Chicago Architectural Exhibition 36: 65-
		1923 67

Detroit (MI) Holtz (F.H.) Residence Albert Kahn, Archt. Inland Arch. 48: pl. fol. p 12 Ag., 1906	Detroit (MI) (Semi-detached) Houses John Scott & Co., Archts. Inland Arch. 28: pl. fol. p 10 Ag., 1896	Detroit (Mich.) Institute of Arts Detroit institute of arts. Art and archaeology 17: 97-104,132 March 1924

Detroit (Mi) Home Telephone Co. Central
    Exchange
Stratton and Baldwin, archts.
 	
West. Archt.
24: 139
Oct, 1916
	Detroit, Mich., Hudson Bldg.
	
	W.I. Smith, Archt.
	
	Inland Archt.
	vol. 23, No. 6, pl.
	      Fol. p. 66
	July 1894
		Detroit (Mich.) Insitute of Arts
		Burroughs, Clyde
		  The new Detroit museum of arts.
		
		Museum work 7: 66-74
		September-October 1925

Detroit, Mich., Hotel Ste. Claire
 	
Donaldson + Meier, Archts.
 	
Inland Archt.
Vol. 25, No. 1, pl.
      Fol. p. 11
Feb. 1895
	720.5
	A67 Detroit (Mich.). Hudson motor-car co.
	      Albert Kahn, archt.; Ernest Wilby,
	associate.
	
	Arch rev 70 (n.s.2): pl I
	D '16
		Detroit (Mich.)Institute of Arts
		Burroughs, Clyde
		  New home of the Detroit Institute of arts.
		
		American magazine of art 18: 544-554
		October 1927

Detroit (Mich.) Institute of Arts Detroit Institute of Arts, Detroit, Mich. Cret, Zanzinger, Borie & Medary, archts. Architect (N.Y.) 9: 305-323 December 1927	720.5 A67a church Detroit (Mich.) Jefferson Ave. Presbyterian Jefferson avenue Presbyterian church, De- troit, Mich. Smith, Hinchman & Grylis,archts. Architecture 56: pl. 143-6 September 1927	Detroit (MI) Kellogg (F.W.) Residence. Sketch by E. C. VanLoyen, Arch. Inland Arch. 22: pl. fol. p 40 N, 1893
Detroit. Institute of Arts Detroit's Institute of Arts; Paul P. Cret, Zantzinger, Borie and Medary, archts. Through the ages 5: front., 4-8 January 1928	Detroit (Mich.) Jefferson Ave. Presbyterian Church Jefferson Avenue Presbyterian Church, Detroit. Smith, Hinchman & Grylls, archts. Arch. forum 50: pl.66-67 March 1929	Detroit (Mich.) Kelvinator Company Building for the Kelvinator Co., Detroit Smith, Hinchman & Grylls, archts. Architectural forum 51: 297-298, September 1929
Detroit (Mich.) Institute of Arts Laprade, A. Le musée de Détroit aux Etats-Unis. (The Detroit museum in the United States.) Plans. Paul Cret, archt. Zantzinger, Borie and Medary, assoc. L'Architecture 42: 403-408 November 15, 1929	Detroit, Mich. Jefferson Intermediate School Jefferson Intermediate school, Detroit, Mich. Malcomson and Higgenbotham, archts. Arch. record 55:442-9 May 1924	Detroit (MI) Kresge Building Albert Kahn, archt. West. Archt. 24: 130,136 Oct, 1916
Detroit (Mich.)Institute of Arts Auditorium Theater Auditorium, Theatre, Detroit Institute of Arts, Detroit, Mich. Cret,Zanzinger, Borie & Medary, asso. archts. Architect (N.Y.) 9:323 December 1927	Detroit (Mich) Jefferson Rouge Jefferson Rouge, the development of Solvay Co., Detroit,Mich. Mann & MacNeille, archts. and town planners Arch for 28: 121-123 Ap 1918	Detroit (MI) Kresge (S.S.) Co. Store Smith, Hinchman and Grylls, archts. West. Archt. 24: 131 Oct, 1916
Detroit (MI) James Scott Fountain, Design Competition West. Archt. 20: p. 2 Jan, 1914	Detroit (MI) Joyce (A,M) School Malcomson and Higginbotham, archts. West. Archt. 24: pls.fol.p. 141 Oct, 1916	Detroit, Mich., Krolik (Mrs. A.) Residence Mason and Rice, archts. Inland archt. vol.28,No.3,pl.fol.p. 30 Oct, 1896
Detroit (Mich.) James Vernor school New type school construction. Eberle M. Smith and associates, archts. [drawing] Nat'l Arch 2:12-13 D '46	Detroit (MI) Juvenile Court Bldg. Stratton and Von Schneider, Archts. West. Archt. 24: pls.fol.p. 141 Oct, 1916	Detroit (Mich.) Kuhn (Frank) house House of Frank Kuhn, Detroit, Michigan. Albert Kahn, archt. No plan. Architectural record 40: p.566-567 December 1916
720.5 A51 Detroit (Mich.) Jefferson Ave. Presbyterian church Jefferson avenue Presbyterian church, Detroit Michigan. Smith, Hinchman & Grylls, architect. American architect 126: 641 December 31, 1924	Detroit (Mich.)Kahn (Albert) office Baldwin, G.C. Office of Albert Kahn, Detroit. Plans. Architectural forum 29:125-130 November 1918	Detroit (MI) Kuhn (James C.) Residence. Rogers & MacFarlane, Archs. Inland Arch. 21: pl. fol. p 18 F, 1893

Detroit (Mich.) La Salle gardens apts. La Salle Gardens apartments, Detroit,Mich. J. Philip McDonnell, architects. Amer. arch. 126:pl.11-13 July 2, 1924	Detroit (Mich.) Liberty theater Liberty theatre, Detroit, Michigan C. Howard Crane, archt. American architect 106: pls. September 23, 1914	Detroit (MI) McAdon (Mrs.) Residence. John Scott & Co., Archs. Inland Arch. 21: pl. fol. p 30 Mr., 1893
Detroit (MI) Lafer Brothers Store Joseph E. Mills, archt. West. Archt. 24: 137 Oct, 1916	Detroit, Mich. Liberty Theater Liberty Theatre, Detroit, Mich. C. Howard Crane, archt. (Plan) Builder 108: 3-5 Ja 1, 1915	Detroit (Mich.) McGraw (Arthur) house Residence of Arthur McGraw, Detroit, Mich. Rogers and MacFarlane, archts. Inl archt 22:pl.fol.p.20 Mr 1892
Detroit, Mich. Lee + Cady Warehouse Mason + Rice, Archts. Inland Archt. Vol. 27, No. 5, pl. Fol. p. 50 June 1896	Detroit, Mich., Livingston (William, Jr.) Residence Mason + Rice, Archts. Inland Archt. Vol. 27, No. 6, pl. Fol. p. 60 July 1896	Detroit (MI) McLaughlin (J.R.) Residence. Edward C. Van Leyen, Archt. Inland Arch. 28: pl. fol. p 30 O, 1896
Detroit (MI) Lee (G.W.) Residence Mason & Rice, Archs. Inland Arch. 20: pl. fol. p 58 D, 1892	Detroit (Mich.) Livingstone lighthouse Livingstone lighthouse on Belle Isle, near Detroit, Michigan. Albert Kahn, inc., archts. Gesu Maroti, sculptor. Through the ages 8: 35-36 November 1930	Detroit (MI) McMillen (J.H.) Residence Mason and Rice, archts. Inland archt. 28:pl.fol.p. 44 Nov, 1896
Detroit (MI) Lee (G.W.) Residence. Mason & Rice, Archs. Inland Arch. 21: pl. fol. p 18 F, 1893	Detroit, Mich. Long Residence Rogers and MacFarlane, Archts. Inland Archt. vol.27,no.1, pl.fol.p. 10 Feb, 1896	790.f A67 rev Detroit (Mich.) Majestic building The Majestic building. D.H. Burnham and co., archts architectural reviewer:14C S 1897
Detroit (MI) Lee (G.W.) Residence, Library Room Mason & Rice, Archs. Inland Arch. 23: pl. fol. p 36 Ap., 1894	Detroit, Mich., Mabley Bldg. D. H. Burnham + Co., Archts. Inland Arch. Vol. 25, No. 6, pl. Fol. p. 64 July 1895	720.5 A67r Detroit. Majestic building The Majestic building,Detroit,Michigan. D.H.Burnham and Company,archts. No plan. Architectural record 15:466 May 1904
Detroit (MI) Leonard (H.R.) Furniture Co. Store Baxter, O'Dell and Halpin, archts. West. Archt. 24: pls.fol.p. 141 Oct, 1916	Detroit (MI) Mabley Bldg. Enameled brick by Tiffany Pressed Brick Co., Chicago. Inland Arch. 26: (xvii) adv. trade supp. #2 1896	Detroit (Mich.) Majestic theatre Majestic theater, Detroit, Michigan, C. Howard Crane, archt. Western architect 24: pl.fol. p.124 September 1916

Detroit (Mich.) Majestic theatre Majestic theater, Detroit, Michigan. C. Howard Crane, archt. Plans. Architectural forum 26: 174-176 June 1917	Detroit (MI) Michigan Central Railway Station Warren and Wetmore, archts. West. Archt. 24: 129 Oct, 1916	Detroit (MI) Morgan and Wright Machine Shop Albert Kahn, archt. West. Archt. 24: pls.fol.p. 141 Oct, 1916
Detroit, Mich., Marlborough Flats (detail view). W.S. Joy, Archt. Inland Archt. Vol. 28, No. 1, pl. Fol. p. 10 Aug. 1896	Detroit (MI) Michigan Central Railway Station (old) C. L. Eidlitz, archt. West. Archt. 24: 128 Oct, 1916	Detroit (Mich.) Morrell Street power plant Morrell Street power plan, Detroit,Mich. Smith, Hinchman and Grylls, archts. Architecture 59: 377-378 June 1929
721 755 Detroit. Marygrove college Interior views Marygrove College buildings, Detroit, Michigan. D.A.Bohlen and Son, archts. Through the ages 8: 19-25 October 1930	Detroit (MI) Michigan State Capitol (1807) West. Archt. 24: 127,128 Oct, 1916	Detroit, Mich., Mount Flats Mason + Rice, Archts. Inland Archt. Vol. 27, No. 6, pl. Fol. p. 60 July 1896
Detroit, Mich. Mason Monument Mason monument, Detroit,Michigan. H.Van B. Magonigle, archt. A.Weinert, sculptor Plan. New York archtect 3:256-257 April 1909	Detroit (Mich.) Michigan theater Michigan Theater, Detroit. C. W. and George L. Rapp, archts. Through the ages 5: 8-10 May 1927	Detroit (MI) Mt. Eliot Fire Engine House Rogers & McFarland, Archs. Inland Arch. 20: pl. fol. p 58 D, 1892
Detroit, Mich., Masonic Temple Mason + Rice, Archts. Inland Archt. Vol. 27, No. 5, pl. Fol. p. 50 June 1896	Detroit (MI) Miller (Sidney T.) Residence West. Archt. 24: 127 Oct, 1916	Detroit (MI) Municipal Court Bldg. Smith Hinchman and Grylls archts. West. Archt. 24: 133 Oct, 1916
Detroit, Mich., Masonic Temple, details of entrance. Mason + Rice, Archts. Inland Archt. Vol. 27, No. 6, pl. Fol. p. 60 July 1896	Detroit (MI) Moore (William S.) Residence Mason & Rice, Archs. Inland Arch. 20: pl. fol. p 70 Ja., 1893	Detroit (Mich.) Myers (E.E.) house Residence of architect E. E. Myers on Woodward Ave. E. E. Myers, archt. Plans. Inland archt 2: 91, 96 1883
Detroit, Mich., Medical College W.I. Smith + Son, Archts. Inland Archt. Vol. 24, No. 6, pl. Fol. p. 64 Jan. 1895	720.5 A67 Detroit (Mich.), Morgan & Wright Machine shop for Morgan & Wright, Detroit Mich. Albert Kahn; Ernest Wilby, associate. Arch rev 20 (n.s.8): pl I D '18	Detroit (Mich.) National bank of commerce National bank of commerce, Detroit. Amer. arch. 113: pl.125-133 Apr. 10, 1918

720.5
A51

Detroit (Mich.) Nat'l bank of commerce.
Doors
  Designed by Albert Kahn for the National Bank of Commerce, Detroit, Mich.

Amer arch 111: 371
Je 15, '17

Detroit (Mich.) Noble (H.W.) house
  Residence of H.W. Noble, Detroit, Mich.
Nettleton & Kahn, archts.

Inl arch 25:pl.fol.p.90
Mr 1899

Detroit (Mich.) Orchestra hall
Orchestra Hall, Detroit, Mich.

Architecture. 42:113-5
Aug. 1920

Detroit (Mich.)National theatre
  National theater, Detroit, Mich.
Albert Kahn, archt., Ernest Wilby, Assoc. archt

American architect 102: pls.fol.p.8
July 3, 1912

Detroit (Mi) Northern High School
Malcomson and Higginbotham, archts.

West. Archt.
24: pls.fol.p. 141
Oct, 1916

720.52
A67

Detroit, Orchestra Hall
  Orchestra Hall, Detroit. C.Howard Crane, archt.

A

Architects journal 53: 676-677
June 1, 1921

Detroit (MI) Nettleton (G.W.) Residence
G. W. Nettleton,Archt.

Inland Arch. 28:
pl. fol. p 10
Ag., 1896

720.5
A67f

Detroit, Mich. Northern high school
  Northern high school, Detroit, Mich.
Malcomson & Higginbotham, archts. Plan.

Arch for 96: pls 62-5
Ap 1917

Detroit (MI)
  (New) Orphan Asylum
Stratton & Baldwin

West. Arch.
13: pl. 10
May 1909

Detroit (MI)
  Newman (Dr.) Residence
H.P. Kirby, Arch.

Inland Arch.
42: pls. fol.p. 40
Dec.1903

Detroit, Mich. Northland shopping center
  Drei amerikanische shopping centers [plans]
Victor Gruen, archt.

Bauen & Wohnen no. 2
p. 73-77
Ap 1954

Detroit, Mich., Osburn (Frank A.) Residence.

John Scott + Co., Archt.

Inland Archt.
Vol. 27, No. 1, pl. Fol. p. 10
Feb. 1896

Detroit (Mich.) news bldg.
  Detroit news building. Albert Kahn, archt.
Ernest Wilby, assoc. archt.

Architectural forum 28: pls.1-5,p.27-28
January 1918

Detroit, Mich. Northland   shopping center
  Northland Regional Shopping Center, Detroit,
Mich. [plans] Victor Gruen, assocs., archts.

Bauen and wohnen
No. 4: 109-112
Ap 1956

Detroit (Mich.) Owen (Mrs.) Residence
Rogers and MacFarlane, Archts.

Inland Archt.
vol.32, No.4,pl.fol.p. 40
Nov, 1898

Detroit (Mi) News Building
Albert Kahn, archt .

West. Archt.
27: 87-8
Oct, 1918

Detroit (Mich.) Oakland Holbrook branch bank
  Dime savings bank (Oakland Holbrook branch)
Detroit, Michigan.
Weary and Alford, archts.
Plans.

Architecture 37:57,61
March 1918

720.5
W52

Detroit (Mich.) Packard motor co. bldg.
  Sales building for Packard Motor Co.
Albert Kahn, inc., archt.

West arch. 34: pls 12-15
Ag '25

Detroit (Mi)   News Bldg.
Albert Kahn, archt.

West. Archt.
28: 22
Mar, 1919

Detroit (Mich) Opera House
  Mason and Rice; J.M. Wood; and A.W. Chittenden;
Archts.

Inland Archt.
vol.35,No.5,pl.fol.p. 44
Jun, 1900

Detroit (Mich.) Palace theatre
  Palace theatre, Detroit, Michigan
G. Howard Crane, archt.

American architect 106: pls.
September 23, 1914

---

v. 4

Detroit, Mich, Palace Theater Palace Theater, Detroit. C. Howard Crane, archt. [Plan] Builder 108: 3-5 Ja 1, 1915	Detroit (MI) Partridge (W.E.) Residence W.E.N. Hunter, Archt. Inland Arch. 48: pl. fol. p 24 S, 1906	Detroit (MI) Perry (Mary Chase) Residence William B. Stratton, Arch. Miss Perry's Models for House-Pewabic Pottery, Plans. West. Arch. 27: pl.1-4 May 1918
Detroit (MI) Palmer Memorial Fountain Carrère and Hastings, archts. Zack Rick, assoc. Inland Architect 33: 52 Jul, 1899	Detroit (MI) Patterson Brothers and Co. Houses Alvin E. Harley, archt. plans West. Archt. 24: 134 Oct, 1916	Detroit (MI) Pittman (S.K.) Residence Charles M.Baker, Arch. Burrowes & Wells, Assoc. Archs. Plans. West Arch 26: pl.12 Aug. 1917
720.5 A67 Detroit (Mich.). Palmer memorial fountain Carrère & Hastings, archts. Plan and elevation. Arch rev 6: pl LXVIII fol 176 O 1899	Detroit (MI) Patterson Brothers Houses Entrances Alvin E. Harley, archt. Terrace, Parker and St. Paul Aves. West. Archt. 26: pl. 16 Dec, 1917	Detroit (MI) Pewabic Pottery Co. Bldg. Stratton and Baldwin, archts. West. Archt. 24: pls.fol.p. 141 Oct, 1916
Detroit (MI) Palmer Park Entrance Competition Gold Medal - Richard Wildner Silver Medal - T. Carl Rollmar Hon. mention - Louis Risper. Inland Architect 38: 31 Nov, 1901	720.5 A67r Detroit (Mich.) Penobscot bldg. Study, Penobscot bldg., Detroit. Smith, Hinchman & Grylls, archts. Architect (N.Y.) 9:300 D '27	720.5 A51 Detroit(Mich.)Phelps(George Harrison)inc. building t' George Harrison Phelps, inc., Detroit. Office building and studio. Smith, Hinchman and Grylls, archts. Plans. A American architect 130:pl.174-9 July 20,1926
Detroit, Mich, Palms (C.L.) Residence Mason and Rice, Archts. Inland archt. vol.28,No.4,pl.fol.p. 44 Nov, 1896	721 T55 Detroit. Penobscot building The Greater Penobscot building in Detroit. Smith, Hinchman and Grylls, archts. A Through the ages 7: 22-30 November 1929	720.5 A67f Detroit(Mich.)Phelps(George Harrison) building (George Harrison) Phelps, inc. building, Detroit. Smith, Hinchman and Grylls, archts Plans. A Architectural forum 45:79-80,pl.17-21 August 1926
Detroit (MI) Palms (C.L.) Residence Dise and Ditchy, Archts. West. Archt. vol. 34: pl. 7-12 Jan, 1925	Detroit (Mi) Peoples State Bank Donaldson and Meier Archts. West. Archt. 24: 131 Oct, 1916	Detroit (MI) Pittman (SK) Residence.Children's Porch Charles M. Baker Archt. Plan. West. Archt. 26: pl. 2 Jul, 1917
Detroit, Mich., Palms (F.F.) Dining Room Mason + Rice, Archts. Inland Archt. Vol. 24, No. 5, pl. Fol. p. 52 Dec. 1894	Detroit. Peoples Wayne County Bank Peoples Wayne County Bank 1912-1913. (Formerly Dime Savings Bank). Detroit, Mich. Graham, Burnham and Co., archts. Graham, Anderson, Probst and White Works. 2 vols. London: B.T. Batsford, 1933. v.2:283-284	Detroit (Mich.) Plan Bennett, E. H. City plan of Detroit, Mich. A.I.A. Jour. 3:264-70 Je '15

Detroit (Mich.) Plan
Phillips, T. G.
The Detroit plan.

Art and archaeology 17: 120-122
March 1924

720.5
A67m

Detroit (Mich.) Pontchartrain hotel
Pontchartrain hotel, Detroit, Michigan
George D. Mason, archt.

Arch & bldrs. mag. 40:182-6
Ja '08

Detroit (Mich.) Public library
The Detroit public library

Architecture, 44:203-12, p193-105
July 1921

Detroit (Mi) Plan (1807)
Woodward Plan

West. Archt.
24: 127
Oct, 1916

720.5
A67

Detroit. Pontchartrain hotel
Hotel Pontchartrain, Detroit, Michigan,
George D. Mason, Plans

Architectural review 19 n.s.2: 94-95
April 1913

Detroit (Mich.) Public library
Detroit public library.

Arch. and building 53: 74 & pl.
150-4. Oct. 1921

Detroit (Mich.) Planning
Blucher, W. H.
City planning in Detroit.

City planning 3: 101-107
April 1927

Detroit, (Mich.) Post Office-Court House
One interior view only. Wm. Martin
Aiken, archt.

Inland Arch.
vol.31, No.3, pl.fol.p. 30
Apr, 1898

Detroit(Mich.)Public library
Paris, W. Francklyn
Italian Renaissance in Detroit, the library

Am architect 123: 15-19, 21
Ja 3, '23

Detroit, Mich. Planning
Un plan urbanistico para Detroit. Norbert
M. Gorwic, archt.

Arquitectura Mexico
65:13-20 Mar 1959

Detroit (Mich.) Prenticw(George H.)Residence
Exterior plus views of Library, Hall and
Dining Room. Rogers and MacFarlane, archts.

Inland Arch.
vol.32, No.5, pl.fol.p. 50
Dec, 1898

720.5
A67a

Detroit (Mich.). Public library
Paris, W. Francklyn
The art of painted windows. I. The windows
of the Detroit Public library. Cass Gilbert,
archt.

Architecture 47: 37-40
F '23

Detroit (MI) Police Station (East Side)
Edward C. Van Leyen, Archt.

Inland Arch. 28:
pl. fol. p 18
S, 1896

Detroit (MI) Public Library. Entrance Hall
Cass Gilbert, archt. sketch.

West. Archt.
29: pl. 8
Apr, 1920

Detroit (Mich.) Public library
Decoration for children's room,
Detroit Public Library

American architect 124:front.
Nov. 7, 1923

Detroit (Mich.) Pond (Ashley) Stables
Stables of Ashley Pond, Detroit,Mich.
Pond and Pond, archt.

Architectural review 9,n.s.4:152
September 1902

Detroit (Mich.) Public library.
Perspective view of entrance hall,
Detroit library. Cass Gilbert, Archt.

Amer. Arch. 119: pl. fcing 506
Ap 20, '21

Detroit (Mich.) Public library
Paris, W. Francklyn
The library, Detroit

Art and archaeology 17:85-96
March 1924

720.5
I55

Detroit (Mich.) Pontchartrain hotel.
Hotel Pontchartrain, Detroit, Mich.
George D. Mason, archt.

Inland archt 48: 9 pls fol p.48
N '06

Detroit (Mich) Public Library.
The Detroit public library. Cass Gilbert
archt.

Amer. Arch. 120: 2:8-33 &
8 pl.fol. 500
S 28, '21

720.5
M59a

Detroit. Public Library
Bronze entrance doors, Detroit Public
Library, Detroit, Michigan. Cass Gilbert,
archt.

Metal arts 3: pl.34
May 1930

Detroit (Mich.) Public library. Addition
    Distinguished addition to Detroit's
main public library.   Francis Keally and
Cass Gilbert, Jr., archts.

                    Nat'l arch 4:7
                    O '48

Detroit (Mich.) Real estate exchange
    Real estate exchange

                Arch. & bldg. 50: pl.75
                Apr. 1918

Detroit, (Mich.) Residence
    Rogers and MacFarlane, Archts.

                    Inland Arch.
                    vol.32, No.5,pl.fol.p. 50
                    Dec, 1898

Detroit (Mich) Public library. Branch
    Branch library for city of Detroit,
Michigan. Mildner and Eisen, archts.

                Amer arch 114; pl 99-100
                S 25, '18

Detroit (Mich.) Recreation building
    Recreation building, Detroit, Michigan.
Smith, Hinchman & Grylls, archts.

                Western architect 27: pl.11-12
                April 1918

Detroit (MI)
    Residence
    A.W. Chittenden, Arch.

                    Inland Arch.
                    42: pls. fol. p. 40
                    Dec. 1903

Detroit (MI) Public Library, Conely Branch
    H.B. Clement, archt.

                West. Archt.
                24: pls.fol.p. 141
                Oct, 1916

Detroit (Mich.) Recreation building
    Recreation building, Detroit, Michigan.
Smith, Hinchman and Grylls, archts.

                American architect 114:pls.9-11
                July 10, 1918

Detroit, (Mich)
    Residence
    Albert Kahn, Arch.

                    Inland Arch.
                    43: pls. fol.p. 32
                    June, 1904

Detroit (Mich.). Public library. Doors
    Bronze entrance doors, Detroit Public
Library, Detroit, Michigan. Cass Gilbert, archt.

                Metal arts 3: pl.34
                May, 1930

Detroit, Mich. Residence

    unnamed architect

                Inland Arch.
                Vol. 25, No. 2, pl.
                    Fol. p. 23
                Mar. 1895

Detroit (MI)
    Residence
    Stratton & Baldwin, Arch.

                    Inland Arch.
                    43: pls. fol.p. 32
                    June, 1904

Detroit (Mich) Public library. Duffield
branch
    Duffield branch library, Detroit, Mich.
Marcus R. Burrowes, archt. Plan.

                Amer arch 116; pl 111-112
                S 17, '19

Detroit, Mich. Residence
    (no further definition).

                Inland archt.
                vol.26, no.3, pl.fol.p. 30
                Oct, 1895

Detroit (MI) Residence
    Joseph E. Mills, Archt.

                    Inland Arch. 48:
                    pl. fol. p 48
                    N, 1906

Detroit (Mich.) Public library, Mosaics
    Detroit Public Library, frontal colonnade

                Arch. rec.49:p. 300-9
                Apr., 1921.

Detroit (MI) Residence

                Inland Arch. 28:
                pl. fol. p 10
                Ag., 1896

Detroit (MI) Residence
    Rogers & MacFarlane, Archts.

                    Inland Arch. 48:
                    pl. fol. p 60
                    D, 1906

Detroit (Mich.) Public library, Schoolcraft
                    branch
    Schoolcraft branch, Detroit public library
Donaldson & Meier, architects

                Amer. arch. 126:311
                Sept. 24, 1924

Detroit, Mich., Residence
    (not named)
    Edw. C. Van Leyen archt.

                Inland archt.
                vol.30,No.5,pl.fol.p. 54
                Dec, 1897

Detroit (MI)   Residence

                    Inland Arch. 49:
                    pl. fol. p 22
                    Ja., 1907

Detroit (MI) Residence
Roland C. Gies, archt. plans

West. Archt.
17: pls.fol.p. 26
Feb, 1911

Detroit, Mich. Roosevelt Group
The Roosevelt group, Detroit, Mich.

Malcomson, Higginbotham & Palmer, architects.

American architect 123:401-4 & 8 pl.
May 9, 1923

Detroit (MI) St. Paul
St. Paul's Cathedral. Cram , Goodhue &
Ferguson, archs.

Inland Arch.
52: 62
Nov. 1908

Detroit (MI) Residence
(duplex)
A.J. Darling, archt.

West. Archt.
24: 135
Oct, 1916

Detroit (Mich.) Rosella (Edward G.) office
Architect builds for future, rental income at present. [plans] Edward G. Rosella,
archt.

Nat'l arch 6:1
Ja '50

720.5   Detroit.Saint Paul
I56   St. Paul's cathedral, Detroit, Mich. Cram
            Goodhue and Ferguson, archts. Renderings.

A   Inland architect 54:pl.fol.p.66
            November 1909

Detroit (MI) Residence Terrace
Albert Kahn, Archt.

Inland Arch. 46:
pl. fol. p 76
Ja., 1906

720.5   Detroit (Mich.) St. Agnes' church
A67a   St. Agnes's church & rectory
            Van Leyen, Schilling & Keough, archts.

Architecture 52: pl. 129-33
Sept. 1925

720.5   Detroit.Saint Paul
A67r   St.Paul's cathedral,Detroit,Mich. Exterior
            and reredos. Cram,Goodhue and Ferguson,
            archts.

A   Architectural record 29:82
            January 1911

Detroit, Mich., Rice (Z. [Architect]) Semi-
detached houses.

Mason + Rice, Archts.

Inland Arch.
Vol. 27, No. 5, pl. Fol. p. 50
June 1896

720.5   Detroit (Mich.) St. Benedict church
A67r   St.Benedict Church and school,Detroit,Mich
            Donaldson and Meir, architects

Arch.record 53:15-16
Jan. 1923

Detroit (MI) Saints Peter & Paul.
Cathedral School. Leon Coquard, arch.

Inland Arch.
25: 32
April 1895

Detroit (MI) Rinaldo Apt. Bldg.
Richard H. Marr, archt.

West. Archt.
24: 135
Oct, 1916

Detroit (Mich.) Saint Florian church
Saint Florian church, Detroit, Michigan.
Cram and Ferguson, archts.

American architect 136: 147-152
August 5, 1929

Detroit, Mich., Saints Peter and Paul Cathedral
                                                    School
(with plans for 4 floors).

Leon Coquard, Archt.

Inland Arch.
Vol. 25, No. 3, Plates
Fol. p. 34
Apr. 1895

720.54   Detroit (Mich.) River Terrace apartments
A67au   Groupe d'immeubles a River Terrace,
            Detroit, Mich. [plans]

L'Arch d'aujourd'hui
18: 97
Jl '47

Detroit (Mich.) St.Francis home for
orphan boys
St. Francis home for orphan boys,
Detroit, Michigan. Albert Kahn, archt.Plans.

American architect 120:436-40 & 3 pls.
December 7, 1921

Detroit (MI) Sarmiento (S.J.) Residence
Rogers & McFarland, Archs.

Inland Arch. 20:
pl. fol. p 58
D, 1892

Detroit (MI) Riverside Storage Co. Warehouse
Stratton and Baldwin, archts.

West. Archt.
24: 139
Oct, 1916

RYERSON LIBRARY
705.1   Detroit. Saint Paul
C55   St.Paul's Cathedral,Detroit,Michigan.
            Cram,Goodhue and Ferguson,archts. Plan.

Christian art 4: 89-92
November 1908

A

Detroit (Mich.) Savoyard Club
Savoyard Club, Detroit, Michigan.
Smith, Hinchman and Grylls, archts.

American architect 136: 31-34
July 5, 1929

706.1 A51a M.B.D. Detroit, Scarab club Detroit Scarabs' new home. View of main lounge. Launcelot W. Sukert, architect American magazine of art 20:534-535 September 1929	Detroit (MI) Scripp (J.E.) Residence, Addition to Mason & Rice, Archs. Inland Arch. 21: pl. fol. p 18 F, 1893	Detroit (Mi) Smith (C.F.) Warehouse Pollmar and Ropes, archts. West. Archt. 24: pls.fol.p. 141 Oct, 1916
Detroit (Mi) Scheinman (I.L.) and Co. Factory Architects mis-identified as A. L. Kahn correct: Pollmar and Ropes, archtects. West. Archt. 24: pls.fol.p. 141 Oct, 1916 correction: 147, XII, Nov. 1916	Detroit, Mich. Seivers and Erdman carriage works Carriage works of Seivers and Erdman, Detroit, Michigan. Mason and Rice, archts. Inland Archt 20: pl. fol. v.70 no.6 Ja 1893	720.5 A51 Detroit(Mich.)Standard savings and loan association Standard savings and loan association, Detroit (Mich.) Views and plans. G.D. Mason and company, archts. A American architect 134:327-40 September 5,1928
Detroit (Mi) Schemansky (Otto) and Sons Monumental Works Mildner and Eisen, archts. West. Archt. 24: pls.fol.p. 124 Sept. 1916	Detroit (MI) Sellick (Mrs.H.) and Parker (Miss) Residence Edw. C. Van Leyen, Arch. Inland Arch. 22: pl. fol. p. 64 Jan. 1894	Detroit, (Mich) State Savings Bank McKim, Mead and White, Archts. Inland Archt. vol.35,No.6,pl.fol.p. 52 Jul, 1900
Detroit, Mich. Schmidt Building Donaldson and Meier, Archts. Inland archt. vol. 28,No.4,pl.fol.p. 44 Nov, 1896	Detroit (Mi) Sheraton Apts. Baxter, Odell and Halpin, archts. West. Archt. 24: 135 Oct, 1916	720.5 A67 Detroit.State Savings bank State Savings Bank building,Detroit,Mich. McKim,Mead and White,archts. Scale drawings. A Architectural review 8:n.s.3:pls.12- February 1901 14
Detroit, Mic. Scott memorial fountain. Competition Cass Gilbert's design...[renderings by Thomas P. Johnson] Pencil points 4: 30,[fig. 27-29] Dec. 1923	Detroit (Mi) Sherbrooke Apts. Pollmar and Ropes, archts. West. Archt. 24: 134 Oct, 1916	720.5 A67 Detroit (Mich). State savings bank Detroit state savings bank, Detroit, Mich. McKim, Mead & White, and Donaldson & Meier. associated architects. Plan. Arch rev 17:95-97 Mr '05
Detroit, Mich. Scott memorial fountain Illustration, Cass Gilbert, architect. Architecture 56: 196 Oct. 1927	720.5 A67c Detroit.Shoppers Parking Deck Rolfe, W.S. Shoppers parking deck-Detroit. Smith, Hinchman and Grylls, Inc., archts. Plan and section. A Architectural concrete 5:24-26 No.2[1939]	Detroit (Mich.) State Theater Interior views-the Francis Palms building and the State theater. C. Howard Crane, archt. Through the ages 5: 7-14 June 1927
Detroit, Mich. Scott memorial fountain. Competition. Competition design. [perspective] Henry Mc Goodwin and Robert Mc Goodwin, architects. American architect 108: pl.fol p. 412 Dec. 29, 1915	Detroit (Mich.) Showroom & garage Show room and garage. Detroit, Michigan. Smith, Hinchman & Grylls, architects. Arch. record 56:143 Aug. 1924	Detroit (Mich.) Statler hotel Hotel Statler, Detroit, Michigan. George B. Post & Sons, archt. Arch. & bldg. 47: 89-101 March 1915

V. 4

720.5 A67r Detroit (Mich.) Statler hotel Hotels, Detroit, Statler Wagner, W. S. The hotel Statler in Detroit. George B. Post and Sons, archts. [plans]. Arch rec. 37:321-339 Ap '15	Detroit (Mi) Stevenson Hotel Joseph P. Jogerst, archt. West. Archt. 24: 134 Oct, 1916	720.5 I66 Detroit. Temple Bethel Temple Bethel, Detroit, Michigan. Albert Kahn, architect. No plan. A Inland architect and news record 42: December 1903 pl.fol.p.40
720.5 B84 Detroit (Mich.) Statler hotel Hotels, Detroit, Statler Statler hotel, Detroit, Michigan. George B. Post and Sons, archt. Brickbuilder 24:pl. 50-55 Ap '15	720.5 B95b Detroit(Mich) Store & Apt. bldgs. 2 two-story store and flat bldgs. Perrien Brothers, archts. Building budget 5:5 in supp Jl 30, 1887	Detroit (Mich.) Temple Beth-El Temple Beth-El, Detroit, Albert Kahn, architect. Architectural forum 40:pl.73-4 May 1924
Detroit (Mi) Statler Hotel Geo. B. Post and Sons, archts. Smith Hinchman and Grylls, Assoc. Archts. West. Archt. 24: 130,136 Oct, 1916	Detroit, Mich., Strelinger Store Rogers + MacFarland, Archts. Inland Arch. Vol. 24, No. 1, pl. Fol. p. 10 Aug. 1894	Detroit (Mi) Tennis Club Marcus R. Burrowes and Dalton R. Wells, Archts. Plan West. Archt. 24: pls.fol.p. 141 Oct, 1916
Detroit (Mich.) Statler hotel Plan of the Statler hotel, Detroit. Geo. B. Post, archt. Architect (Lond.) 117: 988 June 10, 1927	Detroit (MI) Sweeney-Huston Bldg. See Detroit (MI) Recreation Bldg.	Detroit, Mich. Third Church of Christ Scientist Third church of Christ, Scientist, Detroit. Presbyterian Church of the Redeemer, Detroit, George D. Mason and Co., archts. Architectural forum 51: 489-497 Oct, 1929
Detroit (MI) Stephens (A.L.) Residence Mason & Rice, Archs. Inland Arch. 20: pl. fol. p 58 D, 1892	Detroit (Mi) Teal (Frank C.) Residence Preston, Brown and Walker, archts. plan West. Archt. 24: pls.fol.p. 141 Oct, 1916	Detroit, Mich., Thompson (B.S.) Residence Mason + Rice, Archts. Inland Arch. Vol. 27, No. 1, pl. Fol. p. 10 Feb. 1896
Detroit (Mi) Stephens (AL) Residence George D. Mason, archt. Plans West. Archt. 24: pls.fol.p. 141 Oct, 1916	Detroit (Mich.) Telephone Company building Branch offices, Detroit Telephone Co., Detroit, Michigan. Smith, Hinchman and Grylls, archts. Architecture 44: 378-9 December 1921	Detroit, Mich., Thompson Residence, Entrance Detail Only. Mason + Rice, Archts. Inland Arch. Vol. 27, No. 5, pl. fol. p. 50 June 1896
Detroit (MI) Stevens (C.L.) Residence, Library Mason & Rice, Archs. Inland Arch. 23: pl. fol. p. 24 Mr., 1894	Detroit, Mich., Telephone Exchange Bldg. Gordon W. Lloyd, Archt. Inland Arch. Vol. 24, No. 4, pl. Fol. p. 40 Nov. 1894	Detroit, Mich., Trinity Church Mason + Rice, Archts. Inland Arch. Vol. 24, No. 5, pl. Fol. p. 52 Dec. 1894

720.5 B95b Detroit(Mich.) Trumbull Ave. houses 2 two-story residences on Trumbull Ave. McEnhill, Andrew, archt. Building budget 3:3 in supp Jl 30, 1887	Detroit (Mich.) Union Trust bldg. Detroit bank features color and wood. Union Trust Company, Detroit, Mich. Smith, Hinchman and Grylls, archts. Western architect 37: 230-232 November 1928	Detroit (Mi) Victor Theater Smith and Kohner, archts. West. Archt. 24: 141 Oct, 1916
Detroit (Mich.) trust co. Detroit trust co. Amer arch 109: pl 2099 Mr 15, 1916	Detroit (Mich.) Union Trust building Union Trust building, Detroit, Mich. Smith, Hinchman and Grylls, archts. (Interior views). Through the ages 7: front.,15-24 July 1929	Detroit, Mich. W. A. Moore public school W. A. Moore Public School, Detroit, Michigan. Malcolmson & Higginbotham, archts. Western Arch't 13: pl. fol. p. 58 My 1909
Detroit (Mich.) trust company Building for Detroit trust company, Detroit (Mich.). Views and plans. Albert Kahn, Inc. archts. American architect 132:645-55 November 20, 1927	720.5 W52 Detroit. Union Trust building The Union Trust building of Detroit, Smith, Hinchman and Grylls, archts. A Western architect 58: 137,146, August 1929 pl.121-128	Detroit (MI) Walker (Harry) Residence Jenney & Mundie, Archts. Inland Arch. 28: pl. fol. p 10: Ag., 1896
Detroit (Mi) Tuller Hotel West. Archt. 24: 130 Oct, 1916	Detroit (Mich.)Union Trust building Color dominant in design of the Union Trust Building, Detroit, Michigan. Smith, Hinchman and Grylls, archts. American architect 136: 32-39 November 1929	Detroit, Mich., Walker (J.H.) Residence Jenney + Mundie, Archts. Inland Arch. Vol. 24, No. 2, pl. Fol. p. 20 Sept. 1894
Detroit, Mich., Union Trust Bldg. Donaldson + Meier, Archts. Inland Archt. Vol. 27, No. 6. pl. Fol. p. 60 July 1896	Detroit (Mich.) University of Detroit New campus of University of Detroit. Malcomson and Higginbotham, archts. Architecture 55:12 January, 1927	721 T53 Detroit. Water Board Building The new Water Board building in Detroit. Louis Kamper, archt. Interior views. Through the ages 8: 9-13 November 1930
Detroit. Union Trust building New skyscraper for the Union Trust Co. Detroit, Mich. Smith, Hinchman & Grylls & Donaldson & Meier, archts. Architecture 55: 326 June 1927	Detroit (Mi) University of Detroit Building Oscar C. Gottesleben, archt. West. Archt. 24: 133 Oct, 1916	720.5 B95b Detroit(Mich.) Watson St. house 3-story residences on Watson St. Faulconer, A. C., archt. Building budget 3:3 in supp Jl 30, 1887
720.5 M59a Detroit. Union Trust building Working drawings and shop drawings for elevator doors of monel metal in the Union Trust C ompany building, Detroit, Mich. Smith, Hinchman and Grylls, archts. A Metal arts 2: 234-237. June 1929	Detroit (Mich.) University of Detroit. Library New library buildingat the University of Detroit...Harley, Ellington and Day, Inc. Archts. and engineers. Plans. Natl archt 8: 1,4-6 Ja 1952	Detroit (Mi) Wayne County and Home Savings Bank Donaldson and Meier, archts. West. Archt. 24: pls.fol.p. 141 Oct, 1916

Detroit (Mich.) Wayne county & home savings bank Wayne County and Home Savings Bank Donaldson & Meier, arch Architectural record 54:341 Oct. 1923	Detroit (MI) Weiler (J.) Store Harry S. Angell, archt. West. Archt. 24: 131 Oct, 1916	Detroit (MI) Woolley (Geo. H.) Residence George D. Mason, archt. plans West. Archt. 24: pls.fol.p. 141 Oct, 1916
Detroit (Mich.) Wayne County savings bank Wayne Co. Detroit Detroit savings bank Arch. record 43: 82-84 Jan. 1918	Detroit, Mich., Wheelmen Clubhouse. Edw. C. Van Leyen, Archt. Inland Archt. Vol. 27, No. 2, pl. Fol. p. 20 Mar. 1896	Detroit, Mich. YMCA bldg. Young Men's Christian Association bldg., Detroit, Mich. [plans] Mason & Rice, archts. Inland Architect v.11 no.4 Ap 1888 - pls. at end of vol.
727 A51 Detroit (Mich.) Wayne university. Classroom building Wayne university classroom building. Suren Pilafian, archt. Amer. school and univ. yearbook 50:ff1 1948-9	Detroit, Mich. Wills, Childe Harold, house (Project) ...a large commission in Detroit [plans and rendering] H. V. von Holst, architect. Marion M. Griffin, associate. Prairie School review III: 5, 14-15, 18 Second quarter 1966	Detroit, Mich. Y.M.C.A. Bldg. Young Men's Christian Association Building, Detroit, Michigan [plans] Donaldson & Meier, archts. Western Arch't 13: 2 pls. fol. p. 24 F 1909
Detroit. Wayne University. Engineering building Wayne University College of engineering building. Nat'l. Archt. 4:1 D '48	Detroit (MI) Nilson (Marian D.) Residence Wells D. Butterfield, archt. plans West. Archt. 24: 140 Oct, 1916	Detroit, Mich. Y.W.C.A. bldg. The Young Women's Christian Association building, Detroit, Michigan. Donaldson and Meier, archts. Plans. Interiors. Architects' & builders' magazine 37: June 1905 418-421
727 A51 Detroit (Mich.) Wayne university. Group plan Neef, Arthur The new plant plan for Wayne university. [plans] Am. school and univ. yearbook Vol. 90, p. 216-2? 1948-9	Detroit (Mich.) Wolverine hotel Hotel Wolverine, Detroit, Michigan. Fridstein & Company, archts. and engineers. Arch. & building 53: pl.167-8 Oct. 1921	Detti, Edoardo Hotel Minerva, Florenz [plans] Edoardo Detti, archt. Baumeister vol.58: 1224-1226, D 1961
727 A51 Detroit (Mich.) Wayne university Science building Science building, Wayne university. Ralph R. Calder, archt. Amer. school and univ. yearbook Vol. 20:922 1948-9	Detroit (MI) Woodlawn Cemetery Chapel Albert Kahn, archt. West. Archt, 25: pl.fol.p. 22 Mar, 1917	RYERSON LIBRARY 705.3 Dettingen on the Main.Church C55 Lill,Georg West deutschekirchenbaukunst. Dorfkirche in Dettingen a. Main. Dominikus Böhm, archt. A Die Christliche kunst 24: 264-271 June-July 1928 pls.257-259
Detroit (Mich.) Webster Hall Webster Hall, Detroit. Halpin and Jewell, archts. Architecture 51: 175-180 May 1925	Detroit (MI) Woodmere Cemetery, Chapel and Waiting Room Donaldson and Meier, archts. plan West. Archt. 24: pls.fol.p. 141 Oct 1916	711 Deutsche akademie des Städtebaues S77 Der städtebau 18:106-7 Heft 9-10, 1922

Deutsch and Schneider
 	
see
 	
New York (N.Y.) Park ave. synagogue
	720.54
	A67 Deverin, Joseph-Henri 1846-1922
	    Risler, Charles
	      Brief biographical sketch.
	
	                L'architecture 45: 248
	                July 15, 1932
		Devon, Pa. Kuhn (C. Hartman) house
		    Mr. Hartman Kuhn's house, Devon, Pa. Horace
		Trumbauer, archt. No plans.
		
		          Architectural rec
		          21:57-61
		          Ja 1907

Deutsche Bauzentrum
 	
        Baumeister
        52, no. 1: 33-34
        Ja 1955
	Devey, George
	  Cover dedication page
	          Arch Jour 54: 639
	          N 30, 1921
		Devon, Pa. Kuhn (C. Hartman) house & stable
		    Country house and stable, C. Hartman Kuhn,
		Devon, Pa. Horace Trumbauer, archt. Plans
		
		          Architecture 19: 14-15,
		          pl. V fol 16
		          Ja 1909

Deutsche Kampfbahn, Berlin
 	
see
 	
Berlin, Ger. Reichssportfeld. Olympiastadion
	Devey, George
	  George Devey, F.R.I.B.A. (b.1820;d.1886).
	A Biographical Essay. By Walter Hindes Godfrey.
	
	          RIBA Jour 13: 501-25
	          S 29, 1906
		720.5
		A67ar Devon (Pa.) Pepper (G.W.) house
		    Residence of the Hon. George Wharton Pep-
		per, Devon, Pa. Tilden, Register, and Pep-
		per, archts.
		
		          Architect (N.Y.) 12: 175-181
		          May 1929

Deutschen gewerkschaftshaus-bundes bldg.
Hannover, Ger.
 	
see
 	
Hannover, Ger. Deutschen gewerkschaftshaus-
bundes bldg.
	Devices, Competitions
	  A competition for a historical device for
	the Octagon House of the A.I.A., Washington, D.C.
	
	          Architecture 51:82
	          Mr 1925
		Devon,(Pa.) Wilbur (W.N.) House
		    Interior detail drawing of Ingle-Nook
		in Den. Kennedy, Hays and Kelsey, archts.
		
		          Inland archt.
		          vol. 33,No.2,pl.fol.p. 20
		          Mar, 1899

Deutscher bausustellung
 	
see
 	
Berlin (Ger.) Deutsche Bauausstellung 1931
	Devil's Lake, (Wis)
	  Homes among the lakes. photo.
	
	          Inland Architect
	          30: 8
	          Aug, 1897
		Devonport, Eng. Churches
		
		          The Builder 127:plate
		          Aug. 29, 1924

710.5
C85 Devenport. Royal Naval Barracks
    The officers' mess, Royal Naval Barracks.
 	
          Country life (Lond.) 73: 62-63
          January 21, 1933
	Devin, Rasongles and Bart
	
	see
	
	Marseilles (Fr.) Theatre chave cinema
		Devotion, Edward
		
		see
		
		Brookline (Mass.) Devotion (Edward) house

D'Evereux, Natchez (Miss.)(near)
 	
See
 	
Natchez (Miss.)(near) D'Evereux.
	Devlin, W. J.
	
	see
	
	Willesden-Green, Eng. Church of our lady of
	compassion
		790.52
		B95 Dew reservoirs
		    Design for a dew reservoir. S. B. Russell,
		archt.
		
		          Builder 122: 119
		          Ja 20 '22

Dewar, A.L., house (1886), Chicago.

see

Chicago, Ill. Dewar, A.L., house (1886).

Dewsbury (Eng) War Memorial
  Dewsbury war memorial competition, the
winning design. W. Naseby Adams and E.R.
Arthur, architects

Architects Journal 57:861-3
May 16, 1923

Dexter (Wirt) house. Chicago, Ill.

see

Chicago, Ill. Dexter (Wirt) house

Dewar, A.L., stable. Chicago

see

Chicago, Ill. Dewar, A.L., stable

Dewsbury (Eng.) War Memorial
  Dewsbury war memorial competition

Builder 124:813-6
May 18, 1923

DeYevele, Henry, d. 1400
Harvey, John H.
  Henry Yevele reconsidered. (map)

Archeo jrl 108:100-108
1951

Dewes, Villa, Chicago

see

Chicago (Ill.) Dewes (Francis J.) house

Dewsnap, W   S

see

Yonkers (N.Y.) Okamoto (Yonezo) house

---

d'Hooquet

see also

Abbeville (Fr.) Porte Louis XVI

Dewey, F. H. & Co.

see

New York (N.Y.) Robertson-Cole office building

Dexter Brothers' Shingle Stain
  Exhibit at World's Columbian Expo.
Chicago.

Inland Architect
22: 21-3
Sept, 1893

Di Nardo, Antonio, 1889(?)-1948
[Obituary]

Nat'l arch 4:2
Ag '48

Dewitt and Washburn

see

Dallas (Tex) Robert E. Lee school

Dexter, Granville W.

see

Palisade (N.J.) Valentine (D.H.) house
  "   "   Cavagnaro (H.V.) house

Dia del arquitecto, 1947
El dia del arquitecto

Arquitectura Cuba
15: 83-96
Mr 1947

DeWitt (L.V.) office building, Decatur, Ill.

see

Decatur (Ill.) DeWitt (L.V.) office building

Dexter (Mich.) Gordon hall
  Dexter centennial.

Michigan soc of archts weekly
bul: 15:2
Jl 8 '41

Dia del arquitecto 1948
  "Dia del arquitecto"

Arquitectura Cuba
16: 70-78
Mr 1948

Dewitt, Lyle Vinson

see also

Decatur (Ill.) Dewitt (L.V.) office building

Dexter, Robert E.

See

Dayton (OH)   Dayton Nat'l Bank

"Dia del Arquitecto" 1949
  Hernandez Roger, Miguel A.
  El Dia del Arquitecto.

Arquitectura Cuba 17:64-69
Mr 1949

"Dia del Arquitecto" 1949
    El Dia del Arquitecto en Santa Clara. El
Dia del Arquitecto en Matanzas.

        Arquitectura Cuba 17:114-115
        Ap 1949

Diament, Robert

    see

Macsai and Diament

Diana Weathervane, Tower building, Chicago

    see

    "Progress lighting the
pathway of commerce" (weathervane)

Dia del arquitecto. 1950
    El Dia del Arquitecto en Oriente
    El Dia del Arquitecto en Matanzas

        Arquitectura Cuba
        18: 281-282
        Je 1950

720.5
P59   Diamond, Henry R.
        Pencil rendering by Henry R. Diamond of
the First National Bank and Trust Company,
Utica, New York. York & Sawyer, archts.

        Pencil points 7: 190
        March 1926

Diaper ornament.

    Ward, James. Colour decoration of
architecture. London: Chapman and
Hall, Ltd., 1913. pl.25-7.

Dia del Arquitecto. 1950
    El dia del arquitecto; 13 de Marzo de 1950

        Arquitectura Cuba
        18: 214-217
        My 1950

720.5
W52   Diamond, James
    Kimball, Fiske and Wells Bennett
        The competition for the Federal buildings,
1792-1793. pt.1; pt.2; pt.3; pt.4

        American institute of architects' journal 7:
        January 1919   8-12;
        March 1919   98-102;
        May 1919   202-210;
        August 1919   355-361;
        December 1919   521-527

Diaphragm walls

    see

Walls, Diaphragm

Dia del Arquitecto. 1954
    El Dia del Arquitecto.

        Arquitectura Cuba 22:94
        Mr 1954

Diamond, Redfern & partners
    United Kingdom; cottage at Draycott-in-the-
Clay, Staffs. [plan] Diamond, Redfern & Partners,
archts.

        Arch't'l design
        32: 128, Mr 1962

Dias Dorados. Beverly Hills, Cal.

    see

Beverly Hills (Cal.) Dias Dorados

Dia del Arquitecto. 1954
Hernandez Roger, M. A.
    El Dia del Arquitecto.

        Arquitectura Cuba 22:143
        -148
        Ap 1954

Diamond, Redfern & partners
    United kingdom. House at Tettenhall, near
Wolverhampton [plan] Diamond, Redfern & partners,
archts.

        Architectural design
        31: 451-52, O 1961

"Dias felices", Santa Barbara, Calif.

    see

Santa Barbara, Calif. "Dias felices"

Dia del Arquitecto. 1954
Canas Abril, Eduardo
    Funcion social del arquitecto.

        Arquitectura Cuba 22:149-154
        Ap 1954

Diana, Temple of Ephesus

    see

Ephesus (Turkey). Temple of Diana

710.5
H84   Diatom
        "... J. Neutra's home of to-morrow: "One-
Plus-Two" house constructed of slabs of
Diatom. Plans.

        House and garden 74: 22-23
        November 1938 (pt. 2)

Diamanti palace. Ferrara

    see

Ferrara. Palazzo dei diamanti

Diana, Temple of Magnesia

    see

Magnesia. Artemis temple

Dias Morales, Ignacio
Villagran Garcia, Jose
    Concurso de ante-proyecto para el Templo de
Cristo Rey en la ciudad de Torreon, Coah., Mex.
[plans] Vladimir Kaspe; Ignacio Dias Morales;
Federico Alonso y Enrique Mariscal; Benjamin
Burillo; Luis Prieto y Sousa; E. Suares Leroy,
architects.

        Arq Mexico
        17: 101-110
        Ja 1945

Dias Posada, Alberto
    Club deportivo "El Rodeo" - Alberto Dias
Posada, Manuel de Andreis, Jorge Cadavid Lopes,
archts. [plan & section].

Proa no. 90
p. 12-14
Je 1955

Diboll & Owen

see

New Orleans (LA)   Public Library Competition

Dickenson, H.

see

Liverpool (Eng.) Lister drive power station

Dibblee, Henry, Co.
    Exhibit at World's Columbian Expo.
Chicago.

Inland Architect
22: 21-3
Sept. 1893

Diboll, D. C., Boettner and Kessels

see

New Orleans (La.) Bus terminal

Dickerson (William) house. Chicago

See

Chicago. Dickerson (William) house.

Dibblee, Henry, Co.
    Mosaic floor in Chicago Athletic Building
by Henry Dibblee Co.

Inland Architect
21: 77
Jul, 1893

Dick, D. D.

see

Winnipeg (MM)   Bank of Hamilton

Dickey, C. W.

see also

Honolulu (HI)   Royal School
"   "   Strangenwald Building
Oakland (CA)   Alexander (Juliette) Garden

Dibblee, Henry, Co.
    Mosaic walls and ceilings in Auditorium
Hotel annex [now Congress Hotel] by Henry
Dibblee Co.

Inland Architect
21: 76
Jul, 1893

Dick (Edison) house, Lake Forest, Ill.

see

Lake Forest, Ill. Dick (Edison) house

RYERSON LIBRARY
020.5
L69   Dickey, C   W
    Decidedly Hawaiian in design, the Maui
county free library, C. W. Dickey, archt.

Library Journal 55: 784-785
October 1, 1930

Dibelka, James B.

see also

Urbana (IL)   Univ. of Ill. Ceramics Building

720.52
B93   Dick, William Reid
    Bust of Sir Edwin Landseer Lutyens by W.
Reid Dick.

Builder 144: 303
May 19, 1933

720.54
A67au   Dickey, C. W.
    Théatre de plein air a Hawaii.C.W. Dickey,
archt.

L'Arch d'aujourd'hui
9: 76
S '38

Dibelka, James B.
    Sketch for an armory.

West. Archt.
23: 32
Apr, 1916

720.5
A67f   Dickason, L. King
    House in Tulsa (Okla.), L. King
Dickason, archt. Plans.
American Gas Association Competition

Architectural Forum 71:324
October 1939

720.52
A67c   Dickie, Archibald Campbell 1868-
Worthington,J.W.
    Professor A.M.Dickie,M.A.,A.R.I.B.A: an
appreciation.

Architect (Lond.)155: 29-30
July 14,1933

Dibelka, James B.   1869-
    Trustee of the Board of Education of Chicago,
State architect.

Herringshaw, Clark J. Herringshaw's
city blue book of current biography.
Chicago: American Publisher's
Association, 1915.

720.5
A51   Dickens,Charles
    Dickens' haunts to be pulled down.(one
half page text, no illustrations.)

American architect 118: 603
November 10, 1920.

Dickie, George William -1918
    obit.

West. Archt.
27: 82
Sept, 1918

Dickinson, Sir Arthur Loves house
A house near Haslemere for Sir Arthur
Loves Dickinson. A.D. Connell and B.R.Ward,
archts.

Architect (Lond.)133: 314-317
March 10, 1933

Dieppe (Fr.) Fishmarket
Shand, P. Morton
The new fishmarket at Dieppe.

Architects' Jl 67: 234-236
F 8 '28

Dietrich, E.G.W.

see also

Baltimore (MD)   House (near Baltimore) sketches
Cranford (NJ)   House
Jamestown (NY)   Bailey (Clayton E.) House
"   "   House
"   "   Marvin (Robt. N.) House
Lakewood (NJ)   Hall for House
"   "   Residence Hallway
Larchmont (NY)   Smith (Geo. C.) Residence

(See Card 2)

Dickson, Eugenia L.
An American Pottery (Teco Pottery) photos.

West. Archt.
17: 57-9
Jun, 1911

720.52 Dieppe (near). Manoir d'Ango.
A873   Bradwell, Darcy
Manoir d'Ango. 1532. Plans

Architectural review(Lond.) 58: 208-
December 1925   218 & pls.

Dietrich, E.G.W.   (Card 2)

see also

New London (CT)   Newcomb Residence, sketch
New York (NY)   (18) Broadway
Scranton (PA)   Jones (T.E.) House
"   "   Platt (Miss E. J.) Residence
"   "   Platt (F.E.) Residence
"   "   Taylor (D.E.) Residence
Warwick (NY)   Red Swan Inn
"   "   Wilder (V.A.) Residence

(See Card 3)

Dickson Mounds, Ill.
Deuel, Thorne.
Unique chapter of Illinois' past.
Ill. public works
4: 20-24
No. 1, Spring 1946

Dierschke, Werner
Das Ratsgymnasium in Hannover [plans &
section] Werner Dierschke & Annemarie
Bätjer-Kiens, archts.

Bauen & Wohnen
11:386-89 N 1956
Konstruktionsblätter
at end of issue

Dietrich, E.G.W.   (Card 3)

see also

Wyckoff (NJ)   Fuller (Paul) House

Dickson (TN) Dickson Normal College. Sketch by
Thompson & Gibel, Archs.

Inland Arch. 22:
pl. fol. p 12
Ag., 1893

720.5 Dietel and Wade and S.W.Jones
W59c   Metal artistry: Buffalo City Hall. Dietel
and Wade and S.W. Jones, archts.

Metalcraft 8: 160-161
April 1932

720.5 Dietrich, E. G. W.
A87m   Design for parish house and church. E. G.W.
Dietrich, architect.

Arch'ts. & bldgs. mag. 40:
562,563
S 1908

Didden, C.A.
Gardiner Hubbard
Residence, Washington D.C.

Inland Architect
32: 14
Sept, 1898

Dieterle, P

see

Riesenwald, Ger. Sanatorium

Dietrich, E G W
House for Mr. Chamberlain, Chester, New
York. E. G. W. Dietrich, archt.

Inland architect
v. 13 no. 5
pl. fol. p. 75
My 1889

Diedrichson, Hans Peter
Architekten-studio in Kiel [plan, section &
details] Haus Peter Diedrichson & Rüdiger Hoge,
archts.

Architektur & Wohnform
69: 150-53, My 1961

Dietfurt, Ger. St. Ägidius
Neuhofer, Theo
Die Pfarrkirche von Dietfurt; ein Werk von
Gabriel de Gabrieli.

Das Münster
14: 360, S-O 1961

Dietrich, E.G.W., residence
design (with floor plan)

Inland Archt.
Vol. 24, No. 4, pl.
Fol. p. 40
Nov. 1894

Diener, Marcus
Autosilo und Hotel International, Basel
[plan & sections] Marcus Diener, archt.

Baumeister
55:503-5 Jl 1958

Dietrich, A
Kassel; Haus St. Michael; 1960/1961 [plans]
A. Dietrich, archt

Das Münster
vol.14: 424-425, N-D 1961

Dietrich, E G W
Residence for Mr. Waring, Brooklyn, N.Y. E.
G. Dietrich, archt.

Inland architect
v. 12 no. 1
pl. at end of vol.
Ag 1888

Dietrich, E.G.W. Residence (no location given) with 1st and 2nd floor plans.

Inland Arch.
Vol. 27, No. 6, pl. Fol. p.60
July 1896

720.54   Dijon. Architecture
A87   Mayeaux, Albert
XCI congrès de la Société Francaise d'Archéologie. (Ninety first congress of the Société Francaise d'Archéologie at Dijon)

L'Architecture 41: p.321-328
October 15, 1928

Dijon. Maison Milsand
Maison Milsand, 38, rue des Forges, Dijon.
Text in French. Exteriors, bibliography.

Vitry, Paul. Hotels et maisons de la Renaissance Française. 3 vols. Paris:
E. Lévy, 1910 -[?] v.3 pt1:32, v.3 pt 2
pl. 65-66

Dietrich, E   G   W
Semi-detached houses for W. Wagner, Esq.
[plan] E. G. W. Districh, archt.

Inland architect
v. 12 no. 7
pl. at end of vol.
D 1888

Dijon. Cathedral

See

Dijon. Saint Bénigne.

Dijon. Maisons
Maisons du XV siècle à Dijon. Plans.

Verdier, Aymar. Architecture Civile et domestique. 2 vols. Paris:
Bance, 1857-58. vol. 2:111-114, plates

Dietrich, E. G. W.
Sketch of residence for F. P. Hall (no location given) with 1st floor plan.

Inland Arch.
Vol. 27, No. 6, pl. Fol. p. 60
July 1896

Dijon. Hotel Benigne Serre
Hôtel Benigne Serre, 39, rue Vannerie, Dijon.
Text in French. Exteriors, bibliography.

Vitry, Paul. Hotels et maisons de la Renaissance Francaise. 3 vols. Paris:
E. Lévy, 1910 -[?] v.3.pt 1:32,v.3 pt 2:
pl. 64

Dijon. Palais de Justice
Palais de Justice de Dijon, 16th century.
Text in french. Measured details.

Sauvengeot, Claude. Palais, Chateaux, hotels, et maisons de France. 4 vols.
Paris: A. Morel, 1867. v.4:73-83,pls.1-4

Dietrich (E.G.W.) and Henry La Pointe
Design for a Church.

Inland Archt.
vol. 36,No.2,pl.fol.p. 16
Sept, 1900

Dijon. Hôtel de Rochefort
Hôtel de Rochefort, 56, rue des Forges, Dijon.
Text in French. Exteriors, plans, bibliography.

Vitry, Paul. Hotels et maisons de la Renaissance Francaise. 3 vols. Paris:
E. Lévy, 1910 - [?] v.3 pt 1: 31,v.3 pt.2:
pls. 62-63

Dijon (Fr.) Place Darcy
The Treatment of a City Square in France. The Place Darcy at Dijon.

House and garden 5: 123-24
Mr 1904

Dietterlin, Wendel   1550-1599
Alten kanzleigebäude zu Stuttgart

Fritsch, K.E.O., ed. Denkmaeler deutscher renaissance. 4 vols.
Berlin: E. Wasmuth, 1891. v.1:73-74
v.4:18

Dijon. Hôtel de Vogüe
Hotel de Vogüe à Dijon. 17th century. Text in French. Plan, measured detail drawings.

Sauvengeot, Claude. Palais, Chateaux, hotels, et maisons de France.
4 vols. Paris: A. Morel, 1867.
v.1:21-32, pl. 35-60

Dijon (Fr.) Rue des Forges maison
Maison du 16th century: Rue des Forges, à Dijon.
Text in French. Plan, measured detail drawings.

Sauvengeot, Claude. Palais, Chateaux, hotels, et maisons de France. 4 vols.
Paris: A. Morel, 1867. v.2:1-4,pl.1-7.

Jahrbuch der asiatischen kunst
2:101-105
1925

Dijon. Hôtel Fyot de Mimeure
Hôtel Fyot de Mimeure, 23, rue Admiral-Roussin.
Text in French. Exteriors, bibliography.

Vitry, Paul. Hotels et maisons de la Renaissance Francaise. 3 vols. Paris:
E. Lévy, 1910 -[?] v.3 pt 1:33, v.3 pt 2:
pl. 67-68

Dijon (Fr.). Rue Vannerie, 66
Maison, rue Vannerie, 66, Dijon. Text in French.
Exterior, bibliography.

Vitry, Paul. Hotels et maisons de la Renaissance Francaise. 3 vols. Paris:
E. Lévy, 1910 -[?] v.3 pt.1:33 v.3
pt.2 pl.69

Diggle, W. Wrigley

see

Lympe Hill (Eng.) Long Barrow

Dijon. Maison des Cariatides
Maison des Cariatides, 28, rue Chaudronnerie, Dijon. Text in French. Exterior, Bibliography.

Vitry, Paul. Hotels et maisons de la Renaissance Francaise. 3 Vols. Paris:
E. Lévy, 1910 - [?]
v.3 pl: 34 v.3 pt 2 pl

Dijon. Saint Bénigne
Dijon cathedral. Details and working drawings.

King, Thomas H. The Study-book of mediaeval architecture and art. 4 vols. London: H. Sotheran and Co., 1868. v.1:pl.63

Ryerson
Dijon, Fr. Saint Bénigne
Maitre, L.
Les monuments chrétiens d'Autun. L'église
de Saint Bénigne de Dijon et ses cryptes [plans
and sections]

Revue de l'art chrétiens
54:279-291
Jl 1904

Dillon, Arthur

see also

St. Louis, Mo., St. Louis Club House Competition

Dimitrijevic, Jean

see

Dimitrijevic, Jova

790.53   Dijon (Fr.) St. Philibert
A67c   South doorway

Arch & c. rep 73: 144, pl prec
153
Mr 3, '05

720.5   Dillon, Arthur
A67   Competition for the rearrangement of the
University of Minnesota campus. Arthur Dillon
and Henry Beadel, and others, archts. Plans.

Architectural review 15:130
August 1908

Dimitrijevic, Jova
Hotel de France, Conakry, Belgisch-Kongo
[plans & section] Guy Lagneau, Michel Weill &
Jean Dimitrijevic, archts.

Bauen & Wohnen
#4:130-31 Ap 1958

Dilks, Albert W.

see

Williamsport (Pa.) Camble (J.M.) house
Wynnewood, Pa. Dissel (Charles) house
Stratford, Pa. Morton (T.G.) house

Dillon, Arthur
Sketch (unidentifed)

Inland Archt.
50: pl.fol.p. 24
Aug, 1907

Dimmock, M. J.

see

Richmond, Va., Apartment Bldg.

Dillard, Frank G.   -1949
[obit. note]

AIA Chicago chap. bul: 18
Je 1949

Dillon, John Robert

Member of firm:

Bruce, Morgan and Dillon

Dimond, Grover W., jr.

see

St. Paul, Minn. Dimon (G.W. jr.) house

Dillard, Richard

see

Edenton (N.C.) Beverly hall

Dillon, McLennan and Beadel

see

Put-in-Bay (O.) Perry memorial. Competition

720.52   Dinant (Belg.)
B96   Pen and ink sketches by T.R. Davison

British architect 82: plates
for
S 25 '14

Dillingham (Walter) residence, Honolulu, Haw.

see

Honolulu, Haw. Dillingham (Walter) residence

Dimakopoulos, Dimitri

see

Affleck, Desbarats, Dimakopoulos, Lebensold,
and Sise

Dinant, cathedral
Water color by Sir Ernest George.

Builder 107: pl. fol.
S 25, 1914

Dillman, F. C.
Ski cabins. Plans. Design of three cabins
by F.C. Dillman. Plans. Maximum accomodation
comfort and economy.

House and garden 72:70-71,92
December 1937

Dimensional coordination of building materials

see

Building. Standardization of sizes

Dingemans, F. C. J.
Wongingbouw te Maastricht [plan & sections]
F. C. J. Dingemans,

Forum no. 8
p. 308-309
1954

Dingle, Aubrey Hendon Dawes
House at Kingswear [plan & section]
Dawes Dingle, archt.

Archl Design
28:358 S 1958

Dining Rooms
A student's dining hall. B.A.I.D.
Award.

Amer. arch. 103:
2 pls fol 244
My 21, 1913

720.5   Dinkelberg, Frederick Philip 1859-1935
I58   Rhythm in architecture.

Inland architect 51:58
Jun 1908

Dingley Hall (Northamptonshire), Eng.
The Estate market, Dingley hall, in the
Woodland Pytchley country.

Country life (lond.) 80:xxx
December 12, 1936

Dining rooms
Tiravanti, Lanfranco Bombelli
Vita breve della camera da pranzo [history of
the dining room.]

Domus no. 715:17-19
Mr'46

Dinkelberg, Frederick P.
Thoughts on architecture.

Inland Arch.
51: 39-40
May 1908

Dining halls

see

Refectories

Dinkelberg, E. P.

see

Vatican City. San Pietro

720.5   Dinkelsbuhl (Ger.) Architecture
A67   Josellyn, F.M.
            The most picturesque medieval town in Cen-
         tral Europe.

Arch review 21:n.s.4:73-76
My '16

Dining Rooms

see also

Banquet Halls
Hotel dining-rooms

Dinkelberg, Frederick Philip, 1859-1935

see also

Chicago (IL)   Mausoleum, Studies
   "   "   Pure Oil Building

720.5   Dinocrates
A 7r   Frothingham,A.L.
            Greek architects: Dinocrates.

Architectural record 23:80-95
February 1908

720.5   Dining rooms.
A67   Designs for a dining room.

Arch rev 6: pl LXII fol 114
S 1899

Dinkelberg, Frederick Philip
Modern architecture

In SCRAPBOOK ON
ARCHITECTURE p. 945
(on film)

Dinwiddie & Newberry

See

Battle Creek (MI) First Presbyterian Church
Chicago (IL)   Candee Apt. Building

Dining rooms
Dining room furniture

Bajot, Edouard. Encyclopédie
du meuble du XVe Siècle. 7 vols.
Paris: C. Schmid, 1901-09.

Dinkelberg, Frederick Philip, 1859-1935
Obituary

Illinois society of architects
Monthly bulletin
19:4
Ap-My 1935

Dinwiddie, J. H.

see

Chicago, Il., Wells (L.G.) Apartment Bldg.

720.54   Dining rooms
H76   La fonction alimentation dans le logis
         [plans]

L'Homme et L'Arch.
17-48, S-0, 1946

Dinkelberg, Frederick Philip, 1859-1935
obituary notice

In SCRAPBOOK ON
ARCHITECTURE p.724
(on film)

Dinwiddie, John Ekin

see

San Francisco (Cal.) Chevrolet building

Diocletian, emperor, Baths of, Rome

see

Rome, It. Thermae of Diocletian

Dirnhuber, Karl

see

Vienna (Aus.) Housing

Dise, J. Ivan

see

Ann Arbor (Mich.) Walser (J.J.) house
Bloomfield Hills (Mich.) Reichhold (H.) house

Diocletian, emperor. Palace. Split, Yugo.

see

Split (Yugo.) Palace of Diocletian

Dirssar, Leon G
   House in Vancouver, British Columbia
[plans] Leon G. Dirssar & H. Peter Oberlander,
archts.

Archtl Design
29:436-37 N 1959

720.55   Disinfection stations. Germany.
B51   Städtische desinfektionsanstalt, Neukölln.

                Berliner architekturwelt
                16:heft 5-6, 214-7.
                1913

Dionysus theater

See

Athens. Theater of Dionysus

Disabled

see

Handicapped

Dismukes, T   L   d. 1891
   Obituary.

Inland architect
v. 18 no. 1: 12
Ag 1891

Dioramas.

Britton, John and A. Pugin.
   Illustrations of the Public
   buildings of London. 2 vols.
   London: J. Taylor, 1825-28.
   v.1,p. 66-71 and pl.

Dischinger,Fr

See

Ritter,Hubert and Dischinger

Dispensaries

   see also names of dispensaries, i.e:

New York (city) St. John's Riverside hospital,
   Sherman memorial dispensary
Casablanca, Mor. Dispensaire antituberculeux

Dioramas, Chicago

see

Chicago (Ill. Dioramas

Dise.   and   Ditchy

see also

Detroit (Mich.) Cosgrain (C.B.) house
  "   "   Palms (C.L.) house

720.54   Dispensaries, France
A67   Dispensaire d'hygiène sociale

                L'Architecture 37:86-8
                Apr. 25, 1924

Dirksmöller, Hermann
[plans and sections]

Baumeister
52, no.3:156-158,
tafel 24
Mr 1955

Dise & Ditchy

   Members of firm:

   Dise, J.I.
   Ditchy, C.W.

Display of merchandise

see

Show windows

Dirlam, Arband A.

see

Pawtucket,(R.I.) Park Place Congregational

720.5   Dise and Ditchy
P59   House and plan, residence of W. B. Bry-
          ant. Dise & Ditchy, archts.

                Pencil points 6: 81
                January 1925

Display rooms

see

Showrooms

Dissel (Charles) house. Wynnewood, Pa. see Wynnewood, Pa. Dissel (Charles) house	Distel, Hermann - 1946 Ein molkerei-Neubau in Hamburg. (A new dairy building in Hamburg.) Hermann Distel, archt. Plans. Wasmuths monatshefte 15: 322-325 July 1931	Ditchley, Eng. Ditchley park; James Gibbs, archt. Vogue: 112, pt.1: 196-201 S 1 '48
Dissymmetry see also Asymmetry	Distel, Hermann - 1946 Uber bettenpreis und krankenhauskosten. (About bed-prices and hospital expenses.) New hospital of the German-Jewish organ-ization in Hamburg. Plans. Observation station of the children's hospital in Hamburg. Home for cripples in Hamburg. Hermann Distel, archt. Wasmuths monatshefte 15: 119-125 March 1931	Ditchy, Clair W. 1891 - Clair Ditchy re-elected. [biographical sketch] Nat'l arch 1:1 N '45
720.5 A51 Dissymmetry Bosworth, W.W. Some Observations on Architectural Dissymmetry. Amer. archt 98, Pt 1: 93-3 ,pl. pre-ceding 93 S 21, '10	720.53 M68 Distel, Rolf Brückner, F.P. Arbeiten von Rolf Distel, Köln. (Work by Rolf Distel, Cologne.) Plans. Orphan home in Cologne-Mülheim; residence building; interiors. Moderne bauformen 26: 413-426 November 1927	Ditchy, Clair W. 1891- Elected secretary A.I.A. [includes biographical sketch]. Nat'l arch 2:6 L '47
Distel and Grubitz see also Hamburg, Ger. Kontanhof office bldg.	Distilleries see also names of individual distilleries i.e.: Montreal, Que. Meagher bros. co. ltd. distillery etc.	710.5 H84 Ditchy-Farley-Perry Residence of Mr. Elmer E. Kelley, Detroit, Michigan. Ditchy-Farley-Perry, archts. Plans House and garden 74: 44 August 1938
Distel and Grubitz Modern water tower, Germany. Double residence at Hamburg. Modern German residences. Unique design for corner bldg., Hamburg. Moderne bauformen 25: 113-138 1926	720.54 T25 Distilleries Grimaud, G. Les distilleries. [sect.] Tech. et Arch. 3: 144-147 My-Je '43	Ditmars, Isaac E. see Schickel and Ditmar
Distel, Hermann - 1946 see also Hamburg (Ger.) Elektricitätswerke. Verwaltungs-gebaude Bergedorf (Ger.) St. Petri-und-Pauli-gemeindehaus	District heating see Heating from central stations	Dittemore, Leonard D. see Lake George (Col.) Eleven-mile ranch. Houf (Harry) cabin
Distel, Hermann - 1946 Hamburg's neuer seegrenz-schlachthof. (Hamburg's new sea-coast slaughter yard.) Hermann Distel, archt. Plans. Wasmuths monatshefte 14: 120-123 March 1930	720.52 A67ay Ditchingham (Eng.) Housing Terrace houses at Ditchingham (Lodden) Norfolk. [plans] Taylor and Green, archts. Archts' yr. bk 4: 168-169 1951	Dittoe and Wisenall see Covington (KY) First Christian Church

Dittoe, Fahnestock & Ferber
see also
Wilmington (O.) theater

Diving platforms
see also
Lausanne (Switz.) Bellerive plage

Dixon and Brooks
Three residences for George Sunderland
on Forest avenue near 38th street. Dixon
& Brookes, archts.

Inland archt & news rec 20:20
September 1892

Dittoe, Fahnestock and Ferber
Members of firm:
Dittoe, Louis G.
Fahnestock, L.W.
Ferber, C.H.

720.54
T25
Diving Platforms.
Plongeoirs. [sect.].

Tech et Arch 2:65-66
Ja-F'42

Dixon, Francis George
Wohnquartier in Peterlee bei Newcastle [plan]
RJA Gazzard, chief archt, Peter Daniel & Frank
Dixon, archts.

Baumeister
58: 750-55, Ag 1961

Dittoe, Louis G.
see also
Cincinnati (OH) Cincinnati Arch. Club Competition
Lych Gate

Diving platforms
Fabian, D.
Sprungeinrichtungen in frei- und hallen-
badern [plans and sections]

Baumeister
53: Entwurfsblätter 9-24
F 1956

Dixon (Ill.) Dodge library
O.B. Dodge library, Dixon, Ill. W.A.Otis,
archt. Plan.

Architectural review 9,n.s.4:49
January 1902

Dittoe, Louis G.
Member of firm:
Dittoe, Fahnestock and Ferber

Diving platforms, Finland
see
Helsinki (Fin.) Ugnsholmen bathing beach. Diving tower
and grandstand.

720.5
I56
Dixon (Ill.) Farwell (C. N. & Co.) shoe
factory
Shoe factory for C. N. Farwell & Co.,
L. B. Dixon, archt.

Inland archt & news rec 18:28
September 1891

Dittoe, Louis G.   1869(?)-1947
[obituary]

Nat'l arch 5:15
Ar '47

Divus Julius temple, Rome
see
Rome (It.)   Temple of Divus Julius

Dixon, Lavall B.   1834 - ?
see also
Chicago (Ill.) Armour (J.Ogden) barn
"   "   Cohn (Bernard) house
"   "   Fargo (C.H.) & Co.manufacturing co.
"   "   Rothschild (A.M.) house
"   "   Roys (C.D.) house
"   "   South Park Ave.Methodist Episcopal
             Church (ca.1887)
"   "   Stubbs (J.B.) house
"   "   Walker (P.) house
"   "   Witkowsky (Conrad) house
Dixon   (Ill.)   Farwell (C.H.& Co.)shoe
                                    factory

Dives-sur-Mer (Fr.) William the Conqueror Inn
The inn of William the Conqueror at Dives-
sur-Mer.

Country life (U.S.) 56: 53
August 1929

Dixon and Brooks
see also
Chicago, Ill. Syndicate hotel Wabash
"   "   South Park Ave. M. E. church. Par-
sonage
Chicago, Ill. Cornell ave. (no.5431) apt. house

Dixon, Lavall B   1834-
Architect

Andreas, A.T. History of Chicago.
3 vols. Chicago: A.T. Andreas, 1884.
3:68

Dives-sur-Mer (Fr) William the Conqueror Inn
Chambre des Marmoussets, Inn of William
the Conqueror, Dives, Normandy. Drawing by
Edwin H. Denby.

Architectural digest 9: 92
Number 2 [1936-37]

Dixon and Brooks
A block of 5 residences for Louis Keefer
on Prairie avenue, south of 39th street.
Dixon & Brooks, archts.

Inland archt & news rec 19:65
June 1892

Dixon, Lavall B.   1834 - ?
5 Residences for George Sunderland on Forest
avenue near 37th street. L.S. Dixon, archt.

Inland archt & news rec 18:56
November 1891

Dixon, Lavall B
Manufacturing building for C. M. Fargo & co.
L. B. Dixon, archt.

Inland architect
19, no. 4
pl. fol. p. 54
My 1892

Djenan-el-Mufti

see

Mustapha Superieur (Alg.) Djenan-el-Mufti

Dobbs, H. Wilson. Architectural heraldry.
Photos.

Inland Arch.
48: 27-8 Oct. 1906
48: 39-40 Nov. 1906
49: 31-2 Feb. 1907

720.5
B95b
Dixon, Lavall B   1854-
Sketch of residences of Bernard Cohn and
Louis Wampold, Michigan boulevard between
31st and 33rd streets, Chicago. L. B. Dixon,
archt.

Building budget 3: pl.fol.p.166
December 31, 1887

Doane building (1872), Chicago

see

Chicago, Ill. Doane building (1872)

Dobbs Ferry, N.Y. Livingston Apts.
Livingston apartments, Dobbs Ferry, N.Y.

Architecture 45:222-3
Jul., 1921

720.5
B95b
Dixon, Lavall B.   1854-
Sketch of two residences on Michigan Ave.
near 37th St. for Conrad Witkowsky and
Lipman Glick. L.B.Dixon, archt.

Building budget 5: pl.fol.p.22
February 23, 1889

Doane, Ralph Harrington   1886-1941
See also
Walker and Doane

Dobbs Ferry (N.Y.) New York juvenile Asylum.
Competition
General plan - competition for the New York
Juvenile Asylum. York and Sawyer, archts.
Howell and Stokes, archts. Hospital, school
building, cottages, church.

Architectural review 9,n.s.4:pl.40-
August 1902   47

Dixon, Lavall B.   1834 - ?
two 3-story residences on Dearborn
Ave. for Wiley N. Eagan. L.B. Dixon, archt.

Building budget 3:24a
F 28 1887

Doane, Ralph Harrington   1886-1944
see also
Boston (Mass.) Motor Mart garage

Dobbs Ferry (N.Y.) New York Juvenile Asylum
School
School building,N.Y. Juvenile Asylum,
Dobbs Ferry, N.Y. York and Sawyer, archts.

Architectural review 16: 105
August 1909

Dixon (S.B.) house. Detroit, Mich.

see

Detroit, Mich. Dixon (S.B.) house

720.5
F29
Doane, Ralph Harrington 1886-1941
Shepley, H.R.
Modern architecture; the Park Square
Garage, Boston. Ralph H. Doane, archt.; no plan.

Federal architect 7:19
October 1936

Dobbs Ferry, (N.Y.) Misses Masters School
The Misses Masters' school, Dobbs Ferry,
N.Y. Cram and Ferguson, architects

Architectural record 53:136-41,
Feb. Ap. 1923   354-61

Dixon-Spain, J.   E.

see

Gibralter (Spain) Rock hotel

MICROFILM

Doane, Ralph Harrington, 1886-1941
obituary notice

in SCRAPBOOK ON
ARCHITECTURE p. 724
(on film)

720.5
A67
Dobbs Ferry (N.Y.) Tyssowski (J.) house
House of John Tyssowski, Dobbs Ferry,
N.Y. Clinton Mackenzie, archt. Plan.

Architect (N.Y.) 9: 489-491
Ja '28

Djémila (Alg.) Arch of Triumph
Ballu, Albert
Note sur les fouilles de Djémila: L'arc de
triomphe de Djémila (avant et après la restauration) (Note on the excavations of Djémila: arch
of triumph - before and after the restoration.)

L'Architecture 37: 262
October 10, 1924

Dobbins (Cal.) hotels
Hotel at Dobbins, Yuba County, California.

Architect & engineer 118: 29
July 1934

Doberitz, Ger. Evangelische garnisonkirche
Evangelische Garnisonkirche, Doberitz.

Berliner architekturwelt
19:6-10 & col. pl. Heft 1,
1916.

720.5 W52 **Dobie, Samuel** Kimball, Fiske and Wells Bennett The competition for the Federal buildings, 1792-1793. pt.1; pt.2; pt.3; pt.4 American institute of architects' journal 7: January 1919 8-12; March 1919 98-102; May 1919 202-210; August 1919 355-361; December 1919 521-527	**Docks** see also Ferry terminals Wharves	720.5 H97b **Dockstader, Otis** Summer cottage at Lake Hopatcong, N.J. Otis Dockstader, archt. Building budget 6: pl.fol.p.58 May 31, 1890
Dobris, Czechoslovakia Burnap, George The gardens of Dobris near Prague, Czechoslovakia. Architectural record 52: 511-23 December 1922	**Docks** With ship landing. Scribner's 50:570 Nov. 1911	720.5 B97b **Dockstader, Otis** Sketch for Castle Rock hotel, Lake Hopatcong, N.J. Otis Dockstader, archt. Building budget 6: pl.fol.p.70 June 30, 1890
Dobrzynska, J. and Z. Loboda see Istebna (Pol.) Sanatorium for children	720.52 B93 **Docks-England** New cold storage works, Royal Albert Docks Builder 114:67,68 & pl. Jan. 25, 1918	720.5 A67b **Dockyards.** Staten island, Stapleton, N. Y. Arch.& building 53:87-8 & pl.174-80. Nov. 1921.
720.52 A675 **Dobson, Frank.** Bell, C. Frank Dobson. (Lond.) Arch. rev.59:41-45 Feb. 1926	720.52 A67 **Docks,England. Southampton** New graving dock at Southampton. Largest dry dock in the world. Architects' journal 78: 129 August 3,1933	720.52 B93 **Dockyards. England.** Buildings for the Port of London. Builder 119: pl. , p. 487. Oct. 29, 1920.
Dobson, John Glover, Kenneth What Newcastle owes to Dobson. Archts' jour 52:43-47 Jl 8, 1925	720.52 A67 **Docks,France. Cherburg** Dock at Cherburg. Architects' journal 78: 129 August 3,1933	710.5 C85 **Dockyards, England. Liverpool.** The new Gladstone docks. Liverpool. Country life (Lond.) 62: 111-12 July 23, 1927
Dockery, J. see Apartment houses (U.S.) (Mo.) Saint Louis	**Docks, U.S. Chicago.** Chicago's first dock. Andreas, A.T. History of Chicago. 3 vols. Chicago: A.T. Andreas, 1884. v.2,p.329	720.52 B93 **Dockyards,England. London** Staff offices for the Port of London Authority,King George V Dock; Front and back elevations. Sir Edwin Cooper,archt. Builder 144: 59-60,98 January 13,1933 A
Dockhead, Eng. Fire Station The new Dockhead fire station. Architect (Lond.) 121: 364-365 March 15, 1929	720.5 A51 **Docks,U.S.Portland(Ore.)** Hegardt, G.B. The port development at Portland, Oregon. G.B.Hegardt, chief engineer, the commission of Public works. American architect 118:865-867 December 29, 1920	915.08 J36 **Dockyards, Manchuria; Dairen** Japan 19:25 February 1930

"Dr. R." house, Milan (It.)

see

Milan (It.) "Dr. R." house

720.52
A874

Dodd, George
Original designer of Waterloo bridge

Architecture (Lond.) 4: 112-
118.
July 1925

Doddington (Eng.)
Hussey, Christopher
Doddington Hall, Lincolnshire. Seat of
Major Charles Jarvis. Built 1593-1600.
Furniture and pictures at Doddington Hall.

Country Life 80:356-361,382-388,1x
October 3, 1936

Doctors' offices

see

Medical and dental buildings

Dodd, John
see

Madison (N.J.) Eken (A.J.) house

MICROFILM

Dodecagonal houses
[George D. Tesch, archt.]

in BOTA.......
ARCHIT......... p. 10
(on film)

Dod, Harold A.

see

Liverpool (Eng.)University Library (proposed)

Dodd, W. J.

see also

Beverly Hills (Cal.) Hellman (Irving) house

Dodford (Eng.) Church
Views from southeast, northwest, and of the
Transept and side chapel. Arthur Bartlett,
F.R.I.B.A., archt

Arch and con rep 83:
64 and pl;Ja 28, 1910
96 and pl;F 11,   "
pl 8; Mr 4, 1910

Dodd, A.B.C., house. Charles City, Ia.

see

Charles, City, Ia. Dodd, A.B.C., house.

Dodd, W.J.
Member of firm.
McDonald & Dodd

Dodford (Eng.) "The Tower"

"The Tower," Dodford. Mr. Arthur Barlett,
Architect.

Arch & con rep 83: pls
F15, 1910

Dodd, A. H.

see

Manchester-by-the-sea (Mass.) Pratt (W.) house

Dodd, W. J. and Arthur Cobb

see also

Frankfort (KY)   Berry (G.F.) House
Louisville (KY)   Dodd (W.J.) Residence
     "   "   Fourth Ave. M.E. Church
     "   "   Grabfelder (S.) Residence

Dodge and Morrison

see

Coney Island (N.Y.) Brighton theatre
Jersey City (NJ) Peoples Palace

Dodd and Richards

see

Los Angeles (Cal.) Spring st. market
  "   "   "   Pacific finance building
  "   "   "   Jacob Riis Boy's school

Dodd, William J.
Member of firms:
Maury & Dodd
Dodd (W.J.) and Arthur Cobb

Dodge, Edwin S.

See also

Ames, Putnam & Dodge

Dodd and Richards, McNeal . Swasey

see

Los Angeles (Cal.) Architects' building

Dodd, William J.
Forms association with Arthur Cobb.

Inland Arch.
27: 59
July 1896

Dodge, Edwin S.

see

Farmington (Conn.) Bissell (R.M.) house

720.5
A67r
Dodge, F.W.
Babson, R.W.
F.W. Dodge, A tribute

Arch rec 39: fol. p. 98
Ja 1916

Döcker, Richard, 1894-1968
Die Universitäts - Bibliothek in Saarbrücken
1952/53 (plan and section) Richard Döcker, archt.

Architektur and Wohnform
63: 236-243
Ag 1955

Doerr, J.F. and J.P.

see also

Chicago (Ill.) Doerr (J.P.) house
"   "   Stein (Joseph) houses
"   "   Wentworth Ave. (no.2971) bldg.
Naperville (Ill.) S.S.Peter and Paul catholic school
Chicago (IL)   Cottage Grove Ave. (5008 & 5010)
                Apt. Building
"   "   39th St. & Vernon Ave. 4-story
                Store and Flat Building

720.6
C53
Dodge, Colonel Harrison Howell
Colonel Dodge of Mount Vernon.

Federal architect 7:26-27
October 1936

Döcker, Richard 1894-1968
Universitätsbiblithek in Saarbrücken (plan
and section) Richard Döcker, archt.

Bauen and wohnen
No. 5: 329-332
O 1955

Doerr, J. F. and J.P.
Apartment house for Dr. Tucker on
Jackson avenue between 56th and 57th sts.
J.F. & J.P. Doerr, archts.

Inland archt & news rec 20:58
December 1892

720.5
A61
Dodge, William Waldo, Jr.
Unskilled labor and local materials lend
character to house of W. A. Knight, Biltmore
Forest, N. C. William Waldo Doige, Jr., archt.

American architect 136: 26-29
November 1929

Döcker, Richard 1894-1968
Ein wohnhaus für 3 familien in Reichen-
bach/Württ (plan) Richard Döcker, archt.

Architektur and Wohnform
V. 63: 143-150
Ap 1955

Doerr, J.F. and J.P.
Apartment house of C.E.W. Platt on
Berkeley avenue, near 45th st. J.F.
& J.P.Doerr, archts.

Inland archt & news rec 17:73
July 1891

Döcker, Richard, 1894-1968
Biblioteca de la Universidad de Sarrebruck,
Alemania (plan) R. Docker, archt.

Proa
108:21 Ap 1957

Döhnert, Horst
Einfamilienhaus in München [plan & section]
Horst Wöhnert, archt.

Baumeister
58: 758-63, Tafeln 48-52
Ag 1961

Doerr, J. F. and J.P.
Apts. for C. Crede on Wabash avenue corner of 45th
street. J. F. & J.P. Doerr, archt.

Inland archt & news rec 20:29
October 1892

Döcker, Richard 1894-1968
Einfamilienhaus in Bad Cannstatt (plans)
Richard Döcker, archt.

Architektur and wohnform
63: 151-156
Ap 1955

720.53
B35
Döllgast, H
Wettbewerb für eine volksschule in München
Trudering (Competition for a public school
in Munich-Trudering). Plan by H.Döllgast.

Der baumeister 34:54-55
February 1936

Doerr, J.F. and J.P.
Apts for F.Cragin on Wabash avenue
and 41st street. J. F. & J.P. Doerr,
archts.

Inland archt & news rec 18:13
August 1891

Döcker, Richard, 1894-1968
Salle à Stuttgart avec peintures murales
de Willy Baumeister et détail. (Hall at Stuttgart
with mural paintings by Willy Baumeister and detail.)
Richard Döcker, archt.

L'architecture vivante: pl.40
Winter 1927

Doen brothers
Store and Apts. for John Phillips.
Doen Bros., archts.

Inland archt & news rec 13:13
February 1889

Doerr, J.F. & J.P.
Apts. for Patrick Walsh on 37th st. near Wallace
street. J.F. & J.P. Doerr, archt.

Inland archt & news rec 20:53
May 1892

Döcker, Richard, 1894-1968
Sanatorium, à Waiblingen, 1928.
(Sanatorium, at Waiblingen,1928)
Richard Döcker, archt. No plan.

L'Architecture Vivante: pls. 1-3
1929 - Autumn

D'Oench and Yost

see

Sandusky (O.) Carnegie library
Utica (N.Y.) Public library. Competition
New York (N.Y.) Tribune building

Doerr, J.F. and J.P.
Apts for W.C. Polzin at 5118 Wabash avenue.
J.F. & J.P. Doerr, archts.

Inland archt & news rec 20:57
December 1892

Doerr, J.F. and J.P. Apts. for W.J.Doerr on Dearborn street near 24th st. J.F. & J.P. Doerr, archt. Inland archt & news rec 18:56 November 1891	Dörr, Rudolf [plans] Baumeister 52, no.5: 282-286, tafeln 36-7 My 1955	Dog Race tracks, England Greyhound racing track, Townsend-lane, Liverpool. John E. Rowlands, archt. Builder 131: 1086 December 31, 1926
Doerr, J.F. & J.P. Biographical Sketch Industrial Chicago: The Building Interests. 4 vols. Chicago: Goodspeed Pub. Co., 1891-(?) - Vol. 1: Pg. 631	Doerrbecker, Karl P. Erdgeschossige einfamilienhäuser bei Frankfurt/Main [plans] Karl P. Doerrbecker, archt. Baumeister Vol. 51:152-160, pl 26 and 27 My 1954	Doggett building, Chicago see Chicago (Ill.) Doggett building
Doerr, J.F. & J.P. Bldg for John Becker at 3654 Wentworth avenue. J. F. & J. P. Doerr, archts. Inland archt & news rec 18:13 August 1891	Doerrbecker, Karl Ferienhaus im Odenwald [plans & sections] Karl Doerrbecker, archt. Baumeister 57:914-16 D 1960 Tafeln 65 & 66	Dog-trot house Smith, Joseph Frazer. White Pillars: early life and architecture of the lower Mississippi Valley Country. New York: W. Helburn, 1941. p.24-26
Doerr, J.F. and J.P. Bldg. for John O'Hare at 28th and Butler sts. J.F. & J.P. Doerr, archts. Inland archt & news rec 18:56 November 1891	Doerrbecker, Karl P [plans] Baumeister 51, no.11: 702-704 N 1954	Doheny, Edward L. jr., memorial library see Los Angeles, Cal. University of S. California. Edward L. Doheny jr. memorial library
Doerr, J.F. and J.P. Bldg. for R.F.Reedy at 31st and Armour ave. J.F. & J.P. Doerr, archts. Inland archt & news rec 17:73 July 1891	710.5 C85 Dog gate The dog gate at Newton Ferrers, Cornwall. Country life (Lond.) 84: 604-608;628-632 December 17, 1938	Doherty, John M. (delineator) see St. Paul (MN) Brown & Biglow Co. Art Gallery and Sales Room " " Carling Restaurant
Doerr, J.F. & J.P. Five residences for C.Tolman & Co. J.F. & J.P. Doerr, archts. Inland archt & news rec 19:15 February 1892	710.5 C855 Dog kennels Kennels of the Radnor Hunt Club at White Horse, Pa. Mellor and Meigs, archts. Country life (U.S.) 62: 59 October 1932	Dohme, Robert, 1845-1893 Norditalienische centralbauten des XVII. und XVIII. Jahrhunderts. Jahrbuch der K.Preussischē Kunstsammlungen 3:119-135 1882
Doerr, J.F. and J.P. Hotel in Hyde Park. J.F. & J.P. Doerr, archt. Inland archt & news rec 17:28 March 1891	Dog race tracks, England The dog track at Wimbledon. Country life (Lond.) 68: 436 October 11, 1930	720.54 A67 Doillet, Laurent brincourt, A. Immeuble Rue Doillet, 23 et 25, par A. Laurent Doillet. (Apartments 23 and 25, Bobillot Street, Laurent Doillet, architect.) Plans. L'architecture 38:45-50 February 25, 1925

720.54
A67
Doillet, Laurent
Brincourt, M.
Project of a commemorative monument. Laurent
Doillet, archt.

L'architecture 42: 259-260
August 15, 1929

710.5
C85
Doll houses
Edwards, Ralph
A child's wardrobe in the form of a house.

Country life (Lond.) 69: 375
March 21, 1931

Dolsth (Ger.) Waterworks
Waterworks at Dolsth. E.Richard Schmidt,
archt.

Wasmuths 11: 99
Heft 2, 1927

Dolan and Anderson

see

Valparaiso (Ind.) university. Chapel

BURNHAM LIBRARY
D19.05
V88
Doll houses
Doll houses by real architects. No plans

Vogue 80: 57
November 1,1932

Dolza, Francesco, 1925-
Due officine meccaniche a Torino;
stabilimento in corso Traiano [plan & details]
Stabilimento in via Sette Comuni [section]
Francesco Dolza, archt.

Casabella
#228:28-31 Je 1959

Dolch, Herman
Sketches for a chapel. Herman Dolch,
archt.

Der architekt 20: pl.75
Heft 6, 1914

710.5
C85
Doll houses
Tipping, H.A.
An eighteenth century doll's house

Country life 32:936-8
December 28, 1912

Dolzani palace.Brescia

See

Brescia.Palazzina Dolzani

Dole. Belay, Hôtel de
Hôtel de Balay, 7, rue Montroland, Dole.
Text in French. Exterior, Bibliography.

Vitry, Paul. Hotels et Maisons de la
Renaissance Française. 3 vols. Paris:
E. Lévy, 1910- [?] v.3 pt 1:34,v.3 pt.2:
pl.71

710.5
C 85
Doll houses
A late Georgian doll's house

Country life(Lond.)57:581
Apr.11,1925

Dom & Maurice
Wohnbauten der Association Nicolas
Bogueret, Geneve [plans & details] Dom & Maurice,
archts.

Bauen & Wohnen
vol.16: Supp. 1-2, Mr 1962

Dolena, J. E.

see

Bel Air (Cal.) Weber (H.B.) house
"   "   "   Wallace (Richard) house
Beverly Hills (Cal.) Taylor (Robert) house
"   "   "   Powell (William) house
"   "   "   Barr (Ingle) house
Brentwood (Cal.) Gale (B.T.) house
"   "   Dolena (J.E.) house
LaCanada (Cal.) Boddy (Manchester) house
Holmby Hills (Cal.) Bennett (Constance) house

BURNHAM LIBRARY
D15
D45
Doll houses
Unemployed architectural draughtsmen of
New York build dolls' houses. No illus.

Design 34: 204
January 1933

Dome of the rock, Jerusalem

see

Jerusalem. Dome of the rock

Doll, C. Fitzroy

see

London (Eng.) Imperial hotel
"   "   Hotel Russell

Doll houses, U.S. 20th c.
Houses have conveniences. [modern house and
southern colonial mansion]

Life articles on art. 340 E
Dec [?] 1940

Domes

see also

Renaissance domes

and subdivision: Dome, under name of
building, i.e:

Paris, Fr. Pantheon. Dome
New Orleans, La. St. Louis hotel. Dome
etc.

Doll houses

see also

Names of individual doll houses, i.e.:

Queen's doll house
etc.

710.5
C85
Doll houses,20th century
The modern movement in the doll's house.

Country life(Lond.)76: xxxvi
December 22,1934

Domes

Macartney, Mervyn Edmund. Practical
exemplar of architecture....7 vols.
London: Architectural review, 1908-27.
pl. 31-39.

Domes

Neufforge, Jean Francois de.
Recueil élémentaire d'architecture.
8 vols. Paris: L'auteur, 1757-68.
v.4:pl. 596,597,599-600.

Domes
McNamara, J. H.
Domes and Towers.

Building budget
5: 138-140
O 1889

705.8
Z48   Domes
Brinckmann, A. E.
The function of the vaulted ceiling

Zeitschrift für bildende
kunst 59: 10-18
Heft 1, 1925

Domes.
About domes.

Builder 106:717-719
Je 19, 1914

720.5
I56   Domes
McNamara, J.H.
Domes and towers: dimensions of famous towers

Inland archit-ct 14:57-58
November 1889

Domes
Midland bank: dome details. Gotch and
Saunders, archt. Plan

Archts jour
69: 133-5
Ja 16, 1929

Domes
Architecture's portfolio of cupolas.

Architecture 57: 286-292
May 1928

Domes.
The Dome as an Architectural Form.

British archt 57: 75
Ja 31, 1902

Domes
Hamlin, A.D.F.
The modern dome.

Inland Architect
29: 53-5
Jul, 1897

720.52
A67   Domes
Boyd, J. S.
Construction and stone-cutting of a domed
pavilion. Plans, section

Arch. jour 55: 567-75, 614-18
Ap 19, 26, '22

72052
B93   Domes
The dome in architecture

Builder 113:1
Jl 6 '17

Ryerson
Domes
Glück, Heinrich
Östlicher kuppelbau, renaissance und St.
Peter. Plans of domes: Pazzi chapel, Florence
(1430-1443); etc.

Monatshefte für kunst-
wissenschaft
12: 153-165, pl 50-51 fol
192
Jl 1919

Domes
Sanpaolesi, Piero
La cupola di Santa Maria del Fiore ed il
mausoleo di Soltanieh. Rapporti di forma e struttura fra la cupola del Duomo di Firenze ed il
mausoleo del Ilkhan Ulgiaitu a Soltanieh in
Persia. [illus., sum. in Ger.]

Florence. Kunsthistorisches
Institut. Mitteilungen.
v. 14, Heft 3: [221]-260
1972

Domes
Toy, Sidney
The dome: its history and construction,
Plans, sections. 4 pts.

Builder 125:
282-83; Ag 24, 1923
330-31; Ag 31, "
400-01; S 14, "
448-50; S 21, "

720.6
R88   Domes
Traquair, Prof. Ramsay
The origin of the pendentive.

R.I.B.A. 35: 185-7
January 26, 1928

Domes
The cupola that crowns the barn.

Country life (U.S.) 61: 52
April 1932.

729
T67   Domes
Ecclesastical domes

Topical architecture
V.1:No.11,pls 1-8, 1900
V.1:No.12,pls 1-8, 1900
V.2:No.16,pls 1-8, Ap '01
V.3:no.19,pls 1-8, Je '01
V.5:No.20,pls 1-8, Ag '01
V.5:No.29,pls 1-8, Ap '02
V.5:No.30,pls 1-8, Je '02
V.5:No.36,pls 1-8, D '02
V.6:No.44,pls 1-8, Ag '03
V.7:F 51,pls 1-8, F '04

Domes, Aluminum
Dôme en alliage léger, sans nervures, à
grande porté

Techniques & architecture
14e ser 1-2:10-11
1955

Domes
Decoration

Cassina, Ferdinando. Le Fabbriche più
cospicue di Milano. 2 vols. Milan:
F. Cassina and D. Pedrinelli, 1840-64.
pl. 65, K.

Domes
Brinckmann, A. E.
The function of the cupola

Zeitschrift für bildende kunst 59:43-48
Heft 2, 1925

720.6
A512j   Domes, Bulbous
Born, Wolfgang
The origins and the distribution of the
Bulbous Dome. Illus.

ASAH jl 3 no 4: 32-48
O '43

Domes, Coffered Birch, George H. London Churches of the XVIIth and XVIIIth centuries. London: B.T. Batsford, 1896. pl. 20	720.8 R88 Domes, India Longhurst, A. H. The developpment of the Stupa. R.I.B.A. 36: 135-149 December 22, 1928	Domestic architecture Card 2 Dodecagonal houses Glass houses Dymaxion houses Half-timbered houses Double houses Hexadecagonal houses Duplex houses Hexagonal houses Expansible houses Hillside architecture Four-Family houses Historic houses (see card 3)
Domes, Construction Detail of gymnasium carpentry cupola at Manhattan College. J. W. O'Connor, archt. Plan. Pencil points 6:79-80 January 1925	720.5P B93 Domes. India Metta, V.B. The dome in India Builder 125, pt. 2: 563 O 12 '23	Domestic architecture card 3 Lake Dwellings Log cabins Plastic houses Manor houses Plaster houses Metal houses Prefabricated houses Model houses Remodeled houses Octagonal houses Round houses Oval houses Saddle-back houses Plantation houses (see card 4)
Domes, England Cupolas. English detail. Builder 144: 194 February 3, 1933	Domes, Persia Burlington 26:146-155; 208-13 Jan., Feb. 1915	Domestic architecture Card 4 Steel houses Stone houses Stucco houses Villas Wooden houses Weekend houses
Domes, England, Georgian. Gibbs, James. Bibliotheca Radcliviana. London: The author, 1747. pl. 19.	Domes, Persia Origin of the Persian double dome Burlington 24: 94-99 Nov. 1913	710.5 C855 Domestic architecture Baum, D.J. The architecture of houses. Country life (U.S.)52:53 October 1927
Domes, England. London Selected examples of architecture. The cupola of the Horse Guards, Whitehall, London. Architectural rev. 53:220-1 June 1923	705.8 T55 Domes, Sweden Åberg, Gustaf Korrlundestaplarnas "lökar" en studie i deras forhistoria. (the onion dome in Sweden) Tidskrift for konstvetenskap 24, pt.4. 105-119 1942	710.5 C855 Domestic architecture Cross, John Walter The architecture of houses. Country life (U.S.)52:66-7 September 1927
Domes. France Planat, Paul. Le Style Louis XIV. Paris: Librairie de construction moderne, [c.1912] pl.35-6,71-3.	Domestic architecture see also City. Name of owner (Name of street and number when owner is not known)	710.5 H84 Domestic architecture Before you actually decide to buy a place. House and garden 63: 32-33 January 1933
Domes, France Enlart, C. Churches with cupolas in Aquitania and Cyprus Gazette des beaux-arts Per, 5, v.13: 129-152 March 1926	Domestic architecture See also Architects' homes Chalets houses Cinder concrete block Concrete houses Copper Houses Aluminum houses Coral houses Cottages Castles Country houses Cellular houses Conical houses (see card 2)	710.5 C855 Domestic architecture The budget idea in building. A country house on Main Street. Country life (N.Y.)49: 70-2 April 1926

710.5
C855
Domestic architecture
Harriman, E.E.
Building for best results. Pt.2 - Where to
look for trouble. Pt.3 Avoiding errors.

Country life 49: 44-46; 36-38
November-December 1925

Domestic architecture
Lanchester, H. V.
The ideal home [plans]

Western Arch't
13: 40-1
Ap 1909

Ryerson

Domestic architecture
Willson, Corwin
Shelter and mobility - an address given
the Yale - Life Conference on House Building
Technics, Feb 1, 1939

Delphian quarterly
22: 12-17, 37/
Ap 1939

720.5
A67a
Domestic architecture
Walsh, H.V.
Construction of the small house.

Arch 44:387-90
D '21

720.5
A79
Domestic architecture
Price, Matlack
The ideal of dignity in domestic architecture

Arts and decoration 23:24-26
July 1925

720.5
A51
Domestic architecture
Small dwelling construction - minimum
requirements recommended by the U.S. Dept.
of Commerce.

Amer archt 123, 285-90
Mr 28 '23

705.f
A644
Domestic architecture
Adams-Acton, Murray
Domestic architecture and decoration;
the decoration and general aspect of the
interior at various periods in the past.
Parts I-XX.

Apollo 1-8
Jan.1925- July 1928

720.5
A67f
Domestic architecture
The integrated house: it takes more than
30,000 parts to build a typical house.

Architectural forum 66: pp.fol.244
April 1937

Domestic architecture
Small house [General types and costs]

Architecture 42: 308-11
O 1920

Ryerson

Domestic architecture
Carver, Humphrey
The family house

Canadian art
4: 94-97
My 1947

Domestic architecture
Maison Standart pour le logement d'une
famille. (Standard house for the lodging of a family.)
Hugo Häring, archt. Plans.

Encyclopedie de l'architecture;
constructions modernes. 12 vols.
Paris: Albert Morancè, 1928-39.
4:no. 4 pl. 82-84

A

710.5
C855
Domestic architecture
Hering, Oswald
Smaller and better homes.

Country life (N.Y.) 50: 51
October 1926

720.54
T25
Domestic architecture
Sonrel, Pierre
Les fonctions de l'habitation:
1. L'Alimentation 2. Distraction-Conversation
3. Sommeil 4. Puériculture 5. Rangements
6. Hygiène 7 Circulations

Techniques et architecture
7:242-266
No. 5-6, 1947

710.5
C855
Domestic architecture
Beveridge, I.A.
Modern British and American houses, and plan
From church to residence, an unusual altera-
tion. Hanson & Altfillisch, archts.

Country life (N.Y.) 50: 60-2
October 1926

Domestic Architecture. Jenkins, C.E.
Style in residential architecture.

Inland Arch.
28: 5-6
Aug. 1896

Domestic architecture
A formal small house

House beautiful
88: 198-201
N 1946

720.52
B93
Domestic architecture
A modern house for a modest income. From
a correspondent.

Builder 144: 804
May 19,1933

Domestic architecture
Unità e variabilità della casa. Luigi
Fratino, archt. [plans, models, sections]

Domus no. 214:4-8
O'46

D13.1
H84
Domestic architecture
Holden, A.C.
A home for the man with a $7,000 income

House beautiful 65:158-160
February 1929

710.5
C855
Domestic architecture
Crane, C.B.
"The most convenient house in the world"
Gilbert Worden, archt. Plans.

Country Life 47:70-76
Ap '25

Domestic architecture
The walls begin to rise. The house assumes
its basic form

House and garden
50:124
O 1926
50: 114-15
N 1926

Card 1
713.1
H34   Bogner, W. F.
Wise economy in building.

House beautiful 69: 148-150,180;
February;March 1931 276-277,292-303

Card 2
Domestic architecture, 20th century.
H84   Morrison, Theodore
The house of the future

House beautiful 66:292-293,324,
September 1929   326,328,330

Card 3
713.1
H84   Domestic architecture, 20th century
Our modern home

House beautiful 64:724-725
December 1928

Card 4
Domestic architecture
Die Wohnhäuser. Von Albert Gessner.

Berliner Architekturwelt 10:447-72
Heft 12, 1908

Card 5
Domestic architecture. 20th century
Sexton, R.W.
The house of today. 5 pts.

House beau
67:596-8 , 744-5
68:58-9 , 136-7 , 262-3
My-S 1930

Card 6
Domestic architecture, 20th century.
Smith, Howard Leland
The postwar house.

Northwest archt v.no.6-7: 9
1944

Card 7
Domestic architecture. 15th cent.
Villefranche-de-Rouergue (Aveyron) maison
xve siècle.

Encyclopedie de l'architecture,
constructions de Style. 2 vols.
Paris: Albert Morancé, 1928 - [?]
Tome 1:pl.40

Card 8
710.5
H84   Domestic architecture, 20th century
If you're planning to build - analyses of
4 new American homes: Regency influence; modern Expression; Western type; early American
design. Allman Fordyce and William Hamby,
archts.

House and garden 70:56-61
September 1936

Card 9
710.5
H84   Domestic architecture, 20th century
Two degrees of modernism: a modified type,
and a straight interpretation. Albert Lee
Hawes, archt.

House and garden 64: 22-23
July 1933

Card 10
Domestic architecture. 20th century
Robertson, Howard M.
The domestic scene: contemporary trends.

RAIC jrl 15:254-255
N 1938

Card 11
720.5
H76   Domestic architecture, 20th century
La maison familiale. [plans, sect.]

L'Home et L'Arch
19-39
N/D '45

Card 12
Domestic architecture. 20th century. Exhibitions

see

New York (city) Museum of modern art. Exhibitions.
1945 ("Tomorrow's small house")

Card 13
Domestic architecture. 20th Cent.
Ramírez de Lucas, Juan
"Habitat 67". [illus.]

Goya
83: 306-308
Mr - Ap 1968

Card 14
051
V37   Domestic architecture. 20th century
Taylor, Helen Louise
A modern house plan for a family of four.

Vassar journal 9:1-4 and
plates I - IV. 1935

Card 15
910.5
N27   Domestic architecture, Africa
Kano builders in baked mud have developed
their own style of architecture...the dwelling of the Lamido of Rei Bouba...Potters
mould the conical huts of Logone river villages...

National geographic 74: 339,352,356
September, 1938

Card 16
Domestic architecture, 20th century
Gunn, Edwin
The house of the future.

Architect (Lond.) 119:3, 254,262
Ja 6, F 17, F 28, 1928

Card 17
Domestic architecture. 20th cent.
Maurer, Hans
Neue einfamilienhäuser.

Bauen & wohnen
#3:73 Mar 1957

Card 18
Domestic architecture, Africa, North

see also

Domestic architecture, Morocco
Domestic architecture, Algeria

Card 19
720.52
A67   Domestic architecture, 20th century
Bird, Eric L.
The house of the future.

Architects' journal 67: 321-322
February 29, 1928

Card 20
711
S77   Domestic architecture, 20th century
Klein, Alexander
Neues verfahren zur untersuchung von
Kleinwohnungs-grundrissen. (New procedure for
the investigation of small house ground plans.)
Particular attention paid to division of space
for comfortable room arrangements. Plans.

Städtebau 23: 16-21
January 1928

Card 21
Domestic architecture, Africa, North
Trigg, H.I.
Ancient Arab houses and gardens, northern
Africa

Country Life
38: 392-399
S 18, 1915

Domestic architecture, Africa, South

see also

Dutch colonial architecture, Africa, South
Domestic architecture, Transvaal

Domestic architecture, Argentine republic
Case unifamiliari a Buenos Ayres. [plan
and section] Valerio Peluffo, archt.

Metron 39:42-45
D 1950

720.52
A67c
Domestic architecture, Austria
Ground floor plan, basement plan, exteri-
or and interior views of house near Vienna.
Prof. Maxim Monter, archt.

Architect 115: 167-9
February 26, 1926

710.5
C85
Domestic architecture, Africa (South)
An English house in south Africa.
The new home of the High Commissioner.

Country life (Lond.)85:1xii,1xiv
May 7,1938

Domestic architecture, Argentine Republic.
Mar del Plata
Los chalets de Mar del Plata.

Plus ultra 1: 13-16
December 1916

710.5
C85
Domestic architecture, Austria
Lukin, Robert
Wild flowers in Tyrol.

Country life (Lond.)76: 166-167
August 18, 1934

Domestic architecture, Africa, South
South African houses

Archt
108: 19-20
Jl 14, 1922

Domestic architecture, Argentine republic
Moreno, Mercedes
The home of Dona Elvira Soto of Castro

Plus ultra 13:8-11
January 1928

720.52
A67c
Domestic architecture, Austria.20th century
Robertson, Howard
A viennese villa by Helmut Wagner-Freysheim.

Architect (Lond.) 131: 72-74
July 15, 1932

Domestic architecture, Algeria

see

Mustapha-Supérieur (Alg.) El Bardo
"   "   Djenan-El-Mufti

710.5
H84
Domestic architecture.Argentine republic.
20th century
Modern in the Argentine...designed by
Daniel Duggan.

House and garden 72:34-35
August 1937

720.52
A67
Domestic architecture, Austria. 20th century
A villa in brick at Innsbruck, Austria;
designed by Lois Welzenbacher.

Architects' journal 74: 407-408,pls.
September 23, 1931

720.52
A67
Domestic architecture, Alsace
An Alsatian home

Architects' Jour. 62: 505
Oct. 7, 1925

705.6
A76
Domestic architecture,Argentine Republic
A Spanish house in Buenos Ayres.

Arte Espanol 6:256
No.5,1923

Domestic architecture, Austria. Roman influence

see

Litslberg (Aus.) (near) Villa Lindenhof

Domestic architecture, Arabs

see also

Mustapha-Superieur, Alg. El Bardo
"   "   "   Djenan-El-Mufti

720.52
A67c
Domestic architecture, Australia
House in Toorak, Melbourne. Rodney A.
Allsop, archt.

Architect 115: 556
June 11, 1926

Domestic architecture, Austria. Vienna
The house of the citizen of Vienna in the
time of the Empire and Vormärz.

Der architekt 22:109-119.
Heft 8,1919.

Domestic architecture. Arabs
Van Beek, Gus W.
A new interpretation of the so-called
South Arabian house model. [illus]

American journal of
archaeology
63: [269]-273; pls. 69-70
Jl 1959

720.55
B35
Domestic architecture,Austria.
Mayr,Otto
Berghöfe in Tirol. (Mountain peasant homes
in Tirol.) Compared with Spanish buildings.

Baumeister 32: 16-27
January 1934

Domestic architecture, Austria, Vienna
Imbert, Charles
Popular lodgings in Vienna.

L'architecture 42: 261-272
August 15, 1929

Domestic architecture, Basque

see

Basque architecture

720.52
A67c
Domestic architecture, Bermuda
Eberlein, A.D.
Bermudian domestic architecture.

Architect 103: 227-8
Ap 9'20

Domestic architecture, Canada
Traquair, Ramsay
The cottages and houses of French Canada;
Their architecture and native peculiarities.

House and garden 36: 24-25,52,54
July 1919

720.55
W31
Domestic, Architecture, Belgium
Apartments and houses of Belgium.

Wasmuths 11:299-302
Heft 7, 1927

RYERSON LIBRARY
051
T72
Domestic architecture, Bermuda
Kaltbaum, H.K.
The coral houses.

Touchstone 6:231-237
January 1920

710.5
H84
Domestic architecture, Canada
Houses in French Canada.

House & garden 53: 66-7
January 1928

720.55
B35
Domestic architecture, Belgium
Lechner, Theo
Bürgerliche wohnhäuser in Belgien. (Civil
homes in Belgium.) Sketches by Theo Lechner.

Der Baumeister 28: 232-236
June 1930

710.5
H84
Domestic architecture, Bermuda
Heaton, J.T.
Coral-stone and palm. The homes of Bermu-
da.

House and garden 2:165-74
Ap '02

710.5
C855
Domestic architecture, Canada
The old inspires the new: three Canadian
manor houses that served as inspirations for
four modern homes.

Country life 55: 58-9
March 1929

Ryerson
Domestic architecture, Belgium
Cloquet, L.
Les Maisons anciennes en Belgique

Revue de l'Art Chrétien
58: 30-36,93-101, 170-179,
328-337
59: 95-103, 245-250, 311-316
Ja, Mr, My, S 1908
Mr, Jl,S 1909

Domestic architecture, Bosnia
Peasant's homes

Kunst und Kunst handwerk 17:518,532
Kleft 11 & 12, 1914

720.52
A67
Domestic architecture, Canada
Some Canadian houses by Septimus Warwick

Architects jour. 57: 473-81
Mr 14 '23

720.54
A67
Domestic, Architecture, Belgium
Maisons Belges

L'Architecture 38:57-62
Mr 10, '25

Domestic architecture. Brazil. 18th cent.
Saia, Luis
A casa bandeirista.

Habitat 6:
7-10 no.25
D 1955

710.5
C855
Domestic architecture, Canada
Nobbs, P.E.
Some developments in Canadian architecture

Country life 43: 35-41, 57-60
Ja '23

Domestic architecture, Bermuda

see also names of individual houses, i.e:

Gray Gables, Bermuda
Point Mouse, Spit Head, Bermuda

Domestic architecture. Brazil. 20th cent.
Oito residéncias no Bairro de Boacava,
São Paulo [plans]

Habitat
6:43-4 F 1956

Domestic architecture. Canada. Manitoba.

RAIC jrl 16:102
My 1939

RYERSON LIBRARY
D15.1
H84
Domestic architecture, Bermuda
Nutter, M. A.
Bermuda and its houses.

House beautiful 66: 700-703
December 1929

Domestic architecture. Brazil 20th cent.
Residéncia no Sumare, bairro de S.Paulo
[plans & section]

Habitat
6:73 Je 1956

Domestic architecture. Canada. Manitoba
Parfitt, Gilbert
Ukranian cottages

RAIC jour 18: 152-153
Ag 1941

Domestic architecture. Canada. Ontario.

RAIC jrl 16:107-113
My 1939

720.55
B35   Domestic architecture. Caucasia
     Kessner, Helmut
       Reiseskissen aus dem Kaukasus. (Travel
sketches from Caucasia.)

Baumeister 32: 124-128
April 1934

Domestic architecture, Classic revival

see

Classic revival

Domestic architecture, Canada.(Ontario) Toronto

RAIC jrl 14:109,111
Je 1927

Domestic architecture, Celebes
Bekker, Johannes and Bertild
   Wood carving in the Toradja highlands.

Asia
40: 534-538
O 1940

Domestic architecture, Cliff dwellers

see

Cliff dwellings

Domestic architecture. Canada. Quebec.

RAIC jrl 16:114
My 1939

705.18
R45   Domestic architecture. Chile
     Secchi, Eduardo
       Arquitectura rural. Dibujo a pluma. por
Eduardo Secchi

Revista de arte 7: 6-9
No.12,1938

Domestic architecture, Colonial, see

Colonial architecture (State or region)

Domestic architecture, Canada. Ukrainian influence
Parfitt, Gilbert
   Ukranian cottages

RAIC jour 18: 137-133
Ag 1941

720.5
A67r   Domestic architecture, China
     Mathews,C.T.
       Eastern Asia: or China,Corea and Japan:Intro-
duction.

Architectural record 5:288-297
January-March 1896

Domestic architecture. Color

see

Color in architecture

Domestic architecture, Can. Vancouver.

RAIC jrl 16:99-101
My 1939

720.5
A67c   Domestic architecture, China
       New house in Shanghai. Stewardson, Spence
and Watson.

Architect (Lond.) 121: 883-885
June 28, 1929

Domestic architecture, Competitions

see also

American gas asso. small house competition
   "   "   " competition for completed houses
Cement marketing company's competition
Chicago Tribune small house competition
Concrete houses. Competitions
Detroit free press better homes competition
House Beautiful small house competition
Ladies' home journal small house competition

(more)

720.55
W31   Domestic architecture. Canary Islands
     Zechlin,H.J.
       Spanische bauernhäuser auf den Kanarischen
Inseln. (Spanish peasant houses on the Canary
Islands.)

Wasmuths monatshefte 14: 381
August 1930

720.5
A67   Domestic architecture, China
       Views about the home of an American
gentleman in Pekin.

Arch rev 11: 157
My '04

Domestic architecture, Competitions

see also

National better homes architectural competition
Pencil Points. Competitions. 1927
White Pine Architectural Competitions
Own your own home competition

720.52
A67c   Domestic architecture, Canary Islands
       Two typical examples of domestic archi-
tecture,Santa Cruz, Teneriffe. Block of
offices, flats and shops at Santa Cruz.

Architect (Lond.) 137: 96
October 27,1933

Domestic architecture, China. U. S.
   influence

see

Peiping (China) Lum (Bertha) house

720.5
A67   Domestic architecture. Competitions
       A competition for a residence of limestone.

Arch review 22 (n.s.s.):181-273
b '17

Domestic architecture. Competitions £1,000 All-British house competition. Builder 143: 556-561 September 30, 1932	Domestic arch. Competitions 1929 Two prize houses submitted by two California architects, H.Roy Kelley and Gordon B. Kaufmann. House beautiful 65: 177-180 February 1929	Domestic architecture. Competitions. 1959 Junge architekten entwerfen einfamilienhäuser; wettbewerb der Bausparkasse Schwäbisch-Hall AG. [plans] Alfred Geller, Ulrich Klauss & Bertram Perlia, Karlheinz Tillmann, Frans Gärtner, Otto Geiger, Wilhelm von Wolf, archts. Baumeister 56:575-78 Ag 1959
Domestic Architecture. Competitions 1912 Brickbuilder 21:116 Apr. 1912	720.6 A5loc Domestic architecture. Competitions 1930 Small house architectural competition under the auspices of Better Homes in America. The Octagon 2: 5-7 September 1930	Domestic architecture. Conferences see White house conference on home building and home ownership
Domestic Architecture. Competitions 1920 Labour-saving house competition. Architect. 103:3-5. Jan.2, 1920	720.52 A67 Domestic architecture. Competitions 1932 The Competition promoted by the Incorporated Association of Architects and Surveyors. Architects' journal 76: 437- October 5, 1932 439	Domestic architecture. Conservation and restoration. Bestrebungen der Forschungsgesellschaft für den Wohnungsbau zur Schaffung eines Ortskernerhaltungsgesetzes. Österreichische Zeitschrift für Kunst und Denkmalpflege 21, Heft 2: 131-133 1967
Domestic architecture. Competition 1920 Labour-saving house competition. Arch. Jour. 51:13-14. Jan.7, 1920.	Domestic architecture. Competition 1933 "E & O.E." Competition for the design of small villa property. Plans. Architect (Lond.) 137: 105-108 October 27, 1933	Domestic architecture. Conservation and restoration. Italy. Rome. 15th cent. Corbo, Anna Maria I contratti di locazione e il restauro delle case a Roma nei primi anni del secolo XV. Commentari Anno 18: 340-342 O-D 1967
720.5 A67 Domestic architecture. Competitions. 1921. Prize-winning designs in the "Own a Home" competition. Arch. Rev. 12: 85-7. Mar. 1921.	720.52 A67c Domestic architecture. Competitions 1933 The I.A.A.S. £ 1,000 All-British house. Edward H.Banks,archt. Plans. Architect (Lond.)137: 78-79 October 20,1933	Domestic architecture. Cost see Building costs
Domestic architecture, Competitions 1927 Competition for residence and garage. Pencil points 8: 262-285 May 1927	Domestic architecture, Competitions 1933 Small villa property competition. Organized by architectural association. Elevations and plans ## prize winning homes. Builder 145: 662-663,667 October 27, 1933	720.6 R88 Domestic architecture, Crete Eaton, A.R.C. Minoan architecture: a study of pre-Hellenic art in Crete. Plans and chronological table. R.I.B.A.21:667-678 September 26, 1914
720.5 P59 Domestic architecture. Competitions 1929 "A bachelor's retreat." Pencil points 10: 274-276 April 1929	Domestic architecture. Competitions. 1956 see Lisle, Ill. Morton arboretum. Small house competition. 1956	Domestic architecture, Crete Minoan houses. Plans Rider, Bertha Carr. The Greek house. Cambridge, Eng.: Cambridge University Press, 1916. 142-165

Domestic architecture, Czechoslovakia
Neue wohnhäuser in der Tschechoslowakei.
(New residences in Czechoslovakia.)
Bohuslav Fuchs, J.F.Koula,Otto Eisler, and
Friedrich Weimwurm,archts.

Baumeister 28: 142-149
April 1930

Domestic architecture. Design
The Cleveland architectural advisory
bureau. Small house design.

Architecture, N.Y. 44: 226-8
Jl '21

Domestic architecture. Design.
Green, J. M., Jr.
Small house design - an analysis (7 parts)
Pt.1-The dream house; pt.2-The site;pt.3-The
plan; pt.4-Elevation design;pt.5-details;
pt.6-The interior design.
Archt (N.Y.) 4:
143-46; My. 1925
253-58; Je "
271-375; Jl "
487-90; Ag "
601-04; S "
Archt (N.Y.) 5: 33-38; Oct. 1925

Domestic architecture, Czecho-Slovakia
Proposed House at Heleneuthal,
Iglau, Czecho-Slavakia

Builder 125:288-9
Aug. 24, 1923

Domestic architecture, Design
The evolution of a house; working up the
idea in the architect's office.

House beautiful 71: 122-124,149
February 1932

Domestic architecture, Design
Houston, F.
Some principles of house planning.

House & garden.49:120
Apr. 1926

RYERSON LIBRARY
910.5
M27
Domestic architecture,Czechoslovakia
...village houses...

National geographic 74: 214
August 1938

Domestic architecture, Design
Abbottswood, Lutton
Evolving a house plan: some suggestions
on what to do before you consult an
architect. Plans
Examples of Georgian, Spanish, and Dutch
Colonial styles.

House & garden 42:50-1,122
November 1922

Domestic architecture, Design
Boyd, J.T.
Some principles of small house design.
6 pts.
Arch.rec. 46:
402-18; Nov 1919
556-66; Dec. "
Arch.rec. 47:
58-76; Ja 1919
133-80; F "
233-64; Mr "
291-322; Ap. 1919

Domestic architecture, Czechoslavokia,
20th Century
Modern housing at Baba, new suburb of Prague.

Architect and Building News 149:3
January 1, 1937

MICROFILM

Domestic architecture. Design
Wurster, William
From log cabin to modern house.

...BOOK OF
...CHITECTURE p- 545-547
(on film)

Domestic architecture, Design
Holden, A.C.
What is good planning?

House beautiful 67:60-61
January 1930

Domestic architecture,Czechslovakia.20th Century
The Tugendhat house at Brno,Czechoslovakia
Mies van der Rohe, archt.

House and garden 61: 56-57
April 1932

Domestic architecture, Design
Allen, Gordon
How the plan grows

House beautiful 69: 483,530
May 1931

Domestic architecture, Design
Scroggs, P.P.
What size rooms for my house.

House and garden 62: 35
November 1932

Domestic architecture, Denmark
Denmark's old merchant mansions.
Photographs.

American-Scandinavian-Review.
8:274-278
April 1920

Domestic architecture, Design
Lincoln, A. B.
How to build your personality into your
new home. Plans.

House and garden 62: 41,58
July 1932

Domestic architecture, Design
Sexton,R.W.
Your individuality in the design of
your house.

House and garden 57:114-115,156
April 1930

Domestic architecture. Denmark
Pirrone, Gianni
Il problema dell'abitazione in Danimarca
[plans]

Casabella
#247:10-19 Jan 1961

Domestic architecture. Design
Betts, B.F.
Planning the small house

Home information service. Bul2
no. 31:1-31
Jl '37

720.52
A67c
Domestic architecture. Designs and plans
Explanatory sketches for a client by
P. D. Hepworth, archt. Plans, interiors and
exteriors.

Architect 115:pls. fol. p.94
Ja 29, '26

Domestic architecture. Design & Plans.
Five good small houses.

House and garden. 38:27-32.
July,1920.

710.5
H84
Domestic architecture. Designs and plans
We complete a little house. House
and garden's little house for beginners.
[plans] Howard and Frenay, archts.

House and garden 65:77-75
N '39

Domestic architecture, Egypt

see also

Mohammedan domestic architecture, Egypt

Domestic architecture. Designs & plans
Peters, Paulhans
Gartenhof-häuser [plans]

Baumeister
57:EB 1-EB 6 Jan 1960

Domestic architecture. Details.
Detail charts: later Colonial Georgian,
Greek revival, French provincial, English,
Regency.

House beautiful 77: 62-63; 52-53; 62-63
October-December 1935

House beautiful 78: 50-51; 54-55; 64-65
January-March 1936

Domestic Architecture, Egypt
Desroches, Christiane
L'habitation civile Égyptienne. (Illus:
type de maison citadine du nouvel empire; une
partre du quartier commercant d'el-Amarna.)

Musées de France, bulletin 7:118-120
October 1935

Domestic architecture, Design & Plans
A house that grows with the years -
adaptable to changing needs. Blue prints,
etc.

House and garden 59:
48-53; Je 1931
House and garden 60:
42-49; Jl 1931
60-63; Ag "
58-62; S   "

Domestic architecture. Details
Wohnhausbau - details.

Baumeister
57:EB 19-EB 22 My 1960

AVERBUR LIBRARY
705.2
B96
Domestic architecture,Egypt
Briggs,M.S.
The Saracenic house.

Burlington 38:228-238;289-301
May 1921

Domestic Architecture. Designs and plans.
Kinney, Nina C.
A housekeepers house plan.

House beau 3:
119; Mr 1898
5:
103; F 1899
257; My "
6:
69; Jl 1899
166; S   "

Domestic architecture. Double houses

see

Double houses

Domestic architecture, Egypt.
Fairman, H. W.
Town planning in Pharaonic Egypt.
[Bibliography] [plans, drawings].

Town planning rev. 20:32-51
Ap '49

Domestic architecture. Designs & Plans
Lincoln, A. B.
Planning the first floor for a house; II-
The second floor for a house.

House and garden: 58:64-5, 118,
80-1, 106
N/D '30

Domestic architecture. Duplex houses

see

Duplex houses

710.5
C85
Domestic architecture, Egypt, Cairo
A Mameluke house in old Cairo. The Bayt
el Kredlea.

Country life (Lond.) 84: 654-658
December 31, 1938

Domestic architecture. Designs and plans

[plans]

Baumeister   no.8:
52, no. 7:458-463,* 534-539
Jl, Ag 1955

Domestic architecture, Dutch colonial influence

see also

Domestic architecture, U.S. Dutch colonial influence

Domestic architecture, Elizabethan influence
Yewell, J.F.
Know your architecture before you plan to
build. (Characterization of various styles of
domestic architecture).

House and garden 58: 44
July 1930

710.5
C855
Domestic architecture, Design and plans
Two designs for houses for the man
of moderate means. [plans] Archts, Small Home
Service

Country life 46:61
My '24

Domestic architecture, Easter Island
Ferdon, Edwin N.
Easter Island house types [illus]

El Palacio (bulletin of
New Mexico museum)
68: [28]-46, Spring 1961

Domestic architecture, England

see also

Castles, England
Cottages, England
Country houses, England
Half-timbered houses, England
Historic houses, England
Manor houses, England
Norman domestic architecture, England

Domestic Architectures, England.

The architect 111:60-8 and 10 pl.fol.
Jan. 25, 1924   48

710.5   Domestic architecture, England
C85   Hussey, Christopher
The English house; a resume' of types.

Country life(Lond.)79:iii,iv,vi
May 16, 1936

Domestic Architecture, England   (card no. 4)
Lloyd, Nathaniel. A History of the English house.
28 parts.
                Arch rev (Lond) 68:
                15-20; Jl, 1930
                165-170; O,   "
                205-210; N,   "
                236-241; D,   "
                Arch rev (Lond) 69:
                37-42; F, 1931
                115-120; Ap,   "
                153-169; My,   "

720.55   Domestic, Architecture, England
W31

Wasmuths, (Heft 5-6)8:246-67
1924

720.5   Domestic architecture, England
A67r   Sturgis, Russell
English house architecture.

Architectural record 20:81-91
August 1906

Domestic architecture, England
Morrison, Kathrine
The homelike character of the English house:
Pt.1 As found in certain types of the late Gothic
and early renaissance. Pt.2. As found in certain
types of late renaissance architecture.

House beautiful 65:
70-71, 105-108; Ja 1927
172-174,217-220; F   "

---

728   Domestic architecture, England
T92   Gunn, Edwin
Architecture of East Anglia: Lavenham,Stoke-
by-Nayland, Thaxted, Norwich, Higham, Clare,
King's Lynn, Bumpstead, Walberswick, Woodbridge,
Long Melford, Blythburgh.

Tuileries brochures 1:18-31;
March; May 1930   34-47

710.5   Domestic architecture, England
C85   Hussey, Christopher
The Englishman's home, the destiny of the
roof-tree.

Country life(London)88:166-171
August 24,1940

Domestic architecture, England. 19th--20th
centuries
The house (plans and sections)

Harling, Robert. Home: a Victorian
vignette. London: Constable, 1938.
(pp.15-40)

Domestic architecture, England
Belton house, Bridgwater house

Arch & con rep 99: pl
Je 14, 1918

---

728   Domestic architecture, England
T92   La Beaume, Louis
From Chipping Campden to Bath: Painswick,
Tormarton, Bradford-on-Avon, Stroud, Wotton-under
Edge, Norton St.Philip, Mailsworth.

Tuileries brochures 1:82-95
November 1929

720.52   Domestic architecture, England
A67   A house without a bathroom: bath in connection with every room.

Architects' journal 68: 882
December 19, 1928

Domestic architecture, England
Gentili, Eugenio
La Casa inglese

Domus no. 208:9-14
Ap '46

Domestic Architecture, England
Lloyd, Nathaniel. A history of the English house.
28 parts.
                Arch rev (Lond) 63:
                4-11; Ja, 1928
                50-57; F   "
                93-97; Mr   "
                130-137; Ap "
                172-179; My "
                212-219; Je "

                        (more)

Domestic Architecture, England
Houses of the county towns of England.

(London) Country Life 51: 372-80.
Mar. 18, 1922.

720.5   Domestic architecture, England
A67r   Fletcher, Banister
The decoration of the smaller suburban house
in England. Illustrated.

Architectural record 11: 642-65
October 1901

Domestic Architecture, England   (card no.2)
Lloyd, Nathaniel. A history of the English house.
28 parts.
                Arch rev (lond) 64:
                3-10; Jl, 1928
                142-150; O   "
                179-187; N   "
                Arch rev (Lond) 65:
                4-12; Ja, 1929
                70-79; F   "
                118-127; Mr "
                165-213; Ap "
                227- 231; My "
                        (more)

Domestic architecture, England
Nash, Joseph
The mansions of England in olden time

Architecture
vols 9-13:pls 1-52
F 15,1904-Mr 15,1906

---

728   Domestic architecture, England
T92   Embury, Aymar II
English architecture as scarce material.

Tuileries brochures 1:3-15
January 1929

Domestic Architecture, England   (card no. 3)
Lloyd, Nathaniel. A History of the English
house. 28 parts.
                Arch rev (Lond.) 66:
                155-162; O, 1929
                209-216; N,   "
                227-286; D,   "
                Arch rev (Lond) 67:
                11-13; Ja, 1930
                83-89; F   "
                135-140; Mr   "
                187-192; Ap   "
                        (more)

Domestic Architecture, Eng.
Eberlein, H. D.
Old houses of interest to see in England (and
Normandy).

House and garden 60: 71-72,92
July, 1931

Domestic Architecture, England Some Southgate Seats. Arch and con rep 86: 244-46 O 27, 1911	Domestic architecture, England. 19th century Fletcher, Banister The smaller houses of the English suburbs and provinces. Part 1. Work of: Ernest George and Peto, R.N. Shaw, Basil Champneys, T.E. Collcutt, and George Devey. Pt. 2; construction Architectural record 5:321-338 Apr-je; 1896 6:114-125 O-D "	710.5 Domestic architecture,England.20th century C85 Marshall,C.J.E. A new house on the Cotswolds. Country life(Lond)81:208-209 February 20,1937
720.52 Domestic architecture. England A673 Special number on recent English domes- tic architecture from Tudor style through present day modern - plans, elevation,cost, etc. Architectural review 64: 253-356 December 1928	720.5 Domestic architecture,England.20th century A67f British building boom. $7500 house in England. Interiors, exteriors and plans. Architectural forum 65: sup.34,36 August 1936	Domestic architecture, England. 20th century Una piccola casa. F. R. S. Yorke, archt., con la collaborazione degli arch. E. Rosen- berg e C.S. Mardall. Lomus no. F19:64 My '47
Domestic Architecture, England A Successful House in England. By Gertrude Jekyll. House beau 13: 151-60 F 1903	Domestic Architecture, England,20th Century Great Britain Adopts American House Construction Methods. West. Archt. 29: 19 Feb, 1920	Domestic architecture, England. 20th century Warren, H. Langford Recent domestic architecture in England. Arch rev 11: 5-12 Ja '04
Domestic architecture, England. 17th /18th century A survey of 17th and 18th century English domestic architecture. Arch. rev. 62:112-115;150-154 September; October, 1927	Domestic architecture, England. 20th century A Group of Modern English Houses. By Michael Bunney. Brickbuilder 16:66-68 April, 1907	Domestic Architecture, England, 20th century Recent English domestic architecture by M. W Frohne. Arch record 25 : 259-270 no. 4, April, 1909
Domestic Architecture. England. 18th cent. Late Eighteenth Century. Arch. Jour. 52:392. Oct. 13, 1920	710.5 Domestic architecture,England.20th century C85 Williams-Ellis, Clough Houses after the war- pt.2. For a site on the Welch coast. A project by Clough Williams- Ellis. Plans. A Country life(Lond.)89:16-17 January 4,1941	720.5 Domestic architecture, England. 20th W52 century A review of recent English domestic architecure - illustrated West. arch. 31:92-8 Ag '22
720.52 Domestic architecture. England.18th century A675 A survey of 17th and 18th century English domestic architecture. Ormeley lodge. Arch. rev. 62: 112-15;150-4 September;October;1927	Domestic architecture, England. 20th century Das moderne Englische wohnhaus. (The modern English residence.) Plans of country house by E.L. Lutyens; residence by Robert Lowry, country house by Allan Brace; bungalow by Cheriton and Whitby; etc. Moderne bauformen 26: 309-312 August 1927	720.52 Domestic architecture. England.20th century A674 Special number. Architecture (Lond.)6: spec. no. March-April 1928
Domestic architecture. England. 18th/19th cent. Wrightson, Priscilla The English picturesque: villa and cottage, 1760-1860. [illus.] Indianapolis museum of art. Bulletin, v.1, no.3 (n.s.) Summer 1973	710.5 Domestic architecture, England. 20th century H84 Modernist architecture in an English suburb. Prof. Behrens, architect. A House & garden 51: 100-01 June 1927	Domestic architecture, England. 20th century Special number. Arch. rev. (Lond.) 51: 135-262. Jun., 1922

Domestic architecture, England. 20th century
Special number on modern English houses.

Architecture (Lond.) 7: 142-80
November-December 1929

Domestic Architecture, England. Elizabethan
Sumptuous simplicity - A note on the Elizabethans

American architect: 123:223-5
March 14, 1923

---

ff
720.52
A67c Fletcher, Banister
Domestic architecture, England. Georgian
Georgian domestic architecture.

Architect and contract reporter 79:
April 3, 1908   230-232

RYERSON LIBRARY
705.1
A79 Price, C.M.
Domestic architecture, England. 20th century
The trend of modern domestic architecture in
England. Pt.1 - the influence of the work of two
great architects, C.F.A. Voysey; pt.2 - E.L. Lutyens,
designer of houses and gardens.

A
Arts and decoration 2:323-326; 384-
July; September 1912   387

Domestic architecture. England. Exhibitions

see also

London (Eng.) "Ideal home" exhibition. 1933
Gidea Park, Eng. Exhibitions. 1934

Domestic Architecture, England. Georgian
Selected examples of architecture

Arch. Rev. 57: 122-25
Mar. 1925

705.37
V92 Domestic architecture. England 20th century
Vila: Vila v Amershan, Anglie. A.T. Connell
archt.

Volne smery 29:209-213
1932, no. 9-12

Domestic architecture, England. Exhibitions. 1928
Domestic architecture at the Royal Academy 1928.

Architect (Eng.) 119: 692-3, 695
May 11, 1928

720.5
A51 Domestic architecture, England. Georgian
Small English houses of the late Georgian
period.

American architect 110: 43-44
July 19, 1916

Domestic architecture, England. Birmingham
An 18th Century residence, now demolished in
Birmingham-measured drawing

Arch. journal 56:809
Dec. 6, 1922

Domestic architecture, England. Exhibitions 1929
Domestic architecture at the Royal Academy.

Architect (Lond.) 121: 616-620
May 10, 1929

720.5
A51 Domestic architecture, England. Georgian
The small house of the Georgian period.
Photos of various houses in England.

American architect 116: 163-167
August 6, 1919

Domestic architecture, Eng. Chinese influence

Tipping, Henry Avray. English homes.
9 vols. London: Offices of Country
Life; New York; Charles Scribner's
Sons, 1920-37
Vol. 1:30-1,180-1,270 Period VI,
vol. 1:xxx,15,159,182,184,185

Domestic Architecture, England. Georgian

Country Life 45: 211-212
239-240
267-268
Feb. 22 and Mar. 1, 1919.

720.52
A67 Thompson, W.H.
Domestic architecture, England. Hampstead
Some recent work at Hampstead.

Architects' jour. 63:689-700
May 19, 1926

Domestic architecture. England. Competitions

see

Daily Mail concrete house competition
"   " labour saving house competition
English cottage competition

Domestic Architecture, England. Georgian
The Duke of York's new home

Country life (Lond.) 53:526-7
April 21, 1923

720.52
B86 Gotch, J.A.
Domestic architecture, England. History
Domestic architecture in England from the
twelfth to the eighteenth century

British architect 57: 24-34
Ja 10 '02

Ryerson

Domestic architecture, England. Elizabethan
English house at time of Elizabeth and the
first Stuarts.

L'art decor.
20: 121-133
Ap 1909

Domestic Architecture, England. Georgian
Eberlein, H. D.
Georgian and Regency houses of interest to see in
England.

House and garden 60: 72-73
August, 1931

RYERSON LIBRARY
913
A65 Wheatley, H.B.
Domestic architecture, England. History
History and development of the house: the
hall; the living room; bedrooms.

Antiquary 9: 1-7; 101-106;
" 10: 185-190
January, March; November 1884

Domestic architecture. England.Ipswich
McDowall, R. W.
The domestic architecture of Ipswich [plans]

Archaeo jrl 108:147-144
1951

Domestic architecture. England. London. 19th cent.
Some artists' houses.

Amer arch
1: 350-351
O 28, 1876

710.5
H84

Domestic architecture,England.Regency
Fifth avenue country house displays
Regency taste. W. and J. Sloane display.

House and garden v.64: .26-29,68,82,96
October 1933

Domestic architecture, England
Italian influence

see also

Brighton (Eng.) Atree house

913
A66j

Domestic architecture,England.Norman period
Wood,Magaret
Norman domestic architecture.

Archaeological journal 92: 167-242
Part 2, 1935

710.5
C85

Domestic architecture,England.Regency
Hussey,Christopher
Four Regency houses.

Country life(Eng.) v.69:450-456
April 11,1931

Domestic architecture, England. Italian influence
Kaufmann, G.B.
A house of Tuscan inspiration

Arts and decoration 28:36-38,
February, 1928   95

Domestic Architecture. England. Plymouth
Late Eighteenth Century, examples at Plymouth.

Arch. Jour. 52:627.
Dec. 8, 1920

710.5
C855

Domestic architecture,England.Regency
A house that turned backward.

Country life(U.S.)v.51: .63-65
April 1927

Domestic architecture, England. Jacobean
Lloyd, Nathaniel
A history of the English house. X-The sixteenth
century. XIV-The seventeenth century (Jacobean).
Arch rev (Lond.) 65:
    4-12; Ja 1929
    70-79; F "
    118-27; Mr "
    165-73; Ap "
    227-31; My "

710.5
C85

Domestic architecture,England.Queen Anne
Falkner, Harold
The creator of "modern Queen Anne": the
architecture of Norman Shaw.

A   Country life(Lond.)89:??-??5
March 15,1941

710.5
C85

Domestic architecture,England.Regency
Mr. Luke Forman and the Empire style.

Country life(Eng.)v.67: .694-698
May 10,1930

720.52
B86

Domestic architecture, England.London
White, Henry
Ancient and modern town houses; or, the
evolution of domestic architecture in London

British architect 59: 252-4
Ap 3 '03

710.5
H84

Domestic architecture, England. Queen Anne
Geerlings, G. K.
Formal English houses of Pre-Georgian times.

House and garden 59: 70-73
June 1931

720.52
A673

Domestic architecture,England.Regency
Rogers,J.C.
The real English tradition.

Architectural review v.70: .151-154
November 1931

Domestic architecture, England. London.
Housing in medieval London

Architect 108: 348
Nov. 10, 1922

Domestic architecture, Eng. Regency

see also

Melford hall, Eng. Library

720.5
A67f

Domestic architecture,England.Regency
The Regency house at Farnhurst.

Architectural forum v.49: .241-248
August 1928

913
A67

Domestic architecture, Eng. London
Kingsford, Charles Lethbridge
On some London houses of the early Tudor
period.

Archeo 71: 17-54
1921

710.5
H84

Domestic architecture,England.Regency
Eberlein, H.D.
Backgrounds of English Regency rooms.

House and garden v.62: .28-39,73-74
December 1932

Domestic architecture, England. Regency
Gunn, Edwin
Regency houses - a record of some that are in danger
of demolition. Drawings by Alison Shepherd.

Architect 129-33. Supp plates for:
1932:Jan 8,Feb. 5, Mar 4, May 6,
    June 3, July 1, Aug 5, Sept 2,
    Oct 7, Nov. 4, Dec. 2
1933: Jan 6, Feb 3, Apr 7, May 5, July 7
1934: April 6, Aug 3, Oct 5
1935: Jan 4
1937: Feb 5

710.5 C85 A.C.
Domestic architecture,England.Regency
 	
Regency Plymouth - designed by John Foulston, archt.
 	
A   Country life(Lond)82:129
      July 31,1937
	Domestic architecture, England. St. Albans
	  Richardson, H.E.
	Small houses and cottages at St. Albans.
	Photographs by W.R.L. Love and others.
	
	Architectural review (London)42:21-25
	August;October, 1917 pl.1;71-76
		913 A67
		Domestic architecture, Eng. Tudor
		Kingsford, Charles Lethbridge
		  On some London houses of the early Tudor period.
		
		     Archeo 71: 17-54
		     1921

710.5 C85
Domestic architecture,England.Regency
  A regency terrace in Cheltenham.
 	
     Country life(Lond.)79:449
     May 2, 1936
	Domestic Architecture, England. Shrewsbury
	  Tipping, H.A.
	Houses of the county towns of England. 1.Shrewsbury.
	
	Country life 47:268-273;300-306;334-40
	Feb. 28; March 6,13, 1920
		710.5 C85
		Domestic architecture, England . Tudor
		Tipping. H. Avray
		  Tudor houses in Northeast Essex.
		
		     Country life(Lond.)54:14-21
		     July 7, 1923

710.5 C855
Domestic architecture,England.Regency
Hussy, Christopher
  Regency, the nineteenth century modern.
 	
     Country life(U.S.)68:24-26
     October 1935
	Domestic architecture. England. Silver End
	  Modern houses at Silver End, Essex.
	
	     Architect (Lond.) 121: 16-19
	     January 4, 1929
		Domestic architecture, England. Winchester
		  A house at Winchester
		
		     Arch rev (Lond) 59: 65
		     F 1926

710.5 C855
Domestic architecture,England.Regency
Barrender.B.H.
  Restoring a Regency country house.
 	
     Country life(U.S.)v.53: 35-40
     February 1928
	Domestic Architecture, England. Stokesley
	  Stokesley. A typical Yorkshire market town.
	
	     Arch. Jour. 54: 399-401.
	     Oct. 5, 1921
		710.5 C855
		Domestic architecture,English influence
		Humphrey,Henry,Jr.
		  What type of house shall I build? Pt.2 The English house.
		
		     Country life 49: 61-63
		     November 1925

Domestic architecture, England. Regency influence
  A modern expression of Regency style.
 	
     Architectural forum v.48: 45-63
     January, 1928
	Ryerson
	Domestic architecture, England. Stuart
	  English house at time of Elizabeth and the first Stuarts.
	
	     L'art decor.
	     20: 121-133
	     Ap 1909
		Domestic architecture. Exhibitions
		
		     see also
		
		Model houses

720.52 A67
Domestic architecture. England. Ruislip
  The brick house,Ruislip-ground and first floor plans
 	
     Architects' journal 57:522-3
     March 21, 1923
	Domestic architecture, England. Tudor
	  The Development of House Design in the Reigns of Elizabeth and James, as Illustrated by Contemporary Architectural Drawings. By J. Alfred Gotch, F.S.A. (Kettering).
	
	     RIBA Jour. 16:41-60
	     N 21, 1908
		Ryerson
		708.1 N533 pre
		Domestic architecture. Exhibitions. 1945.
		  Race of Lilliputian New Yorkers invited to view exhibition of tomorrow's small house opening at Museum of Modern Art My 29
		
		     N.Y. Museum of modern art
		     press releases:202-205
		     1945

Domestic architecture, England. St. Albans
  Roberts, H.V.M.
Old domestic architecture of St. Albans.
I.Mediaeval and early renaissance.
II. The later renaissance
 	
     Builder 129:384-385;838-839
     September 11; December 11, 1925
	Domestic arch., Eng., Tudor
	  The English House of the Tudor Period.
	
	     Amer. archt 100: 29-33
	     Jl 26, 1911
		Domestic architecture, Finland
		
		     see also
		
		Domestic architecture, Karelia

Card 1 (row 1, col 1):
720.52
A674 Domestic architecture. Finland
The home of the Finnish musical composer,
Sibelius, Finland.

Architecture (Lond.)4: 361
March 1926

Card (row 1, col 2):
Domestic architecture. Four-family houses

see

Four-family houses

Card (row 1, col 3):
Domestic architecture, France
Ganay, Ernest de
Official residences, France

Revue de l'art 49: 217-225
April, 1925

Card (row 2, col 1):
720.571
A79 Domestic architecture, Finland, 20th century
Heinola Fanerfabrik, Zachariasen & Co.
Paavo Riihimäki, archt. [plans]

Arkitekten no. 12:187-8
1938

Card (row 2, col 2):
Domestic architecture, France

see also

Brickwork, France
Farmhouses, France
Brittany, Architecture
Basque Architecture

Issues of Country Life mag.

Card (row 2, col 3):
Domestic architecture, France
Ferree, Barr
Pictures, old houses in France.

House beautiful
17: no. 1
D 1904

Card (row 3, col 1):
720.571
A72 Domestic architecture, Finland. 20th century
[special number]

Arkitekten 129-143
1939

Card (row 3, col 2):
Domestic Architecture, France
Homes, farm buildings

Amer. arch.
112: 257-269, pl.154-161
O 10, 1917

Card (row 3, col 3):
RYERSON LIBRARY.
D13.1
H84 Domestic Architecture, France.
Hitchcock, H.R., Jr.
Six modern European houses that represent
current tendencies in France and Germany

House beautiful 64:253-255
September 1928

Card (row 4, col 1):
720.571
A79 Domestic architecture, Finland. 20th
century. Competitions
Socialministeriets Tävlan om
typritningar för egnahemsbyggnader
[one-family houses]

Arkitekten:142-144
1939

Card (row 4, col 2):
710.5
H84 Domestic architecture, France
House styles in six French provinces:
Basque, Béarnaise, Alsace, Normandy, Breton, and
Provence.

House and garden 70:30-31
August 1936

Card (row 4, col 3):
D10.5
A786 Domestic architecture, France
Vaillat, Léandre
Sketches of houses on the Loire by Skyrian-
oe.

RYERSON LIBRARY.

Art et décoration 45:57-64
Feb. 1924

Card (row 5, col 1):
Domestic architecture, Finland. Exhibitions
1939

see

Helsinki (Fin.) Bostadsutställningen 1939

Card (row 5, col 2):
Domestic Architecture, France
Houses and plans at small cost, France.

L'Architecture 40:142-9
May 15, 1927

Card (row 5, col 3):
Domestic architecture. France. 12th cent.
Metz; maison, Rue des Trinitaires; xiie siècle

Encyclopedie de l'architecture,
constructions de Style. 2 vols.
Paris: Albert Morancé, 1928- [?]
Tome 2, pl 3

Card (row 6, col 1):
720.571
A79 Domestic architecture. Finland. History
Laine, Yrjö
Drag ur utvecklingen av de Finska
allmogebostädernas planform under 1700-
och 1800- Talen [plans]

Arkitekten:129-133
1939

Card (row 6, col 2):
D13.1
H 84 Domestic architecture, France
Individual expression in architecture

House beaut. 43:282-284
Ap 1918

Card (row 6, col 3):
Domestic architecture. France. 13th cent.
Figeac (Lot) Rue Hortabadial; maison (xiiie
siècle) (plan and section)
Lavardin (Loir-et-Cher) maison du xvie
siècle; Charlieu (Loire) maison du xiiie siècle.

Encyclopedie de l'architecture,
constructions de Style. 2 vols.
Paris: Albert Morancé, 1928- [?]
Tome 1: pls 37 and 38,39

Card (row 7, col 1):
Domestic architecture. Fireproofing

see

Fireproof construction. Domestic architecture

Card (row 7, col 2):
STACK
720.44 Domestic architecture. France
A79 Muller, H
Notes brèves sur le Queyras (Hautes-Alpes).

L'art populaire en France.
1:57-62. 1929.

Card (row 7, col 3):
Domestic architecture. France. 13th cent.
Montréal (Yonne) maison double (debut du
xiiie siècle). (plan).

Encyclopedie de l'architecture,
constructions de style. 2 vols.
Paris: Albert Morancé, 1928- [?]
Tome 1: pl.90

Domestic architecture, France. 15th century
Maisons du XV siècle àDijon, a Tours et a
Verneuil.

Verdier, Aymar. Architecture Civile
et domestique. 2 vols.
Paris: Bancé, 1857-58. vol.2:111-117
plates.

Domestic architecture.France.20th century
Storez, M.
Maisons de France: Les villas provençales
d'aujourd'hui. Examples of work of M. Storez,
Nenot, Dardi, Louis Bonnier.

L'Art et les artistes n.s.v.6:192-197
February 1928

Domestic architecture, France. Louis XIII
style

see

Saint Nom-la-Brèteche (Fr.) (near) La Ranchère

Domestic architecture. France. 15th cent.
Mont-Ferrand; maison; fin du xve siècle.

Encyclopedie de l'architecture,
constructions de style. 2 vols.
Paris: Albert Morancé, 1928- [?]
Tome 1: pls. 95-96

Domestic architecture.France.20th century
Porcher, Jean
The new house in France

Art et décoration 32:1-16;
January 1928   sup.p.
1-2

Domestic architecture. France.Mediaeval
Forster, J. J.
The appeal of the minor domestic architecture
of mediaeval France.

House beautiful 62: 255-257; 380-385
September-October 1927

Domestic architecture, France.15th century influence
Un Petit Hotel dans le Genre du XV Siecle.
A. Albert (Somme) Architecte: M.H. Mignan. By I.C.
Boileau.

L'Arch Hebdomadaire 19, no. 13
31 Mr 1906

720.52   Domestic architecture, France.20th century
A673   Robertson, H.
Some recent French developments in domestic
architecture.

Arch. rev. 61: 2-7
January 1927

720.5   Domestic architecture,France. Mediaeval
AG7r   Schopfer,Jean
Wooden houses in France during the Middle
Ages.

Architectural record 9:331-362
April 1900

Domestic architecture. France. 15th cent.
Rouen; maison Rue Engène-Duthuit; fin du xve
siècle. (section).

Encyclopedie de l'architecture,
constructions de Style. 2 vols.
Paris: Albert Morancé, 1928- [?]
Tome 1:pl.93

Domestic architecture, Fr. Albi

Ach Jean
Notes sur les vieilles maisons d'Albi.
Paris. Université. Institut
d'art et d'archéologie
Travaux des étudiants du
groupe d'histoire de l'art
de la Faculté des lettres de
Paris. Paris: Institut d'art
et d'archéologie, p. 1-5
1928.

Domestic architecture, Fr. Neuilly
Zahar, Marcel
L'architecture nouvelle...un hotel à Neuilly

L'art vivant 9:262-264
Je 1933

Domestic architecture. France. 16th cent.
Lavardin (Loir-et-Cher) maison du xvie siècle;
Charlieu (Loire) maison du xiiie siècle.

Encyclopedie de l'architecture,
constructions de style. 2 vols.
Paris: Albert Morancé, 1928 - [?]
Tome 1: pl. 39

Domestic Architecture, France, Cluny
Maisons.

Verdier, Aymar. Architecture civile
et domestique. 2 vols. Paris:
Bance, 1857-58. v.1,p.69-92 and pl.

Domestic architecture, France. Orleans
Maisons à Orleans: Rue du Chatelet no. 3;
Place du Marche à la Volaille; Maison dite de
François 1er; Maison dite Du Cerceau; et Rue
des Hôtelleries no.17. 16th and 17th centuries.
Text in French. Plans, measured detail drawings.

Sauvengeot, Claude. Palais, chateaux,
hotels, et maisons de France.
4 vols. Paris: A. Morel, 1867.
v.3:1-23,pls.1-16

Domestic architecture, France, 16th century
Maisons du XVI siècle à
Orleans, à Lisieux, à Halberstadt
et à Verneuil.

Verdier, Aymar. Architecture Civile
et domestique. 2 vols. Paris:
Bance, 1857-58. vol.2:118-124,plates

Domestic architecture, France. Directoire

see

Versailles (Fr.) Rue royale no. 93

Domestic architecture, France. Paris
Architecture privée, grande médaille d'argent.
Work of A. Pellechet in Paris - who was awarded
the Gold Medal in 1930.

L'Architecture 43: p.326,328-335,347,
September 15, 1930   350.

A

Domestic architecture. France.20th century
Badovici, Jean, C
The house of today, and Interior architec-
ture: Pierre Chareau; J. de Andrada; Le Corbusier

Cahiers d'art 7:12-15
January 1926

Domestic architecture, France. Exhibitions
The exhibition of regional architecture in
the invaded provinces of France

AIA jour
5:107-114
Mr. 1917

Domestic architecture, France. Paris
Fouquières, Andre de
L'elegance des grands hôtels de Paris.

L'art vivant
9: 41-42, 141-142
Jy Mr 1933

Domestic Architecture, France. Paris
Flagg, Ernest
Influence of the French School on architecture in the United States. Illustration of residences in Paris.

Architectural record 4:210-228
October-December, 1894

Domestic architecture. France. Rouen
Rouen; maisons.

Encyclopedie de l'architecture,
constructions de Style. 2 vols.
Paris: Albert Morancé, 1928- ?
Tome 1: pl. 89

720.5
A67r

Domestic architecture, Germany
Design for residence. Oskar Dedreux, architect. Drawing.

A

Architectural record 1:48
July - September 1891

Domestic architecture, France. Paris
Modern gardens in Paris. Patterned gardens by Jean-Charles Moreux and Albert La Prade, archt.

A

House and garden 70:42-43
September, 1936

Domestic architecture, France. Spanish influence
see
Mandelieu (Fr.)(near) house

Domestic architecture, Germany
Pechmann, Günther
Dwellings

Deutsche kunst 56:185-199
June, 1925

Domestic architecture, France. Paris
Schuyler, Montgomery
Nouveautés de Paris: private residences of Paris.

Architectural record 10:361-392
April, 1901

STERSON LIBRARY Domestic architecture, Gaul
Blondel, L.
Habitation gauloise de l'oppidum de Genève.

Genava 4: 97 - 110
1926

Domestic architecture, Germany
(Editorial and German house plans)

Amer. archt. and bldg. news
53: 82
S 12, 1896

Domestic architecture, France. Paris
Imbert, Charles
Romantic houses in Paris.

L'Architecture 42: 13-22
January 15, 1929

Domestic architecture, Georgian
see
Domestic architecture, England. Georgian Colonial architecture

---

STERSON LIBRARY
D10.5
W32

Domestic architecture, Germany
Wolfer, Oskar
Exhibition of dwellings by the Werkbund in Stuttgart

Dekorative kunst 31:57
December 1927

720.5
A67r

Domestic architecture, France. Paris
Lees, Frederick
Some sixteenth and seventeenth century Parisian mansions: Hôtel de Beauvais; Hôtel de Sully; Hôtel d'Aumont; Hôtel Lamoignon; Hôtel de Châlons. Plans.

Architectural record 26:210-230
September 1909

Domestic architecture, Germany
see also
Eitel, Albert
Volkart and Trüdinger
Krüger, Willy
Zucker, Paul

720.5
Ed8

Domestic architecture, Germany.
C. M.
German half-timber houses.

Brochure series 7: 26-34
February 1901

STERSON LIBRARY
704.5
A78v

Domestic architecture, France. Paris
Fouquieres, Andre de
La tradition de l'elegance dans les grands hotels de Paris et de Londres

L'art vivant 8:256-60
My '32

Domestic architecture, Germany   see also
Issues of
Berliner Architekturwelt

Deutsche Baukunst

D15.1
1613

Domestic architecture, Germany
Locher, Robert
Germany builds a house.

Interior architecture 39: 283-286
December 1931

Domestic architecture, France. Rouen
Maisons à Rouen, 16th and 17th century.
Text in french. Measured drawings.

Sauvengeot, Claude. Palais, chateaux, hotels, et maisons de France. 4 vols.
Paris: A. Morel, 1867.v.4:33-39,pl.1-6

Domestic Architecture. Germany

Wasmuths Monatshefte. für baukunst.
4:319-350. 1919-20.
Heft 11-12

720.5K
B35

Domestic architecture, Germany
Harbers, Guido
Das kleine und mittlere einfamilienhaus. (The small and medium one-family house. Work of six architects.

Der Baumeister 28: 49-57
February 1930

Domestic Architecture, Germany
Ein kleines haus am see, Paul and Jürgen Emmerich, archt.
WohnhÄuser in Köln, W. Wucherpfennig, archt.
Ein landhaus bei Meran, J. Ludwig, archt.

Die Kunst 47:
228-238, S '49.

Domestic architecture, Germany
Workmen's houses, Essen, Germany

Dekorative kunst 26:185-203
June, 1923

720.52
A67c
Domestic architecture, Germany. 20th century.
A house at Stuttgart. H.P.Schmohl, archt.
Plans.

A   Architect and Building News 149:44-45
January 8, 1937

720.54
A67
Domestic architecture, Germany
Badovici,Jean
Les Maisons Métalliques en Allemagne (The metallic houses in Germany).

L'Architecture Vivante: p.5-15
1929- Autumn-Winter

720.53
B35
Domestic architecture, Germany. 17th century
Ein aussterbender Bauernhaustyp in Süd-deutschland. (A disappearing house-type in South Germany.) Chalet style.

Der Baumeister 34:294-298
September 1936

Domestic architecture. Germany. 20th century
Modern German domestic architecture

Arch. Journ. 61:216-23
Feb. 4, 1925

720.5
A67
Domestic architecture. Germany
Bragdon, Claude
Modern German domestic architecture.

Architectural review 14: 197-200
September 1907

Domestic architecture, Germany. 20th century
Country house in North Germany. Hellmut Lubowski, archt.

Encyclopedie de l'architecture;
constructions modernes. 12 vols.
Paris: Albert Morancé, 1928-39
5:pl.59-60

720.52
B93
Domestic architecture, Germany. 20th century
Modern German domestic architecture.

Builder 138: 659
April 4, 1930

720.53
B35
Domestic architecture, Germany
Neue einfamilienhäuser in der ausstellung "Haus und Heim",München - 1933. (New one-family houses in the exhibit "House and Home" Munich - 1933.) Plans.

Der Baumeister 31: 348-361
October 1933

Domestic architecture. Germany. 20th cent.
Doppelhaus in Hannover [plans] Architek-tengemeinschaft Dipl.-Ing. Kloppelberg, Dipl.-Ing. Lichtenhahn, archts.

Baumeister
53: 26-28
(Tafeln 6-8 at end of issue)
Ja 1956

710.5
C85
Domestic architecture, Germany. 20th century
Towndrow,Frederic
Modernism in house design. An experiment in Germany.

Country life (Lond.) 67: 842-844
June 7, 1930

720.53
B35
Domestic architecture, Germany
Harbers, Guido
Neue arbeiten von architekt, Rudolf Fröhlich Burghausen. (Recent work by architect Rudolf Fröhlich, Burghausen.) Painted figures on outside houses.

Der Baumeister 34: 114-119, pls.37-38
April 1936

Domestic architecture. Germany. 20th cent.
Exterior and interior views of modern German architecture.

Moderne bauformen 25:73-112
Band 25, 1926

720.53
B35
Domestic architecture, Germany. 20th century
Harbers,Guido
Neue arbeiten von Lois Welzenbacher,Inns-bruck. Haus Schulz in Westfalen. (Schulz house.) Plans and interior views.
Haus Buchroithner in Zell am See. Plans.

Der Baumeister 28: 1-18
January 1930

720.5
W52
Domestic architecture. Germany
Woltersdorf, Arthur
Patrician houses of old north Germany from Cologne to Danzig.

Western architect 36:32-38 pl.37-41,
March 1927   front.

720.53
B35
Domestic architecture. Germany. 20th century
Ein familienhausentwurf Buff. (Plans for one-family houses.) Plans by: Tessenow; Pfuhl; Karl Keppler; Adolf Schneck; Trostler; Lauterbach.

Der Baumeister 28: 67-74
February 1930

720.5
B35
Domestic architecture. Germany 20th century
Neue einfamilienhäuser in der ausstellung "Haus und Heim",München - 1933. (New one-family houses in the exhibit "House and Home" Munich - 1933.) Plans.

Der Baumeister 31: 348-361
October 1933

720.52
A675
Domestic architecture. Germany
The work of Dr. Paul Zucker.

Arch. rev. 63: 12-13
January 1928

720.53
B35
Domestic architecture, Germany. 20th century
Haus Radicke in Harburg. Derossen and Averhoff,archts. Plans.

Der Baumeister 28: 358-359
September 1930

710.5
H84
Domestic architecture. Germany 20th century.
A new expression of Teutonic modernism: house of F.Dannenbaum,Berlin,Germany. Hans Wormann,archt. Plan.

House and garden 65: 54
January 1934

Card 1 (col 1, row 1):

710.5
A786   Domestic architecture, Germany, 20th century
Porcher, Jean
        The new foreign house exhibited at Stuttgart

                                    Art et décoration 31:183-
                                    December 1927   192

Card (col 2, row 1):

720.53   Domestic architecture, Germany. Berlin
M468   Völter, Ernst
        Vom bauen in Berlin. (About building in
Berlin.) Residence buildings by Wilhelm Keller
and Rudolf Frümmel, archts. Plans.
        Domestic work by Hans Jessen, Brothers Luck-
hardt and Alfons Anker, Otto Firle, Emil Fahrenkamp,
Friedrich Benoit and others.

                                    Moderne bauformen 26: 201-207
        A   June 1927

Card (col 3, row 1):

Domestic architecture, Germany, Munich
        Neue einfamilienwohnhauser (New one-family
houses), Munich. Plans. Work of:
Franz Ruf
Kurt Marohn
Richard Kesseler

                                    Der baumeister 32:423-429
        A   December, 1934

Card (col 1, row 2):

720.52   Domestic architecture, Germany, 20th century
A67c   The real modern: the house of Mr. Karl
Bertsch, near Berlin.

                                    Architect (Lond.) 121: 672-676
                                    May 17, 1929

Card (col 2, row 2):

Domestic architecture, Germany. Cologne
        Residences at Cologne, Germany. Theodor
Merrill, archt. Plans.

                                    Moderne bauformen: 53-66
                                    Band 25, 1926

Card (col 3, row 2):

Domestic architecture, Greece

        see also

Domestic architecture, Macedonia

Card (col 1, row 3):

Domestic architecture, Germany. 20th century
        Some modern German residences.

                                    Wasmuths 11:106-11,116-23
                                    Heft 3, 1927

Card (col 2, row 3):

Domestic architecture, Ger. Cologne
        Some residences at Köln-Marienburg.

                                    Wasmuths 11: 125-8,132
                                    Heft 3, 1927

Card (col 3, row 3):

Domestic architecture, Greece

                                    Arch. and contr. reporter 96:119-
                                    Sept. 1, 1916.

Card (col 1, row 4):

720.53   Domestic architecture, Germany. 20th century.
B55   Harbers, Guido
        Ein zeitgemässer wohnsitz. (A residence
premature for this age.) Martin Elsässer, archt.
Plans.
        Estate has: riding garden, rose garden with
terraces, park with wild-flower garden, bathing pool
with showers, sand-beach, lawn, playground, etc.

                                    Der Baumeister 31: 203-216, pl.64-70
        A   June 1933

Card (col 2, row 4):

Domestic architecture, Germany. Competitions
Joedike, Jürgen
        Vorbildliche initiative einer bausparkasse;
architekten-wettbewerb für wohnhaus-entwürfe,
ausgeschrieben von der Bausparkasse Schwäbisch
Hall A.G., Schwäbisch Hall [plans]

                                    Arch & Wohnform
                                    67:*27*-*30* Ag 1959

Card (col 3, row 4):

Domestic architecture, Greece
        A one-family house in the lowlands.

                                    Der baumeister 28: 241
                                    June, 1930

Card (col 1, row 5):

720.52   Domestic architecture, Germany, 20th century
A67   Villa at Altona-Othmarschen. Karl
Schneider, archt. Plan.

                                    Architects' Journal 74: 54
                                    July 8, 1931

Card (col 2, row 5):

Domestic architecture, Germany. Competitions
        Das zeitgemässe eigenheim. (The contemporary
one-family house: a contest in designing one-
family house: a contest in designing one-family
houses.) Plans.

                                    Wasmuths monatshefte 15:113-118
                                    March, 1931

Card (col 3, row 5):

720.53   Domestic architecture, Greece, 20th century
B55   Harbers, Guido
        Bauten von architekt Angelo Siagas - Athen
(Buildings by Angelo Siagas, archt. Athens). Plans.
        Zwei kleine landhaüser für Griechland (Two
small country houses for Greece). R. Coste,
archt. Plan.

                                    Der baumeister 34:62-67
        A   February 1936

Card (col 1, row 6):

Domestic architecture. Germany. 20th cent.
Wolff, J.
        Uber die qualität im Wohnungsbau

                                    Baumeister
                                    53: 33-34
                                    Ja 1956

Card (col 2, row 6):

Domestic architecture. Germany. Exhibitions

                                    see

Munich (Ger.) Haus und heim austellung. 1933
Stuttgart (Ger.) Werkbund austellung 1927

Card (col 3, row 6):

Domestic architecture, Greece. 20th cent.
        Modern

                                    Wasmuths 7:91-3
                                    Heft 3-4
                                    1923

Card (col 1, row 7):

720.53   Domestic architecture, Germany. 20th century
B55   Harbers, Guido
        "Was ist modern?" (What is modern,)
        The house on the Alb near Urach: a vacation
home for commerce and industry. Adolf G. Schneck,
archt. Plans, interiors, drawings of furniture, etc.

                                    Der Baumeister 28: 377-411, pls.52-55
                                    October 1930

Card (col 2, row 7):

Domestic architecture, Germany. Münster
        Maison à Munster, XV siècle.

                                    Verdier, Aymar. Architecture Civile
                                    et domestique. 2 vols. Paris:
                                    Bance, 1857-58. v.1:159-160, plate

Card (col 3, row 7):

Domestic architecture, Greek revival

                                    see

Classic revival

Domestic architecture, Half-timbered
 	
see
 	
Half-timbered houses
	710.5
	H84 Domestic architecture. History
	       Elevations and plans of houses through
	the ages.
	
	     House and garden 74: 24-25
	     November 1938
		Domestic architecture, Indians of North America
		
		see
		
		Indians of North America. Architecture

Domestic architecture, Hawaiian Islands
   Designs for houses to be built in Hawaii.
G.R. Miller, archt.
 	
     Pencil points 8:388
     June, 1927
	Domestic Architecture. History
	   The Evolution of Domestic Architecture.
	By R.P.S. Twizell (A.)
	
	     RIBA 12:537-48
	     Je 24, 1905
		Ryerson
		
		   Domestic architecture, Iraq
		Muller, Valentin
		   Types of Mesopotamian houses
		
		      Amer oriental soc jour
		      60: 151-180
		      Je 1940

Domestic architecture. Hawaiian Islands.
   Freese, E.I.
Hawaiian houses of other days.
 	
     Art and archaeology 8:215-223
     July-August, 1919
	Domestic architecture, Holland
	
	see
	
	Domestic architecture, Netherlands
		710.5 Domestic architecture, Ireland
		C85 G. R. S.
		     Celtic daylight, idle thoughts of a soldier
		in Ireland. Exterior and interior of a cottage.
		
		     Country life(London)88:250-251
		     September 21,1940

Ryerson
 	
   Domestic architecture, Hawaiian islands
   Houses of other days.
 	
     Arts & arch
     8: 215-223
     Ag 1919
	720.52 Domestic architecture. India.
	B68 Development of domestic work.
	
	     Builder 121: 521.
	     Oct. 21, 1921.
		720.52 Domestic architecture, Ireland
		A674 Abram, J. F.
		     Domestic architecture in Ireland.
		
		     Architecture (Lon1.) 5: 394-397
		     May 1927

Domestic architecture, Hawaiian Islands.Chinese
                influence.
   A Chinese house in Honolulu. Hart Wood,
archt.
 	
     House and garden 51:129-131
     March, 1927
	Domestic Architecture, India
	   Indische gärten
	
	     Wasmuth's 7:1-11
	     Heft 1-2
	     1923
		711.05 Domestic architecture, Ireland. Cork
		T77 Docking, S. J.
		     The city of Cork. Its residential quays.
		
		     Town planning rev 17: 212-14, pls
		     39-40
		     J1 '37

Domestic architecture. Heating
 	
see
 	
Heating, Domestic
	Domestic architecture. India
	   What is a home? [plans]
	
	     Marg 1.no.2:35-95+
	     Ja. 1947
		710.5 Domestic architecture,Ireland.Regency
		C85 Hussey,Christopher
		     Caledon,Co.Tyrone, seat of the Earl of
		Caledon - begun from designs by Thomas Cooley in
		1779 for the first Earl. Additions.. by second
		Earl in 1812 with John Nash as archt. Plan.
		
		     Country life(Lon1)81:224-229;250-255
		A February 27;March 6;1937

Domestic architecture. History
 	
see also
 	
Domestic architecture. Primitive
        etc.
	Domestic architecture, India, New Delhi
	   Residence plans
	
	     Archt's and Bldr's jour. 37:512-514
	     May 14, 1913
		Domestic architecture, Italian influence
		
		see also
		
		Domestic architecture, U.S., Italian influence

Card 1 (row 1, col 1):
710.5
C855 Lockwood, O. M.
Domestic architecture. Italian influence
    If I had an Italian house. No plan.

        Country life (U.S.) 58: 49-51,78
        August 1930

Card (row 1, col 2):
720.53
B35 Harbers,Guido
Domestic architecture. Italy. 20th century
    Das einfamilienhaus und landhaus in Italien.
    (The one family house and country house in Italy)
    Plans.

        Baumeister 32: 58-64, pl.28
        February 1934

Card (row 1, col 3):
Domestic architecture. Italy. Veneto(province)
Puppi, Lionello
    Un letterato in villa: Giangiorgio Trissino
a Cricoli. [illus.]

        Arte veneta
        v. 25: 72-91
        1971

Card (row 2, col 1):
710.5
H84 Yewell, J. F.
Domestic architecture. Italian influence
    Know your architecture before you plan to
build. (Characterization of various styles of
domestic architecture).

        House and garden 58: 43
        July 1930

Card (row 2, col 2):
Domestic architecture. Italy. 20th cent.
Bettonica, Franco & Gianfranco Frattini
    Recenti tendenze dell'architettura civile in
Italia.

        Zodiac
        1:77-88 O 1957
        Eng. trans. p. 267-69

Card (row 2, col 3):
Domestic architecture, Italy. Venice
    Old palazzina near the Grand Canal in Venice
restored and refurbished by Mr. Mortimer Levintrett,
decorator.

        House and garden 53: 93-95
        February, 1928

Card (row 3, col 1):
710.5
C855 Humphrey, Henry, Jr.
Domestic architecture. Italian influence
    What type of house shall I build? IV-Italian
style.

        Country life 49: 43-45
        January 1926

Card (row 3, col 2):
Domestic architecture, Italy. 20th century
Chessa, Paolo A.
    Strapaese e stracittà.

        Domus no. 216:4-9
        D '46

Card (row 3, col 3):
Ryerson
                Domestic architecture, Iviza (island)
Herzberg, Max
    Habitations à Ibiza

        Aujourd'hui
        2:64-5, Ja 1957

Card (row 4, col 1):
RYERSON LIBRARY
D13.1
H84 Rogers, E. M.
Domestic architecture. Italy
    Antecedents of the American house

        House beautiful 61:50-51
        January, 1927

Card (row 4, col 2):
Domestic architecture. Italy. Castiglione
delle Stiviere
Fattori, Lionello Costanza
    Le opere di Rodolfo Vantini in Castiglione
delle Stiviere. [illus.]

        Arte lombarda
        v.7, I: 75-81
        1962

Card (row 4, col 3):
Domestic architecture, Iviza (Island), Sp.
    Baeschlin, Alfredo
Das bauernhaus der insel Ibiza (The peasant house
of the island Ibiza). Drawings - types of
construction.

        Der baumeister 32:B71-72
        May 1934 (Supplement)

Card (row 5, col 1):
Domestic architecture, Italy.
    Melani, Alfredo
Modern Italian architecture.

        Architectural record 12:357-374
        September, 1902

Card (row 5, col 2):
Domestic architecture, Italy. Fregene
    Rifugi al mare di Fregene (plans)

        Spazio no. 2:45-49
        Ag 1950

Card (row 5, col 3):
Domestic architecture, Jamaica
    Residence at Jamaica, B.W.I. An example of
reinforced concrete. No plan.

        Architectural record 23:255
        April, 1908

Card (row 6, col 1):
RYERSON LIBRARY
910.5
T77 Raffalovich, George
Domestic architecture,Italy.15th century
    The stone tents of Apulia

        Travel 48: 28,60
        April 1927

Card (row 6, col 2):
Domestic architecture, Italy. Rome

            see

Roman domestic architecture, Italy, Rome

Card (row 6, col 3):
Domestic Architecture. Japan

        Wasmuths Monatshefte für Baukunst
        6:249-60.
        Heft 7-8 1921

Card (row 7, col 1):
Domestic architecture. Italy. 15th-16th c.
Puppi, Lionello
    Le residenze di Pietro Bembo "in padoana."
[illus., sum. in Eng.,Fr.& Ger.]

        L'Arte
        v.2: 30-65
        D 1969

Card (row 7, col 2):
Domestic architecture, Italy. Sienna
    Chierici, Gino
La maison siennoise du moyen age.

        Congrès d'histoire de l'art,
        Paris, 1921. 3 vols. Pairs: Les
        Presses universitaires de France,
        1923-24. 2:148-157

Card (row 7, col 3):
RYERSON LIBRARY
D13.1
H84 Lewis, Ethel
Domestic architecture. Japan
    Homes in other lands: The gardens and houses
of Japan

        House beautiful 68:626-
        627, 648-650
        December, 1930

Card 1 (top-left):

RYERSON LIBRARY

705.9
I61   Domestic architecture, Japan
C.M.P.
    The house beautiful of Japan. (Text discusses
the Japanese house. Illustrations are of Japanese
garden and tea house at Tuxedo Park, N.Y., designed by S. Mori.)

    A   International studio 48:p.XV-XVIII
    No.189,November,1912

Card 2 (top-middle):

RYERSON LIBRARY

91A.08   Domestic architecture, Japan
A83   Kuck,L.E.
    My neighbor builds a house.

    Asia 38: 544-548
    September 1938

Card 3 (top-right):

Domestic architecture, Japanese influence

see also

Domestic architecture, U.S., Japanese influence

Card 4 (row2-left):

RYERSON LIBRARY

705.2   Domestic architecture, Japan
G64   Murdoch, N.G.B.
    How Japan lives - native type of home in
Nippon passing. No plans.

    Good furniture 14:229-237
    June 1920

Card 5 (row2-middle):

Domestic architecture, Japan
    Style of home adapted by west. [color]

    Life articles on art 1951:696
    D 31, 1951   697

Card 6 (row2-right):

Domestic architecture. Japanese influence
Jay, M.R.
    A bungalow in Japanese spirit. No plan.

    House beautiful 32:72-73
    August, 1912

Card 7 (row3-left):

Domestic architecture, Japan

Rein, Johann Justus.
Japan: travels and researches...
New York: A. C. Armstrong, 1884.
p. 414-419

Card 8 (row3-middle):

Domestic architecture, Japan. 20th century

see also

Yoshida, Tetsuro

Card 9 (row3-right):

720.971   Domestic architecture, Karelia
A79   En gård från gränskarelen i
friluftsmuseet på Fölisön
[plans, photos, sections]

    Arkitekten no. 2:17-19
    1941

Card 10 (row4-left):

720.5   Domestic architecture, Japan
A67r   Mathews, C.T.
    Japanese architecture: Temple of Shibi: Pal-
ace of Nagoya; Shinto Temple of Izumo.

    Architectural record 5:384-387
    April-June 1896

Card 11 (row4-middle):

Domestic architecture. Japan. 20th cent.
    Casa en el Japon - construccion en concreto
[plans]

    Proa
    #139:12 O 1960

Card 12 (row4-right):

Domestic architecture. Lighting

see

Lighting, Domestic

Card 13 (row5-left):

Domestic architecture. Japan
    Japanese houses.

    Amer arch
    1: 26-27
    Ja 22, 1876

Card 14 (row5-middle):

Domestic architecture, Japan. 20th cent.
Clute, Eugene
    Japanese homes to today.

    House and garden 35:39-41
    June, 1919

Card 15 (row5-right):

Domestic architecture. Lots

see

Building sites

Card 16 (row6-left):

720.5   Domestic architecture, Japan
A67r   Budd, K.C.
    Japanese houses. Exteriors and interiors.

    Architectural record 19: 1-26
    January 1906

Card 17 (row6-middle):

Domestic architecture. Japan. 20 th cent.
    Kleines einfamilienhaus in Tokio;
entwarf 1959, gebaut 1959 [plans & section]
Forschungsinstitut für architektur in Tokio,
archts.

    Bauen & Wohnen
    14: 461-466 D 1960

Card 18 (row6-right):

720.95   Domestic architecture, Macedonia
A67r   Walér-White, E.
    The Macedonian house. Plans.

    Architect 100: 154-156
    September 20. 1918

Card 19 (row7-left):

720.52   Domestic architecture, Japan
A67   Middle-class house

    Arch & bldrs jour 45:84-86
    F 14 '17

Card 20 (row7-middle):

Ryerson
Domestic Architecture, Japan. 20th century.
Exhibitions, 1954
    Art museums being prepared for summer's
tourist influx

    CAI Scrapbook
    89:90
    1954

Card 21 (row7-right):

RYERSON LIBRARY

910.5   Domestic architecture, Malay states
N27   ...sharp-roofed homes of a Kampong, or jungle
village, at Prapat.

    National geographic magazine 73: 690
    June 1938

Domestic architecture. Mechanical equipment see Mechanical equipment	Domestic Architecture, Mexico. Mexico City Residences of the Avenida Bucareli, Mexico City. Architectural record 32:408,413-414,416-418, November, 1912 420-421	Domestic architecture, Mountain Pica, Agnoldomenico Architetture di montagne. Spazio no. 2:40-44 Ag 1950
Domestic architecture, Mediaeval see Windows, Medieval	Domestic architecture, Mexico. Mexico City Burden, Shiela Three weeks in Mexico Vogue 73:90-91,172 April 13, 1929	720.55 Domestic architecture, Mountain D67 Case semplice per una vita felice e semplice- linee d'architettura in montagna. Domus No. 147 1940
Domestic architecture, Mexico Rivera, Diego The new Mexican architecture: a house of Carlos Obregon. Mexican folkways 2: 19-25 October-November, 1926	Domestic architecture, Modern see Domestic architecture, 20th century	720.55 Domestic architecture, mountain D67 Linee d'Architettura in Montagna. Ettore Tam, archt. Domus 147:37-39 1940
Domestic Architecture, Mexico Hill, Winifred S. A patio house in Mexico House beautiful 57:558 May, 1925	Domestic architecture, Mohammedan see Mohammedan domestic architecture	Domestic architecture, mountain, Spain Cossio y Gomez-Acebo, Manuel de La "casona" montañesa, Arte español 6: 16-37, no. 1 '22 104-115 no. 2 '22 136-154 no. 3 '22 210-218 no. 4 '22 278-285 no. 5 '23
Domestic architecture. Mexico. 20th c. Dos bungalows campestres. [plans and section] Artecnica, archts. Arq Mexico 16:29-32 Ag 1944	Ryerson Domestic architecture, Mongolia Mongols - Tent houses of the Steppes Nat geog 82:633 N 1942	Domestic architecture, Navaho Indians see Navaho Indians. Architecture
710.5 Domestic architecture,Mexico. 20th century H84 Modern in Mexico: house of Juan José Bar- ragán at Guadalajara,Jalisco..J.J.Barragán, archt.; home of José Villagram Garcia in Mexico City..J.V.Garcia,archt.; home of Fran- cisco Martinez Negrete,built by the owner and designed by his brother Luis Martinez Negrete; home of Carlos Palomino,Mexico City, the Negrege brothers,archts. House and garden 72:40-41 A August 1937	Domestic architecture, Morocco Gardens and houses of Morocco House and garden 52: 78-83 N 1927	Domestic architecture, Netherlands see also Huis ten bosch
Domestic architecture, Mexico. Mexico City see also Mexico City. Casa de los azulejos Mexico City. Casa Alvarado	Domestic architecture, Mountain see also names of houses, i.e.: Cortina d'Ampezzo, It. Tabiá di Crignes Cortina d'Ampezzo, It. Tabiá del bosco	Domestic Architecture, Netherlands Apartments and houses of Holland. Wasmuths 11:299-302 Heft 7, 1927

RYERSON LIBRARY
705.942   Domestic architecture, Netherlands
W46   Boterenbrood, J.
      Architecture of Holland.

          Wendingen 9: 22-24
          No.1, 1926

720.5   Domestic architecture,Netherlands
A67   Penfield,Edward
      The narrow house.

          Architectural review 15:101-103
          June 1908

720.52   Domestic architecture, New Zealand
A675   The English tradition in New Zealand. R.K.
Binney, archt.

          Arch. rev. 61: 172-6
          May 1927

RYERSON LIBRARY
705.2   Domestic architecture, Netherlands
A644   Adams-Acton, Murray
      Domestic architecture and decoration

          Apollo 1: 275-279
          May 1925

RYERSON LIBRARY
705.942   Domestic architecture, Netherlands
W46   Special number of domestic architecture
in Holland.

          Wendingen 12: 2-18
          #4, 1931

Domestic architecture, New Zealand.
  House in Auckland [plans] Peterson, archt.

          Architectural design
          31: 474, O 1961

720.52   Domestic architecture, Netherlands
A675   Phillips, R.R.
      Dutch house-fronts

          Arch. rev. (Lond.) 36:11-14, pl.
          7-9
          Jl '14

705.942   Domestic architecture,Netherlands
093   Wijdeveld,H.Th.
      Woningbouw Netherlands. (Domestic archi-
tecture of Holland by various architects.)

          Wendingen 3: 2-20, 22-38
          March-April 1920
          No.3-4

Domestic Architecture, Norway

          Wasmuths, (heft 2) 9:59-66
          1925

710.5   Domestic architecture, Netherlands
H84   Milman,Helen
      Dutch houses and gardens. J.G.Voldheer and
Frederica Hulswit,archts. Plans.

          House and garden 2: 501-514
          October 1902

RYERSON LIBRARY
705.942   Domestic architecture, Netherlands,century
W46   Dwelling at Dottingen; J.L.M.Lauweriks,
architect.   20th

          Wendingen 10:20
          Number 8, 1929

Domestic architecture, Norway
  Nordische bürgerhäuser

          Wasmuths monats hefte fur baukunst 8:175-
          heft 5-6, 1924   189.

720.54   Domestic architecture, Netherlands
A67   A few houses and villas in Holland. D.
Smit, jr., archt.

          L'Architecture 41: 407-414
          December 15, 1928

Domestic architecture, Netherlands. 20th century
  Modern Dutch houses

          Architect 108:303-4
          Oct. 27, 1922

720.5   Domestic architecture,Norway
A67r   Norwegian cottage. No plan.

          Architectural record 3:55
          July-September 1893

Domestic architecture, Netherlands.
  The houses of the people.

          L'Architecture 40:247-53
          August 15, 1927

Domestic Architecture, Netherlands. Hurensgracht
  Amsterdam: House in Hurensgracht

          Architects journal 58:272
          Aug. 22, 1923

720.5   Domestic architecture,Norway
A67r   Some timber houses in Norway. Plans.

          Architectural record 21:475-482
          June 1907

720.52   Domestic architecture, Netherlands
A67   Modern cottages and houses in Holland.

          Architects' journal 74: 833-835
          December 23, 1931

Domestic architecture, New Zealand.
Sheppard, N. & J.
  Domestic architecture in New Zealand.

          Architectural design
          31: 471, O 1961

Domestic architecture, Norway (Project)
  Villa in Norvegia. [plan] Ivo Pannaggi, archt.

          Domus 255: 1
          Fe 1951

720.52
A67c
Domestic architecture, Palestine. 20th century
House near Tel-Aviv, Palestine. Joseph
Neufeld, archt. Plan.

A   Architect and Building News 148:229
November 20, 1936

710.5
C85
Domestic architecture, Poland
De Wiart, Major-General Carton, F.C.
A peasant's room in Podolen, Fisherman's
hut on the Chollske, Polesia.

Country life(London)86:301-303
September 22,1939

Domestic architecture, Roman

see

Roman domestic architecture

720.55
B55
Domestic architecture, Panama
Brunner,K.H.
Neue bautypen in den Amerikanischen tropen.
(New building types in the American tropics.)

Baumeister 32: 122-123
April 1934

910.5
N27
Domestic architecture, Portugal
Pre-Roman people built circular houses
within rectangular walls

Nat geog mag 73:161
F '38

Domestic architecture. Row houses

see

Row houses

Domestic architecture, Peru
Some houses of Peru

House beautiful 53:46-47
Jan. 1923

Domestic architecture, Primitive
Thesiger, Wilfred
Marsh dwellers of southern Iraq
[illus]

National geographic 113:
205-239
F 1958

720.55
W51
Domestic architecture. Rumania
Way, Ernst
Rumänische bauernhäuser aus holz und lehm.

Wasmuth's monatshefte 4:111-119
Heft 3-4, 1919/1920

Domestic architecture, Philippine Islands
Curious Philippine house

House beautiful
16: 24-25
O 1904

Domestic architecture, Pueblo Indians

see

Pueblos

720.54
A67av
Domestic architecture, Rumania, 20th century
Habitation en Roumanie. R. Fraenkel,
archt. [plans].

L'Arch d'aujourd'hui
9: 40-41
F'38

Domestic architecture. Philippine Islands
Linsenbach, Fred
Hausbau in den Philippinischen tropen

Bauen & Wohnen
15: Suppl8, Je 1961

Domestic architecture, Puerto Rico
Bartholomew, E.C.
Porto Rican building.

Architecture 39:147-149
May, 1919

Domestic architecture. Russia.

Quarenghi, Giacomo. Fabbriche
e disegni di Giacomo Guarenghi.
2 vols. Mantua: Fratelli Negretti,
1844-45. pl. 27

Domestic architecture. Planning

see

Domestic architecture. Design

Domestic architecture, Queen Anne

see

Domestic architecture, England. Queen Anne

Dom. Architecture, Russia.
House in Russia: View from Southeast. M.H.
Baillie Scott, Architect.

Builder 95: pl.
Oct 31, 1908

Domestic architecture. Plans

see

Domestic architecture. Designs and plans.

Domestic architecture, Renaissance

see

Renaissance domestic architecture

Domestic architecture, Russia
2 examples of Russian timber houses (2 photos)

Archts. jour. 50:469
Oct. 15, 1919

705.7 L879 Domestic architecture, Russia Loukomsky, G Les vieux hôtels de Plioss, près Kostroum. Old houses of Plioss, near Kostroma. Illus. (In Russian.) Starye gody 1915, v.1, p.63-64.	Domestic architecture. Serbia Zdravković, I.M. Denkmäler der serbischen Volsarchitektur. [illus.] Österreichische Zeitschrift für Kunst und Denkmalpflege v.24, Heft 1/2: 79-82 1970	Domestic architecture, Spain see also Basque architecture
Domestic architecture, Rus. Leningrad Homes in St. Petersburg. Alexander Klein, archt. Wasmuths 10:342-345,351,353 Heft 8, 1926	Domestic Architecture. Sites see Building sites	RYERSON LIBRARY. D13.1 Domestic architecture, Spain H84 Rogers, E. N. Antecedents of the American house House beautiful 61:50-51 January, 1927
Domestic archtiecture. Scandanavia Peters, Paulhans Vom wohnen in Dänemark und Schweden. Baumeister 57:1, 44 Jan 1960	Domestic architecture, South America Plus ultra 3 p. 8-17 June, 1918	RYERSON LIBRARY. 705.1 Domestic architecture, Spain A79 Davis, Felice The Basque house Arts and decoration 26:42-43 November, 1926
Domestic architecture, Scotland see also Renaissance domestic architecture, Scotland	Domestic architecture, South America Plus ultra 3:11 Sep. 1918	720.52 Domestic architecture, Spain A67c Cnnr E. de Anchorena, El Socuéron, Mar Del Plata. Stanley Hamp, archt. House in the Basques. Oliver Hill, archt. Architect 115: pls., 554 June 11, 1926
Domestic architecture, Scotland William Bruce house. House at Kuiross Archts jour 70: 463-7 S 25, 1929	Domestic Architecture, South America Plus ultra 4:2-5 Jan. 1919	705.6 Domestic architecture, Spain S67 Vaguer, S Concurso de la antigua casa española Arte español 2:97-9 y '14
720.52 Domestic architecture, Scotland. 1800 A67? Lloyd, Nathaniel Gems of architecture: a Scottish example: Earlshall, Louchars, Fife. No plans. Architectural review (Lond.)45:111-114,pl Architectural review (Lond.)46:14-18 June-July 1919	Domestic architecture, South America Plus ultra 5:2-4 June, 1920	720.5 Domestic architecture, Spain A51 Cram, R. A. Domestic architecture in Spain Amer archt 125: 371-8 Ap 23, '24
Domestic Architecture, Scotland, 20th century see Bearsden (Scot) Kilmardinny	72 . Domestic architecture. South America A67r Art in South America. Architectural record 28:229 September 1910	RYERSON LIBRARY. 705.6 Domestic architecture, Spain S67 Mountain houses of Spain Arte Español 6: 156-164 No. 3, 1922

705.1 A722 Roberts, M. F. Domestic architecture, Spain Spain for beauty, America for comfort Arts and decoration 28:52-54, February 1928 92,94	Domestic architecture, Sweden Villiers-Stuart, C.M. Gardens of Sweden: Sturefors, Sandemar, Oveds Kloster, Eriksberg, Gunnebo, Lidingö. Country Life (London) 77:38-44 January 12, 1935	770.53 B35 Domestic architecture, Switzerland. Neve einfamilienwohnhäuser der Schweiz, Interiors and plans. Artaria und Schmidt, Ernst F. Burckhardt, archts. Der Baumeister 28: 195-204, pl. 38 My' 30
Domestic architecture, Stuart see Domestic architecture, England. Stuart	710.5 H84 Domestic architecture, Sweden Schmidt, Harriet von A holiday home in the heart of Sweden: "Sveden", home of Margareta Johnson, in the vill- age of Leksand, Delecarlia. House and garden 72:22-25 July 1937	705.1 A78a Domestic architecture. Switzerland Lutz, W.A. Photographs of reconstructions. Art and archaeology 17:189-193 April 1924
720.5 A67f Domestic architecture, Suburban Current American suburban homes. Arch for 38:115-31,147-67 Mr '23	710.5 H84 Domestic architecture, Sweden. 20th century A house in the Stockholm exhibition. Carl G. Bergsten, archt. House and garden 58: 91-93 September 1930	720.53 B35 Domestic architecture. Switzerland Harbers, Guido Schweizer wohnhäuser von architekt Franz Scheibler, winterthur mitarbeiter architekt H. Schnabel. (Swiss residences by the architect, Franz Scheibler; assistant architect, H.Schnabel.) Plans. Der Baumeister 31: 430-434 A December 1933
710.5 H84 Domestic architecture, Suburban Mitchell, G. B. An ideal suburban house. House & Garden 15: 172-5 My 1909	710.5 C85 Domestic architecture, Sweden 20th century Carrington, Noel The small Swedish house. Country life (Lond.) 68: 356-357; September 20;27;1930 389-390	720.53 H31 Domestic architecture, Switzerland Hippenmeier, K. Swiss buildings. Wasmuths 13: 7-29 January 1929
Domestic Architecture, Suburban, England Modern English Suburban Houses. plans 2 pts. Brickbuilder 15:222-226 N 1906 Ja 1907 16:8-11	710.5 H84 Domestic architecture, Sweden. 20th century Sweden creates a group of one-family houses with past and present mingled. House and garden 58: 94-95 November 1930	720.53 B35 Domestic architecture. Switzerland.20th cent. Neve einfamilienwohnhäuser der Schweiz. (New one family houses in Switzerland.) Interiors and plans. Artaria and Schmidt, Ernst F.Burckhardt,archts. Der Baumeister 28: 195-204, pl.38 May 1930
Domestic architecture, Sumatra Residence and dove cote. Arch & bldg 51:56 Jl 1917	Domestic architecture, Switzerland see also Bauen & Wohnen (magazine) Chalets, Switzerland Wooden houses, Switzerland	705 W48 Domestic architecture, Switzerland. 20th cent. Vier kleine wohn - und drei ferienhauser. [plans, sect.] Das Werk 33:193-201, 205-211 Je '46
Domestic architecture, Sweden Ein haus aus Schweden an der Exposition de l'urbanisme et de l'habitation. [plans, sect.] Bauen & Wohnen 2:21-24 1948	720.53 A67c Domestic architecture, Switzerland A house decorated in Sgraffito at Andeer Architect 111:pl. Feb. 1, 1924	720.5 A67r Domestic architecture, Switzerland Schopfer, Jean Wooden houses in Switzerland. Architectural record 6:415-428 April-June 1897

Domestic architecture, Switzerland. Basel
  Harbers, Guido
Neue arbeiten von Bräuning, Leu und Dürig in Basel.
(New works by Bräuning, Leu and Dürig in Basle.)
Plans.

Der Baumeister 31: 293-322,pl.89-93
September, 1933

A

Domestic architecture, Turkey. Priene
Stevens, G.P.
  A trip in Asia Minor: the students side
travel in connection with Athens and Constantinople. [plans and drawings]

Archl record
31: 131
F 1912

720.5
A51   Domestic architecture, United States
           The artistic development of the standard-
           ized house. Plans by George Gilbert, Aymar
           Embury II and others.

A   American architect 117: 571 pl.fol.p.
             May 12, 1920   6008

Domestic architecture, Switzerland.Basel
  Neue arbeiten von Hans Volkart (New works of
Hans Volkart)

A   Der baumeister 34:12-13
         January, 1936

Domestic architecture, Two-family houses

see

Double houses
Duplex houses

Domestic architecture. U.S.
  Arts in reference to dwellings (and
illustrations of houses 609-636)

Knight, Charles. Knight's pictorial
gallery of arts. 2 vols. London and
New York: London Printing and
Publishing Co., Ltd., n.d. 1:144-195

Domestic architecture, Switzerland. Luzern
  Painted houses at Lucerne

Architect 109:358-60
May 25, 1923

Domestic architectue, U.S.

see also

Dutch colonial   architecture, U.S.

705.1   Domestic architecture. United States
A792   Thompson, J.R.
           Building a house around Americana

             Arts and decoration 28:46-47,86
             February 1928

Domestic architecture, Switzerland. Zurich
  G.H.
Einfamilienhäuser der architekten Laubi und
Bosshard - Zürich. (One-family houses by Laubi and
Bosshard, archts. - Zurich). Plans.

A   Der baumeister 34:381-386
         November, 1936

Domestic architecture, U.S.

Architecture. 43:137-70 and pl.61-76.
May, 1921.

720.5   Domestic architecture,United States
A67r   Spencer,R.C. Jr.
           Building a house of moderate cost.

             Architectural record 31:608-615
             June 1912

910.5   Domestic architecture,Syria
N27   Assyrian refugees...windowless with one
           low door, their thickwalled beehive huts...
           sugarloaf houses,..

             National geographic magazine 74: 712,714
             June-December 1938

Domestic architecture, United States

Greber, Jacques. L'architecture
Aux Etats-unis... 2 vols. Paris:
Payot, 1920. v.1,p. 37-72.

720.5   Domestic architecture. United States
A51   Hunt, Myron
           Domestic architecture in the United States.

             Amer.arch. 107: 81-87, pl 242
             February 10, 1915

720.52   Domestic Architecture, Transvaal
A67e   Sloper, E W
           Domestic Architecture in the Transvaal

             Arch & con rep 72: 25-6
             Jl 8,'04

Domestic Architecture U.S.
  American domestic architecture through
French Eyes.

Inland Architect
20: 52-3
Dec, 1892

720.5   Domestic architecture, United States
B84   Elevations and plans in creating the
           very small home. Daniel Neilinger, archt.

             House and garden 48:45-51,65
             July 1925

Domestic architecture, Tudor

see

Domestic architecture, England. Tudor

Domestic architecture, United States
  Embury, Aymar, II
Architectural impressions;- the large American
house; notes on plan; how your house will look
personality in the city house.
             Arts and decoration 12:
                 171-73; Ja. 1920
                 240-41; F   "
                 312-13; Mr   "
                 398-99; Ap   "

705.1   Domestic architecture. United States
A79   Simons,E.A.
           The evolution of American domestic architec-
           ture

             Arts and decoration 26:78-80
             March, 1927

720.5
F29
Domestic architecture, United States
Federal Housing Administration's
suggested plans for small houses: plans.

Federal architect 7:36-38,44,46
July 1936

710.5
H84
Domestic architecture, United States
Cram, R. A.
The promise of American house building.

House and garden 29: 9-12
January 1916

720.5
A67r
Domestic architecture, U. S. 19th century
Bonta, Edwin
Along the Seneca turnpike. Introducing a
distinct type of Post-colonial house.

Arch rec 40: 505-15
D '16

710.5
C855
Domestic architecture, United States
Taylor, C.S.
The high cost of architectural eccentricity.

Country life (U.S.)52:41-43
October 1927

Domestic architecture, U.S.
"The quality house": That's what we are building
today in America.

Craftsman 31: 148-153, 185-86
Nov., 1916

Domestic architecture. United States. 19th century
Cottage and village architecture. Plans.

Peterson's Mag. 23:
96-97; Ja 1853
156-57; F "
Peterson's mag. 24:
23-24;Jl 1853
116-17; Ag "
162-63; S "
211-12; O "
255-56; N "

D10.5
C88
Domestic architecture, United States
Goodhue, Bertram
The home of the future: a study of America in
relation to the architect. No plans.

Craftsman 29:449-455,543-544
February 1916

710.5
H84
Domestic architecture, United States
Mason, Roger L.
Three small houses of today.

House and garden 54: 45-48
July 1928

Domestic architecture, United States. 19th century
Fallon, J.F.
Domestic architecture of the early nineteenth
century. 2 pts.

Amer. arch
110:139-144,167-171,pl.2126
S 6,20, 1916

710.5
H84
Domestic architecture, United States
Taylor, C. S.
How much house for your money?

House and garden 53: 113-117
May 1928

720.5
A67ar
Domestic architecture, United States
Newcomb, Rexford
The whitherward of American architecture.

Architect (N.Y.) 7:702-05
March 1927

Domestic architecture, United States. 19th century
Model cottages.

Godey's mag. and Lady book 34:
44-46; Ja 1847
54-60; F "
108-09; Mr. "
169-70; Ap. "
pl.prec.p.177,183,259-60;My 1847
307-08; Je 1847

(see card 2)

Domestic architecture, United States
Ideas for small houses

Amer inst of arch jour
6: 174-181
Ap 1918

Domestic Architecture U.S.
Fitzpatrick, F.W.
Women and domestic architecture.

Inland Architect
33: 2-3
Feb, 1899

Domestic architecture, United States. 19th century
Model cottages.   (continued-card 2)

Godey's mag and Lady book 35:
pl.prec.p.5, 11;Jl 1847
95-96; Ag 1847
142-44; S "
207-08; O "
pl.prec.217;N 1847

720.53
W51
Domestic architecture,United States
Bugge, Andreas
Der moderne Amerikanische kleinhaus. (The
modern American small residential house.)
Die drei Amerikanischen fachwerkkonstruktion-
en: Balloon-Frame, braced-frame and Western-frame.
(The three American frame-work construction.)

Wasmuths monatshefte 14: 59-64
February 1930

Domestic architecture. U.S. 18th cent.
Glassie, Henry
Eighteenth-century cultural process in
Delaware valley folk building. [illus]

Winterthur portfolio
v. 7: [29]-57, 1972

Domestic architecture. United States. 19th century.
Model cottages. Plans.

Godey's Lady's Book 38:
pl.prec.p.1; Ja 1849
pl.prec.p.73; F "
122; Mr. "
363-65; Ap. "
301-02; My "
348-49; Je "
373-74; Jl "
416; Ag "
(see card 2)

705.2
A79
Domestic architecture, United States
Cram, R. A.
The pre-eminence of our own domestic
architecture

Arts and decoration 22: 21-23
April 1925

Domestic architecture. U. S. 19th cent.

see also

Domestic architecture. U. S. Victorian

Domestic architecture. United States. 19th century.
Model cottages. Plans.

(Card 2)

Godey's 39:
1-2,pl. prec. p. 1; S. 1849
144; Oct "
215; N "
358-59,461; D 1849

Domestic architectures. United States. 19th century
Model cottages. Plans.

Godey's 42:
4;Ja, 1851
126;F "
180;Mr "
212;Ap "
283;My "
pl.prec.340; Je 1851
(see card 2)

Domestic architecture (U.S.) 20th c.
Best houses under £15,000. Eight fine mass-
produced examples show buyers what they can get in
low-priced homes. [plans]

Life articles on art 1951:471-475
Sept. 10, 1951

Domestic architecture, U.S., 20th century
A house designed for the business woman.

House beautiful 69: 160
February, 1931

Domestic architecture. United States. 19th century
Model cottages. Plans.

Godey's 43:
4; Jl 1851
117; Ag "
pl.prec.197;0 "
260; N 1851
324; D "

Domestic architecture, U.S., 20th century
Brown, F.C. Designs for some smaller wooden
houses by younger American architects.

Architectural review 21 n.s.4:109-155
August, 1916

D15.1
H84   Domestic architecture, U. S. 20th century
Sexton, R. W.
The house of today. Pt I. Plan Pt. II
Exterior design.

House beautiful 67:
596-598, 636, 744-745, 788
My, Je '30

D19.05   Century
G58   Domestic architecture. United States. 19th
Model Cottages. Plans.

Godey's Lady's Book 52:530-531
June - 1856   v.53:263-354;
Oct.,Dec. 1856   542-543

Domestic architecture, U.S., 20th century
Designs for small houses.

Builder 143: 449-460
September 16, 1932

Domestic architecture, U.S. 20th c.
Nelson, Geo. and Wright, Henry
Ideas for houses. U.S. must accept a lot of
unfamiliar ones to make its new homes genuinely
up-to-date.[condensation of book Tomorrow's House]

Life articles on art 1945 pt. 2:
479-489
Dec [?] 1947

Domestic architecture (U.S.) 19th century
Fitzpatrick, F. W.
The modern woman and domestic architecture.

Inl archt 33: 2-3
F 1899

D10.5
C99   Domestic architecture,U.S. 20th cent.
Development of home-building in America; illustrated by the work of the Architectural League for 1914

Craftsman 26: 35-51
Ap '14

Domestic architecture, U.S. 20th c.
Life presents a portfolio of ideas for home
planning.

Life articles on art 1945 pt.
1: 398-422
May 28, 1945

Domestic architecture. U.S. 19th cent.
Notes from our French exchanges; American
domestic architecture through French eyes.

Inland architect
20, no. 5: 52-53
D 1892

Domestic architecture, United States. 20th century
The East and West prize houses

House beautiful 57: 672
June, 1925

705.1
L72   Domestic architecture, U.S. 20th century
Minimum house. Pietro Belluschi, archt.
[plans, sect.]

Life (Art. on art): 199-203
Ag 21 '47

705.1
C91   Domestic architecture, U.S. 20th century
Norton, O.T.K.
American model homes

Creative art 4:41-44
January 1929

Domestic architecture. U.S. 20th cent.
Pütz, Friedrich
Haus and heim im amerikanischen bildungs-
wesen.

Architektur and Wohnform
64: * 26-30 * no.4
Ap 1956

720.5   Domestic architecture, United States   20th century
W52   Bennett, Wells;Ludlow, W. O.
Modern materials and the American house.
Another view on the modern house.

Western architect 40: 7-9
January 1931

D15.1
H84   Domestic architecture,U.S.20th century
American modern architecture.Three ex-
amples.

House beautiful 80: 22-25
September 1938

Domestic architecture, U.S. 20th century
Wright, Richardson; McElroy, Margaret
House and Garden designs its own modernist house.
Francis Keally, archt.
The interiors of House and Garden modernist
house.
Grounds and gardens of the modern house.

House and garden 57:
58-65; Ja 1930
72-75,122,138; F 1930
93-95,150,154,156; Mr. 1930

Domestic architecture, 20th century
Beresford, A. E.
Modernist tendencies in domestic architecture.

Builder 141: 460
September 18, 1931

Domestic architecture, U.S., 20th century
A number of small homes and their plans.
 	
House and garden 58: 67-79
July, 1930
	RYERSON LIBRARY.
	D13.1 Domestic architecture, U.S, 20th century
	H84 Price, Matlack
	      Progress and precedent in small house design
	
	House beautiful 58:202-218
	Sept. 1925
		Domestic architecture. United States. 20th cent.
		Blake, Peter
		   The vanishing American house.
		
		Zodiac
		1:89-94 O 1957

D13.1   Domestic architecture, U.S. 20th century
H84   Our home builders service designs a
    modern house
 	
House beautiful 67:80-81
January 1930
	710.5 Domestic architecture, U.S. Twentieth cent.
	H84 Fistere, J.C.
	    Skyline architects turn to houses: models of
	small houses by Leonard Schultze, Harvey Wiley Cor-
	bett, Raymond Hood, William Van Alen, and Lawrence
	White, archts.
	
	House and garden 65: 35-37,70
	January 1934
	
	A
		Domestic architecture, U.S., 20th cent.
		Barringer, Anna
		When no architect was available.
		
		House beautiful 69:520-521,544,546
		May, 1931

Domestic architecture, U.S. 20th cent.
Gunn, Edwin
The planning and equipment of the small house.
pts. 1-4
     Builder 130:
        64; Ja 8, 1926
    125-26; " 15, "
     154;   " 22, "
     187;   " 29, "
     273;   F 12, "
     312;   " 19, "
          (see card 2)
	RYERSON LIBRARY.
	D13.1 Domestic architecture, U.S. 20th century
	H84 Bonta, Edwin
	    The small-house primer
	
	House beautiful 57:238-240
	March 1925
		Domestic architecture, U.S. 20th century.
		Dutch colonial influence
		Price, C.M.
		   "Dutch Colonial" - a native style of
		country house architecture
		
		Arts and dec
		3:118-119
		F 1913

Domestic architecture, U.S. 20th cent.
Gunn, Edwin
The planning and equipment of the small house.
pts. 1-4
 	
     Builder 130:
     352; F 26, 1926
   401-02; Mr. 5, 1926
     431; " 12, "
     510; " 19, "
     548; Ap 2, "
	Domestic architecture, U.S. 20th century
	Small houses
	
	House beautiful 48:357-388
	Nov. 1920
		Dom. arch., U.S. Alabama. 19th century
		Curtis, N.C.
		Ante-Bellum houses of Central Alabama.
		
		A.I.A. journal 8:388-397
		November, 1920

710.5 Domestic architecture, United States. 20th H84 century Planning the minimum home. Plans. Modern interpretations of small houses by William Lescaze, Eleanor Pepper and Henry P. Staats. House and garden 72:39-41,88 October 1937	Domestic architecture, U.S. 20th century Small houses. House beautiful 50:357-361,376-379. Nov. 1921	Domestic architecture, U.S., Bavarian influence Brandt, M.S. A Bavarian farm house in New York State. House and garden 60: 74-75,90 July, 1931

Domestic Architecture. U.S., 20th century
   Portfolio of current architecture featuring
the small house.
 	
Architectural record 65: 339-386
April, 1929
	Domestic architecture, U.S. 20th century
	Special number
	
	Architectural forum 38:79-106
	March, 1923
		720.5 Domestic architecture, U.S. (Cal)
		A67r An architectural innovator: some houses
		in Berkeley, Piedmont and Claremont, Cal. by
		Louis Christian Mullgardt, archt.
		
		     Architectural record 30: 117-135
		A August 1911

D13.05   Domestic architecture, U.S. 20th century
V88   Draper, Mrs. George
    The problem of the smaller city house
 	
Vogue 67:120-121
April 15, 1926
	Domestic architecture, U.S. 20th Century
	Unusual American residences.
	
	Country life (U.S.) 51: 57-9
	February, 1927
		Domestic architecture. U.S. California.
		Gebhard, David
		   The case study houses. [illus.]
		
		Artforum
		v.2:24-25
		O 1963

Domestic architecture, U.S. California
Desert homes. A new type of country life developed in California.

Country life (U.S.) 55:54-55
November, 1928

710.5
C855
Domestic architecture, U.S., California
Kaleidoscopic California, whose houses and gardens owe their inspiration to many lands.

Country life (U.S.) 58: 55-57
September 1930

720.5
W52
Domestic architecture, U.S. California
Wight, P.B.
Residential architecture of Southern California.

Western architect 29: 91-96
September 1920

Domestic architecture, U.S. California
Kent, W.K.
Domestic architecture of California:
Influence of the Spanish and Italian Renaissance.

Architectural forum 32:95-100;151-156
March; April, 1920

Domestic architecture, U.S. Calif.
A Mediterranean house in California

Arts and decoration 28:64
April, 1928

705.1
A79
Domestic architecture, U.S., California
Ackermann, Phyllis
A Spanish palace by the sea

Arts and decoration 23:33-35
October 1925

Domestic architecture, U.S. California
Four California houses submitted in the House beautiful third annual small-house competition.

House beautiful 69:138-144
February, 1931

720.5
W52
Domestic architecture, U.S. California
Duell, Prentice
The new era of California architecture, Los Angeles.
Plates of residences in Los Angeles region.

Western architect 32: 87-90, pls.1-16
August 1923

705.1
A79
Domestic architecture, U.S., California
Spanish houses in California landscape

Arts and decoration 26:66-67
March, 1927

Domestic Architecture. U.S. California
A group of California residences near Los Angeles, Spanish style.

American Country Houses of Today.
8 vols. New York: Architectural Book Publishing Company, 1922
pp.84-103

D13.1
H84
Domestic architecture. U.S. California
Kellogg, Mary
Ojo del Desierto, home of Mr. and Mrs. Thomas A. O'Donnell in Southern California.

House beautiful 64: 29-32
July 1928

D13.1
H84
Domestic architecture. U.S., California
Two western houses

House beautiful 65: 39-41
January 1929

D10.5
C88
Domestic architecture, U.S. California
Gill, I.J.
The home of the future: the new architecture of the West: small homes for a great country.

Craftsman 30:140-151,220
May 1916

708.1
L872
Domestic architecture, U.S., California
Parks, Marion
The oldest houses in Los Angeles county.

Masterkey 1: 25-30
November-December 1927

Domestic architecture, U.S. California
The Y for California [plan] Paul Laszlo, archt.

Interiors
104; pt. 1: 60-61
Ja 1945

720.5
W52
Domestic architecture, U.S. California
[Homes in Hollywood and San Diego]

Western arch. 26: 7 pl.fol.p.8
July 1917

Domestic Architecture U.S. California
(winter) Residence in Southern Calif. for D.R. Cameron, D.M. Smyth, A. McNally and Dr. Fenyes.

Inland Archt.
vol.32, No. 6, pl.fol.p. 60
Jan, 1899

Domestic architecture, U.S. Calif. Exhibition
see also
Los Angeles (Cal.) Cal. house and garden exhibition

D13.1
H84
Domestic architecture, U.S., California
The house in good taste

House beautiful 42: 137-140
August 1927

Domestic Architecture U.S. California
Residence in So. Calif.

Inland Archt.
vol. 33, No.1, pl.fol.p. 8
Feb, 1899

720.5
W52
Domestic architecture, U.S., Cal. Los Angeles
Duell, Prentice
The new era of California architecture, Los Angeles.
Plates of residences in Los Angeles region.

Western architect 32: 87-90, pls.1-16
August 1923

Domestic architecture, U.S. Cal. Los Angeles
    Two residences and gardens at Los Angeles,
Cal.
 	
West archt 13-14:11 pls.
fol. p.58
May 1909
	Domestic architecture, U.S. Chinese influence
	
	see
	
	New port (R.I.) Belmont (O.H.) tea house
		Domestic architecture, U.S., Cotswold influence
		    Hopkins, Alfred
		House of Alfred Hopkins done in a Cotswold manner.
		Alfred Hopkins, archt.
		
		House and garden 64:23-25,62,64
		November, 1933

Domestic architecture, U.S. Cal. Santa Monica
    Traditional design at Santa Monica.
 	
House and garden 54: 115-117
November, 1928
	Domestic architecture, U. S. Churrigueresque
	influence
	
	see names of individual houses, i.e:
	Pasadena, Calif. "Mi Sueno"
		Domestic architecture, U.S., Cotswold influence
		    Yewell, J. Floyd
		In the manner of the Cotswolds. Designed by
		J. Floyd Yewell.
		
		House and garden 54:86-87
		November, 1928

Domestic architecture, U.S. Cape Cod influ- ence see also Egypt (Mass.) Ward (James A.) house Harrison (N.Y.) House Lake Forest (Ill.) Cottage Riverside (Conn.) Spence (Hartzell) house New Canaan (Conn.) "Little Farms" Annisquam (Mass.) Norton (Charles L.) house	Domestic architecture, U.S. Classic revival see Classic revival, U.S.	Domestic architecture, U.S., Cotswold influence Yewell, J.F. Know your architecture before you plan to build. (Characterization of various styles of domestic architecture). House and garden 58:44 July, 1930

Domestic architecture, U.S. Cape Cod influence
    Willis, C. M.
Effective economies in building a house.
Plans.
 	
House beautiful 70:228-232,252
September 1931
	Domestic architecture, U. S. Colonial
	
	see
	
	Colonial architecture
		Domestic Architecture, U.S., Cotswold influence
		    Modern Cotswold at St. Martins, Pa.
		
		Arch. Forum. 33:7-16.
		July, 1920.

Domestic architecture, U.S. Cape Cod influence
    Chaffee, G.E.
For less than nine thousand dollars: a house
built from the House Beautiful stock plans of a
Cape Cod Cottage.
 	
House beautiful 71:110-114,144-145
February, 1932
	Domestic architecture, U.S. Cotswold influ-
	ence
	see also
	Great Neck (L.I.) Hammerstein (Oscar) house
		Domestic architecture, U.S., Cretan style
		    For the design of our Fourth Little House we
		choose the ancient modernism of Crete. Plan.
		Harvey Stevenson, archt.
		
		House and garden 63:56-59,62
		March, 1933

Domestic architecture, U.S. Cape Cod influence
    New England furnishes the inspiration for
House and garden's Third Little House. Plan.
Francis Keally, archt.
 	
House and garden 63:60-63
February, 1933
	Domestic architecture, U.S., Cotswold influence
	    Hopkins, Alfred
	Applying the Cotswold style to America.
	
	Country life (U.S.)56:70,72,74,76.
	May, 1929
		Domestic architecture, U.S., Danish influence
		    House in Danish quarter Philadelphia
		William Lauritzen, archt.
		
		The architect 114:297
		Oct. 23, 1925

Domestic Architecture, U.S. Cape Cod influence
    Three more houses that grow: designed after
Mediterranean, Cape Cod and Cotswold styles by
Leigh French, Jr. Plans.
 	
House and garden 60:48-51
November 1931
	Domestic architecture, U.S., Cotswold influence
	    Cotswold architecture on Long Island
	
	Vogue 92:94-95
	December 1, 1938
		Domestic architecture. U.S., Danish influence
		    Reproduced in Riverside, Il.
		
		House beaut. 45:68-69
		Feb. 1919

Domestic architecture, U.S. Designs and plans
Robinson, J.B.
Architects' houses. Parts 1-4
(Architect-designed)

Arch rec 3:
188-206; O 1893
299-340; N "
354-83; D "
Arch rec 4:
45-74; Ja 1894

Domestic architecture, U.S., Dutch colonial
influence
The Dutch Colonial as suited to the present
day. Designed by Lewis E. Welch.

House and garden 66:28-29
November, 1934

A

Domestic architecture. U.S., English influence
An English cottage for a suburban site.
Lyle Boulware, archt. Timber work.

House and garden 58:72
August 1930

Domestic architecture, U.S., Directoire influence
Residence in the manner of the Directoire
at Jamaica, N.Y. Newton Bevin, archt.

House and garden 53:96-97
January, 1928

Domestic architecture, U.S., Dutch Colonial
influence.
Early Dutch Colonial outlines interestingly
adapted.

Arts and decoration 28:70
December, 1927

720.5
A51

Domestic architecture, U.S. English influence.
The English Derived Treatment of the Small
American Dwelling. Frank Chouteau Brown, Archt.

Amer archt 98 pt 1 : 57-62, pls
4-8 fol 68
Ag 24, '10

Domestic architecture, U.S., D.C., Washington
Residence at Washington, D.C.

Inland architect
v.12 no. 7
pl. at end of volume
D 1888

Domestic architecture. U.S., Dutch Colonial
influence
Abbottswood, Lutton
Evolving a house plan: some suggestions on what
to do before you consult and architect. Plans.
Examples of Georgian, Spanish, and Dutch Colonial
styles.

House and garden 42:51
November 1922

Domestic architecture. U.S., English influence
Nelson, F.A.
English home adapted to an Old Connecticut town.
English house of unusually pleasing contour.
Timber work.

Arts and decoration 30:
74-75,114,118
February, 1929

Domestic architecture, U.S., D.C., Washington
Residences, Washington, D.C.

Inland Architect
v.11 no. 6
pl. at end of vol.
My 1888

Domestic architecture. U.S., Dutch colonial
influence
A house in Wellesley Hills, Mass. of Dutch
Colonial style

House beautiful 67:609
May 1930

710.5
C855

Domestic architecture, U.S. English influence
Stillman, Michael
English tradition in American houses. Illus-
trations and plans. Country house style.

Country life (U.S.) 60: 35-41,78
October 1931

Domestic architecture, U.S. Dutch colonial
influence
see also

Augusta (Ga.) Prichard (Gilman) house
Beechurst (L.I.) Stewart (Gordon) house
Brookline (Mass.) Daitch (J.J.) house
Fieldston (N.Y.) Griffen (J.W.) house
Great Neck (L.I.) Young (O.S.) house
Lansdowne (Pa.) Roberts (W.W.) house
Riverdale (N.Y.) Evans (Charles) house
Springfield (O.) McCulloch (Hugh) house
Tenafly (N.J.) Cooke (Frederick) house
Terra Haute (Ind.)   Oakley (F.D.) house

Domestic architecture, U.S. Egyptian influence
see

Key Biscayne (Fla.) "Mestha"

Domestic architecture, U.S., English influence
Scheffer, Alfred
Gracious type of house on a small lot. (Timber
work).

Arts and decoration 30:66,68
January, 1929

720.5
A67r

Domestic Architecture, U.S., Dutch colonial influence
Embury, Aymar II
Conservatism in design. Residences in Kensington, Great Neck, L.I. Aymar Embury, II, archt.

A   Architectural record 32:328-335
October 1912

Domestic architecture, U.S., Elizabethan
influence
see

Harrison (N.Y.) Mittendorf (A.D.) house

Domestic architecture. U.S., English influence
Geerlings, G.K.
Informal English houses.

House and garden 59:94-97,120
May, 1931

Domestic architecture, U.S., Dutch Colonial
influence
The Dutch Colonial in modern dress.

House and garden 45:58-9
May 1924

Domestic architecture, U.S. English influence
see also

Colonial architecture
Half-timbered houses, U.S.
Domestic architecture, U.S. Elizabethan influence
"   "   "   Jacobean   "
"   "   "   Tudor   "
"   "   "   Regency   "
"   "   "   Cotswold   "

720.5
B84

Domestic architecture, U.S. English influence
Brown, F.C.
The relation between English and American
domestic architecture.

Brickbuilder 15: 138-44
Jl '06

Domestic architecture. U.S., English influence Stone and stucco in a house of English precedent at Haverford. Timber work. Arts and decoration 30:44-45 January, 1929	Domestic architecture, U.S. French influence see also Domestic architecture, U.S. Normandy influence and names of individual houses, i.e.: Stanford, Conn. Marion (F.J.) house Winnetka, Ill. Hussagh (R.D.) house Santa Barbara, Calif. Le petit manoir St. Louis, Mo. Ferrières	710.5 Domestic architecture, U.S. French influence H84 The Gallic trend in domestic architecture. House and garden 42: 54-5 N '22
Domestic architecture. U.S., English influence A studio-house built on old English lines. Plans. Country life (U.S.) 58:42-43,76 October, 1930	705.1 Domestic architecture, U. S. French A79 influence Adaptation of the French chateau type Arts & decoration 7:124-127 Ja '17	Domestic architecture, U.S., French influence A house in the French style designed by Francis Keally House beautiful 64:401 A October 1928
Domestic architecture. U.S., English influence Humphrey, Henry, Jr. What type of house shall I build? II-The English house. Country life 49:61-63 November, 1925	Domestic architecture. U.S., French Influence The farmhouse of France modernized. Plans. Country life (U.S.) 58:36-37,76 October, 1930	Domestic architecture, U.S., French influence Geerlings, G.K. Informal French houses give hints to American architects. House and garden 59:86-89,114 March, 1931
915 Domestic architecture,U.S.Exhibition P15 Houses old and new: New York museum of Science and Industry exhibit. No illustrations. El palacio 40:127-128 May 27-June 10,1936	710.5 Domestic architecture, U.S., French influ- H84 Geerlings, G. K. ence The formal French manner for America. House and garden 59: 88-91,132 April 1931	710.5 Domestic architecture, U.S. French influence H84 Yewell, J. F. Know your architecture before you plan to build. (Characterization of various styles of domestic architecture). House and garden 58: 44 July 1930
Domestic architecture, U.S. Federal Federal Interiors Kimball, Fiske. Domestic architecture of the American Colonies and of the early Republic. New York: Charles Scribner's Sons, 1922. 232-261	Domestic architecture, U.S., French influence Howard, E.L. A French farmhouse enters the American scene. Arts and decoration 29:44-45,88 June, 1928	Domestic architecture, U.S., French influence Mansart recurs in New Orleans. House and garden 55: 83 January, 1929
Domestic Architecture, U.S. Federal Newcomb, Rexford. Architecture in Old Kentucky. Urbana: University of Illinois Press, 1953. pls 49-56	710.5 Domestic architecture, U.S. French influence H84 Price, Llewellyn A French farmhouse set on a Quaker country hillside. Designed by Walter Durham of Durham and Irvine, archts. House and garden 59: 72-73,92 January 1931	Domestic architecture, U.S.French influence Hungerford, Edward An old French house built by James and Vincent LeRay at Cape Vincent, New York. House beautiful 64:38-39,79 July, 1928
Domestic Architecture, U.S. Federal Federal interiors Newcomb, Rexford. The Colonial and Federal house. Philadelphia and London: J.B. Lippincott, 1933.112-116	Domestic architecture, U.S., French influence A French provincial interpretation. Herbert T. Johnson, archt. House and garden 59: 102-103 April, 1931	710.5 Domestic architecture,U.S. French influence H84 Sophisticated provincial: the Norman home of Mr.Ralph E.Clifford,at Greenwich,Conn. Frank Forster,archt. Plan. House and garden 72:46-48 A July 1937

Domestic architecture. U.S. French influence
Humphrey, Henry, Jr.
What type of house shall I build? III-French style.

Country life 49:80-82
December, 1926

Domestic architecture, U.S. History
Domestic architecture in United States:
early days to Victorian.

Butterworth, Benjamin, Comp.
The growth of industrial art.
Washington, D.C.: U.S. Gov.
Printing office, 1888. p.60

710.5
H84
Domestic architecture, Italian influence-
For New England or California; a stucco
residence in the Italian manner especially
designed by J. Floyd Yewell, archt.

House and garden 55: 60-61
January 1929

A

Domestic architecture, U.S. French-Canadian
influence
Suggested rooms for a house of the habitant
style of Montreal and Quebec (French provincial).

House and garden 57:108-111
May, 1930

Domestic architecture, U.S., IL. Park Ridge
Park Ridge
Residences in Park Ridge IL.

Western arch. 34:13-16
Jan. 1925

Domestic architecture, U.S. Italian
influence
Meeks, C.L.V.
Henry Austin and the Italian villa
[bibliography]

Art Bull. 30:145-149
Je. '48

Domestic architecture, U.S. Ga., Atlanta
Atlanta homes. They are among the nation's
most beautiful

Life articles on art 1948 pt.
1:517-524
June 7, 1948

Domestic architecture, U.S., Indians of North
America Influence
Henderson, Rose
A primitive basis for modern architecture
Taos; Sante Fe; Alburquerque, New Mexico.

Architectural record 54:189-96
August, 1923

710.5
H84
Domestic architecture, U.S. Italian influence
Lowell, Guy
Is "Italian" architecture really Italian?

House & garden 38:18-21
N 1920

Domestic architecture, U.S. German influence
Downs, Joseph
A Pennsylvania-German house

Philadelphia. Pennsylvania
museum   Bulletin 22:265-275
Dec., 1926

Domestic architecture, U.S. Italian influence

see also names of individual houses, i.e.:

Hartsdale, N.Y. Hilhouse
San Francisco, Calif. Leighton (J.H.) house
Sarasota (Fla.) Ringling (John R.) house

Domestic architecture. U.S. Italian influence
Italian precedent in American domestic
architecture

American magazine of art 14:231-239
May, 1923

Domestic architecture, U.S. Gothic influence

see

Gothic revival, U.S.

Domestic architecture, U.S. Italian influence
Adaptation of the Italian villa

Arts and decor 6:165-167
Feb. 1916

Domestic architecture, U.S., Italian influence
Geerlings, G.K.
Old-world precedent applied to Italian houses in
America.

House and garden 59:75-77,94
January, 1931

Domestic architecture, U.S. Greek revival

see

Classic revival, U.S.

Domestic architecture, U.S. Italian influence
A bungalow in the Italian manner

House and garden 45:71
Jan. 1924

Domestic architecture, U.S. Jacobean influence

see also

Mt. Kisco (N.Y.) Boissevain (G.L.) house
Lenox (Mass.) Frothingham (Samuel) house

713.5
H84
Domestic architecture, U.S., Hawaii
Roosevelt, Jr., Col.and Mrs. Theodore
Hawaiian holiday "La Pietra", home of Walter
Dillingham, Fagan house, home of Mrs. Harold Erd-
man, and Harold Castle residence.

House and garden 72:29-31,88
January 1938

Domestic architecture, U.S. Italian influence
Newcomb, Rexford
"Bungalows" in the Spanish and Italian style.

Architectural forum 44:191-200
March, 1926

Domestic architecture U.S., Jacobean influence
McCabe, L.R.
Darlington, a Jacobean Manor in New Jersey,
in the Ramapo hills of New Jersey. James Brite,
archt.

A   Architectural record 32:496-509
December, 1912

Domestic architecture, U.S. Japanese influence

see also

Fall River (Mass.) Knapp (Rev.) house
Santa Monica (Cal.) Bernheimer (A.L.) house

Domestic architecture. U.S. Maryland
Roth, Rodris
   Interior decoration of city houses in
Baltimore: the federal period. [illus]

   Winterthur portfolio
   v.5: [59]-86, 1969

Domestic architecture, U.S., Mexican-Spanish
   influence
   By selecting Mexican-Spanish, Ernst Lubitsch
breaks a spell. Walter G. Willrich, archt.
H.W. Grieve and Jetta Gondal Grieve, decorators.
No plan.

A   House and garden 66:52-53
           December, 1934

Domestic architecture, U.S. Japanese influence

   Country Life 41: 48-50.
   Mar. 1922.

Domestic architecture, U.S. Md. Baltimore
   Residence at Baltimore, Md.

   Western architect 14:pl.prec.p.39
   October, 1909

720.5   Domestic architecture, U.S. Michigan
A67r   Kimball, Fiske
             The old houses of Michigan

             Arch rec 52: 227-40
             S '22

AVERSON LIBRARY
706.2   Domestic architecture.U.S.Japanese influence
I61   C.M.P.
             The house beautiful of Japan. (Text discusses
          the Japanese house. Illustrations are of Japanese
          garden and tea house at Tuxedo Park, N.Y., design-
          ed by S. Mori.)

A   International studio 48:pp.XV-XVIII
          No.189,November.1912

Domestic architecture. (U.S.) Mass.

   see also

Belmont (Mass.) TAC house

720.6   Domestic architecture,U.S.,Middle Western
A67r   Sturgis,Russell   States.
             Dwellings of the Middle West. American resi-
          dences of today. Plans.

          Architectural record 16:297-406
          October 1904

Domestic architecture, U.S. Japanese influence
   Japanese style bungalow

   House and garden 35:42
   Jan. 1919

720.5   Domestic architecture. U.S. Mass
A67r   Brown, F.C.
             Boston suburban architecture.

          Architectural record 21: 245-290
          April 1907

Domestic architecture, U.S., Mission influence
   The architecture of California.

   House and garden 51:104-5
   February, 1927

Domestic architecture, U.S., Japanese influence
Keith, H. P.
The trail of Japanese influence in our modern
domestic architecture.

   Craftsman 12: 446-451
   July, 1907

Domestic architecture. U.S. Massachusetts.
Boston. 19th century
Blackall, C. H.
   Boston sketches - private work.

   Inland architect
   v. 13 no. 1: 6-7
   pl. fol. p. 14
   v. 13 no.3: 40-41
   pl. fol. p.48
   no.4 Ap: 53-4
   1889

Domestic architecture, U.S. Mohammedan influence

   see also

Santa Barbara (Cal.) Cotton (D.D.) house
Palm Beach (Fla.) Pennock (H.H.) house
Palo Alto (Cal.) Hoover (Herbert) house
Palm Beach (Fla.) Barkbrausen (H.G.) house

                   Competitions
Domestic architecture, U.S., Japanese influence.
   Results of Yamanaka competition...open for
young architects and draftsmen in Japan to show
adaptability of Japanese architecture to a
suburban house in America, costing not more than
$50,000. Plans.

   Architecture (N.Y.) 35: 77-8
   F'17

Domestic architecture. U.S. Mass. Boston
Cummings, Abbott Lowell
   The domestic architecture of Boston, 1660-
1725. [illus.]

   Archives of Amn. art. Journal
   v.9, no.4: 1-16
   1970

Domestic architecture, U.S., Moorish influence

   see

Domestic architecture, U.S., Mohammedan influence

D15.1   Domestic architecture. U.S. Louisiana
H84   Yeager, Mollie Harrop
             Louisiana plantation homes

          House beaut 49: 294-296, 334,336
          Ap '21

Domestic architecture U.S., Mexican influence

   see also

Domestic architecture, U.S. Churrigueresque influence

Pasadena (Cal) Behr (O.M.) house

D15.1   Domestic architecture, U.S., New England
H84   Smith, G.R.
             Regarding our New England "Castles in Spain"

          House beautiful 60:52-53
          July, 1926

Domestic architecture, U.S., N.Y., New York

see also

Town houses, U.S., N.Y., New York

Domestic architecture, U.S., New York (city) 19th century

Fallon, J.T.
Domestic architecture of the early nineteenth century.

American architect 110:139-144;
Sept. 6, 1916   167-171

Domestic architecture, U.S. N.Y. Scarsdale
Houses being built at Scarsdale, N.Y.

Architecture 41:20-22.Jan. '20.

Domestic architecture, U.S. New York (city)

Inl archt 33:pl.fol.p.8
F 1899

Domestic architecture, U.S., N.Y. (city)
1902
Croly, Herbert
The contemporary New York residence

Arch. rec. 12:704-722
D '02

Domestic architecture, U.S., Normandy influence

see also

Bronxville (N.Y.) Scannell (R.N.) house
Great Neck (L.I.)Coote (A.W.) house
Greensboro (N.C.) Morton (J.R.) hosue
Greenwhich (Conn.) Khakum Wood
Johnstown (Pa.) Swank (A.M.) house
King's Point (L.I.) Williams (E.L.) house
Montclair (N.J.) Hatfield (Milton) house
New Canaan (Conn.) Bailey (J.H.) house
                    (see card 2)

Domestic architecture, U.S. New York (city)
Willauer, A. S.
The modern home in New York.

Amer archt 96:no. 1774.
D 1909

Domestic architecture, U.S. New York (State)
Bonta, Edwin
Along the Seneca turnpike. Introducing a distinct type of Post-colonial house.

Arch rec 40: 505-15
D '16

Domestic architecture, U.S. Normandy influence
(card 2)

see also

New Haven (Conn.) Edgerton (Franklin) house
Philadelphia (Pa.) Bell (Samuel) house
"   "   "Brightwood"
"   "   Button (J.P.) house
"   "   "   (Conyers) house
"   "   Welsh (H.S.) house
"   "   Woodward (George) house
Santa Barbara (Cal.) Mitchell (C.B.) house
                      (see card 3)

Domestic architecture, U.S., New York (city)
New York city houses by various architects:
McKim, Mead and White, Grosvenor Atterbury,
Warren and Whetmore, Charles Platt, etc.

Brickbuilder 17:187-210
September, 1908

710.6
C855
Domestic architecture, U.S. New York (State)
Hungerford, Edward
Old houses of our north country. Hungerford homestead at Watertown, N.Y.; the old Peugnet house at Cape Vincent. Old house at Watertown built by Micah Sterling, Landmark of Sacketts Harbor, house built by Colonel Elisha Camp in 1816; great house of James Donatian Le Ray de Chaumont at LeRaysville near Watertown, N.Y.

Country life 45:60-2
April 1924

Domestic architecture, U.S. Normandy influence

see also

Silvermine (Conn.) Barnum (J.H.) house
South Norwalk (Conn.) Sheldon (Waldo) house

Domestic architecture, U.S. N.Y. City
Rowe, H. W.
Post colonial architecture of New York.

Am arch 107: 193-9, 203
3rd & 5th pl. fol. p. 204
Mr 24,'15

Domestic architecture, U.S., New York. Long Island
Old houses on Long Island

A.I.A. jour 9: frontis-
Piece, 161-8
My 1921

Domestic architecture, U.S., Normandy influence
An architect choose Norman and puts his house upon a picturesque hillside. Staats, archt.

House and garden 66: 26-27
August, 1934

720.5
A67m
Domestic architecture, U.S. N.Y.N.Y.
Private residences in N.Y. city [plans]

Arch. & Bldrs. mag. 41:
465-74
Aug. 1909

Domestic architecture, U.S. N. Y. Long Island
Eight old Long Island houses

A.I.A. jour
12: 110-17, Mr 1924

710.5
H84
Domestic architecture, U.S. Normandy
influence
Creating the very small home.
Design for Norman house. [plans, elevations, perspective] O.L. Gowman, arch't.

House & Garden 48: 45-52
July 1925

Domestic Architecture, U.S., N.Y. (city) 17th century
Seventeenth Century Houses, still occupied in Greater New York. By Henry Wysham Lanier.

House and gard 5: 26-32
Ja 1904

Domestic Architecture, U.S. New York.
Long Island
Kellogg, A. M.
A Long Island house and garden

House and garden
7: no. 3, Mr 1905

Domestic architecture, U.S., Normandy influence
A French village, Chestnut Hill, Pa.
R.R. McGoodwin, archt.

A   American architect 135: 499-509
        April 20, 1929

Domestic architecture, U.S., Normandy influence Taylor, C.S. A luxurious home of medium size Arts and decoration 28:64-66 January, 1928	Domestic architecture, U.S., Ohio Early domestic architecture of Ohio American architect 123:307-12 April 11, 1923	Domestic architecture. U.S. Ohio. Columbus A group of houses in Columbus, Ohio. R.G. Hanford, archt. American archt. 135: 297-308 Mr 5, 1929
710.5 N84 Domestic architecture, U.S. Normandy influence In the Normandy manner. R.S. Walcott, archt. House & garden 52:112-13 Sept '27	Domestic architecture. U.S., Ohio., Cleveland The C.F. Brush house, Cleveland. Architect not given. Sheldon, George William. Artistic Country Seats. 2 vols. New York: D. Appleton and Co., 1871. v.2,pt.4. pp.81-83,pl.23	D10.5 c88 Domestic architecture, U.S. Pacific Coast States Pacific. coast. houses Craftsman, 13:450-457 Jan. 1908
Domestic architecture. U.S., Normandy influence Yewell, J.F. Know your architecture before you plan to build. (Characterization of various styles of domestic architecture). House and garden 58:45 July, 1930	Domestic architecture. U.S. Ohio. Cleveland. The Colonel J.H. Ammon house, C.F. Schweinfurth, archt. Sheldon, George William. Artistic Country Seats. 2 vols. New York: D. Appleton and Co., 1871. v.2,pt.3,pp.29-30,pl.9	720.5 A67r Domestic architecture,U.S. Pennsylvania Embury,Aymar II Pennsylvania farmhouses: examples of rural dwellings of a hundred years ago. Architectural record 30:475-485 November 1911
Domestic architecture. U.S., Normandy influence Home of Mr. and Mrs. Gilbert Browning. Forster and Gillimore, archts. A House and garden 60:52-55 December, 1931	Domestic Architecture. U.S., Ohio Cleveland. The Dr. J.H. Salisbury house, C.F. Schweinfurth, archt. Sheldon, George William. Artistic Country Seats. 2 vols. New York: D. Appleton and Co., 1871. v.2,pt.3 pp. 15-16,pl.5	708.1 P54b Domestic architecture, U.S. Pa. Downs, Joseph A Pennsylvania German house. Philadelphia, Penn. Museum bulletin 22: 265-275 D 1926
Domestic architecture, U.S., Normandy influence A "Modern Instance" of the Feudal (in wood). Architectural record 14:136 August, 1903	Domestic architecture, U.S., Ohio, Cleveland English and early American homes in favor Good furniture 27:73-75 August, 1926	Domestic architecture, U.S. Pa. Recent suburban architecture in Philadelphia and vicinity. arch. rec 19:167-193 Mr 1906
Domestic architecture, US., Normandy influence Various materials combine in a house of Norman type. Bernhardt E. Müller, archt. Plan. House and garden 60:74-75 November, 1931	Domestic architecture. U.S., Ohio. Cleveland The N.S. Posson house, C.F. Schweinfurth, archt. Sheldon, George William. Artistic Country Seats. 2 vols. New York: D. Appleton and Co., 1871. v.2,pt.3, pp. 17-19, pl.6	Domestic architecture. U.S. Pa. Philadelphia Portfolio of current architecture. Phila- delphia houses. Archl. record 52: 212-18 S 1922
Domestic architecture, U.S. Norwegian influ- ence see also Oakland (Cal.) Crandall (H.L.) house	Domestic architecture, U.S., Ohio. Cleveland Frary, I.T. The small house illustrated with examples of the work of Bohnard and Parsson. A Architectural record 44:187-198 September, 1918	Domestic architecture, U.S., Pa. Philadelphia Nolan, Thomas Recent suburban architecture in Philadelphia and vicinity. Cope and Stewardson, archts.; Brockie and Hastings, archts., and others. No plans. A Architectural record 19:166-193 March, 1906

Domestic architecture. U.S. Pa. Philadelphia
Typical secondary street of two-story houses,
21st St. and Pemberton Streets, Philadelphia, Pa.

Archl.rec
29: 235,249
Mr 1911

Domestic architecture, U.S. Regency influence
Modified regency, the home of Mr. and Mrs.
J.Linerd Conarroe in Chestnut Hill, Pa...
designed by Mr. Conarroe.

A   House and garden 72:43
July, 1937

Domestic architecture, U.S., S. Carolina.
Charleston
Kennedy, J.R.
Examples of Georgian work in Charleston, South
Carolina. Plans of "Mulberry Castle"; Horry
house; Witte house.

Architectural record 19:282-294
April, 1906

Domestic architecture. U.S. Pa. Philadel-
phia
Willard, Julian
The work of Wilson Eyre.

Archl.rec
14: 283-325
O 1903

Domestic architecture, U.S., Regency influence
Regency character lends itself to the modern:
an all-metal house in a traditional style.
Robert B. Carr, archt. Plan.

A   House and garden 66:26-27
July, 1934

Domestic architecture, U.S., S. Carolina
Charleston
Miles Brewton house; Ralph Izard house; William
Blacklock house; Daniel Blake houses; Henry
Manigault house; Brewton-Sawter house; Nathaniel
Russell house; houses at 25 and 27; 35 Meeting
street; house at 301 East Bay, South, Charleston,
South Carolina.

White pine 14: pls.
no. 4, 1928

720.5
A87r   Domestic architecture, U.S., Pa., Pittsburgh
Schuyler,Montgomery
The building of Pittsburgh: 1 - The terrain
and the rivers. 2 - The business quarter and
commercial buildings. 3 - A real civic center.
4 - A modern auditorium church. 5 - The homes of
Pittsburgh.
Architectural record 30: 264-282
September 1911

Domestic architecture, U.S., Regency influence
Residence in Westchester County, N.Y.
Perry M. Duncan, archt. Plans. First prize winner
in class 1 of the House and garden's architects'
competition, 1937.

A   House and garden 72:16-17
September, 1937 (Sect. 2)

Domestic Architecture. U.S., Southern States.
Classic Houses of the South. By Mrs. Thaddeus
Horton.

House beau 13: 388-93
My 1903

Domestic architecture, U.S. Regency influence

see also

Bedford village (N.Y.) Fuller (C.F.) house
Bellingham (Wash.) Stanton (F.C.) house
      "   Wahl (H.) house
Bethayres (Pa.) Kenwood
Farnhurst (Del.) Swanwick manor
Grosse Point (Mich.) Johnston (G.O.) house
Houston (Tex.) Hill (Gillette) house
Mansfield (O.) La Dow (J.E.) house
                  (see card 2)

Domestic architecture, U.S., Regency influence
Victorian yields to Regency.

House and garden 64: 46-47
August, 1933

Domestic Architecture, U.S., Southern States
A Group of Southern Suburban Houses.
De Buys, Churchill and Labouisse, Architects.

Arch. rec. 30: 388-400
O, 1911

(card 2)
Domestic architecture, U.S., Regency influence

see also

South Norwalk (Conn.) Cowell (E.I.:) house
Tenafly (N.J.) Moser (J.R.) house

Domestic architecture, U.S., Regency influence
W. and J. Sloane's two story Regency house at
their Fifth Avenue Shop, New York City. Henry
Otis Chapman, Jr., and Harold W. Beder, archts.

House and garden 64: 26-29,68-69,82,96
October, 1933

D10.5
C88   Domestic architecture, U.S. Southern states
Ziegler, C.A.
Home of the future: What will be the con-
tribution of the south in the development of
American architecture?

Craftsman 30: 41-52
Ap '16

Domestic architecture., U.S., Regency influence
A Cleveland boulevard displays this Regency
house inspired by a Sussex example.
Clarence Mack, archt.

House and garden 59:90-92
May, 1931

Domestic architecture, U. S. Russian
influence

see

Oyster Bay (N.Y.) Levienne (Sonia) house

Domestic architecture, U.S., Southern States
Whitehead, R.F.
The old and new south; a consideration of
architecture in the southern states. Illustration
of residences in Virginia, Maryland.
The new south. Various illustrations and plans
in Tenn, and Alabama, etc.
Domestic architecture. Examples of residences
in Georgia and Tennessee. Plans.

Architectural record 30:1-12,13-43,44-56
July, 1911

Domestic architecture, U.S., Regency influence
If you're planning to build - analyses of
4 new American homes: Regency influence;
modern Expression; Western type; early American
design. Allman Fordyce and William Hamby, archts.

A   House and garden 70:56-61
September, 1936

710.5
C855   Domestic Architecture (U.S.) South Carolina
Wright, Hamilton
Carolina: Camden - old and new. Residences
of Mr. and Mrs. Charles P. Knight, and of Ward
C. Belcher's Horse Branch Ha 11.

Country life (N.Y.) 69: 31-33; 66,81
March 1936

Domestic architecture, U.S., Southern States.
Ronin, E.E.; Willy, D.A.
Quaint houses of the South. Colonial homes of
Natchez. "Westover", an historic Virginia
mansion.

House and garden 11:59-64,230-235
F, Je '07

Domestic architecture, U.S., Southern States
Major, H.
Southern plantation homes.

House and garden. 50:112-113
Nov. 1926

Domestic architecture, U.S., Spanish influence
Wren, H.R.
Architecture indigenous to California: home of
Mr. and Mrs. John E. Barber.

Arts and decoration 30:50-52
April, 1929

Domestic architecture, U.S. Spanish influence
A house of Spanish type

House beautiful 64:535
November 1928

D15.1   Domestic architecture. U.S. Southern states
H84   Edgerton, Gurdon I
        Southern variations

House beaut 49: 297, 336, 338
Ap '21

720.5   Domestic architecture, U.S., Spanish influ-
A67f   Newcomb, Rexford   ence.
        "Bungalows" in the Spanish and Italian style.

Architectural forum 44: 191-200
March 1926

Domestic architecture, U.S., Spanish influence
Houses for Witmer Brothers Company, Los
Angeles, California. David J. Witmer, archt.
Residence for Davidson Construction Company,
Los Angeles, California. Plans.

Western architect 29: pls.14-16
October, 1920

Domestic architecture, U.S. Spanish influence

    see also

Flintridge (Cal.) Cass (Louis) house
Hillsborough (Cal.) Neiman (Alma) house
Linda Vista (Cal.) Booth (J.S.) house
Los Angeles (Cal.) Eltinge (Julian) house
Orinda (Cal.) Johnson (C.B.) house
Palm Beach (Fla.) McGinley (H.P.) house
Pasadena (Cal.) Armstrong (E.V.) house
   "   "   McCarthy (L.A.) house
                 (see card 2)

Domestic architecture, U.S., Spanish influence
California residences by John Byers, archt.

Western archt. 38:pls.1-16
January, 1929

A

Domestic architecture, U.S., Spanish influence
Wren, H.R.
Informal charm of old Spain in a city home,
Los Angeles

Arts and decoration 29:44-47,88
October, 1928

Domestic architecture, U.S. Spanish influence

    see also   (card 2)

Pasadena (Cal.) Morse (W.S.) house
Pleasanton (Cal.) Hacienda del Pozo de Verona
San Gabriel (Cal.) Marmon (W.F.) house
Santa Barbara (Cal.) "Casa Dorinda"
   "   "   " Smith (G.W.) house (second)

Domestic architecture, U.S., Spanish influence
Geerlings, G.K.
Characteristics of the Spanish style interpreted
for America.

House and garden 59:82-85
February, 1931

710.5   Domestic architecture, U.S.Spanish influence
H84   Yewell, J. F.
        Know your architecture before you plan to
        build. (Characterization of various styles of
        domestic architecture).

House and garden 58: 42
July 1930

Domestic architecture U.S., Spanish influence

    see also

Domestic architecture, U. S. Churrigueresque
    influence
Spanish colonial architecture, U.S.

Domestic architecture. U.S. Spanish influence
Wingage, Amelia
A country home refashioned in the Spanish manner

Arts and decoration 27:58-59,102
September, 1927

Domestic architecture, U.S., Spanish influence
Byers, C.A.
Modern version of Spanish architectural style

Arts and decoration 30:79,122
March, 1929

Domestic architecture,U.S., Spanish influence
Adjusting Mediterranean architecture to
Illinois

Arts and decoration 31:68-69
May, 1929

710.5   Domestic architecture, U.S., Spanish influ-
H84   Abbottswood, Lutton   ence
        Evolving a house plan: some suggestions on
        what to do before you consult an architect. Plans
        Examples of Georgian, Spanish, and Dutch Colonial
        styles.

House & garden 42:51
November 1922

Domestic architecture, U.S., Spanish influence
Quinn, Lucile
A picturesque castle in Florida

Arts and decoration 28:45-47
January, 1928

Domestic architecture, U.S., Spanish influence
Adopting the Spanish peasant type of house.
Plans.

Country life (U.S.) 58: 40-41,76
October, 1930

Domestic architecture, U.S., Spanish influence
Home of Miss M. Burke, Santa Barbara.
George Washington Smith, archt.
    Home of J.B. Alexander, Montecito, Cal.
James Osborne Craig, archt.

House and garden 47:81-83
April, 1925

A

Domestic architecture, U.S., Spanish influence
Reflecting old Spain. E.J. Lang, archt.

House and garden 51:79
April, 1927

Domestic architecture, U.S., Spanish influence
   Residence of E.V. Armstrong, Pasadena,
California. Johnson, Kaufmann and Coates,
architects. Residence of E.R.Richardson, Los
Angeles, California. C.M. Winslow, archt.
Residence of S.W. Bixby, Los Angeles, California.
Elmer Grey, archt.

         Architectural forum 38:163-9
         March, 1923

Domestic architecture, U.S., Spanish influence
   Dashwood, Wyona
Spanish estate in Colorado

         Arts and decoration 30:74
         April, 1929

Domestic architecture, U.S., Swiss influence
   Cottage near Lake Harriet, Minneapolis, Minn.
L.A. Lamoreau, archt. Plan.

A   Architectural review 14:70
         March, 1907

Domestic architecture, U.S., Spanish influence
   Residences at Santa Barbara, California:
F.L. Baxter; W.S. Spaulding; Miss Elise Hodges;
Eleanor M. Semmelmeyer. Soule, Murphy and Hastings,
archts.

         Architecture 48:pls.107-122,p.225-8
A   July, 1923

Domestic architecture, U.S., Spanish influence
   Humphrey, Henry, Jr.
What type of house shall I build? IV-Spanish
style.

         Country life 49:43-45
         January, 1927

Domestic architecture, U. S. Swiss influence
   Design for a house in Cincinnati. L.F.
Plympton, archt.

         Arch rev
         3: 46-47, pl. 33
         O 1894

Domestic architecture, U.S., Spanish influence
   Smaller houses in the sunshine of Florida.

         Country life (U.S.) 51: 50-1
         January, 1927

720.5
I56   Domestic architecture, U.S. Spanish mission
                  influence.
Jenney, W.L.B.
   The old California missions and their influence
on modern design.

         Inland archt 47: 75, 71-2
         Ap, Je'06

Domestic architecture, U. S. Swiss influence
   Influenced by the Swiss chalet.

         Craftsman
         28: 220-223
         My 1915

Domestic architecture, U.S., Spanish influence
   Some recent works of Marston and Van Pelt

         Architectural record 52:17-38
A   July, 1922

Domestic architecture, U.S., Spanish
              mission influence
Baum, G.C.
The Spanish mission style of house, the architec-
tural style that is being developed from the old
Spanish missions.

         House and garden 21:11-13
         March, 1912

Domestic architecture, U.S., Swiss influence
   Stellman, L.J.
Swiss chalet type for America. No plans.

         House and garden 20:288-292
         November, 1911

720.5
W52   Domestic architecture, U.S.Spanish influence
Newcomb, Rexford
   Some Spanish residences in Southern Califor-
nia by George Washington Smith, archt.

   A   Western architect 31:58-61,pl.6-16
         May 1922

710.5
H84   Domestic architecture,U.S. Swedish influence
    Scandinavia in Connecticut. A peasant
home, inspired by native Swedish design, of
Mrs.Mengel Grew, at the Longshore Country
Club,Westport,Conn. William F.Todé and C.L.
Nutt,archts.

         House and garden 72:26-27
  A   July 1912

720.6
A51j   Domestic architecture. U.S. Texas
Gideon, S.E.
   The architecture and incidents of a Texas
frontier town.

         American institute of architects 5:
                   285-289
         June 1917

Domestic architecture, U.S., Spanish influence
Stacy-Judd, R.B.
Spanish and Aztec architectural forms combined

         Arts and decoration 29:74,126
         May, 1928

Domestic architecture, U.S., Swedish influence
Priddy, Jane
Vikingsborg, the house with the grass roof.
Home of Mr. and Mrs. Lennart Palme

         House beautiful 65:615-618
         May, 1929

720.5
A51   Domestic architecture. U.S. Texas
Gideon,S.E.
   Early architecture in Texas.

         American architect 111:49-53
         January 24,1917

Domestic architecture, U.S., Spanish influence
Major, Howard
Spanish architecture in tropical America.

         Country life (U.S.) 53:40-1
         January, 1928

Domestic architecture, U.S. Swiss influence

        see also names of individual bldgs.

Lake Geneva (Wis.) "Northwoodside"
Santa Barbara (Cal.) Dennison (C.S.) estate
Summit (N.J.) "Kingdor"

        etc.

Domestic architecture, U.S., Texas
   House for Texas, cheap to build, it is
especially adapted to state's hot climate

         Life, articles on art: 194-5
         S 3, 1945

Domestic architecture. U.S. Texas.
Texas house [plan] Mackie and Kamrath, archs.

Interiors
104; pt. 1: 74
Ag. 1944

710.A Domestic architecture, U.S. Victorian
C855 Stuart, Betty and Edward
An artist reverses the hour glass: Robert
Locher restores a Victorian house. Emerson house
on Staten Island, New York.

Country life (U.S.) 60: 55-59
September 1931

D10.5 Domestic architecture, U.S. Western states
C88 Gill, I.J.
Home of the future: The new architecture
in the west: small homes for a great country.

Craftsman 30: 140-151
My '16

Domestic architecture U.S. Tudor influence

see also

Des moines (Ia.) Salisbury house

Bacon's castle, Va.

Domestic architecture, U.S., Victorian
Bright, Eleanor
Footnotes in wood and stone: Staten Island
houses cover periods from 17th century.

House and garden 66: 60-61
November, 1934

Domestic architecture, western states
Some country house architecture in the far
west.

Architectural record 52: 309-44
October, 1922

710.5 Domestic architecture, U.S. Tudor influence
H84 A little Tudor house in Roseland, N.J.
Michael Stillman, archt.

House and garden 47:59
Ja 1925

Domestic architecture, U.S., Victorian
Parlor of the Price Mansion at Jefferson City.

Bryan, John Albury, ed.
Missouri's contribution to
American architecture. St. Louis,
Missouri: St. Louis Architectural
Club, 1928. p.30

Domestic architecture, U.S., West Indies, British,
influence
see

Palm Beach (Fla.) Kennedy (J.H.) house

Domestic architecture, U.S. Tudor influence
Tudor homes of colonial days

International studio
77:345-8
Jl 1923

---

domestic architecture, U.S., Victorian
Richardson, A.E.
Small town house of the early Victorian period.

Architects' and builders' journal
Jan. 31, 1917   45:56-58

Domestic architecture, West Indies influence

see

Domestic architecture, U.S., West Indies influence

Domestic architecture, U.S., Utah. Salt Lake City
Some early domestic architecture in and near
Salt Lake City, Utah.

Amer. arch. 125:473-6
May 21, 1924

Domestic architecture, U.S., Victorian
Victorian revival in Illinois, a new
home in the local tradition on Somonauk, near
Chicago, for W.P. Paepcke, Esq. Walter S. Frazier,
archt. plan.

House and garden 74:50-51,63
July, 1938

Domestic architecture, Wales
R.P.
Timber house building in North Wales.

Country life (Lond.) 84: lvii
October 29, 1938

Domestic architecture. Ventilation

see

Ventilation, Domestic

Domestic architecture, Virginia
Baldwin, F.C.
Early architecture of the valley of the
Rappahannock: Kenmore, Cleve Manor, Gay Mont and
Belle Grove. Plans

AIA jour
3:113-18, 234-40, 329-36
Mar, Je, Ag 1915

Domfront, Fr. Saint-Julien
Louvet, A
Les églises modernes: L'église Saint-Julien, à
Domfront (Orne) (Modern churches: church of
Saint-Julien at Domfront (Orne). Albert Guilbert
archt. Plan.

A   L'Architecture 49:241-252
July, 1936

770.6 Domestic architecture, U.S. Victorian
A512j Brumbaugh, Irvin
The American house in the Victorian period.

ASAH j1 2 no 1: 27-30
Ja '42

Domestic architecture, U.S., Western States
Garden, N.H.G.
Country homes of the western plains. F.L. Wright,
W.B. Griffen, archts.

House and garden 18:230-233
October, 1910

Dominguez, Calif. Dominguez School
Dominguez school, Dominguez, Cal. W.L. Risley,
archt.

Architectural digest 6:56
Number 4 [1930]

Dominican college of St. Thomas Aquinas,
River Forest, Ill.

see

River Forest, Ill. Dominican house of studies

Dominion public building, Winnipeg

see

Winnipeg (Manit.) Dominion public building

Donaldson and Meier   (Card 2)

see also

Detroit (MI)   First Unitarian Church
    "   "   Hotel Ste. Claire
    "   "   Ingleside Club
    "   "   Peoples State Bank
    "   "   Public Library. Schoolcraft Branch
    "   "   St. Benedict Church
    "   "   Schmidt Building
    "   "   Union Trust Building

                                (See Card 3)

Dominican house of studies, River Forest, Ill.

see

River Forest Ill. Dominican house of studies

Dominioni, Luigi Caccia

see

Caccia Dominioni, Luigi

Donaldson and Meier   (Card 3)

see also

Detroit (MI)   Wayne County and Home Savings Bank
    "   "   Y.M.C.A. Building
    "   "   Y.W.C.A. Building
    "   "   Woodmere Cemetery Chapel and
                       Waiting Room
Port Huron (MI)   St. Joseph Church
Trenton (MI)   Church (Austin) Residence

Dominican Republic   see

Cuidad Trujillo

720.5   Dommey, Étienne Théodore 1801-
B93b   Palace of justice entrance hall and stairs
         transverse section, principal facade and
         plan. Paris. Duc and Dommey, archts.

             Building budget 5: pls.fol.p.62
             May 31, 1899

720.5   Donaldson and Meier
A67rev   Jenkins, C.E.
                 Donaldson and Meier

             architectural reviewer:116-137
             S 1897

Dominick, William F.

see

Greenwich (Conn.) Dominick (W.F.) house
    "   "   Root (F.C.) house
    "   "   Siedenburg (R. jr.) house
Bayshore (L.I.) Thorne (L.K.) house
New York (N.Y.) Cammann (H. L.) house

Domskov, Peter R.

see

Eugene (Ore.) Larsen (Hart) house

Donaldson, John M.

see

Donaldson and Meier

Dominion housing act. Competition. 1938
Mathers, A. S.
    Dominion housing competition. [plans]

             RAIC jrl 15:81-91
             Ap 1938

Donahue, James P. house

see

Palm Beach (Fla.) "Cielito Lindo"

Donaldson, W. house, Minneapolis, Minn.

see

Minneapolis, Minn. Donaldson (W.) house

720.5   Dominion of Versailles
A51   A new Versailles project for cooperative
         buildings on the shores of Manhasset Bay,
         on Long Island, New York. Plans and illus-
         tration. Thomas Hastings architect of
         buildings and gardens. Frederick MacMonnies
         Paul Bartlett and Robert Aiken, sculptors.

             American architect 109:412-413
             June 21, 1916

Donahue, John W.
             SEE
Lenoxdale (MA)   Roman Catholic Chapel

Donan house, El Paso

see

El Paso, Tex. Donan house

Dominion public bldg., London, Ont.

see

London (Ont.) Dominion public bldg.

Donaldson and Meier

see also

Ann Arbor (MI)   Stevens (F.W.) Residence
Detroit (MI)   Acme White Lead Works
    "   "   Bagley Building
    "   "   Church of the Holy Redeemer
    "   "   Detroit Boat Club House
    "   "   Donaldson (John M.) Residence
    "   "   Fire Dept. Headquarters
    "   "   Fire Engine House

                                (See Card 2)

Donatelli, Romolo, 1923-
Santini, Pier Carlo
    The focus is on the young architects;
Romolo Donatelli, Ippolito Malagussi-Valeri &
Ezio Sgrelli [plans]

             Zodiac
             4:149-59 Ap 1959

Donatelli, Romolo, 1921-
    Prototype prefabricated house, Fiera
di Milano, 1960 [plan] Romolo Donatelli, archt.

    Archtl Design
    30:483 N 1960

Doncaster (Eng.). Royal Infirmary.
    Doncaster Royal Infirmary. Wm. Pite, Son
and Fairweather, archts.

    Architect 116: pl.
    August 20, 1926

Donjons, England. Colchester.

    Antiquary 7:157-162
    April, 1883

STACK
708.2
B51j
    Donatello, i.e. Donato Niccolo di Betto Bardi,
    1386-1466
Geymüller, Heinrich von
    Die architektonische entwickelung Michelozzos
und sein zusammenwirken mit Donatello.

    No illustrations.
        Jahrbuch der k. preussischen
        Kunstsammlungen 15: 247-259
        1894

Doncaster (Eng.). Royal infirmary
    Doncaster Royal Infirmary. William A. Pite,
Son, and Fairweather, archts.

    Builder 131:486
    September 24, 1926

Donjons, England. Colchester.
    Norman architecture.

    Antiquary 7:45-48.
    Feb., 1883

Doncaster (Eng.) Bank
    Bank premises, Doncaster

    Builder 126:pl.
    Mar. 21, 1924

Doncaster (Eng.). Royal infirmary
    New Royal infirmary, Doncaster. William A.Pite,
Son and Fairweather, archts.

    Builder 136:726-727
    April 19, 1929

Donjons. England. Tattershall
    Tattershall Castle

    Country life 38: 18-21
    July 3, 1915

Doncaster (Eng.) infectious diseases hospital
    Plans for the proposed infectious disease
hospital at Doncaster, England. Adshead, Topham
and Adshead, archts.

    Architects' jour. 64: supp.pls.
    August 11, 1926

Doncaster (Eng.) Westminster Bank
    Wesminster Bank, Doncaster

    Builder 128:792 and pl.
    May 22, 1925

Donjons. France. Coucy
    Great Keep, Château de Coucy

    Arch. and builders jour. 45:pl.for.
    May 30, 1917

Doncaster (Eng.) infectious diseases hospital
                            Competition
    The Doncaster infectious diseases hospital
competition.

    Architect 116: 185-91, pls.
    August 13, 1926

720.5
A67r
    Dongan Hills (S.I.) Simons (C.D.) house
        Residence of C.D.Simons, Dongan Hills,
    Staten Island. Renwick,Aspinwall and Owens,
    archts. No plan.

A   Architectural record 16:73
        July 1904

Donjons. Norman
    Houses of English country towns: Rochester

    Country life Lond. 55:322-3
    Mar. 1, 1924

Doncaster (Eng.) infectious diseases hospital
                            competition
    Infectious diseases hospital, competition.

    Builder 131:245-9
    August 13, 1926

720.5
A67r
    Dongan (N.Y.) Flagg (Ernest) house
        Residence of Ernest Flagg, Dongan, N.Y.
    Ernest Flagg, archt. Plan.

A   Architectural record 11: 76-81
        April 1902

Donjons. Scotland.

    MacGibbon, David and Thomas Ross.
    The castellated and domestic
    architecture of Scotland from the
    Twelfth to the eighteenth centuries.
    5 vols. Edinburgh: D. Douglas,
    1887-92.v,3,p.115-137,162-253,372-
                            389.

Doncaster (Eng.) National Provincial Bank
    A single-story provincial bank building.
Designed by Brierley and Rutherford, archts.

    Architects' journal 71: 387-389
    March 5, 1930

Donjons

    Ruprich-Robert, Victor Marie
    Charles. L'architecture
    normande...2 vols. Paris:
    Librairie des imprimeries
    réunies, 1889. v.2 pl. 146-149.

Donjons. Scotland.
    Scottish keeps.

    Country life (Lond.) 60:164-71
    July 31, 1926

Denkelaar, Bodegraven & Vroman
   Melchviehhof als Mustergut (plans)& section)
Denkelaar, Bodegraven & Vroman, archts.

Baumeister
58: 536-37, Tafel 34, Je 1961

Donon (Fr.) Monument Aux Morts
   Schommer, Pierre
Le monument aux morts du Donon. (War memorial at
Donon) Paul Célis, archt. No plan.

L'Architecture 37:170
July 25, 1924

Dooley (Major) James H., house

see

Afton (Va.) (near) Swannanoa

Donnellan and Burrows

see

Chicago (Ill.) Graham & Son hotel and bank
   building

Donovan, John J.

   see also

Eureka (CA)   Stadium
Oakland (CA)   Clawson School
   "   "   McChesney Elementary School

Dooly Block, Salt Lake City, Utah

see

Salt Lake City, Utah, Dooly block

Donnellan and Nothnagel
   2-story store and flat building for Wm.
Fitzgerald at Western Ave. and Van Buren.
Donnellan and Nothnagel, archts.

Building budget
3:65
Ap 30, 1887

720.5   Donovan, John J
A51   Auditorium for the city of Oakland, Cal.
   John J. Donovan, srcht. Plans.

American architect 102:15,pls.fol.p.16
July 10, 1912

Door (unidentified)

Inland Archt.
Vol. 25, No. 3, pl.
   Fol. p. 34
   Apr. 1895

706.5   Donner,Georg Raphael   1693-1741
D48   Pretzell, Lothar
   Treppenhaus des Erzbischoflichen lusts-hlsses
Wirsbell in Salzburg 1791-1797. Johann Lucas von
Hildebrandt (1668-1745) und Georg Raphael Donner
   (1693-1741).

Deutsche kunst fitext prec.pl.,pl.99
No.9,1936

Donovan, John J.
   Relations between Boards of Education, their
Superintendents and the Architect.

West. Archt.
26: 13-15
Aug, 1917

Doors and doorways

   see also

Church doors and doorways
Entrances
Gates
Gothic doors
Renaissance doors and doorways
Romanesque doors and doorways
Colonial doors and doorways
Norman doors and doorways

Donohue, E. J.

see

Jamestown (ND)   Stutsman County Jail
St. Paul (MN)   Cleary (James) Residence
   "   "   St. Stanislaus Parochial School

MICROFILM

Donovan, John Joseph, 1876-1949
   obituary notice

in SCRAPBOOK ON
ARCHITECTURE p. 722
(on film)

Doors and doorways

Cyclopaedia of architectural
illustration....10 vols. Boston:
ticknor and Co. (n.d.)v.5.pl.441-480.

Donohue, John William

   see also

Northampton,(Mass.) St. John's Cantius church
   "   "   Church of the Sacred Heart
Springfield (Mass.) Church of the Holy Family
   "   "   Elk's club

Donsieders, Ger. Kirche
   Harbers, Guido
Kirche in Donsieders (Pfalz). Entwurfsmodell.
(Church in Donsieders.) Albert Bosslet, archt.
Plans.

Der Baumeister 31:118
April, 1933

A

Doors and doorways

House beaut. 27:50-52
F '10

Donohue, John William
   Old colonial house, West Springfield,
Massachusetts.

Western archt
15: 29
March 1910

720.54   Donzenac
A87   Mayeux,Albert
   Sainte-Madeleine de Donzenac (Saint-Madeline
of Donzenac).

L'Architecture 43: p.252
July 15, 1930

Doors and doorways

House beaut. 28: 154-155
Oct. 1910

Doors and doorways	720.6 B38 Doors and doorways Beaux-arts institute of design, competition: "Doorway at the end of a hall." Awards. B.A.I.D. 2: 16 March 1926	Doors and doorways Doors of many materials. House & Garden 53:88-9 Ja 1928
Doors and doorways House beaut. 36:188-190 Nov., 1914		

Doors and doorways House beaut. 40:13 June, 1916	705.2 C75 Doors and doorways Carved door of Eridge castle, England Connoisseur 16:222 December 1906	D13.1 H84 Doors and doorways Doors that invite whether closed or open House beautiful 74:202 November 1933

710.5 H84 Doors and doorways House & Garden 41: 39-41. Feb. 1922.	Doors and doorways Colonial houses with 2 front doors, even though occupied by only one family, are by no means unusual... Cousins, Frank and Phil M. Riley. The colonial architecture of Salem. Boston: Little Brown and Co., 1919. 29	D13.1 H84 Doors and doorways Doors under cover House beautiful 81: 69-72 March 1939

Doors and doorways Neufforge, Jean Francois de. Recueil élémentaire d'architecture. 8 vols. Paris: L'auteur, 1757-68. v.4:pl.541-546.	710.5 H84 Doors and doorways Different periods House & garden 48:76-79 Sept. 1925	720.6 B38 Doors and doorways "A doorway." Beaux-Arts Institute of Design awards. B.A.I.D. 5: 10-12 August 1929

770.5 P67 Doors and doorways Photo-era magazine 65:164-167 September 1930	720.5 A51 Doors and doorways Doors and doorways [nos.1,2,3,4] Amer archt & bldg news 56: pls fol 32, Ap 24 pls fol 72, My 29 1897	720.52 A67c Doors and doorways The doorway-its rise and fall Architect 113:185-88. Feb. 27, 1925

720.5 A67a Doors and doorways Architecture's portfolio Arch. 65: My '32 67: F '33 71: Je '35 57: Mr '28	710.5 H84 Doors and doorways Gregory, Julius Doors inside the house. This important detail is capable of vastly diversified treatment. House and garden 60: 42-47 September 1931	720.6 B38 Doors and doorways "Doorway to an architects' building." B.A.I.D. 6: 11 December 1929

705.1 A79 Doors and doorways Beautiful doors designed for period decoration Arts and decoration 29:62-63 October 1928	705.1 P41 Doors and doorways Doors. Large and small Pennsylvania arts and sciences 2: 155-157 No. 3, 1937	710.5 H84 Doors and doorways Higgins, J.F. Doorways for the small house. House & garden 51: 58-63 July 1927

705.4 A79 Doors and doorways Taylor, C.R. The entrance to your home Arts and decoration 25:54-55 May 1926	Doors and doorways Harvey, William Little things that matter - Diagrams Architects' jour 62: 971-73 D 30, 1925	705.1 A79 Doors and doorways Unique doorways with matching lighting fixtures Arts and decoration 29:50-51 October 1928
D13.1 H84 [Doors and doorways Robinson, T.P. Entrances to houses: doorways for small houses – some guides to choice. House beautiful 41:129-131 February 1917	720.52 A67c Doors and doorways Gunn, Edwin Local variations in construction--windows, doorways and porches. Architect 115: 590-591 June 18, 1926	Doors and doorways Vine-clad doorways, old and new Craftsman 26:179-186 May, 1914
710.5 H84 Doors and doorways Exterior doors. House and garden 74: 18-19 September 1938 (pt. 2)	Doors and doorways Mediaeval and modern House beaut. 47:82-84 Feb., 1920	Doors and Doorways. Adam A fine Adam doorway now in the Boston Museum International studio 90:71 August, 1928
Doors and doorways Fermetures [special issue]. Tech. et arch. 14, no. 5-6: 86-101 1954	720.5 A51 Doors and doorways Memorial doorway. BAID design award. Amer archt 122: 525,529 D 6 '22	Doors and doorways, Africa An Ivory coast door Pennsylvania university. Museum Bulletin 1:21-23 April, 1930
710.5 H84 Doors and doorways Has your door an architectural pedigree? House and garden 43: 83-5 May 1923	D13.1 H84 Doors and doorways Nichols, K. S. The revival of the doorway House beautiful 66:46-47 July 1929	Doors and doorways, Alsace. Doorways, Haute Alsace. Builder 117:180-1,184 Ag 22, 1919
710.5 H84 Doors and doorways Roberts, M.F. If you are going to build (Consider the Interior Door) House and garden 42: 72-3, 124,126 O '22	705.1 A792 Doors and doorways Technically fine entrances to some modern homes Arts and decoration 28:48-49 February 1928	Doors and doorways, competitions Beaux-arts institute of design, competition: "A monumental doorway". Awards. B.A.I.D. 2: 20-31 May, 1926
D13.1 H84 Doors and doorways Interior doors House beautiful 81:56-57 September 1939	705.1 A79 Doors and doorways Byers, C.A. Tile borders make decorative doorways Arts and decoration 30:58-59,100 February 1929	Doors and doorways, Concrete Country life in Amer 22:46, O 1, 1912

Doors and doorways, Dutch

see

Doors and doorways, Netherlands

Doors and doorways, England. 16th century
T.S.
XVI century oak door from Sussex

Toronto university. Royal
Ontario museum. Bulletin
9:11-13 January, 1930

Doors and Doorways. France
Four simple French doorways

Architecture 49:186
June, 1924

Doors and doorways, Dutch colonial

see

Dutch colonial doors and doorways

708.1
C53b
Doors and Doorways, England. 18th century.
Carved English doorway from Lombard
Street, London. Early eighteenth century.
English doorway reflecting the Gothic-
Chinese taste, 1745-1770. The Howard
Van Doren Shaw memorial [reproductions]

Chicago art institute bulletin 28:
1, 4
Ja '34

Doors and doorways, France
Pillement, Georges
Portes à Paters (illus)

Art et style
No. 6:36-43, D 1946

Doors and Doorways. England
Doorway from Mollington hall, Cheshire, England.
The Howard van Doren Shaw memorial collection.

Chicago art institute
Masterpiece of the month
Notes and biblio. p. 74-77
April 1938-Dec. 1941

Doors and Doorways, England. 18th century.
Catalogues
Picture books ... illustrating important
objects in the permanent collections. English
doorways and woodwork of the eighteenth century

Chicago art institute
Bulletin 34: 100
November, 1940

Doors and Doorways, France. Louis XVI
Details of elevation to a hotel
(Louis XVI style) César Daly. archt

Architects' journal
50:751 Dec. 17, 1919

Doors and doorways, England
Bullock, A.E.
English architectural decoration: Doorways and
fanlights.

Arch rec 46: 569-82
D '19

Doors and Doorways, England. London
Morrison, Kathrine
London doorways

House beautiful 58:490-491
Nov. 1925

Doors and doorways, France, Paris. 18th century
Sturgis, Russell
Parisian doorways of the eighteenth century.

Architectural record 19:123-134
February, 1906

Doors and doorways, England
Ionides, Basil
Interior doors and doorways

Architects' jour 62: 492-93
S 30 '25

Doors and Doorways, England. Regency
Doorways of the English Regency style

House and garden 46:84-85
Nov. 1924

Doors and doorways, French style.
Huard, F.W.
The etiquette of French doors.

House and garden 49:118-19
Apr. 1926

Doors and Doorways, England.
(Old Doorway from Mollington Hall, Cheshire,
England)

Chicago art institute
Masterpiece of the month
Releases p. 39
1938-1940

Doors and doorways, Etruria
Hanfmann, George M. A.
Etruscan doors and windows

ASAH jl 2 no 1:8-16
Ja '42

Doors and doorways, Georgian
Drawings by the architects' Student Sketch
Club

Arch and con rep 94: pl fol
N 26, 1915

Doors and doorways, England.
Old English doorways

Craftsman 21:603-611.
March, 1912

705.1
A79
Doors and Doorways, France
Famous old doorways in ancient Paris.
Hotel Cluny (1485). Hotel de Chateaubriand.
Louis XVI doorway in the rue de Clery.
Hotel de Chimay

Arts and decoration 32:61
November 1929

Doors and doorways, Germany.

Zetzsche, Carl.Zopf und Empire.
Berlin: Kanter and Mohr, [1906?]

Doors and doorways, Germany
Remington, Preston
Doors after the designs of François de Cuvilliés

New York. Metropolitan museum of art
Bulletin 22:292-294
December, 1927

Doors and doorways, Italy
Doors and doorways, no. 1:door of a house
on the Piazza S. Andrea in the Mercato Vecchio,
Florence, Italy.

Amer. archt and bldg news
56: pl fol 32
Ap 24, 1897

Doors and Doorways, Italy. Florence
Doorway and hood, Florence

Archts and bldrs. jour 48: pl.fol 192
Oct. 23, 1918

Doors and doorways, Germany
Portal einer Verwaltungsgebäudes, architect
Werry Roth

Moderne bauformen 21:288
Sept. 1922

Doors and doors, Italy
(Fine pictures)

Amer. arch and bldg. news
March 16, 23, 1907

Ryerson

Doors and doorways, Italy. Milan
Albissati, Carlo
Um Portale d'Età Romana a Milano.

La Critica d'Arte 2:55-65
F-D 1937

Doors and doorways. Germany
Hagemann, Ernst
Zur Ikonographie des Ronnenberger "Bonifa-
tius-Portals". [illus.]

Niederdeutsche Beiträge zur
Kunstgeschichte
Bd 11: 24-48
1972

Doors and doorways, Italy
The Forum studies of European precedents

Arch. forum 41:pl.10-16
Dec. 1924

Doors and doorways, Italy, Venice
Oraffice, P.
Di alcune porte in legno intagliate dei
secoli XIV e XV esistenti in Venezia (illus.)

Arte italiana decorativa ed
industriale, 1:text 18-20,pl.5
1890-91

Doors and doorways, Germany. Empire

Sauermann, Ernst. Alt-Schleswig-Holstein.
Berlin: Verlag für kunstwissenschaft,
1912. p. 69-73, 129.

Doors and doorways, Italy
From architecture Toscane in Burnham
library (reproduction)

Chicago Art Institute
bulletin 14:89
October, 1920

Doors and Doorways, Italy. Venice
Venice. Doorway of fourteenth century

Architects' jour. 61: front pl. 800
May 27, 1925

Doors and doorways, Greece. 20th cent.
Modern

Wasmuths 7:95
Heft 3-4, 1923

Doors and Doorways. Italy.
Meas. drawings. 11 pl.

Cicognara, Leopoldo.
Le Fabbriche e i monumenti
Cospicui di Venezia.
Venice: G. Antonelli, 1858

Doors & Doorways, Jacobean

Douglas, John. Abbey square sketch book.
3 vols. Liverpool: A. Macgregor, 1872-[907].
v.1, pl.23.

Doors and Doorways, Hungary
Gal, Ladislas
Portails romans en Hongrie.

Paris. Université. Institut
d'art et d'archéologie. Travaux des étudiants du groupe d'histoire de l'art de la
Faculté des lettres de Paris. Paris:
Institut d'art et d'archéologie, 1928.
p. 61-70

Doors and doorways. Italy
Erffa, Hans Martin von
Das Programm der Westportale des Pisaner
Domes. [illus.]

Florence. Kunsthistorisches
Institut. Mitteilungen
Band 12: [55]-106
D 1965-S 1966

Doors and doorways, Moravian

see

Moravian doors and doorways

Doors and doorways, Italy.
Bronze?

Salazaro, Demetrio. Studi Sui
monumenti della Italia Meriodionale....
Napoli: A. Morelli, 1871-77.
v.1,pl.16;v.2,pl.11.

Doors and Doorways, Italy. 16th century
A sixteenth century doorway

Antiquarian 10:45
June, 1928

Doors and doorways, Neo-Classic
House at Paterson (N.J.) Doorway.
W.L. Stoddart, archt.

Arch and bldg 48:cover, pl fol 108
Je '16

Doors and doorways, Netherlands see also "Dutch" doors	Doors and doorways, Rome Albizzati, Carlo Un portale d'Età Romana a Milano Critica d'arte 2:55-65 April, 1937	Doors and doorways, Spanish style In Spanish style Architecture 38:pl.135 Aug. 1918
Doors and doorways, Netherlands Amsterdam: Entrance to an old house on a canal Architects journal 58:522 Oct. 10, 1923	705.6 B69 Doors and doorways, Sicily Samona,Guiseppe L'influenza mediaevale par la formazione degli elementi architetonici del sec.xvi nella Sicilia orientale. Bolletino d'arte 25: 517-524 May 1932	Doors and doorways, Spanish style Barker, Ruth Laughlin Old Spanish doorways House beaut 42: 166-167,179 Ag '17
Doors and doorways, Netherlands Deur met beslagwerk van een wandkast of "Spinde", XV de eeww. Elaborate Dutch door. Keuken in de Lakenhal ti Leiden. XVII de eeww etc. Sluyterman, Karel. Huisraad en binnenhuis in Nederland... Hague: M. Nijoff, 1918. 4, 35, 45, 51, 56	Doors and Doorways, Spain Arte y decoración en Espagna: pls. 2,9,13,22,23,27; v.1, 1917. pls. 11, 19-20, 51-52, 54, 59; v.2,1918. pls. 24, 36-37, 43, 66, 81; v.3, 1919. pl.18; v.4, 1920.	Doors and doorways, Sweden Wrangel, Ewert Mediaeval ironwork in Småland. Tidskrift för konstvetenskap 12:83-93 No. 3, 1928
Doors and doorways, Netherlands Robertson, Howard and Yerbury, F.R. Dutch doorways; ancient and modern. Architect 120:439-442 October 5, 1928	D10.5 A788 Doors and doorways, Spain Puerta de madera tallada del siglo XVI estilo renacimiento Arte y decoración en Espagna 4: plate 12 1920	Doors and doorways, U.S. see also Colonial doors and doorways
Doors and doorways, Netherlands 2 examples Archts' and bldrs' jour. 46:pl.for Dec. 19, 1917	Doors and Doorways, Spain Spanish doorways School arts magazine 29:28-29 September, 1929	Doors and doorways, U.S. McQuade, Walter. Architecture series of measured details. New York: Charles Scribner's Sons, 1922. pl. 11-12,14-16,18-22,24.
Doors and doorways, Persia A lacquered door from a Persian palace. Providence, Rhode Island School of design. Bulletin 15:27-30 July, 1927	Doors and Doorways, Spain, Toledo An Arab doorway of Alcántara in Toledo Arte Español 13:18-24 No. 1, 1924	Doors and Doorways, U.S. Dow, J.W. American renaissance doorways. Architects' and builders' magazine 39: February, 1907 208-216
Doors and doorways, Persia Palace doors from the throne room of Shah Abbas, now in the Detroit Museum Detroit institute of arts bulletin 7:49-52 Feb., 1926	Doors and Doorways, Spanish style American doorways influenced by Spain House beaut. 49:306-307 Apr., 1921	Doors & doorways. U.S. 19th cent. Entrance to "The Shoreham" apartment house, Washington, D. C. Hubert, Pirsson & Hoddick, archts. From residence of Mr. Chaffin, Washington, D. C. H. L. Page, archt. Inland architect v. 16 no. 3 pl. fol. p. 36 O 1890

Doors and doorways, U.S., Dutch Colonial
Architecture's portfolio of exterior doors of wood.

Architecture 65:296,298-299,306
May, 1932

Doors and Doorways, U.S., N.Y., 1840
Second floor hall arch, Dibble house built about 1840, Lima, N.Y.
Measured drawings by Benjamin F. Betts.

Architecture 33: pl.17
February, 1916

Doors and doorways, U.S., Spanish influence
Doors of old Spain in modern California

House and garden 42:56
Ag '22

Doors and doorways, U.S. Dutch Colonial
3 examples

Eberlein, Harold Donaldson. Historic houses of the Hudson Valley. New York: Architectural Book publishing Co., Inc., 1942. pp.40, 152, 195.

Doors and Doorways, U.S., N.Y., City. 20th century
Some entrances to the skyscraper

Arch rec 9: 363-374
Ap. 1900

Doors, Bronze
see also
Names of building having bronze doors, i.e.:
Wellesley,(Mass) college. Library doors
Hildesheim, Ger. Dom. Berwardtür

Doors and Doorways. U.S., Georgia, Savannah
Savannah doorways, drawn by Christopher Murphy, Jr.

Country life (U.S.) 52:61
October, 1927

Doors and doorways, U.S., Pennsylvania
Five original doorways from houses in Buck's county, Penn.

House and garden 70:58-59
August, 1936

Doors, Bronze

Builder
105:538-540 & pl., 695-698
N 21, D 26, 1913

Doors and doorways, U.S., Georgian influence
see also
Lloyds Neck (L.I.) Field (Marshall) estate

Doors and Doorways, U.S., Pennsylvania
Pennsylvania doorway dated "1819" and showing German influence. The Howard Van Doren Shaw memorial (reproduction)

Chicago Art Institute
bulletin 28:5
January, 1934

Doors, Bronze

Builder
106:38-39 & pls., 285-286, pls
Ja 9, Mr 6, 1914

Doors and Doorways, U.S., Georgian influence
Doorways of drawing-rooms.

Country life (U.S.) 52:43-44
June, 1927

Doors and doorways, U.S., Rhode Island, Bristol
Dow, Joy Wheeler
Doorways of the Bristol renaissance.

Arch rev 8:28-30
Mr '01

Doors, Bronze

Dalton, Ormonde Maddock.
Byzantine art and archaeology.
Oxford: Clarendon Press, 1911.
p.616-621

Doors and Doorways, U.S., New England
Some Century-Old Doorways in Rural New England.

Arch rec 30: pls.
D 1911

Doors and Doorways. U.S., S. Carolina. Charleston
Charleston doorways.

Architecture. 43:181-2 and pl.86-8.
June, 1921

Doors, Bronze.

Hittorff, Jacob Ignaz. Architecture modern de la Sicile. Paris: P. Renouard, 1835. pl.66.

Doors and doorways, U.S., New Mexico
Barker, Ruth Laughlin
Old Spanish doorways

House beaut 92: 166-167,179
Ag '17

Doors and Doorways, U.S., South Carolina,Charleston
Casey, William
Charleston doorways, entrance motives from a South Carolina city.

White pine 14:243,pl.126-138
Number 5, 1928

Doors, Bronze

Kowalczyk, Georg. Denkmaeler der Kunst in Dalmatien. 2 vols. Berlin: Verlag für Kunstwissenschaft, 1910. pl.27-8

720.54
A67
Doors, Bronze
Age d'Or. Henri Fairer & Max Blondat

L'Architecture 36:371
Dec. 10, 1923

Doors, Bronze
Rhind, J. Massey

Monumental news 12:397
July, 1900

Doors, "Dutch"

see

"Dutch" doors

720.5
B38
Doors, Bronze
Beaux-arts institute of design, department of sculpture, competition: "A pair of bronze doors".

B.A.I.D. 4: 18-20
January 1928

910.5
N27
Doors, Bronze
Rogers doors of the rotunda

National geographic magazine 43:635
June 1923

Doors, Elevator

see

Elevator doors

Doors, Bronze
B.A.I.D. award. Bronze doors.

Amer archt 119: 314, 316
Mr 16, 1921

720.5
W52
Doors, Bronze
Special number of modern bronze and iron-work doors.

Western arch.37: pl.163-170,173-180
October 1928

Doors, Fire

see

Fire doors

720.5
A51
Doors, Bronze
Fullerton, C. A.
Bronze doors.

Amer arch 112: 113-20, 143, 155
Ag 15, 29, '17

705.1
S93a
Doors, Bronze
St. Joseph door, bronze, at Bell tower, Woods Hole, Mass. Dante door, bronze, 1930

Studio news 1:4-5
October 1930

720.5
A67f
Doors, Glass
Interior doorway, apartment in New York. Donald Deskey, designer. Pittsburgh plate glass institute competition.

Architectural forum 67:133
A   August 1937

705.1
A78a
Doors, Bronze
Bronze doors by Henry Wilson for the Salada Tea company

Art digest 2:10
Mid-April 1928

705.5
I29
Doors, Bronze, Italy
Margotti, Marc
La sculpture romane dans les portes de bronzes italiennes

L'Illustrazione vaticana 9:65-70
February 1938

Doors, Glass
The painted glass door

House and garden 43:94
April, 1923

705.5
K98
Doors, Bronze
Masse
Mediaeval bronze doors

Die kunst für alle 42:187-191
March, 1927

705.1
A78a
Doors, Bronze, United States
Masonic doors

Art digest 4:18
No.8, January 1930

Doors, Gold, U.S.

see

New York (N.Y.) Guggenheim (Isaac) house. doors

Doors, Bronze
Renaissance & modern

Amer arch 98: 145-148
N 2, 1910

Doors, Decorated

see

Decorated doors

Doors, Heck

see

"Dutch" doors

Doors, Iron
   Iron doors

      Gailhabaud, Jules. L'architecture
     du V au XVII siècle. 4 vols. Paris:
     A. Morel, 1869-72.
     v.2 pl. 36-38.

Doors, Screen

    see

Screen doors

720.52   Dorchester-on-Thame
B93   Roberts, H. V. M.
      Dorchester-on-Thame, Oxfordshire.

      Builder 139: 378
      September 5, 1930

Doors, Mechanically operated
   The revolving door, its characteristics,
design and installation in two parts. Plans

     American architect 118:327-331;355-359
     September 8; 15, 1920

Doors, Steel
   Steel doors adorn the Wright memorial

     National geographic magazine 64:728
     December, 1933

720.54   Dorat (Fr.) La Lanterne des Morts
A67   Doillet, Laurent
      La lanterne des morts du Dorat (The lantern
    tower for the dead of Dorat). No plan. Mm.Elie
    Berteau,and Coutheillas,archts.

     L'Architecture 43: p.11-12
     January 15,1930
    A

Doors, Metal

   see also

Doors, Bronze
Doors, Iron
Doors, Steel

720.5   Doors, Steel
M59a   Steel door for a mausoleum. Oscar B.
    Bach, craftsman.

     Metal arts 3: pl.7
     January 1930

---

729   Dore (Abbey) England
L84   Meas. drawings by G. Frisch and C.
    Henman.

     Lond. Arch. Assoc. sketch
     book 1873-4 pl 1.
     1872-3 pls 1-5.

Doors, Metal
   Kremp, Conrad
Distinctive doors in hollow metal.

     Metal arts 3:192-194
     May, 1930

Doorways

    see

Doors   and Doorways

720.2   Dore (Abbey) England
B93   Abbey Dore

     Builder 82:327
     April 19, 1902

Doors, Metal
   Metal doors

     Arch rev 61: 116-122
     Mr 1927, supp.

Dopff, M.   Paul

    see

Strasbourg (Fr.) housing

---

726   Dore (Abbey) England
C55   Dore abbey, England.

     Christian art v. 1 p. 214-218
     Ag. 1907

Doors, Painted
   A pair of painted doors by Eyre de Lanux
(Mrs. Pierre de Lanux).

     Architecture 45:198
     June, 1922

Dorbay, Francois, 1634-1697
Hautecoeur, Louis
   Projet d'une salle de spectacle (Project for
a play-house) Plans. Designs by D'Orbay, Potain, (
Cochin.

     L'Architecture
     37:31-36, F 10, 1924

720.52 Dore (Abbey) England
B93 Paul, Roland
    Abbey Dore church, Herefordshire.

     Builder 141: 500-501, pls.
     September 25, 1931

Doors, Revolving

    see

Doors, Mechanically operated

Dorchester, Mass.

    see

Boston, Mass.

Dore (Eng.). Golf club house
   Golf club-house at Dore, England. Chapman
and Jenkinson, archts.

     Architects' jour. 64:679
     December 1, 1926

Doria-Tursi palace. Genoa

see

Genoa.   Palazzo municipale.

913
A67
    Doric order
        Jeffery, George
            Notes on the origin of the Doric style
        of architecture.

        Archaeologia, 78: 57-60
        1928

Dorking (Eng.) Pippbrook Filling Station
    Pippbrook Filling station, Dorking, Surrey.
Designed by Imrie and Angell. Plans.

        Architects' journal 77: 7
        January 4, 1933

Doric order

        Antiquities of Ionia. 5 vols.
        London: Society of Dilettanti.
        vol. 1, 1769; vol.2, 1797; vol.3,
        1840; vol.4, 1881; vol.5, 1915:
        v.2

913
A51
    Doric order
        Origin of the entablature

        Amer jour of arch 21: 117-158
        Ap/Je '17

Dorking (Eng.) "Spotted Dog" Inn
    The "Spotted Dog" at Dorking.

        Arch. review 52:144-6
        Nov., 1922

705.1
A79
    Doric order

        Art world & Arts & decoration :
        9 :38-41
        My '18

720.5
B95b
    Doric order
        Thiersch, Prof. A
            Proportion in Doric architecture - Handbuch
        der architektur, div. 4, vol.1 - sed. ? - trans-
        lated by N.C. Ricker.

        Building budget 6:7-9;17-18;29-31;
                        41-45
        Ja/ Ap 1890

Dormer Windows

        Dollman, Francis Thomas. An analysis
        of ancient domestic architecture.
        2 vols. London: B.T. Batsford,
        1861-63. v.2 pl. 22.

720.5
A67a
    Doric order
        Swartwout, Egerton
            The classic orders of architecture; -Pts.
        2-4 the Doric order.

        Architecture 34:229-235;253-5
        N/D '16
                    35: 1-6
        Ja '17

720.6
R88
    Doric order
        Masey, F.E.
            Some thoughts upon the possible origin
        of the Doric order of Greek Architecture.

        RIBA jour 17: 590-592
        My 28 '10

Dormer Windows

        Raguenet, Alphonse. Matériaux
        et documents d'architecture et
        de sculpture... 10 vols. Chicago:
        G. Broes Van Dort Co., [1915 ?]
        v. 5: 48 p. section on Dormer-
        windows (Lucarne)

720.5
B95
    Doric order
        The development of the Greek Doric style

        Brochure series 7: 11-16
        Ja '01

720.52
A67
    Doric order
        Students' drawings, Doric order, temple
        at Cori, by Emanuel Brune.

        Archts and bldrs' jour 40:
        pl 30 fol p 186
        S 9 '14

Dormer Windows
    Architecture's Portfolio

        Architecture 54: 349-54
        N 1926
        Architecture 71: 226-40
        Ap 1935

720.52
B95
    Doric order
        Doric origins and development

        Builder 118:277-8
        Mr 5 '20

Dorilton apartments, New York city

    see

New York (city) Dorilton apartments

720.52
A67c
    Dormer Windows
        Details of dormer window and stonework.

        Architect (Lond.)121: supp.pl.opp.p.732
        June 7, 1929

720.52
B95
    Doric order
        Elements and theory of architecture

        Builder 122: 482
        Mr 31 '22

Dorion, C. N., house (1886), St. Paul

    see

St. Paul, Minn. Dorion, C. N., house (1886).

710.5
C855
    Dormer Windows
        Jack,E.G.
            Dormer windows in house of old New Orleans.

        Country life (U.S.) 49: 70
        March 1926

710.52
A67o
Dormer windows
Gunn, Edwin
Dormers and their design: variations of a
feature which is sometimes misused.

Architect (Lond.) 120: 466-470
October 12, 1928

Dormer Windows
Salomonsky, V.C.
An exemplar of old and new colonial details:
various types of dormers

House beautiful 61:669-671
May, 1927

Dormer Windows
Porch with dormer window above. Scale drawing.
Designed by J. D. Clarke.

Architects' journal 72:641-642
October 29, 1930

710.5
C855
Dormer windows
Brinckle, W.D.
Porches and dormers.

Country life in America 21: 34-36
March 15,1912

Dormer Windows
Three pages of unusual dormer windows:
Dormers from French, English and American houses.

House and garden 45:57-9
Jan. 1924

Dormitories

see also

Residence clubs

Dormitories

Arch. rev. 21:n.s.v.4:91
June, 1916

Dormitories
Sheppard, Richard & William Mullins
The design of university halls of residence
[plans & section]

Architectural design
vol. 30: 125-127, Ap 1960

Dormitories.
Johnson, Marjorie G.
A home in one room.

Northwest archt 9.:No.5-6: 12
1945

720.53
W31
Dormitories
Studentenhäuser in Deutschland, Schweden
und der Tschechoslowakei. (Dormitories in
Germany, Sweden and Czechoslovakia.)
The new dormitory in Leipzig-Dölitz.
Walther Beyer, archt. Plans.

Wasmuths monatshefte 15: 207-208
May 1931

A

Dormitories, College

see

College dormitories

Dormitories, Czechoslavakia, Brno

see

Brno (Czech) Masarykav Studentsky domov

Dormitories, England

see also

Cambridge (Eng.) Wesley hostel
Gloucester (Eng.) Rotton house
Newcastle-on-Tyne (Eng.) Armstrong college

720.52
A67o
Dormitories, England.
Crosby Hall Settlement scheme.

Architect 105:20-1 & pl.
Jan. 14, 1921

Dormitories, Finland

see

Turku (Fin.) Abo Akademi. Kårhus

Dormitories, France

see also

Paris. Université. Cité universitaire. Pavillon
suisse
Paris. Université. Cité universitaire. Maison
des étudiants danois
Paris. Université. Cité universitaire. Maison
des étudiants l'Indo-chine
Paris. Université. Cité universitaire. Maison
des étudiants japonais
(see card 2)

Dormitories, France   (card 2)

see also

Paris. L'Ecole centrale des artes et manufacture
Maison des éleves
Limoges (Fr.) Ecole professionelle

720.54
A67
Dormitories. France
House for Canadian students, France.

L'Architecture 39: 351-54
October 25, 1926

720.54
A67
Dormitories, France. Paris
Student lodging houses. P. Tournon, archt.

L'architecture 44: 297-301
September 15, 1931

Dormitories, Germany

see also

Jena (Ger.) University. Studentenhaus
Tübingen (Ger.) Deutsche burse

Dormitories. Germany
Rotkreusheim für studenten und jungarbeiter
in Hannover [plans and sections] Staatshochbau-
amt Hannover, archt.

Baumeister
53: 10-13
(Tafeln 2-4 at end of issue)
Ja 1956

720.53 W31 Dormitories, Germany Teacher's house, Berlin. Ludwig Hoffman, archt. Wasmuths 11: 319-21,329-31 Heft 8, 1927	705 W48 Dornach (Swits.) Kirche Kirche Dornach (Solothurn) H. Baur, archt. Vincent Bühlmann, associate archt. [plans, sect. S] Das Werk 28:10-14 Ja '41	Dorpfeld, Wilhelm Dr. Wilhelm Dorpfeld, Royal Gold Medalist, Institute of Architects, 1911. Builder 100: 802-03, pls. Je 30, 1911
720.52 W31 Dormitories, Germany. Berlin Dormitories, Berlin. Ludwig Hoffmann, archt. Wasmuths 11: 322-328, 319-321,329,331 Heft 8, 1927	Dornach, Switz. Metallwerke AG factory Fabrikationshalle der Metallwerke Ag, Dornach. Suter and Suter, archts. Bauen and Wohnen No. 1 P. 14-15 Konstruktions blätter (end of issue) F 1954	Dorr, A. L. see also Minneapolis (MN) Apt. Building Design " " Keller (C. E.) Residence " " Residence
Dormitories, Sweden see Stockholm (Swe.) Technischen hockscule studenten-haus	Dornbusch and Fuller see Chicago (Ill.) Medical center. Institution for tuberculosis research.	Dorr, A.L. Architect Perspective Sketch for Residence. West. Archt. 3: pls.fol.p. 26 Jan, 1904
Dormitories, Switzerland see Erlenhof (Swits.) Zöglings-pavillon	Dornbusch, Carl see Genesee Depot (Wis.) Lunt (Alfred) house	Dorr & Dorr see also Minneapolis (MN) Chase (E. S.) Residence
Dornach, Goetheanum Le Goetheanum at Dornach designed by Rudolf Steiner Le Bulletin de l'art 55:111,115 March, 1929	Dornbusch, Charles H. see also Cone and Dornbusch	Dorr and Dorr Residences of hollow-tile construction. West. Archt. 18: 66 Jun, 1912
Dornach, Goetheanum Robertson, Howard and Yerbury, F.R. The Goetheanum at Dornach. Rudolf Steiner, archt. Architect (Lond.) 121:359-363 March 15, 1929	Dornette, E. H. see Cincinnati (O.) Central Fairmount public school	Dorr, Louis L. see Phoenix (Ariz.) Westward Ho hotel
720.53 W31 Dornach. Goetheanum Das Goetheanum. Wasmuths monatshefte 13: 200 May 1929	Dorp, Ernst Van Umgestaltung der Büroräume der Fa. Soennecken, Bonn [plans] Franz Schmidt, Ernst van Dorp, archts. Bauen & Wohnen no. 6 p. 380-381 Konstruktionsblätter at end of issue D 1954	Dorr, William Grey Log Cabin Competition Winner. West. Archt. 20: p. 60 Jun, 1914

Dorrenbach, Franz
    Walter Dodde in der schlacht bei Worringer equestrian statue.
 	
    Berliner architekturwelt
    18:heft 5-6,pl.274,p.221.
    1916-17
	720.53
	W31 Dortmund. Children's clinic
	    Children's clinic in Dortmund. W.Eckenrath and W. Schurig, archts.
	
	    Wasmuths monatshefte 14: 446-447
	    October 1930
		Dortmund (Ger.) Planning
		    Hartleb, Walter
		Great Dortmund, the city plan of an industrial city of the Ruhr district.
		
		    Stadtebau 24: 213-218
		    Heft 8, 1929

T22
T92 Dorset, Architecture
Barney, M. G.
    The towers of Dorset.
 	
    Tuileries brochures 2: front.,179-199
    November 1930
	720.53 Dortmund. Commerce and industry building
	W31 Gegemann,Werner
	    Die neue Dortmunder handelskammer. (The new building of commerce and industry in Dortmund.) Pinno and Grund,archts. Plans.
	
	    Wasmuths monatshefte 15: 151-154
	A April 1931
		711 Dortmund (Ger.) Planning
		877 Siedler,E.J.
		    Städtebauliches aus Dortmund. (City building of Dortmund.) Plan. Reconstruction suggestions by Pinno and Grund,archts.
		
		    Der städtebau 22: 17-20
		A February 1927

710.5   Dorset. Athelhampton hall
C85   Atholhampton hall,Dorset,England. Estate market.
 	
    Country life (Lond.)71: 756
    December 31,1932
	720.52 Dortmund (Ger.) Flughafen
	A67c Dower,John
	    The airport of Dortmund,Germany. L.Franzius, archt.
	
	    Architect (Lond.) 133: 283-285
	    March 3, 1933
		720.53 Dortmund (Ger.) Planning
		W31 Vorschlage zur bebauung der Dortmunder Innenstadt nördlich der Reinoldikirche. (Plans for buildings of the Dortmund inner city, north of Reinoldi Church.) Emil Pohle, archt.
		
		    Wasmuths monatshefte 14: 454-455
		A October 1930

Dorset (Eng.). Eastbury Park.
    Archways at Eastbury park, Dorset, England.
 	
    Country life (Lond.) 62:330-32
    September 3, 1927
	Dortmund (Ger.) house
	    Paul Bonatz and F.E. Scholer, architects: two new residences in Dortmund and Bochum.
	
	    Moderne bauformen 29:43-47
	    Heft 1, January, 1930
		Dortmund, Ger. Stadt-theater. Competition. 1955
		    Wettbewerb Stadt-theater Dortmund [plans] Z.h.Heinrich Rosskotten and G. Graubner, prize-winning archts.
		
		    Baumeister
		    52:846-847 no.12
		    D 1955

720.53   Dortmund. Architecture
W31   Hegemann,Werner
    Arbeiten von Pinno und Grund,Dortmund.(Works by Pinno and Grund,Dortmund.) Plans for commerce building; trolley car station and residences in Dortmund.
 	
    Wasmuths monatshefte 13: 346-349
A   August 1929
	720.53 Dortmund (Ger.) Housing
	W31 Eine siedlung und ein gemeindehaus. (A settlement and a community house.) Pinno and Grund,archts. Plans.
	
	    Wasmuths monatshefte 14: 542-544
	A December 1930
		Dortmund (Ger.) Strassenbahnhof
		    Hegemann, Werner
		    Arbeiten von Pinno und Grund, Dortmund. (Works by Pinno and Grund, Dortmund.) Trolley car station in Dortmund. Plans.
		
		    Wasmuths monatshefte 13: 346-349
		A August 1929

720.53   Dortmund,Architecture;
M68   Cemeteries,Germany
 	
    Moderne Bauformen 24:145-176;pl.39
    May 1925
	Dortmund, Ger. Nikolai Kirche
	    Cirkon, Paul
	Die Nikolai-kirche in Dortmund. (The Nichols Church in Dortmund.) Pinno and Grund, archts. Plans.
	
	    Wasmuths monatshefte 14: 489-496
	A November, 1930
		Dortmund, Ger. Westfalenhalle
		    Westfalenhalle in Dortmund. [plans & sections] Walter Höltje, archt.
		
		    Bauen & Wohnen No 1
		    p. 15-21 Konstruktions-
		    blätter (end of issue)
		    F 1954

720.53   Dortmund. Architecture
W31   A settlement and a community house at Dortmund. Pinno and Grund, archts.
 	
    Wasmuths monatshefte 14: 542-544
    December 1930
	Dortmund (Ger.) Odeon Theater
	    "Odeon" theater, Dortmund. Strunck and Wentzler, archts.
	
	    Moderne bauformen 22: 105-107,pl.27
	    April, 1923
		Dosic, G D, see
		Dosio, Ciovnnantonio

Dosi,Giovanantonio

See also

Dosio,Giovanantonio 1533-c.1609

720.52 Douai. Architecture
A67c Randolph, John A
       Douai

Architect and contract reporter
97: P55-6   May 4, 1917

720.5 Double houses
A67a

Architecture 31: 60,pl. 1-2
Feb. 1915

Dosio, Giovanantonio, 1533-c. 1609.
Luporini, Eugenio
Un libro di disegni di Giovanni Antonio
Dosio. [illus.]

Critica d'arte
Anno 4, no.24: 442-467
N-D, 1957

Douai. Hôtel de Goy
Hôtel de Goy, ou, Ancien hotel de la Tramerie.
Douai. Photographs.

Martin, Camille. La renaissance
en France. 2 vols. Paris: C. Eggiman
c.1913-21   1:14,pls. 88-89

720.53 Double houses, Belgium
W31 Some modern double houses in Belgium.

Wasmuths 11: 13
Heft 1, 1927

Dosio, Giovanantonio 1533-c.1609
Palazzo Arcives-covale in Florence.
Giovanni Antonio Dosio, archt. Photograph, plan.

Palast Architektur. 6 vols. in 11
bks. Berlin: E. Wasmuth, 1886-1911
2:pt.2:11,pl.67

Douai. Hôtel de Tramerie

See

Douai. Hotel de Goy

Double houses, Germany

see also

Berlin (Ger.) Double house

Dosio, Giovanantonio 1533-c.1609
Palazzo Larderel in Florenz. (Via de
Tornabuoni no. 19). Giovanni Antonio Dosio,
archt. Photograph.

Palast Architektur. 6 vols in 11 bks.
Berlin: E. Wasmuth, 1886-1911
2:pt.1:14,pl.18

Douai. Maison des Remy
Maison de Remy. Douai. Photographs.

Martin, Camille. La renaissance en
France. 2 vols. Paris: C. Eggiman
c.1913-21   1:14-15,pl.90-91

720.53 Double houses, Germany
W31 A double house in Aachen. Otto Karow,
archt.
  A double house in Düsseldorf-Lohausen.
Hanns Hübbers, archt.

Wasmuths 11: 361-363
Heft 9, 1927

Dosio,Giovanni Antonio

See

Dosio,Giovanantonio 1533-c.1609

Douaumont hill monument

see

Verdun (Fr.) Douaumont hill monument

720.53 Double Houses, Germany
W31 Frans Scheibler, archt., Winterthur.

Wasmuth's Monatshefte 12: 192-3
Heft 5, 1928

720.5 Dothan (Ala.) Newton (W.F.) House
A67f House for W. F. Newton. Moreland
Griffith Smith, archt. John David Sweeney,
associate. Plan.

A   Architectural Forum 71:302
     October 1939

720.5 Double arcades
A67a Lincoln, choir aisle.

Architecture 51:pl.97
June 1925

720.53 Double houses,Switzerland
B35 Harbers,Guido
  Schweizer wohnhäuser von architekt Frans
Scheibler,winterthur mitarbeiter architekt H.
Schnabel. (Swiss residences by the architect,
Frans Scheibler; assistant architect,H.Schnabel.)
Plans.

Der Baumeister 31: 430-434
December 1933
A

Dothan, Ala. School
McCauley, C.H.
School - Dothan, Ala.

A   Architectural concrete 6:32-33
     No.4 1940

720.52 Double doorways
A67a Lawrence St., Cheyne Row, Chelsea

Arch. Rev. (Lond.) 58:118-19
Sept. 1925

720.53 Double houses,Switzerland. Zurich
B35 Doppelhaus in der Kierbrecht,Erlenbach-
Zürich. (Double house in Kierbrecht,Erlen-
bach-Zürich.) Werner Moser,archt. Plans
and interior.

Der Baumeister 31: 74-76
February 1933
A

Double houses, U.S.
see also
Cincinnati (O.) Highland Ave and MacMillan St.house
Chicago(IL.) Blake (N.N.) house
Evanston (IL.) Tobey houses
Knoxville (Tenn.) Yeager-McDowell house
Mariemont (O.) Mackenzie group house
Los Angeles (Cal.) Pyke (C.F.) house
New York (N.Y.) Gould (Edwin) house
Philadelphia (Pa.) Girard estate development

Douglas & Fordham
see
Port Sunlight (Eng)   Bridge
"   "   "   Schools

720.52   Douglas, John
D95   Memorial to John Douglas, architect

                              Builder 124:923
                              June 8, 1923

D19.06   Double houses_U.S.19th century
G58   Plans.

          Godey's Lady's book 53:353-354;54:-543
          Oct.,Dec.1856

Douglas & Hartman
see
Los Angeles (CA)   Bungalow
Los Angeles (CA)   Residence

Douglas, R.H.
see
Beverly Hills (Cal.) Douglas (R.H.) Residence

Douden, William   1869[?]-1946
[obituary]

          Nat'l arch 2:15
          Jl '46

Douglas and Minshull
see
Chester (Eng.) Abbott's park. Clare lodge

Douglas (Scot.) Castle
Douglas Castle. Plans

          Adam, William. Vitruvius
          Scoticus. Edinburgh: Adam
          Block and J.J. Robertson;
          London: J. Taylor, n.d.
          pl. 135-136

Dougherty & Gardner
see
Knoxville (Tenn.) First Baptist church

720.5   Douglas, Donald
P39   Adams, Rayne
         The architectural aquatints of Donald Douglas

          Pencil points 8: 652-661
          November 1927

Douglas, Stephen, memorials
see
Chicago, Ill. Douglas (Stephen) monument.

720.5   Dougherty, Floyd E
A67f   The Chicago taxpayer. Facts and figures
         about four Chicago taxpayers. Plans

          Architectural forum 67: 232
          September 1937

710.5   Douglas, Donald
H84   Modern house designed by Donald Douglas..
         Plan.

          House and garden 70:42-43,80b
          November 1936

Douglas, Tom
see
Beverly Hills (Cal.) Francis (Kay) house

Doughoragan Manor, Md.
   Buckly, J.A.
Doughoragan Manor, Howard Country, Maryland.
A fine example of Neo-Greek architecture, built
about 1830.

          Arch rev 14:238-240
          D '07

Douglas (Eng.) St. Mary's Church
   Altar and Reredos, St. Mary's Church, Douglas,
England. G.Gilbert Scott, archt.

A   Architectural review 19 n.s.2:pl.111
          August, 1913

Douglas, Volk
Muralist: work in Minnesota State Capitol
Photo

          West. Archt.
          4: 4
          Oct. 1905

Dougill, Wesley, 1895-1945
Abercrombie, Patrick
   Wesley Dougill [obit.]

          Town plnng. rev 19: 9
          No. 1 Autumn 1945

Douglas hall, Montreal, Que.
see
Montreal (Que.) McGill university. Douglas hall

720.5   Douglas, Wilmot C.
A67f   House by the Celotex Corporation,
         Plainfield (N.J.). Wilmot C. Douglas, archt.
         Harrison and Foulhoux, consultants. Plan

          Architectural Forum 71:255
          October 1939

720.5
A51

Douglas (Wyo.) Converse county court house
Converse county court house, Douglas, Wyoming. W. N. Bowman, archt. Plans.

Amer. archt. 108:pl. 2128
O 6, '16

Dove cotes
see also

Individual examples, i.e.:

East Lothian, Scot. Dirleton castle. Dovecot etc.

Dove Cotes, Egypt
"The beasts that perish".

Country Life (Lond.) 50:488.
Oct. 15, 1921.

Douglass, Lathrop, 1907-
Edificio Esso, Bogota [plans] Lathrop Douglas & Martinez Cardenas & Cia., archts.

Proa
#133:20-21 O 1957

710.5
H84

Dove cotes
The bird on the roof

House & Garden 47:88-89
June 1925

Dove Cotes, England

Northampton, William, Fifth marquis of. Compton Wyngates. London: A.L. Humphreys, 1904: 36

720.5
A67ar

Douglaston (L.I.) Brownell (Mable) house
House of Miss Mable Brownell, Douglaston, Long Island. O.Preis, archt.

Architect (N.Y.) 5:pl.158-59
March 1926

Dove Cotes
Wilder, L.B.
Dovecotes.

House and garden 60:64-65,104
November, 1931

Dove Cotes, England
Greenwood, G.B.
Dovecotes in the Lothians.

Builder 141:50,56-57
July 10, 1931

Douglaston (L.I.) Brundage (Wilbur) house
Residence of Wilbur Brundage, Douglaston, Long Island. Frank J. Forster, archt. Plans.

Architect 4: pls.fol.p.268
December, 1925

710.5
H84

Dove cotes
The dove cote's place in the garden.

House and garden 39:54-5.
Jun.,1921.

Dove Cotes. France
Columbiers: Boos (Seine-Inferieure xvie siècle) L'Ile Bouchard (Indre-et-Loire xviie siècle).

Encyclopedie de l'architecture, constructions de Style. 2 vols. Paris: Albert Morancé, 1928 - [?] Tome 1: pl.6

Douglaston (L.I.) house
Residence at Douglaston, L.I. Frank J. Forster, archt.

Architect (N.Y.) 4:Detail pl.25
December, 1925

Ryerson

Dove cotes
Drawn and designed by Mallows, C.E. Garden store and pigeon-house

Intl studio
41:200
S 1910

Dove Cotes, France
Un pigeonnier breton

L'architecture 35:312
Oct. 10, 1922

Douglaston (L.I.) North Hills Golf Club
North Hills Golf Club, Douglaston, L.I. C.C. Wendehack, archt.

Architect (N.Y.) 7: 446
January, 1927

Ryerson

Dove cotes
Mesple, Paul
Les pigeonniers de la terre d'Oc

L'art populaire en France
2:11-33
1930

Dove Cotes, U.S.
Pigeonnier at Uncle Sam - near Convent (1841).

Louisiana; a guide to the State. comp. by the Writers' program of the WPA. New York: Hastings House, 1941. 6th pl.fol.p.188.

Dourges, Fr. Tours de Chargement de silo
Tours de Chargement de Silo, à Dourges, 1924. (Towers for loading the grain pit at Dourges, 1924) E. Freyssinet (Limousin et Cie)

L'Architecture vivante :pl.25
Autumn 1926

Ryerson

Dove cotes
The tithe barn, which incorporates a dovecote at South Stoke, near Bath. A fine example of restoration

Country life (Lond.)
123: 168
Ja 23, 1958

Dovecotes
see
Dove cotes

Dow, Alden B., 1904 - Alden Dow, his modern homes are not monastic. [color] Life articles on art 1948 pt. 1: 19?-196 March [15?] 1948	Dow, J. Wheeler The Bates Cottage, Wyoming, N.J. J.Wheeler Dow, architect. Architecture 18:116 Jl '08	720.5 I56 Downers Grove, (Ill.) Fish (J.T.) house Residence for J.T. Fish in Downers Grove. Beman & Parmentier, archts. Inland archt & news rec 18:56 November 1891
Dow, Alden B., 1904- Houses in Midland, Michigan. [plans] Archl forum 65: 191-200 S 1936	Dow, J. Wheeler "Eastover," Wyoming, N.J. J. Wheeler Dow, architect. Architecture 17:102 Je '08	Downers Grove (IL.) Kindergarten Downers Grove kindergarten, Downers Grove, Illinois. Perkins, Fellows, and Hamilton, archts. Plans. Brickbuilder 24:pl.103-105 July, 1915
Dow, Alden B office see Midland (Mich.) Dow (A.B.) office	Dower, John see London (Eng.) Burbage house	MICROFILM Downers Grove (Ill.)Rinaldo (P.J.) house Schweikher and Elting, archts.] in CHICAGO BOOK ON ARCHITECTURE p. 11,12 (on film)
Dow, Arthur W. Architectural Education. Inland Architect 37: 36-8 Jun, 1901	Dowling (John M.) stable. Chicago, Ill. see Chicago, Ill. Dowling (John M.) stable	Downey A.H. Member of firm: Downey and Deegan
Dow, John K. see also Spokane (WA) Club " " Patterson (R. B.) Residence	Dowling, William M. see New York (N.Y.) 88th Street (east) No. 19	Downey and Deegan Members of firm: Downey, A.H. Deegan, John E.
720.5 A67r Dow, John K The suburban residence of the Pacific Northwest: a few examples of recent work in Spokane, Tacoma and Seattle by Cotter and Malmgren, Russell and Babcock, John K. Dow, Somervell and Cote. Architectural record 28: 51-59 July 1910	Downe (Eng.). Buckston Browne Farm Buckston Browne Farm, Downe, Kent. Built for Royal College of Surgeons, England. E.C. Frere, archt. Plan. Builder 145:182-184 August 4, 1933	720.5 A67d Downey (Cal.) Johnson (Parley) house Residence of Mr. and Mrs. Parley Johnson, Downey (Cal) Roland E. Coate, archt. Plan A Architectural digest 7:77-79 Number 4
Dow, Joy Wheeler see also Summit (N.J.) "Kingdor" Marquetec (Mich.) "Keepsake"	MICROFILM Downers Grove, Ill. First Methodist church Tallmadge & Watson , archts. First Methodist church, Downers Grove, Ill. Roll 31, frames 152-161	720.5 A67d Downey (Cal.) Our Lady of Perpetual Help Our Lady Of Perpetual Help church, Downey, Cal. Newton and Murray, archts. Architectural digest 9: 68 Number 2 1932-33

Downey, Joseph
    Appointed Chicago Commissioner of buildings.

    Inland Arch.
    25: 41
    May 1895

Downing, Burke
    see
Downing, Henry Philip Burke

Downs & Eads
    see
Minneapolis (MN)   Hoffman (Charles L.) Bungalow

Downham, Eng. Rangefield School
    Rangefield Elementary School, Downham Housing
Estate. G. Topham Forrest, archt.

    Builder 131:861-2
    November 26, 1926

Downing, Henry Philip Burke
    see also
Beddington, Eng. All Saints (church)
London, Eng. Cannon Greene memorial church.
    Parish hall.
Mitcham, Eng. St. Barnabas church
Wimbledon, Eng. Pelham road schools
Worthing, Eng. St. Paul's church, War Memorial

Downs, G. A.
    G. A. Downs [biog. note]

    Natl arch 6: 6
    Ag 1950

Downieville (Cal.) Churches
    Church in Downieville, Sierra County, California.

    Architect and engineer 118: 28
    September, 1934

Downing, Henry Philip Burke
    House at Burgh Heath, Surrey. H.P. Burke
Downing, F.R.I.B.A., Architect.

    Arch. and contract reporter 80:
    232, 2 pls. preceeding 241
    O 9 '08

Downside Abbey, Somerset
    Downside Abbey, England.

    Christian art v.1,p.135-146
    July, 1907

710.5 1 Downing, Andrew Jackson
L28 Pattee, S.L.
    Andrew Jackson Downing and his influence on
Landscape architecture in America.

    Landscape architecture 19:79-85
    January 1929

Downing, Henry Philip Burke
    A Mission church and hall in Surrey. H.P.
Burke Downing, archt.

    Archt and con rep 84:248
    O 14, 1910

Downside Abbey, Somerset
    Downside Abbey, near Bath
Sir Giles Gilbert Scott, R.A., arch.
Plans, elevations, sections

    Builder 129:178 and pl.
    July 31, Aug. 7, 1925

705.1   Downing, Andrew Jackson
A51m Blossom, H.H.
    Andrew Jackson Downing, landscape architect

    American magazine of art
    8:263-268
    May 1917

Downing, Paul Cook house
    see
Palm Beach (Fla.) "Little Parland

Downside Abbey. Gasquet (Cardinal) Tomb
    The tomb of Cardinal Gasquet, Downside Abbey,
near Bath. Sir Giles Gilbert Scott, archt.

    Architect (Lond.) 134: 160-161 supp.
    May 12, 1933

Downing, Andrew Jackson
    Andrew Jackson Downing, the First American
Landscape Architect. By Richard Schermerhorn, Jr.

    House and garden 16: 43-45
    Ag 1909

Downing, W. T.
    see
Chattanooga (Tenn.) Patten hotel
Atlanta (Ga.) Craigellachie

Dows, Tracy, house near Rhinebeck, N.Y.
    see
Foxhollow farm, N.Y.

710.5   Downing, Andrew Jackson
H84 Pratt, Richard
    In the days of Downing.

    House and garden 52: 102-5
    December 1927

790.5   Downington (Pa.) Brown (E.Y.) house
A67r   Alterations and additions for house of
Ellis Y. Brown, Jr., Downington, Pa. Mellor
and Meigs, archts. Original (farm) house
was built before 1700. Plan

A   Arch rec 40: 372-375
    O '16

Dowson, Philip Manning
    House at Coldharbour, Pangbourne, Berkshire
[plan, section & details] Philip Dowson, archt.

    Architectural design
    vol. 30: 232-233, Je 1960

MICROFILM

Dowswell, Harry Royden, 1884-1955

obituary notice

in SCRAPBOOK ON
ARCHITECTURE p. 722
(n film)

Drach, Gustave W.

see

Cincinnati (O.) Gibson hotel

Draftsmen
"T" Square
Architects draughtsmen. No illus.

Inland architect 4: 55-56
November, 1884

Doyle, A. E. and Associate

see

Portland (Ore.) Watzek (A.R.) house

Drafting

see

Architectural drawing

Draftsmen's Unions
Progress of the idea, with reference to
New York City.

Amer. inst. of arch. Jour.
8:158-9.
Apr. 1920.

Doyle and Patterson

see

Portland (Ore.) Northwestern national bank bldg.
"   "   Morgan building
"   "   Architecture
"   "   Oregon hotel
"   "   Reed college
"   "   Public library. East side branch

Drafting boards, tables, etc.

see

Drawing boards, tables, etc.

RYERSON LIBRARY
913   Dragon houses, Euboea
A51   Johnson, F. P.
        Dragon houses of southern Euboea

American journal of archaeology
29: 398-412
Oct. - Dec. 1925

Doyle, J. Francis

see

Liverpool (Eng.) Royal insurance building
Wallasey, Eng. St. Nicholas church

Draftsmanship
S., M.
Draughtsmanship and architecture
Arch rec 25: 215-217
Mr 1909

Drainage
The drainage of a house.

Inland Architect
44: 14-15
Sept, 1904

Doyle-Jones, F. W.

see

War memorials, England
Ossett (Eng.) Ossett war memorial
Zeebrugge (Belg.) war memorial

Draftsmen
Credit to the designer in the office of the
official architect.

West. Arch.
11: 66
June 1908

720.52   Drainage
A67c   The housing tragedy

Architect 109:325
May 11, 1923

721.97   Doylestown(Pa) Bucks County Historical Soc.   museum
A67c   Wendell,G.F.
        Bucks county historical society museum.
Designed by H.C.Mercer. No plan.

A   Architectural concrete 2:28-31
        No.1,1936

Draftsmen
Moore, F   W
        The draughtsman.

Arch rec   25: 103-105
F 1909

720.8   Drainage.
A67f   Land drainage.

Arch. forum 35: 55-8.
August 1921.

Doylestown (Pa.) Mercer (Wm.). Garden house
    The garden of William Mercer at Doylestown,
Pennsylvania, designed on geometric lines. Willing,
Sims, and Talbutt, archts.

House and garden 63:26-27
February, 1933

Draftsmen. A practical hint to draftsmen.

Inland Arch.
49: 35-6
March 1906

Drainage.
    The Nature of Sewage

Builder 82: 116-17
Feb. 1, 1902

720.8 A67f Drainage Problems in large buildings. Architectural forum 31:211-4 Dec. 1919.	Drake hotel.Chicago see Chicago.Drake hotel	Drake-Farwell building, Chicago (second) see Chicago, Ill. Drake-Farwell building (1871)
711 S77 Drainage,Germany. Berlin Adler,Leo Berliner städtentwässerung. (City drainage in Berlin.) Plans. Städtebau 25: 43-45 February 1928	Drake, Lindsey Alexander Thompson Webster, 1910- see Tecton, Architects	720.52 B93 Drawbridges Bodiam Castle,Sussex: aerial view as in 1395. From a drawing by A.E.Henderson. (Separate plate.) Builder 145: Plate July 7,1933
Drake and Lasdun see London (Eng.) Bishop's bridge road. Housing project	Drake, Samuel Davis, house. Mason City, Ia. see Mason City, Ia. Drake, Samuel Davis, house.	Drawbridges Château de Chaumont..Le Pont-levis. Photograph. Saint Sauveur, Hector. Chateaux de France. 10 vols. Paris: Librairie génerale de l'architecture et des arts decoratifs, 1922. v.2:pl.2
Drake block, Chicago see Chicago, IL. Drake-Farwell building 1871	Drake, W. H. see also Chicago (IL.) Fay (A.R.) house " " Hutchinson (George C.) house " " Payne (W.S.) Laundry Fox Lake (Wis.) Rawson house La Grange (IL.) Babbitt (C.M.) house	Drawing, Architectural see Architectural drawing
Drake, Sir Francis Memorials Sketch design for a monument to Sir Francis Drake, from a drawing by the late F. Derwent Wood. Builder 130:691 April 23, 1926	Drake, W. H. Bldg. for H. E. Bennett on the corner of Armour and 27th Sts. W.H. Drake, archt. Inland archt and news rec. 19:77 July, 1892	Drawing boards, tables, etc. A letter on drafting Pencil points 4:64 July, 1923
Drake, Gordon see Los Angeles, Cal. Drake (Gordon) house	Drake, W. H. Bldg. for W. H. McDonald on the corner of 27th and Dearborn Streets. W.H. Drake, archt. Inland archt and news rec 19:77 July, 1892	Drawings see also Measured drawings Working drawings Architectural drawing
Drake, N. A. see Kansas City (Mo.) Newman theater	Drake, W. H. Hotel for Thomas Conlan and W.S. Foley on Stony Island Avenue and 69th place. W.H. Drake, archt. Inland archt and news rec 18:80 January, 1892	Drawings Architects' drawings ruled works of art Inland Architect 43: 17 Apr, 1904

Drawings
Important customs ruling on architects'
drawings.

Inland Architect
43: 23
Apr, 1904

Drebin and Scott

see

San Marino (Cal.) Stewart (F.A.) house

Dresden (Ger.) Andreaskirche und pfarrhäusen
Andreaskirche mit zwei Pfarrhäusen und
Konfirmandensaal zu Dresden. Otto Schubert, archt.

Moderne bauformen 21: pl. 65 fol.268
Sept., 1922

Drawings,Ownership. Copyright for the
architect.

Inland Arch.
51: 2
July 1908

Dredgers,

see

Caters

Dresden (Ger.) Architecture

see also

Baroque architecture, Germany, Dresden

Drawings, Ownership. Institute (A.I.A.)
asked to recover lost drawings.

Inland Arch.
25: 56
July 1895

Dreieck-Streben-Bauart
Stoy, Wilhelm
Die entwicklung der Dreieck-Streben-Bauart

Baumeister No. 10
51: 562-663
O 1954

720.53 .   Dresden. Architecture
W31   Dresden house groups, Erich Hempel,archt.

Wasmuths 14: 201-206
May 1930

Drawings. Ownership
The ownership of drawings.

Amer archt & bldg news 55:2y
Ja 23, 1897

Dreitausend (Ger.) Theater
Frey, Dr. Dagobert
Sketches for the theater of Dreitausend.
Hoppe, Kammerer, and Schonthal, archts. Plans.

Der architekt 23: 45-48
Heft 5-6, 1920

720.52   Dresden. Architecture
A67   Haussenstein, Dr. Wilhelm
          Dresden, the home of Baroque.

Architects' journal 69: 937-940
June 19, 1929

Drawings
Ownership of drawings; what is architecture?

Inland Architect
44: 25
Nov, 1904

Dreker, Frederik W. and Son

see

Ardmore (Pa.) Planning

D10.5   Dresden. Architecture
D32   Haenel, Erich
         Dwellings in Dresden, 1925

Dekorative kunst 29: 135-146
March 1926

Drayton House, Eng.
Webb, G. F.
Drayton House

Archaeological Jour
v.110:188-89
1953

Dresden, Ger. Akademie der bildenden kunsten
(1894)
The new Academy of fine-arts [Koenigliche
Kunstakademie], Dresden, Ger.

Amer archt
56: 39-40, pl fol 4
in supp.
My 1, 1897

720.52   Dresden. Architecture
W31   Grossgarage und kesselhaus des Dresdener
          Konsumvereins Vorwärts. (Garage and boiler
          house for Dresden Konsumvereins Vorwärts.)
          Karl Schmidt,archt. Plans.

Wasmuths monatshefte 15: 385-389
September 1931

A

"Dreamwold", Egypt, Mass.

see

Egypt Mass. Dreamwold

---

ff
720.53   Dresden, Ger. Andreaskirche
M68   Bauamtmann a.D.Dr.Ing.Otto Schubert - B.D.
          A. Andreaskirche mit zwei Pfarrhäusen und
          Konfirmandensaal zu Dresden. Sketch and plan.

Moderne bauformen 21: pl. 65
September 1922

720.53   Dresden. Architecture
W31   Wolf,Paul
             Neue bauten von Paul Wolf-Dresden. (New
          buildings by Paul Wolf.)
             City hospital;clinic for children; public
          school;city power works;house and other buildings.
          Plans.

Wasmuths monatshefte 14: 1-12
January 1930

A

Dresden, Architecture
   Schilling u. Graebner, arch.

        Moderne Bauformen 8:49-96
        F '09

Dresden, Ger. Gemälde-galerie

  For material between 1918 - 1955 see

  Dresden, Ger. Staatliche gemäldegalerie

Dresden, Ger. Hoftheater (1878)
   New Grand Theater at Dresden, erected 1871-8.
Gottfried Semper, archt.

        Building budget
        5:102, pl fol 98
        Ag 1889

720.53 Dresden. Architecture
W31   Some modern buildings in Dresden. Paul Wolf,
archt.

        Wasmuths 11: 176-82
        Heft 4, 1927

Dresden, Ger. Gemälde-Galerie
   Dresden: Der entwurf zu einem Gebäude
für die moderne Abteilung der königlichen.
Gemälde Galerie in Dresden. Architekten:
Finanz und Baurat O. Kramer und Bauamtmann
B.O. Pusch in Dresden. (landscape plans, plans,
photograph)

     Deutsche bauzeitung 48:
      373-76; My 16, 1914
      381-87; " 20, "
      402; " 27, "

Dresden, Ger. Hoftheater (1913)

        see

Dresden, Ger. Schauspielhaus

Dresden, Ger. Court theater (1841)

        see

Dresden, Ger. Hoftheater (1841)

Dresden.Georgenschloss

      See

  Dresden.Schloss.

711.05 Dresden (Ger.) Ilgen-kampfbahn
877   Die Ilgen-Kampfbahn (Stadion) in
Dresden.

        Städtebau 19:119, pl 44
        Heft 11-1f, 1923

Dresden, Ger. Court theater (1878)

        see

Dresden, Ger. Hoftheater (1878)

Dresden (Ger.) German Hygiene Museum
   Plans for the German Hygiene Museum at Dresden.

     Wasmuths monathshefte für baukunst 6:
                 39-64
     Heft 1-2. 1921

Dresden, Ger. Internationalen hygiene-austellung
1911.
Haenel, Erich.
   Die bauten der Internationalen hygiene-austel-
ung, Dresden. 1911.

        Dekorative kunst 14:481-504
        Ag 1911

Dresden, Ger. Court theater (1913)

        see

Dresden, G r. Schauspielhaus

Dresden (Ger.) German Municipal Exposition. 1903
   The German Municipal Exposition in Dresden.
By Max Floessel

        House and gard. 4:188-196
        O 1903

                    1930
720.53 Dresden. Internationalen hygiene-ausstellung
B35   Ausstellungsquerschnitt 1930 Dresden.
(International Hygiene Exhibit,Dresden,1930.)
Restaurant by H.Richter,archt.,also Hall for
physical culture.
   State Tower on exhibit. Kreis,archt.

        Der Baumeister 28: 500-501
        December 1930

720.53 Dresden. Deutsches Studentenbund
B35   Harbers, Guido
   Das Haus des N. S. Deutschen Studentenbundes
in Dresden. (The house of the National Socialist
Student Union in Dresden.) Professor Jost, archt.
Plans.

A   Der Baumeister 34:426-431
       December 1936

Dresden, Ger. Hoftheater (1841)
   Theatre at Dresden, 1835. Gottfried Semper,
archt. Burned down 1870.

        Bldg. budget
        5:101-2, pl fol 98
        Ag 1889

Dresden.Königliches schloss

      See

  Dresden.Schloss.

720.53 Dresden, Ernemann plant
W31

        Wasmuths, heft 9-10, 8:313-14
        1924

Dresden, Ger. Hoftheater (1841)
   Biermann, F.B.
   Karl Friedrich Schinkel und Gottfried Semper
als reformatoren des theaterbaues. (Karl F. Schinkel
and Gottfried Semper as reformers of theater
buildings.) Court theatre in Dresden. Plans.

        Wasmuths monatshefte 13:254-255
        June, 1929

A

720.53 Dresden, Ger. Konsumvereins vorwärts Kessel-
W31   haus.
   Grossgarage und kesselhaus des Dresdener
Konsumvereins Vorwärts. (Garage and boiler
house for Dresden Konsumvereins.Vorwärts.)
Karl Schmidt,archt. Plans.

        Wasmuths monatshefte 15: 385-389
        September 1931

A

D10.5 H96 **Dresden (Ger.) Krematorium** Haenel, Erich Das krematorium in Dresden Dek. kunst 15:105-26 D'11	**Dresden (Germany) A Protestant Church Interior** Fritz Schumacher, Arch. Selections from Pittsburg Architectural Club Exhibition, 1907. Inland Arch. 50: pl. fol. p 76 D, 1907	Ryerson 708.Z B51j **Dresden. Schloss** Sponsel, Jean Louis The "Georgenschloss" in Dresden, Germany. Berlin.Jahrbuch der preussischen kunstsammlungen 45: 214-228 Heft 4, 1924
Dresden (Ger.) Landstaendische Bank Landstaendische Bank, Dresden. Lossow and Kühne, archts. A Architectural record 27:247 March, 1910	720.53 W31 **Dresden (Germany) Rathus** Röseiger, H.D. Drawing for town hall in Dresden;Wilmersdorf. Friedrich Ostendorf, archt. Wasmuths 10: 282, 289 Heft 7, 1926	**Dresden, Ger. Staatliche gemäldegalerie** For material before 1918 and after 1955 see Dresden, Ger. Gemälde-galerie
720.5 A51 **Dresden (Ger.) Market-house (new)** Side entrance ...Rettig & Fischer, archts. Amer archt and bldg news 53: pl fol 4 in supp S 5, 1896	**Dresden.Residenz-schloss** See Dresden.Schloss.	720.53 M68 **Dresden.Staatliche gemäldegalerie** Städtliche gemälde gallerie.Dresden Hygiene-museum, Dresden Moderne bauformen 21:269 Sept. 1922
Dresden (Ger.) Open-Air Kindergarden Schütte, W. Grundsätzliches über neue volksschulen. (Fundamentals about new public schools.) Special number. School in Dresden: Open-Air Kindergarden. Paul Wolf, archt. Der Baumeister 28: 461-476,pl.66-69 Dec, 1930	720.53 A67as **Dresden. Restaurant Italienisches Dörfchen** Gurlitt, Cornelius Hans Erlwein, das Italienische dorfchen in Dresden. Hans Erlwein, archt. Plans. A Architektur des XX jahrhunderts : 3-54 12 Sonderheft. 1913	**Dresden, Ger. Staatliche kunstsammlungen. Gemälde galerie** see Dresden, Ger. Gemälde-galerie
Dresden, Ger. Opera house (1841) see Dresden, Ger. Hoftheater (1841)	**Dresden.Royal palace** See Dresden.Schloss.	**Dresden (Ger.) Technical High School** Inland Archt. 45: pl.fol.p. 44 May 1905
Dresden, Ger. Opera house (1878) see Dresden, Ger. Hoftheater (1878)	**Dresden, Ger. Schauspielhaus** The new Court Theater at Dresden, Germany. Prof. William Lossow and Max Hans Kühne, archts. Plans Archl rev 19, N.S. 2:263, 266, pls 144-147 N 1913	720.53 A67as **Dresden. Theater. Plats** Gurlitt, Cornelius Hans Erlwein, das Italienische dorfchen in Dresden. Hans Erlwein, archt. Plans. Architektur des XX jahrhunderts :3-54 12 Sonderheft. 1913
705.5 D48 **Dresden. Palais im Grossen Garten** Keller, Harald Das palais im Grossen Garten su Dresden. Built 1679. Deutsche kunst 6:235-257 Lieferung 6, 1940	**Dresden. Schloss** Schloss zu Dresden: Ostseiteum 1550, Westseiteum 1590. Stallhof, 1586. Hans Buchner archt. No plan. Fritsch, K.E.O., ed. Denkmaeler deutscher renaissance. 4 vols. Berlin: E. Wasmuth, 1891. v.1:25-29 v.3:pls.70-72	**Dresden (Ger.) Third German Exposition of Crafts-manship, Dresden 1906 - Selections from.** (1) A Bremen Antechamber, Emil Hogg, Arch. (2) A Window Seat - Prof. Schumacher, Decorator Inland Arch. 48: pl. fol. p 48 N, 1906

Dresse and Oudin

see also

Paris (Fr.) École de puériculture de la faculté
de médecine de Paris.

Drews, Hans

see also

Robledo, Drews, Castro, Ltda.

720.5
A67a   Drexel Park (Pa.) Anderson (G.B.) house
    Residence of G.B. Anderson, Drexel Park,
    Pa. Wallace & Warner, archts.

Architecture. 53: pl.97-98
May, 1926

720.54
A67   Dresse and Oudin
    Duval, Charles
     The Mathilde-Henri de Rothschild Foundation,
    197 and 199, Rue Marcadet, Paris. Dresse and
    Oudin, archts.

L'architecture 43: 53-61
February 15, 1930

Drews, Hans
   Casa en Medellin [plan & section]
   Casa en Bogota [plans & sections]
   Casa en Bogota [plans & sections] Hans
Drews & Arturo Robledo, archts.

Proa
#139:8-11, 16-17 O 1960

Drexhage, G
   Burohaus in Rotterdam [plan] J. P. van
Bruggen & G. Drexhage, archts.

Baumeister
58:527 Je 1961

Dreux, Fr.
   Dreux, Châteaudun, and Les Andelys

Archite curre 49:67-70
Mr 1924

Drews, Hans
   Colegio en Cartagena [plans & sections]
Arturo Robledo & Hans Drews, archts.

Proa
#129:14-17 Ag 1959

Dreyer, E. S. house, Chicago

see

Chicago (Ill.) Dreyer (E.S.) house

Dreux.Chapelle royale

See

Dreux.Chapelle Saint Louis

Drews, Hans
   Nuevo barrio en Belencito [plans] Arturo
Robledo & Hans Drews, archts, with Cuellar,
Serrano, Gomes & Cia., archts.

Proa no. 78: 16-17
Ja 1954

Dreyer, Jorgen (Sculptor)

see

Kansas City (MO)   Rushton (George) Baking Co.

705.4
GP8   Drwux.Chapelle Saint Louis
    Roux, Alphone
     La chapelle de la famille d'Orleans à Dreux
    et ses monuments funeraires.

Gaz.des beaux arts Per.5,v.7,p.189-199
August;September 1920

Drexel bldg. Philadelphia, Pa.

see

Philadelphia, Pa. Drexel bldg.

Dreyer, Otto

see

Lucerne (Swits.) St. Joseph
   "   "   Cinema moderne

Drew, Jane B

see

Fry, Maxwell, Jane Drew & partners

Drexel fountain, Chicago

see

Chicago, Ill. Drexel fountain

Dreyfuss, Henry, 1904-1972

see

Philadelphia (Pa.) Western Union Telegraph Co.
New York (city) World's fair 1939. Perisphere

Drew, Joyce Beverly

see

Cliftonville (Eng.) house

Drexel Hill (Pa) Residence
E.E. Hendrickson, archt. plan

West. Archt.
22: pls.fol.p. 14
Aug, 1915

720.5
A67f   Driesler, Benjamin,
    $2500 for house and land, also house for
    $7400. Hillside Heights, Long Island, N.Y.
    Benjamin Driesler, Jr. archt. Plans

Architectural forum 66: 70-72
January 1937

720.52 B93 — Drill halls New Infantry drill hall, Dumbarton. Denny & Blain, architects Builder 125:580b Oct. 12, 1923	Driver, A. J. see Blomfield, Arthur and A. J. Driver	Driveways Checklist on driveways. Northwest archt 14: 40 No. 1 1950
720.52 A67c — Drinkwater, G.C. Boat house for Christ church, Oxford. Architect, G.C. Drinkwater. Plans. Architect(Lond.)150:380-381 June 25,1937	Driveways New country life 33:48 Nov. 1917	710.5 C855 — Driveways. Constructing the driveway. Country Life 41: 70. Jan. 1922
Drischler, Francis see St. Louis (MO) Lewis Residence	720.5 A51 — Driveways Approach to a country house at Brookline, Mass. Vitale, Brinckerhoff & Geiffert, landscape architects. Amer. arch. 126:pl.14 July 2, 1924	710.5 H84 — Driveways Stanton, Carl Designing a drive. House and garden 53: 68-9 June 1928
Drive-in and curb services see also Drive-in theaters	Driveways The approach to the house. Country Life. 39:44. Jan. 1921.	710.5 H84 — Driveways Designing the entrance drive. House & garden 52: 122 September 1927
Drive-in and curb services A roadside supermarket; shopping without standing. Interiors 104, pt. 1: 64-65 N 1944	710.5 H84 — Driveways The approach to the house House and garden 42: 47-9 Oct. 1922	720.5 A51 — Driveways A driveway through a public bldg. B.A.I.D. problem. Amer. arch 102: pl fol 226 D 25, 1912
Drive-in Theaters, World's first see Camden (N.J.) Drive-in theater	720.5 A67a — Driveways Architecture's portfolio Arch. 68: 112-26 Ag. '33	710.5 H84 — Driveways. Garage sites and entrance drives. House & Garden 40: 46-7. Nov. 1921
Drive-in theaters, The theatre-community; the automobile brings a major change to theater design. Interiors 104, pt. 2:66 Mr. 1945	720.5 A67f — Driveways Rogers, Tyler Stewart The automobile and the private estate. Arch forum 32: 113-116, 171-174, 253-254 33: 23-5, 69-79 Mr, Ap, Je, Jl, Ag '20	710.5 L26 — Driveways Head, F. Garage turns. Landscape architecture 15:160-170 April 1925

710.5 L26 Driveways Taylor; A. D. Notes on stone pavements for entrance courts and driveways. Landscape architecture 21: 30-37 October 1930	720.52 B95 Droitwich (Eng.) Uplands "Uplands", Droitwich, Worcestershire. Baron C. S. Underhill, archt. Plan. Builder 139: 736,743-744 October 31, 1930	Drottningholm (Swe.) Theatre Drottningholm theatre restored Amer. Swedish mon. 40:11-12 Ag. 1946
Driveways Turns for automobiles Amer. arch. 115:699-704,777-782 May 21, 1919; June 4, 1919	Droitwich (Eng.) Westwood Westwood Park, Worcestershire, England. The seat of Lord Doverdale. Country life (Lond.) 64:50-57;94-100 July 14;21, 1928	Drovers' Journal building (1889), Chicago see Chicago, Ill. Sun and Drovers' Journal building (1889).
Drogheda (Ire) library Drogheda Library competition. Selected design, Finian N. Tallan, Drogheda, archt. - design placed second. J. J. Hazlett, Dublin, archt. British archt 60: 94 and pl. Ag 7, 1903	Droitwich (Eng.) Westwood Westwood, residence of Lord Doverdale, Droitwich, England. Country life (Lond.) 75: xxvi February 3, 1934	Dros and Marrast see also Vincennes (Fr.) St. Louis
Drogo Castle, Devonshire Castle Drogo, Devonshire. Sir Edwin L. Lutyens, R.A., architect. Architect 111: 2 pl. May 2, 1924	Dropmore (Buckingham), Eng. Dropmore. Country life (Lond.) 84: xxxiv September 3, 1938	720.54 A67 Dros and Marrast Louvet,A. Les églises modernes. L'Église Saint-Louis de Vincennes. (Modern churches. Saint Louis of Vincennes church.) M.M.Dros and Marrast, archts. L'Architecture 37: 89-96 May 10, 1924
Drogo Castle, Devonshire Castle Drogo, Devon Builder 126:pl. May 9, 1924	Drottningholm (Swe.) Theater Beijer, Agne The Drottningholm theatre, Sweden. Country life (Lond.) 64:641-644 November 10, 1928	Dros, Jacques see also Huningue (Fr.) Eglise du Christ Roi Nice (Fr.) Sainte Jeanne d'Arc St. Eloi-les-Mines (Fr.) Sainte Jeanne d'Arc Vendhuile (Fr.) St. Martin
710.5 C85 Droitwich (Eng.) Railton, Joanna In praise of Droitwich. Country life (Lond.) 80: xxx,viii N 14 '36	Drottningholm (Swe.) theater Ewer, Monica The player king and the theater at Drottningholm, built by Gustave III of Sweden in 1766. (Interior) Theatre arts monthly 15:228-232 March, 1931	720.54 A67 Dros, Jacques Church architecture by Jacques Dros: St.Eloi-les-Mines; Vendhuile; Vincennes; Nice Huningue; Sainte-Jeanne d'Arc at Saint-Eloi- les-Mines; St.-Martin at Vendhuile; St.Louis de Vincennes; model of church of Saint- Jeanne d'Arc at Nice; model of church of Christ Roi at Huningue; private chapel-pro- perty of Count of Ussel. L'architecture 44: 302-311 September 15, 1931
Droitwich (Eng.) Churches Droitwich. Arch. Jour. 55: 254,262-7. Feb. 15, 1922	Drottningholm (Swe.) Theater Beijer, Agne Gustaf III's theater restored. Drottningholm Castle, Sweden. Interiors. American Scandinavian review 20:32-35 January, 1932	720.54 A67 Dros,Jacques Louvet,A. Les églises modernes, l'oeuvre de Jacques Dros,archt. (Modern churches, the work of Jacques Dros.) Plans. Church of Sainte-Jeanne d'Arc at Saint-Eloi-les-Mines. M.Dros,archt. L'Architecture 43: p.89-100 March 15,1930

721.97 A67c	Dros, Jacques Roset, Charles Saint Joan of Arc church, Nice, France. Jacques Dros, archt. Plan. Condensed from an article by Charles Roset which appeared in the October 1935 issue of La Technique des Travaux, Brussels, Belgium Architectural concrete 2:10-13 No.1,1936	710.5 C85	Drumlanrig Castle, Dumfriesshire Hussey, Christopher The homes of the Duke of Buccleuch: Drumlanrig Castle, Dumfriesshire. Dalkeith Palace, Edinburgh, Boughton house, Northamptonshire. The Duke of Buccleuch's furniture. Country life (London) 78:246-251;268- September 7;14;1935 269	Drummond, William, 1876-1946 Letters to the Editor, following Miss Ganschinietz's article. [by John Lloyd Wright and Alan M. Drummond] Prairie school review VI: 25 Third quarter 1969
	Drübeck, Ger. Stiftkirche Feldtkeller, Hans Neue forschungen zur baugeschichte der Drübeck stiftskirche [plans, sect.] Zeitschrift für kunstwissenschaft 4: 105-124, Heft 3/4 1950		Drummond, David D. -1912 Obit. West. Archt. 18: 49 Apr, 1912	Drummond, William, 1876-1946 On things of common concern. [reprinted from Western architect, Feb. 1914] Prairie School review I: 8-11 Second Quarter, 1964
	Drug Stores see also names of individual drug stores, i.e.: Helsinki, Fin. Kaisaniemi Apothek Etc.	710.5 C855	Drummond, E Lynn Old-time manner in a new-time garden: the gardens of the residence of Mrs.James N. Andrews, Aiken, S.C. Garden designed by Mrs. Lloyd Richards. E.L.Drummond, archt. Erick in a South Carolina setting: the residence of Mrs.Lloyd Richards at Aiken, S.C. E.L.Drummond, archt. Country life(U.S)69:16-17;22-23 January;April 1936	Drummond, William 1876-1946 Perspective and plot plan for house on Lake Shore: William Drummond, archt., Chicago; plan. Chicago architectural club 25:20 1912
	Drug Stores, Denmark Elevation for apothecary shop in Denmark. Wasmuths 11:44 Heft 1, 1927	750.6 R889	Drummond, George Fairly G.F. Drummond Royal arch'l inst. of Can. Jour. 19: 157 Jl '45	Drummond, William, 1876-1946 Project for an American embassy [perspective]. House on Lake Shore, and Fireproof house projects [elevation]. Grower apartment project [perspective]. Prairie school review VI: 6;8-9;16,18 First quarter, 1969
710.5 C85	Druid remains, Hebrides, Outer Hindmarsh, H. H. The Islands of Thule: in the home of the spinning wheel. Country life (London) 78:436-438 October 26, 1935		Drummond, William, 1876-1946 see also Chicago, Ill. Shedd park. Recreation building Chicago, Ill. Tribune Tower. Competition Grosse Pointe, Mich. Ferry, Dexter, house River Forest, Ill. Badenoch, Benjamin, house River Forest, Ill. Library River Forest, Ill. Vilas, , house Mason City, Ia. Yelland, Curtis, house	Drummond, William, 1876-1946 Ganschinietz, Suzanne William Drummond: I. Talent and sensitivity. [portr., illus., plans, renderings] Prairie school review VI: 1-19, 27 First quarter 1969
710.5 C85	Druid temples.Reconstructed Carpenter, J.A. On the Yorkshire moors - model of a Druids' temple, erected by William Danby about 1890. Country life(London)88:106 August 3,1940		Drummond,William, 1876- 1946 See also Guenzel and Drummond	Drummond, William, 1878-1946 Ganschinietz, Suzanne William Drummond: II. Partnership and obscurity. [illus., plans, renderings] Prairie school review VI: 1-19 Second quarter, 1969
	Druiding, A. see Assisium, Wis. St. Francis convent (1887). Buffalo, N.Y. Church of the Seven Dolors (1886). Cincinnati, O. St. Lawrence church (1886). Delaware, O. St. Mary's church (1886). Princeton, Wis. Polish church (1887). South Bend, Ind. St. Patrick's church (1886).		Drummond, William 1876- Brief biography. Herringshaw, Clark J. Herringshaw's city blue book of current biography. Chicago: American publisher's association, 1915.	Drummond (William) house. River Forest (Ill) See River Forest (Ill.) Drummond (William) house.

Drumsheugh (Eng.) Swimming baths
    The work of Sir John Burnet, Royal Gold
medalist. Drumsheugh Swimming baths.

Archts.' jour. 57: 1074-8
June 27, 1923

720.8
B88
    Dryrot.
        Professor Groom on.

Jour. Royal Inst. of Brit. Arch. 29: 58-60.
Nov. 28, 1921.

720.52   Drymen (Scot) Cottages
    Cottage homes, Drymen, N. B.
J. A. Campbell, Architect

Arch & con rep 67: pl 1, 8
28 in Supp
Ja 17, '02

MICROFILM

Drury, John
    Chicago's little streets.

In SCRAPBOOK ON
ARCHITECTURE p. 239-41
(on film)

Dry Rot
    Report on Dry Rot.
By Paul Ogden

RIBA jour 15: 475-77
Je 6, 1908

Drysdale, George

see

Birmingham (Eng.) Church of Our Lady and St.
Hubert

MICROFILM

Drury, John
    Historic Chicago sites.

In SCRAPBOOK ON
ARCHITECTURE p. 44-171
(on film)

Dryburgh Abbey.

Wheatley, Richard. Cathedrals and Abbeys
of Great Britain and Ireland. New York:
Harper and Bros., 1890 p. 257-263

723.6
A67f
    Dryton, John C., Jr.
      House for A. J. Timmerberg, Brentwood
(Mo.). John C. Dryton, Jr., archt. Plan

Architectural Forum 71:291
October 1939

915.05
A83
    Druses, Architecture
Seabrook, W. B.
      The marriage dagger of the Druses - tales of
the Druse code for women and a visit to the "Veil-
ed Lady of Mukhtara." (Examples of architecture).

Asia 26: 311-315
April 1926

Dryburgh Abbey
    Dryburgh given as monument.

Archt's and bldrs.' jour. 47:270
June 12, 1918

Du Buys, Rathbone E.

see

New Orleans (LA)   Public Library Competition
      Top 4 designs

Drusus, Arch, Rome, It.

see

Rome (It.) Arch of Drusus

720.52
B93
    Dryburgh Abbey

Builder 127:6-8,10
July 4, 1924

Du Page Co. (Ill.) Hippach Memorial Chapel
    Hippach Memorial chapel, Green Ridge cemetary
Arthur Woltersdorf, archt. Plans.

American architect 134:573-582
November 5, 1928

720.52
B93
    Dry rot
Findlay, W. P.
      Dry rot.

Builder 144: 420
March 10,1933

Dryden, D. W.

see

Denver (CO)   (New) High School

720.5
W52
    DuPage county (Ill) Rogers (W.A.) farm
      Sketch of farm home in DuPage County for
W. A. Rogers. John S. Van Bergen, archt.
Plan

West archt 21: 28
Ap '15

720.52
B93
    Dry rot.
      In wood.

Builder 121: 651-3.
Nov. 11, 1921.

Dryden, G. B., house. Evanston

see

Evanston, Ill. Dryden, G.B., house.

Duarte, Helio de Queiros, 1906-
    Escola de Engenharia de São Carlos;
caracteristicas do planejamento e dos projetos
[plans & sections] Helio de Queiroz Duarte &
E. R. Carvalho Mange, archts.

Habitat
6:44-9 Ag 1956

Duarte, Hélio de Queiros, 1906-
Plano da Cidade Universitária de Santa
Catarina. Hélio de Queiros Duarte & Ernesto
Roberto de Carvalho Mange, archts.

Habitat
7:1-16 Jl-Ag 1957

Dublin (Ire.)
Dublin of the future

Architect 109:163 and pl.
March 9, 1923

Architect 107:52, pl.
Ja 20, 1922

720.53   Dubach and Gloor
235   G.H.
Evangelisch. Reformiertes Kirchengemein-
dehaus in Bern. (Evangelist-reform church community house in Bern.)

Der Baumeister 34: 109-113
April 1936

Dublin (Ire.) airport terminal

see

Collinstown, Ire. Dublin airport terminal

Dublin, Ire., Christ Church Cathedral
Christ church cathedral.

Antiquary 7:203-206.
May, 1883.

Duban,Félix Louis Jacques

See

Duban,Jacques Félix, 1797-1870

Dublin, Ire. Architecture

see also

Churches. Ireland. Dublin

Dublin (Ire.) Christ Church cathedral
Christ Church Cathedral, Dublin.

Wheatley, Richard. Cathedrals
and Abbeys of Great Britain and
Ireland. New York: Harper and
Bros., 1890. p.265-269

720.5   Duban,Jacques Felix   1797-1870
A67r   Flagg,Ernest
The École des Beaux Arts, Paris. Debret and
Duban,archts of two principal buildings.

Architectural record 3:302-313;419-428
January-March; April-June 1894

Dublin, Ire. Architecture
Dickinson, P. L.
Georgian Dublin.

Architects' and builders' journal 39:
February 18, 1914   117-120

Dublin (Ire) Christ Church Cathedral.
A great architect - a great mistake.
George Edmund Street - arch. of restoration.

Inland Arch.
51: 37-8
May 1908

Duban, 1797-1870
Tomb of Mme. Delaroche neé Vernet, Montmatre
Cemetery, Paris, France. F. Duban, archt.

Building budget
5: pl.fol.p.74
Je 1889

Dublin (Ire.) Architecture
A vision of Dublin
H.V. Lanchester

Architecture 16:286-290
Apr. 1923

720.52   Dublin (Ire.) Custom house
A67   Custom house, Dublin. James Gordon,
archt.

Archt's jour 50: 185
Ag 6 '19

Dubin, George H   , 1890-1958
obituary notice

In SCRAPBOOK ON
ARCHITECTURE p. 720
(on film)

720.52   Dublin (Ire.) Blue Coat school
A67   Bluecoat school

Arch & bldrs. jr 44: 28-30
Jl 19 '16

Dublin (Ire.) Custom house.
Custom house, Dublin and its architect.

Architect 106:38-41, 92
Jul. 15, 1921.
Ag. 12, '21

Dublin (Ire.)
Notes from Ireland.

Architect. 105:178-82
Mar. 11, 1921.

Dublin (Ire.) Botanic Garden
Taylor, G.C.
A national garden: The Botanic Garden, Glasnevin,
Dublin.

Country life (Lond.) 79:148-150
February 8, 1936

Dublin (Ire.) Dawson Street Club
Dawson Street Club. Dublin.

Arch. Jour. 53:223.
Feb. 23, 1921

Dublin (Ire.) Dawson Street Club
    Dawson Street Club, Dublin.

Architect 107:55.
Jan. 20, 1922.

Dublin (Ire.) Howth Castle
    Hussey, Christopher
    Howth Castle, Dublin.

Country life (Lond.) 68: 286-292;316-321
September 6, 1930

Dublin, Ire. Plan
    A new town plan for the city of Dublin

Arch. and contr. rep. 97:55-58
Jan. 26, 1917

Dublin (Ire.) Four Courts
    The Four Courts, Dublin. Thomas Cooley,
architect.

Architects journal 61: 2
July 5, 1922

Dublin (Ire.) Hibernian Branch Bank
    The Hibernian Branch Bank, Sackville St.,
Dublin. Wm. H. Burne and Sons, architects.

Architects journal 58:535-539
Oct. 10, 1923

Dublin (Ire.) Plan
    Smith, F. A. Cushing
    A town plan for Dublin, Ireland.

Arch. record 41: 403-422
May, 1917

Dublin (Ireland) Gresham Hotel
    Gresham Hotel, Dublin. Robert Atkinson, archt.

Builder 130: 4 pls., 229, 234-5
February 5, 1926

Dublin (Ire.) Marino housing scheme
    Marino housing scheme, Dublin.

Builder 118:247,248-249
February 27, 1920

Dublin (Ire.) Planning competition
    Contest for replanning

Arch. and bldrs' jour. 44:147-148
Sept. 27, 1916

Dublin (Ireland) Gresham Hotel
    Rebuilding of the Gresham Hotel, Dublin.
Robert Atkinson, archt. F.B.M. Woodhouse, del.

Architect 115:pl.
May 7-21, 1926

Dublin (Ire.) Municipal buildings

Builder 104:439-440
April 11, 1913

Dublin (Ire.) Planning Competition
    The Dublin town planning competition.
Re-building of Dublin.

Builder 112:14-16, 20-21
January 5, 1917

Dublin (Ireland.) Gresham Hotel
    Gresham Hotel, Dublin. Robert Atkinson, archt.

Architect (Lond.) 117:30-31
January 7, 1927

Dublin (Ire.) Municipal buildings. Competition.
    Dublin Municipal Buildings Competition.

Archts & builders jour 37: 369-70
Ap 9, 1913

Dublin (Ire.) Post Office
    Dublin general post office

Arch. and bldrs. jour. 43:194-196 and
May 10, 1916   plates

Dublin (Ireland) Gresham Hotel
    Wornum, G. Grey
The Gresham Hotel, Dublin. Robert Akinson, archt.

Architect (Lond.) 117: 725-731,pls,
Ap. 29; May 6, 1927   785-6.

Dublin, Ire. Parliament house (old)
Craig, Maurice
    A parliament and its extensions. (illus.)

Country life
138: 552-553
S 2, 1965

Dublin (Ire.) Reconstruction

Builder 115:17
July 12, 1918

Dublin (Ire.) Gresham Hotel. Winter Gardens
    Winter Gardens at the Gresham Hotel, Dublin.
Designed by Robert Atkinson.

Architects' journal 74:pls.
November 25, 1931

Dublin (Ire.) Plan
    A new town plan

Arch. and contr. reporter 97:35-36
and plates
Jan. 19, 1917

Dublin (Ire.) Royal College of Science
    ground floor plan

Arch. review 46:26
July, 1919

Dublin (Ire.) St. Patrick's cathedral Wheatley, Richard. Cathedrals and Abbeys of Great Britain and Ireland. New York: Harper and Bros., 1890. P.263-265	DuBois (PA) Presbyterian Church. Sketch by W. J. East, Arch. Inland Arch. 21: pl. fol. p 66 Je., 1893	Dubris see Dover (Eng.)
Dublin, Ire. University. Trinity college The Chapel, Trinity college, Dublin. Measured drawings by Wm. N. Spence, archt. Archts' journal 57: 528-31; 581-3 Mr 21; 28, 1923	DuBois (Pa.) Salvation Army Quarters Quarters for the Salvation Army, DuBois, Pa. Edward Kent, archt. Architectural review 8:n.s.3:pl.10 February, 1901	RYERSON LIBRARY. 705.1 Dubrovnik.Architecture A79 Khrabroff,Irina Villas and gardens of old Dubrovnik: garden of Palazzo Pozza,Palazzo bonda,Palazzo Gorgo. Arts and decoration 30: 52-54,86 January 1929
Dublin (Ire.) Views. 1916 Views after rebellion 1916 Arch. rev.(Lond.) 39:133-137 June, 1916	Duboy and Stroughton see New York (NY) Riverside Park, Soldiers & Sailors Monument	microfilm Dubuis, O. F., landscape architect Garfield park plans, Chicago, 1885, 1888. Roll 13, frames 43-4
720.5 Dublin (N.H.) Chapman (J.G.) house A67 The summer home of Mrs.J.G.Chapman, Dublin,N.H. Mauran,Russell and Garden,archts A Architectural review 8:n.s.7:141 December 1901	Duboy, Paul E. see also New York (N.Y.) Ansonia Hotel New York (N.Y.) Riverside Park, Soldiers and sailors monument	Dubuisson, J S.H.A.P.E. village St. Germain en Laye [plans] J. Dubuisson, archt. Forum No.3: 56-60 My 1955
Dublin (N.H.) Hitchcock (Hon. E.A.) Summer House Mauran Russell and Garden, Archts. Inland Archt. 46: pl.fol.p. 60 Dec, 1905	Dubrae see Dover (Eng.)	Dubuisson, René see Chicago (IL) World's Columbian Exposition 1893 Manufacturers & Liberal Arts Building Facade of French Court
720.5 Dublin (N.H.). Our lady of the snows A67 Our lady of the snows, Roman catholic chapel, Dublin, N.H. Frank A. Bourne, archt. Plan. Arch rev 12: 257 O '05	Dubreuil and Hummel see Maisons Alfort, Fr. Condorcet Schools	720.5 Dubuque, Edward W P39 Dubuque, E. W. Fresco painting and the frescoes in Christ Church, Cranbrook, Michigan. Painted by Edward W. Dubuque and Miss McEwen. Pencil points 10: 572-575, August 1929 575,577
Dubois, G. P. & Eschenmoser see Eschens (Switz.) Unipektin A. G.	Dubreuil, André, 1895- Groupe d'Habitations de l'Office du Department de la Seine, Groupe scolaire "Jules-Ferry", Groupe Scolaire "Condorcet", à Maisons-Alfort. Plans. A Dubreuil et R. Hummel, archts. Encyclopedie de l'architecture; constructions modernes. 12 vols. Paris: Albert Morancé, 1928-39. 10:pls.26-36	720.6 Dubuque. Architecture A51q List of buildings designed by F. J. Heer in Dubuque. American institute of architects-Quarterly October 1910 bulletin 11: 198-199

720.5
B95b
Dubuque(Iowa) Crane(D.C.) house
Residence for D. C. Crane.
Hyde, F. D., archt.

Building budget
3:4 in supp.
Ap 30, 1887

Dubuque, Iowa, Y.M.C.A. auditorium and gymnasium facade.

T. T. Carkeek, Archt.

Inland Archt.
Vol. 24, No. 3, pl.
Fol. p. 30
Oct. 1894

Dudley (Eng.) castle
Simpson, W.D.
The castles of Dudley and Ashby-de-la-Zouch. Plans

Archael Jour
96: 142-158
Ja 1940

Dubuque (IA) German Bank Bldg.
Williams and Spencer, archts.

West. Archt.
2: pl.fol.p. 24
Nov, 1903

Duc, Louis Joseph, 1802-1879
Tomb of Felix Duban, Paris. Duc, archt.
Triumphal column of July, 1830, Paris.

Building budget
5: pl. fol. p. 62
My 1889

Dudley (Eng.) Housing
Dudley

Architects' Jour. 48:
Suppl. pl.
Dec. 11, 1918

Dubuque, Ia. Municipal swimming pool
Krajewski, C.I.
Elegant - as anticipated. Dubuque, Iowa bath
house. C.I. Krajewski, archt. No plan.

Architectural concrete 4:30-31
No. 3 [1938]

Ducassi y Mendieta, Francisco, 1879-1953
In memoriam Francisco Ducassi y Mendieta;
ingeniero civil y arquitecto

Arquitectura Cuba
Vol. 22:45-46
Ja 1954

Dudley (Eng.) Housing
Silcock, H.
Housing accommodation in the county borough
of Dudley. [graphs]

Town planning rev 22: 146-162
No. F Jl 1951

720.5
A67r
Dubuque (Iowa.) Planning
Awakening of Dubuque.

Architectural record 24:74-75
July 1908

Burnham

Duchess of Bedford (ship)
Problems of a floating hotel: architectural
and decorative details in a great new liner;
duchess of Bedford.

Architect (Lond.)
120: 76-81, Jl 20, 1928

Dudley (Eng.) Public Buildings
City Halls, England. Dudley
Public buildings, Dudley, Staffordshire.
Harvey and Wicks, archts.

Architects journal 72:48-51
July 9, 1930

Dubuque (Ia.) planning
Nolen, John and Hartzog, J.R.
Dubuque plans anew.

City planning 8: front.,145-153
July, 1932

Duckworth, J.A.

see

Carbondale (IL) St. Rose of Lima cathedral

Dudley (Eng.) Public buildings.
Dudley public buildings.

Architect (Lond.) 121: 785-789
June 14, 1929

720.5
B95b
Dubuque(Iowa)Staples & Vibber building
Brick business block for Staples & Vibber.
Hyde, F. D., archt.

Building budget
3:4 in supp
Ap 30, 1887

Ryerson

Dudley castle, Scot.
Simpson, W. Douglas
Dudley castle: the Renaissance buildings

Archaeological Jour 101:
119-125
1944

Dudley (Eng.) zoo. Entrance.
Tecton, archts.

Raic jrl 15:144
Je 1938

Dubuque (Ia.) Wartburg Theological Seminary
Wartburg Seminary at Dubuque, Iowa.
Perkins, Fellows and Hamilton, archts.

Western architect 29:77-80, pl. 1-10
August, 1920

Dudley, Eng. Brewery Fields Estate,Competition
Proposed new school, Brewery Fields
Estate, Dudley. Scott and Clark, archts.

Builder 139: 344-347,349
August 29, 1930

720.52
A67
Dudley memorial competition
A criticism of the designs.

Architects journal 59:231-5
Jan. 30, 1924

720.52
A67   Dudley memorial competition

Architects journal 59:312-15
Feb. 13, 1924

705.942
W46   Dudok,Willem Marinus
       Wijdeveld,H.Th.
         Inleiding voor architect Dudok. (Work of M.
       Dudok.)

Wendingen 6: 3-24
No.8, 1924

Dübendorf (Switz) Airport

see

Dübendorf (Switz) Flugplats

---

ffo
750.6   Dudley,W   J   H
C55   Ingle Nook in stone; sketch by W.J.H.
        Dudley: Sketch Club of New York:Class problem

Chicago architectural club 7: 48
Annual exhibit 1894

705.94
W46   Dudok, Willem   Marinus
         Interiors by the architect W. M. Dudok

Wendingen 8:3-18
No. 2, 1927

Dübendorf (Switz) Flugplats. Werkstattgebäude.
  Die heisungsanlage im werkstallgebäude mit
grossflugzeughalle in Dübendorf bei Zürich.

Das werk 12:xvi-xviii
Mai 1925

Dudok, Willem Marinus

  see also

Hilversum (Neth). Raadhuis
  "   "   Architecture

The Hague (Neth.) house
  "   "   planning
Hilversum (Neth.) Baths

Dudok, Willem Marinus, 1884-
    1921 Hilversum - scuola "Dott. Bavinck"
  [plans]
    1926 Hilversum - Scuola "Fabritius" [plan]
  W. M. Dudok, archt.

Casabella
#245:13-14 N 1960

Düblin, Jacques
    Entwurf für ein wandbild in einem
  ruheraum auf den Hörnli-Gottesackers

Werk 28:108
April 1941

Dudok, Willem Marinus
    Architectural work

Maanblad voor beeldende
kunsten 4:116-122
April, 1927

Dudok, Willem Marinus
  Pluym, Willem van der
    Willem Marinus Dudok, architect

Maanblad voor beeldende
kunsten 4:163-182
May 1927

Dülfer, Martin, 1859-

Architektur dex XX
Jahrhunderts,
Sonderhefte.
[v. 1] no.4, entire issue
1910

705.942
W46   Dudok, Willem Marinus
         Boterenbrood, J.
           Architecture of Holland

Wendingen 9:3-24
No.1, 1928

720.52
W51   Dudok, Willem Marinus
         Work of W. Dudok.

Wasmuths monatshefte 8: 87-94
Heft 3-4, 1924

Duell, Randall

see

North Hollywood (Cal.) Kane (J.I.) house

Dudok, Willem Marinus, 1884-
  Snellebrand, J.A.
    Berlage, Dudok en "De Nederlanden van
1845" [plans] H.P.Berlage, archt., completed
by W.M.Dudok.

Forum
No.12: 446-449
Mr 1955

Dudok, Willem Marinus. Portraits

Maanblad voor beeldende
kunsten 4:115
April 1927

705.3   Düren, Ger. Katholische kirche
C55   Hoff,A.
          Die erweiterung der katholisch en kirche der
        provinzial-heil und pflegeanstalt in Düren durch
        landesoberbaurat Rühl.

Die Chrigtliche kunst 28: 161-165
March 1932

720.52
B93   Dudok, Willem Marinus
         Summerson, J. N.
           A cubist architect; some recent schools at
         Hilversum by W. M. Dudok.

Builder 139: 1038-1039
December 19, 1930

Dudovitch, Marcello
  Frenzel, H. K.
    M. Dudovich

Gebrauchsgraphik 6:22-29
June 1929

Dürig,

see

Basel (Switz.) Bürgerspital

Dürnstein, Austria. Church
Koller, M.
Dürnstein sur Dokumentation.
[illus.]

Österreichische Zeitschrift
für Kunst und Denkmalpflege
21, Heft 2: 124-130
1967

D10.8
D32
Düsseldorf. Architecture
Budde, Illa
The buildings by Wilhelm Kreis at the Gesolei exposition

Dekorative kunst 39:253-269
August, 1926

720.53
W31
Düsseldorf. Ausstellung Gesolei
Place of honor and the art museum,
Wilhelm Kreis, archt.

Wasmuths 10: 477-489
Heft 12, 1926

Dürr, Otto
Strandbad Tiefenbrunnen, Zürich. [plans & section] Josef Schütz, Otto Dürr, & Willy Roost, archts.

Bauen & Wohnen no.2
p.77-86 Konstruktionsblätter at end of issue
Ap 1955

D10.8
D32
Düsseldorf. Architecture
Budde, Illa
The Düsseldorf building and the Firemen's tower

Dekorative kunst 39:296-300
September, 1926

720.52
A67c
Düsseldorf. Ausstellung Gesolei
Robertson, Howard and F.R.Yerbury
Town planning for amenity: The Dusseldorf art center, Wilhelm Kreis, archt.

Architect (Lond.) 121: 556-558
April 26, 1929

720.53
M66
Dürrenberg(Ger.)Architecture
A large settlement - Dürrenberg baths.

Moderne bauformen 29: 294-303, adv.129-132
July 1930

720.54
A67v
Dusseldorf. Architecture
Halle à Dusseldorf,1926. (Hall at Dusseldorf,1926.) Max Taut,archt.

L'architecture vivante : pl.54
Winter 1927

Dusseldorf, Ger. Ausstellung "Schaffendes volk"
L'Exposition de Dusseldorf 1937. Peter Grund and Emil Fahrenkamp. archts.

L'Arch. d'aujourd'hui
9:26, O 1938

720.53
W51
Dürrenberg (Ger.) Housing
Guske
Die 1000 wohnungen der siedlung bad Dürrenberg. (The 1000 homes of the colony-resort, Dürrenberg.) Alexander Klein,archt. Plans.

Wasmuths monatshefte 13: 284-291
July 1929

720.54
A67
Dusseldorf. Architecture
The halls of science and art at the exposition of Dusseldorf. Wilhelm Kreis, archt.

L'Architecture 39: 315-322
October 10, 1926

Düsseldorf, Ger. Ausweichtheater
Das Dusseldorfer Ausweichtheater [Plans and section] Arthur Garard, archt.

Baumeister No. 7
51: 430-435
Jl 1954

Duesberg, A. C.
Villa, à Heusy-Verviers (Belgique). Plans.
A.-C. Duesberg, archt.
Villa, à Embourg-Liége (Belgique). Plans.
A.-C. Duesberg, archt.

Encyclopedie de l'architecture;
constructions modernes. 12 vols.
Paris: Albert Morancé, 1928-39.
6:pls. 12-14, pls. 15-17

Düsseldorf (Ger.) Art Center
Place of honor and the art museum.
Wilhelm Kreis, archt.

Wasmuths 10: 485-7
Heft 12, 1928

Düsseldorf (Ger.) Bank
Lud. Lony, archt. Rendering

West. Arch.
17: pls.fol.p. 68
Jul, 1911

720.53
W31
Düsseldorf. Architecture.
Architecture and academy. A sketch of the history of the Düsseldorf Academy.

Wasmuths monatshefte für baukunst. 4:195-259. pl.
Heft 7-8,1919.

720.52
A67c
Dusseldorf. Art centre
Robertson, Howard and Yerbury, F. R.
Town planning for amenity: The Dusseldorf art center, Wilhelm Kreis, archt.

Architect (Lond.) 121: 555-558;587-590
April 26; May 3; 1929

Düsseldorf, Ger. Evangelische kirche
Plans, elevations and studies for Evangelist Church at Dusseldorf. E. Fahrenkamp, archt.

Moderne bauformen 27:39-43
January, 1928

720.53
W31
Düsseldorf. Architecture
Archetekt Fritz Becker, Dusseldorf:
Wettbewerbnenturerf bürohaus Alleeplatz,
Düsseldorf, 1921; bürohaus Gelsenkerchen;
gebäude des einen forschungs, instituts,
Dusseldorf, 1921. Plan.

Wasmuths, 7:191-95
Heft 7-8, 1925

Dusseldorf.Ausstellung,1926

See also
Dusseldorf.Ausstellung Gesolei
Dusseldorf.Planetarium

720.52
A67c
Dusseldorf Exhibition, 1926
Sports hall at the Dusseldorf Exhibition, 1926. E. L. Wehner, archt.

Architect (Lond.) 117: 487
March 18, 1927

Düsseldorf, Ger. Exhibition 1937

see

Düsseldorf, Ger. Ausstellung "Schaffendes Volk"

720.53 W31 — Düsseldorf.Kunstakademie (Neue)
Hegeman,Werner; Leo Adler
Warnung vor "akademismus" und "klassizismus"
(Düsseldorf art museum,Germany. Karl Wach,archt.)

Wasmuths 11: 1,8,9
Heft 1, 1927

Düsseldorf (Ger.) Palast Hotel Bridenbacherhof.
The barber shop at the Palast Hotel, Dusseldorf,
Germany. E. Fahrenkamp, archt.
Bar in Palast Hotel.

Moderne bauformen 27:13, 19
January, 1928

720.53 W31 — Düsseldorf. Exposition. 1926
Düsseldorfer Kunst-Ausstellung 1926
Entwurf von Wilhelm Kreis

Wasmuth 9: Heft 8; 351
1925

Düsseldorf, Ger. Manna factory

see

Düsseldorf, Ger. Mannesmannröhren-werke AG factory

720.53 M68 — Dusseldorf. Phoenix, A. G.
New building for Phoenix, A. G. Karl
Wach, archt.

Moderne bauformen 27: 401-409
Heft 10, October 1928

720.53 W31 — Dusseldorf. Exhibition 1926
The buildings for the large exhibition
at Dusseldorf, 1926.

Wasmuths 10: 477-489
Heft 12, 1928

Düsseldorf, Ger. Mannesmannröhren-werke AG
factory
Werk- und fabrikationshallen der deutschen
Mannesmannröhren-werke AG, Dusseldorf, Hartwig
Dams, archt.

Bauen & Wohnen No. 1
P.22-23
F 1954

Düsseldorf, Ger. Phoenix-Rheinrohr AG bldg.
Competition
Wettbewerb hochhaus Phoenix-Rheinrohr AG,
Düsseldorf

Baumeister
53: 175-179
Mr 1956

Düsseldorf. Gesolei exposition   see
Düsseldorf. Ausstellung Gesolei

Düsseldorf (Ger.) Michel Dept. Store
Michel Department store, Dusseldorf. C.
Fahrenkamp and G. Shafer, archts.

Moderne bauformen 29: 449-452, adv.
October, 1930   209, 211

720.53 M68 — Düsseldorf.Planetarium
New observatory at Dusseldorf, Germany.
Wilhelm Kreis, archt.

Moderne bauformen 25: 275-279
Heft 8, 1926

Düsseldorf. Grossen ausstellungen für gesund-
heitspflege, soziale fürsorge und leibes-
übungen   see
Düsseldorf. Ausstellung Gesolei

Düsseldorf, Ger. Oberkassel kirche
Church, parsonage and community house in one
building. Rudolph W. Verheyen and Julius Stobbe,
archts.

Wasmuth's monarchefte fur baukunst
3:pl.62-70
Heft 2/3, 1916

720.54 A67 — Düsseldorf:Planetarium
New planetarium at Dusseldorf, Prof. Wilhelm Kreis, archt.

L'Architecture 39: 316-319
October 10, 1926

720.53 M68 — Düsseldorf (Ger.). Haus Rheinmetall. Leidig-
heim.
Das Leidigheim "Haus Rheinmetall".
Willy Krüger, archt. Plan.

Mod bauformen 19, heft 4: 121-128
Jl '20

Düsseldorf, Ger. Opernhaus.
Opernhaus Düsseldorf [plans and section]
Städtisches Hochbauamt Düsseldorf, Prof. Schulte-
Frohlinde, Prof. Paul Bonatz and Ernst Kuhn,
archts.

Baumeister
53: No.9: 609-619
Tafeln 65-68 at end of
issue.
S 1956

720.53 W31 — Düsseldorf:Planetarium
The buildings for the large exhibition at
Dusseldorf, 1926.

Wasmuths 10: 478-482,486
Heft 12, 1928

720.53 W31 — Dusseldorf.Kunstakademie
Klapheck,Dr.Richard
Baukunst und kunstakademie - Ein Umriss zur
geschichte der architekturabteilung der Kunst-
Akademie zu Düsseldorf. Zum hundertjährigen
jubiläum der akademie-neugründuun am 1.November
1919.

Wasmuth monatshefte für baukunst 4: 195.
Heft 7-8, 1919   258

Düsseldorf (Ger.) Palast Hotel
Hotel Palast at Dusseldorf. Emil Fahrenkamps,
archt.

Moderne bauformen 27:1-19
January, 1928

720.53 A67a — Düsseldorf.Planetarium
Dusseldorf planetarium. Wilhelm Kreis,
archt.

Architect (Lond.) 121: 583-589
May 3, 1929

720.52 **A67e** Düsseldorf.Planetarium A main entrance, the Planetarium, Düsseldorf, Germany. Wilhelm Kreis, archt. Architect (Lond.) 123: supp. January 24, 1930	Düsseldorf (Ger.) Rheinischen Metallwaren und Maschinenfabrik Settlement of the Rheinisnsen Metallwaren und Maschinenfabrik, Düsseldorf. Willy Krüger, architect. Mod. bauformen 19, heft 4;123-30. July, 1920.	Düttmann, Werner Interbau 1957. Objekt 23: volksbücherei mit jugendleseraum [plan & section] Werner Düttmann, archt. Architektur & Wohnform 65:169 Je 1957
Düsseldorf (Germany) Rathaus Zur Rathausfrage in Düsseldorf. E.L. Wehner, archt. Sketch and plan. Deutsche Bauzeitung 48:p.241 March 25, 1914	Düsseldorf, Ger. Schauspielhaus. Competition. 1960 Gedanken zum wettbewerb:Schauspielhaus Düsseldorf [plans & sections] Richard Neutra, archt.; Bernhard Pfau, archt. Arch & Wohnform 68:*17*-*20* My 1960	DuFais & Canfield The Genesee Valley Club House, Rochester, N.Y. DuFais & Canfield, archts. Inland architect v. 15 no. 5 pl. fol. p. 78 Je 1890
720.53 **W31** Düsseldorf, Rathaus Düsseldorfer Rathaus-Wettbewerb Wasmuth 9: Heft 8; 347-50 1925	Düsseldorf (Ger..) Theater Theater in Düsseldorf, designed by Dr. Wilhelm Kreis. Moderne bauformen:286-94 Band 25, 1926	**720.5** **A67r** Du Fais and Cass Gilbert The new building of the Union Club, Northeast corner of 5th Avenue and 51st Street, New York City. Du Fais and Cass Gilbert, archts. No plan. Architectural record 12:34: June 1902
Düsseldorf (Germany) Rathaus Klopheck-Strumpell, Dr. Anna Model of the city hall. Karl Wach, archt. Moderne bauformen 27: 399-400 Heft 10, 1928	Düsseldorf (Ger.) Zoological Garden Neue bauten im Düsseldorfer zoologischen garten. (New buildings in the Zoo of Düsseldorf. Reissinger, archt. Plans.) Der Baumeister 28: 189-193 May, 1930	Dufais, John see Chicago, (IL) World's Columbian Exposition Manufacturers Building, Tiffany and Gorham Ct.
Düsseldorf, Ger. Reichausstellung 1937 see Düsseldorf, Ger. Ausstellung "Schaffendes Volk"	Düsseldorf-Benrath. Ger. Volksschule Volksschule in Düsseldorf-Benrath. (Public school in Düsseldorf-Benrath.) Georg Schmalz, archt. Plans. Wasmuths monatshefte 15: 248-250 June, 1931 A	Du Fais, John See Du Fais & Canfield
Düsseldorf, Ger. Rhein Restaurant The Rhine restaurant, Düsseldorf. Wilhelm Kreis, archt. Architect (Lond.) 121:587, 590 May 3, 1929	Düttmann, Werner Altersheim in Berlin-Wedding [plans and col. illus.] Werner Düttmann, archt. Architektur and Wohnform 64: 58-65 no.2 D 1955	Dufayels' dept. store, Paris see Paris (Fr.) Palais de la nouveauté
Düsseldorf.Rheinhalle See Düsseldorf.Planetarium.	Düttmann, Werner Interbau 1957. Die neue Berliner Kongresshalle [plans & sections] Hugh A. Stubbins & Werner Düttmann, archts. Architektur & Wohnform 65:171 Je 1957	**720.5** **A67b** Duff, Thomas J New West side bank. Thomas J. Duff, archt No plans. Architecture & building 43: 176-178 January 1911

710.8
C855
Dufner, Edward
An interpreter of nature. Portrait, and col.pl. of his "Old house in sunlight."

Country life 38:41. Jun.1920

710.5
H84
Duggan, Daniel
Modern in the Argentine...designed by Daniel Duggan.

House and garden 72:34-35
August 1937

Duhring, Okie and Ziegler
Developing a suburban community. St. Martins, Pa.

American architect
112: 79-81, pl.2171
Ag 1, 1917

Dufour-Berte palace. Florence
See
Florence.Palazzo Guadagni.

Duhring, H.   Louis
see also
Philadelphia (Pa.)   -Gehringer (F.W.)
  house
Philadelphia (Pa.) St. Martin's Green houses

Duhring, Okie & Ziegler
A double house at St. Martin's, Pennsylvania. Plans.

American architect
102: 2 pls.fol.p.92
S 4, 1912

Dufournet, Paul
see
Le Bosquel (France)

Duhring, Louis Herman
see also
Rome (ITALY)   Arch of Titus Restoration

Duhring, Okie & Ziegler
Eberlein, H.D.
A group of stone houses at St. Martin's Green, Philadelphia. Plans

Arch for
28: 181-6, pl.46-64
My 1918

720.53
M68
Dufrène, Maurice
Some sketches by Maurice Dufrène.

Moderne bauformen 1:pls.33,68,81
1902

Duhring, Louis Herman
Receives Stewardson Memorial Scholarship 1897.

Inland Architect
29: 59
Jul, 1897

720.5
B84
Duhring, Okie and Ziegler
House at Bryn Mawr, Pennsylvania. Duhring, Okie & Ziegler. archts., plans.

Brickbuilder 19: pls.87-89 (fol.178)
July 1910

Dufresne, Adrien
see
Beauport (Can.) St. Therese church

Duhring, Okie & Ziegler
see also

Allen Lane (PA)   Residence
Bryn Mawr (PA)   Blabon, Walter D., Stable
Philadelphia (PA)   Canby (W. Marriott) Residence
    "   "   Baker, F., Jr., House
    "   "   Inasmuch Mission
    "   "   Residence
    "   "   Scott, R.W., House
    "   "   Smith, J.L., House

(See Card 2)

720.5
A51
Duhring, Okie and Ziegler
A house at Germantown, Philadelphia, Pennsylvania. Duhring, Okie and Ziegler, archts. Plans.

American architect 102: pls.fol.p.90
September 4,1912

Dugand, Roberto
See
Noguera & Dugani, Ltda

Duhring, Okie & Ziegler   (Card 2)
see also

Philadelphia (PA) Wentz, C.R., House
St. Martins (PA)   Williams, I.J., House
Valley Forge (PA) Knox, Reed, House

720.5
A67r
Duhring, Okie and Ziegler
The Pennsylvania type: a logical development. Work of Duhring, Okie and Ziegler,archts

Architectural record 30:322-336
October 1911

Dugdale,Michael, 1905-
See
Tecton, architects

Duhring, Okie & Ziegler
Colonial houses near Philadelphia. Plans.

House and garden
5: 22-26
Ja 1904

720.5
A67r
Duhring,Okie and Ziegler
Some domestic architecture by Duhring,Okie and Ziegler,archts. - in Pennsylvania.

Architectural record 19:173,175-178
February 1906

V 4

720.5
A67r

Duhring, Okie and Ziegler
Some recent suburban houses. Their planning, designing and interior decoration:
work of Duhring, Okie and Ziegler, plans;
Walter Burly Griffin, plans; Robert C.Coit,
plans; Oswald C.Hering.

Architectural record 23:478-485
June 1908

Duiker, W

see also

Amsterdam (Neth.) Volkschule

Duke house

See

New York. Duke house

Duhring, Okie and Ziegler
A studio workshop. Duhring, Okie and
Ziegler, archts.

Arts and decoration
5:361-3
Jl 1915

Duintjer, H   F
"Buitenwoel" te Veendam [plan & section]
M. F. Duintjer, archt.

Forum
13:138-42 Ap 1958

Duke university

see

Durham (N.C.) Duke university

Duiffobrucart, Gaspar, see
Duiffoprugcar, Gaspar

Duintjer, M.F.
Gebouwen voor het Gem. Energiebedrijf en het
Vervoerbedrijf Arnhem. [plans] M.F.Duintjer,
archt.

Forum 9:133-135
Mr 1954

Dukenfield, Eng. Senior Girl's School
Dukenfield Senior Girls School.
Percy Howard, archt.

Architect (Lond.) 133: 251-252
February 24, 1933

Duiffoprugcar, Gaspar
B.,D.J.
Een viola da gamba, van Gaspar Duiffobrou-
cart

Hague. Dienst voor kunsten en
wetenschappen. Mededeelingen
4,pt.2:131-137
1937

Duisburg, Ger.Bahnhofsvorplatz
Adler, Leo
Wettbewerb zur bebauung des bahnhofsvor-
platzes in Duisburg. (Competition for building
up the railway station plaza in Duisburg.)
Plans by Joseph Fredemann,Paul Bonatz, F.E.
Scholer, H. Mertins,E.Fahrenkamp and others.

Städtebau 22: 81-85
June 1927

The Dukeries (area), England
Christian, Roy
Changes in the Dukeries. [illus]

Country Life
V. 137: 1580-1582
Je 24, 1965

720.5
A67f

Duiker and Bijvoet
Horner, E. A.
Modern architecture in Holland.

Architectural forum 50: 205-212
February 1929

Duisburg, Ger. Duisburger hof
Hofmann, Herbert
Hotelzimmer im geiste unserer zeit. Duisburger
Hof, Duisburg [plans]

Arch & wohnform
62:136-141
Ap 1954

Duke's farm, Somerville, N.J.

see

Somerville (N.J.) "Duke's farm"

Duiker, J.

see also

Hilversum (Neth.) Hotel Gooiland

Duisburg Ger. Einschornsteinsiedlung
Die "Einschornsteinsiedlung" bei Duisburg. [The "Einschornstein" settlement near
Duisburg.] No chimney. Kramer and Kremer,
archts.

Der Baumeister 28: 153-162,pls.21-
April 1930   25

720.5
A67a

Dulles Allen J. H.
The polychrome grilles of the Singing Tower.

Architecture 59: col.pl. 205
April 1929

Duiker, Johannes, 1890-1935
1930 Amsterdam, Olandia - Scuola all'
aria aperta [plan & section] J. Duiker, archt.

Casabella
#245:18 N 1960

Duisburg, Ger. Housing

see

Duisburg (Ger.) Einschorsteinsiedlung

Duluth (MN) Academy for the Sisters of St. Benedict.
Sketch by G. A. Tenbush, Arch.

Inland Arch. 21:
pl. fol. p 78
Jl., 1893

Duluth. Alworth Building
   Alworth building, Duluth, Minn. 1909.
D.H. Burnham and Co., archts.
 	
        Graham, Anderson, Probst and White.
        Works. 2 vols. London: B.T. Batsford,
        1933. v.2:368.
	Duluth (MN) Congdon Residence
	   Oak Hall carvings by Wm. A. French & Co.
	
	        West. Arch.
	        12: pl.fol.p. 20
	        Aug. 1908
		Duluth (MN) Lansdale Office Bldg.
		   Palmer, Hall & Hunt, archs.
		
		        Inland Arch.
		        25: adv. trade supp.
		        #6, July 1895

Duluth (MN) Black (D.R.) Residence
 	
   Photo
Louis Lockwood, archt.
 	
        West. Archt.
        2: pl.fol.p. 20
        Jun, 1903
	Duluth, Minn. Cotton, J.B., house
	   Residence of J.B. Cotton, Duluth, Minnesota
	[plans] Kees and Colburn, archts.
	
	        Western Arch't
	        13: 3 pls. fol. p.12
	        Jan. 1909
		Duluth (MN) Lansdale Office Bldg.
		   Contract taken by Pioneer Fireproof
		Construction Co., Chicago.
		
		        Inland Arch.
		        26: (xvii) adv. trade supp.
		        #3, 1896

Duluth. (MN) Brewer (Frank H.) Residence
   photo
Palmer Hall and Hunt archts.
 	
        West. Archt.
        2: pl.fol.p. 22
        Mar, 1903
	Duluth (MN) Crosby (Geo. H.) Residence
	   Rendering I. Vernon Hill, Archt.
	
	        West. Archt.
	        1: pls.fol.p. VIII
	        Oct, 1902
		Duluth (MN) Loeb (Mr. L.S.) Residence
		   photo.
		
		        West. Archt.
		        2: pl.fol.p. 22
		        Mar, 1903

Duluth (MN) Cathedral of the Sacred Heart.
   G.A. Tenbusch, Arch.
 	
        Inland Arch. 21:
        pl. fol. p 42
        Ap., 1893
	Duluth (Minn.) Hartman (A.W.) house
	   House of A.W. Hartman, Duluth, Minn.
	Frederick W. Perkins, archt. Plans.
	
	        Architectural record 40:568
	        December 1916
		Duluth (MN) Lutes (Chas. H.) Residence
		   photo.
		Palmer, Hall and Hunt, archts.
		
		        West. Archt.
		        2: pl.fol.p. 24
		        Nov, 1903

720.5
B97b   Duluth, Chamber of Commerce
      Chamber of Commerce, Duluth, Minnesota.
   Henry Raeder, archt.
 	
   A   Building budget 5: 1.fol.p.6
        January 31, 1899
	Duluth (MN) Hunter (James) Residence
	   photo. Charles McMillan Archt.
	
	        West. Arch.
	        1: pl.fol.p. 22
	        Dec, 1902
		Duluth (MN) Olcott (W.J.) Residence.
		   Bray & Nystrom, Arch.
		
		        West. Arch.
		        12: pl.fol.p. 78
		        Dec.1908

720.5
I56   Duluth, Commercial bank and office building
      Sketch of Commercial bank and office
   building for George Spencer and Company.
   Duluth, Minn. W.L.B. Jenney, archt.
 	
   A   Inland architect 7:23,pl.fol.20
        March 1886
	Duluth (MN) Jefferson Public School
	   Rendering, Radcliffe and Willoughby, archt.
	
	        West. archt.
	        1: pl.fol.p. 20
	        Nov, 1902
		720.5
		B97b Duluth, Palladio building
		      The Palladio, office building, Duluth,
		   Minnesota. Henry Raeder, archt.
		
		   A Building budget 5: pl.fol.p.6
		        January 31, 1899

Duluth (MN) Commercial Club Building
   Rendering, John R. de Waard, archt.
 	
        West. Archt.
        1: pl.fol.p. VIII
        Oct, 1902
	Duluth (Minn.) Kitchi Gammi Club
	   Kitchi Gammi club, Duluth, Minn. Cram,
	Goodhue and Ferguson, archts.
	
	        Architectural forum 26: pl.37-39 fol.p.80
	        March 1917
		Duluth (MN) Patrick (F.A.) and Co. Wholesale
		     Building
		   Rendering, Palmer, Hall, and Hunt, archts.
		
		        West. Archt.
		        1: pl.fol.p. VIII
		        Oct, 1902

Duluth (MN) Patrick (F.A.) Residence
Photo., I.V. Hill, archt.

West. Archt.
2: pl.fol.p. 22
Feb, 1903

790.5
B93b
Duluth, Spalding hotel
Design of Spalding Hotel, Duluth, Minn.
J.J.Egan, archt. Chicago.

A
Building budget 3: pl.fol.p.100
August 31, 1887

Dulverton (Eng.) Brushford Church Chapel
Memorial Chapel, Brushford Church, Dulverton;
Sir Edwin L. Lutyens, archt.

Builder 130: pls.,
January 1, 1926

790.1.
A67c
Duluth(Minn.)Pilgrim congregational church
Pilgrim congregational church, Duluth,
Minn. German and Jensen, archts. Plans.
Interior.

A
Architectural forum 29: pl.58-59
October 1918

Duluth (MN) Superior and Lake, Office Bldg.
Rendering, Palmer, Hall and Hunt, archts.

West. Archt.
1: pl.fol.p. 22
Nov, 1902

Dulwich college picture gallery, London
[for arch. of], see
London, Eng. Dulwich college picture gallery

Duluth (MN) Pressentin (Warner)
Residence
Bray & Nystrom

West Arch 10:
pls. fol. p. 108
Oct. 1907

Duluth (MN) Suspended Car Ferry

West. Archt.
3: p. 21 and pl.fol.p. XV
Feb, 1904

Dulwich (Eng.) College. Memorial Library
Memorial Library, Dulwich College

Builder 83: 606 and pl
D 27, 1902

Duluth (MN) Residence
Charles W.Leavitt, Landscape Arch.
Clarence H. Johnston, Arch. Grounds Plan.

West. Archt.
15: 46-8
pls. fol.p. 48
April 1910

Duluth (MN) Tischer Creek Bridge

West. Archt.
17: 76
Aug, 1911

Dulwich gallery, London
see
London, Eng. Dulwich college picture gallery

Duluth, (MN) St.Louis County Courthouse.
St.Louis County Courthouse, Duluth, MN.
D.H. Burnham & Co., Archs.

West. Arch.
15: 10, pls. fol. p.12
Jan, 1910

Duluth (MN) Washburn (J.L.) Barn& Garage
Frank L. Young & Co., Arch. Plans.

West. Arch.
11: pl.fol.p. 42
April 1908

Dumas, F. and D. Honegger
see also
Fribourg (Switz.) Université
Fribourg (Switz.) Cité Paroissiale [project]

Duluth. St. Louis County Courthouse
St. Louis County courthouse, Duluth, Minn.1909.
D.H. Burnham and Co.,archts.

Graham, Anderson, Probst and White.
Works. 2 vols. London: B.T. Batsford,
1933. v.1:110-111

Duluth (MN) Wolvin Building
Rendering
Palmer, Hall and Hunter, Archts.

West. Arch.
1: pl.fol.p. VIII
Oct, 1902

705.944
K48
Dumas, F and D. Honegger
Posca, Francois
Projet d' hotel particulier. Plan, ele-
vation, section.

Das werk 32: 153-155
My '45

Duluth (Minn) Soldiers' and Sailors' Monument
Sculpture
"Patriotism Guarding the Flag"
Paul Bartlett, Sculptor.

West. Archt.
29: 47, pl. 1-2
May, 1920

Duluth, (MN) Y.M.C.A. Bldg.
Y.M.C.A. Bldg., Duluth, MN. German & Lignell,
Archs. Plans.

West. Arch.
15: pl.fol.p. 12
Jan, 1910

Dumbarton Oaks, Washington, D.C.
see
Washington, D.C. Dumbarton Oaks

710.5
M64
Peyser, E.R.
Giving the house a lift: dumbwaiters, electric and otherwise.

House & Garden 47:74 ,106
June 1925

Dumont television center, New York (city)

see

New York (city) Dumont television center

Dunblane, Scot. Keir chapel
Barman, Christian
A new mosaic decoration: Chapel at Keir,
Dunblane, Scotland. Decorations by Boris Anrep.

Architects' Journal 67: 252-254
February 15, 1928

Dumez company

see

Société Dumez

Dumsky, Hans
Parkhaus in Nürnberg; Vorentwurf [plans]
Gerd Wiegand & Hans Dumsky, archts

Architektur & Wohnform
69: 47-9, F 1961

Duncan, Herman J.

see

Cameron Parish (La.) Court house

Dumfried (Scot) Townhall
Dumfries town hall competition.

Architects' Journal 71: 137
January 15, 1930

Dun building, New York

see

New York (city) Dun building

Duncan, Hugh, house. Cobden, Ill.

see

Cobden, Ill. Hugh Duncan house

Dumfries, Frederick, 1871-1941
Obituary

RAIC jour 18: 209
D 1941

Dun, R G   and co. office building, New York

see

New York (city) Dun building

Duncan, J.   K

see

New York (N.Y.) Nathan Straus pasteurized milk
laboratory

DuMond, F. V.
see also

Lake Forest (IL)   Residence Murals

Dun, Robert G. house, Narragansett Pier

see

Narragansett (R.I.) pier. Dun (Robert G.) house

Duncan (J.S.) house, Toronto, Ont.

see

Toronto (Ont.) Duncan (J.S.) house

DuMond, F.V.
Murals in residence at Lake Forest, IL

West. Arch.
12: pl.fol.p. 20
Aug. 1908

Dunbar, William McLeish, 1895? - 1951

see

Ithaca (N.Y.) Phi Delta Theta fraternity
Burlington, Vt. Phi Delta Theta house

Duncan, John

see

Chicago (Ill.) Groveland Apartment Bldg.
Chicago (Ill.) Temple Court bldg.

Dumont (N.J.) Camp Merritt inn
Camp Merritt inn, N.J. Edward L. Tilton
& Alfred Morton Githeus archts. Plan.

Architecture 38: 345, pl.196-198
D'18

Dunbarton, N.H. Stark homestead
Stark homestead, Dunbarton, N.H. Measured &
drawn by Murray P. Corse. Date 1785.

Architecture 47: pl.62-4 & p.123
April 1923

Duncan, John H.

see

New York (NY)   Clyde's Cafe
  "   "   Knox Building

710.5
H84
Duncan, Perry M
  Residence in Westchester County, N.Y.
Perry M. Duncan, archt. Plans. First prize
winner in class I of the House and garden's
architects' competition, 1937.

House and garden 72:16-17
September 1937 (Sect.2)

Dundee (Scot.) Civic center
  Plan for Dundee

Arch & bldrs. Jour. 43:pl. for
Apr. 26, 1916

Dundee, Scotland, **Secondary School**
  Dundee Secondary school competition
Messrs. Thoms & Willie, archts.

Builder 129: 392-95
Sept. 11, 1925

MICROFILM
Dundee (Ill.) Magnuson (Dr. Paul B.) House
  1933.
David Adler, archt. plans.

Roll 34, frames 294-304

Dundee (Scot.) Housing
  Housing and town planning, Dundee,
Scotland.

Builder 112:375-376
May 18, 1917

Dundee (Scot) Secondary school
  Dundee secondary school. Gall & Hay
archts.
  Alfred Bossom Studentship:winning design,
Miss Doris Lewis, archt.

Builder 130: pls., 151-2
January 22, 1926

Dundee (Scot.) Caird hall
  The Caird Hall, Dundee. James Thomson,
city architect

Architects Journal 58:638-642
Oct. 31, 1923

Dundee (Scot) library
  Dundee

Builder 108: pl. for
June 25, 1915

Dundee (Scot) Townhall
  The old town house, Dundee, Scotland. The
Elder Adam, archt. (1734). Plan.

Builder 142: 213
January 29, 1932

Dundee (Scot) Caird hall
  Caird Memorial Hall, Dundee. J.Thomson,
architect

Builder 125:684 & 5 pls.
Nov. 2, 1923

Dundee (Scot) Planning
  City plans of Dundee.

Architect 101: 164-165
March 14, 1919

Dundrum (Ire.) Carnegie free library
  Carnegie Free Library, Dundrum, Ireland.

Architect's Jour.53-p.657
May 25, 1921

720.52
A67
Dundee. (Scot.) Caird hall
  Caird Hall, Dundee. James Thomson, city
architect

Architects Journal 58:716-24
Nov. 14, 1923

Dundee. Scot. School
  Schools, England
The Dundee School competition
The assessor's report

Arch.Journal 60:586-589
Oct. 15, 1924

Dunedin (FL) Club House
  Patton & Fisher, Archs.

Inland Arch. 20:
pl. fol. p 10
Ag., 1892

720.52
A67c
Dundee. (Scot.) Caird Hall
  The Caird Hall, Dundee.Jas. Thomson,arch.

Architect 110:319-20
Nov. 16, 1923

Dundee (Scot.) School.Competition
  Dundee school competition
design by Maclaren,Soutar & Salmond

Builder 127:595-596 and plates
Oct. 17, 1924

Dunedin (N.Zeal.) Cathedral
  Dunedin Cathedral,New Zealand.
E. W. Sedding and B. Stallybrass, archts.
No plan.

Builder 120: 316,pl.
March 11, 1921

Dundee (Scot) Civic Center
James Thomson; Archt.

Builder
108:585,pl.fol..p.588
June 25, 1915

Dundee (Scot.) Schools
  New school, Blackness road, Dundee.
Maclaren, Soutar, & Salmond, archts.

Architects' Jour. 62:974-78
Dec. 30, 1925

Dunes   see

Sand dunes

720.52
A87e
Dunfermline abbey
    Dunfermline abbey, text and development
of plan.

                    Arch & contr rep 95:256-7
                    Ap 7 '15

708.1
P69m
Dunfermline (Scot.) Carnegie, (Andrew)
                        memorial building
Shearer, James
    The Andrew Carnegie birthplace memorial
building. James Shearer, archt.

                    Pittsburg. Carnegie mag
                    2:99-105
                    D '28

Dunfermline (Scot.) Library.
    Extension of the Dunfermline Central
Library, James Shearer, architect.Plan.

                Architects' Journal 57:723-30
                April 25, 1923

Dunham, C. A.
    see also
Algona (Ia.)   Cowles (Gardner) house
Burlington (Ia.)Choate (H.) store
Burlington,(Ia.)Congregational church (1886)
Burlington,(Ia.)McFarland (W.C.) house
Burlington,(Ia.)Theatre (project), 1886.
Fort Madison(Ia.)Altee(S & J.C.) apt.houses
                    and office bldg.
Fort Madison(Ia.)Case (Mrs.) double house
Huron (S.Dak.)National bank of Dakota
Monmouth (Ia.) U.P. church

Dunham, Charles A   , 1830-1909
    Obituary.

                    Western Arch't
                    13: 36
                    Mar. 1909

Dunham, Charles B.
    see
Watertown (Mass.) First Baptist church
Arlington (Mass.) First Baptist church

Duni theatre, Matera (It.)
    see
Matera (It.) Cinema Duni

Dunkel, W.
    see
Country houses, Switzerland. Solothurn

Dunkerly, F. B.
    see
Windermere (Eng.) "Cragwood"

Dunkerque, Fr. Architecture
Laprode, Albert
    L'Architecture dans nos provinces. L'oeuvre
de Jean Morel, à Dunkerque (Architecture in our
provinces: the work of Jean Morel, at Dunkerque).

                L'Architecture 49:15-26
                January 1936

Dunkirk, Fr.
    see
Dunkerque, Fr.

720.5
A51
Dunkirk (N.Y.) Railroad station
    Passenger station at Dunkirk, N.Y.
Price and McLanahan, archts.

                Am. arch 100: pl. fol. 137
                O 4, '11

Dunlap, Francis E.
    Member of firm:
    Holabird and Roche

Dunlap, Francis E.
    Open Office in Chicago.

                West. Archt.
                31: 109
                Sept, 1922

Dunn and Copper
    see also
Shaker Heights (O.) Rogers (Nelson) house
 "   "   "   Driver (J.R.) house
Kirtland Hills Village (O.) Wick (K.B.) Gate
    lodge

710.5
H84
Dunn and Copper
    Pennsylvania architecture in old Ohio
residence. Dunn and Copper, archts.

                House and garden 58: 106-107
                September 1930

Dunn and Copper
    Sport center - delightful grouping on
estate near Cleveland,Ohio. Dunn and
Copper, archts.

                Country life (U.S.) 63: 40-41
                April 1933

710.5
H84
Dunn and Copper
    Two small residences in brick.

                House and garden 58: 88-89
                December 1930

Dunn and Watson
    see
London (Eng.) British bank of South America
Maidenhead (Eng.) Schottesbrooke Park

Dunn, H. H.
    New county hall at Cambridge. Designed
by H.H.Dunn.

                Architects' Journal 76: 397-400
                September 28, 1932

Dunn, J.F.
    Watercolor sketch for hotel & surroundings near
Santa Cruz, CA.

                West. Arch.
                9: 77
                July 1906

Dunn, James Bow, 1861-1930

see also

Hawick (Scot.) war memorial
Lockerbie (Scot.) war memorial
War memorials, Scotland

Dunning hospital, Chicago

see

Chicago (Ill.) state hospital

Dunning, Nelson Max
Winner of Traveling Scholarship Competition,
Chicago Architectural Club, 1901.

Inland Architect
37: 24
Apr, 1901

720.52 Dunn, James Bow   1861-1930
B95   James Bow Dunn obituary.

Builder 139: 334
August 29, 1930

Dunning, N. Max 1873-1945

see also

Capra ola (IT)   Garden Termination-Sketch
Chicago (IL)   American Book Company
   "   "   American Furniture Mart
Evanston (IL)   Pruitt (A.J.) House
Glencoe (IL)   House
Highland Park (IL)   Mavor (M.R.)
Kenilworth (IL)   Thayer (F.C.) house
Lake Forest (IL)   Thorne (R.J.) House

Dunning, N.Max 1873-1945
The work of N.Max Dunning: Building for
American book Co.,Kenosha Cemetery associa-
tion, Kenosha hospital, Dixon Home Telephone
Co., Dixon National bank building,Stromberg
motor device building.

American architect 119: 111-116,
                       pl.fol. p.194
February 2; 16; 1921

Dunn, James B
Proposed Scottish national war memorial,
design by J.B. Dunn.

Builder 117: pl for
D 19, 1919

Dunning, N. Max, 1873-1945
Dunning steps up.

Illinois society of architects
monthly bulletin.
2:1
April 1918

Dunnotar castle, Kincardineshire
Simpson, W.D.
Development of Dunnottar castle. Plan.

Archaeological Journal 98:87-98
1941   pl.1-4

720.52 Dunn,John 1850-1932
B95   Obituary

Builder 142: 339
February 19,1932

Dunning, N. Max.
French building sketch.

Inland Archt.
Vol. 26, No. 5, pl.
   Fol. p. 54
Dec. 1895

Dunrobin castle, Scot.
Ceiling of Dunrobin castle,Sutherland

London Country Life 50: 321
Sept. 10, 1921

Dunn, W.
Ferro - Concrete

Inland Architect
44: 31-2
Nov, 1904

Dunning, N. Max, 1873-1945
Obituary

Illinois society of
architects bulletin
29-30:8
Jn.-Jl., 1945

Dunstable (Eng.) Chiltern road estate
Borough of Dunstable,Chiltern Road estate.
T. Alwyn Lloyd,archt. Layout.

Builder 145: 778,784
November 17, 1933

Dunn, W   N

see

London, Eng. Streatham cemetery. Chapel

Dunning, Nelson Max
Photo-President of Architectural League
of America (1905).

Inland Architect
45: 8 page supp. foll.
Apr, 1905 issue

Dunstable Eng. Northfields School
Northfields school, Dunstable.
O.P. Milne, archt. Plans.

Architect and building news 148:288-
December 4, 1936   290

Dunnell, W. B.

see

Minneapolis (MN)   Douglas School

Dunning, N. Max
Summary of the Accomplishment of the Post - War
Committee.

West. Archt.
29: 46-7
May, 1920

Dunton, William Herbert
F. Warner Robinson
Dunton-- Westerner

American magazine of art 15:501-508
Oct. 1924

Dunwoodie (N.Y.) Catholic seminary
Catholic seminary, Dunwoodie, N.Y.
William Schnickel & Compnay, architects.

Architectural record 1:344
January-March 1892

---

du Pont (Alfred I.) Carillon Tower

see

Nemours, Del. Carillon Tower

Dupuy, Carlos
Biblioteca Nacional de Caracas [plans]
Julian Ferris, Carlos Dupuy & Jaime Hoyos, archts.

Proa
#128:11-13 Jl 1959

Dupee (H.M.) house. Chicago, Ill.

see

Chicago, Ill. Dupee (H.M.) house

Dupont, Alfred I., house

see

Nemours, Del.

Duque, Gustavo Galvan

see

Galvan Duque, Gustavo

Dupin, M.

see

Hussein-Dey (Alg.) Marché municipal

Du Pont, Alfred V.

See

Massean and DuPont

720.5
AG7r   Duquesne
            The "Prix de Rome", 1897(first prize), M.
            Duquesne.

Architectural record 7:170
October-December 1897

Duplex apartments

See

Apartments.Duplex

Dupont and Guilbert
Detail of a hotel de ville. Dupont & Guilbert,
archts.

Amer archt & bldg news 55: pl fol
104
Mr 27, 1897

Duquesne, M. Eugene

Appointed to Harvard Univ. faculty

West. Archt.
17: 16 Feb 1911
: 51 June 1911

720.8
B58   Duplex houses
            Design of a duplex house.

B.A.I.D. 11: 19-26
December 1934

Duprat, Alfred
Aérogare a Bordeaux-Mérignac (France). Plans.
Alfred Duprat, archt.

Encyclopedie de l'architecture;
Constructions modernes. 12 vols.
Paris: Albert Morancé, 1928-39.
10:pls. 12-13

Duquesne, (PA)
Carnegie Library. Music Hall, Clubhouse
Alden & Harlow, Arch.

Inland Arch.
43: pls. fol. p. 32
June 1904

Duplex houses
Zweifamilienhaus. Plan. Hartwig Lensch,
archt.

Deutsche baukunst
13:195
My 10, 1914

Dupré, Pierre

see

Le Bosquel (France)

Du Quoin (Ill.) high school
Du Quoin School, Du Quoin, Ill. Charles
K. Illsley, archt.

Inland architect
20, no. 4
pl. fol. p. 46
N 1892

Duplex houses. Competition
Competition, Portland Cement association
for duplex houses. Awards.

Architect (N.Y.)10: 454-456
July 1928

Dupuis, Jacques
Habitation d'un collectionneur à Uccle,
Belgique [plan] Jacques Dupuis, archt.

Aujourd'hui
Vol.1:28-29
no. 5
N 1955

Durand, A. H. and Allison W.

see

London (Eng.) Ambassador club

Durand, Asher Brown, 1796-1886 Cowdrey, Bartlett Asher Brown Durand, 1796-1886. [illus] Panorama V. 2, no. 2: [15]-24 O.1946	Durer, H. G. see Toronto, Ont. Creed's storage vaults ltd.	Durham (Eng.) Castle Tipping, H. Avray Durham castle in danger. Country Life (Lond.) 63: 396-399 March 24, 1928
Durand, George F d. 1889 Death of architect George F. Durand. Inland architect v. 14 no. 8: 87 Ja 1890	Duret, Jean, 1926- "Eisstadion in Genf" entwurf 1955, gebaut 1957-58 [plans & sections] A. Cingria, F. Maurice & J. Duret, archts. Bauen & Wohnen 14:250-54 Jl 1960 Konstruktionsblätter at end of issue	Durham, (Eng.) Cathedral Durham Cathedral, England. Text and illustrations. King, Richard John. Handbook to the Cathedrals of England. 6 vols. London: J. Murray, 1861-69. vol. 6 p. 229
Durant (Miss.) Yazoo and Mississippi Valley R.R. Station Frank D. Chase Archt . West. Archt. 23: 45 May, 1916	Durham Abbey, Eng. see Durham (Eng.) cathedral	Durham (Eng.) cathedral Fowler, J.T. Account of the excavations made on the site of the chapter-house of Durham cathedral in 1874. Fragments of vestments, crosiers found. Plan of chapter-house. Archaeologia 45: 385-404 1880
Duraug, E. F. see Philadelphia (Pa.) Church of Our Lady of Mercy	710.5 H34 Durham and Irvine Price, Llewellyn A French farmhouse set on a Quaker country hillside. Designed by Walter Durham of Durham and Irvine, archts. House & garden 59:72-73, 92 Ja '31	Durham (Eng.) Cathedral Exterior, interior views. Allen, Fred Hovey. Great Cathedrals of the World. 2 vols. Boston: Haskell and Post, c1886 -88. 4 pls.fol.p.184. Pl.prec.p.93.
Durban [Eng.] War Memorial Upper part of decoration for war memorial; Durban. Harold and Phoebe Stabler,sculptors. Architect (Eng.) 117:151 January 21, 1927	720.52 A67c Durham castle Durham Castle. Arch & con rep 71: 417-419 Je 24 '04	Durham (Eng.) Cathedral London. Architectural association Sketchbook.Ser. 3, v. 1. pl. 5-7 1894-95
Durbar manufacturing co. Minneapolis, see Minneapolis, Minn. Durbar manufacturing company.	Durham (Eng.) Barnard castle. Butter market The butter market, Barnard Castle, Durham. Field, Horace and Michael Bunney. English domestic architecture of the 17th and 18th centuries. London: G. Bell and Sons, 1905. p.48, pl 50.	Durham (Eng.) cathedral Leaves from the sketch-book of A.E. Newcombe. International studio 35: 197-203 S 1908
Durden, James F Habitation, Pasadena, California [plan] James Durden, archt. Aujourd'hui 2:77 Ap.1957	Durham Eng. Castle Durham Castle. Builder 119:311-14 & pl. Sept. 17, 1920	Durham Cathedral Curtis, Adelaide Durham cathedral, England. Architectural review 17:13-16 February 1910

Durham (Eng.) Cathedral
Brock, A.C.
Durham Cathedral.

Country life(Lond.) 42: 208-212;233-236
September 1; 8, 1917

Durham (Eng) cathedral. Cloister
Hope, W. H. St. John
Recent discoveries in the cloister of
Durham Abbey with an introduction by Canon
J. T. Fowler

Archaeologia
58, pt.2:437-457
1903

Durham light infantry memorial chapel

see

Durham, (Eng.)cathedral. Durham light infantry
memorial chapel

Durham (Eng.) Cathedral
Sedding, E.H.
Durham Cathedral. Plan.

Builder 117: 288-290
September 19, 1919

Durham (Eng.) Cathedral
Durham Cathedral font.

Architect 143:234
August 30, 1935

Durham (N.C.) Duke University
Duke university, former Trinity College,
Durham, North Carolina. Horace Trumbauer,
archt.

Through the ages 6: 14-17
January 1929

Durham (Eng.) Cathedral
Ely, Durham and ST. Bartholomew's.
Photographs.

A.I.A. Journal 12:501,507,510-512
December 1924

Durham (Eng.) Finchale Abbey hotel
Finchale Abbey hotel, Durham.
Percy L. Browne & Son, arch. Plans.

Architect(Lond.)149:364-365
March 19, 1937

Durham (N.C.) Duke university
Lee, A.C.
The use of marble in the buildings of
Duke University. Horace Trumbauer, archt.

Through the ages 9: 23-24
February 1932

Durham cathedral
Northumbria

Builder 129: 51-59
July 10, 1925

Durham (Eng.) school. War memorial chapel
Durham School chapel. Walter H.Brierley,
architect

Architects Journal 58:541-544
Oct. 10, 1923

Durham (N.C.) Duke university. Library
Breedlove, J.P.
New Duke University library building.
Horace Trumbauer, archt.

Library Journal 56: 691-693
September 1, 1931

Durham (Eng.) Cathedral
Gostling, F.M.
The cathedral where women were barred:
Durham Cathedral.

Travel 47:10-13,54
May 1926

Durham (Eng.)school. War memorial chapel.
Durham school war memorial chapel.
Brierley and Rutherford, archts.

Architect (Lond.) 121: 742-743
June 7, 1929

720.5
A67a
Durham(N.C.)Fidelity bank
Fidelity bank, Durham, (N.C.) A. C.
Bossom, archt, Plan.

A   Architecture 37:pls.50-51
March 1918

Durham Cathedral Library
Oswald, Arthur
Durham Cathedral Library: - Monks' dormitory,
and relics of St. Cuthbert.

Country life (London) 85:168-173
Fedrary 18, 1939

Durham (Eng.) University. Armstrong college.
Library competition.

Builder 125:363-4,397,402,pl
Sept. 7,14, 1923

720.5
A67a
Durham(N.C)Merchants bank
Merchants' bank, Durham, (N.C.) A. C.
Bossom, archt. Plan

A   Architecture 37:64
March 1918

Durham (Eng.) Cathedral. Durham light infantry
memorial chapel
Durham light infantry memorial Chapel,
South screen, Durham Cathedral.W.D.Caroe, archt.

Architect 115: pls
January 29, 1926

Durham (Eng.)university. Armstrong college
Weightman, F. N.
Armstrong college, University of Durham.

R.I.B.A. 36: 285-288
February 9, 1929

720.5
A67f
Durig,
Hitchcock,H.R.Jr.
Paris, 1937: Swiss pavilion, Durig
Plan.

Architectural forum 67: 172A
September1937

Durrant & Bergquist

see

Viroqua, Wis. Vernon county memorial hospital

Dusseldorf,

see

Düsseldorf

Dustin (Ross) house. La Grange, Ill.

see

La Grange, Ill. Dustin (Ross) house

Dutch colonial architecture, Africa, South
Hunter, R.W.
Dutch architecture in South Africa

House beau
34:30-32
Je 1913

Dutch colonial architecture, Africa, South
Fairbridge, Dorothea
Old Dutch houses in South Africa

House beau
60:709-711
D, 1926

Dutch colonial architecture, U.S.

see also names of individual houses, i.e.:

Bronxville, N.Y. Schieren (G.A.) house
New York (city) Vanderveer house

Dutch colonial architecture, U.S.
The Dutch Colonial farm-house

Architecture
48: 401-3
D 1923

Dutch colonial architecture, U.S.
Ray, J.E.
Dutch colonial house

Ind arts mag
20:59-61
F 1931

Dutch colonial architecture, U.S.
Slocum, S. E.
Early Dutch Colonial architecture

Amer arch
105: 1-10,12
Ja 7, 1914

Dutch colonial   architecture. U.S.
A group of three houses, by Dwight James
Baum: a small suburban home with a Dutch roof,
residence of Charles Evans at Riverdale-on-Hudson;
home of John W. Griffen at Fieldston, New York.

House and garden 39:50
J 1921

Dutch colonial architecture, U.S.
Saylor, H.H.
Know the real Dutch Colonial

House & garden
66: 27-29
N 1934

Dutch Colonial architecture, U.S. New Jersey
Black, W. N.
Colonial building in New Jersey:
The First Dutch Reform church
Furley Place
Washington's headquarters
The Mansion house
The Zabriskie homestead
The Vanderbeck homestead
The Van Lorn homestead
The Brinkerhof homestead
Mantel in Hopper homestead
Architectural record 3:247-
January-March 1894   262

Dutch colonial architecture, U.S. New Jersey
Gambrel slopes of New Jersey

Architecture
55: 61-6
F 1927

Dutch colonial   architecture.
U.S. New Jersey
Boyd, J. T. Jr.
Some early Dutch houses in New Jersey: an
architectural study of origin, evolution and
detail. Measured details of some New Jersey
houses.

Arch rec 36: 31-48;
pls fol 148-158; 220-230,pls.
,Jl - S 1914

Dutch colonial architecture, U.S. New York

see also

Rensselaerwyck, N.Y. Architecture

Dutch colonial architecture, U.S. New York,
Long Island
Eight old Long Island houses

AIA jour
12: 110-17
Mr 1924

Dutch colonial doors and doorways

see also

"Dutch" doors

Dutch Colonial doors and doorways,U.S.

see also

Needham (Mass.) Cutler (Leslie B.)
South Norwalk (Conn.) house
Nordhoff (N.J.) Vreeland house
East Marion (L.I.) Webb house
Wernersville (Pa.) (near) Fort Zeller

"Dutch" doors
origin, construction, etc.

Waterman, Thomas Tileston.
The dwellings of colonial
America. Chapel Hill:University
of North Carolina Press. 1950.
222-3

Dutch East Indies. Architecture.

see

Indonesia. Architecture.

Lutcher, John E
[brief biographical sketch]

Nat'l arch 5:8
Ja '40

Dutchess hill cottage, Hyde Park, N. Y.

see

Hyde Park (N.Y.) Roosevelt (F.D.) estate.
Dutchess hill cottage

Dutton

See

Beers, Clay and Dutton

Duyster, Willem Cornelisz
"Fastnachtsnarren"

Amtliche berichte 37:17, 21-22
November 1915

710.5
C855   Dutel, Pierre
        Room of the month; Pierre Dutel, designer.

Country life (U.S.) 64: 56
October 1928

Duval and Gonse

see also

Paris (Fr.) École de puériculture de la
Faculté de médecine de Paris
Biarritz (Fr.) Villa
Beuvraignes (Fr.) Église
Moreuil (Fr.) Église
Rouvroy-Mines (Fr.) Saint Louis

d'Welles, Jacques

see

Bordeaux (Fr.) Stade municipal
   "   "   Cité universitaire
   "   "   Bourse du travail
Malleau-la-Dune, Fr. Preventorium

Dutert, Charles Louis Ferdinand   1845-1906

see also

Paris (Fr.) Exposition   1889--Palais
des machines

720.54
A67   Duval and Gonse
       Louvet, A.
       The town hall of Montdidier. Duval and
       Gonse, archts.

L'architecture 45: 95-105
March 15, 1932

Dwellings

see

Domestic architecture
Remodeled houses

720.5
A67r   Dutert, Charles Louis Ferdinand 1845 - 1906
Schopfer, Jean
        Natural History Museum at Paris. C.L.F.Dutert
        archt. No plan.

Architectural Record 10:55-75
July 1900

Duval, C.
        Ecole de Puériculture, à Paris. Plans.
C. Duval et E. Gonse, archts.

Encyclopedie de l'architecture;
Constructions Modernes. 12 vols.
Paris: Albert Morancé, 1928-39.
6:pls. 90-95

Owen and White

see

Chicago (Il) Michigan Ave. near 38th St. 3 Story
Residence
Wilmette (Il) Crane (F.A.) Residence

Duthoit, Edmund Clément Marie, 1837-1889
   Basilique de Notre-Dame de Brebieres, Albert.
Edmund Duthoit, archt. Robert Cronie, A.R.I.B.A.
archt. Drawings & sketches fol. p.84. Plan.

Architects & builders jour
47: 78-80, pl.
F 20, 1918.

Duxbury, Mass. Alden house
        Alden house at Duxbury, Mass.

Arch.Rec. 49:398-407.
May 1921

Dwight and Chandler

see

Boston (Mass.) Congress street building

Duttler, Andreas
   Haus eines glaskünstlers in München [plan
& section]
   Wohnquartier im osten Münchens [plans]
Wolfgang Horny & Andreas Duttler, archts.

Baumeister
58:16-17, 24-29 Jan 1961
Tafeln 2-7

Ryerson
D13.1
H94   Duxhurst (Eng.) Somerset (Lady Henry)
           cottage
Tooley, (S. J.)
        The cottage homes of Lady Henry Somerset.
Butler and Paul, archt. [of Duxhurst cottage]

House Beau 4:19f
N 1898

MICROFILM
        Dwight, Ill. C & A railroad station
Cobb, Henry Ives, archt.
        C & A railroad station, Dwight, Ill.
[n.d.]

Roll 37, frames 427-428

Duttler, Andreas
   Miethausgruppe in München [plans] Wolfgang
Horny & Andreas Duttler, archts.

Baumeister
vol.58: 1227-1231, Tafeln
75-78, D 1961

Duyn, A   Fokke van
   Haus in den dünen [plan] A. Fokke van Duyn,
archt.

Bauen & Wohnen
14:Supp. 4 My 1960

Dwight (IL) Judd (C.J.) House
A. W. Cole, Arch.

Inland Arch. 19:
pl. fol. p 42
Ap., 1892

Dwight (Timothy, Jr.) house. Evanston, Ill.

see

Evanston, Ill. Dwight (Timothy, Jr.) house

MICROFILM

Dyer, John Milton, 1870-1957
obituary notice

In SCRAPBOOK ON
ARCHITECTURE p. 718
(on film)

720.5
A51   Dynamic symmetry.
Eisen, G.A.
Criticism and comment: dynamic symmetry and
its reviewer.

American architect 118: 701-702
December 1, 1920

Dworsky, Daniel Leonard, 1927-
Restaurante en Deep Well Ranch. Daniel
L. Dworsky, archt.

Arquitectura Mex
no.56:244-6 D 1956

720.5
A67r   Dyer, John Milton, 1870-1957
The work of Mr.J.Milton Dyer,archt.Plans.

Architectural record 20:384-403
November 1906

720.5
A67r   Dynamic symmetry
Bragdon, Claude
A dissertation on dynamic symmetry.

Architectural record 56: 305-315
October 1924

MICROFILM

Dwyer, Thomas, 1862(?)-1943
obituary notice

In SCRAPBOOK ON
ARCHITECTURE p. 720
(on film)

720.53 Dykes
W58   Walsenwehr porjus im lule Elf, schweden, man

Wasmuths monats hefte fur baukunst 8:150
heft 3-5, 1924

720.5
A51   Dynamic symmetry.
Southwick, A.A.
Dynamic symmetry.

American architect 121: 54-57
January 18, 1922

Dyer and Nadherny

see

Park Ridge (IL)   Reed (J.H.) Residence

Dymaxion house

see also

Fuller house

720.5
A67a   Dynamic symmetry.
Hambidge, Jay
Dynamic symmetry and modern architecture.

Architecture 44: 343-5.
November 1921

Dyer, John Milton, 1870-1957

see also

Cleveland (OH)   Athletic Club
  "   "   City Hall
  "   "   Coast Guard Station
  "   "   Dodge (Samuel) Residence
  "   "   Euclid Ave. M.E. Church
  "   "   First Methodist Church
  "   "   First National Bank
  "   "   Johnston (H.H.) House

(See Card 2)

Dymaxion house
The Dymaxion house conceived by R.
Buckminster Fuller.

Architecture 59: 335-340
June 1929

720.5
A51   Dynamic symmetry.
Goodyear, W.H.
Dynamic symmetry and the Greek vase.

American architect 118:669-674
November 24, 1920

Dyer, John Milton, 1870-1957   (Card 2)

see also

Cleveland (OH)   Silver (M.T.) House
  "   "   Sterling & Welch Co. Building
  "   "   Wickham (D.O.) House
  "   "   Windermere Presbyterian Church
Wellington (OH)   Herrick Library

710.5
H84   Dymaxion house
Dymaxion house. R. Buckminster Fuller,
arch't. Plan.

House and garden 74: 31,43
November 1938 (pt. 2)

720.52
B93   Dynamic symmetry
Dynamic symmetry in ancient architecture.

Builder 120:279-80.
March 4, 1921

720.5
B84   Dyer, John Milton, 1870-1957
G., A.
J. Milton Dyer. [Biography. Photograph]

Brickbuilder 24: 127
My 1915

Ryerson

Dymaxion house.
For fuller living. [plan] R. Buckminster
Fuller, archt.

Interiors
105:pt.2:66-69
My 1946

720.52
A67   Dynamic symmetry
Hambidge, Jay
Dynamic symmetry in ancient architecture.

Architects' journal 53:301
March 9, 1921

720.6
R88
Dynamic symmetry
Bjorne, F. R.
Dynamic symmetry in ancient architecture.
(Letter in regard to Hambidge's theory.)

Jour.Royal Inst.of Brit.Arch. 28:297.
March 19, 1959

720.6
R88
Dynamic symmetry
Fyfe, Theodore
Mr. Hambidge's discoveries: dynamic symmetry

Jour.Royal Inst.of Brit.Arch.27:491-2.
Oct. 23, 1921

720.53
B55
Dyrssen and Averhoff
Flughafen Hamburg. (Airport,Hamburg.)
Dyrssen and Averhoff,archts. Plans.

Der Baumeister 28: 367-373
September 1930

720.52
A67a
Dynamic symmetry
Hambidge, Jay
Further evidence for dynamic symmetry in
ancient architecture.

Architect. 105:171.
March 11, 1921

720.6
R88
Dynamic symmetry
Hubbard, P. W.
Mr. Jay Hambidge on dynamic symmetry in an-
cient architecture.

Jour. Royal Inst.of Brit.Arch.28:266-7.
March 5, 1921

720.6
R88
Dynamic symmetry
Hambidge, Jay
Further evidence for dynamic symmetry in
ancient architecture.

Jour. Royal Inst. of Brit. Arch. 28:597-606
October 22, 1921

720.5
A67a
Dynamic symmetry
Southwick, A.A.
A study in dynamic symmetry.

Architecture 47:111-3
April 1923

720.6
R88
Dynamic symmetry.
Hambidge, Jay
Greek design.

Royal Inst.of Brit.arch.
Jour. 27:213-24.
March 20, 1920

720.5
A51
Dynamic symmetry
Hambidge, Jay
Symmetry and proportion in Greek art.

American architect 116: 597-605
November 12, 1919

720.5
A51
Dynamic symmetry.
Swartout, Egerton
Greek proportions..theoretically and other-
wise.

American architect 120: 579-583
November 23, 1921

720.6
R88
Dynamic symmetry
Brereton, Cloudesley
True inwardness of Mr. Hambidge's theory
of dynamic symmetry.

R.I.B.A. Journal 27:455.
September 25, 1920

720.5
A51
Dynamic symmetry.
Kane, J.A.
Hambidge theory of symmetry and proportion
in Greek architecture as relating to architectur-
al design.

American architect 120:261-265
October 12, 1921

Dynevor castle, Wales
Webb, Michael
New role for a Welsh castle. [illus.]

Country life
143:1740-1741
Je 27 1968

720.6
R88P
Dynamic symmetry
Fryer, Bryant
The mathematical bases in Greek de-
sign.

Royal arch. inst. of Canada.
Journal 24: 368-73
O '47

Dyrssen and Averhoff
Aeroport de Hambourg. Plans. Dyrssen et
Averhoff, archts.

Encyclopedie de l'architecture;
Constructions Modernes. 12 vols.
Paris: Albert Morancé, 1928-39.
7:pls.16-22

E	Ealing, Eng. Churches Builder 123: pl Sept. 8, 1922	Eames and Young (Card 2) see also St. Joseph (MO) Robidoux Hotel St. Louis (MO) Agusta Building " " Allen (George L.) Residence " " Bent (Mrs. E.) Residence " " Boatmen's Bank (1915) " " Brookings (Robert S.) Residence " " Bunge Store and Apt. Bldg. " " Chapman (J.G.) Residence (See Card 3)
E. C. DeWitt & Co. warehouse. Chicago, Ill. see Chicago (Ill.) E. C. DeWitt & co. warehouse	Ealing (Eng.) Cinema studios Anderson, A.F.B. New cinema studios, Ealing, England. Robert Atkinson, archt. Plans. Builder 142: 392-396 February 26, 1932	Eames and Young (Card 3) see also St. Louis (MO) Clark (C.T.) House " " Clark (Mrs. K.) House " " Ely and Walker Store Bldg. " " Ferguson & McKinley Building " " Francis (D.R.) Residence " " Frisco Building " " Humphrey, (F.W.) Residence " " Liggett Building (See Card 4)
Eager, Alvin Residence of Mr. and Mrs. R.R. Bush, Pasadena, Robert H. Ainsworth, archt. Alvin Eager, landscape archt. Architectural digest 9: 55-58 Number 2 [1936-37]	Ealing, Eng. St. James' Church Church of S. James, Ealing. Mr. Wm. Pywell, A.R.I.B.A., Architect. Builder 88: 209 and pl. 7 25, 1905	Eames and Young (Card 4) see also St. Louis (MO) Lincoln Trust Co. Building " " Louisiana Purchase Exposition " " McMillan (William) House " " Medical School " " Mississippi Valley Trust Co. " " National Bank of the Republic " " Nicholson (Peter) and Sons Building " " Pierce (H.C.) Mausoleum (See Card 5)

Eager and Eager
 	
see
 	
Los Angeles (Cal.) 'Leven Oaks hotel
	Ealing, Eng. St. Matthews Church
	St. Matthew's church, Ealing Common, W.
	A memorial stained glass window, designed by
	Reginald Hallward.
	
	Builder 127: plate and p.681
	October 31, 1924
		Eames and Young (Card 5)
		see also
		St. Louis (MO) Public Library Competition
		" " Public Library. Frederick M.
		   Cruden Branch
		" " Residence
		" " St. Louis Club House Competition
		" " St. Louis Shoe and Monarch Rubber
		   co. bldg.
		" " St. Louis Trust Co. bldg.
		   Competition design.
		
		(See Card 6)

Eagle exchange tavern. Chicago See Chicago. Sauganash hotel.	Eames and Saarinen see Santa Monica, Cal. Entenza (John) house	Eames and Young (card 6) see also St. Louis (MO) Simmons (E.C.) Residence, Remodeling " " Sterling (G.E.) Residence " " Studio Building " " Telephone Co. Branch Building " " Thornburg (W.H.) Residence " " University Club " " Victoria Building " " Warehouses (See Card 7)
Eagle Rock Valley (Cal.) Occidental College Various Buildings Myron Hunt, archt. Plan. West. Arch. 27: pl. 2-6 Jun, 1918	Eames and Saarinen Members of firm: Eames, Charles, 1907- Saarinen, Eero, 1910-	Eames and Young (Card 7) see also St. Louis (MO) Washington University Warehouse " " Wright Building " " Y.M.C.A. Building Competitive Design San Francisco (CA) Custom House Seattle (WA) Alaska Building " " Washington Hotel University City (MO) Studio Building Washington (DC) Pan-American Union Building Competition West Point (NY) U.S. Military Academy

Eagle tower. Carnarvon (Wales)
 	
see
 	
Carnarvon (Eng.) Carnarvon castle.
Eagle tower
	Eames and Young
	see also
	Atlanta (GA) Federal Penitentiary
	Galveston (TX) Rosenberg Library
	Indianapolis (IN) Courthouse and Post Office
	   Competition Design
	New York (NY) Ely-Walker Dry Goods Company
	Omaha (NB) Trans-Mississippi Exposition, Fine
	   Arts Building
	St. Joseph (MO) Corby-Forsee Office Building
	
	(See Card 2)
		Eames & Young
		
		Members of firm:
		
		Young, Thomas Crane
		Eames, William Sylvester

770.5
A67rev   Eames and Young
Jenkins, C.E.
    Eames and Young

Architectural reviewer:86-102
June 1897

Eames (Charles) house, Santa Monica, Cal.

see

Santa Monica (Cal.) Eames (Charles) house

Earle and Fuller
    Building on Main Street, Worcester, Mass.
[plans] Stephen C. Earle and James E. Fuller,
archts.

Amer arch
1: 109, pl.fol.p.108
Ap 1, 1876

Eames and Young
    Examples of architecture.in St. Louis:
residences, Eames and Young, archts.

Archi record
5: 405-406, 409
Ap-Je 1896

Eames, Ray (Kaiser)

special issue

Architectural Design
36: 432-471
Sept. 1966

Earle, Stephen Carpenter 1839-1913

Member of firms:

Earle and Fuller
Earle and Fisher

Eames and Young
    Park View, St. Louis. Messrs. Eames and Young,
architects.

Builder 101:362 and pl.
S 29, 1911

Eames, W. S.

see

St. Louis (MO) Frances (David R.) Residence

Earls Barton,Eng. All Saints (church)
Radford, C.A.R.
    Earl's Barton church [plan]

Archaelogical Jr.
110:196-97
1953

Eames, Charles

see also

Santa Monica (Cal.) Eames (Charles) house

Eames,William Sylvester, 1857-

see

Eames & Young

Earls court, London

see

London. Earls court

Eames, Charles, 1907 -
Santi, Carlo
    Charles Eames e la tecnica

Domus 256: 11-14
Mr 1951

Earl Stonham (Eng.) St. Mary's church
Rahbula, E.A.R.
    Earl Stonham church [plan]

Archaeo jrl 108:156-157
1951

Early American architecture

see

Colonial architecture

Eames, Charles, 1907 -
    Particolari della casa-studio di Eames e
della sede della "Miller furniture"

Domus 256: 15-23
Mr 1951

Earle and Fisher

Members of firm:

Fisher, Clellan Waldo
Earle, Stephen Carpenter, 1839-1913

Early Christian architecture

see also

Basilicas

Eames, Charles, 1907-

Special issue

Architectural Design
36: 432-471
Sept. 1966

Earle and Fuller

Members of firm:

Fuller, James E. ,   1836-1901
Earle, Stephen Carpenter, 1839-1913

723.5   Early Christian architecture
A67r Longfellow,W.P.P.
    The Early Christian architecture of Rome.

Architectural record 4:395-403
April-June 1894

Burnham Library
Early Christian architecture.
Vorläufer und anfänge Christlicher architektur.
Früher Deutscher Kirchenbau.

Kunstchronik 6:229-266
S 1953

Burnham Library
Early christian architecture, Spain
Ainaud, Juan
Notas sobre iglesias prerrománicas.

Anales y Boletín de los museos
de arte de Barcelona 6: 315-320
Jl - D '48

770.5
A67b
Earthquakes and building
    Earthquake resistant construction

arch & bldg. 55:172
D '23

Early Christian architecture.
Heliot, Pierre
    Les murs-diaphragmes longitudinaux dans
l'architecture religieuse du Bas Empire e
du Moyen Age. [illus.]

Arte lombarda
v.8, I: 111-130
1963

Early, John J.

see

Washington (D.C.) Meridian hill park.
Menlow Park (N.Y.) Edison tower

Earthquakes and building
    "Expert opinion on earthquake-proof
structures"

West Arch 10:
70-72
July 1907

Early Christian architecture. Italy. Lombardy
Roberti, Mario Mirabella
    Quattro edifici di età tardoantica in
Lombardia. [illus.]

Arte lombarda
v.15, II: [111]-116
1970

Earswick, Eng.
Weaver, Lawrence
    Cottages at Earswick, photographs and
plans.

Country life (London)58:68-81
October 31,1925

770.52
A67
Earthquakes and building
    The Japanese earthquake

Architects jour 58:849-50
D 5 '23

Early Christian architecture
Ehrensperger-Katz, Ingrid
    Les représentations de villes fortifiées
dans l'art paléochrétien et leurs dérivées
byzantines. [illus.]

Cahiers archéologiques
v.19: [1]-27
1969

Earth construction

see

Pisé

770.5
A51
Earthquakes and building
    A scheme for an earthquake proof house.
Plan

Amer. archt. 95: 504-5
Je 23 '09

Early Christian architecture. Italy. Milan.
Gengaro, Maria Luisa
    Significato del valore classico nella
architettura paleocristiana in Milano. [illus.]

Arte lombarda
v. 9, I: 49-54
1964

Earthquakes and building

see also

Palo Alto (Cal.) Hanna (P.R.)house

Earthquakes and building
Cetto, Max
    Un tremblement de terre; lettre de Mexique.

Zodiac
1:206 O 1957

Early Christian architecture. Italy. Milan
Kleinbauer, W. Eugene
    Toward a dating of San Lorenzo in Milan.
Masonry and building methods of Milanese Roman
and early Christian Architecture. [illus.]

Arte lombarda
v.13, II: 1-22
1968

Earthquakes and building

Kidder, Frank Eugene. Building
construction and superintendence.
3 vols. New York: W.T. Comstock,
1897-1906. pt.1,p.587

770.52
B95
Earthquakes and building, Japan. 1923
Davison, Charles
    The effects on buildings of the Japanese
earthquake of 1923.

Builder 127:895
D 5 '24

Early christian architecture, Spain

see also

Vega del Mar, Sp. San Pedro de Alcantara Malaga

Earthquakes and Building
    "The Earthquake in Sicily", w/ illus.
by Robt. C. McLean.

West. Archt.
vol. 13; p. 8-9
Jan, 1909

770.5
W57
Earthquakes and building, Japan. 1923
    The effect of the earthquake in Japan
upon construction

west archt 37:117-8
O '23

710.5
C85
East Africa
The land of the giant craters

Country life Lond.53: 74-7
Jan. 20, 1923

East Cliff, Gloucestershire. Designed by
E.C. Francis.

(Lond.) Arch. rev.59:102-05 & pl.4
Mar. 1926

East Gloucester (Mass.) Fassett,(J.S.)garage
Garage for Mrs. J. Sloat Fassett, East
Gloucester, Mass.
Edwin J. Lewis, Jr. Archt.

Architectural review 18 n.s.1: pl.100
November 1912

710.5
C85
East Anglia.
A Voyage of Discovery.

Country Life. 48:442-3.
Oct. 9, 1920.

East Croydon (Eng.)

see

London. (Eng.)

710.5
H84
East Gloucester (Mass.) Hall house
Views of the Hall residence, East Gloucester
Mass.

House & garden 51: 97-9
January 1927

720
E93
East Anglia. Architecture
Gunn, Edwin
Architecture of East Anglia: Lavenham,Stoke-
by-Nayland, Thaxted, Norwich, Higham, Clare,
King's Lynn , Bumpstead, Walberswick, Woodbridge,
Long Melford, Blythburgh.

Tuileries brochures 1:18-31;
March; May 1930   34-47

East Dean, England. Gayles Orchard
Hussey, Christopher
An invisible house. Gayles Orchard, Eastdean,
Sussex. [illus.]

Country life
143: 334-335
F 15 1968

E. Greenbush (N.Y.) Breese (Jan) house
Jan Breese House, East Greenbush,
Rensselaer county, New York

Architectural forum 63:39-41
July 1935

720.5
A67r
East Avon (Conn.) Congregational church
Embury,AymarII
Early American churches. Pt.8. East Avon
Congregational church.

Architectural record 32:95-88
July 1912

East Derby (Conn.) Gilbert (Trueman) house
Stivers, M.P.
The Trueman Gilbert house

Old time New England 19:75-79
October 1928

East Grinstead, Eng. "Ardmillan"
"Ardmillan",East Grinstead, Sussex,Eng.
E.T. Powell, archt. Plan.

Architectural review 17:pls.27,36;
March 1910   supp.fol.p.48

East Boston, Mass.

see

Boston, Mass.

STILSON LIBRARY
D15.1
H84
East Gloucester (Mass.) Atwood (W.E.) house
Cram,R.A.
Noteworthy houses by well-known architects.
III. Mr. and Mrs. William E. Atwood's house and
studio at East Gloucester, Mass. Cram and Ferguson,
archts. Plan.

A
House beautiful 46:129-132
September 1919

720.52
A67c
East Grinstead (Eng.) Fire brigade station
New fire brigade station at East Grinstead,
Sussex. H. Huntley Gordon, A.R.I.B.A., archt.

Arch & con rep 68:
3rd pl after 32
D 5 '02

East Cambridge (Mass.)Thorndike School
Thorndike School

Brickbuilder 23: pl.83-84
June 1914

East Gloucester (Mass.)Atwood (W.E.) house
"The House on the Moors," home of
Mr. and Mrs. William E. Atwood.

American magazine of art 16:414-417
Aug. 1925

East Grinstead (Eng.) Great house court
Entrance Hall, Great House Court, East
Grinstead, Sussex, England.
F. Turner Powell, Architect.

Arch rev 1:pl.
Jl, 1912

East Chicago (Ind.) Kennedy hotel
Sketch of "The Kennedy" East Chicago, Ind.
Treat and Foltz, archts.

Building budget 5: pl.fol.p.22
February 28, 1889

720.5
A67
East Gloucester (Mass.). Beaux (Cecilia) house
Charles K. Cummings, archt.

Arch rev 20 (n.s5): pls XXXII-
D '15   XXXIV fol 116

720.5
A67r
East Haddam (Conn.) Library
East Haddam Library. Orr & Del Grella,
archts.

Arch. Rec 49: 166-7
F '21

720.5 A67r   East Hampton(L.I.)Architecture
 deKay,Charles
     Summer homes at East Hampton,N.J.
 	
 Architectural record 13:19-33
 January 1903
	East Hampton, (L.I.) houses
	 deKay, Charles
	     Summer homes at East Hampton, N.Y.
	
	 Arch rec 13: 19-33
	 Ja '03
		720.5 A67a East Hampton (L.I.) St. Luke's church
		     St. Luke's church, Easthampton, Long
		 Island. Thomas Nash, archt.
		
		 Architecture 26: p.167-169
		 September 1912

East Hampton (L.I.) Cottage
    A Cottage and Garden at East Hampton, L.I.
 Designed by Grosvenor Atterbury, Architect.
 	
 House and gard 3: 213-14
 Ap 1903
	705.1 A79 EastHampton (L.I.) James (E.S.) house
	 Bullard, R.H.
	     A house especially designed for the dunes
	 of East Hampton. Home of Mr. and Mrs. Ellery S.
	 James. Roger Bullard, archt.
	
	 A Arts and decoration 31: 68-70,112
	 October 1929
		RYERSON LIBRARY
		
		 East Hampton, L.I. Wiener (Paul Lester) house
		    Maison de Paul Lester Wiener à East
		 Hampton [plan] no archt given
		
		 Aujourd'hui
		 5:70-1 Ja 1960

705.1 A79   East Hampton (L.I.) Golf Club House
     New golf club at East Hampton, Long
 Island
 	
 Arts and decoration 21:15-7
 Jl '24
	East Hampton (L.I.) Jenney,W.S. house
	    Residence, William S. Jenney, East
	 Hampton, L.I. Polhemus & Coffin, Architect
	
	 Architecture 48: 3 pls
	 O '23
		East Harling (Eng.) Church
		    Meas. drawing by L.Stokes. Flèche.
		
		 Lond. Arch. Assoc. sketch book:pl. 18
		 1881.

East Hampton (L.I.) Guild hall
    The Guild Hall at East Hampton, L.I.
 Aymar Embury II, archt. No plan.
 	
 House and garden 61: 70-71
 May 1932
	RYERSON LIBRARY
	 705.1 A79 EastHampton (L.I.) King (Hamilton) house
	 Castells, barman
	     An artist's home of unique charm. Home of
	 Mr. and Mrs. Hamilton King at Easthampton.
	
	 Arts and decoration 29: 56-57
	 June 1928
		East Haven (Conn.)Hagaman Memorial Library
		    Hagaman memorial library, East Haven, Conn
		 Davis & Waldorff, archts.
		
		 Architect 10:310
		 June 1928

720.5 A51   EastHampton (L.I.) Herter (Albert) house
    House of Albert Herter,Easthampton,Long
 Island. Grosvenor Atterbury,archt. Plans.
 	
 American architect 94: 4pls.fol.p.80
 A   September 2,1908
	720.5 A67a EastHampton (L.I.) Library
	    Easthampton, Long Island library. Aymar
	 Embury II, Archt. Plan and elevation.
	
	 Architecture 28: 216-217
	 S '12
		East Haven (Conn.) Hagaman Memorial Library
		    Hagaman memorial library,East Haven,Conn.
		 Davis and Walldorff, archts.
		
		 American architect 135:785-788
		 June 20, 1929

RYERSON LIBRARY
 D15.1 H84   EastHampton (L.I.) Herter (Albert) house
 Barrington,A.L.
     "A fielde of delite": the country home of two
 well-known artists—Mr. and Mrs. Albert Herter,
 at Easthampton,L.I. No plan.
 	
 House beautiful 45:188-191
 April 1919
	EastHampton (L.I.) library
	    Library, Easthampton, L.I. Aymar Embury
	 II, archt. Plans
	
	 Brickbuilder 22: pls 28-9
	 F 1913
		East Indies. Architecture
		    Raffles college, Singapore.
		
		 Architect (Eng.) 119: 729
		 May 18, 1928

East Hampton, (L.I.) Herter,(Albert) house
    Country estate of Albert Herter, East
 Hampton, Long Island, New York.
 Grosvenor Atterbury, archt.
 	
 Arch 40: pls. 135-139
 S '19
	720.5 A51 EastHampton (L.I.) Rice (C.C.) house
	    House of Dr. C.C. Rice, Easthampton,
	 Long Island. Grosvenor Atterbury, archt.
	 Plans.
	
	 American architect 94: 4pls.fol.p.72
	 A August 26,1908
		East Kirby (Eng.) St. Thomas' church
		    New Church of St. Thomas, East Kirby,
		 Nottinghamshire.
		 Louis Ambler, F.R.I.B.A., Architect.
		
		 Arch & con rep 74: pls & plan
		 O 27, 1905

East Linton, Eng. Rennie (John) memorial
John Rennie Memorial, East Linton
(East Lothian)

Architect and Building News 148:91
October 23, 1936

710.5
H84
East Meon.Court house
Oswald,Arthur
The court house,East Meon,Hampshire,the home
of Mr.P.Morley Horder. Plan.

Country life(Lond)81:510-515
May 8,1937

East Orange (N.J.) Christ church
Study for Christ Church, East Orange,
New Jersey. R. H. Robertson, archt.

Inl. archt 34 pl. fol. p. 8
Ag 1899

East Liverpool (O.) Carnegie library Competition
Competition for Carnegie library,East
Liverpool, Ohio. Myers and Fisher, archts.
Plan.

Architectural review 9 n.s. 4:39
January 1902

720.6
A67ar
East Meon,Court house
The East Meon court house

Architecture.journal 3:303-306
Apr.1925

East Orange (N.J.) cooperative bldg.
East Orange Co-operative building,East
Orange, N.J. John B Peterkin, archt.

Architect (N.Y.) 13: 95-101
October 1929

East Liverpool (OH) Public Library
Rendering and Floor Plan.
David C. Myers and Mahlon H. Fisher.

West. Archt.
4: pls.fol.p. 12
Dec, 1905

713.1
N84
East Norwich (L.I.) Hammond (Paul) house
The house of Mrs. Paul Hammond at East
Norwich, Long Island. Delano and Aldrich,
architects

House beautiful 67:594-595
May 1930

East Orange (N.J.) Essex County trust co.
Essex County Trust Co., East Orange, N.J.
Dennison & Hirons, architects

Architecture 50:408,pl.183-185
Dec. 1924

East Lothian, Eng. Whitekirk Church
Restoration of Whitekirk church.
East Lothian

Archts' bldrs. Jour 46:pl. for
Dec. 19, 1917

East Norwich (L.I.) Swann (Arthur)house
House for Mrs. Arthur Swann,East
Norwich, Long Island.
Tennis court and swimming pool for
Harrison Williams, Bayville, N.Y.

Architectural record 66: 420-423,
497
November 1929

East Orange (N.J.) French (C.S.) house
The C.S. French house, W.H. Wood, architect.

Sheldon, George William. Artistic
Country Seats. 2 vols. New York:
D. Appleton and Co., 1871.
v.1,pt.1:17-21 and pl.6

East Lothian (Scot) Dirleton Castle,Dovecot
The Dovecot, Dirleton Castle, East
Lothian, Scotland. From the Ancient Monu-
ments Exhibition at the R.I.B.A.

Builder 144: 568
April 7, 1933

East Orange,N.J. Ashland School
Ashland School, East Orange, N.J.
W.B. Tubby, Architect.

Architecture 21: pls.
F 1910

East Orange (N.J.) Geiger (F.C.) house.
The F.C. Geiger house, W.H. Wood, archt.

Sheldon, George William. Artistic
Country Seats. 2 vols. New York:
D. Appleton and Co., 1871.
Vol. 1, pt 1: 35-37 and pl. 9

East Lothian (Scot) Yester house
Yester House, East Lothian. James Smith
and Alexander McGill, archts.

Country life (Lond.) 72: 94-100;
July 23, 1932   126-132

East Orange (N.J.) Bayard Dod (s.) house
The S. Bayard Dodd house, A.B. Jennings, archt.

Sheldon, George William. Artistic
Country Seats. 2 vols. New York:
D. Appleton and Co., 1871.
vol 1, pt. 2:147-50,pl.34

East Orange (N.J.) houses
Residence, East Orange, New Jersey.

Inl archt 33:pl.fol.p.44
Je 1899

East Marion (L.I.) Webb house Door
The Webb house, East Marion. L.I.
Detail of doorway. Built c. 1790.

White pine series 5:front
April 1919

East Orange (N.J.) Burgess (John W.) house
The John W. Burgess house, W.H. Wood, architect.

Sheldon, George William. Artistic
Country Seats. 2 vols. New York:
D. Appleton and Co., 1871.
vol.1,pt.1:pp 29-33,pl.8

East Orange (N.J.) Lincoln School
Lincoln School, East Orange, N.J.
William B. Tubby and Son, Archts.

Western Archt.
15: pl. fol p. 12
Jan 1910

East Orange (N.J.) National Bank Bldg. Accepted design...Ludlow and Valentine, Archts. [plans] Amer archt and bldg news 53: 80, pls. fol. 4 in supp. Sept. 5, 1896	**720.5 B98b** East Saginaw (Mich) Caskey (J. C.) house Stone and frame residence at East Saginaw (Mich) for J. C. Caskey. George Beaumont, archt. Building budget 3:56a Mr 31, 1887	**720.5 W58** East Taunton (Mass.) Deane-Barstow house The Deane-Barstow house, East Taunton, Mass. 1800. White Pine 14:155-158,Pls.79-85 Number 1, 1928
720.5 A67ar East Orange (N.J.) Our Lady of All Souls Church Study of Our Lady of All Souls Church, R.C. East Orange, N.J. Architect (N.Y.) 8: pl.456 July 1927	E. St. Louis (Ill.)Cahokia power station Cahokia Power Station, E.St. Louis, Ill. Mauran, Russell & Crowell, architects Power provisions and steam plant design. Architectural forum 39:front & 137-143 Sept. 1923	East, W. J. see also Dubois (PA) Presbyterian Church Sewickley (PA) St. Stephen's Church
720.5 A67a East Orange (N.J.) Park ave. and 18th st. apts. Park ave. and 18th st., East Orange, N.J. Edward V. Warren, archt. Architecture 47: 89-92 pl 48 Mr 1923	East Sharon, Mass., Inn (Old-Time Roadside) sketch E. Eldon Deane, sketcher Inland Archt. Vol. 24, No. 3, pl. Fol. p. 30 Oct. 1894	East, W J Design for residence of E. P. S. Wright, Sewickley, Pennsylvania. W. J. East, archt. Inland architect 20, no. 5 pl. fol. p. 58 D 1892
East Orange (NJ) Residence Lamb & Rich, Archs. Inland Arch.38: pls. fol.p.16 Sept. 1901	East Sheen, Eng. All Saints Church All Saints' church, East Sheen, Surrey. Newberry and Fowler, archts. Architects Journal 71: 461-465 March 19, 1930	East Williston (L.I.) Pashley (Bertram) house House for Bertram Pashley, East Williston, L.I. N.Y. Porter O. Daniel, archt. Architectural forum 66: 40-41 January 1937
East Orange (NJ) Residence Robert T. Lyons, Arch. Inland Arch. 50: pl. fol. p 76 D, 1907	East Sheen (Eng.) End house End House, East Sheen, England. Basil Oliver, archt. Architect 119: 935-9 June 29, 1928	East Youngstown (O.) see Youngstown (O.)
East Orange (N.J.)Schweinler (C.L.) estate. gate lodge The gate lodge on the estate of Mr. and Mrs. Carl L. Schweinler at East Orange, New Jersey. Bernard E. Muller, archt. Country life (U.S.) 61: 40 November 1931	East Smithfield (Eng.) see London (Eng.)	Eastbourne (Eng.) The Royal visit to Eastbourne,England. A planned seaside town. Country life (Lond) 77:135-137 February 9, 1935
720.5 B84 East Orange (N.J.) Wise (C.L.) house House for C.L.Wise,East Orange,New Jersey. Percy Griffin,archt. Plans. Brickbuilder 15: 2pls.fol.p.154 July 1906	East Sussex (Eng.) house Phillips, Randal Georgian and modern, A house in East Sussex, Designed by H. T. B. Barnard. Plan. Country Life (Lond.) 84: 662-663 December 31, 1938	Eastbourne (Eng.) College. War memorial bldg. Eastbourne college war memorial building. Sydney Tatchell and Geoffrey C. Wilson, archts. Plan. Builder 139: 682,690,697-700 October 24, 1930

Eastbourne (Eng.) St. Mary the Virgin
St. Mary. Meas.drawing by R.C.Page.
Arcade, etc.

Lond. Arch. Assoc. Sketch book:12
1872-73

Easter Island
Schulze-Mainier, Friedrich
Die Entdeckung der Osterinsel
(illus.)

Du
18:54-59, D 1958

Easthampton (L.I.)

see

East Hampton (L.I.)

Eastbourne (Eng.) Technical Institute
Eastbourne Technical Institute. Mr. Philip A.
Robson, A.R.I.B.A., Architect.

Builder 87: 252 and pl.
S 3, 1904

Easter Island. Architecture

see

Domestic architecture. Easter Island

Eastman, C. E.

see also

Des Moines (IA)   Drake University, Chancellor's
Residence

"Eastbourne"(Sussex)
Esdaile, K.A.
A georgian sculptor discovered: Charles
Stanley and his English colleagues.

Country life (Lond) 82:348-349
October 2, 1937

Easter sepulchre.

Bowman, Henry and J.S. Crowther.
The churches of the middle ages.
2 vols. Lond: G. Bell, 1857. v.2.1 pl.

Eastman, C.E.
Drawings for Modern Square House floor plans.

West. archt.
2: 7 pls.fol.p. 20
Jun, 1903

Eastbury manor

see
Barking. England. Eastbury manor

710.5   Easter sepulchres
C85   Haxton church, Newark

Country life (Lond) 51:517
April 15, 1922

Eastman, George, House, Rochester, N.Y.,

see

Rochester, N.Y. Eastman (George) house

720.5   Eastchester (N.Y.) St. Pauls' church
W58   Upjohn, R.B.
St. Paul's church (1768), Eastchester, N.Y.

White pine series 15: 4; pl.3-4
Number 1, 1929

720.52   Easter sepulchres
A67c   Parish church of Haxton, Newark

Architect 109:276
April 20, 1923

Eastman national business college, Chicago
(c.1866)

see

Chicago, Ill. Eastman national business college
(c.1866)

Eastcote, Eng. St. Lawrence church
St. Lawrence Church, Eastcote, Middlesex.
Sir Charles Nicholson, archt. Plan.

Architect (Lond.)136: 352-354
December 29, 1933

Eastern state penitentiary, Graterford, Pa.

see

Graterford (Pa.) Eastern state penitentiary

Eastman school of music

see

Rochester (N.Y.) University. Eastman theater and
school of music

Easter Island
Ferdon, Edwin N.
Easter Island house types [illus]

El Palacio (bulletin of
New Mexico museum)
68: [28] - 46, Spring 1961

Eastern states exposition

see

West Springfield, Mass. Eastern states exposition

Eastman, Sidney, house. Kenilworth, Ill.

see

Kenilworth, Ill. Barratt, Edgar G., house.

Eastman theater

see

Rochester (N.Y.) University. Eastman theater
and school of music

Easton, Hugh

see

Clifton (Eng.) Clifton College. Chapel

Easton Neston, Eng.
Whinney, Margaret
Easton Neston.

Archaeological Jr.
110:209-211
1953

Eastman, W.R.
Library Buildings

Inland Architect
39: 22-3
Apr, 1902

Easton, J. Murray, 1889-1975

see

Easton and Robertson

Easton Neston, Eng.
The staircase at Easton Neston, seat of
Sir Thomas Hesketh, England.

Country life (Lond.) 62:297,299
August 27, 1927

Easton and Robertson

see also

Bishopsgate (Eng.) Financial news bldg.
London (Eng.) Royal horticultural hall
London (Eng.) Belgrave place house

Easton, John Murray

see

Easton, J. Murray, 1889-1975

790.5
A51

Easton,(Pa.) Knapp,(R.S.) house
Rollo S. Knapp, Easton, Pennsylvania.
Thomas, Martin & Kirkpatrick, archts.

Amer archt 122: 5 pl
O 25 '22

Easton and Robertson

Member of firm:

Robertson, Howard Morley, 1888-
Easton, J Murray, 1889-

720.5
A67a

Easton (Md.) "Auburn"
Alterations to "Auburn", residence,
Barclay H. Trippe, Easton, Maryland.
Henry P. Hopkins, architect. Plans.

Architecture 49:pl.85-87
June 1924

790.5
A51

Easton(Pa.)Lafayette college.Chapel
Chapel for Lafayette college, Easton, Pa.
Carrère and Hastings, archts.

American architect 112:pl.174-177
October 17, 1917

Easton & Robertson
The new facade to the Financial News building.
Stanley Hall and Easton & Robertson, archts.

Architect (Lond.)
150: 5
Ap 2, 1937

720.5
A67ar

Easton (Md.) "Cape Centaur"
"Cape Centaur", House of Glenn Stewart,
Easton, Md. Bradley Delehanty, archt.

Architect(N.Y.)5:pl.106-12
Feb. 1928

Easton (Pa.) Parsons-Taylor house
Fackenthal, Dr. B.F., Jr.
Homes of George Taylor, signer of the Declaration
of Independence; Parsons-Taylor house, Easton, Pa.
1753-1757. George Taylor house at Lower Catasauqua,
Lehigh County, Pa.

Bucks County Historical Society Papers.
1926. (Vol V.) Meadville, PA:Tribune
Publishing, 1926.5:113-133,pl.opp.p.113

720.6
R88

Easton and Robertson
Royal Institute of British Architects
The R.I.B.A. London architecture medal and
diploma 1928. With discussion. Presentation to
Easton and Robertson.

R.I.B.A.Journal 37: 164-165
January 11,1930

Easton, Md. Stewart (Glenn) house

see

Easton, Md. Cape centaur

"Easton", Syosset, L. I.

see

Syosset, L. I. "Easton"

917.4
O44

Easton(Conn.)Bennett(James)log house
Kelly,J.F.
A seventeenth century Connecticut log house:
James Bennett house, Easton, Conn. Plan.

Old time New England 31:front.,29-40
October 1940

Easton, Murray

see

Easton, J. Murray, 1889-1975

Eastriggs (Eng.) Housing

Arch. and contr. reporter 100:257 and
Nov. 8, 1918   pl.

Eastwood, J.   H.

see

Bridgeford (Eng.) Church of St. Joseph

Eau Claire, Wis. First Congregational Church.
Community house
    Illustration. Purcell and Elmslie, archts.

Northwest archt.
10: 8
No. 2,1946

Eber, Dietrich Heins
    Funkhaus und unterhaltungsstudio des
Südwestfunks in Baden-Baden   [plans & sections]
Dietrich Heins Eber, archt.

Bauen & Wohnen no.2
p. 105-107 Konstruktions-
    blätter at end of issue
Apr 1955

Eaton and Robertson

see

Milton (Eng.) Parish church

---

microfilm Eau Claire, Wis. Congregational church parsonage
Purcell, Feick and Elmslie, architects
    Parsonage and community house for the First
congregational church, Eau Claire, Wisconsin, 1914.

Roll 22, frames 230-8;239-45

720.63   Eberhardt, Hugo.
M68   Work of Hugo Eberhardt

Moderne bauformen 7: 497-544
December 1908

Eaton (O.) Preble County Court house
    The Preble County Court House, Eaton, O.
H.H. Hiestand and Richards, McCarty and Bulford,
Assoc. archts. Plans.

Amer. arch. 117:511
April 28, 1920

Eau Claire, Wis., Steven, J.D.R., house.
    Illustration and plan. Purcell and Elmslie
architects.

Western architect
21: pl. 20
January 1915

Eberhart, John F. house, Chicago

see

Chicago, Ill. Eberhart (J. F.) house

Eaton Socon, Eng. St. Mary the Virgin Church
    Church of St. Mary the Virgin, Eaton Socon,
Hunts. Richardson and Gill, archts.

Builder 143:90-94
July 15, 1932

Eau Claire, Wis. Steven, J.D.R., house.
    Plan. Purcell and Feick, architects.

Prairie School review
II:7
First quarter 1965

Eberl, Michael
    Ein kleiner industriebau in München[plans
& sections] Michael Eberl, archt.

Baumeister
57:470-72 Jl 1960
Tafeln 33 & 34

Eatontown, N.J., Monmouth County Country Club
    Monmouth County Country Club, Eatontown, N.J.
Scott and Teegen, architects.

Architectural forum 65:327
October, 1936

720.5   Eaves
A67a   Architecture's portfolio

Arch.67: 356-70
Je '33

Eberl, Michael
    Wohnhausumbau am Starnberger See [plan]
Michael Eberl, archt.

Baumeister
57:628-29 S 1960

Eau Claire, Wis. First Congregational Church.
Community house
    Plan and illustration. Purcell and Elmslie,
architects.

Western architect
21: pls. 16-17
January 1915

Eaves.
    Measured drawings.

Der architekt 22:190-4.
Heft 12,1919

720.5 Eberlein, Harold Donaldson
A67f   Shop fronts in country towns and smaller
cities.

Architectural forum 50: 869-884
June 1922

Eau Claire, Wis. First Congregational Church.
Parsonage
    Illustration. Purcell and Elmslie, archts.

Western architect
22: 11
July 1915

720.5   Eaves.
C855   Watch your Gutters.

Country Life. 38:65-6.
Oct. 1920.

720.5 Eberlein, Harold Donaldson
A67f   Twickenham House, Abigdon, Berks.

Architectural forum 50: 733-748
May 1929

720.5 A67m Eberlein, H.D.; French, L.H. Jr. Numero 147, Boulevard de la Reine, Versailles. Plan. Architectural record 54:277-285 September 1928	7P0.5 A51 Eberson, John Niels Esperson building, Houston, Texas. John Eberson, archt. Views and plans. American architect 132:583-8 November 5, 1927	Ebert, Wils Grundschule in Berlin-Spandau [plans] Wils Ebert, archt. Architektur & Wohnform vol. 69: 312-317, N 1961
Eberson, John see also Dallas (Tex.) Majestic theater Brooklyn (N.Y.) Laemmle theater Houston (Tex.) Niels Esperon bldg. Jamaica (N.Y.) Valencia theater	MICROFILM Eberson, John, 1875-1954 obituary notice In SCRAPBOOK ON ARCHITECTURE p. 718 (on film)	Ebert, Wils Interbau 1957. Objekt 7: 8 geschossiges hochhaus mit 61 wohnungen [plans] Walter Gropius & Wils Ebert, archts. Architektur & Wohnform 65:155 Je 1957
720.5 A67ar Eberson, John Capitol theater, Chicago, Illinois. John Eberson, archt. Architect (N.Y.) 6: pls.91-96 fol.p.436 July 1926	720.721 T53 Eberson, John Richmond, Virginia, has a new twenty-four story building. John Eberson, archt. Through the ages 8: 40-42 September 1930	Ecclesiastical architecture see Churches
720.5 N52 Eberson, John Lobby, Avalon theater, Chicago, Illinois. John Eberson, archt. Western architect 38: pl. 23 February 1929	720.5 P39 Eberson, John Murphy, E.C. A special type of motion picture theatre. John Eberson, archt. Pencil points 9: 704-711 November 1928	Eccleston (Eng.) St. Mary's Church From East End of South Aisle Looking into Chancel. The Nave, looking east. G.F. Bodley, archt. Arch and c. rep 67:2 pl fol 26,28, in Ja. 10,17, '02 supps.
720.5 A67b Eberson, John Loew's Paradise theatre, Bronx, N.Y. John Eberson, archt. Architecture and building 61: 332,347- November 1929 350,356	720.5 A51 Eberson, John Vestibule, Rivieria Annex theatre, Detroit Mich. Foyer & promenade, Avalon theatre, Chicago. Promenade & entrance lobby, Paradise theatre, Chicago, Ill. American architect 135: 825-828 June 20, 1929	Eccleston (Eng.) St. Mary's Church St. Mary's Church Eccleston. From South Aisle, Looking Northeast. Arch and con rep 67:pls. Ja 24; Ja 31, 1902
720.5 A67b Eberson, John Loew's Valencia Theatre, Jamaica, Long Island, New York. John Eberson, archt. Arch. and bldg. 61: 59 February 1929	MICROFILM Eberson, John and Drew New York Telecity planned. In SCRAPBOOK ON ARCHITECTURE p. 401 (on film)	Echagüe, César Ortiz- see Ortiz-Echagüe, César, 1026-
720.5 A67b Eberson, John Majestic theatre, Dallas, Texas. John Eberson, archt. Architecture and building 53: 88,pls.189- November 1921 191 fol.p.90	Ebert, Brückner & Gabriele Würzburg: Das "Ferdinaudeum," ein wohnheim für 175 studierende; baujahr 1960/1961 [plans] Dornbaumstr. Schädel, archt. with Brückner & Gabriele Ebert, assoc. archts. Das Münster vol.14: 414-415, N-D 1961	Echeverria, Luis Dos obras del arq. Luis Echeverria; Edificio comercial y de apartamentos "Trinidad" de la Insular Trading Co. Edificio de apartamentos en la calle 17 y 6, Vedado frente al Parque Menocal [plans and sections] Luis Echeverria, archt. Arquitectura Cuba Vol. 22:56-63 F 1954

Echevarria, Luis
    Residencias pol el Arq. Luis Echevarria.
    [plans]

        Arquitectura Cuba 18:464-467
        O 1950

Eckel and Mann
    Members of firm:
        Mann, George R
        Eckel, Edmond Jacques, 1845-1934

Eckel, E. J.
    see also
    Albany (MO)   Library
    St. Joseph (MO)   Corby-Forsee Office Building
        "   "   Elks Club Building
        "   "   (New) High School
        "   "   Hotel
        "   "   Krug (H.W.) Retail Store Building
        "   "   Live Stock Exchange Building

            (See Card 2)

Eckbo, Royston and Williams
    Le jardin d'une habitation en Californie
    [plan] Eckbo, Royston and Williams, land.archts.

        Aujourd'hui
        2: 42-43
        S 1956

720.5
A67   Eckel and Mann
            House at St.Louis. Drawing by Ellis.Eckel
        and Mann,archts.
            Perspective of tomb by Ellis. Eckel and
        Mann,archts.

            Architectural review 15:pls.85-86
            December 1908

Eckel, E. J.   (Card 2)
    see also
    St. Joseph (MO)   Mt. Mora Cemetery, J.B. Collins
                       Mausoleum
        "   "   Public Library
        "   "   Richardson Dry Goods Co. Building
        "   "   Robidoux Hotel
        "   "   St. Francis Xavier Church
        "   "   Scottish Rite Cathedral
        "   "   Tootle (J.J.) Residence

            (See Card 3)

Eckel & Aldrich
    see
    Memphis (TN)   Isele (Joseph A.) Residence
    St. Joseph (MO)   City Hall
        "   "   Methodist Episcopal Hospital
        "   "   St. James Roman Catholic Church
        "   "   Wyatt Park Baptist Church
    Wichita (KS)   Buckingham (S.J.) Residence

Eckel & Mann
    Residence for C.M. Carter, St. Joseph, Missouri.
    Eckel and Mann, archts.

        Inland archt.
        19, no.1
        pl. fol. p. 16
        F 1892

Eckel, E. J.   (Card 3)
    see also
    St. Joseph (MO)   Tootle-Lemon National Bank Bldg.
        "   "   (New) Union Station
        "   "   Wheeler-Motter Dry Goods Co. Bldg.
    Tarkio (MO)   Rankin (F.W.) Residence

Eckel and Aldrich
    Members of firm:
        Eckel, Edmond Jacques
        Eckel, George R
        Aldrich, Will S

Eckel & Mann
    Residence of T.D. McNeeley. St. Joseph,
    Mo. Eckel & Mann, archts.
    Residence of J. W. McAlister, St. Joseph,
    Mo. Eckel & Mann, archts.

        Inland architect
        v. 15 no. 4
        pl. fol. p. 64
        My 1890

Eckel, E.J.
    Beaux arts studies.

        West. Archt.
        17: 80,pls.fol.p. 86
        Sept, 1911

Eckel and Boschen
    see
    St. Joseph, Mo. First Presbyterian church
        "   "   McCord Mausoleum
        "   "   Robidoux School

Eckel & Mann
    Residence for S. M. Nave, St. Joseph,
    Missouri. Eckel & Mann, archts.

        Inland architect
        19, no. 6
        pl. fol. p. 78
        Jl 1892

720.5
N52   Eckel, Edmond Jacques, 1845-1934
            Contemporary architects and their works:

            Western architect 17:79-84 & pl.fol.p.
            September 1911   86

Eckel and Boschen
    Members of firm:
        Eckel, Edmond Jacques, 1845-1934
        Boschen, Walter

Eckel & Van Brunt
    Richardson, Roberts, Byrne & co. wholesale
    dry goods house. Eckel & Van Brunt, archts.

        Inland architect
        19, no. 4
        pl. fol. p. 54
        My 1892

Eckel, E.J.
    Design for "Bridge of the Republic."

        West. Archt.
        17: 82
        Sept, 1911

Eckel and Mann
    see
    Albany (MO)   Carnegie Library
    Jefferson City (MO)   Missouri State Penitentiary
    St. Joseph (MO)   Bartlett (D.L., Jr.) Residence
                          Carter Residence
    St. Louis (MO)   City Hall
    St. Joseph (MO)   McAlister (J.W.) Residence
        "   "   Moss (J.B.) Residence
        "   "   Tootle (J.J.) Residence

Eckel, Edmond Jacques, 1845-1934
    see also:
        Eckel and Mann
        Eckel and Boschen
        Eckel and Aldrich

720.53
W31   Eckenrath and Schurig
            Kinderklinik in Dortmund. (Clinic for
        children in Dortmund.) W.Eckenrath and W.
        Schurig,archts. Plans.

            Wasmuths monatshefte 14: 446-447
            October 1930

Eckert, Günther
    Internationales Studentenhaus in
München [plans] Günther Eckert & Werner
Wirsing, archts.

            Bauen & Wohnen
            #1:18-19 Jan 1957

Eclecticism in architecture. U.S.
Kimball, Fiske
    Development of American architecture; pt.
3: Eclecticism and functionalism

            Arch. for. 29: 21-25
            Jl 1918

Ecouen, Fr. Chateau
Cailleux, Gaston
XLVII Congrès des architectes Francois.
(47th Congress of French architects.) Paris

            L'architecture 36:239-265
            September 10, 1923

Eckland and DeArmant
    dissolved.

            West. Archt.
            24: XIV fol.
            Dec, 1916 issue

Ryerson
Ecochard, Michel
    Le Musee de Mohenjo Daro [plans] Michel
Ecochard, archt.

            Aujourd'hui
            Vol. 2:no. 8:37
            Je 1956

Ecouen. Chateau
    Château d'Ecouen. Text in French. Engravings.

            Eyries, Gustave. Les Chateaux
            Historiques de la France. 3 vols.
            Paris: Poitiers, H. Oudin Frères,
            1877-81 v.3:145-175

Eckland, Fugard and Knapp
    Members of firm:
        Eckland, Henry
        Fugard, J.R.
        Knapp, G.A.

Ecole de Nancy (group)
Nicolas, Émile
    L'Ecole de Nancy et ses concours [illus.]

            L'Art décoratif
            16: 191-194
            Nov. 1906

Ecouen (Fr.). Chateau
    Escovan. French text. Plan, engravings.

            Androuet du Cerceau-Les plus excellents
            bastiments de France. 2 vols. Paris:
            A. Lévy, 1868-70. vol.2:11,pls.47-51

Eckland, Fugard and Knapp
    Firm Dissolved.

            West. Archt.
            28: VI
            Jan, 1919

Ecole des Beaux-Arts

            see

Paris (Fr.) Ecole des Beaux-Arts

Ecouis.Nôtre Dame
    Ecouis church.

            Archaeological journal 95:386-387
            Part 2,1938

Eckland, Henry
    Member of firm:
        Eckland, Fugard and Knapp

Economy, Pa.

            see also

Ambridge, Pa.

Écuries. Chantilly

            See

Chantilly. Château. Écuries.

Eckstorm, Christian A.

    see also

Chicago, Ill. Harvester building (1907)

Economy, Pa. Architecture. Conservation
    and restoration.
Stotz, Charles Morse
    Threshold of the golden kingdom: the
village of Economy and its restoration. [illus]

            Winterthur portfolio
            8: [133] - 169
            1973

Edberg, Gösta, 1918-
    Gosta Edberg [biog. note][photo]

            Northwest arch 16. no. 4:41-2
            Jl-Ag 1952

Eclecticism in architecture. U.S.
Tallmadge, T   E
    American architecture: eclecticism, 1893-1917

            Building for the future
            1930: 1-4

Economy (Pa.) Church
    The tower of the church at Economy,
Pennsylvania.

            American-German review 6:cover
            August 1940

Edbrooke and Burnham
    see also

Atlanta, Ga. Y.M.C.A. building (1886)
Chicago (IL.) Chase (H.G.) house
    "   "   Englewood M.E. Church
    "   "   Grimes (F.R.) house
    "   "   Herrick (L.A.) house and stable
    "   "   Hill (William) house
    "   "   Mecca Apts.
    "   "   Oakland M.E. Church (1886)
    "   "   Wolff (M.) stable
                        (see card 2)

Edbrooke and Burnham (card 2)

see also

Clinton (Ia.) Gardiner (S.B.) house
" (Mo.) Henry County Court House (1886)
Evanston (IL.) Kirk (J.B.) house
Kansas City (Mo.) Calvary Baptist Church
Pontiac (IL.) Cook (A.L.)house

720.5
B93b   Edbrooke and Burnham
Sketch of Leavitt Street Congregational
Church, corner of Leavitt and Adams Streets.
Edbrooke and Burnham, archts. Plan.

Building budget 3: pl.fol.p.40
March 31, 1887

Edbrooke, J. H.

see

Chicago (Ill.) Randolph building

Edbrooke & Burnham
Members of firm:
Edbrooke, W. J.
Burnham, Franklin Pierce

Edbrooke, F. E. & Co.

see

Denver (CO)   Cooper Building
             McMurtrie Building

Edbrooke, W. J.

see also

Chicago (IL)   World's Columbian Exposition
             United States Govt. Building

Edbrooke & Burnham
Amateur athletic association building &
lyceum theater, Memphis, Tenn. Edbrooke &
Burnham, archts.

Inland architect
19, no. 5
pl. fol. p. 66
Je 1892

Edbrooke, Frank E.

see also

Denver (CO)   Denver Gas & Electric Building

Edbrooke, Willoughby J., 1843 - 96

See also

Edbrooke and Burnham.

Edbrooke and Burnham
Block of 6 stories on Indiana St. for Wm.
Johnson. Edbrooke and Burnham, archts.

Building budget
3:86b
Je 30, 1887

Edbrooke, Frank E. 1840-1921
obit.

West. Archt.
30: 65
Jun, 1921

Edbrooke, Willoughby J. 1843-1896
Biography and list of works of Willoughby J.
Edbrooke.

Andreas, A.T. History of Chicago.
3 vols. Chicago: A.T. Andreas, 1884.
v.2:p.566

720.5
I56   Edbrooke and Burnham
Ware, W. R.
The Exchange building Association of Kansas
City.
Results of competition. Designed by Edbrooke
and Burnham.

Inland architect 8:4-6,pl.fol.14
August 1886

Edbrooke, George H., d.1894

see also

Chicago, Ill. College of physicians and surgeons
(1881)
Chicago, Ill. Hiram Sibley & Co. warehouse (1883)
" " homoeopathic college (1881)
" " Republic life building (1870)
Detroit, Mich. American building
St. Louis, Mo. Commercial building

720.6
A51   Edbrooke, Willoughby J.   1843-1896
In memoriam. Willoughby J. Edbrooke.

A.I.A.Proceedings 30:152
1896

Edbrooke and Burnham
Remodelling five-story building on Wabash Ave.
for D.T. Loring. Edbrooke and Burnham, archts.

Building budget 3:86b
Je 30, 1887

MICROFILM

Edbrooke, George H   archt.
South Congregational church, Drexel blvd.
and 40th st., Chicago,.Ill. 1905.

Roll 26, frames 250-256

Edbrooke, Willoughby J. 1843-1896.
Obit.

Inland Arch.
27: 28
April 1896

Edbrooke and Burnham
School house in Jefferson, IL.
Edbrooke and Burnham, archts.

Building budget
3:86b
Je 30, 1887

Edbrooke, H. W. J.

see

Denver (CO)   Kistler (W.N.) Stationery Co.

Eddy, A.J.
see

Pasadena (CA) Eddy residence

Rde, G J P van Zuiderhoek, D 　Information; V.V.V. bureau te Arnhem (plans and section) C. Nap and G.J.P. van Rde, archts. 　Forum 　No. 7: 220-223 　S 1955	790.5 A67r　Edgartown (Mass.). Architecture 　Road, Grace Norton 　Doorways of an old whaling village. 　Arch rec 33: 55-65 　Ja '13	Edgewater, Ill. 　see Chicago, Ill. Edgewater.
Edelman, A. M. 　see Los Angeles (CA)　B'nai Brith Synagogue	Edgbaston (Eng.) Cedars 　The "Cedars", Calthorpe Road, Edgbaston. Bateman and Bateman, archts. Plans. A　　Architectural record 5:339-346 　　April-June 1896	720.5 A51　Edgewater Park (N.J.)Terry (J.H.) house 　House of J.Hermon Terry,Edgewater Park, New Jersey. J.Fletcher Street,arcbt. Plans. 　American architect 101: pls.fol.p.236 　May 22,1912
Eden, F. C. 　see Ipswich (Eng.) "Field of Honor"	Edgbaston, Eng. Dalecross Grange 　Bunney, Michael Dalecross Grange and other houses: House in Pritchatts Road, Edgbaston, Crouch and Butler, archts. 　Brickbuilder 17:97-100 　May, 1908	Edgewater Presbyterian church. Chicago 　see Chicago, Ill. Edgewater Presbyterian church
Edens plaza shopping center. 　see Wilmette, Ill. Edens plaza shopping center.	Edgbaston (Eng.) Golf Club House 　Golf Club house, Edgbaston, Birmingham. Buckland, Haywood and Farmer, archts. 　Architects' and Builders' journal 44;pl.for 　September 6, 1916	Edgewood (IN) Messich (Harry) Residence 　Johnson and Miller, archts. 　West. Archt. 　24: 146 　Nov, 1916
Edenton (N.C.) Beverly Hall 　Beverly Hall: a bachelor's old Colonial home on King Street, Edenton, North Carolina. Originally a bank - built 1810. Richard Dillard, archt. 　House and garden 10: 27-29 　July 1906	720.52 A67c　Edgbaston (Eng.) house 　House at Edgbaston, Birmingham. Messrs. Cossins, Peacock & Bewlay, Architects. 　Arch. & contract reporter 81: 　416, last pl. fol 424 　Je 25 '09	Edgware (Eng.) Convent of St. Mary of Nazareth. 　　　　　　　　Chapel. 　Memorial Chapel, Convent of S. Mary of Nazareth, Edgware. Messrs. Brook, Son and Adkins, architects. 　Builder 99:pl. 　Jl 9, 1910
720.5 A67r　Edenton (N.C.) Saint Paul's episcopal church Embury,Aymar II 　Early American churches. Pt.8. St.Paul's, Edenton,N.C. and others. No plans. 　Architectural record 32:80-82 　July 1912	Edgecliff, Winnetka, Ill. 　see Winnetka, Ill. Edgecliff	720.5 B93b　Edinburgh(Ind.)　　Christian Church 　Edinburgh Christian Church at Edinburgh, Ind.　Daggett, R. P. & Co., archts. 　Building budget 　3:3 in supp 　My 31, 1887
720.5 Up75　Edenton (N.C.) St. Paul's Episcopal church Upjohn, H.B. 　St. Paul's church (1736)Edenton, N.C. 　Monograph series 15: 4, pl 2 　No 1 '29	Edgewater Beach hotel.Chicago 　See Chicago.Edgewater Beach hotel	Edinburgh School of architecture 　see Edinburgh (Scot.) College of Art. 　School of architecture

Edinburgh.

Nouveau Theatre de la Grande
Bretagne. 5 vols. London:
D. Mortier, 1708, 1715-28.
v.4,pl.43.

Edinburgh (Scot) America's Tribute to Scotland
America's tribute to Scotland.

Country life (Lond.) 62:315,319-23
September 3, 1927

720.6
R88   Edinburgh. Architecture
      "Edinburgh: its rise and progress"

      Royal Inst.Brit.Arch. 30:518-22
      Jun. 30, 1923

710.5
C85   Edinburgh
      The charm of Edinburgh.

      Country life (Lond.) 68: lxviii
      July 26, 1930

710.5
C85   Edinburgh.Archers Hall
      Archers Hall - interiors only.

      Country life(Lond)82:61-63
      July 17,1937

710.5
C85   Edinburgh. Architecture
      Maclehose, Alexander
      Edinburgh revisited.

      Country Life 80): lxii, lxiv, lxvi
      July 1936

720.52
A67c   Edinburgh
       "Edinburgh: its rise and progress"

       Architect 109:447-9
       Jun. 29, 1923

720.52
A67   Edinburgh. Architecture
      Architectural travel. Edited by F.R.
      Yerbury. Edinburgh.

      Architects Journal 57:993
      June 13, 1923

710.5
C85   Edinburgh. Architecture
      "The modern Athens"

      Country life (Lond.) 58:172-79
      Aug. 1, 1925

720.6
A51j   Edinburgh
       Planned cities-II-Edinburgh

       American institute of architects
       12:1-12
       Jan. 1924

Edinburgh, Scotland. Architecture
Rowan, Alistair
   The Athens of the north explored.
Georgian Edinburgh -- II.
[illus.]

   Country life
   142: 1052-1055
   O 26, 1967

720.6
R88   Edinburgh. Architecture.
      Old Edinburgh and some of its buildings,
      by Henry F. Kerr.

      Royal Inst. of Brit.arch.J.
      27:93-105. Jan.10,1920.

720.52
B93   Edinburgh
      The town-planning institute, annual
      conference. York

      Builder 125:575-7
      Oct. 12, 1923

Edinburgh, Scotland. Architecture
Rowan, Alistair
   Bicentenary of a classical city. Georgian
Edinburgh -- I. [illus.]

   Country life
   142: 956-959
   O 19, 1967

Edinburgh, Scotland. Architecture
Murdoch, W.G.B.
Recent ecclesiastical and domestic architecture in
Edinburgh, Scotland

   American magazine of art 17:9-19
   Jan. 1926

Edinburgh (Scot.) Academy
Edinburgh academy

Country life 42:supp 8,10,12
N 3, '17

710.5
C85   Edinburgh. Architecture
      The courts and wynds of old Edinburgh

      Country Life (Lond.) 57:22-29
      Jan. 3, 1925

720.52
A67   Edinburgh. Architecture
      The Royal High school, the City Chambers,
      Charlotte Square.

      Architects Journal 57:1041-3
      June 20, 1923

710.5
C85   Edinburgh.Acheson house
      Stuart, M.K.
      "Acheson House, Edinburgh": the restoration
      of an old mansion.

      Country life(London)85:20-21
      January 7,1939

720.52
B93   Edinburgh. Architecture
      Edinburgh.

      Builder 135: 583,585
      October 12, 1928

Edinburgh (Scot.) Caroline Park house
Caroline Park house, Edinburgh.

      Arch. Jour. 55:431,433.
      Mar. 22, 1922.

Edinburgh (Scot.) Castle
The Scottish National War Memorial.
Sir Robt. Lorimer, archt.

Arch. rev. 62:101-107
September, 1927

Edinburgh, Scot. George Watson's Boys' College
Competition for new secondary school,
George Watson's Boys' College, Edinburgh.

Architects' journal 67:831-834
June 13, 1928

Edinburgh, Holyrood Palace and Abbey. Gates.
National Scottish Memorial to King Edward VII,
Holyrood Palace.

Arch. jour. 52:123-5.
Aug. 4, 1920

Edinburgh (Scot.) Castle
Special number.

Architecture (London) 5
August 1927

Edinburgh, Scot. Holyrood house

see

Edinburgh, Scot. Holyrood palace and abbey

Edinburgh (Scot.) King (Dr.) house
House for Dr. King, Murrayfield, Edinburgh,
Kininmonth and Spence, architects. Plan.

Architect 143:227
August 23, 1935

Edinburgh (Scot.) Castle. Scottish National War
Memorial
The Scottish National War Memorial.
Sir Robert Lorimer, archt.

Builder 133:118-119,122-3
July 22, 1927

Edinburgh. Holyrood Palace and Abbey
The Palace and Chapel of Holyrood.

Billings, Robert William. The baronial and
ecclesiastical antiquities of Scotland.
4 vols. London: W. Blackwood and Sons
for the author, 1845-52
3:pls 16-20 and 8 pages of text.

Edinburgh, Scot. Leith

This heading is used for articles about the
town or area of Leith.

For specific buildings in this area, see under
Edinburgh, Scot., i.e.: Edinburgh, Scot. Leith
town hall and library

Edinburgh (Scot.) Castle. Scottish National War
Memorial.
The Scottish National War Memorial. Special
number. Sir Robert Lorimer, archt.

Country life (Lond.) 62: supp.
July 16, 1927

Edinburgh. Scot. Holyrood palace and abbey.
Dunbar, J. G.
The palace of Hollyrood house during the
first half of the sixteenth century.
[illus]

Archaeological Journal
V. 120: [242]-254
1963

Edinburgh, Scot. Leith Town Hall and Library
The new town hall and library, Leith.
Bradshaw, Gass and Hope, archts.

Builder 143: 358-360
September 2, 1932

Edinburgh, Scot. Church of Christ Scientist
Inverleith Terrace, Edinburgh

Archts. and bldrs' jour. 47: pl.for
May 8, 1918

Edinburgh, Scot. Holyrood Palace and Abbey
Easton, J.
The Royal Palace of Holyrood House.

Architects' journal 69:277-281
February 13, 1929

Edinburgh, Scot. Leith Town Hall and Library
Leith town hall and library. Bradshaw, Gass
and Hope, archts.

Architect (Eng.) 131:357-363
September 16, 1932

Edinburgh (Scot.) College of Art. School of
Architecture.
Begg, J.
School of architecture, Edinburgh College of
Art.

R.I.B.A. 36: 199-203
January 12, 1929

Edinburgh, Scot. Holyrood palace & abbey
Ceiling

Builder 124: 1013-15
Je 22, 1923

720.52
A67c
Edinburgh (Scot.) life assurance company building
The Edinburgh life assurance company's
new offices, George street, Edinburgh.
J.M. Dick Peddie, architect. Illus. of
exterior and interiors of board room and
public office.

Architect and contract reporter 81:209,
March 26, 1909   pl.fol.p.216

Edinburgh, (Scot.) George Heriot's School War
Memorial
George Heriot's School Edinburgh, War Memorial.

Builder 126:980
June 20, 1924

Edinburgh (Scot.) Holyrood Palace and Abbey. Chapel
Interior of Holyrood Abbey Chapel.
Drawn by G.S. Aitken, F.S.A. (Scot.)

Arch and con. rep. 81:400,pl.
Je 18, 1909

720.52
A67c
Edinburgh. McEwan Hall
McEwan Hall, Edinburgh.

Architect 67: pl.fol.p.32 of supp.
January 3, 1902

Edinburgh, Scot. Order of Thistle Chapel
Chapel for Order of Thistle, Edinburgh

West. arch. 19,n.s. 2:pl.71-72-74
June 1913

Edinburgh (Scot.) Planning
Planned cities--II-Edinburg

American institute of architects
12:1-12
Jan. 1924

Edinburgh, Scot. St. Gile's Cathedral Chapel of the
Thistle
L.,W.
The Thistle Chapel. Plan.

Country life 30:81-85
July 15, 1911

Edinburgh, Scot. Orthopaedic Center
Orthopaedic Center. Edinburgh

Archts' and bldrs' jour. 48:pl.for
Nov. 20, 1918

Edinburgh (Scot.) Planning
Summerson, J.N.
The terrace houses of Edinburgh.

Builder 141:264-265;302-303
August 14; 21, 1931

Edinburgh, Scot. St. Gile's Cathedral Chapel of the
Thistle
Chapel of the Thistle, Edinburgh.
Mr. R. S. Lorimer.

Builder 101:6 pls.
July 21, 1911

Edinburgh (Scot.) Outlook Tower
Outlook Tower, Edinburgh

Museums jour. 16:103-113
Nov. 1916

Edinburgh, Scot. Prince's Street
Geddes, Alasdair
The picture palaces of Princes street, Edin-
burgh. The last chapter in a century of "Progress".

Town planning rev 5:55-6,pls
22-23
Ap 1914

Edinburgh, Scot. St. Gile's Cathedral Chapel of the
Thistle
Chapel of the order of the thistle, St. Giles
Cathedral, Edinburgh. R.S. Lorimer, archt. Plan.

A   New York architect 5:465-467
August, 1911

Edinburgh (Scot.) Planning
Hurd, Robert
Clearing the slums of Edinburgh; some typical
reconditioning and rebuilding schemes.

Architects' journal 71:491-494;542-545
March 26; April 2, 1930

720.52   Edinburgh (Scot.) Register house
A67   Architecture of the 18th century. The
Register house, Edinburgh. Robert Adam,
architect

Architects jour. 57: pl 1039
Je 20 '23

Edinburgh, Scot. St. Gile's Cathedral Chapel of the
Thistle
The Thistle Chapel, Edinburgh, by Sir Robert
Lorimer, archt.

A   Architectural review 19 ns.2:202,pl.
June 1913   77-80

Edinburgh (Scot.) Planning
Hughes, T.H.
An early nineteenth century town planning scheme.

Town planning review 13: 69-79
December, 1928

Edinburgh (Scot.). Royal College of Physicians.
Royal College of Physicians, Edinburgh.
Thomas Hamilton, archt. Plan and elevation.

Builder 121:286-7.
Sept. 2, 1921

Edinburgh, Scot. St. Giles Cathedral. Lorimer
(Sir Robert) Memorial
Memorial to Sir Robert Lorimer, St. Gile's
Cathedral, Edinburgh.

Builder 143:202,204
August 5, 1932

Edinburgh (Scot.) Planning
Edinburgh.

Builder 135:583,601-606
October 12, 1928

Edinburgh. Royal Scottish Academy Buildings
The Royal Scottish Academy Building,
Edinburgh. Playfair, archt.

Builder 130:742-4
April 30, 1926

Edinburgh, Scot. St. Giles Cathedral. 16th Royal
Scots. Memorial
War memorials, 32-The 16th Royal Scots Memorial,
St. Giles Cathedral. Sir Robert Lorimer, archt.

Architects' journal 57:179
January 24, 1923

Edinburgh (Scot.) Planning
"Edinburgh: its rise and progress"

Jour. Royal Inst. Brit. Arch. 30:518-22
Jun. 30, 1923

Edinburgh, Scotland. St. Cecilia's hall.
Fenwick, Hubert
St. Cecilia's hall restored. [illus.]

Country life
144: 401-402
Ag 15 1968

Edinburgh, Scot. St. Mary's Cathedral
St. Mary's Cathedral, Edinburgh.

Arch and con rep 73: 17-20
Ja 6, 1905

Edinburgh (Scot.) St. Paul's church.
Memorial chapel. Reredos
The memorial chapel, St. Paul's church,
Edinburgh.W.O. Tarbolton. archt.

Architects' jl. 58: 847-9
Je 21, '39

Edinburgh (Scot.) Usher Hall
Usher Hall. Edinburgh

Builder 106:496
Apr. 24, 1914

Edington, Eng. (Wilts) Priory church
Edington and its monastic church

Arch & rep   85: 264-267
April 28, 1911

720.52
A67c
Edinburgh. "(The)Scotsman"
New offices of "The Scotsman", Edinburgh.
James B. Dunn, archt. Photographs.

Architect and contract reporter 75:pl.
March 16,1906   Fol.p.184

Edinburgh (Scot.) Usher Hall
Usher Hall, Edinburgh

Arch. and Bldrs. jour. 40:357-8
May 20, 1914

Edirne, Turkey
Vogt-Goknil, Ulya
Die Külliye von Bayazit II. in Edirne,
Aufnahmen von Eduard Widmer. [illus]

Du
V. 25: 612-623
Ag. 1965

Edinburgh University
Designs for buildings

Adam, Robert. Works in architecture.
3 vols. London: Priestley and Weale,
1822. v. 3

Edinburgh (Scot.) War Memorial
Edinburgh War Memorial

Builder 117:616
Dec. 19, 1919

Edis, Robert W.

see

London (Eng.) Imperial hotel
Chicago (Ill.) World's Columbian exposition.
Victoria house

Edinburgh (Scot.) University
The University, Edinburgh. Robert Adam
architect.

Architects journal 57:pl.1026
June 20, 1923

Edinburgh. Scot. Wardie Elementary School
Wardie Elementary School, Edinburgh.
signed by J. M. Johnston. Plan.

Architects' journal 76: 355-357
September 21, 1932

Edison building, Chicago

see

Chicago (Ill.) Edison building (1898)
"   "   Edison building (1907)

720.52
A675
Edinburgh. University.
The university, Edinburgh; Robert Adam,
archt.

Architectural review 64: pl 3
July 1928

Edinburgh, Scot. Young Men's Christian Assn.
The Edinburgh Y.M.C.A. G.W. Browne, architect.

Architect 103:60-2
January 23, 1920

Edison building, New York city

see

New York (city) Edison building

Edinburgh University Housing Research Unit
Prestonpans development [site plan &
plan] Edinburgh University Housing Research
Unit, archts.

Archtl Design
30:351 S 1960

Edinburgh (Scot.) Zoological Garden
Stebbing, E.P.
The zoological park at Edinburgh.

Country life (Lond.) 34: 417-419
September 27, 1913

Edison Company power houses, Chicago

see

Chicago (Ill.) Edison company power
house (1887)

Edinburgh (Scot.) Usher Hall
Usher Hall, Edinburgh

Arch. rev. (Lond.) 36:18-20
pl. 12-14

Edington, Eng. Churches
Edington Church, Wilts. Drawn by Mr. T.F.W. Grant.

Builder 101:274 and pls.
S 8, 1911

Edison electric appliance co., Chicago

see

Chicago (Ill.) Edison electric appliance co.

Edison institute, Dearborn, Mich.

see

Dearborn, Mich. Henry Ford museum

Edmonds and Jackson

see also

London, Eng. Crystal palace (new) Competition

Edmonton (Alb.) Packing House
Abattoir a Edmonton. E.R.Arthur, archt.(plan)

L'Architecture d'aujourd'hui
11:38
No. 3-4, 1940

Edison laboratory

see

West Orange (N.J.) Edison laboratory

Edmonton (Alberta) Architecture

West. Archt.
19: p. 110-113
Dec, 1913

Edmonton, Alberta. Provincial museum
and archives of Alberta.
Harrison, Raymond
Planning for action and growth. [illus.]

Museum news
v. 51: 21-24
N 1972

Edison service bldg., Detroit

see

Detroit (Mich.) Edison service bldg.

Edmonton (Alberta) Canada packers ltd. Building
Plans for Canada Packers ltd.,Edmonton,Alberta.
E. R. Arthur and A.P.C. Adamson, archts.

RAIC jrl 14:70 F 1937
158-60 Ag '37

Edmonton, Alb. Public Library
Edmonton Public Library, Alberta. Macdonald
and Magoon, architects. Plan.

Architecture 49:17-18
Jan. 1924

Edison shop, Chicago

see

Chicago (Ill.) Edison shop

Edmonton, Alberta. Eaton company western limited.
Building
The T. Eaton company western limited. Edmonton,
Alberta. Northwood and Chivers, archts.

RAIC jrl 16:257
Dec 1939

Edmunds, James R.

see

Baltimore (Md.) Civic Center [proposed]

Edison Shop. Kansas City

see

Kansas City, Mo. Edison Shop.

Edmonton (Alberta) Empire Theater
Empire Theater, Edmonton, Alberta.
Major and Stacy-Judd, archts.

Western architect 30: pl.13-14
December 1921

Edna's Mill house, Charles City County, Va.
Edna's Mill house near Raxbury, Charles City
County.

William and Mary Quarterly, ser.2,18:pl.
April 1938

Edison shop, San Francisco, Cal.

see

San Francisco, Cal. Edison shop

Edmonton, Alberta. General hospital(1941)
New General hospital, Edmonton, Alberta.
[plans] McDonald and Magoon, archts.

RAIC jour 18: 157
Ag 1941

Edo, Jap.

see

Tokyo, Japan

Edison, Thomas Alva, memorial

see

Menlo Park, N.Y. Edison tower

720.5
A67b   Edmonton (Alb.) MacDonald hotel
Hotel McDonald, Edmonton, Alberta,
Canada. Ross and MacDonald, archts. Plans.

Arch & bldg 48: 89-91
My '16

720.52
E93   Edstrom, David
A maker of monuments

Builder 128:479-80
Mar. 27, 1925

Education, Architectural see Architectural education	Edward Nicholl Home for Babies The Edward Nicholl home for babies. Builder 120:798 and pl. June 24, 1921.	Edwards, Arthur Trystan, 1884- Geoffrey Scott. Architect (Lond.) 122:221-222,227-228 August 23, 1929
Education, Industrial See Technical education.	Edwards and Green see Camden (N.J.) county court house	Edwards, Arthur Trystan, 1884- Ornament and mouldings A. Trystan Edwards, archt. Architects Jour. 62:818-819 Dec. 2, 1925
Education, Technical see Technical education	720.5 A67f Edwards & Hoffman House for Matthew W. Black, Berwyn, Pa. Edwards & Hoffman, archts. Plan. Architectural forum 65: 448 November 1936	Edwards, E. Nelson see Philadelphia (Pa.) Lea & Febiger office building
720.52 B93 Edward VII, Monument. -- Sir Bertram Mackennal, Sculptor. Builder 121:128. July 29, 1921.	Edwards & Plunkett see Santa Barbara, Calif. Mitchell (C.B.) house	Edwards, F. E. P. see Sheffield (Eng.) Public baths Baths, England
Edward, Black Prince, Tomb see Canterbury (Eng) cathedral	Edwards and Sayward see Columbia (S.C.) Heath (M.C.) house	Edwards, Harry. C. Died May 9, 1922. American art news 20: 6 May 13, 1922.
Edward, King of England. Memorials The London Memorial to King Edward. RIBA jour. 18: 389 Ap 1, 1911	Edwards & Sunderland see Kansas City (MO) Apartment Building " " " "Maples" Apt. Bldg. " " " New England Apt. House	Edwards Place, James City County, Va. Edwards place, owned by Mrs. Marcus Cottrell. William and Mary Quarterly, ser.2,18:pl.69c July 1938
Edward L. Doheny jr. memorial library see Los Angeles, Cal. University of S. California. Edward L. Doheny jr. memorial library	Edwards and Walter see Bishopville (S.C.) Lee county court house Savannah (Ga.) Southern railway station	Edwards, Reid and Booth see Ceylon (Ind.) The Chartered Bank Colombo Colombo (Ceylon) Villa Venesia

Edwards, S. J. Colombo town hall and municipal offices. S.J. Edwards (Booty and Edwards), archts. Architecture (Lond.) 5:103 August 1926	Effingham, Eng. Robins Wood. Phillips, Randal Robins Wood, Effingham, Surrey. Country life (Lond.) 66:659-660 November 9, 1929	720.5 B92b Egan, James J Design of Spalding Hotel, Duluth, Minn. J.J.Egan, archt. Chicago. Building budget 3: pl.fol.p.100 August 31, 1887
Edwards, W. B. see Pasadena (CA) Stratton Apt. Building	Effingham, IL. School Royer, J.W. School for Effingham, Illinois, Royer and Davis, archts. Plans. A Architectural concrete 7:15-17 No. 1 [1941]	720.5 B92b Egan, James J Sketch of new Roman Catholic church, Des Moines, Iowa. James J. Egan, archt. Building budget 6: pl.fol.p.22 February 28, 1890
Edwards-Ficken, H see Ficken, Henry Edwards, d. 1929	Efflorescence see Bricks. Efflorescence	720.5 I56 Egan, James J Sketches of cathedral for Roman Catholic Society of San Francisco, California. by J. J. Egan, archt. Plans. Inland architect 7:43,pl.fol.52 April 1886
Edwardsville (Il.) Griffin (R.D.) House Walter Burley Griffin, archt. Roll 33, frame 16	Egan and Prindeville see Chicago (IL) F. J. Geraghty Residence " " Holy Angels Church " " St. Vincent de Paul Church " " St. Xavier's Academy (1899) Lake Forest (IL) Academy of the Sacred Heart Notre Dame (IN) St. Mary's Academy Pittsburgh (PA) St. Paul's Cathedral	Egandale, Chicago see Chicago (Ill.) Egandale

Edwardsville(IL.) Griffin (R.D.) house
Residence of Ralph D. Griffin, Edwardsville,
Illinois. Walter Burley Griffin, archt.
 	
A   Architectural record 32:380-381
October, 1912
	Egan, James J., 1839-1914
	
	see also
	
	Chicago (IL) Breevort Hotel
	" " Calvary Cemetery. Keeley, M.
	    Mausoleum (1886)
	" " Cook County Court House and City Hall
	    (1887-85)
	" " St. Elizabeths Church
	" " St. Vincent de Paul Church
	" " St. Jarlaths Church (1886)
	Clinton (IA) St. Marys Church (1886)
		STEVENS LIBRARY.
		705.6
		A67 Egas, Enrique
		Architecture in the chapel of Granada
		
		Archivo Español de arte y arqueologia
		1: 248-250
		Sept.- Dec. 1925

Edwardsville (Ill) Residence Walter Burley Griffin, Archt. West. Archt. 19: pls.fol.p. XV Aug, 1913	Egan, James J., 1839-1914 see also Egan & Prindiville Armstrong & Egan	Egeler, Ernst see Erlenhof (Switz.) Zöglings-pavillon Stables, Switzerland Bettingen (Switz.) Haus Binningen (Switz.) Haus
720.5 A51 Edwardsville (Ill.) Warnock (W.M.) house House of Mr. W.M. Warnock...F.C. Bonsack, archt. Amer archt and bldg news 55: pl fol 88 & 1F, 1896	720.5 B92b Egan, James J DeLaSalle Institute, Chicago, Illinois. James J. Egan, archt. Building budget 5: pl.fol.p.22 February 28, 1889	Egender, Karl see also Zürich (Switz.) Zum Sihlgarten " " Schweizerischen Landesausstellung 1939. Modetheater.

Egender, Karl
Projekt für bungalows der Messrs. Baur & Co.
in Kelaniya (Ceylon). K. Egender & W. Müller,
archts.

Das werk
32: beilage 2 fol sup 36
Nr 1945

Eggen, Karen & Jan
Bâtiment administratif, Herning, Danemark
Aagaard Andersen & Karen & Jan Eggen, archts.

Aujourd'hui
3:54-5 Jl 1958

Eggers Otto R.

see also

Yorkship Village (N.J.)

Egender, K. and E. Burkhardt

see

Basel (Switz.) St. Johanneskirche

Eggeriex, J. J.

see

La Panne (Belg.) house

720.5 | Eggers, Otto | 1889-
A67ar | Constitution Hall, Daughters of the
American Revolution, Washington, D.C.
John R. Pope, archt. Otto Eggers, del.

Architect (N.Y.)10:438,446
July 1928

Egender, K. and W. Müller
see
Colombo (Ceylon) A. Baur and Co., Ltd. building

Eggers & Higgins

see

Great Kills (N.Y.) Church of St. Clare
Bloomington (Ind.) Indiana university
New York (N.Y.) Worlds Fair. 1939 Schaefer center

720.5 | Eggers, Otto R | 1889-
P80 | Design submitted by John R. Pope, archt. for
Harding memorial. Rendering by Otto Eggers.

Pencil points 8: 23
January 1927

Egeskov Castle, Denmark
Egeskov, Island of Fyn

Amer. Scand. review 8:opp.823
Nov. 1920

Eggers and Higgins

members of firm
Higgins, Daniel Paul
Eggers, Otto R

720.5 | Eggers, Otto R. | 1889-
A51 | Doorway to Fairfax house, Alexandria, Va.
Sketch by O. R. Eggers.

American architect 119: 584
May 25, 1921

Eggeling, H
Bürogebäude "Bismarckhaus" in Essen [plan]
H. Eggeling, archt.

Baumeister
56:640-42 O 1959

Eggers, George W.
Review of Irwing Pond's "The meaning of
architecture"

Western arch 27:111-114
Nov. 1918

720.5 | Eggers, Otto R | 1889-
C855 | Entrance; drawing by Otto Eggers.

Country life (U.S.) 52:49
August 1927

Eggeling, Wilhelm
Ein druckereigebäude in Essen [plans]
Wilhelm Eggeling, archt.

Architektur and Wohnform
64: 105-109 no.3
F 1956

Eggers, Otto C.
Architect - "shipbuilder"

Natl arch 6: 5
D 1960

720.5 | Eggers, Otto R. | 1889-
A67ar | Hendricks Chapel, Syracuse University,
Syracuse, N. Y. Office of John Russell Pope,
archts. Otto R. Eggers, del.
Scottish Rite Temple of Baltimore, Md.
Clyde N. Friz, archt., Office of John Russell
Pope, consulting archts., Otto R. Eggers, del.

Architect (N.Y.) 11: 630,632
March 1929

Eggen, Jan

see

Eggen, Karen & Jan

Eggers, Otto R | 1882-

See also

Eggers and Higgins
Pope, John Russell - Office of

Eggers, Otto R. | 1882-
Interior studies of residence of George G.
Sicard, Larchmont, New York. Office of John
Russell Pope, archt. Otto R. Eggers, del.

Architect (N.Y.) 12:20-22
April 1929

720.5
B84

Eggers, Otto R.   1882-
Monographs on architectural renderers.
Being a series of articles on the architec-
tural renderers of to-day, accompanied by
characteristic examples of their work: Pt.1.
The work of O.R.Eggers.

Brickbuilder 23:7-9
January 1914

720.5
A67a

Eggers, Otto R   1882-
Sketch of entrance side of a country house
by O.R. Eggers.

Architecture 55: front.
January 1927

720.5
A67ar

Eggers, Otto R.   1882-
Study, Savings Investment and Trust Co.,
Newark, N. J. Elliott Lynch, archt. Otto
R. Eggers, del.

Architect (N.Y.) 11: 44
October 1928

720.5
A51

Eggers,Otto R   1882-
Old State house, Philadelphia, Pa.
Building started 1729. Tower added about
1751. Sketch by O.R. Eggers.

American architect 119:452 & pl.opp.p.
April 27,1921   452

720.5
A67a

Eggers, Otto R   1882-
Sketch of interior by Otto Eggers.

Architecture 55: front.
April 1927

720.5
A67ar

Eggers, O.R.   1882-
Study, Tack room, Stable, residence of Mr.
Marshall Field, L.I. J.R. Pope, archt. O.R.
Eggers, del.

Architect (N.Y.)9:290
December 1927

720.5
A51

Eggers,Otto R   1882-
Old Stock exchange, Philadelphia, Pa.
designed by William Strickland. Built in
1831. A "Greek revival" building. Sketch
by O.R. Eggers.

American architect 120:116 & pl.opp.p.
August 17,1921   116

720.5
A67ar

Eggers, O .R.   1882-
Studies by O.R. Eggers of the Baltimore Art
museum and Hotel Annapolis.

Architect (N.Y.)8:448,450,
July 1927   452

Eggers, Otto R.   1882-
Twenty-one sketches of Early American
architecture in New York and Connecticut.

Amer. archt. 118, Aug-Dec. 1920:
opp.p.144;176;212;250;284;320;352;380;
410;442;472;500;534;576;604;642;
670;704;736;788;822;860.

720.5
A67r
Boyd,J.T.,Jr.

Eggers,Otto R   1882-
Otto R.Eggers,architectural renderer and
designer.

Architectural record 43: 420-425
May 1918

720.5
A67ar

Eggers, Otto R.   1882-
Study by Otto Eggers, house of Mr. M.Lew-
is, Sterlington, N.Y.

Architect (N.Y.) 9: 554
February 1928

Egham, Eng. Great Fosters
Great Fosters, Egham

(Lond) Country life 52:640
Nov. 18, 1922

720.5
A67ar

Eggers, Otto R.   1882-
Pencil sketches of the University club,
Milwaukee, Wisc. Office of J. R. Pope,archt.

Architect (N.Y.) 7:558,560,562
February 1927

720.5
A67ar

Eggers, Otto R.   1882-
Study, Holy Trinity Church, parish house
and rectory, New York City. Office of John
Russell Pope, archts. Otto R. Eggers, del.

Architect (N.Y.) 11: 282
December 1928

Egidien-kirche, Nuremberg, Ger.
see
Nuremberg, Ger. Egidien-kirche

720.5
A67ar

Eggers, Otto R   1882-
Renderings of the Tuxedo country club &
Memorial hospital, Syracuse, N.Y.

Architect (N.Y.) 8:176,182,188
May 1927

720.5
A67ar

Eggers, Otto R.   1882-
Study, Miss Spence's School, New York
City. Office of John Russell Pope, archts.
Otto R. Eggers, del.
An entrance lodge. The Office of John
Russell Pope, archt. Otto R. Eggers, del.

Architect (N.Y.) 12: 146,152
May 1929

Egina,
see
Aegina

720.5
A67ar

Eggers, O.R.   1882-
Renderings (pencil) of a gate lodge and house
by O.R. Eggers. Office of J.R. Eggers, archts.

Architect (N.Y.)8:pl.328,330
June 1927

720.5
A67ar

Eggers, Otto R.   1882-
Study, new building for the Junior League
New York. Office of John Russell Pope,archts.
Otto R. Eggers, del.

Architect (N.Y.) 12: 380,382
July 1929

720.55
B55

Egli,Ernst
Harbers,Guido
Neue bauten von Ernst Egli - Ankara (New
buildings by Ernst Egli in Ankara). School of
music,high school,country house,etc. Plans.

Der baumeister 34:68-71
February 1936

7P0.5P B95 Egremont (Eng.) Manor house hospital Manor house hospital. Lewis & Smith, archts. Builder 129:741 N 20, 1925	720.5 A67r Egypt.Architecture Dennond,H.F. The alphabet of architecture. Data of Egyptian architecture. Architectural record 4:477-506 April-June 1895	Egypt. Architecture Creswell, A.C. The evolution of the minaret with special reference to Egypt Burlington 48:134-140,252-258,290-298 Mr.,May,Je, 1926
720.52 B95 Egremont, Eng. War memorial annex War memorial Annex, Egremont. Lewis & Smith, arch'ts. Builder 129: 740 Nov. 20, 1925	720.5 B86 Egypt. Architecture The architecture of Egypt. Brochure series 8: 122-144 June 1902	Egypt. Architecture Pottier,E The lotus in Egyptian architecture. Gazette des beaux-arts Per.3.v.19:77-86 1898.
Egypt. Architecture see also Mohammedan architecture, Egypt Cairo. Architecture Domestic architecture, Egypt Pyramids Churches, Egypt Coptic architecture Thebes, Eg. Architecture Akhetaten, Eg. " Sakkara, Eg. "	Egypt. Architecture Conway, Sir Martin The beginnings of the Egyptian style of architecture. RIBA jrl 10: 371-91 My 23, 1903	720.52 B95 Egypt. Architecture. Origin, evolution and construction. Builder 121: 454-6. Oct. 7, 1921.
Egypt. Architecture Bancroft, Hubert Howe. Achievements of Civilization.... 10 vols. New York: The Bancroft Company, Publishers. 1896 1:chap.2	710.5 C85 Egypt. Architecture The call of Egypt. Country Life 60:xcviii October 10, 1.26	Egypt. Architecture Portico of temple of Edfou paintings in color of Karnak by David Roberts Amer Inst. of Arch. 2:175, 177 Apr. 1914
Egypt. Architecture British arch 84: pl. for Oct. 29, 1915	Egypt. Architecture Egyptian antiquities Arch and con rep 71, no. 1844: 277-78 Ap 22, 1904	720.5 P39 Egypt. Architecture Clark, Kenneth Selections from the field sketches of David Roberts, lithographed by L.Haghe, to illustrate "Egypt and Nubia". Pencil points 7: 2-18 January 1926
Egypt. Architecture Noack, Ferdinand. Die Baukunst des Altertums. Berlin: Fischer and Franke, 1910. pl.30-32	Egypt, Architecture Egyptian Antiquities Inland Architect 43: 26-8 May, 1904	Egypt. Architecture Hegemann, Werner Weimarer bauhaus und Egyptische baukunst Wasmuths Monatshefte für baukunst v. 8, heft 3-4:69-86 1924
Egypt. Architecture Roy. Inst. of Arch. 23:217-222 May 6, 1916	720.52 B95 Egypt. Architecture Egyptian architecture. Builder 136: 604 March 29, 1929	Egypt. Architecture, 20th century Gabr, Labib Contemporary architecture L'art vivant 16,No.134:563-566,582 July 15, 1930

Egypt. Architecture. Classic influence
Vogel, Hans
Egyptian architecture with classic influence

Zeitschrift für bildende kunst
62:160-165
October 1928

Egypt (Mass.) Lawson (T.W.) farm

see

Egypt (Mass.) Dreamwold

Eich, George B., architect

see

Adler and Eich

710.5
C855
    Egypt. Views
        Egypt - a series of pictures

Country life(U.S.)70:55-56
September 1936

720.5
A67f
    Egypt(Mass.) Lorenz (F.E) house
      House for William E. Lorenz. George R.
Paul, archt. Plan.

A   Architectural Forum 71:308
      October 1939

7P1.97
A67c
    Eichberg, S.Milton
      The Illinois armories. Plan of typical
first floor.

Architectural concrete 5:20-29
No.4[1939]

Egypt. Views
    Photographic views

Country life 31:313-317
Mar. 2, 1912

720.5
A67f
    Egypt (Mass.) Ward (J.A.) house
      House for Mrs. James A .Ward, Egypt,Mass.
Royal Barry Wills, archt. Plan

A   Architectural forum 66: 212-213
      March 1937

Eichberg, Werner

see also:

Eichberg, Werner and Otto Roth

MICROFILM

    "Egypt" (Illinois)

in SCRAPBOOK ON
ARCHITECTURE p. 883-884
(on film)

Egyptian legation, London

see

London, Eng. Bute house

Eichberg, Werner
    Druckerei Kastner and Callway, München
[plans and section] Werner Eichberg and Otto
Roth, archts.

Baumeister
52: 570-575
    Tafel 65 at end
    of issue
S 1955

Egypt (Mass.) Beals (F.A.) house
    House for Fred A. Beals, Egypt, Mass.
Royal Barry Wills, archt. Plan

A

Architectural forum 66:46-47
January 1937

720.5
A67f
    Ehlers, A   H
      House for Lloyd A. Springett. Salt Lake
City, Utah. A. H. Ehlers, designer. Plan

Architectural forum 66: 211
March 1937

Eichberg, Werner
    Grosseres einfamilienhaus bei München [plans]
Werner Eichberg, archt.

Baumeister
Vol. 51:146-147, pl 22-25
Nv1954

D15.1
H34
    Egypt (Mass.) "Dreamwold"
Baldwin, Maurice
      The country estate of Thomas W. Lawson.
"Dreamwold", Egypt, Mass. Architect not given.
Illustrated.

House beautiful 13: 296-312
Ap '03

720.53
K91
    Ehn, Karl
      New mortuary chapel, Classic in style

Baumuths 10: 369
Heft 9, 1976

Eichberg, Werner and Otto Roth

see

Munich, Ger. Tiefbau-berufgenossenschaft bldg.

720.5
A67
    Egypt (Mass.) Dreamwold (farm)
      "Dreamwold" the farm of Thomas W. Lawson,
Egypt,Mass. Coolidge and Carlson,archt.
Plans.

A   Architectural review 9,n.s.4:248-260
      October 1902

Eia, Manor of
Button, Wm. Loftie
    The Manor of Eia or Eye next Westminster.
Illus.

Archaeologia 62, pt. 1: 31-58
1910

Eichholzer, Fredi, 1922-
    Überbauung Vogelsangstrasse, Zürich; entwurf
1958-1960, gebaut 1960-1961 [plans & reciton]
Hans Fischli & Fredi Eichholzer, archts.

Bauen & Wohnen
vol.16: 120-123, Nr 1962

Riehholzer, Fredi
Uitbreiding electrische apparatenfabriek
Ad. Feller A. G. te Horgen [plans] Hans Fischli,
archt. with Fredi Riehholzer Y Eduard Frans,
archts.

Forum no.5: 204-205
1954

720.5
A67r

Eidlitz, Cyrus L .   W   1853-1921
Accepted design for Bleecker Street Sav-
ings bank, N.Y.C. C.L.W.Eidlitz, architect.
No plan.

Architectural record 2:209
October-December 1892

720.5
A67r

Eidlitz, Cyrus L   W   1853-1921
The New York Times building, Broadway and
42nd Street, New York City. C.L.W.Eidlitz,
archt. Plan.

Architectural record 14:152-153
August 1903

Rickanrcht and Cooke
see
San Antonio (Tex.)   Fine Arts
Auditorium. Little theater

720.5
A67r

Eidlitz, Cyrus L   W   1853-1921
American Society of Civil Engineers, New
York City. C.L.W.Eidlitz,archt. No plan.

Architectural record 7:357
January-March 1898

720.5
B52

Eidlitz, Cyrus L.W.   1853-1921
Obituary.

Western Arch. 30: 114.
Oct. 1921.

Eidelweis tavern, Ky.
see
Kenton county (Ky.) Eidelweis tavern

720.5
A67r

Eidlitz,Cyrus L   W   1853-1921
Country residence. C.L.W.Eidlitz,archt.

Architectural record 4:pl.4 prec.p.
April-June 1895   379

720.5
I56

Eidlitz, Cyrus L   W   1853-1921
Passenger station of the Chicago and West-
ern Indiana Railroad. Polk and Third and
Fourth Avenue, Chicago, Illinois. Cyrus L.W.
Eidlitz, archt. Sketch.

Inland architect 3:89,pl.fol.38
July 1884

Eidlitz and McKenzie
see also
New York (city) Times building

720.5
A67r

Eidlitz,Cyrus L.   W 1853-1921
Schuyler,Montgomery
Cyrus L.W.Eidlitz. (Son of Leopold Eidlitz.)

Architectural record 5: 412-435
April-June 1896

720.5
A67r

Eidlitz, Cyrus L   W   1853-1921
David,A.C.
Private residences for banking firms: Liberty
national bank building, New York City. Cyrus L.W.
Eidlitz,archt.

Architectural record 14:14
July 1903

720.5
A67f

Eidlitz and McKenzie
[firm succession]

Arch forum 70: supp p 76
F '39

720.5
A67r

Eidlitz, Cyrus L   W   1853-1921
Design for Fine Arts Academy, San Diego,
Cal. C.L.W.Eidlitz, architect. No plan.

Architectural record 1:176
October-December 1891

720.5
A67r

Eidlitz, Cyrus L   W   1853-1921
Racquet club, N.Y.C. C.L.W.Eidlitz,
architect. No plan.

Architectural record 2:145,164
October-December 1892

Eidlitz, C. L.
see
Detroit (MI)   Michigan Central RR Station (old)

720.5
A67r

Eidlitz,Cyrus L   W   1853-1921
Schuyler,Montgomery
The evolution of a skyscraper: illustrations
of New York Times building. C.L.W.Eidlitz,archt.
Plans.

Architectural record 14:329-343
November 1903

720.5
A67r

Eidlitz, Cyrus L   W   1853-1921
The tall office building section of
New York City. Washington Life building,
southwest corner of Broadway and Liberty.
Cyrus L. W. Eidlitz, archt.

Architectural record 8: 183;247-
January-March 1899   250,258
October-December 1898

Eidlitz, Cyrus L. W.
See also
Buffalo (NY)   Library and Art Building
New York (NY)   Bank for Savings
   "   "   "   Bar Association Building
   "   "   "   Telephone Co. Building (1890)
   "   "   "   Washington Life Building
San Antonio (TX)   National Bank

720.5
A67r

Eidlitz,Cyrus L   W   1853-1921
Reynolds,Cuyler
The New York Capitol building. Thomas Fuller,
archt. C.L.W.Eidlitz archt. who completed struct-
ure. No plan.
Electric lighting in Albany Capitol.

Architectural record 9:142-157,211-
October-December 1899   225

720.5
A67r

Eidlitz,Cyrus L .   W   1853-1921
Washington Life building, Broadway, New
York City. C.L.W.Eidlitz,archt. No plan.

Architectural record 7:377
April-June 1898

<table>
<tr><td>

Eidlits, Leopold, 1823-1908

see also

New York (city) Produce exchange (1861)
Albany, N.Y. State capitol
New York (city) Continental bank bldg.

</td><td>

720.5
A67r   Eidlitz, Marc and Son
     An historic firm: history of the house of
Eidlitz.

Architectural record 5:454-455
April-June 1896

</td><td>

Eiffel tower, Paris

see

Paris. Tour Eiffel

</td></tr>

<tr><td>

720.5
A67r   Eidlitz, Leopold 1823-1908
Schuyler, Montgomery
     A great American architect: Leopold Eidlitz.
Pt.1 - Ecclesiastical work. Pt.2 - Commercial
and public. Pt.3 - The Capitol at Albany. Portrait.

Architectural record 24: 163-179; 277-292;
September;October;November,1908   385-378

</td><td>

Eiermann, Egon, 1904-
     [biographical note]

Bauen & Wohnen
12:(290) N 1958

</td><td>

Eijkelenboom, W
     Bürobäude für zwei schleppschiffahrtsdienste in
Rotterdam [plans & sections] J.W.C. Boks, W. Eijkelenboom & A. Middelhoek, archts

Baumeister
58: 404-5, My 1961

</td></tr>

<tr><td>

720.5
A67r   Eidlitz, Leopold, 1823-1908
     An historic firm: history of the house of
Eidlitz.

Architectural record 5:454-455
April-June 1896

</td><td>

Eiermann, Egon, 1904-
     Projekte für zwei verwaltungsgebäude in
Mannheim und Karlsruhe [plans & section] Egon
Eiermann, archt.

Bauen & Wohnen
16: 187-188, Ap 1962

</td><td>

Eijkelenboom, W
     House at Oostvoorne [plans] J.W.C. Boks,
W. Eijkelenboom & A. Middlehoek, archts.

Archtl Design
30:453 N 1960

</td></tr>

<tr><td>

Eidlits, Leopold, 1823-1908
Leopold Eidlitz, F.A.I.A.

West archt
11; no.6: 74
Je 1908

</td><td>

Eiermann, Egon, 1904-
     Neubau der Essener Steinkohlenbergwerke
AG in Essen [plans & section] Egon Eiermann,
Robert Hilgers, Heinz Kuhlmann et al., archts.

Bauen & Wohnen
15: 181-186, Ap 1962
Konstruktionsblätter at
end of issue

</td><td>

Eijkelenboom, W
     Pathologishh-anatomisches und bakteriologisch-serologisches laboratorium in Deventer
[plans] J. W. C. Boks, W. Eijkelenboom & A.
Middelhoek, archts.

Baumeister
58:532-33 Je 1961

</td></tr>

<tr><td>

ff o
720.6
A51q   Eidlits, Leopold   1823-1908
Eidlits, C. L. W.
Leopold Eidlits, F.A.I.A.

American institute of architects quarterly
April 1955   bulletin 3: 57

</td><td>

Eiermann, Egon, 1904-
     Wohnhaus der familie des Grafen Hardenberg in
Baden-Baden [plans & details] Egon Eiermann & Georg
Pollich, archts.

Architektur & Wohnform
vol.70: 1-12; Ja 1962

</td><td>

711.05
T75   Eindhoven (Neth.) Planning
De Casseres, J. M.
     Eindhoven, Holland. The planning of an
industrial town.

Town planning rev 16:171-81,
pls. 27-31
Je '55

</td></tr>

<tr><td>

Eidlitz, Leopold   -1908
Obit.

Western Architect
11:74
Je 1908

</td><td>

Eiffel, Alexandre Gustave,

see

Eiffel, Gustave, 1832-1923.

</td><td>

Einfeldt (Henry) house, River Forest, Ill.

see

River Forest, Ill. Einfeldt (Henry) house

</td></tr>

<tr><td>

720.5
A67r   Eidlitz, Leopold, 1823-1908
     The vicissitudes of architecture.

Architectural record 1:471,474,476,
April-June 1892   479,482,484

</td><td>

Eiffel, Gustave, 1832-1923
see

Garaby, Fr. Viaduc
Paris, Fr. Tour Eiffel

</td><td>

Einstein tower, Potsdam

See

Potsdam. Einsteinturm.

</td></tr>
</table>

Eire see Ireland	Eisendrath, Simeon B., -1935 Obituary Illinois society of architects Monthly bulletin 20:8 F-Mr 1936	Eiskonditorei Venezia. Munich, Ger. see Munich, Ger. Eiskonditorei Venezia
720.5 P39 Eiseman, Albert, jr. "A housing development". Albert Eiseman, jr. Pencil points 10: 496-497 July 1929	Eisendrath (Simeon B.) and Company see Chicago (Il) Jefferson and Maxwell Sts. 3 Story Bldg. Chicago (Il) Evans Ave. near 47th St. 4 Story Apt. Bldg.	720.53 M68 Eisler, Otto Work of Otto Eisler in Brünn; Phönix. Moderne bauformen 29: 304-306 July 1930
Eisen & Son see Whittier (CA) Residence	Eisenhower museum, Abilene, Kan. see Abilene (Kan.) General Dwight D. Eisenhower museum	Eisman, Ferdinand 1924 scholarship Illinois society of architects monthly bulletin 8:7 Apr. 1924 9:5, 9:3 Jan., Feb-Mr 1925 10:3, 10:5 Jan., Mar. 1926 11:7, 11:3, 11:7 Jul., Aug. Sept. 1926
Eisen, P.A. Member of firm: Walker and Eisen	Eisenlohr & Pfennig Zwei kindergärten in Sindelfingen [plan & section] Eisenlohr & Pfennig, archts. Baumeister 55:864-66 D 1958	Eitel, Albert Moderne Bauformen 9:149-183 1910
Eisenbach (Ger.) Savings Bank Savings Bank, Eisenach. By H. Jenssen. Berliner architekturwelt 21:157-9 Heft 5-6, 1919.	Eisenlohr and Weigle see Friedrichshaferr (Ger.) Kurgartenhotel	720.53 M68 Eitel, Albert The houses by Albert Eitel, Stuttgart, Germany. Moderne bauformen 24: 177-97 June 1925
Eisenberg and Feer see Boston (Mass.) Netoco Egyptian theater	Eisenmaun, John Cleveland Architect receives award for building code. Inland Architect 45: 49 Jun, 1905	720.53 M68 Eitel,Albert May,Bruno Neue bauten für die gemeinde Oberlenningen/ Teck. (Buildings for the new community house for Oberlenningen.) Albert Eitel,archt. Gymnasium, club rooms. Plans. Moderne bauformen 26: 136-150 April 1927
Eisendrath, S. B. see also New York (N.Y.) Criterion club " " " Free synagogue	Eisinger, D. W. see Pocantico Hills (N.Y.) Union church	720.53 M68 Eitel,Albert New building for Karl-Olga hospital in Stuttgart, Albert Eitel, archt. Moderne bauformen 29:233-238 Heft 6, June 1930 adv.101-104

710.8 **Eitel, Albert** 928 Schürer, O. New dwelling houses by the architect, Albert Eitel, Stuttgart. Dekorative kunst 31: 249-258 August 1928	El molino viejo. Pasadena (near) See San Gabriel (calif.) San Gabriel Arcángel. Old mill.	El Paso, Texas. Architecture West. arch. 19: pl. fol. p. 88 Oct., 1913
Ekelund, Hilding see also Children's Homes, Finland Olympic Games. Housing Gothenburg (Swe.) Planning.	El Monte, Calif. Cherry Lee School Culver, W.L., Jr. Concrete details for modern schools: Cherry Lee School, El Monte School District, San Bernardino County, Calif. Architectural concrete 5:21-24 No. 3 [1939]	El Paso, Tex. Bassett tower Illustration. Trost and Trost, architects. Western architect 39: 126 Ag 1930
Ekelund, Hilding and Martti Välikangas see also Olympic games. Housing	El Monte (Cal.) Rominger (H.H.) house House for H.H. Rominger, El Monte, Cal. Kenneth A. Gordon, archt. Plan Architectural forum 66:298-299 April, 1937	El Paso, Tex. Bassett tower ...near twin of Luhrs tower. Trost and Trost, architects. Prairie school review VI: 28 Fourth quarter 1969
Eklund, Jarl see Helsinki (Fin.) (near) Fiskartorpet Tampere (Fin.) Kraftwerk	Ryerson El Morro national monument, N. Mex. El Morro national monument El Palacio 12: 161-168, Je 15, 1922	El Paso, Tex. Brazos apartments ...similarity to the Charnley house. [illus.] Trost and Trost, architects. Prairie school review VI: 31 Fourth quarter 1969
Elcran, Sylvio Jaguaribe see Jaguaribe Elcran, Sylvio	El Pardo. Sp. Casita del principé Ezquerra del Bayo, Joaquín The house of the Prince, in El Pardo. Arte espanol 10:87-89, No. 3, 1930	El Paso (Tex.) Carrol & Daeuble office Architects' office in El Paso, Texas. Nat'l Arch 5:1-2 D '49
"El Dorado", Columbus, Ga. see Columbus, Ga. St. Elmo	Ryerson El Pardo. Sp. Casita del principé Villa, J. M. Edificación de la Casita del Principé, de el Pardo: fecha y autor. (plans) Juan de Villanueva, arch'ts. Archivo espanol No. 24:259-263, S-D 1932	El Paso (Tex.) Donan Residence Trost and Trost, Archts. West. Archt. 20: pls.fol.p. 23 Feb, 1914
El mirasol, Palm Beach, Fla. see Palm Beach, Fla. El mirasol	El Pardo. Sp. Prince's cottage, see El Pardo, Sp. Casita del principé	El Paso, Tex. Donan house ...unique among all of Trost's oeuvre. [illus., plan] Trost and Trost, architects. Prairie school review VI: 23-24 Fourth quarter 1969

El Paso, Tex. Grey, Douglas, house
...now somewhat altered. [illus.]

Prairie school review
VI: 23
Fourth quarter 1969

El Paso, Tex. Paso del Norte hotel
Illustration and plans. Trost and Trost,
architects.

Architectural review
19: 119
Ap 1913

El Paso, Tex. Swartz, Adolph, house. 1914
...more traditional. [illus.]

Prairie school review
VI: 22-23, 31
Fourth quarter 1969

El Paso, Tex. Lawton house.
Illustration.

Prairie school review
VI: 31
Fourth quarter 1969

El Paso, Tex. Paso del Norte hotel
Paso del Norte hotel. [illus. & plans]
Trost and Trost, architects.

Western architect
19: 95 and 4 plates
N 1913

El Paso, Tex. Trost, Henry C., house. 1908
...the most remarkable building of Trost's
career. [illus., plans, measured drawings]

Prairie school review
VI: 3, 15-21
Fourth quarter 1969

El Paso (Tex.) Liberty Monument
Liberty monument, El Paso, Texas.
O.H. Thorman, archt. Plan

Western architect 29:pl.13
June, 1920

A

El Paso, Tex. Poe, A. B., house
...the other Prairie School house.
[illus.] Trost and Trost, architects.

Prairie school review
VI: 1, 22
Fourth quarter 1969

El Paso, Tex. Turney, W.W., house. 1906
...the largest private house Trost ever
designed. [illus.] Trost and Trost, architects.

Prairie school review
VI: 14
Fourth quarter 1969

El Paso, Tex. McGregor, Malcolm, house

see

El Paso, Tex. Trost, Henry C., house. 1908

El Paso (Tex.) Presbyterian Church
Trost and Trost, Archt.

West. Archt.
19: pls.fol.p. XIX
Oct, 1913

El Paso (TX)
YMCA Bldg.
Trost & Trost, Arch.

West. Arch.
14: pl. 6
Aug. 1909

El Paso (Tex) Masonic Temple
Trost and Trost, Archts.

West. Archt.
20: pls.fol.p. 23
Feb, 1914

El Paso, Tex. Roberts-Banner building
...Trost's first venture in reinforced
concrete. [illus.] Trost and Trost, architects.

Prairie school review
VI: 24-25
Fourth quarter 1969

El Paso, Tex. Young men's Christian association
building. 1907.
...achieves interest. [illus.]

Prairie school review
VI: 14-15
Fourth quarter 1969

El Paso, Tex. Mills building. 1910
Illustrations and plan. Trost and Trost,
architects.

Western architect
19: two plates
O 1913

El Paso, Tex. Stevens, B.F., house. (First)
Illustration and plan. Trost and Trost,
architects.

Western architect
19: two plates
O 1913

El Saguero

see

Westwood (Cal.) El Saguero

El Paso, Tex. Mills building. 1910
...one of Trost's most important buildings.
[illus., plan] Trost and Trost, architects.

Prairie school review
VI: 24-25
Fourth quarter 1969

El Paso, Tex. Stevens, B.F., house (First)
...relied very heavily on a local bungalow
tradition. [illus., plan] Trost and Trost,
architects.

Prairie school review
VI: 21-22
Fourth quarter 1969

El Sur Rancho (Cal.) Hunt (Harry C.) House
(Monterey County)
David Adler, archt. plans.

Roll 34, frames 389-391

Klan, Gervase house, Portsmouth, R.I.

see

Portsmouth, R.I. Vaucluse

Eleanor Clubs (one), Chicago

see

Chicago, Ill. Eleanor Clubs (one),

---

electric equipment
Abbott, Arthur Vaugn
Electrical engineering for architects.
[plans, sections]

Inl archt 34:17-23
Ja 1900 sup

Klan, Samuel house, Portsmouth, R.I.

see

Portsmouth, R.I. Vaucluse

Electe. Centrale Hemweg. Amsterdam, Neth.

see

Amsterdam, Neth. Electe Centrale Hemweg

Electric Equipment
Adams, Alton A.
The physical limits of electric - power
transmission (from Engineering News, Oct, 1902).

Inland Architect
40: 18-20
Oct, 1902

Elberon, New Jersey

see

Long Branch, New Jersey

Electric apparatus

see

Electric equipment

Electric equipment
Comstock, L. K.
The poor man's lamp.

Inland architect
v. 18 no. 2: 19-20
S 1891

Elcock & Sutcliffe

see also

Runwell (Eng.) Hospital for mental and nervous
diseases

Electric appliances

see

Electric equipment

Electric plants

see

Electric power-plants

Elcock and Sutcliffe
The "Daily Telegraph" building, Fleet st.,
E. C., Elcock and Sutcliffe, archts. and Sir
John Burnet & partners, assoc. archts.

Builder
139: 522-23, pls fol 518
S 26, 1930

Electric company buildings

see

Public utilities buildings

Electric power-plants.

see also

Hydroelectric plants

Eldem, Sedar Hakki

see

Yalova (Tur.) Hotel Thermal

Electric   equipment
Conduits for electric wires in buildings.

Inl archt 34:15
S 1899

Electric Power-plants
Habasque, Guy
Art, science et technique; electricité,
dualité des formes.

Aujourd'hui
V.1: 44-49   no.4
S 1955

Eldridge, Charles William
Moves office.

West. Archt.
18: 10
Jan, 1912

790.52   Electric equipment
A67ay   Hemsley, S. H.
Electrical developments

Architects' yearbook 1: 295-304
1945

Electric power plants
Hochdruckkraftwerk der papierfabrik
Dachau [plan & section] Allgemeine Elektricitäts-
Gesellschaft, designer
Hochdruckkraftwerk papierfabrik Reishols
[plan & section] Allgemeine Elektricitäts-
Gesellschaft, designer

Baumeister
56:142-42,145 Mar 1959

Electric Power - Plants
Peach, C. Stanley
Design and construction of electrical
supply buildings.

Inland Architect
44: 20-1
Oct, 1904

Electric power - plants
A temporary electric transformer station,
designed by Henri Sauvage for 1925 Exposition
des Arts Décoratifs.

Architects' journal
71:4, Ja 1, 1930

Electric Power-plants, England
Electricity sub-station, Back Hill, Holborn.
Ernest Gale, Heath and Sneath, archts.

Builder 138:578
March 21, 1930

Electric power - plants, England.
Usine de la "Electro Flo" L. T. D.
Adie et Button, arch'ts. (plans, sect.)

L'Arch d'aujourd'hui
10:87, Je 1939

Electric power - plants, France
see

Asnières (Fr.) Novion poste electrique
Aubervilliers (Fr.) Société nord-lumière. Poste
de coupure
Malakoff (Fr.) Société ouest-lumière. Sous-station.
Saint Denis (Fr.) "Pleyel" poste electrique

Electric power-plants. Switzerland
R., A
Elektrische Kraftentrale Lucendro. Carlo
and Rino Tami, arch'ts.

Werk
32:289-299, O 1945

Electric Power-plants. U.S. 19th cent.
Sweet, James F.
Steam plant for isolated electric light plants.

Inland architect
v.14 no. 5:50-51
N 1889

Electric power-plants, U.S., IL. Chicago,

see

Chicago, IL. Commonwealth Edison Co. Generating
station (S. Crawford Ave.)

720.6   Electric signs
B53   Beaux-arts institute of design, competition: "An illuminated electric sign". Awards.

B.A.I.D. 2: 19
April 1926

720.5   Electric wiring.
A67b   Adequate wiring for a small house.

Architecture & building 53:14-
20. Mar. 1921:

Electric Wiring
Conduits for electric wires in buildings

Inland Architect
34: 15
Sept. 1899

720.52   Electric wiring
A67   Diagrammatic layout of electric conduits
and of systems of electric supply. Plans.
Sir John Burnet, Tait and Lorne, archts.

Architects' journal 78: supp.
August 31, 1933

720.5   Electric wiring
A67a   Electric wiring and elevators. By D.B.Em-
erson.

Architecture 41:120-1.
Apr. 1920.

720.5   Electric wiring
A67f   Electric wiring layouts for modern buildings. Pt.4.

Arch. forum 36: 151-4
Apr. 1922.

720.5   Electric wiring
A67f   Electrical wiring layouts for modern buildings. pt.5.

Arch. forum 36: 185-6
May 1922.

720.5   Electric wiring
A67f   Electric wiring layouts for schools

Arch. forum 37: 227-30
Nov. 1922

720.5   Electric wiring
A51   Electricity in the house, pt.5. The bed
room.

Amer.arch 121: 49-56
May 10,1922

720.5   Electric wiring
A51   Electricity in the house. VII.- Halls,
stairs and porch.

Amer.arch.122: 37-9
Jul. 5, 1922.

Electric Wiring. Standard symbols for
wiring plans.

Inland Arch.
48: 34
Oct. 1906

720.5   Electric wiring
A51   Wire distribution in industrial buildings

Amer.architect 123:163-4
Feb 14, 1923

Chicago.
Electrical building. Century of progress.

See

Chicago. Century of progress international exposition. 1933-34. Electrical building.

7P0.571 A79 Lindbohm, R [engineer] Electrical codes, Finland Förändringar i Helsingfors elektriska installations-föreskrifter. Arkitekten no. 5:79-90 1938	710.5 H84 Electricity in the home The electrically equipped house House & Garden 43: 37-9 Ja '23	7P0.5 A67 Moses, P.R. Electricity in the home Some data on Electricity in apartment houses. Arch rev 10 (n.s.5): 111-115 Ag '03
720.5 A51 Electrical equipment Special electrical requirements. American architect 125:118-22,123-6 Jan. 30, 1924	720.5 A51 Electricity in the home Electricity in the home Amer arch 121: 234-5 Mr 15 '22	720.5 A67f Klerbe and Co. Bars. Plans Architectural forum 7:437 November 1927
720.5 A67a Electrical equipment. More light on panel boards. Architecture.53:121-22 Apr. 1926	720.5 A51 Electricity in the home Electricity in the home. Amer arch 125: 99-106 Ja 30 '24	Elevated railways Designs for stations, bridges, etc. Amer. arch. 104: 161-167 October 29, 1913
Electricity Hayward, Albert W. Electricity in the province of the architect. Inland Architect 31: 4-5 Feb, 1898	Electricity in the home Electric lighting and heating: sizes of switch and junction boxes, etc. Diagrams. Sir John Burnet, Tait and Lorne, archts. Architects'journal 78: supp. September 7, 1933	(720.5) M59a Elevator cabs Elevator entrance and interiors of ele- vator cars in the Chrysler building, New York City. William Van Alen, archt. Metal arts 3: 198 May 1930
Electricity in the home see also Lighting, Domestic	Electricity in the home Electricity in a modern residence. Inland archt. 20, no. 1: 5-6 Ag 1892	720.6 A51j Elevator construction Ups and downs in the modern building. A.I.A. journal 12:328-31 July 1924
710.5 C855 Electricity in the home Decorating the small house, V-the use of electricity. Country life 44: 54-6 My '23	720.5 A67r Lees,Frederic Electricity in the home A French electric villa: M.Georgia Knap's Villa Feris. Electra,Troyes,France. Portrait of M.Knap, and plans of electric houses designed by him. A Architectural record 22:215-226 September 1907	Elevator doors see also issues of Metalcraft magazine.
720.5 A51 Electricity in the home Department of architectural engineering- electricity in the house. Amer arch't 121: 188-191 Mr 1 '22	728.6 H76 Electricity in the home Planning the electrical installation for greatest use. Home information service. Bul.f no. 29:1-30 My '37	720.5 A67a Elevator doors Architecture's competition: Design for elevator cab. Architecture 55: 330 June 1927

720.5 Elevator doors
A67a   Architecture's portfolio

Arch. 61: 313-20
My '30

720.5   Elevator doors
M59a   Elevator doors of bronze, Park Avenue
building, New York City. Buchman and Kahn,
archts.

Metal arts 2: 56
January 1929

Elevators

Amer. arch. 102: 93-95
Sept. 11, 1912

720.5   Elevator doors
M59a   Bronze elevator doors, Fisher building,
Detroit, Mich. Albert Kahn, archt.

Metal arts 2: pl.8
February 1928

Elevator doors
[of ornamental iron]

Ornamental iron, vols. 1 & 2:
many plates
1893-1895

720.5   Elevators
I56   Discussion of new passenger elevators.

Inland architect 4: 69
December 1884

720.5   Elevator doors
M59a   Bronze elevator doors, 535 North Michigan
Avenue, Chicago, Illinois. Holabird and
Root, archts.

Metal arts 1: pl.11
December 1928

720.5   Elevator doors
A67b   Pershing Square building, New York City.
York & Sawyer and John Sloan, architects

Architecture & building 55: pl.140
June 1923

Elevators
The elevator influence
in extra high buildings

West. Arch.
12:41
O 1908

720.5   Elevator doors
W52   Courtesy of the Gorham Company.

Western arch.37: pl.173
October 1928

720.5   Elevator doors
A67r   Baker, Cecil F.
Types of elevator lobbies in office buildings

Arch. rec. 38:631-640
Dec. 1915

720.5   Elevators
A67f   Elevator installation. I.

Arch. forum 36: 181-4
May 1922.

720.5   Elevator doors, U.S. Baton Rouge
M59c   Doors of the Governors. Elevator doors
in the Louisiana State Capitol building at
Baton Rouge. Weiss, Dreyfous and Seiferth,
archts.

Metalcraft 8: 84;front.
February 1932

720.5   Elevator doors
M59a   Working drawings and shop drawings for
elevator doors of monel metal in the Union
Trust Company building, Detroit, Mich.
Smith, Hinchman and Grylls, archts.

Metal art 2: 234-237
June 1929

720.5   Elevators.
A67f   Electric and hydraulic elevators in modern buildings, Part I

Architectural forum 39:169-74
Oct. 1923

720.5   Elevator doors
M59a   Detail of the entrance lobby of the Film
Centre, New York City. Buchman and Kahn,
archts.

Metal arts 2: pl.25
May 1929

720.5   Elevator equipment
A51   The selection of elevator equipment.

Amer. arch. 126:31-32
July 2, 1924

720.52   Elevators.
B93   Electric passenger lift equipment for
modern buildings.

Builder 122: 51-2.
Jan. 6, 1922.

720.5   Elevator doors
M59a   Elevator doors, International Telephone
company building. Buchman and Kahn, archts.

Metal arts 1: pl. 5
November 1928

Elevator Shafts.

Popp, Joseph. Bruno Paul,
mit 319 abbildungen. Murich:
Bruckmann, [1910-1921] p. 125

720.54   Elevators
A67   Chanut, M.Ferdinand
L'importance actuelle des élévateurs dans
l'architecture américaine et ce qu'elle devrait
être dans l'architecture européenne (The actual
importance of elevators in American architecture
and in European architecture).

L'Architecture 43: p.315-326
1930

V 4

720.5
A67r
Elevators
A new type of elevator.

Architectural record 11: 115-117
April 1902

Elevators, Grain

see

Grain elevators

720.5
B95b
Elgin (Ill.) Jennings. House. Alterations.
Alterations on Jennings House at Elgin,
Ill. Clarence L. Stiles, archt.

Building budget
3:86b
Je 30, 1887

770.5P
A67ay
Elevators
Fethergill, J. R.
Post-war development of lift design

Architects' yearbook 1: 358-62
1945

710.5
C855
Elevators, Private
The treatment of the elevator

Country Life 47:52
Jan. 1925

Elgin (IL.) Northern Illinois State Hospital
New female infirmary, Illinois Northern Hospital
for the insane, Elgin: Robert Bruce Watson, archt.;
sketch, no plan.

Chicago architectural club 13:35
1900

720.5
M58c
Elevators
James,H.D., Yearsley,E.W.
Today's elevator saves space and weight.
Vertical transportation development now ahead
of building requirements.

Metalcraft 8: 17-22
January 1932

Elffers, Corns
Zentrallabor der Sikkens' Farbenwerke
Sassenheim (Holland) [plans & sections] Corns
Elffers, archt.

Baumeister
vol. 59: 317-21, Ap 1962

720.5
A51
Elgin (Ill.) Post office.
United states post-office, Elgin, Ill.
James K. Taylor, archt. [plan]

Amer archt & bldg news
70:pl fol 4 in supp
D 1, 1900

710.5
E84
Elevators,Domestic
Elevators for the home.

House and garden 70:66-67
November 1936

Elgin house, Lake Joseph, Ont.

see

Lake Joseph, Ont. Elgin house

Elgin (Ill.) school
Schoolhouse at Elgin, Ill. Clarence L. Stiles,
archt. Plan.

Inland arch 2: 111, 114
1883

720.52
B95
Elevators, Electric.

Builder 122: 530-33.
Apr. 7, 1922.

Elgin (IL.) Academy
Louis Guenzel and H. F. Robinson, arch.

Architect (N.Y.) 4:47-48
May, 1925

720.5
I56
Elgin (Ill.) Sherman hospital
Sherman hospital in Elgin. A. E.
Daniels, archt.

Inland archt & news rec 20:19
September 1892

Elevators, Electric
Atkinson, A.S. Electric elevators.

Inland Arch.
48: 40-1, Nov. 1906
49: 33, Feb. 1907

Elgin (IL.) Acute Disease Hospital
Acute Disease hospital, Elgin, IL. Edgar Martin,
architect

Arch. record 52: 495
Dec. 1922

720.5
A67r
Elgin marbles
Gale, Edward
The great buildings of the world: the Erech-
theum.

Architectural record 12:498-513
October 1902

720.52
B95
Elevators, Electric
Electric lifts

Builder 124:194-5
Jan. 12, 1923

Elgin, Ill. High schools (1886).
Two buildings of this character. [illus.]
Clarence L. Stiles, architect.

Building budget
II: 69 and plate
June 1886

Elgin Marbles
Reich, Emil
Early Greek Art and the Elgin Marbles.

Inland Architect
44: 34-5
Dec. 1904

Elgin, Scot. Cathedral
Measured drawings by G. Holt of Elgin Cathedral.
Vaulting to Chapter house; detail of East front facade.

Architect 46:pl.fol.p.22;pl.fol.p.34
July 11; 18, 1917

Eliot, Charles, 1859-1897

Member of firm:

Olmsted, Olmsted & Eliot

---

ff
724.5915
V81W

Elizabeth City County(Va.)Cloverdale house
Cloverdale, located five miles from
Hampton on Back River road toward Yorktown.

William and Mary Quarterly,ser.2,v.18:
April 1928   pl.62

Elgin, Scot. Cathedral
Cooper, Prof.
The Elgin Cathedral.

Architect 99: 117-120
February 22, 1918

Eliot, Charles
The Civic Plan

Western Architect
12:66
D1908

---

ff
724.5915
V81W

Elizabeth City County(Va.)Gumwood farm.
Gumwood Farm, owned by heirs of
J.W. Cummings.

William and Mary Quarterly,ser.2,v.13:pl.
April 1928   64

El-Hanani, Arieh, 1898-
Bibliothek des naturwissenschaftlichen Institutes in Rehovet; entwurf 1957, gebaut 1958/9
[plans] Arieh El-Hanani, archt.

Bauen & Wohnen
15: 330-32, S 1961

Eliot, Charles W.
Industrial education.

Inland Arch.
51: 7-8
Feb. 1908

720.5
A67r

Elizabeth (N.J.) Davis (F.H.) house
House of F.H. Davis, Elizabeth, N.J.
C.P.H. Gilbert, archt. No plan.

A   Architectural record 14: 107-116
August 1906

El-Hanani, Arieh
The Wix Library of the Weizmann Institute of
Science, Rehooth, Israel [plans] Arieh El-Hanani,
archt.

Architectural Design
31: 210, My 1961

Eliot (Mass.)

see

Newton (Mass.)

Elizabeth (N.J.). Elizabeth Town and Country Club
Auditorium, Elizabeth Town and Country Club,
Elizabeth, N.J. C.C. Wendehack, archt.

American architect 134:253-6
August 20, 1928

Elias of Dereham
Thompson, A. Hamilton
Master Elias of Dereham and the King's works.

Archaeological jl 98: 1-35
1941

Elisabethville (Fr.) Ste. Thérèse de l'Enfant Jésus
Varenne, Gaston
The church of Elisabethville

Art et décoration 55:55-60
February, 1929

Elizabeth (N.J.) Housing.
Veiller, Lawrence
Industrial housing developments in America:
a development at Elizabeth, New Jersey. Murphy and
Dana, archts.

Architectural record 44: 49-58
July, 1918
A

Eliassen, G.

see

Bjerke, Arvid and G. Eliassen

Elisabethville (Fr.) Ste. Thérèse de l'Enfant Jésus
Louvet, A.
Les églises modernes. L'église d'Elisabethville.
(Modern churches. The church of Elisabethville)
Plans. Paul Tournon, archt.

A   L'Architecture 42:249-258
August 15, 1929

Elizabeth (N.J.) National State Bank
National State Bank, Elizabeth, N.J.

Arch. Rec. 50: 462-4.
Dec. 1921.

720.53
B35

Elingius, Erich and Gottfried Schramm
Harbers, Guido
Neues Bürohaus in Hamburg. (A new office
in Hamburg) Erich Elingius and Gottfried Schramm
archts. Plan.

Der Baumeister 34:234-239,pls.77-79
July 1936

Elisabethville (Fr.) Ste. Thérèse de l'Enfant Jésus
Church at Elisabethville. P. Tournon, archt.

L'architecture 44: 292,295
September 15, 1931

Elizabeth (N.J.) National State Bank
National State Bank of Elizabeth, N.J.

Architecture 45:81-2 and pl. 33-7.
Mar. 1922

Elizabeth Town (Pa.) Grand Lodge Hall
   Grand lodge hall, a home for aged members of the
Masonic order in Elizabeth Town, Pennsylvania.
Zantzinger, Boris and Medary, archts.

Architectural forum 32:231-234,pl.81-84
June, 1920

Elks' clubs

see

Name of city followed by;Elks' club

Ellerbe & Round

see

St. Paul (MN)   Oppenheim (Greve) Residence

Elizabethan architecture

see

Domestic architecture. England. Elizabethan

Elks national memorial headquarters, Chicago

see

Chicago, Ill. Elks national memorial headquarters

Ellerton, Homer E.

see

Tryon (N.C.) "El Taarn"

Elizabethan theaters

see

Theaters, England. Elizabethan

ELLEM spa pharmeceutical laboratory, Milan,
It.

see

Milan (It.) Laboratorio farmeceutico ELLEM spa

Ellett, Thomas Harlan

see also

Glen Head (L.I.) Alken (C.A.) house
 "   "   "   Barnes (E.M.) house
New Brunswick (N.J.) Johnson (J.S.) Estate
New York (N.Y.) Cosmopolitan Club
 "   "   "   World's fair 1939. Terrace Club
Wilton (Conn.) Long House

720.5
I56
   Elk Grove (Ill.) St. John's church
   St. John's church, Elk Grove, Illinois,
Fred Ahlschlager, archt.

Inland archt & news rec 19:27
March 1892

Ellen Wilson Memorial Homes

Jour. Amer. Inst. of arch. 3:352-6
Aug., 1915

Ellicott and Emmart

see also

Annapolis (MD)   Court of Appeals Bldg. Competition
Baltimore (MD)   Bauernschmidt (W.) House
 "   "   Colonial Trust Co. Bldg.
 "   "   Custom House. Competition
 "   "   Ellicott House
 "   "   Enoch Pratt Free Library
 "   "   Roland Park House

(See Card 2)

Elk Point (S.D.) Union County Court House

West. Archt.
17: XXIX
Apr, 1911

Ellenberger, Jean

see

Geneva (Switz.) Université. Auditorium

Ellicott and Emmart   (Card 2)

see also

Roland Park (MD) Corkram (B.W.) House
 "   "   Gremer (J.E.) House
St. Louis (MO)   Louisiana Purchase Exposition,1904

Elkhart (Ind.) Harter (Dr. George E.) Residence
   E. Hill Turnock, Archt.

West. Archt.
19: pls.fol.p. 40
Apr, 1913

721
T53
   Ellerbe and Company
   The Mayo Clinic building in Rochester,
Minn. Ellerbe & Co. archts. (interior views).

Through the ages 7: 13-19
October 1920

720.5
B84
   Ellicott and Emmart
   Hampden branch of the Provident Savings
bank, Baltimore, Md. Ellicott and Emmart,
archts.

Brickbuilder 25:118
May 1916

Ryerson
Elkouken, B.
   Un immeuble de rapport, Rue de Theâtre

L'art vivant
8:190, 192
Ap 1932

721
T53
   Ellerbe and company
   The Northern States Power building in St.
Paul, Minneapolis. Ellerbe and company,
archts. No plan.

Through the ages 9: 19-25
August 1931

Ellicott City (Md.) Doughoregan Manor

see

Doughoregan Manor, Md.

Ellicott square building (1892), Buffalo

see

Buffalo, N. Y. Ellicott Square building (1892).

720.5
A87r   Ellington, Douglas D.
      The new senior high school of Asheville,
N.C. Douglas D. Ellington, archt.

      Architectural record 66: 195-204
      September 1929

720.5
A67   Ellis,A   Raymond
      Two designs for country houses. A.Raymond
Ellis,archt. Plan.

      Architectural review 14:67-69
      March 1907

Ellicott, William M

See

Ellicott and Emmart

Elliot (F.M.) house. Evanston, Ill.

see

Evanston, Ill. Elliot (F.M.) house

Ellis and Clarke

see

London (Eng.) Associated newspapers, ltd.
Bristol (Eng.) Northcliffe house
Birmingham (Eng.) Richmond house
London, Eng. Daily Express Bldg.

720.53
W31   Ellingen, Architecture

      Wasmuths heft 11-12,8:347-49
      1924

720.5
W52   Ellipse
    Thayer, E. R.
      The ellipse in design.

      Western architect 38: 142-144
      August 1929

Ellis and Wells

      Members of firm:
        Ellis, H.G.
        Wells, William A.

Ellingsen and Erickson

      Members of firm:
      Ellingsen, Willeik E.
      Erickson, Ernest R.
      Manley, Frank J.

Elliptical churches

see

Oval churches

720.5
A67   Ellis, Charles and Harvey
      Water color sketch for plaster house by
Harvey Ellis, Charles and Harvey Ellis, archt

      Architectural review 15: pl.91
      December 1908

Ellingsen, Willeik E.

      Member of firm:
        Ellingsen and Erickson

Ellis, A. L.

see

San Francisco (California) Memorial [proposed]

Ellis, Charles S

see

Rochester, N.Y. Stein manufacturing block

720.5
A87r   Ellington, Douglas D.
      City Building, Asheville, N.C.
Douglas D. Ellington, archt.

      Architectural Record 64: 125-136
      August 1928

Ellis, A.   Raymond

see also

Alexandria Bay (N.Y.) Thousand islands country
club

Ellis college, Newtown Square, Pa.

see

Newton Square (Pa.) Ellis college

721
T55   Ellington, Douglas D.
      The new City building in Asheville (N.C.)
Douglas D. Ellington, archt.

      Through the ages 7:front.,5
      June 1929

Ellis,A. Raymond
      Hon- mention - design for $6,000 house. AIA
Columbus Chapter Competition.

      West. Archt.
      28: pl. 15
      May, 1918

Ellis, Curran R.

see

Eufaula (AL)   Shorter Residence

Ellis, Edmund Lewis

see

New York (NY)   Park Central Hotel
" " "   29th St. (East) (116) Display Rooms

---

microfilm Ellis, Harvey, del.
Buffington, Leroy S., architect
A. L. Wilston house, Lynchburg, Virginia,
1888. Harvey Ellis, del.

Roll 21, frame 191

Ellis, Harvey, 1852-1904
Kennedy, Roger
Long dark corridors: Harvey Ellis. [illus.,
port.]
[also reprint of articles by Claude Bragdon and
Hugh Garden] Bibliography.

Prairie School review
V: 1-3, 5-18;19-19;51
First-second quarter 1968

Ellis, Edmund L. and Hugh M.G. Garden
Establish office at Real Estate
Board Building, Chicago.

Inland Architect
21: 16
Feb, 1893

---

microfilm Ellis, Harvey, del.
Buffington, Leroy S., architect
Aragon apartments, Chicago, 1888. Harvey Ellis,
del.

Roll 21, frame 211

Ellis, Harvey
Pen and ink renderings for L.S. Buffington.

West. Archt.
18:pls.fol.p.39 Mar, 1912
pls.fol.p.51 Apr, 1912
pls.fol.p.61 May, 1912
pls.fol.p.73 Jun, 1912

720.5 Ellis, F   M
I56   Sketch of residence at Peoria for K. G.
Sloan, F. M. Ellis, archt.

Inland architect 5:79,pl.fol.94
May 1896

720.5 Ellis, Harvey . 1852-1904
A67 brown, F.C.
The architectural renderings of F.L.Griggs,
also discussion of others who have done fine renderings particularily in America.

Architectural review 19 n.s.2: 2,3
August 1913

Ellis, Harvey
Pen and ink sketches for L.S. Buffington.

West. Archt.
18:pls.fol.p.82 Jul, 1912
.pls.fol.p.112, Oct, 1912
.pls.fol.p.176 Nov, 1912
.pls.fol.p.XVIII Dec, 1912

Ellis, George A., Jr, estate, S.C.,

see

"Richmond", S.C.

---

microfilm Ellis, Harvey, del.
Buffington, Leroy S., architect
Bank and office building [Minneapolis, Minne-
sota] 1887. Project. Harvey Ellis, del.

Roll 21, frame 128

Ellis, Harvey
"A revival of pen and ink rendering: the work
of Harvey Ellis."

West. Archt.
18: 36-37; pls.fol.p. 39
Mar, 1912

Ellis, H.G.

Member of firm:
Ellis and Wells

Ellis, Harvey
Drawings for L.S. Buffington, archt.

West. Archt.
19: pls.fol.p. 33
Mar, 1913

---

microfilm Ellis, Harvey, del.
Buffington, Leroy S., architect
S. C. Gale house, Minneapolis, Minnesota, 1888.
Harvey Ellis, del.

Roll 21, frames 166-90

Ellis, Harvey, 1852-1904

see also

Menomonie, Wis. Mabel Tainter memorial building
Minneapolis, Minn. University of Minnesota.
Chemistry building.
Minneapolis, Minn. University of Minnesota Pills-
bury Science Hall.
St. Louis, Mo. Compton Heights water tower
St. Paul, Minn. Merriam, John L., house
" " "   Germania bank bldg.
" " "   Noyes brothers & Cutler bldg
" " "   West   publishing co. bldg.

720.5 Ellis, Harvey . 1852-1904
A67 Bragdon, Claude; H.M.G.Garden
Harvey Ellis: a portrait sketch with illus-
trations of the work of L.S.Buffington, Eckel and
Mann and others.
Harvey Ellis, designer and draughtsman.
Water color sketch for plaster house by
Harvey Ellis, Charles and Harvey Ellis, archts.

Architectural review 15:173-186,pls
December 1908   84-86,91-
92

---

microfilm Ellis, Harvey, del.
Buffington, Leroy S., architect
Soldiers' and sailors' monument, Indianapolis,
Indiana, 1888. Project. Harvey Ellis, del.

Roll 21, frames 192-203

---

microfilm Ellis, Harvey, del.
Buffington, Leroy S., architect
A. G. Kennedy house, Minneapolis, Minnesota,
1888. Harvey Ellis, del.

Roll 21, frames 212-3

Ellis, Harvey, 1852-1904
Harvey Ellis drawings. [work done for
L. S. Buffington]

Western Architect
18: two plates each
Mr. Apr. My. Je. Jl. Ag.
Oct. Nov. Dec. 1912

---

microfilm Ellis, Harvey, del.
Buffington, Leroy S., architect
Spencer library, Penn college, Oskaloosa, Iowa,
1888. Harvey Ellis, del.

Roll 21, frame 163

Ellis, Harvey, 1852 - 1904
To Harvey Ellis. A great architect. [illus.]

Northwest archt 8:No.6-7:
1,8
1944

Ellis Island, (N.Y.) U.S. Immigrant Station
Front (2) and end Elevations; six
floor plans; one section; and Block plan.
Boring and Tilton, Archts.

Inland Archt.
vol.31,No.3,pl.fol.p.. 30
Apr, 1898

MICROFILM
Ellison Bay, Wis. Jensen (Jens) house

in SCRAPBOOK ON
ARCHITECTURE p. 72,73,74
[on .:lm]

---

microfilm Ellis, Harvey, del.
Buffington, Leroy S.,   architect
    Tomb for archbishop Ireland, Minneapolis,
Minnesota, 1888. Harvey Ellis, del.

Roll 21, frame 204

Ellis Island, (NY) U.S. Immigrant Station
Perspective of entire building. Boring
and Tilton, archts.

Inland Archt.
vol.31,No.4,pl.fol.p. 40
May, 1898

Ellsworth building, Chicago

see

Chicago, Ill. Terminals building

---

microfilm Ellis, Harvey, del.
Buffington, Leroy S., architect
    Unidentified office building, 1883. Harvey
Ellis, del.

Roll 21, frames 203-10

Ellis Island (N.Y.). U.S. Immigration Station.
Model...Boring and Tilton, archts.

Arch rev 6:40
Ap 1899

Ellsworth, James W., house (1892), Chicago

see

Chicago, Ill. Ellsworth, James W., house (1892).

---

microfilm Ellis, Harvey, del.
Buffington, Leroy S., architect
    Unidentified tall building, project, 1888.
Harvey Ellis, del.

Roll 21, frame 207

Ellis Island (N.Y.) U.S. Immigration Station
    Architecture appreciations, no. 3: the New York
immigrant station on Ellis Island. Boring and
Tilton, archts.

Architectural record 12:726-733
December, 1902

Ellsworth (MN) Public Library
Omeyer and Thori, archts.

West. Archt.
3: p. 12
May, 1904

Ellis, Herbert O.

see also

Ellis and Clarke

720.5   Ferry house
F29   Ellis Island(N.Y.)U.S.Immigration station.
         Ferry house United States Immigration
Station, Ellis Island, N.Y. No plan.

Federal architect 9:27
October 1938

Ellwood, Craig   1922-
    Apartmenthaus mit vier Wohnungen in Hollywood
[plans] Craig Ellwood, archt.

Bauen & Wohnen no.2
p. 89-93
Ap 1955

Ellis, Herbert O
    "Daily Express" building, Fleet St., E.C.
Designed by Herbert O. Ellis & Clarke. Robert
Atkinson, archt. of entrance hall.

Architects' jour
76: 2, 5-9
Jl 6, 1932

Ellis Island (N.Y.) U.S. Immigration Station Hospital
    Hospital Building for Immigrant Station for the
U.S. Government, Ellis Island, New York Harbor.
Boring and Tilton, Architects.

Brickbuilder 2:pls.
July, 1902

Ellwood, Craig, 1922 -
    Deux immeubles commerciaux à Los Angeles:
Bureaux - banque [plans] Craig Ellwood, archt.

Aujourd'hui
3:80-1 S 1957

Ellis Island (N.Y.) U.S. Immigration
    Station
Ellis Island Emigrant Building.Boring
and Tilton, Archts. 2nd Competition
under Tarsney art.

Inland Architect
31: 26-7
Feb, 1898

Ellis, Manfred Maria [pseud]

see

Hegemann, Werner, 1881-1936

Ellwood, Craig, 1922 -
    Ferienhaus in Malibu [plan] Craig Ellwood,
archt.

Bauen & Wohnen
13:208-12 Je 1959

Ellwood, Craig, 1922-
Blake, Peter
   The focus is on the young architects;
Craig Ellwood.
   The following are exerpts from various lec-
tures [by Craig Ellwood]

         Zodiac
         4:160-67 Ap 1959

Ellwood, Craig, 1922 -
   Haus in Beverly Hills; entwurf 1956,
ausgeführt 1957/58 [plan] Craig Ellwood, archt.

         Bauen & Wohnen
         13:61-68 F 1959
         Konstruktionsblätter at end
         of issue

Ryerson
   Ellwood, Craig, 1922 -
      Projet d'un club de golf en Californie
   [plans] Craig Ellwood, archt.

         Aujourd'hui
         Vol. 2:78-79
         N 1956

Ellwood, Craig   1922-
   Habitation à Beverly Hills, California
[plan and col. Illus.] Craig Ellwood, archt.

         Aujourd'hui
         2: 56-61
         S 1956

Ellwood, Craig, 1922-
   House in California [plan] Craig Ellwood,
archt.

         Architectural design
         vol. 30: 229-231, Je 1960

Ellwood, Craig, 1922-
   Ein postgebäude - nicht nach schema F;
entwurf 1957, gebaut 1958-59 [plan] Craig
Ellwood, archt.

         Bauen & Wohnen
         15:58-60 F 1961

Ryerson
   Ellwood, Craig, 1922-
      Habitation à Malibu, Californie [plan]
   Craig Ellwood, archt.

         Aujourd'hui
         Vol. 2:No. 8: 68-71
         Je 1956

Ellwood, Craig, 1922 -
   Hunt House, Malibu Beach, California
[plan]
   Johnson House, Crestwood Hills, California
[plan]
   Pierson House, Malibu Beach, California
[plan] Craig Ellwood, archt.

         Archtl Design
         29:475-80 N 1959

Ellwood, Craig, 1922-
   Recent work of Craig Ellwood Associates:
South Bay Bank, Manhattan Beach, California
[plans]; Airline office, Beverly Hills [plan];
Photographes's studio, Beverly Hills [plan]
Post office, Westchester, Los Angeles [plan]
Craig Ellwood Associates, archts.

         Archtl Design
         30:505-9 D 1960

Ellwood, Craig, 1922 -
   Habitation au bord de la mer à Malibu,
California [plan] Craig Ellwood, archt.

         Aujourd'hui
         4:62-5 Mar-Ap 1959

Ellwood, Craig, 1922 -
   Machines and architecture.

         Bauen & Wohnen
         13:297 S 1959

Ellwood, Craig, 1922-
   Stahlhaus in Hillsborough, Kalifornien;
entwurf 1961 [plan] Craig Ellwood & I.E. Lomax,
archts.

         Bauen & Wohnen
         16: 176-177, Ap 1962

Ellwood, Craig, 1922 -
   Habitation aux environs de Los Angeles
[plan] Craig Ellwood, archts. with J. S. Lomax,
assoc. archt.

         Aujourd'hui
         5:74-7 F 1960

Ellwood, Craig
   Maison experimentale en Californie [plan]
Craig Ellwood, archt.

         Aujourd'hui
         1: 44-47
         Mr-Ap 1955

Ellwood, Craig, 1922-
   Stahlskeletthaus an einem hang; entwurf
1955, gebaut 1958 [plan] Craig Ellwood, archt.

         Bauen & Wohnen
         14:162-65 My 1960

Ellwood, Craig, 1922 -
   Habitation experimentale, Beverly Hills,
California [plan & colored illus.] Craig
Ellwood, archt.

         Aujourd'hui
         4:56-61 Mar-Ap 1959

Ellwood, Craig 1922-
   Maypole apartment house (4 unit.) at Hollywood
(Calif.) [plans] Craig Ellwood, archt.

         Forum no. 9/10
         p. 362-363
         1954

Ellwood, Craig, 1922 -
   Le studio d'un photographe à Los Angeles,
Californie [plan] Craig Ellwood, archt.

         Aujourd'hui
         3:84-5 Jl 1958

Ellwood, Craig, 1922-
   Haus einer reklame-agentur in Los Angeles;
entwurf 1959, gebaut 1961 [plans] Craig Ellwood,
archt.
         Bauen & Wohnen
         vol.16: 137-142, Mr 1962
         Konstruktionsblatt at end
         of issue

Ellwood, Craig, 1922 -
   Prefabrication et avenir de l'architecture.
Projet de bâtiment à usage industriel
[plan] Craig Ellwood, archt. & landscape archt.

         Aujourd'hui
         4:80 Mar-Ap 1959

Ellwood, Craig
   "Unity by the sea" à Santa Monica Californie
[plan] Craig Ellwood, archt.

         Aujourd'hui v.1
         p.48-49
         Mr-Ap 1955

710.5 C85 Elm Stillwell,S.T.C. Elm as a decorative wood. Country life (Lond.) 76: lviii,lx December 1, 1934	Elmhurst (Ill) Church of Our Savior E. Norman Brydges, archt. West. Archt. 23:pls.fol.p. 37 Apr, 1916	MICROFILM Elmhurst, Ill. Lathrop, J.H., house Bauer & Loebnitz, archts. J.H. Lathrop house, Elmhurst, Ill. Additions. [n.d.] Roll 37, frames 105-108
Elmes, Harvey Lonsdale see also Liverpool (Eng.) St. George's hall	MICROFILM Elmhurst (Ill.) College in SCRAPBOOK ON ARCHITECTURE p. 13,14 (on film)	MICROFILM Elmhurst, Ill. Lathrop, J.H., house Holabird & Roche, archts. J.H. Lathrop house, Elmhurst, Ill. Alterations for Bryan Lathrop [n.d.] Roll 37, frames 109-124
Elmes, Harvey Lonsdale Harvey L. Elmes, designer of St. George's Hall, Liverpool in 1841. Country life (Lond.) 62:127-31 July 23, 1927	Elmhurst, Ill. Emerson elementary school Escuela elemental en Illinois [plans] Cone & Dornbusch, archts. Arquitectura Mexico 14:80-3 Je 1958	MICROFILM Elmhurst, Ill. McCormick (Robert H., Jr.) house]Ludwig Mies van der Rohe, archt.] in SCRAPBOOK ON ARCHITECTURE p. 40 (on film)
720.52 Elmes,Harvey Lonsdale A675 Jones,R.P. The life and work of Harvey Lonsdale Elmes. Architectural review 15: 231-245 June 1904	Elmhurst (IL.) Emery house Emery house, Elmhurst, IL. Walter Burley Griffin, arch. Plans. A Architectural record 23:443,486-487 June, 1908	Elmhurst (Ill) Residence Walter Burley Griffin, Archt. West. Archt. 19: pls.fol.p. XV Aug, 1913
710.5 Elmsford,(N.Y) Kelly, (Henry) house C855 Country home of Henry Kelly, Jr. at Elmsford, N.Y. Patterson and Willcox, archts Country life (N.Y.) 49: 64 Ap '26	Elmhurst, IL. Emery, William H., house H.A.B.S. sheet. illus McKee, Harley James, comp. Recording historic buildings. Washington, D.C.: Historic American buildings Survey, 1968. pages 26-29	Elmhurst, Ill. Sturges (Frank) house Residence for Frank Sturges, Elmhurst, Ill- inois. F. R. Schock, archt. Inland architect 20, no. 3 pl. fol. p. 30 O 1892
MICROFILM Elmhurst, Ill. in SCRAPBOOK ON ARCHITECTURE p. 13 (on film)	720.5 Elmhurst (Ill.) Hogans (L.A.) house I56 Residence for L.A. Hogans, Elmhurst,Ill. Fiedler and Penner, archts. Plan. Inland architect 4: 68,pls.fol.7f A December 1884	microfilm Elmhurst, Ill. Wilder (T.E.) subdivision Griffin, Walter Burley, architect Subdivision, Elmhurst, Illinois, n.d. Plot and landscaping plans. Roll 8, frames 25, 30
Elmhurst (Ill) Brydges (E. Norman) Residence E. Norman Brydges, archt. Plan. West. Archt. 32: pl. 1-3 Dec, 1923	Elmhurst, Ill. Lathrop, Bryan, house see Elmhurst, Ill. Lathrop, J.H., house	Elmira (N.Y.) Chemung Canal Trust Co. Chemung Canal Trust Co., Elmira, N.Y. Architecture. 45:6-7 and pl. 1-6. Jan. 1922.

Elmira, (N.Y.) City Hall
Pierce and Bickford, Archts.

Inland Architect
vol. 35, No.4, pl.fol.p. 32
May, 1900

Elmira, (N.Y.) Y.M.C.A. and Steele Memorial
Library
Pierce and Bickford, Archts.

Inland Arch.
vol. 35,No.5,pl.fol.p. 44
Jun, 1900

Elmslie, George Grant, 1871-1952
...the Angell loving cup - and testimonial
book [illus.]

Prairie school review
VI: 22-23
Second quarter 1969

720.5
A51
Elmira (N.Y.) D.L.and W. railroad station
Station on line of D.L.and W. railroad
at Elmira, N.Y. Kenneth M. Murchison, archt.

Amer. archt. 104: pls. fol. 106
S 10, '15

Elms, Newport, R.I.

see

Newport, R.I. Berwind, E.   J., house

microfilm
Elmslie, George Grant, architect
Capitol building and loan association building,
Topeka, Kansas, 1922.

Roll 7, frames 14-28

Elmira, (N.Y.) Gillett (Mrs. S.L.) Residence
Exterior plus view of dining room.
Pierce and Bickford, Archts.

Inland Architect
vol. 35, No.4, pl.fol.p. 32
May, 1900

(The) Elms, North Ferrisburgh, Vt.

see

North Ferrisburgh, Vt. The Elms

microfilm
Elmslie, George Grant, architect
Dormitory for men, Yankton college, Yankton,
South Dakota, 1931.

Roll 7, frames 144-53

Elmira (N.Y.) Rathbone (J.A.) Residence
Considine and Haskell, archts. plans

West. Archt.
23: pls.fol.p. 26
Mar, 1916

Elmslie, George Grant 1871-1952

see also

Purcell, Feick, and Elmslie
Purcell and Elmslie

Elmslie, George Grant, 1871-1952
Hasbrouck, W. R.
Elmslie drawings [review of David Gebhard's
book; illus.]

Prairie school review
VI: 27
Third quarter 1969

Elmira, N.Y. Steele memorial library

see

Elmira, N.Y. Young men's Christian association
and Steele memorial library

Elmslie, George Grant, 1871-1952

see also

Topeka (Kas.) Capitol bldg. and loan assn' bldg.
Adams (Minn.) Bank
Western Springs (Il.) Congregational Church

Elmslie, George Grant, 1871-1952
Purcell, W.G.
Elmslie Orchestration - a letter to the Forum

Arch forum 86:22
F '47

720.5
A67ar
Elmira (N.Y.) Tompkins (Ray) house
Residence of Mrs. Ray Tompkins, Elmira,
N.Y. Charles A. Platt, archt. Ferruccio
Vitale and Alfred Geiffert,Jr., landscape
archts.

Architect (N.Y.) 11: 673-679
March 1929

MICROFILM

Elmslie, George Grant, 1871-1952

in SCRAPBOOK ON
ARCHITECTURE p. 323
(on film)

microfilm
Elmslie, George Grant, architect
Forbes hall of science, Yankton college,
Yankton, South Dakota, 1929.

Roll 7, frames 116-32

Elmira, N.Y. Young men's Christian association and
Steele memorial library
Y.M.C.A. and Steele memorial library, Elmira,
N.Y. Pierce and Bickford, archts.

Amer archt & bldg news
55: pls fol 24, Ja 16, 1897

microfilm
Elmslie, George Grant, architect
Alterations for the Henry B. Babson house,
Riverside, Illinois, 1925.

Roll 7, frames 65-71

Elmslie, George Grant, 1871-1952
Hamlin, Talbot F.
George Grant Elmslie and the Chicago scene.

Pencil points
22: 575-586
S 1941

microfilm
Elmslie, George Grant, architect
The Healy chapel, Aurora, Illinois, 1927.

Roll 7, frames 72A-87B

Elmslie, George Grant, 1871-1952
...a rare holograph letter. [illus.]

Prairie School review
II: 27
First Quarter 1965

Elmwood Park, Ill. Nuger house
Maison d'habitation à Elmwood Park, Illinois.
Crombie Taylor et Robert Bruce Tague, architectes.

Tech. et arch.
14, no. 7-9: 18-19
1955

---

microfilm
Elmslie, George Grant, architect
Institutional building, Aurora, Illinois, 1924

Roll 7, frames 29A-39B

---

microfilm
Elmslie, George Grant, architect
Redfield-Peterson house, Glenview, Illinois,
1929.

Roll 7, frames 109-17

Elne. Cathedral

see

Elne. Sainte Eulalie

---

microfilm
Elmslie, George Grant, architect
James J. Montgomery house, Evanston, Illinois,
1922.

Roll 7, frames 1-13

---

microfilm
Elmslie, George Grant, architect
St. Charles country club, St. Charles, Ill.,
1925.

Roll 7, frames 40-5

705.1
I61
Elne.Sainte Eulalie
Elne cathedral and town

International studio 79:264-271
July 1924

---

microfilm
Elmslie, George Grant, asso. architect
Von Holst, Hermann Valentin, architect
Maxwelton Brace clubhouse, Bailey's Harbor,
Wisconsin, 1930. George Grant Elmslie, associate
architect.

Roll 7, frames 133-43

Elmslie, George Grant, 1871-1952
[re. the six drawings for the Owatonna
bank: letter to the Editors by David Gebhard]

Prairie school review
IV: 33-36
Third quarter 1967

7~0.F71
A7r
Elovaara, Torsten, 1890-
Torsten Elovaara

Arkitekten: supp 15
1940

Elmslie, George Grant, 1871-1952.
A new addition to the collections of
architectural ornament. [illus.]

Chicago. Art institute
calendar.
v. 66: 12-13
Ja 1972

Elmslie, George Grant, 1871-1952
... the six surviving drawings for
ornamental details [for the Owatonna bank]

Prairie School review
IV: 7-10, 16-17
Second quarter 1967

Elsaesser, Martin, 1884-1957

see also

Frankfurt-am-Main, Ger. Konrad Haenisch school

Elmslie, George Grant, 1871-1952
Newly elected fellows of the A. I. A.
[brief biographical sketch and photograph]

A. I. A. Journal
7: 216
My '47

---

microfilm
Elmslie, George Grant, architect
Western Springs congregational church, Western
Springs, Illinois, 1928-9.

Roll 7, frames 88-108

Elsaesser, Martin, 1884- 1957
Garden room with electrically controlled
sliding windows, Hans K. in O. Martin Elsaesser,
archt.

Arch jour 78:640
N 16, 1933

MICROFILM
Elmslie, George Grant, 1871-1952

obituary notice

in SCRAPBOOK ON
ARCHITECTURE p. 716
(on film)

---

microfilm
Elmslie, George Grant, architect
William H. Graham building, Aurora, Illinois,
1925.

Roll 7, frames 46-64

720.53
W51
Elsaesser,Martin, 1884-1957
Hallenschwimmbad in Frankfurt a.M. (Swimm-
ing pool pavilion in Frankfurt a.M.-Fechen-
heim. Martin Elsaesser,archt.

Wasmuths monatshefte 14: 296
June 1930

Elsaesser, Martin, 1884-1957
   Les Halles à Francfort-sur-le-Main. Plan.
Prof. Elsaesser, archt.

   Encyclopedie de l'architecture;
   Constructions modernes. 12 vols.
   Paris: Albert Morancé, 1928-39.
   4:pls. 58-61

Elsinore, Denmark

   see

Helsingör, Denmark

Eltham (Eng.) palace
   Eltham Palace, interior of hall. Drawings
by Mr. Ion Elton

   Archt & con rep 71:96
   F 5, 1904

Elsaesser, Martin, 1884-1957
   Kulturelle nachrichten. Martin Elsaesser

   Architektur und Wohnform
   No. 5 - 62: #27#
   Je 1954

Elson, C. H., and partners
   Eastbourne Terrace redevelopment, London
W2 [plot plan & details] C. H. Elson & Partners,
archts.

   Archtl Design
   29:236-38 Je 1959

Eltham (Eng.) Palace
   Plan and great hall of Eltham Palace, Kent.

   Architectural review 64:147-8
   October, 1928

Elsaesser, Martin, 1884-1957
   Martin Elsaesser [obit.]

   Architektur & Wohnform
   66:#22# O 1957

Elson and Stone
   see

Welwyn garden city, Eng. Council offices

Eltham (Eng.) Palace
   The Old Palace, Eltham.

   Architect (Lond.) 137: 181
   November 17, 1933

720.55 Elsässer, Martin , 1884-1957
B55   Harbers,Guido
   Ein unzeitgemässer wohnsitz. (A residence
premature for this age.) Martin Elsässer,archt.
Plans.
   Estate has riding garden,rose garden with
terraces,park with wild-flower garden,bathing
pool with showers,sand-beach,lawn,playground,etc.
   Der Baumeister 31: 203-216,pl.64-70
   June 1933

720.52 Elsworth, W.
B95   Design of a National Theater (plan). W.
   Elsworth, archt.

   Builder 119: 575 and pls fol p
   575; pls fol p 602
   N 19, 26, '20

720.52 Eltham (Eng.) Palace
A67   Photograph of the Royal Palace,Eltham.
The surviving Great Hall built 1479. To be
restored and rebuilt for Mr.Courtauld. Sir
Charles Peer,architectural adviser.

   Architects' journal 78: 651
   November 23,1933

Elsässer, Martin and Körte, Walther

   see

Frankfurt-am-Main (Ger.) School

Eltham (Eng) College. Chapel

Eltham College

   Builder
   95: 376,pl. fol. p. 390
   Oct, 10, 1908

Eltham (Eng.). Parish Hall
   Selected Design for Proposed Parish Hall, Eltham.
Messrs. Moscrop-Young and Glanfield and Percy J.
Waldram, architects.

   Builder 97:556 and pls.
   N 20, 1909

Elsässer, Martin and Schütte, W.

   see

Römerstadt (Aust.) school

Eltham, Eng. King John's barn

   see

Eltham (Eng.) palace

Eltham, Eng. St. Saviour's Church
   The churches of St. Saviour, Eltham, and St. Alban,
Southampton, Welch. Cachemaille-Day and Lander, archts.
Plans.

   Architect (Lond.) 134:384-391
   June 30, 1933

Elsau. Switz. Neue Schulhaus
   Hohloch, H
Das neue schulhaus in Elsau (The new school house in
Elsau). H.Hohloch, archt. Plans.

A   Der baumeister 34:393-395,pl.133
   November, 1936

Eltham (Eng.) Palace
   Elton, P. I.
   Eltham Palace

   Arch and c. rep 69:161-2,1 pl
   prec. p. 169
   Mr 6, '03

720.52 Eltham (Eng.) St Saviour's church
A67c   Interior of the brick church of St.
   Saviour's Church. Eltham Welch, Cachemaille-
   Day and Lander, archts.

   Architect (Lond.) 135: supp.
   S 15 '33

Eltham (Eng.) Ye Old Kings Arms Inn Ye Old Kings Arms, Eltham. Builder 123: 829, 831 Dec. 1, 1922	Elwes, Guy see London (Eng.) Devonshire Place W. (no.8) house	720.8P A67c Ely (Eng.) Cathedral Cathedral series: Ely, south screen of Bishop Alcock's chapel from retro-choir. Choir triforium, nave. Architect 8d: 94, plu. preced- ing 32; 70, pl. preceding 77; 87, pls preceding 39 Jl 14, Ag 4, 11, 1911
Eltham Hall, Kent Hussey, Christopher Eltham Hall, Kent..the residence of Mr. Stephen Courtauld. John Seely and Paul Paget, archts. of reconstruction. Country life (Lond.) 81: 534-39; My 15, 1938 568-73; " 22, " 594-99; " 29, "	Ely (C. Morse) house, Lake Bluff, Ill. see Lake Bluff, Ill. Ely (C. Morse) house	Ely (Eng.). Cathedral Curtiss, Adelaide Ely Cathedral. Plan. Architectural review 19:n.s.2: 1-7 January, 1913
Elting, Winston see also Schweikher and Elting	Ely (Eng.) Air Views Ely and the Cathedral. Arch. Jour. 52:343. Sept. 29, 1920.	Ely (Eng.). Cathedral Ely and the cathedral. Architect's journal 52:343 September 29, 1920
720.6 I29 Elting, Winston An all steel plate welded restaurant building: Chicago Bridge and Iron Co. restaurant. Plan and section. Illinois society of architects 6-7:1, pl. Monthly bulletin October-November 1941	Ely (Eng.). Cathedral Ely Cathedral, exterior, interior. Allen, Fred Hovey. Great Cathedrals of the World. 2 vols. Boston: Haskell and Post, c1886 -88.	Ely (Eng.). Cathedral Ely, Durham and St. Bartholomew's. Photographs. A.I.A. journal 12:502,504-505 December, 1924
MICROFILM Elting, Winston, 1907-1968 Obituary in SCRAPBOOK ON ARCHITECTURE p. 143 (on film)	Ely (Eng.). Cathedral Ely cathedral, elevations. Wheatley, Richard. Cathedrals and Abbeys of Great Britain and Ireland. New York: Harper and Bros., 1890. p.117-129	Ely (Eng.). Cathedral Cathedrals, England. Ely The church plan in England. Interiors. Architectural review (London) 62:1-3 July, 1927
Elveden, Eng. St. Andrew's and St. Patrick's Church Church of St. Andrew and St. Patrick, Elveden. W.D. Caroe, architect. British archt 64: 345 and pl. N 17, 1905	Ely, Eng. Cathedral The west front; the octagon, the choir from the octagon: north aisle, looking west; general view of choir Ely Cathedral. Amer archt & bldg news 55:pls fol 8 in supp, fol 88 Mr 6, 13, 1897	Ely (Eng.). Cathedral Drawing by Sir George Gilbert Scott of his proposal for the restoration of Ely Lantern. Architect (Lond.) 123: 571 May 2, 1930
Elwell, R. E. (Sculptor) see New York (NY) (New) Custom House	Ely (Eng.). Cathedral The Octagon, Ely Cathedral. Photograph. Architectural record 12: 354 August, 1902	Ely (Eng.) Cathedral. Chantry of Bishop Alcock. Door Bishop Alcock's Chantry, Ely. Builder 121: pl. Dec. 16, 1921.

Ely (Eng.) Cathedral. Lady Chapel
Nos. 682 and 683.—Ely: Lady Chapel, Eastward;
Arcading in Lady Chapel.

Arch and con rep 86: pls.
S 8, 1911

Ely, John H. & Wilson C.

see

Newark (N.J.) City hall

Elzner, A. O.   (Card 2)

see also

Cincinnati (OH)   Lancaster Building
    "   "   Lawson (Mrs. Fenton) Residence
    "   "   Literary Club
    "   "   Odd Fellows Temple Competition
    "   "   Phoenix Club Bldg. Competitive Design
    "   "   Plant (Nathan) Residence
    "   "   Reinstrom Residence
    "   "   Sykes (G.S.) Residence

(See Card 3)

Ely (Eng.). Cathedral, Prior's Door
Sketch by Mr. Leslie Wood of the Prior's Door,
Ely.

Architecture (Lond.) 5: 403
May, 1927

Ely's furnishing house, Chicago (1864)

see

Chicago, Ill. Ely's furnishing house (1864)

Elzner, A. O.   (Card 3)

see also

Cincinnati (OH)   Western German Bank
    "   "   Whitman & Barnes Mfg. Co. Warehouse
Clifton (OH)   Forword (William H.) Residence

Ely (Eng.) Cathedral, Screen
Hope, Sir William St. John
Quire screens in English churches with special
reference to the twelfth century quire screen
formerly in the cathedral church of Ely.

Archaeologia 68: 43-110
117

Elzas, A
Klug, Hanswietmar
Der "BIJ ENKLPF" in Rotterdam [plans]
Marcel Breuer & A. Elzas, archts.

Bauen & Wohnen
12:257-62 Ag 1958
Konstruktionsblatt at end
issue

Elzner, A. O.
"On the Artistic expression
of Concrete"

West Arch 10:
121-127
Dec. 1907

Ely (Eng.). Cathedral. War Memorial Chapel
War Memorial chapel, Ely Cathedral. Reginald
Blomfield, archt.

A   Builder 121:10 and pl.
           July 1, 1921

Elzas, A
Grand magasin à Rotterdam [plans]
Marcel Breuer and A. Elzas, archts.
Bâtiment provisoire pour l'organisation
du chantier d'un grand magasin à Rotterdam
[plan]

Aujourd'hui 1:
60-63 no.5
N 1955

Elzner, A. O.
Residence of A. Offner, Avondale, Cincinnati, Ohio.
A. O. Elzner, archt.

Inland architect
19, no. 6
pl. fol. 78
J1 1892

720.5   Ely. Prior Cranden's Chapel
R92b   Prior Cranden's Chapel, Ely England.
        Sketches and plan made by John T. Hetherington

Building budget 3: 89-90
July 3, 1887   pl. fol. p. 90

Elzas, A
Habitation individuelle à Andover,
Massachusetts [plans] Marcel Breuer, archt.

Aujourd'hui 1:
64-67 no.5
N 1955

Elzner, A   O
Residence of Charles Mendenhall. East Walnut
Hills, Cincinnati, Ohio. [plans] A.O. Elzner,
archt.

Inland architect
19, no. 4
pl. fol. p. 54
My 1892

Ely (Eng.) St. Mary's St. House
House (c.1780) in St. Mary's Street, Ely.

Arch. Rev. 51: pl. 3.
Feb. 1922

Elzas, A
Sandberg, d.
Les grands magasins de Rotterdam [plan]
Breuer, Elzas & Schwarzman, archts.

Zodiac
1:145-58 O 1957

Elzner, A. O.
Residence of Dr. A. Springer, Norwood,
Cincinnati, Ohio. [plan] A. O. Elzner,
archt.

Inland architect
19, no. 6
pl. fol. p. 78
J1 1892

Ely, Frank O., house. Kenilworth, Ill.

see

Kenilworth, Ill. Ely, Frank O., house.

Elzner, A. O.

see also

Armdale (OH)   Kellogg (C.H.) House
Cincinnati (OH) Baldwin Piano Factory
    "   "   Baldwin Piano Factory
    "   "   Bullock (J.W.) Residence
    "   "   Chester Park Club House
    "   "   Cincinnati Club
    "   "   Country Club House
    "   "   Elzner (A.O.) Residence
    "   "   Foster (Mr.) Residence

(See Card 2)

720.5   Elzner, A.O.
B84   The town hall series. Pt. I. For a western
        town. A.O. Elzner, archt. [plan]

Brickbuilder 11: 7-9
Ja '02

Elzner & Anderson

see

Avondale (OH)	Presbyterian Church
Cincinnati (OH)	Anderson (L.W.) House
" "	Anderson (Robert) Residence
" "	Banning (L.G.) Residence
" "	East Walnut Hills Country Club
" "	Hoadley (George) Residence
" "	Ingalls Building
" "	Livingood (C.J.) House

(See Card 2)

Embassies (buildings), Brazil
One of the first of the permanent foreign embassy buildings to be built by the United States government. Frank L. Packard, archt.

Amer archt
122:183-4, Ag 30, 1922

Embassies (buildings). Morocco
Palais du Résident Général au Maroc.
(Residence for the General Minister to Morocco.)
Prost and Laprade, archts. Plan.

Encyclopedie de l'architecture;
constructions modernes. 12 vols.
Paris: Albert Morancé, 1928-39.
1:26-27, No. 2

Elzner & Anderson   (Card 2)

see

Cincinnati (OH)	Morton (W.) House
" "	Ramsey (Robt.) Residence
" "	Residence
" "	Sattler (Dr. Eric) Residence
" "	Woods (H.F.) Residence
Kansas City (MO)	Terminal Warehouse

Embassies (buildings). Competitions
Risler, Charles
Le Concours du Prix de Rome 1923: La residence du representant de la France au Maroc. (Competitions for the Grand Prix de Rome: An embassy for the representative of France in Morocco.) Plans.

L'architecture
36:323-328, 0.10, 1923

Embassies (buildings), U.S.

see

Washington, D.C.,	Iranian Embassy
" "	Royal Italian Embassy
" "	Pan-American Union Building
" "	British Embassy

INFORMATION CARD

Elzner and Anderson

Drawings of approximately fifty Cincinnati buildings by this firm are in the private collection of Al Geiser, 3427 Whitfield Avenue, Cincinnati, Ohio. A list of the buildings included is in the Burnham Pamphlet File housed in the Ryerson and Burnham Librairies, Art Institute of Chicago.

Embassies (buildings). Competitions
Risler, Charles
Academie des Beaux-arts concours pour le Grand Prix de Rome de la section d'architecture en 1928. (Academie des Beaux-arts competitions for Grand Prix de Rome, architectural section 1928.) Subject: An Embassy for construction in a large oriental country. Plans.

L'architecture
41:353-358, N.15, 1928

Embden, S. J. van
Arbeiderscantine te Rotterdam [plans & section] S. J. van Embeden, archt.

Forum no.7
p. 292-295
1954

720.52 Emanuel, Frank L.
A67E   Work of Frank L. Emanuel. Pencil sketches and etchings.

Architectural review 33:65-67 pl.1-3
April 1913

Embassies (buildings). Competitions
Beaux-arts institue of design, competition:
"A French Embassy at Washington." Awards.

B.A.I.D.
2:3, Mr 1926

720.52 Embden, Walter
A87c   "Newspaper Buildings," Portugal Street,
London, W.C., England. Walter Emden, archt.

Architect 69: pl.fol.p.26 of supp.
April 3,1903

720.52 Embankments
A87c   Blackpool. South Shore improvement
Thomas H. Mawson & Son, architects

Architect 110:pl
Aug. 3, 1923

Embassies (buildings). Competitions
Beaux-arts institute of design, competition:
"An embassy."

B.A.I.D.
3:2-8, Mr 1927

Embden, Walter
Romano's restaurant, Strand, London, Eng.
W. Emden, archt.

Amer archt & bldg news 55:pl
fol 40
Ja 30, 1897

720.52 Embankments
B93   Chiswick River Embankment and Promenade
competition. Winning design, A.B.Elliott, architect

Builder 125:680-1
Nov. 2, 1923

Embassies (buildings). Competitions
"An embassy of the United States near the capital of a great South American Republic."
Rotch travelling scholarship for 1929.

Pencil points
10:414-415, Je 1929

Emberton, Joseph

see

Burnham-on-Crouch, Eng. Yacht club
London, Eng. Magazine Simpson
London, Eng. Olympia garage
London, Eng. Universal house

Embassies (buildings)

see also

Names of individual embassies, i.e.:

Rio de Janeiro, Braz. U.S. embassy

Embassies (buildings). Egypt
New Consulate-General, Alexandria.

Builder
135:550, 0.5, 1928

Embury, Aymar II

see also

Aberdeen (NC)	Public School
" "	Sand Hill Fruit Growers Assn. Bldg.
Atlanta (GA)	Richardson (Hugh) House
Bellport (LI)	Memorial Library
Birmingham (AL)	Mountain Brook Country Club
Bound Brook (NJ)	Doty (Douglas Z.) Residence
East Hampton (LI)	Guild Hall
" "	Library
Englewood (NJ)	Barber (St. George) Residence

(See Card 2)

Embury, Aymar II   1880-1966
  Architectural impressions:- the large American
house; notes on plan; how your house will look,
personality in the city house.

         Arts and decoration 12:
         171-73; Ja 1920
         240-41; F   "
         312-13; Mr   "
         398-99; 436; Ap. 1920

720.5   Embury, Aymar II   1880-1966
A67a   Cullman Brothers. Aymar Embury II. Exterior, base and tower photographs.

         Architecture 35:pl.17-20
         February 1917

720.5   Embury, Aymar II   1880-1966
A51   The artistic development of the standardized house. Plans by George Gilbert, Aymar Embury II & others.

       American architect 117: 571 and pl.fol
May 12, 1920   p.600B

Embury, Aymar II   1880-1966   (1)
     Early American Churches.
Parts 1-11.
     Architectural record
     30:584-[59], Dec 1911
     31:57-68, Jan 1912
     :153-[163], Feb 1912
     :256-[26], Mar 1912
     :417-[42], Apr 1912
     :547-556 May 1912

               see card 2

720.5   Embury, Aymar II   1880-1966
B84   A biography of his life.

         Brickbuilder 24:128
         May 1915

Embury, Aymar II   1880-1966   (2)
     Early American Churches.
Parts 1-11.
         Architectural record
         31:629-[638], Jun 1912
         32:80-90 Jul 1912
         :158-170 Aug 1912
         :256-266 Sept 1912
         :453-463 Nov 1912

710.5   Embury, Aymar II   1880-1966
C855   "Coeur de reve", the dream house of
Aymar Embury, II.

         Country life (U.S.) 37: 36-37
         November 1919

726   Embury, Aymar II   1880-1966
T92   English architecture as source material.

         Tuileries brochures 1:3-15
         January 1930

720.5   Embury, Aymar II   1880-1966
A67r   Conservatism in design. Residences in Kensington, Great Neck L.I. Aymar Embury, II, archt.

         Architectural record 32: 328-335
         October 1912

720.5   Embury, Aymar II   1880-1966
A67a   Examples of work of Aymar Embury II.

         Architecture 30:pls.160-189
         August 1914

705.1   Embury, Aymar II   1880 - 1966
A79   Architectural impressions: Are we on our
way?

         Arts and decoration 14:284-285
         February 1921

D13.1   Embury, Aymar, II   1880-1966
B84   Cooperative building

         House beau 33:116-118
         Mr '13

720.5   Embury, Aymar II 1880-1966
B84   From Twenty-third Street up. Article on
New York architecture.

         Brickbuilder 25:281-288 pl.170-74
         November 1916

705.1   Embury, Aymar II   1880-1966
A79   Architectural impressions: Public buildings
reflect community spirit.

         Arts and decoration 13:158-161
         August 1920

Embury, Aymar II, 1880-
     The Country House. By Aymar Embury II,
architect.

         West archt 17: 52-54
         Je, 1911

Embury, Aymar II   1880-1966
     House at Garden City, Long Island. Aymar Embury, II,
archt. Plans.

         Brickbuilder 21: pl.fol.p.60
         February, 1912

720.5
A67b   Embury, Aymar II   1880- 1966
     Houses - designed by Aymar Embury. II.
Ten homes, photographs and plans.
 	
      Architecture & building 48:191-197
      May 1914
	710.5
	C855 Embury, Aymar II 1880- 1966
	     The reincarnation of an old Long Island
	barn. Aymar Embury II, archt.
	
	      Country life (N.Y.)53:55
	      November 1927
		Emdrup (Den.)
		
		    see
		
		Copenhagen (Den.) Emdrup

720.5
W58   Embury, Aymar II   1880- 1966
    Embury, A. II
    Houses in southeastern Massachusetts.
 	
     White Pine 14: 14: 147-52
     No. 1, 1928
	Embury, Aymar II
	   Sage Foundation Cottage. plan
	
	     West. Archt.
	     17: pls.fol.p. XV
	     Jun, 1911
		720.5
		A67d Emerald Bay (Cal.) Coate (R.E.) house
		     Beach residence of Mrs.Roland E.Coate,
		Emerald Bay,Roland E.Coate, archt.Plans
		
		     Architectural digest 9: 70-71
		A Number 3 [1936-37]

Embury, Aymar II, 1880-1966
    Impressions of three cities
1. Chicago 2. Detroit 3. Pittsburgh
 	
     Architecture 31: 49-53
     77-80, 105-109
     F, Mr, Ap, 1915
	720.5
	A67r Embury, Aymar II .. 1880- 1966
	    Whitehead, R.J.
	     Some work of Aymar Embury, II in the sand
	hills of North Carolina. Elevations and plans.
	
	     Architectural record 55:505-568
	     June 1924
		Emerald Bay (Cal.) Coate (R.E.) house
		    The beach home of Roland E. Coate, Emerald Bay,
		California.
		    R. E. Coate, archt. Plans.
		
		     House and garden 72:96
		     October, 1937

Embury, Aymar II   1880-1966
   In the middle colonies tradition. Aymar Embury II,
archt.
 	
     House and garden 59: 86-87
     April, 1931
	710.5
	H84 Embury,Aymar II 1880- 1966
	     Town house: georgian rebirth of a staid
	brownstone front. Aymar Embury II,archt. of
	remodelling.
	
	     House and garden 72:44-45
	     October 1937
		Emergency housing
		
		    see
		
		Housing of refugees

720.5
W58   Embury, Aymar II   1880- 1966
     The New England influence on North Carolina
architecture.
 	
     White Pine 13: 4-6
     No.2, 1927
	720.5
	A67a Embury,Aymar II 1880- 1966
	     The work of Aymar Embury II.
	
	     Architecture 28:189-219
	     September 1913
		Emerson, Ernest
		
		    see
		
		Lowestoft (Eng.) Royal Norfolk and Suffolk yacht
		club

Embury, Aymar, II·   1880-1966
Crisp, Arthur
     Panels in dining room of Seward Prosser
house
 	
     N.Y. Arch' league. Annual
     29:72, 80, 89
     1914
	Emck, J. H.
	Stout, A.J. vander
	     Een bontzaak met wonigen aan de Grote Markt
	te Groningen [plans and section] J.H.Emck and H.
	Salomonson, archts.
	
	     Forum
	     10: no.7, p.213-215
	     S 1955
		Emerson, W. P.
		
		    see
		
		Boston (MA) Residence (Jamaica Plain)

720.5
A67r   Embury, Aymar II   1880- 1966
     Portfolio of country residences:
residence of Louis Stare, Jr. Tenafly, N.J.;
residence at Englewood, N.J.; residence of
Mr. Embury, Englewood, N.J. House of Stanley
G. Flagg III. Stowe, Pa. and others.
     Architectural record 78:584-587
     October 1910
	Emck, J H
	     Magasins: immeuble et magasin à Groningen
	[plans and section] H. Salomonson and J.H.Emck,
	archts.
	
	     Aujourd'hui 1:
	     68
	     Mr-Ap 1955
		720.52
		B93 Emerson, Sir William
		     The late Sir William Emerson
		
		     Builder 128:5
		     Jan. ?, 1925

Emerson, William, 1873-1957

see also

New York (N.Y.) 70th St., East (No.159) house
Lake George (N.Y.) Moffat (G.B.) summer home
New York (N.Y.) Beaux-arts institute of design.
    building. 1915

Emerson, William Ralph,   - 1917
    Residence at Jamaica Plain. Boston, Mass.
W. R. Emerson, archt.

Inl archt. 43:
6 pls pre 1
Jl 1904

Emery, Thomas, Offices, Cincinnati, O.

see

Cincinnati, O. Emery (Thomas) offices

MICROFILM

Emerson, William, 1873-1957

obituary notice

In SCRAPBOOK ON
ARCHITECTURE p. 716
(on film)

720.5   Emerson,William Ralph,   - 1917
A51   Rich,C.A.
    William Ralph Emerson: an appreciation.

American architect 112: 475-476
December 26, 1917

Emery, William H., house, Elmhurst, Ill.

see

Elmhurst, Ill. Emery, William H., house

Emerson, William 1873-1957
    Public Bath and Gymnasium

Amer. arch. 111: pl 2147
F 14, 1917

Emery, Amos Barton
    Amos Barton Emery [biog note]

Natl arch 6: 5
Ag 1950

Emeryville (Cal.) Pacific Manifolding Book Co.
    Factory, Pacific Manifolding Book Co.,
Emeryville, California. The Austin Company,
engineers. No plan.

Architectural forum 65: 342
October, 1936

720.5   Emerson,William, 1873-1957
B84   C.H.W.
    William Emerson. Photograph and brief
sketch.

Brickbuilder 24: 254
September 1915

Emery and Webb

see

Honolulu (Haw.) Hawaii theater

711.05   Eminent domain
T73   Clarke, J. J.
    Acquisition of land and assessment of com-
    pensation.

Town planning rev 15: 261-78
D '33

Emerson, William Ralph,   -1917

see also

Mount Desert,Me. Howard (W.B.) house
Manchester-by-the-sea, Mass. Hemenway house
Chicago, Ill. Willits (G.S.) house
Hartford, Conn. Collins (W.E.) house

Emery, John J. house, Bar Harbor, Me.

see

Bar Harbor, Me. The Turrets

---

711   Eminent domain
C58   Bassett,H.W.
    Some problems in excess condemnation.

City planning 9: 114-120
July 1933

Emerson , William Ralph -1918
    obit.

West. Archt.
27: 53-4
Jan, 1918

Emery, M.L. & H.G.

see

Greenwich, Conn. Young men's Christian ass'n

Emmerich, Paul 1876 -

See also

Mebes and Emmerich

Emerson, William Ralph, -1917
    Residence at Bar Harbor, Maine.
W.R. Emerson, archt.

Inland architect
v. 12 no. 3
pl. at end of vol.
O 1888

720.5   Emery,M   L   and H   G
A67   House for Mr.Jacob Fuhs,Highmount,N.Y.
M.L. and H.G.Emery,archts.

Architectural review 14:87
March 1907

720.53   Emmerich,Paul 1876 -
B35   Laubenganghäuser in Berlin-Steglitz. (Ar-
    cade houses in Berlin-Steglitz.) Paul Mebes,
    Paul Emmerich,Anton Brenner,archts. Plans.

Der Baumeister 28: 444-446
November 1930

Emmons, J.N.

see also

Chicago (Il) Ritchie Place and Goethe St. Three
3 Story Residences.

Empire palace of varieties, Middlesbrough, Eng.

see

Middlesbrough, Eng. Empire palace of varieties

Empress of Austria's memorial chapel, Geneva

see

Geneva (Swits.) St. Elisabeth's chapel

Emmons, J. N.

Biographical Sketch

Industrial Chicago: The
Building Interests. 4 vols.
Chicago: Goodspeed Pub. Co.,
1891-(?) - Vol. 1: Pg. 617

Empire period

see

Name of country. Architecture. Empire period

Encinas, Antonio
Edificio de departamentos [plans] Antonio
Encinas, archt.

Arq. Mex.   no.50
p.96-98
Je 1955

Emory university

see

Atlanta (Ga.) Emory university

Empire trust building, New York

See

New York.Empire trust building

Enders, Oscar

see also

Chicago (IL)   Architectural Club Exhibitions. 1900
St. Louis (MO)   Louisiana Purchase Exposition. 1904
Transportation Building

Emory, W.   H.

see

Baltimore (Md.) Smith (E.L.R.) house
Princeton (N.J.) McKay (S.) house

720.6
B38
Employment bureaus.
"A municipal employment bureau." Beaux-
Arts Institute of design awards.

B.A.I.D.,5:5-15
July 1926

720.5
P39
Enders, Oscar 1865-1926
Death.

Pencil points 8: 508
August 1927

Ryerson
Empalme, Mex. Planning
Proyectos de planificacion de Guaymas-
Empalme, Son. [plans] Mario Pani, Domingo Garcia
Ramos, Victor Vila, Miguel de la Torre, planners

Arquitectura Mexico
Vol. 43:128-160
S 1953

720.5
P39
Employment bureaus
"A municipal employment bureau".

Pencil points 10: 194-195
July 1929

720.6
C57
Enders,Oscar 1865-1926
Sketch by Oscar Enders in 1899:
store front.

Chicago architectural club 13:114
1900

Empire building. New York (city)

see

New York (city) Empire building

Employment Bureaus, Germany. Kiel
Employment office at Kiel. Hahn and Schroeder,
archts.

Encyclopedie de l'architecture;
Constructions modernes. 12 vols.
Paris: Albert Morancé, 1928-39.
5:pl. 69-75(no. 3)

Enders, Oscar
Sketch for cemetery entrance. Philadel-
phia. T-Square exhibition, 1899.
Cemetery entrance.

Inland Archt.
33: pl.fol.p. 20
Mar. 1899

Empire exposition, Glasgow, Scot.

see

Glasgow (Scot.) exposition. 1938

Emporium dept store, San Francisco, Cal.

see

San Francisco (Cal.) Emporium department store

---

ffo
720.6
C57
Enders,Oscar 1865-1926
Sketch for residence,Oscar Enders,archt.

Chicago architectural club 7: 59, 60
Annual exhibit 1894

Enders Oscar.
    Sketch of a suburban residence.

            Inland Archt.
            vol.33, No. 3,pl.fol.p. 28
            Apr. 1899

7P0.571 Engel, Carl Ludwig
A79   Hichberg, N.E.
            Den första boken om Engel [by] Carl
         Meissner. [illus. review]. Engels stilhist-
         oriska ställning.

            arkitekten no. 4:69-4
                       no. 5:65-70
            1938

Engelking, Roberto
    Asociacion nacional de actores. [plans]
Roberto Engelking & Mateo Ortiz, archts.

            Arq Mexico
            29: 220-223
            O 1949

721.97   machines corporation
A67c   Endicott (N.Y.) international business
        Kirk, C.A.
            I B M builds another in concrete. Plans

            Architectural concrete 8: 71-73
            No 1 [1942]

7P0.571 Engel, Carl Ludwig, 1874-1840
A79   W., N.E.
            Till hundraårsminnet av Engels död

            Arkitekten no. 1:4-7
            1940

Enghauser and Brandhorst

    see

Minneapolis (Minn.) Palmer (R.) house

Endo, Arata, 1891-1951
    ... more uncertainty as to the exact
relationship between Wright and Arata Endo...

            Prairie school review
            III: 22
            Third quarter 1966

Engelbrekt church, Stockholm

    see

Stockholm, Swe. Engelbrekt church

Engis,

    see

Aegina

Enfant, Pierre Charles

    see

L'Enfant, Pierre Charles

Engelhardt, Hannes
    Sporthalle in Köln [plan & section] Hannes
Engelhardt, archt.

            Baumeister
            56:548-49 Ag 1959

Engineering
    see also

Architecture and engineering
building
Structural engineering

710.5   Enfield, Eng. Windrush
C85   Phillips,Randal
            In the modern style: "Windrush",Enfield,de-
        signed by P.D.Hepworth. Plan.

    A   Country life(Lond.)79:lxii,lxiv
            May 30, 1936

720.5   Engelhardt, Theobald H.
A67ar   Manhasset Bay Yacht Club, Manhasset, Long
        Island, N.Y. T.H. Engelhardt, archt.
        Schell Lewis, del.

            Architect (N.Y.) 13: 142,144,159-171
            November 1929

Engineering. Sloan, M.M. Architectural
    and Structural Engineering.

    Inland Arch.
    49: 27-28, Feb. 1907   50: 5, July, 1907
    49: 43,   March 1907   50: 28, Sept. 1907
    49: 55,   April 1907   51: 86,Jan. 1908
    49: 61,   May 1907
    49: 77-8, June 1907

Enfield place, Evanston, Ill..

    see

Evanston, Ill. Enfield place

Engelhardt, Walter
    Der Städtische Saalbau Essen [plans]
Walter Engelhardt, archt.

            Baumeister
            55:471-79 Jl 1958
            Tafeln 41-48

7P0.5   Engineering
AF1   Architectural engineering

            amer arch 155: 11-12
            Ja 5 '24

Engel, Carl Ludwig
    see also

Helsinki (Fin.) Universitetsbiblioteket
    "   "   Storkyrkan

Engelhardt, Walter
    Wohnhaus und arztpraxis in Essen [plans]
Walter Engelhardt, archt

            Baumeister
            58: 319, Ap 1961

Engineering
    Constructional engineering up-to-date:
for architect and constructor

            Builder 124:706-8
            April 27, 1923

720.59
A67ay
Engineering,
Samuely, Felix
The co-ordination of engineering services
[includes a bibliography]

Architects' yearbook 1: 146-63
1945

Engineering and industrial exhibition, 1948.
Madras

see

Madras (India) Engineering and industrial exhibition.
1948. Permanent house

720.55
I67
Engineers' offices
Studio per un inivesore meccanico.
Merio Tedeschi. archt. [plans, sect.]

Domus no. 230:8-9
1949

Engineering
Alderson, Victor
The Engineer in the 20th Century.

Inland Architect
38: 6-7
Aug. 1901

Engineering Association for the South.
Engineering Association for the South.
Annual Meeting. 1895.

Inland Arch.
26: 64-5
Jan. 1896

720.52
B93
England. 19th century
"Springtime, 1820": a drawing by A.E. Rich-
ardson, dealing with England in the 19th
century.

A   Builder 142: 306, pl. fol. p. 306
February 12, 1932

720.52
A674
Engineering
Lethaby, W.R.
Engineering as an art

Architecture (Lond.) 4:119-
170
Jl '25

Engineering laboratories

see also names of specific laboratories, i.e:

National research council of Canada, Ottawa. Division of mechanical engineering. Laboratories

---

England. Aerial views

see

England. Views, Aerial

Engineering
Pond, D. C.
Engineering for architects. 12 pts.

Architecture (NY)
30:138-41   Jl 1914
:156-9   Ag 1914
:193-5   Sep 1914
:246-8   Oct 1914
:254-6   N   1914
:276-9   D   1914
31:43-6   Ja   1915

see Card 2

Engineering (theme)
Noble memorial, Engineering Societies
building, New York City, Willard D. Paddock,
sculptor

Architecture 50: 380
N 1924

720.5 2
A673
England. Antiquities.
Caerleon museum, Monmouthshire.

Arch. Rev. 44:114-19.& pl. 3
Dec. 1918

Engineering   Card 2
Pond, D. C.
Engineering for architects. 12 pts.

31:53-7   F 1915
:80-3   Mar 1915
:109-11   Ap 1915
:140-3   My 1915
:163-5   Jun 1915

"Engineering" (theme)
Sculpture by F.W. Pomeroy

Builder 105: pl.
Nov. 7, 1913

England. Antiquities
Keep great Hedingham. St. Botolph's Priory etc.

Architect 102:99-102
Aug. 15, 1919

Engineering.
Engineering principles in house design.

Northwest archt 1Pi.4
No. 3. 1948.
12: 7
No. 4. 1948

Engineers and architects

see

Architects and engineers

England, Antiquities
The Royal archaeological Institute. II.
Bishop's Canning. The Wansdyke. Avebury.
Silbury Hill.

Architect 104:100-1.
Aug. 13, 1920.

Engineering
Genesis of architectural engineers.

Arch & bldg
53: 69-70
S 1921

Engineers' buildings, U.S.

see

New York (N.Y.) Engineering Societies building

720.52
A67e
England. Antiquities.
Royal Archaeological Institute.
Forest of Dean.

Architect 106: 123-5.
August 26, 1921.

720.52
A67e   England. Antiquities.
     Royal Archaeological Institute. Glou-
   cester.

         Architect 106: 98-100.
         August 12, 1921.

705.2
B96   Webb, Geoffrey
     England. Architects
     John and William Bastard

       Burlington 47:144-150
       September 1925

913.1
H84   Smith, D.H.
     England. Architecture
     'And others'. English background for homes
   of the early colonies.

       House beautiful 64:264-266
       September 1928

England, Architects

   see also

Mitchell, Arnold

720.52
A67   England. Architects
     R. I. B. A. Presidents-elect.

       Architects' journal 69: 558-559
       April 10, 1929

England. Architecture
   The Charm of the country town.

       Arch. Rev. 49:35-42.
       Feb. 1921

720.5
A67a   England. Architects
     The architect-at-large in England
     Lorenzo Hamilton

       Architecture 50:335-337
       Oct. 1924

710.5
C855   Perrett, Antoinette
     England. Architects .18th century
     Amateur architects of the 18th century.

       Country life(U.S.)71:46-47,110
       April 1937

England. Architecture
   Classic architecture

       Amer. arch. 105:307-310
       June 17, 1914

England, Architects
   Architects from George IV to George V.
   By Mr. Maurice B. Adams.

       Arch and con rep 87:
       115-118
       Feb. 16, 1912

720.52
A673   Verney, Lady M.M. & P. Abercrombie
     England. Architects.18th century
     Letters of an 18th century archt. Sir Thomas
   Robinson, Bart., to Ralph, 2nd earl Verney. Pts.
   I, II, III, IV.

       Architectural review 59:259-263
       June 1926   60:1-3;50-53;
       July and August   92-93
       1926

720.52
A67c   England. Architecture
     Contemporary British architecture and
   its immediate ancestry.

       Architect 105:507-10;526-28
       March 25;April 1;1921

720.6
R88   Adams,M.B.
     England. Architects
     Architects from George IV to George V.Paper
   read before the Glasgow ins institute of archts.
   February 14,1912.(In two parts)

       R.I.B.A journal 19:598-607;
       June 29;July 27, 1912

England. Architects. Conferences

   see

British architects conference

720.5
A67r   Blockall, R.M.
     England, Architecture
     Early English detail and design.

       Architectural record 52:387-400
       November 1922

720.6
R88   England. Architects
     Exhibition of seventeenth century archi-
     tectural drawings.

       R.I.B.A. 29: 435-40
       May 20,1922.

England. Architects. Georgian

   see also

Hawksmoor, Nicholas
Gibbs, James
Vanbrugh, Sir John
Chambers, Sir William
Soane, Sir John
Adam Brothers

720.6
R88   England, Architecture
     English architecture

       R.I.B.A.journal 31:97-103
       Dec. 22, 1923

720.52
A67   England.Architects
     From Inigo Jones to William Chambers.

                  260
       Architects' and builders journal 38:258-
       September 10,1913

England. Architects. Georgian
   (Biographies of architects of the late
Georgian Period: 1760-1820)

Tipping, Henry Avray. English Homes.
9 vols. London: Offices of Country
Life, New York: Charles Scribner's
Sons, 1920-37.

England. Architecture.
   Taut, Bruno.
English architecture as I see it.

       Creative art. 5:763-68
       November 1929

England, Architecture
Buckly, Julian A.
English house at Medmenham Buckinghamshire

House beau 4:pl.p. 151
O 1898

720.52
A67
England, Architecture.
Newport Pagnell.

Arch. Jour. 54:275-7.
Sept. 7, 1921

705.2
S92
England.Architecture
The work of Messrs. Falconer, Baker and
Campbell, architects.

Studio 89:25-27;86-89
January,February 1925

England. Architecture
Blomfield, R. T.
Half-timber houses in the Weald of Kent and
neighborhood.

Portfolio 18:1,39,45
1887

720.5
A67r
England. Architecture
Fletcher, B.F.
Recent development of early Renaissance in
England.

Architectural record 2:31-43
July-September 1892

England. Architecture. 16th cent.
French influence.
Blunt, Anthony
L'influence française sur l'architecture
et la sculpture décorative en Angleterre pen-
dant la première moitié du XVIe siècle.
[illus.]

Revue de l'art
no.4: 17-29
1969

720.5
A67
England. Architecture
Brown, Frank Chouteau Brown
A journey in search of the picturesque.
P. A devious road to London

arch rev 10 (n.s.5): 49-53
My '03

720.52
A67c
England. Architecture
Recording britian: second series of topo-
graphical pictures at the National gallery.

Architect 171: 5
July 3, 1942

705.2
P84
England,Architecture. 1550-1650
Blomfield,R.W.
Some architects of the English renaissance.
Part 1,general comments; part P, Thorpe and Abel;
part 3, Thomas Holt and the stones.

Portfolio 19:86-92;145-153;185-191
1888
A

720.5
A67a
England. Architecture
Monthly pictorial review of our English
contemporaries

Architecture
13:36-9
Mr '06

720.6
R88
England.Architecture
Goodhart-Rendel, H.W.
A talk about contemporary British architect-
ure and its immediate ancestry.

Royal institute of British architects-journal
March 5,1921   28:249-256

720.52
A67
England. Architecture.18th century
Architecture of late 18th century. Nelson
house,Devonport.
Architecture of St. Neots.

Arch.jour.51:143-146.
Feb.4,1920.

720.5
A67
England. Architecture
Prior, Edward S.
The movement of English architecture

arch rev 10 (n.s.5): 42-44
Ap '03

England. Architecture
Transition from Norman to gothic

Art and arch. 5:33-37
Jan., 1917

England. Architecture. 18th cent.
Wittkower, Rudolf
English neo-Palladianism, the landscape
garden, China and the enlightenment. [illus.,
sum. in It.,Fr.& Ger.]

L'Arte
v.2: 18-35
Je 1969

England. Architecture
Lethaby, W.R.
National architecture.

Builder 115:
213; O 4, 1918
229; O 11, "
243; O 18, "
261; O 25, "
279-80; N 1, "

England. Architecture
Brakspear, Sir Harold
A West country school of masons.

Archaeologia 81:1-18
1931

England. Architecture. 18th Century.
Sigworth, Oliver F.
The four styles of a decade. (1740-1750)
[illus.]

New York. Public Library. Bulletin
Vol. 64: 407-431
1960

England, Architecture
Clay, H.V.
The New English Country House of Mr. Nat Goodwin

House beau 4:51
Jl 1898

England. Architecture
Richardson, A. E.
The work of English architects of the 18th century
and 19th century.

Archs. and builders jour 39:
10-12; Ja 7, 1914
28-30; " 14, "
46-48; " 21, "

England. Architecture. 19th century

see also

London. Architecture. 19th century

England. Architecture. 19th cent.
Architecture at the Royal Academy.

Amer arch
1: 182 - Je 3, 1876
1: 189 - Je 10, 1876
1: 197-198 - Je 17, 1876

720.52
A67c
England.Architecture.19th-20th century
Last 50 years, 1869-1919.

Architect 101:200-202,267-270,281-285.
March 28;April 18;25,1919

720.52
A67
England. Architecture.20th century
Contemporary British architecture.

Arch. Jour. 53:319.
Mar. 15, 1921.

720.5
A67r
England.Architecture.19th century
Adshead,S.D.
A comparison of modern American architecture
with that of European cities - following the
renaissance.

Architectural record 29:113-125
February 1911

720.52
A67c
England.Architecture.20th century
Hitchcock,Henry-Russell Jr.
An American critic in England. Photograph
p.112.

Architect(Lond.)149:67-70,112
January 15;22,1938

720.6
R88
England. Architecture. 20th century
A debate as to what constitutes modernism.

R.I.B.A. 35:511-523
June 9, 1928

England. Architecture. 19th cent.
Hughes, J. Quentin
La costa di ghisa: Liverpool nel secolo
XIX.

Casabella
#246:50-55 D 1960

England. Architecture. 20th century.
Exhibitions. 1927
Wellesley, Gerald
Architecture at the Academy and at the R.I.B.A.
galleries.

Country life (Lond)
61: 912-914, Je 4, 1927

205
W48
England. Architecture. 20th century
Roth, Alfred
England plant und baut

Das Werk 34:105-155
Sup 37-40
Ap '47

720.6
A673
England.Architecture.19th century
The dark age in England.

Architectural journal of S. of A. 2: 110-
January 1924   116

710.5
C85
England.Architecture.20th century(1910-1935)
Reilly,C.H.
The architecture of the Reign: influences in
English architecture during King George's reign.

Country life(Lond)77:456-462
May 4,1935

England. Architecture 20th Cent.
Willmott, E.C. Morgan English Commercial
Architecture and Shop Fronts. Photos.

West. Archt.
17: 28-34
Mar, 1911

720.52
A67
England.Architecture.19th century
Early 19th century architecture.
5.Post office,Queen street,Exeter.

Arch.Jour.51:336.Mar.17,1920

England. Architecture. 20th century
Lewis, David
Architettura e urbanistica in Gran Bretagna

Casabella
#250: 29-47, Ap 1961

720.52
A67c
England. Architecture. 20th century
Exhibition of modern British architecture.

Architect (Lond.) 117: 738-743
April 29, 1927

720.52
B98
England.Architecture.19th century
Simpson, Prof. F.M.
English architecture in the 19th century.

Builder 118:222
February 20,1920

England. Architecture. 20th century
Jordan, Robert Furneaux
Bilancio dell'architettura inglese

Casabella
#250: 3-11, Ap 1961

England. Architecture. 20th century
La generazione del 1947

Casabella
#250: 27-8. Ap 1961

720.52
A67
England.Architecture.19th century
Royal George hotel, Rugby. Early 19th
century.

Architects' journal 51:574
May 5,1920

720.52
A67c
England. Architecture.20th century
British architecture in 1926.

Architect (Lond.) 117: 54-64
January 7, 1927

720.52
A67
England. Architecture, 20th century
Fisher, A.B.K.
Modern architecture.

Architects journal 67:584-586
April 25, 1928

Card 1 (row 1, col 1):

720.52
A883
England. Architecture. 20th century
Modern English architecture.

Builder 136: 603-4
March 29, 1929

Card 2 (row 1, col 2):

720.52
A674
England. Architecture. 20th century
Edwards, A. Trystan
Twenty years of British architecture

Architecture 16:279-285
Ap 1923

Card 3 (row 1, col 3):

England. Architecture. Elizabethan

see

Domestic architecture, England. Elizabethan

Card 4 (row 2, col 1):

720.52
A674
England. Architecture. 20th century
Robertson, Howard
The modern movement in architecture--England.

Architecture (Lond.) 5: 10,12
May 1926

Card 5 (row 2, col 2):

720.52
A873
England. Architecture. 20th century.
Twenty years of British architecture- the
Architecture Club.

Architectural review 53:132-4
April 1923.

Card 6 (row 2, col 3):

England. Architecture. Empire period
DeJong, F.
Empire style in decoration.

Architects' journal 58:654-5
October 31, 1923

Card 7 (row 3, col 1):

720.52
A67
England. Architecture. 20th century
Reilly, Prof. C.H.
1925 its achievements.

Architects' jour. 63:8-13
January 6, 1926

Card 8 (row 3, col 2):

710.5
C85
England. Architecture. 20th century
Lutyens, Sir E.L.
What I think of modern architecture. Illustrated.

Country life(Lond.)69:775-777
June 20, 1931

Card 9 (row 3, col 3):

720.52
A67
England.Architecture. Exhibitions
Corlette, H.C.
Modern architecture at Wembley.

Architects' journal 59:974-975
June 11,1924

Card 10 (row 4, col 1):

England, Architecture. 20th c.
Kaspe, Vladimir
La nuova arquitectura en Inglaterra [plans]

Arq Mexico 20:269-281
Ap 1946

Card 11 (row 4, col 2):

England. Architecture 1920
Summary of chief events of the year.
Including R.I.B.A. ; Exhibitions;housing; etc.

Arch jour 52: 703-4
D 29, 1920

Card 12 (row 4, col 3):

England. Architecture. Exhibitions. 1924
Architecture at the Royal Academy, 1924.

Builder 126:750-1
May 9, 1924

Card 13 (row 5, col 1):

England. Architecture, 20th century
McLeod, James
The present State of English architecture

Drawing and design 5:39-40
February, 1929

Card 14 (row 5, col 2):

England. Architecture. Bibliography.
Wood, Charles B.,III
A survey and bibliography of writings
on English and American architectural books
published before 1895.

Winterthur portfolio
v.2:127-137
1965

Card 15 (row 5, col 3):

England. Architecture. Exhibitions.1927
Blomfield, Sir Reginald
The exhibition of modern British architecture.

R.I.B.A. 34: 449-452
May 7, 1927

Card 16 (row 6, col 1):

720.52
A67c
England. Architecture. 20th century
Dickinson, P.L.
Some thoughts on modern architecture. Illustrations of work of G.G.Kornus.

Architect 114:313-316
October 30, 1925

Card 17 (row 6, col 2):

England, Architecture. Chinese influence

Tipping, Henry Avray. English homes.
9 vols. London: Offices of Country
Life, New York: Charles Scribner's
Sons, 1920-37. vol.1:6-8

Card 18 (row 6, col 3):

England. Architecture. Exhibitions. 1937
Byron, Robert
Technique and tradition in British architecture as
illustrated in the Royal Academy Exhibitions.

Country life (Lond) 81:70-75
January 16, 1937

Card 19 (row 7, col 1):

RYERSON LIBRARY
705.944
W48
England. Architecture. 20th century
Otten, Frank
Tendances actuelles de l'architecture moderne en Angleterre.

Das werk 32: 339-344
N '45

Card 20 (row 7, col 2):

England, Architecture. Egyptian influence

see

London (Eng.) Arcadia works

Card 21 (row 7, col 3):

720.5
A67r
England.Architecture.French influence
Swales, F.S.
Influence of Ecole des beaux-arts on recent
architecture in England.

Architectural record 26:417-427
December 1909

England. Architecture. Georgian

see also

Domestic architecture, England. Georgian

720.5f
A67c

England. Architecture. Medieval
Kent, G.H.
A comparison between the medieval architecture of England and France

Architect and contract rep. 75:
113-15, 179-71
F 16, 23, '06

England. Architecture, Queen Anne

See also

Domestic architecture, England. Queen Anne

---

ffo
720.5
A67r

England. Architecture. Georgian
Middleton, G.A.T.
English "Georgian" architecture: the source of the American "Colonial" style.

Architectural record 9: 87-108
October 1899

England. Architecture. Mediaeval
Clough and A. Williams-Ellis
The dark age in England.

Architecture 2: 110-116
January, 1924

England. Architecture. Queen Anne
Concerning Queen Anne

Amer archt
1:404
D 16, 1876

728
E93

England. Architecture. Georgian
Ackerman, F.L.
Georgian architecture at King's Lynn, Buckingbamshire, Beaconsfield, Woodbridge, Bungay, Amersham, Thaxted, Norwich, Missenden.

Tuileries brochures 2:115-127
March 1930

England. Architecture. Mediaeval
Prior, E.S.
English mediaeval architecture, pt. 1-10.

Arch. and con rep 86:
230; O 20, 1911
253-54; O 27, 1911
262-63; N 3, "
283-84; " 10, "
295-96; " 17, "
310-11; " 24, "
(see card 2)

720.52
B93

England. Architecture. Regency (1810-1820)
The architecture of the Regency.

Builder 144: 405
March 10, 1933

---

ff
720.52
A67c

England. Architecture. Georgian
Esdaile, Mrs.
The growth of architectural amenities in the reign of George III.

Architect 111:406-8
June 6, 1924

England. Architecture. Mediaeval   (card no. 2)
Prior, E.S.
English mediaeval architecture. pt.1-10.

332-33; D 1, 1911
345; D 8, 1911
382; " 22, "
394-95; D 29, 1911

England. Architecture. Regency (1810-1820)
English Empire or Regency 1800-1830

Newcomb, Rexford. Outlines of the history of architecture. rev. ed. 4 vols. New York: John Wiley and Sons, 1931-39. pt.IV.p.227,230,235

---

ff
720.52
A674

England. Architecture. Georgian
Richardson, A.E.
Late Georgian: Its values and limitations.

Architecture 16: 545-547
September 1923

England. Architecture. Medieval.
Faulkner, P. A.
Medieval undercrofts and town houses.
[illus.]

Archeological journal
123: [120]-135
1966

710.5
C855

England. Architecture. Regency (1810-1820)
Lenygon, Jeannette
George IV: called Regency - also a study of architecture in George's time.

Country life(U.S.)68:18-21,77
September 1935

720.5
A67f

England. Architecture. Georgian
Phillips, R.R.
Small English buildings of the late Georgian period.

Architectural forum 26: 11-16
January 1917

England. Architecture, Medieval
Norman, Philip
Recent discoveries of medieval remains in London.

Archaeologia 67:1-26
1916

England. Architecture. Regency 1810-1820
Regency and early Victorian (1810-1850).

Richardson, Sir Ablert Edward.
Regional architecture of the West of England. London: E. Benn, Ltd., 1924. p.126-137

---

ff
720.52
A67

England. Architecture. Georgian
Richardson, A.E.
The zenith of the Georgian era. 1763-1820.
No illus.

Architects' and builders' journal 38: 558-560
December 24, 1913

England. Architecture. Medieval.
Oswald, Arthur
The royal works in the middle ages.
[illus.]

Country life
v. 137: 305;307
Feb. 14, 1965

710.5
C855

England. Architecture. Regency (1810-1820)
Hussey, Christopher
Regency - the nineteenth century modern

Country life(U.S.)68:24-26,67
October 1935

England. Architecture. Stuart

see

Domestic architecture, England. Stuart

Englewood, Ill.

see

Chicago, Ill. Englewood [district]

720.5
A51

Englewood (N.J.) Flannagan (H.N.) house
   Residence of H.N.Flannagan,Englewood,New
Jersey. Davis,McGrath and Kiessling,archts.
Plans.

American architect 109: 220-224, pls.
April 5, 1916   fol.p.232
A

England. Architecture. Viking influence.
Wood, G. Bernard
   1066 in the North of England. [illus.]

Country life
139: 1267-1268; 1270
My 19, 1966

Englewood (NJ) Barber (St. George) Residence
Aymar Embury II, archt. plans

West. Archt.
17: pls.fol.p. XV
Jun, 1911

Englewood (N.J.) Graeme (E.R.) Residence
Aymar Embury II , archt. plans

West. Archt.
17: pls.fol.p. XV
Jun, 1911

England. Description and travel.

see

England. Views

720.5
A51

Englewood (N.J.) Blake (H.N.) house
   H.N. Blake, Englewood, New Jersey.
Davis, McGrath and Kiessling, archts. Plans

Amer arch 98: 1 pl. fol.p. 144
O 26 '10

720.5
A67a

Englewood (N.J.) Graham (H.S.) house
   Residence, H.S. Graham, Englewood, N.J.
R.C. Hunter, archt. [plans]

Arch 53: 147
My '26

720.6
R88

England. Office of Works.
   Ancient monuments and historical buildings in the charge of H. M. Office of
works.

Jour. Royal Inst.of Brit.Arch. 29: 27-8.
Nov. 12, 1921.

Englewood (N.J.) Coe (E.P.) Residence
Embury, Aymar II, Archt.

West. Archt.
17: 53,pls.fol.p. XV
Jun, 1911

720.5
A67r

Englewood (N.J.) Helicon Hall
   Helicon Hall,Englewood,N.J.- residence of
Rev.J.Craig. No plan. Archt. not given.

Architectural record 5:505-506
January-March 1896

England. Theaters

see

Theaters, England

720.5
A67a

Englewood (N.J.) DeVine (N.J.) house
   Residence, N.J. DeVine, Englewood, N.J.
R.C. Hunter & Bro. archts. [plans]

Arch 53: 148
My '26

Englewood (N.J.) Hillcrest
Aymar Embury II, Archt.

West. Archt.
17: pls. fol.p. XV
Jun, 1911

710.5
C 85

England. Views. Aerial
Tipping, H. A.
   English homes as seen from an aeroplane

Country life
48:429; O 9, 1920

Englewood (N.J.) Embury (Aymar II) Residence
Aymar Embury II., archt. plans

West. Archt.
17: pls.fol.p. XV
Jun, 1911

720.5
A51

Englewood (N.J.) House (proposed)
   Proposed house, Englewood, N.J. Mowray
& Uffinger, archts.

Amer archt and bldg news
55: pl fol 32
Jl 25, 1896

Engleberg (Switz.) Abbey
Lafontaine, P. Cart de
The Abbey Church and Monastery of Engelberg.

Architecture (Lond.) 5:24-6
May, 1926

720.5
A51

Englewood (N.J.) Englewood neighborhood
house
   Englewood neighborhood house, Englewood,
New Jersey. Mann & MacNeille, archts.

Amer arch 116: pls 53-60
Ag 13, '19

720.5
A67a

Englewood (N.J.) Jeffrey (O.W.) house
   House of O.W.Jeffrey, Englewood, New Jersey. E.K.Benedict, archt., plans.

Architecture 26: 178-179
September 1912

710.5 N84 — Englewood (N.J.) Johnson (G. L.) house House of G. Leonard Johnson, Englewood, N. J. Aymar Embury, II, archt. [plans] House and garden 43:92 Ap '23	720.5 A51 — Englewood (N.J.) Platt (D.F.) house Residence of: Dan Fellows Platt, Englewood, New Jersey. [plans]. Davis, McGrath and Kiessling, archts. Amer archt 96:2 pls fol. p.152 O 13, '10	Englund, Dag see also Helsinki (Fin.) Rake Oij: s Ritningstävlan Enso (Fin.) Kyrka. Competition
720.5 A67ar — Englewood (N.J.) Johnson (G.L.) house Detail, house, Mr. G. Leonard Johnson, Englewood, N.J. Aymar Embury II, architect. Architect 1:pl.70 Dec. 1923	720.5 A51 — Englewood (N.J.) Richardson (W.R.) house House of W. R. Richardson, Englewood, N.J. R.C. Hunter and Brother, archts. Amer arch 124: 3 pls J1 18 '23	Englund, Dag. and Kaj. see also Helsinki (Fin.) Englund (Dag and Kaj) house
Englewood (N.J.) Neighborhood House Englewood, N.J. neighborhood house. Architectural forum 29:pl.65-67 November, 1918	Englewood (N.J.) St. John's Episcopal Church A Stained Glass Window. Designed and Executed by J.A. Holzer. For St. John's Episcopal Church at Englewood, N.J. House and gard 6: 9-11 July, 1904	Englund, Dag. and Martti Talvi Oja see Kemi (Fin.) Planning. Competition.
Englewood (N.J.) Palisades Trust and Guaranty Co. Aymar Embury II, Archt. plan West. Archt. 17: pls.fol.p. XV Jun, 1911	MICROFILM English channel. Tunnel, Proposed In SCRAPBOOK ON ARCHITECTURE p. 15 (on film)	Englund, Kaj see Helsinki (Fin.) Granroth house " " Bostadsutställningen
720.5 A67a — Englewood (N.J.) Perkins (T.I.) house house, T.I.Perkins, Englewood, New Jersey. W.K.Benedict, archt., plans. Architecture 26:p.180-181 September 1912	English Cottage Competition English Cottage competition. Builder 143: 98a-98d; 404-411 July 15; September 9; 1932	Engoabe, Dom. Rep. Architecture Palm, Erwin Walter Engombe; una quinta senorial del siglo XVI en el tropico. Arq Mexico 20:304-308 Ap 1946
Englewood (N.J.) Phelps Manor Country Club Phelps Manor Country Club, Englewood Teaneck, N.J. C.C. Wendehack, architect. Amer. arch. 125:pl. May 21, 1924	English, Jay I. see Toronto (Ont.) Fairlawn theater	Engstrom, Alf, 1932- Crematorium in Gävle, Sweden [plan & section] Alf Engstrom, Gunnar Landberg & Bengt Larsson. archts. Architectural Design 31: 220-21, My 1961
720.5 A51 — Englewood (N.J.) Platt (D.F.) house House of Dan Fellows Platt,Englewood,New Jersey. Davis,McGrath and Kiessling,archts. Plans. American architect 96: 2 pls.fol.p.152 October 13,1909	710.5 C35 — English Lake District Hodge, E.W. Houses of the romantic period in the Lake District. Country life(London)88:374-375 October 26,1940	Engstrom, Alf, 1932- Krematorium in Gävle; entwurf 1954, gebaut 1958-60 [plans & section] Alf Engstrom, Gunnar Landberg, Bengt Larsson & Alvar Torneman, archts Bauen & Wohnen 15: 168-71, My 1961

Ennis, G. P. see New York (N.Y.) Church of all Nations	790.871 A79 Enso (Fin.) Kryka. Competition Enso kyrkotävlan. Dag Englund, archt. [plans, sections] Arkitekten no. 8:1Pl-8 1938	Entasis Method of determining Bragdon, Claude F. The Beautiful Necessity. Rochester, New York: Manas Press, 1910. p.44
720.5 W52 Enniskillen (Ire.) Convent chapel Convent chapel, Enniskillen, Ireland. W.A. Scott, archt. Plans. A Western architect 18:pl.18-19 July 1912	Entablatures. Meas. drawings. Cicognara, Leopoldo. Le Fabbriche e i monumenti Cospicui di Venezia. Venice: G. Antonelli, 1858. p. 194	"Ente Mutualita Scolastica" vacation colony, Formia, It. see Formia (It.) Colonia Ente Mutualità Scolastica
720.52 A675 Ensembliers. France. The modern movement in continental decora- tion: The evolution of the ensemblier. Arch.rev.(Lond.)59:243-51 May 1926	720.5 A51 Entablatures. Rome Measured drawing. Entablature in the Ba- silica of Constantine, Rome. American architect 125:17-18 Jan. 2, 1924	MICROFILM Entenza, J. D., In SCRAPBOOK ON ARCHITECTURE p. 31 (on film)
Ensenada (Mex.) Playa Ensenada Hotel Playa Ensenada Hotel and Casino, Ensenada, Old Mexico. Gordon E. Mayer, archt. Architectural digest 8:72-74 A Number 2 [1932-33]	Entasis Goodyear, William Henry. Greek refinements. New Haven: Yale University Press, 1912. p.83-104	Entenza (John) house. Santa Monica, Cal. see Santa Monica, Cal. Entenza (John) house
Ryerson Enshō-ji temple, Jap. Shaka-do chapel Amanuma and Ito Architecture of the chapel Shaka-do of the Enshō-ji temple, Nagano prefecture. On some Buddhistic architecture...India. Bukkyo bijutsu No 12: 49-92 Mr 1929	720.52 B93 Entasis. Architectural design. Builder 122: 143. Jan. 27, 1922	Entraigues (Fr.) Saint-Michel Église de Saint-Michel d'Entraigues. Plan, drawings. France. Commission des monuments historiques. Archives....4 vols. Paris: Gide and J. Baudry, 1855-72. v.2:49-51,pl.39-40.
Enskede (Swe) Church The church at Enskede... Carl Bergsten, archt. Arch rev 56:28 Jl'24	720.5 A51 Entasis Calculation of entasis on profile of a column. Amer.arch.119:p.550-1. May 11,1921.	Entrance, English (no further definition given). Inland Archt. Vol. 25, No. 4, pl. Fol. p. 44 May 1895
720.871 A79 Enso (Fin.) Enso-Outseit mills Utvidgning av Enso-Gutzeits Huvudkontor... Bostad för Chefdirektören...Klubbhus för Tjänstemännen...Bostad för fabriksläkare. Väinö Vähäkällio, arkitekt. [office building, dwellings, staff clubhouse] Arkitekten no. 2:cover, 17-32 1937	720.5 A67r Entasis Goodyear,W.H. A discovery of the entasis in medieval Itali- an architecture. Pisa cathedral. Plan. Architectural record 7:63-96 July-September 1897	Entrance, French (no further definition given) Inland Archt. Vol. 25, No. 5, pl. Fol. p. 54 June 1895

Entrance Gates
    Entrance to the estate.

Country Life (U.S.) 66: 68-71
October, 1934

Environmental design
Elms, Patrick d'
    A problem of environment -- the French
1 percent example. [illus., text in Fr. &
Eng.]

Cimaise
Sér 17: 54-65
S-O 1970

705.4   Epau.Abbaye
B38   Verrier, Jean
            The abbey of Epau, Sarthe.

Beaux-arts 4:36
February 1,1936

Entrance halls

        see

Halls
Lobbies

Environmental design
Rasmusson, Torkel
    Villa naturen, fotografierna togs av
Sven Hemmel hösten 1958. [illus.]

Konstrevy
v.45, NR 4: 148-149
1969

Epfig, Fr. Saint Georges (church).
Lehni, Roger
    L'église d'Epfig dernière oeuvre de
Pierre Michel Dixnard. [illus.]

Information d'histoire
de l'art
An. 15: 60-67
Mr-Ap 1970

Entrances   see also

Architectural school entrances Gates
Arsenal entrances   Garden entrances
Bank entrances   Subway entrances
Bridge entrances
Cemetery entrances
Doors and doorways
Exhibition entrances
Museum entrances
Office building entrances
Theater entrances

Environmental design. Exhibitions
Lindberg, Berndt
    Gott nytt år? [illus.]

Konstrevy
v.48, NR 1: 44
1970

Ephesus, Turkey. Artemision

    see

Ephesus, Turkey. Temple of Diana

Entrances.
    Entrances through a colonnade. Beaux arts
institute of design award.

Amer arch 120:347-
N 9, 1921

Environmental policy.
Denson, Eley P., Jr.
    Endangered species and public law 91-135.

Museum news
v. 48: 22-23
My 1970

Ephesus, Turkey. Churches
Guyer, S.
    Die Kirchen von Ephesos.

Christliche Kunst
31: 282-288
Je 1935

Entwistle, Clive Ernest
    Liverpool Roman Catholic Cathedral
competition: commended project [plan & section]
Clive Entwistle, archt.

Archtl Design
30:423-24 O 1960

Environmental policy.
McGrath, Kyran M.
    Environmental education act.

Museum news
v. 49: 22-25
D 1970

Ephesus, Turkey. Temple of Artemis

    see

Ephesus, Turkey. Temple of Diana

Environmental design.
Webb, Michael
    Museum architecture - to better the city
...or escape it. [illus.]

Museum news
v. 48: 12-14
My 1970

Environmental policy.
Grobman, Arnold B.
    Museums and the biosphere. [illus.]

Museum news
v. 48: [24]-28
Ap 1970

Ephesus, Turkey. Temple of Diana
    The temple of Diana, Ephesus.

The Archt and contract
reporter
v.LXXII, no.1867
S 30, 1904

Environmental design.
Oliver, James A.
    Museum education and human ecology.
[illus.]

Museum news
v. 48: 28-30
My 1970

Eosander von Goethe

        see

Berlin (Ger.)   Charlottenburg

Ephesus, Turkey. Temple of Diana
    The temple of Artemis.

British archt
62, no.17
O 21, 1904

Ephesus, Turkey. Temple of Diana
Temple of Artemis (Diana) at Ephesus.

Builder
95, no.3433
N 21, 1908

Epidaurus (Greece) Greek Theater
Tallant, Hugh
Ruins of theater at Epidaurus, Greece (photo).

Brickbuilder 24:18
January, 1915

720.62
A67c
Epitaph
Architectural...

Arch. 114:334-335
Nov. 6, 1925

Ephesus, Turkey. Temple of Diana
Henderson, A.E.
The Croesus (VIth c. B.C.) Temple of
Artemis (Diana) at Ephesus.

RIBA Journal
v.16, 3rd series,no.3
D 5, 1908

Epidaurus (Greece) Greek Theater
Fossum, Andrew
Harmony in the theatre at Epidaurus.

American journal of archaeology 30:70-75
January-March 1926

Epitaux, George

see also

Geneva (Switz.) International labor office

Ephesus, Turkey. Temple of Diana
Temple of Artemis at Ephesus.

RIBA Journal
22: 130-134
Ja 23, 1915

Epidaurus (Greece) Greek Theatre
The Greek theatre at Epidaurus.

Theatre arts monthly 12:609
August, 1928

720.53
W51
Epitaux, George
The building of the International workers
in Geneva. George Epitaux, archt.

Wasmuths 10: 422-425
Heft 10, 1928

Ephesus. Temple of Diana
Banks, E.J.
Seven wonders of the ancient world.
Pt.4--the fourth wonder, the Temple of
Diana at Ephesus.

Art and archaeology
5: 13-19
Ja 1917

720.54
A67au
Epinay (Fr.) Compagnie générale des eaux.Usine
Usine de la compagnie générale des eaux.a
Epinay (Seine). Charles Auray, archt. en
collaboration avec le bureau d'études techni-
ques Dufour.

L'Arch d'aujourd'hui
10: 56
Je '39

720.52
A67c
Epitaux, George
Robertson, Howard
An office building of the nations: The Geneva
International Labour Bureau. George Epitaux,
archt.

Architect (Lond.) 121: 518-521
April 9, 1929

Ephesus, Turkey. Temple of Diana
Lethaby, W.R.
The Hellenistic temple at Ephesus.

Builder
119: 147-150
Ag 6, 1920

Ryerson
Épis, France
Dufournet, Paul
Épis de faitage en fer-blanc de la Savoie

L'art populaire en France
4:167-184
1932

Époisses (Fr.) Château
Château d'Époisses, à M. le Comte de Guitant.
Text in French. Engravings.

Eyries, Gustave. Les Chateaux
Historiques de la France. 3 vols.
Paris: Poitiers, H. Oudin Frères,
1877-81. v.2:131-150.

Ephesus, Turkey. Temple of Diana
Temple of Diana at Ephesus.

Archl review
52: pl.1
D 1922

Ryerson
Épis, France
Pietri, Jean
Épis de faitage et autres ouvrages en
fer-blanc a Die (Drôme)

L'art populaire en France
6:141-5
1934-5

Époisses (Fr.). Chateau
Château d'Époisses. Text in French.
Exteriors and interiors.

Saint Sauveur, Hector.
Chateaux de France. 10 vols. Paris:
Librairie générale de l'architecture
et des arts decoratifs, 1922.
v.7:9-10,pls.30-35

Epidaurus (Greece) Greek Theater
Article discussing Greek Comedy and Tragedy.
View of amphitheatre at Epidaurus.

Stobart, John Clarke. The glory that
was Greece. London: Sidgwick and
Jackson, Ltd., 1911. p.172-187

Episcopal palaces

see names of individual episcopal palaces, e.g:

Uppsala (Swe) Ärkebiskopsborg

Eppenstein, James F.

see

Ravinia (Ill.) Weinfeld (G.F.) house

Chicago, Ill. Eppenstein (James F.) house
"   "   Ourley (Wm. W.) house
"   "   Shoreland hotel (remodelled)
Pittsburgh, Pa. Roosevelt hotel. Bar

Epping, Eng. Churches

Arch. rev. 23:n.s. 6:pl.
104-105
May, 1918

720.5
A67ar

Epstein, A
Stock Yard Nat'l. Bank, Chicago. A. Epstein.

The Architect (N.Y.) 4: pl. 68-72
June 1925

Equitable building (40 N Dearborn St) Chicago
see
Chicago (Ill) real estate exchange building

Eppinghausen, C.F.
Sketch.

Inland Arch.
47: 41
April 1906

MICROFILM

Epstein, Abraham. 1887-1958
obituary notice

in SCRAPBOOK ON
ARCHITECTURE p. 714
(on film)

Equitable bldg (29 S LaSalle st) Chicago
see
Chicago, Ill. Equitable bldg (29 S LaSalle st)

Epsom (Eng.) College. Memorial chapel
Epsom College Memorial Chapel,
Arthur Blomfield, F.R.I.B.A., architect

Builder 128:pl.
Feb. 27, 1925

Epstein, Abraham and Sons
see also
Chicago, IL. Borg-Warner building
  "   " Mt.Sinai Hospital Medical Center.Research
  laboratories and professional services bldg.
Chicago, IL. Twin Towers Trust Apts.

Equitable trust company,Atlantic City,N.J.
See
Atlantic City (N.J.) Equitable trust company

Epsom (Eng.) West Park Mental Hospital
London County Council West Park Mental
Hospital, Horton Estate, Epsom.

Architect 111:434-7 and pl.
June 20, 1924

MICROFILM

Epstein, Abraham and Sons
Plan office building tentatively named
LaSalle-Jackson building (Union tank car building).

in SCRAPBOOK ON
ARCHITECTURE p.449
(on film)

"Ercole Marelli" houses. Sesto San Giovanni
see
Sesto San Giovanni (It.) Case economiche "Ercole Marelli"

Epsom (Eng.) West Park Mental Hospital
West Park Mental Hospital, Epsom.

Builder 126: 1030-2
June 27, 1924

720.52
A674

Epstein, Jacob
The Epstein panel

Architecture (Lond.) 4: 87-88
June 1925

Erdi, Louis, 1909-
Coach Hotel, Dover [plans] L. Erdi, archt.

Bauen & Wohnen
#4:134 Ap 1958

720.52
A67e

Epstein
A last word on...

The Architect 114: 426
Dec. 11, 1925

Epstein, Max house, Winnetka, Ill. (Hubbard Woods)

see

Winnetka, Ill. Edgecliff

Erdington (Eng.) Municipal offices and free library
Erdington municipal offices and free library.
Design. Crouch and Butler and R. Savage, architects.

British architect 61: 402 and pl.
June 3, 1904

721
755

Epstein, A
The bank that grew up with Englewood,
Illinois. Chicago City Bank and Trust Co.
A. Epstein, archt. Interiors only.

Through the ages 9: 18-22
January 1932

Epworth M.E. church. Chicago, Ill.

see

Chicago, Ill. Epworth M.E. church

Erdman, William
3-story store and flat building.
Erdman, William, archt.

Building budget
3:3 in supp
Jl 30, 1887

Erechtheion. Athens

See

Athens. Erechtheum.

Ericson, Sigfrid
Pearson, Charlotte
Interior of Mastchuggschurch, Gothenburg, Sigfrid
Ericson, archt.

Studio 94:142-144
August, 1927

Erie (Pa.) Kawkwa Club
Kawkwa Club, Erie, Pa., Meade and Garfield,
archts. Plans.

A

New York architect 2:206, 209
April, 1908

720.55 Erfurt. Frederick-William plaza
W51   Plessmer,Hans
        Neugestaltung des Friedrich-Wilhelm-Platzes
        in Erfurt. (Reconstruction of the Friedrich-
        William plaza in Erfurt.) Plans.

        Wasmuths monatshefte 14: 535-538
        July 1930

Ericsson, Henry, 1862-1947
Obituary

Illinois society of
architects bulletin
31:8
Mr-Ap 1947

Erie (Pa.) Mutual Telephone Company Bldg.
The mutual Telephone Company Building of Erie,
Pennsylvania.

Through the ages 6:24-25
September, 1928

706.5 Erfurt.Predigerkirche
D48   Rosemann, H.P.
        Die Predigerkirche in Erfurt.
        Dominikanerklosterkirche.(Exterior and interior
                                        views.)

        Deutsche kunst Sp:l.112,113 and text
        No.10,1940

Erie (PA) Atlantic Refining Co. Filling Station
Joseph Franklin Kunz, Architect. Illus.

West. Archt.
vol. 34, p. 30
Mar, 1925

Erie (PA) Public Library
Alden & Harlow, Archs.

Inland Arch. 38:
pl.fol.p.16
sept. 1901

Erfurt (Germany). Rathaus
Sketch for a town hall in Erfurt, Germany,
Willy Harder and Fritz Schock, archts.

Der Städtebau 16: pl.60-6
Heft 9-12, 1919

Erie (Pa.) Custom house
The Old Erie, Pennsylvania, Custom house is
nearly a century old.

Through the ages 5:13-15
December 1927

720.5 Erie, Pa. Second national bank
A67b   Second national bank, Erie, Pa., W.L.
        Stoddard architect.

        Arch. & building 54: 48 & pl.79-81
        May 1922.

Erickson, Arthur
Canada; House on Vancouver Island, B.C.
[plans] Arthur Erickson, archt.

Arch't'l design
32: 143-144, Mr 1962

Erie (Pa.) Custom house
Old custom house, Erie, Pa.
Built in 1836.

Federal architect 2:10
October, 1931

720.5 Erie. Pa. Second national bank
A51   Second national bank, Erie, Pa., W.L.Stod
        dard, architect.

        Amer. arch. 122: 15-16 & 3 pl.
        Jul.5, 1922.

Erickson, Don

see

Glen Ellyn, Ill. Mayes (Jack) house

720.5 Erie(Pa.)Erie trust company
A67f   Erie trust company, Erie(Pa.). Views
        and plans. Dennison and Hirons, archts.

        A   Architectural forum 47:135-9
            August 1927

Eriksdal hall

see

Stockholm (Swe.) Eriksdal hall

Erickson, Ernest R.

Member of firm:
Ellingsen and Erickson

720.5 Erie (Pa.). Housing
A67b   Housing development of American Brake
        Shoe and Foundry Co., Erie, Pa. No archt.
        given.

        arch & bldg 51: 4
        Ja '19

Erikson,Carl A

See also

Schmidt,Garden and Erikson

Erikson, Carl A   ,1888-
    [brief biographical sketch]

            Nat'l arch F:8
            Ja '46

Erlwein, Hans.
    Das italienische dörfchen in
Dresden.
    Architektur des XX jahrhunderts.
    Sonderhefte [v.2] no.12 entire issue
    1913

Erskine, Ralph, 1914-
    Building in the Arctic [diagrams]

            Architectural design
            vol. 30: 194-197, My 1960

720.52   Eriksson, Nils Einar
E31   Competition drawings for the Palace of
           the Society of Nations.

            Wasmuths 11: 457
            Heft 11, 1927

Ernst, Klaus H
    Wohnbauten am Ruhwald-Park in Berlin-
Neuwestend [plans, section & details] Klaus
H. Ernst, archt.

            Arch & Wohnform
            67:244-50 O 1959

Erskine, Ralph, 1914-
    Hotel le montagne en Laponie [plans &
section] Ralph Erskine, archt.

            Aujourd'hui
            3:68-69 Mar 1958

720.5   Erkins, Henry
A67   Louis Martin's restaurant, New York,
         Henry C. Pelton and Henry Erkins, assoc. a
         archts.
             Murray's restaurant, N.Y.C. Henry Erkins,
         archt.

            Architectural review 19 n.s.176-178
            April 1913

Errard
    see
Paris (Fr.) Eglise de l'assomption

Erskine, Ralph 1914-
    Maison de campagne, Ile de Lison, Suède
[plans & section] Ralph Erskine, archt.

            Aujourd'hui
            5:70-3 F 1960

720.5   Erkins,Henry
A67r   Murray's Roman Gardens,New York.Hotel and
         Restaurant.John McKiernan,builder,Henry Erkins,
         archt. Interior and exterior views.

            Architects' and builders' magazine 39:
            September 1907   574-579

720.54   Errazuriz
A67v   Errazuriz,Maison en Amerique du Sud,1930.
            (Errazuriz.,house in South America,1930.)
            Plans and perspectives. Le Corbusier and
            Pierre Jeanneret,archts.

            L'Architecture Vivante: p.37-39.
            Spring-Summer,1931   pl.42

Erve, W   S   van de
    Polizeipräsidium in Den Haag [plans]
W. S. van de Erve, archt.

            Baumeister
            57:460-61 Jl 1960

720.5   Erkins,Henry
A67m   Price,C.M.
             A renaissance in commercial architecture:
         some recent buildings in uptown New York. Detail
         of the first two stories,No.305 Madison Avenue.
         Henry Erkins,archt. No plan.

            Architectural record 31:468
            May 1912

Erskine and American United church, Montreal
    see
Montreal, Que. Erskine and American united church

Ervi, Aarne
    see also
Heinola (Fin.) Heinolan Lüke O.Y.

Erl Dorf farm house, Mansfield, Mass.
    see
Mansfield (Mass.) "Erl Dorf farm" house

Erskine, Ralph
    see also
Lidingö (Sw.) Molin (Villa) house

Ervi, Arne, Aarne, 1910 -
    Bibliothek der Universität Turku; entwurf 1952,
gebaut 1953-54 [plans & section] Arne Ervi, archt.

            Bauen & Wohnen
            15: Supp 6-10, S 1961

705.944   Erlenhof (Swits.). Zöglings-pavillon
W48   Artaria, Paul
               Zöglings-pavillon im landheim "Erlenhof".
           Plans. Ernst Egeler, archt.

            Das werk 32: 321-323
            N '45

Erskine, Ralph, 1914-
Cocchia, Fabrizio
    Un architetto inglese in Svezia: opere di
Ralph Erskine [plans & sections] Ralph Erskine,
archt.

            L'Architettura
            4:196-109 Je 1958

Ervi, Aarne, 1910-
    Eigen huis bij Helsinki [plans & section]
Aarne Ervi, archt.

            Forum
            #1:10-11 Jan 1958

Ervi, Aarne, 1910– Ferienhaus in Finnland [plan and section] Aarne Ervi, archt. Baumeister 53; No.9: 634–639 S 1956	Erwarton, Eng. Gatehouse The gatehouse at Erwarton. Country Life (Lond.) 82:486 November 13; 1937	Escalators Arch and Bldg. 44:509–514 Dec. 1912.
Ervi, Aarne, 1910– Gartenstadt Tapiola bei Helsinki: Tapiola- zentrum und hochhaus mit kino. Aarne Ervi, archt. Bauen & wohnen #9:316–20 S 1957 Konstruktionsblätter at end of issue	Erwin, C.R., house. Oak Park, Ill. see Oak Park, Ill. Erwin, C.R., house.	720.5 A67f Escalators Escalator,Emporium department store,San Francisco,Calif. Eleanor Le Maire,designer; John R.Ember,archt. Pittsburgh Glass insti- tute competition. Section drawing. Architectural forum 67:130 A August 1937
Ervi, Aarne, 1910– "Mäntytorni" torenflat in tuinstad Tapiola [plan] Aarne Ervi, archt. Forum #1:17–18 Jan 1958	720.5 A67r Erwin (Tenn.) Veiller,Lawrence Industrial housing developments in America: a colony in the Blue Ridge mountains at Erwin, Tennessee. Grosvenor Atterbury,archt. Plan. Architectural record 43: 547–559 June 1918 A	Escalators A novel stair – lift invention – invented by Link – Belt Engineering Co. and Dodge Coal Storage Co. Illus. Inland Architect 36: 23 Oct, 1900
720.54 T28 Ervi, Aarne, 1910– Restaurants, Finland. Un café-restau- rant a Helsinki. Tech et arch 6:374–376 No. 7–8, '48	710.5 H84 Erwinna (Pa.) Lindley (E.K.) house Mr. Ernest K. Lindley's house, Erwinna, Pa. Emil J. Szendy, archt. Plan. – House and garden 74: 45 October 1938	Escalier (archt.) Town house, façade. Escalier, architect. Arch. jour. 51:583. May 5, 1920
Ervi, Aarne, 1910– Universiteitsbibliotheek te Turku [plan] Aarne Ervi, archt. Forum #1:28–29 Jan 1958	720.53 B55 Erwitte (Ger.) Harbers, Guido Erwitte, eine alte Burg, als Schulungslager. (Erwitte, an old castle, as a training camp.) Schulte-Fröhlinde, Rogler, Görres, Koch, Kornowsky Schuhknecht, archts. Der Baumeister 34:145–159,Pls.47–53 May 1936	Escalier de la Reine Berthe,Chartres See Chartres.Maison consulaire
Ervi, Aarne, 1910– Villa Koivikko, Helsinki [plan] Aarne Ervi, archt Archtl Design 29:445–46 N 1959	Esbig, Arthur H see Rockville Center (L.I.) Williams (Cy) house	720.5 B93b Escanaba (Mich) Irwin (W.R.) house Residence of W. R. Irwin in Escanaba. M. L. Beers, archt. Building Budget 3:16a January 31 1887
Erwin, Raymond Harry see Denver, Colo. J. C. Penney co.	720.571 A75 Esbo (Fin.) Suomen teknillinenkorkeakoulu Arkitekturklubbens stuga Arkitekturklubbens Stuga i Sibbo, Seppo Hytonen, arkitekt [photos, sections] Arkitekten no. 8:124 1937	Esch, Vincent see Calcutta (India) Bristol hotel

TO6.942
W46
Eschauzier, F   A
    Country house at Wassenaar, Kundekerke,
Rotterdam, Holland. F.A.Eschauzier,archt.
Plans.

        Wendingen 12: 2-7
        #4, 1931

Eschweiler,Alexander C., Sr. 1865- 1940

    See also

Eschweiler and Eschweiler

Escorial. El real monasterio de San Lorenzo
    del Escorial, see
Escorial

Eschauzier, Frits Adolf, 1889-
Rietveld, G.
    Professor F. A. Eschauzier.
Tijen, W. van
    Een persoonlijke herinnering aan Eschauzier.
Röell, D. C.
    Eschauzier als museum-architect.
Eschauzier, Frits
    Het karakter van het werk van Prof. Eschau-
zier. [plans & sections]

        Forum
        13:216-50 Jl 1958

Eschweiler, Alexander C., 1865-1940
Ilsley, Samuel
    The work of Alexander C. Eschweiler,
Milwaukee, Wisconsin: residences of John S.
Batchelor, Clement C. Smith; the Cottril
residence; houses of Clarence Falke and Judge
Carpenter; the houses of Mr. S. A. Goodrich
and of Mr. A.L. Kern; the Black residence;
the houses of Ferdinand Schlesinger, William
Bigelow, Sherburn Becker, and Frank Ward Smith.
[plan of the Schlesinger house]

        Architectural Record
        17: 209-230
        Mr 1905

Escurial
    see
Escorial

Eschenbach, Benson
    see
Hartsdale (N.Y.) Radebaugh (W.H.) house
    "   "   Snyder (G.R.) house

Eschweiler and Eschweiler
    see also
Milwaukee (Wis.) Arena

Escutcheons, Spain
    Escutcheon of Charles V.

        Byne, Arthur. Spanish
        architecture of the sixteenth
        century. New York and London:
        G.P. Putnam's Sons, 1917. Illus.p.73
                    Text p.72

705
W48
Eschens (Swits.) Unipektin A. G.
    Obstverwertungs - Anlage der Unipektin
A. G. in Eschenz. [plans, sect.] G. P. Dubois
& Eschenmoser, archts.

        Das Werk 33:330-33P
        O '46

706.1
M662b
Eschweiler & Eschweiler
    Perspective drawing of Milwaukee gas
light company building

        Milwaukee art institute
        Bulletin 3:cover
        March 1930

Esenwein and Johnson
    see also
Buffalo (NY)   Curtiss (Harlow C.) House
    "   "   Iroquois Hotel
    "   "   Mayer and Weill Building
New York (NY)   Statler Hotel

Escher, Hans
    Reihenhäuser für Holland, Escher and
Weilenmann, archts. [plans, sect.]

        Bauen & Wohnen
        p. 12-13
        no. 3, 1948

Esclimont (Fr.) Chateau
    Château d'Esclimont. Text and photographs.

        Saint Sauveur, Hector.
        Chateaux de France. 10 vols. Paris:
        Librairie génerale de l'architecture
        et des arts decoratifs, 1922.
        v.4:pl.16-21

Esenwein and Johnson
    Temple of music. Pan-Amer. Expo.
1901, Buffalo N.Y.

        Inland Architect
        34: 8 Aug, 1899
          :16 Sept, 1899

Escher Wyss AG. Administration bldg. Zurich,
Swits.
    see
Zurich, Swits. Escher Wyss AG. Administration
    bldg.

Escorial
    [whole issue; illus; part col.]

        Goya
        No.56/57:70-207
        S & D, 1963

Esfahan, Iran
    see
Isfahan, Iran

Eschweiler, Alexander C., Sr.
    see also
Milwaukee (WI)   Black (Elizabeth) House & Stable
    "   "   Cottrill Residence
    "   "   Eschweiler (Alexander) Residence
    "   "   Greene (Howard) House
    "   "   Milwaukee-Downer College
    "   "   St. Thomas Aquinas Church
Pine Lake (WI)   Vogel (Augustus) Residence
Racine (WI)   St. Rose's Church

720.9P
A673
Escorial.Architecture
Elton,L.S.
    In Spain, some examples of brick, plaster
and granite in the Spanish renaissance, pt. 4.
Granite at the Escorial.

        Architectural review 61:8-15
        January 1927

Ryerson
Esguerra & Herrera
    Edificio en Bogota [plan] Esguerra and
Herrera, archts.

        PROA
        No. 67:26
        Ja 1953

Esguerra Garcia, Rafael

Member of firm:

Esguerra, Saens, Urdaneta, Suares

Esher, Lionel Gordon Baliol Brett, 4th vicount

see

Brett, Lionel

Espinosa, Roberto Alvares

see

Alvares.Espinosa, Roberto

Esguerra, Saens, Urdaneta, and Suares

see also

Pereira, Col. Banco de Bogatá

710.5
C85

Esher.Wolsey's tower
Lambert, Clive
  A historic building in danger - Wolsey's tower at Esher, built middle 15th century by Waynflete, founder of Magdalen College, Oxford.

Country life(Lond.)86:77
July 22,1939

Esquiros, Mario
  Inauguracion del nuevo edificio del Colegio Provincial de Arquitectos de La Habana. Mario Esquiros & Fernando de Zarraga Moya, architects.

Arq Cuba
16: 2 - 12
Ja 1948

Esguerra, Saens, Urdaneta, Suares

Members of firm:

Esguerra Garcia, Rafael
SaensCamacho, Alvaro
Urdaneta Holguin, Rafael
Suares Hoyos, Daniel

Esherick, Joseph

see

Oakland (Cal.) Grill (Joaquin) house

Esquivelzeta, A
  Casa habitacion [plans] Vladimir Kaspé & A. Esquivelzeta, archts.

Arquitectura Mexico
no.56:231-3 D 1956

Esguerra, Saens, Urdaneta, Suares
  Casa en Bogata [plans] Esguerra, Saens, Urdaneta, Suares, archts.

Proa no. 86
p. 14-15
F 1955

710.5
C855

Esherick, Wharton
Yarnall, Sophia
  Sculptured wood creates the unique interiors of the Curtis Lok house. Residence of Judge and Mrs. Curtis Loy, Rosemont, Pa.

Country life (U.S.) 74: 67-74
June 1938

720.53
M68

Essen. Architecture
Küstner-Wilhelm,Dr.
  Alfred Fischer-Essen: Hans-Sachs-Haus in Gelsenkirchen; office building of the Union Settlement Ruhr coal district in Essen.

Moderne bauformen 29: 157-162
Heft 4, April 1930

Esguerra, Saens, Urdaneta, Suares
  Edificio comercial en Bogota [plans] Esguerra, Saens, Urdaneta, Suares, archts.

Proa no. 83
p. 18-21
Ag. 1954

D15.1
H84

Espalier
  Espalier orchards on the wall.

House beautiful 77:18-21
August 1935

720.53
B35

Essen. Architecture
Harbers,Guido
  Vorstädtische kleinsiedlungen in Essen. (Small suburban colonies in Essen.) Faber,archt. Illus. Plans.

Der Baumeister 31: 405-417,pl.117-122
December 1933

Esguerra, Saens, Urdaneta, Suares ltda.
  Edificio de renta - Bogota [plans & section] Esguerra, Saens, Urdaneta, Suares Ltda., archts.

Proa
#129:8-9 Ag 1959

710.5
H84

Espalier
Davison,Irene
  The orchard on the wall through the use of espalier trees.

House and garden 52: 114,210
October 1927

Essen, Ger. Cathedral

see

Essen, Ger. Münster

Esguerra, Saens, Urdaneta & Suares
  Edificio de renta en Bogota [plans] La Biblioteca del Banco de la Republica [plans & sections] Esguerra, Saens, Urdaneta & Suares, archts.

Proa
#115:12-21 Jan 1958

Esperson (Neils) building, Houston

see

Houston (Tex.) Esperson (Neils) building

720.53
B35

Essen. Deutschnationalen Handlungsgehilfen-verband Häuser
  Häuser des Deutschnationalen Handlungsgehilfenverbandes in Essen und Stuttgart. (Houses of the German National Commercial Aid Society in Essen and Stuttgart.) Albert Hauschildt,archt.

Der Baumeister 31: 5-8
January 1933

Essen (Ger.) Dinoswerke Ausstellungshalle
Die ausstellungshalle der Dinoswerke in
Essen von Regierungsbaumeister Jung-Essen,
architekt, B.D.A.

Moderne bauformen 21:143-5
May, 1922

Essen, Ger. Krupp iron works, housing

see

Margarethenhöhe, Ger.

Essen (Ger) Münster
Der Westbau des Essener Münsters

Deutsches kunst 5:
O 1939
taf. 107, 108

Essen, Ger. Folkwang Museum

see

Essen, Ger. Museum Folkwang

720.53 Folkwang
W51 Essen.Kunstmuseum der stadt Essen und Museum
Hegemann, Werner
Die architektur-ausstellung im Folkwang-Mu-
seum zu Essen. (The architectural exhibit in the
Folkwang Museum at Essen.) Edmund Körner, archt.
Plans.

Wasmuths monatshefte 14: 441-444
A October 1930

Essen, Ger. Museum Folkwang
Gosebruch, Ernst
Art and technique in the exposition in
the Folkwang museum in Essen.

Der Kunstwanderer
10: 518-523
Ag 1928

Essen (Ger.) Housing

see also

Essen (Ger.) Siedlung Heimaterde

Essen, Ger. Margarethenhöhe

see

Margarethenhöhe, Ger.

Essen, Ger. Museum Folkwang
Waldstein, Agnes
The new Folkwang museum in Essen

Museumskunde
n.s. 1: 107-110, plates,
Heft 2-4, 1929

720.53 Essen (Ger.) Housing
W51 Ein hörsaal, eine siedlung und eine reit-
bahn. (An auditorium of the Coal Research
Institute in Mülheim-Ruhr, a residential col-
ony in Essen, and a riding school in Mulheim-
Ruhr.) Pfeifer and Grossmann,archts. Plans.

Wasmuths monatshefte 14: 376-380
A August 1930

Essen (Ger.) Market Hall
Mauritz, M.
Zu den arbeiten des Reg.-baumeisters Ernst
Bode, Essen. (The works of Ernst Bode, Essen.)
Market Hall in Essen. Plans.

Moderne bauformen 26: 279
A July, 1927

Essen, Ger. Museum Folkwang
Waldstein, Agnes
Opening of the new Folkwang museum (no illus)

Cicerone
21: 321, pt. 1, Je 1929

Essen (Ger.) Housing
Siedlung neudorf des gemeinnützigen bauvereins.
Kramer and Kremer, archts.

Der Baumeister 28: pl.26-27
April, 1930

720.53 Essen.Marktplatz
W51 Neugestaltung des burgplatzes in Essen.
Die entwurfe von Josef Rings. E. Fahrenkamp,
Brocke. und Bode-Schroetz. Drawings and plans.

Wasmuths 9, heft 1:10-25
1925

Essen, Ger. Museum Folkwang
Klapheck-Strumpell, Anna
The new Folkwang museum in Essen

Die kunst für alle
44: 385-386, plate, S 1929

720.53 Essen (Ger.) Housing
B35 Harbers, Guido
Vorstädtische kleinsiedlungen in Essen.
(Small suburban colonies in Essen.) Faber,
archt. illus. Plans.
Der Baumeister
31: 405-17, pl. 117-19
D '33

Essen (Ger.) Moving Picture Theater
Buildings by G. Metzendorf and J. Schneider;
a studio apartment; a sanatarium "Haardheim",
moving picture theater in Essen.

Wasmuths monatshefte 14: 450-451
October, 1930

720.53 Essen. Ger. Museum Folkwang
W51 Hegemann, Werner
Die architektur-ausstellung im Folkwang-Mu-
seum zu Essen. (The architectural exhibit in the
Folkwang Museum at Essen.) Edmund Körner,archt.
Plans.
Wasmuths monatshefte 14: 441-444
October 1930

Essen (Ger.) Housing
Workmen's houses, Essen, Germany

Dekorative kunst 26:185-203
June, 1923

Essen (Ger.) Mülheim

see

Mulheim-an-der-Ruhr

Essen, Ger. Museum Folkwang
Holzinger, Ernst.
Neue erwerbungen des Folkwang museums.

Museum der gegenwart
3: 8-24, Heft 1, 1932-1933

Essen, Ger. Museum Folkwang Museum Folkwang, Essen Wallraf-Richartz jahrbuch 15: 239-241, 1953	Essen, Ger. Sport-und Kongresshalle. Competition Sport- und kongresshalle auf den Grugage- lände in Essen [plans and sections] Brockmann and Lichtenhahn, archts. Baumeister 53: 100-103 F 1956	Essex and Goodman see Birmingham (Eng.) Lancaster house
Essen, Ger. Opernhaus. Competition. 1959 Zietschmann, Ernst Wettbewerb für ein neues opernhaus in Essen [plans] Alvar Aalto, archt. first prize. Bauen & Wohnen 14:Supp. 18-23 Jan 1960	Essen, Synagogue Die neue synagoge in Essen a.d. Ruhr erbaut von Professor Edmund Körner. Architektur des XX. Jahr hunderts. Sonderhefte [V.1] no. 13: entire iss. c. 1913 [?]	ff 724.5915 V81W Essex County(Va.) Vauter's church West and south doorways Vauter's church: Essex County: 1719,1731. Measured drawing. William and Mary Quarterly ser.2,18: October 1938 pl.112-113
Essen (Ger.) Opernhaus (project) Sketch for an opera house in Essen. Moderne bauformen 23; pl.63 opp.p.276 September, 1924	720.55 M68 Essen, Town Hall Mauritz,W Zu den arbeiten des kn:.-baumeisters Ernst Bode,Essen. (The works of Ernst bode,Essen.) Town hall extension: representatives assembly hall Officer. Plans. Moderne bauformen 26: 271-275 A July 1927	Essex, Eng. (county) Architecture Historical monuments in Essex Builder 126:373,378, My 7, 1924
Essen. Ger. Realgymnasium. Realgymnasium in Essen. (School in Essen.) Wahl and Rödel, archts. Plans. Der Baumeister 28: 495 December, 1930	MICROFILM Essen, Ger. Villa Hugel. in SCRAPBOOK ON ARCHITECTURE p. 15A,16 (on film)	Essex, Eng. (county). Architecture. Dent, A. R. Old Thames-side haunts in Essex. Builder 144:616,617, Ap 14, 1933
720.55 W31 Essen. Reinoldi house Das "Reinoldihaus" in Essen. (The Reinoldi house in Essen.) Emil Pohle,archt. Wasmuths monatshefte 14: 454-455 October 1930 A	Essen-Ost (Ger.) Strassenbahnhof Strassenbahnhof in Essen-Ost. (Street car station in Essen-Ost.) Emil Jung, archt. Plan. Wasmuths monatshefte 14: 456 October, 1930	Essex, Eng.(county). Architecture. Pen and ink sketches by Miss Tynne Smith of Butler's Hall, Great Leighs, Essex, England. Remains of a chapel in Old Barn at Little Dunnow, Essex, England. St. Clere's Hall, St. Osyth, Essex, England. Builder 144:444,445, Mr 17, 1933
720.55 W31 Essen (Ger.) Siedlung Heimaterde Siedlung "Heimaterde" in Essen-Mülheim. (Residential settlements: settlement "Heima- terde" in Essen-Mülheim.) Theodor Suhnel, archt. Plans. Wasmuths monatshefte 14: 486-488 October 1930	720.5 A67r Esser, H Public Service Corporation building, Mil- waukee, Wisconsin. H.J.Esser, archt. No plan. Architectural record 23:322-325 April 1908	710.5 H84 Essex Falls (N.J.) Westerfield (J.R.) house Nantucket Colonial in New Jersey; home of John R. Westerfield at Essex Falls,N.J. Goodrille and Moran, archts. House and garden 61: 66 January 1932
720.55 W31 Essen. Siemens Haus Das Siemens-Haus in Essen. (The Siemens Building in Essen.) Hans Hertlein,archt. Plans. The building contains stores,showrooms, offices,storage and factory. Wasmuths monatshefte 15: 294-297 July 1931 A	705.4 G28 Esserent.Saint Leu La premiere floraison de l'art gothique: Église de Saint-Leu-D'Esserent. XII siècle. (The first flowering of Gothic art. The church of Saint Leu of Esserent.) Gazette des beaux-arts 25:305-317 Per.3,1901	MICROFILM Essex (Mass.) First meeting house in SCRAPBOOK ON ARCHITECTURE p. 16,17 (on film)

Esso building, New York (city)

see

New York (city) Esso building

710.5   Estates
'855   Edgar, A. C.
        Creating the country estate.

                Country life (U.S.) 58: 35-37
                August 1930

Estates, U.S., Lake Forest (IL.)
    Airplane views of four estates in Lake
Forest: Louis F. Swift, Cyrus McCormick,
T. Ogden Armour, Edith Rockefeller McCormick.

                Arts and decoration 18:20-21
                January, 1923

720.5   Estate buildings
A67ar   Study for seashore estate. Treanor &
        Fatio, archts.

                Architect (N.Y.) 9: 556
                February 1928

710.5   Estates
R84   Eberlein, H. D.
        Designing the dependencies: stables,garage,
        laundry,chauffeur's quarters.

                House & garden.50:95-97
                Oct. 1926

Estates, U.S., Lake Forest (IL.)
        Root, R. R.
Country place types of the middle west: Mrs. Edith
R. McCormick; T. E. Donnelley; Mrs. J. M.
Patterson; Mrs. Chas. A. Pike; Walter J. Brewster;
H.J. McBirney; L.E. Laflin; Severett Thompson;
A.M. Day; Francis C. Farewell; Mrs. C. Morse Ely;
J. Ogden Armour; and E. J. Ryerson.

                Architectural record 55: 1-32
                January, 1924

710.5   Estate buildings
A67a   Superintendent's cottage, estate Mrs. W. H.
        Harkness, Glen Cove, N.Y.
            Charles S. Keefe, architect

                Architecture 50:344
                Oct. 1924

Estates
    Fleming, M.C., Jr.
Planning a 20-acre estate

                Country life (U.S.) 70:
                    29-30; S 1936
                    22-24; O   "
                    42-43; N   "
                    65-66, 114-15; D   "

Estates, U.S. New Jersey
        Country life in America. II. "Vernon Manor,"
the New Jersey estate of Richard V.N. Gambrill,
Esq. III. "Skylands Farm," the New Jersey
estate of Clarence Lewis, Esq. Plans, photos

                Country life 72:45-54
                J1, 1937

710.5   Estate offices
C855   Mrs.Oakleigh Thorne sets up an office
        Interior view of office in home.

                Country life(U.S.)71:35
                November 1936

10.5   Estates, Mexico
C855   Perrett, Antoinette
        History of the country estate,part 9:Spanish
country estates in Mexico.

                Country life(U.S.)70:47-49,81
                June 1936

720.57   Estates.U.S.N.y.
A67f   An estate development at Rye, New York,
        Dwight James Baum, architect.

                Arch.forum 36: 281-4 & pl.90-5
                Jun. 1922.

710.5   Estates
L26   Wheelwright, Robert
        Character and style in estate planning.

                Landscape architecture 20: 311-314
                July 1930

720.5   Estates,United States
A67r   Croly,Herbert
        The American country estate.

                Architectural record 18:1-7
                July 1905

710.5   Estates,U.S. Ohio
C855   Sport center - delightful grouping on
        estate near Cleveland,Ohio. Dunn and Coppen,
        archts.

                Country life (U.S.)63: 40-41
                April 1933

710.5   Estates
C855   Breed,F.N.
        The compact country estate. Illus. Plan.

                Country life (U.S.)63: 35-36,77
                April 1933

710.5   Estates. U.S.
L26   An estate at Westbury, L.I.
          An estate at Greenwich, Conn.

                Landscape architecture 14:178-9
                Apr. 1924

Estelita, Lúcio
        Clube Social [plans & sections] Lúcio
Estelita, archt.

                Modulo
                vol.5: 16-19, Ag 1961

710.5   Estates
C855   Pope, J.R.; Vitale, Ferruccio
        The complete country estate: I. The house
and farm buildings. Illustrations by Otto R.
Eggers. II. The grounds and gardens.
                Country life(U.S.)38:34-41
                October 1920

710.5   Estates. U.S.
C855   The farm as a picturesque asset

                Country life 43:53-8
                April 1923

Estep, Joe

    see also

Kelly, Arthur and Joe Estep

720.5
A67d
  Estep,Joe
    California House and Garden Exhibition
Los Angeles.English cottage,Arthur Kelly
and Joe Estep,archts.Plan. Seymour Thomas
landscape archt.

    Architectural digest 9: 28-29
    Number 3 [1937]

Esteves, Nauro Jorge
  Prasa municipal de Brasília [plans & section]
Nauro Jorge Esteves, archt.

    Módulo
    vol 4: 8-12, D 1960

705.944
W48
  Esthetics
  Baud, François
    De la construction à l'architecture.

    Das werk 35: 14-17
    Ja '48

720.5
A67d
  Estep, Joe
    Residence of Mr. and Mrs. Joe Estep,
Santa Monica,Cal.Arthur Kelly,archt. Joe
Estep,assoc.archt.Plan
    Residence of Mr. and Mrs. A.H.Tichener,
Los Angeles,Cal.Arthur Kelly,archt.Joe
Estep,assoc.archt. Plan

    Architectural digest 7:124-125;128-129
    Number 2 , 1928

Esthetics
  Seidler, Harry
    Aesthetics in modern architecture

    Royal arch'l Institute of Canada
    Jour. 23:245-249
    O '46

720.5
A67
  Esthetics
  Blackall,C.H.
    Esthetics of constructive design: defining
the esthetic rules of architecture.

    Architectural review 9,n.s.4:85-89
    April 1902

720.5
A67d
  Estep, Joe
    Residence of Mr. and Mrs. O.b.English,
Beverly Hills, Cal. Arthur Kelly, archt. Joe
Estep, assoc.archt. Neville R. Stephens, land
scape archt. Plans
    Residence of Mr.& Mrs.Joe Estep,Santa Mon
ica,Cal.Arthur Kelly,archt.Joe Estep,assoc.
Plan

    Architectural digest 7: 102-107;124-
    Number 2, 1928   125

Esthetics
  The Aesthetice of Architecture

    Arch. Rev. 57:29-33, 76-79
    Jan.; Feb., 1925

Esthetics
  Ethics and Esthetics.

    Arch and con rep 73:79
    Feb. 3, 1905

720.5
A67d
  Estep,Joe
    Residence of Mr. and Mrs.P.H.Young,Holly
wood.Arthur Kelly and Joe Estep,archts.Plans

    Architectural digest 9: 120-121
    Number 4 [1937]

720.5
156
  Esthetics
  Brown, Glenn
    Architecture and Dress Reform

    Inland Archt. 50: 17 A'07

Esthetics
  Laeuger, M.
    Grundsätzliches über kunsterziehung und kultur
des farbengefühls.

    Der Baumeister 31:
      1-5, pls. 1 and 2; Ja, 1933
      3-4; F, 1933
      pls 5 and 6; Mr., 1933
      pls 7 and 8; Ap., "

720.5
A67d
  Estep,Joe
    Residence of Mr. and Mrs. W.b.Cline,Bever
ly Hills,Cal. Arthur Kelly,archt.Joe Estep,
assoc. archt. Plans

    Architectural digest 8: 33-37
    Number 1 , 1932

Esthetics
  Baroet, Gaston
    La arquitectura del amor

    Arquitectura Cuba
    17: 196-203
    Jl 1949

705
W48
  Esthetics
  Stockmeyer, E.
    Mass und Zahl in der Baukunst

    Das werk
    30:353-360
    pt. 2 N'43

720.5
A67d
  Estep, Joe
    Residence of Mr. and Mrs. William Channey
Brentwood, Cal. Arthur Kelly, archt.Joe
Estep, assoc. Plans
    Residence of Mr. and Mrs. Arthur Letts,
Holmby Hills, Los Angeles.Arthur Kelly,archt.
Joe Estep,assoc.Plans

    Architectural digest 7: 16-17;85-
    Number 1. 1928   93

Esthetics
  Beauty in Architecture. By B. R. Gribbon.

    Arch. + con rep.
      83: 13, Jan. 7, 1910
      : 30, Jan. 14, 1910
      : 47-48, Jan. 21,
      1910

Esthetics
  The Origin of the Sense of Taste in Art.
By Mr. Felix Clay.

    Arch. and c.reporter 80:313-316,330-
    Nov. 13; 20, 1908   332

Esteves, Nauro Jorge
  Hotel nacional-Brasília [plans & section]
Nauro Jorge Esteves, archt.

    Módulo
    vol. 4: 30-35, O 1960

Esthetics
  Les créations de l'Homme. (extract from
Eupalinos)

    Tech et arch
    5: 1-11
    1-2, 1945

Esthetics
  Over de techniek en de aesthetica van het bou
wen.

    Forum 9:138
    Nr 1954

720.5   Esthetics
B98b Marshall, H.R.
            The science of aesthetics.

            Building budget 6: 124-127
            October 31, 1890

Estorff and Winkler

    see also

Estorff (Mrs. Otto von) house, Ger.

720.52 Etchells, Frederick
A67   A house in Surrey. Designed by Frederick
        Etchells. Plans.

            Architects' journal 78: 194,207
            August 17, 1933

Esthetics
Marshall, Henry Rutgers
    The science of esthetics.

            Inland architect
            v. 16 no. 4: 36-40
            O 1890

Estorff and Winkler

    Members of firm:

Estorff, Otto von,
Winkler, Gerhard

720.52 Etchells, Frederick
A67   Showroom for Messrs. John Smedley Ltd., in
        Mayfair. Frederick Etchells, archt. Plans.

            Architects' journal 78: 665-667
            November 23, 1933

Esthetics
    Von der gemeinsamen der Architektur und
Philosophie.

            Das Werk 29:204-208
            Ag '42

720.53 Estorff (Mrs. Otto Von) house, Ger.
W31   Hegemann, Werner
            Otto von Estorff und Gerhard Winkler. (Work
        of Otto von Estorff and Gerhard Winkler, archts.)
        Country home for Mrs. von Estorff near Potsdam.
        Plans.

            Wasmuths monatshefte 13: 292
            July 1929
        A

Etchers, Architectural

    see

Griggs, Frederick Landseer Maur, 1876-1938

720.5   Esthetics
A67ar Newcomb, Rexford
            What indeed is beauty?

            Architect(N.Y.)7:167-171
            November 1926

Estudillo house, Oldtown (Calif.)

    see

Oldtown (Calif.) Estudillo house

Etching, Architectural
    How to etch.

            Architect 112:126-27
            Aug. 29, 1924

Esthetics
    Lethaby, W. R.
What shall we call beautiful? A practical view of
aesthetics.

            Lethaby, W.R. Form in civilization.
            London: Oxford University Press,
            1922. 147-68.

Esty, A   R
            Congregational Church on Columbus Avenue,
        Boston, Mass. A.R.Esty, archt.

            Amer arch
            1: 77, pl.fol.p.76
            Mr 4, 1876

720.5   Etching, Architectural
A67r Weitenkampf
            Architectural etching

            Architectural record 44:551-557
            December 1918

720.6   Esthetics, Greece
R66   Chambers, F.P.
            The aesthetic of the ancients.

            R.I.B.A. journal 32:241-252
            February 21, 1925

Etampes (Fr.) Notre Dame
            Nôtre Dame. Meas. drawing by A.W. Tanner.

            Lond. Arch. Assoc. sketch book. 3-4:pls.
                                            46-49
            1869-70.

Etching, Architectural
    Architecture. Engineering and Etching.
    Art and the Antique.

            Arch. Rev. 44:119-27.
            Dec. 1918.

Estimates

    see

Building. Estimates

Etchells, Frederick

    see also

Lansdowne (Eng.) house
London (Eng.) High Holborn st. (no. 253)

Etching. Italy. Lombardy. Exhibitions
Mezzetti, Amalia
    Una mostra dell'acquaforte lombarda.
[illus.]

            Arte lombarda
            v.2: 201-202
            1956

Ethics

see

Architects. Ethics

Etrepy, Fr. Chateau
Angus, L.M.
The chateau of Etrepy, Marne, France.

Builder. 119:661-662 and pl.
Dec. 10, 1920.

Euboea, Gr. House of Dystus
Plan and reconstruction of house of Dystus,
Euboea, Greece.

Architects' journal 74:218
August 12, 1931

Ethiopia. Architecture

see

Cave churches, Ethiopia

RYERSON LIBRARY
913
A66j
Etretat. Nôtre Dame
Etretat church. Plan.

Archaeological journal 95:405-407
Pt.2, 1938

Euclid (O.) Pickands (H.S.) house
Country House, H.S. Pickands, Euclid, O.
Meade and Garfield, Architects.

Architecture (NY) 8:pls.
Ag. 1903

Ethnological Museums, Switzerland
Competition for ethnological building in
Genf.

Wasmuths 11: 345-352
Heft 8, 1927

Etruria. Architecture

see

Doors and doorways, Etruria
Windows, Etruria

Eufaula (AL)
Shorter (Hon. E.S.) Residence
Curran R. Ellis, Arch.

West. Arch.
14: pl. 8
Sept. 1909

720.6
E882
Etobicoke (Can.) Planning
Etobicoke, Ontario. [plans]

Royal arch inst of Canada
23: 295-
N '46

Etruscan architecture

see also

Orvieto, It. Etruscan temple

Eugene Field memorial, Lincoln park, Chicago

see

Chicago, Ill. Lincoln park. Eugene Field memorial

Eton (Eng.) College. Memorial Chapel
Eton Memorial Chapel, designed by
Walter H. Godfrey

Arch. Rev 57: 74-75
Feb. 1925

Etton (Eng.) Church
Measured drawing of West door of Etton
Church, East Yorks. Example of Norman work.
E. Julian White, archt.

Builder 145:606,607
October 20, 1933

720.5
A67f
Eugene (Ore.) Larsen (Hart) house
House for Hart Larsen, Eugene, Ore.
Peter R. Domskov, archt. Plan.

Architectural forum 65: 425
November 1936

Eton (Eng.) College. Memorial Chapel
Eton College Memorial Chapel. Messrs.
Wratten and Godfrey, archts.

Architecture (Lond.) 5:385
May, 1927

Etsel, A.   E.   Wilhelm

see

Schreckenstein (Ger.) Friedhofhalle

Eureka block, Chicago

see

Chicago, Ill. Eureka block

720.54
A67
Etrépilly (Fr.) Eglise
Satin, Marcel
Eglise d'Etrépilly, Aisne. E.Sellé,archt.
Plans. (Church of Etrépilly,Aisne.)

L'Architecture 46: 25-26
January 15, 1933

Eu (France) Eglise abbatiale
Eglise abbatiale d'Eu. Text in French.
Drawings, sections, plan.

France. Commission des monuments
historiques. Archives....4 vols.
Paris: Gide and J. Baudry, 1855-72.
v.1:33-37, pl. 15-19

MICROFILM
Eureka (Calif.) Carson house

in SCRIPBOOK
ARCH 1718
(on film)

Eureka (Calif.) Housing
   A California rental project: arrangement of
small houses for privacy. Illustrations and
plans.

   Architectural forum 67:72-73
A   July, 1937

Europe, Architecture
   Cleveland, Ralph
Photographing Architecture in Europe.
Photos.

   Inland Architect
   36: 26-7
   Nov, 1900

720.52   Europe. Architecture. 20th century
B95   Goodhart-Rendel, H.S.
            Modern European architecture.

   Builder 141: 824-825
   November 20, 1931

Eureka (Cal.) Stadium
   Plot plan of school group, including stadium,
Eureka, Cal. J.J. Donovan, archt.

   Western architect 36:pl.134
   August, 1927

720.5   Europe. Architecture. 19th century
A67r   Adshead, Stanley D.
            A comparison of modern American architecture
with that of European cities.

   Architectural record 29:113-125
   February 1911

720.52   Europe. Architecture. 20th century
A674   Robertson, Howard
            The modern movement in architecture — Eu-
ropean countries.

   Architecture (Lond.) 5: 104
   August 1926

Europa, Miss. School
   Malvaney, E. L.
School for Europa, Mississippi.
   E.L. Malvaney, archt. Plans.

   Architectural concrete 7:24-25
   No. 4 [1941]

Ryerson

            Europe. Architecture. 20th Century
   Samonà, Giuseppe
            L'architettura contemporanea nel ventennio
razionalista in Europa

   Critica d'arte 8:89-104
   Jl 1949

720.5   Europe. Architecture. 20th century
AC7r   Recent European architecture.

   Architectural record 27:241-248;311-323
   March; April; 1910

Europe. 1878-1879
   Bacon, F. H.
Extracts from "The Log of the Dorian" parts 1-6 being
the account of an European voyage in a small boat made
in the year 1878-79 by Joseph T. Clarke, and Francis
H. Bacon, taken from the personal journal and notes
made by the latter.

   Arch rev 18:
      73-77; Jl 1912
      85-89; Ag "
      97-101; S "
            (see card 2)

910.5   Europe. Architecture. 20th century
277   Parker, R.A.
            Creating a new Europe

   Travel 51:7-12
   October 1928

"European palaces" of Yüan Ming Yüan

   see

Peking. Yüan Ming Yüan. "European palaces"

Europe. 1878-1879   (card 2 continued.)
   Bacon, F. H.

   Arch rev 18:
      109-115; O 1912
      121-125; N "
      133-136; D "

720.55   Europe. Architecture. 20th century
D67   Pica, Agnoldomenico
            Crisi dell' architettura europa.

   Domus no. 233: 26-27
   1949

European War, 1914-18. Destruction and pillage
   Bombardment of Arras.

   Architectural review (London)37:11
   January, 1915

910.5   Europe. Architecture
277   Parker, R.A.
            Creating a new Europe

   Travel 51:7-12
   October 1928

Europe. Architedture. 20th cent.
   Elemente der zeitarchitektur.
   Konstruktives bauen.
   Romantisches bauen.
   Kristallines bauen.
   Plastisches bauen.
   Dekoratives bauen.
   Die architekten unseres heftes.
[col. illus.]
            Du
            20:2-52 N 1960

European War (1914-18) Destruction and Pillage
   Damages

   L'Architecture 33:246-52,
      279-82
   N. 1; D. 1, 1920

705.5   Europe. Architecture
D29   Piacentini, Marcello
            Dove e irragionevole l'architettura ra-
zionale.

   Dedalo 11: 527-540
   January 1931

720.5   Europe. Architecture. 20th century
K52   Berlage, H.P.
            Modern Architecture.

   Western architect 18:29-36
A March 1912

European War, 1914-18. Destruction and Pillage
   Tallmadge, T.E.
The destruction of historic buildings as revealed
by the official French war photographs. Pt. 1
Cathedral of Soissons. Pt. 2 Arras. Pt. 3 Parish
churches

   Arch rec 42: 248-258; 458-467
         43: 131-147
   S, N, '17
   F, '18

European war 1914-18. Destruction & pillage
Riggs, Arthur Stanley
Great cathedrals of the war zone. Pts 1-4

Art and archaeology 8:
5-16; Ja-F, 1919
67-69; Mr-Ap, "
203-14; Jl-Ag, "
311-27; N-D, "

European war, 1914-1918. Destruction and
pillage. France
Alexandre, Arsène
L'exposition du vandalisme au Petit
Palais. [illus.]

Les arts
14, no.157: 20-28
1917-1918

European War (1914-18) Reconstruction

see

Reconstruction (1914-1939)

705.1
A78a
European war 1914-18. Destruction and Pillage
Reinach, Col. Theodore
Martyred monuments of France. Pt.1 Castle of
Coucy. Pt.2. Town hall of Arras

Art and arch 9: front, 107-118
Mr '20   11: front, 85-94
Mr '21

European War, 1914-18. Destruction and pillage,
France.
Homes in the neighborhood of war lines

L'Illustration 75:47-51
Jan. 20, 1917

705.4
E98
Eustache, Henri
Vitry, Paul
The architect Henri Eustache

Beaux-arts 1:132-134
May 15,1923

European War (1914-18) Destruction and pillage
Ruins

Architectural rev
46:166-72
D 1919

European War, 1914-18. Destruction and pillage,
France.
In the invaded regions

Les arts no. 157:12-19
1917

720.54
A67
Eustache, Henri
Exposition de l'OEuvre peinte de Henri
Eustache

L'Architecture 36:387-90
Dec. 25, 1923

European war, 1914-1918. Destruction and
pillage
Clemen, Paul
Der Zustand der Kunstdenkmäler auf dem West-
lichen Kriegsschauplatz. [illus.]

Zeitschrift für bildende Kunst
27: 49-96
1915/16

European War, 1914-18. Destruction and pillage.
France
France. Ruins of Reims.

L'Illustration 73:593-95
D 4, '15

Eustache, Henri. Concours

see

Concours Henri Eustache. [date]

European War (1914-18) Destruction and Pillage.
Belgium
Barron, Oswald
The German sack of Dinant

Country life 36:416-19,437
S 26, '14

720.5
A67a
European war, 1914-18. Destruction and
pillage, France
Porter, A. Kingsley
What the Huns have done for French art.

Architecture 40:307-8
D 1919

Eutaw savings bank bldg. Baltimore, Md.

see

Baltimore, Md. Eutaw savings bank bldg.

European War 1914-1918. Destruction and pillage,
France.
see also
Coucy-le-Château, Fr.
Arras, Fr. Reconstruction
Soissons. Cathédrale

European War (1914-18) Destruction and pillage,
France
What the Huns have done for French art.

Architecture 41:13-16.
Jan. 1920.

Evangelical lutheran Lord Jesus Christ church,
Chicago

see

Chicago (Ill.) Evangelical lutheran Lord Jesus Christ
church, Missouri synod

European war (1914-18) Destruction and pillage,
France
Architecture damaged in the war.

L'Architecture
27: 301-306
O 10, 1914

European War 1914-18. Drawings
Sales, John
Landscapes of Hell, by Lieutenant Paul Nash.

Country life 43:67-68
January 19, 1918

Evans, Alfred P.

See

Architectural League of New York, 1892. Competition

Burnham Index to Architectural Literature

Evans, Allen
see also:
Furness, Evans and Co.

Evans, David
Parkes, Kineton
A Prix de Rome sculptor: David Evans
Studio 94:79-85
August 1927

Evanston (Il.) Abrahamson (Allen) House plans.
Bertha Yerex Whitman, archt.
Roll 38, frames 125-126; 143-146

Evans, Allen
Member of firm:
Furness, Evans and Co.

Evans, Frank R.
see
Winnipeg (MAN) Somerset Building

Evanston (Il.) Ahlstrom (John) House
Bertha Yerex Whitman, archt.
Roll 38, frames 64-67

720.5 Evans, Allen
N56 Girard Trust Co., Philadelphia, Pa. Allen Evans, McKim, Mead, and White, assoc. archts. Plans.
New York architect 2:246-251, 274-279
November 1908

Evans, James Carey, house. Lake Forest, Ill.
see
Lake Forest, Ill. Evans, James Carey, house.

Evanston (Ill.) All Souls' Unitarian church
Illustrations and plan. Marion Mahony Griffin, architect.
Western architect
18: pl. 51-53
S 1912

729 Evans and Bright
A51 Competition for the Springfield Municipal Building, Springfield, Massachusetts.
American competitions 2: pl.148-150
1908

720.5 Evans, Moore and Woodbridge
A67f Two houses in Princeton (N.J.). Evans, Moore and Woodbridge, archts. Plans.
Architectural Forum 71:310-312
October 1939

Evanston, Ill. All Souls' Unitarian church.
... Marion's earliest major independent commission. [illus. plans, section] Marion Mahony Griffin, architect.
Prairie School review
III: 6-10
Second quarter 1966

Evans, Arthur John.
The royal gold medal, 1909.
RIBA jrl 17:1-10
N 6, 1909

720.5 Evans, Randolph
A67f Nassau Shores, Nassau Co., Long Island, New York. Harmon National Real Estate Corp. Randolph Evans, archt. Plan.
Architectural forum 65: 387
October 1936

MICROFILM
Evanston (Ill.) "Anchorfast"
in SCRAP BOOK ON ARCHITECTURE p. 18,19,20
(on film)

Evans, Clifford
Member of firm:
Miller, Wooley and Evans

Evans, Mrs. Robert D. house, Beverly Cove, Mas:
see
Beverly Cove, Mass. Dawson hall

720.5 Evanston (Ill.) Anthony (Elliott) house
I56 Residence for Judge Elliott Anthony, Evanston, Ill. Pond and Pond, archts. Plan.
A Inland architect 25: pls.fol.38
May 1895

Evans, David
See Also
Philadelphia (PA) - Bourse Bldg. Competition

710.5 Evans, Rudolph
C855 A Century of Progress garden: American Radiator and Standard Sanitary Exhibit. Hood and Foulihoux, archts. Vitale and Geiffert, landscape archts. Rudolph Evans, sculptor.
Country life (U.S.)64: 51
September 1933

Evanston (Il) Apartment Bldg.
For Erickson and Sandegren. Plan
Andrew Sandegren, archt.
West. Archt.
25: pl.fol.p. 14
Feb. 1917

V. 4

246

Evanston (Ill) Apt. Bdg. Myron H.Hunt, Arch Inland Arch. 38: pl.fol.p.48 Jan. 1902	720.6 C53 Evanston (Ill.) Armstrong (H.W.) house Exterior views - residence - Mr. H.W. Armstrong, Evanston, Ill. (Photos.); Chatten and Hammond, archts.; no plan. A Chicago architectural club 26:77 1913	Evanston (IL.) Biggs (M.H. and F.H.) houses Residences for M.H. and F.H. Biggs in South Evanston. W.D. Cowles, archt. Inland archt and news rec. 19:77 July, 1892
720.5 A51 Evanston. Architecture Tallmadge,T.E. Architectural history of a western town: Evanston,Illinois. American architect 115: 443-451 March 26,1919	Evanston (Il.) Arseneau (A.J.) House Bertha Yerex Whitman, archt. plans. Roll 38, frames 70-71	Evanston (IL) Blanchard (William) Houses Holabird & Roche, Archs. Inland Arch. 20: pl. fol. p 70 Ja., 1893
051 G76 Evanston.Architecture Evanston, Illinois. Views. The graphic 7:468-472 December 24, 1892	Evanston (Ill) Asbury Avenue.Two-Family Apt. House Walter Burley Griffin, Archt. West. Archt. 19: pls.fol.p. XV Aug, 1913	Evanston, (IL) Boll (E.H.) Residence Ernest A. Mayo, Arch. Inland Arch. 44: pls. fol.p. 32 Nov. 1904
720.5 I56 Evanston (Ill.) Armour (M.C.) house Residence for M.C. Armour. H.R. Wheelock, archt. Inland architect 39: 2 pls.fol.p.70 March 1902 A	720.5 I56 Evanston (Ill.) Barry (A.) cottages Twenty frame cottages for A. Barry in Evanston. August Bessler, archt. Inland archt & news rec 18:55 November 1891	720.5 A67r Evanston (Ill.) Bovee,(M.H.) house Portfolio of country residences; Some houses by Walter Burley Griffin: residence for Mrs. Mary H. Bovee, Evanston, Illinois. A Architectural record 28:308 October 1910
720.5 I56 Evanston (Ill.) Armsby, (J.K. Jr.) house Residence of J.K. Armsby, Jr. W. Henri Adams, archt. Inland archt & news rec 18:13 Ag 1891	Evanston, Ill. Bartlett (W.H.) house Residence for W. H. Bartlett, Evanston, Ill. [plan] J. L. Silsbee, archt. Inland architect v. 18 no. 4 pl. fol. p. 56 N 1891	Evanston, Il., Bradley (Prof. Chas. F.) Residence 2 exterior views. Bosworth + Chase, Archts. Inland Archt. Vol. 26, No. 5, pl. Fol. p. 54 Dec. 1895
Evanston (IL.) Armsby (J.K., Jr.) house Sketch of residence for J.K. Armsby, Jr. Evanston, Illinois. Pond and Pond, archts. Inland architect 18:pl.fol.34 October, 1891	Evanston, Il., Bassett (Dr. Jared) Residence John T. Long, Archt. Inland Arch. Vol. 25, No. 2, pl. Fol. p. 23 Mar. 1895	Evanston, (Il.) Bradley (Mrs. Frank) Residence W. Chester Chase, Arch. Inland Arch. Vol. 31,No.3,pl.fol.p. 30 April, 1898
Evanston (Il) Armstrong (F.H.) Residence, Hall Chatten and Hammond, archts. West. Archt. 23: 34 Apr. 1916	720.5 I56 Evanston (Ill.) Bennett estate, houses Bennett estate, six double two-story frame houses. Wesley A. Arnold, archt. Inland archt & news rec 17:73 Jl 1891	Evanston, Il., Bradley (Mrs. Frank)Residence W. Chester Chase. Inland Arch. vol.31,No.4,pl.fol.p. 40 May 1898

720.5
I56   Evanston (Ill) Brown (A.K.) house
     Sketch of residence of A.K. Brown, Asbury
    Avenue, Evanston. G. Isaacson, archt. No plan.
 	
    A   Inland architect 5th,pl.fol.16
           February 1888
	Evanston (Il.) Burnett Residence
	   Frank P. Burnham and Co., Archts.
	
	          Inland Arch.
	          vol. 31, No.3,pl.fol.p. 30
	          Apr, 1898
		Evanston (Ill) Church of All Souls
		   Marion Mahony Griffin, Archts.
		
		          West. Archt.
		          18: pls.fol.p. 102
		          Sept, 1912

Evanston, Ill. Brown (E.) house
   Residence of E. Brown, Evanston, Illinois.
   [plan] Frederick Baumann & J. K. Cady, archts.
 	
        Inland architect
        19, no. 3
        pls. fol. p. 42
        Ap 1892
	MICROFILM
	   Evanston (Ill.) Burnham (Hubert) house
	
	       in SCRAPBOOK ON
	       ARCHITECTURE p. 37,38
	       (on film)
		BURTON LIBRARY
		061
		G76 Evanston. City hall
		       Evanston town hall.
		
		       The graphic 6: 97,56
		       January 9, 1897

Evanston (Il.) Brown (Edwin F.) Residence
   2 exterior views. Handy and Cady
   archts.
 	
        Inland Arch.
        vol.31,No.4,pl.fol.p. 40
        May, 1898
	Evanston (IL.) Burt (Wm. G.) house
	   Residence for Wm. G. Burt, Evanston.
	   Clark and Walcott, archt.
	
	       Western architect 31:pl.7-9
	       Oct., 1922
		Evanston (Ill.) club
		   Evanston club house, Evanston, Ill. Holabird
		   and Roche, archts.
		
		       Inland archt
		       16, # 8; pl fol 96,
		       Ja 1891

Evanston (Il.) Brown (Edwin F.) Residence
   Handy and Cady, Archt.
 	
        Inland Arch.
        vol.31,No.3,pl.fol.p. 50
        Jun, 1898
	MICROFILM
	   Evanston (Il.) Cannon (C.A.) House
	     plans.
	   Bertha Yerex Whitman, archt.
	
	      Roll 38, frames 119-120
		MICROFILM
		   Evanston (Ill.) club
		   [Holabird and Roche, archts.]
		
		       in SCRAPBOOK ON
		       ARCHITECTURE p. 36
		       (on film)

Evanston (IL)
   Brown (W.L.) Residence
P.C. Stewart, Arch.
 	
        Inland Arch.
        41: pls. fol.p. 12
        Feb. 1903
	MICROFILM
	   Evanston (Il.) Carter (F.B., Jr.) House
	   Walter Burley Griffin, archt.
	
	      Roll 33, frame 17
		Evanston, Ill. College for ladies (1874)
		
		      see
		
		   Evanston, Ill. Northwestern university. Willard
		   hall (1874)

Evanston, Ill. Brown, William H., house.
   Illustration. G. Isaacson, architect.
 	
        Building budget
        II: 10
        Jan., 1886
	Evanston, Ill. Chandler (Charles H.) house
	   Residence of C. H. Chandler, Evanston, Ill.
	   [plan] Raeder, Coffin & Crocker, archts.
	
	       Inland architect
	       v. 18 no. 2
	       pl. fol. p. 24
	       S 1891
		microfilm
		   Evanston, Ill. Comstock (Hurd) house
		   Griffin, Walter Burley, architect
		    H. Comstock house, Evanston, Illinois, 1912.
		   Landscaping plan.
		
		     Roll 8, frame 35

Evanston, IL. Browne (Charles E.) house
   Residence of Charles E. Browne
 	
       Chamberlin, Everett. Chicago
       and its suburbs. Chicago: T.A.
       Hungerford, 1874. p.380
	Evanston, Il., Church
	
	   Burnham + Root, Archts.
	
	       Inland Arch.
	       Vol. 24, No. 3, pl.
	         Fol. p. 30
	       Oct. 1894
		MICROFILM
		   Evanston (Il.) Comstock (Hurd) Houses
		   Walter Burley Griffin, Archt.
		
		      Roll 33, frame 18

Evanston (Ill) Comstock (Hurd) Houses Walter Burley Griffin, Archt. West. Archt. 19: pls.fol.p. XV Aug., 1913	720.5 A67r Evanston (Ill.) Dawes (H.M.) house House of H. M. Dawes, Evanston, Ill. E. A. Mayo, archt. Plan. A Architectural record 40:p.565 December 1916	Evanston, Ill. Elliot (F.M.) house Residence of F.M. Elliot, Evanston, Ill. J.K. Cady, archt. Inland architect v. 14 no. 7 pl. fol. p. 86 D 1889
Evanston, (IL) Condict, (L.) Residence E.A. Mayo, Arch. Inland Arch. 44: pls. fol.p. 24 Oct.1904	Evanston (Ill) Dempster St. School D.H. Burnham & Co., Arch Inland Arch 38: pl.fol.p.40 Dec. 1901	Evanston, Ill. Emmanuel M.E. church M.E. Church, Evanston, Illinois. Burnham and Root, archts. (called Emmanuel M.E. church in Monroe--J.W. Root--724.81 / R78m, p.285\ 1894 Inland archt & news rec 21: pl.fol.p.4 April 1893
Evanston, Il., Congdon (C.B.) house views of exterior, Library, Dining Room and Hall A.M.F. Colton + Son, Archts. Inland Archt. Vol. 25, No. 6, Plates Fol. p. 64 July 1895	720.5 I56 Evanston (Ill.) Dickinson (J. Spencer) house Residence of J. Spencer Dickinson in Evanston. Beers, Clay & Dutton, archts. Inland archt & news rec 17:73 July 1891	MICROFILM Evanston, Ill. Enfield place in SCRAPBOOK ON ARCHITECTURE p. 28 (on film)
Evanston (Il.) Cottages Robt. C. Spencer, Jr., Archt. Inland Archt. vol.31,No.4,pl.fol.p.40 May, 1898	MICROFILM Evanston (Ill.) Dryden (G. P.) house in SCRAPBOOK ON ARCHITECTURE p. 29,30,31 (on film)	Evanston, Il., Evanston Boat Club House Henry Ives Cobb, Archt. Inland Archt. Vol. 26, No. 5, pl. Fol. p.54 Dec. 1895
Evanston, Ill. Country club house The County Club House, Evanston, Illinois [plans] Holabird & Roche, archts. Inland architect 20, no. 5 pl. fol. p. 58 D 1892	Evanston, Ill. Dryden, G.P., house Illustrations, plans and elevations. G. W. Maher, architect. Western architect 29: 10, plates 1-6, 11,12 January 1920	720.5 B93b Evanston (Ill.) Fabian (W. J.) house Sketch of residence for W.J.Fabian, Evanston, Ill. Raeder, Coffin and Crocker, archts. A Building budget 6: pl.fol.p.150 December 31, 1890
720.5 I56 Evanston (Ill.) Cummings (Joseph) house Residence for Prof. Joseph Cummings, Evanston. Sketch. Plan. A Inland architect 4: 45 October 1884	720.5 I56 Evanston (Ill.) Dunoon (George) house Sketch of residence of George Dunoon at Evanston, Illinois. G. Isaacson, archt. Plan. Inland architect 5:39,pl.fol.44 April 1885	720.5 I56 Evanston (Ill.) Fabian (WJ.) house Residence of W.J.Fabian. Raider,Coffin and Crocker,archts. Inland architect 21: pl.fol.p.18 A February 1893
Evanston (IL) Daniels (Henry E.C.) Residence. Pond & Pond, Archts. Inland Arch. 21: pl. fol. p 42 Ap., 1893	Evanston, Ill. Dwight (Timothy, Jr.) house Residence of Timothy Dwight, Jr., Evanston, Illinois. S.A.Jennings, archt. Inland Archt 20: pl. fol. p.70 no.6 Ja 1893	microfilm Evanston, Ill. Felton house Griffin, Walter Burley, architect Felton house, Evanston, Illinois, n.d. Roll 8, frame 18

720.5
A51
Evanston (Ill.). Ferguson (L.A.) house
House of Louis A. Ferguson, Evanston,
Illinois. Holabird and Roche, archts.

Amer arch 119: pl fol p 442
Ap 6 '21

Evanston (IL)
Fowler (E.L.) Photographic Studio
P.C. Stewart, Arch.

Inland Arch.
41: pls.fol.p. 12
Feb.1903

720.5
A67ar
Evanston. Garrett Biblical Institute (ca. 1924)
Garrett Biblical Institute, Evanston, Ill.
Holabird & Roche, architects

A

Architect 2:pl. 115-117
August 1924

Evanston (IL.) First Baptist Church School
First Baptist Church School, Evanston, IL.
Tallmadge and Watson, architects.

Architectural record 55: 153-5
Feb., 1924

Evanston, (IL)
French, (F.E.) House, entrance detail
E.A. Mayo, Arch.

Inland Arch.
44: pls. fol.p. 24
Oct.1904

720.5
W52
Evanston, Ill. Garrett Biblical Institute (ca. 1925)
Rolfs.M.A.
Garrett Biblical Institute at Evanston, Illinois. Holabird and Roche,archts. Plans.

Western architect 54: 89-90, pl.1-12
September 1925

Evanston (IL.) First Congregational Church
First Congregational Church, Evanston, Illinois.
Tallmadge and Watson, archts.

Architect (N.Y.) 11: 333-339
December, 1928

Evanston (IL)
French (F.E.) House
E.A.Mayo, Arch.

Inland Arch.
44: pls.fol. p.32
Nov.1904

Evanston (Il) Garrett Biblical Institute (ca. 1919)
Educational Bldg. (proposed)
Sketch
Holabird and Roche, archts.

West. Archt.
25: pl.fol.p. XVI
Apr, 1917

720.5
A51
Evanston (Ill.) First Methodist church
First Methodist church, Evanston. Tallmadge and Watson, architects. Plan.

A

American architect 101:54,56 pl.fol.
January 31,1912   p.56

720.5
I56
Evanston (Ill.) French (F.E.) house
Residence of F. E. French, Evanston, Ill.
Ernest A. Mayo, archt.

Inland archt 44: pls 2 & 6
preceding back cover of vol.
Ja '05

Evanston, IL. Garrett Biblical Institute.
Heck Hall (1867)
Heck Hall. (illus.)

Commercial and architectural
Chicago. (Chicago): G.W. Orear,
1887. pp. 83, 87.

720.5
W52
Evanston.First methodist episcopal church
First methodist episcopal church, Evanston
(Ill.)Tallmadge and Watson,archts.plan.

A

Western architect 22:pls.fol.p.52
December 1915

Evanston, Ill. Garland (Mae O.) house,

see

Evanston, Ill. Enfield place

Evanston, IL. Garrett biblical institute.
Memorial Hall (1887)
One of the group of Northwestern University Campus.
(illus.)

Commercial and architectural Chicago.
(Chicago): G.W. Orear, 1887. pp. 87-88.

Evanston Il., First Presbyterian Church.

D. H. Burnham + Co., Archts.

Inland Archt.
Vol. 26, No. 5, pl.
Fol. p. 54
Dec. 1895

Evanston (Il) Garrett Biblical Institute (Ca. 1919)
Sketch
Holabird and Roche, archts.

West. Archt.
27: pl. 5
Apr, 1918

Evanston, IL. Garrett Theological seminary

see

Evanston, IL. Garrett Biblical Institute

Evanston (IL.) Foster (George) house
Sketch of residence of George Foster,
Evanston, Illinois. G. Isaacson, archt.

A

Inland architect 7:23,pl.fol.30
March, 1886

Evanston. Garrett Biblical Institute (ca. 1919)
The Garrett Biblical Institute, Evanston,
Illinois. Holabird and Roche, archts. Plans

Amer. archt. 118:
231-39, 241-42; Ag 25, 1920
pl fol p. 522; O 20, 1920

720.5
W52
Evanston (Ill) Georgian apartments
Georgian apartments, Evanston. A.S.
Hecht. archt.

Western architect 36: pls.53-4
March 1927

Evanston (Il) Golf Club
Perspective Detail. Walter W. Alschlager, archt.

West. Archt.
27: pl. 10
Apr, 1918

Evanston (Ill) High School
Charles R. Ayars, Arch

Inland Arch 38:
pl.fol.p.48
Jan. 1902

720.5
I56
Evanston (Ill.) Howe (C.W.) house
Residence for .C.W. Howe, Evanston, Ill.
Pond and Pond, archts.

A
Inland architect 31: pls.fol. 40
May 1898

Evanston, Il., Grape (J. Stanley) Residence

Robert C. Spencer Jr. and R. R.
Kendall, Associated Archts.

Inland Archt.
Vol. 26, No. 5, pl.
Fol. p. 54
Dec. 1895

MICROFILM

Evanston, Ill. Hillel foundation bldg.
[Max Abramovits, archt.]

in SCRAPBOOK ON
ARCHITECTURE p. 27
(on film)

Evanston, Ill. Hunt, Myron, house.
Illustration. Myron Hunt, architect.

Architectural review
9: 101
Apr 1902

Evanston, Il. Gross (A.W.) Residence
Flanders and Zimmerman, Archts.

Inland Archt.
vol.31,No.3,pl.fol.p. 30
Apr, 1898

Evanston, Ill., Hospital (1898)
Illustration. George L. Harvey, architect.

Inland architect
31: plate following p.50
June 1898

720.5
B93b
Evanston (Ill.) Hurd (H.B.) house
Residence for H.B.Hurd, Evanston, Ill.
W.W.Boyington and Co. archts. Plans.

A
Building budget 6: pl.fol.p.150
December 31, 1890

MICROFILM

Evanston, Ill. Grosse Point lighthouse

in SCRAPBOOK ON
ARCHITECTURE p. 35
(on film)

Evanston, Ill. hospital. (1921)
Illustrations and plans. Schmidt, Garden
and Martin, architects.

Architectural forum
37: 250-1; 285; plates 91-92
December 1922

Evanston (IL.) Ingleside Club house
Sketch of Ingleside Club House, Evanston,
Illinois. Pond and Pond, archts.

Inland architect 17: pl.fol.16
February 1891

Evanston (Ill.) Hamline (Leonida) house

see

Evanston (Ill.) "Anchorfast"

Evanston, Ill. hospital (1941)
Schmidt, Garden and Erikson are architects
for Evanston hospital.

Nat'l. arch.
4: 5
O 1948

Evanston (Il.) Jenks (Chancellor L., Jr.) Residence
Exterior plus view in Living Room.
Myron Hunt, Archt.

Inland Architect
vol. 35, No.2, pl.fol.p. 16
Mar, 1900

Evanston, Il., Harper (Wm. Hudson) Residence.

Handy + Cady, Archts.

Inland Archt.
Vol. 26, No. 5, pl.
Fol. p. 54
Dec. 1895

Evanston, (Il.) House
(One-Half of Double House)
Myron Hunt, Archt.

Inland Architect
vol. 34,No.4, pl.fol.p. 32
Nov, 1899

MICROFILM

Evanston (Il.) Johnson (Oscar) House
plans.
Bertha Yerex Whitman, archt.

Roll 38, frames 24-27;57-63;131-132;
137-140

Evanston (IL) Haugan (Oscar H.) Residence
John A. Nyden, archt. plans

West. Archt.
24: pls.fol.p. 124
Sept, 1916

720.5
A67r
Evanston (Ill.) Howe house
The Howe house, Evanston, Ill. Pond and Pond
archts. No plan.

A
Architectural record 17:165
February 1905

Evanston, Ill. Kirk, John B., house (1886).
Illustration. Edbrooke and Burnham,
architects.

Building budget
II: 10 and plate
Jan., 1886

720.5
I56
Evanston (Ill.) Kirk (John B.) house
    Residence of John B. Kirk, Evanston,
Illinois. Edbrooke and Burnham, archts.
No plan.

Inland architect 13: 48, pl.fol.p.48
March 1889

Evanston (Il) Llewellyn (S.J.) Residence
    Alterations
Tallmadge and Watson, archts. Plans.

West. Archt.
28: pl. 7-10
Aug. 1919

Evanston (Il.) Madison (Wm.) House
    plans.
Bertha Yerex Whitman, archt.

Roll 38, frames 83-84

Evanston (Ill) Klee (Simon) Residence
Ottenheimer, Stern and Reichert, Archts.

West. Archt.
18: pls.fol.p. XVIII
Dec. 1912

Evanston, Ill. Lord, Thomas, house
    Residence of Thomas Lord, Evanston, Ill.
Burnham & Root, archts.

No identification on it; attributed to
Burnham & Root

Inland archt.
13: 90, pl.fol.p.92
Je 1889

Evanston (Il.) Madison (Wm.) House
    plans.
Bertha Yerex Whitman, archt.

Roll 38, frames 147-151

Evanston (Il.) Kurzawa (August) House
    plans.
Bertha Yerex Whitman, archt.

Roll 38, frames 72-73

720.5
W52
Evanston. Lucas building
    H. J. Lucas building, Evanston, Illinois.
Pierre Blouke, archt.

Western architect 39: 146
September 1930

720.5
W52
Evanston (Ill.) Mallers (C.E.) house
    Residence of C. E. Mallers, Evanston, Ill.
Mayo & Mayo, archts.

Western architect 37: pl., 211
December 1928

Evanston (Il.) Lawrence (Brynolf) House
    plans.
Bertha Yerex Whitman, archt.

Roll 38, frames 127-128

Evanston (Ill.) Lunt (Orrington) house

see

Evanston (Ill.) "Anchorfast"

720.5
T15b
Evanston (Ill.) Mallers (C.E.) house
    Home of C.E. Mallers, 2750 Sheridan
road, Evanston. Mayo and Mayo, archts.

Building for the future 5-6
December 1921

720.5
A51
Evanston (Ill.) Lincoln school
    Lincoln school, Evanston, Ill. J.T.W.
Jennings & H.J. Ross, archt.

Amer archt and bldg news
55: pl fol 3F,
Jl 25, 1896

Evanston (Ill.) McGowen (Vera) house

see

Evanston (Ill.) "Anchorfast"

Evanston, Ill. Mallory, H   H   house
Tallmadge & Watson, archts.
    H. H. Mallory house, Evanston, Ill.

Roll 31, frames 237-244

Evanston, (Il) Lincoln School
Jennings and Ross, archt.

Inland Architect
vol. 49, No. 1 pl.fol.p. 8
Feb, 1902

Evanston, Ill. McGrew (Orville) house.

see

Evanston, Ill. Enfield place

Evanston (Il) Milhenning (Frank) Residence
Arthur Howell Knox, archt. Plan

West. Archt.
34: pl. 15-16
Dec, 1922

Evanston ((L)
    Little (C.G.) Residence
Ernest A. Mayo, Arch.

Inland Arch.
44: pls.fol.p. 32
Nov.1904

Evanston (Il) McMullin (D.S.) Residence
L.T. Shipley archt.

Inland Architect
25: 11
Feb, 1895

Evanston (Ill.) Miller (H.H.C.) house
    Residence of H.H.C. Miller, Evanston, Ill.
W. A. Otis, archt.

Inl archt 34:pl.fol.p.16
S 1899

720.5
D93b

Evanston (Ill.) Mitchell (G.P.) house
Residence of G. P. Mitchell, Evanston,
Illinois. Henry Raeder, archt. Plan

Building budget 5: pl. fol. 114
3 1889

Evanston (Ill) Noble (L.C.)
Residence
Pond & Pond, Arch.

Inland Arch 38:
pl.fol.p.48
Jan. 1902

720.6
C53

Evanston. Northwestern university
Perspective sketch of dormitories and
fraternity buildings, Northwestern University.
Evanston. Ill.: Palmer, Hornbostel and
Jones, archts.; no plan.

A   Chicago architectural club 26:38
1915

Evanston, Ill. Mitchell (C.P.) house
Residence of C.P. Mitchell, Evanston, Ill.
Raeder, Coffer & Crocker, archts.

Inland architect
v. 16 no. 3
pl. fol. p. 36
O 1890

Evanston, (Il.) Nolan (J.E.) Residence
Exterior plus view in Living Room.
Myron Hunt, Archt.

Inland Architect
vol. 35, No. 2,pl.fol.p. 16
Mar, 1900

720.5
B84

Evanston. Northwestern university
Foster,W.D.
The new dormitories of Northwestern university
Evanston,Illinois.General plan and winning design
for future development - fraternity houses,dormi-
tory - quadrangle.Palmer,Hornbostel and Jones,
archts. Plans

Brickbuilder 23: 269-270 pls.174-176 fol.
A   November 1914   p.2d2

Microfilm
Evanston, Ill. Montgomery (James J.) house
Gmelin, George Grant, architect
James J. Montgomery house, Evanston, Illinois,
1922.

Roll 7, frames 1-13

720.5
A67f

Evanston (Ill.). North shore apts.
North Shore apts., Evanston, Illinois.
Robert S. DeGolyer, archt.

Arch forum 32: 71
F '20

720.5
P39

Evanston. Northwestern university
Woodblock of new Northwestern university
building by Charles Turzak, at Evanston,
Illinois.

Pencil points 8:vol.15 fol.p.250
April 1927

720.5
I56

Evanston (Ill.) Moore (Mrs. Julia) house
Residence of Mrs. Julia Moore in Evanston. A. W. Cole, archt.

Inland archt & news rec 19:27
March 1892

Evanston, Ill. North Shore hotel (1920)

see

Evanston, Ill. North Shore apartments

MICROFILM
Evanston, Ill. Northwestern university. Alice
S. Millar chapel

in SCRAPBOOK ON
ARCHITECTURE p. 25,26
(on film)

Evanston (IL.) Mullen (T.H.) house
House for Thomas H. Mullen, Evanston, Illinois.
Bertrand Goldberg, architect.

The architectural forum book of small
houses. New York: Simon and Schuster,
1940. p. 44-45

Evanston (Ill.) Northwestern university

see also

Chicago. Northwestern university. Chicago
campus
Chicago. Northwestern university settlement

Evanston, (IL) Northwestern University. Campus.
Northwestern University Campus - an
American ideal. Proposed plan. (plan and
sketch) G.W. Maher, arch.

Inland Arch.
51: 15-17, pl. X,
March 1908

Evanston (IL.) Nance (Willis D.) house
House remodeled for Willis D. Nance,
Evanston, Illinois. Jerome Robert Cerny,
architect. Plan.

Architectural forum 65:292-293
October, 1936

MICROFILM
Evanston, Ill. Northwestern university

in SCRAPBOOK ON
ARCHITECTURE p. 934-937
(on film)

Evanston (Ill) Northwestern University, Campus
George W. Maher, Arch.

West. Arch.
20: p. 25-26
Mar, 1914

720.5
A51

Evanston (Ill.) Wellis (Frank) house
House of Frank Wellis, Evanston, Ill.
Russell S. Walcott, architect

Amer. arch. 126:553-555
Dec. 3, 1924

Evanston (Ill.) Northwestern university
Northwestern university

Moran, George E. Moran's
dictionary of Chicago and
its vicinity... Chicago: G. E.
Moran, 1892-1912.
61-62, 152-154

Evanston, Il., Northwestern Univ., Cumnock School
of Oratory.

Charles R. Ayars, Archt.

Inland Archt.
Vol. 26, No. 5, pl.
Fol. p. 54
Dec. 1895

Evanston, Ill. Northwestern university. Dear-
born Observatory.
Observatory for the Northwestern University,
Evanston, Ill. [plan] Cobb & Frost, archts.

Inland archt.
v. 11 no.6
pl at end of issue
My 1888

Evanston (IL.) Northwestern Univ. Orrington Lunt
Library
Orrington Lunt Library, Northwestern University,
Evanston, IL. W.A. Otis, archt. Plans.

A   Architectural review 9 n.s.4:40
January, 1902

Evanston (Il.) Northwestern Univ. Settlement
Dwight Heald Perkins, Archt.

Inland Architect
vol. 35, No. 3, pl.fol.p. 24
Apr, 1900

720.5
B84   Evanston (Ill.) Northwestern univ. Dormitories
Foster, W.D.
The new dormitories of Northwestern university.
Palmer, Hornbostel and Jones, archts.

Brickbuilder 23:269-70, pls
174-176
N'14

Evanston, Ill. Northwestern university. Patten
Gymnasium.
Rendering and plans. G.W. Maher, architect.

Inland architect
52:42, plate VII
September 1908

Evanston, Ill. Northwestern university. Swift
hall of engineering.
Rendering. George W. Maher, architect.

Inland architect
51: pl. IX
March 1908

Evanston, Ill. Northwestern University.
Fayerweather hall. (ca. 1887)
Science Hall, North Western University.
[illus.] Holabird & Roche, architects.

Building budget
II: 99 and plate
August, 1886

Evanston, Ill. Northwestern university. Patten
Gymnasium.
[Illustrations and plans] G.W. Maher, archt.

Western architect
20: p.27, plates V-VII
March, 1914

Evanston, Ill. Northwestern university. Swift
hall of engineering.
Illustration and plan. George W. Maher,
architect.

Western architect
20: pl. VIII
March 1914

Evanston, IL. Northwestern University. Fayerweather
Hall (ca.1887)
Science Hall. (illus.)

Commercial and architectural
Chicago. (Chicago): G.W. Orear, 1887.
p. 84

Evanston, Ill. Northwestern university. Patten
Gymnasium.
Illustration. George W. Maher, architect.

American architect
99:116
March 22, 1911

Evanston, IL. Northwestern University. University
Hall (1873)
College of Liberal Arts. (illus.) Gurdon P. Randall,
archt.

Commercial and architectural
Chicago. (Chicago): G.W. Orear, 1887.
pp. 83

Evanston, Ill. Northwestern university.
Garrett biblical institute

see

Evanston, Ill. Garrett biblical institute

Evanston (Ill.) Northwestern University, Patten
Gymnasium
George W. Maher, Archt.

West. Archt.
20: p. 24-27
Mar, 1914

Evanston, IL. Northwestern University. Willard Hall
(1874)
Women's College, Northwestern University campus.
(illus.) Gurdon P. Randall, archt.

Commercial and architectural
Chicago. (Chicago): G.W. Orear, 1887.
p. 85

Evanston, Ill. Northwestern university. Laboratories of the medical & pharmaceutical schools.
Laboratories of the medical & pharmaceutical
schools, Northwestern University, Chicago. S. S.
Beman, archt.

Inland architect
19, no. 5: pl. fol. p.66
Je 1892

Evanston, Ill. Northwestern University. Patten
Gymnasium. MacNeil Sculpture Groups
Illustrations. G.W. Maher, Architect. Herman
A. MacNeil, Sculptor.

West. Archt.
26: 3-4, plates 3-5
Jul, 1917

Evanston (Ill.) Norton (L.D.) residence
Perspective view of residence for L. D. Norton,
Esq. & Baumann, archt. Plans.

Inland archt 1: 35,38
1883

Evanston (Il) Northwestern Univ. MacNeil
Sculpture Groups.

See

Evanston (Il) Northwestern Univ. Patten Gymnasium.
MacNeil Sculpture Groups

Evanston, Ill. Northwestern university.
Science hall (ca.1887)

see

Evanston, Ill. Northwestern university. Fayerweather hall (ca.1887)

Evanston (Il) Off (Clifford) Residence
Clark and Walcott, archts. Plan.

West. Archt.
31: pl. 5-6
Oct, 1922

Evanston (IL.) Original Manufacturing Co.
Building for Original Manufacturing Co.
Evanston, Illinois. Tallmadge and Watson, archt.

Western architect 19:pl.fol.p.33
March, 1913

Evanston (Il.) Patten (James A.) Residence
Photos
Thistle motif. interior.   George W. Maher, archt.

West. Archt.
3: pls.fol.p. XV
Mar, 1904

720.5
A67r

Evanston (Ill.) Perkins (D.H.) house
A group of Western residences: The residence of Dwight H. Perkins; D.H.Perkins, archt. No plans.

A   Architectural record 18:71-78
July 1906

720.5
I56

Evanston (Ill.) Orr (A.) house
Residence at Evanston for A. Orr. J. L. Silsbee, archt.

Inland archt & news rec
15:61
Ap 1890

Evanston, Ill. Patten, James A., house
Residence of Mayor Patten. [illus.]
G.W. Maher, architect.

Architectural record
15:371-380
April 1904

720.5
A67r

Evanston (Ill.) Pirie (J.T.) house
Interiors in the house of J.T.Pirie,
Evanston,Ill. Myron Hunt,archt.

A   Architectural record 16:312,334,368,
October 1904   373,376

Evanston, Ill. Orr (Arthur) house
Residence of Arthur Orr, Evanston, Illinois.
J.L. Silsbee, archt.

Inland architect
v. 15 no. 6
pl. fol. p. 92
Jl 1890

Evanston, Ill. Patten, James A., house
Illustrations. George A. Maher, architect.

Architectural record
21:437,439,440
June 1907

720.5
A67r

Evanston (Ill.) Pirie (J.T.) house
Three houses of Myron Hunt: John T.Pirie,
Jr,Evanston; Healy house,Sheridan Road,Chicago; residence in Oak Park.

A   Architectural record 17:154-157
February 1905

720.973
T15b

Evanston (Ill.) Osborne (W.I.) house
Residence of W.Irving Osborne, Evanston.
Jarvis Hunt, architect.

Building for the future:4
April 1930

Evanston (Ill) Patten (James A.) Residence
George W. Maher, Archt.

West. Archt.
20: p. 26
Mar, 1914

Evanston (Ill.) Pittman (C.K.) house
Residence of C. K. Pittman, Evanston, Ill.
a. A. Otis, archt.

Inl archt 34:pl.fol.p.16
S 1899

720.5
A67f

Evanston (Ill.) Parks (W.R.) house
House of Dr. W. R. Parks, Evanston,Illinois.Tallmadge and Watson,archts. Plans

A   Architectural forum 33: pl.48
September 1920

Evanston, Ill. Patten, James A., house.
Interior of the James A. Patten house,
Evanston, Illinois, 1901. Designed by George
W. Maher and Louis J. Millet. [rep.]

Chicago. Art institute.
Bulletin.
v. 67: 17
Mr-Ap 1973

Evanston (IL.) Plan
Plan of Evanston.

Amer. inst. of arch. jour. 5:pls.foll.
July, 1917   p.344 and 345

Evanston, Ill. Patten, James A., house.
Description of Mr. James A. Patten's house,
Evanston, Illinois. [illus.] G.W. Maher,
architect.

Inland architect
42: 6-7; plates III,IV,VII,
VIII,XIII,XV,XVI,XIX,XX
August 1903

Evanston, Ill. Patten, James A., house.
Portiere, 1901, designed by George W.
Maher and Louis J. Millet for the James A.
Patten house. Cotton and silk velvet
with design appliqued in cotton damask. Height
80 1/2 in. and width 47 7/16 in. Gift of
the Antiquarian society, 1971.680. [rep.]

Chicago. Art institute.
Bulletin.
V. 67: 18
Mr-Ap 1973

720.5
I56

Evanston.Post Office
Post Office,Evanston,Ill.J.Knox Taylor,
supervising archt.

A   Inland architect 48: pls.fol.p.48
November 1906

Evanston, (IL)
Patten, (James A.) Residence
Geo. W. Maher (Arch.)

Inland Arch.
42: pls. fol. p. 32
Nov. 1903

Evanston, Ill. Peabody, F.F., house (1886).
Illustration. A.M.F. Colton, architect.

Building budget
II: 44 and plate
April 1886

720.6
C53

Evanston (Ill.) Pruitt (A.J.) house
Residence for Mr.A.J.Pruitt. Evanston.
Ill.. N. Max Dunning. archt.; no plan.

A   Chicago architectural club 25:13
1912

Evanston (IL) Public Library James Gamble Rogers & Charles A. Phillips, Archts. Inland Arch. 48: pls. fol. p 24 S, 1906	Evanston (IL) Residence Inland Arch. 41: pl.fol.p. 52 July 1903	Evanston (IL.) St. Luke's Church Figures in the reredos of St. Luke's Church, Evanston, Il. Tallmadge and Watson, archts. Carved by U. Langenegger from cartoons by John W. Norton. Architectural record 65:485-488 May, 1929
790.5 A67r Evanston (Ill.) Reckitt (Ernest) house House of Ernest Reckitt, Evanston, Ill. F. A. Keys, archt. Plan. A Architectural record 40:514 October 1916	Evanston (Il) Residence Clark and Walcott, archts. West. Archt. 32: pl. 3 Oct, 1922	Evanston (Ill.) St. Mary's church St. Mary's. (Murals by O'Shaughnessy and an interior). Inland printer 44: 45-47. Oct. 1909.
720.5 R93b Evanston (Ill.) Reese (Harvey H.) house Residence of Harvey H. Reese, Evanston, Illinois. Beman and Parmentier, archts. Building budget 5: pl. fol. 98 Ag 1889	Evanston, (IL) Residence Ernest A. Mayo, Arch. Inland Arch. 44: pls. fol.p. 40 Dec. 1904	MICROFILM Evanston (Ill.) St. Matthews episcopal church. St. Mary's chapel. [Armstrong, Furst and Tilton, archts.] in SCRAPBOOK ON ARCHITECTURE p. 22 (on film)
Evanston, Ill. Reese (H.H.) house Residence for H.H. Reese, Evanston, Ill. Beman & Parmentier, archts. Inland architect v. 16 no. 3 pl. fol. p. 36 O 1890	Evanston (Il) Residence Naid and Cranford, Archts. Inland Archt. vol.36,No.3,pl.fol.p. 16 Sept, 1900	Evanston (IL) St. Matthew's Episcopal Church E. Norman Brydges, archt. plan. West. Archt. 33: pl. 13-15 Dec, 1924
Evanston (IL) Residence Inland Arch. 23: pl. fol. p 24 Mr., 1894	microfilm Evanston, Ill. Ridge quadrangles Griffin, Walter Burley, architect Ridge quadrangles, Evanston boundary, Chicago, Illinois, n.d. Plot plan. Roll 8, frame 28	720.973 T15b Evanston (Ill.) Sargent (F.W.) house nt A modern "Early Georgian." Residence of F.W.Sargent. Tallmadge and Watson,archts. Building for the future:4 A February 1930
Evanston, Il., Residence Inland Archt. Vol. 26, No. 6, pl. Fol. p. 68 Jan. 1896	Evanston, IL. Roycemore School McLean, Robert Craik Growth of the American School Building as Illustrated by the Roycemore Private School for Girls. Lawrence Buck and Tallmadge and Watson, archts. West. Archt. 26: pl. 1-6;p. 37-8 Nov, 1917	MICROFILM Evanston (Ill.) Schulz (Otto) House plans. Bertha Yerex Whitman, archt. Roll 38, frames 39-45; 158-160
Evanston, Il., Residence Inland Archt. Vol. 27, No. 4, pl. Fol. p. 40 May 1896	Evanston (IL.) St. Luke's Church St. Luke's Church, Evanston, Illinois. (drawing) John Sutcliffe, archt. Christian art 1: 60 My, 1909	Evanston, Il., Sheppard (R.D.) Residence Front and Rear Exteriors. H. Edwards Ficken, Archt. Inland Archt. Vol. 27, No. 4, Plates Fol. p. 40 May 1896

720.5
A67a
Evanston (Ill.) State bank and trust company's building
State bank and trust company's building, Evanston, Ill. Views and plans. Childs and Smith, archts.

A   Architecture 57:43-8
January 1928

720.5
A67a
Evanston (Ill.) Terry (A.G.) house
Residence, A.G.Terry, Evanston, Illinois. Granger, Lowe and Bollenbacher, archts. Plans.

A   Architecture 51:pl.81-85
June 1925

Evanston (IL) Ward, (C.A) Residence
View in hall, Dn.Rm., entrance detail
G.L. Harvey, Arch.

Inland Arch.
42: pls.fol.p. 24
Oct. 1904

Evanston (IL.) State Bank and Trust Company Building
The State Bank and Trust Company building, Evanston, IL. Childs and Smith, archts. (interior views).

Through the ages 7:38-42
March, 1930

Evanston (IL.) Tobey houses
Semi-detached dwellings designed for Mrs. Tobey, Evanston, IL. A.M.F. Colton, archt.

A   Building budget 3:pl.fol.p.60
April 30, 1887

Evanston (IL.) Warmington (L.R.) House
plans.
Bertha Yerex Whitman, archt.

Roll 38, frames 141-142

Evanston (IL.) Stiles (F.C.) house
House for Fred C. Stiles, Evanston, Illinois. White and Weber, architects. Plan.

The architectural forum book of small houses. New York: Simon and Schuster, 1940. p. 33.

Evanston, Ill. University building.
Exterior [illus.] G.W. Maher, architect

Architectural record
21: p. 429, 439.
June 1907

Evanston (Ill) Washington School
includes plan
Patton, Fisher & Miller, Archs.

Inland Arch. 38;
pl.fol.p.8
Aug. 1901

720.5
B93b
Evanston (Ill.) Stockham (A.B.) house
Sketches of residence at Evanston for Dr. A.B.Stockham. Frederick Baumann and J.K.Cady, archts. Plan.

A   Building budget 6: pl.fol.p.150
December 31, 1890

Evanston, Ill. University building.
Exterior and entrance [illus.] G.W. Maher, architect.

Western architect
20: plate XXIV
March 1914

Evanston (IL) Webster (Dr. E.H.) Residence
Holabird & Roche, Archs.

Inland Arch. 20:
pl. fol. p 70
Ja., 1893

Evanston (Ill.) Strom (John) House.
plans.
Bertha Yerex Whitman, archt.

Roll 38, frames 20-23; 28-31

Evanston Il. Van Deusen (A.S.) Residence
Myron Hunt, Archt.

Inland Archt.
vol.31, No.4, pl.fol.p. 40
May, 1898

Evanston (Ill.) Welch (Walter) House
plans.
Bertha Yerex Whitman, archt.

Roll 38, frames 115-116;117-118;121-124;
129-130;133-134;152-153

Evanston (Ill.) Sweet (Frances M.) house
Residence for Mrs. Frances M. Sweet, Evanston, Illinois. Myron Hunt, archt.

Inl archt 84:pl.fol.p.82
N 1899

Evanston (Ill.) Victor (David) House.
plans.
Bertha Yerex Whitman, archt.

Roll 38, frames 135-136

Evanston, Ill. Wheeler (C.P.) house
Residence of C.P. Wheeler, Evanston, Ill. Frederick Baumann & J. K. Cady, archts.

Inland architect
v. 18 no. 1
pl. fol. p. 14
Ag 1891

Evanston (Ill.) Sweet (John M.) house
Residence for John M. Sweet, Evanston, Ill. Myron Hunt, archt.

Inl archt 84:pl.fol.p.82
N 1899

Evanston (Ill.) village hall
Village Hall, Evanston, Illinois. Holabird & Roche, archts.

Inland architect
v. 18 no. 1
pl. fol. p. 14
Ag 1891

Evanston, Ill. White, Catherine, house.
Illustration; one-half of house. Myron Hunt, architect.

Inland architect
34: plate following p. 32
Nov 1899

v. 4

257

Evanston, Ill. White, Catherine, house.
Illustrations. Myron Hunt, architect.

Architectural review
9: 102, 103
Apr 1902

Evanston, Ill. Wilson, H.R., house
Residence of H.R. Wilson, Evanston, Ill.
Burnham & Root, archts.

Inland arch.
v.13, no.1: pl.fol.p.14
F 1889

Evansville (IN)
Cutsinger (F.M.) Residence

West. Arch.
14: pl.8
Sept. 1909

Evanston, Ill. White, Catherine, house.
...Marion Mahony claimed to have
designed this building [illus.] Myron
Hunt, architect.

Prairie School review
III: 10
Second quarter 1966

Evanston, (Ill.) Wilson (M.H.) Residence
Beers, Clay and Dutton, Archt.

Inland Arch.
vol.31,No. 3,pl.fol.p. 30
Apr, 1898

720.5
A67r
Evansville(Ind.)Government building
Government building(1875). Evansville,
Ind. W. A. Potter, archt. No plan.

A
Architectural record 26:179
September 1909

720.5
A67f
Evanston (Ill.) Will (Philip) house
House for Philip Will, Jr., Perkins,
Wheeler and Will, archts. Plans.

A
Architectural Forum 71: 242-243
October 1939

Evanston, (IL)
Wilson (Oliver T.) Residence
Ernest A. Mayo, Arch.

Inland Arch.
44: pls. fol.p. 32
Nov. 1904

720.5
B93b
Evansville(Ind.) Jones(J.N.) office building
Office building for J. N. Jones. Reed
Bros., archts.

Building budget
3:3 in supp.
Ap 30, 1887

Evanston (IL.) Williams (N.W.) house
House of N.W. Williams, Esq. Evanston, IL.

Arch. Forum. 33: 15-16 pl.
July, 1920

Evanston (Ill.) Z Products Co. Machine shop
Barancik, Conte and assos., archts...Z Products
Co., in Evanston.

Natl archt 8: 8
Ap 1962

Evansville, Ind. memorial airport
Evansville memorial airport - exterior and con-
course. Albert Kahn assoc. archts. & eng. ins.

Interiors 105, pt. 1:85
Ja 1946

720.5
W52
Evanston (Ill.) Williams (N.W.) house
Residence of Mr. Natnan R.Williams,Evan-
ston,Illinois.Spencer and Powers,archts.Plans

A
Western architect 29: pls. 1-10
September 1920

720.5
W52
Evansville (Ind.) Bosse high school.
Stadium
View of stadium of Bosse high school,
Evansville, Ind. J.C. Llewellyn co.,
archts.

West. archt. 36:pl 144
Ag '27

Evansville (IN) Municipal Market
Clifford Shopbell and Co., archts.

West. Arch.
28: pl. 15-16
Mar, 1919

Evanston (IL.) Williams (Mrs. Nony) Apt. Bldg.
Apartment building in Evanston for Mrs. Nony
Williams; Myron Hunt, archt.; no plan.

Chicago architectural club 13:57
1900

---

microfilm
Evansville, Ind. City national bank
Jenney, Mundie and Jensen
City national bank, Evansville, Indiana, 1913.

Roll 10, frames 160-73

720.5
B93b
Evansville,(Ind.)Orr(James L.)store & office bldg
Store and office building for James L. Orr
(will contain a Masonic Hall). Reed Bros.,archt

Building budget
3:3 in supp.
Ap 30, 1887

Evanston, Ill. Wilson, H.R., house
Residence for H.R. Wilson at Evanston, Ill.
Burnham & Root, archts.

Building budget
3: 2 in supp.
Jl 30, 1887

Evansville (IN) City National Bank
Mundie and Jensen, archts. plan

West. Archt.
24: pls.fol.p. 109
Jul, 1916

Evansville (Ind.) planning
An attractive Evansville.

City planning 4:141-2,150
April, 1928

Evansville (Ind.) Planning
Blachard, R.W.
Ten years of city planning in Evansville.

City planning 8: front. 65-78
April, 1932

Evening journal building, Chicago (1872)

see

Chicago, Ill. Evening journal building (1872)

720.5
A67f
Everett(Wash.) Weyerhaeuser Timber Co.
Pulp division, Weyerhaeuser Timber Co.,
Everett, Washington. O.C.Schoenwerk, consul-
ting engineer.

Architectural forum 66: 171-174
March 1937

720.5
W68
Evansville (Ind.) Soldiers and Sailors monument
Soldiers and sailors memorial. Coliseum,
Evansville, Indiana. Clifford Shopbell and
Co..archts. Plan.

West arch 28: pl 12-14
Mr '19

Evening post building, Chicago (1928)

see

Chicago (Ill.) Sun-Times building (1928)

Everett, Wash., White (C. Ferris) house

Floor plan and sketch of hall.
C. Ferris White, Archt.

Inland Arch.
Vol. 24, No. 5, pl.
Fol. p. 52
Dec. 1894

Ryerson

Evansville, Ind. Soldiers' and Sailors' memorial coliseum
The soldiers' and sailors' memorial coliseum at Evansville, Ind. Clifford, Shopbell & Co., architects.

House beau 47: 124
F 1920

Everard and Pick

see

Leicester (Eng.) Parr's bank

Evergreens

see also

Hedges, Yew
Box (shrub)

720.5
B95b
Evansville(Ind.) Wood(A.J.) house
Residence for A. J. Wood.
Reed Bros., archts.

Building budget
3:3 in supp.
Ap 30, 1887

Everett, Arthur J.

see

Ottawa, Ont. Imperial bank of Canada

Evergreens
Broadleaved evergreens.
By Henry Teuscher.

House and Garden 72:82
Aug., 1937

720.5
A67r
Evelyn,John. 1620-1706
Goodyear,W.H.
An echo from Evelyn's diary: spreading piers in: St.Mark's,Venice(plan); St.Maria della Pieve at Arezzo; S.Ambrogio,Milan(plan).

Architectural record 7:180-213
October-December 1897

Everett, Ill. Lasker (Albert Davis) farm

see

Everett, Ill. Mill Road farm

710.5
H84
Evergreens
Evergreens for flowering
Emile Mardein

House and garden 46:84-85
Oct. 1924

711
273
Evelyn, John 1620-1706
Peets, Elbert
Famous town planners. Pt. 4. The plan for rebuilding London in 1666: John Evelyn, 1620-1706; Christopher Wren; Robert Hooke; Valentine Knight.

Town planning review 14: 13-17,pls.2-3
May 1930

---

microfilm
Everett, Ill. Mill Road farm
Adler, David and Robert Work
House for A. D. Lasker, Everett, Illinois, 1926.

Roll no. 34, Frames 123-148
Roll 1, frames 131-5

710.5
H84
Evergreens.
Wilson, E. H.
Evergreens from east to west.

House & garden.50:60-61
August 1926

710.5
H84
Evelyn, John. 1620-1706
Wilder, L. B.
The garden books of John Evelyn.

House and garden 56: 94-95,154
December 1929

720.8
A51
Everett (Mass.) Woodlawn cemetery. Gate and lodge
Entrance gate and gate lodge for Wood-
lawn cemetery, Everett, Mass. W.H. Taylor, archt.

Amer archt and bldg news
56: pl fol 4 in supp
My 1, 1897

710.5
L26
Evergreens
The future for hardy evergreens in America as affected by Quarantine 37.

Landscape arch.10: 175-80.
Jul.1920.

720.R **N84** Lemmo, R.S. Evergreens. Some conifers of easy culture. House & garden. 50:85-87 July, 1926	Evreux (Fr.) Ancien hôtel de ville Avant corps de l'Ancien Hôtel d'Evereux du coté de la cour. Blondel, Jacques Francois. Décorations extérieures et intérieures des XVIIe and XVIIIe Siècles....Paris: Ch. Massin (n.d.) v.8:p.19	Ewing & Allen see also New York (City) Architects' building
Evergreens Use in landscape gardening Amer. homes and gardens 9:318-319 Sept. 1912	**913** **A66j** Evreux.Notre Dame Evreux cathedral. Plan. Archaeological journal 95:393-395,pl. Pt.2,1938 facing p.394	**720.5** **A67** Ewing and Allen Warner, R.F. Muscle Shoals. A new industrial town in Alabama. Ewing and Allen, archts. Architectural review 25:n.s.8:18-23,pls. January 1919 15-16
720.5 **F29** Everman,T.B.and W.E.Humphrey House for two architects: Belle Haven, Va.; Tox B. Everman and W.E. Humphrey, archts.; no plan. Federal architect 8:20-22 July 1937	Evreux (Fr.) St. Taurin St. Taurin. Meas. drawing by G. H. Birch. Shrine. Lond Arch. Assoc. Sketchbook 1:pls 38-39 1867-8	Ewing and Chappell see Cedarhurst, L.I. Lord (S.B.) house Muscle Shoals, Ala New York (city) Bristol hotel. Addition. Portsmouth, R.I. Oakland Farm. Riding Academy " " Sandy Point Farm Riding Academy Poughkeepsie, N.Y. Vassar College. Sanders Chemical laboratory Tarrytown (N.Y.) Cobb Lane house
Everton, Eng. Barker and Dobson's factory Barker and Dobson's new factory, Everton Architect 107:pl Je 30, 1922	Evreux (France) St. Taurin Church (sketch) J. F. Jackson, Arch. Inland Arch.20: pl. fol. p 46 N, 1892	Ewing, Whitley L. see Scroggs and Ewing
Evian (Fr.) "La Folie Amphion" Satin, Marcel The villa "La Folie Amphion" at Evian (Haute Savoie). Maurice Gras, archt. L'architecture 44:341-348 September 15, 1931	**913** **A66j** Evreux.Saint Taurin St. Taurin abbey, Evreux. Plan. Archaeological journal 95:393,pl.facing Pt.2,1938 p.393	Excelsior (Minn.) Medical building Modern medical building for the group practice of four doctors: two internists-obstretician- surgeon. Undergraduate thesis submitted by James F. Bofferding to the School of Architecture, U. of Minn. Plans. Northwest archt 14: 14,16-18 No. 5 1960
Evian-les-bains (Fr.) Casino Plan and view of the Casino d'Evian. Jean Hébrard, archt. L'Architecture 41:175 June 15, 1928	Ewen, Harper brothers see Birmingham (Eng.) Phoenix offices	Exchange bldg. Boston, Mass. see Boston, Mass. Exchange bldg.
Evill, Norman see Wilton (Eng.) housing scheme	Ewhurst, Eng. Prawles Prawles, Ewhurst, Sussex. Alterations and additions by Nathaniel Lloyd. Country life (Lond.) 65:919-921 June 22, 1929	Exchanges see also Names of individual exchanges, i.e.: Pistoia, It. Borsa Merci Manchester, Eng. Royal exchange etc.

Ryerson Exchanges Leathems, Charlotte The development of the exchange Ciba rev 19: 672-680 Mr 1939	Exergian, Manoug see Manhasset, L.I. hospital center	Exeter (Eng.) Cathedral Exterior, details, interior; Allen, Fred Hovey. Great Cathedrals of the World. 2 vols. Boston: Haskell and Post, c1886 [-88.] 5 pls. fol. p.80; p.71-80 4 plates after p. 80
Executive house, Chicago, see Chicago, Ill. Executive house	Exeter (Eng.) The city of Exeter. Architectural review 47:63-8,pl.2,3 March, 1920	Exeter (Eng.) Cathedral Exeter Cathedral. Builder 84:183-184 February 21, 1903
Executive mansions see Governors' houses Presidents' houses	Exeter, England Phillips-Birt, D. A museum of sail for Exeter. [illus.] Country life v. 140: 1215-1219 N 10, 1966	Ryerson Exeter, Eng. Guild hall Exeter guild hall. Ciba rev No. 1: 15 S 1937
Exedras. Bliss, Harry Augustus. Memorial Art, Ancient and modern. Buffalo, New York: The Author, 1912. p.95-113.	Exeter (Eng.) Cathedral. Wheatley, Richard. Cathedrals and Abbeys of Great Britain and Ireland. New York: Harper and Bros., 1890. p. 47-54.	Exeter (Eng.) Planning Brown's map of Exeter, 1835. Arch. rev. 47: pl.2.Apr., 1920.
720.5 A87 Exedras Design for an exedra,M.I.T. Architectural review 2:pl.38 August 1895	(1) Exeter (Eng.) Cathedral Exeter Cathedral, plan Arch and con. rep. 70: 2-4, Jul 3, 1903 :pl., Jul 10, 1903 :40, pl., Jul 17, 1903 :56, Jul 24, 1903 :72, Jul 31, 1903 :88, Aug 7, 1903 :pl., Aug 14, 1903 see card 2	Exeter (Eng.) War Memorial Exeter war memorial. John Angel, sculptor Architect 110:124-5 Aug. 24, 1923
720.5 P39 Exedras Beaux-arts institute of design. Pencil points 8: 316 May 1927	(2) Exeter (Eng.) Cathedral Exeter Cathedral, Plan Arch and con. rep. 70:120, Aug 21, 1903 :pl., Sept 4, 1903 :168, Sept 11, 1903 :200-3, Sept 25, 1903 :pl., Oct 9, 1903 :pl., Oct 16, 1903 :pl., Oct 23, 1903 see card 3	Exeter (N.H.) Davis Memorial Library The Davis Memorial Library at Exeter, N.H. Cram, Goodhue and Ferguson, archts. (no plans) Through the ages 7:7 July, 1929
720.5 A58 Exedras Beaux-arts institute of design, competi- tion: "An exedra". B.AII.D. 3: 12-18 April 1927	(3) Exeter (Eng.) Cathedral Exeter Cathedral, Plan Arch and con. rep. 70:280, Oct 30, 1903 :296, Nov 6, 1903 :312, Nov 13, 1903 :pl., Nov 20, 1903 :pl., Nov 27, 1903 :pl., Dec 4, 1903 :376, Dec 11, 1903 :407-8 Dec 25, 1903	720.5 A67 Exeter (N.H.). Phillips church Phillips church (second congregational), Exeter, N.H. Cram, Goodhue & Ferguson, archt. Plan. arch rev 12: 239 O '05

Exeter (N.H.) Phillips Exeter Academy. Academic
          Building
 New Academic Building, Exeter, N.H. Cram and
Ferguson, archts.

    Architectural review 20: n.s.3:112,pls.
  Dec., 1915 75-80, 82 fol.p.116

720.52 Exhibition booths
A67   An architect at the building exhibition

     Architects Journal 59:671-7
     Apr. 16, 1924

720.52 Exhibition booths
B93   Exhibition stand, empire marketing board,
  Holland park rink. Richardson & Gill,
  archts.

     Builder 131: 766
     November 12, 1926

720.5 Exeter (N.H.) Phillips exeter academy. Davis
B94   library
 Davis library, Phillips Exeter Academy,
Exeter, N.H. Cram, Goodhue, and Ferguson,
archts. [plans, elevation, section]

    Brickbuilder 23: pl 12-13
    Ja '14

---

705 Exhibition booths
W48   Aus einzelnen abteilungen-détails
  d'aménagements de pavillons. [special no. on
exhibition display].

     Das Werk
     26:Special Number
     S '39

720.54 Exhibition booths
A67   Exhibition stand for the Portuguese colonies. Vicente de Pedralva Seal de Camarra,
archt.

    L'architecture 43: 363
    September 15, 1930

Exeter (N.H.) Phillips Exeter Academy. Dormitories
 Exteriors, interiors, and details to dormitories
for Phillips Exeter Academy. Exeter, N.H.
Cram and Ferguson, archts.

    Architecture. 53:pl.101-06
    June, 1926

Exhibition booths
 Austellungsstand Kunststoffmesse in
Düsseldorf, 1959 [plans]

    Baumeister
    57:198-203 Ap 1960

720.52 Exhibition booths
A673   Exhibitors' architecture.

    Arch. review 55:222-29
    June 1924

Exeter (N.H.) Phillips Exeter Academy. Dunbar Hall
 Dunbar Hall, Exeter, N.H.
Cram, Goodhue and Ferguson, archts. No plan.

    Architectural record 29:40
    January, 1911

Exhibition booths
 Booths designed by Kurt Hoppe and Martin
Weinberg, Otto Amtsberg

    Gebrauchsgraphik 6:49-64
    April, 1929

Exhibition booths
 Some further notes on the exhibition stands

    Architects' Jour. 55:629-33
    Apr. 26, 1922.

720.5 Exeter (N.H.) Phillips Exeter academy.
A67r   Phillips Exeter hall.
   Phillips Exeter hall, Exeter, N. H. Cram,
Goodhue and Ferguson, archts. No plan.

    Arch rec. 29:40
    Ja '11

Exhibition booths
 Building exhibition, Olympia

    Archts jour 76:
    289-302; S 7, 1932
    327-31,334; S 14, 1932
    371-77; S 21, 1932
    Suppl; S 28, 1932

Exhibition booths. England
 Exhibition stands at the Building Exhibition.

    Architect (Eng.) 119: 578-581,585
    April 20, 1928

Exhibition Boats
 A travelling exposition boat, designed by
Marcel Chappey and winning Third Annual French
travelling fellowship of the American Institute of
Architects.

    Pencil points 10: 425-429
    June, 1929

720.52 Exhibition booths
B93   The building exhibition.

    Builder 130: 655-665; 713-719
    April 16, 23, 1926

Exhibition booths, England
 Stands at electrical exhibition.

    Architect. 105: pl.
    Mar. 4, 1921

Exhibition booths

   see also numbers of

 Art and Industry

720.52 Exhibition booths
A67   The exhibition stand: an architectural
  treatment.

    Architects' Jour.56: 127-8.
    Jul.26,1922.

Exhibition booths, Germany
 Exhibition booths, Germany

    Dekorative kunst 24:228-238
    August, 1921

Exhibition buildings see also Names of individual exhibition buildings, i.e.: London, Eng. Crystal palace Sacramento, Cal. State agricultural exhibit bldg. etc.	720.54 A67 Exhibition buildings Imbert,Charles Stands d'exposition (Exposition stands). L'Architecture 43: p.363-364 September 15,1930	Exhibition Bldgs., France, Paris Hall de l'Exposition du Centenaire de l' Aluminium. Tech et arch 14: 3-4 9-11 1954
Exhibition Buildings Olbrich, Josef Maria. Architektur von Olbrich. 6 vols. Serie I-III. Berlin: E. Wasmuth, (1901-13). Bd.2 Teil 2. pl. 91-97. Bd.3, pl. 1-8	720.5 A51 Exhibition buildings. Competition An exhibition center. Beaux-arts insti- tute of design competition. Amer Arch 120: 196-200 S 14 '21	Exhibition Bldgs. Germany Künstlerische Hallenbauten Wasmuths 7:109-17 Heft 3-4 1918-1919
Exhibition buildings Nestler, Paolo Ausstellungen und architektur. Bauen & Wohnen #1:1-2 Jan 1958	Exhibition bldgs., England Architectural treatment for the Fashions Fair exhibition, 1924; W. Braxton Sinclair, archt. Builder 130: 790 May 14, 1926	Exhibition bldgs., Germany Wasmuths 7:172-7 Heft 5-6 1920-21
Exhibition buildings Beaux-arts institute of design competition: An exposition building. B.A.I.D. 4:5-8 November 1927	Exhibition bldgs., England Architectural treatment of interior of Fashions Fair exhibition hall. W.B. Sinclair, archt. Architect 116:pls. October 1, 1926	Exhibition bldgs., Germany Mod. bauformen 24,heft 4:122 Apr. 1925
720.54 Exhibition buildings A67 Risler,Charles Concours de nouveau Palais des Expositions - Le concours de l'O.T.U.A. (Competitions for new exposition palace- the competition designs of the Technical Office for the Utilization of Steel.) Tournon and Chappey,winners of competition. Plans. L'Architecture 47: 161-184 May 15, 1934	Exhibition bldgs. England Modern exhibition hall Wasmuth's Monatshefte 12: 322-323 Heft 7, 1928	Exhibition bldgs., Germany Wasmuths, (heft 2) 9:69 1925
720.5 Exhibition buildings B93b Wyatt, Sir Digby Exhibition buildings. Building budget 6: 53-54 May 31, 1890	720.52 Exhibition bldgs., England. Liverpool A67 Perspective drawing of the proposed £ 330,000 exhibition hall,Liverpool. Ernest Shennan,archt. Architects' journal 78: 409 October 5,1933	Exhibition bldgs., Germany Der Bau Des Hauses Der Deutschen Funkindustrie Wasmuths 9: Heft 3; 103-19 1925
720.54 Exhibition buildings A67 Pavillon Demontable Pour Les Foires Com- merciales,1928. (Building Which Can be Taken Apart for Commercial Fairs,1928.) Le Cor- busier and Pierre Jeanneret,archts. L'Architecture Vivante: pl.28-29 1929 - Summer	720.52 Exhibition bldgs., England,Newcastle A67c Bird, E. L. The north-east coast exhibition. Architect (Lond.) 121: 635,639-647 May 17, 1929	Exhibition Bldgs. Germany. Berlin Wireless exhibition hall, Berlin; Heinrich Staumer, archt. Architect (Eng.) 119: 652 May 4, 1928

Exhibition bldgs. Germany. Essen
Exhibition Halls in Essen, Josef Rings, archt.

Wasmuth's Monatshefte 12:256-62
Heft 6, 1928

720.52 Exhibition entrances
A67   An entrance to an exhibition. Student
work at Liverpool.

Architects' journal 76: 12
July 6, 1932

720.53 Exhibition rooms
M68   Stained glass exhibition rooms

Mod. bauformen 24
heft 4:124
Ap 1925

Exhibition Buildings, Germany
Die Architektur auf der diesjahrigen
Grossen Berliner Kunstausstellung.
Von Hans Schliepmann.
Berliner architekturwelt
vol.4:115-120
Heft 4, 1901

Exhibition entrances
Grille d'entrée d'un parc des expositions.

L'Architecture 37:109
June 10, 1924

Exhibition Rooms, Denmark. Copenhagen
Exhibition Halls in Copenhagen.

Wasmuths 10: 240-1
Heft 6, 1926

Exhibition buildings. Germany
Dreigeschossige ausstellungshalle in
Düsseldorf [plan] Städtisches Hochbauamt, archt.

Baumeister
55:555-56 Ag 1956
Tafeln 54-56

Exhibition Grounds
Pearse, R. J.
The use of fair grounds as recreational centers.

Landscape architecture 16:40-44
October, 1925

720.5   Exhibition rooms, U.S. New York
A67f   The French exposition, Grand Central
Palace, New York. Howard Greenley, architect.

Arch. forum 41:;1.10-12
July 1924

Exhibition bldgs. Germany
Fritz Voggenberger, Frankfurt a.M.

Wasmuths 7:42-7
Heft 1-2
1923

Exhibition halls

see

Exhibition rooms
Exhibition buildings

Exhibition stands

see

Exhibition booths

720.54 Exhibition buildings,Germany
A67   Pavillon Démontable en Bois Pour Exposition,1929. (Exposition building in wood com-
partments,1929.) Walter Gropius and Moholy-
Nagy,archts.

L'Architecture Vivante: pl.14
1929 - Autumn

Exhibition houses

see

Model houses

Exhibitions

see also

Fairs and names of individual exhibitions, i.e.:
Glasgow, Scot. Exposition. 1938
Gothenburg, Swe. Jubilee exhibition. 1923
etc.

Exhibition Bldgs., Netherlands, Amsterdam.
Tennis und ausstellungshalle "Apollo".
Amsterdam 1933/34. Ing. A. Boeken, archt.
Plans.
Photograph and brief biographical account of
architect.
Roth, Alfred. La Nouvelle Architecture.
Erlenback, Switzerland:
Editions de Architecture, 1946.
p:157-166

720.89 exhibition planting
A67ay   Clark, W.J.
Indoor and exhibition planting

Archts' yr bk 3: 143-154
1949

720.54 Exhibitions
A 67au

L'Architecture d'aujourd
'hui 11: No. 1-2, 1940

Exhibition entrances
Beaux-arts institute of design, competition:
"The entrance to a small exposition". Awards.

B.A.I.D. 2: 25-28
March, 1926

Exhibition Rooms.

Popp, Joseph. Bruno Paul, mit
319 abbildungen. Munich: Bruckmann,
[1910-1921] p.13-16

Exhibitions
Bill, Max
Ausstellungen.

Das Werk 35: 65-71
Mr '48

790.54
A67au
Exhibitions
Tournant, Jacques
Éléments et décors de fêtes.

L'Arch d'aujourd'hui
9: 89-93
S '38

Exhibitions
Pros. J. V. Cissarz, architect

Moderne bauformen 22:213-18
July, 1923

Exhibitions, Germany
Krockow, L. von
German achievements in exhibitions.

Amer archt & bldg news 55:35-6
Ja 30, 1897

Exhibitions
McLean, R.C.
Expositions and our architectural
renaissance.

West. arch. 35:80-81
Jul. 1926

Exhibitions
Aalto, Alvar
Världsutställningarna: New York
World's Fair. The Golden Gate Exposition.

Arkitekten 113-117
1939

Exhibitions. Installation
Björklund, Eva
Mot en ny utställningsform, av Eva
Björklund, Sture Balgård och Jöran Lindvall.
[illus.]

Konstrevy
41, Häfte NR6: 195-198
1965

Exhibitions
Fairs: their lusty ancestry, their vigorous
maturity, their present indecisiveness; and what
of New York, 1939?

Architectural forum 65: front, 171-190
September 1936

Exhibitions. Bibliography
Davis, Julia Finette
International expositions, 1851-1900,
compiled by Julia Finette Davis.

American association of
architectural bibliographers
Papers.
4: [47]-130
1967

Exhibitions. Installation
Lehmann, A.
Sacred white walls.

Midwestern art reviews
II:7-8
Ja 1966

Exhibitions
The great industrial and art exhibitions of
Europe and America.

Knight, Charles. Knight's Pictorial
gallery of arts. 2 vols. London and
New York: London Printing and
Publishing Co., Ltd., n.d. :1-XL

Exhibitions. Competitions
Beaux-arts institute of design, competition:
"An exposition". Second preliminary competition
for the 19th Paris prize. Awards.

B.A.I.D. 2: 20-24
April, 1926

720.52
A67
Exhibitions, Italy, Rome. 1923
Exhibition architecture in Rome.

Architects' journal 57: 947-8,950,953,959
June 6, 1923

Exhibitions
Due Mostre d'arte alla Fondazione Cini in
San Giorgio [illus]

Arte Veneta
V. 9: 280-281, 1955

720.52
A67
Exhibitions, England. London
Exhibition of modern living at Whiteley's
Queen's Road,W. Selected and displayed by
Serge Chermayeff. Plans.

Architects' journal 78: 691-695
November 30,1933

Exhibitions. Sweden. Gothenburg

Architectural rev. 54:201-7
Dec. 1923

720.5
B93b
Exhibitions
A national system of classification of
the exhibits of a world's fair. Charts and
plans.

Building budget 6: 89-90
August 30, 1890

720.54
A67
Exhibitions, France. Paris 1923
Verrier, Jean
L'Exposition de dessins d'architecture au
Pavillon de Marsan. (The exposition of architec-
tural designs at the Pavillon de Marsan.) Musée
des Arts Decoratifs. Plans. Original designs by
French architects: Mansart, Vauban, Gabriel,
Rousseau, Mique and others.

L'architecture 36:1-12
January 10, 1923

Ryerson
Exhibitions, U. S.
Photographs (some in color) of expositions
of 1853, 1876, 1893, 1915, 1926, 1939

Life articles on art:
67-83
Mr 13, 1939

711
T75
Exhibitions
Budden,L.B.
The relation of exposition planning to civic
design.Plans of expositions in various cities in
the U.S. and Panama.

Town planning review 6: 153-165
January 1915   pls. 34-44

720.54
A67
Exhibitions, France. Rouen
Louvet, A.
Exposition of modern religious art at Rouen.

L'architecture 45: 267-282
August 15, 1932

720.5
B84
Exhibitions. United States
Githens,A.M.
Recent American group plans. pt.1,
Fairs and expositions: Alaska-Yukon-Pacific ex-
position; Pan American exposition, Buffalo; New
York state fair, Syracuse; Tennessee state fair,
Nashville; Panama exposition, San Diego.

Brickbuilder 21:267-260
October 1912

Exhibitions, U.S. Ill. Chicago

see

Chicago (Ill.) Exhibitions

Expert, Roger H.
Iglesia de Sta. Teresita del Nino Jesus en
Metz, Francia. (plan) Roger H. Expert, archt.

Arquitectura Cuba 17:13-14
Ja 1949

Exposition halls

see

Exhibition rooms
Exhibition buildings

720.3   Exits
A51   Safety exits for school buildings

American architect 123: 128-31
Jan. 31, 1923

Expo 67, Montreal

see

Montreal. World's fair, 1967

Exposition internationale des materiaux et
equipments du batiment et des travaux publics,
1955

see

Paris, Fr. Exposition. 1955

Expansible houses
Homes that grow; designed especially for
House and Garden by Leigh French, Jr.

A   House and garden 61: 64-65
January, 1932

Expo '70, Osaka, Japan

see

Osaka, Japan. World's fair, 1970

Exposition of architecture and allied arts

see

New York (N.Y.) Exposition of architecture and
allied arts. 1925.

Expansible houses
Holden, A   C
House that will expand. [plans]

Country life 39: 68-9
D 1920

Exposicion de arquitectura contemporanea mexicana.
1949

see

American institute of architects. Conventions.1949.
Exposicion de arquitectura contemporanea mexicana

Exposition of the fascist revolution

see

Rome (It.) Exposition 1933.

Expansible houses
The plan is flexible [plan] Ernst Payer,
archt.

Interiors
104; pt.1: 62
Ja 1945

Exposicion de arquitectura Mexicana. 1955
Una exposicion de arquitectura Mexicana en
Londres.

Arq. Mex. no.50
p. 115-116
Je 1955

Expositions

see

Exhibitions

Experiments.
Experiments in Architecture.

Architecture 22: 113
Jl 1910

Exposition boats

see

Exhibition boats

Express highways

see

Roads

Expert, Roger H.

see also

Paris (Fr.) Ecole nationale supérieure des beaux-
arts, bldgs.

Belgrad (Yugo) French legation

Exposition buildings

see

Exhibition buildings

Exterior stairways,

see

Stairways, Outdoor

V. 4

Eychmüller, Hans Frieder
    Geschäftsräume des S. Fischer Verlags,
Frankfurt/Main [plan] Hans Frieder Eychmüller,
archt.

        Bauen und wohnen
        64: 235-237
        Ag 1956

Eyre, Wilson, Jr.   (Card 4)

    see

Philadelphia (PA) Barring St. & 36th St.
   "   " Chestnut at 22nd St. Residence
   "   " City Trust, Safe Deposit & Surety
            Building
   "   " Cooke (Jay) House
   "   " Double House
   "   " Drexel (A.J., Jr.) Residence
   "   " Germantown Cottage

        (See Card 5)

Eyre, Wilson, 1858-1944
    Obituary

        Illinois society of
        architects bulletin
        29:10
        D 1944- Ja 1945

Eyck, Aldo van
    The Children's House, Amsterdam, Aldo van
Eyck, archt.

        Architectural design
        vol. 30: 179-180, My 1960

Eyre, Wilson, Jr.   (Card 5)

    see

Philadelphia (PA) Harrison Bros. Offices
   "   " Jayne (H. LaBarre) Residence
   "   " Kelsey Oriental Bath Co.
   "   " (Lansdown Station) PA
   "   " Leidy (Dr. Joseph) House
   "   " Mask and Wig Club
   "   " Moore (C.B.) Residence
   "   " Newhall (Charles A.) House

        (See Card 6)

    Eyre, Wilson, 1858-1944
    Wallick, Frederick
        The rational art of Wilson Eyre

        Craftsman 17: 527-551
        F '10

Eyck, Aldo van
    Kindergaten in Amsterdam (plan & section) Aldo
van Eyck, archt.

        Baumeister
        58: 538-43, Tafel 35, Ja 1961

Eyre, Wilson, Jr.   (Card 6)

    see

Philadelphia (PA) Potter (Charles A.) House
   "   " Residence
   "   " St. Anthony's Club (Entrance Detail)
   "   " Starr (Dr.) Residence
   "   " Store Building
   "   " University Club House
   "   " University of Pennsylvania
   "   " Univ. of Pennsylvania, Univ. Museum

        (See Card 7)

Eyre, Wilson, Jr.
    Receives Gold Medal at Pan-Amer. Expo.
Buffalo N.Y., 1901.

        Inland Architect
        38: 32
        Nov, 1901

Eynsham Hall
    Eynsham Hall, Oxfordshire. Messrs. Ernest
George and Yeates, Architects.

        Arch and con rep 71:320 and pl.
        My 13, 1904

Eyre, Wilson, Jr.   (Card 7)

    see

Philadelphia (PA)   Williams (John) House
   "   Wistaفs (Rodman) House
Quogue (LI)   House
Rydal Station (PA) Borie (Chas. L.) House
   "   Borie (B.) Garden Houses
Short Hills (NJ) Schultz (B. Van H.) House
Spring Lake (NJ) Rogers House

Eyre, Wilson, 1858-1944
    Residence at Philadelphia. Wilson Eyre, Jr.,
archt.

        Inland architect
        v. 18 no. 6
        pl. fol. p. 80
        Ja 1892

Eyre, Wilson, Jr.

    see

Albany (NY)   House Sketch
Ardmore (PA)   Ladd (J.B.) House
Camden (NJ)   Taylor (Dr. H. Genet) Residence
Camp Hill Station (PA) Herbertson (Craig) Residence
Detroit (MI)   Detroit Club
Huntington (LI)   Rosemary Farm
Jenkintown (PA)   Bone (Chas.) House
   "   "Fairacres"

        (See Card 2)

720.5
A67   Eyre, Wilson, 1858-1944
        From Liverpool to London. [Sketcher]

        Arch rev 4: 5-8
        Ja 1896

Eyre, Wilson, 1858-1944
    Residence of C. L. Freer, Detroit, Michigan.
Wilson Eyre, archt.

        Inland architect
        20, no. 5
        pl. fol. p.58
        D 1892

Eyre, Wilson, Jr.   (Card 2)

    see

Jenkintown (PA)   Pepper (J.W.) House
Jersey City (NJ) Bennet (H.C.) House
   "   House
Kingston (NY)   Freer (Miss.) House
Lenox (MA)   Clarke (Thomas Shields) House
   "   Residence
New York (NY)   West End Ave. and 58th St. Houses

        (See Card 3)

Eyre, Wilson, 1858-1944
    Houses by Wilson Eyre and Grosvenor Atterbury
in Forest Hills Gardens, L.I.

        House beaut 33:116, 118
        Mr 1913

Eyre, W., Jr.
    Sketch for T-Square Club
Exhibition.

        Inland Architect
        35: 4
        Feb, 1900

Eyre, Wilson, Jr.   (Card 3)

    see

Orange (NJ)   Cornell (Charles) House
Paris (FR)   Exposition 1900 House Designs
   "   Exposition 1900. U.S. Exhibit
        Palace of Mines and Metallurgy
Philadelphia (PA) Architects' Office
   "   Ashhurst (R.L.) House
   "   Borie Building
   "   Chestnut Hill (PA) architecture

        (See Card 4)

720.5
A67   Eyre, Wilson, 1858-1944 .
        New front to a banking house, Philadel-
phia. Wilson Eyre, Jr., archt. Elevation.

        Arch rev 7 (n.s.2): pl VII fol 12.
        Ja 1900

Eyre, Wilson Jr.
    Sketches of interiors, 2 Libraries and
1 dining room, and of a bench with chairs.

        Inland Archt.
        vol. 31,No.2,pl.fol.p. 20
        Mar, 1898

Eyre, Wilson
Sketch of House at "Little Orchard Farm"

Selection from Brooklyn Chapter A.I.A.
Fifth Exhibition, 1905.

Inland Archt.
46: pl.fol.p. 24
Sept, 1905

Eyre, Wilson and McIlvaine

see also

Bryn Mawr (PA)   Ellis (WM. S.) House
Philadelphia (PA) "Brookfield"
  "   "   Church of St. Giles
  "   "   University of Pa. University
                  Museum Addition
Radnor (PA)   Townsend (John Baines) House

720.5   Eyre, Wilson   1858-1944
F35   Some of his drawings & sketches

Pencil points 6:45-54 &
pl.
July 1925

Eyre, Wilson and McIlvaine

see also

Eyre, Wilson, 1858-1944

Eyre, Wilson , 1858-1944
Store alterations, Philadelphia, Pa.
Wilson Eyre, Jr., archt.

Inland Architect
v. 11 no. 6
pl. at end of vol.
My 1888

Ezekiel, Moses Jacob, 1844-1917
Soria, Regina
Moses Ezekiel's studio in Rome. [illus.]

Archives of American art
Journal
4: 6-9
Ap 1964

Eyre, Wilson
At Univ. of Penn., Phila. Photo.

Inland Architect
34: supp.p. 24
Jan, 1900

MICROFILM

Ezekiel, Moses Jacob, 1844-1917
Statue of Columbus.

in SCRAPBOOK ON
ARCHITECTURE p. 274-275
(on film)

D10.5   Eyre, Wilson, 1858-1944
C88   Wilson Eyre: a pioneer in American
domestic architecture.

Craftsman 18: 367
Je '10

720.5   Eyre, Wilson   1858-1944
A67r   Wilson Eyre: in appreciation. Photograph.

Architectural record 18: 314
October 1905

720.5   Eyre,Wilson   1858-1944
A67r   Willard,Julian
            The work of Wilson Eyre.

Architectural record 14:283-325
October 1905

F

Fabricius, Eugen, 1871-1960
Eugen Fabricius [obit.]

Arch & Wohnform
68:°22a My 1960

Façades. Cleaning

see

Cleaning of buildings

FHA

see

U.S. Federal housing Administration

ATACK
708.3 Fabricsy,G von
B81j   Das landhaus des Kardinals Triulisie am
       Salone.

       Jahrbuch der k. preussischen
       kunstsammlungen
       17:186-205
       1896

Facades, England
    Garden Front to a London Residence. Arthur J.
Yale.

    Arch. and c.reporter 84:408,2 pls.
    Dec. 23, 1910   fol p. 416

---

726   Fabbri, Egisto
L78   LaFarge, L.B.
       A contrast in romanesque. Canterbury School
Chapel, New Milford, Conn. Raphael Hume, archt.
and Church of Serravalle di Casentino, near Florence, Italy. Built from plans by Egisto Fabbri,
archt.

       Liturgical arts 1: 138-145
       October 1932

Fabro, Eduard del

see

Del Fabro, Eduard

Facades, Eng. London
    A Facade in Kingsway, London. Edwin L. Lutyens,
F.R.I.B.A., architect.

    Arch and con rep 82: 168,pl.
    S 10, 1909

790.52   Faber
B85   Harbers, Guido
       Vorstädtische kleinsiedlungen in Essen.
(Small suburban colonies in Essen.) Faber,
archt. illus. plans.

       Der Baumeister
       81: 405-17, pl.117-55
       D '55

Facades
Hager, Hellmut
    Il modello di Ludovico Rusconi Sassi del
concorso per la facciata di San Giovanni in
Laterano (1732) ed i prospetti a convessità
centrale durante la prima metà del Settecento
in Roma.   [illus.]

       Commentari
       Anno 22: 36-67
       Ja-Mr 1971

Facades (famous)

    Brochure series 4:215
    1898

Faber, Frederick E.

    Biographical Sketch

    Industrial Chicago: The
    Building Interests. 4 vols.
    Chicago: Goodspeed Pub.Co.,
    1891-(?) - Vol. 1: Pg. 626

Facades, Austria
    Some Old Austrian Facades.

    House and garden 3:pls.
    F, 1903

Façades. France. 16th cent.
Béguin, Sylvie
    L'hotel du Faur, dit Torpanne, [par] Sylvie
Béguin et Bella Bessard. [illus.]

       Revue de l'art
       no.1-2: 38-56
       1968

790.59   Faber,Oscar
A67a   New warehouse for the Southern railway
at Nine Elms. Designer and engineer:
Dr. Oscar Faber.

       Architect(Lond.)149:359-355
       March 19,1957

720.52   Facades, Brick
A67   Lloyd, Nathaniel
       The urban brick facade.

       Architects' jour. 63: 517-524
       April 7, 1926

Facades, France. 20th century.
    Robertson, Howard and Yerbury, F.R.
Modern French Facades.

    Archt 120:
       111-115; J1 27, 1928
       149-51,153; Ag 3, 1928
       188-191; Ag 10, 1928

Fabricated houses

See

Prefabricated houses

Facades, Cast iron

see

Cast iron fronts

Facades - Italian

    Amer arch & bldg. news 91: p 18
                Jan. 19 '07

Facades, Italy
Botto, Ida Maria
Proposte per la storia di una facciata.
[illus.]

Florence. Kunsthistorisches
Institut. Mitteilungen
Band 10: 128-134
My 1961-F 1963

720.5
W52   Factories
             Architects' standpoint designing indus-
             trial buildings

                         Re.t. arch. 34:80,81-84
                         ,l.
                         Aug. 1916

Factories
Factory stairs and stairways

Amer arch
117:129-134, 161-164, Ja 28,
F 4, 1920

Facades, Italy, Genoa
A Renaissance Leaning Facade at Genoa.

Arch rec 12:600-19
N, 1902

Factories.
Design and construction of industrial
premises

Architects Jour
50:802
D 31, 1919

720.5
A67a   Factories
              The Gleason works; a plant planned for
              the future.

                         Architecture 42:221-4.
                         Jul.1920.

720.52
A67ay   Facings, Building
         Howe, Jack
             The external facing of building

                         Archts' yr bk 3: 308-317
                         1947

---

ff
720.52
A67   Factories
         Goldenberg, M.
             The design and construction of modern
         industrial buildings. A comparison - old and new.

                 Architects' & builders' journal 46: 106-
                 September 5, 1917   108

720.5
A67c   Factories
             Industrial buildings. Concrete con-
         struction. Sections and plans.

                 Architectural concrete 4:17-20
                 No.3[1938]

Factories

    see also

Airplane factories
Automobile assembly plants
Cement plants
Chemical plants

Fireproof construction. Factories
Food factories
Machine shops
Mills
Potteries   (cont.)

720.5
A51   Factories
         Chapman,Howard; K.S.Timmins;
             Design of industrial buildings.

             Factory construction and equipment.

                 American architect 107: p.113-118
                 February 24, 1915   153-198,

Factories. Brill, George M. Manufacturing
     plants. Diagram. Photos. Plan.

             Inland Arch.
             52: 5-7 July 1908
             52: 18-21 Aug 1908

Factories

    see also

Textile mills

    and also names of individual factories, i.e:

Detroit, Mich. Dodge brothers factory
Kahn, Albert

720.54
A67v   Factories
             Ecole Supérieure d'art et industrie à Mos-
         cou; dessin d'une construction,1925. (Stu-
         dent work done by the Ecole Supérieure; de-
         sign of a construction,1925.)

                 L'architecture vivante : 14. pl.8-11
                 Spring 1926

---

ff
720.52   Factories
A67   Kahn, Moritz
             Modern factory buildings.

                 Architects' & builders' journal 45: 125-
                 March 7, 1917   126

720.54   Factories
A67au

                 L'Arch d'aujourd'hui
                 10: special number
                 Je '39

---

ff
720.6   Factories
R88   Buckland,H.T.
             Factory building chiefly in relation to the
         welfare of the worker.

                 R.I.B.A.journal 26: 145-153
                 May 1919

720.52   Factories.
A67   Some essentials in factory building.

                 Arch.jour.52:105-6.
                 Jul.28,1920.

Factories
Aesthetic Consideration in Factory Designs.

         Amer archt 99: 216-18
         Je 14, 1911

720.52   Factories
A67   Wallis,Thomas
             Factory planning and construction.

                 Architects' journal 77: 263-266
                 February 22, 1933

720.5   Factories.
N76   Technique structures. [drawings]

                 L'Homme et L'Arch.
                 41-48
                 My-Je '46

720.52
A67 — Factories
A Turbine manufacturing workshop.

Arch. Jour. 54: 569-70.
Nov. 9, 1921.

720.53 Factories, Czechoslovakia
M58 — Schraubenfabrik in Tyrnau (Tscaecoslowakei)
S. Theiss and Hans Jaksch, architects

Moderne bauformen 23:214
July 1924

720.52 Factories, England
B93 — Wallis, Thomas
Factories: a paper read at the R.I.B.A. meeting.

Builder 144: 320-322
February 24, 1933

720.53 Factories
W81 — Schmidt, Hans
Werke der technik und industrie im landschaft sbilde. (Technical and industrial developments in the country scene.)

Wasmuths monatshefte 14: 195-198
April 1930

Factories, England
see also

Bournville, Eng. Cadbury Bros. Factory
Brentford, Eng. Coty Factory
"   "   Firestone Factory
"   "   H.G. Products, Ltd.
"   "   Sperry's gyroscope factory
Brighton, Eng. Oppenheimer diamond factory
Brimsdown, Eng. Congoleum, Ltd.
Broadheath, Eng. Automatic Scale Co., Ltd.
Clerkenwell, Eng. Winstone house
Everton, Eng. Barker and Dobson's factory
(see card 2)

720.52 Factories, England
B93 — Factory in reinforced concrete. Wallis, Gilbert & Partners, archts.

Builder 130: 55
January 8, 1926

720.52 Factories, Austria. Linz
A67 — Cigarette factory, Linz. Austria. Dr. Peter Behrens and Alexander Popp, archts. Plan.

A   Architects' journal 77: 277-279,sup.
February 22, 1933

Factories, Eng.   (card 2)
see also

Greenford, Eng. Alladin Industries, Ltd.
Hayes, Eng. Orchestrelle Co. Factory
Hounslow, Eng. Tyre factory
Leicester, Eng. Thomas Morley and Son factory
London, Eng. Carrerras, Ltd.
"   "   Gillette Industries, Ltd. factory
"   "   Napier and Sons Works
"   "   Pyrene Factory
"   "   Solex Carburettor Factory
"   "   Staples and Co. Factory
(see card 3)

710.5 Factories, England
C85 — Welchett, F. C.
Idealism in industry.

Country life (Lond.) 65: 473-477
April 6, 1929

720.54 Factories, Belgium
A67v — Usine en Belgique. (Factory in Belgium)

L'Architecture vivante :pl. 34
Winter 1926

Factories, Eng.   (card 3)
see also

London, Eng. W. H. Smith and Son factory
Luton, Eng. Skefko ball-bearing factory
Maidstone, Eng. Tilling Stevens factory
Marfleet, Eng. W. R. Todd Factory
Nottingham, Eng. Raleigh Cycle Co. Offices
Peckham Rye, Eng. Roberts Capsule Stopper Co., Ltd.
Perivale, Eng. Hoover Factor
Silver End, Eng. Crittall Manufacturing Co.
Slough, Eng. Berlei, Ltd. factory
Southall, Eng. Daimler factories

720.52 Factories, England
A67 — Imperial typewriter co's factory. Pick, Everard, Keay & Gimson, archts.

Architects' jour. 63: 790
June 9, 1926

Factories. Building sites
Surveying a .. site
3 - Plotting

Architects' Jour. 62:771-72
Nov. 18, 1925

720.52 Factories, England.
A67c — New factory for Messrs. Burgoyne, Burbidges & Co., East Ham.   Searle and Searle, archts.

A   Architect 102: pl.fol.p.338
October 17, 1919

720.52 Factories. England
A67 — The industrial work of Wallis, Gilbert & partners.

Architects' jour. 63: 553-564
April 14, 1926

Factories. Chimneys
see
Chimneys, Factory

720.52 Factories, England
A67 — Clothing factory, designed by Hobden and Porri.

A   Architects' journal 71: 874-875
June 4, 1930

720.52 Factories. England
A57 — Manufacturing premises, Birmingham. Harvey & Wicks, architects

Architects' journal 57:397
March 21, 1923

Ryerson
706.57 Factories, Czechoslovakia
V99 — Factory for articles made of India rubber
A.Korn, archt. No plan.

A   Volnésměry 29: 20-21,24
No. 1, 1931

720.52 Factories, England.
B93 — Electric apparatus factory.

Builder 121:42 & pl.
Jul 8, 1921.

720.52 Factories. England
B93 — Model factory buildings and out-buildings

Builder 124: 274 & pl
Feb. 16, 1923

720.52 A67 Factories, England. New Multi-storey building for Messrs. G. A. Vanderbilt & Co. Arch. Jour. 54: 720-3. Dec. 14, 1921.	720.52 B93 Factories, England. Bushey A factory at Bushey, Watford. H.Guy Hall, archt. Plan. Builder 142: 227 January 29, 1932	ff 720.52 A67 Factories, England. Manchester Wartime factory construction - Engineering shops, Trafford Park, Manchester. Architects' & builders' journal 47: 105- March 6, 1918 105
720.52 B93 Factories. England. New Reinforced concrete factory. Builder. 120: 413-4. Apr. 1, 1921	720.52 A67 Factories, England. Croydon Factory at Croydon. T.Graham Crump, archt. Plan. Architects' journal 78: 458-459 October 12, 1933	720.52 A67c Factories, England. Middlesex The Firestone Tyre Factory. Architect (Lond.) 121: 29-33 January 4, 1929
720.52 B93 Factories. England. Reinforced concrete factory construction. Builder 118:88. Jan.16, 1920.	720.52 A67 Factories, England. Ellesmere Port Thesis design for "Tobacco Factory, Elles- mere Port," School of Architecture, Liverpool. Design by H.F. Vincent. A Architects' journal 78: (117 pl.) July 27, 1933	720.52 A67 Factories, England. Norwich Shoe factory at Norwich. A.F.Scott & sons, AA.R.I.B.A., archts. A Architects' journal 62: 375-83 September 9, 1925
720.52 A674 Factories, England Special number on factory planning and examples in England. Architecture (Lond.) 7: spec. no. May-June 1929	720.52 A67 Factories, England. Enfield A factory in steel at Enfield: by Donald Hamilton. Architects' journal 76: 673 November 23, 1932	720.52 A67 Factories, England. Nottingham Factory at Nottingham. F.A.Broadhead, archt. Plan. Architects' journal 78: 490-491 October 12, 1933
720.52 A67e Factories, England Some modern factories: facades. Architect 119: 961-965 June 29, 1928	720.52 B93 Factories, England. Garston Match factory, Garston, near Liverpool. Mewes and Davis, archts. Builder 117: pl.fol.p.36 July 11, 1919	720.52 A67 Factories, England. Peckham Rye Factory at Peckham Rye. Wallis, Gilbert and Partners, archts. Plans. Architects' journal 78: 771 A December 14, 1933
710.5 C85 Adam Factories, , England. A 300 Year old factory, the home of Wilton carpets. No plan. Country life (Lond.) 78: 13-19 July 6, 1935	720.52 B93 Factories, England. Kettering Boot factory, Kettering; R.J.Williams, archts. A Builder 130: 77 January 8, 1926	720.52 B93 Factories, England. Perivale New factory, Perivale, England. Wallis, Gilbert and Partners, archts. Builder 142: 386, 389-391 A February 26, 1932
720.5 A51 Factories. England. Brantham Factory design in England. Brantham. Amer.arch. 117:116 & pl. Jan.28, 1920.	720.52 A67e Factories. England , London New factory, Wood Green, London. P.J.Westwood & Emberton, architects Architect 109:250 & 4 pl. April 13, 1923	720.52 B93 Factories, England. Stepney Photograph of new business premises, Turner Street, Stepney, E., for gown manufac- turing and showrooms. H.Victor Kerr, archt. Plan. Builder 145: 7, 22 July 7, 1933

720.52 A87e Factories, England. Welwyn Garden City. Design for factory at Welwyn Garden City. Louis de Soissons, archt. Architect 116: 103-05 July 23, 1926	Factories, France. Puteaux Usine de parfums, à Puteaux (Seine) Perfumes factory at Puteaux, (Seine). R. Nicolas, archt. Plan. Encyclopedie de l'architecture; constructions modernes. 12 vols. Paris: Albert Morancé, 1928-39. 4:no.4 pl. 91-95	**720.53 M68** Factories, Germany Entwurf architekt Philipp Schäfer, Hamburg Verwaltungsgebäude der Gebr.Schöndorff A. G.,Düsseldorf.Ausführung Gebr.Schöndorff A.G.,Dusseldorf A Moderne bauformen 22:60-1 Feb. 1923
710.5 C85 Factories, England. Wilton Adam A 300 year old factory, the home of Wilton carpets. No plan. Country life (London) 78:18-19 July 6, 1935	Factories, Germany see also Frankfort am Main, Ger. H. Fuld & co. telephon-fabrik Essen, Ger. Siemens haus	**720.53 B35** Factories, Germany Eine fabrikerweiterung. (A factory extension for Paul Jenisch.) Naidla,archt. Plan. Der Baumeister 31: 88 March 1933
Factories,Fires and Fire Prevention Correspondence: E. V. Johnson re: Factory Construction (Use of hollow tile as fireproofing). Inland Architect 45: 30-1 Apr, 1905	Factories. Germany Wasmuths 5:131-89 1920	**720.53 W31** Factories. Germany Industrial plant. E.H. Richard Schmidt,archt Wasmuths 11: 98 Heft 2, 1927
Factories. Fires and fire prevention Wentworth, F.H. Factories and their fire protection. Architectural record 27: 218-226, Mr 1910	Factories, Germany Wasmuths, (heft 7-8) 7:207 1923	**720.53 W31** Factories,Germany Koksseparatiohsanlage. (Coke-separation plant.) Curt von Brocke,archt. Wasmuths monatshefte 13: 135-136 March 1929
Factories, France see also Paris, Fr. Meccano factory	**720.53 W31** Factories, Germany Arteiten von Hans Kiesinger und Franz Münerfeld Wasmuths 9: Heft 7; 267-78 1925	Factories, Germany Modern German factory, designed by Emil Fahrenkamp, archt. Moderne bauformen 27: 26-31 January, 1928
705.4 A79a Factories,France Usine du "Jouet de France", Ile de Puteaux. Plan. Section. Les arts francais 20:159-162 August 1918	Factories. Germany Burohausprojekt an der königstrasse in Stuttgart Wasmuths 7:146 Heft 5-6, 1923	**720.53 W31** Factories. Germany New industrial plant. Erwin von Quittner, archt. Wasmuths 11: 91-4 Heft 2, 1927
720.53 W31 Factories,France. Mentataire Dormoy,Marie Neue bauten von A.und G.Perret,Paris. (New buildings in France by A.and G.Perret,archts.) Factory in Mentaire. No plan. Wasmuths monatshefte 13: 193 May 1929 A	**720.53 W31** Factories, Germany Electric apparatus and radios. Wasmuths 10: 129-133 Heft 4, 1926	**720.53 M58** Factories. Germany Walter Gropius, Weimar. Mitarbeiter Adolf Meyer. Schuhfabrik Alfeld Wasmuths 7:48-50 Heft 1-2, 1923

720.53 W31 **Factories, Germany** Work by Curt von Brocke. Wasmuths 10: 315-317 Heft 8, 1926	720.53 W31 **Factories, Germany. Dortmund-Huckarde** Von Stegmann, Helmuth Industriebauten der Vereinigten Stahlworks. (Buildings of the United Steel industry, Dortmund-Eving, Dortmund-Huckarde.) Helmuth von Stegmann, archt. Wasmuths monatshefte 13: 49-57 A February 1929	720.53 M68 **Factories. Germany. Hamburg** Schröder, Dr. Hans Hamburger architekten. Plans. Moderne bauformen 23:1-8 Jan. 1924
720.53 M68 **Factories, Germany** Working drawings of new factory at Helmet Hill. Moderne bauformen 24: 206-8 June 1925	**Factories, Germany. Frankfort-on-the-Main** see also Frankfort-on-the-Main I.G. Farben Administration building	720.53 W31 **Factories, Germany. Heidelberg** Nathan, Fritz Ein fabrikbau. (a factory building: illustrations and plans of a cigar factory in Heidelberg.) Fritz Nathan, archt. a Wasmuths monatshefte 15: 109-112 March 1931
Factories, Germany. Alfeld See Alfeld. Faguswerke	720.53 Br5 **Factories, Germany. Frankfort-on-the-Main.** Telephon-fabrik H. Fuld & Co. Wettbewerb Frankfurt a. Main. (Telephone-factory H. Fuld and Company competition, Frankfurt a. Main.) Example of factory organization and city planning possibilities. Der Baumeister 28: 129-140 April 1930	790.53 M69 **Factories, Germany. Kempten** Kästner, Dr. Wm. Furniture factory - Zu den arbeiten der architekten L. Heydecker. A Moderne bauformen 23: 129-140 May 1924
Factories, Germany. Berlin Dépôt Central des Machines Singer à Berlin. (Central office of Singer Machines at Berlin.) Zerbe and Harder, archts. No plan. Encyclopedie de l'architecture; constructions modernes. 12 vols. Paris: Albert Morancé, 1928-39 5:pl. 25(Number 1)	720.54 A67v **Factories, Germany. Frankfort-on-the-Main.** Usine Fuld, à Francfort-sur-Mein, 1929. (Factory at Franckfort-on-the-Main, 1929) Marcel Breuer, Hassenpflug and Samueli, archts. L'Architecture vivante: p.34 A Autumn-winter, 1931	720.54 A67v **Factories, Germany. Luckenwalde** Usine à Luckenwalde, Allemagne, 1922. (Factory at Luckenwalde, Germany, 1922.) Erich Mendelsohn, archt. L'architecture vivante : 14,17,19, pl. A Spring 1926 22-25
720.54 A67v **Factories, Germany. Berlin** Fabrique d'outils, à Berlin, 1923. (Tools factory at Berlin, 1923.) Designs by Hans et Wassili Luckhardt and by Max Taut. A L'Architecture vivante :pl.43 Winter 1926	720.53 W31 **Factories, Germany. Gelsenkirchen** Väth, Hans Neuere bauten der Mannesmannröhren-Werke. (New buildings of the Mannesmannröhren Factory.) Hans Väth, archt. Plans. Wasmuths monatshefte 15: 390-394 September 1931	720.53 W31 **Factories, Germany. Mannheim** Die lebendige stadt Mannheim. (The living city, Mannheim.) Oil tanks; closing apparatus for water supply; pressure lye containers of the celluloid factory, Waldhof. Wasmuths monatshefte 14: 356-357 August 1930
720.54 A67v **Factories, Germany. Berlin** Fabrique, 1913 à Berlin, Allemagne. (Factory, 1913, at Berlin, Germany.) Walter Gropius, archt. Plans. L'architecture vivante : 19 A Spring 1927	720.53 W31 **Factories, Germany. Grossaubeim** Ochs, K. W. Fabrikbauten. (Factory buildings.) Karl Wilhelm Ochs, archt. Plans. Wasmuths monatshefte 14: 249-255 A June 1930	790.53 W31 **Factories, Germany. Oberstein on the Nahe** Ein fabrikbau von Paul Pott, Köln. (A factory building in Oberstein on the Nahe river.) Paul Pott, archt. Plans. Wasmuths monatshefte 14: 256 A June 1930
720.53 W31 **Factories. Germany. Berlin** Industrial plant at Charlottenburg, Germany. Hans Hertlein, archt. Wasmuths 11: 94-7 Heft 2, 1927	720.52 A67 **Factories. Germany. Hamburg** Cigarette factory, Hamburg; perfume factory, Berlin. Fritz Hoger, archt. A Architects' journal 74: 99 July 22, 1931	720.53 W31 **Factories, Germany. Stuttgart** Zechlin, H. J. Neubauten der Boschwerke in Stuttgart. (New buildings of the Bosch factory in Stuttgart.) Hans Hertlein, archt. Plans. Wasmuths monatshefte 13: 350-352 A August 1929

720.54
A67v
Factories, Italy

Usine en Italie. (Factory in Italy)

L'Architecture vivante :pl. 54
Winter 1926

Factories. Lighting
Dodington, E. L.
Natural and artificial lighting of
industrial plants. Bibliography.

Royal arch'l institute of Canada
Jour 23: 26-29
F '46

---

ff
720.52
A67
Factories, Munition

A guncotton factory. Plan. Sections.

Arch.jour.51:153-7.Feb.4,
1920.

720.54
A67au
Factories. Lighting
L'Éclairage des Locaux industriels.

L'Arch d'aujourd'hui
10: 80-82
Je '39

Factories. Lighting
Night-lighting the factory (3 parts) Table

American architect 113:835-842;871-875
June 19; 26, 1918   114:59-66
Jl 10, 1918

---

ff
720.5P
A67
Factories, Munitions, England
Munitions factory. Buckland, Haywood and
Farmer, archts. Plans.

A   Architects' and builders' journal 45: 75-
February 7, 1917   77

Factories, Lighting
Electricity. Factory lighting

Architect 102: 280
Nov. 7, 1919.

720.5
A67f
Factories. Lighting
Fogg, William
Natural lighting of industrial buildings.

Arch forum 39:117-121
S '23

720.53
B35
Factories,Netherlands. Rotterdam
Neue fabrikbauten in Holland und Schweden.
(New factory buildings in Holland and Sweden)
Tobacco factory "Van Nelle",Rotterdam.
H.A.Bruckmann,and V.D.Vlugt,archts.
Bread factory in Sweden. Kontoret,archt.
Plans.

Der Baumeister 28: 326-327
August 1930

Factories. Lighting.
Gooch, John W.
Facts on industrial daylighting.

RAIC jrl 16:201
S 1939

Factories. Lighting
North light roofs.

Arch. jour. 51: 297-9.
Mar. 3, 1920.

705.37
V92
Factories,Netherlands. Rotterdam
Továrna Van Nelle v Rotterdamu. (Les
Usines Van Nelle.) J.A.Brinkman and L.C.
Van der Vlugt, archts.

Volné Směry 29: 40-46
No. 2, 1931

Factories. Lighting
Saxer, Hans
Künstliche beleuchtung in industriebauten
[plan & sections]

Bauen & Wohnen
#5:157-60 My 1957

Factories, Munitions

Archt's jour 45: pl for
Apr. 4, 1917

720.5
A67a
Factories,Pharmaceutical,U.S.Quincy.
Monroe Drug Co., Lockwood, Greene, &
Co., Inc., architects and engineers

A   Architecture 51:pl. 13-14
Jan. 1925

Factories. Lighting
Lighting in factories and workshops.

Arch. Jour. 54: 221-2.
August 24, 1921.

Factories, Munition

Archt's jour. 46:42
July 25, 1917

720.5
A51
Factories, Piano
Building for Baldwin Piano Mfg. Co.,
Cincinnati, Ohio. Lockwood, Greene & Co.,
architects.

A   American architect 123: 2 pl.
January 17, 1923

Factories. Lighting
Lighting in factories and workshops.

Architect 106:164-5.
Sept. 16, 1921

---

ff
720.5
A67b
Factories, Munitions
Starrett, Theodore
Building the Remington Arms plant.

Architect and builder 48: 37-47
March 1916

720.53
W31
Factories, Poland. Warsaw
Factory at Warsaw, Poland. Jankowski & Lil-
pop, archts.

Wasmuths 11: 211
Heft 5, 1927

705.87 V92 — Burnham Library Factories, Rubber Factory for articles made of India rubber. A.Korn,archt. No plan. Volné směry 29: 20-21,24 No.1, 1931	Factories, Sugar Planning of a beet sugar factory RIBA jour. 23:161-167 Mar. 18, 1916	720.52 A67 Factories, Tobacco, Germany. Hamburg Cigarette factory, Hamburg; perfume factory, Berlin. Fritz Hoger, archt. A Architects' journal 74: 99 July 29, 1931
720.54 A67v Factories,Russia Projet de filature à Ivanovo-Voxniessenks. (Spinning factory project at Ivanovo-Voxniessenks.) G.B.and M.B.Barchine,archts. plan. L'architecture vivante : pl.22 Spring 1927	720.53 B35 Factories,Sweden Neue fabrikbauten in Holland und Schweden. (New factory buildings in Holland and Sweden) Tobacco factory "Van Nelle",Rotterdam. H.A.Bruckmann and V.D.Vlu*t,archts. Bread factory in Sweden. Kontoret,archt. Plans. Der Baumeister 28: 398 August 1930	720.53 N31 Factories, Tobacco, Germany.Heidelberg Nathan,Fritz Ein fabrikbau.(A factory building: illustrations and plans of a cigar factory in Heidelberg) Fritz Nathan, archt. A Wasmuths monatshefte 15: 109-112 March 1931
720.54 A67v Factories, Russia. Moscow Maison centrale du textile, à Moscou, 1925. (Central textile office at Moscow,1925, 1926) Designs by Guinsbourg, archt. and by Golossof and Oulinits. A L'Architecture vivante :pl.40-41 Winter 1926	720.53 B35 Factories,Sweden Schwedische industrie bauten aus "Byggmästaren. (Swedish industrial buildings.) Der Baumeister 28: 164 April 1930	720.5 A51 Factories, Tobacco, U.S. Peoria Lewis Cigar Co., Peoria, Ill. Hewitt and Emerson, archts. A American architect 122: pl.fol.p.484 November 22, 1922
720.54 A67v Factories, Russia. Moscow Maison du textile à Moscou. (Textile factory at Moscow) Kokorine, architect. No plan. Tour pour l'utilisation des lessives dans une fabrique de produits chimiques, à Moscou, 1923. (Tower for the utilisation of lye washing in a chemical fabrics factory at Moscow, 1923) Ladowski, archt. No plan. A L'Architecture vivante :pl.27 Winter 1926	Factories, Tobacco Box, C.W. Carreras' new tobacco factory. M.E. and O.H. Collins, archts. Archt's jour 67: 729-33; My 23, 1928 761-65; " 30, " 799-801;Je 6, 1928 915-19; " 27, "	Factories, United States see also names of individual factories, i.e.: Chicago, Ill. Kuppenheimer B and Co. Bldg. Cleveland, O. Richman Bros. Co. factory
720.53 N31 Factories, Russia. Moscow. Factories in Moscow. Wasmuths 10: 331-333 Heft 8, 1926	720.52 A67 Factories,Tobacco,Austria.Linz Cigarette factory,Linz,Austria. Dr.Peter Behrens and Alexander Popp,archts. Plan. A Architects' journal 77: 277-279,supp. February 22, 1933	720.5 A67f Factories. U.S. Architectural forum 39:83-151 Sept. 1923
720.6 R882 Factories. Sanitation Gibson, C. Grant Personal service facilities for industrial employees. Bibliography. Royal arch. institute of Canada. Journal: 20:74-77 My '43	720.52 A67 Factories, Tobacco,England.Ellesmere Port Thesis design for "Tobacco Factory,Ellesmere Port," School of Architecture,Liverpool. Design by H.F. Vincent. Architects' journal 78:pl.117 July 27,1933	720.5 A67r Factories. U. S. American Chicle Co's factory. Arch. Rec. 48:553-6. Dec. 1920.
720.52 A67 Factories. Shoe,England.Norwich Shoe factory at Norwich A.V. Scott & sons,AA.R.I.B.A., archts. A Architects' Jour. 62: 375-88 Sept. 9, 1925	720.52 B95 Factories, Tobacco, England. London New factory for Carreras, Hampstead Road N.W., M. E. & O. H. Collins, archts. A Builder 135: 807-810 November 16, 1928	720.5 A67a Factories, U.S. Architectural expression in a modern piano factory Lockwood, Greene & Co., arch. Architecture 50:257-8 July, 1924

720.5 A67a — Factories, U.S., Green, James M. Jr. Design &industrials. Planning for their economical and efficient operation. Architecture 53: 35-42 February 1926	720.5 A67a Factories, U.S. Monroe Drug Co., Lockwood, Greene & Co., Inc., architects and engineers. A Architecture 51: pl.17-14 January 1925	720.5 A67f Factories, U.S. Mich., Detroit Precision Spring Corporation, and the Par tool Machine Company, Detroit, Michigan. Architectural forum 66: 185 March 1937
Factories, United States Tracy, Everts The growth and development of modern manufacturing buildings. Frohne, H.W., factory and warehouse. Plates and plans. American architect 101: 261-264;273-83, June 19, 1912 pl.fol.284	720.5 A67f Factories, United States Photographs and plans of various factory buildings in the United States. Architectural forum 31 pls.10-16 July 1919	720.5 A67f Factories, U.S., Wis., Milwaukee Ice cream factory and sales space, Mil-waukee, Wisconsin. Grassold and Johnson, architects. Plan. A Architectural forum 65: 344 October 1936
Factories, U.S. Gurney Electric Elevator Co. Hickok Mfg. Co. Knabe Piano Co., etc. Amer. arch. 109:pl.2107 May 10, 1916	720.52 A67 Factories, United States Wallis, D. T. Single-story factory roofs of America. Architects' journal 68: 269-272 August 22, 1928	Factory Entrances Gardiner, F.M. Factory entrances. American architect 111:117-120,123 February 21, 1917
720.55 W31 Factories, U.S., Iron work factory in St. Charles. Wasmuth's Monatshefte 12: 36 Heft 1, 1928	720.5 A51 Factories, United States Dolke,R.F.Jr.; F.M.Gardiner; Some essentials in the construction of an industrial building. Factory entrances - The architectural oppor-tunities offered in the design of entrances to factories and similar buildings. American architect 111:Pt.1:111-116 February 21,1917. 117-119,173 pls.fol.p.178	Factory fires see Factories. Fires and fire prevention
720.5 A67 Factories, U.S. Wallis, Frank E. Is American architecture a live art ? Arch rev 20 (n.s.7): 83-88 O '15	Factories, U.S. Illinois. Chicago see Chicago (Ill.) Factories	Fadigati, Vasco see Rome, It. Stazione di Termini. Fabbricato viaggiatori
720.5 A67b Factories, U.S. Manufacturing building for the Baldwin Piano Co. Arch. & building 53:72 & pl. 138-40. Sept. 1921.	ff 720.52 A67 Factories, U.S., Mich., Bay City. Perkins, N.R. Modern factory buildings - Industrial works, Bay City, Michigan. Architects' & builders' journal 46: 17-19 July 11, 1917	MICROFILM Faelten, Otto, 1884-1945 obituary notice 710
ff 720.5 A67a Factories , U.S. Briggs, W.R. Modern American factories. Architecture 38: 231-234 September 1918	ff 720.5 W52 Factories, U.S. Mich., Detroit Factory architecture in Detroit. Western architect 24: 158-159 October 1916	Faenza, It. Cathedral see Faenza, It. San Pietro

Faenza, It. Cattedrale
 	
see
 	
Faenza, It. San Pietro
	Fagiuoli, Ettore, 1884 -
	  Solarium - Villa "Girasole", a Marcellise
	(Italie). Plan. A. Invernizzi, ing. et E.
	Fagiuoli, archt.
	
	      Encyclopedie de l'architecture;
	      constructions modernes. 12 vols.
	      Paris: Albert Morancé, 1928-39.
	      9:pls.81-84
		Fahrenkamp, Emil 1885-1966
		
		  see also
		
		Berlin (Ger.) Platz der Republik (Comp.)
		Bochum (Ger.) Parkhotel Haus Rechen
		Düsseldorf (Ger.) Evangelische kirche
		   " " Michel dep't. store
		   " " Palast hotel
		   " " Palast hotel. Bridenbacher hof.
		Duisberg (Ger.) Bahnhofsvorplatzen
		Hamburg (Ger.) K (Dr.) house

Faenza, It. Duomo
 	
see
 	
Faenza, It. San Pietro
	Faglia, Vittorio
	  Mobelzentrum in Lissone [plans] Vittorio
	Faglia & Gualtiero Galmarini, archts.
	Entwurf 1955, gebaut 1957/58.
	
	      Bauen & Wohnen
	      14:62-64 F 1960
		720.53
		W31
		  Fahrenkamp,Emil 1885-1966
		    Der Berliner Platz der Republik. (The Ber-
		liner Plaza of the Republic.) Competition for
		planning of Plaza in front of Imperial build-
		ing. Plans by Peter Behrens,Emil Fahrenkamp
		and other archts.
		
		      Wasmuths monatshefte 14: 51-56
		      January 1930

Faenza, It. San Pietro
Grigioni, Carlo
Documents concerning the Duomo of Faenza
 	
    L'Arte 26:161-174
    July-August, 1923
	Fagnano Olona, Italy. Sant'Anna (chapel)
	Perer, Maria Luisa Gatti
	  Dionigi Maria Ferrari - Oratorio di S. Anna,
	Fagnano Olona - 1762. [illus.]
	
	    Arte lombarda
	    v.12,11 95-99
	    1967
		D10.5
		D48
		  Fahrenkamp, Emil, 1885 - 1966
		  Kraft, L.
		    Entwürfe von E. Fahrenkamp
		
		      Deutsche kunst und
		      dekoration 44: 143-153
		      Je '19

Faesulae
 	
see
 	
Fiesole, It.
	Fagnoni, Rafaello
	
	see
	
	Florence (It.) Scuola di Applicazione Aeronautica
		705.942
		W46
		  Fahrenkamp,Emil 1885-1966
		  Lauweriks,Jan
		    Fahrenkamp: special number on his work.
		  (Text in Dutch.)
		
		      Wendingen 12: 2-18
		      No.10, 1931

Fagan & McLeod
  2-story dwelling on Portland Ave., Minneapolis
Minn.
 	
    Building budget
    3: 4 in supp.
    My 31, 1887
	Faguswerke, Alfeld
	
	see
	
	Alfeld, Faguswerke
		Fahrenkamp, Emil, 1885-1966
		  Kunz, Fritz
		The Kurhotel on Mount Verità in Ascona.
		Emil Fahrenkamp, archt.
		
		    Moderne bauformen 29:349-355,adv.161
		    August, 1930

Fagin building, St. Louis, Mo.
 	
see
 	
St. Louis (Mo.) Fagin building
	Fahnestock, L.W.
	  Member of firms:
	    Fahnestock and Robinson
	    Dittoe, Fahnestock and Ferber
		Fahrenkamp, Emil 1885-1966
		  Lill, Georg
		On modern church architecture. Mary's Church in
		Mulheim. E. Fahrenkamp, arch.
		
		    Die christliche kunst 25:353-356,380
		    September, 1929

Fagioli, Ettore
 	
see
 	
Fagiuoli, Ettore, 1884-
	Fahrenkamp, Emil
	
	see also
	
	Grund and Fahrenkamp
		Fahrenkamp, Emil, 1885-1966
		  Die neuesten bauten von Emil Fahrenkamp.
		(The latest buildings by Emil Fahrenkamp.)
		Plans. Insurance Company in Berlin. Emil
		Fahrenkamp, archt.
		
		    Wasmuths monatshefte 15: 147-148
		    April, 1931

720.52 A67c — Fahrenkamp, Emil 1885-1966 "Shell House," Berlin. Professor Fahrenkamp, archt. Architect (Lond.) 131: 155 August 5, 1932	D10.5 D48 — Fahrenkamp, Ernst Fahrenkamp, E. Country house in Ascona Deutsche kunst und dekoration 64:80-83 April 1929	Fair grounds see Exhibition grounds
720.52 A67 — Fahrenkamp, Emil 1885-1966 The Shell-Mex Building, Berlin. Designed by Emil Fahrenkamp. Architects' journal 77: 18-19 January 4,1933	Fahy's building. New York (city) see New York (city) Fahy's building	Fair Oaks (Cal.) Bramhall (Frank J.) house House for Frank J. Bramhall, Fair Oaks, Cal. C. F. Hogeboom, Jr., archt. Inl archt 33:pl.fol.p.44 Je 1899
720.53 W31 — Fahrenkamp, Emil 1885-1966 Some modern work of Emil Fahrenkamp in Nuremburg,Stuttgart and Dusseldorf and other cities. Wasmuths 9: 1-19 Heft 1, 1925	Faidy, Abel see also Chicago (Ill.) Herman Nelson Corporation. Show room.	Fair store, Chicago see Chicago, Ill. Fair store
720.53 M68 — Fahrenkamp,Emil 1885-1966 Volter,Ernst Vom bauen in Berlin. (About building in Berlin.) Residence buildings by Wilhelm Keller and Rudolf Prömmel,archts. Plans. Domestic work by Emil Fahrenkamp and others. Moderne bauformen 26: 219 June 1927	720.5 A67f — Faidy,Abel Hedrich-Blessing studio,Chicago.Abel Faidy,architectural designer.Plans Architectural forum 65: 21-28 July 1936	720.5 F29- — Fairbanks(Alaska)Architecture Collier, W. N. Inspection trip to Fairbanks, Alaska...Final inspection of the Federal building before its acceptance. Federal Architect 5:16-18 July 1934
Fahrenkamp, Emil 1885-1966 Wenhold house, Bremen. E. Fahrenkamp, architect Dekorative kunst 32:17-19 October 1928	720.5 A67f — Faidy,Abel Hedrich-Blessing studio,Chicago,Ill. Winner,Pittsburgh glass institute competition. Abel Faidy,designer. Architectural forum 67:80-81 July 1937	Fairbanks, Alaska. Federal building New federal building, Fairbanks, Alaska Architectural concrete 1:21-22 No. 1, 1935
720.53 M68 — Fahrenkamp, Emil 1885-1966 Work of the atelier of Emil Fahrenkamp. Moderne bauformen 27: spec. no. January 1928	720.5 A67f — Faile, E H Apartments.77th Street and 3rd avenue, New York City. E.H.Faile, engineer. Plan Architectural forum 67:510-511 December 1937	Fairbanks, C.W. house, Indianapolis see Indianapolis, Ind. Fairbanks (C.W.) house
720.53 W31 — Fahrenkamp, Emil and Deneke, Albert Competition drawing for the Palace of the Society of Nations at Geneva. Wasmuths 11: 455 Heft 11, 1927	Failures, Building see Building failures	Fairbanks, Douglas house see Beverly Hills, Cal. "Pickfair"

Fairbanks, Greenleaf and co., Chicago

see

Chicago (Ill.) Fairbanks, Greenleaf & co.

"Fairfield"

see

Morristown (N.J.). Waterbury (John I.) house

720.5
A51

Fairfield (Conn.) St. Michael's P.E. church
St. Michael's P.E. (Italian) church, Fair-
field, Conn.
Edward B. Caldwell, Jr., architect

Amer. arch. 126:643-644
Dec. 31, 1924

Fairbanks, Nathaniel K., house (ca. 1890),
Chicago

see

Chicago, Ill. Fairbank, Nathaniel K., house
(ca. 1890)

Fairfield, Conn. Allis (Mary) house

see

Fairfield, Conn. Ogden (David) house

710.5
H84

Fairfield (Conn.) Van Kirk (William) house
A Connecticut version of the Early
American farmhouse. Residence of William
Van Kirk at Fairfield, Conn. Walter Bradnee
Kirby, archt.

House and garden 57: 98-99
March 1930

Fairbanks-Morse building, Chicago

see

Chicago, Ill. Harvester building (1907)

Fairfield, Conn. Auchincloss (H.D.) house
Country house of Mrs. Hugh D. Auchincloss,
Fairfield, Conn. Roger H. Bullard, archt.

House and Garden
48: 73-5
J1 1925

Fairfield, Ia. Clarke, J. F., house
... a tendency to break with the manner of
the past. [illus. and plan] Barry Byrne, architect.

Western architect
33:31 and plates 5-10
Mar. 1924

Fairclough, Stanley.D.,   -1950
Obituary

Illinois society of
Architects bulletin
34-35: ?
Nov. 1949- Oct. 1950

Fairfield (Conn.) Auchincloss (H.D.) house
House of Mrs. Hugh D. Auchincloss, Fairfield,
Conn. Roger H. Bullard, archt.

Architectural forum 51:141-155
August, 1929

Fairfield, Ia. Clarke, J. F., house
... Byrne breaking away from Wright. [illus.,
plan] Barry Byrne, architect

Prairie School review
III: 1,2,13,16
Fourth Quarter 1966

720.5
A75

Fairfax. County court house
Fairfax county court house, Fairfax,
Virginia.

Monograph series 16: pl.181
Number 6, 1930

720.5
A67f

Fairfield (Conn.) Burr (Thaddeus) house
Major, Howard
The Thaddeus Burr house, Fairfield, Connecti-
cut, 1790. A Greek revival house. No plan.

Architectural forum 40: 49
February 1924

Fairford (Eng.) Burdocks
"Burdocks," Fairford, Gloucestershire.
E. Guy Dawber, archt.

Builder 101:12, pl.fol.p.30
July 7, 1911

A

Fairfax County (Va.) Manour house farm

See

Mount Vernon (Va.) Mansion.

710.5
C855

Fairfield (Conn.) Burr (Thaddeus) house
The Thaddeus Burr house (1790), Fairfield,
Connecticut. One of first instances of Greek
revival. No plan.

Country life 47: 41
February 1925

Fairford, Eng. Churches
Meteyard, H.G.
Fairford Church and its windows.

Architectural review 13:133-135
October, 1906

Fairfax County (Va.) Washington (George) house

See

Mount Vernon (Va.) Mansion

Fairfield, Conn. Ogden (David) house
Ormsbee, T.H.
Rescuing a fine old house

American collector
4:1, 4-5
Ag 22, 1935

779
L84

Fairford (Eng.) S. Mary the Virgin
Meas. drawings by J. H. Bryan & A.
Reeve; J. Gillespie, and J. Stewart. Church,
stall and screen.

Lond. arch. Assoc. sketch book
1872-3_____pl.15
1899_____pl.f7
1904 --   --pls. 5-8

Fairgrounds see Exhibition grounds	Fairhurst, Harry S. and Son see Manchester (Eng.) Rylands and sons	Fairmount park art building, Philadelphia see Philadelphia, Pa. Fairmount park art building
Fairhaven (Mass.) Millicent library Millicent Library, Fairhaven, Mass. Charles Brigham, archt. Inl archt 35:pl.fol.p52 Jl 1899	Fairley, J. Graham see Bathgate (Eng.) St. David's church Cooperative society, ltd.	Fairmount parkway See Philadelphia.Fairmount parkway
Fairhaven (Mass.) Rogers (H.H.) house Residence for H.H. Rogers, Fairhaven, Mass. Charles Brigham archt. Inl archt 34:pls.fol.p.74 O 1899	Fairlie, Reginald Francis Joseph, 1883-1952 see Rothesay, Eng. St. Andres' church and house	Fairmont (West VA.,) Marion County Courthouse Yost and Packard, Archts. Inland Archt. vol.35,No.6,pl.fol.p. 52 Jul, 1900
720.5 A67r Fairhaven (Mass.) Rogers (H.H.) house Interiors in the house of H.H.Rogers, Fairhaven,Mass. Architectural record 16:328,366 October 1904	Fairmount College. Wichita, Kan. see Wichita (Kan.) Fairmount College	Fairs, see also Exhibitions Festivals
Fairhaven (Mass.) Rogers (H.H.) house. Stable Stable for H. H. Rogers, Fairhaven, Mass. Charles Brigham archt. Inl archt 34:pl.fol.p.74 O 1899	710.5 C855 Fairmont (Ill.) Olin (J.M.) house Estate of John M.Olin,at Fairmont,Alton, Ill. C.H.Walcott,archt. Country life(U.S.)68:20-23 August 1935	720.52 B93 Fairs Design for a fashions fair. Builder 126:259-60 Feb. 15, 1924
720.5 A67 Fairhaven (Mass.). Rogers memorial church The Rogers memorial church (Unitarian), Fairhaven, Mass. Charles Brigham, archt. No plan. Arch rev 12: 226-227 O '05	Fairmont (N.Y.) Church Gillespie and Carrel,Archts. Selection from Brooklyn Chapter, A.I.A. Fifth Exhibition, 1905. Inland Archt. 46: pl.fol.p. 24 Sept, 1905	Fairs. Dezarnaud, Adrien Peintures forraines Arts et métiers graphiques no.55:31-35 November 15,1936
720.6 A51q Fairhaven (Mass.) Rogers memorial church. Doors Memorial church, Fairhaven, Mass. Bronze doors Amer. Inst. of Arch. Quar Bull. 11: 304 Ja '11	Fairmount Park. Philadelphia, Pa. see Philadelphia, Pa. Fairmount Park	Fairview, Ky. Davis (Jefferson) Memorial The Jefferson Davis Memorial, an obelisk at Fairview, Ky. Architecture 60:20 July, 1929

Falaise, Fr. Chateau
     Falaise, a Norman Gothic chateau of Ile-de France

               Arts and decoration 24:38,70
               March, 1926

Falconetto, Giovanni Maria c.1468-c.1534
     Palazzo Giustiniani, Padua. Giovanni Maria
Falconetto, archt. Measured drawings, Photographs.

          Italian Renaissance: Sixty measured
          drawings with details. 3 vols. New York:
          The architectural book publishing
          Company, n.d. 2:pl.3-6
               3:pl.46

Fall River (Mass.) Highland Hospital
     The Highland Hospital, Fall River, Mass.
Parker Morse Hooper, archt. Plan.

               Architectural record 32:129-132
               August, 1912

Falaise (Fr.) Monument Aux Mort
     Monument Aux Mort de la Ville de Falaise
(War memorial for the city of Falaise - Angué,
sculptor.)

               L'architecture 36:31
               January 25, 1923

Falconetto, Giovanni Maria c.1468-1534
     Palazzo Giustiniani, Padua. Giovanni
Maria Falconetto, archt. 1524. Photograph, Plan.
Measured drawings.

          Palast Architektur. 6 vols. in 11 bks.
          Berlin: E.Wasmuth, 1886-1911
          4:pt.1:20-21
               pt.2:pls.85-90

Fall River (Mass.) Knapp (Rev.) house
     C., R.A. An architectural experiment: Japanese
style house from the Rev. Mr. Knapp at Fall River,
Massachusetts. Plan. Archt. not given

               Architectural record 8:82-91
               July-September, 1898

Falaise, France; St. Trinité Church

E. C. Jensen, Sketcher

               Inland Archt.
               Vol. 24, No. 3, pl.
                    Fol. p. 30
               Oct. 1894

Falkenau, Victor, houses
          see
Chicago, Ill. Falkenau, Victor houses (1890).

Fall River (Mass.) Plan
     Preliminary general plan showing thoroughfares,
parks, playgrounds and schools. Arthur A.
Shurtleff, town planner.

               Amer. arch. 126: 85
               July 30, 1924

720.5   Falcini,Treves and Micheli
A67r   Modern synagogue,Florence,Italy. Falcini,
        Treves and Micheli,archts.

               Architectural record 19:744
               April 1931

720.5   Falkenberg,Arthur
A67f   Drug stores - planning techniques for new
        and remodeled buildings,no.5:Miner and Carter
        Atlanta,Ga. Arthur Falkenberg,designer.

               Architectural forum 87:47
               July 1957

Fall River (Mass.) Public Library
     Public Library, Fall River, Mass.
Cram, Goodhue and Ferguson, archts. Plan.

               Architectural Review 9 ns.4: 15
               January, 1902

Falco, Luis Guillermo Rivadeneyra
          see
Rivadneyra Falco, Luis Guillermo

720.5   Falkentorp, Ole
M59c   Copenhagen's copper clad building: Vester-
        port, designed by Ole Falkentorp.

               Metalcraft 8: 157
               April 1937

720.5   Fall River (Mass.). Public library (proposed)
A67   Cram, Wentworth & Goodhue, archts.
        Plan, elevation, detail, section.

               Arch rev 4: pl 1-V fol 9
               Ja 1896

Falconer, Baker and Campbell
     Summer house at Great Rissington Manor,
Gloucestershire. Falconer, Baker and Campbell,
archts. Plans, sections, details.

               Architects' journal 69: 136-137
               January 16, 1929

720.52 Falkner, Harold
A67   Pencil sketch of the town of Guildford by
        Harold Falkner.

               Architects journal 61:172
               January 28, 1925

720.5   Fall River(Mass.) St. Mary's cathedral
A67   St. Mary's Cathedral, Fall River, Mass.
        Maginnis & Walsh, archts.

               Architectural review 19 n.s.2: pl.38
          A   March 1913

Falconetto, Giovanni Maria, c. 1468-c. 1534
Schweikhart, Gunter
     Eine Fassadendekoration des Giovanni Maria
Falconetto in Verona. [illus.]

               Florence. Kunsthistorisches
               Institut. Mitteilungen.
               Band 13, Heft III-IV
               pp. [325]-342
               O 1968

720.5   Fall River (Mass.) Court house
B93b   New court house, Fall River, Mass. R. H.
        Slack, archt.

               Building budget 5:pl. fol. 98
               Ag 1889

720.5   Fall River (Mass.) St. Stephen's church
A51   St. Stephen's church, Fall River, Mass.
        Cram & Wentworth, archts.

               Amer archt and bldg news
               56: pl fol 48
               My 8, 1897

Fall River, Mass., Saints Peter and Paul
    Parish of Saints Peter and Paul

        Architecture 52:330 and pl.134-135.
        Sept. 1925

Fallingwater (house), Pa.
    "Fallingwater," house for Edgar J. Kaufman.
    1937-39 [plan]. Frank Lloyd Wright, archt.

                N.Y. Museum of Modern Art.
                Built in U.S.A., p. 26-27,
                1932-44

Fallows, Huey and Macomber

    Members of firm:
        Fallows, E.T.
        Huey, G.T.
        Macomber, Wm.

Fall River, Mass. U.S. custom house and post
office
    U. S. Custom House and Post Office. Wm.
A. Potter, archt.

            Amer arch
            1: 181, pl.fol.p.180
            Je 3, 1876

Fallingwater (house), Pa.
    Laporte, Paul, Jr.
        Architecture and democracy [plans]

            Architects' year book 3:
            12-19, 1949

Falls Church, Va. Pope, Loren, house.
Pope, Loren
    The love affair of a man and his house.
[illus.]

            House Beautiful
            90: 32-34+
            Ag 1948

Fall River (Mass.) Women's Union
    Women's Union, Fall River, Mass. Parker Morse
Hooper, archt.

        Brickbuilder 20:pls.24-25 fol.p.44
        February, 1911

Fallis, E. O.

    see also

Castle Park (MI)   Godfrey (May L.) Residence
Sandusky (OH)   Donahue Residence
Toledo (OH)   Chapman Residence
                     Peoples Savings Assn. Building
   "   "   St. Paul's Methodist Church
   "   "   State Hospital Tower
   "   "   State Hospital Women's Hospital
   "   "   Ursuline Sisters of the Sacred Heart
                     Convent School

                     (See Card 2)

Falls Church, Va., Pope, Loren, house. Restoration

    see

Woodlawn plantation, Va. Pope-Leighey house.
    Restoration

720.55   Fallen Leaf Lake (Cal.) Felton (Morris) house
D87   I secondi pionieri. John Campbell,
         designer, Worley K. Wong, archt.

            Domus
            256:1
            1949

Fallis, E. O.   (Card 2)

    see also

Toledo (OH)   Y.M.C.A. Building

720.5   Falmouth (Mass.). Free public library
A67   Bacon & Mears, archts. Memorial
         library

            arch rev 7 (n.s.2): 142. pl LXXXIII
            D 1900   fol 148

Fallingwater (house), Pa.
    The prophet honored in his own country
[Frank Lloyd Wright, archt.] [illus.]
from Esquire, 1949

            Frank Lloyd Wright scrapbook,
            p. 26

Fallis, E.O.
    Member of firm:
        Becker and Fallis

720.54   Falun (Swe.) Museum
A67au   Petit musée a Falun. Hakon Ahlberg, archts.
         [plans, sect.]

                L'Arch. d'aujourd'hui
                9: 72
                Je '39

Fallingwater (house), Pa.
    Mumford, Lewis
        The Sky Line: at home indoors and out. Frank
Lloyd Wright, archt. from The New Yorker, Feb.
12, 1938

            Frank Lloyd Wright scrapbook,
            p. 183

Fallis, E.O.
    Work of E.O. Fallis, F.A.I.A., photo

                West. Archt.
                17: 99
                Nov, 1911

Falus, E.

    see

Budapest (Hung.) Cinema Corso

Fallingwater (house), Pa.
    [Illustrations]. Frank Lloyd Wright, archt.

        Frank Lloyd Wright scrapbook,
        p. 11, 22, 25, 29, 54

Fallows, E.T.

    Member of firm:
        Fallows, Huey and Macomber

Famagusta, Cyprus. Cathedral
    The orthodox cathedral of Famagusta, Cyprus.
Plan.

            Builder 87: 31-34
            July 9, 1904

Famagusta, Cyprus. Cathedral The orthodox cathedral of Famagusta, Cyprus. Inland architect 44: 2-3 August, 1904	Faneuil Hall Boston, Mass. see Boston, Mass. Faneuil Hall	720.5 Fanning, E F A67b Knights of Columbus club hotel, New York. E.F.Fanning, archt. Architecture and building 59: pl.61- March, 1927. 65
Famagusta, Cyprus. Cathedral Byron, Robert Famagusta Cathedral, now a mosque. Country life (Lond.) 75: 152,153 February 10, 1934	710.5 Fanlights C85 Country life (Lond.) 58:331-33 Aug. 23, 1915	Fantastic architecture see Architecture, Fantastic
Famagusta, Cyprus. St. Nicolas St. Nicholas, now known as St. Sophia, 16th century Greek Gothic. Famagusta, Cyprus. Country life (Lond.) 75: 153,154 February 10, 1934	720.52 Fanlights. A57 French metalwork. Arch.Jour.51:337.Mar.10,1920.	Fantuzzi palace. Bologna see Bologna. Palazzo Cloetta
Fan Vaulting Builder 104: pl. fol. p. 596 May 23, 1913	720.52 Fanlights A57b Selected examples of decoration Architectural review 53:94-5 Feb 1923	Fanzolo, It. Villa Emo Eberlein, H.D., and R.B.C.M. Carrère Villas of the Veneto. Pt. 1. Villa Emo, at Fanzolo. Designed by Andrea Palladio. Architectural forum 34:1-8 January, 1921 A
Fan Vaulting Arch and contract reporter 93:pl.for Mar. 12, 1915	720.5 Fanlights A67a Fanlights and other over-door treatments. Architecture 55: 283-88 May 1927	"Far hills" see Dayton (O.). Patterson (John H.) house
Fan Vaulting. Vallance, Aymar. The old cottages of Oxford. London: B.T. Batsford, 1912. p.xxii.	720.5 Fanning and Shaw A67b Church of St. Rose of Lima, Newark, N.J. Fanning and Shaw, archts. Architecture and building 61: 265,277- September 1929 278	720.5 Far Hills (N.J.) Frothingham (T.H.) house A67ar House of Mrs. Thomas H. Frothingham, Far Hills, New Jersey. John Russell Pope,archt. The architect (N.Y.) 1: pls 46-47 N '23
Fane, R. P. Estate, Eng. Chapel Chapel on estate of R.P. Fane, England. Country life (Lond.) 61:722-4 May 7, 1927	Fanning, Edward F. see also New Rochelle (N.Y.) Tully (C.J.) house White Plains (N.Y.) Chisholm (Angus) house New Rochelle (N.Y.) Iona school for boys	720.5 Far Hills (N.J.) Frothingham (T.H.) house A51 House of Thomas H. Frothingham, Far Hills, N.J. John Russell Pope, architect. Amer archt 125: 11 pl Ap 9 '24

Far Hills (N.J.) houses House at Far Hills, New Jersey, Cross and Cross, architects. Amer. arch. 122: 110 and 8 pl. Aug. 2, 1922.	**Far Readingley (Eng.) Iveson house** Iveson House, Far Readingley, Leeds: Staircase, corridor. Wilson and Oglesby, archts. Architect 67:pls.fol.p.26;pl.fol.p.26 March 7; April 11, 1902	720.5 A67r **Far Rockaway (L.I.) Sage memorial church** The Sage memorial church, Far Rockaway, N.Y. 1909. Cram, Goodhue and Ferguson, archts. Plans A Architectural record 29:65-69 January 1911
Far Hills (N.J.) house House at Far Hills, N.J. Renwick, Aspinwall and Owen, archts. (plan). Amer. archt and bldg. news 70:pl fol 24 O 20, 1900	**Far Rockaway (L.I.) Benjamin (G.G.) house** Country House, George G. Benjamin, Far Rockaway, N.Y. Edward I. Shire, Architect. Plan. Architecture 19:pls.XXVII-XXVIII fol 48 Mr '09	720.5 A51 **Far Rockaway (L.I.) St. Joseph's hospital** St. Joseph's Am. arch. 114:995-6, pl.61-65 Ag 21, '15
720.5 A67ar **Far Hills (N.J.) houses** Residence at Far Hills, N.J. Edward S. Hewitt, archt. Architect (N.Y.) 12: 321-31 Je '29	**Far Rockaway (L.I.) Cowden (John) house** The Mrs. John Cowden house, Far Rockaway, Long Island, N.Y. McKim, Mead and White, archts. Plan. Sheldon, George William. Artistic Country Seats. 2 vols. New York: D. Appleton and Co., 1871. v.2,pt.5:p.121-123, pl.33	**Faraway, Conn. Cooper (Wyatt) house** Private world--the Connecticut house of Mr. and Mrs. Wyatt Cooper--which Mrs. Cooper "invented and then found." [col. illus.] Vogue 147: [182]-[192] F 1, 1966
710.5 C855 **Far Hills (N.J.) Newcombe (C.N.) house** The residence of Charles N. Newcombe, at Far Hills, N.J. Country life (U.S.) 60: 52-53 October 1931	720.5 B84 **Far Rockaway (L.I.) First Presbyterian church** First Presbyterian church, Far Rockaway, L.I. Cram, Goodhue and Ferguson, archts. Brickbuilder 19: pls.153-155 November 1910	**Farey, Cyril A.** see Hounslow (Eng.) Holy trinity parish hall Tekyngton, Eng. St. Michael's church Torquay, Eng. Planning
710.5 C855 **Far Hills (N.J.) Pyle (D.N.) house** House of David N. Pyle, Far Hills, N.J. Hyde & Shepherd, archts. Country life 54: 62-63 May 1928	720.5 N56 **Far Rockaway (L.I.) Sage memorial church** Woodman, H.R. Some current church architecture by Cram, Goodhue, and Ferguson. Russell Sage Memorial, Far Rockaway, Long Island. Plan. A New York architect 4:136-157,152-165, March 1910 183	**Farge and Guerry** see Paris (Fr.) Theatre Empire
720.5 A67f **Far Hills (N.J.) Schley (Reeve) house** House of Reeve Schley, Far Hills, N.J. Peabody, Wilson & Brown, architects. Arch forum 32: pl 85-9 Je '20	720.5 B84 **Far Rockaway (L.I.) National bank** National bank at Far Rockaway, L.I. Joseph L. Steinam, archt. Plan. A Brickbuilder 24:pl.116 August 1915	**Fargo (ND) I.O.O.F. Building** Orff & Joralemon, Archs. Inland Arch. 23: pl. fol. p 46 My., 1894
STINSON LIBRARY 705.1 A79 **Far Hills (N.J.) Sibley (Reeve) house** Reeves Sibley house, Far Hills, N.J. Peabody, Wilson and Brown, archts. A Arts and decoration 12:317-319 March 1920	720.5 A67a **Far Rockaway (L.I.) Sage Memorial church** Sage Memorial church, Far Rockaway. L.I. Cram, Goodhue and Ferguson, archts. Architecture 31: pl.29-32 April 1910	**Fargo (N.Dak.) N. Dak. Agr. Coll. Lib.** Stallings, H. Dean A new pattern for economy, utility and beauty: The North Dakota Agricultural College Library. (no illus.) [Wm. F. Kurke & assoc., Fargo, N. Dak. architects]. College & research libraries 11:135 Ap 6, '50

Faribault (Minn.) C.M. and St. P. Railroad Station
Sketch of C.M. and St. P. Ry. station at
Faribault, Minn. Cobb and Frost, archts.

A   Building budget 3:pl.fol.p.128
October 31, 1887

Farkas, George

see

Miami, Fla. 36th st. Airport. Officers' club

Farm buildings

see also

Swine houses
Dairy farms

Stables
Barns
Farmhouses

Faribault, Minn. Seabury divinity school
Divinity-hall and warden's residence,
Seabury-Mission, Faribault, Minn [plan] H. M.
Congdon, archt.

Amer arch
1: 157, pl.fol.p.156
Ap 29, 1876

Farkas, Molnar
Immeuble a Budapest. Molnar Farkas, archt.
(plans).

L'Arch. d'aujourd'hui
9:32-33
F '38

Farm buildings

Brickbuilder 23:51-54
Mar. 1914

Faribault (MN) Shattuck School
Armory (proposed)
Cass Gilbert, Arch.

West Arch 10:
pl. fol. p.24
Feb. 1907

Farleigh castle
Wright, Reginald & M
Farleigh castle.

Walpole Society. Annual volume.
10: 71-74 and plates LXXXVIII-
XCI

Farm, buildings

Amer. arch. 109:17-24 and pl. 2090
Jan. 12, 1916

Faribault (MN) Shattuck School
Shumway § Morgan Halls
W.H. Wilcox; and Wilcox § Johnson, Arch.

West Arch 10:
pl. fol. p. 24
Feb. 1907

710.5
C85   Farleigh castle. Office of works.
Peto, H. A.
Restoration of Office of Works
at Farleigh castle.

Country Life (Lond.)
50: 593
N 5, 1921

Farm buildings

Amer. arch. 114:pl.136-144
Nov. 6, 1918

Faribault, Minn. Waterworks
Tyrie, W.W.
Waterworks at Faribault, Minnesota. Long and
Thorshov, Inc. archt. No plan.

Architectural concrete 7:10-11
No. 1 [1941]

Farleigh Hungerford Castle, Somerset
Castle of Farleigh Hungerford and its preservation

(London) Country Life 50: 692.
Nov. 26, 1921.

Farm buildings

Archts' and bldrs. mag. 45:268-270
June 6, 1917

720.52
B95   Farington
Watkins,N.G.
Farington's diary and its interest to archi-
tects.

Builder 145: 10-11
July 7,1933

Farley, Eng. Churches
A problem of chronology in stone: Farley
Church, Surrey

Builder 127:852-853
Nov. 28, 1924

Farm buildings

Amer. arch. 114: pl. 199.
Dec. 25, 1918

Farinholt House, York County, Va.
Farinholt House, York County. First military
balloon ascension made near here in April, 1862.

William and Mary Quarterly, ser.2.v.18:
January, 1938   pl.9

Farlin, J   W   house, Chicago

see

Chicago, Ill. Farlin (J.W.) house

Farm buildings

House beaut. 47:88-89
Feb. 1920

720.5
H8C
Farm buildings
Holbrook, E. C.
Agricultural architecture: out-buildings for a country estate; interiors of cow barns.

Western architect 17: 70-74, pl.fol.p. 75.
August 1911

710.8
N84
Farm buildings
Farm buildings of Charles M. Schwab, Loretto, Pa. illus.

House and garden 37:28-9.
Feb.1920.

Farm Buildings
On estate of Dr. C. Fahnestock

House and garden 32:40-41
Dec. 1917

720.54
T25
Farm buildings
Amenagement rural. [special no.]

Tech et arch 6:special no.
No. 3-4, '46

Farm buildings
Weingartner, Hans
Frischluftstall für alpenlandische betriebe
[sections & details]

Baumeister
vol.58: 1239-40, D 1961

720.5
A51
Farm buildings.
(Pigeon tower, etc)

Amer. Arch. 121: pl.
Feb. 15, 1922.

Farm Buildings
Bailiff's House, Dairy and Farm Buildings, Hever, Kent. F.L. Pearson, F.R.I.B.A. Architect.

Builder
95:622,pl.fol. p.636
no.3435
Dec 5, 1908

MICROFILM

Farm buildings
Morgan, Charles L.
Igloos are cheaper and easy to build.

In SCRAPBOOK ON
ARCHITECTURE p.796
(on file)

710.5
C855
Farm buildings
Random thoughts on farm buildings
Alfred Hopkins

Country Life 46:66-7
July, 1924

Farm buildings
The Buildings of a Model Farm. Shadow Brook Farm, Shrewsbury, N.J. Albro & Lindeberg, Architects.

Int. Studio 42: xxxvii
D 1910

710.5
C855
Farm buildings
An interesting farm group designed by Frank R. Mead for Edward D. Libbey, Ojai, Calif.

Country life 47:63
Nov. 1924

720.54
T25
Farm buildings
Techniques et architecture rurales.

Techniques et architecture
7:595-405
No. 7-8, 1947

710.5
C855
Farm buildings.
Efficient and Attractive.

Country Life. 38:56-7.
Oct. 1920.

Farm building
Modern

Brickbuilder 23:91-95
Apr. 1914

Farm buildings. 20th century

Arch. forum 30:63-76,pl.33-48
Mar. 1919

710.5
C855
Farm buildings
The farm as a picturesque asset

Country life 43:53-8
April 1923

710.5
C85
Farm buildings
Dominy,J.M.
Modern farm buildings: dairies for the accredited farm. Plan.

Country life(Lond)82:xxxiv
September 18,1937

Farm buildings, 20th century

Arch. forum 30:109-114
Apr. 1919

710.5
N84
Farm buildings
Keefe, Charles S.
Farm buildings for the small place

House beautiful 57: 368
April 1925

720.52
B93
Farm buildings
New buildings at Barrington Court, Somerset

Builder 126:872
May 30, 1924

720.6
A51j
Farm buildings, Belgium.
Reconstruction.

Amer. inst.of arch. journal
8:261-5.July,1920.

Farm buildings, Cape colony
Martienssen, Rex
Wine cellars and minor farm buildings of the Cape.

Architectural review 64:131-137
October 1928

Farm buildings. England.
Fryer, Norman T.
Ingenuity of the Dartmoor builders. Long houses for farm and family, written and illustrated by Norman T. Fryer. [illus.]

Country life
143: 1862-1862
My 23, 1968

Farm buildings, England
Small holdings; construction and equipment.
illus.

Architects' journal
50:783 and pl., Dec. 24,1919.

720.54
T25
Farm buildings, Czechoslovakia
Snajdr, S.
Projet pour une ferme
[cattle raising].
d'élevage en Tchécoslovaquie [plans, sect.]

Tech et arch 6:383-385
No. 7-8, '46

720.6
R88
Farm buildings, England.
Land settlement building work, ministry of agr. and fisheries.

R.I.B.A. 28:307-21.
Apr.9, 1921.

720.52
B93
Farm buildings, Eng land
Somerset County,.

Builder. 120 pl.
Jan. 21, 1921.

Farm buildings, England

Landscape arch. 5:120-123
Apr. 1915

720.52
A67
Farm buildings, England. Dorking
Leladone, Dorking. Heaton Comyn, archt.

Architects' journal 67: 6 pls.
April 18, 1928

720.52
A673
Farm buildings, England
A Sussex estate, by Barry Parker

Arch. Rev. 57:106-13
Mar. 1925

Farm buildings. England.
English Farmsteds. G.A.T. Middleton, A.R.I.B.A.

Arch rec 12: 514-27
O, 1902

710.5
C85
Farm buildings, England
Lord Bledisloe's great agricultural experiment

(London) Country Life 56:282-84
Aug. 23, 1924

710.5
C85
Farm buildings,England
Timber for agricultural buildings - a modern farmstead in Cambridgeshire. Plan.

Country life(Lond)82:389-390
October 16,1937

710.5
C855
Farm buildings,England
Dominy,J.N.
Farm buildings: future developments in planning and construction.

Country life(Lond)81:xxxii,xxxiv
February 27,1937

710.5
C85
Farm buildings. England
The manor farm and village, Gloucestershire.

Country life (Lond.)62: 736-42
November 19, 1927

Farm buildings. France
Entrées de ferme; Abbaye de Maubuisson; ferme de la Valouine.

Encyclopedie de l'architecture,
constructions de style. 2 vols.
Paris: Albert Morancé, 1928- ?
Tome 1:pl.11

720.52
B93
Farm buildings, England.
Farm buildings at Dulwich: Shortly to be demolished.

Builder 125:918
Dec. 14, 1923

720.52
A67
Farm buildings. England
Modern domestic architecture

Architects journal 59:529
Mar. 26, 1924

720.54
A67
Farm buildings, France
Imbert, Charles
The farms of "The Friends of the People" in the various sections of France. Ch.E.Mewes, archt. Plans.

L'architecture 44: 157-168
May 15, 1931

710.5
C85
Farm buildings. England
Farm buildings at Poynings,Sussex.

Country life.Lond. 51: 587
Apr. 29, 1922.

710.5
C85
Farm buildings, England.
Outbuildings at Barrington Court, Somerset, England.

Country Life (Lond.) 64: p 332-337
September 8, 1928

720.54
T25
Farm buildings, France
La ferme. [plans].

Tech et Arch 2:Special Number
N-D. 1942

720.5 Farm buildings,France
A67r Girard,Anatole
  French farms. Plans.
 	
  Architectural record 13:298-321
  April 1903
	Farm buildings, France. 13th century
	Ferme de Meslay, Près de Tours.
	Treizième siècle. Plan.
	
	  Verdier, Aymar. Architecture civile
	et domestique. 2 vols. Paris: Rance,
	1857-58. v.1:27-35,plates
		Farm buildings. Germany
		Euting, H. H.
		Holz im landwirtschaftlichen bauwesen
		[plans & sections]
		
		  Baumeister
		  55:804-8 N 1958

720.54 Farm Buildings, France
T25 Habitat rural
 	
  Tech et arch
  4: 105-108
  Ma/ Je '44
	Farm buildings, France. Moulis
	  Ferme de "l'ami du peuple" à Moulis (Tarnet-
	Garonne). "Friend of the people farm" at Moulis
	(Tarn and Garonne). Ch. Mewes, archt. Plan.
	
	  Encyclopedie de l'architecture;
	  constructions modernes. 12 vols.
	  Paris: Albert Morancé, 1928-39.
	  4: no. 4 pl. 86
		Farm buildings. Germany
		Arbeitsblätter der Staatsbauschule
		München, Akademie für Bautechnik. Landwirts-
		schaftliches entwerfen [plans & sections]
		
		  Baumeister
		  55:Tafeln 73-80 N 1958

Farm buildings, France
Homes, farm buildings
 	
  Amer arch
  112: 257-260, pl. 154-
  161
  O 10, 1917
	Farm buildings, France. Nohic
	  Ferme de "l'ami du peuple" à Nohic (Tarnet-
	Garonne) "Friend of the people" farm, at Nohic
	(Tarn and Garonne). Ch. Mewes, archt. Plan.
	
	  Encyclopedie de l'architecture;
	  constructions modernes. 12 vols.
	  Paris: Albert Morancé, 1928-39.
	  4: no. 4 pl. 85
		Farm buildings. Germany
		Landwirtschaftliches bauwesen; wettbe-
		werbsteil "Familienbetrieb im ebenen gelände"
		[plans & sections]; wettbewerbsteil "Familien-
		betrieb im hängigen gelände" [plans & sections];
		wettbewerbsteil "Nebenerwerbsstelle im ebenen
		belände" [plans & section]
		
		  Baumeister
		  55:EB85-EB92 N 1958

STEWART LIBRARY
D10.994 Farm buildings, France
A78a Desaymard, Joseph and
  Desforges, Emile
  Les maisonettes des champs dans le massif
central
 	
  L'art populaire en France
  5: 15-24
  1933
	Farm buildings, France. Piecegrande
	  Ferme de "l'ami du peuple" à Piecegrande
	(Tarn-et-Garonne) "Friend of the people farm" at
	Piecegrand - (Tarn and Garonne). Ch. Mewes,
	archt. Plan.
	
	  Encyclopedie de l'architecture;
	  constructions modernes. 12 vols.
	  Paris: Albert Morancé, 1928-39.
	  v.4:no.4 pl. 87
		Farm buildings, Germany, Tyrol
		
		  [plans]
		
		  Baumeister
		  52, no.6:365-374, 384-385
		  Je 1955

720.54 Farm buildings. France
A67 Plan, elevation and views of farm buildings
near Alsace.
 	
  L'Architecture 39: 307-8
  December 10, 1926
	Farm buildings, France. Villemade
	  Ferme de "l'ami du peuple" à Villemade
	(Tarn-et-Garonne) "Friend of the people" farm at
	Villemade (Tarn and Garonne). Ch. Mewes, archt. Plan
	
	  Encyclopedie de l'architecture;
	  constructions modernes. 12 vols.
	  Paris: Albert Morancé, 1928-39.
	  4:no.4 pl. 88
		Farm buildings, Switzerland
		
		  [plans]
		
		  Baumeister
		  52, no.6:350-364, tafel- 41-45
		  Je 1955

720.54 Farm buildings, France
A67 Plans for modern farm groups, France.
 	
  L'Architecture 41: 182
  June 15, 1928
	Farm buildings, Germany.
	
	  Baumeister 52, no.6:
	  375-383, tafeln 46-48
	  Ja 1955
		Farm buildings. Switzerland. 20th cent.
		  Het aandeel van de SVIL in de ontwikkeling
		van de bouw van boerderijen in Zwitserland
		[plans] Carlo & Rino Tami, archts.
		
		  Forum no. 5
		  p. 200-203
		  1954

Farm buildings. France.13th cent.
  Ferme a Meslay, près de Tours, xiiie siècle;
greniers de l'Hopital d'Angers, xiiie siècle.
 	
  Encyclopedie de l'architecture,
  Constructions de Style. 2 vols.
  Paris: Albert Morancé, 1928- ?
  Tome:1 pl. 20
	720.53 Farm buildings, Germany
	B35 Harbers, Guido
	  Alte Landarbeiter- und Kleinbauernstellen der
	Nordmark. (Old farms and peasant dwellings of
	Nordmark.) Plans.
	
	  Der Baumeister 34:432-435,Pl.146
	  December 1936
		Farm buildings, U. S.
		
		  see also
		
		  Perrysburg (O.) Secor (J.K.) estate

Farm buildings, U.S.

Greber, Jacques. L'architecture
aux Etats-unis...2 vols. Paris:
Payot, 1920. v.1,p.127-32.

720.5
A51

Farm buildings. U.S.
The evolution of farm life in America

American architect 125:379-82
Apr. 23, 1924

720.5
A67r

Farm buildings, United States
Klaber, J.J.
The grouping of farm buildings: examples
from the work of Alfred Hopkins.

Architectural record 37:341-359
April 1915

720.5
A67r

Farm buildings. U.S.
Barns-Estate of E.S.Clarke,Esq.,Cooperstown
N.Y. Frank V. Whiting,architect.

Arch.record 52: 115-18
Aug. 1922

720.5
A67

Farm buildings, U.S.
Fahnestock

Arch. Rev. 23:plates 24-26
March, 1918

720.5
A67a

Farm buildings, U.S.
J.K. Socor estate
Alfred Hopkins, arch.

Architecture 52: pl. 188-92
Dec. 1925

710.5
C855

Farm buildings. U. S.
Beauty that is utilitarian

Country life 44:51-3
Sept. 1923

720.5
A67

Farm buildings,United States
Hopkins,Alfred
Farm barns. Plans.

Architectural review 9,n.s.4:237-264
September 1902

720.5
A67a

Farm buildings, U. S.
Residence, Estate Mrs. W. A. Slater,
North Castle, N. Y.   Bradley Delehanty,
architect

Architecture 51:49-52
Apr. 1925

710.5
C855

Farm buildings. U. S.
Dairy buildings on the Fuller estate

Country life 45:64
Nov. 1923

710.5
C855

Farm buildings .U.S.
The farm group beautiful. Green Lane
farm.

Country life 48:67
June 1925

720.5
A67

Farm buildings, United States
Some interesting farm buildings. Alfred
Hopkins, archt. Charles S. Keefe, associate
archt.

A   Architectural review 26:n. s.9:105-108
October 1919   pl.53-54

720.5
A67

Farm buildings,United States
"Dreamwold" the farm of Thomas W.Lawson,
Egypt,Mass. Coolidge and Carlson,archts.
Plans.

A   Architectural review 9,n.s.4:248-
October 1902   260

720.5
A67f

Farm buildings. U.S.
Farm buildings of Walter Douglas, Esq.,
Dobbs Ferry,N.Y. Alfred Hopkins, archt.

Architectural forum 38:pl.21-2
Feb. 1923

720.5
A67

Farm buildings, United States
Cramer, E.C.
Some observations on the grouping of farm
buildings, with especial relation to the six
groups illustrated.

Architectural review 23:n. s.6:33-36:pl.
March 1918   24-41

720.5
A67a

Farm buildings, U. S.
Estate Arthur E. Newbold, Jr., Laverock,
Pa.
Mellor, Meigs & Howe, Architects

Architecture 50:plates 126-7
Aug., 1924

720.5
A67ar

Farm buildings. U.S.
Farm group, estate of Mr. Arthur James,
Newport, R.I. Grosvenor Atterbury,archt.

Architect (N.Y.) 9: 713-15
March 1928

720.5
A67r

Farm buildings, U.S.
Stable group, Estate of Seth Thomas, Jr.,
Esq., Morristown, New Jersey.
Stable group, Estate of Mrs. Amasa S. Ma-
ther, Chagrin Falls, Ohio.

Architectural record 55:337,369
April 1924

720.5
A67ar

Farm buildings, U. S.
Estate of Mr. Donald H. Cowl, Port
Washington, L. I. Thomas Harlan Ellett,
N. Y., architect

Architect (N.Y.) 3:pl.121-28
Mar. 1925

720.5
A67

Farm buildings. U.S.
Garage and farm building,Glen Head, Long
Island. Thomas H.Ellet, architect.

Architectural review 10: pl.
3-4. Jan.1920.

710.5
C855

Farm buildings. U.S.
Surprise Valley Farm.

Country life 45:51-3
Apr. 1924

720.5 **A67** Farm buildings, United States Three interesting farm groups on Long Island. J.W.O'Connor,architect. Arch. rev. 10:97-104.Apr.1920 & pl.55-64.	720.5 A67f Farm buildings, U.S. Newport(R.I.) Anderson, W.F. Farm buildings of Arthur Curtis James, Newport, R.I. Grosvenor Atterbury and Stowe Phelps, associate archts. Architectural forum 34:55-58 and February 1921 pl. 22-24	720.53 B55 Farm labor. Housing. Germany. Borkallen Harbers, Guido Werkbauernsiedlung Borkallen (Ostpr.) (The Borkallen agricultural settlement. East Prussia) Theodor Petzold, archt. A Der Baumeister 34:253 August 1936
Farm buildings.U. S. 18th cent. Glassie, Henry Eighteenth-century cultural process in Delaware valley folk building. [illus] Winterthur portfolio v.7: [29]-57, 1972	710.5 C855 Farm buildings,U.S.,Pennsylvania Mayhill farms; the estate of Mr.and Mrs. Quincy Bent, at Bethlehem,Pa. J.P.Sinklor, archt. Country life(N.Y.)69:52-58,79 November 1935	Farm labor. Housing, India see also Punjab (Pakistan)Vanhar farm center (project)
710.5 C855 Farm buildings,U.S.,Babylon(L.I.) Firenze Farm,and more especially:Firenze Stables. Country life(U.S.)65:21-23 October 1956	706.1 A79 Farm buildings, U.S., Rhode Island Boyd, J.T., jr. Picturesque farm architecture on Newport estate Arts and decoration 30: 60-61, 100, 126 March 1929	Farm labor. Housing, Italy. 20th century Case per contadine. Piero Bottoni, Gabriele Mucchi, Marco Pucci, archts. [plans] Domus no. ?:319-11 A. '46
710.5 C855 Farm buildings,U.S.,Illinois Field day at St.James farm,Naperville,Ill Farm of Mr.and Mrs.Chauncey McCormick. Country life(U.S.)68:53-55 October 1936	Farm communities, U.S. Arizona Cooperative farm community. Chandler, Ariz. 1936/67. Vernon DeMars, Burton D. Cairns, archts. Plans. Photographs and brief biographical sketch. Roth, Alfred. La nouvelle Architecture. Erlenbach, Switzerland: Editions de Architecture, 1946. 61-70	Farm labor. Housing, U.S. see also Chandler (Ariz.) Farm Security Administration community for agricultural workers Woodville (Calif.) FSA Community
710.5 C855 Farm buildings,U.S.,Indiana Yarnall,Sophia "Corner Prairie Farm" - the estate of Mr.and Mrs.Eli Lilly at Noblesville,Ind. Country life(N.Y.)69:63-66,107-110 April 1936	710.5 C855 Farm groups Hoffman, R. W. Managing the estate. Country Life (U.S.) 65:54-58 December 1933	Farm labor. Housing, U.S. De Mars, Vernon Social planning for western agriculture. Task no. 2: 5-9 '41
720.5 A67a Farm buildings. U.S. Mariemont (O.) Farm buildings, Resthaven Demonstration farm. Mariemont, O. Planned by J. Nolen & P.W. Foster. Hubert E. Reeves, archt. Architecture.54: pl.172-173 Sept. 1926	Farm houses see Farmhouses	Farm Security Administration see also Chandler (Ariz.) Farm Security Administration Community for agricultural workers Taft (Cal.) FSA community for agricultural workers Yuba City (Cal.) FSA Community for agricultural workers
710.5 C855 Farm buildings, U.S. New York State A model farm, example of education. Milton H. McGuire, archt. Julia Dyckman Andrus Memorial Farm at Yonkers, N. Y. (U.S.) Country life 74: 42-43 August 1938	Farm labor. Housing Stewart, J. M. The new land settlement. Country life (Lond.) 82:595-597 December 11, 1937	720.5 T19 Farm security administration De Mars, Vernon Social planning for western agriculture. Task no.2: 5-9 '41

Farmers' and mechanics' bank, Minneapolis, Minn.

see

Minneapolis, Minn. Farmers' and mechanics' bank

720.6
C53

Farmhouses
Spencer, J.C.Jr.
The farmhouse problem: elevations and plans of two farmhouses, Robert C. Spencer, Jr., archt.

A   Chicago architectural club 13:78-41
1900

710.6
H84

Farm houses, Denmark
Danish farm house, old style.

Country life (London)   84: 6
July 2, 1938

Farmers' and merchants' state bank, Hector, Minn.

see

Hector, Minn. Farmers' and merchants' state bank

Ryerson

Farm houses
Percival Goodman's symbiotic farm. [plan]
Percival Goodman, archt.

Interiors
105:pt.2:63-65
My 1946

720.5
A67r

Farmhouses. Designs and plans.
Planning the farm house.

Arch.record 47:558-60.
Jun.1920.

(Wis.)
Farmers' and merchants' union bank, Columbus

See

Columbus(Wis.)Farmers' and merchants' union bank

720.6
A51oc

Farmhouses
Brickloe, W. D.
The problem of the farm house.

The octagon 2: 12-13
November 1930

720/5
A67r

Farm houses, Dutch colonial
Stapley,Mildred
The last Dutch farmhouses in New York City.

Architectural record 32:23-36
July 1912

Farmers loan and trust company, New York

See

New York.Farmers loan and trust company

Farmhouses
A $3500 farmhouse.

American arch. 107:367-369
June 9, 1915

Farmhouses, England

see also

Cotswold cottages

Farmhouses
see also
Plantation houses
and names of individual farmhouses, i.e.:

Haslemere, Eng. Valewood farm
etc.

Farmhouses, Alsace-Lorraine
Ferme Jacob à Busvillier (XVI e siècle).
Cour de ferme à Zoberswdorf.

L'Art francais moderne
No 11: pl 1-2, 5
1919

Farmhouses, England

Arch. rev. (Lond.) 39:127-130
June, 1916

710.5
H84

Farmhouses
Advantages of remodeling.

House and Garden 41: 15-17.
Jan. 1922.

051
T72

Farmhouses, Canada

Touchstone 3: 43-49
April 1918

Farmhouses, England.

Dawber, Edward Guy. Old cottages, Farm-houses, and other stone buildings in the Cotswold district. London: B.T. Batsford, 1905. 18 pl.

Farmhouses
American Farmhouses. By Robert C. Spence, Jr.

Brickbuilder 9:177-78, 179-86
S 1900

Farmhouses, Cotswold hills (Eng.)

see

Cotswold cottages

705.2
S93

Farmhouses, England
Adaptation of an old farm house into a residence.

Studio 85:72-79
Feb. 1923

710.5
C 85
Farmhouses- England
    Chapel farm, Buckinghamshire

        Country life(Lond.) 57:908-915
        June 6,1925

720.52
D03
Farmhouses, England
    Old Dairy farm, Edenbridge.

        Builder 121: 195-4 & pl.
        August 12, 1921

720.5 4
T75
Farmhouses, France
    Architecture régionale. [special number -
comparison of architecture of regions in
France.]

        Techniques et Architecture
        7: no. 1-2 [special no.]
        1947

710.5
C85
Farmhouses. England.
    Cotswold.

        London Country Life 50: 343-4
        Sept. 17, 1921

720.52
A67
Farmhouses. England
    Prinsted farmhouse, West Sussex. Oliver
Hill, architect

        Architects Journal 58:318-23
        Aug. 29, 1923

720.5
A67f
Farmhouses, France
    Farmhouses near the Riviera.

        Architectural forum 40:209-12
        May 1924

710.5
C85
Farmhouses. England.
    Cotswold farmhouses and others.

        Country Life. Lond.48:304-11.
        Sept. 4, 1920.

710.5
C85
Farmhouses, England.
    Twatling farm, Barnt Green, Birmingham.

        (London)Country Life 51: 278-80.
        Feb. 25, 1922

720.5
A67a
Farmhouses, France
    XIVth century farmhouse, Aisne, France.

        Architecture 44: pl.,154
        September 1921

720.5
A67r
Farmhouses,England
Middleton,G.A.T.
    English farmsteads. Plans.

        Architectural record 12:514-527
        October 1902

710.5
C85
Farmhouses,England
    A Wiltshire farmhouse. Woodfolds.
Oaksey.

        Country life(Lond.)89:420-421
        May 10,1941

720.51
A673
Farmhouses, France
    Manoir d'Ango.

        Arch. Rev. 58: 209-13 & pl. 2
        Dec. 1925

Farmhouses, England
Harper, Charles G.
Farmhouses.

        Archt 115:
            71-75; Ja 22, 1926
            145-147;F 19,   "
            230-231;Mr 19,   "
            290-291;Ap 2,   "
            316-317; " 9,   "
            360-61;   " 16,   "

705.1
A79
Farmhouses, England, Sussex
Gillespie, A.B.
    Tudor farmhouse transformed into a week-end
cottage

        Arts and decoration 30:
        66-67; 82,126
        December 1928

705.4
A72a
Farmhouses, France
    Rural architecture after the war.

        Les arts francais no. 23:
        203-226
        1918

720.52
A67a
Farmhouses, England
    North farm, Ropley, near Winchester.
Philip Evans Palmer, archt.
    Floor plan for house at Peter's Farm,
near Chippingham. E.Guy Dawber, archt.

        Architect 115: 537; 617
        June 4; 25; 1926

710.5
C85
Farmhouses,England.Tifters
    Tifters farm,Charlwood,Surrey..the resi-
dence of the Hon.Sir Gerald Chichester. Plan.

        Country life(Lond)82:lxviii,lxxx,
        November 27,1937   lxxxii

720.52
B93
Farmhouses, France.
    Sketches in northern France.

        Builder 126:136-137,144
        Jan. 25, 1924

720.5
b86
Farm houses, England
    Old cottages and farm houses in Kent
and Sussex, England.

        Brochure series 7: 132-144
        June 1901

Farmhouses, France

    see also

Farmhouses, Provence

720.5
T25
Farm-houses, France
    Villages et Fermes. de montagne. La recon-
struction dans les Hautes-Alpes.

        Techniques et arch
        8: 105-113
        No. 1-2, 1948

Farmhouses. France. 18th cent.
Projet de ferme; dessin de Lavoignat, fermier
(epoque de la Revolution) plans

Encyclopedie de l'architecture,
constructions de style. 2 vols.
Paris: Albert Morancé, 1928- ?
Tome 1: pl.25

720.53
B55
Farmhouses, Germany. Bavarian
Ein aussterbender Bauernhaustyp in Süd-
doutschland. (A disappearing house-type in
South Germany) Châlet style.

Der baumeister 34:294-298
September 1936

720.52
B75
Farmhouses, Spain
Baeschlin, Alfredo
Ein katalanischen landhaus aus dem XVII jahr
hundert. Das bauernhaus der region Valencia

Der baumeister 34: sup 91-94
F '36

720.5
A67a
Farmhouses, France. Aisne
XIVth century farmhouse, Aisne, France.

Architecture 44: pl.,154
September 1921

RYERSON LIBRARY
Farmhouses. Italy
Samminiatelli, Bino
Case coloniche in Toscana.

Civiltà
3: 85-93
Je 1942

710.5
C855
Farmhouses, U.S.
The evolution of the American country house

Country life 42: 55-7
July 1922.

RYERSON LIBRARY
D10.5
A78a
France
Farmhouses, Burgundy
Jeanton, Gabriel
Habitations rustiques de la Bourgogne
de Sud

L'art populaire en
France 4:43 - 50
1922

720.5
A67a
Farmhouses, Italy
North Italian farmhouses

Architecture 48:298-300
Sept. 1923

D10.5
C88
Farmhouses, U.S.
Planning for beauty and comfort in the new
American farmhouse.

Craftsman 30: 55-65
Ap '16

RYERSON LIBRARY
D10.994
A78a
France
Farmhouses, Brittany
Gauthier, J.
La Maison Bretonne

L'art populaire en
France 4:27 - 42
1932

720.52
A673
Farmhouses, Italy, Florence
Maraini, Yoi
A tuscan farmhouse; Torre di opra, Florence;
residence of Signor Antonio Maraini.

Architectural review 64: 102-105
September 1928

710.5
C855
Farmhouses, U.S., California
An Andalusian farmhouse in California;
residence of Mark Daniels at Santa Monica.

Country life (U.S.) 55: 49-51
December 1928

Ryerson
Farmhouses, Brittany
Gauthier, Joseph
Les maisons du Marais Breton
France

L'art populaire en France
2:1-9
1930

Farmhouses. Italy. Lucca
Marchetti, Giorgio
Il problema delle Corti nella Piana di
Lucca. [illus.]

Critica d'arte
Anno 18: 57-67
J1-D 1971

720.5
A67d
Farmhouses,U.S. California. Santa Barbara
Farmhouse of Mr. and Mrs. Benjamin R.
Meyer,Hope Ranch,Santa Barbara,Gordon B.
Kaufmann,archt. Plans

Architectural digest 8: 16-21
Number 3 [1932-1933]

720.53
B55
Farmhouses,Germany
Der Adolf-Hitler-Koog an der Elbemündung
als beispiel für friedliche landgewinnung und
seine besiedlung (The Adolf-Hitler-Hoog on
the mouth of the Alba as a beginning of
peaceful acquisition of land and its coloni-
zation). Ernst Prinz,archt. Plan.

Der baumeister 34:102-104,pls.35,
March 1936   36

Farmhouses. Normandy)
Livarot (Calvados) Ferme de la Pipardière;
Crevecoeur (Calvados) Manoir, façade aterale et
façade principale.

Encyclopedie de l'architecture,
constructions de style. 2 vols.
Paris: Albert Morancé, 1928- ?
Tome 1: pl.22

D13.1
R34
Farmhouses, U.S. Carlisle (Mass.)
Thayer, Morris
A remodeled farmhouse that speaks for it-
self, - residence of Mr. and Mrs. Henry V.
Greenough in Carlisle, Mass.

House beautiful 67:586-592
May 1930

720.53
B35
Farmhouses, Germany
Harbers, Guido
Forsthauswettbewerbe fur niedersachsen und
Oetpreussen. (Competition for ranger's house for
lower Saxony and East Prussia.) Hermann Tuch,
archt.

Der Baumeister 34: 132-138, pl.42-43
April 1936

RYERSON LIBRARY
D10.994
A78a
Farmhouses, Provence
Algoud, Henri
La maison rurale en Provence et ses
accessoires

L'art populaire en
France 1:43 - 56
1929

Farmhouses, U.S. Colonial

see

Colonial farmhouses

720.5 W52 — Farmhouses, U. S., Colorado. Ranch house for Mr. Penrose, Turkey Creek farm, Colorado. Western Arch. 30: 90. August 1921.	710.5 C855 — Farmhouses, U.S., Italian style. Estate of A.V. Davis, Long Island. Guy Lowell, archt. Country life (U.S.)52:57 October 1927	710.5 H84 — Farmhouses, U. S., New Jersey. Pretty Brook farm, Princeton, N. J. Arthur C. Holden and associates, archts. Vitale and Geiffert, landscape archts. House and garden 56: 95-97 October 1929
710.5 C855 — Farmhouses, U.S. Connecticut. Farm group ideal at Menbrook, the estate of Frederick Rentschler at West Hartford, Connecticut. Chester A. Patterson, archt. Country life (U.S.) 65:66-67 January 1934	710.5 C855 — Farmhouses, U.S., Maine. Marbury, Elisabeth. My rural paradise, Lakeside farm, Belgrade Lakes, Maine. No plan. Country life (U.S.) 58: 38-40 August 1930	720.6 A51j — Farmhouses, U.S., New York. Eight old Long Island houses, New York. A.I.A. journal 11:plates Sept. 1923
710.5 H84 — Farmhouses, U.S., Connecticut. Maramoko Farm, country place of Charles Wesley Dunn at Wilson's Point, South Norwalk, Connecticut. Frank J. Forster, archt. House and garden 55: 140-145 April 1929	D13.1 H84 — Farmhouses, U.S., New Hampshire. Mayo, W. H. The house that fulfilled all requirements. House beautiful 67:39-44 January 1930	720.5 A67r — Farmhouses, U.S. New York. Farm group, Oyster Bay, L.I.N.Y. Alfred Hopkins, archt. Architectural record 51:241-3 March 1922
710.5 H84 — Farmhouses, U.S., Connecticut. Wright, Richardson. The Norman invades Connecticut. Provincial farmhouse designed by Frank J. Forster for James E. Bailey, at New Canaan, Conn. House and garden 54: 74-79,96-97 November 1928	710.5 C855 — Farmhouses, U.S., New Jersey. Holden, Arthur C. The evolution of a farmhouse: Pretty Brook, near Princeton. Arthur C. Holden & assoc.archts. Ferruccio Vitale and Alfred Geiffert, Jr., landscape archts. Country life (U.S.) 64: 51-53 October 1928	720.5 A67r — Farmhouses,U.S. New York. Stapley,Mildred and A.G.Byne. The last Dutch farmhouses in New York City. Architectural record 32: 23-36 July 1912
720.5 A67r — Farm houses. U.S. Connecticut. Residence of Miss Mary T. Bradley, New Canaan, Connecticut. Richard H. Dana, Jr., architect. Architectural record 55:163-71 Feb. 1924	D13.1 H84 — Farmhouses, U.S., New Jersey. Sexton, R. W. A farmhouse plan adapted to modern needs. House of W. B. Ruthrauff in Red Bank, N. J. House beautiful 68: 587-591,634 December 1930	705.1 A79 — Farmhouses, U.S., New York. Normandy farmhouse in Manhasset Bay, Long Island, New York. Home of Mr. Edward L. Williams. Alfred A. Scheffer,archt. Arts and decoration 30: 71,108 March 1929
Farmhouses, U.S., French influence. Ramsdell, R.W. and Eberlein, H.D. Bringing back architecture. House and Garden. 50:73-75 Nov. 1926	720.5 A67r — Farmhouses, U.S., New Jersey. Pretty Brook Farm, Princeton, N. J. Arthur C. Holden & Associates, archts. Ferruccio Vitale and Alfred Geiffert, Jr., landscape architects. Architecture (N.Y.) 11: 289-303 December 1928	710.5 C855 — Farmhouses, U.S., New York. Kaufman, G. L. The barn that became a mansion. Farm house at Orienta Point, Mamaroneck, N. Y. Plan. Country life (U.S.) 58: 49-50,78 October 1930
720.5 A67r — Farm houses,U.S.,Illinois . Oregon. Herbert,William. Sinnissippi Farm - house of Colonel Frank O. Lowden, at Oregon,Ill. Pond and Pond,archts. Plans. Architectural record 22:299-310 October 1907	710.5 C855 — Farmhouses, U.S., New Jersey. Pretty Brook farmhouse at Princeton, N. J. Arthur C. Holden and associates, archts. Country life (U.S.) 55: 64-66 November 1928	710.5 H84 — Farmhouses, U.S., New York. At "Thimble Farm". Walter S. Gifford's house at North Castle, New York. House and garden 55: 133-135 March 1929

710.5
H84
Farmhouses, U.S., New York
Brandt, M. S.
A Bavarian farm house in New York state.

House and garden 60: 74-75,90
July 1931

720.53
W51
Farmhouses, U.S., Pennsylvania
Early farmhouses in Pennsylvania.

Wasmuth 9: 256-58
Heft 6, 1925

720.5
A67f
Farmington (Conn.) Bissell (R.M.) house
House of Mrs. R. M. Bissell, Farmington,
Conn. Edwin S. Dodge, architect.

Architectural forum 40:pl.39-42
March 1924

1013.1
H84
Farmhouses, U.S., New York
Priddy, Jane
Mill farm, the home of Mr. and Mrs. Edward
C. Oude in Harrison, New York.

House beautiful 65: 181-185
February 1929

710.5
H84
Farmhouses, U. S., Pennsylvania
A farmhouse home in Pennsylvania.
E. S. Paxton, archt.

House & garden.49:105-07
Jun. 1926

720.5
A67r
Farmington (Conn.) Meeting House
Embury, Aymar, II.
Early American churches. Meeting House.

Architectural record 31: 57,61,62
January. 1912

710.5
C855
Farmhouses, U.S., New York
Sweetwater Farm, residence of Thomas
Talmage, Long Island, New York. F. B. Hoff-
man & H. Hoffman, archts.

Country life (N.Y.) 49: 57-9
April 1926

710.5
H84
Farmhouses. U.S., Pennsylvania
Farmhouse in the tradition of Pennsylvania.

House & garden 51: 77-79
January 1927

720.5
A67r
Farmington (Conn.) Pope (A.A.) house
Alfred A.Pope's house at Farmington. McKim
Mead and White,archts.

Architectural record 20: 122-127
August 1906

A

Farmhouses. U.S., Normandy influence
Howard, E.L.
A French farmhouse enters the American scene.

Arts and decoration 29:44-45,88
June, 1928

720.5
A67r
Farmhouses,U.S. Pennsylvania
Embury,Aymar II
Pennsylvania farmhouses: examples of rural
dwellings of a hundred years ago.

Architectural record 30:475-485
November 1911

720.5
A67
Farmington (Conn.) Pope (A.A.) house
House of Alfred A.Pope, Farmington,Connec-
ticut. McKim,Mead and White,archts.

Architectural review 9: 282-283
November 1902

A

Farmhouses. U.S., Normandy influence
A Norman farmhouse. F.J. Forster, archt.

House and garden 51:110-11
February, 1927

770.5
A67d
Farmhouses,U.S.Texas
Residence of Mr. Robert L. More, Jr.,
Vernon, Tex. E. Gilbert Mason and assoc.,
archts.

A   Architectural digest 10:57-59
No.7[1940]

Farmington (Me.) Abbot School. Howard Hippach
Memorial Athletic Field

Howard Hippach Memorial Athletic Field, Abbot School,
Farmington, Me. Arthur Woltersdorf, archt.

American architect 111:pls.fol.p.180
March 14, 1917

Farmhouses. U.S., Normandy influence
Residence of E.C. Duble, Forest Hills,
L.I. Frank Forster, archt.

House and garden 52:85,117-119
October, 1927
also p. 100: Dec. 1927

710.5
H84
Farmhouses,U.S. West Virginia
Home of Plus E.Levi, New England type,
near Charleston,West Virginia. Lewis E.
Welsh,archt. Plan.

House and garden 65: 46-47
March 1934

720.5
A67ar
Farmington (Mass.) Macomber (John) house
Residence of Mr. John Macomber, Farming-
ton, Mass. Parker, Thomas & Rice, archts.

Architect (N.Y.) 9: 761-5
Mr '28

720.5
W52
Farmhouses, U.S., Ohio
Early architecture of the state of Ohio

Western architect 31: 127-9 & pl.
Nov. 1922   11-16

Farmingdale (L.I.) Methodist Episcopal Church
Methodist Episcopal Church, Farmingdale, L.I.
Julius Gregory, archt.

Architectural record 65:445-451
May, 1929

Farmington (MI)
Boys' Home
Baxter & O'Dell, Arch.

West. Arch.
13: pl. 10
Mar. 1909

720.5
A67r Farms,England
Middleton,G.A.T.
English farmsteads. Plans.

Architectural record 12:514-527
October 1902

Farnborough, Eng. Houses
A house at Farnborough, Kent. O.P. Milne,
archt. Plan.

A   Architect and Building News 148:50-51
October 9, 1936

720.52
A67c Farnham. Architecture
Farnham: a study in amenities.

Architect (Lond.) 131: 195-198;
August 12; 19; 1932   219-222

720.5
A67r Farms,France
Girard,Anatole
French farms. Plans.

Architectural record 13:298-321
April 1903

Farnese palace. Caprarola

see

Caprarola. Palazzo Farnese

710.5
C85 Farnham (Eng.) Grange
Oswald,Arthur
The Grange,Farnham,Surrey: the residence of
Major-General Sir Edward Perceval. A Queen Anne
house.

Country life (Lond.)76: 90-95
July 28, 1934

720.52
A673 Farms, Italy
The old Italian farm

Arch rev.(London) 57:244-247
June 1925

Farnese palace. Piacenza

see

Piacenza. Palazzo Farnese

Farnham (Eng.) Perceval (Sir Edward) house

see

Farnham (Eng.) Grange

Farms. Spain
His Majesty the King of Spain's farm at El Pardo.

Country life Lond. 53:206-9
Feb. 17, 1923

Farnese theater, Parma

see

Parma, It. Teatro Farnese

Farnham, Eng. St. Joan of Arc Church
Church of St. Joan of Arch, Farnham. C. Nicholas
and J.E. Dixon-Spain, archts.

Architect (Lond.) 121:677
May 24, 1929

Farms. U.S. Illinois
Drawings of farms in Illinois

Atlas of the State of Illinois.
Chicago: Union Atlas Co., 1876.

Farnesina villa. Rome

See

Rome. Villa Farnesina.

Farnhurst (Del.) Swanwick manor
Swanwick Manor, Lander's Lane, Farnhurst,
Del. A regency house. Plan.

Architects' emergency committee.
Great Georgian houses of
America... 2 vols. New York:
Kalkhoff press, inc., 1933 [vol. 1] .
Scribner press, 1937 [vol. 2] . 2:153-158

Farnam, Julian

see also

Minneapolis (Minn.) Kuhlman (J.C.) house

Farnham Chase
Farnham Chase, Buckinghamshire. Alterations
designed by Adshead and Ramsey.

Architectural review (Lond.) 66: 172-173
October, 1929

MICROFILM

Farnsworth (Edith B.) house, Ill.
[Ludwig Mies van der Rohe, archt.]

in SCRAPBOOK ON
ARCHITECTURE p. 30,24,36
(on film) 1,43,49,50,14

720.5
A67f Farnam,Julian
House for J.C. Kuhlman, Minneapolis,
Minnesota. Julian Farnam, architect. Plan.

Architectural forum 65:471
November 1936

720.52
A673 Farnham,England
Falkner,Harold
Farnham,England.Pencil sketches of houses,
streets,entrances and doorways, etc. by Harold
Falkner.

Architectural review (Lond) 40: 45-50
September 1916

720.5
A67f Farnsworth, Edith B. house, Ill.
This is the first house by Ludwig Mies Van
der Rohe since he came to America in 1938....

Arch for 96: 156-62
O 1951

Farnsworth (Edith B.) house
House of Dr. F. at Plano (Illin.) plan
Ludwig Mies van der Rohe, archt.

Forum no. 9/10
p.357
1954

Farradèche, R.
Garage, à Paris. Plans. R. Farradèche, archt

Encyclopedie de l'architecture;
constructions modernes. 12 vols.
Paris: Albert Morancé, 1928-39.
4:pls. 19-24

Farwell block, Chicago (1886)

see

Chicago,(Ill.) Farwell block (1886)

720.5   Farnsworth, James M
A67r   Entrance to Morse building, N.Y.C.
J.M.Farnsworth, architect. No plan.

Architectural record 2:144,155
October-December 1892

Farragut boat club house, Chicago (1884)

see

Chicago, Ill. Farragut boat club house (1884)

Farwell, C   B   house. Chicago

see

Chicago. Farwell (C.B.) house

Farquhar, Robert D.

see also

Beverly Hills (CA) High School
Los Angeles (CA)   California Club
   "   "   Clark (W. A.) House
   "   "   Leimert (W. H.) House
   "   "   McReynolds (Dr. R.P.) Residence
Pasadena (CA)   Fenyes (Adalbert) House
   "   "   House
   "   "   Kellam (E.R.) House
Sierra Madre (CA) House

Farragut houses, Brooklyn, N.Y.

see

Brooklyn (N.Y.) Farragut houses (project)

Farwell (Frank) house. Lake Forest, Ill.

see

Lake Forest (Ill.) Farwell (Frank) house

720.5   Farquhar, Robert David
A67d   Living room in library building of W.A.
Clark, Jr. Los Angeles, Cal. Robert Farquhar,
archt.

Architectural digest 7: 66-69
Number 2 [1931]

Farrant, L   G
Kaufhaus-hochgarage in Salt Lake City
[plan & section] L.G. Farrant, archt

Architektur & Wohnform
69: 56-9, F 1961

Farwell, G., house, (1886), Chicago

see

Chicago, Ill. Farwell, G., house (1886).

720.5   Farquharson, H
A67   The new theatre, Manchester, England. H.
Farquharson and Richardson and Gill, archts.
No plan.

Architectural review 38:pl.10-12
April 1915

Farrar, Benedict

see

St. Louis (Mo.) Farrar (Benedict) house

Farwell hall, Chicago

see

Chicago, Ill. Young men's Christian association
(central) (1867)

Farquharson, Horau, Richardson and Gill

see

Manchester (Eng.) New theater

Farrington, R   M
School buildings, Bogota, Columbia

Architecture
53: 139
My 1926

Farwell, John V. and co. bldg., Chicago (1865)

see

Chicago, Ill. Farwell, John V., and Co. bldg.
(1865)

Farr, Albert

see

Beverly Hills (Cal.) Lewis (C.L.) house
   "   "   "   (W.J.) house
Piedmont (Cal.) Jensen (G.C.) house
San Francisco (Cal.) Lowe (W.H.) house
Monterey (CA) Murray Residence

Farson (John) house. Oak Park, Ill.

see

Oak Park (Ill.) "Pleasant home"

Farwell (John V. and co.) building, Chicago
(1870)

see

Chicago, Ill. Drake-Farwell building (1870)

Farwell (John V. and co.) building, Chicago
(1871)

see

Chicago, Ill. Drake-Farwell building (1871)

Fascist party headquarters, Italy

See

Bollate.Casa del fascio

915.05   Fatehpur-Sikri. Architecture
J36   McCully, Anderson
            The resplendent monument of Emperor Akbar's
        whim: the romance of deserted Fatehpur-Sikri, the
        city of victory - twenty-four miles southwest of
        Agra.

                    Japan 15: 12-14, 50
                    June 1926

Farwell (John V. and co.) building, Chicago
(1872)

see

Chicago, Ill. Drake-Farwell bldg. (1872)

Fasolo, Furio, 1897-

see

Recoaro, It. Church. Competition

Fatehpur-Sikri. Architecture
Terry, John
    Some aspects of the Fatehpur Sikri
Architecture.

            Marg 2: 17-52
            No 5 [1948]

Farwell, J. V., house. Chicago

see

Chicago, Ill. Farwell, J. V. house

Fasse, Charles H. & Edward H. Reed
Form Partnership

            Western Architect
            11:VIII
            Ap 1908

910.8   Fatehpur Sikri. Description and travel
277   Owens, W. R.
            The deserted city of Akbar the Great
        (Fatehpur Sikri, near Agra)

            Travel 54:26-28,48
            March 1930

Farwell (John V., jr) house. Lake Forest, Ill.

see

Lake Forest (Ill.) Farwell (John V., jr) house

Fassett & Tompson
    The Birches, Cushings Island, Maine. To be
occupied by John Kelley Robinson of Chicago.
[plan] Fassett & Tompson, ardhts.

            Inland architect
            v. 14 no. 5
            pl. fol. p. 56
            N 1889

Fatehpur-Sikri. Miriam's Palace
    Miriam's palace at Futtehpore, Sikri, erected
(1556-1605) is one of a group of buildings.
Photograph and drawings.

            Architects journal 58:910-912
            December 19, 1923

Farwell (John V. and co.) warehouse and stables,
Chicago

see

Chicago, Ill. Farwell (John V. and co.) warehouse
and stables

Fassett, Francis H.

see

Yakima (Wash.) Lynch (H.C.) house

Fatimite architecture, Egypt

see

Mohammedan architecture, Egypt

Farwell trust building, Chicago

see

Chicago, Ill. Mallers building (224-26
LaSalle st.)

Fasth, S. E.

see

Minneapolis, Minn. Fasth (S.E.) house

Faulconer, A. C.

see

Detroit (Mich.) Watson St. house

Fasces, Roman

            Archt's and Bldrs' jour. pl. for
            Ap. 14, 1915

Fatehpur-Sikri, India
Terry, John
    Architecture: 3. Mughal architecture:
synthesis of Hindu and Islamic forms-
Fatehpur Sikri [section]

            MARG
            11:12-20 Je 1958

Faulhaber, J.M., house (1886), Chicago

see

Chicago, Ill. Faulhaber, J.M., house, (1886).

Faulkner, Charles Draper
see also
Chicago IL Grow (Fred A.) residence
"   "   Millet (Harold L.) "
"   "   Tudor Apts. 66th St. & Yale Ave.
Christian Science Churches
Cleveland OH First Church of Christ Scientist
Glen Arbor MI   "   "   "   "   "
Hinsdale IL Tousey (Charles A.) residence
New York (NY) Eighth Church of Christ Scientist
San Diego (CA) First "   "   "   "
Tokyo (JAP)   "   "   "   "   "
Wilkinsburg (PA) "   "   "   "   "

720.5
B93b
Faulkton(S.D.)Des Moines Loan & Trust Company
Bank and office building for the Des Moines
Loan and Trust Co. at Faulkton, S. Dak.
Fay, archt.

Building budget 3:3 in supp
My 31, 1867

Favier, Marcel
see
Gennevilliers (Fr.) Chapelle Jeanne d'Arc
Jerusalem, Pal. Hotel consulaire de France

Faulkner, Charles Draper
Charles D. Faulkner, Architect. Chicago.
[plans].

Nat'l Archt.
5:7
Ap '49

Faure-Dujarric, Louis, 1877 -
Groupe d'immeubles a Saint-Cloud, près Paris.
Plans. L. Faure-Dujarric, archt.

Encyclopedie de l'architecture;
constructions modernes. 12 vols.
Paris: Albert Morancé, 1928- 39.
10:pls. 81-84

720.5
B84
Faville, William B.
William B. Faville [Biography. Photograph]

Brickbuilder 24: 75
Mr 1915

720.5
A67r
Faulkner, Charles Draper
Eighteenth Church of Christ Scientist,
Chicago; First Church of Christ,Scientist,
Montclair, N.J.; Fourth Church of Christ
Scientist, Milwaukee, Wis. Charles Draper
Faulkner, archt. Plans.

Architectural record 70:176-182
September 1931

Faure-Dujarric, Louis, 1877-
Hôtel particulier, a Paris. Plan. L. Faure-
Dujarric, archt.

Encyclopedie de l'architecture;
constructions modernes. 12 vols.
Paris: Albert Morancé, 1928-39.
12:pls. 18-20

(La)Favorita, Noto, It.
see
Noto (It.) Chiesetta della Favorita

720.5
A67
Faulkner, Charles Draper
Residence for Mr. Fred A. Grow, Chicago.
"   "   " Mr. Chester A. Tousey, Hins-
dale, Ill.
Residence for Mr. Harold L. Millett, Chi-
cago.
Tudor apartments, Chicago.
Western Arch. 30: pl. 2-12.
Jan. 1921.

Faversham, Eng.
Hussey, Christopher
A cinque port and royal abbey. Faversham,
Kent - I. [illus.]

Country life
139: 6-9
Ja 6, 1966

Favoysey, C.
Bungalow near Bath. C. Favoysey, archt.

Builder 98:268,pl.fol.p.282
March 5, 1910

720.6
C53
Faulkner,Charles Draper
Student work -"A fine arts building" -
Chicago School of Architecture. C.D.
Faulkner. Plan.

Chicago architectural club £6:31-32
1913

Faversham, Eng.
Hussey, Christopher
A record of wise restoration. Faversham, Kent-
III. [illus.]

Country life
139: 237-240
F 3, 1966

Favrot and Livandais
see
New Orleans (LA) Cotton exchange
"   "   " Hibernia bank & trust co.
"   "   " Public Library. Competition

Faulkner, Waldron
see
Greenway (Va.) Madeira school

Faversham, Eng.
Hussey, Christopher
The setting of a notorious murder.
Faversham, Kent - II. [illus.]

Country life
139: 76-79
Ja 13, 1966

720.5
W52
Faw, Abraham
Kimball, Fiske and Wells Bennett
The competition for the Federal buildings,
1732-1735. pt.1; pt.2; pt.3; pt.4

American institute of architects' journal 7:
January 1919   8-14;
March 1919   98-102;
May 1919   202-210;
August 1919   355-361;
December 1919   521-527

Faulks, N.   W.
see
Short Hills (N.J.) Prange (Charles) house

Faversham. Market Place (No.4)
No. 4, Market Place, Faversham.

Dan, Horace and E.C. Morgan
Willmott. English shop-fronts.
London: B.T. Batsford, 1907. pl.10

Faxon, John Lyman
see also
Boston (MA) Kensington apt. hotel
Cincinnati (OH) Univ. of Cincinnati. Competitive
design
Detroit (MI) First Congregational church
Lynn (MA) Shute memorial library
Newton (MA) First Baptist church
Wayland (MA) Public library. Competition.

720.5
I56 Faxon, John Lyman
Ware, W. R.
      The Exchange building Association of Kansas
City.
      Results of competition. Designed by John
L. Faxon.
            Inland architect 8:4-6, pl.fol.14
            August 1886

Fay
    see also
Sioux City (Ia.) school
Faulkton (S. Dak.) Des Moines Loan & Trust Co.

Fay, Addison Grant
see also
Hubbard Woods (IL) Bolte (Mrs. Jesse W.) house

Fay & Dryer
See
Rochester (NY) - First Methodist Church. Entrance.

Fay (C.N.) house. Chicago, Ill.
    see
Chicago, Ill. Fay (C.N.) house

Fayans, Stephens (Dr.)
    see
Vienna (Aus.) Marie Therese theater

Fayerweather hall. Northwestern university.
    Evanston
    see
Evanston, Ill. Northwestern university. Fayerweather hall (ca.1887)

Fayeton, Jean
    Mehrfamilienhäuser mit stahlskelett an der
Porte des Lilas in Paris [plan] J. Fayeton, archt.
            Bauen & Wohnen
            #2:38-9 F 1957
            Konstruktionsblatt
            at end of issue

Fayette(Ia.)Upper Iowa University
    Model of campus and buildings.
            College and university
            business 7:15
            Jl '49

Fayette (MO) Central College
    W. C. Root, Arch.
            Inland Arch. 23:
            pl. fol. p 56
            Je., 1894

720.5
A67ar Fayetteville (N.C.) First Presbyterian church
    First Presbyterian Church, Fayetteville,N.C
Hobart B. Upjohn, architect.
            Architect 2:pl.138-41
            Sept. 1924

D15.1
H84 Fearing (George R.) house
    Set in the midst of an apple orchard:
The house of George R. Fearing. Gordon Allen
archt. for the remodelling.
            House beau 67: 45-47
            Ja '30

Febles Valdés, Manuel
    Hospital municipal de emergencias.
Addition.
    (plan) Manuel Febles Valdés, archt.
            Arquitectura Cuba
            16:246
            O 1948

Febles Valdes, Manuel
    La labor del arq. Manuel Febles Valdes en
el departamento de urbanismo de la Ciud.de La
Habana   [Plans]
            Arquitectura Cuba
            16: 156-172, 185-189
            Jl 1948

Febles Valdés, Manuel
    El nuevo ministro de obras publicas
            Arquitectura Cuba
            16: 247
            O 1948

Febure and Deporta
    see
Nice (Fr.) Notre dame du perpetual secours

Febure, J.
    see also
Nice (Fr.) Monument

913
A66j Fécamp. Trinité, La
            Fécamp Abbey. Plan.
            Archaeological journal 95:407-409
            Pt.2, 1938

Fechheimer, A.   Lincoln
    see
Cincinnati (O.) Hebrew union college

Federal architects association
    see
Association of federal architects

Federal buildings
    see
Public buildings

Federal housing

see

Housing projects, Government
Housing of defense workers

WILSON LIBRARY
705.042
W46   Feenstra, G
       House at Arnhem, Holland. G. Feenstra, archt.

Wendingen 12: 8
#4, 1931

Fehling, Hermann
    Mensa der Freien Universität in Berlin-Dahlem [plan] Hermann Fehling, archt.

Bauen & Wohnen
#7:256-57 Jl 1957

Federal housing administration

see

U.S. Federal housing administration

Feer and Eisenberg

see

Chelsea (Mass.)   memorial stadium

Fehmer & Page. Country House (photo) at Boston Arch. Club Exhibition 1906.

Inland Arch.
48: 54
Dec. 1906

Federal period architecture

see

Domestic architecture, U. S. Federal

Fees, Architects'

see

Architects. Fees

720.5
A67   Fehmer and Page
       Quarter scale of Bell Telephone building Boston. Fehmer and Page, archts.

Architectural review 1: pl. 46
June 15, 1892

Federal period interiors, U. S.

see

Domestic architecture, U. S. Federal

Fehling, Hermann
    House in Dahlem, W. Berlin [plan & section] H. Fehling, D. Gogel & P. Pfankuch, archts.

Archtl Design
29:43J N 1959

Feick, George, 1883-

see

Purcell, Feick and Elmslie
Purcell and Feick

Fedrigolli, Bruno, 1921-
    Hotel Jardin mit kino in Breno, Italien [plans & section] Bruno Fedrigolli, archt.

Architektur & Wohnform
66:9-19 O 1957

Fehling, Hermann
    Berlin-Pavillon für die INTERBAU im Hansaviertel [plan & section] Hermann Fehling, archt.

Bauen & Wohnen
#7:235 Jl 1957

720.5
A51   Feil and Paradise
       Guaranty Building and Loan Association, Los Angeles, California. Feil and Paradise, archts.

American architect 136: 219-222
September 1929

Feehanville (Ill.) Archbishop Feehan Summer Residence
Willett and Pashley, Archt.

Inland Archt.
vol. 29,No.5,pl.fol.p. 50
Jun, 1897

Fehling, Hermann
Lancelle, Annemarie
    Bücherstube Schoeller in Berlin. [plan]
Hermann Fehling, archt.

Arch & Wohnform 62:147-149
Ap 1954

720.5
A67d   Feil and Paradise
       Mandel's Broadway store,Los Angeles. Feil and Paradise,designers.
       Mullen and Bluett Wilshire store,Los Angeles.Morgan,Walls and Clements,archts. Feil and Paradise,store designers.

Architectural digest 8: 64,65
Number 2 [1932-33?]

Feehanville (Ill.) St. Mary's Training School. Central Building
Willett and Pashley, Archts.

Inland Archt.
vol. 29,No.5,pl.fol.p. 50
Jun, 1897

Fehling, Hermann
    Pavillon der glasindustrie auf der INTERBAU am Messedamm [plans] Hermann Fehling, archt.

Bauen & Wohnen
#7:242 Jl 1957

Feiss, Carl
[brief biographical sketch]

Nat'l arch 2:7
N '46

790.55
W31
    Feit and Rüger.
    Zschlin, H.J.
      Laubenganghäuser in Hagen. (Arcade buildings in Hagen.) Feit and Rüger, archts. Plans.

Wasmuths monatshefte 14: 366
Ag '30

720.5
P39
    Felipe, Sanchez
      Pen and ink drawing, Santiago de Composita, Spain, by Sanchez Felipe.

Pencil points 9: pl.1
January 1928

720.5
A67b
    Fellheimer and Wagner
      Chase National Bank, 48th St. branch, New York City. Fellheimer and Wagner, archts.

Architecture and building 61: 361,370-371
November 1929

D10.5
D32
    Felbach.Evangelische kirche
    Riedrich,Otto
      Der neue kirchenbau: Evangelische kirche in Felbach bei Stuttgart.Wilhelm Jost, archt.

Dekorative kunst 32: 237-233
July 1929

    Fellerer, Max
      Grossere mietwohnhausanlage bei Linz (Larger apartment buildings near Linz). Max Fellerer, archt. [plans]

Baumeister
32: 170-171
My 1934

720.5
A67f
    Fellheimer and Wagner
      Corn Exchange Bank Trust Co.,New York City.Fellheimer and Wagner,archts.

Architectural forum 65: 324
October 1936

    Feldman, H.I.
      Apartment house at Hartsdale, N.Y.

Archl forum
66: 410-411
My 1937

    Fellerer, Max
    Harbers, Guido
      Hotelrestaurant auf dem Tulblinger Kogel. (Hotel-Restaurant on the Tulblinger Kogel) Max Fellerer, archt. [plans and interiors]

Baumeister
31: 82-84, pl.24-25
Mr 1933

790.5
A67b
    Fellheimer and Wagner
      Corn Exchange banks 931st street branch and 42nd street branch, New York.Fellheimer and Wagner,archts.

Architecture and building 60:174-5
June 1928   pl.116-19

720.5
A67b
    Feldman, H. I.
      The Pierrepont Club, Brooklyn, N. Y. H. I. Feldman, archt.

Architecture and building 61: 362,375-376
November 1929

Fellheimer and Wagner

see also

Fellheimer, Alfred, 1875-

720.5
A67f
    Fellheimer and Wagner
      Oregon state capitol competition design. Fellheimer and Wagner, New York City. Plan

Architectural forum 65: 7
July 1936

    Feldspausch, Ed.

see

Böhm, Cl. and Ed. Feldspausch

MICROFILM

Fellheimer, Alfred, 1875-

in SCRAPBOOK ON
ARCHITECTURE p. 24
(on film)

720.5
A67r
    Fellheimer and Wagner
      A railway passenger station at Erie, Pa. Fellheimer & Wagner, archts.

Architectural record 65: 468-475
May 1929

705.8
T55
    Feldt,Gustaf Fredrik
    Schwerin,H.H.von
      Gustaf Fredrik Feldt och hans skanska herrgardsbilder.

Tidskrift för konstretenskap 16:67-74
no.2,1932

Fellheimer, Alfred, 1875-

see also

Fellheimer and Wagner

Fellheimer, Wagner and Vollmer

see

Brooklyn, N.Y. Farragut houses (project)

BURNHAM
    Felguerez, Manuel, 1928-
    Rodriguez, Ida
      Manuel Felguerez [illus]

Arquitectura Mexico
vol.17, 175, 178, S 1961

721
T55
    Fellheimer and Wagner
      Buffalo has a new Central Railroad terminal. Fellheimer and Wagner, archts. No plan.

Through the ages 9: front., 28-33
June 1931

Fellner & Helmer

see also

Vienna, Aus. Schnapper (Marie, Freifrau von) house

Fellner & Helmer

members of firm:

Fellner, Ferdinand, 1847-
Helmer, Hermann, 1849-1919

Fellows, William Kinne, 1870-1948
Obituary

Illinois society of architects
bulletin
32-33: 8
My-Ag 1948

Fence-posts

see

Fences

Fellner and Helmer
New Theatre, Zurich, Switzerland. Fellner
and Helmer, archts.

Arch rec
3: 165-8
O-D 1893

Felsenthal, Eli B., house (1886), Chicago

see

Chicago, Ill. Felsenthal, Eli B., house (1886).

Fences

see also

Gates
Hedges

Fellner and Helmer
The theatre at Pesth [plans] Fellner and
Helmer, archts.

Amer arch
1: 293-4
S 9, 1876

Felsheimer, Alfred

see

Macon (Ga.) Terminal station

Fences

House beaut. 41:147-149
Feb., 1917

Fellowes-Prynne, G.H.

see

Bournemouth (Eng.) St. Alban

Felstead, Eng. School
New Library, etc.: Felstead School. Henry
Chetwood and T.F.W. Grant, architects

Builder 124:pl.
Feb. 9, 1923

Fences

House beaut. 49: 110-111
Feb., 1921

Fellows, William Kinne, 1870-

Member of Firms:
Nimmons & Fellows (1898-1910)
Perkins, Fellows & Hamilton (1911-1927)
Hamilton, Fellows & Nedved (1927-1934)

Felstead (Eng.) School. Library
New library Felstead School. Henry Chetwood
and T.F.W. Grant, architects

Builder 124: pl.
Feb. 9, 1923

RYERSON LIBRARY
705.1   Fences
A792   Rothery, Agnes
          Fences and walls for every kind of garden

Arts and decoration 28:72,78
February 1928

MICROFILM
Fellows, William K.

in SCRAPBOOK ON
ARCHITECTURE p. 117
(on film)

Feltham, Eng. St. Lawrence Church
Church of St. Lawrence, Feltham, Middx, by
Thomas H.B. Scott. Plan.

Architects' journal 77: 270-271
February 22, 1933.

710.5   Fences
C855   Fences for every place and purpose

Country Life 47:61-65
Feb. 1925

Fellows, William Kinne   1870-
Brief biography.

Herringshaw, Clark J. Herringshaw's
city blue book of current biography.
Chicago: American Publisher's
Association, 1915

Felton house, Evanston, Ill.

see

Evanston, Ill. Felton house

710.5   Fences
C855   Pearson, H. S.
          Fences for every purpose.

Country life (U.S.) 62: 58-59
June-July 1932

710.5
H84
Fences
Fences that screen and protect. Ruth Dean, landscape archt.

House and garden 53: 62-65
June 1928

710.5
H44
Fences
New fences for old.

House and garden 74: 44-46
September 1938 (pt. 2)

720.5
A51
Fences, Iron
Fences.

Amer. arch. 104: 97-101
September 10, 1913

710.5
A51
Fences
Gaut, H. K.
Fences, walls and hedges.

American homes and gardens 7: 334-337
September 1910

710.5
H84
Fences
..Sketched here and there, by Jack M. Rose.

House and garden 38:26.
July, 1920.

Fences, Jade
see
Washington (D.C.) Pan-American Union building. Jade fence.

Fences
Keally, Francis
Four houses especially designed to show walls and fences used to advantage.

House and garden 59:45-49
January 1931

D13.1
H84
Fences
Sketches by Egbert G. Jacobson

House beautiful 55:129
Feb. 1924

710.5
H84
Fences, Rail
An old rail fence.

House and garden 56: 82
August 1929

710.5
L26
Fences.
From papers of Frederick Law Olmsted, Sr.

Landscape Arch. 11:13-18.
Oct. 1920.

D13.1
H84
Fences
Some suggestions for gates and fences of different types

House beautiful 64:410
October 1928

917.4
O44
Fences, Rail
The "worm" fence

Old time New England 15: 183
April 1925

710.5
C85
Fences
Gates and fences for garden and estate.

Country life (Lon.) 63: clxi,clxii.
March 31, 1928

710.5
H84
Fences
When you plan your garden

House & garden 42: 56
Dec. 1922

Fences. U.S., Mass. Cape Cod.
Old Cape Cod fence-posts

Landscape arch. 13:19-26
Oct. 1922

710.5
H84
Fences
How do you fence-in your yard?

House and garden 44:78-79
Oct. 1923

Fences
Wood fences. Architecture's portfolio

Arch 62: 300-314
N '30

051
A51
Fences, U.S. Wisconsin. Pine Grove.
Stott,C.B.
The white pine stump fences of Pine Grove village, Wisconsin

American-German review
7:14-15
October 1940

720.5
A67a
Fences
Metal fences. Architecture's portfolio.

Arch. 65: 358-72
Je '52

Fences, Colonial
see
Colonial fences

710.5
C85
Fences,Wattle
Wattles.

Country Life (Eng) 56:985-986
Dec. 20, 1924

710.8
C86   Fenders

Country life 55:1vi.
June 14, 1924

Fenton (Eng.) Library
Fenton Library Design. Brooks, Son, Godsell and
Grooms, London and Hereford, architects.

British archt. 60: 276 and pl
O 16, 1903

Ferdinand, Ind. Immaculate Conception Convent and
Chapel
Immaculate Conception Convent and chapel,
Ferdinand, Indiana

Amer. arch. 110:pl. 2135
Nov. 22, 1916

720.52
A67   Fenichel, Irving M.
A laundry in New York, designed by
Irving M. Fenichel.

Architects' journal 77: 127-128
January 25, 1933

Fentress (Anthony) house, Princess Ann County (Va)

See

Princess Anne County (Va.) Fentress (Anthony) house

Ferdinand, Ind. Immaculate Conception Convent
Immaculate Conception Convent, Ferdinand,
Indiana. Victor J. Klutho, archt.

Architecture 35: pl.62-66
April, 1917

Fenner, Burt Leslie
Letter from C.F. McKim. (1/10/1904)

Letters and autographs of famous
architects: A collection started for
Burnham Library by Thomas E. Tallmadge.
Housed in the Burnham and Ryerson
Libraries, The Art Institute of
Chicago. no. 8.

Fenway court, Boston

see

Boston. Isabella Stewart Gardner museum

Ferentino, It. Architecture
Bartoli, Alfonso
L'Acropoli di Ferentino

Bolletino d'arte 34:
295 - 306, O - D '49.

720.5
A67a   Fenner, Burt Leslie   1869-1926
Obituary.

Architecture 53: 85
March 1926

Fenway Garden, Boston

see

Boston, Mass. Fenway garden (proposed)

Feretories.

Bond, Francis. An introduction to
English church architecture. 2 vols.
London and New York: H. Milford, 1913.
v.1. p.77,91.

720.5
F59   Fenner, Burt Leslie 1869-1926
Obituary.

Pencil points 7: 105
February 1926

705.5
A78   Ferabosco, Martino
Beltrami, Giuseppe
Martino Ferabosco, architect

L'Arte 29: 23-36
Jan.-Feb. 1926

Ferguson, Finley Forbes, 1867-1946
obituary notice

in SCRAPBOOK ON
ARCHITECTURE p. 710
(on film)

720.5
W52   Fenner, Burt Leslie
McLean, R. C.
Obituary— Burt Leslie Fenner. F. A. I. A.

West. arch. 35:48
Apr. 1926

Ferber, C.H.

Member of firms:
Holstein, Ferber and Dewpey
Dittoe, Fahnestock and Ferber

Ferguson, Frank William   1861-1926

see also

Cram, Goodhue and Ferguson
Cram and Ferguson

Fenner, Burt L. Portrait

West. Archt.
23: 26
Mar, 1916

Ferdinand, Ind. Chapel of the Immaculate Conception
Immaculate Conception.
Ferdinand, Indiana

Amer. arch. 110: 317 and pl. 2135
Nov. 22, 1916

720.5
A67a   Ferguson, Frank William.   1861-1926
Obituary — Frank W. Ferguson.

Architecture.54:345
Nov.1926

Ferguson, Frank William 1861-1926
Obituary.

Pencil points 7: 686
November 1926

Fermi memorial. Chicago, Ill.

see

Chicago, Ill. Enrico Fermi memorial. Competition

Fernandez, José A

see

New York (city) Modernage building

Ferguson, H. K. Co.

see

Kankakee (Ill.) General foods corn mill

Fermor-Hesketh, Sir Thomas house

see

Easton Neston, Eng.

Fernandes Simon, Abel
Homenaje a los arquitectos Abel Fernandes
Simon y Manuel Angel Gonzales del Valle.

Arq. Cuba
17: 47-51
F 1949

Ferguson, Harry, inc., Detroit

see

Detroit (Mich.) Ferguson (Harry) inc.

Fernald, George Porter   Portal, drawing.
Selection from Boston Architectural Club
Exhibition, 1906

Inland Arch. 48:
pl. fol. p 60
D, 1906

Fernandez, Raul

see

Mexico (City) Universidad nacional.
Casino, Gimnasio y banos (project)

Ferguson, R.C.

see

Los Angeles (CA) Angelos (Mrs. Jessie W.) residence

Fernándes de Henestrosa,
    Football stadium, Barcelona [plan &
sections] J. Soteras Mauri, F. Mitjans Miró
& Garcia-Barbon Fernánves de Henestrosa, archts.

Archl Design
29:80-81 F 1959

"Ferncliff", N.Y.
    Kimbrough, Emily
Mansion on the Hudson. "Ferncliff", the Vincent
Astor estate, Rhinebeck, N.Y.

Country life (U.S.) 74:48-52,72
August 1938

Ferguson, W. H.

see

Bear Mountain (Ark.) hotel

Fernandes, Lygia, 1919-
    Residencia em Maceió, Alagôas [plans &
section] Lygia Fernandes, archt.

Habitat
6:67-9 Je 1956

"Ferncliff" (N.Y.) Sports Building
    Court and pool at "Ferncliff", country
residence of J.J. Astor. No plan. McKim, Mead
and White, archts.

A   Architectural record 18:20-26
July, 1905

Ferme de la Valouine, Fr.
    Ferme de la Valouine (Seine-Inférieure) (plan)

Encyclopedie de l'architcture,
constructions de Style. 2 vols.
Paris: Albert Morancé, 1928- ?
Tome 1: pls. 11-13

Fernandes Saldanha, Firmino,

see

Saldanha, F.F.

"Ferncliff" (N.Y.) Sports Building
    The stables, tennis court and pool of
"Ferncliff", Mrs. J.J. Astor's estate rt Rhinebeck,
N.Y. McKim, Mead and White, archts.
Lounging room. No plan.

A   Architectural record 20:177,208
September, 1906

Fermi, Enrico, 1901-55, competition
    Enrico Fermi Memorial Pavilion design com-
petition.

AIA Chis Chap Bul: p.22
S 1956

Fernández, Carlos Ardavin

see

Ardavin Fernández, Carlos,   -1955

"Ferncliff" (N.Y.) Sports building
    New sports building for Vincent Astor,
Rhinecliff (sic), N.Y. McKim, Mead and White,
archts.

Country life 29:38-39
November, 1915

720.5
A51
Ferndale (Mich.) Evangelical church
Ferndale (Michigan) Evangelical Church.
C. Howard Crane, arch. Elmer George Kiehler,
assoc.

Amer. arch. 126:115-16
July 30, 1924

Fernwood (Cal.) Percy (Mrs. Nelson Mortimer)
Estate,Guest Cabin
Edward W. Cannon, archt.

West. Archt.
29: pl. 11-12
May, 1920

Ferrara. Casa Romei
Casa Romei, Ferrara. Plan (dark) photograph
and interior sketches in text.

Palast Architektur. 6 vols in 11 bks.
Berlin: E. Wasmuth, 1886-1911
5:pt.1:7-8

Ferndale (MN) Bell (J.S.) Residence
William Channing Whitney, archt.

West. Archt.
16: pl.fol.p. 134
Dec, 1910

Ferra.Palazzo_Contabili
See
Ferrara.Palazzo Bentivoglio

Ferrara, It. Cathedrale.
Valentiner, W. R.
Il "Giudizio finale" della Cattedrale di
Ferrara. [illus.]

Critica d'arte
Anno 1, no. 2: 119-[132]
Mr., 1954

Fernekes and Cramer
see
Milwaukee WI. Andrae (J.) residence
" " Esser (Louis) "
" " Hoffman (H.J.) "
" " Poppendieck (John) "
" " Schaaf (Frank) "
" " Spence (Edward R.) "

Ferrand C. (Enrique) house, Miraflores, Peru
see
Miraflores, Peru. Ferrands (Enrique) house

Ferrara. Civica raccolta lapidaria
see
Ferrara. Palazzo dei diamanti

Fernhurst (Eng.). Parish Church. Door
Parish Church, Fernhurst, Sussex

Arch. 114:pl.
Nov. 27, 1926

Ferrante, Alberto
see
Verona (It.) Teatro Filarmonico

Ferrara. Civico lapidario
see
Ferrara. Palazzo dei diamanti

Fernier, Jean Jacques
see
Biro and Fernier

Ferrara
See also
Palaces, Italy. Ferrara

Ferrara. Palazzo Bentivoglio
Palazzo Bentivoglio, Ferrara. Erbaut 1585.
Photograph.

Palast Architektur. 6 vols. in 11 bks.
Berlin: E. Wasmuth, 1886-1911
5:pt.1:8,pl.28

Fernitz, Aus. Maria Trost (church)
Kodolitsch, O.
Maria Trost in Fernitz bei Graz. 200 Jahre
Diagnosen und Therapien an einer Wallfahrtskirche.
[illus.]

Österreichische Zeitschrift
für Kunst und Denkmalpflege
V.19, Heft 4: 164-171
1965

720.52
A67
Ferrara
Molani, Professor Alfredo
The palaces of Ferrara: Palazzo dei diamanti;
Palazzo Magnanini or Hall of the Merchants;
Palazzo Schifanoia; House of Ludovico Aristo;
Palazzo Sacrati;

Architect and contract reporter 97:
April 13;20;1917   213-215,pls.fol.p.224;
228-230,pls.fol.p.238

Ferrara. Palazzo dei diamanti
Palazzo dei Diamanti, Ferrara, Italy.
Biagio Rossetti, archt. Measured drawing,
photograph.

Italian Renaissance: Sixty measured
drawings with details. 3 vols.
New York: The architectural book
publishing company, n.d.
3:pl. 34, 49

Fermucken, Wilhelm
see
Vermuiken, Wilhelm

Ferrara. Arcivescovile
Erzbischöflicher palast, treppenhaus, Ferrara.
Interior photograph in text. Erbaut mitte des 18
Jahr. Photograph of staircase.

Palast Architektur. 6 vols in 11 bks.
Berlin: E. Wasmuth, 1886-1911
5:pt.1:7,pl.20

Ferrara. Palazzo dei diamanti
Palazzo di Diamanti, Ferrara. Biagio
Rossetti, archt. 1492-1567. Gabriel Frisoni
bildhauer. Photograph, Measured drawings.

Palast Architektur. 6 vols in 11 bks.
Berlin: E. Wasmuth, 1886-1911
5:pt.1:8,pls.24-25

Ferrara. Palazzo di Lodovici$_9$il Moro
   Palazzo di Lodovico il Moro, Ferrara, Italy.
Biagio Rossetti, archt. Measured detail drawing,
photograph.

A   Italian Renaissance: Sixty measured
         Drawings with details. 3 vols. New York:
         The architectural book publishing company,
         n.d. 2:pl.25
                 3:pl.49

Ferrara, It. Palazzo Schifanoia
Varese, Ranieri
   Novità a Schifanoia. [illus.]

                 Critica d'arte
                 Anno 17: 49-62
                 S-O 1970

Ferrari, Francesco Bernardino. Collection.
Perer, Maria Luisa Gatti
   Fonti per l'architettura milanese dal
XVI al XVIII secolo: Francesco Bernardino
Ferrari e la sua raccolta di documenti e
disegni - I. [illus.]

                 Arte lombarda
                 v.9, I: 173-222
                 1964

Ferrara. Palazzo di Lodovicio il Moro
   Palazzo Lodovico il Moro (Costabili)
Ferrara. Biagio Rossetti, archt. 1495.
Photograph and measured drawing.

         Palast Architektur. 6 vols. in 11 bks.
         Berlin: E. Wasmuth, 1886-1911
         5:pt.1:8-9,pls.29-30

Ferrara, Italy. Planning
Varese, Ranieri
   Ferrara, una storia e una carta, 2. [illus.]

                 Critica d'arte
                 39:39-46 (20,n.s.fasc.138)
                 N-D 1974

Ferrari, Francesco Bernardino. Collection
Perer, Maria Luisa Gatti
   Appunti per l'attribuzione di un disegno
della Raccolta Ferrari. Giovannino de'
Grassi e il Duomo di Milano. [illus.]

                 Arte lombarda
                 v.10, I: 49-64
                 1965

Ferrara. Palazzo Prosperi
   Palazzo Prosperi, Ferrara, Italy. Measured
drawing.

         Italian Renaissance: Sixty measured
         drawings with details. 3 vols.
         New York: The architectural book
         publishing company, n.d. 2:pl.24

Ferrara, It. Planning. 18th cent.
Varese, Ranieri
   Ferrara, una storia e una carta, 1. [illus.]

                 Critica d'arte
                 An.39,n.s.,fas.137:23-36
                 S-O 1974

Ferrari, Francesco Bernardino. Collection.
Perer, Maria Luisa Gatti
   Fonti per l'architettura milanese dal XVI
al XVIII secolo: Francesco Bernardino Ferrari
e la sua Raccolta di documenti e disegni - II.
[illus.]

                 Arte lombarda
                 v.9, II: 128-158
                 1964

Ferrara. Palazzo Prosperi
   Palazzo Prosperi, Ferrara, erbaut gegen 1500.
Photographs, measured drawings.

         Palast Architektur. 6 vols. in 11 bks.
         Berlin: E. Wasmuth, 1886-1911
         5:pt.1:8,pls.26-27

Ferrari, Dionigi Maria,

   see also

Fagnano Olona, Italy. Sant'Anna (chapel)

Ferrari, Francesco Bernardino. Collection
Perer, Maria Luisa Gatti
   Fonti per l'architettura milanese dal XVI
al XVIII secolo: Francesco Bernardino Ferrari
e la sua Raccolta di documenti e disegni - III.
[illus.]

                 Arte lombarda
                 v.10, I: 139-155
                 1965

Ferrara. Palazzo Roverella
   Palazzo Roverella, Ferrara, Italy. Measured
detail drawing, photograph.

         Italian Renaissance: Sixty measured
         drawings with details. 3 vols. New York:
         The architectural book publishing
         company, n.d. 2:pl.22-23
                 3:pl.49

Ferrari, Dionigi Maria, fl. 1733-1768
Perer, Maria Luisa Gatti
   Dionigi Maria Ferrari - Oratorio di S. Anna,
Fagnano Olona - 1762. [illus.]

                 Arte lombarda
                 v.12,II: 95-99
                 1967

Ferrari, Francesco Bernardino. Collection
Bascapé, Mariarosa
   I disegni di Martino Bassi nella Raccolta
Ferrari. Catalogo. [illus.]

                 Arte lombarda
                 v.12,II: 33-64
                 1967

Ferrara. Palazzo Roverella
   Palazzo Roverella, Ferrara. Erbaut 1508.
Photograph and measured drawings.

         Palast Architektur. 6 vols. in 11 bks.
         Berlin: E. Wasmuth, 1886-1911
         5:pt.1:7,pls.21-23

Ferrari, Dionigi Maria, fl. 1740-1783
Perer, Maria Luisa Gatti
   Fonti per l'architettura milanese dal XVI
al XVIII secolo: Francesco Bernardino Ferrari
e la sua raccolta di documenti e disegni - I.
Tom. (XVII) - Ing. Dionigi Maria Ferrari Mio
Padre. [illus.]

                 Arte lombarda
                 v.9, I; 215-217
                 1964

Ferrari, Lorenzo de, 1680-1744
Gavazza, Ezia
   Lorenzo De Ferrari tra Arcadia e
Neo-classicismo. [illus.]

                 Commentari
                 An.14:266-288;tav.CIV-CVII
                 O-D 1963

Ferrara. Palazzo Sacrati

   see

Ferrara. Palazzo Prosperi

Ferrari, Francesco Bernardino, fl.1770-1818
Perer, Maria Luisa Gatti
   Fonti per l'architettura milanese dal XVI
al XVIII secolo: Francesco Bernardino Ferrari
e la sua raccolta di documenti e disegni - I.
Tom.(XVIII) - De Me Ing.re Francesco Bernardino
Ferrari. [illus.]

                 Arte lombarda
                 v.9, I: 218-220
                 1964

Ferree, A. G.

   see

Chicago (Il) Halsted (South) (5745) Store and Flat
Chicago (Il) 2 Story Residence (Auburn Park)
Chicago (Il) 75th near Webster 2 Story Residence

Ferree, Barr
An "American style" of architecture.

Arhcitectural record 1:39-45
July - September 1891

720.5   Ferree, Barr
A67r   What is architecture?

Architectural record 1:199-210
October-December 1891

Ferrières, St. Louis, Mo.

see

St. Louis (Mo.) Ferrières

Ferree, Barr. Architecture & the allied arts.
    illus.

Inland Arch.
17: 55-7   June 1891   18: 71-83 Jan. 1892
17: 67-70   July 1891   19: 3-4   Feb. 1892
18: 3-5   Aug 1891   19: 19-21 Mar   1892
18: 17-18   Sept 1891   19: 31-2   April 1892
18: 27-9   Oct 1891
18: 37-9   Nov 1891
18: 59-62   Dec. 1891

Ferreira, Carlos Frederico, 1906-
    Armazens e estação de passageiros do Pier
Mauá, Pôrto do Rio de Janeiro [plans & sections]
Carlos Frederico Ferreira, archt. with Sergio
Wladamir Bernardes, archt.

Habitat
5:16-22 O 1955

Ferrin, Charles H.

see

Minneapolis (MN) Twin City Rapid Transit Co.

720.5   Ferree, Barr
A67r   Architecture in London: residences and office
buildings - work of R.N.Shaw;Ernest George and
Peto;T.E.Colcutt;Aston Bebb and others.

Architectural record 5:1-30
July-September 1895

Ferreira, Carlos Frederico, 1906-
    Associacao Atletica do Banco do Brasil
(AABB), Rio [plans & sections] Ante-projeto
premiado: Carlos Frederico Ferreira & Ralf
Cesar Habib, archts.

Habitat
6:24-8 F 1956

Ferris, James D
    Scheletri nuovi per una stadio, un palazzo
per uffici e un ponte [plan & sections]
Myron Goldsmith & James Ferris, archts.

L'Architettura
4:495-97 N 1958

720.5   Ferree, Barr
A67r   The art of the high building.

Architectural record 15:445-466
March 1904

MICROFILM

Ferrenz, Tirrell J.
    Architectural specifications and details.
(Lecture delivered to the Illuminating Engineering Society.)

in SCRAPBOOK ON
ARCHITECTURE p. 1103-1105
(on film)

Ferris, Julian
    Biblioteca Nacional de Caracas [plans]
Julian Ferris, Carlos Dupuy & Jaime Hoyos, archts.

Proa
#128:11-13 J1 1959

720.5   Ferree, Barr
A67r   French cathedrals. Pts. 1-16

Arch rec 2-8
1892-1898

Ferreolus, Saint. Crypte

see

St. Ferjeux, Fr. Eglise. Crypte

Ferriss and Kunse

see

St. Louis, Mo. memorial plaza

Ferree, Barr
    Modern office building. Sections. Plans.

Inland Arch.
27: 4-5   Feb   1896
27: 12-14   Mar   1896
27: 23-5   April 1896
27: 34-5   May   1896
27: 45-7   June 1896

Ferrer, Miguel, Jr.

see

Toro, Ferrer and Torregrosa

720.5   Ferriss, Hugh, 1888-1962
F59.   The Adler planetarium. Ernest A.
Grunsfeld,jr., archt. plans; a rendering by
Hugh Ferriss of facade.

Pencil points 10: pl.37,707-710
October 1929

Ferree, Barr
    Trinity Building, New York. Francis H.
Kimball, archt.

Inland Architect
46: 7-8
Aug, 1905

Ferrier, Claude W.

see

Highbury (Eng.) Arsenal football stand
London (Eng.) Institute for the blind

720.5   Ferriss, Hugh, 1888-1962
A51   Capitol Park, showing the Educational
building and pylons of the Memorial Bridge,
Harrisburg, Pa. From a drawing by Hugh
Ferriss.

American architect 135: 530
April 20, 1929

Burnham Index to Architectural Literature

Ferriss, Hugh, 1888-1962
Hugh Ferriss' vision of aerial terraces.

Woltersdorf, Arthur. Living
Architecture. Chicago: A. Kroch, 1930
160

720.5 A67ar
Ferriss, Hugh, 1888-1962
Study, by Hugh Ferris, proposed office
building, New York. Ludlow & Peabody, archts.

Architect (N.Y.) 10: 56
April 1928

720.53 W51
Ferriss, Hugh, 1888-1962
Hegemann, Werner
Zeichnung von Hugh Ferriss, New York. (Drawings by Hugh Ferriss of New York.)

Wasmuths monatshefte 13: 222-224
May 1929

720.5 A51
Ferriss, Hugh 1888-1962
Methodist Episcopal church, South Dallas,
Texas. Herbert M. Greene Co. archts. Rendering
by Hugh Ferriss.

American architect 120: 401,413
November 23, 1921

720.5 A67ar
Ferriss, Hugh 1888-1962
Study, Detroit branch of Chicago Federal
Reserve bank, Detroit. Graham, Anderson, Probst
& White, archts. Hugh Ferriss, del.
Penobscot bldg. Detroit.
Fisher bldg., Detroit.

Architect (N.Y.) 9: 298,300,302
December 1927

Ferrucci, Francesco di Simone
Palazzo Bevilacqua, Bologna - erbaut 1481-1484,
Portal von Francesco di Simone Ferrucci Bildh.
1438-1493. Photograph, measured drawings.

Palast Architektur. 6 vols. in 11 bks.
Berlin: E. Wasmuth, 1886-1911
5:pt.1:2-3,pls.4-6

720.5 A51
Ferriss, Hugh, 1888-1962
New York Life insurance company building,
New York. Cass Gilbert, Inc., archt. Rendering by Hugh Ferriss.

American archt.135: front
March 20, 1929

720.5 A67ar
Ferriss, Hugh, 1888-1962
Study of final design of the Smith-Young
Tower, San Antonio, Texas. Atlee B. Ayres &
Robert M. Ayres, archts. Hugh Ferriss, del.

Architect N.Y. 10: 86
August 1928

Ferrutius, Saint. Crypt
see
St. Ferjeux, Fr. Eglise. Crypte

720.5 P29
Ferriss, Hugh, 1888-1962
Old Jefferson market, New York city, drawn
on stone ... pulled by Bolton Brown.

Pencil points: 4 pl. Jan. 1923

720.5 A67ar
Ferriss, Hugh, 1888-1962
Study, 1301 Astor Street Apartment building, Chicago. Philip B. Maher, archt.,
Hugh Ferriss, del.

Architect (N.Y.) 12:144
May 1929

Ferry and Clas
see
Indianapolis (IN) Courthouse & Post office. Compet.
design
Madison (WI) Univ. of Wis. Library. Final Compet.
"   " Wisconsin Historical society library
"Compet.
Milwaukee (WI) Apartment bldg.
"   " Auditorium
"   " Clas (A.C.) flat bldg.
"   " Falk (Frank) house
"   " Falk (Messrs.) houses
"   " Frobach (H.) residence
(see next card)

720.5 W52
Ferriss, Hugh, 1888-1962
Pacific edgewater club, San Francisco, Cal.
J.R. Miller & T.L. Pflueger, archts. Rendering by Hugh Ferriss.

Western architect 36: front.
November 1927

720.5 A67
Ferriss, Hugh, 1888-1962
Work of Hugh Ferriss

Arch. review
24:n.s.7:21-25, Ag 1918

Ferry and Clas   (card 2)
see
Milwaukee (WI) Jorgensen (J.C.) studio
"   " Knights Templar bldg.
"   " Library & Museum. Compet. design
"   " Lindsay (Henry) house
"   " Northwestern nat'l insurance co.
"   " Pabst (Fred) house
"   " Pabst (Gustave) residence
"   " Public library
"   " Residences (2)
"   " Seminary

720.52 A67c
Ferriss, Hugh 1888-1962
A picture of the city as it may be, from
a drawing by Hugh Ferriss.

Architect 115: pls
February 5, 1926

Ferris, Hugh, 1888-1962
The world's largest airport.

Nat'l Arch 2:6
N '46

Ferry and Clas
Noteworthy Library Buildings: Milwaukee,
Wis. Public Library. Photo.

Inland Architect
34: supp.p. 14
Jan, 1900

MICROFILM

Ferriss, Hugh, 1888-1962
President's medal of the Architectural
League of New York.

in SCRAPBOOK ON
ARCHITECTURE p.1035
(on film)

Ferriss, Hugh
Youth in architecture

West. Archt.
22: 27-8
Sept, 1915

Ferry and Clas
Receive Gold Medal at Pan-Amer. Expo,
Buffalo N.Y., 1901.

Inland Architect
38: 32
Nov, 1901

Ferry, Dexter, house. Grosse Pointe, Mich.,

see

Grosse Pointe, Mich. Ferry, Dexter, house.

Ferry terminals

Archts & bldrs mag
42: 49-56
N 1909

Festivals
Licht, Margherita
L'influsso dei disegni del Filarete sui
progetti architettonici per teatro e festa
(1486-1513). [illus]

Arte lombarda
18:91-102
1973

Ferry, George B.

see also

Milwaukee (WI) Noyes (Judge George H.) residence

Ferry terminals. Competitions
Beaux Arts competition. Class B. A ferry
house.

Architecture 9: 61-2
Ap 15, 1904

Festivals, France
Fêtes de Versailles

L'architecture 35:57-64
Apr. 10, 1922

Ferry, George B.
Hotel building, Winona, Minnesota. G. B.
Ferry, archt. Sketch

Building budget 5:
pl fol p. 128
O 1889

720.52 Ferry terminals,England. Wallasey
B93   Seacombe Ferry buildings,Wallasey. Wil-
son B.Allison,chief architectural assistant.
L.St.G.Wilkinson,engineer,and surveyor.

Builder 145: 307,312,313
August 25,1933

Festivals. Italy
Arnold, Irene Ringwood
Agonistic festivals in Italy and Sicily.

American journal of
Archaeology
64:[245]-251
Jl 1960

Ferry, George B. -1918
obit.

West. Archt.
27: 16
Feb, 1918

Ferry terminals,U.S.St. George(S.I.)

See

St. George (S.I.)Ferry terminal

Festivals. Italy
Pillsbury. Edmund
The temporary façade on the palazzo Picasoli:
Borghini, Vasari, and Bronzino. [illus.]

U.S.National gallery of art
Report and studies in the
history of art:74-83
1969

Ferry, George B.
Public Libraries and their design and plan.

Inland Architect
37: 42-3
Jul, 1901

720.53 Festival halls, Germany
W31

Wasmuths 9 heft 1:27-32 & pl. 38
1925

Festivals, Italy. Umbria

Corpus Christi in Umbria

Country life Lond. 54:199
Aug. 11, 1923

Ferry, George B
Residence at Milwaukee, Wis. George B.
Ferry, archt.

Inland architect
v. 12 no. 7
pl. at end of vol.
D 1888

Festival of Britain, 1951

see

London (Eng.) Festival of Britain, 1951

Festivals. Italy. Venice
Watson, Ross
Guardi and the visit of Pius VI to Venice in
1782. [illus.]

U.S.National gallery of art
Report and studies in the
history of art:114-131
1968

Ferry, John

see

Panjab, Pakistan. Vanhar farm center (project)

Festivals

see also

Street decorations

Festivals. Sicily
Arnold, Irene Ringwood
Agonistic festivals in Italy and Sicily.

American journal of
Archaeology
64: [245]-251
Jl 1960

Festoons
Bas-relief antique

Tatham, Charles Heathcote.
Etchings, representing the best
examples of ancient ornamental
architecture. London: T. Gardiner,
1803. pl. 17-19

Ryerson
Fettweis, José
Prix d'architecture Van de Ven 1956:
Habitation a Meuay-Verviers, Belgique [plan]
José Fettweis, archt.

Aujourd'hui
Vol. 2:99
N 1956

Fick-Büscher, Catharina
Umbau eines büro- und wohngebäudes in
Nördlingen.

Baumeister
57:91 F 1960

720.82 Festoons
B93   The origin of the Adam festoon

Builder 124:639
April 20, 1923

Feucherolles, Fr. Architecture
Clos de St. Antoine. Three fourteenth
century houses at Feucherolles, Bois de Marly,
recently acquired by Edward Montgomery, architect

House beautiful 66:167-172
August 1929

Ficken, Henry Edwards   d. 1929
see
Evanston (IL) Sheppard (R.D.) residence
Montclair (N.J.) Fenn (Harry) house
New Haven (CT) (The) Cloister

Fêtes
see
Festivals

Feuerstein, Bedrich
see
Prague (Czech.) Krematorium

Philadelphia
Fidelity-Philadelphia trust building,
see
Philadelphia. Fidelity-Philadelphia trust
building

Feth, Dieter
Post- und wohngebäude Rieterplatz, Zürich
[plans and section] Diether Feth, archt.

Bauen and wohnen
No. 3: 166-167, Konstruktions-
blatt at end of issue
Je 1955

720.53 Feulner, Adolf
M68   Adolf Feulner - Color in the interior
decoration in the past.

Moderne bauformen 29: 184
Heft 4, April 1930

Fidenza (It.) Cattedrale
The western facade of the Duomo, Borgo
San Donnino.

Builder 91:16,pl fol 32
Jl 7 '06

Feth, William P.
see
Leavenworth (KS) high school

Fez. Architecture
Unchanging Fez: the ancient capital of Morocco

Country life Lond. 52:718-27;778-784
Dec. 2; 9, 1922

Fidler, Alwyn G. S.
Rome scholarship in architecture, 1933.
Winning design: a Road House. Alwyn G.S. Fidler,
archt.

Builder 144:972,1005-1006
June 23, 1933

Fetherstone and Durnford
see also
Arvida (Can.) Aluminum Company of Canada, Ltd.
Office building
Montreal, Que. Fetherstonhaugh (H.L.) house
"   "   McGill university. Douglas Hall

Fianello, It. Santa Maria.
Chiesa di S. Maria di Fianello in Sabina
(plans and sections)

Rassegua d'arte 16:281-288
Nov-Dec, 1916

Fiebig, M   Schmitt-
see
Schmitt-Fiebig, M

Fetherstonhaugh (H.L.) house, Montreal
see
Montreal (Que.) Fetherstonhaugh (H.L.) house

Fiber board
see
Wallboard

Fieder, F. Wm.
Odd bits from an architect's sketch book. F. Wm.
Fieder, archt.

Inland arch ?: 107,114,145,146
D 1883

Fiedler, August

see

Chicago, Ill. Fiedler (August) house

Field, Eugene, memorial

see

Chicago, Ill. Lincoln park. Eugene Field memorial

Field, Leiter and company store, Chicago (1868)

SEE

Chicago, Ill. Singer building (1868)

Fiedler and Penner

see

Elmhurst (Ill.) Hogans (L.A.) house

Field, Evelyn house, New York (city)

see

New York (city) Field (Marshall, 3rd) house

Field, Leiter and company store, Chicago (1873)

see

Chicago, Ill. Singer building (1873)

Field and Leiter store building (1873)

see

Chicago (Ill.) Singer building

Field, Evelyn house, Syosset, L. I.

see

Syosset, L. I. "Easton"

Field, Leiter and company store, Chicago (1878)

see

Chicago, Ill. Singer building (1878)

Field and Medary

see

Bala (PA) Roberts (G.B.) residence
Merion (PA) St. John's protestant episcopal church
Philadelphia (PA) Butcher (H.C.) house
    "   " Free library. Spring Garden branch.
    "   " Roberts (G. Brinton) residence
Wyncote (PA) Collins (P.L.) house
    "   " Lorimer (G.H.) stable

Field, G.W.E.

see also

Cincinnati (OH) Central union depot & railway bldg.
Hot Springs (VA) Bowling alley
  "   "   " Homestead hotel. Remodeling.
  "   "   " Ingalls (M.E.) cottage
  "   "   " Laundry bldg.

Field, Marshall and Co.

see also

Chicago (Il) Congress Hotel

Field and Simmons

see

London, Eng. Northeastern railway offices
Okehampton, Eng. Lloyds Bank
Wealdstone, Eng. Lloyds Bank

Field, G.W.E.
    Formerly of Read and Field opens
office in Richmond Va.

Inland Architect
21: 63
Jun, 1893

Field, Marshall, house, Chicago

see

Chicago, Ill. Field (Marshall) house

Field building, Chicago (135 S. LaSalle st.)

see

Chicago, Ill. Field building

Field, Horace

see

Field and Simmons

Field, Marshall, 3rd house, New York (city)

see

New York (city) Field (Marshall 3rd) house

720.5   Field, Ephraim
A67f   Le Tourneau steel house(mobile house)
      Ephraim Field, archt.

Architectural forum 67:53-56
July 1937

Field, Horace

see

Southampton (Eng.) Lloyd's bank

Field, Marshall 3rd, house, Syosset, L.I.

see

Syosset, L. I. "Easton"

Field memorial library, Conway, Mass.
 	
see
 	
Conway, Mass. Marshall Field memorial library
	720.5
	A67ar Fieldston (N.Y.) Morris (D.H.) house
	    Residence of Dr. Dudley H. Morris,
	Fieldston, N. Y. Julius Gregory, archt.
	
	    Architect (N.Y.) 12: 545-555
	    August 1929
		Fielitz, Eckhard Schulze-
		
		see
		
		Schulze-Fielitz, Eckhard, 1929-

Fielding, Mantel   1863-1941
 	
see
 	
Philadelphia. Fielding (Mantel) house
	710.5
	C855 Fieldston (N.Y.) Morris (D.H.) house
	    The residence of Dr. Dudley H. Morris at
	Fieldston, N. Y. Julius Gregory, archt.
	
	    Country life (U. S.) 56: 55-56
	    October 1929
		Fiera Campionaria. Milan, It.
		
		see
		
		Milan, It. Fiera Campionaria

710.5
H84   Fieldston, (N.Y.) Bierman (N.J.) house
    House of N.J.Bierman,Fieldston,N.Y.
Dwight James Baum,archt. Plan.
 	
    House and gardens 64: 37
    November 1933
	720.5
	A51 Fieldston,(N.Y.) Rollins,(Frank) house
	    Frank Rollins, Fieldston, New York.
	Dwight James Baum, archt.
	
	    Amer archt 121: 177-180 & pls
	    Mr 1 '22
		Fiera nacional del Campo, Madrid (Sp.)
		
		see
		
		Madrid (Sp.) Fiera nacional del Campo

Fieldston (N.Y.) Country Club
    Dwight James Baum, architect
 	
    Architect 3:pl. 10-12
    Oct. 1924
	Fieldston (N.Y.) Rollins (Frank) house
	    The house of Franke Rollins at Fieldston,
	New York. Dwight James Baum, architect.
	
	    House and Garden 40:54
	    Nov. 1921.
		Fiesole, It. Cathedral
		
		see
		
		Fiesole, It. San Romolo (cathedral)

Fieldston(N.Y.) Griffen (J.W.) house
   ...home of John W. Griffen at Fieldston
New york...Dwight James Baum, archt.
 	
    House and garden 39: 50
    Ja'21
	710.5
	H84 Fieldston (N.Y.) Wheeler (J.M.) house
	    A rock-ribbed house on a rocky knoll.
	Julius Gregory, archt. Plans. Dr. J. M.
	Wheeler, owner.
	
	    House and garden 60: 56-57
	    November 1931
	A
		Fiesole, It. San Francesco.
		    Church of S. Francesco, Fiesole, Italy.
		(drawing)
		
		    American architecture 112:pl.opp.p.381
		    November 21, 1917

720.5
A67ar   Fieldston.(N.Y.) Hoffman (W.P.) house
    House of William P. Hoffman, Fieldston,
New York. Dwight James Baum, archt.
 	
    The architect (N.Y.) 7: pls 36-38
    My '24
	RYERSON LIBRARY
	705.1
	A79 Fieldstone
	    Howe, Samuel
	    Fieldstone for the country house - notes on
	the texture and craftsmanship of informal masonry.
	
	    Arts and decoration 2:354-356
	    August 1912
		Fiesole, It. San Romolo (cathedral)
		    Apsidal treatment, no. 4: the cathedral,
		Fiesole, italy.
		
		    Amer archt & bldg news 55:23, pl
		    fol 24
		    Ja 16, 1897

720.5
A67ar   Fieldston (N.Y.) house
    Study, House, Fieldston, N. Y. W. Stan-
wood Phillips, archt. Plan
 	
    Architect (N.Y.) 3: 216
    D '24
	RYERSON LIBRARY
	705.1
	A79 Fieldstone
	    Price,C.M.
	    Possibilities in picture building: the field-
	stone home-"Storeacres" Bellows and Aldrich,archts
	
	A Arts and decoration 7: 186-189,218
	    February 1917
		Fiesole, It. Villa Benivieni
		    Roberts, M. F.
		    Modern life in an old Tuscany villa: home of the
		American artist, Ben Ali Haggin.
		
		    Arts and decoration 28:32-36,76
		    January 1928

Fiesole, It. Villa Medici
Plan of the Villa Medici at Fiesole, student's
work.

Pencil points 8:115
February, 1927

Figeac, Fr. Hotel de ville Garden
Arcatures dans les jardins de l'ancien
hotel de ville (xiiie siècle.)

Encyclopedie de l'architecture,
constructions de style. 2 vols.
Paris: Albert Morancé, 1928- ?
Tome 1: pl. 35

Figini, Luigi 1903-
Projekt für ein wohlfahrtsgebäude in Ivrea
[plans] Luigi Figini and Gino Pollini, archts.

Bauen and wohnen
No. 8: 285-287
Ag 1956

Fiesole, Italy, Villa Medici
Newton, T.
Villa Medici at Fiesole; its landscape construction,
plans and photographs.

Landscape architecture 17:185-98
April, 1927

Figeac. Maison
Maison à Figeac, XIII siècle.

Verdier, Aymar. Architecture Civile
et domestique. 2 vols. Paris: Bance,
1857-58. v.1:149-152, plates

Figini, Luigi , 1903-
Struttura della Fascia dei Servizi Soci-
ali ad Ivrea [plan] Luigi Figini & Gino Pollini, archts.

L'Architettura
4:641-42 Jan 1959

Fiesso Umbertiano, It. Villa Vendramin-
Calergi
Forlati, Ferdinando
La villa Vendramin-Calergi a Fiesso Umbertiano
(Rovigo) [illus.]

Arte veneta
v.19: 175-178
1965

Figini, Luigi, 1903-

see also

Rome, It. Exposition 1942. Palazzo dell' autar-
chia, del Corporativismo e della Previdenza ed
Assicurazione
Stone houses, Italy

Figueiredo, Bernardo de
Posto na Rio-Petrópolis (service station)
[plan] Bernardo de Figueiredo & Edson de
Cesare Musa, archts.

Módulo
vol.5: 14-15 , Je 1961

Fiestas, see
Festivals

Figini, Luigi, 1903-
Dove far andare l'architettura - edificio in
Milano. Gino Pollini e Luigi Figini, archts.
[plans, sect]

Domus
No. 239:1-9
1949

720.52   Fiji Islands
A67c   The new government house at Suva: modern
architecture and building problems in the
Fiji Islands.

Architect (Eng.) 120: 565
November 2, 1928

Fietz, Hermann, 1898-
Zahnärztliches Institut der Universität
Zürich [plans & sections] R. Steiger, H. Fietz
& M.E. Haefeli, & others, archts.

Bauen & Wohnen
vol.15: Supp.2 & 4, N 1961

Figini, Luigi, 1903-
Kleinkinderkrippe und kinderhort in Ivrea
[plan] Figini and Pollini, archts.

Bauen and wohnen
No. 8: 277-280
Ag 1956

Fikoff, Nicolai
Embaixada da Bélgica em Brasilia [plans]
Nicolai Fikoff, archt.

Module
vol.5: 37-42, Ag 1961

Fife (county), Scot. Pitcorthie house.
Webb, Michael
A versatile holiday house in Fife. [illus.]

Country life
143: 1461-1462
My 30, 1968

Figini, Luigi, 1903-
Maquette pour un garage. Pollini and
Figini, archts.

L'architecture vivante
Pl 42
Winter 1927

Filarete, Antonio di Pietro Averlino,
known as, 1400? - 1469
Canton, Giuseppina dal
Architettura del Filarete ed architettura
veneziana: analisi campione di un palazzo del
"Trattato" filaretiano. [illus]

Arte lombarda
18:103-115
1973

Fifth Avenue Association. awards, year
see
New York (N.Y.) Fifth Ave. Ass'n. Awards. Year.

Figini, Luigi, 1903-
Neues bürogebäude der Olivettiwerks in
Ivrea [plan and section] L. Figini, G. Pollini
and A. Fiocchi, archts.

Bauen and wohnen
No. 8: 256-258
Ag 1956

Filarete, Antonio di Pietro Averlino,
known as, 1400? - 1469
Gatti, Sergio
L'azione del Filarete in un giudizio di
Cesare Cesariano.

Arte lombarda
18:129-132
1973

Filarete, Antonio di Pietro Averlino,
known as, 1400? - 1469
Olivato, Loredana
La città "reale" del Filarete. [illus]

Arte lombarda
18:144-149
1973

Filarete, Antonio di Pietro Averlino,
known as, 1400? - 1469
Sinisi, Silvana
Il Palazzo della Memoria.

Arte lombarda
18:150-160
1973

720.5   Filing systems.
A67ar   "The Architect" index filing system.

Architect (N.Y.).7:56
Oct. 1926

Filarete, Antonio di Pietro Averlino,
known as, 1400?-1469
Carpeggiani, Paolo
Congruenza e parallelismi nell'architet-
tura lombarda della seconda metà del '400: il
Filarete e Luca Fancelli. [illus]

Arte lombarda
18:53-69
1973

Filarete, Antonio Di Pietro Averlino, known
as, 1400?-1469
Foster, Philip
Per il disegno Dell'Ospedale di Milano.
[illus]

Arte lombarda
18:1-22
1973

718/5   Filing systems
L26   Taylor, Albert D.
          Filing system data for landscape architects.

Landscape architecture 19:187-216
April 1929

Filarete, Antonio di Pietro Averlino,
known as, 1400? - 1469
Onians, John B.
Filarete and the "qualità": architectural
and social. [illus]

Arte lombarda
18:116-128
1973

Filarete, Antonio di Pietro Averlino,
known as,1400?-1469
Pigozzi, Marinella
La presenza dell'Averlino a Mantova e a
Bergamo. [illus]

Arte lombarda
18:85-90
1973

Filing Systems. Need of better methods in
filing public documents.

Inland Arch.
27-31
May 1896

Filarete, Antonio di Pietro Averlino,
known as, 1400?-1469
Wakayama, Eiko M. L.
Filarete e il compasso:nota aggiunta all
teoria prospettica albertiana, [illus]

Arte lombarda
18:161-171
1973

Filarete, Antonio di Pietro Averlino, known as,
1400?-1469
Resoconto sommario---corso di specializza-
zione I.S.A.L. sull'arte lombarda:«Il Filarete».
Villa Monastero di Varenna, 17-21 giugno 1972.
[illus]

Arte lombarda
18:196-199
1973

720.5   Filing systems
P59   Numerical index of folios of magazine
          plates and articles.

Pencil points 10: 267-268,270
April 1929

Filarete, Antonio di Pietro Averlino,
known as, 1400?-1469
Puppi, Lionello
Filarete in gondola. [illus]

Arte lombarda
18:75-84
1973

Filarete, Antonio di Pietro Averlino,known
as, 1400?-1469
Levi d'Ancona, Mirella
Il "S. Sebastiano" di Vienna: Mantegna e
Filarete. [illus]

Arte lombarda
18:70-74
1973

720.5   Filing systems
P59   The Pencil Points filing system for archi-
          tectural plate pages.

Pencil points 9: 527-528
August 1928

Filarete, Antonio di Pietro Averlino,
known as, 1400?-1469
Licht, Margherita
L'influsso dei disegni del Filarete sui
progetti architettonici per teatro e festa
(1486-1513). [illus]

Arte lombarda
18:91-102
1973

Filarete, Antonio di Pietro Averlino,
known as, 1400?-1469
Seymour, Charles, Jr.
Some reflections on Filarete's use of antique visual sources. [illus]

Arte lombarda
18:36-47
1973

Filing systems. Uniform sizes for catalogues,
etc. desirable.

Inland Arch.
51: 82
Jan. 1908

Filarete, Antonio di Pietro Averlino, known
as, 1400?-1469
Perogalli, Carlo
Origini e fortuna delle torri considdette
«filaretiane».

Arte lombarda
18:48-52
1973

Filarete, Antonio di Pietro Averlino, known
as, 1400?-1469
Spencer, John R.
Two new documents on the Ospedale Maggiore,
Milan and on Filarete.

Arte lombarda
Anno 16: 114-116
1971

Filling stations

see

Automobile service stations

720.5 W52 **Fillmore (Cal.)(near) Camulos ranch house** Newcomb, Rexford The architecture of the Spanish renaissance in California. Part 26. Rancho Camulos - the home of the fabled Ramona. Western architect 32: 17-20,pl.14-16 February 1923	**Finance, Building** see building, Finance	710.5 C855 **Findlay,Hugh** Spring in a Westchester garden: "Lue Shore",Portchester,N.Y. - home of Mr.and Mrs Walter C.Teagle. Hugh Findlay,archt. Country life(N.Y.)69:54-57 March 1936
720.5 A67ar **Fillmore (Cal.) First church of Christ / Scientist** Study, First Church of Christ, Scientist, Fillmore, Calif. H. Roy Kelley, archt. Architect (N.Y.) 11: 32 October 1928	**Finchcocks (Kent), Eng.** Lloyd, Nathaniel Gems of English architecture. pt. 3, Finchcocks, Goudhurst. Architectural review (Lond.) 45:68-73,pls. April, 1919 3	**Findlay (OH) Linaweaver (Dr. A.H.) residence** Henry Preibisius, archt. Dr. A.H. Linaweaver, designer Photos West. Archt. 4: 8, pls. fol. p. 8 Aug 1905
Filmore (Cal.) First Church of Christ,Scientist First Church of Christ Scientist, Fillmore (Cal.) H. Roy Kelley, archt. Architectural digest 7:138-139 Number 4 [1931?]	**Finchley (Eng.) Fire Station and cottages** Fire station and cottages, Finchley. Percival T. Harrison, engineer and surveyor. Plans. Architect (Long.) 149:160-162 January 29, 1937	**Fine arts academy building, New York city (1892)** see New York (city) Fine arts academy building (1892)
720.5 F29 **Fillmore, Lavius 1767-?** Into Vermont: fraternity house, University of Vermont: Congregational Church, Middlebury, Vermont, said to have Wren characteristics, Lavius Filmore, archt.; Town Hall at Burlington, McKim, Mead and White, archts.; no plans. Federal architect 7:49,50,52-53 January 1937	**Finchley (Eng.) "Glenroy"** "Glenroy," Finchley: exterior from garden front. E.W. Poley, archt. Architect 68: pls. fol. p. 32 August 22, 1902	**Fine arts bureau (proposed). see** United States. Fine arts bureau (proposed)
917.4 044 **Fillmore,Lavius 1767-?** Booth, Rev. Vincent Restoration of the old First Church of Bennington, Vermont. Built 1805 - dedicated January 1, 1806. Lavius Fillmore, archt. Old-time New England 30:front,73-81 January 1940	**Finchley (Eng.) Public Baths** Public Baths, Finchley. A.W.S. and K.M.B. Cross, architects Architect 110:pl Aug. 24, 1923	720.5 I56 **Fine Arts Bureaus** Wide spread desire for fine arts bureaus. Attitude of European societies. Inland arch 51: 49-50 Je '08
710.5 C855 **Filoli, California** Country life in America. On the California estate of W. P. Roth, Esq. [27 m. south of San Francisco] Country Life v. 72: 29-40 June 1937	**Finchley, Eng. Public baths** Public baths, Finchley. Selected design by A.W.S. Cross, arch.. Builder 105: pl fol 442 O 24, 1913	**Fine arts bureaus, United States** see U.S. Fine arts bureau (proposed)
Filtration plants see Waterworks	720.52 B93 **Finchley (Eng.) Public baths** Public baths, Finchley Builder 106:pl. for My 1, '14	**Fine arts institute, Chicago** see Chicago, Ill. Fine arts institute

Finell, Matti
see
Helsinki (Fin.) Snedslund hus

Fingland, William
see
Saskatoon (Sas.) Standard Trusts bldg.
Winnipeg (Man.) Fisher (E.A.) residence

710.5   Finials.
C88   Newel Posts.

Country Life. 48:81042
Oct. 16' 1920.

Finella (Eng.)
Frost, A. C.
Finella - a house for Mansfield D. Forbes.
Raymond McGrath, archt.

Architectural review (Lond.) 66:pl.1-2,
December, 1929   p.264-272

Finials.

Cassina, Ferdinando. Le fabbriche più
cospicue di Milano. 2 vols. Milan:
F. Cassina and D. Pedrinelli, 1840-64.
pl. P.

Finials, England

Ambler, Louis. The old halls and manor
houses of Yorkshire...London: B.T.Batsford,
1913. Fig. 11,12.

Fingask, Scotland
Cox, E.H.M.
A garden of Scottish statues: sculpture and
topiary at Fingask.

Country life (Lond.) 80:62-63
July 18, 1936

Finials.

Cottingham, Lewis Nockalls. Plans,
elevations, sections, details, and
views of the magnificent chapel of
King Henry the Seventh at Westminster
Abbey. 2 vols. London: Priestley and
Weale, 1822-29. v.1 pl. 19,33.

Finishing of woods
see
Wood finishing

Finger and Rustay
Finger and Rustay, Architects distinguished
firm in Houston, Texas.

Nat'l arch file
Jl '46

Finials

Garner, Thomas and Arthur Stratton.
The domestic architecture of
England during the Tudor period.
3 vols. London: B.T. Batsford,
1911. v.2:pl.140-141

Fink, Charles A.
see
Milwaukee (WI) Forest Home cemetery, Mausoleum

Finger, Joseph
see also
Finger and Rustay

Finials

Godfrey, Walter Hindes,. The
English staircase...London:
B.T. Batsford, 1911., plate 22.

720.5   Fink, Robert Kendall
P59   Skinner, J. L.
            The drawings of Bob Fink.

Pencil points 8: 524-34
September 1927

Finger, Joseph, Inc.
see also
Houston (Tex.) Clarke & Courts printing house

Finials

Ysendyck, Jules Jaques Van.
Documents classes d l'art dans les
pays-Bas. 5 vols. Anvers: J. Maes, 1880-89.
B,pl.14;C,pl.23;E,pl.24;F,pl.24
H,pl.17;L,pl.6,9,11;M.pl.6,14,22,34;
P,pl.34;T,pl.5,11,13.

Finkelhor, Robert
see
Beverly Hills (Cal.) Bricker (David) house
      "   "   "   Buckman (Sydney) house
      "   "   "   Krasna (Norman) house
      "   "   "   Loew (D.L.) house

720.5   Finger, Joseph, Inc.
A67f   Printing plant, Clarke & Court, Houston,
            Texas. Joseph Finger, Inc., architects. Plan.

Architectural forum 65: 338
October 1936

Finials
Carved finials on newels of staircase.

Arch and bldrs' jour. 45:pl.for
Mar. 14, 1917

720.5   Finken, John
A67d   Pergola, garden grounds of Archibald
            W. Edes estates Beverly Hills, Cal. Seymour
            Thomas, landscape archt. John Finken, assoc.
            archt.

Architectural digest 7: 64
Number 2 [1931]

Finkler, Adolph

see also

Chicago (IL) City hospital
"   "   Finkler (Adolph) residence

Finland-Architecture

Art et decoration 23:17-32
Jan. 1908

Finland, Architecture
Blomstedt, Aulis
Inleiding.
Schimmerling, André
De ontwikkeling van de Finse architectuur.

Forum
f1:2-9 Jan 1958

720.5
I56   Finkler, Adolph
       City hospital, Chicago. Adolph Finkler,
       archt. Plan

       Inland architect and news record 25:pl.
       April 1895   fol.p.28

Finland, Architecture

L'architecture 40:389-394
N 1927

Finland, Architecture
Lindberg, Carolus.
L'etude de l'architecture nationale en Finlande.

Congrès d'histoire de l'art,.
Paris, 1921. 3 vols. Paris:
Les presses universitaires
de France, 1923-24. 2:143-148

---

711   Finland.
377

Der Städtebau 17: 21-7 & pl.
13-19. Heft 3-4, 1920.

720.52
A67o   Finland. Architecture
       Gaisford, Cassie
       Ancient glories of Finland. Illustrations of
       the castle and cathedral of Abo; the Katherine
       tower, the castle, and the round tower of Viborg;
       the castle of Olafsborg.

       Architect 115: 152-154
       February 19, 1926

720.52
B93   Finland. Architecture
       Mediaeval church architecture in Finland

       Builder 123: 547-50
       Oct. 13, 1922

710.5
C85   Finland
       Beck, Herbert
       The lure of Finland: Abo, an inland town.

       Country life (London) 78:xxx
       November 23, 1935

720.52 Finland. Architecture
A673   The architecture of Finland. 1-the past

        Arch. rev. 56:215-219
        Dec. 1924

720.52 Finland. Architecture
B93   Mediaeval church architecture in Finland

        Builder 123: 582-5
        Oct. 20, 1922

Finland. Architects

        see also

Asplund, E Gunnar   Paatela, Toivo
Blomstedt, P   E   Paalanen, Martti
                      Petrelius, A A
Gustafsson, Ragnar   Rancken, A A
Huttunen, Arikl   Schroderus, Eino
Jäntti, Toivo   af Schultén, Marius
Lindgren, Yrjö   Schults, Sigurd
Meurman, Otto-Iivari Strömmer, Bertal
                      Vähäkallio, Väinö

720.52 Finland, Architecture
A673   The Architecture of Finland.

        Arch. Rev. 57:34-39
        Jan. 1925

720.53 Finland. Architecture
W31   Two new buildings in Helsingfors, Finland.
        Torben Grot, archt.

        Wasmuths 11:233
        Heft 6, 1927

720.54 Finland. Architects
A67   Chauliat, A
       "Constructeurs d'églises finlandaises des
       XVIIe et XVIIIe siècles." (Review of book by
       Heikki Klemetti)

       L'architecture 43: p.31-32
       January 15, 1930

---

705   Finland. Architecture
W48   Doppelnummer. Finnland. [special no. -
       historical and modern].

       Das Werk 27:special no.
       Mr. - Ap. 1940

792.05 Finland. Architecture. 20th century
T37   Losey, Joe
       A new theatre for Finland: for the Kansant-
       eatteri or People's theatre. P.E.Blomstedt, archt.
       Plans.

       Theatre arts monthly 20:33-36
       A   January 1936

720.52 Finland. Architects
A67   The Finnish houses of Parliament. J. S.
       Sirén, archt.

       Architects' journal 76: 725-729
       December 7, 1932

720.52 Finland. Architecture
A67   The growth of a national style

        Architects' journal 57:757-63
        May 2, 1923

MICROFILM
       Finland. Architecture. 20th century. Exhi-
       bitions. 1936
       ... a large exhibition of photographs ...

       Scrapbook of art &
       artists of Chicago
       p. 24
       1936

Finland. Architecture. 20th century. Map
Benson, John
Modern architecture in Helsinki, Finland
[map with numbered key giving archt., address &
date]

Architectural Design
31: 199-200, My 1961

720.571 Finland. Architecture. Russian influence
A72 Viiste, Juhani O. V.
De av Katarina II och Alexander I
påbjudna fasadtypernas inflytande på det
Gamla Viborgs stadsbild

Arkitekten no. 1:8-9
1940

---

705 Finland. Reconstruction
W48 Der Architektenverband Finnlands und der
Wiederaufbau

Das Werk 29:XXVI-XXVIII
Sup. Ap. '42

Finlayson, Adrian C.
see
San Juan (Por.R.) capitol

Finn, Alfred C.
see also
San Jacinto monument

Finney memorial chapel, Oberlin
see
Oberlin, O. college. Finney memorial chapel

Finnish institute of technology
see
Helsinki (Fin.) Suomen teknillinenkorkeakoulu

Finnish sports institute
see
Vierumäki urheiluopisto, Fin.

Finsbury, Eng.
see
London, Eng. Finsbury

Finseth, John
see
Frediksvarn (Nor.) war memorial beacon

720.54 Finsing-on-Isar (Ger.) Power Plant
A67v L'usine hydro-électrique de Finsing-sur-
Isar,Bavière. (The Hydro-Electric Factory
of Finsing-on-Isar,Bavaria.) Archt.not given
No plan.

L'architecture vivante : pl.7
Spring 1927

Fiocchi, Annibale
Angestellten-wohnhäuser der Firma Olivetti
in Ivrea, Italien; erbaut im jahre 1950 [plans]
Annibale Fiocchi & Marcello Nizzoli, archts.

Arch & Wohnform
58:125-29 My 1960

Fiocchi, Annibale
Bürobau Olivetti Mailand [plans and
section] Dr. Gian Antonio Bernasconi, Dr.
Annibale Fiocchi, and Marcello Nizzoli,
archts.

Bauen and Wohnen
No.1: 11-16
Ja 1956
Konstruktionsblätter at
end of issue
F 1956

Fiocchi, Annibale
Kindererholungsstation in Marina di Massa
[plans] A. Fiocchi and O. Cascio, archi.

Bauen and Wohnen
No. 8: 274-275
Ag 1956

Fiocchi, Annibale
Neues bürogebäude der Olivettiwerke in
Ivrea [plan and section] L. Figini, G. Pollini
and A. Fiocchi, archts.

Bauen and Wohnen
No. 8: 256-258
Ag 1956

Fiocchi, Annibale
Le siège de la société Olivetti à Milan.
G. A. Bernasconi, A. Fiocchi & M. Nizzoli,
archts.

Aujourd'hui v.1 no.2
p. 80-83
Mr-Ap 1955

Fiorentino, Mario
see also
Lariano, It. Edificio ente beni demaniali

Fiorentino, Mario, 1918-
Melograni, Carlo
Il collegio universitario della Facoltà d'Agraria
a Portici, dell'architetto[plans, section & details]
Mario Fiorintino, archt.

Casabella
#238: 28-35, Ap 1960

Fire department houses
see
Fire houses

Fire dogs, see
Andirons

720.5 Fire doors
A51 Automatic exit fixtures, or "panic bolts"

American architect 123:471-5
May 23, 1923

Fire doors
    Fire resisting doors and windows.

            Architects' jour. 64:454-457
            October 13, 1926

Fire houses, England
    E. and O. E.
    Current notes on planning. Fire stations. Plans.

            Archt (Lond.) 150:
            161-62;My 7, 1937
            184-85; " 14, "
            287-88;Ja 4, "

Fire houses, U.S. Conn.

            see

    Bridgeport (Conn.) Fire and police station
    Westville (Conn.) Fire engine house

Fire engine houses

    see

Fire houses

Fire houses, England. Redhill.
    (plans)

            Builder 107:455-456
            N 13, 1914

Fire houses, U.S. District of Columbia

            see

    Washington,(D.C.) Fire engine house
        "   "   "   "   "   , no. 2

720.5   Fire escapes
A67r   Pember,C.A.
            The problem of the fire escape:a suggested
        solution. Plans

            Architectural record 32:169-174
            August 1912

Fire houses, Germany

            see

    Berlin (Ger.) Fire station, Stockholm st.
    Karlsruhe (Ger.) Fire station

Fire houses, U.S. Georgia

            see

    Gainesville (Ga.) Fire station

Fire escapes, U.S. Ill. Chicago

            see

    Chicago, Ill. Fire escapes

Fire houses, U.S.
    American fire departments.

            Inland Arch.
            52: 1
            July 1908

Fire houses, U.S. Maryland

            see

    Baltimore (Md.) Fire station

Fire houses
    Fire Department Buildings. By Halsey
Wainwright Parker.

            Brickbuilder 19:117-127
            May, 1910

Fire houses, U.S.
    Plans. A.S. Jenney and C.W. Bixby, arch'ts.

            Brickbuilder 25 pl.
            10-12
            Ja 1916

Fire houses, U.S. Massachusetts

            see

    Boston (Mass.) Fire Station
    Brighton (Mass.) Fire station (central)
    Cambridge (Mass.) Fire station
    Quincy (Mass.) Fire station. Hose house and
                                    wardroom
    Salem (Mass.) Fire station (branch)

Fire houses. Competition
    Beaux-arts institute of design, awards:
"A fire house".

            B.A.I:D. 5: 12-13
            February, 1929

Fire houses, U.S. Alabama

            see

    Gadsden (Ala.) Fire station

Fire houses, U.S. Michigan

            see

    Detroit (Mich.) Fire alarm telegraph building
                                    (central)

Fire houses, England

    see also
    Bristol (Eng.) Fire and police station
    Brighton (Eng.) Fire Station
    Dover (Eng.) Fire Station
    Finchley (Eng.) Fire Station and Cottages
    Hull (Eng.) Fire Station (central)
    Hove (Eng.) Fire Station and electrical offices
    East Grinstead (Eng.) Fire brigade station

Fire houses, U.S. Calif.

            see

    Oakland (Cal.) Fire stations
    San Francisco (Cal.) Fire engine houses

Fire houses, U.S. New Jersey

            see

    Hackensack (N.J.) Fire house

Fire houses, U.S. New York

see .

Albany (N.Y.) Fire house
Garden City (L.I.) Fire house and auditorium
New York (N.Y.) Fire engine house, Vermilye Ave.
"   "   Fire dept. hdqtrs., 68th St.
New York (N.Y.) Fire engine house, Great Jones St
Brookline (Mass.) Fire station

720.5
A87r
Fire prevention
Pond, I.K.
The architect and fire protection. Paper read
at the convention of the National Fire protection
association at Chicago, May 18, 1910.

Architectural record 28: 71-74
July 1910

Fire Prevention
Fire protection in small cities.

Amer. arch. 126:89-94
July 30, 1924

Fire houses, U.S. Ohio

see

Columbus (O.) Fire station, Cleveland ave.
Oakwood (O.) Fire station

Fire prevention
The architects responsibility for fire
safety.

AIA bul
10: 55-60
Mr-Ap 1956

Fire prevention
Fire protection of the dwelling house.

Architecture and building 44: 65-88
Feb. 1912.

Fire houses, U.S. Pennsylvania

see

Philadelphia (Pa.) Fire and patrol station, 22nd
St.

710.5
C855
Fire prevention.
Checkmating the fire god.

Country Life 41: 58-9.
April 1922.

Fire prevention
Fireproof ordinance - editorial note.

Inland arch 3:33
Ap 1884

Fire houses, U.S. Texas

see

Dallas (Tex.) Fire stations
San Antonio (Tex.) Fire station (suburban)

Fire Prevention
Department of Engineering and construction.

Arch. forum 33:139-42.
Oct. 1920

Fire prevention
Fireproof requirements for buildings

Amer architect 122:472
N 22, 1922

Fire houses, U.S. Virginia

see

Richmond (Va.) Fire dept. headquarters

Fire prevention
Exterior openings, and Comparative exposure
table.

Architectural forum 32:41-6.
Jan. 1920.

Fire Prevention
First aid fire appliances

Amer. architect 123:89-90
Jan. 17, 1923

Fire prevention

see also

Factories, Fires and fire prevention
Theaters, Fires and fire prevention
Museums, Fires and fire prevention

Fireproof construction
Fire resisting materials

Fire prevention
Bird, Eric L.
Fire precautions and means of escape.

Archl Design
28:264 Jl 1958

Fire prevention
Installing fire protection

Architecture 42:218-20.
Jul. 1920

Fire Prevention

Arch. Jour. 54:737-9.
Dec. 21, 1921

Fire prevention. Fire protection equipment.

Inland Arch.
52: 71
Dec. 1908

710.5
C855
Fire prevention
Taylor, C.S.
New methods of fire prevention.

Country life (U.S.)63: 72,74
January 1933

Fire Prevention Proposed State Law for fire protection. Inland Architect 46: 38 Nov, 1905	Fire Prevention, England. British Fire Prevention Committee, reports and testing operations 1899-1900 Builder 79: 81; Jl 28, 1900 175; Ag 25, "	Fire Resistance. Testing The Test of Building Materials in the Baltimore Fire. By J.B. Noel Wyatt. Brickbuilder 8: 34-35 Mr. 1904 (extra number)
Fire Prevention Protection against exposure fires American architect 125:347-8 Apr. 9, 1924	Fire prevention, England. London Fire protection in London. Builder 89:65-66 July 15, 1905	Fire resisting materials see also Fireproof construction
Fire Prevention Alfred Hands, F.R. Met. S. "Protection from Lightening." Arch and con rep. 79: 260-62; Ap 17, 1908 270-71; Ap 24, "	720.54 A67 Fire prevention, France Michaut,J. Exposition du Feu. La prévention contre l'incendie, science de l'architecte. (Fire exposition. Prevention against fire, science of the architect.) L'Architecture 42: 319-322 September 15, 1929	Fire resisting materials Burnt clay fireproofing and its substitutes. Archl rec. 8: 111-116 Jl - S 1898
Fire prevention Protection of historic public buildings. Arch. and building 54:13-15 Feb. 1922.	Fire protection see Fire prevention Fire resisting materials Fireproof construction	Fire Resisting Materials "Cement the Remedy for Nation's Fire Losses" by R.L. Humphrey. West. Archt. vol. 13, p. 20-21 Feb, 1909
720.54 T25 Fire prevention Sécurité [special no.] Tech et arch 6:[special number] No. 11-12, '46	Fire resistance Methods of anchoring & safe construction. Inland architect v. 14 no. 1: 8-10 Ag 1889	Fire resisting materials Fire test of a new fire proofing material. [sections] Inland architect v. 17 no. 5: 61 pl. fol. p. 64 Je 1891
Fire Prevention Fitzpatrick F.W. State fire protection. Inland Architect 46: 45-7 Nov, 1905	Fire resistance. Testing Fire tests of brick walls. 2 pts. Amer. Arch. 124: 307-14, 355-62 S 26, O 10, '23	Fire resisting materials Silica and fire clay. Builder 110: 416 Je 9, 1916
Fire Prevention. Congresses The International Fire Prevention Congress. Arch and con rep 69:supp.p.27 Je 5, 1903	720.5 A51 Fire resistance. Testing Committee on fireproofing tests First report...Bulletin no. 5. Amer archt and bldg news 53: 59-61, pls fol 64 Ag 22, 1896	Fire resisting materials Steel and concrete as fire resistants. American architect 92:191-192 December 7,1907

Fire resisting materials.
Vermiculite makers take on under writers for re-examination.

Northwest archt.
14: 28
No. 2 1950

Fireman's memorial, New York city

see

New York (city) Fireman's memorial

Fireplaces. Construction
The modern fireplace and some of its problems.

Arch. record 52:352-6
Oct., 1922

Fire resisting materials.
Versatile vermiculite.

Northwest Arch.
12: 6,8,18
Jl-Ag '48

Firenze, Italy

see

Florence, Italy

Fireplaces, construction
Some essentials of fireplace construction

Amer. architect 122:131-4
Aug. 16, 1922

Fire resisting materials.
Zonolite insulation, also known as Vermiculite. Products and practice.

Architectural forum
65: sup, 48
July 1936

Fireplace (unidentified).

Inland Archt.
Vol. 25, No. 3, Pl.
Fol. p. 34
Apr. 1895

Fireplaces. England. 20th cent.
Denby, Elaine
Keeping the home fires burning.
[illus.]

Country life
V. 136: 726;729;
S. 17, 1964.

Fire stations

see

Fire houses

Fireplaces, see also

Chimneys;

Mantels

Andirons

Fire screens

Fireplaces, gas
Gas fires and their settings.

Architectural rev. 65: 102-4
February 1929

Fire tests

see

Fire resistance. Testing

720.5
A67f
Fireplaces,construction
...Cantilever design open on three sides. Section. Plan of another fireplace...

Arch for 77: 41-2
N° 42

710.5
C855
Fireplaces, Construction
Frear, James
Building a fireplace that draws.

Country life (N.Y.) 49: 44-5
April 1926

Fire vaults

see

Vaults, Safe deposit

720.5
A67f
Fireplaces, Construction
The efficient fireplace. Plan and sections.

Architectural forum 65: sup. 40,
August 1936   42

710.5
H84
Fireplaces, Construction
Mennecke, Harry
Building the smokeless fireplace.

House and garden 40:45
August 1921

Firehouses

see

Fire houses

Fireplaces. Construction
A group of air circulating fireplaces through courtesy of Superior Fireplace Co., Los Angeles.

Architectural digest 10:139-141
No. 3 [1940]

710.5
C855
Fireplaces. Construction
Parsons, Jos. & Brinckle, W.D.
Fireplaces that will not smoke

Country life in America
12: 672-675
October 1907

720.5
I56   Fireplace,construction
     Fireplace construction. No illustration
 	
     Inland architect 7:73
     March 1886
	D13.1 Fireplaces, Outdoor
	H84 Fire burn and cauldron bubble
	
	     House beautiful 79:34-35
	     August 1937
		720.5
		A67m Fireproof construction
		
		     Arch. & bldr's mag. 40: 250-54
		     March 1908

Fireplaces. Construction
   Freese, E.I.
Fires and fireplaces (Proportions and construction).
 	
     House beautiful 36:166-171
     November, 1914
	D13.1 Fireplaces, Outdoor
	H84 The grate outdoors
	
	     House beautiful 80:20
	     August 1938
		Fireproof Construction
		
		     Western Arch.
		     1: p. 10 and p. 19
		     Sept, 1902

710.5
H84   Fireplaces . Construction
     Is there a flue doctor in the house? How
to avoid galloping consumption and ultimate
suffocation by and in your fireplace.
 	
     House and garden 72:65,70
     July 1937
	D13.1 Fireplaces, Outdoor
	H84 Open hearth
	
	     House beautiful 80:76-77,99-102
	     May 1938
		Fireproof Construction
		   Baumann, Frederick
		About fireproof buildings.
		
		     Inland Architect
		     43: 18-19
		     Apr, 1904

Fireplaces, Gas. Construction
     Mantel fireplace units - gas fired...
Blue print of flue for use of gas heaters.
 	
     Building for the future: 6-8,6
     O' 30 Ap'31
	D13.1 Fireplaces, Outdoor
	H84 Outdoor fireplaces
	
	     House beautiful
	     82: 38-41, 83
	     June 1940
		Fireproof construction
		     American methods of construction in Paris.
		
		     Architecture 49:80-1
		     March 1924

Fireplaces, Outdoor
 	
     see also
 	
   Ovens, Outdoor
	710.5 Fireplaces, Outdoor
	L26 Wheelwright, Robert
	     Outdoor fireplaces
	
	     Landscape architecture
	     9: 194-195
	     July 1919
		Fireproof Construction
		     As to the fire resisting qualities of
		gypsum.
		
		     West. Archt.
		     24: 119
		     Sept, 1916

D13.1   Fireplaces, Outdoor
H84   Come and get in
 	
     House beautiful 81:45
     June 1939
	Fireplaces, United States
	   Flagg, Maurice Irwin, "Fireplaces with
	Individuality"
	
	     West. Archt.
	     18: 45-47
	     Apr, 1912
		Fireproof construction
		     The Baltimore fire: a record of achievement.
		Fireproof construction...
		
		     Brickbuilder 13: spec. no.
		     Mr 1904

D13.1   Fireplaces,Outdoor
H84   Done to a turn - outdoors.
 	
     House beautiful 83:34-35
     July-August 1941
	Fireproof construction
	     See Also
	
	   Concrete construction.
	   Fire resisting materials.
	   Fire doors.
	   Fireproofing.
		Fireproof construction. A better quality
		     of fireproofing necessary.
		
		     Inland Arch.
		     27: 2
		     Feb. 1896

Fireproof Construction
    Biological Buildings, University of
Chicago. Henry Ives Cobb, Archt.
Section of Roof.

        Inland Architect
        32:15
        Sept, 1898

Fireproof Construction
    An example of fireproofing-Old Colony
and Manhattan Buildings, Chicago. photos.

        Inland Architect
        31: 28
        Apr, 1898

Fireproof construction
Hutton, W. H.
    Fire-proof construction.

        Amer arch
        1: 43-44
        F 5, 1876

Fireproof construction
Humphrey, Richard L.
    Cement the remedy for nation's fire losses.
Address of the president of the National
Association of Cement Users before its annual
convention at Cleveland, Ohio, January 13, 1909.

        Western Arch't
        13: 20-21
        F 1909

723.5   Fireproof construction
A67r   Failure and efficiency in fire-proof con-
        struction.

        Architectural record 7:395-398
        January-March 1898

Fireproof construction
Dwight, George
    Fire-proof construction.

        Amer arch
        1: 72
        F 26, 1876

Fireproof construction. Atkinson, A.S.
    The commercial value of fireproof construction

        Inland Arch.
        46: 75
        Jan   1906
        47: 74
        June 1906

Fireproof construction. Fitzpatrick, F.W.
    The fire insurance habit.

        Inland Arch.
        48: 56-8
        Dec. 1906

720.5   Fireproof construction
B84   Freitag, J.K.
        Fire-proofing: some inconsistencies in modern
        fire-proof design.

        Brickbuilder 9:149-150;170-171
        July;August 1900

Fireproof Construction
    Controversy over false fireproofing in New
York.

        Inland Architect
        40: 1
        Aug, 1902

Fireproof Construction. Fire insurance vs.
    fireproof buildings.

        Inland Arch.
        48: 50
        Dec. 1906

720.5   Fireproof construction
IF6   Fire resisting construction.

        Inland architect 3:50-51
        May 1884

Fireproof construction
Wight, Peter B.
    Development of the fireproofing of buildings.
[sections]

        Inl archt 34:8-12
        Ja 1900 sup

Fireproof Construction. Fire losses in
    the United States; responsibility of
fire insurance companies; advantages of
fireproof building.

        Inland Arch.
        48: 14
        Sept. 1906

Fireproof construction
    Fire resisting doors and windows.

        Architects' jour. 64:454-457
        October 13, 1926

Fireproof Construction
Fox, Charles E.
The effects of fire upon modern fireproof
buildings.

        West. Archt.
        31: 62-6
        May, 1922

D15.1   Fireproof construction
H84   Peyser, Ethel
            Fire prevention before you build.

        House beautiful 71: 132-133,143-144
        February 1932

Fireproof Construction
    Fire risks to valuable art and book
collections.

        Inland Architect
        45: 10
        Mar, 1905

Fireproof Construction
    Exaggerated reports regarding fires.

        Inland Architect
        32: 41
        Dec, 1898

Fireproof construction
    Fire-proof columns (Experiments by Peter B.
Wight)

        Amer archt
        1: 29-30
        Ja 22, 1876

Fireproof construction. Fire tests on iron
    columns.

        Inland Arch.
        28: 11-12
        Sept. 1896

Fireproof Construction
"Fireproof Buildings"
brochure published by Roebling Construction Co.

Inland Architect
40: 16
Sept, 1902

Fireproof Construction
Fireproofing. Economics of Construction.
By John Lyman Faxon.

Brickbuilder 12:
81-83; Ap 1903
125-27; Je "

7F0.F71   Fireproof construction
A7P   Virtala, Veitto
           Konstruktiv brandsäkerhet

Arkitekten no. 8:175-8
1937

Fireproof construction
Fireproof construction at Earl's Court,
London, England.

Architect 69:362-364
June 5, 1903

Fireproof Construction
Fireproofing and the Chicago Centennial

Inland Architect
42: 23-4
Oct, 1903

Fireproof construction. Label buildings
to indicate construction.

Inland Arch.
52: 56
Nov. 1908

7F0.F   Fireproof construction
AF1   Fireproof construction in the Pittr-
         burgh fire.

omer archt and bldg news
56: 70-71
Ay 29, 1937

Fireproof construction
Fireproofing.

Northwest archt 15:20,32-33
No. 6 1951

Fireproof Construction
Lack of responsibility defeats revised
building laws.

Inland Architect
43: 1
Feb, 1904

Fireproof Construction
Potter, Thomas
Fireproof Construction of Domestic Buildings
Sections.

Inland Architect
31: 16-18 Mar, 1898
   : 34-7 Apr, 1898
   :46-7 Jun, 1898

Fireproof Construction
Folly in building without fireproof
protection.

Inland Architect
37: 41
Jul, 1901

Fireproof Construction
Low percentage of loss in fireproofed
buildings [in Baltimore Md.]

Inland Architect
43: 41
Jul, 1904

Fireproof construction.
Fireproof stair ways as fire escapes.

Inland Arch.
50: 14
Aug. 1907

Fireproof Construction
The folly of constructing Combustible
buildings.

Inland Architect
33: 21
Apr, 1899

Fireproof construction
Materiais novos: madeira "incombustível".

Habitat
6:25-6 N 1956

Fireproof Construction
Walsh, George Ethelbert.Fireproofed
Wood for Architectural use.

Inland Architect
45: 48-9
Jun, 1905

Fireproof Construction
The future fireproofing of Schoolhouses
in Chicago.

Inland Architect
31: 41
Jun, 1898

Fireproof   Construction
Fitzpatrick, F .W.
The national ash heap

West. Arch.
9: 101-3
Oct, 1906

Fireproof Construction
Fireproofed Wood for Interior Work.

Inland Architect
45: 45
Jun, 1905

Fireproof Construction
The great conflagration at Baltimore;
lessons of the Baltimore fire, by F.W.
Fitzpatrick. Map, photos.

Inland Architect
43: 9, 10-14
Mar, 1904

Fireproof Construction
Necessity for Fireproofing Schools and
Residence.

Inland Architect
45: 1
Feb, 1905

Fireproof Construction
Not Building Law but Fireproofed Structures

Inland Architect
43: 6
Feb, 1904

Fireproof construction. Fitzpatrick, F.W.
Requirements of fire proof construction.

Inland Arch.
47: 37
April 1906

Fireproof construction
Special industrial number

Architectural forum 39: 83-151
Sept. 1923

Fireproof Construction
Obsolete methods of fireproofing
condemned.

Inland Architect
41: 21
Apr, 1903

Fire Proof Construction
Resistance to Fire of Floors and Doors.

Arch and con rep 67: 76-78
Ja 31, 1902

Fireproof construction
Standard Fire-Resisting buildings. Two and
one-half columns of text.

British architect 57: 55-56
January 24, 1902

Fireproof construction. Owners should
protect themselves.

Inland Arch.
52: 1
July 1908

Fireproof Construction
Results of test of Vulcanite fireproof
floor system.

Inland Architect
39: 27
Apr, 1909

Fireproof construction
Macdonale, F.A.
Standard fire-resisting construction.

American archt 92:21-23;27-29
July 20-27, 1907

Fire Proof Construction
A really fireproof house [hollow tile house]
Photo.

West. Archt.
16: 88
Aug, 1910

Fireproof Construction
Saved by its fireproofing (Old Colony
Building, Chicago) photos.

Inland Architect
39: 18
Mar, 1902

Fireproof Construction
Steel Buildings after Baltimore Fire.

West. Archt.
3: p. 12
Oct, 1904

Fireproof Construction
Reinforced concrete as a fire-proofing
material.

Inland Architect
42: 47
Jan, 1904

720.5 Fireproof construction
A67r Sturgis, Russell
Simple ways of fireproofing

Arch rec 13: 119-133
F '03

Fireproof Construction
Steel doors and shutters
A fireproof necessity

West. Arch.
11: VII-VIII
Ap 1908

Fireproof Construction
A remarkable advance in fireproofing
methods .

Inland Architect
39: 9
Mar, 1902

Fireproof construction. Adler, Dankman. Slow-
burning and fireproof construction.

Inland Arch.
26: 60-2
Jan. 1896
27: 3-4
Feb. 1896

Fireproof Construction
Taxes on fireproof buildings; financial
returns on fireproof bldgs; insurance rates.

Inland Architect
46: 26,28
Oct, 1905

Fireproof construction
Report of the science standing committee on the
regulations for standard fire-resisting buildings.

RIBA jrl 10: 295-96
Ap 4, 1903

Fireproof construction
Slow Burning Construction.

Brickbuilder 12: 105-109
May, 1903

Fireproof Construction
Testing fireproofing materials at
Columbia [University, N.Y.]

Inland Architect
44: 17
Oct, 1904

Fireproof Construction
The Toronto fire from a fireproof standpoint.

Inland Architect
43: 25
May, 1904

Fireproof construction. Domestic Architecture
David, A.C., Frohne, H.W., Wight, P.B.
The advent of the fireproofed dwelling.
Some structural aspects of the fire-proofed dwelling.
Some fire-resisting country houses.

Architectural record 25: 309-340,364-80
May, 1909

Fireproof construction. Domestic architecture
Walsh, G.E.
Need of fireproof country houses.

Architectural record 17:509-512
June, 1905

720.5   Fireproof construction
A67r   Sturgis, Russell
An unscientific enquiry into fireproof building.

Architectural record 9: 29-253
January 1900

Fireproof Construction. Domestic Architecture
The building of the home. VII, Fire resisting construction
H. Vandervoort Walsh

Country Life 46:60-1
July, 1924

Fireproof Construction. Domestic architecture
Reducing fire risk in residential construction.

Architectural forum 40:197-200
May 1924

Fireproof construction. Apartment houses
Construction of the apartment house

Architecture 48:393-6
Nov. 1923; 49:54-5
Feb. 1924

Fireproof construction. Domestic architecture
Construction of the small house.

Architecture. 43:88-92
Mar. 1921

Fireproof construction. Domestic architecture.
Competitions

see

Fireproof house competition, 1905

Fireproof Construction. Apt. Houses
Destruction of unfireproofed apt. bldgs.

Inland Architect
39: 29
May, 1902

Fireproof construction. Domestic architecture
Brown, F.C.
Fire-proof dwelling interiors.

Architectural review 17:25-29
March, 1910

Fireproof construction. Factories

see also

Factories. Fires and fire prevention
Concrete construction
Fire resisting materials
Fire doors

Fireproof Construction. Domestic Architecture

Amer. architect 96:53
August 11, 1909

Fire Proof Construction. Domestic Architecture
The fire proof house as the American type.
(houses designed by Squires and Wynkoop).
Photos.

West. Archt.
16: 107-8
Oct, 1910

Fireproof construction. Factories
Economical temporary roofs for fire-proof buildings. Double stairways for factories.

American architect 117:351-5
Mar. 17, 1920.

Fireproof Construction. Domestic Architecture

Amer. homes and gardens 7:401-405
October, 1910

Fireproof Construction. Domestic architecture
Fire resistive houses a present reality

Architecture and bldg. 55:126-7
Dec. 1923

720.59   Fireproof construction. Hospitals
A67c   Fire-Proof Hospital Buildings.

Arch & c. rep 72: 21 in supp
Jl 22, '04

Fireproof Construction. Domestic architecture

Arch. and Bldg. 43: 545-579
October, 1911

720.5   Fireproof construction. Domestic architecture.
N58   Flagg, Ernest
Fireproof Tenements and the Building Law.

New York architect 5:86-89
February 1911

Fireproof construction. Museums

see also

Museums. Fires and fire prevention

Fireproof construction. Office buildings
The fireproofing of high office buildings.

Brickbuilder 11: 145
July 1902

Fireproof construction. Theaters
see also
Theaters. Fires and fire prevention

Fireproof houses
see
Fireproof construction. Domestic architecture.

Fireproof construction. Office buildings
A practical test of fire-proofing. [plans]

Inland architect
v. 18 no.1: 7-10
Ag 1891

Fireproof Construction, Theaters
Baumann, Frederick
Fireproof Construction of Theaters.

Inland Architect
45: 4
Feb, 1905

Fireproofing
see also
Fireproof Construction

Fireproof construction. Office buildings
Roebling system of fireproofing test.

Inl archt 34:39
N 1899

770.5
I56
Fireproof construction, theaters
Fireproof theatres.

Inland architect 3:61-62
June 1884

Fireproofing. A committee on fireproofing
tests.

Inland Arch.
26: 15-16
Sept. 1895

Fireproof construction. Schools.
Awakening to need of fireproof schools;
radical measures needed.

Inland Arch.
51: 14
March 1908

Fireproof construction. Theaters.
Safeguards against theater fires.

Inland Arch.
50: 14
Aug. 1907

Fireproofing
Failure of concrete as a fireproofing
material.

Inland Architect
41: 26-7
Apr, 1903

Fireproof Construction, Schools
Extraordinary number of fires in College
Building.

Inland Architect
39: 29
May, 1902

Fireproof Construction, U.S., Ill. Chicago
Wight, P.B.
Recent fireproof building in Chicago.
Inland Arch.
5: 52-53 April 1885   19: 57-8 June 1892
(extra number)   19: 69-72 July 1892
19: 21-2 Mar 1892
19: 32-4 April 1892
19: 45-7 May 1892

Fireproofing
Fire prevention and fire resistance.

R.I.B.A. 10: 285-95
April 4, 1903

Fireproof construction. Schools
Forster, H.   W
Fire protection for schools. 3 pts.

Amer arch
117:264-5, 289-93, 323-26
F 25, Mr 3, 10, 1920

Fireproof Construction, Warehouses
A new system of fireproofing for
warehouses. Details.

Inland Architect
45: 7-8
Feb, 1905

Fireproofing
Inexpensive Methods of Fireproofing.
By Emile G. Perrot.

House and gard. 8: 153-62
N 1905

Fireproof Construction. Schools.
Should school buildings be fireproof?

Inland Arch.
49: 47-8
April 1907

Fireproof house competition. 1905
The fireproof house competition.
Awards by the jury.

Brickbuilder 14:127
Je '05

Fireproofing
Roebling System of fireproofing test.

Inland Architect
34: 32
Nov, 1899

V. 4

331

Fireproofing
Singular resistance
to fire protective methods

West. Arch.
12: 2
Jul 1908

Fireproofing, Theatres
Interview with W.C. Zimmerman.

see

Chicago (Il) Iroquois Theatre Fire

Fires
Reasons for loss investigated by
underwriters.

Inland Architect
45: 9-10
Mar, 1905

Fireproofing
Steel Ceilings and Walls.

West. Archt.
3: p. VI
Feb, 1904

Fireproofing, Use of Reinforced Concrete Floors.

see

Concrete, Reinforced. Concrete Floors. Tests
for Fireproofing.

Fires. Woeful waste of resources. American
wastefulness in figures.

Inland Arch.
51: 50
June 1908

Fireproofing
Well-tested system.

Western Archt.
2: p. VI
Jun, 1903

Fires

see also

Theaters. Fires and fire prevention
Fire prevention
Factories. Fires and fire prevention
Museums. Fires and fire prevention

Fires, U.S. Losses beyond comparison;
some hope in the situation.

Inland Arch.
52: 14
Aug. 1908

Fireproofing.
"What can be reasonably expected of
fireproofing.

Western Archt.
1: p. 15 (also p. 8)
Aug, 1902

Fires. Delusion that insurance prevents loss.

Inland Arch.
52: 2
July 1908

Fires. U.S. Ill, Chicago
Fires due to Combustible Construction

Inland Architect
31: 21
Apr, 1898

Fire-Proofing
wood floor Joists.

Western Archt.
2: p. 17
Oct, 1903

Fires: Fire insurance responsible for
fires; in Europe it is difference.

Inland Arch.
52: 44
Oct. 1908

Fires, U.S. Maryland, Baltimore
The Baltimore Fire and its Lessons.

Builder 86: 381-83
Ap 9, 1904

Fireproofing. Buildings

West. Archt.
3: p. 14
Jun, 1904

Fires
Fire loss still increasing.

Inland Architect
44: 42
Jan, 1905

Fires, U.S., N.Y., New York

see

New York (N.Y.) Asch bldg. Fire

Fireproofing. Steel Construction
Benefits of following Baltimore Fires.

West. Archt.
3: p. 23
Mar, 1904

Fires
Origins of fires and conflagrations.

Amer. Arch. 121: 327.
Apr. 12, 1922.

Firestone, Charles E

see also

Firestone and Motter

Firestone, Charles E
Newly elected fellows of the A.I.A.
[brief biographical sketch and photograph]

Nat'l arch 4:6-7
My '47

Fischer, Alfred, 1881-1950
Kästner-Wilhelm, Dr.
Alfred Fischer (Essen) Hans-Sachs-Haus in
Gelsenkirchen; office building of the Union
Settlement Ruhr coal district in Essen.

Moderne bauformen 29:149-162,adv.70
Heft 4, April 1930

Fischer, Benno
Haus eines schiffsbauers in San Pedro bei
Los Angeles; entwurf 1956-57; gebaut 1957-58
[plans] Richard Neutra, Benno Fischer & Serge
Koschin, archts.

Bauen & Wohnen
vol.1;: 445-50, D 1961

Firestone and Notter
Own office and residence

Nat'l arch 1:6
D '45

RYERSON LIBRARY
741.9
C75
Fischer, Alfred 1881- 1950
Dresdner, Albert
Industrial architecture, the work of Pro-
fessor Alfred Fischer

Commercial art n.s.2:110-115
March, 1927

Fischer, F. William 1861-
Brief biography

Herringshaw, Clark J. Herringshaw's
city blue book of current biography.
Chicago: American Publisher's Association,
1915.

D10.5
D48
Pirle, Otto
Architecture in Berlin

Deutsche kunst 54:222-238
July 1924

720.53
M58
Fischer, Alfred 1881-1950
Klopfer, Paul
Government architect - Alfred Fischer, Dussel-
dorf.

Moderne bauformen 9:184-197
1910

Fischer, Johann Michael, 1691-1766
Freiermuth, Otmar
Die wandpfeilerhallen im werke des
Johann Michael Fischer. [plan.]

Das Münster
V.8: 320-332 no. 9-10
S-O 1955

Firmenish building, Chicago
see
Chicago, Ill. T - R building

720.53
W51
Fischer, Alfred 1881- 1950
Konzertsaal im Hans-Sachs-Haus, Gelsen-
kirchen. (Concert room in the Hans Sachs
House, Gelsenkirchen.) Alfred Fischer, archt.

Wasmuths monatshefte 14: 453
October 1930

705.3
M73
Fischer, Johann Michael 1691-1766
Feulner, Adolf von
Johann Michael Fischer, ein bürgerlicher
baumeister der rokokozeit (1691-1766).

Monatshefte für kunst-wissenschaft
15:222-231
November 1922

First unitarian church, Chicago (first bldg)
see
Chicago (Ill.) First unitarian church (1897)

Fischer, Alfred, 1881-1950
Modern domestic and industrial work by
Alfred Fischer (Essen) architect. Germany.

Moderne bauformen 29:30-42
Heft 1, January 1930

MICROFILM
Fischer, John B., 1875(?)-1951
obituary notice

708

First unitarian church, Chicago (2nd bldg.)
see
Chicago (Ill.) First unitarian church (1931)

Fischer, Alfred, 1881-1950
Volksschule in Bammental [plan] Alfred Fischer
& Reinhard Gieselmann, archts.

Baumeister
vol. 59: 108-110, F 1962
Tafeln 12-15

Fischer, Karl von
see
Munich (Ger.) Nationaltheater

Firstbrook (W. Gordon) house, Toronto
see
Toronto (Ont.) Firstbrook (W. Gordon) house

Fischer, Alonzo G., house
See
Lake Geneva (Wis.) "Blacktoft"

Fischer, Leopold
see
Loos and Fischer

Fischer, Otto
Some modern decorative treatments of interiors by Otto Fischer (Trachau.)

Moderne bauformen:67-70,pls.14-16
Band 25, 1926   (col.pl.)

Fischer von Erlach, Johann Bernhard

see also

Vienna (Aus.) Schloss Schönbrunn
"   "   " Palast der ungarischen leibgarde

Fischli, Hans, 1909-
Hans Fischli, architekt B.S.A. Zürich.

Bauen and wohnen
No. 3: (51)
Mr 1956

Fischer, Raymond, 1898-
Hôtel particulier, à Boulogne-sur-Seine.
Plans. Raymond Fischer, archt.

Encyclopedie de l'architecture;
constructions modernes. 12 vols.
Paris: Albert Morancé, 1928-39.
2:pls. 12-14

720.6
A67   II.V. Lanchester
       Fischer von Erlach

Fischer von Erlach, Johann Bernard 1656-1723

Architecture 2:59-72
December 1925

Fischli, Hans, 1909-
Schweisswerk in Bülach [plan & section]
Hans Fischli, archt.
Entwurf 1957, gebaut 1957-1959.

Bauen & Wohnen
14:275-77 AG 1960

Fischer, Raymond, 1898-
Immeuble de rapport, à Paris. Plan. Raymond Fischer, archt.
Hotel particulier, à Saint-Cloud. Plans. Raymond Fischer, archt.

Encyclopedie de l'architecture;
Constructions modernes. 12 vols.
Paris: Albert Morancé, 1928-39.
1:pl.17,18.

ERIASON LIBRARY
705.3
D48   Möhle,Hans
       Joh.Bernh.Fischer v.Erlach (1656-1723)böhmische Hofkanzlei(jetzt ministerium des Innern) Wien

Fischer von Erlach,Johann Bernard 1656 - 1723

Deutsche kunst 1: 21,pl.21
No.2,1935

Fischli, Hans, 1909-
Sidlung von wertvollen billigen wohnungen; entwurf 1958-59 [plans] Hans Fischli, archt.

Bauen & Wohnen
14:212-14 Je 1960

Fischer, Theo

see

Kaiserlautern, Ger. Pädagogische akademie

ERIASON LIBRARY
705.3
D48   Grimschitz, Bruno
       Johann Bernhard Fischer von Erlach: Das treppenhaus im Winterpalast des Prinzen Eugen in Wien.

Fischer von Erlach,Johann Bernhard 1656-1723

Deutsche kunst 6:pl.84 and text
No.7,1940

Fischli, Hans, 1909-
Überbauung Vogelsangstrasse, Zürich; entwurf 1958-1960, gebaut 1960-1961 [plans & section] Hans Fischli & Fredi Eichholzer, archts.

Bauen & Wohnen
16:120-23 Mar 1962

711
S77   Fischer,Theodor 1862-1939
       Camillo Sitte und die "Fischerschule". (Controversies on building between different architects: Camille Sitte vs. Theodor Fischer and others.). Plans.
       Plans for church plazas by Camillo Sitte, architect.

Städtebau 20:39-44
March-April 1925

Fischer von Erlach, Johann Bernhard, 1656-1723
Frey, Dagobert
Johann Bernhard Fischer von Erlach, eine studie über seine stellung in der entwicklung der Wiener palastfassade.

Jahrbuch für kunstgeschichte 1:
93-214. 1921/22.

Fischli, Hans, 1909-
Uitbreiding electrische apparatenfabriek Ad. Feller A. G. te Horgen [plans] Hans Fischli, archt. with Fredi Eichholzer & Eduard Frans, archts.

Forum no. 5: 204-205
1954

Fischer, Theodor 1862-1939
Behrendt, W.C.
New building.

Kunst und kunstler 26:347-353
June 1928

Fischli, Hans, 1909-

see also

Wädenswil, Swits. Siedlung "Gwad"
Wädenswil, Swits."Zum unteren Leihof"
Trogen, Swits. Pestalozzi village

Fish, Edwin A., house

see

Mill Neck (L.I.) "Airurie"

705
W48   Fischer, Theodor, 1862-1939
       Theodor Fischer, stil und persönlichkeit.

Das Werk
26:90-92
Mr '39

Fischli, Hans, 1909-
Geschäftshaus der Möbelgenossenschaft Basel [plans & section] Hans Fischli, archt.

Bauen & Wohnen
#2:48-53 F 1958

Fish (Stuyvesant) house, New York

See

New York. Fish (Stuyvesant) house

Fish, Stuyvesant houses
 	
see
 	
New York (city) Fish (Stuyvesant) house
Newport, R. I. "Cross Ways"
	ffo
	720.6
	C55 Fisher and Miller
	    Design for a church (Wheaton, Ill.)(?)
	    Fisher and Miller, archts., no plan.
	
	    Chicago architectural club 15:62
	    Annual exhibition 1900
		Fisher, D.K. Eater, Jr.
		(biographical sketch)
		
		Nat'l arch 2:9
		Je '46

720.52
A67   Fish shops. England
    A model fish shop
 	
    Arch.journal 56: 244-52
    Aug. 23, 1922
	Fisher and Porter
	
	Members of firm:
	
	Fisher, Albert
	Porter, H.F.J.
		720.5
		A67r Fisher, Howard T. 1905 -
		    House for Mr. and Mrs. Walter T. Fisher,
		    Winnetka, Illinois. Howard T. Fisher,
		    designer.
		
		    Architectural record 66: 459-464
		    November 1929

Fisher, A.A.
    The Architecture of Denver and Vicinity.
 	
    West. Archt.
    30: 31-6, pl. Apr, 1921
    : 47-8 May, 1921
	Fisher, Arthur Addison
	
	see
	
	Fisher, William L. and Arthur A.
		720.5
		A67f Fisher, Howard T 1905 -
		    House in Lafayette, Ind. Purdue Housing
		    project. Howard T. Fisher, archt. John A.
		    Pruyn, associate. Plan.
		
		    Architectural forum 65: 440
		    November 1936

Fisher, Albert
    Forms partnership with H.F.J. Porter,
Chicago.
 	
    Inland Architect
    23: 22
    Mar, 1894
	Fisher brothers
	
	see
	
	Fisher, William L. and Arthur A.
		Fisher, J. B.
		
		see
		
		Trinidad, Colo., Adobe house sketch.

Fisher, Albert J., 1862?-1938
    Obituary
 	
    Illinois society of
    architects bulletin
    23:8
    D 1938-Ja 1939
	Fisher building, Chicago
	
	see
	
	Chicago (Ill.) Fisher building
		Fisher, Lake and Traver
		
		see
		
		Hollywood (Cal.) Roosevelt hotel

Fisher, Alfred see Gelsenkirchen (Ger.) Hans-Sachs-Haus	Fisher building, Detroit (Mich.) see Detroit (Mich.) Fisher building	Fisher, Mahlon H. see East Liverpool (Oh) Public Library

Fisher and Lawrie
    see
Cheyenne (WY) St. Mary's cathedral
Lincoln (NB) City library
Omaha (NB) Trans-Mississippi Exposition. 1898.
    Liberal Arts bldg.
   "   " Woodmen of the World
   "   " Y.M.C.A. bldg.
	Fisher, Clellan Waldo
	
	Member of firm:
	
	Earle and Fisher
		Fisher, R.
		    Bureau d'un quotidien, à Paris. Villa, à
		    Marnes-la-Coquette. Plans. R.Fisher, archt.
		
		    Encyclopedie de l'architecture;
		    constructions modernes. 12 vols.
		    Paris: Albert Morancé, 1928-39.
		    3:pl 31, 44

Fisher, Reynolds

see also

Patton and Fisher

720.8
B84 Fisher, Richard Arnold
House, Cambridge, Massachusetts, Richard
Arnold Fisher, archt., plans.

Brickbuilder 18: 1 pl.fol.p.44
February 1909

Fisher, William Ellsworth
see also
Denver (CO) Apartment bldg.
"   " Park pavilion
"   " Public library. Henry White Warren branch.
"   " Residence

Fisher, Reynolds

Member of firms:

Patton and Fisher
Patton, Fisher and Miller
Raseman and Fisher

Fisher, Ripley and LeBoutillier

see

Franklin (MA) Garden

720.5
A67 Fisher,William Ellsworth
House in Denver,Colo. W.E.Fisher,archt.
Bungalow in Denver. Plans.

Architectural review 14:78-79
March 1907

Fisher, Reynolds
Formerly of Patton, Fisher and Miller,
now v.p. of Pontiac Brick and Tile, Seattle.

Inland Architect
37: 31
May, 1901

Fisher, William E. and Arthur A.
see also
Denver (CO) Brooks (Charlotte) residence
"   " Colorado National bank
"   " El Tovar apartments
"   " Essex apartments
"   " Evans (John) house
"   " Foster bldg.
"   " Gano (George) house
"   " Hollister house
"   " House (Geo.) residence
"   " Hughes (L.M.) "
"   " International Trust Co. Bldg.
(see next card)

Fisher, William Ellsworth
[Architecture in Denver by W.E. Fisher]
Plans

Amer arch 107: pl 2038
Ja 13, 1915

720.5
B93b Fisher, Reynolds
Sketch of wholesale drygoods home of
Marshall Field & Co. Fifth Ave., Adams,
Franklin and Quincy Sts.. Chicago, Illinois.
H.H. Richardson, archt. Brookline, Mass.
Reynolds Fisher, del.

Building budget 3: pl. fol.p.8
January 31, 1887

Fisher, William E. and Arthur A.   (card 2)
see also
Denver (CO) Johnson (J.) house
"   " Kountze (Harold) residence
"   " National Jewish Hospital for Consumptives
"   " National Safety Vault Co.
"   " Phipps (L.C.) house
"   " Presbyterian hospital
"   " Public library. Branch
"   "   "   Henry White Warren branch
"   " Residence
"   " Security bldg.
"   " Sorrento apartments
(see next card)

Fisher, William Ellsworth, & brother
Residence of E. A. Fatras, Denver, Colorado
[plans] Wm. Ellsworth Fisher & Brother, archts.

Western Arch't
13: 2 pls. fol. p. 46
Ap 1909

Fisher (Reynolds) house. Chicago, Ill.

see

Chicago, Ill. Fisher (Reynolds) house

Fisher, William E. and Arthur A.   (card 3)
see also
Denver (CO) U.S. National bank bldg.
"   " Voorhies memorial
"   " Warren branch library
Idaho Springs (CO) Foster (A.C.) house

Fishers' Hill, Eng.
A sketch study of Fishers' Hill. Sir
Edwin L. Lutyens, archt. Mr. Gerald Balfour's
house

Builder
130:10
Ja 8, 1926

Fisher, Richard Arnold

see also

Lancaster (Mass.) church
Boston (Mass.) Prince (Morton) house
Apartment houses (U.S.) Mass, Boston

Fisher, William E. and Arthur A.
A Colorado bungalow, Denver. W.E. Fisher and
brother, archts. Plan.

Arch rev 14:120
Mr 1907

Fishers Island, N.Y. Brown, John Nicholas,
house

see

"Windshields." Fishers Island, N.Y.

720.5
A67r Fisher,Richard Arnold
Brown,F.C.
Boston suburban architecture. Work of R.A.
Fisher.

Architectural record 21:252-255
April 1907

Fisher, William E. and Arthur A.
Denver residences, Denver. William E. and
Arthur A. Fisher, archts.

Western architect 28: pl.
D 1919

Fishers island, N.Y. "Windshield"

see

"Windshield", Fishers island, N.Y.

720.52
A67e

Fishing villages, England
Some fishing houses on the Lea at Ware,
England.

Architect (Lond.) 121: 861-865
June 28, 1929

Fisker, Kay, 1893 -
Member of firm:
Moller, Fisker and Stegmann

Fisker, Kay
Lo stile funzionale è morto, le ragioni del
funzionalismo non muoiono.

Domus 248-49: 1-3
Jl-Ag 1950

Fishing villages. Holland.
Scheveningen, the new fishing village.

Wasmuths Monatshefte 5:310-9
1920-21

720.53
W31

Fisker, Kay
Domestic architecture, Denmark. Kay
Fisker & C. C. Larsen, archts.

Wasmuth's Monatshefte 12: 194-202
Heft 5, 1928

Fisker, Kay
Schule in Husum, Dänemark. Kay Fisker, arch

Wasmuths monatshefte
13: 461
N 1929

Fisk, D.B. & Co., bldg., Chicago (1857)

see

Chicago, Ill. Fisk, D.B. and Co. bldg. (1857)

Fisker, Kay, 1893-
3-4-geschossiges wohnhaus in Hansaviertel
von Berlin [plans] Kay Fisker, archt.

Arch & wohnform
67:251-53 O 1959

Fisker, Kay and S. C. Larsen

see

Apartment houses, Denmark

Fisk (Harvey) and sons banking house
Banking house Harvey Fisk and Sons.

Bancroft, Hubert Howe.
Achievements of civilization....
10 vols. New York: The Bancroft
Company, Publishers. 1896. 10:1018-19

Fisker, Kay, 1893-
Tintori, Silvano
Kay Fisker, architetto danese. Quartiere
Brøndby a Brøndbyøster 1947-1953 [plans]
Quartiere Nygaard a Brøndbyøster 1957 [plan]
Scuola a Brøndbyøster 1954-58 [plan] Quartiere
Voldparken a Husum 1949-51 [plans] La scuola di
Husum 1951-57 [plan & sections] L'Università di
Aarhus. Kay Fisker, archt.

Casabella
#239:4-21 My 1960

Fissore

see

Monaco (Mon.) Stade Louis II

720.5
A67f

Fisk, Henry L
House for Misses Ada and Delia Hutchinson
Iowa City, Ia. Henry L. Fisk, archt., Paul
Charles Ruth, assoc. Plans

Architectural forum 67: 408-409
November 1937

720.52
A67c

Fisker, Kay
Rasmussen, Steen Eiler
A modern Danish architect, Kay Fisker.

WITHDRAWN-UNL

Architect (Eng.) 119: 189-192
February 3, 1928

Fissore, J

see

Monte Carlo. Planning

Fiske building. Boston, Mass.

see

Boston, Mass. Fiske bldg.

Fisker, Kay, 1893-
Mütterheim und verwaltung der vereinigung
"Mødrehjaelpen" [plans & section] Kay Fisker,
archt.

Baumeister
57:30-32 Jan 1960

Fitch, Clyde house

see

Greenwich (Conn.) "Quiet Corner"

Fisker, Kay

see also

Paris (Fr.) Université. Cité universitaire. Maison
des étudiants davois
Copenhagen (Den.) housing

Fisker, Kay, 1893-
Schule "Voldparken" in Husum [plan]
Kay Fisker, archt.

Baumeister
57:149-52 Mar 1960

Fitch hall of pharmacy, Drake university

see

Des Moines, Ia. Drake university. Fitch hall of
pharmacy

Fitch, Marvin.
   A synagogue that can double its capacity.
[plan] Richard M. Bennett and Marvin Fitch, archts.

                    Interiors 106, pt. 2:80-81
                    Ja 1947

Fitzpatrick, F.W.
   " American Architecture"

                    West. Archt.
                    19: p. 75-77
                    Sept, 1913

Fitzpatrick, F.W.
   Architectural drawings

                    West. Archt.
                    4: 5-8
                    Nov 1905

Fitzalan, William. Tomb
   Tomb of William Fitzalan

                    Country life 41:186
                    Feb. 24, 1917

Fitzpatrick, F.W.
   American Architecture
(Comparison of Buildings at Chicago World's Fair
1893 and St. Louis Louisiana Purchase Expo.
1904). Photos.

                    Inland Architect
                    42: 2-4
                    Aug, 1903

Fitzpatrick, F.W.
   Architecture with the laity.

                    Inland Architect
                    43: 26
                    May, 1904

Fitzgerald, D.
   see
Collinstown, Ire. Dublin Airport Terminal

Fitzpatrick, F.W.
                    the Architect
& the postal savings bank bill

                    West. Arch.
                    15: 52
                    My 1910

Fitzpatrick, F.W.
   Assistant archt. for Chicago Post Office
[Federal Building] Henry Ives Cobbs,
Archt. Cornerstone Laying.

                    Inland Architect
                    34: 17
                    Oct, 1899

Fitz-Gibbon, T. David
   see
Virginia Beach (Va.) Mayflower apartments

Fitzpatrick, F.W.
   The Architects

                    Inland Architect
                    39: 38-9
                    Jun, 1902

Fitzpatrick, F.W.
   Beautifying the Nation's Capital.

                    Inland Architect
                    35: 10-14
                    Mar, 1900

Fitzhugh, Thornton
   see
Clifton (O.) Hauks (Charles) house

Fitzpatrick, F.W.
   Architects and Architects Photos .

                    Inland Architect
                    45: 23-6
                    Apr, 1905

Fitzpatrick F.W.
   The business of Architecture

                    Inland Architect
                    39: 30-1
                    May, 1902

Fitzikowski, John S.
   see
Chicago, Ill. St. Mary Magdalene church and
school (1910)

Fitzpatrick, F.W.
   Architects' responsibilities.

                    Inland Arch.
                    50: 41
                    Oct. 1907
                    51: 87-8
                    Jan. 1908

Fitzpatrick F.W.
   The City Beautiful.

                    West. Archt.
                    17: 13
                    Jan, 1911

Fitzpatrick, F.W.
see also
New Orleans (LA) Southern states exposition. 1913.
Springfield (MA) Municipal bldg. Competition.
Washington (D.C.) Pan-American Union bldg.

Fitzpatrick, F.W.
   "Architectural Design"

                    West Arch 10:
                    76-78
                    July 1907

Fitzpatrick, F.W.
   Chicago's Federal Building. Henry Ives
Cobb, archt. Drawings, Model.

                    Inland Architect
                    36: 18-20
                    Dec, 1900

Fitzpatrick, F.W.
  Chicago
Photos.

Inland Architect
45: 46-8
Jun, 1905

Fitzpatrick, F.W.
  The influence of oriental art.
Illus-Taj Mahal (Agra, India). Fort at Delhi.

Inland Architect
38: 34-6 Dec, 1901
: 42-3 Jan, 1902

Fitzpatrick, F.W.
  "The Safety of our Skyscrapers"

West Arch 10: 101-102
Oct. 1907

Fitzpatrick, F.W.

Buildings: their relation to municipal improvement.

West. Archt.
4: 3-4
Sept. 1905

Fitzpatrick, F.W.
  Lessons of the Baltimore Fire
Photos, map.

Inland Architect
43: 10-14
Mar, 1904

Fitzpatrick, F.W.
  San Francisco: notes after a thorough
investigation of the results of the San Francisco
disaster. Photos.

Inland Arch.
47: 79-81
July 1906

Fitzpatrick F.W.
  The cost of Strikes.

Inland Architect
39: 10-12
Mar, 1902

Fitzpatrick, F.W.
  Municipal supervision
of architecture

West. Arch.
12: 51-2
0 1908

Fitzpatrick, F.W. Ramble. Sketches.

Inland Arch.
27: 15-17   March 1896
27: 36-7   May   1896
27: 55-7   July   1896
28: 20-2   Oct   1896
28: 48-50   Dec   1896

Fitzpatrick, F.W.
  "Design"

West. Archt.
18: 63-65
Jun, 1917

Fitzpatrick, F.W.
  On things of common concern.

West. Archt.
21: 45-8
Jun, 1915

Fitzpatrick, F.W.
  Sketch of Washington D.C. Church

Inland Architect
35: 11
Mar, 1900

Fitzpatrick, F.W.
  Designer of invitations to Cornerstone
Laying of new Chicago Federal Bldg.
(Post Office) Notable penwork by an
architect.

Inland Architect
33: 48-9
Jul, 1899

Fitzpatrick F.W.
  Our Washington Letter.

Inland Architect
40: 10-11
Sept, 1902

Fitzpatrick F.W.
  Sketch of Washington (D.C.) Pennsylvania
Railway Station.

Inland Architect
35:11
Mar, 1900

Fitzpatrick F.W.
  The fire-insurance habit.

Inland Arch.
48: 56-8
Dec. 1906

Fitzpatrick, F.W.
  The Paris Exposition (1900)
Photo of U.S. Bldg.

Inland Architect
37: 18-20
Apr, 1901

Fitzpatrick, F.W.
  State Fire Protection.

Inland Architect
46: 45-7
Nov, 1905

Fitzpatrick, F.W.
  Fraudulent architecture.

Inland Arch.
52: 50
Octo. 1908

Fitzpatrick, F.W.
  Requirements of fireproof construction.

Inland Arch.
47: 37
April 1906

Fitzpatrick,F.W.
  A State's bldg for Washington.
Drawings, plans.

Inland Architect
36: 9, 10-12
Sept, 1900

Fitzpatrick, F.W.
The "Stepped Back" Building.

West. Arch.
30: 108
Oct, 1921

Fitzpatrick, Mark

see also

Minneapolis (MN) Deshler bldg.
St. Paul (MN) Brown & Biglow Co. Art Gallery & Sales room
"   "   "   Carling restaurant
"   "   "   Taylor (George D.) Residence

Flagg, Benson and Brockway
Awarded Silver Medal at Paris.

Inland Architect
36: 16
Sept, 1900

Fitzpatrick, F.W.
"Style"

West. Arch.
14 : p.31-3?
Oct. 1909

Fitzpatrick, Mark
Design for a Church. Rendering.

Western Archt.
1: pl.fol.p. 20
Aug, 1902

Flagg, Ernest   1857-1947
see also
Annapolis (MD) U.S. Naval Academy
"   "   "   "   "   Academy bldg.
"   "   "   "   "   Library
"   "   "   "   "   Memorial chapel
Brooklyn (N.Y.) Apt. houses (Bay Ridge)
Chicago (IL) Tamalpais Apt. bldg.
Concord (N.H.) St. Paul's school
Dongan (N.Y.) Flagg (Ernest) house
Milwaukee (WI) Library & Museum. Compet. design
New York (N.Y.) Automobile club of America
"   "   "   Battery Park. Entrance Gate.
                        (see next card)

Fitzpatrick, F.W.
$10,000 fireproof house
Plan, Elev.

West. Arch.
9: 121-2;pls. fol.
N 1906

Fitzsimmons, James J.

see

Springfield (Mass.) Colonial village

Flagg, Ernest . 1857-1947   (card 2)
see also
New York (N.Y.) Botanical Garden Museum. Design
"   "   "   Clark (A.C.) house
"   "   "   Eleventh Ave. (# 639) loft bldg.
"   "   "   Flagg (Ernest) house
"   "   "   "   office
"   "   "   Mills house number one
"   "   "   Nat'l Acad. of Design. Competition.
"   "   "   Public library
"   "   "   St. Luke's Hospital. Travers
                        pavilion & dome
"   "   "   Singer bldg.
                        (see next card)

Fitzpatrick, F.W.
"Unaccountable"Building Codes and Fire
Prevention.

West. Archt.
19: p. 27-30
Mar, 1913

Fivaz, H.

see

Paris (Fr.) Rue Michel-Auge (no. 9)

720.5 Flagg, Ernest   1857-1947
A67a   Architectural design by the use of a module.

Architecture 44:315-318
October 1921

Fitzpatrick, F.W.
Urban & Civic Improvements

West. Arch.
12: 61
N 1908

Fjelde, Jakob, Sculptor
Sculpture for Minnehaha Park.

West. Archt.
2: p. 15
Feb, 1903

720.5 Flagg, Ernest   1857- 1947
A67r   American architecture as opposed to archi-
        tecture in America.
        Some work of Ernest Flagg and others.

Architectural record 10:178-190
October 1900

Fitzpatrick, F.W.
Why?

West. Arch.
12: 14-16
Ag 1908

720.5 Fjelde, Paul
P39   A portfolio of recent architectural sculp-
        ture.

Pencil points 10: 784-785
November 1929

Flagg, Ernest
    American architecture as opposed to
architecture in America.

Inland Architect
35: 36
Jun, 1900

Fitzpatrick, F.W.
Women and domestic Architecture

Inland Architect
33: 2-3
Feb, 1899

Flad, John J.

see

Madison (Wis.) Erickson (Howard) house

Flagg, Ernest 1857-1947   (card 3)
see also
New York (N.Y.) 64th St. (East) (# 25) house
Oakdale (L.I.) Bourne (F.F.) house
Olympia (WA) Capitol group
"   "   State capitol. Design.
Pittsburgh (PA) St. Margaret memorial hospital
Rockville (CT) Savings bank
Washington (D.C.) (New) Corcoran Gallery of Art
Winchester (MA) Ginn (Edward) house
Woodmere (L.I.) Burton (R.L.) house

Flagg, Ernest 1857-1947
  Competition for Soldier's Memorial, Allegheny
County, Pennsylvania.

    (Philadelphia) T Square Club.
    American Competitions. ed. Adin
    Benedict Lacey. 3 vols.
    Philadelphia: T Square Club,
    New York: W. Helburn, 1907-13.
    1: pl. 10-12

720.5 Flagg, Ernest 1857-1947
A67r Desmond, H. W.
   Introduction and the works of Ernest Flagg,
archt. Plans.

    Architectural record 11: intro, 1-104
    April 1902

720.5 Flagg, Ernest 1857-1947
MB6 Public buildings.

    New York architect 5:355-360
    June 1911

720.5 Flagg, Ernest 1857-1947
A67 Competitve design for New York Clearing
house. Ernest Flagg, archt. Plans

    Architectural review 3: 29-30,37
    October 1894

720.5 Flagg, Ernest 1857-1947
A67a The module system of architectural design.

    Architecture 42-206-209
    July 1920

Flagg, Ernest
  Receives Gold Medal at Pan-Amer. Expo.,
Buffalo N.Y., 1901.

    Inland Architect
    38: 32
    Nov, 1901

Flagg, Ernest
  Corcoran Gallery of Art, Washington,
D.C.

    Inland Architect
    29: 39
    May 1897

720.5 Flagg, Ernest 1857-1947
A67r Schuyler, Montgomery
   Monumental engineering. Illustrated; comple-
tion drawings for the Memorial Bridge across the
Potomac from Washington to Arlington. Ernest Flagg;
Edward Pearce Casey (accepted design); Carrère
and Hastings; Walker and Morris; Paul P. Pelz,
archts.

    Architectural record 11: 615-640
    October 1901

D13.1 Flagg, Ernest method
H84 Kaufman, O. L.
   What is the cost of an $18,000 house? Build-
ing by the Ernest Flagg method

    House beautiful 65:152-53
    January 1929

720.5 Flagg, Ernest 1857-1947
A67r The Ecole des Beaux Arts, part 3.

    Architectural record 4:38-45
    July-September 1894

720.6 Flagg, Ernest 1857-1947
A51j New light on Greek art.

    A.I.A. Journal 13: 1-4
    January, 1925

Flagg, Ernest office

    see

  New York (N.Y.) Flagg (Ernest) office

Flagg, Ernest
  The Future American Style

    West. Arch.
    11: 36
    Ap 1908

Flagg, Ernest, 1857-1947
  Obituary

    Illinois society of
    architects bulletin
    31:8
    My-Je 1947

Flagg, Ernest and W. B. Chambers

    see also

  New York (N.Y.) Jennings (O.G.) house

720.5 Flagg, Ernest 1857-1947
A51 Justification of the architect is architecture.

    Amer. Arch. 121: 245-8.
    Mar. 29, 1922.

Flagg, Ernest 1857-1947
[obituary]

    Nat'l arch 4:9
    My'47

720.5 Flagg, Ernest and Walter B. Chambers
A67r Mills house no.1, Bleeker Street, no.2,
Rivington Street. N.Y.C. Ernest Flagg and
W. B. Chambers, archts. Plans.

    Architectural record 11: 41-47
    April 1902

720.5 Flagg, Ernest 1857-1947
A67r Influence of the French School on architecture in the United States. Illustration of residences in Paris.

    Architectural record 4:210-228
    October-December 1894

720.5 Flagg, Ernest 1857-1947
A67 Dillon, A.J.
   The proposed Tilden trust library for New York
city(later called New York Public Library) Plans
and suggestions for the building by Ernest Flagg,
archt.

    Architectural review 1: 69-72
    September 12, 1892

Flagg, Montague

    see also

  New York (City) Astor trust building

720.5
A67a
Flagg, Montague
Astor Trust building, New York City. Montague Flagg, archt.

Architecture 36:pl.121-125
July 1917

711
T75
Flagstaffs

Town planning rev. 5: 47-48,pl.
Apr. 1914

710.5
B84
Flagstaffs
In the cause of town betterment.

House & garden.49:96-99
Feb. 1926

720.5
A67a
Flagg, Montague
Savings bank of Rockville, Conn. Montague Flagg, archt. Plan.

Architecture 37: 70-71
March 1919

Flagstaffs.

Amer. arch. 106:pl.2013
July 22, 1914

720.5
A67a
Flagstaffs
A memorial flagstaff in Brooklyn, N.Y.
Pratt institute. Willard Paddock, sculptor

Architecture.54:337-8
Nov.1926

Flagler gymnasium, Lake City, Fla.

see

Lake City, Fla. Florida agricultural college.
Flagler gymnasium

Flagstaffs
Beaux-arts institute of design, competition:
"Twin flag poles". Awards.

B.A.I.D. 2:14-15
October 1925

Flagstaffs
Meas. drawings.

Cicognara, Leopoldo.
Le Fabbriche e i monumenti
cospicui di Venezia.
Venice: G. Antonelli, 1858.
pl. 14

Flagler, H.M. house, Mamaroneck, N.Y.

see

Mamaroneck, N.Y. Satanstoe

Flagstaffs
Benches and flag poles for town betterment

House and garden 47:102-103
May 1925

720.6
A67
Flagstaffs
New York Public Library

Architectural league N.Y. catalog 1912
v. 27 p. 28

Flagler, Henry M. house

see

Palm Beach (Fla.) "White Hall"

720.5
A51
Flagstaffs
Emerson prize competition- Beaux-Arts
Institute of Design, student work

American architect 124:112-3
Aug. 1, 1923

Flagstaffs.
David, A.C.
The New York public library. Carrère and Hastings,
archts. Plans.

Architectural record 28:172
September, 1910

Flagpoles

see

Flagstaffs

720.52
B93
Flagstaffs
Flagpole base at Birkdale Central School,
Southport. Grayson and Barnish, archts.

Builder 142: 416
March 4,1932

Flagstaffs.
Simple support for the skyscraper's flagpole.

American architect 117:358
Mar. 17, 1920

720.5
A67a
Flagstaff holders
Architecture's portfolio

Arch. 62: 174-88
S '30

Flagstaffs
Flagpole base for N.J. war memorial.
Gaetano Cecere, sculptor. Helmle and Corbett,
archts.

Pencil points 8:182
March 1927

720.5
A67a
Flagstaffs
Soldiers and Sailors Memorial. Village of
Queen's, Long Island, N.Y. 2 photographs and
plan.

Architecture 45:47-8
February 1922

Flagstaffs
War memorial, Bailiffe Bridge, Yorkshire.
(Flagpole.) Walsh and Maddock, archts.

Architect 107:138 and pl.fol.p.152
February 24, 1922

Flagstone terraces

see

Terraces

Flanagan and Biedenweg
Exhibit at World's Columbian Expo.
Chicago.

Inland Architect
22: 21-3
Sept, 1893

720.5
A51
Flagstaffs. Italy
Flagpole in front of The Arsenal, Venice,
Italy. Measured and drawn by Robert M.
Blackall, 35th holder, Rotch Travelling
Scholarship.

American architect 123:411-2
May 9, 1923

Flagstone walks

see

Walks (paths)

Flanders and Zimmerman
see also
Chicago (IL) Apartment bldg.
  "   "   Crilly (D.F.) house
  "   "   "   (W.M.)   "
  "   "   Greenwood Ave. school
  "   "   Haymarket theater
  "   "   Kimball Carriage factory
  "   "   Market St. (South) (# 224-38)
  "   "   Morton (J.) house
  "   "   Oakley (G.K.) house
  "   "   O'Brien (W.V.) house
  "   "   Park Gate   hotel
                        (see next card)

Flagstaffs, Italy. Venice. Piazza san Marco

Nicolai, Hermann Georg. Das
Ornament der Halienischen
Kunst des XV Jahrhunderts.
Dresden: Gilberssche, 1882. Pl. 75

Flaks, Francis Augustus, 1886-1945
Obituary

Illinois society
of architects bulletin
29:8
Ap-My 1945

Flanders and Zimmerman   (card 2)
see also
Chicago (IL) Peabody (H.B.) factory
  "   "   Turner hall
  "   "   Washington Blvd. (# 858-862) houses
  "   "   Winslow (F.A.) house
  "   "   Zimmerman (W.) house
Evanston (IL) Gross (A.H) residence
Glencoe (IL) McLeish (A.)   "
Hinsdale (IL) Knight (Wm.) "

720.52
A67
Flagstaffs, Italy. Venice. St.Mark's
Bronze mast standard on the piazza of St.
Mark's, Venice, by Alessandro Leopardi.

Architects' & builders' journal 41: pl.
March 10, 1915

Flamboyant Style
List of Foreign examples.

Rickman, Thomas. An attempt to
discriminate the styles of English
architecture, from the conquest to
the reformation... 6th ed. Oxford:
Parker, 1862., p. 424-434

Flanders and Zimmerman
Altering and adding to school house on 14th
Street bet. Union and Desplaines.
Flanders and Zimmerman, archts.

Building budget
3:65
My 31, 1887

Flagstaffs, Italy. Venice. St. Marks
Details of one of the masts erected on the
Place of St. Mark's at Venice.

Gailhabaud, Jules. L'architecture
du V au XVII siècle. 4 vols. Paris:
A. Morel, 1869-72. Vol. 3.pl.58

Flamingo shop, San Juan, P.R.

see

San Juan (Puerto Rico) "The Flamingo Shop"

Flanders and Zimmerman
4 one-story stores for C.E. Pope on
West Madison St. Flanders and Zimmerman, archts.

Building budget
3:65
My 31, 1887

720.5
M59a
Flagstaffs, U.S., New York
Commemorative flag staff in Union Square
Park, New York City and detail of bronze
relief sculpture about the base. Perry
Coke-Smith, archt.

Metal arts 3: pl.49
July-August 1930

Flanagan & Biedenweg.
Art glasswork.

Inland Arch.
28: (XV) adv. trade suppl.
#3   1896

Flanders and Zimmerman
Store building for M. R. Kultchar, Chicago.
Flanders & Zimmerman, archts.

Inland architect
20, no. 3
pl. fol. p. 30
O 1892

Flagstone pavements

see

Pavements, Stone

Flanagan & Biedenweg
Art glasswork production. 57-63 Illinois St.,
Chicago.

Inland Arch.
26: (xvii)-xviii
adv. trade suppl.
No. 1 1896

Flanders and Zimmerman
3-story flat building for Harry Ridgeway
Ogden Ave. near Congress St. Flanders and
Zimmerman, archts.

Building budget
3:65
Ap 30, 1887

Flanders and Zimmerman
2-story apartment for F.J. Waters on Paulina near Polk. Flanders and Zimmerman, archt.

Building budget
3:86b
Ja 30, 1887

Flanders, John J.   1847-1914
Architect

Andreas, A.T. History of Chicago.
3 vols. Chicago: A.T. Andreas, 1884.
3:72

720.5
A87d
Flannery, W   E
Residence of Miss Bebe Daniels, Santa Monica, Cal. W.E.Flannery, designer.

Architectural digest 7: 144
Number 2

710.5
C855
Flanders, Annette Hoyt
Landscape architect for gardens on estate of Mrs. Chas. McCann, Oyster Bay, N.Y.

Country life (U.S.)54: 54-55
June 1928

Flanders, J.J.
The Chicago School Board and its Architect.

Inland Architect
20: 48
Dec, 1892

720.5
F29
Flashing
Flashing on the United States Court House at New York: sections.

Federal architect 7:70-72
October 1936

Flanders. Architecture
No illus.

British arch 83:169-170
Mar. 26, 1915

720.5
I56
Flanders, John J   1847-1914
J. B. Kellers office building. Chicago
J.J. Flanders, archt.

Inland architect 5:94,pl.fol.98
July 1885

720.52
A87
Flashing
Lead flashing to chimneys on pantile roofs.

arch journal 106: 2nd p. fol. 498
D 4 '47

705.2
I61
Flanders.Architecture
Monuments of Flemish architecture from photographs taken by the late Sir Benjamin Stone. No text.

International studio 54:119-130
December 1914

Flanders, John J.   -1914
obit.

West. Archt.
20: p. 58
Jun, 1914

Flat iron building, St. Albans, Eng.
see
St. Albans, Eng. Flat iron building

720.52
A87c
Flanders. Architecture
Cammaerts, Emile
The work of restoration in Flanders--Nieuport

Architect 115: 430-431
April 30, 1926

Flanders, John J., 1847-1914
(Obituary)

A.I.A. Journal 2:347-48
Jl. 1914

Flat roofs
Rogers, Tyler Stewart
Disenos de Azoteas o techos para paises del caribe

Arquitectura Cuba
17: 371-374
D 1949

Flanders, John J.   1847-1914
see also

Chicago (IL) Cottage Grove school
    "   "   Kershaw school
    "   "   Haller's bldg. (old) (224-26 S. LaSalle)
    "   "   Morton (J.) house
    "   "   Tilden School (ca. 1886)
    "   "   West Division high school (1886)

720.5
I56
Flanders, John J   1847-1914
Sketch of houses for J. K. Barry on Washington boulevard. J.J. Flanders, archt.

Inland architect 5:68,pl.fol.72
May 1885

Flat roofs
Henn, Walter
Das flache dach [sections & details]

Baumeister
57:EB 23-EB 32 Je 1960
57:EB 35-EB 42 Jl 1960
57:EB 43-EB 50 Ag 1960
57:EB 51-EB 58 S 1960

Flanders, John J., 1847-1914
See also
Flanders and Zimmerman.

Flanigen and Flanigen
see
Rosemont (Pa.) house

Flat roofs
Flachdachkonstruktionen [details]

Baumeister
56:EB73-EB76 O 1959

Flat roofs
Oisel, Marianne and Ernst
Over het dak

Forum
9:no.1:11-13
1954

Fleetwood (Eng.) Rossall School
New dining room, Rossall School, Fleetwood.
Hubert Worthington, archt.

Builder 135:498,505,507,512,pls.
S 28,0 5, 1928

Fleming bldg. Washington, D. C.

see

Washington, D. C. Fleming bldg.

Flat roofs
Harriman, E.E.
The problem of the flat roof.

Country life (U.S.) 52:60
October, 1927

Fleetwood, Eng. Rossall School
Rossall dining-hall.

Architectural review 64:62-69 pls 4-5
August 1928

705.8
F55 Fleming,Hans
Karling,Sten
Hans Fleming. Ett bidrag till kännedomen om
hans verksamhet i Tyskland och Sverige.

Tidskrift för konstvetenskap 21: 65-86
1938

Flatiron building.

see

New York (N. Y.) Flatiron building

710.5
H44 Fleetwood (N.Y.) Griffith house
Home of the Misses Griffith, Fleetwood,
N.Y. Erik Knever, archt. Plans.

House and Garden   74: 51
August 1938

720.53
W31 Flesche,Hermann
Neubauten in Braunschweig. (New buildings
in Braunschweig by Hermann Flesche and Johannes Kölling: apartment buildings, public
library.) Plans.

Wasmuths monatshefte 15: 106-108
March 1931

720.52
A87e Flaxman, John
The Flaxman exhibition at University Col-
lege

Architect 109:290
April 27, 1923

Flegenheimer,Julius

See

Nénot and Flegenheimer

Fletcher and Dannatt

see also

Fletcher, Sir Bannister Flight, 1866-1953

Flaxman, John, 1755-1826.
Bentley, G.E., Jr.
Notes on the early editions of Flaxman's
classical designs.
[illus]

New York. Public library
Bulletin.
V. 68: 277-307, My. 1964
V. 68: 361-380, Je. 1964

Fleischl, Robert
Working Men's Houses in Hungary.
Architects: Robert Fleischl, A. Arkay and
Geza Kullina, Lawrence Lichner.
Photos, plans, elev.

West. Archt.
16: 67-70
Jul, 1910

Fletcher and Dannatt

see

London (Eng.) Roan school

Flaxman, John, 1755-1826.
Wolfe, Richard J.
Postscript on the duplicating of engravings.
With reference to Flaxman's classical designs.

New York. Public library
Bulletin.
V. 68: 381-383, Je. 1964

Fleming, Bryant

see also

Grosse Point (Mich) Estate and garden views
Nashville, Tenn. Cheekwood

Fletcher, Sir Bannister Flight, 1866-1953

see also

Fletcher and Dannatt

790.53
B51 Fleck, Hermann
Wettbewerb, Kirchliche Gebäude für die
St. Jacobigemeinde in Braunschweig. Johann
Kraas and Hermann Fleck, archts. Sketches and
plans.

Berliner architekturwelt 12: 255-260
Heft 7, 1909

MICROFILM

Fleming, Bryant, 1877-1946
obituary notice

In SCRAPBOOK ON
ARCHITECTURE p. 708
(on film)

Fletcher, Sir Bannister Flight, 1866-1953

see also

Blackheath, Eng. Morden college. Hospital and
staff quarters
London, Eng. Gillette industries, ltd. factory

Card 1 (row 1, col 1):
720.52
A67e
Fletcher, Sir Banister Flight, 1866-1953
The new president of the R.I.B.A.
Photograph.

Architect 122:5
July 5, 1929

Card (row 1, col 2):
Fletcher, H.M.
Plan of house at Campden Hill, London.
H.M. Fletcher, archt.

Architects' jour. 63:119-20
January 13, 1926

Card (row 1, col 3):
Fleury abbey

See

Saint-Benoit-sur-Loire. Sainte Marie.

Card (row 2, col 1):
720.6
R88
Fletcher, Sir Banister Flight, 1866-1953
Architectural education; an address to students; with discussion.

R.I.B.A.Journal 37: 219-224
February 8, 1930

Card (row 2, col 2):
Fletcher, Jean Bodman

see

Northampton, Mass. Smith college. Dormitory
competition

Card (row 2, col 3):
Flewelling, Ralph C.

see

Beverly Hills (Calif.) Connelly (Joseph) house
"   "   "   Hawthorne School
"   "   "   Middleton (Chas.) house
Brentwood Heights (Calif.) Donaldson (J.G.) house
Hermosa Beach (Calif.) Bergin (L.E.) house
Laguna Beach (Calif.) Brodley (Kathryn) house
Los Angeles (Calif.) Stockwell (N.Y.) house
"   "   "   University of Southern
California Seeley W. Mudd Memorial

(see card no.2)

Card (row 3, col 1):
720.6
R88
Fletcher, Sir Banister Flight , 1866-1953
Inaugural address; with discussion. Por.

R.I.B.A.Journal 37: 2-15
November 9,1929

Card (row 3, col 2):
Fletcher, Jean Bodman

Member of firm:

The Architects' Collaborative

Card (row 3, col 3):
Flewelling, Ralph C.   (card no. 2)

see

Pasadena (Calif.) Starr (E.G.) house
Santa Barbara (Calif.) Mudd (Mrs.Seeley G.) house

Card (row 4, col 1):
720.52
A67
Fletcher,Sir Banister Flight. 1866-1953
Photograph.

Architects' journal 78: 230
August 24,1933

Card (row 4, col 2):
Fletcher, Norman Collings

see also

Northampton, Mass. Smith college. Dormitory
competition

Card (row 4, col 3):
Fliether, Paul
Harbers, Guido
Dorfgemeinschaftssiedlung Langenhorst bei
Velbert im Rheinland. (Village community of
Langenhorst near Velbert in the Rhine region)
Paul Fliether, archt.
Grunsätzliches zur dorfsiedlung Langen-
horst. (Some facts about the Langenhorst village
development near Velbert in the mountain district.)

Der Baumeister
34: 289-293, 325, sup.181-182.
pl.97
September 1936

Card (row 5, col 1):
Fletcher, Sir Bannister Flight and sons

see

London, Eng. Deptford town hall
London, Eng. Queen Victoria memorial. Competition.

Card (row 5, col 2):
Fletcher, Norman Collings

Member of firm:

The architects collaborative

Card (row 5, col 3):
720.52
A67
Flint.
Industry of Brandon.

Arch. Jour. 54:327-8.
Sept. 14, 1921

Card (row 6, col 1):
720.5
A51
Fletcher,F.A.
Old town national bank, Baltimore (Md.).
View and plan. F.A. Fletcher, archt.

American architect 132:589-90
November 5,1927

Card (row 6, col 2):
Fletcher, Mrs. Norman Collings

see

Fletcher, Jean Bodman

Card (row 6, col 3):
Flint construction

see

Stone construction

Card (row 7, col 1):
Fletcher, H. L.

see

Little Rock (Ark.) house

Card (row 7, col 2):
Fleuri-sur-Loire. Abbaye

See

Saint-Benoit-sur-Loire. Sainte Marie.

Card (row 7, col 3):
711
T75
Flint, England

Town planning review 10:241-4 &
Feb. 1924   pl.36-9

Flint (Mich.) Baptist church (1st) Year's best large church. Swanson, assos. archts. Natl arch 7: 8 F 1961	720.5 A67a Flintridge (Cal.) Cass (Louis) house House,Louis Cass, Flintridge, Cal. Paul R. Williams, archt. Architecture 49:176 My '24	720.5 A67d Flintridge (Cal.) Leone (J.G.) house Residence of Mr. and Mrs.J.G.Leone, Flintridge.Kemper Noaland,archt. Plan Architectural digest 9: 70-71 A Number 4 [1936-37]
Flint (Mich.) Civic bldg. Co. Housing development Industrial housing development for the Civic Building Company at Flint, Michigan. Davis, McGrath and Kiessling, archts. Plans. American architect 113:623-634 May 15, 1918	720.5 A67d Flintridge (Cal.) Cravens (Robert) house House of Robert Cravens, Flintridge,Cal. Ray Kieffer, archt. Plans Architectural digest 6: 32 A Number 3 [1930]	720.5 A67d Flintridge (Cal.) Millikan (C.B.) house Residence of Mr. and Mrs. Clark B.Milli- kan,Flintridge,Wallace Neff,archt. Plan Architectural digest 9: 20-21 A Number 1 [1936-37]
Flint (Mich.) Civic building co. Housing development Davis, H. E. The Civic Building Company's development. William Pitkin, Jr., landscape archt., Davis, McGrath and Kiessling, archts. Architectural review 22:n.s.5:92-94, April 1917 pls.fol.p.96	Flintridge (Cal) Flintridge County Club Myron Hunt, archt. West.Archt. 32: pl. 15 Aug. 1923	Flintridge (Cal.) Moore (R.T.) house Residence of Prof. and Mrs. Robert T. Moore, Flintridge. Robert H. Ainsworth, archt. Charles Gibbs Adams, landscape archt. Plan Architectural digest 8:58-59, Number 3 [1932-33]
Flint (Mi) High School Malcomson and Higginbotham, archts. Plans, photos. West. Archt. 33: pl. 8-13 Nov, 1924	720.5 A67d Flintridge (Cal.) Gross (Frank) house Residence of Mrs. Frank Gross, Flintridge Robert H. Ainsworth, archt. A. E. Hanson, landscape archt. Plans. Architectural digest 8: 65-67 Number 3 [1932-33]	710.5 H84 Flintridge (Cal.) Robbins (W.S.) house A hilltop garden in California. House of Mr. and Mrs. Hunter S. Robbins at Flintridge, Cal. John Byers, archt., Charles Gibbs Adams, landscape archt. House and garden 57:95-97 February 1930
Flint (Mich.) Industrial Savings Bank Industrial Savings Bank building. Amer. Arch. 119: pl. Apr. 20, 1921	720.5 A67d Flintridge (Cal.) house A Flintridge residence - Marston and Maybury,archts. Seymour Thomas, landscape archt. Architectural digest 8: 122- 125 A Number 1. [1932-33]	720.5 W52 Flintridge (Cal.) Robbins (H.S.) house Residence of Mr. Hunter S. Robbins, Flint- ridge, California. John Byers, archt. Western archt.38: pls.1-5 January 1929
720.5 A67d Flintridge (Near)(Cal.)"Altacanyada" Residence of Mr. and Mrs.C.H.McKelligan, "Altacanyada," near Flintridge,Kelly H.Hudson archt. Architectural digest 8: 87-89 A Number 1. [1932-33]	Flintridge (Cal.) Jutten (L.W.) Residence Myron Hunt, archt. West. Archt. 32: pl. 15 Aug. 1923	Flitcroft, Henry see London (Eng.) St. Giles-in-the-fields " " St. Olave
720.5 A67f Flintridge (Cal.) Beetson (F.C.) house House for Mrs. Frank C. Beetson, Marston and Maybury, archts. Plan A Architectural Forum 71:222 October 1939	720.5 A67d Flintridge (Cal.) Kresser (C.F.) house Residence of Mr. and Mrs.C.F.Kresser,Flint -ridge.Allen Rouff,archt. Architectural digest 9: 122 A Number 4 [1936-37]	Floating airports see Airports, floating

Floating clubhouses

see

Clubhouses, Floating

720.5
A67f

Floor coverings.

Arch. forum 35: 105-4.
Sept. 1921.

Floors
Choosing the floor construction.

Architecture. 54:279-82
Sept. 1926

Flockhart. William

Arch. and Bldr's jour. 37:535-537
May 21, 1913

720.52
A67

Floor loads
Weights of materials and L.C.C.(1932)
floor loads. Sir John Burnet, Tait and Lorne,
archts.

Architects' journal 78: supp.
July 13, 1933

A

720.5
A67a

Floors.
The economy of bottom-slab construction.

Architecture.53:149-50
May, 1926

Floderer, Anton

see

Potsdam (Ger.) Rathaus

Flooring

see

Floors

Floors. An experiment in economic floor
construction. Diagrams.

Inland Arch.
27: 58
July 1896

Floodlighting

see

Light projection

Floors

see also

Floor coverings

710.5
C855

Floors
Taylor, C. S.
Fashions in floors: bringing the floor up-
to-date.

Country life (U.S.) 58:63-64
December 1930

Floor construction

see

Floors

Floors

Gailhabaud, Jules. L'architecture
du V au XVII siècle. 4 vols.
Paris: A. Morel, 1869-72.
au xviie siecle v.2 pl. 45-52.

710.5
H84

Floors
Floor coverings in new designs.

House and garden 53: 130-133
May 1928

720.5
A67f

Floor coverings.

Arch. forum 35: 29-30.
July 1921.

710.5
H84

Floors.

House & Garden 41: 42-3.
Mar. 1922.

Floors
Phillips, Derek, ed.
Floor finishes. The warmth of floor
finishes. Variety in concrete flooring. Some
problems in laying floors. Asphalt floor finishes.
Industrial floors. Notes on cork tiles. Comparative
table of floor finishes.

Arch't'l design
32: Technical Supp. #5,
Mr 1962

720.5
A67f

Floor coverings.

Arch. forum 35: 63-4.
August 1921.

Floors.

Newson, John Henry. Homes of
character. 2nd ed. Cleveland, Ohio:
The John Henry Newson Company, 1913.
p.28-55

710.5
C855

Floors
Floorings for beauty and service.

Country life 42: 104-8
Jun. 1922.

Floors
Floors and floor framing

Freitag, Joseph Kendall. Architectural engineering. New York: J.Wiley and sons, 1895. chap IV p. 54-87

710.5
C855
Floors
Pertinent facts about floors and flooring

Country life 43: 74-82
Dec. 1922

790.5P
AC7ay
Floors, Concrete
Concrete and patent floors

Archts' yr bk 9: 245-246
1947

720.5
F29
Floors
Heavy-duty flooring materials: tests of the Bureau of Standards conducted under the supervision of W.C. Clark of the Procurement Division.

Federal architect 8:34,40,52
April 1938

720.54
A67
Floors
Mayeux, Albert
Précautions à prendre pour l'utilisation normale du parquet sans joint. (Precautions to take for the normal utilization of the jointless floor)

L'Architecture 41: p.96
April 15, 1928

Floors, Concrete
Caws, Frank
The bending stresses on flat rectangular concrete floors

RIBA 7: 421-23
Je 30, 1900

Floors.
How to alter the color of floors.

House and garden 42: 51.
Aug.1922.

710.5
C855
Floors
Variety in floors.

Country life(U.S.)52: 72,74,76
May 1927

Floors, Concrete
Concrete Floors in London Flats.

RIBA 10:528
S 26, 1903

720.5
AC7f
Floors
Industrial flooring materials

Architectural forum 39:115-116
Sept. 1923

710.5
H84
Floors.
Dutel, P.
When floors are decorative.

House & garden.50:49-51
Aug. 1926

Floors, Concrete
Allen, William
Designing concrete floors to reduce the transmission of sound.

RAIC jrl 15:239-242
N 1938

Floors.
Wheeler, Walter H.
Many openings in factory floor lead to choice of flat-slab construction.

Northwest archt 13: 8,7-10
No. 3 1949

Floors
Wilce and - Matched Flooring Patent.

Inland Architect
41: 43
Jun, 1903

Floors, Concrete
Light weight concrete floor and roof deck

Arch. forum
67:supp.88 +, Ag 1937

720.52
A67
Floors
Williams,Ll. E.
Modern floor coverings.

Architects' journal 74: 605-609
November 4, 1931

Floors, Care
Floors and their care

Country Life 47:72
Mar. 1925

Floors, Concrete
New flooring material, by Henry M. Morgan.

West. Archt.
3: p. 19
Apr, 1904

720.52
A67c
Floors
Modern methods in building construction.

Arch 108: 276-7, 412-4, 461-3
O 20/ D 8, 29 '22

710.5
C855
Floors. Care
Taking proper care of floors.

Country life (U.S.)51:72-4,76
January 1927

720.5
A67r
Floors, England
British interior decoration—floors
Albert E. Bullock

Arch. record 56:368-374
Oct. 1924

Floors, Fireproof
The selection of fireproof floors

Amer. architect 123:159-62
Feb. 14, 1923

720.52
A67c
Floors, Soundproof
Eleven types of soundproofed floors
now under investigation by the National
Physical Laboratory and the Building
Research station in conjunction with the
architect John Dower and Hope Bagenal.

Architect(Lond.)150:396
June 25,1937

710.5
C855
Floors, wooden
Platt, R. H. jr
Plank floors redivivus.

Country life (U.S.) 64: 59-60
October 1928

Floors, Hospital
The hospital floor

Amer. architect 123:86-9
Jan. 17, 1923

720.52
A67
Floors, soundproof
Yorke,F.R.S.
Notes on new sound proof floors. Diagram.

Architects' journal 78: 397
September 28,1933

720.6
A51j
Florence
Seven drawings - Florence

A.I.A. journal 11:391-7
Oct. 1923

720.5
A67f
Floors. Industrial buildings
Industrial flooring materials

Architectural forum 39:115
Sept. 1923

710.5
B84
Floors, stone.
The stone floors of Pennsylvania. E.S. Paxson
archt.

House & garden.49:92
Feb. 1926

Florence
and its craftsmen

Archts' and bldrs. jour. 48:178-180,
Oct. 16, 1918   188-189
Oct. 23, 1918

721
T55
Floors, Marble
Standard details for interior marble.

Through the ages 6: 3-6,10
August 1928

731.97
A67c
Floors,Terrazzo
Rennon,A.J.
Color in the floor.

Architectural concrete 2:11-13
No.2,1936

Florence.
J.E.O. Pridmore, architect, Rambles in and
about Florence. Her Art Treasures and the
Campanile.

Inland archt 42:
45-47; Ja 1904
Inland archt 43:
2-3; F 1904

Floors, Parquet

see

Parquetry

721.97
A67c
Floors,Terrazzo
Collins,Edna
Texas history in terrazzo. C.H.Page,archt.

A   Architectural concrete 2:29-32
No.4,1936

Florence (It.) Aeronautical school

see

Florence (It.) Scuola di Applicazione Aeronautica

720.52
A67c
Floors,Removable
Removable floor at the Dome, Brighton.
Robert Atkinson, arch. Plan.

A   Architect(Lond.)149:189
February 5,1937

720.5
B84
Floors, Tile
LeBoutillier, A.B.
Tile floors

Brickbuilder 22:43-46
February 1913

Ryerson

Florence, It. Air views
Detti, Edoardo
Dilemma del futuro de Firenze

Critica d'arte
No. 2 p.161-177
Mr 1954

720.52
A67
Floors,Rubber
Various types of rubber floors. Sir John
Burnet,Tait and Lorne,archts. Examples.

Architects' journal 78: supp.
December 21,1933

A

Floors, Tile. Austria. Medieval
Vongrey, P. Felix
Ornamentierte mittelalterliche Bodenfliesen
in Stift Lilienfeld [illus]

Österreichische Zeitschrift
für Kunst und Denkmalpflege
26,Hft 1/2:9-19
1972

Florence (It.) Andiron Chest Cover
By Michael Angelo. (in the Bargello)
Photo.

Inland Architect
34: supp.p. 31
Jan, 1900

705.B B98 Florence. Architecture Brown, G. B. Florence and her builders. Burlington magazine 13: 18-22 April 1908	Florence, It. Architecture. 11th cent. Beenken, Hermann Die Florentiner Inkrustations-architectur des XI. Jahrhunderts. I. Der Stilgegensats. II. Die Bauten. [illus.] Zeitschrift für bildende Kunst 60: 221-230; 245-255 1926/27	Florence. Banca di Firenze See Florence. Palazzo Pazzi Quaratesi
720.52 B95 Florence. Architecture Micklethwaite,D.M. Mediaeval architecture and Florence. Structure and decoration. Reflections. Builder 145: 138-140; 181-182 July 28; August 4,1933	Florence, It. Architecture. 15th cent. Gilbert, Creighton The earliest guide to Florentine architecture, 1423. Florence. Kunsthistorisches Institut. Mitteilungen Band 14, Heft 1: [33]-46 Je 1969	Florence. Baptistery See Florence. Battistero di San Giovanni.
720.5 A67r Florence.Architecture Viale dei Colli; and the Loggia,Piazzale Michelangelo, Florence. G.Poggi,archt. No plans. Architectural record 10:540-541 A April 1901	720.52 A67 Florence (It.). Arco di trionfo Triumphal arch. Piazza Cavour, Florence. Giadot, archt. Arch & bldrs jl 43: n1 for N 13 '18	Florence. Bargello palace. See Florence. Palazzo del Podestà
Florence. Architecture Zwei fenster von palaesten in Florenz. Via di Servi, no. 10, via Ginori, no. 9. Palast Architektur. 6 vols in 11 bks. Berlin: E. Wasmuth, 1886-1911 2:pt.1:13 pt.2:pl.77	Florence. It. (La.) Badia. La Badia. Meas. drawing by H. Morley. Lond. Arch Assoc. Sketchbook 8:pls.56- 1904. 58	Florence, It. Battistero di San Giovanni Baptistery, Florence Gailhabaud, Jules. L'architecture du V au XVII siècle. 4 vols. Paris: A. Morel, 1869-72. 2:pl.17
Florence. Architecture. Conservation and restoration. Heikamp, Detlef 'Appunti di fiorentino argomento.' Restauri monumentali dell'Ottocento nella critica di Pietro Franceschini. [illus.] Paragone Anno 22: 63-72; pls. 13-20 Jl 1971	Florence. (La) Badia Procacci, Ugo Cosimo de' Medici e la construzione della Badia fiesolana. [illus.] Commentari An.19:80-97 Ja-Je 1968	720.52 A67c Florence.Battistero di San Giovanni Founts. The Baptistery of Florence. Architect and contract reporter 65:79 February 1, 1901
Florence. Architecture. Medieval. Paatz, Walter Die Hauptströmungen in der Florentiner Baukunst des frühen und hohen Mittelalters und ihr geschichtlicher Hintergrund. [illus.] Florence. Kunsthistorisches Institut. Mitteilungen. Band 6, Heft 1/2: 33-72 D 1940	Florence. La Badia. Middeldorf, Ulrich Die gotische Badia zu Florenz und ihr Erbauer Arnolfo di Cambio, von Ulrich Middeldorf und Walter Paatz, mit Zeichnungen von Ludwig Joutz. [illus., part col.] Florence. Kunsthistorisches Institut. Mitteilungen. Band 3, Heft 8: [492]-517 Ja 1932	Florence (It.) Battistero di San Giovanni Baptistery. Florence Pavement. Arch. and Bldr's jour 42:pl.for Sept. 29, 1915
Florence. Architecture, Mediaeval Micklethwaite, D.M. Mediaeval architecture and Florence. Structure and decoration. Reflections. Builder 145:138-140;181-182 July 28; August 4, 1933	Florence (It.). (La) Badia. Door. Doorway, Chiesa di Badia, Florence Arch. journal 56:434 Oct. 4, 1922	Florence (It.) Battistero di San Giovanni Baptistery, Florence, Pavement Archts and bldrs. jour. 48:pl.for Oct. 23, 1918

Florence (It.) Battistĕro di San Giovanni Detail of pavement in Baptistery Florence.1200 Archt's and Bldrs' jour. 42 sup.for Nov. 24, 1915	Florence.Battistero di San Giovanni Horn, Walther Das Florentiner baptisterium. Plans, sections, etc. Mitteilungen des kunsthistorischen institutes in Florenz 5:99-151 Heft 2,December 1938	Florence. Biblioteca Mediceo-Laurenziana Wright, C. H. The Laurentian Library; the great building at Florence designed by Michelangelo for the Medici. Interior views. No plan. Country life (Lond.) 68:485-487 October 18, 1930
Florence. Battistero di San Giovanni Mendes Atanasio, M. C. Documenti inediti requardanti la «Porta del Paradiso» e Tommaso di Lorenzo Ghiberti. [illus.] Commentari An.14:92-103;tav.XXXIII-XXXIV Ap-S 1963	705.5 R45 Florence.Battistero di San Giovanni Excavations around the Baptistry of Florence. Rivista d'arte 9:81-120,161-217 Apr.-July 1916 Aug.-Dec.1916	Florence, It. Biblioteca Mediceo- Laurenziana Wittkower, R. Michelangelo's Biblioteca Laurenziana. Plan, drawings Art bulletin 16; No. 2: 123-218 1934
Florence (It.) Battistero di San Giovanni The Florentine Baptistry. Arch and c. rep 73: 410-11 Je 30, '05	Florence (It.) Battistero di San Giovanni Doors Details from bronze doors of Baptistery, Florence Architect and contract reporter 99: plate 3 following 220 April 12, 1918	Florence, It. Biblioteca Mediceo-Laurenziana Stairway: Biblioteca Medicea, Florence, Italy. Amer. archt and building news 94:pl. S 16, 1908
Florence. Battistero di San Giovanni. Horn, Walther Das Florentiner Baptisterium. [illus.] Florence. Kunsthistorisches Institut. Mitteilungen Band 5, Heft 2: [99]-151 D 1938	Florence, It. Biblioteca Laurenziana see Florence, It. Biblioteca Mediceo-Laurenziana	Florence. Bigallo Bigallo, Florence. Erbaut 1352-1358. Photograph of detail in text. Photograph, measured drawings and details. Palast Architektur. 6 vols. in 11 bks. Berlin: E. Wasmuth, 1886-1911 6:15:pls.89-91
Ryerson 705.1 A78s Florence (It.) Battistero di San Giovanni Anthony, Edgar W. The Florentine baptistery. Art studies 5: 29-111. 1927	Florence. Biblioteca Mediceo-Laurenziana Laurentian Library, Florence. Ruggieri, Fernando. Studio d'architettura civile. 3 vols. Florence: Tartini, 1722-28. v.1,pl.1-14.	Florence,It. Boboli gardens see Florence,It. Giardino di Boboli
Ryerson Florence, It. Battistero di San Giovanni Nava, Antonia Sui disegni architettonici per S. Giovanni dei Fiorentini in Roma La critica d'arte 1:102-8 1935-6	Florence. Biblioteca Mediceo-Laurenziana Biblioteca Laurenziana zu Florenz. Michelangelo Buonarroti, archt. Measured drawings. Colored plates of details. Palast Architektur. 6 vols. Berlin: E. Wasmuth, 1886-1911 2:pt.1:6,pls. 31-37	Florence, It. Capella dei Medici see Florence It. San Lorenzo. Sagrestia nuova
Florence. Battistĕro di San Giovanni Interior of baptistery at Florence. Gebhart, Emile. Florence. Paris: H. Laurens, 1906. p. 39	Ryerson Library Florence (It.) Biblioteca Mediceo-Laurenziana Gronau, Georg Dokumente zur entstehungsgeschichte der neuen sakristei und der bibliothek von S. Lorenzo in Florenz. Jahrbuch der k. preussischen kunstsammlungen 32:beiheft 62-81 1911	Florence, It. Cappella dei Pazzi see Florence, It. Santa Croce. Cappella dei Pazzi.

Florence. Casa Buonarroti
Savelli, Maddalena de Luca
Studi sulla simbologia della «Camera degli
Angeli» nella Casa Buonarroti. [illus]

Commentari
Anno 24:176-192
Jl-S,1973

Florence, It. Description

see

Florence, It. Guide-books
Florence, It. Views

720.5
A67r
Florence.Galleria degli Uffizi
Melani,Alfredo
The ceilings in the Galleria degli Uffizi,
Florence.

Architectural record 23:39-46
January 1908

Florence (It.) Casa dei Mutilati
La nuova "Casa dei Mutilati in Firenze.[plans]
Rodolfo Sabatini, archt.

Architettura 17: 495-502
Ag 1938

Florence.Duomo

See

Florence.Santa Maria del Fiore

Florence, It. Galleria degli Uffizi
Zorzi, Giangiorgio
Le prospettive del Teatro Olimpico di
Vicenza nei disegni degli «Uffizi di Firenze
e nei documenti dell'» Ambrosiana» di Milano.
[illus.]

Arte lombarda
v.10, II: 70-97
1965

Florence. Casino di Livia
Casino della Livia in Florenz. Bernardo
Buontalenti, archt. Photograph.

Palast Architektur. 6 vols in 11 bks.
Berlin: E. Wasmuth, 1886-1911
2:pt.1:16
pt.2:pl.100

Florence, It. Forte de San Giorgio
Bemporad, Nello
Il Forte Belvedere e il suo restauro
(plans and Sections) Bernardo Buontalenti, Archt.

Bollettino d'Arte
42:122-34
Ap-Je 1957

Florence. Galleria degli Uffizi
Hoogewerff, G. F.
Due ritratti fiamminghi nella Galleria
degli Uffizi. [illus.]

Florence. Kunsthistorisches
Institut. Mitteilungen
Band 8: 63-64
O 1957-My 1959

Florence.Cathedral

See

Florence.Santa Maria del Fiore

Florence, It. Forte del Belvedere

see

Florence, It. Forte de San Giorgio.

Florence, It. Giardino di Boboli
Boboli gardens, Florence. Fountains.

Triggs, Harry Inigo. The art of garden
design in Italy. London: Longmans,
Green and Co., 1906. p.71,pls 30,31,71,34

Florence (It.) Certosa
(Carthusian Monastery) Well-head.

West. Archt.
31: front.
Oct, 1922

Florence, It. Fortezza di Belvedere

see

Florence, It. Forte de San Giorgio.

Florence, It. Giardino di Boboli
Fountains and garden views in Boboli gardens,
Florence.

Latham, Charles. The gardens of
Italy. 2 vols. London: Country Life,
Ltd., and G. Newnes , Ltd., 1905.
v.2,p.73-77,80,83

720.5
A51
Florence. Davanzati palace.
The Davanzati Palace, Italy. Pt.VIII.
Interior court.

American architect 102:pl.prec.
December 18, 1912   p.213

Florence, It. Fortezza di S. Maria del
Belvedere

see

Florence, It. Forte de San Giorgio.

Florence (It.) Giovanni Berta stadium

see

Florence (It.) Stadio comunale Giovanni Berta

720.5
A67r
Florence.Davanzati palace
Bombe,Walter
A Florentine house in the Middle Ages: the
Davissi-Davanzati palace. No plans.

Architectural record 31:575-590
June 1912

Florence, It. Galleria degli Uffizi

see also

Florence, It. Palazzo degli Uffizi

Florence, It. Guide-books
Gilbert, Creighton
The earliest guide to Florentine archi-
tecture, 1423.

Florence, It. Kunsthistorisches
Institut. Mitteilungen
Band 14, Heft I: [33]-46
Je 1969

Florence, It. Hall of the great council (old)

see

Florence, It. Palazzo vecchio. Sala di consiglio grande (1495-8)

Florence, It. Loggia dei Lanzi
Loggia des Lances, Florence. Detail drawing and plan

Cromort, George. Choix d'éléments empruntés à l'architecture classique. Paris: A. Vincent, 1927. vol 2, pl 4

Florence.Loggia dell' Orcagna

See

Florence.Loggia dei Lanzi

Florence, It. House of the company of weavers
House of the Company of Weavers

Ciba rev no 1:11
S 1937

729
L84

Florence.Loggia dei Lanzi
Loggia dei Lanzi, plan and details.

Architectural Association Sketch
Book 1-?:pl.41-4?
Series 4,1909-1910

Florence.Loggia della Signoria

See

Florence.Loggia dei Lanzi

Florence. Innocents, Hospital of the

See

Florence. Ospedale degli innocenti.

720.52
B93

Florence. Loggia dei Lanzi
Loggia de Lanzi, Florence,Italy. From the interior, drawn by Mr. A.C.Conrade.

Builder 88: 15 pl.fol.p.28
January 7, 1905

Ryerson
Florence, It. Maps

Mask
13:fol 86
Ap-Je 1927

Florence. Kunsthistorisches Institut.
Brües, Eva
Palazzo Capponi-Incontri, der neue Sitz des Kunsthistorischen Instituts in Florenz.
[illus.]
Florence. Kunsthistorisches
.Institut. Mitteilungen
Band 12: [319]-354
D 1965-S 1966

720.5
A67

Florence (It.). Loggia dei Lanzi
Measured drawing...by H.L. Duhring.

Arch rev 6: pl LXI fol 114
S 1899

Ryerson
Florence, It. Maps
An old map of Florence

Mask
12:opp 170
O 1926

Florence, It. Laurentian library

see

Florence, It. Biblioteca Mediceo-Laurenziana

Florence.Loggia dei Priori

See

Florence.Loggia dei Lanzi

Florence.Market(new)

See

Florence.Mercato nuovo

Florence. Loggia dei Lanzi
Details of Loggia de Lanzi at Florence, formerly called Loge de la Seigneurie.

Rohault de Fleury, Georges. Les monuments de Pise au Moyen age.2 vols.
Paris: A. Morel, 1866. vol.1 33-36 (renumbered) pls. 7-12

Florence.Loggia del Bigallo

See

Florence.Bigallo

Florence (It.) Medici chapel

see

Florence (It.) San Lorenzo. Sagrestia nuova

Florence (It.) Loggia dei Lanzi

Illustrating Article "Art as an Educational Force and Source of Wealth ".

Inland archt.
46: pl.fol.p. 36
Oct. 1905

Florence.Loggia del mercato nuovo

See

Florence.Mercato nuovo

Florence, It. Medici library

see

Florence, It. Biblioteca Mediceo-Laurenziana

Florence. Mercato nuovo
Mercato Nuovo, Florence, Italy. Bernardo
Tasso, archt. Measured detail drawings, plan.

Italian Renaissance: Sixty measured
drawings with details. 3 vols.
New York: The architectural book
publishing company, n.d. 2:pl.53-54

Florence. New market

See

Florence. Mercato nuovo

Florence. Palazzo Bartolini-Salimbeni
Palazzo Bartolini in Florenz. Baccio
d'Agnolo, archt. Photograph.

Palast Architektur. 6 vols in 11 bks.
Berlin: E. Wasmuth, 1886-1911
2:pt.1:4,pl.20

Florence. Mercato nuovo
Mercato nuovo in Florenz. Bernardo Tasso,
archt. Sketch, measured drawings, details, plans.

Palast Architektur. 6 vols in 11 bks.
Berlin: E. Wasmuth, 1886-1911 2:pt.1:11
pt. 2:pl.64-66

720.5
W52

Florence. Ospedale degli innocenti
Arcade, hospital of the Innocents, Florence,
Italy. Ernest Pickering, del.

Western architect 36: pl.17
January 1927

Florence. Palazzo Capponi-Incontri

see

Florence. Kunsthistorisches institut

Ryerson

Florence, It. Mercato vecchio
Mercato vecchio - old marketplace.

Ciba rev.
No. 1: 12
S 1937

Florence. Ospedale degli innocenti
Hof und halle der Innocenti in Florenz.
Brunellesco, archt. Measured detail, photograph.

Palast Architektur. 6 vols in 11 bks.
Berlin: E. Wasmuth, 1886-1911 2:pt.1:11
pt. 2:pls. 68-69

Florence. Palazzo Cataldi
Villa Careggi, Florence, Italy. Plan.

Italian Renaissance: Sixty measured
drawings with details. 3 vols. New York:
The architectural book publishing
company, n.d. 2:pl.52

Florence, It. Michelangelo Monument
Monument dedicated to Michelangelo, Florence,
Italy. Designer M. Poggi.

Architectural record 14:398
November 1903

Florence. Ospedale degli innocenti
Loggia degli Innocenti, Brunellesco, archt.,
and Loggia - Piazzia S. Maria Novella.
Measured drawings.

Italian Renaissance: Sixty measured
drawings with details 3 vols. New
York: The architectural book
publishing company, n.d. 2:pl.55

Florence. Palazzo Ceperello
Palazzo Ceperello in Florenz. Archt. unknown.
Measured drawings.

Palast Architektur. 6 vols. in 11
bks. Berlin: E. Wasmuth, 1886-1911
2:pt.1:13, pt.2:pl.76.

Florence, It. Municipal stadium

see

Florence, It. Stadio comunale Giovanni Borta

720.5
A51

Florence. Palazzo Antinori
Palazzo Antinori, Florence, Italy.
(frontispiece for April 11, 1917)

American architect 111: pl.fac.p.225
April 11, 1917

Florence. Palazzo Cerchi

See

Florence. Palazzo dell'Antella

Florence   Museo nazionale

See

Florence. Palazzo del Podestà

Florence. Palazzo Arcives-covile
Palazzo Arcives-covale in Florence.
Giovanni Antonio Dosio, archt. Photograph, Plan.

Palast Architektur. 6 vols in 11 bks.
Berlin: E. Wasmuth, 1886-1911
2:pt.2:11,pl.67

720.5
A51

Florence. Palazzo Davanzati
The Davanzati Palace, Italy. Pt.VIII.
Interior court.

American architect 102:pl.prec.p.213
December 18, 1912

Florence (It.) National Bank
Entrance door of the National Bank, Florence.
Antonio Cipolla, archt. No plan.

A   Architectural record 10:243
April 1901

Florence (IT) Palazzo
Bartolini-Salembeni

Archs and Bldrs. jour.
41: 40, pl. VIII
Jan 27, 1915

720.5
A67r

Florence. Palazzo Davanzati
Bombe, Walter
A Florentine house in the Middle Ages: the
Davizzi-Davanzati palace. No plans.

Architectural record 31:575-690
June 1912

013.2 **044** Florence. Palazzo Davanzati Reddie, Arthur Italian furniture from the Palazzo Davanzati Old furniture 3:153-160 March 1928	Florence. Palazzo Davizzi, see Florence. Palazzo Davanzati.	720.5 Florence. Palazzo del Podestà A67 Courtyard of the Bargello, Florence (Palazzo Podesta). Measured drawing by Babcock, Jr., sixth winner of Rotch Travelling scholarship. Architectural review 2:13, pl.4 January 2, 1923
720.5 **A67f** Florence. Palazzo Davanzati Italian renaissance details. Chimney- pieces in Palazzo Davanzati, Florence. Measured drawings by Howard Moise. Architectural forum 37:215-218 November 1922	720.5 Florence. Palazzo degli Uffizi A67r Melani, Alfredo The ceilings in the Galleria degli Uffizi, Florence. Architectural record 23:39-46 January 1908	Florence. Palazzo del Podesta Palazzo del Podesta (Bargello), Florence. Erbaut 1255, 1332. Photographs. Palast Architektur. 6 vols in 11 bks. Berlin: E. Wasmuth, 1886-1911 6:14-15:pls.87-88
720.5 **A51** Florence (It.) Palazzo Davanzatti Bach, R. F. The Palazzo Davanzati, Florence Amer arch 111:81-6 F 7, '17	720.52 Florence. Palazzo degli Uffizi A674 The Uffizi palace by night, and colon- nade of the Uffizi palace from pencil sketches by Maxwell Fry. Architecture (Lond.) 5: 139,141 September 1926	Florence, It. Palazzo del Podesta Court Palais de podestate, Florence. Rohault de Fleury, Georges. Les Monuments de Pise au Moyen age. 2 vols. Paris: A. Morel, 1866. v.1,pl.13-26.
705.4 **A79** Florence. Palazzo Davanzati Rusconi, A.J. Le palais Davanzati a Florence (XIV siecle). Les arts 10:9-39 August 1911	Florence. Palazzo degli Uffizi Uffizien, Florence. Giorgio Vasari, archt. Measured drawings, photographs. Italian Renaissance: Sixty measured drawings with details. 3 vols. New York: The architectural book publish- ing company, n.d. 2:pl.45-48 3:pl.52	Florence. Palazzo dell'Antella Palazzo dell' Antella (Florenz), Antonio da San Gallo, d.j. archt. Photograph. Palast Architektur. 6 vols in 11 bks. Berlin: E. Wasmuth, 1886-1911 2:pt.1:10 pt.2:pl.62
705.1 **A51a** Florence. Palazzo Davanzati Brinton, Selwyn The Palazzo Davanzati at Florence American magazine of art 18:254-257 May 1924	Florence. Palazzo degli Uffizi Die Uffizien zu Florenz. Giorgio Vasari, archt. Measured drawings, photographs, colored plate of ceiling. Palast Architektur. 6 vols. in 11 bks. Berlin: E. Wasmuth, 1886-1911 2:pt.1:7,pls.38-44,47,48	Florence, It. Palazzo della Signoria see Florence, It. Palazzo vecchio
Florence. Palazzo Davanzati Palazzo Davanzati, Florence. Erbaut um 1350. Photograph in text. Photograph. Palast Architektur. 6 vols in 11 bks. Berlin: E. Wasmuth, 1886-1911 6:15:pl.92	Florence. Palazzo del Bargello see Florence. Palazzo del Podestà	Florence (It.) Palazzo di Parte Guelfa Dami, Luigi Une oeuvre de Brunelleschi recouvree. L'amour de l'art 6:194,195 My 1925
ff **720.5** **A51** Florence. Palazzo Davanzati Newhall, L.C. The restored palace of the Davanzati, Florence, Italy. American architect 102: 25-27 & pls. July 24; August 14, 28, 1912	720.5 Florence. Palazzo del Podestà A51 Palazzo Podesta. Florence. American architect 115: opp. 447 March 19, 1919	720.52 Florence. Palazzo di Parte Guelfa A673 Marsini, Yoi The restoration of a famous palace: the Palazzo della Parte Guelfa. Architectural review (Lond.)54: 80-82 September 1923

Florence.Palazzo Dufour- Berte

See

Florence.Palazzo Guadagni

Florence. Palazzo Gondi
    Palazzo Gondi, Florence. Giuliano da Sangallo,
archt. Measured detail drawings, photograph.

A

        Italian Renaissance: Sixty measured
        drawings with details. 3 vols. New York:
        The architectural book publishing
        company, n.d. 2:pl. 27
                    3:pl. 52

Florence. Palazzo Larderel
    Palazzo Larderel in Florenz. (Via de Tornabuoni
no. 19). Giovanni Antonio Dosio, archt. Photograph.

        Palast Architektur. 6 vols in 11 bks.
        Berlin: E. Wasmuth, 1886-1911
        2:pt.1:4,pl.18

Florence. Palazzo Ferroni
    Palazzo Ferroni, Florence. Erbaut um 1300.
Photograph.

        Palast Architektur. 6 vols in 11 bks.
        Berlin: E. Wasmuth, 1886-1911
        6:15:pl.92

Florence. Palazzo Gondi
    Palazzo Gondi in Florenz. Giuliano da San
Gallo, archt. Plan.

        Palast Architektur. 6 vols. in 11 bks.
        Berlin: E. Wasmuth, 1886-1911
        2:pt.1:13
            pt.2:pl.80-82

Florence. Palazzo Medici-Riccardi
Büttner, Frank
    Der Umbau des Palazzo Medici-Riccardi zu
Florence. [illus., sum. in It.]

        Florence. Kunsthistorisches
        Institut. Mitteilungen
        Bd.14,Heft4: [393]-414
        D 1970

Florence. Palazzo Frescobaldi
    Palazzo Frescobaldi, Florence. Erbaut um 1650.
Photographs.

        Palast Architektur. 6 vols. in
        11 bks. Berlin: E. Wasmuth,
        1886-1911 6:16:pls. 94-95

Florence. Palazzo Guadagni
    Palazzo Guadagni, Florence. Simone Cronaca,
archt. Measured detail drawings, photographs.

        Italian Renaissance: Sixty measured
        drawings with details. 3 vols. New York:
        The architectural book publishing
        company, n.d. 2:49-51, 3:52

Florence. Palazzo Medici-Riccardi
Bulst, Wolfger
    Die ursprüngliche innere Aufleilung des
Palazzo Medici in Florence. [illus., sum. in
It.]

        Florence. Kunsthistorisches
        Institut. Mitteilungen
        Bd 14, Heft 4: [369]-392
        D 1970

Florence, It. Palazzo Giacomini
    Facade of the Giacomini palace, Florence.

        Architects' journal 50: 177 pl. 173
        August 6, 1919

Florence. Palazzo Guadagni
    Palazzo Guadagni zu Florenz. Simone Cronaca,
archt. Photograph, measured drawings, details.

        Palast Architektur. 6 vols. in 11 bks
        Berlin: E. Wasmuth, 1886-1911
        2:pt.1:8,pls.49-50
        2:pt.2:pls.51-52

Florence.Palazzo Montalvi

See

Florence.Palazzo Pazzi

Florence (It.) Palazzo Giugni-Canigiani
    Palazzo Giugni-Canigiani in Florenz. B.
Ammanati, archt.

        Palast Architektur. 6 vols in 11 bks.
        Berlin: E. Wasmuth, 1886-1911
        2:pt.1:13,pls.78-79
            pt.2:pls.78-79

Florence (It.). Palazzo Guadagni. Door
    Doorway, Palazzo Guadagni, Florence.
Measured by J.K. Smith and Ernest A. Grunsfeld, Jr.
Drawn by Ernest A. Grunsfeld, Jr.

        Pencil points 5:73
        Apr. 1924

Florence (IT) Palazzo
    Nonfinito

        Archs. and bldrs. jour.
        41: 29, pl VII
        Jan 20, 1915

720.5   Florence. Palazzo Gondi
B86   J.G.G.
        Capitals from the Palazzo Gondi, Florence.

        brochure series 7: 142-146
        August 1931

Florence, It. Palazzo Horne
    The Palazzo Horne, Florence

        American magazine of art 15:77-78
        Feb. 1924

Florence. Palazzo Nonfinito
    Die palaeste Quaratese und non Finito in
Florenz. Bernardo Buontalenti, archt. Photograph,
measured drawings, plans.

        Palast Architektur. 6 vols in 11 bks.
        Berlin: E. Wasmuth, 1886-1911
        2:pt.1:14
            pt.2:pls.89-92

Florence (It) Palazzo Gondi Court
    Giuliano San Galleo, archt.

        West. Archt.
        31: front.
        Nov, 1922

Florence, It. Palazzo Horne
    The Palazzetto Corsi, bequeathed to the
Italian government by Herbert Horne

        House beautiful 52:413-416
        Nov. 1922

Florence. Palazzo Nonfinito
    Palazzo non Finito, Florence. Bernardo
Buontalenti, archt. 1592. Obergeschoss. Vincent
Scamozzi, 1602. Photograph.

        Palast Architektur. 6 vols in 11 bks.
        Berlin: W. Wasmuth, 1886-1911
        6:15-16:pl.93

Florence. Palazzo Panciatichi-Ximenes
     Palazzo Panciatichi-Ximenes in Florenz. Archt.
not given. Plan only.

          Palast Architektur. 6 vols in 11 bks.
          Berlin: E. Wasmuth, 1886-1911
          2:pt.1:14,pl.19

720.52
A67
          Florence. Palazzo Pitti
               Florentine palaces, courtyard of the Pitti
          bartolomeo Ammannati, architect.

               Architect's and builder's journal 40:
          A   pl. for December 23, 1914

Florence, It. Palazzo Riccardi

     see also

Florence. Palazzo Medici-Riccardi

Florence (IT) Palazzo Pandolfini

          Archs. and bldrs. jour.
          41: 17, pl. VI
          Jan 13, 1915

720.52
A67   Florence.Palazzo Pitti
              Main staircase, Pitti palace.

              Architect's journal 50:150-151
              July 30,1919

Florence. Palazzo Riccardi
     Palazzo Riccardi in Florenz. Plan, measured
drawing, photograph. Michelozzo Michelozzi archt.

          Palast Architektur. 6 vols. in 11 bks.
          Berlin: E. Wasmuth, 1886-1911
          2:pt.1:14-15
               pt.2:pls.92-94

Florence. Palazzo Pazzi
     Palazzo Montalvi in Florens (Borgo degli Albizi
no. 24). Bartolomeo Ammanati, archt. Photograph.

          Palast Architektur. 6 vols in 11 bks
          Berlin: E. Wasmuth, 1886-1911
          2:pt.1:15, pt.2:pl.95

Florence (IT) Palazzo Pitti

          Archs. and Bldrs. jour.
          41: 5, pl. V
          Jan 6, 1915

Florence. Palazzo Rucellai
     Palazzo Ruccellai in Florenz. Leon Battista
Alberti, archt. Photograph.

          Palast Architektur. 6 vols in 11 bks.
          Berlin: E. Wasmuth, 1886-1911
          2:pt. 1:9, pt.2:pl.59

Florence. Palazzo Pandolfini
     Palazzo Pandolfini in Florenz.
Giovanni Francesco da San Gallo, archt.
(Entwurf von Raffael) Measured drawing, photograph.

          Palast Architektur. 6 vols in 11 bks.
          Berlin: E. Wasmuth, 1886-1911
          2:pt.1:9, pt.2:pls.57-58

Florence. Palazzo Pitti
     Palazzo Pitti in Florenz. Brunellesco, archt.
Photographs.

          Palast Architektur. 6 vols in 11 bks.
          Berlin: E. Wasmuth, 1886-1911
          2:pt.1:11-12
               pt.2:pls.70-74

720.52
A67   Florence.Palazzo Rucellai
              Rucellai palace. Florence.

              Architect's journal 49:4-24
              June 1.,1919

Florence. Palazzo. Pazzi Quaratesi
     Die palaeste Quaratesi und non Finito in
Florenz. Bernardo Buontalenti, archt. Photograph,
measured drawings, Plans.

          Palast Architektur. 6 vols. in 11 bks.
          Berlin: E. Wasmuth, 1886-1911
          2:pt.1:14
               pt.2:pls.89-92

Florence. Palazzo Pitti
     Palazzo Pitti, Florence. Filippo
Brunelleschi, archt. 1440. Fortgesetzt 1550,1568,
1620,1762. Photographs in text. Photographs,
measured drawings.

          Palast Architektur. 6 vols. in 11 bks.
          Berlin: E. Wasmuth, 1886-1911
          6:14:pls.83-86

Florence. Palazzo Serristori
     Palazzo Serristori in Florenz. Baccio d'Agnolo,
archt. Photograph. Plan.

          Palast Architektur. 6 vols. in 11 bks.
          Berlin: E. Wasmuth, 1886-1911
          2:pt.1:10, pt.2:pl.60

Florence, Palazzo Pitti

          Ruggieri, Fernando. Studio
          d'architettura civile. 3 vols.
          Florence: Tartini, 1722-28.
          v.3,pl.1 - 28.

STESSOR LIBRARY
705.5
RSS   Florence.Palazzo Pitti
              Restoration according to the designs
         of Pietro da Cortona - Pitti.

              Rassegna d'arte 7:190-95
              November-December 1920

Florence.Palazzo Spini

     See

Florence.Palazzo Ferroni

Florence. Palazzo Pitti

          Salvatore, Camillo, comp.
          Italian architecture, furniture,
          and interiors. Boston: G.H. Polley
          and Co., 1904 pl.20-21

Florence.Palazzo Quaratesi

     See

Florence.Palazzo Pazzi Quaratesi

Florence, It. Palazzo Strozzi
Leland, C. G.
     The lanterns of the Strozzi palace.

          Amer archt & bldg news 55:30-1
          Ja 23, 1897

Florence (It.) Palazzo Strozzi
Palais Strozzi, Florence. Benedetto de Majano and Simone Cronaca, archts. Measured detail drawings.

Italian Renaissance: Sixty measured drawings with details. 3 vols. New York: The architectural book publishing company, n.d. 2:pls.31-39

720.5
A67

Florence.Palazzo vecchio
Doorway,Palazzo Vecchio,Florence.Envoi of Rotch scholarship. Drawing by C.H.Blackall.

A

Architectural review 2:pl.55
November 1895

Florence, It. Palazzo vecchio. Sala di consiglio grande (1495-8)
Wilde, J.
The hall of the great council of Florence

Warburg and Courtauld institutes journal
7,no. 3-4:65-81
1944

Florence. Palazzo Strozzi
Palazzo Strozzi, Florence, Italy.

Ruggieri, Fernando. Studio d'architettura civile. 3 vols. Florence: Tartini, 1722-28.
v.3:pl.52-58

Florence (It.) Palazzo Vecchio
Doorway and details of ornament on doorway in Palazzo Vecchio, Florence, Italy. Measured and drawn by Ernest A. Grunsfeld, Jr.

Pencil points 7:339-340
June 1926

Florence (It.) Palazzo Vecchio. Tower
Tower (section and plans), measured drawing

Boston Society of Architects. Rotch Scholarship committee. Envois of the Rotch Travelling Scholarship. 2 vols. Boston: Boston Society of architects, 1896-1902. 2:pl 15-16

Florence. Palazzo Strozzi
Palazzo Strozzi in Florenz. Benedetto da Majano und Simone Cronaca, archt. Measured drawings, photogrphs, plans.

Palast Architektur. 6 vols in 11 bks. Berlin:E. Wasmuth, 1886-1911
2:pt.1:1-2,pls.1-14

720.5
A67

Florence. Palazzo vecchio
Drawing of elevation of the Palazzo Vecchio, Florence. Envoi of the Rotch Travelling Fellowship. Walter H. Kilham.

Architectural review 3: pl. 45
December 1894

Florence, It. Pazzi chapel

see

Florence, It. Santa Croce. Cappella dei Pazzi

720.5
A51

Florence. Palazzo Torrigiani
Palazzo Torrigiani, Florence.

American architect 114: opp. p.1
July 3, 1918

Florence. It. Palazzo Vecchio
Old Palace. Perspective view of the grand council chamber

Archts. jour. 49:pl.for
April 2, 1919

Florence (It.) Pergola theater

see

Florence (It.) Teatro della Pergola

Florence. Palazzo Torrigiani
Palazzo Torrigiani zu Florence. Archt. not given. Photograph only.

Palast Architektur. 6 vols. in 11 bks. Berlin: E. Wasmuth, 1886-1911
2:pt.1:7,pl.46

710.5
H84

Florence. Palazzo vecchio
Palazzo Vecchio by night, Florence.

House and garden   74: 61
October 1938

Florence. Planning.
Detti, Edoardo
Dilemma del futuro di Firenze. [illus., part col.]

Critica d'arte
Anno 1, no.2: 161-177
Mr., 1954

720.52
A67

Florence.Palazzo Uguccioni
Palazzo Uguccioni, by Raphael.

Architect's journal 50:774
December 17,1919

Florence. Palazzo vecchio
Palazzo vecchio in Florenz. Giorgio Vasari, archt. Phtographs, plan.

Palast Architektur. 6 vols in 11 bks. Berlin: E. Wasmuth, 1886-1911
2:pt.1:8, 2:pt.2:pls. 53-56

Florence, It. Ponte Santa Trinita
Santa Trinita Bridge, Florence

Parsons, William Barclay. Engineers and engineering in the Renaissance. Baltimore: Williams and Wilkins, 1939. Chap. 31:539-551

Florence. Palazzo Uguccioni
Palazzo Uguccioni (Fenzi) in Florenz. Photograph, measured drawings. Mariotto di Zanobi Tolfi, archt.

Palast Architektur. 6 vols in 11 bks. Berlin: E. Wasmuth, 1886-1911
2:pt.1:15, pt.2:pl.97-98

Florence. Palazzo vecchio
Palazzo Vecchio, Florence. Arnolfo di Cambio, 1298-1314. Photographs, measured drawings, and details.

Palast Architektur. 6 vols in 11 bks. Berlin: E. Wasmuth, 1886-1911
6:13:pls. 77-82

Florence (It.) Ponte vecchio
Pastel drawing of "Il Ponte Vecchio" at Florence, Italy, by Harry Sternfeld.

Pencil points 8:col. pl.
opp 164
Mr '27

Florence. Ponte vecchio Rohault de Fleury, Georges. Les monuments de Pise au Moyen age. 2 vols. Paris: A. Morel, 1866. 1:pl.39-40	Ryerson Florence, It. San Giuseppe (church) Toni, M. I. La chiesa di San Giuseppe [models]. Cecio d'Arnolo, archt. Dedalo 9: 283-289 O 1928	Florence, It. San Lorenzo, Old sacristy see Florence, It. San Lorenzo, Sacrestia vecchia

Florence,It. Regio Giardino di Boboli
 	
see
 	
Florence,It. Giardino di Boboli
	720.5 Florence,San Lorenzo
	A67r Cheney,C.H.
	  The American Academy in Rome: "Watering the plants of genius" Cellini: Interior of San Lorenzo, Florence, Italy - by Brunelleschi.
	
	Architectural record 31:255
	March 1912
		Florence.(It) San Lorenzo, Sagrestia Nuova
		Apollonj, B.M.
		  Opere Architettoniche di Michelangelo a Firenze: Cappella Medicea. Photographs, plan, measured drawings, sections etc.
		
		Accademia d'Italia, Rome. I Monumenti Italiani Relievi Raccolti a cura della Reale Accademia D'Italia; fascicola I-IX, 1934-1936. 2 vol. Rome: LaLibreria Dello Stato, 1934-1936. Vol. 1, fasc. 2:1-4, pls., 13-22

MICROFILM Florence (It.) Restoration In SCRAPBOOK ON ARCHITECTURE p. 45,46 (on film)	720.5 Florence,San Lorenzo A51 Cloister of San Lorenzo, Florence, Amer. Arch. 121: 93-4. Jan. 18, 1922.	Florence (It.) San Lorenzo. Sagrestia nuova Gronau, Georg Dokumente zur entstehungsgeschichte der neuen sakristei und der bibliothek von S. Lorenzo in Florenz. Jahrbuch der k. preussischen kunstsammlungen 32:beiheft 67-81 1911

Florence (It.) Riccardi Palace
  Details - first floor window of Riccardi palace, Florence, Italy.
 	
Pencil points 8:53
January 1927
	Florence. San Lorenzo
	Apollonj, B.M.
	  Opene Architettohiche di Michelangelo a Firenze: San Lorenzo. Model, plans, measured drawings.
	
	Accademia d'Italia, Rome. I Monumenti Italiani Relievi Raccolti a cura della Reale Accademia D'Italia; fascicola I-IX, 1934-1936. 2 vol. Rome:La Libreria dello Stato, 1934-1936.
	v.1, fasc.2 :1-4, pls. 23-26
		Ryerson
		
		Florence, It. San Lorenzo. Sacrestia vecchia
		Carli, Enzo
		  La sacrestia vecchia di San Lorenzo
		
		Emporium
		109:216-221, My 1949

Florence, It. Sala di consiglio grande (old) see Florence, It. Palazzo vecchio. Sala di consiglio grande (1495-8)	Florence. San Lorenzo De Tolnay, Charles I progetti de Michelangelo per la facciata de S.Lorenzo a Firenze: nuove ricerche. [illus.] Commentari Anno 23:53-72 Ja-Je 1972	Florence (It.) San Martino dei Buonomini see Florence (It.) San Martino del Vescovo
Florence (It.) San Francesco al Monte see Florence (It.) San Salvatore al Monte	Florence. San Lorenzo S. Lorenzo. Meas. drawings by P.E. Nobbs and R.W. Schultz. New Sacristy and singing gallery. Lond Arch Assoc Sketchbook Ser 2, v. 12: pl. 60. 1893 ser 3, v. 8: pls. 59-62. 1904	Florence, It. San Martino del Vescovo Tommaso Rosselli Sassatelli del Turco The church of San Martino dei Buonomini in Florence Dedalo 8:610-632 March 1928
Florence.San Giovanni Battista See Florence.Battistero di San Giovanni.	Florence,It. San Lorenzo. Capella dei Medici see Florence,It. San Lorenzo. Sagrestia nouva	Florence. San Miniato al Monte S. Miniato al Monte. Meas. drawings by W.S. George and H. Morley, Chapel, altar, and Chapel of S. Giacomo. Lond Arch Assoc Sketchbook ser 3, v.8:pl.63. 1904 ser 3, v.10:pl.47.1906

720.9 **M63** Florence. San Miniato al Monte Church of San Miniato Al Monte, Florence, Italy. Western Architect 37: 151 July 1928	Florence. Santa Croce Marble inlay: memorial-slabs from Santa Croce, memorial slab, Florence. Waring, John Burley. Examples of stained glass. London: Vincent Brooks, 1858 pl.26-27.	Florence. Santa Maria del Fiore see also Florence. Santa Reparta (church)
Florence. San Salvatore Al Monte San Salvatore del Monte. Anderson, William James. Architectural Studies in Italy. Glasgow: Maclure, Macdonald and Co., 1890. pl. 19-23	**779** **L84** Florence. Santa Croce Measured drawings of tombstones. Santa Croce, Florence. Sketch and details of marble tabernacle at Santa Croce, Florence, and details of central portion of loggia of Pazzi chapel, Santa Croce 1470. Brunelleschi, archt. A London.Architectural assoc.sketch book 1891; 1905. v.2 s.2:pl.53; v.9.s.2:pl. 54-57	Florence (It.) Santa Maria del Fiore Santa Maria del Fiore, Florence. (col.pl.) Walcot, William. Architectural water colours and etchings. London: H.G. Dickins, 1919. pl. 119
Florence, It. San Salvatore al Monte Bastoli, Lando La "generazione" albertiana dei rapporti ne "La Bella Villanella" a Firenze. [illus., sum.in Eng.,Fr.,& Ger.] L'Arte n.s. v.4: 66-81 Mr 1971	Florence, It. Santa Croce Soffit from the cloisters, Santa Croce. Arch. jour. 51:107. Mar. 31, 1920.	Florence. Santa Maria del Fiore Braunfels, Wolfgang Drei Bemerkungen zur Geschichte und Konstruktion der Florentiner Domkuppel. [illus.] Florence. Kunsthistorisches Institut. Mitteilungen Band 11: [203]-226 D 1963-S 1965
Florence (It.) San Stefano in Pane (church) Apsidal treatment, no. 18: church of S. Stefano, Florence, Italy. Amer. archt. and bldg news 56: 23, pl fol 24 Ap 17, 1897	Florence, It. Santa Croce. Cappella dei Pazzi. Door of the Cappella dei Pazzi. F. Brunelleschi, architect. Architectural journal 56: 332 Sept. 13, 1922	Florence. Santa Maria del Fiore. Sanpaolesi, Piero La cupola di Santa Maria del Fiore ed il mausoleo di Soltanieh. Rapporti di forma e struttura fra la cupola del Duomo di Firenze ed il mausoleo dell'Ilkhan Ulgiaitu a Soltanieh in Persia. [illus., sum. in Ger.] Florence. Kunsthistorisches Institut. Mitteilungen. v. 14, Heft 3: [221]-260 1972
720.52 **A67** Florence. Santa Croce Door in the church of Santa Croce, Florence. Arch.journal 56: 640 Nov. 8, 1922	Florence, It. Santa Croce. Cappella dei Pazzi. Pazzi chapel, Florence: 1443-1478 illus., plans, sections Filippo Brunelleschi, architect. Prak, Niels Luning. The language of architecture. The Hague: Mouton and Co., 1968. pp. 100-116	Florence, It. Santa Maria del Fiore The Dome of Santa Maria del Fiore (plans and section) Parsons, William Barclay. Engineers and engineering in the Renaissance. Baltimore: Williams and Wilkins, 1939. Chap. 35: 587-607
720.5 **A67** Florence. Santa Croce In the cloisters of Santa Croce, Florence Architecture 51:8-10 Jan. 1925	Florence. Santa Croce. Memorial Stone Marble inlays: memorial stone, Santa Croce, Florence A.D. 1403 Waring, J.B. Examples of Architectural art in Italy and Spain.... London: McLean, 1850. pl. 43.	Florence. Santa Maria del Fiore Exterior, interior, details. Allen, Fred Hovey. Great Cathedrals of the World. 2 vols. Boston: Haskell and Post. c1886 -88. pl.preceding p.189, 4 pls. following p.200
Florence. Santa Croce Brües, Eva Die Fassade von S. Croce in Florenz, ein Werk des Architekten Matas. [illus.] Florence. Kunsthistorisches Institut. Mitteilungen Band 12: [151]-170 D 1965-S 1966	Florence, It. Santa Maria del Carmine (church). Cappella di Brancacci. Brockhaus, Heinrich Die Brancacci-Kapelle in Florenz. [illus.] Florence. Kunsthistorisches Institut. Mitteilungen. Band 3, Heft 4: [160]-182 Mr 1930	Florence (It.) Santa Maria del Fiore Weinberger, Martin The first facade of the cathedral of Florence Warburg and courtauld institutes jour 4:67-79, pls. 15-18 O '40-Ja '41

Florence (It.) Santa Maria del Fiore
Metz, Peter
Die Florentiner domfassade des Arnolfo di Cambio.
(archt.)

Jahrbuch der Preusszischen kunst
sammlungen 59: 121-160
Heft 3, 1938

Florence. Santa Maria del Fiore. Facade
Becherucci, Luisa
Sculptures on the ancient façade of the cathedral
of Florence

Dedalo 8:719-737
May 1928

Florence, It. Santa Trinità
Salmi, Mario
Nuovi reperti nella Badia Santa Trinita.
[illus]

Commentari
Anno 20:87-89
Ja-Je, 1973

Florence. Santa Maria del Fiore
Morozzi, Guido
Indagini sulla prima cattedrale fiorintina.
[illus.,part col.]

Commentari
An.19:3-17
Ja-Je 1968

Ryerson

Florence, It. Santa Maria del Fiore. Restoration. 1956
Rossi, Ferdinando
La lanterna della cupola di Santa Maria
del Fiore e i suoi restauri [plans and sections]

Bollettino d'arte
41: 128-143
Ap-Je 1956

Florence, It. Sante Apostoli
La restauration de la basilique des saints
Apôtres a Florence.

Informations mensuelles :2
February 1933

Florence. Santa Maria del Fiore.
Matteoli, Anna
I modelli lignei del '500 e del '600 per la
facciata del Duomo di Firenze. (illus.)

Commentari
An.25:73-110
Ja-Je 1974

Florence. Santa Maria Novella.
Wackernagel, Martin
Zur älteren Baugeschichte von S. Maria
Novella. Nachtrag [von] Walter Paatz. [illus.]

Florence. Kunsthistorisches
Institut. Mitteilungen.
Band 3, Heft 6: [349]-353
Ja 1931

Florence, It. Santo Spirito
Church of Santo Spirito. Florence, Italy.

Builder 103: 780
D 27, 1912

790.5
B95b   Florence.Santa Maria del Fiore
        Santa Maria del Fiore - The Duomo of
        Florence, Italy. Completed May 11, 1887.
        De Fabris and Del Moro, archts.

Building budget 3: 76-77 pl.fol.p.78
June 1887

Florence (It.) Santa Maria Novella
Kern, G. Joseph
Das dreifaltigkeitsfresko von S. Maria
Novella: eine perspektivisch-architekturgeschicht-
liche studie.

Jahrbuch der k. prussischen
kunstsammlungen
34:36-58
1913

Florence, It. Santo Spirito
Gronau, Georg
Das Erzengelbild des Neri di Bicci aus
der Kirche S. Spirito. [illus.]

Florence. Kunsthistorisches
Institut. Mitteilungen.
Band 3, Heft 7: 430-434
Jl 1931

790.52
A673   Florence.Santa Maria del Fiore
        Sta Maria Degli Fiore, Florence, Italy.

Arch. Rev. 50: pl. 1.
Sept. 1921

Florence. Santa Maria Novella
Botto, Ida Maria
Proposte per la storia di una facciata.
[illus.]

Florence. Kunsthistorisches
Institut. Mitteilungen
Band 10: 128-134
My 1961-F 1963

790.5
A51   Florence. Santo Stefano
       Interior view of St. Stephen, Florence.

American architect 119: frontispiece
May 25, 1921

790.5
B84   Florence, It. Santa Maria del Fiore,
       Dome.
       Bach, R. F.
       Dome of Santa Maria del Fiore.
       Plans, section.

Brickbuilder 25:
209-215
Ag 1916

Florence.Santa Reparata

See also

Florence.Santa Maria del Fiore

Florence (It.) Scuola di Applicazione Aeronautica
La scuola di applicazione per la R. Aeronaut-
ica a Firenza [plans and sections] Raffaello
Fagnoni, archt.

Architettura 17: 329-369
Je 1938

Florence. Santa Maria del Fiore. Facade
Metz, Peter
Die Florentiner domfassade des Arnolfo di Cambio.

Jahrbuch der Preusszischen kunst sammlungen 59: 121-160
Heft 3, 1938

Florence. Santa Reparta (church)
Salmi, Mario
Considerazioni sui reperti di Santa Reparata.

Commentari
An.19:17
Ja-Je 1968

Florence (It.) Scuola di Applicazione Aeronautica.
Ecole supérieure de l'aéronautique a Florence.
Rafaello Fagnoni, archt. (plans)

L'Arch d'aujourd'hui
9:64-67
Ag '38

Florence (It.) Sede Compagnia Singer
    Nuova sede della compagnia "Singer" a Firenze.
[plans and section] Italo Gamberini, archt.

                Architettura 17: 61P-6PO
    O 1938

Florence. Santissima Annunziata (church)
Casalini, Eugenio
    L'angelico e la cateratta per l'armadio
degli argenti alla SS. Annunziata di Firenze.
[illus.]

                Commentari
                An.14:104-124;tav.XXXV-XXXIX
                Ap-S 1963

7PO.52   Florence (It.). Via Cavour (no.63). Door
A673   Italian doorways: Florence, no.63, Via
    Cavour. Bernardo Buontalente, archt.

                Arch rev 47: pl fol p 154
                My '20

Florence. Spedale degli innocenti

            See

Florence. Ospedale degli innocenti.

Florence (It.) Stazione Centrale
    Railway station, Florence, Italy. Giovanni
Michelucci, Nello Baroni, Pier Niccolo Berardi,
Italo Gamberini, Sarre Guarnieri, Leonardo Lusanna,
architects.

                Architectural forum 65:205-212
                September 1936

Florence. Via porta Rossa
    Fenster eines palastes in der Via Porta
Rossa zu Florenz.

                Palast Architektur. 6 vols. in 11 bks.
                Berlin: E. Wasmuth, 1886-1911
                2:pt.1:7,pl.45

Florence (It.) Stadio comunale Giovanni Berta
    A direct descent from Rome. The Giovanni
Berta Stadium, Florence. Pier Luigi Nervi, archt.
Plans.

                Architect (Lond.) 136: 219-223
                November 24, 1933

792.05   Florence (It.) Teatro della Pergola
M39   An astounding discovery concerning the
    Florentine theatre "La Pergola" Plan. 1652.

                The mask 13: 87-88, pl 12
                Jl/Ag/S '27

Florence. Views
Hülsen, Ch
    Die alte ansicht von Florenz im Kgl. kupper-
stichkabinett und ihr vorbild.

                Jahrbuch der k.
                preussischen
                kunstsammlungen
                35:90-102
                1914

Florence (It.) Stadio Comunale Giovanni Berta
    Municipal Stadium, Florence. P.L. Nervi,
archt. Plan.

                Architects' journal 78: 577
                November 2, 1933

Florence (It.) Tempio degli scolari. Restoration
    La nuova "Casa dei Mutilati in Firenze.[plans]
Rodolfo Sabatini, archt.

                Architettura 17:425-50P
                Ag 1938

Florence. Villa Careggi
    Villa Careggi near Florence. Archt. unknown.
Drawing. Plan.

                Palast Architektur. 6 vols. in 11 bks.
                Berlin: E. Wasmuth, 1886-1911
                2:pt.1:10, pt.2:pl.61

Florence (It.) Stadio comunale Giovanni Berta
Michelucci, Giovanni
    Lo stadio "Giovanni Berta" in Firenze, dell'
Ing. Pier Luigi Nervi. [plans, sections, diagrams]
Pier Luigi Nervi, archt.

                Architettura 11: 105-116
                Mr 1932

Florence (It.) Torre de Rossi
    Lees, D.N.
A tower of old Florence.

                Arch. rev. 61:14-5, pl.3
                January, 1927

Florence (It.) (near) Villa Castello
    Castello and Petraja

                Latham, Charles. The gardens of
                Italy. 2 vols. London: Country
                Life, Ltd., and G. Newnes , Ltd.,
                1905. 2:106-111

Florence, It. Stadio comunale Giovanni Berta
    Stade Giovanni Berta, à Florence. Plan.
P. Luigi Nervi, archt.

                Encyclopedie de l'architecture;
                constructions modernes. 12 vols.
                Paris: Albert Morancé, 1928-39.
                6:pls. 50-57

Florence. Uffizi gallery

            see

Florence. Galleria degli Uffizi

Florence. Villa Castello
    Villa Di Castello. Fountain of Hercules.

                Triggs, Harry Inigo. The art of
                garden design in Italy. London:
                Longmans, Green and Co., 1906. pl.41.

Florence (It.) Stadio comunale Giovanni Berta
    Le stade "Giovanni Berta" de Florence [plan]
Pier Luigi Nervi, archt.

                Tech et Arch 1: 63
                S-O 1941

Florence (It.) Ugolino Golf Club
    The Ugolino Golf Club, Florence, Italy.
Gherardo Bosio, architect. Plan.

A   Architect 143:221-225
            August 23, 1935

Florence (It.) (near). Villa Corsini Castello.
                            Fountain
    Villa Corsini Castello near Florence.
Fountain in the Bosco.

                Triggs, Harry Inigo. The art of
                garden design in Italy. London:
                Longmans, Green and Co., 1906. pl.46

Florence (It.) Villa Fabricotti
Villa Fabricotti - from gate entrance.

Latham, Charles. The gardens of
Italy. 2 vols. London: Country
Life, Ltd., and G. Newnes, Ltd.,
1905. v.2:p.132.

Flores, Anibal & Vidal Vila
Pequenas resedencias por los arquitectos
Anibal Flores y Vidal Vila, [plans]

Arquitectura Cuba
18: 362-368
Ag 1950

705.1
A79
Florida. Architecture
Roberts, M.F.
"Cielito Lindo".

Arts and decoration 29: 35-40
July 1928

Florence (It.) Villa Lauder
Villa Lauder in Florence

House beautiful 52:549-551
Dec. 1922

Flores, Salvador Ortega
see
Ortega Flores, Salvador

Florida. Architecture
Houses should vary with regions. - Florida
house open wide to trade winds. David Anderson,
archt. model

Life articles on art 1945 pt.2:
S 3, 1945   194

Florence, It.   Villa Pazzi
Eberlein, H.D.
Villa Pazzi Pian De' Givllari. Florence.
Plan and photographs of exteriors, interiors and
gardens.

Architectural Record 48:494-511.
December, 1920

Flores Jenkin, Anibal
Programa para el edificio de "El Seguro del
Abogado" Proyecto del Arq. Anibal Flores Jenkin.
[plans]

Arq. Cuba v.23
p.226-232
My 1955

Florida. Architecture
Jacksonville

Western arch. 20: pl.fol.p.59
June 1914

Florence. Villa Salviati
Fountain of Jove. Villa Salviati, Florence.

Latham, Charles. The gardens of Italy.
2 vols. London: Country Life, Ltd., and
G. Newnes, Ltd., 1905. v.2:p.96

Flores Villasenor, Ricardo
see also
Mexico (city) Aeropuerto central de Mexico

705.1
A79
Florida. Architecture
Price, Matlack
Latin architecture in the playgrounds of the
South

Arts and decoration 22:29-31
Jan. 1925

Florence Harkness memorial chapel for women
see
Cleveland(O.) Western reserve university.
Florence Harkness memorial chapel for women.

Flores, Humberto
Casa en Ibague [plans & section] Humberto
Flores & Edgardo Bernal, archts.

Proa
#105:22 N 1956

D13.1
H84
Florida. Architecture
Price, Matlack
The new Mediterranean architecture of
Florida

House beautiful 57: 664-666
June 1925

705.6
025
Florensa, Adolf
Sacs, Joan
The newest academic architecture of Adolf
Florensa.

Caseta de les arts 3: cover,1-5
No.14, 1930

Florida agricultural college [before 1905]
see
Lake City, Fla. Florida agricultural college

061
V26
Florida. Architecture
Ferris, Hugh
The new architecture of Florida

Vanity Fair 26:54-55
April 1926

Florent, Nanquetta
Ecole maternelle, à Pantin. Groupe scolaire,
à Courbevoie. Plans. F. Nanquette, archt.

Encyclopedie de l'architecture;
Constructions modernes. 12 vols.
Paris: Albert Morancé, 1928-39.
7:pls.5-7, 71-75

705.1
A79
Florida. Architecture
Martin, J.W.
Castles in Florida

Arts and decoration 24: 35-39
Jan. 1926

705.1
A79
Florida. Architecture
Old world glamor in new Florida world

Arts and decoration 27:52-53
September 1927

710.5
C855
Florida. Architecture
Residence of H.P. McGinley, Palm Beach.
Addison Mizner, archt.

Country life (U.S.)51: 43-5
March 1927

Florin, Frits
Kreiskrankenhaus Schongau am Lech/Bayern
[plan] Frits Florin, archt.

Bauen and wohnen
No. 4: 130-133
Ap 1956

Flossmoor, Ill. Hunter, Amy Hamilton, house.
Illustration. Purcell and Elmslie, archts.

Prairie School review
II: 23
First quarter 1965

710.5
C855
Florida. Architecture
Smaller houses in the sunshine of Florida.

Country life (U.S.)51: 50-1
January 1927

Florin, Frits
Projekt für eine volksschule in Hausham/
Oberbayern [plan] Frits Florin, archt.

Bauen & Wohnen
#11:400 N 1956

Flossmoor, Ill. Hunter (Amy Hamilton) house
Residence of Mark Ross, esq., Flossmoor,
Ill. Purcell & Elmslie, archts. [illus.]

Arch. rec. 52:300-302
Oct. 1922

710.5
C855
Florida. Architecture
Home of Maitland Belknap. Howard Major, archt.

Country life (U.S.)51: 65-7
February 1927

705.3
B48
Florists' shops
Schl, C.F.W.
Der blumenladen

Neue srat 2:114-116
April 1939

Flossmoor, Ill. Ross, Mark, house

see

Flossmoor, Ill. Hunter, (Amy Hamilton) house

705.2
A79
Florida. Architecture
Spain's architectural gift to Palm Beach

Arts and decoration 28:69
April 1928

Florists' shops, U. S.

see

Los Angeles (Cal.) Margaret's flowers
Cleveland (O.) Jones-Russell Co. flower store

Floto, Julius   1864-1950
[obit. note]

AIA Chicago chap. bul: 50
My 1951

705.2
I61
Florida. Architecture
Robie, Virginia
A Spanish city in Florida

International studio 81:107-112
May 1925

Flossmoor, IL. Homewood Country Club
Nimmons, G.C.
Golf-club houses. Flossmoor, Illinois. George C.
Nimmons, archt.

Architectural review 22:n.s.5:49-50
February, 1917   pl. 3-6 fol. p. 60

Flourtown (Pa.) Carson College for Orphan girls
Carson College for Orphan girls, at Flourtown,
near Philadelphia.

Arch. Rec. 50: 3-25.
July, 1921.

Florida Association of Architects

see

West Palm Beach, Fla. Norton Gallery

Flossmoor (IL.) Homewood Country Club
Homewood Country Club, Flossmoor, Illinois.
Howard Shaw, archt.

Architectural record 26:354-356
November 1909

A

720.5
A67a
Flourtown,(Pa.)Mechling,(B.F.) house
House of B.F. Mechling, jr. Flourtown,
Pa. R.B. Okie, archt.

Architecture 55: 341-4
Je '27

Florida Southern College

see

Lakeland (Fla.) Florida Southern College

Flossmoor, Ill. Hunter (Amy Hamilton) house
Purcell and Elmslie, architects
Amy Hamilton Hunter house, Flossmoor, Illinois,
1916.

Roll 22, frames 387-94

Flourtown, Pa. Morice (Mary H.) house
House for Mrs. Mary H. Morice, Flourtown, Pa.
Harry Sternfeld, archt.

Architectural record 66: 413-417
November, 1929

Flower, Gov. Monument

see

Watertown, N.Y. Governor Flower Monument

Flum, Max
Blechwarenfabrik E. Müller AG, Münchenstein
[plan & section] Max Flum & Ernst Arber, archts.

Bauen & Wohnen
#5:170-71 My 1957

Flynn, Richard
see:
Keefe and Flynn

Flower, Roswell P., memorials

see

Watertown, N.Y. Roswell P. Flower memorial
library

Fluorescent lighting

see

Lighting, Fluorescent

Fodri palace
see
Cremona. Monte di Pietà

Flower rooms

see

Garden rooms

Flushing (L.I.) Carnegie Library. Branch
Carnegie Branch Library, Flushing, Long Island,
N.Y., Lord and Hewlett, architects.

Brickbuilder 16:pl. 13 fol. p. 18
Ja '07

Fogaccia palace.Bergamo
See
Bergamo.Casa dell' Arciprete

Flower sanctuaries

see

Plant sanctuaries

790.5
A67f

Flushing (L.I.) Hamilton (W.J.) house
House of Wm. J. Hamilton, Flushing,
N. Y.

Arch for 40:pls.75-77
fol. 232
My '24

Fogg (William Hayes) art museum

see

Cambridge (Mass.) Harvard university. Wm.
Hayes Fogg art museum

Flower shows, Germany

see

Hamburg, Ger. Gartenbauausstellung "Planten un
Blomen" 1953

Flushing (L.I.) N.Y. and Queens Electric Light and
Power Co. Sub-station
Sub-station at Flushing, L.I. for New York
and Queens Electric Light and Power Co.

Amer. arch. 117:195-204.
Feb. 11, 1920.

Foggia (It.) Opera di San Michele.
Oeuvre de Saint-Michel-Archange a Foggia.
C. Petrucci, archt. plan

L'Arch d'aujourd'hui
9:41
Jl '38

Floyd, Michael Pulsford, 1923-

see

Challen and Floyd

Flying buttresses

Pugin, Augustus Welby Northmore.
The true principles of pointed or
Christian architecture. London: J.
Weale, 1853. 1

Foggia (It.) Planning competition
Lenzi, Luigi
Foggia, Italy, national competition for its
rebuilding.

Town planning review 13:220-227,pls.
December, 1929   58-62

Floyd, W.   H.

see

Chattanooga (Tenn.) Cosby (W. M.) house
"   "   Terrace (E.) house

Flynn, John
see
Columbus (OH) Fire Dept. Engine house

Foggia, It. San Micheli opera

see

Foggia, It. Opera di San Micheli

Peggitt & Addison

see

Leeds (Eng.) Public library. Bramley branch.
competition

Folger Shakespeare library, Washington, D.C.

For the architecture of the building, see

Washington, D.C. Folger Shakespeare library

Folkstone (Eng.) Foreshore. New development
The new Foreshore development, Folkstone,
England. D. Pleydell-Bouverie, archt.

RAIC jrl 15:147-145
Je 1938

Ryerson

Fokker, J   P
Veth, Cornelis
Huis en tuin

Maandblad voor
beeldende kunsten
12:135-139
My 1935

705.6   Folguera, Francesc
625   Bàfols, G. F.
Francesc Folguera, architect

Gaseta de les arts 2:140-142
June 1929

Folkestone (Eng.) Grand Mansions Hotel
Grand Mansions Hotel, Folkestone. Daniel
Baker, archt.

Architect 73: pl.fol.p.56
January 20, 1905

Folembray. Chateau
Folembray, dit le Pavillon, French text, plan,
engraving.

Androuet du Cerceau – Les Plus
excellents bastiments de France.
2 vols. Paris: A. Lévy, 1868-70.
vol. 1. pl. 30-31

Foliage. Gothic.

Sharpe, Edmund. Architectural
parallels. London: J. Van Voorst, 1848.
v.2.pl.118.

Folkestone (Eng.) Housing
The Folkstone housing scheme.

Builder 118:665.
June. 4, 1920.

Foley, John J   -1946
[obituary]

Nat'l arch 7:15
Jl '46

720.5   Folitz and Company
F52   Architect's sketch of Marquette Teal and
Manufacturing company, Chicago. Folitz and
Company, archts.

Western architect 40: pls.8-9
January 1931

Folkwang Museum, Essen,Ger.

see

Essen,Ger. Museum Folkwang

Foley, Max Henry

see

Voorhees, Walker, Foley and Smith

Folklore in architecture

La constr. mod. 29:80-81
Nov. 16, 1913

Follies
Follies.

Architect
108: 282, 299-302, O 20, 1922

Folfi, Mariotto di Zanobi 1521-1600
Palazzo Uguccioni (Fenzi) in Florenz.
Photograph, measured drawings. Mariotto di
Zanobi Folfi, archt.

Palast Architektur. 6 vols in 11 bks.
Berlin: E. Wasmuth, 1886-1911
2:pt.1:15
pt.2:pl.97-98

Folk museums

see

Iona. The shelter

Ryerson

Follies
French, Cecil
Follies with a difference [illus]

Country life [Lond]
123:210, Ja 30, 1958

Folger (Peter) house, Nantucket (Mass.)

See

Nantucket (Mass.) Folger (Peter) house

Folkes & Folkes

see

Wollescole (Eng.) Stevens Park. Bandstand

Ryerson

Follies
Lamborough, W.J.; Quarrell, Charles
Follies with a difference...
In memory of a sailor

Country life
123:462, Mr 6, 1958

Ryerson

Follies
Lewis, W.O.J.
Triangular follies

Country life
123:655, Mr 27, 1958

720.5
A67a
Folsom, Stanton and Graham
House of Phillip Wallis, Bala, Pa.
Folsom, Stanton and Graham, archts.

Architecture 59: 245-248
April 1929

Folts, Frits.

see

Chicago, Ill. Assumption church. School

720.5
A67f
Folly Mills,(Va.) "Folly Farms"
"Folly Farms", home of Joseph S. Cochran,
Folly Mills, Va. Probably designed by
Thomas Jefferson. H.A.B.S. Plans, measured
drawings.

Arch forum 66: 56-57
Ja '37

Folte,

see

Brussels (Belg.) Bibliothèque royale

Folts, Herbert

see also

Fort Wayne (IN) Residence

Folsom and Stanton

see

Merchantville (N.J.) Rowe (John M. Jr.) bungalow

Foltz and Parker
see
Indianapolis (IN) Darlington (F.G.) residence
   "   Long (H.W.) house
   "   Powell (Frank) residence
   "   Residence
   "   Sutherland (J.A.) house

Foltz, Herbert
Moderate Cost Bungalow for Mr. Harry Kahn.

West. Archt.
19: pls.fol.p. 33
Mar, 1913

Folsom, Cal. State Prison
Detail of entrance; main cell building,
State prison, Folsom, California. California
State Bureau of architecture. George B. McDougall,
state archt. No plans.

American architect 116:pl.38
July 30, 1919

720.5
A67f
Foltz, Frederick C
Clearing - the freight yard that became
Chicago's biggest paying subdivision.

Architectural forum 65: 66-70
July 1936

MICROFILM

Foltz, Herbert W., 1867-1946
obituary notice

in SCRAPBOOK ON
ARCHITECTURE p. 706
(on film)

Folsom (Cal.) State Prison
Entrance detail
George B. McDougall, archt.

West. Archt.
2R: 15
Feb, 1919

Foltz, Frederick C., 1889?-1938
Obituary

Illinois society of
architects bulletin
23:8
O-N 1938

Folts, King, and Day, inc.

see

St. Paul(Minn.) gas, Light co. Inland station powe
plant
St. Paul, Minn. A. J. Krank and co.

Folsom (Cal.) State Prison.Main Cell Building
George B. McDougall, archt.

West. Archt.
2R: pl. 7
Feb, 1919

Foltz, Frederick L.

see

Folts, Fritz

Fomine, M.
A pleasure house Neo-Greek on the shores of the
gulf of Corinthe. M. Fomine, archt.

Palast Architektur. 6 vols. in 11 bks.
Berlin: E. Wasmuth, 1886-1911
Je 25 '26

720.5
W52
Folsom, Cal. State prison, Warden's
house
State prison, Warden's house,
Folsom, Calif.

Western arch. 28 pl 5
F 1919

Folts, Fritz, 1843-1916

see also

Treat and Foltz

Fond du Lac (WI) Ebert Residence
A.M.F. Colton & Sons, Archs.

Inland Arch. 19:
pl. fol. p 54
My., 1892

Fondutis, Agostino de
Palazzo Landi, Piacenza. Agostino de Fondutis.
Measured detail drawings, photograph.

Italian Renaissance: Sixty measured
drawings with details. 3 vols.
New York: The architectural book
publishing company, n.d. 2:pl.11
3:pl.53

Fondutis, Agostino di
Palazzo Landi, Piacenza Agostino di
Fondutis, archt. Giovanni Battagio da Lodi,
bildhauer, 1484. Measured drawing, photograph of
doorway.

Palast Architektur. 6 vols in 11 bks.
Berlin: E. Wasmuth, 1886-1911
3:pt.1:11,pls.39-40

Ryerson

Fonseca Menendez, Isabel
Una obra de los arquitectos Isabel Fonseca
Menendez y Julio Hernandez Soler. [plans and
sections]

Arquitectura Cuba
Vol. 21:28-33
Ja 1953

720.54
A67   Font-Rumeu (Fr.). Grand hotel
Veissière, Gabriel
Hotel de Font-Romeu. Tringuesse et Henri
Martin. archts. Plan

L Archts 38: 129-136
My 10 '25

720.54
A67   Fontaine, Jean Louis
Portrait of...architect of Chateau de Bri-
enne.

L'architecture 33:pl.12.
Apr.15, 1920.

Fontainbleau, Fr. Château.
Lossky, Boris
A propos du château de Fontainebleau.
Identifications et considérations nouvelles.
Serlio - escalier du Fer à cheval. Peintures
de Verdier et de Sauvage. Trône de Napoléon.
[illus.]

Société de l'histoire de
l'art français. Bulletin.
Année 1970: [27]-44
1972

RYERSON LIBRARY
913
AG6j   Fontaine-Guérard.Abbaye
Fontaine-Guérard Abbey.

Archaeological journal 95:387,pl.4-5
Part 2,1938

Fontaine - Henri. Chateau
Chateau de Fontaine-Henri (Calvados).
Photographs.

Martin, Camille. La renaissance en
France. 2 vols. Paris: C. Eggiman,
c.1913-21. 1:4-5,pls.22-29

Fontaine-Henri (Fr.) Chateau
Le chateau de Fontaine-Henry

L'architecture 35:282-4
Sept. 10, 1922

Fontainebleau. (Fr.)

Androuet du cerceau - Les plus
excellents bastiments de France.
2 vols. Paris: A. Lévy, 1868-70.
v.2 pl. 9-15.

Fontainebleau. Chateau
Fontainebleau. French text, plans, engravings.

Androuet du cerceau - Les plus excellents
bastiments, de France. 2 vols. Paris:
A. Lévy, 1868-70. vol.2:3 pls. 9-15

720.5
A67f   Fontainebleau.Chateau
End pavilion and wall of the stable
court.

studies)
Architectural forum 41:pl.6(forum
October 1914

720.5
B38   Fontainebleau.Chateau
General plan and views of Palace of Fon-
tainebleau.

B.A.I.D. 4: 21-22
April 1928

720.5
A67r   Fontainebleau.Chateau
Sturgis,Russell
Great buildings of the world,No.1: Palace of
Fontainbleau. No plan. -

Architectural record 10:129-142
October 1900

720.54
A67   Fontainebleau.Chateau
Satie,Marcel
The use of the Rockefeller donation to
Fontainebleau palace.

L'architecture 45: 407-412
November 15, 1932

Fontainebleau. Château
Le château de Fontainebleau. Text in French
Engravings.

Eyries, Gustave. Les chateaux
Historiques de la France 3 vols.
Paris: Poitiers, H. Oudin Frères,
1877-81   v.3:197-238

Fontainebleau. Château.
Johnson, William McAllister
Les débuts de Primatice à Fontainebleau.
[illus., sum. in Eng. & Ger.]

Revue de l'art
no.6: 8-18
1969

Fontainebleau, Fr. Château
Johnson, W. McAllister
Five drawings for the palace of Fontaine-
bleau. [illus.]

Master drawings
v.4: 25-29; pl.16-20
Je 1966

Fontainebleau. Château.
Lossky, Boris
La fontaine de Diane à Fontainebleau.
[illus.]

Société de l'histoire de
l'art français. Bulletin
Année 1968: [9]-21
1970

Fontainebleau, Fr. Château
Thirion, Jacques
Rosso et les arts décoratifs. [illus.,
sum. in Eng.& Ger.]

Revue de l'art
no.13: 32-47
1971

Fontainebleau (Fr.) Groupe Scolaire
Groupe Scolaire à Fontainebleau. J.B. Hourlier
et Delaire, archts. plans

L'Arch d'aujourd'hui
9:32-33
Ag '38

720.5 F69 Fontainebleau, School of Fine Arts Pencil points 5:78 May 1924	720.5 B95b Fontanelle(Iowa) Dunlap(D.N.) house Residence for D. N. Dunlap of Fontanelle, Iowa. Ball, W. K., archt. Building budget 3:3 in supp. My 51, 1887	Food Factories, Germany. Bückeburg Entwurf einer obstverwertungsanloge in Bückeburg. Paul Baumgarten, archt. (Sketch for canning factory.) A Moderne bauformen 24: 233 July 1925
720.6 B38 Fontainebleau, School of Fine Arts Beaux-arts institute of design; "A yacht- ing club; an academy of dance and plastic culture; fresco room; group of students; sketches. B.A.I.D. 3: 22-6 May 1927	Fontanne, Lynn house, See Genesee Depot (Wis.) Lunt (Alfred) House.	Food factories, United States see Los Angeles, Cal. Hoffman candy co. Philadelphia, Pa. American preserve co. Syracuse, N. Y. General ice cream corp. Woodland, Cal. Spreckels sugar plant no. 3 New York (city) National biscuit co. factory
720.5 B38 Fontainebleau School of Fine Arts Explanation concerning school and ex- amples of work done by students there. B.AI.D. 5: 20-28 April 1929	Ryerson Fonte Avellana, It. Sainte-Croix des Ca- maldules abbey Luconi, G. L'abbaye de Sainte-Croix des Camaldules à Fonte Avellana L'illustrazione vaticana 6: 469-470 O 1935	Fooks, Dr. Ernest Leslie Australia; house in Melbourne [plans] House in Melbourne [plans] Dr. Ernest Fooks, archt. Arch't'l design 32: 157-158, Mr 1962
720.6 B38 Fontainebleau School of Fine Arts Scholar- ship 1929 Fontainebleau School of Fine Arts Schol- arship; a masonic temple. Beaux arts in- stitute of design awards. B. A. I. D. 5: 5-22 May 1929	720.52 B93 Fonthill house The courtyard Messrs. Detmar Blow & Fernand Billerey, archts. Builder 129: pl. Aug. 14, 1925	Fooshe and Cheek A small house in Austin, Texas. Fooshe and Cheek, archts. House and garden. 49:105 Mar. 1926
Fontainebleu hotel, Miami Beach, Fla. see Miami Beach, Fla. Fontainebleu hotel	Food factories, England see also York, Eng. Joseph Terry and sons, ltd. Welwyn Garden City, Eng. Shredded wheat factory Wembly, Eng. Wrigley factory	Foot Bridges Decorations for parks and gardens.... London: J. Taylor, [18?]. pl. 40-9.
Fontana, Wisc. School Matson, J. M. School for Fontana, Wis. J.Mandor Matson, archt. No plan. Architectural concrete 5:26-27 No. 4 [1939]	720.52 A67 Food factories, England. Birmingham Two story toffee factory, Birmingham, England. S.N. Cooke, archt. A Architectural journal 68: 46-50 July 11, 1928	Foot Bridges Humphreys, Phebe Wescott. The Practical book of garden architecture Philadelphia and London: J.B. Lippincott Company, 1914. p.215-222
Fontenelle. Abbey see Saint Wandrille. Fontenelle Abbey	720.52 A67c Food Factories, England.North Wembley New factory for food products, North Wembley. Wallis, Gilbert & Partners,archts. A Architect 115: pls. April 30, 1926	Foot Bridges Bridges in the landscape scheme House and garden 43:84-5 Feb. 1923

Foot, Bridges
    Little bridges to span your garden streams

House and garden 65: 26-29
June 1934

Foote, Headley and Carpenter

see

Rochester, N.Y. Lake Ave. Baptist Church

Forbes hall of science, Yankton college

see

Yankton (S. Dak.) college. Forbes hall of science

Foot Bridges
    Some rustic foot bridges in Westchester County Park.

House and garden 50: 100
July, 1926

Foote, Orlando K.

see also

Rochester, N.Y., Third Presbyterian Church

Forbes, Holland

see

Forbes, A   Holland, 1863-1927

Foot Bridges,   England
    Passerelle à Plymouth [section] Drake and Lasdun, archts.

Aujourd'hui 1:
72-73 no.4
S 1955

Foote, Orlando K
    School house at Canandaigua, N.Y. [plans] Orlando K. Foote, archt.

Inland architect
19, no. 4
pl. fol. p. 54
My 1892

Forbes, Ian

see

St. George's Hill (Eng.) Hamstone house

Foot Bridges, U.S.

see

Deal Beach (N.J.) O'Day estate. Brick bridge

720.5   Forbes, A. Holland, 1863-1927
A67ar   Obituary.

Architect (N.Y.)9: 552
February 1928

710.5   Forbes,J   a
C85   Hussey, Christopher
    Vandalism at Cheltenham: Pittville pump room at Cheltenham. Built 1825-1830 by J.B. Forbes, archt.

Country Life(London)85:49
January 14,1939

720.52   Football fields,England
A67   Association football field. Sir John Burnet,Tait and Lorne,archts. Plan.
    Rugby football field. Sir John Burnet, Tait and Lorne,archts. Plan.

Architects' journal 78: supp.
October 19,1933

Forbes, A. Holland. 1863-1927   Portrait
    Photograph

Architect (N.Y.) 4:478
Ag '25

Forbes (Mansfield D.) house

see

"Finella" (Eng.)

Football stadiums

see

Stadiums

Forbes and Tate
    "Dorothy" Cafe, Cambridge, England. Forbes and Tait (sic) archts. Rear elevation and main front.

Builder 144: 952,953,972
June 16, 1933

Ford and Rogers

Members of firm:

Ford, O'Neil, 1906 (?)-
Rogers, Gerald Raymond

Foote and Headly

see

Rochester (N.Y.) Todd (G.W.) House
"   "   Two Residences

Forbes and Tate
    Fish bar. Designed by Forbes and Tate.

Architects' journal 74: 826-828
December 23, 1931

Ford Brothers Glass Company
    Church Windows Designed by

West. Arch.
12: 50
O 1908

Ford, Butler & Oliver

see also

New Marlborough (Mass.) Ogle (Ponsonby) house

Garden City (L.I.) Garden City hotel

Garden City (L.I.) Fire house and auditorium

New York (City) Woodlawn cemetery. Mausoleum. Doors

Ford, Henry, house, Dearborn, Mich. (Project)

see

Dearborn, Mich. Ford, Henry, house (Project)

Fordham (NY)
Public School
Charles B.J. Snyder, Arch.

Inland Arch.
40: pl.fol.p. 24
Oct. 1902

Ford, Butler and Oliver
Fire house and auditorium, Garden City,
L.I. Ford, Butler and Oliver, archts.

Brickbuilder 21: pl.127
October 1912

Ford, Henry-village

see

Dearborn. Henry Ford Museum

Fordham (NY) Roman Catholic Orphan Asylum
Schickel & Ditmars, Archs.

Inland Arch.
40: pl.fol.p. 8
Aug. 1902

711
C56

Ford, George Burdett
Architecture and the new city.

City planning 5:1-24
January 1929

Ford, James house, Lincoln, Mass

see

Lincoln, Mass. Ford (James) house

Fordham university

see

New York (N.Y.) Fordham university

Ford, George B.
City planning in war time.

West. Archt.
26: 19-21
Sept, 1917

Ford museum, Dearborn, Mich.

see

Dearborn, Mich. Henry Ford museum

Fordson (Mich.) Ford Motor Co. Glass Factory
Ford motor company's glass factory, Fordson,
Michigan. Albert A. Kahn, archt.

Architects' journal 68: 271
August 22, 1928

Ford, George B.
Housing problem

Brickbuilder 18:
26; F 1909
76; Ap "
100; My "
144; Jl "
185; S "

Ford, O'Neil, 1906?-

Member of Firms:
Ford and Rogers
Ford, Cocks, and Smith

720.52
A87

Fordwich (Eng.) Architecture
Andrews, P.M.
The port of Canterbury: Fordwich and its
court house.

Architects' journal 69: 842-844
May 29, 1929

711
C56

Ford, George Burdett
Obituary.

City planning 6: 282
October 1930

Forde Abbey
Inigo Jones' work at Forde Abbey. Measured
drawings.

Architects' journal 76: supp.
Oct. 5; 12, 1932

Fordyce, Allmon and W. I. Hamby

see also

Great Neck (L.I.) Hamby (W.I.)

Ford, Henry

see also

Clarenceville (Mich.) Botsford tavern
Dearborn (Mich.) Henry Ford Museum

Fordham national bank, New York

See

New York. Fordham national bank building

720.5
A67f

Fordyce and Hamby
Drug stores - planning techniques for new
and remodeled buildings, no.5: Pennsylvania
Drug Company store at 52nd Street and Lexing-
ton Avenue, New York City. Fordyce and Hamby;
archts. Plans.

Architectural forum 67:44-45
July 1937

710.5
H84   Fordyce and Hamby
            If you're planning to build - analyses of
         4 new American homes: Regency influence; mod-
         ern Expression; Western type; early American
         design. Allman Fordyce and William Hamby,
         archts.

                House and garden 70:56-61
                September 1936

Forest, G   Topham
   The new Lambeth Bridge. Sir George Humphreys,
chief engineer; Sir Reginald Blomfield & Mr. G.
Topham Forest, consulting archts.

                Builder 143: 139-140
                Jl 22 1932

RYERSON LIBRARY
705.1   Forest Hills Gardens (L.I.)
A79   Forest Hills gardens: a model town in
             America

                Arts & decor. 1: 118-120
                Ja '11

710.5   Fordyce and Hamby
H84   Residence of William I.Hamby, Great Neck,
             N.Y. Allman Fordyce and W.I.Hamby, archts.
             Plans.

                House and garden 70:118-119
                September 1936

Forest, Lockwood de

                see

De Forest, Lockwood, 1896-1949

720.5   Forest Hills Gardens (L.I.)
A67a   May, Charles C.
                Forest Hills gardens from the town-planning
             viewpoint. Plans.

                Architecture 34:161-172,pl.119-127
                August 1916

Foreman, Charles U. - 1908

   Obit.

                West. Arch.
                12: 62
                N 1908

Forest Gate (Eng.) Queen's Cinema
   A reconstructed cinema at Forest Gate,
England, the Queen's cinema. Leathart and Granger,
archts.

                Architect (Eng.) 120:523-527
                October 26, 1928

705.1   Forest Hills Gardens (L.I.)
A79   Howe, Samuel
                A forerunner of the future suburb: Forest
             Hills Gardens, New York.

                Arts and decoration 21:414,419-422
                October 1912

Foreman, P.
   4-story store and flat building on First
Ave. Minneapolis, Minn.

                Building budget
                3: 3 in supp.
                Jl 30, 1887

720.5   Forest Hill, (N.J.) Wood (E.L.) house
A67ar   House of Mr. E.L. Wood, Forest Hill, N.J.
             C.C. Wendehack, archt.

                Architect (N.Y.) 8:pl.44,46
                April 1927

720.5   Forest Hills Gardens, L.I.
B84   Forest Hills Gardens, L.I.,N.Y. Grosvenor
             Atterbury, architect. An example of collec-
             tive planning, development, and control.

                Brickbuilder 21:317-320,pl.155-164
            A   December 1912

Ryerson
   Forero Juliao, Enrique
      Edificio de renta [plans] Enrique Forero
   Juliao, archt.

                PROA
                No. 67:20
                Ja 1953

Forest Hill Village (Ont.) preparatory school
   Forest Hill Village preparatory school.
[plan] Forrey Page and Steele, archts.

                PAIC jrl 14:111-112
                Je 1937

720.5   Forest Hills Gardens (L.I.)
B84   Recent houses at Forest Hills Gardens
             from the work of Grosvenor Atterbury and
             Eugene Schoen,archts.
                Houses for Miss Taylor,E.G.Trowbridge,
             J.A.Meeker and Thomas C.Chalmers. Plans.

                Brickbuilder 25: 139-141
                June 1916

Foreshore development, Folkestone, Eng.

                see

Folkestone (Eng.) Foreshore. New development

720.5   Forest Hills Gardens, L.I.
A51   Howe, Samuel
                Forest Hills gardens. Grosvenor Atter-
             bury, archt. in chief. Plans

                American architect 100: 153-156,159-
                October 30, 1911   160. pls.
                                        fol.p.160

Forest Hills Gardens (L.I.) Chalmers (T.C.) house
   House of Dr. T. C. Chalmers, Forest Hills
Gardens (L.I.) Atterbury and Schoen, archts. Plans.

                Brickbuilder 25:139-42
                Jl 1916

720.53   Foresman, Eino
W51   Stadtisches Tuberkulose-krankenhaus in
             Helsinfors. Eino Foresman, archt. (City
             tuberculosis hospital.)

                Wasmuths monatshefte 13: 455,458-459
                November 1929

Forest Hills Gardens, L.I.
   Forest Hills Gardens

                Architecture 26:110-11
                July 1912

Forest Hills Gardens, L.I. Meeker (J.A.) house
   J. A. Meeker house, Forest Hills Gardens,
L. I. Atterbury and Schoen, archts. Plans.

                Brickbuilder 25:139-42
                Jl 1916

Forest Hills Gardens, L.I. Taylor house
House of Miss Taylor, Forest Hills Gardens,
L. I. Atterbury and Schoen, archts. Plans.

Brickbuilder 25:139-42
Jl 1916

Forest lawn memorial park, Glendale,Calif. (Cemetery)

see

Glendale,Calif. Forest lawn memorial park (Cemetery)

Forest park,St.Louis

See

St.Louis.Forest park

Forest Hills Gardens, L.I. Trowbridge (E.O.) house
House of E. O. Trowbridge, Forest Hills
Gardens, L.I. Atterbury and Schoen, archts. Plans.

Brickbuilder 25:139-42
Jl 1916

Forest Park, Ill. Altenheim

see

Forest Park, Ill. German old people's home (1885).

Forest preserves

see

Forest reserves

Forest Hills, L.I. Arbor Close. Architecture
Houses, Arbor Close, Forest Hills, L.I.
Robt. Tappan, archt.

Architect (N.Y.) 6:pl.121-24
Aug. 1926

Forest Park, IL. Forest Home Cemetery
Einfahrt zu Forest Home. Ansicht zu Forest Home

Simon, Andreas. Chicago, die
Gartenstadt. Chicago: F. Gindele
Printing Co., 1893. p.167,171

Forest Reserves
Landscape architecture and the 152 National
forests.

Landscape architecture 11:57-62
Jan. 1921.

720.5
A67 Forest Hills (L.I.) Church in the Garden
The church in the garden at Forest Hills,
N. Y. Grosvenor Atterbury, archt.

Architectural review 9: 57-40,pls.24-26
August 1919 fol.p.64

Forest Park, Ill. German old people's home (1885).
Illustration. Bauer and Hill, architects.

Building budget
II: 150 and plate
Dec. 1886

Forestier, Pierre
France habitations économiques en bois.
P. Forestier, architecte.

Tech. et arch.
14: 1-2: 54
1954

Forest Hills (L.I.) Duble (E.C.) house
House, Mr. E. C. Duble, Forest Hills,
Long Island. Frank J. Forster, New York, archt.
Timbering details.

Architect (N.Y.) 8:p.577-580,607-627.
August 1927

Forest Park, IL. Waldheim cemetery
Einfahrtsthor zum friedhof Waldheim ... im
Friedhof Waldheim views

Simon, Andreas. Chicago, die
Gartenstadt. Chicago: F. Gindele
Printing Co., 1893
p.175,183,191,201

Forestry

see

Forests and forestry

Forest Hills (L.I.) Elementary Public School no.101
Elementary Public School, No. 101, Forest Hills,
N.Y. William H. Gompert, archt.

Architect (N.Y.) 12:301
June, 1929

Forest Park, IL. Waldheim cemetery. F. Karle
monument.
Das Karle - denkmal im friedhof Waldheim

Simon, Andreas. Chicago, die
Gartenstadt. Chicago: F. Gindele
Printing Co., 1893. p. 229

Forests and forestry

see also

Forest reserves

Forest home cemetery, Forest Park (Ill.)

see

Forest Park (Ill.) Forest home cemetery

Forest Park, Il. Waldheim cemetery. John
Bühler monument
Waldheim - John Bühler's familiendenkmal

Simon, Andreas. Chicago, die
Gartenstadt. Chicago: F. Gindele
Printing Co., 1893. P. 178

Forests & forestry. The destruction
of the forests; conservation of the
forests.

Inland Arch.
49: 72
June 1907

Forests and Forestry, Scotland

Country life (Lond.) 58:227-30
Aug. 8, 1925

Forli (It.) Palazzo di Giustizia (project)
Progetto del Palazzo di Giustizia di Forli.
[plans and section] Francesco Leoni, arcnt.

Architettura 17: 696-698
N 1938

Formal Gardens
Formal Gardens.

Arch and con rep 68:323-24
N 21, 1902

---

711 Forests   and Forestry
C58 Pack, Chas.
      The community forest and the community plan.

City planning 2: 278-81
October 1926

Ryerson
Forli, It. Santi Trinità
Il restauro de Campanile della SS. Trinità
e l'inaugurazione della campana Fulcieri

Melozzo da Forli
fasc. 6:280-1
Ja 1939

Formal gardens
Formal Gardens

Builder 83: 491-93, pls
N 29, 1902

Forests and Forestry
Gardening with trees.
By J. D. Curtis and A.M. Davis.

Country Life 72: 44 and pls.
Sept. 1937

Forli (It.) Sede I.N.F. Previdenza Sociale.
Sede dell'Istituto Nazionale Fascista di Previdenza Sociale a Forli. [plans] Cesare Valle, archt.

Architettura 17: 159-163
Mr 1938

710.5 Formal gardens
C855

Country life in Amer. 15:350-3
F 1909

Forests and Forestry.
Notes on practical forest esthetics

Landscape arch. 12: 224-32
July, 1922.

Formal Gardens

Country life in Amer. 15:350-353
Feb. 1909

Formal Gardens
Formal Planting. By George F. Pentecost, Jr.

House and gard. 3: 222-31
Ap 1903

Forests and Forestry
Wisdom of forest renewal.

Country Life. 40:42-3.
Sept. 1921.

Formal Gardens

House and Garden 20:19-21
June 1912

720.52 Formal Gardens
A673   Garden design. The formal garden: large
          and small.

Architectural review 55:186-91
May 1924

Forests, National
see
Forest reserves

Formal Gardens

House beaut. 49: 206-209
Mar. 1921

Formal Gardens
Gardens at Lou Sueil, estate of Col. Balsan.

Country life (Lond.) 61:208-11
February 5, 1927

Forissier, Roger, 1924-
Roger Forissier [illus]

Art-documents: les Cahiers
no 154:[1-17] 1961

Formal Gardens
The formal garden at Villa Cypris, at Cap
Martin.

Country life (Lond.) 61: 344-5
March 5, 1927

710.5 Formal Gardens
C85   Lindsay, Norah
        The Garden: the making of a garden, design
        and planting.

Country life (Lond.) 65: cxxxiii,
March 23, 1929   cxxxvi

Formal Gardens
    Lay, C.D.
Possibilities of the small formal garden.

        Arts and decoration 2:249-251
        May 1912

Formal Gardens, England
    Views of the gardens on Northamptonshire -
the estate of Sir Thomas Hesketh.

        Country life (Lond.) 62:265-7
        August 20, 1927

Formentone, Tommaso c.1440-1492
    Die loggia (Municipio) Brescia. Tomaso
Formentone, 1492, Jacopo Sansovino, 1554, Andrea
Palladio, 1562, Luigi Vanvitelli, 1775. Photograph,
measured drawing and details.

        Palast Architektur. 6 vols. in 11
        bks. Berlin: E. Wasmuth, 1886-1911
        5:pt.1:15-16
        pt.2:pls.58-61

710.5   Formal gardens
C855 Carhart, A. H.
    Linking the garden with the house: the middle
needs careful studying.

        Country Life (U.S.) 85:70-71
        November 1933

Formal gardens, Italy
    Italian gardens [color] Villa la Pietra;
Isola Bella; Villa Torrigiani;Castello di Montalto
Pavase;Villa d'Este.

        Life articles on art 1950:227-233
        May 8, 1950

Formentone, Tommaso c.1440-1492
    Palazzo Vescovile, Vicenza. Tomass
Formentone, archt. 1495. Photograph and measured
drawing.

        Palast Architektur. 6 vols in 11 bks.
        Berlin: E. Wasmuth, 1886-1911
        4:pt.1:13
        pt.2:pls.51-52

Formal Gardens
    Pentecost, G.F., Jr.
The formal and natural style of gardens.

        Architectural record 12:174-194
        June 1902

720.5   Formal Gardens, U.S.
A67ar   Formal garden, estate of Mr. Moses Taylor,
Newport, R.I. Office of John Russell Pope, archt.

        Architect (N.Y.)8: pl.733
        September 1927

Formery
    Olmer, Pierre
Ensemble municipal à Sèvres, Formery, archt.

        L'Architecture 50: 147-152
        My 15, 1937

Formal Gardens
    Rehmann, Elsa
Geometric garden patterns

        House beautiful 57: 242-243
        March, 1925

710.5   Formal Gardens, U.S.
C855   The formal garden in the United States.

        Country life (U.S.) 57: 41-43
        March 1930

Formia (It.) Colonia Ente Mutualità Scolastica
    Colonie de vacances à Formia. [plans] Giulio
Minoletti, archt.

        L'arch d'auj 10: 32-33
        Jl 1939

710.5   Formal gardens
C85   Some points in garden design.

        Country life (Lond.)62:lxi-lxii
        September 24, 1927

710.5   Formal Gardens, U.S.
H84   The garden of William Mercer at Doylestown,Pennsylvania, designed on geometric
lines. Willing,Sims,and Talbutt,archts.

        House and garden 63: 26-27
        February 1933

Formigé and Bevière
    see
Paris (Fr.) Place St. Pierre

Formal Gardens, England
    Formal garden and small house in the Cotswolds.
Falconer, Baker and Campbell, archts.

        Architecture (Lond.) 5:39
        June, 1926

Formenton, Tomaso
    see
Formentone,Tommaso,c.1440-1492

Formigé, Jean Camille, 1845-1926
    see also
Paris (Fr.) Cimitière du Père Lachaise. Cre-
    matorium
Paris (Fr.) Cimétière de Bagneux it de Pantin.
    Entrée
Paris, Fr. Exposition. 1889. Palais des beaux
    arts

Formal Gardens, England
    A formal garden at Great Ote Hall, Sussex.
Pakington, Enthoven and Grey, archts.

        Arch. rev. 61: 216
        June 1927

Formentone, Tommaso   c.1440-1492
    The Loggia, Brescia, Italy. Tomaso Formentone,
Jacopo Sansovino, Andrea Palladio, and Luigi
Vanvitelli, archts. Measured drawings, photograph.
    Palazzo Vescovile, Vicenza. Tomaso Formentone,
archt. Measured detail drawing, photograph.

        Italian Renaissance: Sixty measured
        drawings with details. 3 vols.
        New York: The architectural book
        publishing company,n.d.3:pls.8-10,50,
        42, 1:pl. 46

720.54   Formigé,Jules
A67   Autel votif érigé dans l'ancienne cathédrale de Tarascon.(Modern votary altar erected
in the ancient cathedral of Tarascon.) Jules
Formigé, architect. Raymond Sudre, sculptor.

        L'architecture 36:334
        October 10,1923

Formigé, Jean Camille   1845-1926
Risler, Charles
Brief biographical sketch.

L'architecture 45: 248
July 15, 1932

Fornovo di Taro (It.) Churches (project)
Una chiesa. [plan, models and sections]
Vittorio Gandolfi, archt.

Domus f44:12-13
Mr 1950

Forrest, G. Topham
Wandsworth Technical Institute. G. Topham
Forrest, archt. Plans.

Architect 113:2 pl.
Apr. 24, 1925

Formigé, Jean Camille 1845-1927
Jean Formigé, an appreciation.

L'Architecture 40:49-58
February 15, 1927

Fornaroli, Antonio
Entwurf der hauptverwaltung der Gesellschaft Pirelli, Mailand [plans and sections]
Gio Ponti, Antonio Fornaroli, Alberto Rosselli,
archts.

Baumeister
53: 106-109
F 1956

Forrest, Topham

see

Forrest, G   Topham

Formigé, Jean Camille, 1845-1926
Jean Formigé, architect 1845-1926

Académie des beaux-arts
Bulletin No. 4:171-178
July- December, 1926

Fornaroli, Antonio
Pirelli building, Milan [plans & sections]
Gio Ponti, Antonio Fornaroli & Alberto Rosselli,
archts.

Archtl Design
30:490-96 D 1960

Burnham

Forrester, John
Lewis, David
John Forrester [illus]

Architectural design
31: 416-17, S 1961

Formigine, Giacomo

See also

Bologna.Palazzo Malvezzi-Campeggi

Forrest G. Topham

see also

London (Eng.) Southeast London technical institute
"   "   Wandsworth technical institute
"   "   Bec School
Downham (Eng.) Rangefield School

D10.5
D32

Forst. (Ger.) Krematorium
Entwurf fur ein Krematorium -
in Forst. Stadtbaurat Kühn-Forst,
Lausitz. Plan.

Dekorative Kunst 27:286-7
S '24

Formigine, Giacomo
Palazzo Malvezzi-Compeggi. Giacomo Formigine,
archt. Measured detail drawings, photograph.

Italian Renaissance: Sixty measured
drawings with details. 3 vols. New
York: The architectural book
publishing company, n.d.2:pl.20
3:pl.54

Forrest, G. Topham
Hammersmith School of Building and Arts and
Crafts, Shepherd's Bush. G. Topham Forrest, archt.

Builder 139: 690,701
October 24, 1930

Forster and Gallimore

see also

Gallimore, Roland A.
Forster, Frank Joseph, 1886-

Formigine, Giacomo
Palazzo Malveggi-Campeggi, Bologna.
Giacomo Formigine, archt. 1549. Photograph,
measured drawing.

Palast architektur. 6 vols in 11 bks.
Berlin: E. Wasmuth, 1886-1911
5:pt.1:5,pls.16-17

720.52
A67

Forrest, G. Topham
London County Council Housing,Pilgrim
Court, by Topham Forrest.

Architects' journal 77: 396-397
March 22,1933

Forster and Gallimore

see also
Greenwich (Conn.) Bass (George) house
"   "   Browning (Gilbert) house
"   "   Kaplan (J.M.) estate. Gate lodge
Johnstown (Pa.) Davies (M.J.C.) house
Silvermine (Conn.) Barnum (J.H.) house
Warner (P.J.) estate (Conn.) Guest house

Formosinho Sanches, Sebastião

see

Sanches, Sebastião Formosinho

Forrest, G. Topham
Report on American bldgs. and bldg. laws.

R.I.B.A. Jour. 32:589
Aug. 15, 1925

710.5
H84

Forster and Gallimore.
A Georgian house with traces of Norman influence. Plans.

House and garden 63: 56-59
May 1933

Forster, Frank J.

see also

Beechhurst (L.I.) Stewart (Gordon) house
Douglaston (L.I.) Brundage (Wilbur) house
Forest Hills (L.I.) Duble (E.C.) house
Great Neck (L.I.) Forster (F.J.) house
"   "   "   Kiltham (R.F.) house

720.5
M59a
Forster, Frank J
The use of metal in domestic architecture

Metal arts 3: 52-54, 89
February 1930

Fort Chambrai-Gozo (Malta)
Fort Chambrai-Gozo, Malta. Mewes and Davis
archts.

Architect 115: pls.
April 9, 1926

Forster, Frank J.

see also

Great Neck (L.I.) Siebert (W.W.) house
Greenwich (Conn.) Clifford (R.E.) house
"   "   Tyson (J.R.) house
Johnstown (Pa.) Swank (A.M.) house
Meridan (Conn.) Cuneo (Charles) garage
Montclair (N.J.) Hatfield (Milton) house
New Canaan (Conn.) Bailey (J.H.) house

Forstner, Leopold
High altar of mosaic in the church
"Am Steinhof" in Vienna

Moderne Bauformen 13:381-384
Aug., 1914

729.6
I29
Fort Chartres. Chapel. Restoration.
Booton, J.F.
French craftsmen in early Illinois:researches
while restoring chapel at Fort Chartres, Illinois.

Illinois society of architects.
Monthly bulletin 27-28:8
June-July 1943

Forster, Frank J.

see also

New Haven (Conn.) Edgerton (Franklin) house
New York (N.Y.) Harlem River houses
"   "   Mixsell (H.R.) house
Riverside (Conn.) Tyson (J.R.) house
Scarsdale (N.Y.) Keffer (Karl) house
Silvermine (Conn.) Pons (Lily) house
South Norwalk (Conn.) Cowell (E.I.) house
South Norwalk (Conn.) Dunn (C.W.) house

721.97
A67c
Forsyth, John Duncan
Functional designs in concrete: Bartlesville,
Okla. high school and junior college. John
Duncan Forsyth, archt. No plan.

Architectural concrete 6:8-10
No.3 [1940]

MICROFILM

Fort Chartres state park, Ill.

Scrapbook on Architecture
p. 1003

Forster, Frank J.

see also

South Norwalk (Conn.) house
"   "   "   Sheldon (Waldo) house
Toledo (Ohio) Canaday (Ward M.) house

Forsyth and Maule

see

Berkhamsted (Eng.) School. Memorial library.

720.54
A67
Fort-de-France. Architecture
Sévère, Victor
The urbanism of the colonies. Fort-de-
France. 1839-1931.

L'architecture 44: 275-288
August 15, 1931

Forster, Frank J

see also

Forster and Gallimore

720.5
F52
Forsythe, J.H.
Obituary

Western architect 34:117
Nov. 1925

Fort de Vincennes, Fr.

see

Vincennes, Fr. Château

RYERSON LIBRARY
D13.1
M94
Forster, Frank J.
The house of M.J.C. Davies

House beautiful 67:48-49
January 1930

Fort Astoria
Fort Astoria

Bancroft, Hubert Howe.
Achievements of civilization....
10 vols. New York: The Bancroft
Company, publishers. 1896. 8:704

MICROFILM

Fort Dearborn (1803-1804)

In SCRAPBOOK ON
ARCHITECTURE p. 145, 164
(on film)   and 787

Forster, Frank J.
Two houses by Frank J. Forster

House and garden 44:69
Sept. 1923

Fort Carillon

see

Fort Ticonderoga, N.Y.

Fort Dearborn
Fort Dearborn

McClure, James Baird. Stories
and sketches of Chicago. Chicago:
Rhodes and McClure, 1880. 26-41

Fort Dearborn (1816) Fort Dearborn, as rebuilt in 1816. Andreas, A.T. History of Chicago 3 vols. Chicago: A.T. Andreas, 1884. v.1,p.100	Fort Dearborn Bank Building. Chicago see Chicago Ill. American Trust and Savings Bank Building.	Fort Dodge (IA) Wahkonsa Hotel Liebbe, Nourse and Rasmussen, archts. plan. Interior West. Archt. 17: pls.fol.p. 94 Oct, 1911
Fort Dearborn (1803-1804) Old Fort Dearborn, erected in 1803. Andreas, A.T. History of Chicago. 3 vols. Chicago: A.T. Andreas, 1884. v.1,p.79-84	Fort Dearborn building, Chicago see Chicago, Ill. Monroe street (west) 105 building	Fort Dodge (IA) YMCA Liebbe, Nourse and Rasmussen, archts. plan West. Archt. 17: pls.fol.p. 94 Oct, 1911
Fort Dearborn Fort Dearborn Bancroft, Hubert Howe. Achievements of civilization.... 10 vols. New York: The Bancroft Company, publishers. 1896. 9:820	Fort Dodge, Ia. Band Shell Forms for concrete band shells. Construction drawings. Illustration of forms for band shell at Fort Dodge, Ia. H.L. Kamphoefner, archt. Architectural concrete 3:17-20 No. 3, 1937	720.5 A67a Fort Edward (N.Y.) St. Joseph's church St. Joseph's Roman Catholic Architecture 40: pl.106-108 July 1919
Fort Dearborn, 1803-1804 Early Chicago - soldiers and pioneers, 1803-1830. Building for the future January-February 1936	Fort Dodge (Ia.) Court house Elevation of courthouse at Fort Dodge, Ia. H.C. Koch and Company, archts. A Architectural review 8;n.s.3:pl.80 November, 1901	Fort, Frank Hon. Mention: Chicago Tribune Tower Competition. West. Archt. 32: 7 Jan, 1923
Fort Dearborn (1816) Old block house and light house in 1857. The last of Fort Dearborn. Andreas, A.T. History of Chicago. 3 vols. Chicago: A.T. Andreas, 1884. v.1,628	Fort Dodge (IA) First National Bank Liebbe, Nourse and Rasmussen. West. Archt. 17: pls.fol.p. 94 Oct, 1911	Fort Garry, Manit. Lower Fort Garry, near Winnipeg. RAIC jrl 16:143 Je 1939
705.1 F49 Fort Dearborn (1816) Old Fort Dearborn... 1856 - formerly situated on the south side of the Chicago river at Michigan avenue and river street . . . Fine arts jour 29: 660 N '13	Fort Dodge (IA) Rehder Cadillac Garage Damon and O'Meara, archts. West. Archt. 30: pl. 16 Sept, 1921	720.6 C53 Fort Hamilton (N.Y.) Johnson (A.L.) house House of Mr. Albert L. Johnson, Fort Hamilton, N.Y., Little and O'Connor, archts.; no plan. Chicago architectural club 13:130 1900
Fort Dearborn (1803). Replica see Chicago, Ill. Century of progress international exposition, 1933-34. Fort Dearborn (1803). Replica	Fort Dodge, Ia. Round Prairie Grade School Round Prairie Grade School, Fort Dodge, Iowa. Arch. Rec. 49: 170-1. Feb. 1921.	Fort Henry, Kingston, Ont. see Kingston, Ont. Fort Henry

Fort Johnson (N.Y.) Johnson (Sir Wm.) house
    Early American domestic architecture:
Sir William Johnson House, Fort Johnson,
New York. Measured drawings by William D. Foster
and Lewis E. Welsh.

        Architectural forum 34:47-54
        February 1921

Fort Lennox

        see

Ile aux Noix (Que.) Fort Lennox

720.5
A67a

Fort Montgomery (N.Y.) State prison. Compe-
tition
    New state prison, Fort Montgomery, N.Y.
Warren and Wetmore, archts. Design placed
II

        Architecture 18: 124-5
        Ag '08

MICROFILM

Fort Kaskaskia state park, Ill. Menard, Pierre,
house

        in SCRAPBOOK ON
        ARCHITECTURE p. 1001-1002
        (on film)

NILSSON LIBRARY
910.5
N27   Fort Mackinac
        Well - preserved Fort Mackinac gives mod-
    ern America a glimpse of life in an old
    frontier outpost.

        National geographic 72:578
        November 1937

720.5
A67a

Fort Montgomery (N.Y.) State prison. Compe-
tition
    New state prison, Fort Montgomery, N.Y.
Herts and Tallant, archts. Design placed
III

        Architecture 18: 126-7
        Ag '08

Ft. Knox, Ky. Waterworks
    Water treatment plant, Ft. Knox, Kentucky.

        Architectural concrete 4:34-35
        No. 1 [1938]

720.5
B95b

Fort Madison(Iowa)Altee(S & J.C.) apt. houses
and office building
    Office building and 7 apt. houses for S.
& J. C. Altee at Fort Madison, Iowa. Dunham,
C. A., archt.

        Building budget
        3:5 in supp.
        My 31, 1887

720.5
A67a

Fort Montgomery (N.Y.) State prison
    Competitive Drawings. Placed I. New
State Prison, Fort Montgomery, New York. Wm.
J. Beardsley, Architect.

        Architecture 18: 122-123
        Ag '08

Fort Lauderdale, Fla. Florida Power and Light Co.
                                Plant
    Centrale de Fort-Lauderdale. Florida Power
and Light Cy., archts.

        Encyclopedie de l'architecture;
        Constructions modernes. 12 vols.
        Paris: Albert Morancé, 1928-39.
        2:pl.100

720.5
B95b

Fort Madison(Ia.) Case(Mrs.) double house
    Double residence for Mrs. Case at Fort
Madison, Iowa. Dunham, C. A., archt.

        Building budget
        3:5 in supp.
        Je 30, 1887

Fort Peck. Administration bldg.
Linscott, M   H
    Administration building - Fort Peck
M. H. Linscott, archt.

        Architectural con
        1: 15 No. 6
        1935

Fort Lauderdale (Fla.) Saulnier (W.D.) house
    House for Willard D. Saulnier, Fort Lauderdale,
Fla. Informal, hurricane-proof winter house in
Southern Florida. Courtney Stewart and Robert
Hansen, archts. Plans

A
        Architectural forum 66:334-335
        April, 1937

Fort Marion. Saint Augustine (Fla.)

        see

Saint Augustine (Fla.) Fort Marion

Fort Pitt
    Fort Pitt

        Bancroft, Hubert Howe.
        Achievements of civilization....
        10 vols. New York: The Bancroft
        Company, publishers. 1896. 10:914

Fort Leavenworth (Kan.) Officers' Club bldg.
    Officers' club building, Fort Leavenworth
Kansas. Rich, Mathesius, and Koyl, archts.

        American architect 135:732
        June 5, 1929

Fort Mifflin

        See

Philadelphia(Pa.)Fort Mifflin.

Fort Prince of Wales, Churchill, Manit.

        see

Churchill, Manit. Fort Prince of Wales

Fort Lee (N.J.) Ben Marden's Riviera
    Ben Marden's Riviera, Fort Lee, N.J.
L.A. Abramson, archt. Plans.

A
        Architectural forum 67:380-384
        November, 1937

---

ff
724.5915
V31W

Fort Monroe(Va.)
    Fortress Monroe, Old Point Comfort and
Hygeia Hotel,Va.,1861.

        William and Mary Quarterly,ser.2,13:pl.
        October 1938   108

710.5
L26

Fort Riley(Kan.)
Pray, J.S.
    Planning the cantonments. Plans of Fort Riley
Kansas.

        Landscape architecture 8:1-17
        October 1917

Fort Ross (Calif.) Greek chapel

See

Fort Ross (Calif.) Russian chapel.

Fort Smith (Ark.) Sparks Theater
Sparks Theater, Fort Smith, Arkansas.
Carl Boller, archt.

Brickbuilder 23: 57
Supp. to February 1914

720.5 Fort Ticonderoga, N.Y. Restoration
A67r Restoration of Fort Ticonderoga. Alfred
C. Bossom, archt.

Architectural record 27: 274
A March 1910

720.5 Fort Ross (Calif) Russian chapel
F99 Clar, C.E.
Where Russia colonized California: a
Russian chapel and fort (Fort Ross); no plan.

Federal architect 9:97-30
April 1939

Fort Snelling, Minn. Chapel
Chapel, Fort Snelling, Minnesota. Hewitt and
Brown, archts.

Architecture 59:37-40
January 1929

710.5 Fort Ticonderoga, N.Y. Restoration
C85t Pell, John
Ticonderoga - its ruin and restoration.

Country life(U.S.)63:24-25,73
August 1935

720.6 Fort Sainte Marie, Canada. Architecture
R882 Kidd, Kenneth E.
The Architecture of Sainte Marie [plan]

Royal Arch. Institute of
Canada. Journal 20:71-73
My '43

Fort Snelling (MN) New Post Exchange and
Gymnasium
Rendering

West. Archt.
3: pls.fol.p. 26
Jan, 1904

Fort Vancouver

see

Vancouver (Wash.) Fort Vancouver

Fort Sam Houston, Tex. Post Prison
Marriott, J. M.
Post Prison - Fort Sam Houston. J.M. Marriott
architect. No plan.

Architectural concrete 1:34-35
No. 6 [1935]

Fort Snelling (MN) Restoration

West. ARcht.
4:6
My 1905

Fort Wallington, England
Saunders, A. D.
Hampshire coastal defence since the
introduction of artillery, with a description
of fort Wallington. [illus.]

Archeological journal
123: [136]-171
1966

Fort Shelby hotel, Detroit, Mich.

see

Detroit, Mich. Fort Shelby hotel

---

microfilm
Fort Snelling (Minn.) soldiers' home
Buffington, Leroy S., architect
Fort Snelling soldiers' home [Fort Snelling,
Minnesota] 1887.

Roll 21, frame 129

Fort Washington-Fort Lee Bridge, N.Y.
Proposed Fort Washington-Fort Lee bridge.
New York.

City planning 3:110
April, 1927

Fort Sheridan (Il) Officers' Mess and Bachelors'
Quarters
Holabird and Roche. Architects.

Inland Architect
vol. 39, No. 2, pl.fol.p. 20
Mar, 1902

Fort Street Union depot. Detroit, Mich.

see

Detroit, Mich. Fort Street Union depot

Fort Wayne (fort)
Fort Wayne in 1794

Bancroft, Hubert Howe.
Achievements of civilization....
10 vols. New York: The Bancroft
Company, publishers. 1896. 9:821

Fort Sheridan (IL.). Old Elm Club
Old Elm Club, Fort Sheridan. Marshall and Fox,
archts.

American architect 106:pls.fol. 240
October 14, 1914

Fort Ticonderoga, N.Y. Gate
Iron gate -- from restoration of Fort
Ticonderoga. Alfred C. Bossom, archt.

Architecture 52: 275-9
Ag 1925

Fort Wayne (Ind.) Allen County Court House
The Allen County Court House, Fort Wayne,
Indiana. Brentwood Tolan, archt. No plan.

Architectural record 12:229
A June, 1902

Fort Wayne (Ind) Allen County
Courthouse
Brentwood Tolan, arch.

Inland Arch 38:
pl.fol.p.32
Nov. 1901

720.5
A67f

Co.
Fort Wayne (Ind.). International Harvester
International Harvester Co., Fort Wayne,
Ind. Holabird and Root, archts.

Arch forum 51: 201
S '29

720.5
A67m

Fort Wayne (Ind.) Scottish Rite temple
Fort Wayne Scottish rite cathedral. Mahurin and Mahurin, archts. Plans.

A   Architecture 22: 117, 124-125, 129,pls.
August 1910   76-78

Fort Wayne, Ind. City bldg.
City building, Fort Wayne, Ind. [plans]
Wing & Mahurin, archts.

Inland architect
20, no. 1
pl. fol. p. 10
Ag 1892

Fort Wayne, (Ind.) Jefferson School
Wing and Mahurin, archts.

Inland Architect
vol. 35, No. 4, pl.fol.p. 32
May, 1900

Fort Wayne (Ind.) Strauss building
Architects own office building A. M. Strauss,
archt.

Natl archt 6: 4
Ag 1950

Fort Wayne, Ind. Concordia Lutheran college
Borcherdt, Helmut
Concordia Lutheran College in Fort Wayne
Indiana [details] Eero Saarinen & Associates,
archts.

Baumeister
57:536-39 Ag 1960
Tafel 36

720.5
A67r

bldg.
Fort Wayne,(Ind.) Lincoln national life insur
Lincoln National Life Insurance building,
Fort Wayne, Indiana. Benjamin W. Morris,
archt.

Arch rec 56: 335-346
O '24

720.5
A67ar

Fort Wayne (Ind.) Trinity Lutheran church
Trinity Lutheran church, Fort Wayne, Ind.
B. G. Goodhue, archt.

Architect (N.Y.).7:pl.39-41
Nov. 1926

Fort Wayne (IN) Ft. Wayne Saengerbund Club
Building. Sketch by Wing and Mahurn, Archs.

Inland Arch. 22:
pl. fol. p 40
N, 1893

Fort Wayne, Ind. Mahurin (M.S.) house
Residence of Mr. Marshall S. Mahurin, Fort Wayne,
Ind. (plans) Wing and Mahurin, archts.

Inland architect
v.18 no. 4
pl. fol.p. 56
N 1891

720.5
W52

Fort Wayne,(Ind.)Trinity Lutheran church
Trinity English evangelical Lutheran
church, Fort Wayne, Indiana

West. arch.35:101 & pl.115-19
Aug. 1926

Fort Wayne, Ind. Franke, J. B, house
One of Byrne's first commissions upon returning
to Chicago. [illus., plan] Barry Byrne, archt.

Prairie School review
III:11-12, 27
Fourth Quarter 1966

Fort Wayne, Ind. Peters (John C.) house
Sketch of residence for John C. Peters
Fort Wayne, Ind. Wing and Mahurin, archts.
No plan.

Inland architect 5:79,pl.fol.84
June, 1885

Fort William
Fort William

Bancroft, Hubert Howe.
Achievements of civilization....
10 vols. New York: The Bancroft
Company, Publishers. 1896. 8:705

Fort Wayne, Ind. Franke, J.B., house
... a pupil and follower of Mr. Frank Lloyd
Wright. [illus., plan] Barry Byrne, architect

Western architect
33:21, plates 1-4
Mr 1924

Fort Wayne (Ind.) Residence
Herbert Foltz, Archt.

West. Archt.
19: pls.fol.p. 24
Feb, 1913

MICROFILM
Fort Worth (Tx.) Anderson (Mrs. Neil P.)
House and Garage. 1916
Henry Corwith Dangler, archt. plans.

Roll 34, frames 305-318

720.5
B95b

Fort Wayne(Ind.) Indiana State Industrial
School for Feeble Minded Youths.
Indiana State Industrial School for
Feeble Minded Youths. Wing & Mahurin,archts.

Building budget 5:5 in supp
My 31, 1887

720.5
I56

Fort Wayne(Ind.) St. Joseph's Hospital
St. Joseph's Hospital, a 4-story addition
and remodeling old building. Bauer & Hill,
archts.

Inland archt & news rec 19:40
April 1892

MICROFILM
Fort Worth (Tex.) Berney (Morris E.) House
and Garage. 1915
Henry Corwith Dangler, archt.

Roll 34, frames 3-19

Ft. Worth, Tex. Board of trade bldg. (proposed)
Proposed Board of Trade Building, Fort
Worth, Tex. A. J. Armstrong, archt.

Inland archt.
vol. 12 no. 1
pl. at end of vol.
Ag 1888

721
T55
Fort Worth. Sinclair building
The Sinclair building at Fort Worth,
Texas. W. G. Clarkson Company, archts. No
plan.

Through the ages 9: 6
October 1931

720.52
B95
Fortescue, G. Alan
Model of motor trading premises
designed to be erected at the Motor
Exhibition, Olympia. Plan.

Builder 145: 625
O 20, '53

Fort Worth (Tex.) Bomar (W.P.) House
Adler and Work, archts.

Roll 34, frames 20-23

Fortaleza de Chanquillo, Peru

see

Castillo de Casma, Peru

720.52
A67c
Fortescue, G. Alan
New house on Springhead Estate, Haslemere,
Surrey. Pair of houses, Bridge Road, Maiden-
head, Berks. G.Alan Fortescue, archt. Ne-
ville A. Lyon, del.

Architect 115: pls., 186-7
March 5, 1926

720.5
:67c
Fort Worth.Dr. Pepper Bottling Co.
Crane, H.H.
New plant for "Dr. Pepper". Bottling plant,
Ft. Worth, Texas. Hubert Hammond Crane, archt.
Plan.

Architectural concrete 4:13-15
No.3[1938]

720.55
B67
Forte dei Marmi (It.) Villa Pesenti
Una villa in pineta, Osvaldo Borsani,
archt. [plans].

Domus
148:58-61
1940

Forth Bridge, Scotland
Forth bridge from the south ... from the
north ...

The graphic 6:52-53
January 16, 1892

Ft. Worth, Tex. Elmwood Sanatorium
Geren, Preston
Elmwood sanatorium in Ft. Worth. Preston M. Geren,
archt.

Architectural concrete 3:30-31
No. 3, 1937

Fortescue, G. Alan

see also

Maidenhead (Eng.) houses
Deepdene (Eng.) house
Caterham (Eng.) Cinema
Thames Ditton (Eng.) Houses

Forth Bridge, Scotland
Schuyler, Montgomery
Modern architecture: a lecture delivered at Union
College, Schenectady, New York. (1894).

Architectural record 4:10
July-September 1894

Fort Worth (Tex.) Festival
Fort Worth Festival, Views of amusement
buildings, no plan.

Architectural forum 65:sup.9,39
September, 1936

Fortescue, G. Alan
A bungalow on the Cornish coast. G. Alan
Fortescue, architect; drawn by Neville A. Lyon.

Architect 115:pls.
February 26, 1926

Forti, Giordano
Chemische fabrik CILAG, Milano. [plans and
sections] Giordano Forti, archt.

Bauen & Wohnen
7:167-170
Ag 1953

720.5
W52
Fort Worth. Montgomery Ward building
Brummitt, Wyatt
Merchandise and modernism. Montgomery Ward
buildings in Fort Worth, Texas; Chicago and
Albany.

Western architect 39: 149-150
September 1930

Fortescue, G. Alan
Bungalow (and plans) Surrey. (A.G.) Fortescue,
archt.

Architect 116:325
September 17, 1926

Fortification

see also

Arsenals   Bridge-heads
Blockhouses   Military architecture
Castles
City gates   Walls (fortification)

and names of individual fortifications, i.e.:

Ile-aux-Noix, Que. Fort Lennox
Siena, It. Fighine fortress
etc.

Fort Worth (Tex.) planning
Bartholomew, H.
Fort Worth, Texas.

City planning 4: 31-38
January, 1928

Fortescue, G   Alan
House at Hampton Court, Middlesex. G. Alan
Fortescue, archt. (Plans)

Architect 115: pl fol 202
Mr 12, 1926

Fortification
Bodnar, Edward W., S.J.
The Isthmian fortifications in oracular
prophecy.

American journal of
Archaeology
64:[165]-171
Ap 1960

Fortification
Ehrensperger-Katz, Ingrid
    Les représentations de villes fortifiées
dans l'art paléochrétien et leurs dérivées
byzantines. [illus.]

        Cahiers archéologiques
        v.19: [1]-27
        1969

Fortification. England. The Solent
Phillips-Birt, D.
    Repelling the Solent's invaders.
[illus.]

        Country life
        142: 224; 226-227
        Jl 27, 1967

Fortification, Malta. Competition
    Competition for development of ...
Messrs. James Burford, A.R.I.B.A., and S. Rowland
Pierce

        Builder 129:pl.and 216-17
        Aug. 7, 1925

Fortification. Brazil
    O forte de castelo.

        Habitat
        6:63-6 Jan 1956

Fortification, Germany

        Bergner, Heinrich.
        Handbuch der bürgerlichen
        Kunstaltertümer in Deutschland.
        Leipzig: Seeman, 1906. p.108-33.

Fortification,Malta. Competition
    International competition for ...

        Architect 114: 93-96
        August 7, 1925

Fortification, Colonial

        see

Names of individual forts, i.e.:
    St. Augustine, Fla. Fort Marion

Fortification. Germany.
    The employment of fortifications in the city
plan.

        Der Staedtebau 13:80-3.
        Heft 8-9, 1916.

Ryerson

    Fortification, Manchuria
        "Chinese-style fort"

        Nat geog 82: 629
        N 1942

Fortification. Competitions
    Beaux-arts Institute of Design, award for a
Portal to a Fortress.

        American architect 99:pl.1833,fol.p.64
        February 8, 1911

Ryerson

    Fortification. Iran

        Asia 38:58
        Ja 1938

Ryerson

        Fortification. Mexico
Mancha, Severo de la
    The fortress churches.

        Pemex travel bul.
        S-O 1945

710.5   Fortification. England.16th century
C85   Oswald, Arthur
        Coast defence in 1540 - how Henry VIII
    prepared to meet invasion: Hurst castle,
    Walmer castle, Pendennis castle, Camber castle,
    St. Mawes castle, Brownsea castle.

        Country life(London)88:190-194
        August 31,1940

Fortification, Italy.

        Sanmicheli, Michele. La Fabbriche
        civili, ecclesiastiche, e militari.
        Venezia: Antonelli, 1832.
        pl.28-33, 144-9.

Fortification, Navaho Indians
    Navajo had walled fort.

        El palacio 47:96
        April, 1940

Ryerson

        Fortification. England. Dartmouth Haven
O'Neil, B.H. St. J.
    Dartmouth castle and other defences of
Dartmouth Haven

        Archaeologia
        85: 129-157
        1935

Fortification. Italy
Perer, Maria Luisa Gatti
    Fonti per l'architettura milanese dal XVI
al XVIII secolo: Francesco Bernardino Ferrari
e la sua Raccolta di documenti e disegni - II.
Tomo IX - Cose militari. [illus.]

        Arte lombarda
        v.9, II: 136-151
        1964

Fortification, Sardinia

        see

Nuraghi, Sardinia

    Fortification. England. Hampshire
Saunders, A. D.
    Hampshire coastal defence since the
introduction of artillery, with a description
of fort Wallington. [illus.]

        Archeological journal
        123: [116]-171
        1966

Fortification, Italy. 16th c.
    Scully, Vincent, Jr.
Michelangelo's fortification drawings: A
study in the reflex diagonal.

        Perspecta 1:38-45
        Summer, 1952

Ryerson

        Fortification, Spain
Castaños y Montijano, Manuel
    Corachas, torres albarranas y baluartes.

        Arte español
        4:357-363

Fortification, Spain Stapley, M. A study of romanesque in Spain: the fortress of Lerida. Architectural record 31:483 May, 1912	Forts see Fortification	Fosbrooke, Bedingfield & Grundy see Glasgow (Scot.) Bridgeton. Assembly halls
Fortification. Spain Towers-bastions Arte Español 8:357-363 No.6, 1919	Fortuna Virilis, temple, Rome see Rome (It.) Temple of Fortuna Virilis	Foschini, Arnaldo see also Rome (It.) Exposition 1942. Chiesa dei Santi Pietro e Paolo (project)
705.8 U68 Fortification, Sweden Schnell, Ivar En förteckning över fornborgarna i Uppland [Eng. summary: A cat. of prehistoric forts in western Uppland] Upplands fornminnesforenings tidskrift XLIII, no. 2:f41-74 1929-33	7P6 L78 Fortune, Charlton Saint Angela's church, Pacific Grove, Cal., Charlton Fortune designer of interior. Interior illus. only. Liturgical arts 1: 25-26 Fall 1931	720.55 Foschini, Arnaldo A67 Ingresso alla Citta Universitaria edificio dalla Clinica Ortopedica Instituto di Igiene e Batteriologia. Arnaldo Foschini, arch. Architettura 14:25-33 Numero speciale 1935
Ryerson Fortification. Turkey Asia 38: 58 Ja 1938	Forums, Roman see Names of individual forums, e.g.: Silchester, Eng. Roman Forum Rome, It. Forum of Trajan " " Roman Forum	720.55 Foschini, Arnaldo A67 P.W. Il corso del Rinascimento. (Final project for new artery in Rome, the Corso del Rinascimento. Arnaldo Foschini, arch. Architettura 15:54-78 Numero speciale 1936
MICROFILM Fortin, Joseph T , 1870(?)-1956 obituary notice In SCRAPBOOK ON ARCHITECTURE p. 706 (on film)	Forum Romanum see Rome (city) Forum	Foshay tower, Minneapolis (Minn.) see Minneapolis (Minn.) Foshay tower
Fortis Salmantina. Salamanca. See Salamanca. Catedral vieja.	Forza d'Agró, (Sic.) Santi Pietro e Paolo (church) Cutrera, Antonino The Norman church of the Saints Peter and Paul at Agro. L'Arte 30:227-236 September-October, 1927	708.4 Fossanova. It. Abbazia B51j Dehio, G Zwei Cisterzienserkirchen: ein beitrag zu-geschichte der anfänge des gotischen stils. Jahrbuch der k. preussischen kunstsammlungen 12: 91-105 1891
Fortresses see Fortification	Forsina, inc. see New York (city) Milgrim shop	Fossanova, It. Abbazia. Interior of the church of the Cistercion monks at Fossanova. No plan. Architectural record 26:146 August, 1909

FOS.3
C55
Fossanova. It. Abbazia
Lipinsky, Angelo
An art historical problem

Die christliche kunst 23:235-244
May 1927

Foster and Vassar
see
Whitfield Estates (Fla.) House

Foster, T.   O.
see
Rangoon (Ind.) Law courts
Rangoon (Ind.) Port Trust airport. Passenger
      station

Ryerson
Fossanova, It. Abbazia
Lipinsky, A.
L'Abbaye médiévale de Fossanova rendue au
culte

Illustrazione vaticana
7:186-8
Ap 1936

Foster, Dewey
see
Fresno (Cal.) Post office

Foster, W. Z.
House for Mr. O. C. Smith at Kearney, Neb.
[plans] W. Z. Foster & W. Pell Pulis, archts.

Inland architect
20, no. 5
pl. fol. p. 58
D 1892

Fossati, Giorgio, 1705-1785
Scattolin, Giorgia
Un edificio di Giorgio Fossati. (Contri-
buto allo studio dell'edilizia residenziale del
XVIII° secolo a Venezia), [di] Giorgio Scattolin
[e] Tito Talamini. [illus.]

Arte veneta
v.23: 192-204
1969

Foster, Gade & Graham
see also
Chappaqua (N.Y.) Bishop (H.R.) house

Foster, William Arthur, 1884-1941
Obituary

Illinois society of
architects bulletin
25-26:8
Je-Jl 1941

Foster and Armstrong
see also
Rangoon (India) Law courts
"   "   Port of Rangoon commissioners off.

720.5
A67r
Foster, Gade and Graham
Town houses at nos.121-123 East 79th
Street,New York City. Robins and Oakman,and
Foster,Gade,and Graham,archts.

Architectural record 30:471
November 1911

710.5
C855
Foster, William Dewey
The home of Norr Erby, William Dewey
Foster, archt.

Country life (U.S.) 58: 61
December 1930

Foster and Armstrong
members of firm:
Foster, T. O.
Armstrong, E. W.

Foster (Giraud) estate
see
Lenox (Mass.) Belle Fontaine (estate)

Foster, Wm. E.
see
Santa Monica (Cal.) Shangri-La

Foster & Pulis
Members of firm:
Foster, W   Z
Pulis, W   Pell

Foster, H. Elbert, estate
see
Greenwich (Conn.) Foster (H.E.) estate

Fostoria, Ohio, Presbyterian Church
Crapsey and Brown, Archts.

Inland ARcht.
vol.25,No.6,pl.fol.p. 64
July 1895

Foster and Pulis
United Presbyterian Church, Kearney, Neb.
W.Z. Foster and W. Pell Pulis, archts.

Inland architect v. 16 no. 5
pl. fol. p. 64
N 1890

790.52
R95
Foster, R.C.
Abberley hall school chapel..stained
glass windows. R.C. Foster, archt. Reg-
inald Hallward, designer of windows.

Builder 144: 10, 14-18
Ja 6 '33

Fota, Ire. Garden house
Garden house, Fota, near Cork, Ireland.
A. Hill, archt.....entrance gate.

Amer archt and bldg news
56: pls fol 56
My 15, 1897

ffo
720.6
A51q

Fouchaux, Henri   1856-1910
Malcolm, D. G.
Henri Fouchaux, A.A.I.A.

American institute of architects-Quarterly
October 1910   bulletin 11: 196

720.5
A67f

Fouilhoux, Jacques André, 1879-1945
Oregon state capitol, competition design
W.H.Harrison and J.A.Fouilhoux, archts. New
York. Plan

Architectural forum 65: 9
July 1936

Foundations

Freitag, Joseph Kendall. Architectural engineering. New York: J.
Wiley and Sons, 1895. p. 284-370

720.5
A67f

Fougeres. Architecture
Some alluring cities of old France

Architectural forum 39:1-6
July 1923

720.5
A67f

Fouilhoux, Jacques André, 1879-1945
The Rockefeller apartments, New York.
J.André Fouilhoux and Wallace K.Harrison,
Architect. Plan.

Architectural forum 65: 298
October 1936

720.5
A51

Foundations.

Amer. Arch. 118:579-85.
Nov. 3, 1920.

Fouilhoux, Jacques André, 1879-1945
see also
Harrison and Fouilhoux

Foulkes, S. Colwyn
Llandudno War memorial. S. Colwyn Foulkes,
architect

Arch. journal 56: 804-5
Dec. 6, 1922

720.5
A51

Foundations.

Amer. Arch. 121: 117-3.
Feb. 1, 1922.

720.5
A67f

Fouilhoux, Jacques André, 1879-1945
House of tomorrow, Ladies' Home Journal,
sponsor. W.K.Harrison and J.A.Fouilhoux,
archts. Pittsburgh glass institute competition. No plans.

Architectural forum 67:83-30
August 1937

720.5
A67r

Foulks, A   B
David,A.C.
The new San Francisco: architectural and
social changes wrought by the reconstruction.
The A.M.Robertson building. A.B.Foulks,archt.
No plan.

Architectural record 31:11
January 1912

720.5
A51

Foundations.

Amer. Arch. 121: 148-50.
Feb. 15, 1922.

720.5
A67f

Fouilhoux, Jacques André, 1879-1945
The Ladies' Home Journal House. Model
house, New York Home Show. Archts: Wallace K.
Harrison and J.André Fouilhoux.

Architectural forum 67: 531
December 1937

Foulston, John
see also
Stonehouse (Eng.) Town hall
Plymouth (Eng.) Royal hotel
      "   "   Proprietary library
      "   "   Theatre Royal

720.6
R88

Foundations
Applications in building and foundations
of modern engineering construction

R.I.B.A.32:165-185
Jan. 24, 1925

MICROFILM

Fouilhoux, Jacques André, 1879-1945
obituary notice

in SCRAPBOOK ON
ARCHITECTURE p. 704
(on film)

Foulston, John.

Richardson, Albert Edward.
Monumental classic architecture
in Great Britain...London: B.T.
Batsford, 1914. p. 67-68.

720.6
R88

Foundations
Applications in building and foundations
of modern engineering construction

R.I.B.A.32:224-34
Feb. 7, 1925

Fouilhoux, Jacques André, 1879-1945
Obituary

Illinois society of
architects bulletin
30: 8
Ag - S 1945

710.5
C85

Foulston,John
A.C.
Regency Plymouth - designed by John Foulston,
archt.

Country life(Lond)82:129
July 31,1937

720.5
A67

Foundations.
Building construction and equipment.

Arch. Rev. 12:9-11.
Jan. 1921

710.5 C855 Foundations Building for best results	Foundations. Foundations.	Foundations The foundations of tall buildings.
Country life 48:44-45 Oct. 1925	Amer archt 92: 77-78 S 7, 1907	Architectural record 23:329-331 April, 1908
720.5 A67f Foundations. Building foundations.	720.5 I56 Foundations Boyington, W. W. Foundations.	Foundations Wight, P. B. Gen. William Sooy Smith's paper on high buildings criticised.
Arch.forum 33: 83-4. Sept.1920	Inland architect 8:69-71 December 1886	Inland architect 19, no. 3:34-36 Ap 1892
710.5 C855 Foundations. For the country house.	720.54 T25 Foundations Foundations [special no.]	720.5 I56 Foundations Root, John Wellborn A great architectural problem
Country Life 41: 63-4. April 1922	Tech et arch pt.1 - no. 9-10, 1944 pt. 2 - no. 1-2, 1945	Inland arch 15: 67-71 Je '90
710.5 H84 Foundations. The foundation for a house.	Foundations Raumann, Frederick Foundations , Diagrams.	720.53 K31 Foundations Tóth, Zoltán Grundlagen für das bauen in stadt und land. (Foundations for buildings in city and country.) Sketches.
House & garden.50:106-07 Sept. 1926	Inland Architect 32: 42-5 Dec, 1898	Wasmuths monatshefte 13: 218-221 May 1929
Foundations Foundation from side of wall line.	Foundations Foundations in soft soils.	720.571 A72 Foundations Alenius, P. Grundundersökning och Husbyggnad [diags.]
Inland architect v. 17 no. 5: 61 Je 1891	Architect 107: 314-17; Ap 28, 1922 368-70; My 19, " 410-13; Je 2, "	Arkitekten no. 2:28-32 1938
720.52 A67 Foundations Foundation problems	Foundations Hatch, James N. Foundations of large buildings.	720.52 B93 Foundations A method of erecting foundations and building simultaneously
Arch. Journ. 61:421-22 Mar. 11, 1925	Inland Arch. 45: 26-9 April 1905 45: 38-40 May 1905 45: 50 June 1905	Builder 124:248-50 Feb. 9, 1923
720.52 A67 Foundations Foundation problems	Ryerson Foundations Skinner, Frank W. Foundations of lofty buildings	720.52 A67 Foundations Modern foundations
Arch. Journ. 61:563-64 Apr. 8, 1925	Century 77:771-781 Mr 1909	Arch. Journ. 61:189-90 Jan. 28, 1925

720.52
487e   Foundations.
       Modern methods in building construction.

       Architect 107: 247-8.
       Apr. 7, 1922.

Foundations
Adler, Dankmar
     Piling for isolated foundations adjacent to walls.

       Inland architect
       20, no. 6: 63-64
       Ja 1893

Foundations
Adler, Dankmar
     Tall buildings.

       Inland architect
       v. 17 no. 5: 58
       Je 1891

720.5
I56   Foundations, Asphalt
      Elson, J.F.
           Asphalt foundations

       Inland architect 7:95-96
       June 1886

720.6
R882 Foundations, Canada. Winnipeg
      Moore, R.E.
           The Winnipeg foundation problem.

       Royal arch. institute of
       Canada. Journal 20:19d-9d
       N°43

720.973 Foundations. History
I290ci   Building foundations of the past

       Industrial Chicago 2:
       pl opp 74
       1891

Foundations. Mexico,(city)
Strau, Wolfgang
     Interesantes trabajos de recimentacion;
vuelta a su posición vertical del edificio núm.
37 de las calle de Balsas de la Ciudad de
Mexico.

       Arquitectura Mexico
       no.58:93-7 Je 1957

Foundations. U. S. Illinois. Chicago
         see
Chicago, Ill. Foundations

720.5
N56   Foundations, U.S., New York, New York
      Landers, C.S.
           Architectural engineering: Caisson foundation
      in New York City. Method of sinking caissons.

       New York architect 4:140-142;188-190
       March; April; 1910

Foundations, U.S., N.Y., N.Y.
     Foundations of New York Court House

       Architectural forum 28:201-4
       April, 1923

Foundations, U.S., N.Y., New York. 20th century
     Modern foundations; Royal Queen building ,
U.S. Realty building, Commercial Cable annex,
New York City. Archt. not given. Diagrams.

       Architectural record 21:459-467
       June, 1907

Foundlings' hospitals
         see
Children's hospitals

720.52 Foundries, Denmark. Copenhagen
B93   Circular foundry hall, Copenhagen; Mr.
        Niels Rosenkjar, archt.

       Builder 130: 72
       January 8, 1926

Foundries, Netherlands
         see
Velsen (Neth.) Fonderie de tuyaux

Fountain houses

       Amer. arch. 111:309-311
       May 16, 1917

Fountain Park (MO)
     Congregational Church
     Weber & Groves, Arch.

       Inland Arch.
       44: pls.fol.p. 32
       Nov. 1904

Fountainhall
     Fountainhall, Haddingtonshire.

       Arch. Rev. 51: 69-71 and pl. 5
       Mar. 1922

Fountains

     see also

Memorial fountains

     also name of town followed by name of
     fountain, as :

New York (city) Straus memorial fountain

Fountains

       Gailhabaud, Jules. L'architecture
       du V au XVII siècle. 4 vols. Paris:
       A. Morel, 1869-72. v.2 pl. 99-100

Fountains

       Amer. homes and gardens 9:282-3
       Aug. 1912

720.5 Fountains
A67a   Architecture's portfolio

       Arch. 69:174-88
       Mr. '34

710.5
H84
Fountains
Foster,Agnes
The decorative value of wrought iron work
and tile. A tile wall fountain for a large hallway

House & garden 29:51
June 1916

720.52
A673
Fountains
Parkes, Kineton
Fountains

Architectural review (Lond.) 64: 92-97
September 1928

Fountains.
Brinton, Selwyn
Garden Sculpture. II: In Relation to water and its
decorative treatment, fountains, city ponds, wall
fountains, bird-baths, and dipping wells. (illus.)

Builder 108:503-506
May 28, 1915

Fountains.
Design for a memorial fountain

Builder 116:pl.for
May 23, 1919

RYLANDS LIBRARY
705.1
A78
Fountains
Taft,Lorado
Fountains.Illustrations of many fountains from
all over the world.

Art and progress 4: 892-899
March,1913

Fountains
Gods of the garden come out again
5 illustrations

House and garden 31:36
June, 1917

720.52
B93
Fountains
Design for a monumental fountain

Builder 125:19
July 6, 1923

D13.1
H84
Fountains
Fountain designed by the architect Mr.
John R. Rawley of New York City.

House beautiful 39: 107
March,1916

Fountains
In color

Amer. Inst. of Arch. 3:5
Jan. 1915

720.5
A67r
Fountains
Florentine wall fountain. (Victoria and
Albert Museum.)

Architectural record 27: 423
May 1910

705.1
A79
Fountains
Wheelwright,Robert
Fountains and pools in garden design.

Arts and decoration 1:172-175,197
March 1911

Fountains.
Memorial fountain, project. [Illus.]
J. H. Morton, architect.

Builder
94: 399 and plate
April 4, 1908

720.54
T25
Fountains
Fontaines et bassins.

Tech et Arch 2:120-123
Mr-Ap. 1942

710.5
H84
Fountains
Fountains for town betterment;

House & garden 51: 114-15,172
February 1927

Fountains
Meas. drawings.

Cicognara, Leopoldo.
Le Fabbriche e i monumenti
Cospicui di Venezia.
Venice: G. Antonelli, 1858.
pl. 113.

RYLANDS LIBRARY
D13.1
H84
Fountains
Sturgis, W. R.
For a garden fountain in the country - how
to reuse the water and so prevent waste and ex-
pense.

House beautiful 70: 66,82
July 1931

Fountains
de Martin, Ralph.
The garden fountain
(illus.)

Amer. homes and gardens 7:255-8
July, 1910

721
T53
Fountains
Measured drawings of drinking fountains:
wall and free standing.

Through the ages 7:12-13
June 1929

Fountains.
Fountains

Burges, William.
Architectural drawings.
London: Clowes, 1870. pl.19.

720.52
B93
Fountains
Garden fountain by Felix Joubert.

Builder 144: 275
February 17,1933

710.5
H84
Fountains
Barrington,A.L.
A plea for the wall fountain.

House and garden 35: 50-51,62
June 1919

RYERSON LIBRARY 705.4 A78 **Fountains** Maignan, Maurice Un projet de fontaine monumentale. L'Art et les artistes 22,n.s.:344-350. July 1928	720.6 A67 **Fountains** Wall fountain by Henry Herring, sculptor. Architectural league of New York 27: 31 1912	**Fountains** 20th c. Fontana a muro. Silvio longo and Leo Pariso, archts. Domus 245-49: 90 Jl-Ag 1950
Fountains. Public Fountains. Topical architecture vol. 3, no. 32, pls 1-8, Ja 1902 vol. 5, no. 49, pls 1-8, Ja 1904	710.5 C855 **Fountains** Wall fountains and dipping pools. Country life 42: 52-3. May 1922.	720.52 B93 **Fountains Abbey, Eng.** Builder 125:215 Aug. 10, 1923
RYERSON LIBRARY **Fountains** Singing waters: fountains and pools for modern gardens Touchstone 4: 470-6 F '19	710.5 C855 **Fountains** A wall fountain in a sunroom. Country life in America 36:37 May 1919	**Fountains Abbey, Eng.** Gourlay, Charles Fountains Abbey. Plan. Architectural journal 54: 530-1 November 2, 1921
RYERSON LIBRARY 750.5 M81 **Fountains** Some public drinking fountains in Europe and America.. Monumental news 20:429 June,1908	**Fountains** Wall fountain Country life in America 24: 38-39 August 1913	**Fountains Abbey, Eng.** Henderson, A. E. Fountains Abbey, Yorkshire. The chapel of the nine altars. Builder 144: 651-654 April 21, 1933
710.5 H84 **Fountains** Suggestions for wall fountains House & garden 18:21 Jl '10	729 T67 **Fountains** Wells and fountains Topical architecture V.5:No.32, pls 1-8, Ag '02 V.7:No.49, pls 1-8, Ja '04	**Fountains Abbey, Eng.** (R.A.I. Summer meeting) Architect 108:122-3 Aug. 18, 1922
Fountains Tazza of marble that could be adapted. Tatham, Charles Heathcote. Etchings, representing the best examples of ancient ornamental architecture. London: T. Gardiner, 1803. pl.36-42	RYERSON LIBRARY 705.1 A79 **Fountains** Bishop, Helen Water essential to certain types of intimate gardens Arts and decoration 27:40-43 June 1927	720.52 A67 **Fountains. China.** Details of craftsmanship. Arch. Jour. 53:282. Mar. 9,, 1921.
720.52 A673 **Fountains** Wall drinking fountain of marble. Architectural review (Lond.) 66: 237 November 1929	**Fountains, 17th century** Frontispiece from a 17th c. book Ysendyck Jules Jaques van. Documents classes d l'art dans les pays-Bas. 5 vols. Anvers: J. Maes, 1880-89. vols. 2, pt. F, pl.9	**Fountains. Competitions** see also Detroit (Mich.) Scott memorial fountain

720.5
A51

Fountains, Competitions
Beaux-arts Institute of Design - 1920
Awards - Class "B" - 2 Analytique - "A wall
fountain"

American architect 117:688-689
June 2, 1920

Fountains. Competitions.
First Atelier of architecture: a monumental
fountain.
Designs by L. H. Bucknell, A. B. Hamilton, and
E.R. Jarrett. plans and elevations

Builder
108:292,294 and 3 plates
Mar. 26, 1915

Fountains, England. London.
Fountain in the winter garden, Ritz Hotel,
London, England.

Architectural record 36: 465
November, 1914

Fountains, Competitions.
Beaux-arts institute of design competition:
A decorative fountain

B.A.I.D. 4:20-21
December, 1927

Fountains. Competitions
"A fountain": Beaux-Arts Institute of
Design awards. 5 designs

B.A.I.D. 5:9-11
April, 1929

Fountains, England.
A tile-built fountain, designed by Sir Edwin
Lutyens.

Architects' journal 67:112
January 11, 1928

Fountains. Competitions.
Builder fountain competition: Design for a
public park. Second prize, Harry B. Laycock.
Extra prize, William Freskin. Fourth mention,
Percy May. Plans, elevations, sections.

Builder 97:
46;J1 10, 1909
73, pl; J1 17, 1909
101, pl; " 24, "
161, pl; Ag 7, 1909

Fountains, Competitions.
A monumental fountain. Beaux-arts institute of
design award. renderings

Amer archt
125:389, 394
Ap 23, 1924

710.5
C85

Fountains, England.
Wall fountains in old English garden. Designed by Sir Edwin Lutyens.

Country life (Lond.)61: 598-9
April 16, 1927

Fountains, Competitions.
Competition, Beaux-arts institute of design:
A wall fountain. renderings

B.A.I.D. 3: 4-7
August, 1927

ETERSON LIBRARY

730.5
M81

Fountains, Competitions.
Prize design, drinking fountain by H.
Van Buren Magonigle, archt. Honorable mentions
of drinking fountain designs.

Monumental news 21: 537-53²
July,1909

Fountains. France

Blondel, Jacques Francois.
De la distribution des maisons
de plaisance. 2 vols. Paris: C.A.
Jombert, 1737-38.v.2,pl.16-18.

Fountains. Competitions
Competition for memorial fountain;
Civics Arts Association Competition,
Design by Cyril A. Farey   rendering

Arch. and Bldrs. jour. 44:pl.for
July 26, 1916

Fountains, Competitions.
R.I.B.A. Student's drawings: An important
monumental fountain. Tike prize design by
Trenwith Wills. plan and elevation

Builder
106:164 and 2 plates
Feb. 6, 1914

Fountains, France.

Cook, Sir Theodore Andrea.
Twenty-five great houses of
France. London: Offices of
Country Life; New York:
Charles Scribner's Sons, 1916.
p.290,291,400.

Fountains, Competitions.
Competition for proposed drinking fountain,
Blackheath. Winning design. Plans.

Builder 139:57
July 11, 1930

Fountains. England
English,1400 A.D.

British arch. 81, pl. for.
Jan., 23, 1914

Fountains, France.

Deshairs, Léon. Bordeaux:
architecture et décoration au
dix-huitième Siècle. Paris: A.
Calavas 1907 pl. 44-6.

Fountains. Competitions.
Dillon memorial competition for the Davenport
(Iowa) Levee improvement commission. [eleva-
tions, plans, sections] F.B. and A. Ware, and
Paul Schulz, archts.

Architecture
38: pl.137-140
Ag 1918

720.52
B93

Fountains, England.
A fountain: Pump Hall,Malvern,England.
A fountain erected to the memory of the
work of women in the war, Shaw,Lancs,England.
Memorial to T.P.O'Connor in Kensal Green
Cemetery,Ireland, by Richard Goulden,sculp-
ture.

Builder 144: 612,613
April 14,1933

Fountains. France

École nationale superieure des beaux-arts
(France). Les Medailles des concours d'architecture de l'École...annee 1898/99-Guérinet, 1900-13.
v. 5 pl. 10-20

Fountains. France.

Neufforge, Jean Francois de.
Recueil élémentaire d'architecture.
8 vols. Paris: L'auteur, 1757-68.
v.5: pl. 55-66.

RYERSON LIBRARY
705.4
A78

Fountains   France
Gryar, Paul
     Les fountains sacrées de Bretagne, Leur
Légendas.

        Art et les artistes n.s. 6:125-134
        January 1923

Fountains, France, Paris
Fontaine de l'Abbaye   (Louis XV)

        Archt's jour. 50:205
        Aug. 13, 1919

Fountains. France.

Stein, Henri. Les Jardins de
France des origines à la fin du
XVIII siècle. Paris: D.A. Longuet,
1913 . pl.91-95

Fountains. France
Saint-Jean-d'Angely (Charente-Intferieure)
Fontaine et puits.

        Encyclopedie de l'architecture,
        constructions de Style. 2 vols.
        Paris: Albert Morancé, 1928- ?
        Tome 1: pl.73

721
T53

Fountains, France. Nancy
     A fountain at Nancy.

        Through the ages 5: 16
        May 1927

Fountains, France.

Vitry, Paul. Hotels et Maisons de
la Renaissance Francaise. 3 vols.
Paris: E. Lévy, 1910 - ?
v.3,pt.2,pl.86.

Fountains. France
Juvisy fountains

        La construct. mod. 29:258-60
        Mar. 1, 1914

Fountains. France, Paris
Fountain at Place St. Michel

        Archt's jour. 46:pl.for
        Aug. 29, 1917

RYERSON LIBRARY
705.4
G28

Fountains, France
Roy, Maurice
     Fountain of Diana of the chateau d'Anet.
Illustrations.

        Gazette des beaux arts Per.5.v.4: 113-141
        August-September 1921

720.52
A67e

Fountains France.
     A monumental fountain at the intersection
of two streets.

        Architect 104: pl. Jul.23
        1920.

720.52
A67

Fountains, France. Paris
     Fountain in the Rue de Grenelle. E.Bouch-
ardon, sculptor.

        Architects' journal 52: 102-103
        July 28, 1920

Fountains. France.
Lossky, Boris
     La fontaine de Diane à Fontainebleau.
[illus.]

        Société de l'histoire de
        l'art français. Bulletin
        Année 1968: [9]-21
        1970

720.54
A67

Fountains, France. Alsace
     A street fountain at Alsace.

        L'Architecture 40:pl. 1
        January 15, 1927

720.52
A673

Fountains, France. Paris
     The fountains of Paris.

        Architectural review (Lond.) 37: 36-39;
        February 1915   pls.5-7 fol.p.48

Fountains, France
     Fontaines, lavoirs et abreuvoirs.
Plans only

        Verdier, Aymar. Architecture
        civile et domestique. 2 vols.
        Paris: Bance, 1857-58.
        Vol. 2:179-184

Fountains. France. Louis XIV

     Designs for a fountain

        Le Pautre, Antoine. Les
        oevres d'architecture
        d'Antoine Lepautre. Paris:
        Jombert, 1710. pl. 16, 17.

RYERSON LIBRARY
064
I29

Fountains, France. Paris
     Medici fountain, Luxembourg garden, Paris

        L'Illustration 150:439
        Nov. 4, 1922

RYERSON LIBRARY
705.4
A78

Fountains, France
Varille, Mathieu
     Fountains of Provence

        L'Art et les artistes 20:
        June 1930   311-315

Fountains, France, Louis XIV style
     Fontaine by LeBrun - Louis XIV style.
Fountain Rocaille by Charles Eisen - Louis XIV
style.

        Guilmard, D. Les maitres
        ornemanistes. Paris: E. Plon, etc.,
        c.1880-81. pl. 26, 62

RYERSON LIBRARY
730.5
M81

Fountains, France. Paris
Kreutzer, E.C.
     Public fountains of Paris.

        Monumental news 22: 499-501
        July, 1910

720.52
A67
Fountains, France. Paris. De La Paix
Fontaine de la Paix, Place de Saint-Sul-
pice, Paris. Destournelles and Voinier,
archts.

Architects' journal 53: 215
February 25, 1921

Fountains, Germany

Stiehl, Otto Max Johannes. Der
Wohnbau des Mittelalters. Leipzig:
A. Kröner, 1908. p.370-376.

Fountains. Germany
German

Arch. Rundschau 31: 44, 64
Nov. 1914

720.52
A67
Fountains, France. Paris. Molière
Molière fountain, Paris. Visconti, archt.,
Pradier, sculptor.

Architects and builders journal 43: pl.fol.
May 24, 1916   p.224

Fountains. Germany.
Von deutschen Brunnen in alter Zeit. illus

Wasmuths Monatshefte 5:224-31.
1920-21

RYERSON LIBRARY
705.3
D48
Fountains, Germany
Maulbronn. Brunnenkapelle

Deutsche kunst 3,lief.10: pl.114
No.3,1937

RYERSON LIBRARY
705.1
C55
Fountains, France. Versailles
Basin of Apollo.

Christian art 2: 167
December 1907

710.5
C35
Fountains, Germany. Berlin
Fairy fountain, Berlin.

Country life 35: 672-675
May 9, 1914

Fountains. Germany.
Wettbewerb um Einen Monumentalbrunnen fur Oppeln.

Berliner architekturwelt 3:328- 36
Heft 9, 1900

RYERSON LIBRARY
705.2
I61
Fountains, France. Versailles
Nolhac, Pierre de
Early fountains at Versailles.

International studio 10:21-30
March 1900

D18 b
D18
Fountains, Germany
Fountain at the Swabian waterworks

Deutsche kunst 51: 52
Oct. 1922

Fountains, Ger. Charlottenburg
Wettbewerb fur Einen Brunnen auf dem Steinplatz
in Charlottenburg. 1 Preis. Bildhauer: August Gaul.

Berliner architekturwelt 7:pls.
Jahrgang, 12 Heft, 1905

Fountains, Germany.

Popp, Joseph. Bruno Paul,
mit 319 abbildungen. Munich:
Bruckmann, [1910-1921] 190

Fountains. Germany.
Fountain in a door yard, Emil Freymouth,
archt. Munich

Dekorative kunst 32: pl.opp.p.249
August,1929

720.53
E35
Fountains,Germany.Munich
Die gestaltung eines gartenhofes in der
Deutschen siedlung-ausstellung München 1934
(The formation of a garden-court in the Ger-
man settlement exhibition,Munich,1934). G.
Harbers,archt. Plans, sculpture by Georg
Kolbe.

A

Der baumeister 32:328-333
October 1934

Fountains, Germany

Popp, Hermann. Die architektur
der barock und rokokozeit in
Deutschland und der Schweiz...
Stuttgart: Julius Hoffmann, 1913.
p. 262

720.52
A673
Fountains, Germany
Fountain of "The fighting bisons",
Königsberg, August Gaul, designer.

Architectural review 64: 95
September 1928

720.5
A67r
Fountains,Germany.Munich
Bacon,F.R.
The new development of German architecture

Architectural record 32:209-210
September 1912

Fountains, Germany.

Bergner, Heinrich.
Handbuch der bürgerlichen
Kunstaltertümer in Deutschland.
Leipzig: Seeman, 1906. p. 341-52.

Fountains, Germany.
Fritz Voggenberger, Frankfurt a M.

Wasmuths 7:39
Heft 1-2,1923

Fountains. Germany. Nuremberg

Arch. rec. 36: 447-455
Nov. 1914

Fountains, Germany. Rothenburg
    Fountains near the Johanneskerk and in
the market place Rothenburg ob der Tauber
(1790)

            Wendingen 11:9-10
            No.1 1930

Fountains, Italy

            Cyclopaedia of architectural
            illustration....10 vols. Boston:
            Ticknor and Co. (n.d.)v.3 pl. 208-227

Fountains. Italy
    Fountains in Italian Gardens.

            Ricci, Corrado. Baroque
            Architecture and Sculpture
            in Italy. London: Heinemann,
            1912. p. 96, 248-269.

720.53
B35
Fountains,Germany. Stuttgart
    Wettbewerb für einen marktbrunnen in
Stuttgart. (Competition for a market place
fountain in Stuttgart.)

            Baumeister 32: B94-95
            July 1934

Fountains, Italy

            Scheult, Francois Léonard.
            Recueil d'architecture dessinée
            et mesurée en Italie. Paris: Ainé,
            1840. pl.38-40,45-6,58,68.

720.5
A67
Fountains, Italy
    Melani, Alfredo
    The fountains of Italy

            Arch rev 10 (n.s.5): 1-6
            Ja '02

Fountains, Germany. Wurtemburg
    The Marktbrunnen, Schwabisch-hall, Wurtemburg,
Ger.

            Amer archt & bldg news 55: 95, pl
            fol 96
            Mr 20, 1897

Fountains. Italy

            Thomas, Walter Grant and John T.
            Fallon. Northern Italian details:
            drawings and photographs. New York:
            The American architect, 1916.pl.53-69

D13.1
H84
Fountains,Italy
    LeBlond,E
    Italian fountains.(Illustrations)

            House beautiful 29: 41-42
            January 1911

Fountains, Greece.
    Wayside fountain

            Gulick, Charles Burton. The life of
            the ancient Greeks. New York: D.
            Appleton and Co., 1902. p. 252.

720.53
A67
Fountains   Italy.
    Carved stone fountain, 15th ce ntury.

            Arch.jour.55:872. Jun.21,1922.

Fountains. Italy
    Petraja - Fountain by Il Tribolo.

            Latham, Charles. The gardens of
            Italy. 2 vols. London: Country Life,
            Ltd., and G. Newnes, Ltd., 1905.
            v.2:p.112

705.95
B78
Fountains, India Bombay
    Modern fountain in Bombay following
traditions of Hindu art.(Illustration)

            Roopa-Lakha 1:opp.p.7
            Number 4, 1929

710.5
L26
Fountains, Italy
    Curbings of some Italian pools. Drawing
by Helen Guthrie Kirby.

            Landscape architecture 14: 279
            July 1924

Fountains. Italy
    Villa della Petraja, Florence.

            Triggs, Harry Inigo. The art of
            garden design in Italy. London:
            Longmans, Green and Co., 1906.
            pp. 77-78: pl. 38-39

Fountains, Italy

        see also

Tivoli (It.) Villa d'Este

Fountains, Italy
    Fountains designed by Bartolommeo
Ammannat:

            Ruggieri, Fernando. Studio
            d'architettura civile. 3 vols.
            Florence: Tartini, 1722-28.
            v.3 pl.27,28.

Fountains, Italy
    Village Fountain near Lake Iseo.

            Lowell, Guy. More small Italian villas
            and farmhouses. New York: Architectural
            Book Publishing Co., c.1920. p.139-140

Fountains, Italy.

            Country life (Eng.) 27:374-377
            12 Mr. '10

Fountains, Italy.
    A fountain in a wall.

            Stern, Giovanni. La villa di
            Giulio III. Rome: Fulgoni, 1784.
            Plates 22, 26

Fountains. Italy. Bagnaia
        Fountain in the garden
    Bagnaia, Italy
        (illus. only)

            Amer. arch. 114: front.
            July 24, 1918

Fountains, Italy, Brescia
Italian Renaissance details - two wall fountains
at Brescia, Italy. Measured drawings by F. Nelson
Breed

Architectural forum 38:187-190
April, 1923

Fountains, Italy. Florence. Pitti Palace
see
Fountains, Italy. Florence. Boboli gardens.

705.3   Fountains, Italy. Rome
K96w   Riess, Margot
        The fountain in Rome

Der Kunst wanderer 10:7-10
September 1928

720.52   Fountains, Italy. Florence
A675   The centaur fountain, Florence.

Architectural review 47: pl. 1
April 1920

705.1   Fountains, Italy. Frascati
A51a   Italian villa gardens - fountain and walk
        in Villa Torlonia - Frascati and Villa Lante.

American magazine of art 9: 450-451 pl
September 1918   fol.p.445

720.52   Fountains, Italy. Rome. Trevi
A67   Fountain of Trevi.

Architects and builders journal 39: sup.
to April 29, 1914

Fountains, Italy. Florence.
    Measured details of a wall fountain in
Florence.

Architect (Lond.) 131: 198
August 12, 1932

720.52   Fountains, Italy. Frascati.Villa Aldobrandini
A673   Fountain on the terrace, Villa Aldobran-
        dini, Frascati, Italy. Giacomo Della Porta
        (1541-1604) architect.

Architectural review 48: pl. 4 opp.p.10
July 1920

720.5   Fountains, Italy. Rome. Vatican
A67f   Italian renaissance details. Fountain in
        Piazzetta della Zecca. Vatican, Rome.
        Measured drawings by J. Hunter McDonnell.

Architectural forum 39:2F-24
July 1923

705.1   Fountains,Italy.Florence
161   Teigelt, Hilda
        The minor fountains of Florence.Illustrations
of a few wall fountains.

International studio 94:87-90.;22
December 1929

720.5   Fountains, Italy. Frascati.Villa Aldobrandini
A51   Villa Aldobrandini, Frascati, Italy.

American architect 114: 361-364
September 25, 1918

720.5   Fountains, Italy. Rome. Via Giulia
A67f   Wall fountain, Via Giulia, Rome
        Courtyard fountain, Monte di Pieta,Rome

Architectural forum 39:175-8
Oct. 1923

Fountains, Italy. Florence.
    Wall fountain at Florence, Italy.

Mawson, Thomas Hayton.
Civic Art. London: B.T. Batsford;
New York: Charles Scribners' Sons,
1911. p.143

720.52   Fountains, Italy. Rome
A673   "Four Rivers" in the Piazza Navona, Rome;
        designer: Bernini.
        "Fontana di Trevi", Rome.
        "Tortoise fountain", Rome.

Architectural review 64: 93-94
September 1928

720.5   Fountains, Italy. Rome. Villa Borghese
P59   "Seahorse fountain", Villa Borghese, Rome.

Pencil points 8: 196
April 1927

720.52   Fountains, Italy. Florence. Boboli gardens
A67   Fountain of the Isoletto,Florence.

Arch.Jour.51:718. Jun.9,
1920.

705.3   Fountains,Italy.Rome
K96w   Riess, Margot
        The fountain in Rome

Der Kunst wanderer 10:7-10
September 1928

705.3   Fountains,Italy.Siena
Z48   Lanyi,Jenö
        Some designs for the Gaia fountain in Siena.

Zeitschrift für bildende kunst (old series)
Heft 7,October 1,1927   61:257-268

720.52   Fountains, Italy. Florence. Boboli gardens
A67   Wall fountain in Pitti palace, Boboli
        gardens, Florence.

Architects and builders journal 41: pl.for
January 6, 1915

720.5   Fountains, Italy. Rome
P59   Fountain, Rome. Water color by Harry
Sternfeld.

Pencil points 8: 14
January 1927

720.5   Fountains, Italy. Tivoli. Villa D'Este
A51   Fountain of Villa d'Este.

American architect 113: opp. p.785
June 12, 1918

RYERSON LIBRARY
705.5
I29
Fountains, Italy, Vatican City
Carpaneaco, F. Z. ii
Les fontaines de la Place Saint-Pierre

L'Illustrazione vaticana
5:534-535
August 1-15, 1934

RYERSON LIBRARY
915.08
A88
Fountains, Morocco
Moorish fountain in the Place of Nedjardine. Made of mosaic and tiles.

Asia 30:634
September 1930

710.5
L26
Fountains, Portugal
Arnold, A. F.
Water features in Portuguese gardens and parks.

Landscape architecture 20: 129-135
January 1930

D10.5
C88
Fountains, Italy, Venice
Matson, Esther
The Venetian fountain spell: a study in the relation of the art to utility. Reproductions of two old Venetian fountains.

Craftsman 24: 30-35
April, 1913

Fountains, Oriental
Student designs

Amer. inst. of arch. 3:79-80
Feb., 1915

720.5
A67f
Fountains, Renaissance
Italian Renaissance details

Architectural forum 39:281 & pl.
Dec. 1923

Fountains, Mexico
Chapatepeo, Mexico

Builder 105:625
Dec. 5, 1913

720.5
W52
Fountains, Persian
Persian fountain: courtesy of Claycraft Potteries, Los Angeles, California.

Western archt. 38: front
February 1929

Fountains, Ship
Salon Mauresque Fontaine D'eau Glacée.
(Illustration)

Vaillat, Leandre. S.S. France:
interior decorations. [Paris:
Devambez, 1913.]

RYERSON LIBRARY
705.972
M61a
Fountains, Mexico
Lozada, J. R.
The fountains.

Mexican art and life no. 6:30-32
April 1939

720.53
W31
Fountains. Poland
Memorial fountain at Warsaw, erected, 1823

Wasmuths 11: 201
Heft 5, 1927

Fountains, Sicily

Hittorff, Jacob Ignaz. Architecture
modern de la Sicile. Paris: P.
Renouard, 1835. pl. 16, 24-32, 52.

Fountains, Mexico
The Churriqueresque, Mexico.

Monumental news 15, no. 4
Ap 1903

RYERSON LIBRARY
O57
F76
Fountains, Poland. Poznan
The fountain before the City Hall, Poznan,
Poland. Detail only

Poland 10: frontispiece
June 1929

710.5
L25
Fountains. Spain
A fountain in the Generalife

Landscape architecture 14:13-14
Oct. 1923

RYERSON LIBRARY
Fountains, Mexico
Mexican fountains.

Pemex travel club bul.
O 15 1941.

RYERSON LIBRARY
705.5
369
Fountains, Pompei
Fountain in the Casa dell'Orso made of
mosaic and tiles, Pompei, Italy.

Bolletino d'arte Anno 9:567
June, 1930

720.5
P59
Fountains. Spain
Fountain in the Court of the Lions, Alhambra. From a drawing by R. Nedved.

Pencil points 6: 89
March 1925

RYERSON LIBRARY
705.942
M11
Fountains, Morocco
Fountain Nedjarine of Fez (made of mosaic
and tile)

Maanblad voor beeldende kunsten 7: 41
February 1930

710.5
L26
Fountains, Portugal
Price, T. D.
Moorish fountain basins in Spain and Portugal. Also measured drawings.
The tiled pools of Spain.

Landscape architecture 19:67-68, 250-258
January; July; 1929

Fountains. Spain.
The Gardens at Aranjuez.

House and gard. 2: 519-41
N., 1902

711
L26
Fountains, Spain
    The gardens of the Alcazar, Seville, Spain

            Landscape arch. 15:1-16
            Oct. 1924

720.52
A673
Fountains, Sweden
    "The Susanna Fountain" in the garden of
the designer's house at Lidingö; a playing
fountain; "The Fountain of Industry" (Ceberus
Fountain) at the Polytechnic, Stockholm;
designer, Carl Milles.

            Architectural review 64: 93,96
            September 1928

720.5
B86
Fountains, Turkey. Constantinople
    M.I.A.
        Constantinople's drinking fountains.

            Brochure series 8: 113-116
            May 1902

710.5
C85
Fountains, Spain
    The Lion fountain, palace of the Alhambra.

            Country life (Lond.)61:563-4
            April 9, 1927

Fountains, Sweden.
    Two drinking fountains of ceramic in the large
concert hall, Sweden.

            Architectural review (Lond.) 65: 209,212
            April, 1929

705.95
J25
Fountains, Turkey. Constantinople
    Glück, Heinrich
        Türkische brunnen in Konstantinopel.

            Jahrbuch der asiatischen kunst 1: 26-30
            1924

710.5
L26
Fountains, Spain
Price, T.D.
    Moorish fountain basins in Spain and Portu-
gal. Also measured drawings.
    The tiled pools of Spain.

            Landscape architecture 19:67-68,250-58
            January; July; 1929

Fountains, Switzerland
    see also
Bern (Switz.) Spitalgasse. Brunnen

Fountains. U. S.
    see also under place, as:
Chicago, Ill. Fountain of the Great Lakes.

720.52
W52
Fountains, Spanish style
    Spanish fountain, residence of Mr. A. I.
Root, Los Angeles, Calif. Carleton M. Wins-
low, archt.

            Western arch.36: front.
            December 1927

720.52
A673
Fountains, Switzerland
    A memorial fountain at Zurich; Arnold
Hünerwadel, designer.

            Architectural review 64: 92
            September 1928

Fountains, U.S.
    see also
Boston, Mass. White memorial fountain
Brooklyn, N.Y. Bailey fountain
Chicago, Ill. Buckingham (Clarence) fountain
    "   "   Fountain of the Great Lakes
Denver, Col. Pioneer monument
    "   "   Thatcher memorial fountain
Detroit, Mich. Scott memorial fountain

                        (contd. on cd. 2)

720.52
A67
Fountains, Street
    A street fountain for Mexico City;
student work.

            Architects' journal 68: 110-111
            July 25, 1928

D10.5
K96K
Fountains, Turkey.
    Fountain details in Turkey.(Illustration)

            Kunst und kunsthandwerk 23: 41-46
            Heft 1-3, 1920

---

cd.2
Fountains, U.S.
    see also
Grinnell, Ia. Clark memorial fountain
Indianapolis, Ind. De Pew memorial fountain
Kalamazoo, Mich. Fountain of pioneers
New York (City . Pulitzer memorial fountain
    "   "   "   Straus   "
    "   "   "   Sullivan (Algernon Sydney) fountain
Washington, D.C. Columbus Memorial fountain

710.5
C85
Fountains, Sweden
Palmstierna, Margareta
    Carl Milles' garden, Lidings, Stockholm.

            Country life (Lond.) 64: 18-26
            July 7, 1928

Fountains, Turkey.
    Marmorbrunnen. Türkei, 18, Jahr;Ausstellung,
München. (Mounted photograph of fountain)

            Sarre, Friedrich Paul Theodor.
            Die Ausstellung von Meisterwerken
            Muhammedanischer Kunst in München.
            3 vols. Munich: F. Bruckmann, 1912.
            pl.2134.

Fountains. United States
    Peyton. Boswell
American sculpture for American gardens. illus.

            House and garden 35:28-29,33
            June, 1919

710.5
C85
Fountains, Sweden
Hinks, Roger
    A great Swedish sculptor: some reflections
on the work of Carl Milles.

            Country life (Lond.) 65: 281-283
            March 2, 1929

Fountains, Turkey
Glück, Heinrich
    Türkische brunnen in Konstantinopel.

            Jahrbuch der asiatischen
            kunst
            1: 26-30, pl. 15-22
            1924

720.5
P59
Fountains. U.S.
    Fountain in bronze and mosaic, by Alvin
Meyer: "Peter Pan".

            Pencil points 8: pl.10
            March 1927

Fountains, U.S.
Fountain on the estate of J. C. Baldwin

Arch. rev. 24:n.s.7:2
July, 1918

.721
T53
Fountains, U. S., Atlantic City
Atlantic City's wonder auditorium.
Lockwood, Greene & Co., designers (no illus.
except fountain).

Through the ages 7: 19-21
December 1929

Fountains. U.S., Gloucester (Mass.)
Piping boy fountain in
garden of Mrs. John Hays Hammond.
Illus. Mrs. Gail S. Corbett, Sculptor.

Architectural record 36:442-3
November, 1914

720.5
P39
Fountains. U.S.
Fountain outlet for Julius Fleischman es-
tate.

Pencil points 8: 520
August 1927

Fountains. U.S., Brooklyn
Small figure fountain in a Brooklyn theater.

Through the ages 8:33
September, 1930

720.5
AC7r
Fountains,U.S.,Lakewood(N.J.)
The fountain at Georgian Court, country
place of George G.Gould, Lakewood,N.J. Bruce
Price,archt. J.M.Rhind,sculptor.

Architectural record 13:70-75
January 1903

Fountains, U. S.
Four fountains - designs by Mario Korbel

New country life 32:54
June, 1917

Fountains, U. S., Bryn Mawr.
Details of terrace, estate of W.H. Smith,
Bryn Mawr, Pa. C.A. Platt, archt.

Architect (N.Y.). 7:34
Oct., 1926

Fountains. U.S. Long Branch (N.J.)
Fountain Made of White Glaze Terra-Cotta,
Matt Surface, in the Grounds of John A. McCall, Esq.,
Long Branch, N.J., Henry Edward Cregier, Architect.

Brickbuilder 13: pls.
N 1904

Fountains. U.S.
Illustrations of the De Pew Memorial Fountain;
The Fountain of Energy; the League of Nations
Fountain. A. Stirling Calder, sculptor.

American architect 118:732,774
Dec. 8; Dec. 15, 1920

Fountain. U.S. Camden (N.J.)
Cooper free public library, Camden, N.J.

Amer. architect 122: pl
Dec. 6, 1922

Fountains, U.S., Los Angeles
Wall fountain in patios of residence of
A.I. Root at Los Angeles, Calif. Morgan, Walls and
Clements, archts.

Country life (U.S.) 55: 52
February, 1929

Fountains, U.S.
Public

Country life 28:sup.14-16
Sept. 17, 1910

Fountains. U.S. Claymont (Del.)
Fountain in the home of John J. Raskob,
Claymont, Delaware.

Architecture. 43:pl.opp. p. 137.
May, 1921

721
T53
Fountains, U.S. Nemours (Del.)
One of the statuary groups in the duPont
gardens at Nemours, Delaware. Messena and
duPont,Inc. archts.

Through the ages 9: 2, 23-28
March 1932

Fountains. U. S.
Sculpture by Robert I. Aitken

New country life 34: 57-59
May, 1918

730.5
M81
Fountains,U.S.Denver(Colo.)
Children's fountain,Denver,Colorado.
Illustration.

Monumental news 27: 33
January 1915

Fountains, U.S., New York
Catskill water fountain, Central Park,
New York. Thomas Hastings, archt.
The completion of the Catskill water-supply
system--- plans and section

Landscape architect 8:45-46 and
plates
October, 1917

Fountains, United States
Payne, F.O.   illus.
Some noteworthy American fountains. Pulitzer
Fountain N.Y.; Fountain of Life, N.Y.;
Davidson-Probasco fountain, Cincinnati;
the Washington fountain, Philadelphia;
the Neptune fountain, Washington;
the American fountain, Hartford.

International studio 57:supp.p.71-78
January, 1916

705.1
A79
Fountains,U.S. Greystone(N.Y.)
Mount,N.M.
Fountain at Greystone - in grounds of Samuel
Untermeyer residence. Designed by famous sculptor
Walter Schott.

Arts and decoration 2:296
June 1912

Fountains, U.S. Pasadena.
Design by E.A. Batchelder for Pasadena

Western arch. 27:pl.16
Dec. 1918

Fountains. U.S., Pasadena.
For Pasadena Board of Trade – Design
by Ernest Batchelder [illustration only]

Architecture 38:pl.136
Aug., 1918

Fountains. U.S. Shrewsbury (N.J.)
Wall fountain on the estate of Ernest Fahnestock
illus. and plan   Lewis Colt Albro,
architect.

Architectural forum
26:8
January, 1917

Fountains, U.S. Washington, D.C.
Pan-American building. Wash.

Arch. rec. 34:429-435
Nov. 1913

720.5
W52

Fountains, U.S., Pasadena
Fountain- Pasadena·City Hall, Bakewell
and Broun, archts.

Western architect 38:pl. 96
June 1929

710.5
L26

Fountains   U.S.,Southhampton (L.I.)
Gardens of Charles H.Sabin,Esq.,Southamp-
ton,L.I.Marian C.Coffin, Landscape artist

Landscape architecture 13:front.
Jan. 1923

Fountains, U.S. White Plains (N.Y.).
Wall fountain of tile and marble in the Gedney
Farm Hotel, White Plains, New York. Kenneth M.
Murchison, archt.

Architecture and Building 47:88
March, 1915

720.5
P35

Fountains. U.S. Plymouth (Mass.)
Contract drawings.
McKim, Mead & White, archts.

Pencil points 6:65-68 & pl.
July 1925

Fountains, U.S. Tarrytown, N.Y.
Florentine fountain, Worcester R. Warner
Estate, Tarrytown, N.Y.

Architect (N.Y.) 11: 270
December, 1928

Four-family houses, England
Working drawings. Typical flats to be erected
by Joseph Weekes, archt. This is a double duplex
house.

Architectural journal 52:158-159
August 11, 1920

Fountains, U.S. Rhinebeck (N.Y.)
Wall fountain modelled by Henry Herring,
sculptor. Residence of Tracy Dows, Foxhollow
Farm, Rhinebeck, N.Y. Albro and Lineberg, archts.

American Country Houses of Today.
8 vols. New York: Architectural
Book Publishing Company, 1912
Plate 2

720.5
A51

Fountains, U,S., Washington, D.C.
"Neptune with trident" end of conserva-
tory, house of John R.McLean,Washington,D.C.
John Russell Pope,archt.

American architect 114: pl.opp.277
September 4,1918

4-L Ranch, Col.
A log cabin homestead, the 4-L Ranch near
Denver, Colorado. J.B. Benedict, archt. Plan.

Country life (U.S.) 58:41-44
August, 1930

A

720.5
A67b

Fountains, U.S., Rochester (N.Y.)
Wainscot and drinking fountain of Grueby
tile, Rochester (N.Y.) station. Claude Bragdon, archt. Measured drawing.

Architecture & Building 47:pl.fol.p
December 1915   454

Fountains, U.S., Washington, D.C.
In conservatory of John R. McLean

Arch. rev. 21:pl.92-93
Sept. 1916

Four Oaks (Eng.) Hill Church
Hill Church (Four Oaks) near Birmingham.
C.E. Bateman, archt.

Builder 131:780-1
November 12, 1926

Fountains, U.S., St. Louis
A wall drinking fountain in the Delmar Boulevard
station of the Wabash Railway, St. Louis, Mo.

Through the ages 7:30
October, 1929

Fountains, U.S., Washington, D.C.
Hadleigh apartment hotel, Washington, D.C.
Fountain in end of loggia. Appleton P. Clark, Jr.,
archt.

Architecture 45:pl.18
Feb. 1922

Fournes, M.

see

Vésinet (Fr.) Lanvin (Jeanne) house

720.5
M81

Fountains,U.S.San Francisco
Panama Pacific exposition,San Francisco.

Monumental news 27: 395-396
July 1915

720.5
F79

Fountains,U.S. Washington(D.C.)
Fountain Union Station Plaza;
Washington, D.C.; photograph, no plan.

Federal architect 7:122
April 1927

Fournier and Tisseyre
Hotel Reynolds, à Paris. Fournier et Tisseyre,
archts.

Encyclopedie de l'architecture;
constructions modernes. 12 vols.
Paris: Albert Morancé, 1928-39.
2:pls.65-66

720.54
A67   Fournier, Alex
    Magasins nouveaux - Magasin Pioré-Blanche
Paris. (New stores - Pioré-Blanche store,
Paris.) A. Fournier, architect.
 	
    L'architecture 36:56
    February 25, 1923
	Fournier, P.
	
	see
	
	Paris (Fr.) Ecole de Garcons
		Fowler, Lawrence Hall
		
		see also
		
		Baltimore (Md.) Black (H.C.) house

Fournier, Alex and Pierre
 	
see also
 	
Paris (Fr.) Société finaniere francaise et
coloniale. Immeuble.
Paris, Fr. La Dépréche Colonials
	Fournier, René
	
	see
	
	Besancon (Fr.) Cité universitaire
		720°5
		A673 Fowler, Lawrence Hall.
		    Three Houses at Baltimore, Md.
		
		    Arch. Rev. 11:41-4 & pl.25-28.
		    Aug. 1920.

720.54
A67   Fournier, Alex and Pierre
Cogniat, Raymond
    Salle Hoche,9,avenue Hoche - par Alex et
Pierre Fournier.
 	
    L'Architecture 43: p.387-392
    October 15,1930
	Fowey Hall, Eng.
	    Fowey Hall, Cornwall: corner in drawing room;
	dining room. Archt. not given.
	
	    Architect 67:pls.fol.p.26
	    January 31, 1902
		Fowler, Robert Ludlow
		
		see
		
		Brookville (L.I.) Redmond (G.L.) house

720.54
A67   Fournier, Alex and Pierre
    Some examples of the work of Alex and
Pierre Fournier.
 	
    L'architecture 45: 302-310
    September 15, 1932
	Fowler, Edward M.
	
	see
	
	Pasadena (Cal.) El Circulo Drive. No. 95. house
	" " Fowler (E.M.) house
		Fowler methodist church, Chicago
		
		see
		
		Chicago, Ill. Fowler methodist church

720.54
A67   Fournier, Alex and Pierre
    Two buildings of colonial inspiration.
Alex and Pierre Fournier, archts.
 	
    L'architecture 44: 261-266
    August 15, 1931
	Fowler, Ernest G.
	see
	
	Melton Mowbray (Eng.) Council School
		Fowler, Seamen & Co.
		
		see
		
		Trenton (N.J.) St. James church,rectory

Fournier, Laurence A.
    Fournier's architectural vocabulary --
it became realistic through actual building.
 	
    Northwest Arch.
    10:8,11
    No. 1, 1946
	MICROFILM
	
	Fowler, Geroge S., 1920-
	
	in SCRAPBOOK ON
	ARCHITECTURE p. 19
	(on film)
		Fowler shops, University of Kansas, Lawrence,
		Ka.
		
		see
		
		Lawrence (Ka:) University of Kansas. Fowler shops

Fournier, Maurice
    Bâtiment de la Criée aux abattoirs de la
Villette, à Paris. Plan. Maurice Fournier, archt.
 	
    Encyclopedie de l'architecture;
constructions modernes. 12 vols.
Paris: Albert Morancé, 1928-39.
7:pls. 31-32
	Fowler-Goodell-Walters, block, Chicago
	
	see
	
	Chicago (Ill.) Fowler-Goodell-Walters block
		Fox and Gale
		
		Members of firm:
		
		    Fox, Thomas A , -1946
		    Gale, Edwards J

Fox, Charles

see

London (Eng.) Lansdowne house

Fox, Charles Eli, 1870-1926
Testimonial.

Illinois society of architects
monthly bulletin
11:8
July 1926

720.5   Fox, John A
A67r   Brown, F.C.
Boston suburban architecture. Work of J.A.
Fox.

Architectural record 21:251
April 1907

Fox, Charles Eli, 1870-1926

see also

Marshall and Fox

Fox, Charles James
The decorative qualities of tiling.
Illus.

West. Arch.
11: 5-7
Ja 1908

720.5   Fox, John A.
B84   House located in a Boston suburb. John
A.Fox,archt. Plans.

Brickbuilder 11: 3pls.fol.p.22
January 1902

Fox, Charles Eli   1870-1926
Brief biography.

Herringshaw, Clark J. Herringshaw's
city blue book of current biography.
Chicago: American publisher's
Association, 1915

Fox, Charles James
Durability of baked clay tile.

Inland Arch.
51: 88-9
Jan. 1908

720.5   Fox Lake (Ill.) Lomax (George) cottage
I56   Cottage of George Lomax in Fox Lake.
George H. Boise, archt.

Inland archt & news rec 17:97
March 1891

720.5   Fox, Charles Eli   1870-1926
W52   McLean, R.C.
Charles E. Fox, obituary.

Western architect. 35:141
November 1926

Fox, Charles James.
Unnatural standards of tiling.

Inland Arch.
50: 32
Sept. 1907

720.5   Fox Lake (Wis.) Rawson (Mr.) house
I56   Residence of Mr. Rawson in Fox Lake,
Wisconsin. W. H. Drake, archt.

Inland archt & news rec 20:29
October 1892

Fox, Charles E.
The effects of fire upon modern fireproof
bldgs.

West. Archt.
31: 62-6
May, 1922

Fox, Jenney and Gale

see also

Weston (Mass.) Public library

Fox Point (Wis.) Beech hill cottage
Beech hill cottage, Fox Point, Wisconsin.
Elmer Grey, archt.

Inl archt 34:pls.fol.p.f4
O 1899

Fox, Charles Eli, 1870-1926
Obituary.

Illinois society of architects
monthly bulletin
11:7
Dec. 1926

Fox, Jenney and Gale

Members of firm:

Fox, Thomas A   , -1946
Jenney, Alexander S
Gale, Edwards J

Fox Point (Wisc.) Beech Hill Cottage
Summer residence for Elmer Grey.
Sketch from the lake and from the drive.
Elmer Grey, Archt.

Inland archt.
vol.32, No.4,pl.fol.p. 40
Nov. 1898

---

microfilm
Fox, Charles Eli, architect
Chicago, Ill. Auditorium building trial
Testimony at Auditorium trial, Chicago, 1925:
testimony of Lawrence G. Parker, Louis E. Ritter,
Ernest Robert Graham, Charles Eli Fox, Paul F. P.
Mueller, Henry J. Burt, Frederick J. Thielbar,
Edward Anderson Renwick, Bernard H. Lichter,
Theodore E. Wade.

Roll 6, frames 1-174 (after frame 232)

Fox, John   A.

see also

Tewksbury (Mass.) Female asylum
"   "   State hospital. Men's hospital

Fox Point, (WI) Grey (Elmer) Summer Home
Entrance gateway.
Elmer Grey, Arch.

Inland Arch.
37: No.1,pl.fol.p. 8
Feb. 1901

Fox Point, (WI) Mariner (Wm.) Summer Home.
Two exteriors plus view of dining room.
Elmer Grey, Arch.

Inland Arch.
37: No. 1, pls. fol.p.8
Feb. 1901

720.5
A67r

"Foxhollow Farm," N.Y.
An American manor house: "Foxhollow farm"
a country place of Tracy Dows,Rhinebeck,N.Y.
Albro and Lindeberg,archts.

A   Architectural record 30:310-325
October 1911

Fraenkel and Schmidt
see also

Chicago, Il., Bennett (Frank I.) House
Peru Il., Church

720.5
A67f

Fox Point (Wis.) Schwemer (E.C.) house
House for Evan C. Schwemer, Fox Point,Wis.
Grassold and Johnson, archts. Plan.

A   Architectural forum 65: 472-473
November 1936

710.5
C855

"Foxhollow Farm," N.Y.
Saylor H.H.
Foxhollow Farm, at Rhinebeck, New York:
One of the twelve best country houses in America.
H.T. Lindeberg, designer; Albro and Lindeberg,
archts.

Country life (U.S.) 29: 25-28
F '16

Fraenkel and Schmidt
Two houses. Fraenkel and Schmidt, archts.

A   Inland architect 29: pl.fol.p.50
June, 1897

Fox Point, (WI) Underwood (Herbert) Summer House.
Two views
Elmer Grey, Arch.

Inland Arch.
37: No.2, pl.fol.p. 16
March 1901

"Foxhollow Farm," N.Y.
A house for Tracy Dows. Albro and Lindeberg,
archts. Plans.

American architect 95:112,2 pls.fol.p.120
April 7, 1909

Fränkel, Rudolph
see also

Bucharest (Rum.) Scala theater and cinema
Bucharest, Rum. Textile factory
Berlin, Ger. Lichtburg kino

Fox Ridge State Park (Ill.)
Frison, Dr. Theodore H.
Survey scientists study fish in 18 acre
"laboratory: Fox Ridge Park Lake experimental area.

Illinois public works f: 16-20
No. 3 Winter 1944

Foyers
see also
Halls

Fränkel, Rudolf
Apartment houses and residences in the modern
style. Rudolf Frankel, archt.

Wasmuths 11: 250-7
Heft 6, 1927

Fox, Thomas J.   -1946
Member of firms:
Fox, Jenney and Gale
Fox and Gale

Foyers
Littman, Max. Die Königlichen
hoftheater in Stuttgart. Darmstadt:
Koch, 1912. p.44,45,48

720.53
F31

Fränkel,Rudolf
Doppelhaus-kolonie in der gartenstadt
Frohnau bei Berlin. (Double house colony in
the garden city, Frohnau,near berlin.) Rudolf
Fränkel,archt.

Wasmuths monatshefte 14: 84
February 1930

Foxborough (Mass.) House (project)
House in Foxborough Massachusetts.
Harry Seidler, archt.; R.D. Thompson, associate.
plan

Royal arch inst of Can jour 25:117-120
Ap '48

720.6
B38

Foyers
Beaux-arts institute of design, competition: "A residential foyer hall." Awards.

B.A.I.D. 2: 5
December 1925

720.54
A67au

Fränkel, Rudolph
Habitation en Roumanie. R. Fraenkel,
archt. [plans].

L'Arch d'aujourd'hui 9:30-41
F '38

Foxcote (Eng.) Church
A Georgian village church. Foxcote Church,
Somerset (1721).

Country life (London) 88:241
September 14, 1940

720.6
B38

Foyers
The foyer of an opera house: Beaux-arts
institute of design competition.

B.A.I.D. 4: 4-6
October 1928

720.53
W31

Fränkel,Rudolf
Ein neues altersheim für Berlin. (A new
home for the aged,Berlin.) Rudolf Fränkel,
archt. Plans.

Wasmuths monatshefte 14: 459
October 1930

720.33
MC8
Frankel, Rudolf
New work by Rudolf Frankel, Berlin.

Moderne bauformen 27: 249-260
Heft 7, July 1928

Fraenkel, Theodore Oscar
Rambling sketches (illus.)

Inland Architect
24: 14-16
Sept, 1894

720.5
A67
Framingham center(Mass.)First Baptist church
First Baptist church, Framingham Center,
Mass. Built in 1826. Photographs and measured
drawings.

Architectural review 23n.s.6:spec.pls.41-
May 1918   45

Fraenkel, T. O.[architect]

drawings:(1) Windmill
         (2) Geo. Washington chair
         (3) Cabinet

Inland Arch
Vol. 19: pl.
fol. p. 54
May 1892

720.6
C53
Fraenkel, Theodore Oscar, 1857-
Sketch for an inn by T.O. Fraenkel, del.
Calumet club, Chas. S. Frost, archt.;
T. O. Fraenkel, del. No plan.
Sketch by T.O. Fraenkel

Chicago architectural club 7:10,12,18
1894

720.5
A67
Framingham (Mass.). Dennison (Henry C.)house
Charles M. Baker, archt. Plan, elevation.

Arch rev 20 (n.s.?): pls LXVIII-LXXI
N '15   fol 104
D '15   pls. XLV-XLVI
                             fol 116

Fraenkel, Theodore Oscar, 1857-

see also

Fraenkel and Schmidt

Fraenkel, Theodore O. and Allyn A. Packard
Form Partnership.

Inland Architect
31: 19
Mar, 1898

720.5
A67f
Framingham, Mass. high school
Framingham high school, Framingham ,Mass.
Chas. M. Baker, archt. Plan.

Arch forum 26: pl 58
Ap 1917

Fraenkel, Theodore Oscar   1857-
Houses in New Orleans, Mt. Vernon,
Alexandria and Mackinac.

Inland Archt.
vol.24,No.2,pl.fol.p. 20
Sept, 1894

Fragelli, Marcello
Edificio Gragoatá, Copacabana [plans]
Mauricio Sued & Marcello Fragelli, archts.

Módulo
vol. 5: 14-17, Ap 1961

Framingham (Mass.) High School
Framingham High School, South Framingham, Mass.
C. M. Baker, archt. Plan.

Architectural review 14: pls. 17-19
April, 1907

Fraenkel, Theodore Oscar, 1857-
. . Designs for mantels in Chicago residences.
L.B.Dixon, architect. T.O. Faenkel, delineator.
[illus.]

Building budget
II: 34 and plate
March 1886

Fragelli, Marcello
House near Rio de Janeiro [plan] Marcello
Fragelli, archt.

Arch't'l design
32: 156, Mr 1962

720.5
A67
Framingham (Mass.) house
House in Framingham,Mass. R.E.Sawyer,
archt. Plan.

A   Architectural review 14:33-61
        March 1907

---

ffo
720.6
C53
Fraenkel, Theodore Oscar, 1857-
Mountain home. Fraenkel and Schmidt.archts
Design for fire place for a wealthy club.
T.O.Fraenkel, archt. Plan.

Chicago architectural club 7: 55,56
Annual exhibit 1894

Fraggianni palace. barletta

See

Barletta. Palazzo Fraggianni.

720.5
C855
Framingham (Mass.) Raceland
"Raceland", Framingham, Massachusetts.

Country life (U.S.)66: 88-73
August 1934

---

ffo
720.6
C53
Fraenkel, Theodore Oscar, 1857-
Pen sketches by T. O. Fraenkel.

Chicago architectural club, annual
1894   exhibit 7:41

Frame houses

see

Wooden houses

Framlingham (Eng.) castle
Reynolds, P. K. Baillie
Framlingham castle [plan]

Archaeo jrl 108:181-183
1951

Frampton Court (Eng.) Garden House
    The garden house at Frampton Court, in the
Gothic manner.

                    Country life (Lond.) 62: 509
                    October 8, 1927

France. Architecture

            see also

    Brickwork, France
    Cathedrals, France
    Castles, France
    Churches, France
    Domestic architecture, France
    Palaces, France

        (see next card)

France. Architecture
    Francis I period.

                Architecture francaise 4: pls. 92,
                            102, 105

                [1939?]

Frampton, George J.

        see also

London (Eng.) "Lloyd's Register"

France. Architecture (cont.)

        see also styles of architecture, e.g.
    Gothic architecture, France
    Renaissance architecture, France
    Romanesque architecture, France
    French Colonial architecture
        also architecture of districts and cities
                            of France, e.g.

    Brittany,   Architecture
    Paris, Fr. Architecture

France. Architecture.
    Henry IV period

            Rouyer, Eugène. L'art architectural
            en France. 2 vols. Paris: J. Baudry,
            1866-67. v.2:13-16 Plates 12-14

France. Air views
    Paris, La cité.
    Royan.

                L'Architecture. 33:482-7 and pl. 22-3.
                August 15, 1920.

France. Architecture

            Bancroft, Hubert Howe.
            Achievements of civilization....
            10 vols. New York: The Bancroft
            Company, Publishers. 1896.
            4: Chapter 10

720.6   France. Architecture
AC7   A letter from France

                Architecture 16:509-514
                Aug. 1923

France. Air views
    Parker, L. H.
From farm to table. Countryside views.

                House and Garden. 38:29.
                Oct. 1920.

720.5   France. Architecture
A67r   Allain, Alb.
            The architectural design as it is in France.
        Plans. Apartment house on the corner of Champs
        Elysées and Rue de Berri. Plan and other examples.

            Architectural record 11: 39-41
            January 1902

France. Architecture
    Bragdon, Claude
    "Made in France" architecture

                Arch rec
                16: no. 6
                D 1904

France. Antiquities
    Ancient cities of Southern France

            Architect (London)
            110: 104-105 Aug 17 1923
                135-139 Aug 31, 1923
                177-181 Sept 21, 1923
                246-247 Oct 19, 1923
                283-287 Nov 2, 1923

France. Architecture
    Architectural tour in central France and
Burgundy

                RIBA jour
                21: 557-72
                Je 27, 1914

France. Architecture
    Giedion, Sigfried
Notes on the situation of French architecture

            Der cicerone 19:
                15-24; Ja. 1927
                174-89; Mr. "
                310-17; My. "

France. Architects

            Enlart, Camille. Manuel d'archéologie
            Francaise....3 vols. Paris:A. picard
            et Fils, 1904, 1919, 1920.
            v.2, p. 740-750, 791-6.

France, Architecture
    Brown, Frank Chouteau. A journey in search of
the picturesque.

                Arch rev 10:
                    13-16; F. 1903
                    25-27; Mr. "
                    37-41; Ap. "

720.5   France. Architecture
P59   Zigrosser, Carl
        "Picturesque architecture in France". A
        selection of chromolithographs by Thomas Shotter
        Boys, an English craftsman of the early nine-
        teenth century.

                Pencil points 7: 394-406
                July 1926

France. Architects
    French architects in Sweden

            L'Architecture 26 :   309-313
            Sept. 20, 1913

France. Architecture.
    Development of Architecture in France.
By S. E. Desjardins.

            Western archt. 11: 3-5
            Ja 1908

France. Architecture
    Géraud, Léon
    La section de la France d'Outre-mer à
1'Ile des Cygnes

            L'Architecture 50: 89-98
            Mr 15, 1937

720.5
A67f
France. Architecture
Some alluring cities of old France

Architectural forum 39:1-6
July 1923

France. Architecture. 18th cent.
18th century architecture

RIBA jour
21: 145-158
Ja 17, 1914

RYERSON LIBRARY
France. Architecture. 20th century
Dormoy, Marie
L'architecture francaise moderne.

L'amour de l'art 6:110-124
Mr 1925

705.4
B45
France. Architecture
Lemonnier, Henry
The variations of the Royal academy of architecture: the Gothic and the Utopia of Soufflot

Revue de l'art 51:173-178
March, 1927

720.5
A67r
France. Architecture. 18th century
Sturgis, Russell
Parisian doorways of the eighteenth century.

Architectural record 19:123-134
February 1906

RYERSON LIBRARY
705.4
A78v
France. Architecture. 20th century
Zahar, Marcel
L'architecture nouvelle. Le cinema des
Miracles. L'hotel de M.Ruhlmann.

L'art vivant : 29,31-32
February 1931

France. Architecture
Vingt ans Après

Journal of A.I. of A. 10:276-82
Sept., 1922

MICROFILM
France. Architecture. 18th century.
Exhibitions. 1968.
Visionary architects [illus., p. 134]

Scrapbook of art and artists
of Chicago and vicinity
pp. 131, 134, 146
1968

720.54
A67
France. Architecture. Twentieth century
Badovici, Jean
Entretiens sur L'Architecture Vivante. (Discourse on Contemporary Architecture.) In France
and Germany.

L'Architecture Vivante: p. 11-20
1923

720.54
A87
France. Architects. 14th century
Mayeus, A.
Les maitres de l'oeuvre au XIV me siècle.

L'Architecture 34: 1-2
December 10, 1921

720.5
A67r
France. Architecture. 19th century
Adshead, S.D.
A comparison of modern American architecture
with that of European cities - following the
renaissance.

Architectural record 29:113-125
February 1911

RYERSON LIBRARY
705.4
A78
France. Architecture. 20th century
Tisserand, Ernest
L'evolution de l'architecture moderne.

Art et les artistes n.s.15:238-245
April, 1927

France. Architecture. 15 cent.
An example of French civil architecture of
the XV century. The Lucy Maud Buckingham memorial.

AIC Bulletin
Vol.18: 86 O 1924

720.5
A67r
France. Architecture. 19th century (Late)
Hamlin, A.D.F.
Modern French architecture - work of the
following architects: Davioud;E.Train;Vaudremer;
Visconti and Lefuel;Ballu and Déporthes.

Architectural record 10:150-177
October 1900

France. Architecture. 20th Century
Pietsch, Theodore Wells Modern
French Architecture. Illus.

Inland Architect
34: 45-6
Jan. 1900

France. Architecture. 18th cent.
Moulin, Monique
L'architecture civile et militaire au
XVIIIe siècle en Aunis et Saintonge.

Information d'histoire
de l'art
An. 16: 157-161
S-O 1971

France. Architecture. 19th and 20th cent.
du Colombier, Pierre
Construction et architecture.

L'amour de l'art
10: 53-58
F 1929

720.53
W31
France. Architecture 20th century
Juge baukunst in Frankreich (The city of
the future) Plans and illustratins.

Wasmuths, (heft 9-10) 8: 316-326
1924

France. Architecture. 18th century
Kaufmann, Emil
Architectural designs of the time of the
French revolution

Zeitschrift für
bildende kunst 63:38-46
May 1929

France. Architecture. 20th cent.

R.I.B.A. jour. 20: 317-345
Mar. 29, 1913

Ryerson
France. Architecture. 20th century
Modern architecture and the new materials

Art et décor: 85-96
Jl - Ag 1919

France. Architecture. 20th century
Blake, Vernon
Modern architecture in the Paris schools

Drawing and design 2:174-177
June, 1927

France. Architecture. 20th century
Davis, A. J.
Survey

Architect
101: 322-27, 337-340
My 16 and 23, 1919

France. Architecture. Exhibitions 1914
Lyon-Paris exhibition

L'architecture 27:
177-78; My 30, 1914
195-96; Je 13, "
253-54; Jl 25, "

France. Architecture. 20th century
Billerey, Fernand
Modern French architecture

Archts and bldrs jour.
37: no. 950
Mr 26, 1931

France. Architecture. 20th century
Jirmounsky, Malkiel
Tendances de l'architecture Francaise contemporaine [illus]

L'amour de l'art 9:361-371
O 1928

France. Architecture. Exhibitions 1914

L'Architecture 27: 245-247.
July 18, 1914

720.6
R88
France. Architecture. 20th century
Robertson, Howard
Modern French architecture.

R.I.B.A. 34:323-33
March 19, 1927

705
N48
France. Architecture, 20th Century. Exhibitions
Une exposition d'architecture française contemporaine.

Das Werk 27:226-235
Ag '40

720.54
A67
France. Architecture. Exhibitions.
1921.

L'Architecture 34: 1-12 & pl. 1-32.
May 25, 1921.

720.6
R88
France. Architecture. 20th century
Cart de Lafontaine, H.P.
Modern tendencies in French architecture.

R.I.B.A. 33: 67-72
December 5, 1925

France. Architecture. 1912
La France Monumentale en 1912.

Art decoratif 27: 101-116
Feb. 20, 1912.

720.54
A67
France. Architecture. Exhibitions. 1923
Verrier, Jean
L'Exposition de dessins d'architecture au Pavillon de Marsan. (The exposition of architectural designs at the Pavillon de Marsan.) [Musée des Arts Decoratifs. Plans. Original designs by French architects: Mansart, Vauban, Gabriel, Rousseau, Mique and others.]

L'architecture 36:1-12
January 10, 1923

705.1
A79
France. Architecture. 20th century
Modernistic architecture in mediaeval Riviera

Arts and decoration 29:67
October 1928

Ryerson
France. Architecture. Arabian influence
Enlart, C.
The church of West in Bologne and its Arabian doorway.

Gaz des beaux-arts
per 5, v. 16: 1-11
Jl - Ag 1927

France. Architecture. Exhibitions. 1933
Exposition d'architecture française - organisée par la Société des Architectes diplômés par le gouvernement sous le patronage de l'Association française d'expansion et d'echanges artistiques. (The exposition of French architecture arranged by the Société des architectes Diplomés.)

L'architecture 46:410-464
December 15, 1933

France. Architecture. 20th century.
Où en est l'architecture française?

L'Oeil
#75: 38-47, Mr 1961

France. Architecture Empire period
Street decorations for peace: a French example of the Empire period.

Architects journal 49:pl.preceding
April 2, 1919   p. 212

France. Architecture. Exhibitions. 1933
Hautecoeur, Louis
Exposition d'architecture française organisée par la Société des Architectes diplômés par le Gouvernement sous le patronage de l'Association française d'expansion et d'échanges artistiques. (Exposition of French architecture organized by the Société des Architectes diplômés par le Gouvernement under the patronage of the Association française d'expansion et d'échanges artistiques.)

L'Architecture 46: 411-464
December 15, 1933

720.52
A67c
France. Architecture. 20th century
Goodhart-Rendel, H.S.
Recent architecture in France.

Architect\Lond.)150:128-134
April 30,1937

France. Architecture. Exhibitions

see also

Paris (Fr.) Salons

705.985
C98
France. Architecture. Exhibitions 1946.
Velarde, Hector
A proposito de la exposicion del libro Frances y de la arquitectura en Francia.

Cultura peruana 6: 16-21
S '46

France. Architecture. Francis I period

Guérinet, Armand, ed. L'architecture
en France: Monuments historiques.
12 vols. Berlin and New York: Bruno
Hessling, n.d.

France. Architecture. Mediaeval.
Fray, François
L'habitat urbain médiéval et de type
médiéval à Bergerac, Eymet, Issigeac et
Sainte-Foy-la-Grande. [illus.]

Information d'histoire
de l'art
An. 16: 182-168
S-O 1971

Francelli, Luca, 1430-1495
Carpeggiani, Paolo
Luca Fancelli architetto civile nel con-
tado Gonzaghesco. [illus.]

Arte lombarda
Anno 16: 37-44
1971

France. Architecture. Francis I period.

Pfnor, Rodolphe. Monographie du
Chateau d'Anet....Paris:L'auteur,
1867. pl. 17-19, 72 - 108.

France. Architecture. Spanish influence
Bevan, Bernard
Spanish baroque in northern France

Apollo 5:144-148
April, 1927

---

fl. 1504
Francesco di Castello, called il Tifernate
Wittgens, Fernanda
Francesco di Castello, called il Tifernate

La bibliofilia 39:273-282
July-August 1937

France. Architecture. Francis I period.
Parmentier, F.
Style of Francis I.

Inland architect
v. 14 no. 2: 20-22
S 1889

France. Architecture. Study and teaching
Reed, Frederick
Suggestions for architectural study in
western France. 2 pts.

Brickbuilder
17:279-83
D 1908
18:30-34
F 1909

Francesco di Giorgio Martini 1439-1502
Palazzo Piccolomini, Pienza. Bernardo
Rossellino and Francesco di Giorgio, archts.
Measured drawings.
Palazzo Piccolomini, Siena. Francesco di
Giorgio, archts.
Palazzo Nerucci, Sienna. Bernardo Rosellino
and Francesco di Giorgio, archts.

Italian Renaissance: Sixty measured
drawings with details. 3 vols. New
York: The Architectural Book Publishing
Company, n.d. 2:pl.40-44;3:pl.53;
2:pl. 57

France. Architecture. Louis XIV period.
In the house of the interpreter. (Louis XIV
and Colbert.)

Simpson, John W. Essays and Memorials.
London: Architectural Press, 1923.
p. 3-33.

France. Brittany. Churches
F.C. Eden, Some Breton Chapels

Builder 87: 172-75
Ag 13, 1904

Francesco di Giorgio Martini 1439-1502
Palazzo Piccolomini in Siena. Francesco
di Giorgio, archt. Measured drawing.

Palast Architektur. 6 vols in 11 bks.
Berlin: E. Wasmuth, 1886-1911
2:pt.1:2-3,pl.15

France. Architecture. Mediaeval
Hastings, C.S.
Architectural refinements in Mediaeval churches
computed: Illus. of nave of the church of
St. Ouen Rouen; nave of Reims Cathedral.

Architectural record 26: 132-139
August, 1909

France. Brittany. Churches
F.C. Eden, Some Breton Chapels.

Inland archt 44: 10-12
S 1904

Francesco di Giorgio Martini 1439-1502
Palazzo Nerucci in Siena. Bernardo Rossellino
und Francesco di Giorgio, archt. Sketch only.

Palast Architektur. 6 vols in 11 bks.
Berlin: E. Wasmuth, 1886-1911
2:pt.1:3,pl.17

720.52
A67c
France. Architecture. Medieval
Kest, G.H.
A comparison between the medieval architec-
ture of England and France.

Architect and contract rev. 75:
117-15, 173-71
F 16, 57, '06

France. Sketch of Building
Facade by A.Rouleau.

Inalnd archt
vol.27, No. 4 pl.
fol. p. 40
May 1896

Francesco di Giorgio Martini 1439-1502
Sgraffito decoration, Pienza. Bernardo
Rossellino und Francesco di Giorgio, archt.

Palast Architektur. 6 vols in 11 bks.
Berlin: E. Wasmuth, 1886-1911
2:pt.1:11
pt.2:pl.63

France. Architecture. Mediaeval
Weise, Georg
Deutschland und Frankreich in spiegel ihrer
mittelalterlichen baukunst.

Christliche kunst 23: 269-291
July 1933

France. Sketch of Building Facade
(unidentified).

Inalnd Archt.
vol. 27, No. 4,pl.
fol. p. 40
May 1896

Francis I period

see

France. Architecture. Francis I period

720.52
B93

Francis, C. H.
Design for a golf club-house by C.H.
Francis, Welsh School of Architecture, the
Technical College, Cardiff.

Builder 145: 220,228
August 11,1933

Francisco and Jacobus

see also

Southold (L.I.) Southold Savings Bank
New York (N.Y.) Colonnade Building

Franco, Raul Macias

see

Macias Franco, Raul

Francis, E. C.

see

Fast Cliff

MICROFILM
Francisco and Jacobus
Proposed Graphic Arts Center in New York, N. Y.

in SCRAPBOOK ON
ARCHITECTURE p. 538
(on film)

Franco-British Exposition
(Architecture)

Amer archt & bldg news. 94:65-71
Aug. 26, 1908

Francis, Eric

see also

West Monkton (Eng.) house

Francke, Paul   1537 or 8-1615
Der Universität zu Helmstedt.
Marienkirche zu Wolfenbrüttel.

Fritsch, K.E.O., ed. Denkmaeler
deutscher renaissance. 4 vols.
Berlin: E. Wasmuth, 1891.
vol. 1:45-46, pl. 50
vol. 3:pl.19-20
vol. 4:pls. 79-80

Franco-British union of architects.
Franco-British union of architects.

Arch Rev
50: 113-7
N 1921

710.5
C85

Francis, Eric
Phillips, Randal
Residence in West Monhton, Somerset, from
designs of Eric Francis. Plan.

Country life(Lond)77:436-437
April 27,1935

Franco, Luis Roberto Carvalho
Centro comercial en el Brooklin (Sao Paulo,
Brasil) Rino Levi, Roberto Cerqueira Cesar, and
Luis Roberto Carvalho Franco, archts.

Arquitectura Mexico
No. 54:107-110
Je 1956

Franco-British Union of Architects. Meeting. 1925
Franco-British union of Architects

Builder 128:862-863
June 5, 1925

Francis, G.   E.

see

Khartoum (Sudan) Grand hotel

Franco, Luis Roberto Carvalho
4 projetas de garages coletivas [plans
& sections] Rino Levi, Roberto Cerqueira Cesar
& Luis Roberto Carvalho Franco, archts.

Habitat
7:19-23 Jan 1957

Franco-British Union of Architects. Meeting. 1928
Louvet, A.
VIII assemblée générale de l'Union Franco-
Britannique des architectes. (8th general assembly
of the Franco-British union of architects.)

L'Architecture 41:p.241-246
August 15, 1928

Francis, H   M
Machine shop at Winchendon. Mr. H.M.Francis,
archt.

Amer arch
1: pl.fol.p.76
Mr 4, 1876

Franco, Luis Roberto Carvalho
Instalacion industrial en Sao Paulo, Brasil.
Rino Levi, Roberto Cerqueira César & L. R.
Carvalho Franco, archts.

Arquitectura Mexico
vol 18: 208-210, D 1961

Franco-British Union of Architects. Meeting. 1930
Louvet, A.
Réunion de l'Union Franco-Britannique des
Architectes à Oxford (Reunion of the Franco-British
Union of Architects at Oxford). Plans.

L'Architecture 43: p.451-455
December 15, 1930

Francis Parker school, Chicago

see

Chicago, Ill. Francis A. Parker school

Franco, Luis Roberto Carvalho
Tecelagem Paraiba S. A. Fazenda Monte
Alegre, São José dos Campos [plans & sections]
Rino Levi, Roberto Cerqueira Cesar & Luis
Carvalho Franco, archts.

Habitat 7:60-3
D 1956

Franco-British Union of Architects. Meeting. 1931
The eleventh annual general meeting of the
Franco-British Union of Architects at Paris.

Builder 141: 510
September 25, 1931

720.52
B93   Franco-British Union of Architects. Meeting.
       Cart de Lafontaine,H.P.L.   1933
       Thirteenth annual meeting,Caen.

                Builder 144: 906, 907
                June 27,1933

       Franke, Edward   , house. Mason City, Ia.

       see

       Mason City, Ia. Franke, Edward, house.

720.5
A67   Frankfort (Ky.) Berry (G.F.) house
       House of George F.Berry,Frankfort,Kentucky
       W.J.Dodd and Arthur Cobb,archts. Plans.

                Architectural review 11: 86-87
                January 1904

       A

       Franconia,Ger. Architecture

       see

       Churches. Germany. Franconia

       Franke, J. B., house, Fort Wayne, Ind.

       see

       Fort Wayne, Ind. Franke, J. B., house

       Frankfort (Ky) Berry (Geo F.) res.
       McDonald & Dodd archts.

                West. Arch.
                16: pls. fol. p. 88
                Ag 1910

720.54
A67   Francotte, Oscar
       Ollivier, Felix
           The new city hall of Louvain. Oscar
       Francotte, archt.   Plan.

                L'architecture 44: 423-424
                November 15, 1931

       Frankel, Ross, house
           For Rip Van Winkle's country. [plan] Ross
       Frankel, inc., archt.

                Interiors 106, pt. 2: 116
                Ja 1947

       Frankfort (Ky.) Liberty Hall
           Liberty Hall, Frankfort, Kentucky.

                Architectural forum 61: 205-209
                September, 1934

       Frank, Josef

       see also

       Exhibitions, Germany. Stuttgart

       Frankenmarkt, Aus. Pfarrkirche
       Wibiral, Norbert
           Wandmalereien der reformationzeit im Chor
       der Pfarrkirche von Frankenmarkt [illus]

                Österreichische Zeitschrift
                für Kunst und Denkmalpflege
                16, heft 4: 128-140, 1962

       Frankfort (Ky.) Kentucky State Capitol
           Stairway in the Kentucky State Capitol at
       Frankfort; Frank M. Andrews, archt.

                Through the ages 6: front
       A   October, 1928

720.54
A67v   Frank, Josef
           Habitations à bon marché de la ville de
       Vienne, Autriche, 1924-25. (Inexpensive
       residences in the city of Vienna, Austria,
       1924-25.) Anton brenner, archt. Joseph
       Frank, archt.

                L'Architecture vivante :pl.42
                Winter 1926

       Frankford (Pa.). St. Mark's episcopal church

       see

       Philadelphia (Pa.). St. Mark's episcopal church

       Frankfort on the Main (Ger.),

       see

       Frankfurt-am-Main (Ger.)

720.53
M68   Frank,Josef
           Josef Frank. (Works by Dr.Josef Frank.)
       Community apartment house in Vienna; resi-
       dences in Austria. Plans,interiors.

                Moderne bauformen 26: 170-185
                May 1927

720.52
A673   Frankfort (Eng.). Cathedral. Door
           Doorway, Frankfort cathedral

                Arch rev (Lond.) 35: 60
                Mr '14

       Frankfurt-am-Main, Ger
       Knappstein, K. H.
           Alt-Frankfurt neu

                Die neue saat 1:121-5
                Ap 1938

720.53
M68   Frank, Josef,
       Eisler, Max
           New buildings and interiors by Josef Frank.

                Moderne bauformen 29: 430-431,436, col.pl.
                October 1930   448, adv.212

       Frankfort (Ind.) Carnegie Library
           Carnegie Library, Frankfort, Ind.
       T. Johnson and Company, archts.

                West. Arch.
                15: pls. fol. p. 12
                Ja 1910

711
S77   Frankfurt-am-Main. (Ger.)
       Adler,Leo
           Frankfurter uferstrassen. (Frankfurt river-
       front streets: lower part of the Main Wharf.)

                Städtebau 22: 192-194
                December 1927

Frankfurt-am-Main. Ger. Konrad Haenisch School
The Konrad Haenisch School at Frankfurt.
Martin Elsaesser, archt.

Architects' journal 77: 192,198-202
February 8, 1933

Frankfurt-am-Main (Ger.) Römer
Entrance to imperial staircase in the Römer
(town-hall)

Amer archt and bldg news
53:80, pl fol 4 in supp
S 5, 1896

Frankfurt-am-Main. Town hall
see
Frankfurt-am-Main (Ger.) Römer

Frankfurt-am-Main (Ger.) Konzerthaus
Ochs, K.W.
Ein konzerthaus für Frankfurt am Main. (A concert
building for Frankfurt on Main.) Ochs, K.W.,
archt. Plans.

Wasmuths monatshefte 15: 71-74
February, 1931

RYERSON LIBRARY
705.3 Frankfurt-am - Main. Sankt Bonifatius
C55 Lill, Georg
Neue deutsche kirchenbaukunst; St.Bonifatius-
kirche, Frankfurt A.Main. Martin Weber. Plan.

A Die Christliche kunst 24: front,564-69
June - July 1928

720.53 Frankfurt-am-Main. Ger. Union-druckerei
B35 Verwaltungsgebäude der Union-Druckerei
Frankfurt A.M. (Administration building of
the Union Printing Office in Frankfurt a.
Main.) Lehr,archt. Plans.

Der Baumeister 28: 268-274
July 1930

Frankfurt-am-Main (Ger.) Musikheim
Schmidt, Paul
Das Frankfurter musikheim. (The Frankfurt school of
Music.) Lecture halls; class rooms; reading rooms;
etc. Otto Bartning, archt. Plans.

Wasmuths monatshefte 13: 502-504
December, 1929

Ryerson
D10.5 Frankfort - am - Main.Sankt Bonifatius
D32 Riedrich,Otto
Der neue kirchenbau: St.Banifatiuskirche,
Frankfurt a M.in. Martin Weber. archt.

A Dekorative kunst 32: 227-229
July 1929

720.53 Frankfurt-am-Main, Ger. Volksschule
W31 Volksschule in Niederursel,Frankfurt a
Main. (Public school at Niederursel,Frankfurt
on-Main.) Franz Schuster,archt. Plans.

Wasmuths monatshefte 13: 165
April 1929

Frankfurt-am-Main (Ger.) Ortskrankenkasse
Hegemann, Werner
Die ortskrankenkasse in Frankfurt am Main.
(The city hospital in Frankfurt on Main.) Ernst
Balser, archt. Plans.

Wasmuths monatshefte 15: 49-58
February, 1931

720.53 Frankfurt-am-Main. Ger. Schools
B35 Schütte,W
Grundsätzliches über neue volksschulen.
(Fundamentals about new public schools.) Special
number.
School in Frankfurt a.Main. Martin Elsässer,
Walther Körte,archts. Plans. Interiors.

Der Baumeister 28: 461-476,pl.66-69
December 1930

Ryerson Frankfort-am-Main, Ger. Volkstimme gebäude
Giedion, S.
Batiment pour les services administratifs
du journal "Volkstimme" de Frankfort. J. W.
Lehr, archt.

Cahiers d'art
5:45-51
No. 1, 1930

Frankfurt-am-Main (Ger.) Planning
Frankfurt am Main.

Der Stadtebau 24: 37-45
Heft 2, 1929

Frankfurt-am-Main. (Ger.) Stadion
Robertson, Howard and Yerbury, F.R.
The Frankfurt Stadium.

Architect (Lond.) 119:773-775;805-810
May 25; June 1, 1928

---

711 Frankfurt-an-der Oder.
S77 Wendt,Viktor
Die drei gesichter der stadt Frankfurt an der
Oder. (The three faces of the city,Frankfurt on
Oder.)

Städtebau 22: 195-196
December 1927

Frankfurt-am-Main (Ger.) Planning
Adler, Leo
Frankfurter uferstrassen. (Frankfurt riverfront
streets: lower part of the Main Wharf.)

Städtebau 22: 192-194
December, 1927

Frankfurt-am-Main (Ger.) Stadion
Stadium, Frankfort

Architects' journal 67:545
April 18, 1928

720.53 Frankfurt-am-der-Oder. Music School
W31 Schmidt,Paul
Das Frankfurter musikheim. (The Frankfurt
school of music.) Lecture halls; class rooms;
reading rooms; etc. Otto Bartning,archt. Plans.

Wasmuths monatshefte 13: 502-504
December 1929

A

Frankfurt-am-Main. Rathaus
The Town Hall, Frankfort. Herr Van Hoven
and Herr Neher, joint archts.

The Builder 86: 111 pl.fol.p.124
January 30, 1904

Frankfurt-am-Main (Ger.) Stadion
Stadium, Frankfort

R.I.B.A. 35: 441-2
My 12, '28

Frankfurt-an-der-Oder (Ger.) Planning
Wendt, Viktor
Die drei gesichter der stadt Frankfurt an der Oder.
(The three faces of the city, Frankfurt on Oder.)

Städtebau 22: 195-196
December, 1927

Frankfurt-an-der-Oder. Rathaus
    Rathaus fur Frankfurt an der Oder, Otto Kohtz, archt.

    Berliner architekturwelt 12: pl. 395
    Heft 10, 1910

Franklin and Marshall college

    see

    Lancaster (Penn.) Franklin and Marshall college

Franklin, Roberto L.
    La inauguracion del edificio de la Caja de jubilaciones y pensiones de Colegio Provincial de arquitectos. [plans] Armando Puentes, Luis Bonich y Roberto L. Franklin, archts.

    Arq Cuba 17: 344-50
    D 1949

---

ff
720.6   Frankish architecture, Greece
R88   Traquair, Ramsay
    Frankish architecture in Greece.

    R.i.B.A.journal 31: 33-48; 73-86
    Nov.24; Dec.8; 1923

720.5   Franklin, Benjamin
A67r   Lees, Frederic
    The Parisian suburb of Passy: its architecture in the days of Franklin.

    Architectural record 12:669-683
    December 1902

Franklin, W. W.

    see

    Cincinnati, Ohio, Sherrick (Henry C.)Residence
    "   "   Price (Mrs. J.) Residence

Frankl, Wolfgang
    Mehrfamilien-häuser in Rom [plans]
Mario Ridolfi & Wolfgang Frankl, archts.

    Baumeister
    56:386-87 Je 1959

Franklin D. Roosevelt library, Hyde
    Park, N. Y.

    see

    Hyde Park (N.Y.) Roosevelt (F.D.) estate.

Franklin savings bank, New York

    See

    New York.Franklin savings bank

Frankl, Wolfgang
    Progetto per le carceri giudiziarie di Nuoro, Sardegna [plans, sections & details]
Mario Ridolfi & Volfango Frankl, archts.

    Casabella
    #225:24-35 Mar 1959

720.5   Franklin (Ind.) Public library
A51   Public library, Franklin, Ind.
    Graham and Hill, archts. Plans, section, details, elevation.

    Amer arch 111: pl 2142
    Ja 10, '17

Franssen, J

    see

    Koninck and Franssen

Frankl, Wolfgang
    Scuola materna a Poggibonsi (1960-61)[plan & details] Progetto di asilo nel quartiere C.E.P. di Treviso (1960) [plan, section & details] Progetto per l'asilonido Olivetti a Canton Vesco, Ivrea (1960 [plans & sections] Palazzino in Via Vulci a Roma (1959-60) [plans, section & details]
Mario Ridolfi & Volfango Frankl, archts.
    Casabella
    #249: 4-23, Mr 1961

Franklin (Mass.) Garden
    Fisher, Ripley and Le Boutillier, archts.

    West. Archt.
    25: 30
    Apr. 1917

Frantz and Spence

    see

    Midland (Mich.) Chamberlain (Leonard) house
    "   "   Britten (J.A.) house
    Tryon (N.C.) Flynn (M.F.) house

Franklin (S.) and co. factory building,
    Chicago

    see

    Chicago, Ill. Franklin (S.) and co. factory bldg.

720.5   Franklin (Mass.) Hayward (H.T.) garden
A67   Garden of H.T. Hayward, Franklin, Mass.

    Arch rev 21: (n.s. 4)
    183, pl 1-2
    O '16

Frants, Irwin I.

    see

    Rogers, Gordon J. and Irwin I. Frants

Franklin & Kump and associates

    see

    Lafayette (Cal.) Acalanes Union high school
    Fresno (Cal.) City hall

Franklin (Mass.) Ray Memorial Library
    Ray Memorial Library, Franklin, Mass. Rand and Skinner, archts. Plan.

    Architectural review 9 n.s.4:36-37
    January, 1902

A

Frants, R. and J. M. Thompson

    see

    Roanoke County (Va.) Rogers (Talos) house

Frans, Eduard
    Uitbreiding electrische apparatenfabriek
Ad. Feller A. G. te Horgen [plans] Hans Fischli,
archt. with Fredi Eichholzer & Eduard Frans,
archts.

                    Forum no. 5: p.204-205
                    1954

Frary (Samson) house, Deerfield (Mass.)

see

Deerfield (Mass.) Frary (Samson) house

Fraser, Duncan

see

Bethlehem (Pa.) "Green Pond Farms"

Fransen, Ulrich Joseph, 1921-
    Damenmäntelfabrik in New York; entwurf
1958, gebaut 1958-59 [plan, sections & detail]
Ulrich Fransen, archt.

                    Bauen & Wohnen
                    14:266-69 Ag 1960
                    Konstruktionsblatt at end
                    of issue

Frascati. Antiquities.

                    Rossini, Luigi. Le antichità
                    dei contorni di Roma. Rome:
                    the author, 1824-26. pl.70-72.

Fraser, Gilbert

see

Noctorum (Eng.) "Axholme"
Bootle (Eng.) Breese Hill secondary school for
    girls

Franzheim, Kenneth

see also:

Crane and Franzheim

Frascati. Villa Aldobrandini
    Semi-circular court of the Cascade. Villa
Aldobrandini, Frascati. Fountain

                    Latham, Charles. The gardens of
                    Italy. 2 vols. London: Country Life,
                    Ltd. and G. Newnes, Ltd., 1905.
                    v.1,p.157-8

MICROFILM

Fraser, Juliette May

        (1953)

                    Scrapbook of art and artists
                    of Chicago and vicinity
                    p. 665
                    1969

Franzheim, Kenneth

see

Roosevelt field, L.I.
New York (city) Harris, Forbes and Co.
Houston, Tex. Police Administration Bldg.

Frascati. Villa Aldobrandini
    Villa Aldobrandini, Frascati. Cascade from
the Casino. Fountain in the parterre.

                    Triggs, Harry Inigo. The art of
                    garden design in Italy.
                    London: Longmans, Green and Co.,
                    1906. pl. 103-104

Fraser, P   M

see

London, Eng. Staples and co. factory

Fransi luggage store, Milan (It.)

see

Milan (It.) Valigeria Fransi

Frascati. Villa Mondragone
    The Dragon fountain. Mondragone, Frascati.

                    Latham, Charles. The gardens of
                    Italy. 2 vols. London: Country
                    Life, Ltd. and G. Newnes, Ltd.,
                    1905. v.1:p.140.

Fraser, W.A.

see also

Pittsburgh (PA) Carnegie Library. Competition.
        Premiated design.

Franzi, Mastelli and Torri

see

Oleggio (It.) Palazzo littorio

720.6   Frascati. Villa Mondragone
A51j   Chillman, James Jr.
        The Villa Mondragone at Frascati.

                    A.I.A. Journal 12: 211-16
                    May 1924

Fraser, William S.   1852-1897
    Obit.

                    Inland Architect
                    29: 39
                    May 1897

Franzius, L.

see

Dortmund (Ger.) Flughafen

720.52   Fraser, A. R.
B93   Panels, British Empire Exhibition.

                    Builder 126:673
                    April 25, 1924

Frassi store, Milan (It.)

see

Milan (It.) Negozio Frassi

Fraternity houses see also Names of individual fraternity houses, i.e.: Cambridge, Mass. Delta Upsilon house	Fratino, Cesaro "Roma" Builder 112: pl. for Jan. 19, 1917	Frasier, Blouke and Hubbard see Lake Forest (Ill.) Porter (Gilbert III) house
720.5 A67f Fraternity houses Greek letter fraternity house architecture. Architectural forum 40:97-100 March 1924	Fratino, C. and E. A. Griffini see also Cesenatico (It.) Colonia Lino Redaelli	720.6 I29 Frazier, Clarence Elbert 1882-1942 Obituary notice. Illinois Society of Architects Bulletin 27:8 August-September 1942
720.5 A51 Fraternity houses Proposed fraternity house, sketch. Day & Klander, archts. Amer. arch. 109: pl. 2110 May 31, 1916	Fraunces tavern, New York city see New York (city) Fraunces tavern	Frazier, Walter S. see also Somonauk (Ill.) Poepcke (W.P.) house Lake Forest (Ill.) Hubbard (W.C.) estate
720.5 A67a Fraternity houses. Proposed Fraternity House for Small College. Architecture. 42:242 & pl. Aug. 1920.	Frazer, A.V. see "Standard Bearers"	Fred, Otto see Chemnitz (Ger.) Sparkassengebaude der stadt Chemnitz
720.5 A67f Fraternity houses Special number on club and fraternal buildings. Architectural forum v.45 September 1926	Frazier, A. A. Biographical Sketch Industrial Chicago: The Building Interests. 4 vols. Chicago: Goodspeed Pub. Co., 1891-(?) - Vol. 1: Pg. 639	Frede, Hermann see also Halle (Ger.) Golden Ball hotel
Fraternity houses with detail drawings Arch. review 22: n.s. 5:pl.39-47 June, 1917	Frazier and Raftery see also Lake Forest (Ill.) Hubbard (William) house " " " Williams (Lawrence) house Chicago (Ill.) Casino club	720.53 W31 Frede, Hermann Hegemann, Werner Bauten von Hermann Frede, Halle. (Buildings in Halle by Hermann Frede, archt.) Association bank and hotel in Halle, and other buildings. Wasmuths monatshefte 13: 260-263 June 1929
720.53 W31 Fraternity houses, Germany. Stuttgart Ein verbindungshaus in Stuttgart. (A fraternity club-house in Stuttgart.) Eduard Krüger, archt. Plans. Wasmuths monatshefte 15: 221-223 May 1931	Frazier and Raftery New offices of Frazier and Raftery [Geneva, Ill.] Nat'l arch 4:6 O '48	Fredemann, Josef see Duisberg (Ger.) Bahnhofsvorplatz

Fredensborg, Den. Slot
The castle, Fredensborg, Denmark. Built 1720-1724.

Builder 139: 337
August 29, 1930

720.5
A67f
Fredericksburg (Va.) Washington (Mary) house
Mary Washington house, Fredericksburg, Va.
Restored by Philip N. Stern, archt. H.A.B.S.
measured drawings, plans.

A

Architectural forum 66: 53-55
January 1937

Fredrikavarn (Nor.) War Memorial Beacon
Competition design for a war memorial
beacon at Fredrikavarn, Norway. Rendering by
John Finseth, archt.

Pencil points 9: pl 28
July, 1928

Fredericksburg, Va. (near) Chatham

see

Chatham, Va

Fredericton (New Bruns.) Allen (T. Carlton)
House. R. Brown, Jr., arch.

Inland Arch.
27: 26
April 1896

Freedlander and Dillon

see

New York (city) Baron de Hirsch trade school

720.6
A51j
Fredericksburg(Va.)Kenmore
Baldwin, F.C.
Early architecture of the valley of the
Rappahannock. Kenmore: built about 1752. Plan.

A.I.A. Journal 3: 113-118
March 1915

Fredericton, New Brunswick, Allen
(T. Carlton) House
With plans of Ground floor and 2nd floor.
R. Brown, Archt.

Inland archt.
vol. 27, No. 3, pl.
fol. p. 30
Apr. 1896

Freedlander and Jacobs

see

New York (city) Andrew Freedman home

720.6
A51j
Fredericksburg(Va.)Kenmore
Kenmore. Saving Kenmore for the nation,
Fredericksburg, Virginia

A.I.A. Journal 11:139-40
April 1923

720.52
A67ay
Frederiksberg (Den.) Churches
Church at Frederiksberg. [plan] Erick Møller,
archt.

Archts' yr bk 2: 106-107
1947

Freedlander and Seymour

see also

Put-in-Bay(O.) Perry memorial competition

MICROFILM

Fredericksburg (Va.) Monroe (James) law office

in SCRAPBOOK ON
ARCHITECTURE p. 7
(on film)

Frederiksberg (Den.) Krematorium
Rasmussen, S. E.
Das Krematorium in Frederiksberg, Dänemark.
(The crematory in Frederiksberg, Denmark.) Edvard
Thomsen and Frits Schlegel, archts. Plans.

A

Wasmuths monatshefte 14: 273-276
June, 1930

720.5
A51
Freedlander and Seymour
Public auditorium competition, Portland,
Oregon. Freedlander and Seymour, archts.
Plan.

American architect 100 pt.2:4pls.opp.244
December 6, 1911

720.5
A67a
Fredericksburg (Va.) National Bank building
Doorways of the National Bank building
Fredericksburg, Va. Colonial architecture
early nineteenth century. Built in 1820.
Measured and drawn by Albert P. Ert.

Architecture. 54:pl.186-87
September 1926

Frederiksberg (Den.) Krematorium and Mausoleum
Krematorium und friedhofsanlage für
Frederiksberg, Dänemark. (Crematories and
mausoleums in Frederiksberg.) Thomsen and Frits
Schlegel, archts. Plan.

Wasmuths monatshefte 13: 462-463
November, 1929

A

Freedlander, Joseph Henry   1870-1943
see also
Albany (N.Y.) State educational bldg.
Auburn (N.Y.) Case Library. Competition.
Frankfort (KY) Berry (G.F.) house
Jersey City (N.Y.) Free public library. Competition.
Johnson City (TN) Carnegie library
 "   "   "   Nat'l home for disabled volunteer
                     soldiers. Chapels & memorial hall
Long Branch (N.J)"Ellencourt"
New York (N.Y.) Ansonia hotel. Bachelor apt.
 "   "   "   Baron de Hirsch trade school
 "   "   "   40th st. (East) # 13

(see next card)

720.6
A51j
Fredericksburg (Va.) Washington (Mary) house
The Mary Washington house, Fredericks-
burg, Va. No plan.

A.I.A. journal 3:118
March 1915

720.F4
A67au
Frederiksberg (Den.) Library
Bibliothèque de Frederiksberg (Danemark)
[plans, sect.]

L'Arch d'aujourd'hui
9: 95
kr '38

Freedlander, Joseph Henry   1870-1943 (card 2)
see also
New York (N.Y.) Greystone hotel
 "   "   "   Importers & Traders nat'l bank
 "   "   "   Museum of the city of New York
 "   "   "   Newborg (M.) house
 "   "   "   Piva (Celestino) house
 "   "   "   Residence
 "   "   "   Station & Power house, Hospital.
                     (21st Annual exhibit - Arch. League
                       of New York)
 "   "   "   Union Theological Seminary. Competition
Oakland (CA) City hall. Competition.

(see next card)

Freedlander, Joseph Henry   1870-1943   (card 3)
see also
Piers, Triumphal
Pleasantville (N.Y.) house
Providence (R.I.) Residence
Put-in-Bay (OH) Perry Memorial. Competition.
St. Louis (MO) St. Louis club
"   "   "   "   house. Competition.
San Francisco (CA) house
Washington (D.C.) Pan-American Union bldg. Competition.

Freeman, Alfred

see

New York (N.Y.) Hess, Goldsmith & Co.

720.5
M75
Freemansburg (Va.) Freeman (John) house
Doorway – the John Freeman house, Freemans-
burg, Virginia.

Monograph series 13: pl.44
No.4, 1928

720.5
B84
Freedlander, Joseph H   1870-1943
Biography of his life.

brickbuilder 24:262
October 1915

Freeman and Hasselman

see

Cedarhurts (L.I.) Erhart (W.H.) house
Rye (N.Y.) Villa Aurora
Westbury (L.I.) "Rosemary Hall"
Seabright (N.J.) Rumson Country Club
Morristown (N.J.) Mellon (C.H.) house

Freemasons' hospital, Melbourne

see

Melbourne (Aus.) Freemasons' hospital

Freedlander, Joseph Henry, 1870-1943

see also

Freedlander and Jacobs

Freeman and Price

see also

Malvern (Eng.) library

Freeport (Ill) Carnegie Library
Patton & Miller, Archs.

Inland Arch. 38:
pl.fol.p.8
Aug. 1901

708.1
N551uh
Freedlander, Joseph Henry, 1870? – 1943
New York university
Joseph H. Freedlander, 1870-1943.

Hall of amer artists 6:75-94
1951

Freeman and Price

Members of firm:

Freeman, Albert C.
Price, Francis H.

720.5
A67f
Freeport (Ill.) Clark (J. Manley) house
Huszagh and Hill
House of J. Manley Clark, Freeport, Ill.
[plans]

Arch for 51:513-14
N '29

MICROFILM

Freedlander, Joseph Henry, 1870(?)-1943
obituary notice

in SCRAPBOOK ON
ARCHITECTURE p. 704
(on film)

Freeman, Frank

see

Brooklyn (N.Y.) Crescent athletic clubhouse
"   "   Fire house
"   "   Savings bank
New York (N.Y.) U. S. Leather Co. bldg.
"   "   "   Scandinavian Trust Co.
White Plains (N.Y.) Bayne (S.G.) house

Freeport (IL.) Krape Park Bridge
Ipsen, Mogens
Krape Park Bridge, Freeport, Illinois: a rigid
frame in architectural concrete.

Architectural concrete 1:6-7
No. 3 1935

Freelander, M.
Architecte: M. Freelander.

L'Architecture 21: 102, pls.
fol.104
Mr 28, 1908

Freeman, French and Freeman

see

Burlington (Vt.) St. Marks Roman Catholic Church

Freeport (IL.) Snyder (Dr. Karl F.) house
House of Dr. Karl F. Snyder, Freeport, IL.
Huszagh and Hill, archts.

Architecture 60:225-228
October, 1929

720.59
A67c
Freeman, Albert C.
Design for a Country Residence. Albert
C. Freeman, Architect. Plan.

Arch & c. rep 69: 1 pl preceding
201
Mr 20, '03

Freeman, Philip G.

see.

London (Eng.) Cavendish rd. (No. 12) house

720.5
B93b
Freeport. (Ill.) Zion Episcopal church and   rectory
Design of Zion Episcopal Church and rec-
tory, Freeport, Ill. Henry F. Starbuck, archt.

A   Building budget 3: pl.fol.p.150
November 31, 1897

Freeport, L.I., N.Y. Archer St. School
Study, Archer Street School, Freeport, L.I.
Wesley Sherwood Bessell, archt.

Architect N.Y. 10:584
August, 1928

Freiberg (Saxony) Dom

Shaw, Richard Norman. Architectural
sketches from the continent. London:
Pub. for the proprietors, 1872.
pl. 69-74.

Freiburg im Breisgau. Münster
Freiburg im Breisgau Münster, Liebfrauen.

Hartung, Hugo. Motive der
Mittelalterlichen baukunst in
Deutschland....3 vols. Berlin:
E. Wasmuth, 1896-1902.1:pls.8-10

720.5
A67r

Freeport, L.I., (N.Y.)Freeport national bank
Freeport national bank, Freeport,
Long Island. Purdy and Davis, archts.

A   Architectural record 60:241-5
September 1926

720.53
W51

Freiberg.(Saxony) Krematorium
Das Krematorium der Stadt Freiberg.
George Salzmann,archt.

Wasmuths 12: 172-176
April 1928

Freiburg im Breisgau. Münster
Koch, Erika
Inside the tower - of the Freiburger munster in
south Germany.

Country life (Lond.) 83:436
April 23, 1938

Freer, C.L., house, Detroit

see

Detroit, Mich. Freer, C.L., house

Freiburg (Ger.) universität. Competition.
1955
Erweiterung des Kollegiengebäudes
der Universität Freiburg [plans and section]

Architektur and Wohnform
64 * 4-6 *   no.1
O 1955

Freiburg im Breisgau. Münster
Vorhalle am Südlichen querschiff der Munsters
zu Freiberg im Baden (1620)
Musikenten Choir. No plan.

Fritsch, K.E.O., ed. Denkmaeler
deutscher renaissance. 4 vols.
Berlin: E. Wasmuth, 1891.
v.1:30-31
v.2:pls.22-23

720.59
A675

Freestone
Granite and freestone

Arch rev 62:66-70
Ag '27

Freiburg im Breisgau, Ger. 1500
Freiburg im Breisgau about 1500: typical city of
the middle ages.

Wasmuths 10:293
Heft 7, 1926

Freiburg im Breisgau, Ger. Universität. Stadion
Stadium at the University of Freiburg.

Wasmuths 13: 417-418
October, 1929

Freeways

see

Roads

Freiburg im Breisgau. Cathedral

see

Freiburg im Breisgau. Münster

Freiburg, Switz.

see

Fribourg, Switz.

Fregene (It.) Casa F
Casa nella pineta di Fregene. [plan and sect-
ions] Cino Pennisi and Brando Savelli, archt.

Spazio no. 3:46-49
O 1950

Freiburg im Breisgau. Dom

see

Freiburg im Breisgau. Münster

Freie Architekten Wurm
Atelierhaus in Ravensburg [plans] Freie
Architekten Wurm, archts.

Baumeister
56:646-48 O 1959
Tafel 62

Freibad Schlieren. Zurich, Switz.

see

Zurich, Switz. Freibad Schlieren

Freiburg im Breisgau (Ger.) Housing
Small dwelling house in Freiburg.

Wasmuths 10:300-301
Heft 7, 1926

Die freie deutsche akademie des städtebaues.
conferences, 1927
Adler, Leo
Wissenschaftlicher städtebau auf der Hamburger
tagung der Akademie. (Scientific city planning
at the Hamburg meeting of the Academy.)

Städtebau 22: 126-127
August, 1927

Freight terminals see Terminals	Fréjus (Fr.) Palais archiepiscopal (ancienne) Doors and doorways, no. 3: entrance to the old Episcopal Palace, Frejus, Fr. Amer archt and bldg news 56:pl fol 72 My 29, 1897	French Colonial Architecture Tallmadge, T. E. Spanish and Creole Architecture in America. Building for the future: 1-2 July, 1930
Freihofsiedlung see Housing, Austria, Vienna, Freihofsiedlung.	720.5 Fréjus.Saint Etienne A67r Ferree,Barr French cathedrals: Fréjus. Plan. Architectural record 7:134-140 October-December 1897	French Colonial Architecture Goertz, Arthémise Courtyards à la Créole. House and garden 63:54-55 March, 1933
Freijs, C. T. 4-story flat building for G.W. Murray at Englewood, IL. (Chicago.) Freijs, C.T., archt. Building budget 3:65 My 31, 1887	Fréjus, Fr. Saint Etienne. Cloister. Fréjus (Alpes-Maritimes) le cloître et le puits Encyclopedie de l'architecture, constructions de Style. 2 vols. Paris: Albert Morancé, 1928 - ? Tome 1:pl.44	French colonial architecture. U. S. Louisiana Wilson, Samuel, Jr. Religious architecture in French Colonial Louisiana. [illus] Winterthur portfolio 8: [63]-106 1973
Freising (Ger.) Housing Siedlungswettbewerb (A building enterprise) Competition drawings by Schultz; Schmid; Wiedemann; Burger, archts. A Der baumeister 34:30-31 January, 1936	MICROFILM Frémiet, Emmanuel, 1824-1910 About his art. (source not known, July 15, 1895) [illus., drawing of the artist] Scrapbook of art and artists of Chicago and vicinity p. 606 1969	French, Daniel Chester (sculptor) see also Chicago (IL) World's Columbian Exposition. 1893. "Columbia"statue for water entrance. Cleveland (OH) Federal bldg. Milton (MA) War memorial St. Paul (MN) Minnesota state capitol " " " " " Quadriga Washington (D.C) Lincoln memorial
Freising, Ger. Pallotiner studienheim Lill, Georg Zu Finands studienheim der Pallotiner in Freising. Christliche kunst 27:271-276 May-June 1931	Fremont (O.) Sandusky County Court House The Old Greek Revival Court House (Fremont, Ohio). Cyrus Williams, archt. Architectural forum 45: 221-224 October, 1926	720.5 French, Daniel Chester A67 Bas-relief for the J.N.Clark Monument, Forest Hills Cemetery, Boston,Mass.Daniel French sculptor; Andrews,Jacques and Rantoul, architects. Architectural review 3: 24,pl. 10 July 1894
Fréjus.Cathedral See Fréjus.Saint Etienne	French building, New York see New York. French Building	French, Daniel Chester "Jurisprudence", Minn. State Capitol bldg.; "The Quadriga" with Edw. C. Potter; "History", "Charity", "Truth" and "Wisdom", "Courage" West. Archt. 4: 11, 28-31 O 1905
Fréjus.Notre Dame et St. Etienne See Fréjus.Saint Etienne	French Colonial Architecture Curtis, N. C. The Creole architecture of Old New Orleans. Architectural record 43: 435-446 May, 1918	French, Daniel C. Letter to D.H. Burnham. (8/18/1892) Letters and autographs of famous architects: A collection started for Burnham Library by Thomas E. Tallmadge. Housed in the Burnham and Ryerson Libraries, The Art Institute of Chicago. No. 3

720.5
A67r
French, Daniel Chester
    The new capitol in St.Paul. Cass Gillert,
archt. No plan. Sculpture by D.C.French

Architectural record 10:281-288
January 1901

French exposition 1924, New York (city)
    see
New York (city) Grand central palace. French
exposition 1924

French, Leigh Hill, 1894 ? - 1946
    Garden house in a Regency garden. Leigh French,
archt.

Country life (U.S.) 53:45
April, 1928

720.5
F29
French, Daniel Chester
    Reuse of sculpture: pediment of old
Philadelphia Post office, Daniel Chester
French sculptor - on new base designed by
Paul Cret - in Fairmount Park, Philadelphia.

Federal architect 9:8
No.3,January 1939

French, Fred F. and Co.
    see also
Greenwich (Conn.) Pickwick Arms hotel
New York (N.Y.) Woodstock Tower
    "   "   "   Haddon hotel
    "   "   "   Cloister hotel
    "   "   "   French building

710.5
H84
French, Leigh Hill, 1894 ? - 1946
    Homes that grow; designed especially for
House and Garden by Leigh French, Jr.

House and garden 61:64-65
January 1932

710.5
L26
French, Daniel Chester
    Sculptor and landscape architect: Daniel
Chester French.

Landscape architecture 16: 91-9
January 1926

French, Fred F., and Co.
    Two modern apartments for city and country.
Fred F. French Co., archts.

Architecture
38: 286-9, pl.168-171
O 1918

French. Leigh Hill, house
    (Interior, Leigh French home)

House and garden 47: 85-87
May, 1925

French, Daniel Chester
    Sculptor of "Columbia", at
World's Columbian Expo., Chicago.

Inland Architect
19: 30
Apr, 1892

French, G. Herbert
    see
Pelham Manor (N.Y.) Rogers (M.D.) house

French, Leigh Hill   1894(?)-1946
    [obituary]

Nat'l Arch 2:15
4 '46

French, Daniel C.
    Sculpture Shown in Parlor of W.M.R. French
Residence.

Inland Architect
vol. 34, No. 1,pl.fol.p. 8
Aug, 1899

French influence on American architecture
    See
United States.Architecture,French influence.

French, Leigh Hill, 1894 ? - 1946
    Restoration of "Kenwood", a regency house.
Leigh French, Jr., archt., Harold D. Eberlein,
assoc. archt.

Architectural forum 51: 519-528
October, 1929

French, David C.   (sculptor)
    see
Minneapolis (MN) Univ. of Minn. Pillsbury Memorial.

French legation, Ottawa, Ont.
    see
Ottawa, Ont. Hôtel diplomatique de France

French, Leigh Hill, 1894 ? - 1946
    Small Parisian shop fronts.

Architectural forum 50:885-894
June, 1929

French embassy, Washington, D.C. [until 1936]
    see
Washington, D. C. French embassy (intil 1936)

French, Leigh Hill, 1894 ? - 1946
    see also
Greenwich (Conn.) Bomeisler (D.M.) house
Darien (Conn.) Kelley (S.C.) house

710.5
H84
French, Leigh Hill, 1894 ? - 1946
    Three more houses that grow; designed
after Mediterranean, Cape Cod and Cotswold
styles by Leigh French, Jr. Plans.

House and garden 60: 48-51
November 1931

720.5
B95b

French Lick,(Ind.) Chapel
    Chapel at French Lick, Ind.
Bohlen, D. A. & Son, archts.

Building budget
313 in supp
My 31, 1887

French, William A. & Co.
    Oak Hall Carvings
Congdon residence
Duluth, MN

West. Arch.
12: pls. fol. p. 20
Ag 1908

Freret, James

see also

New Orleans (La.) Church of the Immaculate
    Conception

French Lick (IN) Hotel
    Ground to be broken for new hotel.
Under management of Monon Road, headed by
Maj. Thomas Taggart.

Inland Architect
37: 31
May, 1901

French, William M.R.
    Appreciation

Jour. of Amer. Inst. of Arch.2:347
July, 1914

Freret, James   1838-1897
    Obit.

Inland Architect
31: 8-9
Feb, 1898

French, S. Q.

see also

Woodlawn, L.I. Dodge vault

French, William M. R., 1843-1914
    Letters from Daniel Hudson Burnham.

Letters and autographs of famous
architects: A collection started
for Burnham Library by Thomas E.
Tallmadge. Housed in the Burnham
and Ryerson Libraries, The Art
Institute of Chicago. nos. 26-27

Freret, William A. -1912
    obit.

West. Arch.
18: 26
Mar, 1912

French, W.A.
    Designer Funiture by.

West. Arch.
2: p. 17-19
Apr, 1903

French, William M.R.
    Letters from W.L.B. Jenney. (11/29/1889,
1/5/1897, 7/26/1890, 12/10/1890, 3/7/1892,
3/16/1893, 9/5/1893, 12/1/1893, 12/19/1893,
12/26/1893, 1/22/1894,1/29/1894, 2/23/1894,
9/10/1894, 6/10,1896, and 1/29/1894)
    Letters and autographs of famous architects: A
collection started for Burnham Library by Thomas
E. Tallmadge. Housed in the Burnham and Ryerson
Libraries, The Art Institute of Chicago. no. 27

Fresh-air camps

see

Camps

French, William A. & co.

see also

Minneapolis (MN) French (Wm. A.) & co.

Frensham (Eng.) Chapel of Ease
    Chapel of Ease, Frensham, Surrey.
Mr. W. Curtis Green, A.R.I.B.A., architect.

Builder 97: 315, pl.
S 18, 1909

Fresnedo, Roman
    — is an architect —

House beautiful 83:50,
137-138
October 1941

French, William A. & Co.
    Couch designed by -
Photo

West. Arch.
16: 98
S 1910

Frere, W. Eustace C.

see

London (Eng.) Central council for medical
    education
Oswestry, Eng. St. Oswald's church house
Harrow Weald park, Eng.

Fresnedo, Roman. Portraits
    — is an architect —

House beautiful 83:50
October 1941

French, William A. & Co.
    Interior woodwork & furniture -
Residence in Duluth, MN

West. Arch.
15: pls. fol. p. 48
April 1910

Frères Niermans,

see

Niermans, Jean and Edouard

Fresno (CA)
    Atchison-Topeka & Santa Fe R.R. Station

Inland Arch.
43: pls.fol.p. 8
Feb. 1904

721.97
A67c

Fresno (Cal.). Architecture
Jellick, J.E.
Fresno architects design civic group. Designed
by the Allied Architects of Fresno, Calif.

Architectural concrete 3:30-31
No.1,1937

720.52
A67

Fret
Greek and Roman meander or fret ornament:
Cottingham's designs.

Architect and builder's journal 40:
August 19, 1914   pl.fol.p.140

Frey, Hermann
Schulhaus in Wolfwil/Solothurn [plans &
sections] Hermann Frey, archt.

Bauen & Wohnen no. 3
p. 172-174
Konstruktionsblätter
(end of issue)
1954

Fresno (Cal.). Architecture
Jellick, J.E.
Fresno architects design civic group. Designed by
the Allied Architects of Fresno, Calif.

Architectural concrete 3:30-31
No. 1, 1937

720.52
A67c

Freudenstadt, Ger. Kirche
Twentyman,A.R.
Four continental churches: Church at Freud-
enstadt. Hugo Schlösser,archt. No plan.

Architect (Lond.) 133: 374
March 24, 1933

Frey, Hermann
Verwaltungsbau der Firma W. Franke,
Aarburg. [plans and section] Hermann Frey,
archt.

Bauen and Wohnen
No.2: 53-56
Konstruktionsblatt at end
of issue
F 1956

Fresno (Cal.) City Hall
City Hall, Fresno Street, Fresno, California.
1941. Franklin and Kump and Associates, archts.

Mock, Elizabeth, ed. Built in the USA.
New York: Museum of Modern Art, 1944.
90-91

Freudenstadt, Ger. Reconstruction 1945-
[plans]

Baumeister
52, no.2:73-91, 105-108,
tafeln 9-11
F 1955

Frey, Roland
Vivienda colectiva en Alemania [plans &
sections] Roland Frey, Hermann Schroder &
Walther Piekert, archts.

Proa
#133:16-19 F 1960

Fresno (Cal.) Planning
Jellick, J. E.
Fresno architects design civic group. Designed by
the Allied Architects of Fresno, Calif.

Architectural concrete 3:30-31
No. 1, 1937

Freund, Karl
Interiors

Architectural review
26 (n.s.9):177-81
Dec., 1919

Frey, Werner
Gewerbehäuser beim Bahnhof Giesshübel in
Zürich [plans and sections] Werner Frey, archt.

Bauen and wohnen
No. 7: 236-240, Konstruktions-
blätter at end of issue
Jl 1956

Fresno (Cal.) Post Office
Roemer, F. A.
Post Office for Fresno, California.
Dewey Foster, archt. No plan.

Architectural concrete 7:27-29
No. 1 [1941]

Frey, Albert, 1903-
Member of firms:
Kocher and Frey
Clark and Frey
Clark, Frey and Chambers
Williams, Clark and Frey

Frey, Werner
Neubau der Schweizerischen Betriebskranken-
kasse in Winterthur [plans & section] Werner
Frey, archt.

Bauen & Wohnen
#2:37-42 F 1958

721.5
A67c

Fresno (Cal.) Scottish Rite Temple
Swartz, F.L.
Scottish Rite Temple-Fresno, Calif. Fred
L. Swartz, archt., and H.C. Coates, Jr.,
associate. No plan.

A   Architectural concrete 5:24-25
No.1[1939]

Frey, Albert   1903-
Week end house, Long Island, N.Y. 1934
Lawrence Kocher, Albert Frey, archts. Plans
Brief biographical notes and photographs of
architects.

Roth, Alfred. La nouvelle architecture. Erlenbach, Switzerland:
Editions de Architecture, 1946.
11-16

Frey, Werner
Projekt für ein verwaltungsgebäude in
Winterthur [plans and section] Werner Frey,
archt.

Bauen and wohnen
No. 7: 249-250
Jl 1956

Fresno, Calif. Water tower and library.
Sketch. George W. Maher, architect.

Inland architect
23: plate VII
April 1894

Frey and Schindler
see
Olten (Switz.) Badanlage

Frey, Werner
Projekt für das Basler Stadttheater [plans]
W. Frey & J. Schader, archts.

Bauen & Wohnen
12:306-7 S 1958

Freymüller
see also
Steglitz (Ger.) Planning

Freyssinet, Eugène, 1879 - 1962
see also
Bagneux (Fr.) Ateliers de reparations des chemins de
fer
Dammarie-Les-Lys (Fr.) Compagnie nationale des
radiateurs. Usine
Dourges (Fr.) Tours de chargement de Silo
Luzancy (Fr.) Bridge
Orly (Fr.) Aeroport. Hangars a dirigeables
Plougastel (Fr.) Pont sur l'Elorn

Fribourg, Switz. Eglise du Christ-Roi
Eglise du Christ-Roi à Fribourg. Auteur du
projet: Atelier Denis Honegger

Techniques & architecture
14 ser 1-2:36-41
1955

720.53
M68
Freymüller, Frits
Sports center and playground. Frits
Freymüller, archt.

Moderne bauformen 29:219-222
Heft 5, May 1930

720.54
A67v
Freyssinet, Eugène, 1879-1962
Badovici, Jean
E. Freyssinet

L'arch vivante pp. 5-11,pls.1-
25. Spring-Summer 1931

Fribourg, Switz. Kathedrale
see
Fribourg, Switz. St. Nicolas (cathedral)

Freymuth, Emil
see also
Munich (Ger.) Siedlung Freiland
Grunewald (Ger.) Volksschule

Freyssinet, Eugène, 1879 - 1962
Dormoy, Marie
Les travaux d'art de M. Freyssinet.

L'amour de l'art 9:310-314
Ag 1928. English summary after
p. 320

Fribourg, Switz. St. Nicolas (cathedral)
Steinmann, Martin
Sakraler Jugendstil. Die Scheiben von
Josef Mehoffer in der Kathedrale von Freiburg
im Uechtland. Aufnahmen: Lukas Landmann.
Text: Martin Steinmann. [illus., part col.]

Du
v.31: 538-[551]
July 1971

720.53
B35
Freymuth, Emil
(Two one-family houses.) Emil Freymuth,
archt. Plans. Zwei ein fanilienhauser von
E.Freymuth.

Der Baumeister 28: 508-513
August 1930

720.54
A67v
Freyssinet, Eugène, 1879-1962
Badovici, Jean
E. Freyssinet

L'arch vivante pp. 5-11,pls.1-
25. Spring-Summer 1931

705
W48
Fribourg (Switz.) Université
Die Neubauten der Universität Fribourg.
[plans, sect.] F. Dumas and D. Honegger,
archt.
Das Werk 29:33-55
F-Mr '42

720.53
B35
Freymuth, Emil
Harbers, Guido
Genossenschaftlich errichtete Volkswohnungen
(München) (Cooperatively-built community
dwellings.) Emil Freymuth, archt.

Der Baumeister 34:348-351
October 1936

720.54
A67au
Friberger, Eric. 1889-
Maisons démontables standards. E. Friberger,
archt. [plans]

L'arch d'aujourd'hui 9:70-71
Ja 1938

720.54
T25
Fribourg (Switz.) Université
Les nouveaux batiments de l'université
de Fribourg. F. Dumas and D. Honegger,
archts. [plans, sect.]

Tech. it Arch. 3: 74-85
Mr-Apr '43

Freymuth, Emil
Ein neues Bürohaus in München. [plans and
sections] Emil Freymuth, archt.

Baumeister
Vol. 51:75-81, pl 11
F 1954

Friberger, Eric.   1889-
Prefabricated houses in timber, Sweden.
Eric, Friberger, archt. Plans.
The house "L" at Gothenburg.

Roth, Alfred. La Nouvelle Architecture.
Erlenback, Switzerland:
Editions de Architecture, 1946: p.25-32

Frick building, Pittsburg, Pa.
see
Pittsburg, Pa. Frick building

Freymuth, Emil
[plans and sections]

Baumeister
52, no.4:205-227, tafeln 25-32
Ap 1955

705
W48
Fribourg (Switz.) Cité Paroissiale [project]
Baur, Hermann
Das projekt für eine "Cité paroissiale" in
Fribourg. Dumas and Honegger, archts. [plan]
Das Werk
30:388-389
pt.2, D. '43

Frick, Kurt
see also
Stallupönen (Ger.) Reconstruction

Frick, Kurt
Baltzer, Ulrich
A country house in Königsberg by Architect
Kurt Frick

Dekorative kunst 31:153-157
April, 1928

Friedenburg (Den.) Country House
Country seat in Friedenburg, Denmark.
Maydahl Nielsen, archt. No plan.

A   Architectural record 22:316
October, 1907

Friedman, Alschuler and Sincere

see

Chicago (Ill.) Newman-Rudolph Lithographing Co.

720.58   Fridinger, Egon
B35   Mayreder, F
Ein wohnlicher dachgarten in Wien. (A comfortable roof garden in Vienna.) Egon Fridinger,
archt. Plans.

Der Baumeister 31: 217-219
June 1933

720.5   Friedland, Louis H.
A67b   The Broadway National Bank and Trust Co.,
New York City. Louis H. Friedland, archt.

Architecture and Building 61:360-361,
November 1929   366-369

Friedman house. Tuscaloosa (Ala.)

See

Tuscaloosa (Ala.) Battle house.

Fridstein and Company
see also
Detroit (Mich.) Wolverine Hotel
Chicago, IL. Webster Hotel

720.5   Friedland, Louis H
A67f   Frank Brothers shoe store, New York City.
Louis H. Friedland, archt. Plan

Architectural forum 66:190
March 1937

Friedman, Ralph
see also
Chicago, Ill. Temple Isaiah Israel

MICROFILM

Fridstein, Meyer, 1884-1964
obituary notice

in SCRAPBOOK ON
ARCHITECTURE p. 702
(on film)

720.5   Friedland, Louis H.
A67r   Boyd, J.T. jr.
Milgrim - a fashion shop for women. Louis
H. Friedland, archt.

Architectural record 65:523-533
June 1929

Friedman, Raphael N.   1890-
Brief biography.

Herringshaw, Clark J. Herringshaw's
city blue book of current biography.
Chicago: American Publisher's
Association, 1915

Fried (Howard) house, Winnetka (Ill.

see

Winnetka (Ill.) Fried (Howard) house

720.5   Friedlander, Leo
M59a   Bronze doors, Herman Goldman Mausoleum,
Congregation Rodeph-Sholom Union Fields
cemetery, Brooklyn, N. Y. Designed and
modeled by Leo Friedlander, sculptor.
Leo Friedlander's significant sculptures.

Metal arts 2: pl.21, p.157-160
April 1929

720.5   Friedman, Raphael N   1890 -
A67f   The Chicago taxpayer. Facts and figures
about four Chicago taxpayers. Plans

Architectural forum 67:232
September 1937

Friedberg, Schloss, Aus.
Gritsch, J.
Mittelalterliche Wandmalerei, Funde 1959-
1969. Katalog--die Restaurierung des Ritter-
saales in Friedberg, Tirol. [illus., part col.]

Österreichische Zeitschrift
für Kunst und Denkmalpflege
v.23, Heft 3/4: 212-217
1969

720.5   Friedlander, Leo
P39   Ornamental panels in ceiling of entrance
hall, National chamber of commerce, Washington, D.C.   Cass Gilbert, archt, and Leo
Friedlander, sculptor.

Pencil points 7: 48
January 1926

Friedman, William and Hilde Reiss
see
Minneapolis, Minn. Idea house

Friedenau, Germany. Rathaus
Rathaus fur Friedenau, Germany. Otto Kohts,
archt.

Berliner architekturwelt 12:pl.398
Heft 10, 1909-10

720.5   Friedlander, Leo
P39   Sculpture by Leo Friedlander for American
Bank and Trust building, Philadelphia. Davis,
Dunlap and Barney, archts.
Pier terminal for Edworth Euclid Metho-
dist Episcopal church, Cleveland, Ohio. Leo
Friedlander, sculptor; Goodhue Associates,
archts.

Pencil points 10: Pl.8, p.126
February 1929

Friedman, Yona
The Future; mobile architecture. [plan]
Yona Friedman & R. Aujame, archts.

Archtl Design
30:356 S 1960

720.53
B35
Friedmann, Robert
Wohnungsbauten an der BarmbeckerStrasse.
Wohnungsbauten an der AlsterdorferStrasse
(Apartment houses in Hamburg.) Robert Fried
mann, archt. Plans. Interiors.

Der Baumeister 28: 354-357
September 1930

Friend, James R.

see

Rolling Hills (Cal.) Bates-Lane (Arthur) house

Frinton Park, Eng.
A planned seaside resort: Frinton Park, Essex.
Designed by Oliver Hill. Plans.

Country life (London) 78:182,xxiv,xxvi,
August 17, 1935   xxvii

Friedrich, Edwin

see

Amriswil (Switz.) Evangelische Kirche

Friern Barnet (Eng.) Wesleyan Methodist Church
                    (proposed)
Competition for proposed Wesleyan Methodist
Church, Friern Barnet.

Builder 141:20-21
July 3, 1931

Frisch, Max

see

Zürich (Switz.) Freibad Letzigraben [project]

720.53
B35
Friedrich, H
Harbers, Guido
Die schulungsburg der Deutschen arbeitsfront
in Sassnitz (The training center of the German
workers in Sassnitz). H. Friedrich and others,
archts. Plans.

Der baumeister 34:361-374,pls.125-
November 1936   132

Friesian Islands
Tillema, J.A.C.
De restauratie van een Frieschen toren.

Maanblad voor beeldende kunsten 13:149-54
May 1936

720.5
A67ar
Frisch, Victor
Study, Immigrants' monument, Battery Park,
New York. Thomas Hibben, archt., Victor
Frisch, sculptor.

Architect (N.Y.) 11: 626
March 1929

720.53
B61
Friedrich, Nicolaus
Am poller. Sculpture.

Berliner architekturwelt
18:296-V.Heft 7-8,1915.

720.52
A67e
Friesland. Description and travel.
Hindeloopen on the Zuider Zee.

Architect 107: 225-7.
Mar. 31, 1922.

Fritsch, A. A.

see also

Melbourne (Aus.) University of Melbourne. Newman
college

Friedrichshafen (Ger.) Kurgartenhotel
Baum, Julius
Kurgartenhotel, Friedrichshafen, built by Eisenlohr
and Weigle, archts. Plan.

Modern bauformen 11: 381-387
August, 1912

720.6
B39
Friezes
Beaux Arts institute of design, competition
An astronomical frieze.

B. A. I. D. 3: 3-6
February 1927

microfilm
Fritsch, A. A., architect
Griffin, Walter B. and A. A. Fritsch, architects
Roman catholic college, University of Mel-
bourne, Melbourne, Australia, 1915-7.

Roll 8, frames 89-127;146 A-B

Friedrichshafen, Ger. St. Petrus-Canisius
The new Catholic churches in Friedrichshafen
and Stuttgart; St. Petrus-Canisius and St. Georg.
Hugo Schlösser, archt.

Moderne Bauformen 29:185-191
Heft 5, May 1930

Friezes.
Section of stenciled frieze. Designed
by Louis J. Millet and Louis H. Sullivan in
1894 for the exchange room of the Chicago
stock exchange building. Oil on canvas, 57 1/4
in. x 23 in. Gift of Mr. and Mrs. Arthur D.
Dubin. 1971.747. [rep.]

Chicago.Art institute.
Bulletin.
v. 67: 13
Mr-Ap 1973

Fritwell manor

see

Somerton (Eng.) Fritwell manor

Friedrichstadt (Ger.) Planning
The origin of Berlin Friedrichstadt.

Der Städtebau 19: 82-4
Heft 7-8, 1922

Friis, Knud
8 houses in Rødovre, Denmark: houses nos.
4 and 5 [plan] Knud Friis & Moltke Nielsen, archts.

Archtl Design
29:439 N 1959

Fritz, A
Heidelberg; Albertus Magnus Studentenheim;
baujahr 1956/1957 [plans] M. Schmitt-Fiebig,
archt., with A. Fritz, assoc. archt

Das Münster
vol.14: 416-417, N-D 1961

Fritz, Erwin, 1927-

see

Atelier 5

720.53 Fröhlich, Rudolf
235 Harber, Guido
    Neue arbeiten von architekt. Rudolf Fröhlich-
Burghausen. (Recent work by architect Rudolf
Fröhlich. Burghausen.) Painted figures on outside houses.

Der Baumeister 34: 114-119, pls.37-
April 1936   38

Frohne, William C

See

New York. Ashland building

Fritz, Karl Richard

Member of firm:

Jassoy and Fritz

Frohman and Martin

see

Santa Barbara (Cal.) Trinity church

Frolich, F.H.

see

Seattle (WA) Alaska-Yukon-Pacific Exposition.

Fritz, Karl Richard
    Steps toward a new architecture: design
for a new opera house in Berlin. Competition of
1912. H. Jassoy and Fritz, archts.

Theatre arts mon
5:18
Ja 1921

Frohman, Philip Hubert

Member of firm of:

Frohman, Robb and Little

Frome (Eng.) Longleat

see

Longleat, Wiltshire

720.5 Froberg, Alben Randolph
A67f   Remodeled store building in Oakland, Calif
A.R.Froberg,archt. Plan.

Architectural forum 67:18
July 1937

Frohman, Robb and Little

members of firm:

Frohman, Philip Hubert
Robb, Eccles Donald, 1880-1942
Little, Harry B

Froment-Clavier architectural firm

see

Société d'enterprise Froment-Clavier

Frochot Memorial
    Frochot Monument

Arch and Bldrs. jour. 41:pl.for
Feb. 24, 1915

720.5 Frohman, Robb & Little
A67ar   East Congregational church, Ware, Mass.
Frohman, Robb and Little, archts.

Architect (N.Y.) 7: pls.69-74
December 1926

Frommann & Jebsen

see

Chicago (IL) Princess Theater

Frölich, C
    Projekt für das verwaltungsgebäude der
Kabelwerks Brugg AG, Brugg [plans and sections]
C. Frölich, archt.

Bauen and Wohnen
No.2: 69-70
F 1956

D15.1 Frohman, Robb and Little
H84   Interiors of the new Antiquarian house,
Concord, Massachusetts. Frohman, Robb and
Little, archt.

House beautiful 68: 157-159
August 1930

Frommann, George, architect
    Humboldt park pavilion, Chicago, n.d.

Roll 13, frames 46-7

Froelich, Karl
    Verwaltungsgebäude der Kabelwerks Brugg AG
[plans & section] Karl Froelich, archt.

Bauen & Wohnen
#10:366-68 O 1957
Konstruktionsblatt at
end of issue

720.5 Frohman, Robb and Little,
W52   The National Cathedral, Mt. St. Albans,
Washington, D. C . Frohman,Robb and Little,
archts. Cram and Ferguson, assoc. archts.
No plan.

Western architect 39: pl.143
September 1930

Frommann, H. Emil

see

Chicago (Ill.) Schloesser (Rudolph) house

Frontispieces
Frontispiece for a book on architecture.
Beaux-arts institute of design award.

Amer archt
125: 389-390
Ap 23, 1924

720.5
A51
Frost and Granger
A competitive design for the improvements
at the U.S.Military Academy, West Point,N.Y.
Frost and Granger,archts.
Competitive design for chapel.

American architect 81:pls.fol.p.64
August22;29,1903   pl.fol.p.72

Frost & Raymond

see also

Winchester (Mass.) house

Fronts, Store

see

Store fronts

Frost and Granger
House at Cleveland, Ohio. [plans]

Brickbuilder
10: 2 pls.fol.p.154
Jl 1901

720.5
A67r
Frost and Raymond
House of Eleanor Raymond, Boston.
Frost and Raymond, archts.

Architectural record 65: front.,573-81
June 1929

Frost and Granger
see also
Camden (ME) Keep (Chauncey) house
Chicago (IL) Ames (F.L.) house
"   " Baptist church
"   " Bartlett (F.C.) house
"   " Barton (E.M.) house
"   " Born (M.) house
"   " Chicago & Northwestern R.R. terminal
"   "   " Railway ofc. bldg.
"   " Cook county courthouse & city hall (1906-
11) Competition.
"   " Hibbard, Spencer, Bartlett co. bldg.

(see next card)

Frost and Granger
House at Rockford, Illinois. [plans]

Brickbuilder
16: 2 pls.fol.p.36
F 1907

720.5
A67r
Frost and Raymond
House for James H. Cleaves, Winchester,
Mass. Frost and Raymond, archts.

Architectural record 66: 442-444
November 1929

Frost and Granger   (card 2)
see also
Chicago (IL) Hyde Park, Y.M.C.A. bldg.
"   " Lake Shore & Rock Island terminal
"   " LaSalle Street station
"   " Mandel (Simon) house
"   " National bank bldg. Design competition.
"   " Northern Trust Company
"   " Residence
"   " St. Luke's Hospital. George Smith memorial
"   " Smith house
Highland Park (IL) Railroad station
Lake Bluff (IL)   "   "
(see next card)

Frost and Granger
House, 2301 S St. Washington, D.C. [plans]

Brickbuilder
17: pl.fol.p.44
F 1908

Frost, Briggs and Chamberlain

see

Worcester (Mass.) Torrey (L.H.) Country house
Worcester (Mass.) Freeman (G. H.) house
"   " Kesby (Herbert) house
"   " Slater bldg.
Hubbardston (Mass.) Morgan (P. B.) house

Frost and Granger   (card 3)
see also
Lake Forest (IL) Church of the Holy Spirit
"   "   " City hospital
"   "   " College
"   "   " Ladies'dormitory
"   "   " Library
"   "   " Reid Memorial Chapel
"   "   " Tower (proposed)
"   "   " Women's dormitory
"   "   " Dangler (C.I.) house
"   "   " Durand (Calvin) "
"   "   " Episcopal church
(see next card)

Frost and Granger
Selected for Chicago Nat'l Bank Competition.

Inland Architect
34: 40
Dec, 1899

Frost, Charles Sumner 1856-1931
see also
Cedar Rapids (IA) Chicago & Northwestern Railway. Station
Chicago (IL) Blair (H.A.) house
"   " Calumet club (1894?)
"   " Cobden apts.
"   " Crane (R.T.) house
"   " Drovers Safe Deposit co.
"   " Edinburgh apts.
"   " Foreman (E.) residence
"   " Fuller (George A.) house
"   " Garden homes
"   " Gresham (W.G.) house
(see next card)

Frost and Granger   (card 4)
see also
Lake Forest (IL) Granger (Alfred) house
"   "   " Hubbard (J.D.) house
"   "   " Town hall
"   "   " Underwood house
"   "   " University. Hospital
"   "   " Vilas (James) house

Frost and Granger
Desmond, H.W.
The work of Frost and Granger: the Bartlett house,
2901 Prairie Avenue, Chicago, etc.

A   Architectural record 18:115-145
August, 1905

Frost, Charles Sumner 1856-1931 (card 2)
see also
Chicago (Il.) Home for the Friendless
"   " Hoyt (Mrs. H.W.) Residence
"   " Illinois Steel Co. Laboratory
"   " Illinois Trust and Savings Bank Bldg.
Competitive Designs.
"   " Keith (D.W.) House
"   " Kenwood Apts
"   " " Club
"   " " Hotel
"   " McKinlock Bldg.
(see next card)

Frost and Granger

Members of firm:

Frost, Charles Sumner, 1856-1932
Granger, Alfred Hoyt, 1867-1939

Frost and Henderson

see

Chicago (Ill.) Northern Trust Co.

Frost, Charles Sumner 1856-1931 (card 3)
see also
Chicago (Il.) Miller (Roswell) House
"   " Municipal Pier
"   " Potter (Edw. C.) Residence
"   " St. James M. E. Church
"   " Shaw (G.B.) House
"   " Walker (S.B.) House
"   " Walker (W.S.) House
"   " Western Bank Note Bldg.
"   " Wilson (C.E. or E.C.) House
"   " Winamac Apt. Bldg.

(see next card)

Frost, Charles Sumner 1856-1931 (card 4)
see also
Chicago (Il.) World's Columbian Exposition. 1893. Main
State Bldg.
Geneva (Il.) Chicago and Northwestern Railway Station
Lake Forest (Il.) Frost (Charles S.) House
Madison (Wi.) Wis. State Historical Society Library
Bldg. Design.
Milwaukee (Wi.) Chicago and Northwestern Station
Rockford (Il.) Brown Office Bldg.
" " Chicago and Northwestern Station
" " Nelson Hotel

770.5
A67rev   Frost, Charles Sumner, 1856-1931
          Jenkins, C.E.
               Charles S. Frost

          Architectural reviewer:19-47
          S 1897

720.6
I29   Frost, Harry Talfourd 1886-1943
            Obituary notice.

       Illinois society of architects
       Monthly bulletin 28:8
       February-March 1944

Frost, Charles Sumner, 1856-1931

See also

Frost and Granger

Frost, Charles Sumner, 1856-1931
...has presented his architectural
library...[to the Architects' Club of Chicago]

       Illinois society of architects
       Monthly bulletin
       13:1
       Dec.'28-Jan.'29

MICROFILM

Frost, Harry T., 1886-1943
     obituary notice

            In SCRAPBOOK ON
            ARCHITECTURE p. 702
            (on film)

Frost, Charles Sumner   1856-1931
Architect

       Andreas, A.T. History of Chicago. 3
       vols. Chicago: A.T. Andreas, 1884.
       3:74

MICROFILM
     Frost, Charles S   archt.
        McKinlock building, S. W. corner Wells
     and Jackson, Chicago, Ill. 1898; alterations
     and additions, 1917-1920.

            Roll 26, frames 139-156

Frostburg, Md. School
     Hitchins, R.H.
School for Frostburg, Md. Robert Holt Hitchins,
archt. Plans

       Architectural concrete 7:14-17
       No. 4 [1941]

Frost, Charles Sumner, 1856-1931
     Asylum for feebleminded children, Lincoln,
Ill. [rendering and plans]

       Inland architect
       14: 10 and pl. Ag 1889

Frost, Charles Sumner, 1856-1931
     Morgan Park Library, Chicago (Sketch)

       Inland architect 15: 51 and pl.
       Ap. 1890

Frothingham, Arthur L
     Le modèle de l'église Saint-Maclou a Rouen.

       Academie des inscriptions et
       belles-Letter. Commision de la
       Fondation Piot. Monuments et
       Memoirs, ed. George Perrot. Paris:
       E. Leroux, 1894- [?] 12:211-224.

Frost, Charles S.
     Biographical Sketch

       Industrial Chicago: The
       Building Interests. 4 vols.
       Chicago: Goodspeed Pub. Co.,
       1891-(?) - Vol. 1: Pg. 623

Frost (Charles S.) house. Lake Forest, Ill.

see

Lake Forest (Ill.) Frost (Charles S.) house

Frueh house, Highland Park, Ill.

see

Highland Park, Ill. Frueh house

Frost, Charles Sumner, 1856-1931
     Brief biography.

       Herringshaw, Clark J. Herringshaw's
       city blue book of current
       biography. Chicago: American
       Publisher's Association.

Frost, Frederick G.
     see also

New Rochelle (N.Y.) Aldridge (W.) house
"   "   "   Alexander (James) house
"   "   "   Jones (Rodney W.) house
"   "   "   North Ave. Presbyterian Church.
                       Parish house
"   "   "   Thompson (Emery) house
New York (N.Y.) Friedsam (Michael) house
Port Chester (N.Y.) Berrien (Price) house
Union City (N.J.) St. Michael's Convent

Fry and Chestermann

see

Richmond (VA) State capitol. Remodeled.

MICROFILM
     Frost, Charles S   archt.
     Calumet club, Chicago, Ill.

       Roll 26, frames 135-138

Frost, Harry Talfourd, 1886-1943

See also

Bennett, Parsons and Frost

720.5
A67ar   Fry and Kasurin
            Women's Athletic Building, University of
         Michigan, Ann Arbor, Mich., Fry & Kasurin,
         archts.

            Architect (N.Y.) 12: 506,571-573
            August 1929

Fry, Drew and partners

see

London (Eng.) Lewisham. Housing.

Fry, Mr. & Mrs. Edwin Maxwell. Collection.
Platts, Beryl
    The architect as collector. The modern
collection of Maxwell Fry and Jane Drew.
[illus.]

Country life
140: 782; 785-786
S 29, 1966

720.52
A675
Fry, Roger
    The heresies of a painter, or the archi-
tecture of Roger Fry.

Architectural rev 63: 184-187
May 1928

Fry, Edwin Maxwell, 1889-

see also

London, Eng. Kensal house

Fry, Mrs. Edwin Maxwell.

see

Fry, Jane Beverly (Drew)

Fry, T
    Mehrfamilienhaus in Point Piper, Sydney
[plan] T. Fry, archt.

Baumeister
57:218 Ap 1960

Fry, Edwin Maxwell, 1889-

    Member of firms:

Gropius and Fry
Fry, Maxwell, Jane Drew and partners

Fry, Frank L., 1860?-1939
    Obituary

Illinois society of
architects bulletin
23-24: 7
Je-Jl 1939

Fryer, Walter J.

see

London (Eng.) Fiat showroom

Fry, Edwin Maxwell, 1889-
R.P.
    A modern country house. "Ridge End,"
Wentworth, Surrey. Maxwell Fry, archt.

Country life (Lond.)
71:332-334, Mr 19, 1932

Fry, Jane Beverly (Drew)
    House near Hendon, London [plans] Jane
Drew, archt.

Archtl Design
30:56-7 F 1960

Fuchs, Bohuslav

    see also

Brno (Czech.) Masaryk Studensky domov
    "   "   school for women
    "   "   Kindergarten
    "   "   School (Masaryk section)

Fry, Edwin Maxwell, 1889-
    Premises for Mortimer Gall and Co., Ltd.,
115-117 Cannon St. Gropius and Maxwell, archts.

Archt and bldg news
148:258, supp, N 27, 1936

Fry, Maxwell

see

Fry, Edwin Maxwell, 1889-

720.55
B85
Fuchs, Bohuslav
    Neue wohnhäuser in der Tschechoslowakei.
(New residences in Czechoslovakia.)
Bohuslav Fuchs, J.F.Koula, Otto Eisler, and
Friedrich Weinwurm, archts.

Der Baumeister 28: 142-149
April 1930

Fry, Edwin Maxwell, 1889-
    The Royal Hospital, Chelsea, from the
Royal Avenue. A pencil sketch by E. Maxwell Fry

Architecture (Lond.)
5:393, My 1927

Fry, Maxwell, Jane Drew & partners
Fry, E. Maxwell
    A college in the tropics: Ibadan [section]
Maxwell Fry, Jane Drew & partners,archts.

Zodiac
2:127-36 My 1958

Fuchs, Will L. [Architect]

    Drawing: architectural plate case.

Inland archt.
vol. 19 pl.vol.p. 54
May 1892

Fry, Edwin Maxwell, 1889-
    Town planning in West Africa

Archts' yrbk
2:64-73, 1947

Fry, Nora
Chatterton,Julia
    The little people behind the curtain or the
secret of the marionettes. Drawings by Nora Fry

Architectural review
63:plate 1,169-171
May 1928

705.3
C55
Fuchsenberger, Fritz
Lill, Georg
    Temporarily new church architecture in Bayern
Germany

Die Christliche kunst 25:1-24
October 1928

Fuchsenfeld

see

Housing, Austria, Vienna, Fuchsenfeld.

Füeg, Frans
Schulhaus Wangen bei Olten/wettbewerbs-
projekt 1955 [plans] Frans Füeg, archt.

Bauen & Wohnen
#11:397 N 1956

Füssen (Ger.) Stiftskirche St. Mang, Krypta
Bertram Walther
Die instandsetzung der St. Magnus-krypta in
Füssen [illus]

Österreichische zeitschrift
für denkmalpflege 5:41-45
heft 3-4, 1951

Fuchssteiner, Wilhelm
Technisches überwachungsamt in Darmstadt;
kraftfahrzeugprüfhalle; entworfen 1957, gebaut
1958-59 [section] Wilhelm Fuchssteiner & Hermann
Tuch, archts.

Bauen & Wohnen
vol.15: 409, N 1961

Fuentes and Gonsales
Una casa en Monterrey, Mex. [plans] O. de Fuentes
and A. Gonsales, archts.

Arquitectura Mexico #26:37-40
Ja 1949

Fugard and Knapp

see also

Chicago (IL) Belmont hotel (1924)
"   " Canton tea garden
"   " Moody church (1925)
"   " Walton Place (230) apts.

720.5
A67f
Fudge, Donald G
House in Elmira, New York. Donald G. Fudge
archt. Plan.
Contemporary details-porches by George C.
Whiting; Royal Barry Wills and Hugh A. Stub-
bins; Donald G. Fudge; and Ivan H. Smith.
Plan and sections.

Architectural forum 66: 308-309; 376-
April 1937   377

Fürst, Danilo
Scola a Strasisco [plans] Danilo Fürst,
archt.

Casabella
#255: 21, S 1961

720.5
A51
Fugard and Knapp
Lake shore drive hotel, Chicago, Illinois.
Fugard and Knapp, archts. Plans

American architect 126: 435-437, pls.149-
November 5, 1924   152

Füeg, Frans
Baustoffe, bauweise und rendite [plans &
sections of apartment houses] Frans Füeg, archt.
Entwürfe 1957

Bauen & Wohnen
14:138-40 Ap 1960

Fürstliche Schwarzenberg-Palais. Vienna, Aus.

see

Vienna, Aus. Schwarzenberg Palast

720.5
A67f
Fugard and Knapp
Lake Shore Drive hotel, Chicago, Illinois.
Fugard and Knapp, archts. Plan and interiors.

Architectural forum 41: 217-220 pls. 58
November 1924.   60

Füeg, Frans
Haus einer musikerfamilie [plans & sections]
Frans Füeg, archt. Entwurf 1955, gebaut 1956.

Bauen & Wohnen
13:276-79 Ag 1959

Fuesler, Walter

see

Claremont (Cal.) Colby (F.K.) house

720.5
A67b
Fugard and Knapp
Lake Shore Drive hotel, Chicago. Fugard and
Knapp, archts.

Architecture and building 56: pl.111-
May 1924   112

Füeg, Frans
Maison Aerny, Feldbrunnen-Solothurn,
Switzerland [plans & sections] Frans Füeg, archt.

Archl Design
28:368-69 S 1958

Füssen (Ger.) St. Magnus (church)

see

Füssen (Ger.) Stiftskirche St. Mang

720.5
W52
Fugard and Knapp
Canton Tea Garden, Chicago. Walter E. Perry
and Fugard and Knapp, archts .

Western architect 31: pl.16,17
March 1922

Füeg, Frans
Metallbauwerkstatt in Kleinlützel;
entwurf 1957, gebaut 1958 [plan & section]
Frans Füeg, archt.

Bauen & Wohnen
14:278-81 Ag 1960
Konstruktionsblätter at
end of issue

Füssen, Ger. St. Mang (church)

see

Füssen, Ger. Stiftskirche St. Mang

Fugard, Burt and Wilkinson

see

Urbana (Ill.) University of Illinois. Mechanical
engineering building

Fugard, John Reed, 1886?-1968

see also

Fugard and Knapp
Thielbar and Fugard

Fujikawa, Joseph Y.

in SCRAPBOOK ON
ARCHITECTURE p. 12
(on film)

Fuller and Delano

see also

Uxbridge (Mass.) Thayer memorial library

Fugard, J.R.

Member of firm:
Eckland, Fugard and Knapp

Fujiwara-no-miya Palace. Japan
Adachi, Kō
On the Fujiwara-no-miya palace.

Kokka no. 544:text no. 2
March, 1936

Fuller and Delano

Members of firm:

Delano, Ward P   , -1915
Fuller, James E   , 1836-1901
Fuller, Robert L

MICROFILM
Fugard, John Reed, 1886?-1968
...president of...Illinois Society of Archts.

in Scrapbook on Architecture
p. 10
(on film)

720.52   Fulborn manor
A67c   Interior of the Hall, Fulborn Manor.
           Mr. Dudley Newman, F. R. I. B. A., archt.

Arch & con. rep. 84:72, 2 pls.
fol. 80
Jl 29, '10

Fuller and Dick

see

Islip (L.I.) Dick (A.G.) house

MICROFILM
Fugard, John Reed, 1886?-1968
Obituary.

In Scrapbook on Architecture
p.115
(on film)

Fulham, Eng.

see

London, Eng. Fulham

Fuller and Warren co. (ca.1887), Chicago

see

Chicago, Ill. Fuller and Warren co. buildings
(ca.1887)

Fuggerei, Augsburg, Germany

Der Städtebau 15: 3-9 pl.1-3
Heft 1, 1918

Fuller, A. J.

see

London (Eng.) Fulham power station

Fuller and Wheeler

see also

St. Louis, Mo. Pierce (H. Clay) house

Fugman, Godfrey
Forms Co-Partnership with Harry A. Cone.

Inland Architect
45: 49
Jun, 1905

Fuller, A. W. and W. B. Pitcher

see

Brockville (Can.) Fulford (G.T.) house

Fuller & Wheeler
Residence at St. Louis. Fuller & Wheeler,
archts.

Inland architect
v. 12 no. 3
O 1888

720.52   Fuhrer, Eugene
W52   Remisoff, Nicolas
           The cinema unique. Eugene Fuhrer, archt.
           Nicolas Remisoff, theater consultant and designer.
           The Punch and Judy theatre.

Western architect 39: front.,175-177,182-
November 1930   184;pls.181-186

Fuller and Pitcher

see

Muskegon (MI) Hackley hospital

720.5   Fuller, Arthur Harold
A67f   House for H. Jackson Sillcocks, Tuckahoe,
          N.Y. Arthur Harold Fuller, archt. Plan

Architectural forum 66: 308-309
April 1937

Fuller, Buckminster, 1895- see Fuller, Richard Buckminster, 1895-	720.59 A67c Fuller, Hall and Foulsham Ibex house, the Minories, E.C.1. Fuller, Hall and Foulsham, arch. Plans. Architect(Lond.)150:354-355 June 18,1937	Fuller, Richard Buckminster, 1895- Bucky Fuller nel Pantheon. L'Architettura 4:498 N 1958
Fuller, Charles F. see also New York (N.Y.) Harlem river houses	Fuller house see also Dymaxion house	Fuller, Richard Buckminster, 1895- Comprehensive designing [no.1] Transformation 1:18-23 1950
720.5 A67f Fuller,Charles F The sporting gallery and Book Shop,Inc., New York City. C.F.Fuller,archt. Architectural forum 67:196 September 1937	720.1 L72 Fuller house Fuller house, 1947. Buckminster Fuller, inventor [model] Life (art. on art):197-200 Ap 1 '46	Fuller, Richard Buckminster, 1895- Freitragende aluminiumkuppel in Honolulu/ Hawai. Baumeister 55:572-73 Ag 1958
Fuller, George International studio 75:265-273 July, 1922	MICROFILM Fuller house in SCRAPBOOK ON ARCHITECTURE p. 21 (on film)	Fuller, Richard Buckminster, 1895- New directions 3: Buckminster Fuller [plans] Perspecta 1:29-37 Summer 1952
720.5 A67rev Fuller, George A. company Geo. A. Fuller company. A great building firm. List of work Architectural reviewer:114-17 June 1897	Fuller, James E , 1836-1901 Member of firm: Earle and Fuller Fuller and Delano	Fuller, Richard Buckminster, 1895- McHale, John Richard Buckminster Fuller [plans & details] Architectural Design 31: 290-319, Jl 1961
Fuller (George A.) Company Reorganized. Inland Architect 37: 24 Apr, 1901	Fuller, Richard Buckminster, 1895- see also Dymaxion house Fuller house	Fuller, Richard Buckminster, 1895- McHale, John Universal requirements check list. Architectural design vol. 30: 101-111, Mr 1960
Fuller (George A.) warehouse, Chicago see Chicago, Ill. Fuller (George A.) warehouse	MICROFILM Fuller, Richard Buckminster, 1895- Auction for Buckminster Fuller foundation. in SCRAPBOOK ON ARCHITECTURE p.832 (on film)	Fuller, Robert L Member of firm: Fuller and Delano

Fuller, T.C. and T.W. Pietsch

see

Washington (D.C.) Municipal hospital. Competition design.

---

† MICROFILM

Fulton, Mo. Westminster college. St. Mary Aldermanbury church

In SCRAPBOOK ON ARCHITECTURE p. 22 (on film)

Functionalism
Gropius, Walter
Arquitectura funcional

Arquitectura Cuba
17: 323-325
N 1949

Fuller, Thomas

see also

Albany, N.Y. State capitol

Fulton, Robert
The Robert Fulton Memorial.

Amer architect
97, pt.2: 225-6,pl. fol.
p. 232.
June 15, 1910

720.5   Functionalism
A67f   Kimball, Fiske
        Development of American architecture; pt.3:
Eclecticism and functionalism.

Architectural forum 29:21-25
July 1918

Fuller, Thomas   1823-1898
Obit.

Inland Architect
32: 21
Oct, 1898

Fulton, Robert Memorial

Arch. review 18: n.s. 1:1-6
Jan., 1912

Functionalism
El Doctor Carlos Graef Fernandez dice...

Arq Mexico 31:2-5
My 1950

Fuller (W.A.) house. Chicago, Ill.

see

Chicago, Ill. Fuller (W.A.) house

Fulton, Robert. Memorial.
The competition for the Fulton Memorial.
Won by Mr. Magonigle.

Architecture 21: 82, 83, 90
Je 15, 1910

Functionalism
Cranswick, Phillip.
The idea of functionalism.
[illus]

Country life
V. 136: 1196-1198.
N. 5, 1964

Fuller's tavern, South Walpole, Mass.

see

South Walpole, Mass. Fuller's tavern

Fulton, Taylor and Cahill

see

Rock Creek (OH) School

705.944   Functionalism
F98   Fisker, Kay
          Die moral des funktionalismus.

Das Werk 35: 131-134
Ma '48

Fullersburg, Ill.

see

Hinsdale, Ill.

Fumagalli, Raúl A.
Fumagalli, Raúl A.
    Una obra del arq. Raúl A. Fumagalli [plans
and sections]

Arquitectura Cuba
Vol. 22:70-83
F 1954

Functionalism
The principles of architectural composition
13--The expression of function

Arch. journal 59:975-977
June 11, 1924

Full-sizing
    Chrysler, Evans
Making full-size details: a discussion of the
methods used in the office of Dwight James Baum.

Pencil points 10: 159-171
March, 1929

Fumagalli, Raul A.
    Un proyecto del arquitecto Raul A. Fumagali.
[plans]

Arq. Cuba. v.23
p.268-272
Je 1955

Ryerson
        Functionalism
        Lichtwark, Alfred
        Realistische architektur

Pan:229-234
Heft 4, 1897

Functionalism
Stannus, Hugh
Some principles of form-design in applied art.

Inland Architect
Vol. 32:45-9
D 1898
33:4-6, 24-27
F, A, 1899

Funtanet Marti, Pablo
Edificio para banco y restaurante - bar [plans and section] Pablo Funtanet Mayti, archt.

Arquitectura Mexico
17: 68-73, Je 1961

Furness and Evans

see

Bryn Mawr (PA) Hotel
Haverford (PA) Haverford Grammar school

Functionalism
Purcell, William Gray
"Say it all, Mr. Architect"

Northwest arch 15: 4-5,P5-P7
No. 1 Ja-F 1951

Furbeck (Rollin) house, Oak Park, Ill.

see

Oak Park (Ill.) Furbeck (Rollin) house

Furness and Hewitt

see also

Philadelphia, Pa. Jefferson medical college. Hospital

Functionalism
Kellermann, L.
Utilitetsbouw; bouwen voor het gebruik.

. Forum 9:114-116
Mr 1954

"El fureidis", Santa Barbara, Calif.

see

Santa Barbara, Calif. "El fureidis"

Furness & Hewitt

Members of firm:

Furness, Frank
Hewitt, George W

Funeral chapels

see

Mortuary chapels

Furlong, Thomas J.   -1897
Obit.

Inland Architect
29: 21
Apr. 1897

Furness,   Evans and Co.

see also

Baltimore (MD) Old Parsonage
Philadelphia (PA) Morris bldg.
Wayne (PA) Leaming (Thomas) house

Funeral homes

see

Undertaking establishments

Furnes, Bel. Grand Place
Abercrombie, Patrick
The Grand' Place at Furnes.

Town planning rev 5:279-281 & pls.
Ja 1915

Furness, Evans and Co.

Members of firm:

Evans, Allen
Casey, George W.
Kleinfelder, H.E.
Willing, Charles

Funk and Wilcox

see

Brookline (Mass.) Fire station

Furnes, Bel. Groote markt

see

Furnes, Bel. Grand Place

Furness, Frank.   -1912

see also

Philadelphia, Pa. Preston (George R.) house
   "   "   Penn. railroad. Broad St.
                              Station.

Funk, John

see

Modesto (Cal.) Heckendorf (Marvin L.) house
Garages, Private, U.S. 20th c.

Furness Abbey
Furness Abbey, Lancashire. London, England.
No illustrations.

Builder 82:357-358
April 12, 1902

Furness, Frank   -1912

Member of firm:

Furness & Hewitt
Furness, Evans & Co.

Furniture Twyman, Joseph Furniture. Inland Architect 35: 19-20 Apr, 1900	Furrer, Conrad Domingo, 1903- see also Stuttgart, Ger. Kohlhammer house	Ryerson Furtenbach, Joseph, 1632-1655 Schröder, Albert Zwei Stammblätter für Josef Furttenbach d.Ä. und d. J. Das Schwäbische museum 8: 51-52, Je-Jl 1932
Furniture, French, Louis XVI Paris and Versailles. Chair, couch, Bed and table. Stephen W. Wirts, sketcher Inland Archt. Vol. 26, No. 3, pl. Fol. p. 30 Oct. 1895	Furrer, Conrad Domingo, 1903- Landhaus am Bodensee. Conrad D. Furrer, archt. [plans] Das Werk 34:245-247, Ag 1947	710.5 Furukawa, S H84 Humphreys, P. W. Japanese gardens in America. Pt. 2 Mr. Charles J. Pilling's garden, Lansdowne, Pa. Executed by S. Furukawa. House and garden 15:49-52 February 1909
Furniture. U.S. 20th century Furniture designed by Frank Lloyd Wright. Frank Lloyd Wright Scrapbook p. 39, 40, 58, 59, 62, page following 62.	Furrer, Conrad Domingo, 1903- Wohnhaus W. K. in Stuttgart. Conrad Furrer, archt. [plans] Das Werk 27: 286-290, N 1940	Fuselli, Eugenio see Genoa (It.) Casa dei Mutilati
Furniture. U.S. 20th century Kalec, Donald The Prairie School furniture. [illus., measured drawings, details] Prairie school review I: special number Fourth quarter 1964	Furrer, E Kultur- und wohnzentrum am Bieler See [plans & section] E. Furrer & J. Kyburz, archts. Bauen & Wohnen 13:36-41 F 1959	720.53 Fuss, Fritz M68 Exhibition buildings by Fritz Fuss at "Pressa", Cologne. Moderne bauformen 29: 134-138 Heft 3, March 1930.
Furniture Stores, U.S. New York Mercantile building, New York City, Schwartz and Gross, archts. Arch. and building 53: pl. 55 Apr., 1921.	Furriers' shops see Paris (Fr.) Bourdeau magasin	720.53 Fuss, Fritz M68 Fuhrmann, V. The work of Fritz Fuss at Cologne, Germany. Moderne bauformen 25: 313-52 Heft 9, 1926
720.5 Furniture stores,U.S.New York.Spear and Co. A67f Planning techniques for new and remodeled buildings,Spear and Co.,New York.Robert Hel- ler,designer. Architectural forum 68: 155 A February 1938	Furse, H. E. H. E. Furse, archt. Builder 129: 919-20 and pl. Dec. 25, 1925	Futtehpore Sikri see Fatehpur-Sikri
Furniture Stores, U.S. (Wash.) Seattle Furniture stores - Schoenfeld Standard Furniture Co., Seattle, Wash. McClelland and Jones, William I. Bain, associate architects. A Architectural forum 68:158 February, 1938	Furst, C.J. see Chicago (IL) Heissler (Jacob) residence	Futurama see New York (N.Y.) World's Fair. 1939. Town of Tomorrow

Future Architecture

see

Architecture, Future

705.1
I61

Futurist architecture, Germany
"Star" church by Otto Bartning

International studio 75: 58
Oct. 1922

Fyfe, James L.

see also

von Holst and Fyfe

---

microfilm
    Fyfe, James L., architect
Von Holst, Hermann Valentin and James L. Fyfe, archts.
   Adolph Mueller house, Decatur, Illinois, n.d.
Planting plan. Marion M. Griffin, asso. archt.

   Roll 8, frame 22

"Fynmere," N.Y.
  "Fynmere," house for James Fenimore Cooper,
Cooperstown, N.Y. F.P. Whiting, archt. Plans.

A   Architectural record 30:360-367
    October, 1911

G

Gaast, K. v. d.
    Station Hilversum-Oost [plans] K.v.d.
Gaast, archt.

        Forum no. 7
        p. 288-291
        1954

Gaastra, T. Charles

see

Alcade (N.M.) San Gabriel Rancho
Santa Fe (N.M.) Center Cassell bldg. El Onato theater.
  "   "   "   Gaastra (T. Charles) residence

Gabetti, Roberto, 1925-
Feltre, Vittorino da
    · Una memoria bruciata del liberty;
abitazioni economiche a Torino [plans & sec-
tion] Roberto Gabetti & Aimaro Oreglia d'Isola,
archts.

        L'Architettura
        4:442-49 N 1958

Gable and Wyant

see

Beverly Hills (Cal.) Hodgeman (W.H.) house
   "   "   "   Security-1st Nat'l Bank.
Huntington Palisades (Cal.) Parry (N.S.) house

Gabler, Cornelius L. T.

see

Ann Arbor (Mich.) University of Michigan. Phoenix
                        memorial laboratory
   "   "   "   University of Michigan. Cooley
                        memorial laboratory

Gables

        Ditchfield, Peter Hampson. The
        manor houses of England. London:
        B.T. Batsford, 1910. p.132-139.

Gables

        Snyder, Frank Miles. Building
        details. 2 vols. New York: F.M.
        Snyder, 1906-14. v.1,pl.23.

Gables

        Stiehl, Otto Max Johannes. Der
        Wohnbau des Mittelalters. Leipzig:
        A. Kröner, 1908. p. 304-312

Gables
    Architecture's Portfolio

        Architecture 56:228-34
        O 1927
        Architecture 67: 356-70
        Je 1933

720.5   Gables
A67ar   Entrance gable, details and photograph.
          Measured drawing by Theodate Pope, archt.

        Architect(N.Y.)8:699-702
        September 1927

710.5   Gables
C855   Gables at Capetown, South Africa.

        Country life (N.Y.) 49: 52-3
        April 1926

710.5   Gables
H84   The gable end of F.L.Wursburg residence at
          Bronxville, N.Y.

        House & garden 51: 62
        January 1927

720.52   Gables
A67c   Note book sketches of gables, by Sir Her-
          bert Baker.

        Architect 116: pls.
        July 9, 1926

720.52   Gables
A67c   Edwards, A. Trystan
          The riotous gable.

        Architect 116: 13
        July 2, 1926

Gables, Gothic

see

Gothic gables

Gables, Renaissance

see

Renaissance gables

720.5   Gabor, Laszlo
A67f   Department store, Kaufmann, Pittsburgh,
          Pennsylvania. Laszlo Gabor, designer. Plan

        Architectural forum 65: 308-309
        October 1936

Gabriel, E.
    London and southwestern bank, Wimbledon Common,
London, Eng. E. Gabriel, archt.

        Amer. archt and bldg news 55:pl.
        fol 4 in supp
        Ja 2, 1897

Gabriel, J. and Aubert, J.

see

Paris (Fr.) Biron Hotel

Gabriel, Jacques Anges · 1698-1782

see also

Paris (Fr.) École militaire
  "   "   "   "   chapelle

720.52
A678 Gabriel, Jacques Ange 1698-1782
Bust by Lemoyne of Jacques Ange Gabriel.

Architectural review(Lond.)38:20
July 1915

Gade, Herman, house, Chicago

see

Chicago, Ill. Gade (Herman) house

Gage & Wallace

see

Westbury (L.I.) Tiffany (Perry) house

720.05
T37 Gabriel, Jacques Ange 1698-1782
Squire, Tom
Gabriel 'Architecte du Roi.'

Theatre arts monthly 22: 231-234
March 1938

Gadsden (Ala.) Fire Station
Hofferbert, P.W.
Firesafe fire station, Gadsden, Ala.
Paul W. Hofferbert, archt.

A   Architectural concrete 6:15
No. 1 [1940]

Gage, Asahel, house, Wilmette, Ill.

see

Wilmette, Ill. Gage (Asahel) house

720.52
A67 Gabriel, Jacques Ange 1698-1782
The Pavillon Gabriel. A.J. Gabriel,
architect. Plans. Measured drawings.

Architects' journal 59:378-9
February 27, 1924

Gadsden, Julio.
Laboratorios Vitaminicos en Mexico. [plans]
Julio Gadsden, archt.

Arquitectura Mexico #28:154-157
Jl 1949

Gage building, Chicago

see

Chicago, Ill. Gage building

Gabriel, Jacques Ange 1698-1782
Place de la Concorde, Paris. Gabriel, archt.

Planat, Paul. Le Style Louis XIV.
Paris: Librairie de construction
moderne, [c.1912] .pl. 76-81

Ryerson
Gaebel, Werner
Eine neue Volksschule in Bonn-Süd [plans]
Werner Gaebel, archt.

Architektur und Wohnform
61:192-198
Ag 1953

Gage building, Chicago, Ill. (facade)

see

Chicago, Ill. Gage building (facade)

Gabriel, Werner
Ein freibad in Böblingen bei Stuttgart
[plan] Werner Gabriel, archt.

Architektur und Wohnform
63: 244-247
Ag 1955

Gaebel, Werner
Haus auf kleinstem raum in Köln [plans]
Werner Gaebel, archt.

Arch & Wohnform
66:368-71 N 1958

Gage, Carl A.

see also

Minneapolis (MN) Boutin (Frank) residence
"   " Miller (Mrs. J.M.) "
"   " Residence

Gad, Dvora
Israelisches National-Museum, Jerusalem
[plan] A. Mansfeld & Dora Gad, archts.
Baumeister
59 : 32-33, Ja 1962

Gaebel, Werner
Pavillon-volksschule in Radevormwald bei
Köln [plans, sections & details] Werner Gaebel,
archt.

Architektur & wohnform
vol. 69: 300-305, N 1961

720.5
M52 Gage, Carl A
McLean, R.C.
Architecture in the twin cities of Minnesota.
Residence for Frank Boutin, Carl A. Gage, archt.
Plan.

Western architect 27: pls.13-16
September 1918

Gaddis, John W., 1856-1932
In memoriam [no information]

Illinois society of architects
Monthly bulletin
16:4
May-June 1932

Gaebel, Werner
Ein wintergartenanbau. [plan] Werner
Gaebel, ardht.

Architektur und Wohnform
64: 110-113   no.3
F 1956

Gage, Carl A.
Joined Tyrie and Chapman.

West. Archt.
20: p. 11
Jan, 1911

Gage, E. Edson

see

Rye (N.Y.) Bayne (Paul) house

Gage, William J.

see

Bel-Air (Cal.) Shepherd (W.E.) house
Beverly Hills (Cal.) Payne (E.L.) house
"   "   "   Payne Furnace & Supply Co.
Inc. Plant

Gaillard, Fr. Château
    Château Gaillard. Plot plan.

Archaeological journal 95:385,pl.8-9,
Pt. 2, 1938   opp. p. 385

Gage, Lyman J.
    The retirement of L.G. Gage, Secretary
of the Treasury.

Inland Architect
38: 41
Jan, 1902

Gagès, René
    Bron-Parilly (Rione) 1957. René Gagès, archt.

Casabella
#248: 32-33, F 1961

Gaillard, M.   F.

see

Paris (Fr.) Bois de Boulogne house

720.5   Gage, Samuel   Edson -1943
A67   Corn exchange bank, 28th street branch,
New York. S. Edson Gage, archt. No plans.

Architecture and building 49:pl.158-9
October 1917

Gagfah (Ger.) Housing
    Dwelling house groups of Gagfah.

Wasmuths 11: 425-429
Heft 11, 1927

Gaillon. Chateau
    Le chasteau de Gaillon. French text, plans,
engravings.

Androuet du cerceau-Les plus
excellents bastiments, de France.
2 vols. Paris: A. Lévy, 1868-70.
vol. 1: pl. 60-66

720.5   Gage, Samuel   Edson   -1943
A67b   Corn Exchange Bank, New York City. S.
Edson Gage, archt.

Architecture and building 55:pl.155
July 1923

Gaggin and Gaggin

see

Syracuse (N.Y.) White (C.G.) house
"   "   Pennoch (C.E.) house
Pittsburgh (Pa.) Metropolitan bank building

Gaillon. Château
    Château de Gaillon (Eure) Photographs.

Martin, Camille. La renaissance
en France. 2 vols. Paris: C. Eggiman
c.1913-21 1:12-13 pls.74-82

Gage, Samuel Edson,   -1943
    Obituary

In SCRAPBOOK ON
ARCHITECTURE p. 700
(on film)

Gaggin, T. Walter, 1870 (?) -1945
    obituary

Nat'l arch 1:15
N '45

---

913   Gaillon. Château
A66j   Gaillon Castle. Plan.

Archaeological journal 95:382-383
Part 2,1938   pl.4

720.5   Gage, Samuel   Edson   -1943
A67a   Sheridan Square branch, Corn Exchange
bank, New York. S. Edson Gage, archt. No plan

Architecture 41: pl.35
June 1920

Gaggin, T. Walker, 1870?-1945
    obituary notice

In SCRAPBOOK ON
ARCHITECTURE p. 700
(on film)

Gaillon, Fr. Chateau
    Valleri-Gaillon; jardins, d'apres du cerceau

Encyclopedie de l'architecture,
constructions de style. 2 vols.
Paris: Albert Morancé, 1928 - ?
Tome 2 pl. 49

Gage, Thomas G.,   -1921
    In memoriam [no information].

Illinois society of architects
monthly bulletin
5:11
June 1921

Gagnon, Clarence
    Venice
(Etching)

West. Arch.
11: pls. fol. p. 42
April 1908

Gaillon (Fr.) Chateau. Fontaine
    Gaillon. La fontaine de marbre dans la court.

Androuet du cerceau - Les Plus
excellents bastiments, de France.
2 vols. Paris: A. Lévy, 1868-70.
1:66

Gainesville (Ga.) Fire Station
    Disaster proof fire station. Gainesville, Ga.
Archt. not given.

    Architectural concrete 7:14-15
    No. 2 [1941]

Galdós, Jorge M.
    Perspectiva de la residencia para el Dr.
Ulises Odio... Jorge M. Galdós, archt

                Arquitectura Cuba
                15: 154
                My 1947

Galena depot

    see

Chicago (Ill.)   Galena depot

Gainsborough Old Hall
    Gainsborough Old Hall, Lincolnshire, which has
been scheduled for preservation under the Ancient
Monuments Act.

    Architect (Lond.) 137: 3
    October 6, 1933

Gale, Arthur J.
    Proposed Residence at St. Albans.
Mr. Arthur J. Gale, F.R.I.B.A., F.S.I.

    Arch and con rep 79:337,pl.
    My 22, 1908

720.5   Galesburg (Ill.) Percy house
A67r   A house by Robert Spencer,archt. - house
        of Dr.Percy,Galesburg,Illinois. No plans.

        A   Architectural record 19:302-305
                April 1906

Gaisford, John

see

Memphis (TN) Apartment bldg.
"   "   Y.M.C.A. bldg.

Gale, Edwards J

Member of firm:

        Fox, Jenney and Gale
        Fox and Gale

Galguera III, Hilario
    Pequeno edificio de departamentos [plans]
Salvador Ortega Flores, Hilario Galguero III,
& Luis Ramos, archts.

                Arq. Mex. no. 50
                No. 50: 99
                Je 1955

Gaitán Cortes, Jorge
    Baseball stadium, Cartagena, Colombia.
Gabriel Solano, Jorge Gaitan, Alvaro Ortega,
Edgar Burbano, archts. [plans, sects.]

        Royal arch inst of Can
        Jour 25: 202-205 Je 1948

Gale market, Minneapolis

    see

Minneapolis, Minn. Gale market

720.5?   Galicia (Aus.) Guiewosz (Count de) house
A67c   Proposed Residence, Galicia, Austria, for
        Count de Guiewosz. Messrs. Clare & Ross,
        Architects.

                Arch. & contract reporter 77:
                327, 4 pls. fol 344
                My 24 '07

Gaitan Cortes, Jorge
    Edificio de apartamentos en Bogota [plans &
section] Jorge Gaitan Cortes, archt.

                Proa no. 78
                P 22-23
                Ja 1954

Gale (S. C.) house, Minneapolis, Minn.

    see

Minneapolis, Minn. Gale (S. C.) house

Galicia (Sp.)
    Dobby, E.H.G.
Galicia _ Unspanish Spain.

                Country life (Lond.) 80:254-255
                September 5, 1936

Galdós, Jorge M.
    Una torre residencia campestre. Jorge
M. Galdós, archt.

        Arquitectura Cuba
        15: 121-124
        Ap 1947

Galeazzo Maria chapel

    see

Milan (It.) Castello Sforsesco

Galion (O.). Water Cooling Tank.
    Kammerer, W. C.
Galion wanted something different. Water cooling
tank. W.C., Kammerer and Associates, archts.

                Architectural concrete 3:15
                No. 2, 1937

Galdós, Jorge M.
    Fachada principal de la residencia de la
Sra. Maria Teresa Escarrá de Casares...

        Arquitectura Cuba
        15: 185
        Je 1947

Galena building, Chicago

    see

Chicago, Ill. Monroe street (west) 105 building

Gall and Hay

    see

Dundee (Scot.) secondary school

Gall, Richard
Wohnhausgruppe an der Fürstenrieder
Strasse in München [plan] Richard Gall &
Kurt Lange, archts.

Baumeister
56:400-1 Je 1959

Gallarate (It.) villa
Villa a Gallarate. Luigi Ghidini e
Guglielmo Mozzoni, archt. [plans]

Domus no. 217:5-10
Ja., '47

Gallimore, R   A

see also

Forster and Gallimore

Gallagher (J.W.S.) house. Winona, Minn.

see

Winona, Minn. Gallagher (J.W.S.) house

Gallardo, Ernesto Gomes

see

Gomes Gallardo, Ernesto

720.5
A67f
Gallimore, R   A
Remodeled house for H.W.Shackelford,
Poundridge,N.Y. R.A.Gallimore,archt. Plans.

Architectural forum 67:220-221
September 1957

Gallagher, Percival, 1874-1934

Member of firm:

Olmsted brothers

720.5
N56
Gallatin (Tenn,) Fletcher (S.J.) house
Practical building details of residence of
S.J.Fletcher, Gallatin, Tennessee. G.L.
Lockhart,archt. Plans.

New York architect 4:129-133
February 1910

710.5
C85
Gallipoli
Loyd, Francis
Gallipoli, 1915-1929.

Country life (Lond.) 66: 602-605
November 2, 1929

Gallaher, H. P. house, Minn/
Purcell and Feick, architects
H. P. Gallaher house, Lake Minnetonka,
Minnesota, 1909.

Roll 22, frames 7-9

Gallatin (Tenn) Yale & Towne lock and builders'
hardware plant
Yale & Towne. Marr & Holman, architects and
engineers.

Natl arcnt 8. no. 9: 8
September 1952

Gallipoli (Turkey) Power House
Groszkraftwerk Gallipoli von Lois Welzenbacher.
(Great power house, Gallipoli, by Lois Welzenbacher.)

Der Baumeister 28: 275-277
July, 1930

Gallaher, H.P., house. Minn.
Plan. Purcell and Feick, architects.

Prairie School review
II: 11,21
First quarter 1965

Gallaudet college. Washington, D. C.

see

Washington, D. C. Columbia institution for the
deaf. Gallaudet college

720.52
A67
Gallori, Emilio
Garibaldi monument, Rome. Gallori, sculptor.

Architects' journal 48: 62,pls.fol.
August 7, 1918   p.62

Gallaher, H.P., house. Minn.
Plan and illustrations. Purcell, and Feick,
architects.

Western architect
19: 6-7
January 1913

Gallier, J.

see

New Orleans (La.) City hall

Gallo-Roman Antiquities

Paris. Commission Municipale de vieux
Paris. 17 vols. Paris: Imprimerie
Municipale, 1898-1917. pl. 28,34-41
1904 pl 1-3; 1905 pl 4-7; 1907 pl 11-15,
pl 61; 1909 pl 72.

Gallantay, E   von
Projet d'église [plan and section]
E. von Gallantay, archt.

Aujourd'hui 1:
60 no.4
S 1955

720.5
W52
Gallier, James, Jr. 1827-1868
Curtis, N. C.
New Orleans---The French opera house 1859-
1917. James Gallier, Jr., archt.

Western arch.38: 5-8
January 1929

Galloway store and apartment bldg., Chicago

see

Chicago, Ill. Galloway store and apartment bldg.

Galmanini, Gualtiero
    Möbelzentrum in Lissone [plans] Vittorio
Faglia & Gualtiero Galmanini, archts.
Entwurf 1955, gebaut 1957/58.

            Bauen & Wohnen
            14:62-64 F 1960

Galveston (Tex.) City National Bank
    City National Bank.

            Arch. Rec. 49: 164-5 and 186.
            Feb. 1921.

Galvoz, Ernesto
    Dos casas habitacion [plans] Ernesto Galvoz,
archt.

            Arquitectura Mexico
            14:18-19 Mar 1958

Galmossi, Luciano

        see

Bergamo (It.) Houses

721.97   Galveston. Cotton exchange building
A67c   Milam, Ben
            Cotton Exchange building, Galveston. Ben
        Milam, archt.

            Architectural concrete 8: 26-27
            No. 1 [1942]

        Gambaro palace

            See

        Genoa. Palazzo Gambaro

Galt (Ont.) Gore district mutual fire insurance co.
Building
    Gore district mutual Fire Insurance Company
Building. Galt, Ontario. Marani, Lawson and Morris,
archts.

            RAIC jrl 14:95
            F 1937

Galveston (TX) Hutchings Office Bldg.
    Contract taken by Pioneer Fireproof
Construction Co., Chicago.

            Inland Arch.
            26: (xvii) adv. trade supp.
            #3, 1896

        Gamberini, Italo

        see also

        Florence (It.) Stazione Centrale
        Florence (It.) Sede Compagnie Singer

Galt (Ont.) Gore district mutual fire insurance co.
bldg.
    Gore district mutual fire insurance co.,Galt.
[plans] Marani, Lawson and Morris, archts.

            RAIC jr 14:206-208
            O 1937

Galveston (Tex.) Rosenberg Library. Competition.
    Accepted design for the Rosenberg Library,
Galveston, Texas. Eames and Young, archts.
Other designs by Ackerman and Ross, and by Thomas R.
Kimball. Plans.

A   Architectural Review 9 ns.4:16-19
        January, 1902

720.5   Gamberini, Italo
A67f   Railway station, Florence, Italy. Gio-
        vanni Michelucci, Nello Baroni, Pier Nic-
        colo Berardi, Italo Gamberini, Sarre Guar-
        nieri, Leonardo Lusanna, architects.

            Architectural forum 87: 105-112
            September 1947

Galtrucco store, Milan (It.)

        see

Milan (It.) Negosio Galtrucco

Galveston (TX) Rosenberg Library
    Competition.Accepted design by Eames & Young.
Other entries by Ackerman & Ross; Thomas R.
Kimball; D.N. McKenzie

            Inland Arch 38:
            pls. fol.p.40
            Dec.1901

Gamberley Heath (Eng.) Golf Club
    Golf Club. Gamberley Heath Golf Club.

            Architect and contract reporter 93:pl.
            March 12, 1915   for

Galvan Duque, Gustavo
    Concurso de ante-proyecto para un monumento
a las madres de Mexico. [plans] J. Villagran
Garcia; Mario Pani; Felix Comes Martinez, Enrico
Martinez de Hoyos Y Gustavo Galvan Duque; Vicente
Mendiola G., Francisco J. Serrano, archts.

            Arq Mex 17: 95-100
            Ja 1945

Galveston (TX) Sealy Office Bldg.
    Contract taken by Pioneer Fireproof
Construction Co., Chicago.

            Inland Arch.
            26: (xvii) adv. trade supp.
            #3 1896

Gambier (O.) Kenyon College. Pierce Hall

    Pierce Hall, Kenyon College, Gambier, Ohio.
Granger and Bollenbacher, archts.

            Architect (N.Y.) 13:279-291
            December, 1929

Galveston (Tex.) Brantly Harris municipal pier.
            Stadium
    Stadium at end of Brantly Harris municipal pier,
Galveston, Texas.

            Woodbury, William Nicoll. Grandstand
            and stadium design. New York: American
            Institute of Steel Construction,1947.
            111

Galveston (TX) Seeley Bldg.
    J.C. Clayton & Co., arch.

            Inland Arch.
            25: adv. trade supp.
            #6 July 1895

        Gamble, David, house, Pasadena, Cal,

        see

        Pasadena, Cal. Gamble (David) house

Gamble, G.

see

Vancouver (B.C.) Residences

720.5
A67a
Gambrel roofs
Gambrel slopes of northern New Jersey.

Architecture 55: 61-6
February 1927

Gandolfi, Vittorio

see also

Fornovo di Taro, It. Churches (project)
Salsomaggiore, It. Apartment houses

Gamble, Henry G.

see also

Cleethorpes (Eng.)   secondary school

DIVISION LIBRARY
D13.1
H84
Gambrel Roofs
A gambrel-roof cottage with an old-
fashioned dooryard garden

House beautiful 67:167-169
February 1930

Gandolfi, Vittorio
Eigenheim eines architekten in Salsomaggiore
[plans & sections] Vittorio Gandolfi, archt.

Bauen & Wohnen no.2
p. 101-102
Ap 1955

Gamble, Henry G.
Lindsey County Council Buildings, Lincoln
Henry G. Gamble, archt. Plan.

Builder 143: 767,773-776
November 4, 1932

Gambrel Roofs

New country life 32: 49-52
May, 1917

Gandolfi, Vittorio
Esperienza giapponese. Vittorio Gandolfi,
archt. [plans, sections]

Domus no. 209: 3-8
My 1946

Gamble House, Warwick County, Va.
Gamble Place, on Rt. 60 at Mariner's Museum.

William and Mary Quarterly, ser.2,v.18:
April, 1938   pl.60

Gambrill and Post

Members of firm:

Gambrill, Charles D.
Post, George Browne

Gandolfi, Vittorio
Gutbrod, Rolf
Ein landhaus in Salsomaggiore. [plans]
Vittorio Gandolfi, archt.

Architektur und Wohnform
v. 62:43-46
D 1953

Gamble (James M.) house. Williamsport, Pa.

see

Williamsport, Pa. Gamble (James M.) house

Gambrill and Richardson

Members of firm:

Richardson, Henry Hobson, 1838-1886
Gambrill, Charles D

Gandolfi, Vittorio
Casa collettiva per una persona sola.
[tree house]

Domus 245:1
Ap '50

Gambrel Roofs
The gambrel roof. Line drawing.

Architects' journal 76: 594-595
November 9, 1932

Gambrill, Charles D

Member of Firms:

Gambrill and Post
Gambrill and Richardson

Gandolfi, Vittorio
Due versioni di una casetta di montagna.
[Plans, models and sections] Vittorio Gandolfi,
archt.

Domus 248-9 : 21-22
Jl-Ag 1950

Gambrel Roofs
Eberlein, Harold Donaldson
Ackerman-Brinckerhoff house, Hackensack, N.J.
1704, showing typical Dutch Colonial form of
Gambrel roof.

Country life 42: 56
July, 1922

Game rooms

see

Recreation rooms

720.55
D67
Gandolfi, Vittorio
Soluzione di una facciata. [plans]

Domus 232:5
1949

720.52
A67e

Gandon, James.
Custom house, Dublin.

Architect 106: 92.
August 12, 1921.

Cantner, Josef
Münter, Georg
Josef Cantner's "Ground plans of European cities."

Stadtebau 24: 183-184
Heft 7, 1929

Garages

Amer. Arch. 96 pls.
D 29, 1909

Gandy, E   M

see

Cairo (Egypt) Egyptian state telegraph and
telephone headquarters

Garaby (Fr.) Viaduc
Viaduc de Garaby (Garabit). (Garaby viaduct.)
Eiffel, engineer.

Encyclopedie de l'architecture;
constructions modernes. 12 vols.
Paris: Albert Morancé, 1928-39.
5:pl.50

Garages

Amer. arch. 97: pl
F 23, '70.

720.59
A67c

Gandy, Joseph Michael   1771-1943
Summerson, John
The strange case of J. M. Gandy. Drawings.

Architect and building news 145:38-44
January 10,1936

Garage apartments

see

Shreveport (La.) Ramsey (R.D.) apt. & garage

Garages

Construction moderne 29: 327-9
Apr. 12, 1914

Ganske, Walter
Landwirtschaftliche nebenerwerbsstellen
und landwirtschaftliche bauten in Niedersachsen [plans & section] Walter Ganske, archt.

Baumeister
55:778-83 N 1958

710.8
L855

Garage doors.

Country Life 41: 56-7.
Mar. 1922'

Garages

Western arch. 25: pl. fol. p.16
Mar. 1917

MICROFILM
Ganster, William

in SCRAPBOOK ON
ARCHITECTURE p.8
[on film]

720.5
A67f

Garage doors
Metal roll-up garage door.

Architectural forum 65: sup.52,54
November 1936

720.52
A67

Garages
"Design for a garage." Student work at
Liverpool School.

Architects' journal 70:83
July 10,1929

Ganster, William A. and William L.
Pereira

see

Waukegan (Ill.) Lake County Tuberculosis
Sanitorium

710.5
L28

Garage turns
Head, F.
Garage turns.

Landscape architecture 15: 160-70
April 1925

Ryerson
Garages
Baldwin, H   E
Garages as carefully designed as homes

House beaut 49: 120
F 1921

Gantenbein, Werner
Neubau papierfabrik Versoix [plan &
section] Werner Gantenbein, archt.

Bauen & Wohnen
#2:48-9 F 1957

Garages

see also

Automobile service Stations
Parking Garages
Motor bus lines. Stations.

720.5
A67a

Garages
Garage doors. Architecture's Portfolio.

Arch. 63: 306-20
My '31

720.52
B95

Garages
Plan and elevations for a garage, by
Mr. Oliver Law.

Builder 131: 89-91
July 16, 1926

Garages, Attached
Boyd, J.T., Jr.
The garage in the house. Plans.

Country life 32:56-59
My, 1917

720.5
A67

Garages, Attached
Safe construction of built-in garages
explained by Commerce Department.

Architecture 49:197-201
June 1924

720.5
A67f

Garages
Special number on automotive buildings.

v.46

Architectural forum
March 1927

Garages. Townsend, C.Harrison.
Garages and motor houses.

Inland Arch.
51: 27-8
April 1908
51: 40-2
May   1908

720.52
A674

Garages, Attached
Terrace houses with garages incorporated.
Working drawings by E.K. Rowe & H.W. Binns,
archts.

Architecture (Lond.)6: 87-89
May-June 1928

RYERSON LIBRARY
D10.5
C88

Garages
Marple, Albert
Solving the garage problem. No plans.

Craftsman 28:505-509
August 1915

Garages, Attached
Bugbee, B.A.
The garage's place is in the home.

House beautiful 71: 134-136,151
February, 1932

Garages. Competitions
Beaux-arts institute of design, competition:
"A garage on a private estate".

B.A.I.D. 3: 19-20
November, 1926

720.5
A67r

Garages
Technical news and research featuring
garages.

Architectural record 65: 177-198
February 1929

720.52
A67c

Garages, Attached
House plan, with garage attached.
Hughes, Nicholls & Hughes, archts.

Architect 116: 85
July 16, 1926

Garages, England

see also

Seaford (Eng.) Chauffeur's cottage and garage

Garages, Attached

see also

Hastings-on-Hudson (N.Y.) Luttrell (James) house

and

Garages, Private

720.5
A67

Garages, Attached
House with garage attached, Portland, Ore.
Wade Pipes, archt.

Arch.& building 59:171
May 1927

720.52
A67

Garages, England
Motor garage at Stirchley. H.W.Simister,
archt.

Architects' journal 76: supp.
August 3, 1932

Garages, Attached
The attached garage

House beautiful 52: 189-191
Sept., 1922

720.5
A67b

Garages, Attached
House with garage, Portland, Ore. F. H. Johnson, archt.

Arch. & building 59:99-102
March 1927

720.52
B93

Garages, England. Highroad
New garage at Highroad, Balham.

Builder 120: 284,pl. fol. p.284
March 4, 1921

720.5
P59

Garages, Attached
Design for a residence and garage, by Otho
McCrackin, Hutchinson, Kansas.

Pencil points 8: 634
October 1927

720.52
B93

Garages, attached
House at Letchworth, Herts. Crickmer &
Foxley, archts.

Builder 131: 573,4
October 1, 1926

720.53
M68

Garages, Europe
Müller, George
The garage problem in the large European
cities.

Moderne bauformen 29: adv. 66-70
Heft 4, April 1930

Garages, France see also Paris (Fr.) Garage Fresnel	Garages, Private see also Garages, Attached	Garages, Private American Country houses of Today. 8 vols. New York: Architectural Book Publishing Company, 1912-13. p.78,82-3.
720.52 A67 Garages, France. Paris Shand, P. Morton From town house to garage: the history of a Paris transformation. Architects' Journal 69: 7-12 January 2, 1929	720.5 A51 Garages, Private Garage for Edward C. Schaefer, Premium Point, N. Y. Kelley & Steinback, archts. [plan]. Amer arch 115:pl. 174-5. My 28, '19	Garages, Private. American Country Houses of Today. 8 vols. New York: Architectural Book Publishing Company, 1922. p.82,83.
720.52 A67 Garages, France. Paris A garage in the Rue Fonthieu, Paris, by Auguste Perret and Brothers. Architects' Journal 68: 255 August 22, 1928	720.5 A51 Garages, Private Garage of F. O. Zenke, Riverdale, N. Y. Dwight James Baum, archt. [plan]. Amer. arch 111:pl fol. 16 Ja 3, '17	Garages, Private Amer. Homes and Gardens 7:312-3. 1910
720.54 A67v Garages, France. Paris Garage, Rue Campagne-Première, à Paris, 1926. (Garage, Rue Campagne-Première et Paris,1926.) Henri Sauvage, archt. No plan. L'architecture vivante : pl.1-2 Spring 1927	720.5 A51 Garages, Private Garage for Adam Schantz, Dayton, O. Louis Lott, archt. Amer arch 116:pl 134 O 1, '19	Garages, Private Amer. Homes and Gardens 8: 190-192 May, 1911.
711 B77 Garages, France. Paris Brandt, Jürgen Garage building in Paris. Stadtebau 24: 78-81 Heft 5, 1929	720.5 A51 Garages, Private House & garage of F. A. Schick, Bethlehem, Pa. C. E. Schermerhorn, archt. [plans]. Amer. arch 115:pl 207-3 Je 18, '19	Garages, Private Amer. Homes and Gardens 8:387-392 Nov., 1911
720.53 W31 Garages, Germany Wasmuths, (heft 5-6)8:235-37 1924	720.5 A51 Garages, Private Three private garages on Park Ave, New Yk. Amer.architect 122: 504 Dec. 6, 1922	Garages, Private Amer. Homes and Gard. 12:18-19 Jan., 1915
720.53 W68 Garages, Germany. Essen Garage in Essen. Architect, Bode. Moderne bauformen 23: 275 September 1924	720.5 A51 Garages, Private American architect 124:pl. Dec. 19, 1923	Garages, Private Country life in Amer. 21:31-32. Jan. 1, 1912

Garages, Private

House and garden 17:92-94
Mr 1910

710.5
C855   Garages, Private
        Building the garage

        Country life 44:69-73
        July 1923

Garages, Private.
    Garages and Motor Houses.
By C. Harrison Townsend.

        Inland archt 51:
        27-28; Ap 1908
        40-42; My "

Garages, Private

House and Garden 23:112-114
Feb., 1913

D13.1
H84   Garages, private
       Amos, R. L.
       The car and the country estate

        House beautiful 57:390-391
        April 1925

Garages, Private
    Garage, estate W.V. Lawrence, Bronxville, N.Y.
Bates and How, archt.

        Architecture 40:225-29
        Ag., '19

Garages, Private

House and garden 30:24-25
Aug., 1916

710.5
C855   Garages, Private
        A cottage designed to become a garage

        Country life 43: 72-3
        Dec. 1922

720.5   Garages, Private
A67a   Garage group. Estate of Chas. P.
        Holzderber. Wm. Edgar Moran, archt. [plan].

        Arch.39:150-51
        My '19

Garages, Private

House and garden 31: 24-25
Jan., 1917

Garages, Private
    Equipping the garage
Alexander Johnson

        House and Garden 46:74-75
        Aug., 1924

Garages, Private
    Garages particuliers.

        Tech. et arch.
        14, no. 3-4: 92-3
        1954

Garages, Private

House and garden 34:42
July, 1918

D13.1   Garages, Private
H84   Way, Henry
         Finding a place for your garage: a few ways
    of solving problems arising when there is little
    or no land available.

        House beautiful 45:86-87
        February 1919

D13.1   Garages, Private
H84   Garage planned for House Beautiful home
         no.1.(2 car). Plans.

        House beautiful 46:172
        September 1919

Garages, Private

House and garden 36:34
Aug., 1919

Garages, Private
    A $5,000 Garage. Designed by Andrews,
Jaques and Rantoul.

        House and gard 8: 210
        Je 1908

750.5   Garages, Private
A67a   Garage with attached conservatory,
        Philadelphia, Pa. C. E. Schermerhorn, archt.

        Arch 40:225-29
        Ag '19

Garages, Private
    Sites and entrance drives.

House and Garden 40: 46-7.
Nov., 1921.

710.5   Garages, Private
H84   Mathor, M. W.
         The garage and its construction.

        House and garden 57: 89-89,108
        January 1930

Garages, Private
    The house that will keep a car. Illus.

        Country life 38:67-9.
        May, 1920

Garages, Private
    White, C.E., Jr.
Housing the automobile: garage and garage apparatus.
Plans.

        House beautiful 30:84-87,90
        August, 1911

710.5
C855   Garages, Private
    Shepherd,N.E.
      Storage for how many?

        Country life(U.S.) 65:71-72
        April 1934

Garages, Private, U.S. 20th c.
    Storage garage. It organizes space to make
room for car and many other things. John Funk,archt.

        Life articles on art 1945 pt
                1: 417-418
        My 28, 1945

Garages, Private
    Wheeler, Walter F.
Housing the automobile

        House beautiful 57:139-142
        Feb., 1925

Garages, Private
    Two-car garage

        Country life in Amer. 26:50-51
        May, 1914

720.5
A67b   Garages, U.S. New York

        Arch & building 55:pl.233
        Nov. 1923

710.5
H84   Garages, Private
      Instances of clever designing

        House & garden 48:79
        Nov. 1925

D13.1
H84   Garages, Private
      Two garages. No plans.

        House beautiful 63: 766
        June 1928

Garbage Disposal. Garbage disposal in the
      United States.

        Inland Arch.
        25: 51
        June 1895

720.5
A67   Garages, Private
      One-car garage for Sumner Robinson,West
Newton, Mass. Frank Chouteau Brown, archt.
[plan].

        Arch rev. 21:N.S. 4: pl. 20, 1.
        F '16

720.53
M68   Garages, Private, Germany

        Moderne bauformen 23:107
        Apr. 1924

720.5
A51   Garbage disposal
      Municipal house cleaning.

        Amer. arch. 126:123-26
        July 30, 1924

710.5
C855   Garages, Private
      A page of garages.

        Country life (N.Y.) 49: 68
        April 1926

720.52
A67   Garages, Spiral
      A design for a "spiral" garage, by R. G.
Livingstone.

        Architects' journal 68: 594
        October 31, 1928

720.54
A67au   Garbage disposal plants
      La destruction des déchets.

        L'architecture d'aujourd'hui
        11: 5-70
        No. 3-4, 1940

Garages. Private
    The Private Garage. Its Design, Arrangement
and Cost. By. I. Howland Jones.

        House and gard 9: 158-65
        Ap 1906

720.5
A51   Garages, U. S.

        Amer. arch 96: preceding p.1
        D 29, '09

Garbage disposal plants, France

        see

Belfort (Fr.) Usine d'incinération des ordures

710.5
H84   Garages, Private
      Solving the garage problem

        House and garden 46: 64-5
        Nov. 1922

Garages, U.S.
    Sogni dall' America

        Domus no. 206: 18-23
        F 1946

720.53
B55   Garbage disposal plants,Germany. Cologne
      Die müllverwertungsanstalt in Köln am
Rhein. (The rubbish utilizing institution in
Cologne.) Mehrtens,archt. Plans.

        Der Baumeister 28: 255-264
        July 1930

Garbage disposal plants, U.S.

see

Shreveport (La.) Garbage disposal plant
Columbus (O.))best incinerator

Garber and Woodward

see also

Cincinnati (O.) Dixie terminal bldg.
"   "   Public library. Price Hill branch
"   "   Lafayette Bloom school

Garber and Woodward

Members of firm:
    Garber, Frederick W.
    Woodward, Clifford B.

Garber, Frederick W., 1877 - 1950
    Frederick W. Garber [obit note]

Natl arch 6: 7
O 1950

720.54
A67au   Garches (Fr.) Laboratoires du Docteur Debat
    L'usine heureuse par le Docteur Francois
    Debat...Laboratoires du Docteur Debat à
    Garches. Jean Barot, archt.   [plans]

L'Arch d'aujourd'hui
10: 36-39
Je '59

Garches (Fr.) Villa
    Dormoy, Marie
Le Corbusier. Villa in Garches by Le Corbusier.
Plans.

Wasmuths monatshefte 14: 72-75
February, 1930

A

Garches, Fr., Villa
    Robertson, Howard and Yerbury, F.R.
The quest of the ideal.
The villa at Garches by Le Corbusier and Jeanneret.
Plan and photographs of exterior and interior.

Architect (Lond.) 121:621-624;653-658
May 10;17;1929

Garches (Fr.) Villa
    Villa à Garches 1927. Tracé régulateur
des facades. (Villa at Garches 1927. Regu-
lating Outline of the Sides.) Le Corbusier
and Pierre Jeanneret.

L'Architecture Vivante: 15-17,24,32;
pls. 1-22
Ja 1929

Garcia & Yamhure
    Casa en Bogotá [plan & sections] Garcia &
Yamhure, archts.

Proa
#128:20-21 Jl 1959

Garcia, Jose Villagran

see

Villagran Garcia, Jose, 1901-

Garcia, Samuel
    Banco del Comercio - Cali [plan] Juan
Osorio & Samuel Garcia, archts.

Proa
#101:12-13 Jl 1956

Garcia Alonso, Felix
    Rivero, Nicolas M.
    In memoriam

Arquitectura Cuba
18: 32
Ja 1950

Garcia-Barbón, Lorenzo
    Football stadium, Barcelona [plan & sections]
J. Soteras Mauri, F. Mitjans Miro, Garcia-Barbón
& Fernádez de Menestrosa, archts.

Archtl Design
29:80-1 F 1959

Garcia Barbon, Lorenzo
    Palacio dos esportes, Barcelona, Espanha
[plans and section] José Soberas Mauri, Lorenzo
Garcia Barbon, and Fernandes de Menestrosa,
archts.

Habitat 6:
32-34 no. 25
D 1955

Garcia Collantes, Jesus
    Avenida Sierra Paracaima no. 1045. [plans]
    Avenida Sierra Ventana nos. 379,381. [plans]
    Jesus Garcia Collantes, archt.

Arq. Mexico
#22: 99-104
Ap 1947

Garcia Collantes, Jesus
    Casa en Mexico [plans]

Arquitectura Mexico
No. 47 p. 148-150
S 1954

Garcia Collantes, Jesus
    Casa habitacion [plans] Jesus Garcia
Collantes, archt.

Arquitectura Mexico
no.58;82-3 Je 1957

Garcia Collantes, Jesus
    Edificio para despachos. [plans] Mario Pani
and Jesus Garcia Collantes, archts.

Arquitectura Mexico
No. 44:221-226
D 1953

Garcia Collantes, Jesus
    Un establecimiento industrial [plans]
Jesus Garcia Collantes, archt.

Arq. Mex. no.50
p. 86-89
Je 1955

Garcia Lascurain, Xavier
    Museo de arte y escuela de arquitectura [plans]
Jose Villagran Garcia, Alfonso Liceage & Xavier
Garcia Lascurain, archts.

Arq. Mexico
39: 284-287
S 1952

Garcia Meitin, Antonio
    Una obra de los arqs. Carlos Gomez Millet
y Antonio Garcia Meitin. [plans]

Arq. Cuba
18: 146-149
Ap 1950

Garcia Meitin, Gomes Millet, Puentes y Coroelles
Edificio de Apartamentos situado en la calle 26 entre 21 y 23. Arquitecto Proyectista: Armando Puente. Arquitectos constructores: Garcia Meitin, Gomes Millet, Puentes y Coroalles

Arquitectura Cuba
14: 272
S 1946

Garconnieres, U.S.
...detached chambers for the younger male members of the family or for overnight guests...

Art bul
28:103
Je 1946

Gardella, Ignazio, 1905-
Casa per un viticultore. [plans] Ignazio Gardella, archt.

Metron
37: 31
Jl-Ag 1950

Garcia Ramos, Domingo, 1911-
Instituto de biologia y estudios medicos y biologicos. [plans] Domingo Garcia Ramos & Homero Martinez de Hoyos, archts.

Arq Mexico
39: 302-303
S 1952

Gard, Fr. Saint Gilles
S. Gilles du Gard: a glorious example of Romanesque art. [illus.]

Carnegie magazine
15: 115-119
S 1941

Gardella, Ignazio, 1905-
Una casa riflessa dalla laguna veneziana [plans] Ignazio Gardella, archt.

L'Architettura
4:474-75 N 1958

Garcia Ramos, Domingo, 1911-
El plano regulador de Campeche. [plans] Domingo Garcia Ramos, archt.

Arq Mexico
36: 39-54, D 1951

Gardella and Martini
see
Alexandria (Eg.) Dispensaire

Gardella, Ignazio, 1905-
Un edificio per uffici a Milano [plans, sections, & detail] Anna Castelli Ferrieri & Ignazio Gardella, archts.

Casabella
#247:2-9 Jan 1961

Garcia Ramos, Domingo, 1911-
Plan regulador de Culiacan, Sinaloa. Mario Pani, archt. in collaboration with Domingo Garcia Ramos, archt., Victor Vila, eng., & Miguel de la Torre, archt.

Arquitectura Mexico
No. 48: 233-244
D 1954

Gardella, Ignazio
see also
Gardella and Martini

Gardella, Ignazio, 1905-
La mensa Olivetti a Ivrea [plans, sections & details] Ignazio Gardella, archt.

Casabella
#235: 4-6, 9-13, Ja 1960

Garcia Ramos, Domingo, 1911-
Plano regulador de la ciudad y Puerto de Mazatlan, Sin. Mario Pani, archt. in collaboration with Domingo Garcia Ramos & Miguel de la Torre, archts.

Arq. Mexico
47: 168-180
S 1954

Gardella, Ignazio
see also
Milan, It. Villa Borletti
" " Villa Reale. Reconstruction (project)

Gardella, Ignazio, 1905-
Progetto per il quartiere pilota C.P.E. a Vicenza [site plan, plans, sections & details] Ignazio Gardella, capogruppa archt.

Casabella
#230:23-30 Ag 1959

Garcia Ugarte, Benito
Casa habitacion en la ciudad de Durango, Max. [plans] Enrique Manero Peon & Benito Garcia Ugarte, archts.

Arquitectura Mexico
no.58:84-5 Je 1957

Gardella, Ignazio, 1905-
Apartment in Venice [plan] Ignazio Gardella, archt.

Architectural Design
31: 367-68 Ag 1961

Gardella, Ignazio, 1905-
Massariol, Giuseppe
Umanesimo di Gardella [plans & sections] Ignazio Gardella, archt.

Zodiac
2:91-110 My 1958
Engl. trans. p.205-209

Garconnieres, U.S.

Louisiana; a guide to the State. comp. by the Writers' Program of the WPA. New York: Hastings House, 1941.
7th pl. fol. 188

Gardella, Ignazio, 1905-
Guiducci, Roberto
Appunti sulla progettazione di Gardella

Casabella
#235: 7-8, Ja 1960

Gardella, Ignazio, 1905-
Villa a Milano [plans] Ignazio Gardella, archt.

Domus
263: 28-33
N 1951

Garden apartments

see

Apartment houses. Garden apartments

Garden Architecture
Architectural gardening. 9 pts.
Illustrations by C.E. Mallows and F.L. Griggs

Int studio
35:182-8, S 1908
36:31-42,180-8
N 1908, Ja 1909
37:120-8,266-74
Ap, Je 1909
38:101-9,276-85
Ag, O 1909
40:18-27,186-191
Mr, My 1910

Garden Architecture
Guild, I.T. Details of garden architecture.

Arch rev 9:
91-92; Ap, 1902
97-100; My "
109-13; Je "
121-25; Jl "
136-39; Ag "

Garden architecture

see also

Arbors
Garden houses
Foot bridges

Ryerson

Garden architecture
Roper, Lanning
Architecture in the garden

Country life (Lond)
123:494-496, F 27, 1958

Garden Architecture
Recent work

Arch. review 24: n.s. 7:103-117
Dec., 1918

Garden Architecture

Architecture 39: 34-38
pl. 16-17
Feb., 1919

D15.1
H84   Garden architecture
Humphreys, P. W.
A bath house as a garden feature (not decorative).

House beautiful 30:186-187
N '11

720.52
A67a   Garden architecture
Winterstoke garden, Ramsgate. Sir John
Burnet & Partners, archts.
Coleton, Kingswear, Devon; layout of garden. Oswald P. Milne, archt.
Rheinefield, Brockenhurst. Romain, Walker
& Jenkins, archts.

Architect 115: 345-347
April 16, 1926

Garden Architecture.

Richardson, George. New designs
in Architecture. London: The
author, 1792. pl.27-8.

710.5
C855   Garden architecture
Flanders, A. H.
Bath house architecture in garden design.

Country life (U.S.) 53:40
Ap '28

Garden architecture, Concrete
Sloan, M.M.
Architectural treatment of concrete
structures. Pt. IV - Concrete landscape gardening.

Arch rec 31: 68-79
Ja'12

Garden Architecture
Architectural features

Brickbuilder 25: 119-122
May, 1916

Garden architecture
Concrete accessories

House beau
26:136-8
N 1909

Garden architecture, England

see also

Moor Close (Eng.) Garden architecture

Garden architecture
White, H.P.
The architectural garden. 2 pts

Amer archt
102, pt. 2: 185-8
N 27, 1912
103, pt. 1: 45-48
Ja. 15, 1913

Garden Architecture
Garden peristyles in garden of Samuel Untermeyer

American architect 122: pl
Nov. 8, 1922

Garden architecture, England.

Academy architecture 51:1-16
1919-20

Garden Architecture
Architectural features of a garden - modern
gardens

House beautiful 54:26-30
July, 1923

Garden Architecture
Garden Pier, Atlantic City

Amer. arch. 105: pl. 2003
May 13, 1914

710.5
C85   Garden architecture, England
Hussey, Christopher
Modern garden architecture at Tyringham,
Buckinghamshire; garden temples designed by Sir
Edwin Lutyens.

Country life (Lond.) 65: 740-746;
May 25,June 1,1929   780-786

Garden architecture. England. 18th/19th cent.
Berbiers, J. L.
18th and early 19th century garden features [plans]

Archt & bldg news
212:855-9 D 25,1957

Garden books

see

Gardens. Bibliography

720.52 Garden cities
B95   Bird's-eye view of garden city lay-out.
             Dr. Raymond Unwin,

Builder 131: 795
November 12, 1926

Garden architecture. England. Chinese style
Wittkower, Rudolf
English neo-Palladianism, the landscape garden, China and the enlightenment. [illus., sum. in It.,Fr.& Ger.]

L'Arte
v.2: 18-35
Je 1969

Garden Bridges,

see

Foot Bridges

710.5 Garden cities
L:6   Adams,Thomas
           Community development in wartime.

Landscape architecture 8: 109-124
April 1918

720.53 Garden architecture. Germany.
M58

Moderne Bauformen 21: 22-26.
Heft 1, 1922.

710.5 Garden brooks
B84

House & garden 48:68-69
Dec. 1925

Garden cities
Edwards, A. T.
A criticism of the garden city movement.

Town planning rev 4:150-157
Jl 1913

---

711 Garden architecture. Germany
877

Der städtebau 18:56-58
Heft 11-12, 1921

Garden Cities

AIA jour 2:80-91
Feb., 1914

Garden cities
Reade, Charles C.
A defence of the garden city movement.

Town planning rev 4:245-251
O 1913

Garden architecture. Great Britain.
Hadfield, Miles
The place of trees in British gardens. [illus]

Country life
144: 1580-1581
D 12 1968

720.5 Garden cities.
A67r

Arch. Rec. 51: 175-84.
Feb. 1922.

Garden Cities
The Economy of a Garden City.

Architect 88:177-178
Sept. 27, 1912

720.5 Garden architecture, Japan
M81   Some stonework in Japanese gardens.

Monumental news 16: no. 12
D '04

Garden Cities

Craftsman 19:445-451
Feb., 1911.

Garden cities
Edwards, A. Trystan
A further criticism of the garden city movement.

Town planning rev 4:312-18
Ja 1914

720.5 Garden architecture. Spain
A67r   Andalusian gardens and patios

Architectural record 55:177-93
Feb. 1924

Garden cities

Western arch. 27: 55-57
July, 1918

720.52 Garden cities
A67ay Le Corbusier
           Housing equipment for machinist society.

Archts' yr bk 2: 76-78
1947

Garden cities
On the laying out of garden cities.

Sennett, A.R. Garden cities in
theory and practice. 2 vols. London:
Bemrose and Sons, Ltd., 1905.
vol. 1. pages 63-83

Garden cities, England

see also

Silver End, Eng.

Garden Cities, England
Chelsea Park Gardens

Builder 115:pl. for
Aug. 30, 1918

Garden cities
Unwin, Sir Raymond and Sharp, Thomas
Towards a healthy social life.

RAIC jrl 15:27-28
F 1938

Garden Cities, England

Architect 102:pl.for
Aug. 8, 1919

720.52
A67c   Garden cities, England
Garden city and garden suburb, England.

Architect 120: 12-13
July 6, 1928

Garden Cities, Africa (North)
Pinelands Garden City, Cape Town.
A.J. Thompson, architect

Architect 108:pl
Dec. 8, 1922

Garden-cities, England

L'art decor. 26:33-46
Aug. 1911.

720.52
A67   Garden cities, England
Johnson, Harry
A garden suburb's coming of age.

Arch. jour. 68: 9-14
July 4, 1928

710.5
L26   Garden cities. Belgium.
Winterslag,

Landscape arch. 11: 180-5.
July 1921.

Garden cities, England

Craftsman 17:296-310
Dec. 1909.

Garden Cities, England
(Garden cities)

Country life (Amer.) 17:531-534
Mr., '10

720.53
W31   Garden Cities, Belgium
Modern work in Brussel.

Wasmuths 10: 162-368
Heft 4, 1926

Garden Cities, England

House beautiful 31:161-166
May, 1912.

720.52
B93   Garden cities. England.
Graythorp garden village.

Builder. 120: 406-8.
Apr. 1, 1921.

720.6
R88p   Garden cities, Canada. Montreal
Richard, Jean d'Auteuil
A garden city in the making. [plans]

Royal arch. institute of
Canada. Journal 21:195-9,213
S'44

Garden Cities, England

Scribner's 52:1-19
July, 1912.

720.52
A67c   Garden cities, England
Harvey gardens housing estate,
Charlton Lane. By Mr. Kenneth M. Roberts
under superintendence of Mr. Alfred Roberts.
Plan.

A   Architect(Lond.)150:167
May 7,1937

Garden cities. Competitions
Report of jury of award prize drawings

Amer arch 90:199-200
pl 1-5
D 22, 1906

720.52
A67   Garden cities. England
Cottages at Alderley Edge. J. Hubert
Worthington, architect

Architects journal 57:1014-1016
June 13, 1923

720.52
A67   Garden Cities, England
Swanpool Garden Suburb, Lincoln.

Architects' Jour. 55: 749-58
May 24, 1922.

720.8
A51j.
Garden cities. England.
Unpopulating London.

Amer.Inst. of Arch.Jour.8:354-6.
Oct. 1920.

720.52
A67
Garden cities. England.Welwyn
Recent work at Welwyn ...
Louis De Soissons, F.R.I.B.A.,S.A.D.G.,
arch.

Architects' Jour. 62: 268-75
Aug. 19, 1925

720.52
A67c
Garden cities,England. Wembley
Lawn court flats,Wembley. Welch,Cache-
maille-Day and Lander,archts.

Architects (Lond.)155: 254-256
September 1,1933

720.52
A67
Garden cities, England. Bury Port
Bury Port garden suburb.

Arch.Jour.51:252-3.Feb.25,
1920.

720.52
A675
Garden cities. England.Welwyn
Reiss, R.L.
The significance of Welwyn Garden City.

Arch. rev. 61: 177-82
May 1927

720.52
B95
Garden cities,England.Wembley Hill
Wembley Hill garden suburb

Builder 123: 696,698 & pl.
Nov. 10, 1922

Garden Cities, England. Hereford

Town planning rev. 4:145-149
July, 1913

720.52
B93
Garden cities. England.Welwyn
Welwyn.

Builder. 120:227-8.
Feb. 18, 1921

720.5
A67f
Garden cities. England. Whiteley Village
Phillips, R.R.
Whiteley village, at Burhill, Surrey: an
example of modern English philanthropic housing.
Sir Aston Webb, Sir Ernest George, Sir Reginald
Blomfield, Ernest Newton, Mervyn Macartney, Frank
Atkinson, Walter Cave, archts.

Architectural forum 36:85-90 & pl.39
A   March 1922.

Garden Cities, England. Hull
Hull.

Builder 104:183-185
Feb. 7, 1913

720.52
A67
Garden cities. England.Welwyn
Welwyn Garden City, Herts. C.M.Hennell,
and C.H.James, architects
Rhiwbina Garden Village.T.A.Lloyd,archt

Arch.journal 57: 18-22,53-6
Jan. 3, 1923

Garden Cities, France

L'architecture 27: 237-241
June, 1914

Garden Cities, England. Swanpool
Swanpool Garden suburb, Lincoln

Arch's. jour. 50:88-95
July 16, 1919

720.52
B93
Garden cities. England.Welwyn
Welwyn Garden City

Builder 124:547-58
April 20, 1923

Garden Cities, France

Landscape architecture 14:268-269
July, 1924

720.53
W31
Garden cities, England. (Welwyn)
Arbeiten von Louis De Soissons und Ander-
en für die Gartenstadt Welwyn

Wasmuth 9: Heft 7; 285-303
1925

720.52
B93
Garden cities. England. Welwyn
Welwyn Garden city

Builder 128:979-981
June 26,1925

Garden Cities, France

Town planning rev. 7:251-2
Mar. 1918

711
S77
Garden cities,England. Welwyn
Gartenstadt Welwyn bei London. (Garden
city,Welwyn near London.) Louis de Soissons,
archt. Plan,sketches.

Der städtebau 22: 33-34
March 1927
A

711
T73
Garden cities. England.Welwyn
Welwyn garden city.

Town planning rev. 8: 179-82.
Dec. 1920.

720.54
A67
Garden cities, France
La Cité-Jardin d'Arcueil

L'Architecture 36:391-6
Dec. 25, 1923

720.54
A67   Garden cities, France
    Cogniat, Raymond
      Les cités-jardins de la Compagnie du Nord.
    (Garden cities Of the Compagnie des Chemin de
    Fer du Nord.)

          L'Architecture 37: 49-57
          March 10, 1924

Garden Cities, Germany

    see also

Margarthenhöhe, Ger.
Hellerau (Ger.)

720.53
M58   Garden cities. Germany.Falkenberg
    Stadtbaurat Bruno Taut,Magdeburg.Siedlung
    Falkenberg bei Berlin:Vorprojekt Modell
    1913

          Moderne bauformen 21: 294-7
          Oct. 1922

D10.5
A786   Garden cities, France
      In the north of France

          Art et décoration 42: 111-128
          Oct. 1922

Garden Cities, Germany

          Arch. rev. 20 n.s.3:69-74
          Sep. 1915

720.53
W31   Garden cities, Germany. Freidorf
    Housing in Freidorf, Hans Meyer, archt.

          Wasmuths 10: 8-9
          Heft 1, 1926

720.52
A87e   Garden cities. France
      Progress with the housing problem in
    France

          Architect 110:196-7
          Sept. 14, 1923

Garden Cities, Germany

          Internat. Studio 57:349-50
          Nov., 1915

720.53
W31   Garden cities,Germany. Frohnau
    Doppelhaus-kolonie in der gartenstadt Fro-
    hnau bei Berlin. (Double house colony in the
    garden city,Frohnau,near Berlin.) Rudolf
    Fränkel,archt.

          Wasmuths monatshefte 14: 84
          February 1930
    A

Garden Cities, France
    Two French garden suburbs

          A.I.A. jour. 11:210-2
          May, 1923

711
S77   Garden cities. Germany

          Der städtebau 12: 45-8, & pl. 21-6
          May 1915

720.53
M58   Garden cities,Germany.Hüttenau
    Hüttenau

          Moderne bauformen 13 yr.,p.191-193
          April 1914

720.54
A67   Garden cities, France. Arcueil
    Devienne, Albert
      La Cité - Jardin d'Arcueil. (The garden city
    of Arcueil.) Payret-Dortail, architect. Plans.

    A   L'architecture 36:391-396
          December 25, 1923

Garden Cities, Germany

          Der Städtebau 12:63-64 and pl.35-37
          June, 1915

711
S77   Garden cities. Germany.Ludewigslust
    Ludwigslust, country seat of royalty, a
    small town idyll.(Text in German)

          Der staedtebau 16:11-14. pl.
          5-10. Heft 1-2,1919.

Garden Cities, France. Draveil.
    Draveil, France.

          Art et decor. 35:49-54
          Feb., 1914

711
S77   Garden cities. Germany.Augsburg
      Von der siedlungstätigkeit in Augsburg

          Der stadtebau 18:101-102
          Heft 9-10, 1922

720.53
W31   Garden cities, Germany. Mauenheim
    (Siedlung Mauenheim)

          Wasmuths 9:135
          Heft 4,1925

711
S77   Garden cities, France. Plessis-Robinson
      The garden city Plessis-Robinson near
    Paris. Maurice Payret-Dortail, archt.

          Der Stadtebau 23: 70-72
          Heft 3, 1928

D10.5
A786   Garden cities, Germany, Berlin
    Wittkower, Kate
      Garden cities in Berlin

          Art et décoration 55:145-160
          May 1929

720.53
A67   Garden cities, Germany. Pressburg
      Project for a garden city in Pressburg.

          Der Architekt 23,Heft 1-2:9 -
          12. 1920

720.53
M68
Garden cities, Germany .Rechenberg
Dwellings in the city of Rechenberg, de-
signed by Prof. Schultze-Naumberg, archt.

Moderne bauformen 27: 89-96
Heft 3, March 1928

720.54
A67
Garden cities, Sweden
Lavedon, Pierre
Problèmes d'urbanisme à Stockholm. (Urbanism
problems at Stockholm.)

L'architecture 47: 573-584
October 15, 1954

Garden City (L.I.) Cottage
Aymar Embury II, archt. plan

West. Archt.
17: pls.fol.p. XV
Jun, 1911

D10.5
K96
Garden cities, Germany, Staaken
Staaken

Dekor. kunst 32:221-39
May 1919

Garden cities, U.S.

see also names of individual garden
cities, i.e:

Yorkship village, N.J.
Forest hills gardens, L.I.
Wilmington, Del. Union park gardens

Garden City (L.I.) Country Club
Garden City Country Club, Nassau Boulevard,
L.I. Morrell Smith, architect.

Architecture 40: pl. 115-120
August, 1919

720.54
A67
Garden cities,Germany. Stuttgart-Weissenhof.
La Cité - Jardin du Weissenhof, a
Stuttgart, 1928. (The City - Garden of
Weissenhof, at Stuttgart, 1928.)
LeCorbusier and Pierre Jeanneret, archts.

L'Architecture Vivante: 12,13.
1929

720.5
A67
Garden cities, U.S.
Check list of developments

Arch. rev. 22:n.s.8:83-91
Apr. 1917

720.5
A51
Garden City (L.I.) Country life press.
Country Life Press, Garden City, L.I., N.Y.
Henry P Kirby and John J. Petit, Archts. Plan

Amer. archt 99, pt 2: pls 1-5
fol 244
Je 14, '11

720.53
W31
Garden cities,Germany.Tempelhofer Feldes
Die rettung des Tempelhofer Feldes.(The
recovery of the Templars Field.Garden city).
Fritz Bräuning,archt.

A

Wasmuths 8: 333-346
Heft 11/12, 1924

Garden Cities, U.S.

Art et décor. 36: 59-64
May-June, 1919

710.5
H84
Garden City (L.I.) Crosby (Romain) house
Residence of Romain Crosby,Garden City,
N.Y. R.M.Bischoff,archt. Plans.

A
House and garden 70:123
September 1936

720.53
M68
Garden cities, Germany.Werderau-Nürnberg
Prof.Ludwig Ruff,Nürnberg. Gardenstadt Wer-
derau-Nürnberg

Moderne bauformen 21:359-66
Dec. 1922

Garden Cities, U.S.

Greber, Jacques. L'architecture
aux Etats-unis...2 vols.
Paris: Payot, 1920. v.1, p. 101-26.

720.5
A67
Garden City(L.I.)Doubleday-Page Press
Building for the Doubleday-Page Press,
(Country life Press),Garden City,L.I.,N.Y.
H.P.Kirby and J.J.Petit,archts. Plans and
measured drawings.

A
Architectural review 17:32,pls.30-33
March 1910

720.52
B93
Garden cities. Holland.

Builder 122: 4 pl.
Feb. 3, 1922.

Garden cities, U.S. Massachusetts
Village near Worcester, Mass. Indian village

A.I.A. jour
5:28-30
Ja 1917

Garden City (L.I.) Fire house and Auditorium
Fire house and auditorium, Garden City, L.I.
Ford, Butter and Oliver, archts.

A
Brickbuilder 21:pl.127
October, 1912

720.53
W31
Garden cities. Norway
Harald Hals and Ad.Jensen,architekten,Kris-
tiania

Wasmuths 7:99-105
Heft 3-4 , 1923

Garden City, L.I. Adelphi college. Center of
communicative arts & sciences
Centre of Communicative Arts & Sciences,
Adelphi College, New York [plan & section]
Richard J. Neutra & Robert E. Alexander, archts.

Archtl Design
28:458-59 N 1958

Garden City (LI) Floyd (Nicoll) Residence
Aymar Embury II, archt. plan.

West. Archt.
17: 54
Jun, 1911

Garden City (LI) Garage
Aymar Embury II, archt.
 	
West. Archt.
17: pls.fol.p. XV
Jun, 1911
	720.5
	A51 Garden City (L.I.) Peters (Ralph) house
	     House of Ralph Peters, Esq., Garden City,
	L.I., New York. Aymar Embury II, archt.,
	plans.
	
	American architect 96:5 pls.fol.p.116
	September 22, 1909.
	
	A
		720.6
		C53 Garden, Edward G
		     An elevated railroad terminal station.
		First honorable mention, Robert Clark
		competition, 1892. Edward C. Garden,
		designer and del.
		
		Chicago architectural club 7:24
		1894

Garden City (L.I.) Golf Club Garden City Golf Club. Country life (U.S.) 64: 52 May, 1933	Garden City (LI) Peters (Ralph) Residence Aymar Embury II, archt. West. Archt. 17: 52-3, pls.fol.p. XV Jun, 1911	720.5 B84 Garden, Edward G The town hall series. Pt. II. A town hall in central Missouri. E.G. Garden, archt. [plan, elevation, section] Brickbuilder 11: 51-54 Mr '02

Garden City (L.I.) Garden City Hotel
   The Garden City Hotel, Garden City, L.I.
N.Y. McKim, Mead and White, archts. Plans
Additions by Ford, Butler and Oliver, archts.
 	
        Architectural review 19 n.s.2:142-144
A   April, 1913
	Garden city warehouses, Chicago (1880)
	
	see
	
	Chicago, Ill. Garden City warehouses (ca.1880)
		Garden entrances
		
		see also
		
		Garden gates

Garden City (L.I.) Garden City Hotel Garden City Hotel, Garden City, L.I., 1896. McKim, Mead and White, archts. McKim, Mead and White. A monograph of the work of McKim, Mead and White, 1879-1915. 2 vols. New York: The Architectural Book Publishing Co., 1925. 1:pl. 72, 98-99	Garden court apartments, Toronto see Toronto, Ont. Garden court apartments	Garden Entrances Country life in Amer: 501-506 March, 1907
710.5 G855 Garden City (L.I.) Macomber (H.F.) house Interior of home of H. Francis Macomber in Garden City, L. I. Country life (U.S.) 59: 47-49 March 1931	Garden design see Landscape architecture	Garden Entrances Deutsche Baukunst 13: sup.for Mar. 29, 1914

720.5
A51   Garden City (L.I.) Orr (H.S.) house
     Cottage of Henry S. Orr, Esq., Garden City
L.I., New York. Aymar Embury II. archt.
Plans.
 	
American architect 96:117-114,116. 3 pls.
September 22,1909.   fol.p.116
 	
A
	Garden, Edward G
	
	See also
	
	Mauran, Russell and Garden
		720.52
		A67c Garden entrances
		     Details of garden entrance to drawing
		room.
		
		Architect (Lond.) 121: supp.pl.opp.
		May 17, 1929 p.634

Garden City (LI) Orr (H.S.) Residence Aymar Embury II, archt. plan West. Archt. 17: pls.fol.p. XV Jun, 1911	Garden, Edward G. see also St. Louis (Mo.) Bellerive club	710.5 G855 Garden entrances Framing the garden. Country life (U.S.) 60: 51 August 1931

Garden. F.M.
 	
see
 	
Chicago (IL) Root (J.W.) Memorial competition
	710.5
	C855 Garden-gates
	    ...and their planting
	
	      Country life 48: 72-76
	      Sept. 1925
		Garden Gates
		  Gates for gardens.
		
		      House and garden 70:58
		      August, 1936

Garden fences
 	
see
 	
Fences
	710.5
	H84 Garden gates.
	    The alluring garden gate.
	
	     House & Garden. 39:48-9 & cover
	     design. Apr. 1921.
		Garden Gates
		  Gates in Garden Walls
		
		      Amer. arch. 111:154-157
		      Mar. 7, 1917

Garden fireplaces
 	
see
 	
Fireplaces, Outdoor
	Garden Gates
	  Architecture's Portfolio
	
	     Arch. 57: 352-58
	     Je '28
		Garden Gates
		  Gateway to Garden, Brescia
		
		      Amer. Arch. 109:pl. 2108
		      May 17, 1916

051
T72   Garden fountains
  "Singing waters;" Fountains and pools for
modern gardens.
 	
     Touchstone 4: 470-476
     F 1919
	710.5
	A51 Garden gates
	    Attractive types of garden gates for small
	houses.
	
	     American homes and gardens 11: 126-127
	     April 1914
		710.5
		H84 Garden gates
		    Garden of E. K. Croft at Greenwich, Conn.
		
		     House and Garden 45:54
		     June 1924

Garden gates
 	
see also
 	
Garden entrances
	720.5
	A51 Garden gates
	    Beaux-Arts Institute of Design award for
	an entrance doorway to a garden.
	
	     American architect 101: sup.p.3, pl.fol.
	     April 17, 1912 p.180
		710.5
		H84 Garden Gates
		    An invitation to the garden. Clark & Arms,
		archts.
		
		     House & garden.49:70
		     Mar. 1926

710.5
C855   Garden gates,
 	
     Country Life 41: 62-3.
     Mar. 1922.
	720.52
	A67c Garden gates
	    Building craftsmanship: old and new.
	
	     Architect (Lond.) 117: 52-53
	     January 7, 1927
		720.5
		A67a Garden gates.
		    Making a garden.
		
		     Architecture. 43: pl. 30-2.
		     Feb. 1921.

Garden Gates
 	
     House beaut. 48:172-173
     Sep. 1920
	710.5
	H84 Garden gates.
	    Choice... illus.
	    Engaging a Landscape Architect.
	
	     House & Garden 38: 25, 40.
	     Oct. 1920.
		710.5
		C855 Garden gates.
		    Small garden of rare charm.
		
		     Country Life. 40:52
		     July 1921

Garden Gates
Some back-yard entrances.

Country Life (Amer.) 18: 672-673
O '10

710.5
C855   Garden houses .

Country life 34:44-47
June 1918

720.53
R35   Garden houses
Homann,Richard
    Betrachtungen über pflege und gestaltungaform
unserer hausgärten. (Reflections on the care and
building of our house gardens.) Richard Homann,
archt. Plan.

Der Baumeister 31: 145-148
April 1933

710.5
H84   Garden gates
        When you plan your garden

House & Garden 43: 52-3
Jan. 1923

Garden Houses

Craftsman 26: 21-26
Apr., 1914

720.6
R38   Garden Houses
        Design for a garden pavilion; student
work at Glasgow school of architecture,
England.

R.I.B.A. 35: 683
September 22, 1928

710.5
H84   Garden gates
        Wooden doors for garden rooms.

House and garden 53: 64-5
June 1928

Garden houses

Deutsche Baukunst 12:556
Dec. 21, 1913

710.5
H84   Garden houses
        A door

House & garden 48:63
Dec. 1915

Garden Gates
Henslow, T.G.W.
Wrought iron garden gates

Colour 1: 28-29
Ja '29

Garden Houses

House beaut. 40:160
Aug., 1916

Garden Houses
    Garden architecture. A garden at Little Bognor,
Sussex. Clough Williams-Ellis, architect

Architects journal 58:765
Nov. 21, 1923

Garden houses

    see also

Arbors
Garden temples
Garden tool houses
Pergolas
Tea houses
    and names of individual garden houses, i.e:
Chelton house, Eng. Garden house-
Roslyn, L.I. Whitney (Payne) estate. Summer
    house
etc.

720.5 Garden houses
A67a   Architecture's portfolio

Arch. 61: 247-54
Ap '30

720.52
A673   Garden houses
        Garden design

Arch. Rev. 57:154-59
Apr. 1925

Garden Houses

Architecture 39:137
May, 1919

710.5 Garden houses
H84 Reynolds,James
        Attractive summer houses simply made.

House and garden 63: 34-35
June 1933

710.5
C85   Garden houses
        Garden houses, shelters and summer houses.

Country life (Lond.)61:lxxvi
April 30, 1927

Garden Houses

Brickbuilder 25:122
May, 1916

Garden houses
    Belvedere and Lily Pond, estate Arthur E.
Newbold, Jr., Laverock, Pa.
    Mellor, Meigs and Howe, Architects

Architecture 50:plate 124
Aug., 1924

Garden houses
    Garden houses in wood, stone,
concrete

Gardens and Gardening,
    the studio garden annual
1937: p122-125

720.8
H88
Garden Houses
    A garden pavilion: student work, Manchester school of architecture.

                        R.I.B.A. 38: 70
                        November 24, 1928

Garden Houses
    In an old-fashioned garden

                    House beaut. 45:289
                    May, 1919

710.5
H84
Garden houses
    A wide variety of garden architecture

                    House and garden 45:64-65
                    June 1924

Garden houses
    Garden seats and shelters

                    House & garden 43:45-7
                    Je 1923

710.5
H84
Garden houses
    Le Gallienne, Richard
    On small garden houses and quiet outdoor studies.

                    House and garden 59: 38-39
                    June 1931

Garden houses
    Working drawings

                    Archts. and bldrs. jour. 38:140-141
                    Aug. 6, 1913

Garden Houses
    A Gay Garden Pavilion.

                    Country life (U.S.) 58: 69
                    May, 1930

Garden houses
    Pergolas and tea houses

                    House beaut 28:148-y
                    Jl 1910

720.53
W31
Garden houses, Denmark
    Views and plans of garden houses.

                    Wasmuths 11: 282-89
                    Heft 7, 1927

710.5
H84
Garden Houses
    Eberlein, H.D.
    The gazebo and the garden wall: their relation to each other and to the architectural and landscape scheme. Some examples of how and where they may be used. No plans.

                    House and garden 38:34-35,78
                    December 1920

Garden Houses
    Plans and views of summer houses designed by Ernst Wiesner.

                    Moderne bauformen 27:222-223
                    June, 1928

Garden Houses, England.

                    Gibbs, James. A Book of architecture.
                    London: n.p., 1728. pl. 68-70, 72-8.

Garden Houses
    The Gazebo in the Garden. Several examples in the United States.

                    Country life (U.S.) 65:57-59
                    April, 1934

Garden Houses
    Sketches

                    House beaut. 49:191
                    Mar., 1921

710.5
L26
Garden houses, England
    Some English garden pavilions and summerhouses.

                    Landscape architecture 21: front.,11-18
                    October 1930

720.52
A67
Garden houses
    Gazebo in Portland stone. Plan and measured details.

                    Architects' journal 74: pl.
                    November 18, 1931

710.5
H84
Garden Houses
    Huntington, T.T.
    Some hints on garden shelters.

                    House and garden 70:104-105
                    November 1936

Garden Houses, Fr.
    Versailles

                    Arch. and Bldrs. jour. 41:pl.for.
                    Jan. 27, 1915

710.5
H84
Garden houses
    The house in the garden.

                    House and garden 41: 39-41
                    Jun. 1922.

710.5
C855
Garden houses
    The summer house.

                    Country life (U.S.) 38: 58-59
                    June 1920

Garden House, Germany

                    Olbrich, Josef Maria.
                    Architektur von Olbrich.
                    6 vols. Serie I-III. Berlin:
                    E. Wasmuth, [1901-13].
                    Bd. 3, pl. 86-87

Garden Houses. Germany.

Kerckerinck zur Borg, Engelebert
von. Alt-Westfalen. Stuttgart:
Julius Hoffmann, [1912]. P.212-8.

Garden, Hugh   Block of Stores & Offices in a
Country Town. Selection from Chicago Architectural
Club, Sixth Annual Traveling Scholarship
Competition

Inland Arch. 47:
pl. fol. p 52
Ap., 1906

Garden, Hugh Mackie Gordon, 1873-1961
Greengard, Bernard C.,
    Hugh M.G. Garden [illus., port] Bibliography.

Prairie School review
III: 1-22; 27
First quarter 1966

720.5
A51   Garden houses, Germany
    Designs (from "Moderne Bauformen") photo-
graphs, plans, sections, and elevations.

American architect 107: 587
June 16, 1915

Garden, Hugh Mackie Gordon, 1873-1961

Member of firm:

Schmidt, Garden & Martin
Schmidt, Garden & Erikson

Garden, Hugh Mackie Gordon, 1873-1961
Garden, Hugh
    Modern garden architecture in Germany [illus.]

Architectural review
15: 81-86
May 1908

720.55
M58   Garden houses, Germany
    Kriegerehrung Bulda in Sachsen
    Gartenhaus in Dresden-Loschaitz

Moderne bauformen 21: 270
Sept. 1922

MICROFILM

Garden, Hugh Mackie Gordon, 1873-1961

in ... HBOOK ON
ARCHITECTURE p. 1040-1041
(on film)

MICROFILM

Garden, Hugh Mackie Gordon, 1873-1961
    obituary notice

K ON
RE p. 698

Garden Houses, Italy.

Bolton, Arthur Thomas, ed.
The Gardens of Italy....New York:
Charles Scribner's Sons, 1919.
p. 28-9, 38

720.6   Garden, Hugh Mackie Gordon   1873-1961
I59   An architect visits Bogota.

Illinois society of architects
Monthly bulletin 6-7:16-7
December 1941-January 1942

Garden, Hugh Mackie Gordon, 1873-1961
    Rendering of a residence [from Chicago archi-
tectural club exhibition 1898]

Inland architect
31: plate following p.50
June 1898

Garden houses, U.S.
    (good examples of colonial garden houses)

Howells, John Mead. The architectural
heritage of the Merrimack. New York:
Architectural book publishing Co.,
Inc., 1941.

Garden, Hugh Mackie Gordon, 1873-1961
    A block of stores...in a country town [render-
ing]

Chicago architectural club
19: 37
1906

Garden, Hugh Mackie Gordon, 1873-1961
    Sketch. Design for a church.

Chicago architectural club
7: 32; 42
1894

720.5
A67   Garden houses, United States - Massachusetts
    Minor colonial details: 1.Some old
"summer houses", from Eastern Massachusetts
gardens.

Architectural review 22:n.s.5:169-171;
August, 1917   pl.58-59

Garden, Hugh Mackie Gordon, 1873-1961
    A building devoted to the study of Botany...
Competitive design for the Gold Medal of the
Illinois Chapter, A.I.A. [elevation]

Chicago architectural club
8 :5
1895

Garden, Hugh Mackie Gordon, 1873-1961
    Sketch of residence for Charles H. Hodges.

Chicago architectural club
13: 44
1900

Garden, Hugh Mackie Gordon   1873-1961
    see also
Chicago (IL) Hale (W.S.) house
    "   " Herrick (Robert) house
    "   " Lucien Lelong bldg.
    "   " Third Church of Christ Scientist
Highland Park (IL) McMullin (Frank R.) house
    "   "   "   Putnam (John A.) house
Lake Forest (IL) Evans (James Carey) house
    "   "   " Norton (C.D.) house
Marion (IN) Theater
Marshalltown (IA) First church of Christ Scientist

Garden, Hugh Mackie Gordon, 1873-1961
    Design for library building. Shepley, Rutan
and Coolidge, architects; Hugh M.G. Garden, delineator.
    Library building: sketch. Alfred Hoyt Granger,
architect. Hugh M. G. Garden, delineator.

Chicago architectural club
7: 14; 57
1894

Garden, H.M.G.
    Sketch of residence for Prof. W.S.
Hale, and interior view of Library. For
Chicago Archt. Club. Exhibition of 1898.

Inland Archt.
vol.31,No.5,pl.fol.p. 50
Jun, 1898

Garden, Hugh Mackie Gordon, 1873-1961
Garden, Hugh M.G.
The "Village Block" series; article III.
[illus., plans]

Brickbuilder
14: 76-78
April 1905

Garden ornaments

Craftsman 16: 586-590
Ag 1909

720.52
A473   Garden ornaments
       Garden design

Arch.Rev.57:202-209
May 1925

Garden, Hugh Mackie Gordon and Edmund
T. Ellis.
Establish Office at Real Estate Board
Bldg., Chicago.

Inland Architect
21: 16
Feb, 1893

Garden ornaments

Scheult, Francois Léonard.
Recueil d'architecture dessinée
et mesurée en Italie - Paris:
Ainé, 1840. pl.41 -72.

Garden Ornaments
   Garden Embellishments.
By Lillian Harrod.

House and gard. 16:21-23
Jl 1909

Garden lighting

see

Gardens. Lighting

Garden Ornaments
   Garden Ornaments

Touchstone 5:425-427
August, 1919

710.5
C85   Garden Ornaments
      Garden ironwork at Hinwick Hall, Bedford-
shire, England.

Country life (Lond.)61:492-3
March 26, 1927

Garden Models
   Perrin, H.B.
Gardens by sleight of hand

Home and field 44:44-45,78-79
March, 1934

Garden ornaments
Sloan, M.M.
   Architectural treatment of concrete
structures. Pt. IV & Concrete Landscape gardening.

Arch rec 31: 68-79
Ja'12

710.5
C85   Garden Ornaments
      Garden ornament.

Country life (Lond.) 65: cli-clii
March 23, 1929

Garden niches

see

Niches

720.5
A67   Garden ornaments
      Underwood, Loring
      Concrete for artistic, durable and inexpen-
sive garden accessories.

Architectural review 13: 69-73
May 1906

710.]
C85   Garden ornaments
      Garden ornaments.

Country life (Lond.)61:]xxviii
April 30, 1927

Garden ornaments

see also

Bird baths   Trellises
Fountains   Wellheads
Sundials

Garden Ornaments
   Decorative iron trees as an accessory to the
roof garden.

House and garden 53:93-94
March, 1928

710.5
H84   Garden ornaments
      Garden ornaments of cast iron.

House and garden 51: 126-27
March 1927

Garden Ornaments

Arch. and contract reporter 93:41-43
Jan. 15, 1915

Garden Ornaments
   Formal garden ornament.

Country Life 37:56-7.
Mar. 1920.

705.1
A79   Garden ornaments
      Lounsbery, Elizabeth
      Ornaments and furniture for the garden

Arts and decoration 25:26-7
Je '26

710.s
H84
Garden ornaments
Some recent garden pieces

House and garden 53:57
August 1923

Garden planning

see

Landscape architecture

710.5
H84
Garden pools
Beside the still waters.

House & garden 51: 97,99
January 1927

Garden Ornaments
Statuettes, urns., etc.

Country life 31: supp. p. 15-19
June 29, 1912

Garden pools

see also

Water gardens

710.5
C855
Garden pools
Both useful and decorative

Country life (U.S.) 60: 39-41
August 1931

Garden Ornaments
"Tree of Life", forged iron garden wall
decorations.

Metal arts 2: 320
July, 1929

Garden Pools

Builder 93:503
May 28, 1915

D13.1
H84
Garden Pools
Bush-Brown, James
The design and construction of garden pools

House beautiful 69:263-265,303,
March 1931   (306,308

Garden Ornaments, concrete
Underwood, Loring
Concrete for artistic, durable and inexpensive
garden accessories.

Architectural review 13:69-73
May, 1906

Garden Pools

House beaut. 28:112-3
Sept. 1910

710.5
C85
Garden pools
The diving pool in the garden at Manbard,
Essex, England.

Country life (Lond.)61: 916
June 4, 1927

. Garden paths

see

Walks (paths)

Garden pools.

Northend, Mary Harrod. Garden
ornaments. New York: Duffield
and Co., 1916. p. 125-39.

710.5
C855
Garden pools
Evergreens in tubs accenting the corners
of the square pool. Beatty and Beatty,
landscape archts.

Country life (U.S.) 54: 63-4
September 1928

Garden pavements

see

Pavements

720.5 Garden pools
A67a   Architecture's portfolios

Arch. 59: 382-88
Je '29

710.5
H84
Garden pools.
Five pools in Florida gardens. A. Mizner,
archt.

House & garden.49:69-71
Feb. 1926

Garden pavilions

see

Garden houses

RYERSON LIBRARY
705.1
A79
Garden pools
. Beautiful garden pools in the great
estates of well-known Californians.

Arts and decoration 18:38-39
March 1923

710.5
H84
Garden pools
The focal point of the garden.

House & garden 51: 69
January 1927

720.54
T25
Garden pools
Fontaines et bassins.

Tech et arch 2:120-125
Mr-Ap. 1942

STILSON LIBRARY
705.1
A79
Garden pools
Fits-Gibbons, Costen
The garden pool and the average garden.

Arts and decoration 21:57-58,59
July 1924

710.5
C855
Garden pools
The magic of water in the garden

Country life 43:42-4
March 1923

710.5
H84
Garden pools
Formal and informal garden pools, brook-
lets and watercourses.

House and garden 52:78,80,83,202
October 1927

705.1
A79
Garden pools
Furniss, H.M.
Garden pools, deep and shallow.

Arts and decoration 27:35-37
July 1927

Garden Pools
A natural and artificial pool

House beautiful 53:21
Jan., 1923

RYERSON LIBRARY
705.1
A79
Garden pools
Wheelwright, Robert
Fountains and pools in garden design.

Arts and decoration 2: 172-175,197
March 1912

710.5
C855
Garden pools
Ware,R.B.
Garden pools give constant pleasure. Plans.

Country life (U.S.)63: 55,76
February 1933

710.5
H84
Garden pools
Photographs showing various types of
garden pools.

House and garden 26: 79-81
August 1914

710.5
C855
Garden pools
The gardens at Fairacres, estate of Mrs. B.
F. Jones, jr. Wm. Pitkin, landscape archt.

Country life (N.Y.)49:58-9
February 1926

710.5
H84
Garden pools
Garden pool in California, with Spanish
influence.

House and garden 52: 75,77
December 1927

---

ff
720.5
A67
Garden pools
Photograph of small formal garden pool
at Jericho, New York.

Architectural review 25:n.s.8: pl.66
May 1919

D13.1
H84
Garden Pools
Taylor, Albert D.
Garden construction notes

House beautiful 56:353
Oct. 1924

710.5
H84
Garden pools
How to make a pool

House and garden 44:62
Aug. 1923

710.5
C85
Garden pools
Photograph of a small formal garden pool.

Country life 40: 352
September 25, 1926

710.5
H84
Garden pools
The garden corner of repose

House and garden 39:p.31.
Jun.,1921.

Garden Pools
An ideal setting for a garden pool

House beautiful 65:51
January, 1929

710.5
C855
Garden pools
Planning placid pools.

Country life (U.S.) 60: 58-60
July 1931

710.5
L26
Garden pools
Lay,C.D.
Garden pools. Measured drawings,details.

Landscape architecture 9: 113-124
April 1919

710.5
L26
Garden pools
Landscape construction notes. II. Notes
with reference to the construction of pools.

Landscape architecture 14:126-32
Jan. 1924   & pl.A-D.

720.53
B35
Garden pools
Ein planschbecken. (A water basin.) Sepp
Ruf,archt. Plan and section.

Der Baumeister 31: 99
March 1933

710.5 C855 Garden pools Pools and cascades in Mrs.Oakleigh Thorne's garden at Montecito,California. Country life (U.S.)63: front.,44-45 January 1933	RYERSON LIBRARY 705.1 Garden pools A79 Clark, A.S. Seeking perfection in garden pools. Arts and decoration 25:35-36 June 1926	720.5 A67ar Garden pools, U.S. Pool, garden, Mr. H. H. Rogers, Southampton, L.I. Walker & Gillette, architects Architect 2:pl. 118 Aug. 1924
RYERSON LIBRARY D13.1 H84 Garden pools The pool as a garden feature House beautiful 67:192-193 February 1930	051 T72 Garden pools "Singing waters;" Fountains and pools for modern gardens. Touchstone 4: 470-476 F 1919	710.5 C855 Garden pools,U.S. Rydal (Pa.) Garden pool in Gilbert garden, Rydal, Pa. Exley & Kite, landscape, archts. Photographs. Country life (N.Y.)53: 60-1 November 1927
710.5 C855 Garden pools Pools at night. Photographs - submerged lighting. Country life (U.S.) 57: 45 March 1930	710.5 C85 Garden pools A small formal garden and pool in London. Country life (Lond.)62:706-07 November 12, 1927	710.5 C855 Garden rooms Yarnall,Sophia Dressing rooms for flowers. Country life(U.S.)69:49-51 December 1935
710.5 H84 Garden pools The pool by the doorstep House & garden 43:44 June 1923	RYERSON LIBRARY D10.5 Garden pools C88 Roberts, M.F. The soul of the garden Craftsman 28: 21-24 Ap '15	710.5 H84 Garden rooms Dutel, Pierre Flower rooms in city houses. House and garden 57: 68-69 January 1930
710.5 L26 Garden pools Pool control. Landscape arch. 10: 181-3. Jul.1920.	710.5 L35 Garden pools In Spanish patios & gardens Landscape architecture 16:45-52 Oct. 1925	710.5 H84 Garden rooms Gardening rooms: room of Lake Mahopac Garden Club, New Rochelle Garden Club,Larchmont Garden Club, and the flower rranging room of the Hickox residence in Old Westbury,L.I. House and garden 70:46-47 August 1936
710.5 C855 Garden pools Pools in the garden picture. Country life 55: 64-65 March 1929	720.5 A51 Garden pools Terrace pool - garden of C.S. Walton. St.David's, Pa. D.K. Boyd, archt. American arch. 107:pl.fol.p.404 June 23, 1915	720.52 A67 Garden rooms Garden room with electrically controlled sliding windows,Haus K. in O. Martin Elsaesser,archt. Architects' Journal 78: 640 November 16,1933
720.5 A67a Garden pools Portfolio of photographs Arch.rec.49:p.331-9. Apr., 1921.	Garden pools, Italy Scaled details of pool curbs Landscape arch 14: 279 O 1924	RYERSON LIBRARY 705.944 W48 Garden rooms r., w. Garten halle mit herbarium fur Dr. H.M. in Lucern. Werner Ribary, archt. Plan. Das werk 32: 199-200 Jl '45

710.8
H84   Garden rooms.
      In City houses.
 	
     House & Garden 40: 27.
     Oct. 1921.
	720.5
	P59 Garden Steps
	     Details of construction for plant wall and
	steps in wall.
	
	       Pencil points 8: 512-13
	       August 1927
		Garden Steps
		    Photos.
		
		      Landscape and garden 4:88, 89
		      Summer, 1937

Garden shelters
 	
      see
 	
Garden houses
	RYERSON LIBRARY
	705.1
	A79 Garden Steps
	     Enchantment of the garden stairway.
	
	     Arts and decoration 29:42-43
	     August 1928
		710.5
		H84 Garden steps
		     Steps and stairways in the garden
		
		     House and garden 43:80-1
		     May 1923

Garden Steps
 	
     Bolton, Arthur Thomas, ed.
     The gardens of Italy....New York:
     Charles Scribner's Sons, 1919.
     42 illus.
	720.54
	T25 Garden steps
	     Escaliers de jardins.
	
	      Tech et Arch 2:179
	      My-Je. 1942.
		710.5 Garden steps
		H84 Steps in the garden
		
		     House and garden 45:59
		     June 1924

Garden Steps
 	
     New Country Life 33:45-47
     Feb., 1918
	720.52
	A673 Garden steps
	     Garden design:VII--walls, paths and steps
	
	     Arch. rev. 56:166-171
	     Nov. 1924
		710.5 Garden steps
		C855 Steps from house to garden on estate of
		     John D. King, Millbrook, N.Y.
		
		     Country life (N.Y.)49: 63
		     April 1926

Garden Steps
 	
     House beaut. 49: 202-204
     March, 1921
	710.5
	H84 Garden steps
	     Garden steps.
	
	     House and garden 70:31-33,96
	     October 1936
		710.5 Garden Steps
		L26 Olmsted, Frederick
		     Some further notes on steps.
		
		     Landscape architecture 18: 125-129
		     January 1928

Garden Steps
 	
     Humphreys, Phebe Wescott.
     The practical book of garden
     architecture. Philadelphia and
     London: J.B. Lippincott Company,
     1914. p. 315-323
	710.5
	L26 Garden steps
	     Landscape construction notes.VIII. Notes
	     with reference to the construction of steps
	     and ramps
	
	     Landscape architecture 14:43-58
	     Oct. 1923
		710.5
		H84 Garden steps
		     To link the lawns and garden.
		
		     House and garden 58: 49
		     August 1930

720.5   Garden steps
A67a   Architectural portfolio
 	
     Arch. 59: 260-66
     Ap. '29
	Garden steps
	     Olmsted, Frederick Law
	       Notes upon the sizes of steps required for
	comfort
	
	     Landscape architecture
	     1:84-90
	     Ja 1911
		710.5
		H84 Garden steps
		     Upward lead the garden steps of Belgian
		     blocks. A stairway in the Z.G.Simmons'
		     garden at Greenwich,Connecticut. James Y.Rippin
		     archt.
		
		     House and garden 64: 47
		     October 1933

720.5
A67a
Garden steps. England
 Photographic studies of some English
garden steps.

Architecture 55: 77-90
Februar 1927

720.52
A673
Garden temples
 A garden temple in the formal manner

Architectural review 55:67
Feb. 1924

Garden temples, U. S.

see

Somerville (N.J.) "Duke's farm" Garden temples

710.5
L26
Garden steps, England
Some English garden steps.

Landscape architecture 16:107-10
January 1926

Garden temples
Weibezahn, Ingrid
 Das Leibnizdenkmal in Hannover. [illus.]

Niederdeutsche Beiträge zur
Kunstgeschichte
Bd 11: 191-248
1972

Garden theaters

see

Theaters, Open air

Garden suburbs

see

Garden cities

710.5
C85
Garden temples
 The temple in a grove at Clandon Park, Eng-
land.

Country life (Lond.)62: 439
September 24, 1927

710.5
H84
Garden tool houses.
 An adjunct to the greenhouse.
Chas. S. Keefe, archt.

House & garden.50:85
Aug. 1926

710.5
C85
Garden temples
 Bathing pavilion and temple of music at
Tyringham, Buckinghamshire.

Country life (Lond.) 65: 742-746;
May 25;June 1;1929   780-786

720.52
A673
Garden temples
 Tyringham, Buckinghamshire. Sir John
Soane. Built 1794-1800. Sir Edwin Lutyens.
The residence of F. A. Konig.

Architectural rev.65: 56-64,90,98,
February 1929   and pl.3

710.5
H 84
Garden tool-houses
 Housing the garden tools

House and garden 47: 95
Feb.1925

720.5
A51
Garden temples
 Beaux-Arts Institute of Design, award for
a garden temple to Flora.

American architect 99: pl.fol.p.24
January 11, 1911

720.5
A67r
Garden temples
 Water temple, Spring Valley water com-
pany. Sunol, California. Willis Polk and
company,archts.

A   Architectural record 32:133
August 1912

Garden villages

see

Garden cities

720.52
A67
Garden temples
 Garden temple at Bolesworth castle. Clough
Williams-Ellis, archt.

Architects' jour.63: 53
January 6, 1926

720.52
A673
Garden temples,England
Jourdain, M.
 Formal garden and garden temples, England.

Architectural review 49: 70-72
March 1921

Garden walks

see

Walks (paths)

710.5
L26
Garden temples
 The garden temple at Elm Gate, New England.

Landscape architecture 16:249
July 1926

Garden Temples, Italy. Rome
 Villa Borghese and the Borghese Palace,
Rome, a temple in the garden.
 Villa Albani, Rome, a marble temple.

Bolton, Arthur Thomas, ed.
 The gardens of Italy....New York:
Charles Scribner's Sons, 1919.
69,139

Garden walls

see

Walls, Garden

Gardening

see

Gardens

720.5
A67 Gardens
     Sturgis, R. Clipston
          The garden as an adjunct to architecture.

          Arch rev 5: 21-24
          Ap 1898

720.53
W51 Gardens
     Brandt,G.N.
          Der kommende garten. (The future garden:
     article on garden planning.)

          Wasmuths monatshefte 14: 159-176
          April 1930

Gardens

see also

Botanical gardens   Landscape architecture
Cactus Gardens
Colonial gradens   Memorial gardens

Courtyards   Rock gardens

Desert Gardens   Roof gardens

Formal gardens   Rose gardens

Hillside gardens   Round gardens (see cd. 2)

705.1
A79 Gardens
     Cameron, Alexander
          A garden without flowers

          Arts and decoration 20:38-39
          April 1924

720.52
A67 Gardens
          Layout for a garden. Student work at
     Regent street polytechnic school of archi-
     tecture. London.

          Architects' journal 67: 173
          January 25, 1928

Gardens   (card 2)

see also

Sunken gardens

Tropical gardens
Two-level gardens
Water gardens
Winter gardens
Wall gardens
Wild flower gardens
Zoological gardens

Gardens
     The Gardens of Epicurus.

          Arch and con rep 69: 271
          Ap 24, 1903

705.1
A79 Gardens
     Mayne, Sheila
          The miraculous beauty of the Harter garden

          Arts and decoration 23: 34-35,68
          July 1925

710.5
H94 Gardens
          The charm of the enclosed garden

          House & garden 43:54
          June 1923

Gardens
     The Gardens of Newbattle Abbey. By A.D.
     Richardson.

          House and gard 4: 143-47
          S 1903

Gardens
     Moderne gartenkunst

          Kunst und kunsthandwerk 16:221-248
          1913, Heft. 4.

Gardens
     Nutter, Frank M.
Civic beauty in the formal garden
Illus.

          West. Arch.
          12: 76-8
          D 1908

Gardens.
     The Home Garden at Dreamwold.
By Mary H. Northend.

          House and gard. 15: 38-43
          F 1909

Gardens
     My Garden without Flowers. By Carine Cadby.

          Amer. homes and gard 3: 29-31
          Jl 1906

705*1
I61 Gardens
          Formal and informal.

          International studio 75: 133-137.
          April 1922*

720.5
A67b Gardens.
          How Slidertown was transformed into South
     Park. Illus.

          Arch. & building 52:49-51.
          May,1920.

Gardens
     Nationality in gardens

          Lotus mag. 8:387-396
          June, 1917

720.5
A67r Gardens
     Pentecost,G.F.Jr.
          The formal and natural style of gardens.

          Architectural record 12:174-194
          June 1902

Gardens
     Illus. of paved gardens

          Internat. Studio 59:225-231
          Oct., 1916

705.3
K96w Gardens
          Der neue garten.

          Der kunstwanderer 13:252
          April 1931

RYERSON LIBRARY
D13.1
H84   Gardens
        Nichols, Rose Standish
            Pleasure grounds at Westbury House

                House beautiful 57:229-233
                March 1925

Gardens.

The Villa Garden. By Geo. F. Pentecost, Jr.

                Arch rec 11: 61-68
                Ja, 1902

VD6.4   Gardens, Algeria
I29   The garden of Hamma, Algiers

                L'Illustration 159:361-64
                Apr. 22, 1922

710.5
H84   Gardens
        McFarland, J.H.
            Sanity in gardening.

                House & garden 51: 88-91
                March 1927

Ryerson
        Gardens
        Schweizer, J   E
            Wann und wie umfrieden wir unsere gärten

                Werk
                30: 294-95
                S 1943

Gardens, Alpine

        see

Rock gardens

RYERSON LIBRARY
D10.5
A794   Gardens
            Sketches for gardens by Paul Vera and
            Gabriel Guévrékian

                Arts de la maison 5:pl.26-27
                Winter number

720.53   Gardens
B55   Harbers, Guido
                Der wohngarten, Seine raum-und bauelements.
                (The house garden: its space and building elements)
                Plans of Generalife in Granada.

                Der Baumeister 31: 35-40
                January 1933

Gardens, Andulasia

                Arch. rec. 29: 371-377
                May, 1911.

720.5
A87r   Gardens
            Style gardens

                Architectural record 54:121-36
                August 1923

Ryerson
915
A67   Gardens. 15th century
        Amherst, Alicia M. Tyssen
            A fifteenth century treatise on
            gardening by "Mayster Ion Gardener"

                Archaeologia 54, pt.1:157-172
                1894

RYERSON LIBRARY
D10.5
A786   Gardens, Arabia
        Marcais, Georges
            The Arabian garden at Maroc

                Art et décoration 51:59-64
                February, 1927

710.5
H84   Gardens
            Two city gardens by Ruth Dean, Landscape
            archt.

                House and garden 53: 61-65
                June 1928

Gardens, 18th Century
Eighteenth Century Gardens.

                Arch & Cont. Rep. 68:
                311
                Nov. 14, 1902

RYERSON LIBRARY
059.8   Gardens, Argentina. Buenos Aires
P73   The botanical garden of Buenos Aires

                Plus ultra 12:9-11
                February 28, 1927

710.5
H84   Gardens
            Two gardens for two different sites:
            fan shape and oblong.

                House and garden 61: 54-55
                May 1932

710.5   Gardens, Africa, East
H84   Chesham, Lord
                A Tanganyika garden.

                Country life(Lond)81:492-493
                May 1,1937

710.5   Gardens. Australia
H84   Courtyard garden in Sidney, Australia. G.M.
            Hughes, archt.

                House & garden 51: 105
                March 1927

---

705   Gardens
W48   Unsere Gärten

                Das Werk
                30:275-280
                pt. 2, S '43

Gardens, Algeria
Triggs, H.I.
    Ancient Arab houses and gardens. Northern
Africa. Djenan-el-Mufti and El Bardo. Plans.

                Country life 38: 392-9
                S 18, '15

RYERSON LIBRARY
705.1   Gardens, Austria . Dubrovnik
A79   Khrabroff, Irina
                Villas and gardens of old Dubrovnik

                Arts and decorations 30:52-54
                January 1929

Card 1

Gardens, Austria, Miramar
The Gardens of Miramar, near Trieste, Austria.
The Property of His Imperial Majesty Francis
Joseph I. By M. M. Lowe.

House and gard. 3: 146-51
Mr. 1903

Card 2

D13.1   Gardens. Bibliography
H84   Pates, D.S.
        Books will make your garden grow

House beautiful 69:258,288,290,292
March 1931

Card 3

Gardens, Canada
Gardens to see in Canada.

House and garden 71:109
My., 1937

Card 4

710.5   Gardens,Austria.Salzburg
C85   Villiers-Stuart,C.M.
        The Mirabel gardens,Salzburg.

Country life(Lond)82:214-215
August 28,1937

Card 5

710.5   Gardens. Bibliography
L25   The early garden literature of America

Landscape architecture 13:179-85
April 1923

Card 6

710.5   Gardens. Canada
H84   Some gardens in Victoria, B.C.

House & garden 51: 91-5
July 1927

Card 7

710.5   Gardens,Babylon
C855   Perrett,Antoinette
        History of the country estate,part 2: ancient
estate parks in the Euphrates-Tigris country.

Country life(U.S.)68:34-36,72
October 1935

Card 8

720.52   Gardens, Bohemia
A673   Italian gardens in Prague

Arch.rev.(London) 57:253-255
June 1925

Card 9

710.5   Gardens. Canada
C855   Wonder gardens of the Canadian West

Country life 43: 41-7, 72-3
Jan. 1923

Card 10

710.5   Gardens, Bavaria
H84   A garden at Kulmbach; Paul Bonatz and F.
E. Scholer, archts.

House & garden 54: 100-101
September 1928

Card 11

720.52   Gardens. Bohemia
A673   Italian gardens in Prague-II.

Arch. Rev. (Lond.) 58: 68-72
Aug. 1925

Card 12

710.5   Gardens,Canada.Victoria
C85   Coley,G.E.A.
        The English tradition on the Pacific Coast,
examples from Victoria,Vancouver,Shannon.

Country life(Lond)82:148-149
August 7,1937

Card 13

710.5   Gardens,Biblical
C85   Garden-craft in the Bible

Country life(Lond.)57:941-944
June 13,1925

Card 14

Gardens, Bulgaria
Royal gardens in the Balkans. I. King Ferdinand's
By Irina Khrabroff.
Photos.

Country Life 72: 55
Jl, 1937

Card 15

705.5   Gardens, Capri
R22   Gardens and pergolas of Capri

Rassegna d'arte 22 n.s.9:190-198
May-June 1922

Card 16

710.5   Gardens-Bibliography
C85   Some early eighteenth century gardening
books

Country Life (Eng) 56:1006-1007
Dec. 20, 1924

Card 17

Gardens, California

see

Gardens, U. S. California

Card 18

Gardens, China

see also

Gardens, U. S. Chinese influence

Card 19

Gardens. Bibliography
Teall, Gardner
        Collecting old-time garden books

House and Garden 37:34-5, 68
Je 1920

Card 20

710.5   Gardens,Canada
C85   Coley,G.E.A.
        The English tradition on the Pacific Coast,
examples from Victoria,Vancouver,Shannon.

Country life(Lond)82:148-149
August 7,1937

Card 21

Gardens, China

House beaut. 32: 38-40
July, 1912

Gardens, China

Scribners 62: 383-386
Sept., 1917

710.5 Gardens, China
L26 Elwood, P.H.,jr
Impressions of garden art in China and
Japan.

Landscape architecture 20:192-200
April 1930

RYERSON LIBRARY
915.05 Gardens, China
A83 Spring ... shook down the heavy blossoms
... in the court of the summer palace.

Asia 31:358
June 1931

RYERSON LIBRARY
705.95 Gardens, China
C54 Bathing pool, bird bath, in a Shanghai
garden

China journal 8: plates
opp. p. 160

RYERSON LIBRARY
705.6 Gardens, China
S67r Martorell y Téllez-Girón,Ricardo
Jardines Chinos.

Sociedad de amigos del arte. Revista
espanolo 2: 278-295
March 1933

RYERSON LIBRARY
915.05 Gardens, China
A83 Gilbreath, Olive
Ware the pitcher-plant!

Asia 29:524-531
July 1929

RYERSON LIBRARY
915.05 Gardens, China
A83 Thurston, M. C.
Beauty in Chinese garden courts.

Asia 31:514-521,529-530
August 1931

RYERSON LIBRARY
Gardens, China
E., W.
Nature, feeling and art in the Chinese
garden (1 illus)

Ciba symposia
11:1378-1379
Summer, 1951

710.5 Gardens, China
H84 Youtz,P. M.
Within the moon gate.

House & garden.49:82-83
Mar. 1926

915.05 Gardens, China
A83 Chinese Garden Courts

Asia and the Americas 43:788-9
My '43

RYERSON LIBRARY
705.95 Gardens,China
C54 Boynton,G.M.
Notes on the origin of Chinese private gardens.

China journal 23:17-22
July 1935

Gardens, Circular

see

Round gardens

720.53 Gardens, China
W31 Chinese garden art.

Wasmuths 10: 190-193
Heft 5, 1926

915.05 Gardens, China
A83 Graham, Dorothy
Some Chinese gardens

Asia 37: 441-447, 403
Je '37

710.5 Gardens, Community
H84 From town dump to community garden.

House and garden 74: 64-65,79
November 1938

RYERSON LIBRARY
Gardens,China
Tung,Chuin
Chinese gardens, especially in Kiangsu and
Chekiang: 1.Chinese and Western gardens con-
trasted; 2.The design of Chinese gardens; 3.
Chinese gardens: past and present. Many illus-
trations.

T'ien Hsia 3:220-244
October 1936

RYERSON LIBRARY
D15.1 Gardens, China
H84 Nichols, R. S
Some old Chinese gardens

House beautiful 61:158-159
February, 1927

710.5 Gardens, Competitions
H84 Sloane, T.M.
Garden contests for town betterment.

House & garden 52: 70-71
August 1927

RYERSON LIBRARY
705.95 Gardens, China
R45 Ayscough, Florence
The Chinese idea of a garden

Revue des arts Asiatiques 2:39-49
June 1925

Gardens, China
Of Formal Gardens in China.
By Reginald Wrenn.

House and gard 5:139-42
Mr. 1904

720.5 Gardens. Competitions
P39 The garden architecture competition

Pencil Points 4:37-42
April 1923

Gardens. Conservation and restoration.
Hadfield, Miles
 The problems of garden restoration.
[illus.]

Country life
143: 1382-1383
My 23, 1968

Gardens. Design
 Greely, Rose
 Why should the garden have design?

House beau 70:
 411-13, 444-46,448; N. 1931
 316-19, 527-28; D. 1931
House beau. 71:
 59-61, 73-74; Ja. 1932
 128; F. 1932

Gardens. England.

Loudon, J.C. An encyclopaedia of
gardening. London: Longman, Hurst,
et al, 1825. p.1061-1097.

720.5   Gardens, Czechoslovak republic
A67r   Burnap, George
 The gardens of Dobris near Prague, Czecho-
slovakia.

Architectural record 52: 511-23
December,1922

705.4   Gardens, Egypt
A78V   Zulficar, Mohammed
 The art of the garden - the gardens of Cairo
and Alexandria (modern)

L'art vivant 16,No.154:588-591
July 15, 1930

Gardens, England

Tipping, Henry Avray. English homes.
9 vols. London: Offices of Country
Life; New York: Charles Scribner's
Sons, 1920-37.

D13.3   Gardens, Dalmatia
H94   Garden motives from Dalmatia.

House beautiful 62: 385-388
October 1927

705.4   Gardens, Egypt
M886   Tenaud, Suzanne
 Les jardins dans l'Égypte antique. Thèse.

Musées de France bulletin 8:130-151
October 1936

D19.05   Gardens, England
V88   Anne Boleyn's garden at Hever castle in
Kent.

Vogue 72: 66-67
July 1928

705.8   Gardens, Denmark
A51

American-Scandinavian review 10:622-627
Oct. 1922

Gardens, England

Academy architecture, 52: 17-32
1921

720.52   Gardens, England
A67   Binfield: a recent example of garden design .Oliver Hill,architect

Architects' journal 57:483-9
March 14, 1923

710.5   Gardens, Denmark
H84   Garden of Carl F. Glad at Copenhagen.

House and garden 59: 93
April 1931

Gardens, England

Field, Horace and Michael Bunney.
English domestic architecture of
the 17th and 18th centuries.
London: G. Bell and Sons, 1905.
p. 73.

Gardens, England
 Collingham Gardens, W.

Arch. and con. rep. 65: pls.
Mr. 29, 1901

720.55   Gardens, Denmark
W51   Rosegarden at Hellerup. G.N. Brandt, archt.

Wasmuths 11: 42-3
Heft 1, 1927

Gardens, England.

Jones, Sydney R. The village homes
of England. London and New York:
The Studio, Ltd., 1912 p. 149-163

D13.1   Gardens, England
H94   Court Farm, the estate of Mary Anderson

House beautiful 63:297-300
March 1928

720.55   Gardens, Denmark
W51   Brandt, G. N.
 The common garden.

Wasmuths 14: 161-172
April 1930

Gardens, England

Lotus Mag. 4:261-296
Mar., 1913.

D19.05   Gardens, England
V88   English gardens with paved courts

Vogue 73:80-81
April 27, 1929

720.5
A67r   Gardens, England
David, A.C.
   "English pleasure gardens" - review of a book
by Rose Standish Nichols.

Architectural record 13:335-348
April 1903

720.52
A673   Gardens. England
    Garden design: Lay-out and outlay

Architectural review 55:64-5
Feb. 1924

Gardens, England
Beard, Geoffrey
    A magnificent landscape garden. Studley Royal,
Yorkshire [illus]

Country Life
130: 284-287, Ag 10, 1961

Gardens, England
    English Roadside Cottages with their Doorway
Gardens. By Alex. E. Hoyle.

Arch rec 29: 126-38
F, 1911

705.2
893   Gardens, England
    A garden designed by Percy S. Cane

Studio 87:193-197
April 1924

720.5
M52   Gardens, England
    Manor house gardens of England

Western Arch. 33:39-41
April, 1924

Gardens. England.
    Formal Gardens. By H. Inigo Triggs.
Part I. London. B.T. Batsford.

Arch and con rep 68: 59-60
Ja 24, 1902

Gardens. England.
    Garden View, "Frithcote," Northwood, England.
Walter E. Hewitt, Architect.

Arch rev. 16: pl.
My, 1909

705.2
893   Gardens, England
Stephens, J.W.
    Miss Margery Allen's town gardens

Studio 92:177-180
September, 1926

Gardens. England
Roper, Lanning
    The future of great gardens. [illus.]

Country life
v. 141: 1362-1364
Je 1, 1967

051
543   Gardens, England
    Gardens of Cobden - Sanderson, William
Morris and Rossetti

Scribners magazine 74:25-34
July 1923

720.5
A51   Gardens, England
Sturgis, R. Clipston.
    On English gardens.

Amer archt & bldg news
70:100-102
D 29, 1900

705.2
161   Gardens, England
    Garden and terraces at The Hill,
Hampstead Heath. Photographed by
H.N.King.

Inter. studio 68:pl
Jan, 1913

Gardens, England
    Linfield Gardens, Hampstead, N.W. The
Entrance Hall.

Arch and con rep 69:pls.
Je 5, 1903

Gardens. England
Clark, H. F.
    The romantic garden.

Archtl Design
30:70-5 F 1960

Gardens, England
    The Garden at Broad Campden, Glos.
Mr. C.R. Ashbee, architect.

Builder 96: 441, pl.
Ap 10, 1909

Gardens, England
London

Besant, Sir Walter. South London.
New York: Frederick A. Stokes Co.,
1898. p. 282-300

D13.1
H84   Gardens, England
    St. Catherine's court

House beautiful 59:133-135
February 1926

720.5
A67   Gardens, England
Mawson, T.H.
    Garden design in England.

Architectural review 16: 41-52 pl. 29-30,
April 1909   35-36

Gardens, England.
Margetson, Stella.
    London's lost pleasure gardens.
[illus]

Country life
Vol. 135: 490-492.
Mr. 5, 1964

720.5
A67m   Gardens, England
    Snowshill Manor, Gloucestershire. Charles
Wade, architect

Architectural record 54:353-359
Oct. 1923

710.5 893 Gardens, England Studio year book,1917-p.51-62	710.5 C85 Gardens,England.Grayswood Hill Taylor,G.C. Grayswood hill,Haslemere,Surrey; residence of Mrs. C.M.Whittall. Country life(Lond.)80:226 September 26, 1936	Gardens, England. Kingston-on-Thames Garden views at "The Gazeway" Kingston-on-Thames Architect 109:2 pl. April 20, 1923
Gardens, England Spring-Gardens, Charing Cross, and Whitechapel. 1801-1900. Builder 88: 7-14 Ja 7, 1905	720.5 A67 Gardens,England.Hampstead Heath Mawson,T.H. Garden design in England.Plans Architectural review 13:41-51 pl.29-30,35 April 1909	710.5 C85 A.S.O. Gardens, England. London Sir William Chambers and Kew. Country life (Lond.) 67: 792-794 May 31, 1930
Burnham Library Gardens. Eng. 18th century Fleming, John In search of Landscape gardens [illus] Country Life 130: 200-202, Jl 27, 1961	Gardens, England. High Legh Hall High Legh Hall, Cheshire. Illus. Landscape and garden 4:145 Autumn, 1937	710.5 C85 Gardens,England.London Taylor,G.C. A garden in London: - at Regent's Lodge, Regent's Park. Country Life(London)85:161-164 February 18,1939
710.5 C85 Gardens,England.20th century Jellicoe,G.H. The garden in relation to the house. Country life(Lond.)79:x,xii May 16, 1936	710.5 C85 Gardens,England.Highdown Taylor,G.C. Highdown,Goring-on-Sea,Sussex. Residence of Major F.C.Stern. Gardens. Country life(Lond)81:198-203 February 20,1937	710.5 C85 Gardens, England. London Taylor, G. C. Lady Gladstone's London garden. (Lond.) Country life 84: 326-327 October 1, 1938
710.5 C85 Gardens,England.20th century Dillistone, George Garden design of today:- noting changes from past. Country life(London)85:187-195 February 18,1939	720.5 A67r Gardens,England.Informal Hoyle, A.E. English roadside cottages with their doorway gardens. Architectural record 29: 127-138 February 1911	710.5 H94 Gardens,England.London.Chelsea New gardens in old Chelsea - garden of Dr. Lindley Scotts. Oliver Hill, archt.-designer. A House and garden 72:72-73,102 October 1937
710.5 C85 Gardens,England.20th century Taylor, G.C. The modern garden. Country life(London)38:173-175 August 24,1940	Gardens, England. Italian influence Tipping, H A Anglo-Italian Gardens. Arch & con rep 80: 99-100 Ag 14, 1908	Gardens, England. London A shaded city garden in London House and garden 43:70-1 March, 1923
710.5 C85 Gardens, England. Embley Park Taylor, G. C. The garden at Embley Park, a woodland garden whose plant furnishing is a mirror of recent hor- ticultural discovery. Country life (London) 78:5-7 July 6, 1935	720.5 A67 Gardens,England.Kearsney Court View from terrace,Kearsney Court, England. Thomas H. Mawson, landscape archts. A Architectural review 16: pl.36 April 1909	720.5 A67 Gardens,England.Longleat Nichols,R.S. The Longleat flower garden - a description of the ancient flower garden, its layout and design. Architectural review 8,n.s.3:1-4 January 1901

710.5
C85
Gardens,England.Milford
A Surrey garden: Wo Yuen, Milford
Godalming.

Country life(Lond.)89:10-13
January 4,1941

710.5
C85
Gardens,England.Richmond
Taylor,G.C.
St.Nicholas,Richmond,Yorkshire: the residence
of the Hon. Robert James.

Country life(Lond.)80:626-632
December 12, 1936

Gardens. England. Stuart period
Tipping, H.A.
Garden making in early Stuart times - 1.

Country life (Lond.) 62:495-98
October 8, 1927

710.5
C85
Gardens,England.Mount Usher
Taylor,G.C.
Mount Usher, Ashford County,Wicklow, the re-
sidence of H.Walpole.

Country life(Lond.)80:12-18
July 4, 1936

710.5
C85
Gardens,England.Rowallane
Taylor,G.C.
The garden at Rowallane,Saintfield Co.Down—
the residence of Mr.H.Armytage Moore.

Country life(Lond.)79:220-226
February 29, 1936

710.5
C85
Gardens, England. Sutton Place
Taylor, G. C.
The gardens at Sutton Place, Guildford.

Country life (Lond.) 71: 202-207
February 20, 1932

710.5
C85
Gardens, England. Olympia
The gardens at Olympia.

Country life (Lond.) 47: 519-520
April 5, 1930

710.5
C85
Gardens,England.Stilemans
A country garden: Stilemans,Munstead
Heath,Godalming, originally designed by the
late Gertrude Jekyll.

A   Country life(Lond)81:63-65
January 16,1937

Gardens, England. Sydenham
The Crystal Palace.
By Edward White.
Plan, sketch.

Landscape and garden 4: 26
Spring, 1937

710.5
C85
Gardens,England.Pixholme Court
Taylor,G.C.
A garden transformation: the garden at Pix-
holme Court,Dorking - the residence of Sir
Malcolm Fraser.

Country life(Lond)81:230-272
February 27,1937

710.5
C85
Gardens,England.Stoke Poges
Taylor,G.C.
A garden of remembrance: the Stoke Poges mem-
orial gardens.

Country life(Lond.)80:124-125
August 1, 1936

710.5
C85
Gardens,England.Tittenhurst
Taylor,G.C.
Spring at Tittenhurst: a pageant of blossoms

Country life(Lond)77:268-273
March 16,1935

710.5
C85
Gardens,England.Port Lymne
Taylor,G.C.
The garden at Port Lymne,Hythe,Kent—a res-
idence of Sir Philip Sassoon.

Country life(Lond.)79:276-282
March 14, 1936

710.5
C855
Gardens,England.Stoke Poges
English gardens at Stoke Poges.

Country life(U.S.)71:30-31
April 1937

720.5
A67
Gardens,England. Walmer Place
Gazebo and terrace, Walmer Place,England.
Thomas H. Mawson, landscape archt.

Architectural review 16: 52
April 1939

710.5
C85
Gardens,England.Powis Castle
Hussey, Christopher
Powis castle,Montgomery-Shire—the seat of
the Earl of Powis. Plan.

Country life(Lond.)79:564-572
May 30, 1936

710.5
C85
Gardens,England.Stourhead
Hussey, Christopher
Stourhead, Wiltshire - most beautiful and
least changed of 18th century landscape gardens,
designed by F.M. Piper, Swedish architect, in
1779. House designed by Colin Campbell in 1722.
Reconstructed after fire in 1902. Seat of Sir
Henry Hoare, Bt. Plan and sectional drawings of
gardens and grotto. No house plans.

A   Country life(Lond.)83:608-614;638-642
I—June 11;II—June 18,1938

710.5
C85
Gardens, England. Welbeck Abbey
Taylor, G. C.
The gardens at Welbeck Abbey.

Country life (Lond.) 64: 581-585
October 27, 1928

710.5
C85
Gardens,England.Queen Anne
Tea party in a Queen Anne garden: needle-
work hanging from Stoke Edith.

Country life(Lond)81:586
May 29,1957

D13.1
H84
Gardens, England. Stratford-on-Avon
The gardens at Halls Croft, Stratford-on-
Avon, England

House beautiful 42:130-132
August 1927

710.5
C85
Gardens,England. Windlesham Moor
Taylor,G.C.
Windlesham Moor,Windlesham,Surrey.

Country life(Lond.)75: 566-570
June 2,1934

<table>
<tr><td>

710.5
H84
Fox, H. M.
Gardens, Europe.
Gardens to see in travels abroad.
More gardens to see when traveling abroad.

House and garden 59: 84-85,128;62-63
May-June 1931

</td><td>

STEIGER LIBRARY
705.4
R45
Gardens, France
Canay, Ernest de
Castle and gardens of Montjeu

Revue de l'art 47:197-203
Mar. 1925

</td><td>

Gardens, France
Château du Marais, Commune du Val-Saint-Germain
(Seine-et-Oise)

Vacquier, Jules Felix. Les anciens
châteaux de France. 12 vols.
Paris: F. Contet, 1920-31. v.1-2:pl.10

</td></tr>
<tr><td>

Gardens, Europe
Old world gardens

Art and prog. 5:231-237
May, 1914

</td><td>

Gardens, France
Château de Bevilliers-Breteuil, Commune de Choisel
(Seine-et-Oise)

Vacquier, Jules Felix. Les anciens
châteaux de France. 12 vols. Paris:
F. Contet, 1920-31. v.1-2,pls.49-52

</td><td>

Gardens, France
The chateaux and gardens of France

Country life (Lond.)
v. 20 and following vols.
[see index for pages]
Begins D 8, 1906

</td></tr>
<tr><td>

710.5
C855
Gardens, Europe; 20th century
Steele, Fletcher
Modern gardens: Europe blazes a new and
spectacular trail in horticulture.

Country life (U.S.) 58: 67-68,74,76
November 1930

</td><td>

Gardens, France
Château de Champs (Seine-et-Oise)

Vacquier, Jules Felix. Les anciens
châteaux de France. 12 vols. Paris:
F. Contet, 1920-31. v.1-2:24,pl.60.

</td><td>

STEIGER LIBRARY
705.4
R45
Gardens, France
Canay, Ernest de
The English gardens of the French ladies at
Bellvue and Versailles

Revue de l'art 50:215-228
November, 1928

</td></tr>
<tr><td>

710.5
H84
Gardens, Europe; 20th century.
Jay, M. R.
Modernism goes gardening in middle Europe.

House and garden 60: 54-56
September 1931

</td><td>

Gardens, France
Château de Courance (Seine-et-Oise)

Soulange-Bodin, Henri. Les anciens
chateaux de France. 8 vols. Paris:
F. Contet, 1925. v.5-6:pl.5

</td><td>

STEIGER LIBRARY
705.4
B29
Gardens, France
Duchêne, Achille
Estates.

La Renaissance 10:365-371
August 1927

</td></tr>
<tr><td>

710.5
H84
Gardens. France.

House & Garden 40: 19-21
Dec. 1921.

</td><td>

Gardens, France
Château de Dampierre (Seine-et-Oise)

Vacquier, Jules Felix. Les anciens
châteaux de France. 12 vols. Paris:
F. Contet, 1920-31. v.3-4:62

</td><td>

710.5
H84
Gardens. France
The formality of French town gardens

House & Garden 43: 44-5
Jan. 1923

</td></tr>
<tr><td>

Gardens. France.

Roger-Miles, Leon. Architecture,
decoration et ameublement pendant
la dix-haitième siècle. Paris:
E. Rouveyre, n.d. pl. 46-48.

</td><td>

Gardens, France
Château de Rochefort-en-Yvelines. Text in
French. Photographs of exterior and interior

Saint-Sauveur, Hector.
Chateaux de France. 10 vols. Paris:
Librarie génerale de l'architecture
et des arts decoratifs, 1922.
v.1:6,pl. 31-34

</td><td>

Gardens, France
French gardens exhibited at the International
Congress, Paris.
Photos.

Landscape and garden 4:79-81
Summer, 1937

</td></tr>
<tr><td>

STEIGER LIBRARY
713.1
H84
Gardens, France
Nichols R.S.
Anglo-Italian gardens on the French Riviera

House beautiful 58:497-499
Nov. 1925

</td><td>

Gardens, France
Château de Wideville, Commune de Davron
(Seine-et-Oise). Plan, plates

Soulange-Bodin, Henri. Les anciens
chateaux de France. 8 vols. Paris:
F. Contet, 1925. v.5-6:17-20,pls.30-
40.

</td><td>

STEIGER LIBRARY
705.1
A79
Gardens, France
The garden of the villa Cypris

Arts and decoration 26:24-26
January, 1927

</td></tr>
</table>

710.5
4786
Gardens, France
The gardens of J.C.N. Forestier

Art and decoration 32:85-96
March 1928

Gardens, France
Jardin Francais au Château de Marsat.
(French garden in the Chateau of Marsat.)
Pierre Laprade, archt. Plan.

Encyclopedie de l'architecture;
constructions modernes. 12 vols.
Paris: Albert Morancé, 1928-39.
1: pl.6 Number 1.

Gardens, France. Beauregard
Beauregard. Plan, engravings.

Androuet du Cerceau. Les plus
excellents bastiments de France.
2 vols. Paris: A. Lévy, 1868-70.
vol. 2: pls. 59-60

705.4
B28
Gardens, France
Michon, L.M.
The gardens of the hotel Biron

Gazette des beaux-arts
Per.5,v.17:93-104
February 1928

D18.1
N54
Gardens, France
Nichols, Rose Standish
A little garden hunt in France

House beautiful 54:133-135
August 1923

Gardens, France. Bury
Bury. Plan, engravings.

Androuet du cerceau. Les plus
excellents bastiments de France.
2 vols. Paris: A. Lévy, 1868-70.
vol.2:pls.61-62

710.5
C85
Gardens. France
The garden of the Villa Cypris, Cap Martin.

Country life (Lond.)61:342-6
March 5, 1927

D19.05
V88
Gardens, France
Lord Abercommay's château at Antibes

Vogue 70:88-89
October 15, 1927

720.54
A67
Gardens,France. Cannes
Laprade,Albert
L'oeuvre de Léon Le Bel,à Grasse (A.-M.)
(Work of Léon Le Bel at Grasse.) Plans.

L'Architecture 46: 151-164
May 15,1933

A

710.5
C855
Gardens,France
Berg,Carl
A garden path through France. Illus. Map of
France with itinerary of gardens.

Country life (U.S.)63: 60-61,80
February 1933

O54
I29
Gardens, France
Riviera

L'Illustration 157:198
Feb. 26, 1921

Gardens, France. Charleval
Charleval. Plan

Androuet du cerceau. Les plus
excellents bastiments de France.
2 vols. Paris: A. Lévy, 1868-70.
vol.2:pl.19

710.5
H84
Gardens, France
The gardens of France
J.C.N.Forestier

House & garden 46:59-63
Oct. 1924

Gardens, France: 20th century
An example of garden design in the modernist
manner, at St. Cloud, France
Cubistic landscape architecture on the outskirts
of Paris.

House and Garden 46:62-3
Aug., 1924

Gardens, France. Dampierre
Dampierre. Plans, engravings.

Androuet du cerceau. Les plus
excellents bastiments de France.
2 vols. Paris: A. Lévy, 1868-70.
vol. 2: pls. 52-53

705.4
R45
Gardens, France
The gardens of Harcourt

Revue de l'art 43: 59-64
Jan. 1923

Gardens, France. 20th Century
Robertson, Howard and Yerbury, F.R.
Euclid in the garden. Examples of a new phase of
modernism.

Architect (Lond.) 121: 445-449
April 5, 1929

Gardens, France. Fountainebleau
Fontainebleau. Plans

Androuet du cerceau. Les Plus
excellents bastiments de France.
2 vols. Paris: A. Lévy, 1868-70.
vol. 2: pls. 10-11

710.5
C855
Gardens. France
The intimate garden of Miss Elsie de
Wolfe, at Versailles, France

Country life 43:58-61
March 1923

Gardens, France. 20th century
Steele, Fletcher
New pioneering in garden design.

Landscape architecture 20:158-177
April, 1930

710.5
H84
Gardens. France. Garches.
Garden near Paris. garden of Major A.C.M.
Anderson's home at Garches, suburb near
Paris.

House and Garden 74: 54-55
October 1938

720.54   Gardens,France. Grasse
A67   Laprade,Albert
         L'oeuvre de Léon Le Bel, à Grasse (A.-W.)
      (Work of Léon Le Bel at Grasse.) Plans.

                  L'Architecture 46: 151-164
                  May 15,1933
            A

   Gardens, France. Riviera.
      "Lou Sueil". The Riviera estate of
   Colonel and Madame Balsan at Èze

                  Vogue 71:80-81.
                  May 15, 1928

   Gardens, France. Vaux-le-Vicomte
      Les jardins, château de Vaux-le-Vicomte.

                  Saint Sauveur, Hector.
                  Chateaux de France. 10 vols. Paris:
                  Librarie génerale de l'architecture
                  et des arts decoratifs, 1922.
                  v.e:pls.33-36

BYLABOR LIBRARY
708.4   Gardens,France. Maisons-Laffitte
M96   Vitry,Paul
         Chateau de Maisons-Laffitte: l'art des jar-
      dins classiques.

                  Musées de France 4: 113-116
                  July 1932

710.5   Gardens, France. Paris
H84   A remodelled house and garden in an
      ancient street in Paris.

                  House and garden 54: 76-77
                  August 1928

   Gardens, France. Versailles

      see also

   Versailles. Chateau Gardens

710.5   Gardens,France.Neuilly-sur-Seine
L26   Draper,E.S.
         A modern French suburban estate,near Paris;
      the small estate of M.Potin,Neuilly-sur-Seine,near
      the Bagatelle gardens,Bois de Boulogne,Paris.De-
      signed by M.Vacherot.

                  Landscape architecture 17: 203-210
                  April 1927

D19.05   Gardens, France. Riviera
V88   A Riviera garden

                  Vogue 69:76-77
                  June 1, 1927

STILMAN LIBRARY
705.4   Gardens, France. Versailles
028   Nolhac, Pierre de
         The bosquets of Versailles

                  Gazette des beaux-arts
                  Per.3.v.22:265-282,   1899.
                  v.23:39-54,283-292

720.52   Gardens, France, Nîmes
Ac73   Garden design: a formal garden in France
      The public gardens of Nîmes

                  Arch.Rev. 56:2-7
                  July, 1924

710.5   Gardens, France. Riviera
C85   Riviera gardens: Maria Serena.

                  Country life (Lond.) 66: 562-564
                  October 26, 1929

710.5   Gardens, France. Versailles
H84   Garden of Elsie de Wolfe, Versailles,
      France.

                  House & Garden v.75: 60
                  March 1938

   Gardens, France. Paris

      see also

   Paris. Chateau de Bagatelle.   Jardins
   Paris. Jardin du Luxembourg
   Paris. Jardins des Tuileries

   Gardens, France. Saint Maur
      Sainct Maur. Plan

                  Androuet du cerceau. Les Plus
                  excellents bastiments de France.
                  2 vols. Paris: A. Lévy, 1868-70.
                  vol. 2: pl. 27

D19.05   Gardens,France.Versailles
V88   Sleeping gardens in midwinter beauty:
      garden on Paul Louis Weiller's estate at
      Versailles.

                  Vogue 80:58-59,80
                  December 1,1932

710.5   Gardens, France. Paris
H84   Clark, H. M.
         A backyard garden secluded in Paris.

                  House and garden 57: 82-83,134
                  March 1930

720.54   Gardens,France.Sceaux
A67   Ollivier,Félix
         Le parc de Sceaux et les nouvelles cascades
      (The park of Sceaux and the new waterfalls).Azéma,
      archt.

            A   L'Architecture 49:11-14
                  January 1936

   Gardens, France. Villandry
      Château de Villandry, Indre-et-Loire. Text in
   French. Engravings. Plot plan and gardens.

                  Vacquier, Jules Felix. Les anciens
                  châteaux de France. 12 vols. Paris:
                  F. Contet, 1920-31.
                  v.11-12:17-19,pl.32-40

710.5   Gardens,France.Paris
H84   Modern gardens in Paris. Patterned gardens
      by Jean-Charles Moreux and Albert La Prade,
      archt.

            A   House and garden 70:42-43
                  September 1936

   Gardens, France. Vallery
      Le desseing de l'eleuation du Jardin de
   Valleri avec la gallerie et les pauillons.
   Engraving.

                  Androuet du cerceau. Les plus
                  excellents bastiments de France.
                  2 vols. Paris: A. Lévy, 1868-70.
                  vol.1:pl.44

   Gardens, Germany

      see also

   Veitschöchheim (Ger.) Schlossgarten

D10.5
D32   Gardens, Germany
 	
RYERSON LIBRARY.
 	
Dekorative kunst 26:178-184
May 1923
	RYERSON LIBRARY
	D10.5 Gardens, Germany
	D32 Koenig, Hermann
	     Flower gardens. Gardens of Northern Germany
	
	Dekorative kunst 32:8-12
	October 1928 (129-133
	March 1929
		720.53 Gardens, Germany
		W31 German gardens by Oswald Woelke, Von
		   Hermann Koenig and Harry Maass, landscape
		   archts.
		
		Wasmuths 11: 365-368
		Heft 9, 1927

Gardens, Germany Deutsche kunst 32:299-306 July, 1913	D10.5 Gardens, Germany D32 Koenig-Hamburg Garden art in Germany Dekorative kunst 27:97-100 Feb. 1924	710.5 Gardens, Germany H84 German gardens. House & garden 51: 96-7 February 1927

Gardens, Germany
 	
Kunstgewerbe Blatt 25:91-96
Feb., 1914
	720.53 Gardens, Germany.
	B51 Gardens for small houses. Illus. plans.
	
	Berliner architekturwelt
	18:heft 11-12,p.375-81.
		Gardens, Germany
		   German Houses and Gardens. The Musings of a
		   Native. By A. W. Fred.
		
		House and gard 4:133-42
		S 1903

720.53   Gardens. Germany.
M68
 	
Moderne Bauformen 20: 33-48 & pl.
Mar. 1921.
	RYERSON LIBRARY.
	D10.5 Gardens, Germany
	D32 Haenel, Erich
	     Garden play in Dresden
	
	Dekorative kunst 30:57-65
	December, 1926
		RYERSON LIBRARY
		705.3 Gardens, Germany
		M96 Kreisel, Heinrich
		     The history of the planning of the gardens
		   of Veitshöchsheim
		
		Münchner jahrbuch n.s.3:45-74
		Heft 1, 1926

710.5   Gardens, Germany
H84   Alpines and evergreens in a foreign court-
   yard garden.
 	
House and garden 57: 98
April 1930
	RYERSON LIBRARY
	D10.5 Gardens, Germany
	D32 Naumann, Manfred
	     Gardens laid out by Fr. Gildemeister.
	
	Dekorative kunst 31: 264-268
	August 1928
		RYERSON LIBRARY.
		705.3 Gardens, Germany
		C56 The Jubilee gardens at the Dresden expos-
		   ition. 1926
		
		Der cicerone 18: 417-424
		Heft 18, June 1926

Ryerson
   Gardens, Germany
     Blumengärten von Fr. Gildemeister.
 	
Dekorative kunst 14:153-160
Jan 1911
	RYERSON LIBRARY
	705.3 Gardens. Germany
	W48 Kirchweng, Johannes
	     Garten
	
	Die neue saat 1:220-222
	July, 1938
		711 Gardens, Germany
		S77 Der kleingarten in der gartensystematik.
		     Der Deutsche familiengarten in Vergangen-
		   heitgegenwart und zukunft. (Charts showing
		   development of the small gardens.)
		
		Städtebau 22: 118-121
		August 1927

RYERSON LIBRARY
051   Gardens, Germany
A51   Steckelberg, Mathilda
     Flowers and small gardens
 	
Amer-Ger rev 4: 35-37
D '37
	720.53 Gardens, Germany
	B55 Gartenbauausstellungen in Hannover 1933,
	   Essen 1932-33 und Mailand 1933. (Horti-
	   cultural exhibits in Hanover 1933, Essen
	   1932-33 and Milan 1933.) Plans.
	
	Baumeister 32: 80-91
	March 1934
		RYERSON LIBRARY
		705.2 Gardens, Germany
		S93 Dresdner, A.
		     Kurt Hoppe's gardens
		
		Studio 93: 331-333
		May 1927

061
A51   Gardens, Germany
    Hitchcock, H.R.
        Late baroque German gardens

                        Amer-Ger Rev 1:24-35
                        '35

710.5
C85   Gardens, Germany. Hanover
    Robert, C. L.
        Gardens of Herrenhausen, home of George I
at Hanover.

        Country life (Lond.) 84: 174-176
        August 20, 1938

Gardens, Hanging

      see

Babylon. Hanging gardens

710.5
D32   Gardens, Germany
    Kayser, K.
        New gardens. The work of Kayser & Seibert,
Heidelberg

        Dekorative kunst 32:190-192
        May 1929

720.55
K31   Gardens, Germany. Heidelberg
        Garden by Kayser and Seibert.

        Wasmuths 11: 466
        Heft 11, 1927

710.5
C855   Gardens, Hawaii
        In lovely Hawaiian gardens where scented
breezes blow.

        Country life (U.S.) 65: 56-57
        December 1932

720.53
M68   Gardens, Germany
    Baer, C.H.
        Sachlichkeit und gute form auch im garten.
(Practicality and good form in the garden.) Kayser
and Seibert, landscape archts.

        Moderne bauformen 26: 155-160
        April 1927
A

D13.1
N54   Gardens, Germany. Modernist
    Nichols, R.S.
        The futurist gardens of new Germany.

        House beautiful 62: 390-91
        October 1927

710.5
C855   Gardens, Hawaii. Honolulu
    Fox, H. M.
        Gardens in Hawaii - Lester McCoy residence
in Honolulu. Hardie Phillip, archt.

        Country life (U.S.) 59: 55-56,76
        March 1931

720.5
A67   Gardens, Germany
    Perrett, A.R.
        Some "Back-Yard Gardens" of Germany designed
by F. Gildemeister, garden archt.

        Architectural review 19 n.s.2: 195-197
A   June 1913

Gardens. Germany. Potsdam
Hitchcock, Henry-Russell, Jr.
    The romantic gardens of Potsdam. [illus.]

        American-German Review
        Vol.2: 19-23
        Sept. 1935

Ryerson Gardens. History
        Exposition sur l'art des jardins (1730-1830)
au Château de Maisons-Lafitte

        Bibliofilia 37:132
        F-Mr 1935

Gardens, Germany
    Vegetable gardens as units in park systems

        Städtebau
        17, heft 1-2: 14-6 & pl
        1920

710.5
C85   Gardens, Germany. Veitshöchheim
    Villiers-Stuart, C.M.
        Masterpieces of German baroque: Veitshöchheim.
Johann Mayer, landscape archt. Plan.

A   Country life(Lond.)80:436-440
        October 24, 1936

Gardens. History
    L'evolution du jardin

        Gaz. d.beaux arts (n.s.) 10:218-234
        Sept., 1913

Gardens, Germany. 20th century
    Huntington, G.T.
    Modern gardens as the Germans do them.

        House and garden 62: 44-45
        July, 1932

Gardens, Greece
    Royal gardens of Greece

        House beautiful 52: 109-111
        Aug., 1922

Gardens. History
    History of garden craft

        Kunst und Kunsthandwerk 18:163-176
        1915, Heft 3-4

D10.5
D32   Gardens, Germany. Düsseldorf
        Notes on the gardens of Oswald Woelke,
Düsseldorf

        Dekorative kunst 31:74-77
        December 1927

710.5
H84   Gardens, Guatemala. Antigua
        Garden in Guatemala-"House in Antigua",
garden of William Popenoe.

        House and garden 74: 44-45
        November 1938

Gardens in art
    "In the gardens of our forefathers"--old prints
showing gardens

        Bookman's journal 11:70-73
        Nov., 1924

Gardens in art
    Maeterlinck, L.
As represented in French miniatures, ivories
tapestries, etc.

L'art et les artistes v.s.v.9:329-
June 1924   335

915.05   Gardens, India
A83   Wilson, Margaret
                Garden homesickness

Asia. 31:284-289,329-331
May 1931

D13.1   Gardens, Ireland
N64   Nichols, R.S.
                An island garden in Glengarriff Harbor

House beautiful 65:
304-305, 345-346
March 1929

Gardens in art
    Ely, C.B.
Gardens in great paintings

House beautiful 58:352-353
October, 1925

710.5   Gardens, India
C85   Kashmir's most famous garden

Country Life (Lond.) 57:153-54
Jan. 31, 1925

710.5   Gardens, Ireland. Dublin
C85   Taylor, G.C.
                A national garden: The Botanic Garden, Glas-
            nevin, Dublin.

Country Life(Lond.)79:148-150
February 8, 1936

710.5   Gardens in art
C85   Villiers-Stuart,C.M.
                Persian gardens and persian art

Country life (London) 69:230-232
February 21,1931

Gardens, India
    India.
    By Mavis Dillon.
    Photos.

Landscape and garden 4:49-51
Spring, 1937

Gardens, Italy

see also

Vatican. Giardino vaticano

Formal gardens, Italy

Gardens, in art
    Rusiñol

International studio 32: 98-103
Jl. 1907

Gardens, India
    Gardens and cement

Marg 2. no. 2:17-19
1948

Gardens. Italy

Country life 41:306-309
Mar. 31, 1917

Gardens in art
    Watercolor drawings by G.S. Elgood

Internat. Studio 22:209-215
May, 1904

720.53   Gardens. India
W31   Shalimar at Kashmir.

Wasmuths 7: 1, 9-10
Heft 1, Januar 1923

Gardens, Italy.

Falda, Giovanni Battista. La
Fontane di Roma. 4 vols.
Roma: Giacomo de Rossi, [1675-91?]
pl.15,sup pl.4-6,10,13,14,16,18,
19,21,22.

Gardens, India

Arts and decor. 11:271
Oct., 1919

Gardens. India. English influence
Archer, Mildred
    English gardens in India. [illus.]

Country life
112: 1120-1123
N 2, 1967

Gardens, Italy

Inter. studio 16:181-192
May, 1902

Gardens. India

Lotus Mag. 5:465-470
Ap., 1914

710.5   Gardens, Ireland
H84   Moonlight gardens of Ireland.

House and garden 74: 48-49
November 1938

Gardens, Italy.

Nebbia, Ugo. La Brianza,Bergamo:
Istituto Italiano d'arti grafiche,
1912.

Gardens, Italy.

Salvatore, Camillo, comp.
Italian architecture, furniture
and interiors. Boston:G.H.
Polley and Co., [1904] .

Gardens, Italy
The Gardens of Italy.

British archt 64: 305
N 3, 1905

D13.1   Gardens, Italy
H84   Nichols, R.S.
               The new Renaissance of gardens in Italy

House beautiful 60: 276-277
Sept. 1926.

Gardens. Italy.

Scheult, Francois Léonard.
Recueil d'architecture dessinée
et mesurée en Italie. Paris:
Ainé, 1840.

Gardens, Italy
The Gardens of the Villa Lante, at Bagnaia,
near Viterbo, Italy. By George Walter Dawson.

House and gard. 2: 579-93
D 1902

Ryerson Library
705.5   Gardens, Italy
B69   Ballardini,Gaetano
               Per la mostra del giardino Italiano: Villa
               d'Ippolito d'Este à Tivoli. Villa Italiana.

Bollettino d'arte 25: 14-17
July 1931

Gardens, Italy
A Book of Italian Gardens.

Builder 91: 2-4
Jl 7, 1906

710.5   Gardens. Italy
L25   Gardens of Villa Palmieri, Florence

Landscape architecture 13:244-252
July 1923

Gardens, Italy
Remodelling an Old Italian Garden in the
Eighteenth Century. Translated from the Italian.

House and gard 2: 266-70
Je., 1902

710.5   Gardens, Italy
C85   Jellicoe, G. A.
               The exhibition of Italian gardens at Florence:
               A representative collection of models.

Country life (Lond.) 69: 654-656
May 23, 1931

710.5   Gardens. Italy.
H84   Wright, R.
               In a Saracen garden.

House & garden.49:100-01
May 1926

720.5   Gardens, Italy
A67f   A Renaissance garden at San Domenico,
               Florence

Arch. Forum 41:293-300
Dec. 1924

Gardens, Italy.
A 14th century garden.

Dedalo. 368-91.
Nov. 1920.

Gardens, Italy
Italian architectural gardens

Arch and con rep 68: 404-05
D 26, 1902

710.5   Gardens. Italy
C85   Riviera gardens.

Country life (Lond.)62: 745-9
November 19, 1927

710.5   Gardens,Italy
C855   Berg,Carl
               A garden path through Italy. Illus. Map of
           Italy and vicinity with itinerary of gardens.

Country life (U.S.)63: 44-45,78
April 1933

Gardens, Italy
Italian Gardens.

Arch and con rep 73: 59-60
Ja 27, 1905

710.5   Gardens, Italy
C85   Riviera gardens: the villa Fiorentina.

Country life (Lond.)62:912-15
December 17, 1927

720.6   Gardens. Italy
R88   Thomas, F. Inigo
               Gardens.

R.I.B.A. 33: 430-9
June 12, 1926

Gardens, Italy
Italian Landscape Gardener

House beaut. 40:15-17
June, 1916

Gardens, Italy
Some Gardens in Italy.
By Richard Davey.

House beau 13: 84-92
Ja 1903

BURNHAM LIBRARY.
708.4
M23 Gardens, Italy
Fauchier-Magnan, Adrien
Some Italian gardens

La renaissance 9:329-338
June, 1926

Gardens, Italy
Villa Gardens

Amer. Mag. of Art 9:446-451
Sep., 1918

710.5
L26 Gardens,Italy. Gamberaia. Settignano
Hubbard,H.V.
Note taking in Italian gardens: Villa Gamberaia at Settignano. Plans.

Landscape architect 5: 56-66
January 1915

710.5
H84 Gardens, Italy
A terraced garden in Tuscany.

House and garden 41: 54-5.
Jun.1922.

BURNHAM LIBRARY.
705.1
A79 Gardens, Italy
The Villa Lante, Italy's most famous sixteenth century garden

Arts and decoration 25:34-38
July, 1926

720.5
A67r Gardens,Italy.Rome
Cheney,C.H.
The American Academy in Rome: "Watering the plants of genius" Cellini.

Architectural record 31:245,247,249
March 1912

710.5
H84 Gardens. Italy
Carrère, R.
The three graces of the garden.

House & garden 51:114-5
May 1927

Gardens, Italy
Villa Lante at Bagnaia

House and garden 36:44-45
Sep., 1919

720.52
B86 Gardens,Italy. Rome
In the Western garden: The Quirinal,Rome.
Sketch.

British architect 64: 310, pl.fol.p.311
November 3,1905

D13.1
H84 Gardens, Italy
Tuscany

House beaut 50:93-6
Aug. 1921

D19.05
V88 Gardens, Italy
Villa Leopolda

Vogue 69:66-67
June 15, 1927

720.52
B93 Gardens, Italy. Rome
Harbron, Dudley
The Roman garden.

Builder 121: 542-3
October 28, 1921

BURNHAM LIBRARY.
D13.1
H84 Gardens, Italy
Nichols, R.S.
Unknown Italian gardens

House beautiful 58: 625-627
Dec. 1925

710.5
C85 Gardens, Italy. Boccanegra
Riviera gardens: Boccanegra.

Country life (Lond.) 66: 714-717
November 23, 1929

720.5
A67r Gardens,Italy.Rome
Reynolds,M.T.
The villas of Rome,part 2. Plans.

Architectural record 7:1-32
July-September 1897

BURNHAM LIBRARY.
D13.1
H84 Gardens, Italy
Nichols, R.S.
Unknown Italian gardens: Caserta

House beautiful 59:636-638
May 1926

710.5
L26 Gardens, Italy. Como
Hubbard, H.V.
Palazzo Giovio, Como. Plan

Landscape architect 5:115-119
April 1915

710.5
L26 Gardens, Italy, Rome. Bosco Parrasio
Lawson, Edward
Bosco Parrasio, Rome

Landscape architecture 19: 170-174
April 1929

BURNHAM LIBRARY.
D13.1
H84 Gardens, Italy
Nichols, R. S.
Unknown Italian gardens: La Pietra

House beautiful 59: 48-50
Jan. 1926

Gardens, Italy. Florence
Un Piccolo giardino a Firenze. P. Porcinai, ldsp. archt. [plans]

Domus no. 209:26-27
My '46

720.5
A67r Gardens, Italy. Villa Lante
The Villa Lante. No plan.

Architectural record 8: 117-124
October-December 1898

Gardens, Japan, see also Gardens, U.S. Japanese influence	Gardens, Japan Holme, Charles Artistic gardens in Japan [illus] Studio 1:128-135 July 1895	705.2 Gardens, Japan S93 Harada, Jiro The garden of Shoren-In, Kyoto Studio 94:261-262 October 1927
Gardens, Japan Art jour. 62:301-304,345-350 Oct. 1910 - Nov. 1910	710.5 Gardens, Japan H84 Phillips, H. A. Concerning gardens of illusion in Japan. House and garden 62: 42-43,58 August 1932.	720.52 Gardens, Japan A67 Harada, Jiro Garden-art in Japan. Architects' journal 69: 162-165 January 23, 1929
Gardens, Japan. Challaye, Félicien. Le Japon illustré. Paris: Larousse, 1915. p. 145-8.	915.05 Gardens, Japan J36 Stone, J.K. The dream gardens of Nippon Japan 14:22-25 Sept.1925	915.05 Gardens, Japan J36 Popham,W.D. The gardens of Japan. Japan 21: 22-31 August 1932
Gardens. Japan Good furniture 8:192,193 Apr. 1917	Gardens, Japan Famous Gardens of Japan. By Anna C. Hartshorne. House and gard 5: 76-81 F 1904	710.5 Gardens, Japan C855 Lockwood,S.M. A garden path through Japan. Map of Japan with itinerary of gardens. Country life (U.S.)64: 55-56,79 August 1933
Gardens, Japan The Iris Garden at Horikiri Near Tokio, Japan. By Anne H. Dyer. House and gard 3: 32-38 Ja 1903	705.95 Gardens, Japan C54 L.L. The garden: Dwarf firs and pines; other shrubs; flowering shrubs China journal 12:173-175 March 1930	Gardens, Japan The gardeners put nature in a frame. [color] Life articles on art 1951:698-99 Dec [?] 1951
915.05 Gardens, Japan J36 RYERSON LIBRARY. Japan 13:12-17 Nov. 1923	Gardens, Japan The Garden Club of America visits Japan. Kokusa bunka shinkokai quarterly 1:29-33 No. 1. April, 1935	710.5 Gardens, Japan C855 Lockwood, S. M. Gardens of Japan: symbolism is the keynote of their design. Country life (U.S.) 59: 61-63 March 1931
910.5 Gardens,Japan N27 Kuck, L.E. The art of Oriental gardens. Sung painting- gardens in Japan. Modern Japanese gardens. Asia 40:248-254;314-319;383-387 May-July 1940	705.95 Gardens, Japan K79 The garden of the Saihōji temple.Article in Japanese Kokka 33:121-212;247-259 October,November 1922	710.5 Gardens, Japan C855 Woods, Mrs. C.E. The glorious gardens of Japan. Country life (U.S.) 56:48-49 July 1929

710.5
C85
Gardens, Japan
The grace of Japanese gardens.

Country life (Lond.) 63: 975
June 30, 1928

Gardens. Japan
Nakajima, Ken
Japanese gardens.
A brief list of characteristic plants with
their botanical names.

Archtl Design
29:409-15 O 1959

RYERSON LIBRARY
Gardens, Japan
Newsom, Samuel
Secrets of Japanese gardens

Asia and the Americas
46:263-8
Je '46

RYERSON LIBRARY
915.05
J36
Gardens, Japan
Roorbach, Eloise
Japanese gateways to beauty.

Japan 16: 4-7
September 1927

RYERSON LIBRARY
705.95
E13
Gardens, Japan
Kinoshita, Tatsuya
Japanese gardens: Development of Japanese
gardens; examples of famous gardens; Characteris-
tics of Japanese gardens.

Bulletin of eastern art 3-18
Number 17, May 1941

Gardens. Japan
Spirit of the Garden

Scribners 62:703-711
Dec., 1917

RYERSON LIBRARY
915.05
J36
Gardens, Japan. Tokyo
An historic garden opened (Dempo-in
garden, Asakusa Park, Tokyo)

Japan 19:23
September 1930

Gardens, Japan
Toyama, Yeisaku
The Japanese gardens in the Momoyama age
(text in Japanese)

Kokka 36:
169-72; Je 1926
214-27; Ag "
283-87; O "

RYERSON LIBRARY
915.05
A83
Gardens, Japan
Matsuno, Keizo
The spirit of the Japanese garden.

Asia. 31:384-389,400
June 1931

710.5
L26
Gardens, Japan
Elwood, P.H., jr
Impressions of garden art in China and
Japan.

Landscape architecture 20:192-200
April 1930

705.95
K79
Gardens, Japan
Toyama, Eisaku
Notes see the garden of the Jogwan - ji,
Yugwara.

Kokka 41:no.492
November, 1931

RYERSON LIBRARY
705.95
K79
Gardens. Japan
Eisaku Toyama
The Tokugawa Shogunate and landscape gardens
belonging to the imperial household.

Kokka 45, no.537
August 1935

RYERSON LIBRARY
913.05
J36
Gardens, Japan
Wrenn, Sara
In the garden of an empress

Japan 17:14
August 1928

705.95
K79
Gardens, Japan
Toyama, Eisaku
On the garden of the Sioku-ji temple,
Maruko Shizuoka prefecture (text in Japanese -
no illustration)

Kokka 40:No.478
September, 1930

RYERSON LIBRARY
705.1
C91
Gardens, Japan
Harada, Jiro
Viscount Shibuzawa's garden

Creative art 2:184-187
March 1928

Gardens, Japan
in color

Printing art 26: opp.p.448
Feb., 1916

RYERSON LIBRARY
705.95
K79
Gardens, Japan. Kyoto
Eisaku Toyama
On the gardens laid out by Priest Mokuan.

Kokka 45, no.537, March 1935, pt.I
March 1935

RYERSON LIBRARY
705.2
S93
Gardens, Japan. Tokyo
The garden of Marquis Asano's home
in Tokyo

Studio 93:414-417
June 1927

RYERSON LIBRARY
913.1
B84
Gardens, Japan
Pope, H.N.
A japanese garden

House beautiful 58:367-368
October 1925

Gardens, Japan
Toyama, Yeisaku
A refutation of the general opinion concerning the
gardens of the Katsura Palace   The gardening art of
Dōshaku Yamamoto

Kokka 37:
138-47; My 1927
313-17; N "
316-38; D "
Kokka 38:
55-59; F 1928
80-86; Mr "
185-90; Jy "

Gardens. Java
Lombard, Denys
Jardins a Java. [illus.]

Arts asiatiques
t.20: [135]-[183]
1969

710.5
H84
Gardens,Kitchen
A kitchen gardenette.

House and garden 72:46-47,93
September 1937 (Sect.2)

D13.1
H84
Gardens, Majorca
Nichols, Rose Standish
Old gardens at Majorca

House beautiful 56:585-587
Dec. 1924

Gardens, Mexico

House beaut. 48:450-451
Dec. 1920

Gardens. Lighting
Neue gartenleuchten.

Bauen und wohnen
No. 3: 196
Je 1955

710.5
C85
Gardens, Majorca
Villiers-Stuart, C. M.
Spanish Mediterranean gardens: Some gardens in Majorca.

Country life (Lond.) 66: 482-485
October 12, 1929

706.972
M61a
Gardens,Mexico.Cuernavaca
Flandrau, C.M.
Borda gardens in Cuernavaca.

Mexican art and life no.5:28-29
January 1939

Gardens. Lighting
Brittain, J.V.
Electricity in the garden.

Country life (London) 84:1
July 2, 1938

Gardens, Malta
Malta.
By George J.D. Cousin and Salvino J. Zammitt.
Plan, photos.

Landscape and garden 4:40
Spring, 1937

Gardens, Mexico. Cuernavaca
Rendon, Edouardo
Tres jardines en Cuernavaca. [plans]

Arq Mexico 18:156-161
Jl 1945

Gardens. Lighting
Night-lighted gardens.
By Barbara Hill.
Photos.

Country life 72:30
Oct., 1937

710.5
C85
Gardens, Malta
Congreve, Celia
The Villa Frere, Malta.

Country life (Lond.) 68: 12-18
July 5, 1930

Gardens. Mexico (city)
Moreno Villa, José
Un jardin mexicano [plan] Proyecto y ejecución de Adam Rubalcava.

Arquitectura Mexico
no.57:53-60 Mar 1957

Gardens. Lighting
Stiles, E.C.
Lighting the garden.

House and garden 51:80-81
June, 1927

710.5
C85
Gardens,Malta. San Antonio
C.C.
The gardens of San Antonio: the Palace of the Grand Master of the Knights of Malta.

Country life (Lond.)73: lxii,lxiv,
June 3,1933   lxvi

710.5
C85
Gardens, Moraine
Moraine gardens.

Country life (U.S.) 52: 61-63
June 1927

Gardens. Lighting
Chavance, René
M. Sabino et le luminaire moderne.

La renaissance 9: 183-185
March, 1926

710.5
C85
Gardens, Mediaeval
Parrott, Antoinette
History of the country estate: pt.7. The Middle Ages in Europe.

Country life (U.S.) 70:72-73,96-96,98
June 1936

Gardens, Morocco
Gardens and houses of Morocco

House and garden
52: 78-83
N 1927

Gardens, Majorca
Algunos jardines en Mallorca.

Arq Mexico 18:141-147
Jl, 1945

710.5
C85
Gardens, Mediaeval
The mediaeval pleasure garden.

Country life (Lond.)61:316-17
February 26, 1927

D13.1
H84
Gardens, Morocco
Nichols, R. S.
The garden of the Oudayas at Rabat

House beautiful 67:69,104-105
January 1930

910.5
T77   Gardens,Morocco
    Embury,Lucy
       The gardens of Barbary.

Travel 58: 18-21,57
January 1932

Gardens, Norway
   Christensen, Victor P.
   Nordmandsdalen og dens figurer;
Norske haven illus

Copenhagen Statens Museum for
Kunst. Kunstmuseets Aarsskrift
(4) 171-175
1917

D13.1
N84   Gardens, Pompeii
    Nichols, R.S.
      Pompeian gardens

House beautiful 64:398-399,446-449
October 1928

Gardens, Morocco
  Gallotti, Jean
   Les jardins indigènes au Maroc.

L'amour de l'art 8:205-8 Je
1927

Gardens, Persia

see also

Gardens, U. S. Persian influence

D13.1
N84   Gardens, Porto Rico
    Garden spots in Porto Rico

House beautiful 54:592-594
Dec. 1923

915.05
A85   Gardens,Morocco.Rabat
    Bickerstaffe,Elaine
      Thanks for a Moorish garden.

Asia 33: 17
January 1933

Gardens, Persia
  Byron, Robert
  Between Tigris and Oxus: The Plateau of Iran.
  Monuments of the Great Kings. Brick and stucco.
  Color and glaze (illus. in color).
    Country life (Lond.) 76:
     435-38; O 27, 1934
     491-94; N 10, "
     541-44; " 24, "
     584-91; D 1, "

Gardens, Portugal
  A Portuguese Garden at the University of Coimbra.

House and garden 2: pl
S 1902

Gardens, Netherlands
  Jay, M.R.
Dutch gardens.

House beautiful 70:152-53,162
August, 1931

705.1
A78   Gardens, Persia
    Kashmir

Art and archaeology 15:22-30
Jan. 1923

D13.1
N84   Gardens, Portugal
    Nichols, Rose Standish
      Some Portuguese gardens

House beautiful 56:469-471
Nov. 1924

710.5
N84   Gardens,Netherlands
    Milman,Helen
      Dutch houses and gardens. J.G.Veldheer and
Frederica Hulswit,archts.

House and garden 2: 501-514
October 1902

915.05
A83   Gardens, Persia
    Villard, Mariquita
      Of Persian gardens.

Asia 31:420-425,467-468
July 1931

710.5
L26   Gardens, Portugal
    Arnold, A. F.
      Water features in Portuguese gardens and
parks.

Landscape architecture 20: 129-135
January 1930

720.5
A67   Gardens, Netherlands.Lage Voorsche
    Prince Henry's garden, Lage Voorsche, Hol-
land. D.F.Tersteeg, landscape archt.

    Architectural review 19 n.s.2: pl.67-69
A   June 1913

Gardens, Persia
  Villiers-Stuart, C.M.
  Persian gardens and Persian art.

Country life (Lond.) 69:230-232
February 21, 1931

051
843   Gardens, Provence
    Lambert, Jacques H.
      Rustic gardens of old Provence

Scribners 76:11-16
July 1924

Gardens, Netherlands. Loo
    The palace and gardens of Loo, near Daventer
in Gelderland.

Architectural review (Lond.) 39:4-5
January, 1916

D13.1
N84   Gardens, Persia
    Nichols, R.S.
      The pleasure gardens of the great moguls

House beautiful 61:318-319
March,1927

D13.1
N84   Gardens, Riviera
    Nichols, R.S.
      Anglo-Italian gardens on the French Riviera

House beautiful 58:341-344
October 1925

710.5 C85 Gardens, Riviera The garden of Les Bruyeres, Cap Ferrat. Country life (Lond.)61:270-75 February 19, 1927	710.5 C85 Gardens, Riviera A Riviera garden: Fanfarigoule. Country life (Lond.) 63: 289-292 March 3, 1928	710.5 C85 Gardens, Riviera Sainte-Claire le Chateau, Hyeres. Country life (Lond.) 64: 610-616 November 3, 1928
710.5 C85 Gardens, Riviera Garden of Mon Caprice, Eze. Country life (Lond.) 65: 114-118 January 28, 1928	710.5 C85 Gardens, Riviera A Riviera garden: Isoletta. Country life (Lond.) 64: 829-31 December 8, 1928	710.5 C85 Gardens, Rhodesia Moiser, B. A Rhodesian garden. No plans. Country life (Lond.)83:484-485 May 7, 1938
710.5 C85 Gardens, Riviera Lou Suell. Country life (Lond.) 64: 900-903 December 22, 1928	710.5 C85 Gardens, Riviera R. H. Riviera gardens: La Berlugane. Country life (Lond.) 68: 747-749 December 6, 1930	Gardens. Roumania Royal gardens in the Balkans. II. Queen Marie's. By Irina Khrabroff. Photos. Country life 72:55-56 Jy, 1937
710.5 C85 Gardens, Riviera Primavera. Country life (Lond.) 65: 173-176 February 9, 1929	710.5 C85 Gardens, Riviera A Riviera garden: La Leopolda. Country life (Lond.) 65: 78-81 January 19, 1929	Gardens, Scotland see also Glasgow (Scot.) Pollok house, Garden
710.5 C85 Gardens, Riviera. Riviera gardens: Boccanegra. Country life (Lond.) 66: 714-717 November 23, 1929	710.5 C85 Gardens. Riviera E.C. Riviera gardens; the Prince of Monaco's cactus garden. Country life (Lond.) 67: 115-117 January 25, 1930	Gardens. Scotland. Roper, Lanning Visiting gardens by sea. The cruise of the Scottish national trust. [illus.] Country life 137: 125-126; 129 Ja 21, 1965
710.5 C85 Gardens, Riviera A Riviera garden: Champ-Fleuri, Californie, Cannes. Country life (Lond.) 64: 546-549 October 20, 1928	710.5 C85 Gardens, Riviera A Riviera garden: Souleiadou. Country life (Lond.) 64: 695-697 November 17, 1928	Gardens, Scotland. Crathes Hussey, Christopher Crathes castle, Kincardineshire..the seat of Sir James Burnett. Begun in 1553 - one of the finest "Jacobean" Scottish castles. Early Scottish furniture at Crathes castle. Country life (Lond.) 82: 272-76; S 11, 1937 296-301,306-07; S 18, 1937 322; S 25, 1937
710.5 C85 Gardens, Riviera Riviera gardens, Clairfontaine. Country life (Lond.)62: 807-810 December 3, 1927	710.5 C85 Gardens, Riviera. Riviera gardens: Villa Mohbrillant. Country life (Lond.) 66: 837-839 December 7, 1929	710.5 C85 Gardens,Scotland. Devonhall Taylor,G.C. The garden at Devonhall,Perthshire. Country life(Lond.)76: 640-645 December 15, 1934

710.5 C85 Gardens,Scotland.Fingask Cox,E.H.M. A garden of Scottish statues: sculpture and topiary at Fingask. Country life(Lond.)80:62-65 July 18, 1936	720.5 A51 Gardens, Spain. Amer. Arch 121: 287-94 & 4 pl. Apr. 12, 1922.	710.5 H84 Gardens, Spain An appreciation House & garden 48:88 Sept. 1925
710.5 C85 Gardens,Scotland. Edinburgh Taylor,G.C. The Edinburgh Botanic Garden. Country life (Lond.)74: 306-311 September 23, 1933	720.5 W52 Gardens. Spain Western architect 34: 51-54 & pl.9 May 1925	Gardens, Spain Drawings by Peixotto Scribners, 71:720 June, 1922
710.5 C85 Gardens,Scotland. Glasgow Taylor,G.C. The gardens at Pollok House,Glasgow. Country life (Lond.)76: 388-393 October 13, 1934	Gardens, Spain Whittlesley, Austin. The minor ecclesiastical, domestic, and garden architecture of southern Spain. New York: Architectural book publishing Co., [1917] . pl.91-103,105,107.	D13.1 H84 Gardens, Spain Heilprin, Frances The garden of Joaquin Sorolla House beautiful 64:373-377 October 1928
710.5 C85 Gardens,Scotland. Lochinch Taylor,G.C. Lochinch and Castle Kennedy gardens,Wigtownshire: the seat of the Earl of Stair. Country life (Lond.) 76: 300-305 September 22, 1934	720.5 A67r Gardens. Spain Byne, A.G. Andalusian gardens, Spain's contribution to the beautiful gardens of the world. Architectural record 29: 370-377 May 1911	710.5 C855 Gardens,Spain Berg,Carl A garden path through Spain. Illus. Map of Spain with itinerary of gardens. Country life (U.S.)64: 53,78 June 1933
Gardens, South Africa South Africa By W.M. Jones. Photos. Landscape and garden 4:53 Spring, 1937	720.5 A67r Gardens,Spain Stapley,Mildred and Arthur Byne Andalusian gardens and patios(10 parts) pt. 1-Foreword;pt.2-Types of gardens;pt.3-Garden accessories;pt.4-Patios of Cordova,Seville and Granada; pt.5-The garden "del Rey Moro," Ronda;pt.6-The Generalife,Granada;ot.7-The Alhambra,Granada. Architectural record 54:489-506 December 1923 Architectural record 55:65-80;177-194;277-292 January-June 1924 373-381;479-492;589-585	D10.5 A786 Gardens, Spain The gardens of J.C.N. Forestier Art and decoration 32:85-96 March 1928
710.5 C85 Gardens, South Africa. Kirstenbosch Compton, R. H. Kirstenbosch, the National Botanic garden of South Africa. Country life (Lond.) 67: 561-565 April 19, 1930	720.5 A67r Gardens,Spain Stapley,Mildred and Arthur Byne Andalusian gardens and patios.Pt.8- The Alcazar Gardens,Seville;Pt.9-The garden of the Duke of Medinaceli,Seville; Pt.10 - Patios and gardens of Seville and Cordova. Architectural record 56: 74-88;161-177; July-September 1924 257-275	705.1 A79 Gardens, Spain Le Gourmet, Guy Gardens in Spain Arts and decoration 20:9-11 April 1924
Gardens, Spain see also Gardens, U. S. Spanish influence	720.5 A67 Gardens, Spain Kiessling, Calvin Glimpses of Spanish gardens. Architectural review 14: 186-189 August 1907	710.5 H84 Gardens. Spain. Gardens in Spain and Portugal. By Thomas Walsh. No illus. House & Garden 40: 37. December, 1921.

OVERSIZE LIBRARY
D13.1
H84   Gardens, Spain
Prellsitz, Edwin Mitchill
   The gardens of southern Spain
 	
House beautiful 56:17-20
July 1924
	Gardens, Spain. Barcelona
	Villiers-Stuart, C.M.
	   A baroque garden at Barcelona: Casa Gomis,
	the seat of the marquess de Gomis.
	
	Country life (Lond.) 76: 424-426
	October 20, 1934
		710.5
		C85 Gardens, Spain. La Granja
		Villiers-Stuart, C. M.
		   The garden palace of La Granja.
		
		Country life (Lond.) 66: 930-935
		December 28, 1929

710.5
L25   Gardens, Spain
   The Generalife
 	
Landscape architecture 14:1-14
Oct. 1923
	720.5
	A67r Gardens, Spain. Cordova
	Stapley, Mildred and Arthur Byne
	   Andalusian gardens and patios, pt.4 - Patios
	of Cordova, Seville and Granada.
	
	Architectural record 55:277-292
	March 1924
		720.5
		A67r Gardens, Spain. Ronda
		Stapley, Mildred and Arthur Byne
		   Andalusian and patios: Pt. 5: The gardens
		"del Rey Moro," Ronda.
		
		Architectural record 55: 375-387
		April 1924

710.5
C85   Gardens, Spain
Villiers-Stuart, C. M.
   El Laberinto, Barcelona.
   Spanish Mediterranean gardens; Raxa, Majorca.
 	
Country life (Lond.) 65: 554-560;
April 20;June 1;1929   776-778
	720.5
	A67r Gardens, Spain. Cordova
	Stapley, Mildred and Arthur Byne
	   Andalusian gardens and patios, pt.10 - Patios
	and gardens of Seville and Cordova.
	
	Architectural record 56:257-275
	September 1924
		720.5
		A67r Gardens, Spain. Seville
		Stapley, Mildred and Arthur Byne
		   Andalusian gardens and patios, pt.4 - Patios
		of Cordova, Seville and Granada.
		
		Architectural record 55:277-292
		March 1924

OVERSIZE LIBRARY
D13.1
H84   Gardens, Spain
Nichols, Rose Standish
   El Labertino: a Spanish garden of the
eighteenth century
 	
House beautiful 57:37-39
Jan. 1925
	720.5
	A51 Gardens, Spain. Cordova
	   A private garden, Cordoba, Spain
	
	American architect 124:front
	Oct. 24, 1923
		720.5
		A67r Gardens, Spain. Seville
		Stapley, Mildred and Arthur Byne
		   Andalusian gardens, and patios: pt.8 - The
		Alcazar gardens, Seville.
		
		Architectural record 56:74-88
		July 1924

710.5
L26   Gardens, Spain
Fox, H. M.
   Moorish gardens in Spain, described in source
books.
 	
Landscape architecture 20: 12-20
October 1929
	720.5
	A67r Gardens, Spain. Granada
	Stapley, Mildred and Arthur Byne
	   Andalusian gardens and patios, pt.4 - Patios
	of Cordova, Seville and Granada.
	
	Architectural record 55:277-292
	March 1924
		720.5
		A67r Gardens, Spain. Seville
		Stapley, Mildred and Arthur Byne
		   Andalusian gardens and patios, pt.9 - The gar-
		den of the Duke of Medinaceli, Seville. Plan.
		
		Architectural record 56:161-177
		August 1924

720.5
A67a   Gardens, Spain
   Studies in Spain. 4 photographs.
 	
Architecture 45: 123
Apr. 1922.
	720.5
	A67r Gardens, Spain. Granada
	Stapley, Mildred and Arthur Byne
	   Andalusian gardens and patios: Pt. 6 - The
	Generalife, Granada. Plans
	
	Architectural record 55: 479-492
	May 1924
		720.5
		A67r Gardens, Spain. Seville
		Stapley, Mildred and Arthur Byne
		   Andalusian gardens and patios, pt.10 - Patios
		and gardens of Seville and Cordova.
		
		Architectural record 56:257-275
		September 1924

710.5
C855   Gardens, Spain
Fox, H. M.
   What Spain can teach us about gardening.
 	
Country life (U.S.) 57: 52-54
November 1929
	720.53
	B55 Gardens, Spain. Granada
	Harbers, Guido
	   Der wohngarten, seine raum-und bauelemente.
	(The house garden: its space and building elements)
	Plans of Generalife in Granada.
	
	Der Baumeister 31: 35-40
	January 1933
		710.5
		H84 Gardens, Spain. Seville
		Bates, K.L.
		   The gardens of the Alcazar at Seville, Spain.
		   Plans.
		
		House and garden 6: 1-9
		July 1904

711
L26
Gardens,Spain.Seville
Whitney,J.F.
The gardens of the Alcazar,Seville, Spain.
Plans.

Landscape architecture 15:1-16
October 1924

RYERSON LIBRARY
705.4
B93
Gardens,Sweden
Bröchner,Georg
The garden of Professor Carl Milles

Studio 90:3-9
July 1925

720.53
W31
Gardens, Switzerland
Garden and outdoor swimming pool in Baden,
Switzerland. Carl Sattler, archt.

Wasmuth's Monatshefte 12: 54
Heft 2, 1928

720.5
A51
Gardens, Spain. Seville
Staircase to the water garden, Seville.

American architect 124:front.
Oct. 10, 1923

RYERSON LIBRARY
D13.1
H84
Gardens, Sweden
Lee, M.B.
The garden of a sculptor. Carl Milles

House beautiful 65:294-295
March 1929

RYERSON LIBRARY
D10.5
D48
Gardens, Switzerland
Gardens of Zürich

Deutsche kunst 59:82-83
October, 1926

720.5
A67r
Gardens,Spain.Tarragona
Stapley,M
A study of romanesque in Spain: The cathe-
dral and garden of Tarragona.

Architectural record 31:470,473-474
May 1912

705.8
A51aw
Gardens, Sweden
Heinberg, Aage
Railway gardening.

Amer Swe monthly 42:12-13
Jl '48

705
K48
Gardens, Switzerland. 20th century
Keller, Heinz
[Gartenbau].

Das werk 33:82-97
F '46

710.5
C85
Gardens, Sweden
Carl Milles' garden, Stockholm.

Country life (Lond.)64:18-26
July 7, 1928

Gardens, Sweden
Stockholm Gardens: Public and private enterprise.
By Lady Allen of Hurtwood.
Photos.

Landscape and garden 4:207
Winter, 1937

RYERSON LIBRARY
D13.1
H84
Gardens, Syria
In an Eastern garden

House beautiful 64:705-707
December 1928

RYERSON LIBRARY
705.8
A51
Gardens, Sweden
Goodwin, H. B.
Gardens and gardening in Sweden

American Scandinavian
review 16:99-102
February 1928

710.5
H84
Gardens,Sweden. Basted
A Swedish garden that overlooks the Katte-
gat: home of Eric Haakon-Petersson. De-
signed by Karl Guettler,archt. No plan.

House and garden 65: 38-39
May 1934

A

Gardens, Topiary

see

Topiary work

720.55
A673
Gardens, Sweden
A Garden near Stockholm

Arch. Rev. 57:56-60
Feb. 1925

720.53
W31
Gardens, Sweden. Stockholm
Unus, Walter
Garden of sculptor Carl Milles on the
island of Lidingö.

Wasmuths monatshefte 3: 286-295
Heft 8/10, 1917

910.5
T77
Gardens, Tunisia
Embury,Lucy
The gardens of Barbary.

Travel 58: 18-21,57
January 1932

710.5
C85
Gardens, Sweden
Villiers-Stuart,C.M.
Gardens of Sweden: Sturefors, Sandemar, Ovods
Kloster, Eriksberg, Gunnebo, Lidingö.

Country Life (London) 77:38-44
January 12, 1935

Gardens, Switzerland
Formal garden in Baden

Die kunst 19:73-81
Dec. 1915

720.52
A673
Gardens, Tuscany
Einstein, Lewis
The Tuscan gardens.

Arch. rev. 61: 46-49
February 1927

Gardens, U. S.,
see also
Colonial gardens

Gardens, U.S.
An estate development at Rye, New York,
Dwight James Baum, architect.

Arch. forum 36:231-4 and pl.90-5
Jun., 1922.

Gardens, U.S.
J.P. Morgan's iris garden.

House and garden 72:42-43
October, 1937

705.1
A78s   Gardens, U.S.

Art world 2:196-99
May 1917

705.1
A79   Gardens, United States
            Fine detail in beautiful gardens

Arts and decoration 31:58-59
September 1929

Gardens, U.S.
The Martha Washington Garden
By John W. Hall.

House and gard. 15: 46-47
F 1909

051
C39   Gardens, U.S.

Century 100:244-252
June 1920

Gardens, U.S.
Furniss, R.M.
Gardens designed by a sculptor

International studio 81:89-94
May, 1925

710.5
H84   Gardens , U.S.
            May days in a Westchester garden.

House & garden 51: 117-19
May 1927

Gardens. United States

Inter. studio 17:122-128
Aug., 1902

Gardens, U.S.
The Garden of "Aysgarth" at Abington, near
Philadelphia.

House and gard 6: 34-39
Jl 1904

Gardens, U.S.
The most beautiful garden in America

Arts and decoration 19:20-21
August, 1923

Gardens, U.S.
City Garden in California.

House and Garden. 38:54-5.
August, 1920.

Gardens, U. S.
Garden and studio of Mrs. Harry Payne Whitney.

Arch review n.s. 8:4-5
Ja 1919

705.1
A78   Gardens, U.S.
            New England

Art & prog. 5:238-44
May 1914

Gardens, U.S.
A Cottage and Garden at East Hampton, L.I.
Designed by Grosvenor Atterbury, architect.

House and gard. 3: 213-14
Ap 1903

720.5
A67r   Gardens. U.S.
            The gardens of Charles M. Schwab. Illus.

Arch. rec. 47:387-408. May,
1920.

Gardens, U.S.
The New Garden of the Yondotega Club.
Designed by Charles A. Platt.

House and gard. 5: 83-85
F 1904

705.1
L88   Gardens, U.S.

Lotus mag. 7:349-360
June 1916

Gardens, United States
Greystone, "Boscobel", etc.

Arch rev 24:n.s. 7: 103-117
Dec 1918

720.5
A67r   Gardens. U. S.
            Of the country house.

Arch. Rec. 50: 295-336.
Oct. 1921.

710.5
C855
Gardens. U.S.
...of the northwest

Country life 49: 65-88
Nov. 1925

720.5
W52
Gardens. U. S.
Special number.

West. arch.55:pl. 81-96
Jun. 1926

RYERSON LIBRARY
705.1
A78
Gardens, U.S., California
California

Art & prog. 5:254-58
May 1916

710.5
C88
Gardens, U.S.
On the Hudson

Craftsman 24:480-93
Aug. 1913

RYERSON LIBRARY
D13.1
H84
Gardens, United States
Strange, E. L.
Three exhibition gardens. A city garden

House beautiful 63:306-309,345
March 1928

RYERSON LIBRARY
705.1
A79
Gardens, U.S., California
Roberts, M.F.
An enchanting garden on a California
estate - "Cuesta Sinda," garden of Mrs. E. Palmer
Gairt

Arts and decoration 32:frontis-
December 1929 (piece,57-60,115

710.5
C855
Gardens , U.S.
Our country and our gardens. Illus(4 col)

Country life 37:35-41.
April 1920.

720.5
A67a
Gardens. U.S.
A Tudor garden in New England.

Architecture.53:134-36
May, 1926

Gardens, U.S., California
Goodnow, M.N., and Yoch, Florence
Gardens of the far west. California patios,
cloisters and walled gardens. California houses
with shadow decoration

Arts and dec. 29:
73; My 1928
48-49, 84; Je 1928
46-48; S 1928

Gardens, United States.
Plans of Jacques Gréber.

Revue de l'art 40:172-181.
Sept. - Oct., 1921

720.5
A67r
Gardens, United States
Pentecost, G.
The Villa garden. Plans.

Architectural record 11: 61-68
January 1902

Gardens (U.S.) California
Loring garden, Pasadena

Arch. record 43:65-73
Jan., 1918

710.5
C855
Gardens, United States
Yarnall,Sophia
Potted gardens

Country life(U.S.)71:62-65
April 1937

710.5
H84
Gardens, U.S., 18th century
Wilson, E. H.
Gardening's renascence in the 18th and 19th
centuries.

House and garden 57: 86,162
May 1930

710.5
H84
Gardens. U.S. California

House and garden 42: 50-1
Oct. 1922

720.5
A67
Gardens, United States
Underwood,Loring
Private gardens for suburban homes.

Architectural review 14:34-36
March 1907

710.5
H84
Gardens, U.S., 18th century
Wilson, E. H.
Plants of our great-grandmother's day.

House and garden 57: 80-81,164,166,
April 1930   168,170

RYERSON LIBRARY
D13.1
H84
Gardens, U.S., California
Harrier, J. V.
Boisfleury

House beautiful 67:621-653
May 1930

710.5
H84
Gardens. U.S.
Shadows in garden design.

House & garden 51: 62
June 1927

Gardens, U.S., Ariz., Santa Fé
A garden in Santa Fé.

House and garden 55: 91-93
January, 1929

RYERSON LIBRARY
D13.1
H84
Gardens, U.S., California
Yoch, Florence, and Council, Lucile
California gardens. The house in good taste

House beautiful 62:378-379
October 1927   (137-140
August 1927

720.53
N68
Gardens. U.S. California
California gardens, designed by Florence Yoch, landscape architect.

Moderne bauformen 27: 96-105
Heft 3, March 1928

720.5
A67d
Gardens,U.S., Cal., Bel-Air
Garden on the estate of Mrs. Harry R. Callendar, bel-Air,Cal. A.E.Hanson, landscape archt.

A   Architectural digest 7: 42
Number 2 [1931]

710.5
C855
Gardens,U.S., Cal., Montecito
Craig,Margaret
Garden on the edge of a canyon,belonging to Miss Emily Martindale, foothills of Montecito, California. Stuart Chisholm,landscape archt.

A   Country life(U.S.)70:46-47
May 1936

RYERSON LIBRARY
708.1
L872
Gardens, U.S., California
Ring, Mildred
Flora for an Indian garden (California) without useful illustrations.

Masterkey 4: 69-77
August-September 1930

720.5
A67d
Gardens,U.S., Cal., Beverly Hills
Pergola, garden grounds of Archibald W. Edes estate, Beverly Hills,Cal.Seymour Thomas, landscape archt. John Finken, assoc. archt.
A
Architectural digest 7: 64
Number 2 [1931]

710.5
C855
Gardens. U.S., Cal., Montecito
House and gardens of G.W. Smith, Montecito, Calif. G.W. Smith, archt.

Country life (U.S.) 52: 60-1
September 1927

RYERSON LIBRARY
708.1
L872
Gardens, U.S., California
Adams, C.G.
The gardens of old Spanish California

The Masterkey 2:4-8
March 1929

710.5
L26
Gardens, U.S., Glendale
Chesterwood, residence of Daniel C. French, sculptor.

Landscape architecture 16:91-9
January 1926

710.5
C855
Gardens,U.S., California, Montecito
Pools and cascades in Mrs.Oakleigh Thorne's garden at Montecito,California.

Country life (U.S.)63: front.,44-45
January 1933

710.5
H84
Gardens,U.S. California
The plants of California gardens

House & Garden 46:53-55
Dec. 1924

710.5
A51
Gardens, U.S., Cal., Hollywood
Saut,H.L.
Individuality in western architecture: home of Gurdon W. Wattells, Hollywood, California.

American homes & gardens 12:197-200,
June 1915   216

710.5
C855
Gardens,U.S., Cal., Montecito
Dunbar,D.L.
Lesson from the Japanese: Japanese style garden on estate of Mrs.J.J.Mitchell in Montecito, California.

Country life (U.S.)66: 75-77
September 1934

710.5
L26
Gardens, U.S., California
Some California gardens designed by John William Gregg.

Landscape arch.18: front.,200-203
April 1928

720.5
A67
Gardens,U.S., Cal., Los Angeles
Stoll,H.F.
A western city garden; formal garden for Mr. Dan Murphy, Los Angeles, Cal. Wm David Cook, Jr. landscape archt. Plan

Architectural review 19 n.s.2:198 pl.69
A   June 1913

710.5
C855
Gardens, U.S., Cal., Pasadena
The garden of J.L.Severance,Esq.,Pasadena, Calif.

Country life 44:55-6
July 1923

RYERSON LIBRARY
D13.1
H84
Gardens, U.S., California
Galli, Anne
What we accomplished in three years in our garden in southern California

House beautiful 69:270-272,294,
296-297
March 1931

710.5
H84
Gardens, U.S., Cal., Montecito
The canyon that is always green.
Adjuncts to a California garden.

House & garden 52: 77-9
August 1927

720.5
W52
Gardens. U. S. Cal. Pasadena
Garden of Mr. Henry W. Schultz, Pasadena, Calif. E. W. Neff, archt.

West. arch.35: pl. front.
Feb.1926

RYERSON LIBRARY
D10.5
C88
Gardens,U.S., Cal., Bakersville
Byers, C.A.
A garden showing careful thought throughout, in the adaptation of native beauty and in the romantic appeal of its appearance: Los Puertas"- home of Mrs. W.J. Tevis, near Bakersville,Calif.

Craftsman 16:338-345
June 1909

710.5
C855
Gardens, U.S., California, Montecito
Gardens of Mrs. Margaret Carrington in Montecito.

Country life(U.S.) 65: 38-39
April 1934

720.5
W52
Gardens, U.S., Cal., Pasadena
A group of gardens in Pasadena and Altadena, Calif. Florence Yoch, landscape archt.

Western archt.34: pls,1-9
May 1925

720.5 W58 Gardens, U.S., Cal., Pasadena Wight, P. B. Some gardens in Southern California. Western architect 30: 101-102,pls.1-4 September 1921	Gardens, U.S., Conn., Cannondale The gardens of Warren F. Lynch at Cannondale, Conn. Country life 39:58-9 Mar., 1921.	721 T53 Gardens, U.S., Del., Nemours One of the statuary groups in the duPont gardens at Nemours, Delaware. Messena and duPont, Inc., archts. Through the ages 9: 2, 23-28 March 1932
710.5 C855 Gardens, U.S., Cal., Pasadena The year 'round in a California garden Country life 45:64-5 Dec. 1923	RYERSON LIBR. D19.05 V88 Gardens, U.S., Conn., Greenwich A connecticut garden on the estate of Mr. and Mrs. Stanley Resor, Greenwich, Conn. Vogue 77:72-73 April 1, 1931	710.5 L26 Gardens, U.S., Del, Wilmington Wheelwright, Robert The garden at "Goodstay". Landscape architecture 20: 5-12 October 1929
RYERSON LIBRARY 705.1 A79 Gardens, U.S., Cal., San Gabriel Mission Roorbach, Eloise The Padres path in the garden of "Glen-Orr"-San Gabriel Mission Arts and decoration 27:48-49 June 1927	Gardens, U.S., Conn. Litchfield County Munroe, Henry S. Litchfield wild garden. Landscape architecture 16:1-5 October, 1925	710.5 C855 Gardens, U. S., Del, Wilmington The gardens of Mr. and Mrs. J. Simpson Dean, Wilmington, Delaware. Noel Chamberlin, landscape archt. Country life (U.S.) 56: 54-55 August 1929
710.5 C855 Gardens,U.S., Cal., San Marino Dunbar,D.L. Lessons from the Japanese: Japanese garden of the Henry E.Huntington estate at San Marino, California. Country life (U.S.)66: 75-77 September 1934	Gardens, U.S., Conn. Riverside Gardens on the estate of Mrs. J. Langeloth. Country life (U.S.) 64:65-67 October, 1928	720.5 F29 Gardens,U.S., D.C., Washington Washington Cathedral, Washington, D.C.: Bishop's Garden and the Choir of the Cathedral; no plan. Federal architect 7:54-55 April 1937
RYERSON LIBRARY 705.1 M98m Gardens, U.S., Cal., Santa Barbara Bissell, E.B. The Blaksley botanic garden Museums 1:14,15,16 May 1930	710.5 C855 Gardens,U.S., Conn., Riverside Gardens at Walhall,Riverside,Conn. Mr. and Mrs.Frederick T.Bonham's home on Long Island Sound. Country life(U.S.)71:31-37 March 1937	Gardens, U.S., D.C., Washington Bratenahl, Florence A garden for the ages. The Bishop's garden of Washington cathedral House beautiful 64:682-689 December, 1928
710.5 C855 Gardens, U.S., Cal., Santa Barbara A garden of Santa Barbara. El Mirador, the estate of Mr. and Mrs. John J. Mitchell. Country life (U.S.) 59: 54-55 January 1931	Gardens, U.S., Conn., Salisbury Greely, Rose Within garden walls. The garden of Mrs. C.C. Lansing at Salisbury, Connecticut House beautiful 65:286-290 March, 1929	710.5 L26 Gardens, U.S., D.C., Washington Vitale, Ferruccio The Washington Monument gardens. Landscape architecture 20:234-235 April 1930
Gardens, U.S., Chinese influence Haight, M.T. Bringing China to Connecticut: the charm of a Chinese garden in America. Country life (U.S.) 59:40-42 March, 1931	RYERSON LIBRARY D13.1 H84 Gardens, U.S., Conn., Simsbury Steele, Fletcher A dooryard garden with intimate planting: the house of John S. Ellsworth, Simsbury, Conn. House beautiful 69:274-275 March 1931	Gardens, U.S., D.C., Washington. Georgetown Goodwin, I.M.G. Gardens of Old Georgetown House beau 62: frontispiece, 369-72; O 1927 526-27; N " 661-63; D " House beau 63: 36-37, 84-86; Ja 1928 155, 201; F 1928

Gardens, U. S., English influence

see also

Wilmington (Del.) "Goodstay" Garden

710.5
H84
Gardens, U. S., Fla., Palm Beach.
The Moorish invasion. A. Mizner, archt.

House & garden.49: 114-15
Mar. 1926

Gardens, U.S., Ga., La Grange
The Ferrell gardens at La Grange, Georgia

House and garden 47: 76-77
Feb. 1925

Gardens, U.S., English influence
Peck, F.W.G.
English gardens for American estates. Plan.

Country life (U.S.) 65:68-70,82
March, 1934

Gardens, U.S., Fla., Palm Beach
Major Alley, Palm Beach

House beautiful 60:570-571
November, 1926

Gardens, U. S. Ill.

see also

Libertyville (Ill.) Armour estate
Highland Park (Ill.) Williams (L.M.) gardens

720.5
A67a
Gardens,U.S. Exhibitions
Exhibition New York chapter American
society of Landscape architects

Architecture 51:188-190
May 1925

710.5
C855
U.S.
Gardens,French influence
Peck,F.W.G.
French gardens for American estates: Le
Notre, genius of the French garden.

Country life (U.S.)66: 80-82,92
June 1934

710.5
L26
Gardens, U.S., Ill., Ravinia
Garden at Ravinia, Illinois. Jens Jensen,
landscape archt.

Landscape architecture 16:158-60
April 1926

720.5
A67a
Gardens. U.S. Exhibitions
Review of the fourth exhibition of lands-
cape gardening, March & April 1927.

Architecture 55: 321-4
June 1927

710.5
C855
Gardens,U.S.,Georgia
Garden in Georgia. The grounds of the
John W.Herbert residence.

Country life(U.S.)68:16-17
August 1935

Gardens, U.S., Islamic influence
A Moorish garden in California

House and Garden 46:69
Sept., 1924

710.5
H84
Gardens. U.S., Florida
Garden features in our tropics.

House & garden 49: 84-85
January 1926

705.1
A79
Gardens, U.S., Georgia
Magnificent gardens made according to
Georgia's traditions

Arts and decoration 24:40-41,78
February 1926

Gardens, U.S., Italian influence
An Italian garden at Groton, Conn., Guy Lowell,
architect and A.R. Sargent, landscape architect.

Arch. forum 36: 221-2 and pl. 81-3
Jun., 1922.

D13.1
H84
Gardens, U.S., Florida
Wight, S. B.
Gardening in Florida

House beautiful 58: 648,664
Dec. 1925

710.5
C855
Gardens,U.S.,Ga., Augusta
In a Georgia garden: the estate of Mr.and
Mrs.Alfred S.Bourne,Georgia.

Country life (U.S.)66: 38-41
August 1934

Gardens, U.S., Italian influence
Edgerton, Giles
An Italian garden blossoms in Westchester.

Arts and decoration 29:40-42
June, 1928

D13.1
H84
Gardens, U.S., Florida
Wight, S. B.
Three types of Florida gardens

House beautiful 59:312-314
March 1926

710.5
H84
Gardens,U.S.,Ga., Atlanta
Shuey,M.W.
Solving problems in the Southern garden of
Mrs.J.J.Goodrum. Hentz,Adler, and Schutze,archts.

House and garden 63: 38-39
February 1933

Gardens, U.S., Islamic influence
The Moorish invasion. A. Mizner, archt.

House and garden. 49:114-115
March, 1926

710.5
C855
Gardens,. U.S., Italian influence
Garden of Samuel Sloan,Garrison,New York.
(Italian formality.) Fletcher Steele,land-
scape archt.

Country life (U.S.)64: 48-49
July 1933

A

Gardens, U.S., Japanese influence
Japanese gardens in America.

House beautiful 44:125-127
August, 1918

Gardens, U.S., Japanese influence
On estate of P.D. Saklatvala, Plainfield, N.J.

House and garden 34: 10-11
August, 1918

Gardens, U.S., Italian influence
Peck, F.W.G.
Italian gardens for American estates. Plan.

Country life (U.S.) 65:47-49,78
January, 1934

Gardens, U.S., Japanese influence
Saylor, H.H.
The Japanese garden in America...garden of
John S. Bradstreet, Minneapolis, Minn.

Country life in Amer. 15:481-85
March 1909

Gardens, U.S., Japanese influence.
Precedents of Nippon come to Newport. No plan.

House and garden 66:34
December, 1934

710.5
H84
Gardens, U.S. Italian influence
Italy in New England.

House & garden 51: 76-7
June 1927

710.5
H84
Gardens, U.S., Japanese influence
Humphreys, P.W.
Japanese gardens in America. pt. 1, Matthias
Homer's garden.

House and garden 14:17-21
July 1908

Gardens, U.S., Japanese influence
Tea gardens - Ritz Carlton Hotel

Arch and building 49:pl.35-36
Feb., 1917

Gardens, U.S. Japanese influence

see also

Names of specific gardens, i.e.:

Hollywood, Cal. Wattles (G.W.) estate. Garden
etc.

Gardens, U.S., Japanese influence
Humphreys, P.W.
Japanese gardens in America. Pt. 2
Mr. Charles J. Pilling's garden. Lansdowne, Pa.
Executed by S. Furukawa.

House and garden 15:49-52
February, 1909

710.5
C855
Gardens, U.S., Italian influence
McLean, F.T.
The tranquil charm of the Japanese garden...
at Sonnenberg, home of E. W. Clark, at Canandai-
gua, N.Y.

Country Life (U.S.) 54: 59-61
August, 1928

Gardens, U.S., Japanese influence
A bit of Japan in America. The garden of
Milton Tootle, Mackinac Islanc, Mich.

Country life (U.S.) 45:50-1
Nov., 1923

Gardens, U.S., Japanese influence
Japanese style gardens in America.

Art world 2: 571-574
September, 1917

710.5
C855
Gardens,U.S., Ky., Glenview
Melcombo Bingham, country estate of
Honorable Robert Worth Bingham at Glenview,
Kentucky.

Country life (US.)64: 40-41
October 1933

Gardens, U.S., Japanese influence
A Japanese garden created in the Catskill
mountains.

House and garden 56:106-107
October, 1929

Gardens, U.S., Japanese influence
Japanese Tea Garden. Golden Gate Park,
San Francisco

Art and archaeology 28:opp.p. 199
December, 1929

710.5
H84
Gardens, U.S., Ky., Louisville
Goodloe, A. C.
In southern gardens: the log of a wandering
through some of the old and new gardens of
Louisville.

House and garden 32: 13-15
October 1917

Gardens, U.S., Japanese influence
Street, J.F. and Stevenson, Collier.
Japanese gardens in America.

House and garden 29: 11-13
June, 1916

710.5
C855
Gardens, U.S., Japanese influence
Dunbar,D.L.
Lessons from the Japanese: Japanese garden
of the Henry E.Huntington estate at San Marino,
California.
Japanese style garden on estate of Mrs.J.J.
Mitchell in Montecito.

Country life (U.S.)66: 75-77
September 1934

Gardens, U.S., Me., South Berwick
A garden by the river's edge belonging to
Mrs. Henry G. Vaughan in South Berwick, Maine

House beautiful 65:313-316
March, 1929

D13.1
H84

Gardens, U.S., Md., Chevy Chase
A garden at Chevy Chase, Maryland, de-
signed for Mr. and Mrs. Whitman Cross by Ross
Greely, landscape architect.

House beautiful 65:626-627
May 1929

Gardens, U.S., Mass., Nantucket
Nantucket's doorstep gardens.

House and garden 51:112-3
March, 1927

D13.1
H84

Gardens, U.S., Mich., Grosse Pointe Farms
The garden of Mr. and Mrs. Edwin Scott
Barbour, Grosse Pointe Farms, Michigan, Ellen
Shipman, landscape architect

House beautiful. 67:738-740
June 1930

D13.1
H84

Gardens, United States, Mass., Boston
Two gardens in the heart of Boston. The
garden of Mr. and Mrs. Frank E. Bourne.
The garden of Mr. and Mrs. Edward R. Warren

House beautiful 66:558-561
November 1929

720.5
A67

Gardens, U.S., Mass., Stockbridge
Russell, B.F.W.
The works of Guy Lowell - garden of Mrs. Oscar
Iasigi, Stockbridge, Mass.

Architectural review 13: 16
A   February 1906

Gardens, U.S., Mich., Mackinac Island
A bit of Japan in America. The garden of
Milton Tootle, Mackinac Island, Mich.

Country life (U.S.) 45:50-51
November, 1923

D13.1
H84

Gardens, U.S., Mass., Brookline
Cunningham, M.P.
A Massachusetts garden at the height of the
season. Variety of form and abundance of bloom
Garden of Mrs. Henry V. Greenough, Brookline,
Mass. Ellen Shipman, landscape archt.

House beautiful 69:257,259-262
March 1931

D13.1
H84

Gardens, U.S., Mass., Wellesley
Lee, G.H.
An easily cared for garden (of Mrs. F.
Murray Forbes, Wellesley, Massachusetts)

House beautiful 69:40-42,83
January 1931

Gardens, U.S., Minn., St. Cloud.
A home and garden on the Mississippi river:
Mrs. Jennie Brower's home in St. Cloud, Minn.

Arts and decoration 31:48-50
June, 1929

D13.1
H84

Gardens, U. S., Mass., Hingham
Strang, E. L.
Good design plus good personality: Garden
of Mrs. John I. Hollis at Hingham, Mass.
Elizabeth Leonard Strang, landscape architect

House beautiful 67:282-286
March 1930

710.5
H84

Gardens, U.S., Mass., Worcester
Sessions, W.E. III
A secluded Eden replaces chaos in a Worcester
backyard.

House and garden 66: 66-67,84,86
December 1934

710.5
C855

Gardens, U.S., Mo. St. Louis
The Mortimer Burroughs garden in St. Louis.

Country life (U.S.) 66: 47-49
October 1934

D13.1
H84

Gardens, U.S., Mass. Cambridge
Cunningham, M.P.
A breathing space in the city. Mary P.
Cunningham, landscape architect.

House beautiful 70: 316-317
October 1931

Gardens, U.S., Mich. Grosse Ile
The garden of C.T. Fisher, Esq. at Gross Ile,
Michigan.

House beautiful 66:174-175
August, 1929

710.5
C855

Gardens, U.S., Mo., St. Louis
Gardens of Mrs. Samuel W. Fordyce of St.
Louis.

Country life (U.S.) 68:53-55
September 1935

720.5
A67

Gardens, U.S., Mass., Magnolia
Russell, B.F.W.
The works of Guy Lowell - garden of Mr. T.
Jefferson Coolidge, Magnolia, Mass.

Architectural review 13: 21
A   February 1906

720.5
A67f

Gardens, U. S., Mich., Grosse Pointe
Lee, Anne
Three gardens at Grosse Pointe, Michigan.
Ruth Dean, landscape archt.

Architectural forum 51: 505-512
October 1929

Gardens, U.S., New England

Amer. arch. 110 pl. 2137
Dec. 6, 1916

Gardens. U.S., Mass., Nantucket.
Two Nantucket Gardens. By Arthur A. Shurtleff.

House and gard. 2: 310-18
J1, 1902

710.5
L26

Gardens, U.S., Mich., Grosse Pointe
Views in estates and gardens at Grosse
Pointe, Michigan, designed by Bryant Fleming.

Landscape architecture 19:84-90
January 1929

Gardens, U.S., New England
The garden of John Taylor Arms.

House beautiful 59:470-471
April, 1926

Gardens, U.S. New Hampshire A small new Hampshire garden. House and gard 2: 199-204 My, 1902	710.5 H84 Gardens,U.S., N.Y., Buffalo The house and garden of S.M.Flickinger at Buffalo, New York. House and garden 64: 60-61 October 1933	710.5 C855 Gardens,U.S., N.Y. Locust Valley Garden on the estate of Paul D.Cravath, Locust Valley. Illus.of the garden by day and illuminated at night. Isabella Pendleton,landscape archt. Country life (U.S.)64: 38-39 September 1933
Gardens, U.S., N.H., Cornish Garden of Mr. Platt at Cornish, N.H. Charles A. Platt, archt. Architectural review 16:pl.31,34 April, 1909	710.5 C855 Gardens,U.S., N.Y., Garrison Garden of Samuel Sloan,Garrison,New York. (Italian formality.) Fletcher Steele, landscape archt. Country life (U.S.)64: 48-49 A July 1933	Gardens, U.S., N.Y., Long Island Roberts, Mary Fanton The enchantment of Long Island gardens Arts and decoration 22:19-21 Mar. 1925
Gardens, U.S., N.H., Peterboro A garden in Peterboro, New Hampshire House beautiful 63:432-433 April, 1928	Gardens. U.S., N.Y., Fort Ticonderoga Residence of Mr. and Mrs. Stephen H. Pell Fort Ticonderoga, N.Y. Country life 45:49-51 Mar., 1924	Gardens, U.S., N.Y., Long Island A Long Island garden of rare beauty Arts and decoration 29:63 September, 1928
710.5 C855 Gardens,U.S., N.J., Gladstone Garden of Mrs.C.Suydam Cutting,Gladstone, New Jersey. Ellen Shipman,landscape archt. Country life (U.S.)64: 42-43 June 1933	720.5 A67 Gardens, U.S. N.Y., Greystone Varner, R. F. Recent garden architecture. The gardens at Greystone. N.Y.residence of Mr. Samuel J. Tilden, Wolles Bosworth archt. Plan Architectural review 24: 106-109 December 1918	705.1 A79 Gardens, U.S., N.Y., Long Island Gillespie, H.S. Architectural beauty among the Wheatley hills Home of Philip Gossler Arts and decoration 30:56-57,92 November 1928
705.1 M333a Gardens, U.S., N.J., Newark A garden number devoted to the museum garden, Newark, New Jersey The Museum 1:145-152,154-155, November 1927 (158-159	720.5 A67 Gardens,U.S., N.Y., Katonah The garden of Mr.George L.Nichols,Katonah, N.Y. C.A.Platt,archt. Architectural review 15:96 A May 1908	710.5 C855 Gardens. U.S., N.Y., Long Island Some lessons to be learned from a Long Island garden Country life 43:35-9 March 1923
Gardens, U.S., N.J., Newark A.S.Z. Sculpture and other objects in the Thomas L. Raymond walled garden, Newark, N.J. Museum 2:22-24 December, 1928	Gardens, U.S., N.Y., Larchmont A small suburban property proves the case for landscaping. Garden of Carl O. Geissler. House and garden 61:50-51 May, 1932	710.5 C855 Gardens, U.S., N.Y., Long Island Gardens on estate of Sydney Mitchell at Locust Valley, Long Island. Olmsted Bros. Landscape archts. Country life (N.Y.) 50: 46-7 October 1926
710.5 H84 Gardens, U.S., N.Y., Buffalo Garden of Ernst J. Rawleigh, Buffalo,N.Y., showing various stages of its development. House and garden 57: 118-119 May 1930	710.5 C855 Gardens, U.S., N.Y., Locust Valley Pools and paths on the estate of William A. Greer, Locust Valley, N. Y. Country life (U.S.(58: 66-67 October 1930	710.5 C855 Gardens, U.S., N.Y., Long Island The gardens of Samuel A. Salvage, Long Island. Roger Bullard, arch't. Ellen Shipman, landscape architect. (U.S.) Country life 74: 48-49 September 1938

051
T72
Gardens, U.S., N.Y., Long Island
Foster, O.H.
    Some typical Long Island gardens.

Touchstone 6:3:1-7??
May 1920

Gardens, U.S., N.Y., L.I., Southampton
    Garden, Mr. H.H. Rogers, Southampton, L.I.,
Walker and Gillette, archts.

Architect 3: pl.48
November, 1924

Gardens, U.S., N.Y., N.Y.
    Gardens in Central Park

Amer. arch. 112:105-108
Aug. 8, 1917

710.5
C855
Gardens,U.S., N.Y., L.I., Glen Cove
Forbes,E.B.
    Meandering in a famous garden. The estate,
Welwyn,of Mr.and Mrs.Harold Irving Pratt, Glen
Cove,Long Island.

Country life (U.S.)63: 35-39
March 1933

710.5
C855
Gardens,U.S., N.Y., L.I., Stony Brook
    Gardens at Sunwood,estate of Mr.and Mrs.
Frank Melville,Stony Brook,Long Island Sound.

Country life (U.S.)64: 66-67
August 1933

D13.1
H84
Gardens, U.S., New York, New York
    The garden in good taste. The garden of
Carll Tucker. Ellen Shipman, landscape ar-
chitect

House beautiful 64:372,389-392
October 1928

710.5
C855
Gardens; U.S.,N.Y.,L.I., Great Neck
    A cool retreat on summer days. The garden
of R.D. Wyckoff, Great Neck, L.I.

Country life (U.S.) 52: 66-67
June 1927

710.5
C855
Gardens, U.S., N.Y., L.I., Westbury
    The gardens on the estate of Mrs.
Robert Bacon in Westbury.

Country life(U.S.) 65:68-70
April 1934

710.5
H84
Gardens,U.S. New York, New York
    Garden in town: Russell A. Pettengill's
garden.

House and garden 72:37
September 1937 (Sect.2)

Gardens, U.S., N.Y., L.I., Huntington
    The naturalistic garden of S.A. Everitt,
Huntington, L.I.

Country life (U.S.)64: 47-49
May, 1933

710.5
C855
Gardens,U.S., N.Y., Mt. Kisco
    Gardens on the estate of Mrs.W.A.M.Burden
at Mt.Kisco,N.Y.

Country life(U.S.)68:42-43
June 1935

Gardens, U.S., N.Y., New York
    Plan for a sunken garden on site of old reservoir

Amer. inst. of arch. 5:399-400
Aug., 1917

Gardens, U.S., N.Y., L.I., Oyster Bay
    On the estate of H.S. Shonnard, Oyster Bay,
L.I., N.Y. Donn Barber, archt.

American architect 122: 9 pl.
August 16, 1922

720.5
A67
Gardens,U.S., N.Y., New Rochelle
    The rose garden of C.Oliver Iselin, New
Rochelle,N.Y.

Architectural review 15:90-91
May 1908

720.5
A67r
Gardens,U.S., New York, New York
Colton, A. W.
    Turtle Bay gardens, New York City. Edward
Dean and William L. Bottomley, associate archts.

Architectural record 48:467-94
December 1920

Gardens U.S., N.Y., L.I., Oyster Bay
    The gardens on the estate of William Coe,
Oyster Bay, L.I. Walker and Gillette, archts.
and Olmsted Bros. landscape archts.

Country life (U.S.) 53:30-56
March, 1928

Gardens, U.S., New York City
    see also

New York City. 38th Street (east) no. 115 garden
   "   "   "   Metropolitan Museum of Art. The
                      Cloisters.

Gardens, U.S., New York, New York
    Proposed sunken garden in Central Park

Arch. review 22:n.s.5:p. 244:pl.68-69
Nov., 1917

Gardens. U.S., N.Y., L.I., Oyster Bay
    Garden of H.S. Shonnard, Oyster Bay, N.Y.

House and Garden 41:18-19,21.
Jan., 1922.

D19.06
V88
Gardens,U.S.,New York, New York
    Gardens and roof gardens in the heart of
New York

Vogue 68:56-59
July 15, 1926

D13.1
H84
Gardens, U.S., New York, New York
Wheeler, W. F.
    A prized oasis in the heart of the city

House beautiful 62:534-536
November 1927

Gardens, U.S., N.Y., New York. World's Fair
Gardens on parade. The horticultural display at the New York World's Fair.

House and garden 74:38-39
October, 1938

---

ff
720.5
AO7
Gardens, U.S., N.Y., Tarrytown
Warner, R.F.
Recent garden architecture: garden of John D. Rockefeller, Tarrytown, N.Y. Welles Bosworth archt

Architectural review 24: 103-105
December 1918

710.5
C855
Gardens, U.S., O., Cleveland
The garden at the home of Mr. & Mrs. F.F. Prentiss, Cleveland, O.

Country life 54: 44-46
July 1928

Gardens, U.S., N.Y., Nyack
Helen Hayes reigns in a garden above the Hudson River. Fountain by H.V. Poor.

House and garden 72:52-53
August, 1937

705.2
I61
Gardens, U.S., N.Y., Tarrytown
Moulton, R.H.
Wonderful gardens at Pocantico Hills.

International studio 69:sup.19-2}
November 1919

710.5
H84
Gardens, U.S., Pa., Doylestown
The garden of William Mercer at Doylestown, Pennsylvania, designed on geometric lines. Willing, Sims, and Talbutt, archts.

House and garden 63: 26-27
February 1933

Gardens, U.S. N.Y. Pocantico Hills
The Garden at Pocantico Hills, estate of John D. Rockefeller, Esq., By William W. Bosworth.

Amer archt 99: 3-8, 10
Ja 4, 1911

Gardens, U.S., N.Y., Tuxedo
Tranquility reigns at "Boulder Point", the residence of Samuel Sloan Colt, at Tuxedo, N.Y.

Country life (U.S.) 60:44-45
September, 1931

Gardens, U.S., Pa., Philadelphia, Chestnut Hill
Peck, F.W.G.
"Boxly", the Frederick W. Taylor estate at Chestnut Hill, Pa. House built by the Count du Barry in 1833, gardens date 1803.

Country life (U.S.)68:48
August, 1935

Gardens, U.S., N.Y., Pocantico Hills
Japanese garden on the estate of J.D. Rockefeller, Jr., at Pocantico Hills (N.Y.)

Country life (N.S.) 58:67-68,78,80
July, 1930

Gardens, U.S., N.Y., Yonkers
Detail, Greystone Garden, Yonkers, N.Y.

The architect 1:pl.37
Nov. 1923

Gardens, U.S., Pa. Philadelphia
Rothe, Richard
Transforming an embankment.

Landscape architecture 20:117-124
January, 1930

051
T72
Gardens, U.S., N.Y., Pocantico Hills
Genthe, Arnold
"Lookout" or"Kijkuit", the great and lovely garden of John D. Rockefeller, illustrated from photographs by Arnold Genthe.

Touchstone 6:front..348-356
March 1920

Gardens, U.S., N.Y., Yonkers
Greek gardens at Greystone, the estate of Mr. Samuel Untermeyer, Yonkers, N.Y.

Country Life   72: 59-62
May, 1937

710.5
C855
Gardens,U.S., Pa., Rosemont
Castana: the Alba B.Johnson estate in Rosemont,Pennsylvania,has five separate gardens.

Country life (U.S.)66: 56-57
May 1934

710.5
C855
Gardens,U.S., N.Y., Portchester
Spring in a Westchester garden: "Lee Shore",Portchester,N.Y. - home of Mr. and Mrs Walter C.Teagle. Hugh Findlay,archt.

A   Country life(U.S.)69:54-57
March 1936

Gardens, U.S., N.Y., Yorktown Heights
Estate of Arthur H. Marks, Yorktown Heights, N.Y., Andrews, Rantout and Jones, archts.

American architect 120:pls.opp.p.492
December 21, 1921

Gardens. U.S., Pa., St. Martins

House and garden 48:54-55
Aug., 1925

Gardens. U.S., N.Y., Scarsdale.
Roses for restfulness.
A garden of varied aspect.

House and garden. 50:83-85
Dec., 1926

720.5
A78a
Gardens, U.S., O., Cleveland
Garden, W. Hays, Cleveland, Ohio. Wm. Pitkin, Jr., landscape archt.

Architecture 50: pl.176,p.373
November 1924

710.5
H84
Gardens, U.S., Pa., Sewickley Heights
Garden of Mrs. Walter S. Mitchell at Sewickley Heights, Pa. William Pitkin,Jr. and Seward H. Mott, landscape archts.

House and garden 59: 85
May 1931

710.5
H84
Gardens. U.S. Pa., Uniontown
Wright, Richardson
Pages from a garden diary.

House & garden 52: 76
August 1927.

710.5
H84
Gardens, U.S., S.C., Charleston
Briggs, L.W.
Little patterned gardens of Old Charleston.
Plans.

House and garden 65: 72-73,85
May 1934

710.5
C855
Gardens, U.S., Virginia
Wood, Warni
F.F.V.: old gardens of Virginia.
"The Maze" at Tuckahoe, Va., owned by Mrs.N.A.
Baker. 1689-1730.

Country life(U.S.)71:20-23
February 1937

Gardens, U.S., Pa. Villa Nova
Gardens of Mr. George McFadden, Jr., Villa Nova,
Pa.

Country life 42:72-4
Oct., 1922

Gardens, U.S., Spanish influence
Wren, H.R.
Informal charm of old Spain in a city home,
Los Angeles

Arts and decoration 29:46
October, 1928

Gardens, U.S., Va., Mount Vernon
Mount Vernon: the garden and outbuildings.

Architectural review 15:88-89
May, 1908

Gardens, U.S., Persian influence
Persian garden in California

Amer. homes and gard. 10:426-7
Dec., 1913

710.5
C855
Gardens, U.S., Spanish influence
Peck, W.G.
Spanish gardens for American estates.
Plan for an American garden in the Spanish
manner.

Country life(U.S.) 65: 72-74,81
February 1934

710.5
H84
Gardens, U.S. Va., Williamsburg
Gardens of John Curtis Tenescent,Gover-
nor's palace,and Coke-Garrett.

House and garden 72:42,48-53
November 1937

720.5
A67
Gardens,U.S., R.I., Newport
The garden of H.D.Auchencloss,Newport,R.I.
and others.

Architectural review 15:pls.25-32
May 1908

710.5
H84
Gardens, U.S., Spanish influence
Miss Elisa Galban's patio garden,River-
dale on Hudson,New York. Dwight James Baum,
archt.

House and garden 65: 62-63
March 1934.

A

710.5
C855
Gardens, U.S., Wash., Seattle
A wildwood garden on the estate of Gilbert
LeBaron Duffy at Seattle,Washington.

Country life (U.S.) 62: 61-63
May 1932

720.5
A67
Gardens,U.S., R.I., Newport
Garden of Mrs. Kells, Newport, R.I. John
Russell Pope, archt.

A   Architectural review 19 n.s.2: pl. 65-66
June 1913

D18.1
H84
Gardens, U.S., Spanish influence
Strang,E.L.
The making of a Spanish-American garden.Plan.

House beautiful 44:94-95,103
July 1918

710.5
C855
Gardens,U.S.,Wash., Seattle
The gardens of Mr.and Mrs.Chester Thorne
at Seattle,Washington. Omsted Brothers,
landscape archts.

Country life(U.S.)68:44-46
October 1936

A

Gardens, U.S., S.C., Charleston (near)
Garden with more than a hundred sculptures

Country life (U.S.) 70:23-25
September, 1936

710.5
C855
Gardens, U.S., Tennessee
Barron, Leonard
The Plaisance at the Sanford Arboretum.

Country life (U.S.) 69:17-19
November 1935

710.5
H84
Gardens, U.S., Wash., Seattle
Perkins, Mrs. J.C.
Quiet gardens in the Northwest.

House & garden 51: 63-67
June 1927

720.5
F29
Charleston, S. C. St. Michael's Church
"The City" Charleston, S.C.: St.
Michael's Church (1752); James Gibbs, archt.;
St. Philip's, first church of England estab-
lished in South Carolina (1836); pineapple
gates of the Smythe house; Miles Brewton
house - now called the Pringle house; old
Post Office; Record building, Robert Mills,
archt.; and St. John's Lutheran Church; no
plans.
Federal architect 8:10,13-23
October 1937

Gardens, U.S., Tenn., Nashville
Gardens at Cheekwood, Harpeth Hills, Nashville,
Tenn.

Country life (U.S.) 68:42-43
June, 1935

Gardens, U.S., Wash., Tacoma
Perkins, Mrs. J.C.
Thornewood on American lake: residence of
Mr. and Mrs. Chester Thorne, Tacoma, Washington.

House beautiful 59:273-277
March, 1926

Gardens, U.S., Wis., Milwaukee
Sunken garden of Mitchell Park, Milwaukee.

National geographic 72:18
July, 1937

Gardiner, Stephen

see

Stratton park, Eng. Baring (John) house

Gardner, Francis, 1720-1800
Hughes, G. Bernard
An English potter's triumph in imperial
Russia [illus]

Country life
133: 408-410, F 28, 1963

720.5
A67r
Gardens, Wales
The gardens at Duffryn near Cardiff,
South Wales.

Arch. record 56:17-27
July 1924

720.5
A67r
Gardiner's Island(N.Y.)Gardiner house
Gardiner house (1774) Gardiner's Island,
N.Y.

Architectural record 40:84
July 1916

Gardner, George C.
The Obligation of the Architect
to his profession.

Inland Architect
33: 50
Jul, 1899

Gardens, Yugoslavia
Royal gardens in the Balkans. III. King
Alexander's. By Irina Khrabroff.
Photos.

Country life 4:55-56
July, 1937

Gardner, A. McInnes & Robert Whyte

see

Glasgow (Scot.) Clydebank public library

Gardner, Gilbert T.

see

Oxford (Eng.) Headington school for girls

Gardens, Zoological,

see

Zoological gardens

721.97
A67c
Gardner, Albert B
Broadway store for Pasadena.

Architectural concrete 7: 12-14
No. 3 [1941]

Gardner, H. A.
The protection of steel
& iron surfaces

West. Arch.
12: IV
O 1908

720.52
A67t
Gardet, G.
Bronze figures in legislative chamber.

Arch. Rev. 51: 9-10.
Jan. 1922.

Gardner and Bartoo

see

Binghamton (N.Y.) Bayliss house and stable
"   "   Leighton residence

Gardner, Horace C.   1856-1936
Brief biography.

Herringshaw, Clark J. Herringshaw's
city blue book of current biography.
Chicago: American Publisher's
Association, 1915.

721.97
A67c
Gardiner and Mercer
Gardiner, Frank
New hospital in Vancouver: St. Vincent's
hospital. Gardiner and Mercer, archts. No plan.

Architectural concrete 6:24
No.4[1940]

Gardner, E. C. and G. C. Gardner

see

Marietta,(O.) First Congregational church

MICROFILM

Gardner, Horace Chase, 1856-1936
obituary notice

In SCRAPBOOK ON
ARCHITECTURE p. 696
(on film)

Gardiner, Frank G.

see

Chilliwack (Can.) Chilliwack general hospital

Gardner, F.S., house. Chicago

see

Chicago, Ill. Gardner, F.S., house.

Gardner house (1872) Chicago,

see

Chicago, Ill. Stratford hotel (1872)

Gardner, Isabella Stewart collection, see Boston. Isabella Stewart Gardner museum	Gardner museum, Boston see Boston. Isabella Stewart Gardner museum	Gardner-Medwin, Robert Joseph, 1907- Engineering building & theatre, Edinburgh University [site plan] Robert Gardner-Medwin, archt. Arch't'l design 32: 19, Ja 1962
Gardner, Mrs. Jack collection, see Boston. Isabella Stewart Gardner museum	Gardner, Robert W. see also Miami (Fla.) James (A.C.) house	Garfield, Abram, 1872- Member of firm: Meade and Garfield Garfield, Harris, Robinson & Schafer
Gardner (James P.) house. Chicago, IL. see Chicago, IL. Gardner (J.P.) house	720.5 .A67 Gardner, Robert R Apartment at 540 Park Avenue, New York City. R.W.Gardner, archt. Architectural review 17:53-31. March 1910	Garfield, Abram, 1872-1959 Cleveland pays tribute to Abram Garfield. Nat'l Arch 1:6 N '45
Gardner, John L., house See Boston (Mass.) Fenway Court	MICROFILM Gardner, Robert Waterman, 1866-1937 obituary notice in SCRAPBOOK ON ARCHITECTURE p. 696 (on film)	Garfield, Harris, Robinson and Schafer see also Cleveland, O. Ass'n for crippled and disabled. School and shop bldg.
Gardner, Mrs. John Lowell collection, see Boston. Isabella Stewart Gardner museum	Gardner Sash Balance Co. Exhibit at World's Columbian Expo., Chicago Inland Architect 22: 21-3 Sept, 1893	Garfield, Harris, Robinson and Schafer Members of firm: Garfield, Abram, 1872- Harris, George R Robinson, Alexander Cochrane, 1891- Schafer, Gilbert Pierson
Gardner, John Starkie Arch. rev. (Eng.) 45:39-42 Feb., 1919	Gardner, W. R. H. see Margate (Eng.) Housing	Garfield park, Chicago see Chicago, Ill. Garfield park
720.5 Gardner(Mass.)First national bank A51 First national bank, Gardner(Mass.) Hutchins and French, archts. Plan. A American architect 129:389-90 March 20,1926	Gardner-Medwin, Robert Joseph, 1907- see also Old Coulsdon (Eng.) Town hall	"Gargoyle", Chicago see Chicago (Ill.) Hoyt (W.H.) house